The Nonprofit Organization Handbook

The Nonprofit Organization Handbook

Second Edition

Tracy Daniel Connors
Editor in Chief

McGraw-Hill Book Company

New York   St. Louis   San Francisco   Auckland
Bogotá   Hamburg   London   Madrid   Mexico
Milan   Montreal   New Delhi   Panama
Paris   São Paulo   Singapore
Sydney   Tokyo   Toronto

Library of Congress Cataloging-in-Publication Data

The Nonprofit organization handbook/Tracy Daniel Connors, editor in
  chief.—2nd ed.
    p.   cm.

  Includes index.
  ISBN 0-07-012432-9
    1. Charities—United States—Handbooks, manuals, etc.
  2. Corporations, Nonprofit—United States—Handbooks, manuals, etc.
  3. Voluntarism—United States—Handbooks, manuals, etc.
  I. Connors, Tracy Daniel.
  HV91.N58   1988
  361.7′63′068—dc19   87-26276
                                                                           CIP

  234567890   DOC/DOC   89321098

ISBN 0-07-012432-9

*The editors for this book were William A. Sabin and Nancy Young, the
designer was Naomi Auerbach, and the production supervisor was Thomas
G. Kowalczyk. It was set in Meridian. It was composed by the McGraw-Hill
Book Company Professional & Reference Division composition unit. Printed
and bound by R. R. Donnelley & Sons Company.*

To My Parents

MIRIAM MORRIS CONNORS
WOODROW DANIEL CONNORS

*Two outstanding people whose hallmark has been dedicated service
to community, church, family, and each other
throughout their 50-plus year marriage.*

Contents

Part 1 Organization and Corporate Principles

Part 2   Leadership, Management, and Control

Part 3   Volunteers: An Indispensable Human Resource in a Democratic Society

Part 4 Sources of Revenue for the Nonprofit Organization

Part 5   Public Relations

EDITOR IN CHIEF

Tracy Daniel Connors, M.A.

Senior analyst, Kapos Associates, Washington, D.C.; former
staff action officer, Office of the Chief of Naval Operations,
Washington, D.C.; former administrative assistant, U.S. House
of Representatives; former manager of corporate
communications, Gould Electronics, Defense Systems Business
Section; director, Greater Washington Chapter, Surface Navy
Association; vice commander, National Capitol Commandery,
Naval Order of the United States; regional vice president,
Naval Reserve Association; member, Reserve Officers
Association and National Eagle Scout Association; editor,
Financial Management for Nonprofit Organizations and *Dictionary
of Mass Media and Communication.* (CHAPTERS 10, 11, 12, 15, 21,
35, 36, 40, 41, 43)

Contributors

Adler, Madeleine Wing, Ph.D.   Professor of politics and vice president for academic affairs, Framingham State College; author of numerous articles and monographs on urban and state politics. (CHAPTER 9)

Anthony, William P., Ph.D.   Professor and former chairman, College of Business, The Florida State University; conducts seminars, workshops, and conferences on topics such as strategic planning, managing change, participative management, upward management, and managing problem employees; author of numerous articles in the field of management, personnel, and labor relations. (CHAPTER 8)

Baldwin, Burt R., Ph.D.   Professor, Department of Sociology, Central Connecticut State University; member, Association of Voluntary Action Scholars; board member and editor, *Citizen Participation and Voluntary Action Abstracts;* coauthor, *Voluntary Action Research Annotated Bibliography*. (CHAPTER 1)

Berger, Ira   Former associate dean for public affairs, New York Law School; worked with the National Huntington's Disease Program to establish a program of fund raising among corporations; former director of development, Mannes College of Music. (CHAPTER 13)

Campbell, Donald A., Jr., CFRE   President of Campbell and Company, a Chicago-based firm specializing in not-for-profit fund-raising, marketing, and communications services; past chairman of the board of the NSFRE Institute Board; past chairman of the Development Committee of United Way of Chicago; past president of the Chicago Chapter of the National Society of Fund Raising Executives. (CHAPTER 32)

Carlson, Diane M., CFRE   President, IDC; former officer of the national board of the National Society of Fund Raising Executives; past president of the New Jersey Chapter, NSFRE; founder and cochairman, the New Jersey Conference on Philanthropy, 1982 and 1983. (CHAPTER 28)

Connor, Robert C. President and chief executive officer, Community Service Bureau, Inc., and an officer of the firm for 26 years; member, Executive Board of the American Association of Fund-Raising Counsel, Inc.; member, board of directors, AAFRC Trust for Philanthropy. (CHAPTER 26)

Corrick, George W., Ph.D. Faculty member, Graduate Program in Educational Leadership, University of North Florida; graduate faculty, Educational Leadership, University of Florida; former vice president, University Relations, University of North Florida; former assistant to the president, director of development, University of Florida. (CHAPTER 42)

Daly, John Jay President, John Jay Daly Associates, Inc.; former senior vice president, Direct Mail/Marketing Association; former member, Government Relations and Legal Committee, American Society of Association Executives; past president, National Capital Chapter of the Public Relations Society of America and past chairman of its National Government Relations Committee. (CHAPTER 44)

Freyd, William P., CFRE Chairman and founder, IDC; former officer, the National Society of Fund Raising Executives; former officer and current board member, the American Association of Fund-Raising Counsel; author of many articles on fundraising topics. (CHAPTERS 23, 24, 25)

Gaertner, James F., CPA Professor and director, Division of Accounting and Information Systems, University of Texas at San Antonio; former associate professor of accounting and director, University of Notre Dame London MBA program; author and coauthor of several books, including *Financial Accounting,* and of articles of publications such as *The Journal of Accountancy, Management Accounting,* and *The CPA Journal.* (CHAPTER 8)

Hankin, Michael D. Assistant to the vice president for finance and administration, The Florida State University; national administrator, Sigma Iota Epsilon National Management Fraternity; coauthor and coresearcher of many articles on topics such as employee turnover, management training, and membership retention in professional and trade associations. (CHAPTER 6)

Hart, Robert R., Jr. Partner, Wiethe & Hart Attorneys at Law; member, American Bar Association, Ohio State Bar Association, Cincinnati Bar Association, Federal Bar Association, and American Trial Lawyers Association; president, Cincinnati Chapter of Governors, Salmon P. Chase College of Law Alumni Club; member, Salmon P. Chase College of Law Fund committee. (CHAPTERS 11, 12, 15)

Harvey, Barron H., Ph.D., CPA Associate professor of accounting and chairperson, Department of Accounting, School of Business and Public Administration, Howard University; past coordinator of MBA programs, Howard University; former faculty member, University of Miami, University of Nebraska, and Georgetown University; author of numerous articles about business and accounting. (CHAPTERS 45, 46, 49)

Hodge, B. J., Ph.D. Vice president for finance and administration and professor of management, The Florida State University; educational consultant to the Chamber of Commerce of the United States; national president of Sigma Iota Epsilon National Management Fraternity; coauthor of *Management and Organizational Behavior and Organization Theory* and of numerous articles. (CHAPTER 6)

Jarvis, A. Kenneth   Executive director, West Virginia Public Broadcasting; board member, Southern Educational Communication Association; advisory council member, WWVU-FM; commanding officer, Navy Broadcast Service, Fleet Support Detachment 206, USNR; former faculty member, Department of Communications, Texas Tech University. (CHAPTER 43)

Kuhta, Candace   Consultant and freelance provider of foundation research and proposal writing services to nonprofit organizations in St. Lawrence County, NY; former coordinator of public services and former director, New York Library, The Foundation Center; author of articles and teacher of classes on foundations. (CHAPTER 34)

Lane, Frederick S.   Professor and chairperson, Department of Public Administration, Bernard M. Baruch College of the City University of New York; former director, The Executive MBA Program, Baruch College, CUNY; teacher of graduate and continuing education courses in the management of nonprofit organizations; executive vice president. The Nova Institute, Inc.; vice chair, board of directors, National Charities Information Bureau. (CHAPTER 14)

Lentz, Eileen R.   President, Events Management, Inc.; former director of special events, Institutional Development Counsel; member, board of directors, Family Service and Child Guidance Center of The Oranges, Maplewood and Millburn; president, Rutgers Panhellenic Housing Task Force; member, National Society of Fund Raising Executives; frequent speaker on special events. (CHAPTER 31)

McConkey, Dale D.   Professor of management in the School of Business, Management Institute, University of Wisconsin-Madison; former president of his own management consulting firm; former group vice president, United Fruit Company; former vice president, Beech-Nut Life Savers, Inc.; author of numerous books and articles on corporate management, including *How to Manage by Results, Planning Next Year's Profits,* and *Updating the Management Process.* (CHAPTER 7)

Maxwell, James L.   Director of development and public relations, Houston Metropolitan Ministries; former regional vice president, American Cancer Society; former associate director of development, Johns Hopkins University and Hospital; past executive head, the National Society of Fund Raising Executives; chair, 1978 International Conference on Philanthropy. (CHAPTER 29)

Milani, Ken, Ph.D.   Arthur Young faculty fellow in taxation, University of Notre Dame; former assistant chairman of the department of accountancy, University of Notre Dame; author of articles in *The Accounting Review, The Journal of Accountancy, Management Accounting, Cost and Management, Managerial Planning,* and *TAXES—The Tax Magazine.* (CHAPTERS 3, 5, 38, 47)

Richardson, James L., Jr., CFRE   Executive vice president and chief operating officer, Community Service Bureau, Inc.; former development director, School of Law, Southern Methodist University; former executive director, Dallas County Community College District Foundation; former development director, Boys Clubs of America, Southwest Region; former state director, Easter Seals Society of Michigan, Inc.; former associate executive director, Easter Seals Society of Texas. (CHAPTER 30)

Rosso, Henry A., CFRE   Director, The Fund Raising School, a program of the Indiana University Center on Philanthropy and associate director for public service of the Center of Philanthropy; former senior vice president and member, board of directors, G. A. Brakeley & Co., Inc.; past president, Development Executives Roundtable, San Francisco; member, Golden Gate Chapter of the National Society of Fund Raising Executives; member, American Management Association. (CHAPTERS 22, 39)

Schindler-Rainman, Eva, D.S.W. International organization and community consultant; adjunct professor, University of Southern California Schools of Public Administration and Social Work; member and founder, International Association for Volunteer Effort; member, Association of Voluntary Action Scholars, National Training Laboratories, Academy of Certified Social Workers, and Association for Volunteer Administration. (CHAPTERS 16, 17, 18, 19, 20)

Smith, David Horton, Ph.D. Professor of sociology, Boston College; former director of research, Center for a Voluntary Society; author of many articles and book chapters on voluntary action and voluntary groups; founder, Association of Voluntary Action Scholars and first editor of its journal, *Journal of Voluntary Action Research.* (CHAPTERS 1, 2)

Sorkin, Horton L., Ph.D. Faculty member, School of Business Administration, Howard University, teaching about EDP systems and applications, auditing, and managerial accounting. (CHAPTERS 45, 46, 49)

Stanley, Frank L. Portfolio director, Phoenix Mutual Life Insurance Company, former senior vice president, Investment Management Group, Connecticut National Bank; former vice chairman and president of Travelers Investment Management Company; former president, Travelers Equities Fund; former trustee, The Pension Trust, Bethlehem Steel Corporation. (CHAPTER 37)

Sturm, Arthur C., Jr. President and founder, The Sturm Communications Group; former marketing executive for a national consulting firm; author of articles on hospital marketing in *Hospitals, Modern Healthcare,* and *Advertising Age;* national columnist on health-care marketing for *Advertising Age.* (CHAPTER 27)

Van Batenburg, Scott Vice president, Commercial Division, Connecticut National Bank; former international economist, U.S. Treasury Department, and assistant treasury attaché, Rome, Italy; author of articles on electronic banking and short-term asset management; president, Shelter for Women. (CHAPTER 37)

White, Eugene D., Jr. Research associate and former executive officer, Association of Voluntary Action Scholars. (CHAPTER 1)

Wise, Stephen R., Ed.D. Vice president, Institutional Advancement, and former executive director, Educational Resource Development, Florida Community College at Jacksonville; board member, National Council for Resource Development; member, College Advisory Board of CASE. (CHAPTERS 33, 35)

Wittenbach, James L. Professor of accountancy and assistant department chairman, University of Notre Dame and director of the MBA program with a concentration in taxation; author of articles in journals such as *Journal of Accountancy, The Financial Executive, TAXES—The Tax Magazine,* and *Journal of Consumer Research.* (CHAPTER 38)

Wood, Creston C. Case manager, Internal Revenue Service; adjunct professor in accounting, Benjamin Franklin University; temporary faculty member, Gallaudet University. (CHAPTER 4)

Foreword

The nonprofit sector could well be in the early stages of a major sea change. Cutback moves throughout the country from federal, state, and local government entities are having a strong impact on the nonprofit sector and, in turn, on the millions of people who depend on the services that nonprofit organizations and agencies provide. Couple this with the harsh reality of finite philanthropic sources, and one could easily become disheartened and resigned to what appear to be negative trends. But such attitudes are only self-defeating.

What is needed in these times is a clear assessment of the situation and a *will* to deal with that reality in creative ways. All efforts need to move toward maximizing precious resources and seizing control over the nonprofit sector's future.

Nonprofit leaders nationwide, those representing the whole nonprofit spectrum, need to resolve to strengthen their individual and collective capacities and to meet the challenges head-on.

The most pressing challenges and issues affecting the nonprofit sector, issues that must be addressed through appropriate and timely responses, are listed below.

Sectorwide Issues

- On the national level, there is no apparent consistent stance about the value and import of the nonprofit sector. It is not clear whether the nonprofit sector is held as a cherished national asset or as a second-class sector that is not carrying its own weight and that needs to be held in check. These mixed signals only compound the unease and uncertainty that is felt in many nonprofit organizations.

- Because of massive government cutbacks, increasingly the nation is turning to nonprofit organizations to meet the real and growing need for human services, placing such organizations in a most difficult situation; more demand for services and, for many nonprofits, fewer dollars to provide those services.

- Beyond the pervasive lack of an open sharing of known ways to advance nonprofit organizations, a great deal of basic research and development of little-known but potentially widely applicable operating concepts and approaches is badly needed. These communications, research, and development problems must be addressed and solved if important information, ideas, and approaches are to be brought to the attention of and implemented by leaders of these organizations.

- Many nonprofit organizations, particularly the smaller ones, have staff and volunteers who need a broad base of education and training programs in order to have the necessary skills to meet their daily responsibilities. Although there are numerous program offerings specifically targeted for those in the nonprofit sector, there is a general lack of coherence to these programs, resulting in disjointed and incongruent learning. Further, not enough is being done (other than in a few institutions of higher learning) to predetermine the essential content areas nonprofit managers and aspiring managers need to master to become effective practitioners. Also, most of the existing education and training programs fail to offer follow-up evaluations of knowledge acquired and skills developed and applied. And there are numerous subject voids that need to be filled.

- Because of the general absence of clearinghouses of information for nonprofit organizations, it is very common for one organization to grapple with and to work through a particular problem area without first determining whether there are other nonprofit organizations that have worked through a similar problem. Without such a clearinghouse of information, each nonprofit organization fends for itself. These continuous "reinventions of the wheel" by individual organizations are both wasteful and unnecessary.

- There is a lack of up-to-date information about job openings for those seeking employment and those seeking more challenging positions in the nonprofit sector. The paucity of job opportunity listings leads to many people stagnating in their present jobs, moving out of the sector altogether, or never entering the nonprofit field at all.

- Although there exist many potentially valuable leadership, management, and organizational advancement resources which could be used by nonprofits—books, periodicals, pamphlets, position papers, abstracts, audio-visual materials—such resources are often most difficult to locate. The result is that those who most need these educational resources go without them.

- While there is an abundance of organizations, firms, and individuals who serve or could serve nonprofit organizations as outside technical assistance providers, it is difficult for nonprofit decision makers to know where to go to find the best and the specific assistance their organizations need. Too often, the result is that the organization never secures outside assistance or, perhaps even worse, retains the services of those who are less than adequate.

- Certain special service areas within the nonprofit sector (hospitals, educational institutions, and a few national umbrella organizations) have for years been involved in group purchasing arrangements for the purpose of effecting cost savings for participating members. But other nonprofit service areas have lagged behind in this regard. Only recently have a few local and regional group purchasing arrangements surfaced, but these efforts are not enough to meet the needs of most nonprofit organizations throughout the country. Much still needs to be done in creating national and regional group purchasing arrangements, especially for the most isolated nonprofits—all in an effort to help maximize the use of their precious resources.

Individual Nonprofit Organization Issues

- The pressures of running an effective and efficient nonprofit organization in recent years have intensified dramatically. As a result, the complexities of leadership, management, and governance have expanded greatly, calling for new and better management practices and approaches.

- Nonprofit organizations face increasing competition—from other nonprofits, from for-profit firms, and, to some extent, from government entities. No longer can nonprofit organizations assume they have a lock on constituent market segments or service areas. And there is no sign that this competition will lessen in the foreseeable future.

- In response to increased competition among nonprofit organizations for fund support, many nonprofit organizations are turning to generating their own funds through enterprise activities. While there are success stories of nonprofits producing earned income for their causes through new enterprise activities, others have failed, thereby weakening the organization's financial base. And, in some cases, the organization's exempt status has been threatened by inappropriate enterprise choice.

- While virtually all nonprofit organizations need additional funds to fulfill their missions and to meet their highest objectives, many organizations jump too quickly into unrealistic fund-raising programs without first undergoing a strategic planning process or even a fund-raising feasibility study. Such a planning process would help identify problem areas and establish a clear understanding about why the organization exists and what is required to move it forward. As a result of the planning process, the organization would know what outside funds are *really* needed and would in all likelihood be in an improved position to secure such funding support.

- Since resources are becoming more scarce in nonprofit organizations, this means that there is now less margin for error by boards and managers. Wrong, unwise, ill-timed moves in an organization can cause great, sometimes irreversible, damage. In the more fragile nonprofits, poor decisions can result in the organization's demise. Especially in times such as these, sound decision-making processes need to be widely known and applied. But little in the way of instructional materials or education and training programs are available to nonprofit leaders and managers in this critically important area.

- Many nonprofit organizations do not carry their excess revenues over expenditures forward from one fiscal year to the next. A "spend it or lose it" mentality is not uncommon in such organizations. Under this practice, success may partially be determined by the percentage of budget increases which a department or the entire organization is able to garner. Practices such as these, especially with limited resources, are totally unacceptable and must be changed.

- Productivity in many nonprofit organizations is not close to what it should—indeed, must—be. One of the primary reasons for this low productivity is a short planning horizon and the often *ad hoc* nature of management practices. Higher productivity in nonprofit organizations is a key to better meeting client and constituent needs. Nothing short of significantly increasing productivity can be acceptable.

- Accountability of nonprofit organizations is increasingly being sought by funding sources, constituencies, the IRS, state agencies, and the public at large. The criticisms that have been leveled at nonprofits in the area of lack of accountability have, in some cases, been harsh. Unfortunately, a good deal of this criticism is justified. But the answers here are not easy to find.

While the leaders of many nonprofit organizations realize the importance and appropriateness of accountability, they find it difficult to evaluate and measure how successful they are at what they do. Because of the existence of divergent goals and objectives, because of the many constituencies being served and catered to, goal ambiguity often exists. Goal ambiguity results in imprecise measurement of outcomes and in large discrepancies between stated mission and goals and what actually occurs. Although it is admittedly far more difficult to evaluate and measure performance in nonprofit organizations than it is in many for-profit firms, there is a growing expectation from all quarters for nonprofits to be held accountable for what they do and do not do.

- There is some indication of modest improvement in what nonprofit organizations provide in the way of salaries and benefits to their employees. But it is still altogether too common for nonprofit employees to receive much less for their efforts than would be true in comparable positions in both the for-profit and government sectors. While there are some perceived or felt compensating factors for those who work within nonprofit organizations (a more positive work environment, often more flexible working arrangements, and a clearer commitment to the organization's purpose), many nonprofit organizations lean too heavily on their employees in the area of financial reward for work, some even to the point of exploitation.

  As the competition for service people becomes more keen, nonprofit leaders will need to address this problem. This will present a double bind: Just when nonprofit organizations can least afford to provide improved compensation to their employees, they must find ways to do so or lose the capacity to attract and to retain valuable employees.

- Large numbers of nonprofit boards are failing to perform in some of the most important functions. Basic but still extremely important is the failure of many boards to enact broad policies and goals for the organizations they serve and to see to it that those policies and goals are met by the chief executive officer and staff.

  In addition, numerous boards have not been particularly strong in initiating and participating in the strategic planning function. Rather, many board members tend to preoccupy themselves with daily operational problems and issues, things that should be delegated to and handled by the executive director and key staff.

  And too many nonprofit boards do not see to it that their organization's funds (short-term and long-term) are properly managed and invested. This has nothing to do with a strict interpretation of prudent or conservative fund management practices. What is lacking and what must be done is for the board, or a designated board committee, to see to it that the appropriate investment philosophy and policies for the organization's funds are established and then to make sure that those funds are managed and invested in accordance with the established philosophy and policies. The loss of revenue or assets that comes from poorly managed or mismanaged funds in nonprofit organizations is a shameful waste. No nonprofit organization can afford such waste.

These, then, are just some of the challenges and issues confronting most nonprofit organizations nationwide. Obviously, there are many other problems or issues that could have been discussed here, but many are transitory and the result of cyclical market forces and aberrations. A case in point is the liability insurance crisis that has had a negative effect on the nonprofit sector and the entire country. And now there are strong indications of an impending crisis in the area of health insurance. While there are no quick or easy solutions to the challenges and issues identified here; the good news is that much is being done and can be done to improve the situation for all nonprofit organizations. For example, many of the sectorwide issues discussed above are beginning to be addressed through efforts of various national, regional, and local initiatives.

But the most significant responses to the preponderance of the issues identified, particularly those under the heading "Individual Nonprofit Organization Issues" presented above, must necessarily come from the individual organizations themselves. Since most of these issues directly or indirectly relate to the reality of limited resources, what follows focuses on measures and approaches that individual nonprofit organizations have the capacity to take, not only to sustain but also to further develop and empower them.

As this writer sees it, a nonprofit organization can choose from among three approaches to help meet the challenges and issues: (1) become an opportunistic, entrepreneurial, competing organization, (2) become a constrained, defensive, conserving organization, and (3) become an open, cooperating, and collaborating organization, one that actively seeks to develop working relationships and partnerships with other organizations.

While it is anticipated that most nonprofit organizations will assume the more entrepreneurial role, it is certainly possible for organizations to take on some of each of the other two approaches as well, depending on the program, service, or functional area. These three approaches (entrepreneurial, defensive, cooperative), then, are not exclusive and may actually be complementary. And no one approach is more valid than another approach, this being particularly true in the nonprofit sector, a sector that is, for example, generally more open to cooperative and collaborative arrangements than the for-profit sector. But there are drawbacks and factors that merit careful review with each approach before any approach is adopted.

The Entrepreneurial Approach

Those organizations considering taking on the entrepreneurial, more highly competitive approach must have especially strong leadership and management skills in place, skills that are attuned to this mode of operation. To successfully assume a highly competitive stance, the organization must have at least these skills and attitudes: the ability to conduct effective strategic planning; the ability to establish a strong and sophisticated marketing program; the ability to establish and to maintain efficiency of operation in order to compete on the basis of pricing and quality of service; the ability to function with flexible financial resource allocations from one service area to another; the ability to provide appropriate information systems to track service lines over their life cycles; and the ability to establish suitable reward systems for the more risk-accepting personnel.

Further, in the entrepreneurial approach the organization must be willing and able to carefully identify the areas in which it can successfully compete, marshall necessary external and internal resources, assume responsibility for a "down side" result and then make timely adjustments to chart a positive new course of action, and anticipate and appease disgruntled constituents who feel that a highly competitive organization is inappropriate.

The Defensive,
Conserving Approach

The organization that is contemplating meeting its challenges through a defensive, conserving posture has its own set of issues to consider before committing to such an approach. Perhaps the greatest potential threat in this approach is unwittingly to destroy the organization's capacity to operate at all, spiraling down and out of business. An organization can become so risk-adverse and conserving of its resources that it puts a stranglehold on the organization. A cut-back, retrenchment attitude can pervade the entire organization, resulting in a negative, self-fulfilling prophesy of defeatism and decline. But this scenario need not be the case if there is careful planning and an awareness of the warning signs of impending loss of the organization's ability to function.

The leadership of an organization that chooses to take on a defensive, conserving stance will also have to develop a whole array of special skills and talents in order to sustain the organization. What was acceptable management in a time of more resources will no longer be adequate. Operating an organization during a time of scarce resources, while assuming a defensive posture, calls for just as much acumen as managing an organization while taking the entrepreneurial approach.

Here are just some of the skills the manager will need in order to function in a defensive mode: the ability to determine causes of limits to resources, whether they are environmental, internal, or technological limits; the ability to respond appropriately to the realities of limited resources, through sensitivity, imagination, and resolve; the ability to sustain motivation of employees and volunteers who, even in nonprofit organizations, are conditioned to respond to limited resources through planning for growth; the ability to set priorities and to lead others in the creation of appropriate response strategies and plans; the ability to gain or to retain acceptance within the community network; the ability to maintain credibility with the organization's various constituencies; the ability to justify questions from clients and others related to service and program offerings and to any associated cost changes; the ability to gain the willing involvement of more people in planning for needed adjustments to programs and services, thereby increasing their awareness of the issues and the rationale behind the defensive, conserving moves; and the ability to make hard decisions, especially as they relate to personnel.

It is important also to note that the organization which assumes a defensive, conserving posture will be more vulnerable to other organizations seeking to claim portions of its service area(s). This is why it is so critical to gain the understanding and support of the local community network of outside organizations. By so doing, "turf" issues will be less likely to present a threat to the organization in a conserving or constrained posture.

The Cooperative,
Collaborative Approach

Finally, during a time of limited resources, nonprofit organizations can legitimately opt for seeking cooperative and collaborative relationships or partnerships with clusters of compatible organizations.

Faced with mounting pressures to make ends meet or even to survive, the tendency is to become more competitive. While the inclination to compete is an understandable response, many of today's critical concerns facing nonprofit organizations can be addressed through cooperative and collaborative endeavors.

Actually, competition and cooperation need not be contradictory positions; self-interest is often the primary motivation to collaborate.

Nonprofit organizations have a long history of cooperation and collaboration. They conduct joint projects, participate in client referral services, join in combined funding activities, share personnel and information, and belong to umbrella organizations for the benefits which are derived from such associations. Therefore, given this long-standing willingness on the part of many nonprofit organizations to join together, it is quite natural for such organizations to decide in favor of cooperative and collaborative approaches for the purpose of organizational survival and perhaps growth during a time of scarce resources.

However, just as is true with the entrepreneurial and defensive approaches, organizations choosing a cooperative, collaborative, linking operational stance must realize there are trade-offs that will come as a result. And here, too, the managers and leaders of organizations that believe they see opportunities through building interorganizational relationships must realize that many special skills will be required to achieve the desired outcomes.

Managers of cooperative, collaborative-focused organizations must develop at least these skills: the ability to forge and to maintain interorganizational networks; the ability to compromise and to seek a common ground of mutual interests and pay-offs with the leadership of other cooperating organizations; the ability and willingness to trust that, through the development of collaborative relationships, each organization will gain; the ability realistically and objectively to determine the potential or proposed collaborative projects and programs without first seeking to know what is in it for one's own organization; the ability to move from an organizational to an interorganizational mind-set and attitude; the ability to see opportunities with the enlarged interorganizational service area(s) for new resource acquisitions, domain expansion, and linkages; the ability to help effectively represent and promote the interorganizational interests above the parochial interests of one's own organization; the ability and sincere desire to seek to solve interorganizational problems; the ability and desire to help coordinate and facilitate delivery of services to the entire interorganizational client base; and, in sum and above all, the ability to be a true team participant and, when necessary, to give up immediate personal or organizational gain for the betterment and enhancement of the interorganizational whole.

To develop and to implement these skills and attitudes is a tall order, even for nonprofit leaders and managers with a predisposition for such an approach. This approach requires an abiding faith in the best of human qualities. But the rewards for successful interorganizational initiatives can be great for the participating organizations themselves, and for the whole nonprofit sector and those who are served by it. Effectively run cooperative and collaborative programs will clearly help to eliminate duplication of efforts, services, and programs, thereby saving precious resources—resources that can be applied elsewhere for the public good. In a time of limited resources, this approach, properly run, simply makes sense.

No matter whether an organization chooses to become entrepreneurially focused, defensively focused, cooperatively focused, or a mixture of all three approaches as a strategy to meet the challenges of scarce resources, sound leadership, management, and governance practices are the real keys to organizational survival and impact. Required are the combined efforts of the organization's board, the chief executive, the staff, the volunteers, and the broad-based support constituency.

Yes, nonprofit organizations may well be in the throes of a major sea change. And the challenges they face are great. While being subjected to tremendous pressures and jostling in recent years, some of which are beyond their control, there is every indication nonprofit organizations are here to stay. They are here to stay because, collectively, they represent a truly significant force for good. These organizations have had a commendable record of providing much-needed services in this country, long before the governmental and for-profit sectors entered the picture. Thinking, informed people in the country realize and appreciate the great importance of the nonprofit sector and how diminished this country would be without it.

Nonprofit leaders and those who serve these organizations in voluntary and supportive capacities owe it to the many millions of people they serve to see to it that the challenges and issues the sector now faces are turned into opportunities—opportunities to better meet the untold human needs and to enhance the quality of life for all. But this movement from challenge to decisive, purposeful, and productive response will only come about through the efforts of well-trained, motivated, and committed leaders, managers, staff, and volunteers. They must all be vigilant in remaining responsive to the ever-changing environment, in finding ways to secure the resources their organizations need to operate effectively, and in assuring that those resources are judiciously managed and allocated where they can do the most good.

Even though resources are scarce, given the comprehensive array of services being provided by the nonprofit sector, the aggregated expenditures are large. Many billions of dollars flow to and through nonprofit organizations annually to help meet the diverse needs of the population in this country and around the world. The stakes are high for the nonprofit sector to deliver on the vast monetary and human investment being made. There is a growing expectation, even a mandate, that these resources will be employed in purposeful and productive ways.

In order to measure up to this mandate, each nonprofit organization must clearly determine why the organization exists, its purpose and reason for being; develop appropriate goals and objectives derived from the organization's stated mission; establish priorities and selected target areas for services and products; set standards and measurements of performance; set deadlines for projects; hold individuals (staff, board, and volunteers) accountable for defined areas of responsibility; use measurements as feedback in programs, thereby promoting adjustments and fine-tuning mechanisms into the system; and audit the objectives and their results in an effort to identify the objectives that no longer serve a purpose or that have proven unattainable.

Also, it is believed that nonprofit boards are going to have to focus their efforts on what they are best equipped to do and should do rather than dabbling in areas that ought to be the responsibility of management. More boards should concentrate their efforts on setting broad policies and goals; seeing to it that the organization had adequate resources to function properly; assuming responsibility for strategic long-range planning; committing to their fiduciary responsibilities; serving as a bridge between the larger community and society and the organization; and hiring the executive director, delegating the total day-to-day running of the organization to her or him, monitoring and evaluating her or his performance, and, based on a fair and objective performance appraisal, retaining or removing her or him. (It is realized that some nonprofit organizations are run only by volunteers. Obviously, in such organizations this latter point would not apply.)

It is believed that such a clear division of responsibilities between the board and the executive director will be a key factor to secure the future success of nonprofit organizations.

The job of effectively and efficiently operating nonprofit organizations will never be quite the same again. Yet the opportunities remain great for those who have the capacity and the will to take on that challenge.

While there are those who question the very concept and legitimacy of nonprofit organizations in this society, this writer, looking ahead to the 1990s, sees many promising signs for a strong, vibrant, and dynamic nonprofit sector. Such a prospect can materialize. What is required is for the leaders of the millions of individual nonprofit organizations nationwide to be assisted in finding ways to further develop their capacities in order to move to new and higher levels of expertise, productivity, and achievement.

This bright prospect is one reason why I was so willing to accept the invitation extended to me by Tracy Connors to write the foreword to this newly revised and expanded edition of *The Nonprofit Organization Handbook.* When the first edition of the *Handbook* was published in 1980, it was then a long overdue and sorely needed volume. Given the dramatically increasing challenges facing nonprofit organizations and their leaders today, this new edition of the *Handbook* will surely receive a warm welcome.

Anyone interested in helping to advance nonprofit organizations will find the *Handbook* a valuable educational resource, one of the few "must have, must read" publications of its kind. This comprehensive volume will help to assure a healthy and vigorous nonprofit sector.

James R. Burnham
PRESIDENT
THE SOCIETY FOR NONPROFIT ORGANIZATIONS
MADISON, WISCONSIN

Acknowledgments

The overall quality of life in America is created in large part by volunteers, tens of thousands of dedicated and concerned citizens who give so remarkably of their time, talent, and money to improve public health, the arts, education, and religion to name a few. We owe an enormous debt to them for their vital contributions to the spirit of America.

In the same spirit, the contributors to this edition of the *Handbook* are special people who have shared their wealth of experience in voluntary action organizations to help improve the overall quality of management by nonprofit organizations. Maintaining our quality of life in the face of growing demands for more services while government funding trends are falling will be an enormous challenge in coming years. More effective management by NPO volunteers and professional staff will be necessary if these needs are to be met—and our country's quality of life maintained.

Since publication of the first edition of the *Handbook* in 1980, the voluntary action sector has grown and changed to reflect the times and needs of our people. Expanding the *Handbook* and refocusing its coverage to meet changing needs was a major consideration during planning for the second edition. Thanks to the support of editor William Sabin, and to the professional guidance and highly effective coordination applied by Faith Raymond Connors and Nancy Young, that reorientation has taken place. The second edition contains more relevant material for NPO leaders and should be an even more valuable reference than its predecessor.

Tracy Daniel Connors

The Nonprofit
Organization
Handbook

PART 1

Organization and Corporate Principles

1
The Nonprofit Sector

David Horton Smith

Ph.D., Professor of Sociology, Boston College

Burt R. Baldwin

Ph.D., Professor, Department of Sociology, Central Connecticut State University

Eugene D. White

Research Associate, Association of Voluntary Action Scholars

Defining the Nonprofit Organization

Nonprofit organizations (NPOs) vary widely in structure and purpose. This makes it difficult to formulate a definition that embraces them all. Most people believe that they understand what nonprofit organizations are because they hear about them so often or have worked for or belonged to one or more of them. Our experience, however, has been that most people have a very narrow and restrictive view of the NPO.

The essential element of an NPO is voluntary action. Voluntary action is what one is neither paid to do nor made to do. In their broadest sense, NPOs are simply the collective forms of individual voluntary action. That is, NPOs are the vehicles by means of which people pursue together goals that are not primarily remunerative and that they are not forced to pursue.

NPOs, therefore, are significantly different from *for*-profit organizations, in which people together pursue remunerative goals. They are different, too, from governments, which are based ultimately on coercion. And they are different from families, which are socialized manifestations of physiological compulsions.

NPOs may be either informal—unstructured groups and associations—or formal—structured organizations with an explicit leadership, a proper name, and clear membership boundaries. This handbook deals only with the more formal or organized groups. Even so, formally organized NPOs are more numerous and varied than the average NPO leader generally assumes. Most NPO leaders tend to see the term NPO as referring mainly, if not exclusively, to the larger, well-established, incorporated, tax-exempt organizations. This is far too narrow a view to do justice to the reality of the nonprofit sector in America.

There are, in fact, probably 7 to 8 million NPOs in the United States today. The vast majority of these NPOs are not separately incorporated, let alone registered with the Internal Revenue Service as exempt organizations (EOs). Most of these NPOs are local units of some larger, usually national, NPO. As such, they either do not feel the need for separate incorporation or they consider themselves to be covered by the incorporation of their national association (e.g., local Red Cross chapters and the American National Red Cross).

Local NPOs that are small associations with little or no wealth and no connection with any state or national association often find it simply a waste of time and money to go through the formal incorporation process in their state. Such NPOs nevertheless often have constitutions, by-laws, or articles of association. There are advantages to obtaining legal incorporation, of course, but there are also disadvantages. The decision to incorporate is one that each NPO must make for itself. And it is a decision that should be reconsidered periodically in the light of NPO growth, even if the initial decision is *not* to incorporate. This whole issue of incorporation will be dealt with in more detail in Chapters 3 to 5.

Even when an NPO has legally incorporated, as relatively few do generally, it may still not apply for exempt status from the Internal Revenue Service. The IRS has listings for only about one-tenth or fewer of American NPOs. Again, it is the small NPO and the NPO that is a local unit of some national NPO that seldom registers with the IRS and obtains formal EO status. The IRS is simply not concerned with NPOs that have annual budgets under $10,000. Although all NPOs are supposed to register with the IRS, whatever their size, most smaller NPOs simply do not bother, and the IRS does not have the resources or, at present, the inclination to do anything about it. For larger NPOs—those with budgets in excess of $10,000 and with significant assets—registration with the IRS is strongly advised, and the obtaining of formal EO status is recommended.

An NPO Typology: Development and Use

Nonprofit organizations are developing in an ever more bewildering variety. For both student and practitioner, it is important to have a means by which to categorize NPOs in general or in particular. The typology which follows has been derived and revised several times over the past decade from the authors' research on NPOs, from the local level through national and international levels.

The main thrust of the typology is to capture in a relatively modest number of broad categories the general purposes that an NPO has been formed to pursue. The typology can be used in two basic ways:

1. *Central purpose.* The typology can be used to classify NPOs according to their single most central purpose, given that most NPOs have more than one purpose. Used this way, however, the typology can capture only somewhat crudely what an NPO is all about.

2. *Primary purpose.* The typology can be used to classify NPOs according to their

primary purposes, or even in terms of *all* their basic purposes, whether primary or secondary. This is a more sophisticated and accurate approach.

In using the typology the second way, each NPO being classified would be allowed to fall into *more* than one (although usually only a few) of the major categories of the scheme. For example, the nonprofit organization CARE might be classified under the categories of International and Transnational Affairs, Other-Helping Social Welfare, and Fund-Raising and/or Fund Allocation-Distribution NPOs, since CARE is heavily involved in all three of these purposive areas. To classify it, or many other complex and multipurpose NPOs, in a *single* category of the typology fails to do it justice.

We recommend, therefore, that the typology be used generally in the second manner, allowing each NPO to receive at least three or four category designations, where relevant. The last category, Multipurpose, General, and Other NPOs, should be used *only* when the number of type designations allowed is inadequate to describe a given NPO (as will happen with significant frequency if only one type of designation is allowed for each NPO).

Note that certain "commonsense" categories of NPOs are omitted from the typology as major categories, although they will always fit into a subcategory. For instance, no broad category appears for NPOs that deal with the aged or with children or youth because the *type* of client or member of an NPO does not determine its purpose. NPOs *of* and *for* both the aged and youth cover the full range of major purposes in the typology. Therefore, to state that an NPO deals primarily with or has as members the aged, youth, or children says little about its real purposes.

For other reasons, we do not list as broad-purpose categories veterans organizations or Greek letter societies, which are often used as major-purpose categories by some authorities (e.g., the *Encyclopedia of Associations* published by Gale Research Company, Detroit, Michigan). Though quite common in the United States and meaningfully distinct from other types of NPOs, such groups are simply commonsense subcategories of our much broader-purpose category, Expressive-Leisure NPOs. In fact, both commonsense types fall into one of five major subtypes within the Expressive-Leisure category (i.e., sociability and fellowship groups). The point is that these two commonsense kinds of Expressive-Leisure NPOs have more common elements with other sociability and fellowship groups than they have differences as far as their basic purposes and operations are concerned.

In short, although often guided by commonsense, or "natural," (conventionally used) categories in creating the present typology, we went beyond that and did some hard thinking about whether certain kinds of *apparently* different commonsense categories of NPOs are *really* and basically different in their purposes. When careful examination, including empirical studies over the years, showed difference to be more apparent than real, commonsense distinctions were overruled. In creating the typology, distinctions that make no difference were eliminated.

It is important in applying the typology to note carefully the variations in purposes *within* a given NPO—a matter that becomes clear only when substantial information about the NPO is considered, not merely its name. For instance, the *original,* officially stated purposes of an NPO and the *present* actual objectives usually differ. Times change, and the circumstances and functions of NPOs change with them. Even *currently stated objectives* may differ from *actual objectives* of an NPO as pursued through the allocation of its resources of money, personnel, and the like.

Like individuals, NPOs do not always practice what they preach; nor are they always what they think they are or would like to present themselves as being. The best (or worst) examples of this are NPOs pretending to be charities that are really fraudulent organizations with schemes to bilk the public (and there have been a few examples in recent years). Similarly, there have been, and probably still are, some NPOs that are really "fronts" for government-related intelligence-gathering agencies, whether of the U.S. government or other governments. Quite aside from these stark examples, it is fairly common to find milder discrepancies between stated and actual objectives of NPOs. Often, NPO leaders themselves are unaware of the discrepancy. It would be enlightening in many cases if each member of the board of directors of an NPO used the typology independently to classify the organization and then compared answers. The differences in perceiving the goals and/or objectives of the organization (i.e., its type) might vary considerably. The extent of variation would be the degree to which the organization needed a major reevaluation of goals and objectives, or at the very least, a more effective communication of goals and objectives among its leaders.

A final point regarding variations in purposes *within* an NPO has to do with different levels of NPO organization. This point is especially germane to the approximately 14,000 national voluntary organizations and associations currently existing in the United States. These NPOs are "national" in the sense that they attempt to deal with problems or address issues that affect the whole nation, and/or that they have members, participants, or contributors from more than ten states. In such NPOs, there are often state and local branches of the organization, whether they are called chapters, divisions, or whatever. Such lower-level units of national NPOs often have considerable autonomy; indeed, they may even be separately incorporated in their various respective states.

The purposes of the national NPO perceived or defined at its national headquarters may therefore be quite different from the purposes perceived and defined at lower unit levels. This means that although it may be quite correct to classify a particular *local* Sierra Club chapter solely in the Expressive-Leisure category, the *national* Sierra Club must be classified in the *additional* categories of Environmental and Ecological Welfare NPOs and Political Action NPOs. Similar variations by territorial level of inclusiveness of the NPO unit also apply as one moves from national NPOs to international NPOs, where purpose discrepancies often appear.

The principal categories of our typology of broad NPO purposes, include examples of subtypes for each category. It is important to note, however, that the subtype examples are intended to be *representative of volunteer NPOs, not of paid-staff NPOs.*

An NPO Typology: Principal Categories

1. Community Service and Action NPOs

Community service and action NPOs aim primarily toward improving or sustaining either the general physical characteristics of a community or the general economic and social life of its residents. Although particular programs may be quite specific and focused, these organizations tend to view and legitimate their programs not merely as ends in themselves, but rather to see such programs within a broader community perspective.

The programs involved are often multipurpose, and tend to try to improve the overall quality of life of people in a specific community. The territory encompassed by the term "community" can vary greatly—from a neighborhood to a large city or metropolitan area. The NPOs categorized here differ from other problem-oriented NPOs in being more multipurposive (i.e., cutting across problem areas) and more clearly focused on a particular *territory* and its residents. There are several basic subtypes of community service and action NPOs.

Volunteer NPO examples include:

  a. Civic service groups (service group activity of general community relevance
   but without necessary focus on a single problem; includes youth and school-
   related civic service clubs as well as adult clubs such as Rotary and
   Soroptimists)

  b. Community development groups (groups concerned with general institutional
   and socioeconomic improvement of community)

  c. Neighborhood-improvement groups (groups concerned with the preservation
   and enhancement of social and other characteristics of a neighborhood or
   community improvement)

  d. Governance groups with citizen participation (direct involvement of neighborhood and/or resident groups in local decision making)

  e. General policy discussion and planning groups with citizen involvement (conferences, meetings, media, and/or mail-facilitated systems for citizens to make
   their ideas known to local leaders; health and welfare planning councils)

  f. Community protection groups (law enforcement and crime prevention NPOs
   in a community; vigilante groups; volunteer fire departments; community volunteer patrols)

2. Other-Helping Health NPOs

Other-helping health NPOs aim primarily at preserving and enhancing
nonmembers' physical and/or mental health in a broad sense, including illness and
accident prevention, treatment of health problems (medical or paramedical roles),
aftercare, and rehabilitation. (Social welfare problem organizations are classified
under category 7.)
   Volunteer NPO examples include:

  a. Programs in institutional in-patient settings (such as general, psychiatric, and
   other kinds of hospitals, clinics, and nursing homes)

  b. Programs in community settings (such as residential aftercare facilities, rehabilitation centers, community mental health centers, and mental retardation
   facilities)

  c. Health research- and treatment-supporting agencies and organizations (such
   as the American Heart Association, March of Dimes, American Cancer Society,
   and Easter Seal Society)

  d. Groups operating special health care or rehabilitation programs autonomously
   (such as crisis and suicide hotlines, volunteer ambulance corps, storefront
   health care drop-in centers, community health-monitoring programs,
   homebound handicapped- and invalid-care programs, and the Visiting Nurse
   Association volunteer staff/board)

  e. Illness- and accident-prevention groups (such as safety groups)

3. Other-Helping Educational NPOs

Educational NPOs have as their primary goal the education or increased learning
and knowledge of nonmembers; these groups are either included directly in the
educational process or contribute to it in some way, as in helping with the administration of that process.

Volunteer NPO examples include:

a. School educational programs (such as teachers' aides)

b. School-related tutoring programs

c. School-serving student groups (such as student government and school service clubs)

d. Preschool and nursery school programs (*not* mere day care or baby sitting which are classified under category 7)

e. General adult education programs (such as free schools, free universities, street colleges, folk schools, alternative schools, community schools, adult literacy training and right-to-read programs)

f. Workplace-related or union-related adult education programs

g. Church, synagogue, or other religious education programs for youths or adults (such as Sunday schools and Hebrew day schools)

h. Political party or other political education programs

i. School- or college-related general scholastic honorary societies (such as Phi Beta Kappa and Phi Kappa Phi)

j. School or college alumni associations

k. Parent-Teachers' Associations (PTA)

l. Parents' or citizens' advisory councils for schools

m. School boards (usually for all schools in town or other area)

4. Personal-Growth, Self-Development, Self-Improvement NPOs

Personal-growth NPOs focus on the character, personality, and skill development of individual members in a broad sense, principally through self-help and experiential learning rather than formal education.

Volunteer NPO examples include:

a. Youth self-development organizations (such as Boy Scouts, Girl Scouts, Camp Fire Girls, 4H, Boys and Girls Clubs, and YMCA/YWCA)

b. Adult self-development organizations (such as Toastmasters, Toastmistresses, encounter groups, meditation groups, Great Books discussion groups, and consciousness-raising and self-awareness groups)

5. Communication- and Information-Dissemination NPOs

Communication- and information-dissemination NPOs focus on transmitting information to nonmembers through the mass media, documents, or personal consultation.

Volunteer NPO examples include:

a. Public relations, public awareness, and informal public education groups which deal with the public at large *b.* Technical-assistance information groups which provide information to the public in contact (such as libraries and other document-providing organizations)

c. Information-referral groups which direct the public in contact to technical-assistance information sources or other sources of help

6. Scientific, Technical, Engineering, and Learned NPOs

Scientific, technical, engineering, and learned NPOs aim primarily toward accumulating or reorganizing existing knowledge and producing new knowledge, inventions, or discoveries regarding the natural world. (Study of the supernatural world is classified under category 15.) The natural world includes physical and biological as well as social and psychological systems and events. Members of these groups are, in general, involved directly in research and development. Amateurs and hobbyists may be included *only* if the production of new knowledge through search and experimentation (rather than mere practice of the activity) is crucial to the involvement.

Volunteer NPO examples include:

a. Professional associations of specialists in a particular scientific or technical field, including engineering

b. Professional associations in fields of humanistic studies

c. Honorary scientific or learned societies

d. Nonprofit research centers or groups with voluntary staff or boards

7. Other-Helping Social Welfare NPOs

Other-helping social welfare NPOs (dealing with social services, social concerns, and social problems) are oriented primarily toward providing for the general welfare (survival, satisfaction, improvement, etc.) of some category of nonmembers facing serious social problems and dissatisfactions because of their social situation. Although these organizations may validly see themselves working for the good of and the improvement of the whole community (as in category 1), their prime focus and the prime legitimation of their activity is not the community as a whole but rather service to particular categories of persons seen as having special needs, problems, or requirements. (Health-problem organizations are classified under category 2; self-help groups under category 8.)

Volunteer NPO examples include:

a. Basic survival problem groups (such as those dealing with jobs and employment, food and nutrition, shelter and housing, clothing, transportation, travel assistance, traffic safety, maintenance, repair, and construction, poverty and dependency, and cemetery facilities)

b. Emergency survival problem groups (such as those providing aid to refugees, immigrants, homeless people, and disaster victims or assisting in civil defense emergency preparedness and emergency monitoring)

c. Marriage and family problem groups (such as those dealing with family counseling, marriage counseling, emergency child care, day care, baby sitting, adoption, foster parents, population control, youth and children's counseling, counseling for family planning, birth control, or abortion, and shelter for runaways and unwed mothers)

d. Friendship relations problem and social isolation problem groups (such as Big Brothers, Big Sisters, and Foster Grandparents; and others providing friendly visiting; personal relationships with children, youth, adults, and aged with special needs; general therapeutic friendship programs; and neighborhood houses)

e. Intergroup relations problem groups (such as those dealing with civil rights and interracial and interethnic problems)

f. Legal aid and legal rights problem groups (such as public interest law groups)

g. Crime and delinquency problem groups (such as those working in courts and prisons)

h. Drug and alcohol abuse groups (such as those providing assistance to the abusers)

i. Other personal problem adjustment or rehabilitation groups (such as those providing counseling for homosexuals, the mentally retarded, the deformed, the very tall, the obese, midgets or dwarfs, and others; as well as halfway houses of various kinds)

j. Volunteer recruitment, training, placement, or screening groups (such as volunteer bureaus or voluntary action centers)

k. Consulting and technical-assistance groups (such as those giving aid to individuals or groups)

8. Self-Help Disadvantaged and Minority NPOs

Self-help disadvantaged and minority NPOs have members from racial and ethnic minorities, the poor, women, and other disadvantaged groups. Examples of disadvantaged persons represented by such NPOs include blacks, Chicanos (Mexican-Americans), Cubans, other Latin Americans, Native Americans (American Indians), some white ethnics (Poles, Slavs, Germans, French-Canadians, Swedes, etc.), the unemployed, tenants in poor housing, the aged (senior citizens), the handicapped (including the disabled or sick), mental patients, former mental patients, the uneducated and illiterate, the mentally retarded, convicts, ex-convicts, delinquents, drug addicts, former drug addicts, alcoholics and others with alcohol problems, obese and overweight people, very short or very tall people, homosexuals, transvestites, transsexuals, atheists, agnostics, other religious minority groups often discriminated against (Jews, new sects, small sects), the disenfranchised, abused children, neglected children, separated or divorced fathers or mothers, unwed mothers or fathers, the separated, the divorced, the widowed in general, migrant workers, and immigrants.

These NPOs are generally oriented toward improving the common welfare and quality of life of their members either through changing themselves (in the case of behavioral, social, or psychological deviance from societal norms) or through changing society's perceptions and treatment of people like themselves (usually, but not always, in the case of physical or biological deviance from societal norms), or both.

These NPOs differ from deviant or criminal NPOs (category 16) in that the latter are not trying to change their deviant status. These NPOs also differ from the self-improvement NPOs (category 4) in that, unlike the members of the present kind of disadvantaged self-help NPOs, the members of self-improvement self-help groups are *not* generally disadvantaged persons trying to deal with a generally recognized and serious personal problem. The self-help disadvantaged groups may or may not be political action groups as well.

9. Political Action NPOs

Political action NPOs, as defined here, are concerned primarily with influencing the legislative, executive, or judicial aspects of the political process in their social system or society at some territorial level. Such groups may participate directly in legislative, executive, or judicial roles in the system or attempt to influence directly or indirectly (i.e., by affecting public opinion) those who participate directly in such roles. Attempts to influence the political process may take many forms, ranging from conventional letter writing and lobbying, to symbolic protest and civil disobedience, to public demonstrations and protest of all sorts, including violence and other extreme and unconventional or illegal protest activity.

Volunteer NPO examples include:

a. Political awareness and general political involvement groups (such as the League of Women Voters)

b. Partisan political clubs and political parties

c. Political campaign programs, groups, or committees (whether for a recognized party slate or party candidate or for a candidate without party affiliation)

d. Political issue advocacy, political pressure and influence, public interest, civil rights, lobbying and other similar political-social action groups (whether advocating change or stability)

e. Underground, resistance, and terrorist political action groups

10. Environmental and Ecological Welfare NPOs

Environmental and ecological welfare NPOs include those that aim primarily toward preserving, limiting further damage to, restoring, and improving the prehuman, "natural" state of affairs in parks, forests, and wilderness areas. This category also includes NPOs that attempt to deal with problems humans create (pollution and destruction of natural states of the environment in urban areas or elsewhere) and those concerned with land use and other resource- and energy-conservation problems. (Population control NPOs are classified under category 7*c.*)

Volunteer NPO examples include:

a. Natural area and wilderness preservation groups; wetlands, forest, and soil conservation groups; fish, game, and wildlife preservation groups; parks groups, and domestic animal protection (humane society, etc.) groups

b. Environmental pollution abatement groups (air, water, noise, heat, radiation)

c. Recycling, sanitation, solid-waste-disposal groups

d. Environmental beautification and cleanup groups; rat control and other pest control groups *e.* Land use planning and control and facility siting groups; highway and public transportation groups

  f. Energy system development and resource conservation, planning, or management groups; large-scale or world ecosystem preservation groups (such as those dealing with ozone layer preservation, preventing desertification, and controlling biological warfare)

11. Consumer Welfare NPOs

Consumer welfare NPOs are concerned with aiding the consumer in various ways to redress the balance of power in a mass industrial society in which large producers or providers of materials, goods, or services are usually operating on a *caveat emptor* principle without sufficient regard for the rights or well-being of the customers, clients, and purchasers involved.

  Volunteer NPO examples include:

  a. Personal consumer advice and counseling (prepurchase and postpurchase) groups and consumer debt and financial counseling groups

  b. Consumer advocacy and activism groups and consumerism groups

  c. Consumer protection research and public education groups (such as Consumers Union)

  d. Consumer cooperatives

  e. Credit unions (volunteer boards) and nonprofit mutual life insurance associations (volunteer boards)

12. International and Transnational Affairs NPOs

International and transnational affairs NPOs are concerned with people in countries other than their own and with their own country's relations with the people and institutions of other countries. Transnational affairs NPOs may be concerned with only one other country, whereas international affairs NPOs are concerned with the transnational relations of three or more countries. A variety of aspects of other countries and one's own may be of central interest.

  Volunteer NPO examples include:

  a. Development assistance and technical transfer and assistance groups

  b. Humanitarian assistance and relief aid groups and medical assistance groups

  c. Cultural exchange, understanding, and friendship groups, scientific or technical exchange groups, and student exchange groups

  d. Foreign affairs and foreign policy analysis, discussion, or study groups

  e. Peace groups (both general pacifist or antiwar groups and groups opposed to specific wars)

  f. Conflict, war, rebellion, and related transnational disruption groups

  g. Religious missionary groups working abroad

  h. Political advocacy and exile political action groups

  i. Expansion of trade and commerce abroad groups

13. Occupation-Related NPOs

Occupation-oriented NPOs are all concerned basically with the restoration, preservation, or enhancement of socioeconomic conditions and the general welfare of members of a particular kind of paid or profit-seeking work activity, including paid workers in the government, voluntary, and business sectors.

Volunteer NPO examples include:

a. Business, trade, industrial, government, paraprofessional, and professional associations (volunteer boards and sometimes volunteer staff)

b. Agricultural and husbandry owner or manager associations

c. Labor unions and employee associations such as farm labor or peasant unions, blue-collar unions and white-collar workers' groups (all are lower-level employee associations)

14. Expressive-Leisure NPOs

Expressive-leisure NPOs' main goal is to have fun or facilitate having fun and enjoying an activity for its own sake. The subtypes vary in *how* this enjoyment is achieved, but all involve expressing the need for play and personal expression during leisure time as part of an organized group of like-minded people.

Volunteer NPO examples include:

a. Sports, athletic, and recreational groups (such as sports teams and leagues, country clubs, community centers, and outdoor recreation groups for hunting, fishing, hiking, and other activities)

b. Hobbies and games groups (such as collectors of various items; clubs for playing cards and other indoor parlor games; and groups for gardening and plants, for raising, breeding, or showing domestic animals, or for making things)

c. Entertainment and spectatorship groups (such as movie, theater, concert, or lecture attendance clubs; tourism and travel clubs; sports events attendance clubs; reading clubs; fan clubs; and other associations of *consumers* of entertainment)

d. Artistic, literary, musical, cultural, and other esthetic groups (such as "little theater" groups; chorales and other musical groups; literary discussion groups; graphic and plastic arts societies; local historical societies; ethnic or folk art or music groups; and other associations of *producers* of entertainment and esthetic experience)

e. Sociability and fellowship groups (such as military and veterans' groups; lodges and fraternal groups; school social fraternities and sororities; genealogical and kinship-based associations with a social orientation; pen pal clubs; groups of retired occupational specialists; miscellaneous social clubs; general associations of notables; other associations in which interpersonal relations are primary; and nationality or ethnic social groups)

15. Religious and Related NPOs

Religious or ideological-ethical NPOs have as their primary purpose the understanding, affirmation, and ritualized practice of an ideological belief-sentiment system (e.g., theology, cosmology) regarding the universe as a whole or some significant subsector thereof. The guiding theology or ideology, whether it be religious or secular, pervades all aspects of group activity. An ethical ideology may replace or accompany the cosmology (or theology) usually involved.

Volunteer NPO examples include:

a. Churches, synagogues, and associated committees

b. Church- or synagogue-connected religious concern, study, or worship clubs, societies, and groups

c. Philosophical, ideological, and ethical groups

16. Deviant and Criminal NPOs

Deviant and criminal NPOs are those whose primary purpose is to engage in activities (e.g., violence or damage to other people or property) that have been defined as inappropriate or illegal by the larger society (usually by legislative, administrative, regulatory, or judicial agencies) and that are done *not* primarily as an occupational (profit-seeking) activity. These NPOs thus differ from "professional" (i.e., occupational) criminal gangs or syndicates. Deviant NPOs need not necessarily operate covertly but generally tend to do so; otherwise their members tend to be caught and legally sanctioned or made to conform, and the NPO is disbanded.

Volunteer NPO examples include:

a. Youth or adult gangs concerned primarily with theft, violence, or other illegal activity for its own sake

b. Underground resistance, terrorist, or guerrilla groups

c. Sexually or morally deviant groups

17. Fund-raising and Fund Allocation or Distribution NPOs

Fund-raising and fund allocation or distribution NPOs are those whose central purpose is either to obtain charitable contributions from individuals and/or organizations for a given general or specific purpose(s), or to distribute charitable funds to individuals and/or groups (usually NPOs, sometimes families) for a given general or specific purpose(s); or to do *both* fund-raising and fund distribution.

Volunteer NPO examples include:

a. Groups concerned with helping individuals or other groups to raise funds

b. Fund allocation or distribution groups involving volunteers (such as foundation or trust boards of directors and volunteer staff; special funding disbursement projects or groups; and United Ways and United Funds or equivalent federated fund-raising campaigns using volunteers in the fund *allocation* process)

c. Broad, federated, multipurpose fund-raising agencies involving volunteers (such as United Ways, Combined Jewish Appeals, Catholic Charities, and Black United Funds)

d. Single-purpose federated fund-raising agencies involving volunteers (such as Combined Health Agency drives, United Negro College Fund, and International Aid drives)

e. Single-purpose *non*federated autonomous fund-raising agencies (such as American Cancer Society, March of Dimes, Easter Seal Society, and scholarship-providing funds)

f. Fund-raising volunteer groups associated with an institution for which they are raising the funds (such as a hospital, church, school, or museum)

g. Ad hoc groups raising funds for some particular person(s) thought to have special problems or needs (such as groups raising funds for certain widows, a sick person needing special expensive care, or a political candidate needing campaign funds)

18. Multipurpose, General, and Other NPOs

Multipurpose, general, and other NPOs include those that cannot be adequately or meaningfully classified as belonging primarily to one of the foregoing specific types of NPOs but place relatively equal emphasis on two or more different goal types. This category is used particularly when the NPO has more than three main goals in terms of the foregoing categories. In this case, two specific goal types plus the present category are used if relevant. In some cases, *only* the multipurpose category may be relevant.

2

The Impact of the Nonprofit Voluntary Sector on Society*

David Horton Smith

Ph.D., Professor of Sociology, Boston College

There are many ways of looking at the impact of nonprofit voluntary organizations (NPOs), from the level of the individual up to the highest currently applicable level of impact of voluntarism, on society as a whole. In looking at the impact of NPOs, it is all too easy to get lost among the *trees,* thus losing sight of the *forest.* In our view, the "forest" is the larger context of social meaning that nonprofit organizations and voluntary action both have in human society. By "social" we mean to include all aspects of the structure and culture of our society, and by "society" we mean to include not just American society or any other particular society, but all of humankind, past, present, and (hopefully) future.

The "voluntary sector," or "nonprofit sector," refers to all those persons, groups, roles, organizations, and institutions in society whose goals involve primarily voluntary action, particularly all nonprofit organizations. The term "voluntary action," roughly speaking, includes what one is neither made to nor paid to do but rather what one does out of some kind of expectation of psychic benefits or because of commitment to some value, ideal, or common interest. The voluntary sector may be roughly delineated in a negative way by contrasting it with the commercial or business sector (sometimes called the "private sector") and with the government or "public sector." Another way of describing the voluntary sector is to say that it is the total persisting social embodiment (in the form of norms, ex-

*From chap. 14 (with revisions) of David H. Smith (Ed.), *Voluntary Action Research: 1973,* Lexington Books, Lexington, Mass., 1973. This is one of the annual review volumes sponsored by the Association of Voluntary Action Scholars, Lincoln Filene Center, Tufts University, Medford, Mass. 02155. Reprinted here with permission of the publisher.

2.1

pectations, customs, and ways of behaving) of voluntary action in society, mainly organized in the form of not-for-profit organizations.

Our question here is, simply: What impact does the nonprofit, voluntary sector as a whole have on society? Because of insufficient research information, we can only do the sketchiest global analysis, based on a loose inductive logic and general theoretical considerations.

Another way of looking at what we shall call the impacts of the voluntary sector is to see the processes behind these impacts and to term them the "functions," or "roles," of the voluntary sector. These processes are not *necessary* features of the voluntary sector in any given nation, let alone in all nations. However, they do show what the voluntary sector *can* do and often *has* done in the past in particular societies at particular times. This is an attempt to help delineate more clearly *why there is a voluntary sector in society,* much as one might elsewhere discuss the role of government institutions or business or even the family in society. Like all the latter, of course, the role of the voluntary sector changes over time in a given society and even in human society as a whole. Nevertheless, the impacts of the voluntary sector we discuss briefly below are suggested as very general aspects of the voluntary sector in human society, and hence they are present to at least some degree as long as there is a voluntary sector and nonprofit organizations.

The Positive Side

Social Innovations

First, one of the most central impacts of the voluntary sector is to provide society with a wide variety of partially tested social innovations, from which business, government, and other institutions can select and institutionalize those innovations which seem most promising. The independent voluntary sector is thus the prototyping test bed of many, perhaps most, new social forms and modes of human relations. Whereas business and government and science and technology are active in the creation and testing of *technological innovations,* the independent voluntary sector specializes in the practical testing of new *social ideas.* Nearly every function currently performed at various levels by governments was once a new social idea and the experiment of some voluntary nonprofit group, formal or informal. This is true for advances in education, welfare, care for the aged, building roads—even fighting wars (volunteer citizen militias).

In sum, the voluntary sector has tended to be the social risk "capital" of human society. It has remained sufficiently free of the kinds of constraints that bind business (the constant need to show a profit) and government (the need to maintain control and, in societies with effective democracies, the need to act in accord with a broad consensus) so that its component elements (particular nonprofit, voluntary groups or individuals) can act simply out of commitment to some value or idea, without needing to wait until the payoffs for that kind of activity can be justified in terms appropriate to mobilizing economic or governmental institutions. It is thus the most error-embracing and experimental component of society (see Smith with Dixon, 1973).

Countervailing Definitions of Reality and Morality

A *second* central impact of the voluntary sector on society is that it provides a forum for countervailing definitions of reality and morality—ideologies, perspectives, and world views—that frequently challenge the prevailing assumptions about what exists and what is good and what should be done in society. The voluntary sector is that part of society which collectively is most likely to say that "the emperor has no clothes." Voluntary nonprofit groups of various kinds are distinctive among human groups in the extent to which they develop their own ideologies and value systems. If these definitions of reality and morality are sufficiently compelling to people, voluntary nonprofit groups grow into huge social movements and can change the course of history, both within a given nation (e.g., the abolitionist movement in the early and middle nineteenth century in the United States) and across human society as a whole (e.g., Christianity, Buddhism, democracy, communism).

This kind of impact of the voluntary sector is related to the previous one, but whereas the former kind of impact emphasized experimentation with social innovation in practice, this impact emphasizes instead ideological and moral innovation. Whereas the previous point focused on the role of the voluntary sector as the social risk capital of society, the present point focuses on the role of the voluntary sector as a gadfly, dreamer, and moral leader in society. Voluntary nonprofit groups of various kinds are concerned with the generation and allocation of human commitment in the deepest sense. In the process of doing this, the voluntary sector as a whole provides moral and ideological leadership to the majority of human society and often calls into question the legitimacy of existing structures and the accepted social definitions of reality in particular societies.

The "Play Element"

A *third* major impact of the voluntary sector on society is that it provides for the recreational, or play, element in society: The search for novelty, beauty, recreation, and fun—each for its own sake—may be collectively organized in nonprofit organizations. Again, because the voluntary sector is not constrained generally by such values as profit, control, and broad social consensus, voluntary nonprofit groups can organize to represent literally thousands of different kinds of common interests. A full array of common-interest groups (for leisure-related purposes) in an elaborated but still evolving voluntary sector permits (in principle) nearly all individuals to find at least one nonprofit group that will provide enjoyment. If there is no such group, one or more individuals may form one, if they wish, to reflect their own needs and vision of the play element. Such a group may be formal or informal, large or small, permanent or transient, open or closed, and so forth.

To speak of the play element here is not to speak of something trivial and unimportant. As society becomes increasingly complex and as work activity grows increasingly structured within the large bureaucracies, people's unsatisfied needs for play, novelty, new experience, and all manner of recreation tend to increase. The kind of easy interchange and blending of play and work that could be present in more traditional economies tends to be lost. Under such circumstances voluntary nonprofit groups often provide a window of variety and intrinsic satisfaction in an otherwise rather boring, or at least psychically fatiguing, world of work and responsibility.

Social Integration

Fourth, the voluntary sector also has a major impact on the level of social integration in society. Partly through directly "expressive" nonprofit groups, whose aims are explicitly to provide fellowship, sociability, and mutual companionship, and partly through the sociability aspects of all other kinds of collective and interpersonal forms of voluntary action, the voluntary sector helps in a very basic way to satisfy some of the human needs for affiliation, approval, and so on. In advanced industrial and urbanized societies, where the family and kinship as well as the local community and neighborhood play a markedly reduced role in providing social integration, affiliations based on common interests can become very important to the individual. Indeed, without the latter kind of common-interest affiliations rooted in the voluntary sector, the resulting increase in social isolation of the individual in society would lead to even more anomie, or alienation, and a variety of attendant social and psychological problems than are now the case.

Obviously, the voluntary nonprofit sector is not the whole solution to the root problem of social isolation in modern society, and yet nonprofit groups do play a demonstrable and important role in the solution. These groups can provide the individual with a sense of being accepted as a person. Thus, the voluntary sector can provide a significant proportion of the population in modern society with positive feelings, a major component of human happiness and of enhanced quality of life.

Another aspect of the role of the voluntary sector in providing social integration is the social adjustment "buffering" function that many kinds of nonprofit voluntary groups provide. When numerous individuals of a certain social and cultural background are for some reason uprooted from their customary societal positions, new voluntary nonprofit groups frequently emerge to provide these individuals with an insulated (or buffered) special environment for part of their time. Typical examples would be the numerous immigrant associations that sprang up in the United States as a result of successive waves of immigration from various countries (Handlin, 1951) or the kinship-oriented voluntary associations that emerged to ease the adjustment of rural west Africans to life in large cities (Little, 1965).

These kinds of social-adjustment-oriented voluntary nonprofit groups do not, however, emerge only in the case of physical and geographical changes on a large scale. The voluntary sector also provides a social adjustment mechanism to ease the shocks of a variety of social dislocations and rapid social changes. The voluntary nonprofit groups involved may cater to a former elite that has been disenfranchised or deprived of its former holdings (e.g., the association of maharajahs of India, which arose to fight for the rights of maharajahs after the Indian Congress had stripped them of their traditional privileges and land, substituting only a moderate annual stipend). On the other hand, the voluntary nonprofit groups involved may represent a deprived category of persons who are attempting to change social conditions so that they may share more equitably in the good life as lived in their society (e.g., the early labor unions or black power groups, striving for recognition of the right to exist as a group and to fight for the betterment of conditions).

On another level, the voluntary sector plays an important integrative role by linking together individuals, groups, institutions, and even nations that otherwise would be in greater conflict (or at least in greater competition) with one another. (This and other impacts of voluntary groups are discussed further in Smith, 1966.) At the community level, a variety of voluntary nonprofit associations tend to have as members a set of two or more individuals representing differing and often opposing political, religious, cultural, or social perspectives and backgrounds. The coparticipation of this set of individuals in the same voluntary association can have significant moderating effects on any possible conflict relationships among these individuals. Similar integrative effects can be found at national levels, where several groups from different parts of the country and/or different social and cultural perspectives participate together in a common federation or other national nonprofit voluntary organization. On the international level, the joint participation of voluntary groups from otherwise conflicting or competing nations in some transnational, federative nonprofit organization may well have important long-term effects on the relations between the countries involved and on the possibilities of peace in the world (Skjelsbaek, 1973).

Preservation of Tradition

A *fifth* kind of general impact of the voluntary sector involves the opposite of the first one, which dealt with the social innovation role of voluntarism. In addition to providing a wide variety of new ideas about social behavior, the voluntary sector also is active in preserving numerous old ideas. Voluntary action and voluntary nonprofit organizations have played a major role in history in preserving the values, ways of life, ideas, beliefs, artifacts, and other productions of the mind, heart, and hand of peoples of earlier times so that this great variety of human culture is not lost to future generations. For example, numerous local historical societies in the United States specialize in preserving the history of particular towns and areas. Nonprofit voluntary organizations run local museums, libraries, and historical sites. Moreover, a number of voluntary organizations function primarily to preserve the values of cultures or subcultures that no longer have any substantial power or importance in American society but that nevertheless represent a way of life of significant numbers of people at some period in history or somewhere around the world (e.g., American Indian groups, in some instances, or immigrant ethnic associations that persist long after the ethnic group involved has been thoroughly assimilated into American culture). The role of municipal, state, and national governments in supporting museums and historical sites grows from the roots of earlier nonprofit, nongovernmental support of such "islands of culture."

Another aspect of the role of the voluntary sector in the preservation of beliefs and values involves voluntary nonprofit associations as sources of educational experiences. These experiences are especially valuable where the NPOs are attempting to pass on to their members or to the public at large some body of beliefs and values originating in the past. In part this would include many of the activities of most religious sects and denominations (all nonprofit organizations), especially when one focuses on their socialization and indoctrination activities (e.g., catechism classes, Sunday schools, Hebrew day schools, etc.). In part this function also includes all manner of more strictly educational voluntary organizations from Plato's Academy (see Peterson and Peterson, 1973) to modern Great Books discussion groups and so-called free universities, all nonprofit elementary and secondary schools and all nonprofit institutions of higher learning.

The various levels of government in the contemporary world have largely taken over the task of education on a broad scale, and yet voluntary nonprofit organizations are still important at the level of higher education. These groups supplement government-run educational systems by filling in the gaps and by prodding these systems to improve or to take on responsibility for the preservation of additional knowledge or values.

For instance, voluntary civil rights and black liberation organizations have taken the lead in educating both blacks and whites in the United States regarding black history and accomplishments. Gradually over the past several years, under the pressure of such voluntary associations, the public educational system in the United States has been changing to accommodate a more accurate and complete picture of black history—although the process is by no means finished. Similar examples could be given with regard to other content areas as well (e.g., women's history, American Indian history, etc.).

A Sense of Mystery

A *sixth* major impact of the voluntary sector is its embodiment and representation in society of the sense of mystery, wonder, and the sacred. Neither the business nor the government sector in modern society has much interest in such matters. Religious groups are almost invariably nonprofit organizations. Many would say that religion today is very much a big business, and both business and government support science in a substantial way. Yet precisely in those areas where religion and science almost meet, where the borders of religion are receding under the pressure of an ever-expanding science, the business and government sectors are often least involved. Voluntary nonprofit associations and nonprofit foundations or research organizations are the only groups experimenting seriously with new forms of worship, non-drug-induced "consciousness expansion" and "religious experience," the occult, investigation of flying saucers, extrasensory perception, and so on.

The "heretics" of both science and religion are seldom supported in their work directly and consciously by the business or government sectors. Only through non-profit organizations and the support of the voluntary sector have the major changes in the world's view of the supernatural and its relation to the natural tended to come about in the past. The same has also been true, by and large, for major changes in the world's view of human nature and of the natural universe in the past. The dominant economic and political (and religious) systems of any given epoch are seldom very receptive to the really new visions of either the natural or supernatural world (e.g., Galileo and Copernicus; Jesus). Voluntary action embodied in nonprofit organizations is thus the principal manner in which a sense of the sacred, the mysterious, and the awesome can be preserved and permitted some measure of expression in our otherwise hyperrational contemporary society.

Self-Fulfillment

A *seventh* impact of the voluntary sector results from its ability to liberate the individual and permit the fullest possible measure of expression of personal capacities and potentialities within an otherwise constraining social environment. All societies have their systems of laws, customs, roles, and organizations that tend to "box" people in and limit their opportunities for personal expression and personal development. The full extent of societal limitations on people is only gradually being recognized in recent decades, spurred in part by the "liberation" movements of women, blacks, the poor, the Third World peoples, and other disadvantaged or disenfranchised groups. The primary embodiments of these societal barriers and boxes have generally been the economic and governmental systems, although other major institutions of society have played a role as well (e.g., education, the family, religion).

Voluntary nonprofit associations and groups, on the other hand, have long been a primary means of at least *partially* escaping these societal barriers and boxes. Through participation in nonprofit organizations, a wide variety of people have been able to find or to create special social groups that would permit them to grow as individuals. This kind of personal growth has many relevant aspects but can be summed up generally as "self-actualization," to use a term from Maslow (1954). For some this means intellectual development, the process of becoming increasingly analytical, informed, and self-conscious about the nature of one's life situation and problems. When this occurs for a whole category or group of people, the process is often referred to as "group conscienticization" or consciousness-raising (e.g., among blacks, women, the poor). Seldom does such special personal growth occur on a broad scale outside voluntary nonprofit groups and movements.

For others, self-actualization through voluntary action takes the form of developing otherwise unused capacities, talents, skills, or potentials of a more active and practical sort. For many kinds of people—depending on the stage of social, economic, and political development of a society—NPOs, voluntary associations, and voluntary action offer the only feasible opportunity for leadership, for learning to speak in public, for practicing the fine art of management, for exercising analytical judgment, and so on. Until very recently in American society, for instance, neither blacks nor women nor the members of certain other disadvantaged groups could hope to develop fully their capacities through the occupational system of the economic or government sectors. Only in voluntary nonprofit groups of their own making could they seek any kind of fulfillment and self-expression, bound as they were (and, in part, continue to be bound) by the prejudices and discrimination of the dominant white, male, Anglo-Saxon Protestants in American society. This situation, however, is not unique to the United States. Similar and even different forms of prejudice and discrimination exist in all other societies, varying only in degree and in reference to the particular social groups singled out for attention. In all societies, voluntary nonprofit associations also offer the disadvantaged some chance of enhanced self-development, although these associations must sometimes meet in secret as underground groups if they are operating in an oppressive society that does not respect the right of free association.

Voluntary action potentially offers unique opportunities for personal growth and realization of personal potentials not only for those people whom society otherwise deprives, but also for all the members of society in certain directions. No matter how free, open, egalitarian, and highly developed the society, limitations of some sort are always placed on the development of each person by the particular social environment. Any major decision to follow a certain line of personal occupational or educational development, for instance, automatically diminishes or forecloses the outlook for a number of other alternatives. Voluntary nonprofit associations, however, exist (or can exist) in such profusion and variety that they can provide opportunities for missed personal development to almost any person at almost any stage of life. This is as true for the school teacher who always wanted to learn to fly (and who can join a flying club to do so even at age 60) as it is for the airline pilot who always wanted to write novels (and who can join a writer's club to work toward this end).

Not every person, however, will find the appropriate voluntary nonprofit association to suit personal growth needs at the particular time it is needed. Nevertheless, the voluntary sector as a whole serves in some significant degree this general role of providing substantial numbers of individuals in society with otherwise unavailable opportunities for self-actualization and self-fulfillment.

Negative Feedback

An *eighth* major impact of the voluntary sector in society is one of overriding importance, relating directly to the first and second types of impact discussed above. We are referring to the impact of the voluntary sector as a source of "negative feedback" for society as a whole, especially with regard to the directions taken by the major institutions of society such as government and business. Without negative feedback any system is dangerously vulnerable to destroying itself through excesses in one direction or another. Thus, however uncomfortable and irritating they may be at times, NPOs and the voluntary sector are absolutely vital to the continuing development of a society.

This systematic corrective role of the voluntary sector is, of course, *not* carried out by *all* voluntary nonprofit organizations, any more than all such organizations are concerned with the play element, value preservation, or the sacred. Yet the small cutting edge of the voluntary sector that does perform the role of social critic is extremely important, usually bearing the responsibility for the continued existence and future growth of the rest of the voluntary sector. In societies where a sufficient number and variety of NPOs are unable to play their roles effectively as social critics, the dominant governmental and economic institutions may well take over control and suppress the entire voluntary sector (e.g., Allen, 1965).

In the United States today numerous voluntary nonprofit organizations play this systemic corrective role. All the cause-oriented, advocacy, and issue-oriented groups tend to fall into this category, from the environmental movement to the civil rights and women's liberation movements. The tactics and strategy of such groups cover a broad range from rather traditional lobbying, through demonstrations and "be-ins," to direct remedial action such as "ecotage" (sabotage of notable corporate polluters and other "environmental undesirables").

Some of the more imaginative and innovative approaches have been developed in an attempt to modify the business sector, rather than focusing solely on the government sector. There have been in-depth investigations by Ralph Nader and his associates of particular companies' practices and their relationship to the public interest (e.g., of First National City Bank of New York and of DuPont), countermanagement stockholder activity in the public interest (e.g., Project G.M.), dissenting annual reports written to present a full public accounting of a corporation's activities that are harmful to the general public interest and welfare, class action suits brought by voluntary NPOs against manufacturers and developers, etc.

When examined carefully, such activities (which vary markedly in their success) often seem fruitless and doomed to failure, given the power of the business and government organizations and systems being challenged. Yet when we see the activities of voluntary nonprofit groups in a larger context, when we sum up these numerous activities attempting to modify and improve the dominant systems and organizations of our society, they take on a very important *general meaning*. Even if many, or most, of such system correction attempts by nonprofit organizations should fail, the continual and expanding pressure being brought to bear by the voluntary sector on the central institutions of society is still likely to have a positive long-term modifying influence. When the leaders of the business and governmental sectors know that "someone is watching" and that they may eventually have to account to the public for their actions, they are usually encouraged to give greater attention to the public interest rather than merely to narrow private interests.

When for one reason or another the voluntary sector is not able to operate effectively as a systemic corrective (either because of its own inadequacies or the failure of the leaders of dominant institutions to listen and change accordingly), the usual result in human history has been a broad social revolution (not just a palace revolution or simple coup). When the dominant institutions of any society have ignored for too long or too often the voices of the public interest as expressed by elements of the voluntary sector, revolutionary and usually underground voluntary nonprofit groups arise and make concrete plans to overthrow the existing system completely. The American, French, Russian, Chinese, Cuban, and other revolutions *all* attest to this pattern.

Thus, when the voluntary sector cannot make itself heard adequately through the permissible communication and influence channels in society, certain nonprofit voluntary groups and movements tend to arise to revamp the whole system, establishing whole new institutional arrangements with their corresponding new channels of influence and communication. Not surprisingly, these new channels generally favor persons and groups who were not heard previously (although those *formerly dominant* often end up in as bad a position as, or worse than, that faced by the *formerly disadvantaged*).

This cycle tends to repeat itself until a society reaches a point (1) where it is effectively and continuously self-correcting through the activities of a strong voluntary nonprofit sector that is oriented toward social change and (2) where its major institutions are operating primarily in the public interest of *all* citizens (not only the prosperous, white, male, Anglo-Saxon Protestants or their equivalents in societies other than the United States and the British Commonwealth).

Support for the Economic System

The *ninth* major impact of the voluntary sector is the support that the sector gives specifically to the economic system of a society, especially in a modern industrial society. A variety of nonprofit associations provide crucial kinds of social, intellectual, and technical linkages among workers in numerous occupations: Professional associations increase the effectiveness of most kinds of scientists, engineers, technicians, etc., just as manufacturers' and trade associations support the growth of whole industries. Various kinds of labor unions play their part as well, although many businesspeople would question the degree to which they "support" the economic system. However, labor unions only seem nonsupportive of the economic system when the latter is viewed narrowly from the point of view of the employer interested solely in profit maximization. Labor unions ultimately have to be deeply concerned with the viability of the economic system and the productivity of their own members if they are to survive as nonprofit organizations with the current system.

This economic support role of the voluntary sector is usually lost sight of because so many people tend to view all kinds of economic self-interest and occupationally related voluntary nonprofit associations as integral parts of the business sector. In fact, these kinds of nonprofit organizations are quite distinct from the business sector itself, however close their relationship might be to business corporations and occupational activities. These associations are the most numerous type of *national* nonprofit organization. The primary purpose of business corporations is to make a profit for their owners, whether the latter are actually involved in running the corporation or not. On the other hand, economic self-interest nonprofit organizations have as their primary purpose the enhancement of the long-term occupational and economic interests of their member-participants. While corporation employees and professionals are paid in salaries, wages, or fees for their participation, the members of economic self-interest nonprofit organizations themselves *pay* for the privilege of belonging to and benefiting from these associations. The members may be individuals *or* corporations, or both.

Provision for General Welfare

A *tenth* major impact of the nonprofit voluntary sector on society is the one most people would think of first: This sector plays a major role in providing for the general welfare of society through all manner of social services, many of which are or have been unique to nonprofit voluntary organizations (though many other such services have been adopted and institutionalized by the business sector and especially the government sector). Nonprofit social service organizations collectively now have, and always have had, a very great impact on health care, preventive health activities, and health-related rehabilitation. Similarly, NPOs have long been in the vanguard in providing services relating to (1) the basic survival problems of people (jobs and employment, food and nutrition, shelter, clothing, transportation, etc., for the poor or disadvantaged), (2) emergency survival problems (and to refugees, migrants, immigrants, homeless people, disaster victims), (3) marriage and family problems (family counseling, adoption, day care, family planning, birth control, etc.), (4) friendship and social isolation problems (Big Brothers; Big Sisters; friendly visits to shut-ins; personal relationships with children, youth, adults, or the aged with special needs or problems, etc.) and in other areas of human problems and needs.

Societal Goal Attainment

The *eleventh* major impact of the voluntary sector we shall note is a rather subtle one: The voluntary sector constitutes an important *latent resource* for all kinds of goal attainment in the interests of the society as a whole. Put another way, the voluntary sector represents a tremendous reservoir of potential energy that can be mobilized under appropriate circumstances for broad societal goals. The role of the voluntary sector in revolutionary situations is but one example of this latent potential. The activity of voluntary association networks in more limited disaster situations is a more common example (Barton, 1970). The voluntary nonprofit sector and its component organizations, associations, groups, and channels of communication and influence make possible the mobilization of large numbers of people on relatively short notice for special purposes (usually in the common interest) without requiring economic rewards or legal coercion as activating forces. Such a latent potential in the voluntary sector is especially important when neither economic nor political-legal forces can feasibly be brought to bear (quickly enough) to resolve some widespread problem situation.

The latent potential of the voluntary sector can be viewed in another way as well. The nonprofit voluntary sector is largely based on a *charitable grants economy* (donations of time, money, etc.) as contrasted with the *coercive grants economy* (taxation) on which the government sector operates or the *market economy* on which the business sector operates. The last two types of economy work well for certain purposes, but neither works well for the accomplishment of *all* kinds of purposes in society. For certain purposes and activities (several of which are implicit in the ten major impacts of the voluntary sector cited above) the charitable grants economy tends to work best.

Now the important latent potential of the voluntary sector is that, under appropriately compelling circumstances (i.e., for the "right" value, goal, or ideal), the money, goods, real property, and services mobilized by the voluntary nonprofit sector through the charitable grants economy can completely overwhelm all considerations of the coercive grants economy and the market economy. For certain goals and ideals, a large majority of society can be induced to "give their all" and to do so gladly, willingly, and voluntarily. This does not occur very often, and it usually does not last very long. But the latent potential support is present in any society at any time. With the right spark—usually a charismatic leader with an idea and an ideal—the course of history can be changed during these brief, rare periods of almost total societal mobilization through the leadership of the voluntary sector and nonprofit organizations.

The Negative Side

In describing the foregoing eleven types of impact that the voluntary nonprofit sector tends to have in some degree in any society, we have emphasized the positive contributions that voluntary action makes to society. However, as with any form of human group or activity, voluntary action, nonprofit organizations, and the voluntary sector are by no means *always* positive in their impacts.

Every positive impact noted above can have negative consequences under certain circumstances and with regard to certain values. Thus, when voluntary nonprofit associations experiment with new social forms, the failures can often be harmful to specific people and organizations. At times, alternative definitions of reality and morality have become an evil tool in the hands of others, as with the ideology generated in Germany by the Nazi party, a voluntary nonprofit organization. Further, when NPOs focus on the play element, their "fun" can become mischievous or even criminal, as in the case of a boys' gang that wrecks a school "just for kicks." When social clubs provide a warm and close sense of belonging to their members, they can also create deep dissatisfaction in people who would dearly like to belong but are excluded from a particular club or kind of club.

In the same way, voluntary groups striving to preserve certain beliefs or values from the past may be holding on to anachronisms that would be better left to the pages of history books. Clubs whose members chase around seeking flying saucers and little green people from Mars might more profitably spend their time and energy elsewhere with more satisfying results. Nonprofit organizations that arouse the awareness of the full potentials of black people—who must then go out into the real world and face a harsh reality of bigotry and discrimination—may not always be doing them a favor. The kinds of systemic corrections being suggested by cause-oriented and advocacy nonprofit groups may not be conducive to the greatest good of the greatest number. Economic self-interest voluntary groups often tend to ignore the public interest in favor of an exclusive and selfish private interest. And the latent potentials of the voluntary sector can be mobilized to do evil as well as to do good.

Conclusion

The impact of the nonprofit voluntary sector on society is very significant in terms of types of roles or functions played by nonprofit organizations. Several types of impact are relatively unique to this sector and may be considered as the essential and most distinctive functions of the nonprofit sector in society. Particular nonprofit organizations and their leaders need to be aware of these facts as a broader context of their own planning, goal-setting, and operations.

The greater the focus of an NPO on the more distinctive and characteristic functions of the nonprofit voluntary sector in general, the greater its own chances of surviving and being effective in the long run. Conversely, the wise nonprofit organization will realize when the time has come to relinquish certain *less* distinctive and characteristic nonprofit functions to the business sector or government sector as social innovation becomes accepted and institutionalized. There are always new needs and problems of people that must be addressed by NPOs just as there are always new ways of approaching old problems and needs.

Hence, the relinquishing of certain functions by a nonprofit organization should not be seen as a failure or loss but as a sign of success. Getting the business or government sector sufficiently interested to take over frees the nonprofit sector and its organizations to focus on still other tasks in the public interest and thereby contribute to the general welfare. The failure of some NPOs to see and understand this broader picture is perhaps their greatest limitation. To survive and to be effective, nonprofit organizations, as all other organizations, must be flexible enough to adapt to changes in their environment (see Smith with Dixon, 1973). This is a major challenge to the leadership of the voluntary nonprofit sector.

Suggested Reading

Allen, William Sheridan, *The Nazi Seizure of Power*, Quadrangle Books, Chicago, 1965.

Barton, Allen H., *Communities in Disaster*, Anchor Books, Doubleday, Garden City, N.Y., 1970.

Handlin, Oscar, *The Uprooted*, Grosset and Dunlap, New York, 1951.

Little, Kenneth, *West African Urbanization: A Study of Voluntary Associations in Socal Change*, Cambridge University Press, Cambridge, England, 1965.

Maslow, Abraham H., *Motivation And Personality*, Harper and Row, New York, 1954.

Peterson, Sophia, and Virgil Peterson, Voluntary Associations in Ancient Greece, *Journal of Voluntary Action Research*, vol. 2, no. 1, pp. 2–16, 1973.

Skjelsbaek, Kjell, The Growth of International Non-governmental Organizations in the Twentieth Century, in *Voluntary Action Research: 1973*, David Horton Smith (Ed.), Lexington Books, Lexington, Mass., 1973, chap. 5.

Smith, David Horton, The Importance of Formal Voluntary Organizations for Society, *Sociology and Social Research*, vol. 50, pp. 483–492, 1966.

Smith, David Horton, with John Dixon, The Voluntary Sector, in Edward Bursk (Ed.), *Challenge to Leadership: Managing in a Changing World*, The Free Press, New York, 1973, chap. 7.

Smith, David Horton, Richard D. Reddy, and Burt R. Baldwin, Types of Voluntary Action: A Definitional Essay, in David Horton Smith et al. (Eds.), *Voluntary Action Research: 1972*, Lexington Books, Lexington, Mass., 1972, chap. 10.

3

Tax Consequences for Nonprofit Organizations

Ken Milani

Ph.D., Arthur Young Faculty Fellow in Taxation, University of Notre Dame

Taxes have been described as the price we pay for a civilized society. Part of the tab for civilization is paid by nonprofit organizations (NPOs) that generate "unrelated business income." The Internal Revenue Code (IRC) defines unrelated business income as

> Gross income derived from any "unrelated trade or business" that is "regularly carried on" less deductions directly connected with the carrying on of such trade or business

An unrelated trade or business is an undertaking by the NPO which involves activities that constitute a trade or business. These activities which are not substantially related to the NPO's exempt function must display a frequency and continuity that is similar to a profit-making entity's approach. The manner in which the activities are carried out is also considered in determining whether unrelated business income is being produced by the NPO. For example, the following would not be activities subject to taxation.

- Spaghetti and meatball dinner served annually on St. Joseph's Day as part of the day's festivities. The charge is $1.50 per plate or $6 per family. A parish sponsors the event. Radio and newspaper advertising is conducted in conjunction with the event.

- Parking deck operated by university for use of faculty, staff, and students. A per-semester fee is charged for use of the facility.

On the other hand, the activities listed below would generate unrelated business income.

- Pharmacy operated by an exempt hospital for patients, staff and the general public. Ads promoting the operation are carried by the mass media.

- Restaurant operated by members of a religious organization who are trying to encourage the public to adopt simpler lifestyles.

- Laundry service operated by an exempt hospital for its own use plus revenue-producing activity made available and promoted to other health care agencies in the area which are also exempt. The charges are typically set at 80 percent of the going market rate for similar services.

Use of the proceeds or profits from an activity to support an NPO is not a sufficient reason to avoid being taxed. Thus, the pharmacy profits above will be subject to taxation regardless of their disposition within the hospital.

Gross Income

Several sources of gross income are available to the NPO. The major categories are described below. In many instances, major contrasts between the treatment of gross income for profit-seeking enterprises and the unrelated business activities of an NPO will be noted.

Gross Profit

Sales of products or merchandise reduced by cost of goods sold and any returns and allowances represents gross profit. A computation of the cost of goods sold can reflect allowed accounting procedures which include first-in first-out (FIFO), last-in first-out (LIFO) and other methods. Returns and allowances are also calculated using standard accounting procedures.

Where services are the source of sales or revenue (e.g., laundry), no computation of the cost of goods sold is involved. However, allowances must still be recognized.

Investment Income

Generally, investment income (e.g., dividends, interest, and earnings from annuities) is *not* included in the gross income of an NPO. This treatment represents a significant tax break for the NPO since most taxpayers report and pay taxes on investment income.

However, the NPO must include investment income in gross income for tax purposes in two specific situations. The first instance occurs when the NPO is drawing investment income from a controlled corporation (i.e., an organization in which the NPO has at least 80 percent control through stock holdings or through representation on a board of directors or trustees). The other circumstance involves debt financing, or the acquisition of assets with borrowed funds. This latter topic will be covered later in this chapter.

The example below illustrates the investment income provisions as they apply to NPOs.

Healing Light Hospital, an exempt organization, reports the following investment income during the year:

$3000 from American Micro Corporation. This represents dividends on 6000 shares of stock. American Micro has over 1.4 million shares of stock outstanding.

$6000 from Healing Light Gift Shop. This is a dividend on 300 shares of stock. The gift shop has 600 shares of stock outstanding.

$7200 from Healing Light Pavilion. A dividend paid per a directive from the Pavilion Board of Directors. Nine of the ten directors are staff physicians or administrators at Healing Light Hospital.

$3400 from Healing Light Parking Deck Corporation. Represents interest on a loan to the parking deck firm. Healing Light Hospital owns 850 of the 1000 corporate shares of stock.

The first two items will not be reported as unrelated business income since the greater than or equal to 80 percent control factor is not present. However, the third and fourth items, $7200 and $3400, will be reported on the income tax return of Healing Light Hospital since in both instances it maintains at least 80 percent of the control of the organizations making the payments—90 percent of the Pavilion and 85 percent of the Parking Deck Corporation.

Royalty Income

The approach of the IRC to royalty income is similar to its stance on investment income. Royalty income from a controlled organization or generated by debt-financed holdings will be taxed while all other royalty income will not be reported for tax purposes. Consider the following royalties collected by Healing Light Hospital.

$10000 from McIrwin Publishing, Inc.—Royalty income on a book written by a benefactor who instructed McIrwin to pay the royalty directly to the hospital

$4000 from H. L. Book Ministry, Inc.—Book royalties from an organization that is owned 100 percent by Healing Light Hospital

Of the $14,000 received, only the $4000 will be taxed since it came from a controlled organization.

Royalty income received by a profit-seeking entity is fully taxed. Thus, the treatment of royalty income by NPOs represents favorable treatment.

Rent

Another source of income which can qualify for favorable treatment by the income tax law is rent. None of the rent income will be reported for tax purposes if the NPO occupies more than half of the space in a rented facility. Where the rent represents payment for space and the use of tangible personal property (e.g., machinery, equipment, furniture), if less than 10 percent of the rent pertains to the property, none of the rent income will be subject to taxation.

All rental income from the following situations will be included in gross income for tax purposes:

1. More than half the rent is attributable to tangible personal property.

2. Profits from the leased property are the basis for the rent.

3. Personal services, other than routine and ordinary maintenance activities, are rendered as part of the rental.

Only a portion of the rental income will be reported for income tax purposes if the rented property is debt-financed or when the portion of rent allocated to tangible personal property is at least 10 percent but not over 50 percent. Debt-financed situations involve the use of borrowed funds (e.g., mortgages, bonds) to acquire the property. Full treatment of this topic is beyond the scope of this book. Suffice it to say that if any debt remains on a rental property, part of the rent must be reported for federal income tax purposes.

The rent provisions are illustrated by the following example.

An exempt organization reports the following receipt from rentals during the current year:

$6000—Rent for the use of space in a convention center owned by the exempt organization.

$3800—Rent on the Adrian Avenue Building at $200 per month plus 1 percent of gross sales.

$12,000—Rent on Bengal Boulevard Apartments. The apartments are furnished and 20 percent of the rent is attributable to the furnishings.

$7000—Rent on Cavalier Complex composed of building (40 percent) plus printing presses (60 percent) used by tenant.

$2400—Rent on Dantley Drive Offices. The exempt organization occupies 75 percent of the office space while various nonexempt tenants occupy the remainder of the facility.

$9700—Rent on Ara's Acres, a farm, which represents 25 percent of the profits generated by the tenant's operations.

None of the $6000, $3800, or $2400 rents will be included in gross income for tax purposes because of the type of property involved (in the $6000 and $3800 examples) and the exempt organization's use of the facility (in the $2400 example). All of the $7000 in the fourth example (rent for tangible personal property exceeds the 50 percent plateau) and the $9700 in the last example (rent tied to tenant's profit) will be taxable, while only 20 percent of the $12,000 will be added to gross income since the tangible personal property portion falls between the 10 and 50 percent limits.

Gains

If an NPO disposes of property via a sale, trade, or exchange at a gain, none of the gain will be reported for income tax purposes unless the property is debt-financed. A situation involving debt will find the NPO only including a portion of the gain in its tax computation.

This treatment provides a substantial tax break to an NPO as it sells off surplus land or buildings. When properly planned, all of the gain will go unreported. For example,

> Leahy University acquires a building, the Rockne Road Complex (RRC), with borrowed funds. RRC is rented to corporate tenants, and the mortgage is paid off before the building is sold at a substantial gain to one of the tenants. None of the gain on the sale of RRC is taxed.

Other Income

Many other sources of income can be reported by an NPO. Several of these (e.g., advertising, research, partnership agreements) are highly complex arrangements, which are beyond the scope of this effort. A competent tax consultant should be engaged when dealing with these rigorous situations.

Deductions

To determine "unrelated business taxable income (UBTI)," NPOs are permitted to deduct ordinary operating expenses, special deductions, and a specific deduction. This portion of the chapter will focus on situations that are most pertinent or especially applicable to NPOs that will report UBTI.

Ordinary Operating Expenses

Expenses of an NPO involved in a trade or business are treated similarly to the expenses of a profit-seeking organization. To be deductible in the computation of UBTI, the expense must be incurred in the unrelated trade or business. In many cases, this is easy to determine. For example, salaries paid to employees of the unrelated unit, depreciation of machinery used in the unrelated entity, and other expenses can be readily identified and determined. However, some expenses may have to be allocated between exempt functions and unrelated business functions (e.g., facility used for all activities of an NPO, automobile used in a variety of ways by an NPO). An illustration is presented below.

> United Spiritual Conference (USC) is an exempt organization. USC owns and operates a printing business, Pronto Printing Organization (PPO), which generates unrelated business income. The following expenses have been analyzed and their treatment for tax reporting purposes determined.
>
> $18,000—Secretary's salary for the year. Since the secretary spends approximately 40 percent of her time on PPO matters, $7200 will be deducted in determining UBTI.
>
> $40,000—Depreciation of printing presses. All this will be deducted in determining PPO's tax liability since the machinery is used exclusively for PPO activities.
>
> $3600—Operating expenses of a delivery vehicle. Since 75 percent of the delivery vehicle's usage applied to PPO, $2700 will be deducted in determining UBTI.
>
> $30,000—Salary of USC's development director. None of this will be reported when determining UBTI since the development director devotes all of his time to fund-raising activities for USC.

Special Deductions

As a corporate entity, the unrelated business segment of a NPO would be entitled to some special deductions including a dividends-received deduction and a write-off for charitable contributions. The latter is fully deductible but a limit of 10 percent of UBTI places a ceiling on the amount that can be written off yearly. The dividends-received deduction has limited applicability within an NPO and will not be covered in detail.

Specific Deduction

In determining unrelated business taxable income (UBTI), the IRC allows each NPO a $1000 specific deduction. Thus the first $1000 of UBTI will not be taxed as shown below:

Two NPOs report the following information about their unrelated business activities:

	NPO Alpha	NPO Omega
Gross income	$120,000	$250,000
Less operating expenses	(90,000)	(248,800)
Special deductions	(2,000)	—0—
Specific deduction	(1,000)	(1,000)
UBTI	$ 27,000	$ 200

Tax Liability

Unrelated business taxable income (UBTI) is the basis for the tax liability of an NPO. The following tax rates applied to UBTI as of January 1, 1988:

UBTI	Tax rate, %
Greater than $0 to $50,000	15
Greater than $50,000 to $75,000	25
Greater than $75,000 to $100,000	34
Greater than $100,000 to $335,000	39
Greater than $335,000	34

As an illustration of, the above rate schedule, consider the following:

UBTI	Tax	Computation	
$ 20,000	$ 3,000	15% × $ 20,000 =	$ 3,000
$ 60,000	$ 11,250	15% × $ 50,000 =	7,500
		25% × 10,000 =	2,500
			$ 10,000
$120,000	$ 30,050	15% × $ 50,000 =	7,500
		25% × 25,000 =	6,250
		34% × 25,000 =	8,500
		39% × 20,000 =	7,800
			$ 30,050
$535,000	$181,900	15% × $ 50,000 =	$ 7,500
		25% × 25,000 =	6,250
		34% × 25,000 =	8,500
		39% × 235,000 =	91,650
		34% × 200,000 =	68,000
			$181,900

The above rates are always subject to change. An updated tax service should be consulted for the present rate schedule in effect.

Paying the Tax

There are two basic ways of handling the tax liability of an NPO: (1) use credits to reduce the taxes or (2) disburse cash to the Internal Revenue Service. A wide variety of credits is available to the NPO engaged in an unrelated trade or business. These credits (e.g., targeted jobs, building rehabilitation) will be a direct reduction to the tax liability within specific limits. Because of the variety and vagaries of the various credits, they will not be dealt with in any detail in this book. Competent counseling from a tax professional is strongly advised for the NPO that is creating credits as a result of its activities.

Disbursements to the federal government to satisfy any tax liability remaining after credits may have to occur five times for any taxable year. Four of these payments would be estimated payments made before a tax return is filed. The fifth and final cash outlay would occur as the return is filed. Estimated tax payments must be made or the NPO may pay a penalty for underpayment of tax. These payments are due on the fifteenth day of the fourth, sixth, ninth, and twelfth months of the NPO's taxable year (e.g., October 15, December 15, March 15, and June 15 for an NPO with a July 1 to June 30 fiscal year). The tax return of the NPO is filed on Form 990-T and is due on the fifteenth day of the third month following the close of the exempt organization's taxable year (e.g., September 15 for an NPO which closes its year on June 30).

Conclusion

This chapter has focused on a rigorous subject, the federal income tax provisions that apply to an NPO. Illustrated were the activities and specific elements leading to determination of UBTI. Also covered were the tax rate structure applied to UBTI and ways of handling the tax liability.

Planning is an imperative activity for the NPO. In the area of taxation, planning is critical since taxes can be minimized with proper procedures and practices. Some tax trimming tips were included. However, a competent tax professional should be consulted if significant savings are sought.

4

Securing Tax Exemption for Exempt Organizations

Creston Wood
Consultant

The Tax Reform Act of 1969 was aimed particularly at the private foundation area, which Congress believed contained a number of abuses. In addition to new amendments to the Internal Revenue Code (IRC), a number of procedures and revenue rulings affecting private foundations were issued. Accordingly, this chapter is confined primarily to procedures for obtaining exemption from federal income tax under Section 501(c)(3) IRC and related private foundation and public charity statutes.

Domestic Organizations

An organization applying for exemption under Section 501(c)(3) of the IRC must file Form 1023, with the district director for the key district in which the organization's principal office or place of business is located. (See Figure 4.1; addresses for the ten key districts are given in the instructions on page 2 of Form 1023.) If organized after October 9, 1969, the organization must file for exemption within 15 months from the end of the month in which they were organized.[1] If the application is filed within this 15-month period, your organization's exemption will be recognized retroactively to the date it was organized. An extention of time for good cause may be granted. Otherwise exemption will be recognized only for the period after the application is received. Contributions made to a late-filing organi-

Department of the Treasury
Internal Revenue Service

Instructions for Form 1023
(Revised March 1986)

Application for Recognition of Exemption

Under Section 501(c)(3) of the Internal Revenue Code

(Section references are to the Internal Revenue Code, unless otherwise noted.)

Retain a copy of the completed Form 1023 in the organization's permanent records.

General Instructions

For additional information, see **Publication 557,** Tax-Exempt Status for Your Organization, and **Publication 578,** Tax Information for Private Foundations and Foundation Managers.

Purpose of Form.—Form 1023 is used:

● To apply for a ruling or determination letter on an organization's exempt status under section 501(c)(3). (If you are applying for a ruling or determination letter under any other provision of section 501(c), see Publication 557 for the appropriate application form.)

● To apply for a ruling or determination letter under section 501(e) for organizations that claim to be cooperative hospital service organizations.

● To apply for a ruling or determination letter under section 501(f) for cooperative service organizations of operating educational organizations.

● To apply for a ruling or determination letter under section 501(k) for child care organizations.

● To notify the Internal Revenue Service as required by section 508(a) that the organization is applying for recognition of exempt status under section 501(c)(3).

● To notify the Internal Revenue Service as required by section 508(b) that the organization is claiming not to be a private foundation.

Note: *Generally, Form 1023 is **NOT** used to apply for a group exemption letter. For information on how to apply for a group exemption letter, see Rev. Proc. 80-27, 1980-1 C.B. 677, or later revisions.*

Paperwork Reduction Act Notice.—We ask for this information to carry out the Internal Revenue laws of the United States. We need it to determine whether you meet the legal requirements for tax-exempt status. If you want to be recognized as tax-exempt by IRS, you are required to give us this information.

Requirement of Notice Under Section 508.—Section 508(a) provides that an organization organized after October 9, 1969, will not be treated as an organization described in section 501(c)(3) unless it has given notice to the IRS that it is applying for recognition of such status. Section 508(b) provides that any organization described in section 501(c)(3) will be presumed to be a private foundation if it has failed to notify the IRS that it is not a private foundation.

Properly completed, this application constitutes the required notice under section 508(a) and also constitutes the notice under section 508(b). If the organization does not file the notice under section 508(a) within 15 months after the end of the month in which it was created, it will not qualify for exempt status during the period before the date of actual notice. However, in certain circumstances an organization may be eligible for relief from the 15-month deadline provided in section 508(a). The Service has the authority under regulations section 1.9100 to extend the time for filing applications for tax relief provided under other sections of the regulations. Rev. Proc. 79-63, 1979-2 C.B. 578, provides organizations detailed instructions for preparing requests for such relief, and describes factors taken into consideration by the Service to determine whether to grant relief. If a late filer qualifies for

exempt status under section 501(c)(3), and is granted relief under regulations section 1.9100 according to the procedures described in Rev. Proc. 79-63, the organization's exempt status will be recognized before the date of its application.

Exceptions.—You are not required to give notice to the IRS within 15 months if the organization:

(a) Is a church, interchurch organization, local unit of a church, a convention or association of churches, or an integrated auxiliary of a church;

(b) Is not a private foundation (as defined in section 509(a)) and normally has gross receipts of not more than $5,000 in each tax year; or

(c) Is a subordinate organization covered by a group exemption letter, but only if the parent or supervisory organization timely submits a notice covering the subordinates.

Governing Instrument Requirements for Private Foundations Under Section 508(e).—In order for a private foundation to be exempt from income tax, its governing instrument must include provisions that require it to act or refrain from acting so as not to engage in an act of self-dealing (section 4941) or subject the foundation to the taxes imposed by sections 4942 (failure to distribute income), 4943 (excess business holdings), 4944 (investments that jeopardize charitable purpose), and 4945 (taxable expenditures). A private foundation may satisfy these requirements either by express language in its governing instrument or by application of State law that effectively imposes these requirements upon the foundation or treats these requirements as being contained in the governing instrument.

See Rev. Rul. 75-38, 1975-1 C.B. 161, for a list of States that have legislation that satisfies the requirement of section 508(e) relating to governing instruments.

If, however, the State statute by its terms does not apply to a governing instrument that contains a mandatory direction conflicting with any of the statute's requirements, and, if for tax years beginning after March 22, 1973, the organization has such mandatory directions in its governing instrument, then the organization has not satisfied the requirements of section 508(e) by virtue of the passage of such legislation.

Attachments.—Every attachment should state that it relates to Form 1023 and should show the date completed and the organization's name, address, and employer identification number.

In addition to the required documents and statements, you should file any additional information citing court decisions, rulings, opinions, etc., that will expedite processing of the application. Generally, attachments in the form of tape recordings are not acceptable unless accompanied by a transcript.

Language and Currency Requirements.—Form 1023 and attachments must be prepared using the English language. If the organizational document or bylaws are in any other language, an English translation must be furnished. (See conformed copy requirements in the Specific Instructions for Part II.) If the organization produces or distributes foreign language publications that are submitted with the application, you may be asked to provide English translations for one or more of them during the processing of your application.

Report all financial information in U.S. dollars (state conversion rate used). Combine amounts from within and outside the United States and report the total for each item.

Figure 4.1.

zation prior to the date of approval will not be allowed as a deduction to the contributors.[2]

If organized before October 9, 1969, an organization which has no determination or ruling letter granting it exemption under Section 501(c)(3) dated on or before July 13, 1970, is not precluded from obtaining exemption by filing Form 1023. The organization should include statements of receipts and disbursements for at least 3 years. If exemption is granted, it has a good chance to be retroactive.

Signature Requirements.—An officer who is authorized to sign or another person authorized by a power of attorney must sign this application. Send the power of attorney with the application when you file it.

Where to File.—File the completed application, and all information required, with the key district office for your principal place of business or office as listed below. As soon as possible after the complete application is received, you will be advised of IRS's determination and of the annual returns which the organization will be required to file.

When the principal place of business or office of the organization is in one of the districts or locations shown below ▼	Send your application to the key district listed below ▼
Atlanta, Birmingham, Columbia, Greensboro, Jackson, Jacksonville, Little Rock, Nashville, New Orleans	Internal Revenue Service EP/EO Division P.O. Box 941 Atlanta, GA 30370
Baltimore, District of Columbia, Pittsburgh, Richmond, any U.S. possession or foreign country	Internal Revenue Service EP/EO Division, P.O. Box 17010 Baltimore, MD 21203
Brooklyn, Albany, Augusta, Boston, Buffalo, Burlington, Hartford, Manhattan, Portsmouth, Providence	Internal Revenue Service EP/EO Division, P.O. Box C-9050 General Post Office Brooklyn, NY 11202
Chicago, Aberdeen, Des Moines, Fargo, Helena, Milwaukee, Omaha, St. Louis, St. Paul, Springfield	Internal Revenue Service EP/EO Division, P.O. Box A-3617 Chicago, IL 60690
Cincinnati, Cleveland, Detroit, Indianapolis, Louisville, Parkersburg	EP/EO Division, P.O. Box 3159 Cincinnati, OH 45201
Dallas, Albuquerque, Austin, Cheyenne, Denver, Houston, Oklahoma City, Phoenix, Salt Lake City, Wichita	EP/EO Division Mail Code 306, 1100 Commerce St. Dallas, TX 75242
Los Angeles, Honolulu, Laguna Niguel	Internal Revenue Service EO Application Receiving P.O. Box 486 Los Angeles, CA 90053-0486
Newark, Philadelphia, Wilmington	Internal Revenue Service EP/EO Division, Box 1680 Newark, NJ 07101
San Francisco, Las Vegas, Sacramento, San Jose	Internal Revenue Service EP/EO Division P.O. Box 36040, Stop 3-2-29 450 Golden Gate Ave. San Francisco, CA 94102
Seattle, Anchorage, Boise, Portland	Internal Revenue Service EP/EO Division Mail Stop 554, 915 Second Ave. Seattle, WA 98174

Public Inspection of Form 1023.—The application, if approved, and any supporting papers will be open to public inspection as required by section 6104. In addition, any letter or other document issued by the IRS with regard to the application will be open to public inspection at the time and in the manner prescribed by regulations. However, information relating to a trade secret, patent, style of work, or apparatus, which if released would adversely affect the organization, or any other information which if released would adversely affect the national defense, will not be made available for public inspection. You must identify this information, by clearly marking it "**NOT SUBJECT TO PUBLIC INSPECTION**" and attach a statement explaining why the organization asks that the information should be withheld.

Appeal Procedures.—Your application will be considered by the key district office which will either refer the case to the National Office, issue a favorable determination letter, or issue a proposed adverse determination letter denying the exempt status you requested. Within 30 days from the date of a proposed adverse determination, you may appeal through the key district office to the Regional Director of Appeals. In the case of a National Office adverse ruling, you may appeal directly to the Conference and Review Branch of the Exempt Organizations Technical Division.

If you decide to appeal a proposed adverse determination or ruling, be sure the appeal contains all the information listed in **Publication 892**, Exempt Organization Appeal Procedures for Unagreed Issues, since incomplete appeals will be returned for completion. Publication 892 will be mailed with any proposed adverse determination or ruling.

If a conference is requested in a key district determination case, it will be held at an office of the Regional Director of Appeals, unless the applicant requests that the meeting be held at a district office convenient to both parties.

If no appeal is filed within the 30-day period, the proposed adverse determination or ruling letter will become final.

For additional details on appeals also see Publication 557.

If there is a controversy involving an IRS determination (or failure to make a determination) concerning the organization's qualification for exemption under section 501(c)(3), after the organization files an appropriate suit, the U.S. Tax Court, U.S. Claims Court or the District Court of the United States for the District of Columbia may make a declaration regarding the organization's qualification for exemption. The court may not grant jurisdiction unless the organization has exhausted its administrative remedies. Failure to apply for relief under regulations section 1.9100 (see the instructions under the heading Requirement of Notice Under Section 508) may be regarded by the court as failure to exhaust administrative remedies available within the Service for an organization that has been recognized as exempt on a prospective basis due to the provisions of section 508(a). The Court's judgment regarding the organization's qualification for exemption will have the force and effect of a decision of the Tax Court or a final judgment or decree of the Claims Court or the District Court, as the case may be, and will be reviewable as such. The declaratory judgment remedy is also available with regard to the Service's initial or continuing classification of the organization as a private foundation, as a private operating foundation, or as a public charity described in a part of section 170(b)(1)(A) other than the part under which the organization claims it is described.

Annual Information Return.—If the annual information return for tax-exempt organizations becomes due while your application for recognition of exempt status is pending (including any appeal of a proposed adverse determination) with IRS, you should file a **Form 990**, Return of Organization Exempt From Income Tax, and Schedule A (Form 990) or **Form 990-PF**, Return of Private Foundation, if a private foundation, and indicate that an application is pending.

Special Rule for Canadian Colleges and Universities.—A Canadian college or university that has received a **Form T2051**, Notification of Registration, from Revenue Canada (Department of National Revenue, Taxation) and whose registration has not been revoked, does not have to complete all parts of Form 1023 that would otherwise be applicable. Such an organization must complete only Parts I and II and Schedule A (Schools, Colleges, and Universities). The organization must also attach a copy of its current Form T2051 and a copy of its **Form T2050**, Application for Registration, together with all the required attachments that it submitted to Revenue Canada. If any attachments were prepared in French, an English translation must be furnished. (See the conformed copy requirements in the Specific Instructions for Part II if the attachment is an organizational document or bylaws.)

Other Canadian organizations seeking a determination of section 501(c)(3) status must complete Form 1023 in the same manner as U.S. organizations.

Specific Instructions

Except as described above, all applicants must complete Parts I through V of the application. Additional parts and schedules must be completed by certain applicants.

Part I.—Identification

Line 1. Full name of organization.—Enter the organization's name as it appears in its creating documents, including amendments. If the organization will be operating under another name, show the other name in parentheses.

Line 2. Employer identification number.—If the organization does not have an employer identification number, enter "none" and attach a completed **Form SS-4**, Application for Employer Identification Number, to the application. If the organization has previously applied for a number, attach a statement giving the date of the application and the office where it was filed.

Line 5. Month the annual accounting period ends.—Enter the month the organization's annual accounting period ends (see regulations section 1.441-1(b)(3)).

Page 2

Figure 4.1. (*Continued*).

When filing for exemption under Section 501(c)(3), an organization must indicate whether it is a private foundation, private operating foundation, or a public charity, indicating the type of public charity described in Section 509(a)(1), (2) or (3). If it does not so indicate and exemption under Section 501(c)(3) is issued, the organization will be considered to be a private foundation.[3]

A ruling or determination letter will be issued in advance of operations if your organization can describe its proposed operations in sufficient detail to permit a

Line 7. Activity codes.—Select up to three of the code numbers listed on the back cover that best describe or most accurately identify the organization's purposes, activities, or type of organization. Enter the codes in the order of their importance.

Part II.—Type of Entity and Organizational Documents

One of the basic requirements for exemption is that the organization be "organized" for one or more exempt purposes. If the organization does not have an organizing instrument, it will not qualify for exempt status. The organizing instrument must contain a proper dissolution clause. Regulations section 1.501(c)(3)-1(b)(4) requires the dedication of assets to one or more exempt purposes on dissolution. If your organizing instrument does not contain a proper dissolution clause and if State law does not provide for distribution of assets for one or more exempt purposes on dissolution, the organization will not qualify for exempt status. If you rely on State law, please cite the law and briefly state its provisions on an attachment. An organizing instrument is any of the following: Articles of Incorporation, Constitution, Articles of Association, Trust Indenture. Each of these documents that is submitted must be properly signed. The bylaws of an organization alone are not an organizing instrument. See Publication 557 for more detailed instructions and for sample organizing instruments that satisfy the requirements of section 501(c)(3) and the related regulations.

Before submitting a copy of the Articles of Incorporation to the IRS, you must have them approved by the Secretary of State or other appropriate State official.

We will not return any of the documents submitted in support of this application, including organizational documents. Therefore, instead of the originals, submit "conformed" copies of these documents. A "conformed" copy is one that agrees with the original document and all amendments to it. An unsigned copy of the organizational document must be accompanied by a written declaration signed by an officer authorized to sign for the organization, certifying that it is a complete and accurate copy of the original document. Chemically or photographically copied articles of incorporation that show evidence they were filed with and approved (certified) by the appropriate State official need not be accompanied by such a declaration. See Rev. Proc. 68-14, 1968-1 C.B. 768, for additional information.

If the organization has no written bylaws or similar internal rules of operation, submit a statement to this effect signed by an authorized officer of the organization.

Part III.—Activities and Operational Information

Line 1.—If it is anticipated that the organization's principal sources of support will increase or decrease substantially in relation to the organization's total support, attach a statement describing anticipated changes and explaining the basis for the expectation.

Line 2.—For purposes of this question, "fund-raising activity" includes the solicitation of contributions and both functionally related activities and unrelated business activities. Include a description of the nature and magnitude of the activities.

Line 4d.—For purposes of this application, a "disqualified person" is any person who, if the applicant organization were a private foundation, would be a disqualified person with respect to the organization within the meaning of section 4946(a). Thus, if a person's relationship to the applicant organization corresponds to one of the relationships described in section 4946(a), such person should be considered to be a disqualified person even though the applicant organization may not, in fact, be a private foundation.

Under section 4946(a), a disqualified person with respect to a private foundation is:

(1) a "substantial contributor" to the foundation (a "substantial contributor" is any person (including a corporation, trust, etc.) who contributed or bequeathed a total amount of more than $5,000, if such amount is more than 2% of the total contributions and bequests received by the foundation from its creation through the end of the tax year of the foundation in which the contribution or bequest is received by the foundation. The creator of a trust is a substantial contributor regardless of the size of the creator's contribution or bequest);

(2) a foundation manager;

(3) an owner of more than 20% of the total combined voting power of a corporation, the profits interest of a partnership, or the beneficial interest of a trust or unincorporated enterprise which is a substantial contributor to the foundation;

(4) a "member of the family" (as defined in section 4946(d)) of any person described in (1), (2), or (3), above;

(5) a corporation in which persons described in (1), (2), (3), and (4), above, own more than 35% of the total combined voting power;

(6) a partnership in which persons described in (1), (2), (3), and (4), above, hold more than 35% of the profits interest;

(7) a trust or estate in which persons described in (1), (2), (3), and (4), above, hold more than 35% of the beneficial interest; and

(8) for purposes of section 4943 only, any other private foundation that is effectively controlled by the same persons who control the first mentioned private foundation or any other private foundation whose contributions were made by the same contributors.

Line 13e.—An organization that does not submit Form 1023 timely and does not meet the conditions for relief under regulations section 1.9100 (described in Rev. Proc. 79-63, 1979-2 C.B. 578) cannot qualify as a section 501(c)(3) organization for any period before its application is received by the Service. However, the organization may still be able to qualify for exemption under section 501(c)(4) for the periods preceding the effective date of its exemption as a section 501(c)(3) organization. See Rev. Rul. 80-108, 1980-1 C.B. 119, for more information.

Section 501(e) and (f) Organizations.—If you are applying under section 501(e) or 501(f), complete questions 5, 6, 8, and 10 to show the relationship between your organization and the organizations you serve, as well as the services you provide for them. In completing question 5, attach a schedule listing each organization served, its address, and exempt status.

Part IV.—Statement as to Private Foundation Status

Line 1.—Unless an organization meets one of the exceptions provided in section 509, it is a private foundation. In general, an organization is not a private foundation if it is

(a) a church, school, hospital, or governmental unit;

(b) a medical research organization operated in conjunction with a hospital;

(c) an organization operated for the benefit of a college or university (which is owned or operated by a governmental unit);

(d) an organization that normally receives a substantial part of its support from a governmental unit or from the general public as provided in section 170(b)(1)(A)(vi);

(e) an organization that normally receives not more than one-third of its support from gross investment income and more than one-third of its support from contributions, membership fees, and gross receipts related to its exempt functions (subject to certain exceptions) as provided in section 509(a)(2);

(f) an organization operated solely for the benefit of, and in connection with, one or more organizations described above (or for the benefit of one or more of the organizations described in sections 501(c)(4), (5), or (6) of the Code and also described in (e) above), but not controlled by disqualified persons other than foundation managers, as provided in section 509(a)(3); or

(g) an organization organized and operated to test for public safety as provided in section 509(a)(4).

See Publication 578 and the instructions for Part VI-A for more information about determining whether an organization is one of the above types of organizations or if it is a private foundation.

Line 2.—Private operating foundations should see the instructions for Part VII.

Line 3.—The IRS will issue a definitive or advance ruling on foundation status to an organization that makes proper application for recognition of its exempt status under section 501(c)(3).

Definitive ruling.— If you request a "definitive ruling," the letter will also constitute a ruling or determination on whether the organization is a private foundation. A newly created organization, basing its claim to non-private foundation status on either section 509(a)(1) (by reason of section 170(b)(1)(A)(vi)) or section 509(a)(2), cannot get a definitive ruling before the close of its first tax year consisting of at least 8 months. Until this condition is met, an organization must apply for an advance ruling.

Advance Ruling.—If a newly created organization can reasonably be expected to meet the requirements of section 509(a)(1) (by reason of section 170(b)(1)(A)(vi)) or 509(a)(2), it may request non-private foundation treatment for an advance ruling period consisting of its first five tax years. During that period the organization will be treated as a publicly supported organization; however, at the end of that period the IRS will determine if the organization has met the statutory tests for

Page 3

Figure 4.1. (*Continued*).

conclusion that it will clearly meet the particular requirements of the section of the law under which exemption is claimed.[4]

Page 3 of Form 1023 asks for a description of the proposed activities. The reply should be in the greatest detail in language that *paraphrases* the purposes set forth in the articles of incorporation. A restatement of an organization's purposes or a statement that it will operate in furtherance of such purposes will *not* satisfy the publicly supported organizations from its history of operations during the advance ruling period. If the organization does not meet the public support tests, it will be liable for the excise tax on investment income under section 4940 for the period covered by its advance ruling.

If the organization requests an advance ruling or determination, it must file **Form 872-C**, Consent Fixing Period of Limitation Upon Assessment of Tax Under Section 4940 of the Internal Revenue Code, in duplicate. (Forms are included in this package.) The consent extends the period of limitations for assessment of section 4940 tax of all tax years until one year beyond the normal expiration date of the last tax year within the advance ruling period.

If you are requesting a definitive ruling based on section 170(b)(1)(A)(iv) or (vi), or an advance ruling, your answers to questions 1 through 11 of Part III will determine both the organization's claim of exemption and its non-private foundation status. Therefore, be sure to answer those questions completely.

See Rev. Proc. 79-8, 1979-1 C.B. 487, for rules relating to the temporary relief from sections 6651 and 6652 penalties granted to applicants for public charity status under sections 509(a) and 170(b)(1)(A).

Part V.—Financial Data

Provide the financial data in enough detail to show how your organization's activities are financed.

The Statement of Support, Revenue, and Expenses and the Balance Sheet must be completed for the current year and each of the three years immediately before it (or the years the organization has existed, if less than four). **Any applicant that has existed for less than 1 year should give financial data for the current year and proposed budgets for the following 2 years.** We may request financial data for more than four years if necessary. All financial information for the current year must cover the period ending within 60 days of the date of application. Prepare the balance sheets as of the last day of each year or period.

Prepare the statements using the method of accounting the organization uses in keeping its books and records. If the organization uses a method other than the cash receipts and disbursements method, attach a statement explaining the method used.

Line 3. Gross amounts derived from activities related to organization's exempt purpose.—An example of such income would be the income derived by a symphony orchestra from the sale of tickets to its performances.

Line 5. Gross amount received from sale of assets, excluding inventory items.—Attach a schedule that shows a description of each asset, the name of the person to whom sold, and the amount received. In the case of publicly traded securities sold through a broker, the name of the purchaser is not required.

Line 6. Investment income.—Include on this line the income received from dividends, interest, payments received on securities loans (as defined in section 512(a)(5)), rents, and royalties.

Line 7. Other revenue.—Enter the total revenue from all sources not reportable on lines 1 through 6. Attach a schedule that lists each type of revenue source and the amount derived from each.

Line 10. Contributions, gifts, grants, and similar amounts paid.—Attach a schedule showing the name of the recipient, a brief description of the purposes or conditions of payment, and the amount paid. The following example shows the format and amount of detail required for this schedule:

Recipient	Purposes	Amount
Museum of Natural History	General operating budget	$9,000
State University	Books for needy students	4,500
Richard Roe	Educational scholarship	2,200

Line 11. Disbursements to or for benefit of members.—Attach a schedule showing the name of each recipient, a brief description of the purposes or condition of payment, and amount paid. Amounts entered on this line should not be included on line 10. The following example shows the format and amount of detail required for the schedule:

Recipient	Purposes	Amount
Herman Hoe	Health insurance premium	$800

Line 12. Compensation of officers, directors, and trustees.—Attach a schedule that shows the name of the person compensated; the office or position; the average amount of time devoted to business per week, month, etc.; and the amount of annual compensation. The following example shows the format and amount of detail required for this schedule:

Name	Position	Time devoted	Amount
Philip Poe	President and general manager	16 hrs/wk	$7,500

Line 23. Bonds and notes.—Attach a schedule that shows the name of the borrower, a brief description of the obligation, the rate of return on the principal indebtedness, the due date, and the amount due. The following example shows the format and amount of detail required for this schedule:

Name of borrower	Description of obligation	Rate of return	Due date	Amount
Hope Soap Corporation	Debenture bond (no senior issue outstanding)	10%	Jan. 1999	$7,500
Big Spool Company	Collateral note secured by company's fleet of 20 delivery trucks	12%	Jan. 1998	62,000

Line 24. Corporate stocks.—Attach a schedule listing the organization's corporate stocks. For stock of closely held corporations, the statement should show the name of the corporation, a brief summary of the corporation's capital structure, the number of shares held and their value as carried on the organization's books. If such valuation does not reflect current fair market value, also include fair market value. For stock traded on an organized exchange or in substantial quantities over the counter, the statement should show the name of the corporation, a description of the stock and the principal exchange on which it is traded, the number of shares held, and their value as carried on the organization's books. The following example shows the format and the amount of detail required for this schedule:

Name of corporation	Capital structure (or exchange on which traded)	Shares	Book amount	Fair market value
Little Spool Corporation	100 shares nonvoting preferred issued and outstanding, no par value; 50 shares common issued and outstanding, no par value.			
	Preferred shares:	50	$20,000	$24,000
	Common shares:	10	25,000	30,000
Flintlock Corporation	Class A common N.Y.S.E.	20	3,000	3,500

Part VI.—A.—Basis for Non-Private Foundation Status

(Check the line that shows why you are not a private foundation.)

Line 1. A church or convention or association of churches.

Line 2. A school.—See the definition in the instructions for Part VIII, line 1.

Line 3. A hospital or medical research organization.—See the instructions for Schedule D.

Line 4. A governmental unit.—This category includes a separately incorporated instrumentality of a State, or of the United States, a possession of the United States, the District of Columbia, or any political subdivision of any of the above.

Line 5. An organization testing for public safety.—An organization in this category is one that tests products to determine their acceptability for use by the general public. It does not include any organization testing for the benefit of a manufacturer as an operation or control in the manufacture of its product. See Rev. Rul. 65-61, 1965-1 C.B. 234.

Line 6. Organization for the benefit of a college or university owned and operated by a governmental unit.—The organization must be organized and operated exclusively for the benefit of a college or university that is an educational organization within the meaning of section 170(b)(1)(A)(ii) and is an agency or instrumentality of a State or political subdivision of a State, is owned or operated by a State or political subdivision of a State, or is owned or operated by an agency or instrumentality of one or more States or political subdivisions. The organization must also

Page 4

Figure 4.1. (*Continued*).

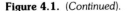

requirements for an advance ruling. The description of proposed operations must describe *fully* the activities in which the organization expects to engage. This includes standards, procedures, or other means adopted or planned by the organization for carrying out its activities, expected sources of funds, and the nature of its contemplated expenditures.

Regarding expected sources of funds, it should show whether support will be from public or private sources. Also, the nature of the support (contributions, grants, etc.) should be explained. If income from fund-raising events, ticket sales, normally receive a substantial part of its support from the United States or any State or political subdivision of a State, or from direct or indirect contributions from the general public or from a combination of two or more of such sources. An organization described in section 170(b)(1)(A)(iv) will be subject to the same publicly supported rules that are applicable to 170(b)(1)(A)(vi) organizations that are described in 7 below. Complete Part VI-B, Analysis of Financial Support, to show whether the organization has the necessary support from required sources.

Line 7. Organization receiving support from a governmental unit or from the general public. — The organization must receive a substantial part of its support from the United States or any State or political subdivision thereof, or from direct or indirect contributions from the general public or from a combination of these sources. The organization may satisfy the support requirement in either of two ways. It will be treated as publicly supported if the support it normally receives from above described governmental units and the general public equals at least one-third of its total support. It will also be treated as publicly supported if the support it normally receives from governmental or public sources equals at least 10% of total support and under the facts and circumstances the organization is set up to attract new and additional public or governmental support on a continuous basis. Complete Part VI-B, Analysis of Financial Support, to show whether the organization has the necessary support from required sources. If the organization's governmental and public support is at least 10% but not over one-third of its total support, questions 1 through 11 of Part III will apply to determine both the organization's claim of exemption and whether under the particular facts and circumstances it is publicly supported. Preparers should exercise care to assure that those questions are answered in detail.

Line 8. Organization described in section 509(a)(2). — The organization must satisfy the support test under section 509(a)(2)(A) and the gross investment income test under section 509(a)(2)(B). In order to satisfy the support test, the organization must normally receive more than one-third of its support from (a) gifts, grants, contributions, or membership fees and (b) gross receipts from admissions, sales of merchandise, performance of services, or furnishing of facilities, in an activity which is not an unrelated trade or business (subject to certain limitations discussed below). This one-third of support must be from organizations described in section 509(a)(1), governmental sources, and persons other than disqualified persons. In computing gross receipts from admissions, sales of merchandise, performance of services, or furnishing of facilities in an activity which is not an unrelated trade or business, the gross receipts from any one person or from any bureau or similar agency of a governmental unit are includible only to the extent they do not exceed the greater of $5,000 or one percent of the organization's total support. In order to satisfy the gross investment income test, the organization must not receive more than one-third of its support from gross investment income. Complete Part VI-B, Analysis of Financial Support, to show whether the organization has the necessary support from required sources.

Line 9. Organizations operated in connection with or solely for organizations described in 1 through 4, or 6, 7 and 8 above. — The organization must be organized and operated for the benefit of, to perform the functions of, or to carry out the purposes of one or more specified organizations described in section 509(a)(1) or (2). It must be operated, supervised, or controlled by or in connection with one or more of the organizations described in the instructions for lines 1 through 4, or 6, 7, and 8 above. It must not be controlled directly or indirectly by disqualified persons (other than foundation managers or organizations described in section 509(a)(1) or (2)). In order to show whether the organization satisfies these tests, complete Part VI-C, Supplemental Information Concerning Organization Claiming Non-Private Foundation Status Under Section 509(a)(3).

Part VI.—B.—Analysis of Financial Support

Lines 1 and 3. — Refer to regulations sections 1.170A-9(e)(8) and 1.509(a)-3(f) and (g) to determine whether a grant from a governmental unit or other grantor represents a contribution (reportable on line 1) or income from the performance of services (reportable on line 3) if the services constitute an exempt function of the organization; otherwise, the amount may be reportable on line 5 as unrelated income.

Page 5

Line 4. — "Investment income" means: interest, dividends, rents, amounts received after December 31, 1976, with respect to securities loans (as defined in section 512(a)(5)), royalties, and unrelated business taxable income (less section 511 tax) from businesses acquired or begun by the organization after June 30, 1975.

Line 12. — Unusual grants generally consist of substantial contributions and bequests from disinterested persons, which contributions and bequests:

(1) are attracted by reason of the publicly supported nature of the organization;

(2) are unusual and unexpected as to amount, and

(3) would, by reason of their size, adversely affect the status of the organization as normally meeting the support test of section 170(b)(1)(A)(vi) or section 509(a)(2), as the case may be.

Subject to the above conditions, if the organization is awarded a grant and the terms of the granting instrument provide that the organization will receive the funds over a period of years, the amount received by the organization each year under the grant may be excluded. See the regulations under sections 170 and 509.

Part VII.—Basis for Status as a Private Operating Foundation

A "private operating foundation" described in section 4942(j)(3) is a private foundation that spends substantially all of the lesser of its adjusted net income (as defined below) or its minimum investment return directly for the active conduct of the activities constituting the purpose or function for which it is organized and operated. The foundation must satisfy the income test under section 4942(j)(3)(A), as modified by regulations section 53.4942(b)-1, and one of the three supplemental tests: (a) the assets test under section 4942(j)(3)(B)(i); (b) the endowment test under section 4942(j)(3)(B)(ii); or (c) the support test under section 4942(j)(3)(B)(iii).

Certain long-term care facilities described in section 4942(j)(5) are treated as private operating foundations for purposes of section 4942 only.

"Adjusted net income" is the excess of gross income for the tax year over the sum of deductions determined with the modifications described below. Items of gross income from any unrelated trade or business and the deductions directly connected with the unrelated trade or business will be taken into account in computing the organization's adjusted net income:

Income modifications (adjustments to gross income). —

(1) Section 103 (relating to interest on certain governmental obligations) does not apply. Thus, interest that otherwise would have been excluded should be included in gross income.

(2) Except as provided in (3) below, capital gains and losses are taken into account only to the extent of the net short-term gain. Long-term gains and losses will be disregarded.

(3) The gross amount received from the sale or disposition of certain property should be taken into account to the extent that the acquisition of the property constituted a qualifying distribution under section 4942(g)(1)(B).

(4) Repayments of prior qualifying distributions (as defined in section 4942(g)(1)(A)) will constitute items of gross income.

(5) Any amount set aside under section 4942(g)(2) that has been determined to be "not necessary for the purposes for which it was set aside" will constitute an item of gross income.

Deduction modifications (adjustments to deductions). —

(1) Expenses for the general operation of the organization according to its charitable purposes (as contrasted with expenses for the production or collection of income and management, conservation, or maintenance of income producing property) should not be taken as deductions. If only a portion of the property is used for production of income subject to section 4942 and the remainder is used for general charitable purposes, the expenses connected with that property should be divided according to those purposes and only expenses related to the income producing portion will be allowed as a deduction.

(2) Charitable contributions, deductible under section 170 or 642(c), should not be taken into account as deductions for adjusted net income.

Figure 4.1. (*Continued*).

rentals, or other business or investment sources is anticipated, the nature of the venture or revenue-producing enterprise should be explained.

Where an organization does not supply the information previously mentioned, or fails to furnish a sufficiently detailed description of its proposed activities to permit a conclusion that it will clearly be exempt, a record of actual operations will be required before a ruling or determination letter is issued. If insufficient information is provided, the application will be considered incomplete and returned to the organization and a "No Ruling" letter issued.

(3) The net operating loss deduction prescribed under section 172 should not be taken into account as a deduction for adjusted net income.

(4) The special deductions for corporations (such as the dividends-received deduction) allowed under sections 241 through 250 should not be taken into account as deductions for adjusted net income.

(5) Depreciation and depletion should be determined in the same manner as under section 4940(c)(3)(B).

(6) Section 265 (relating to the expenses and interest connected with tax-exempt interest) should not be taken into account.

You may find it easier to figure adjusted net income by completing Column (c), Part 1, Form 990-PF, according to the instructions for that form.

An organization that has been held to be a private operating foundation will continue to be such an organization only if it meets the income test and either the assets, endowment, or support test in later years. See the regulations under section 4942(j)(3) for additional information. No additional request for ruling will be necessary or appropriate for an organization to maintain its status as a private operating foundation. However, data related to the above tests must be submitted with the organization's annual information return.

Part VIII.—Required Schedules for Special Activities

Line 1.—A "school" is an organization that has the primary function of presenting formal instruction, normally maintains a regular faculty and curriculum, normally has a regularly enrolled body of students, and has a place where its educational activities are carried on. The term generally corresponds to the definition of an "educational organization" in section 170(b)(1)(A)(ii). Thus, the term includes primary, secondary, preparatory and high schools, and colleges and universities. The term does not include organizations engaged in both educational and non-educational activities unless the latter are merely incidental to the educational activities. A school for handicapped children would be included within the term, but an organization merely providing handicapped children with custodial care would not.

For purposes of this question, "Sunday schools" that are conducted by a church would not be included in the term "schools," but separately organized schools (such as parochial schools), universities, and similar institutions would be included in the term. Child care organizations described in section 501(k) generally are not included in the term "school."

Line 3.—A "for profit" institution includes any organization in which a person may have a proprietary or partnership interest, hold corporate stock, or otherwise exercise an ownership interest. The institution need not have been operated for the purpose of making a profit.

Schedule A.—Schools, Colleges, and Universities

A private school that otherwise meets the requirements of section 501(c)(3) as an educational institution will not qualify for exemption under section 501(a) unless it has a racially nondiscriminatory policy as to students. This policy means that the school admits students of any race to all the rights, privileges, programs, and activities generally accorded or made available to students at that school, and that the school does not discriminate on the basis of race in the administration of its educational policies, admissions policies, scholarship and loan programs, and athletic, or other school-administered programs. The Service

considers discrimination on the basis of race to include discrimination on the basis of color and national or ethnic origin. A policy of a school that favors racial minority groups in admissions, facilities, programs, and financial assistance will not constitute discrimination on the basis of race when the purpose and effect is to promote the establishment and maintenance of that school's racially non-discriminatory policy as to students. See Rev. Proc. 75-50, 1975-2 C.B. 587, for guidelines and recordkeeping requirements for determining whether private schools that are applying for recognition of exemption have racially nondiscriminatory policies as to students.

Line 1. An instrumentality of a State or political subdivision of a State may qualify under section 501(c)(3) if it is organized as a separate entity from the governmental unit that created it and if it otherwise meets the organizational and operational tests of section 501(c)(3). (See Rev. Rul. 60-384, 1960-2 C.B. 172.) Any such organization that is a school is not a private school and, therefore, is not subject to the provisions of Rev. Proc. 75-50.

Schools that incorrectly answer "Yes" to line 1 will be required to furnish the information called for by lines 2 through 9 in order to establish that they meet the requirements for exemption. To prevent delay in the processing of your application, be sure to answer line 1 correctly and complete lines 2 through 9 if applicable.

Schedule D.—Hospitals and Medical Research Organizations

Cooperative hospital service organizations (section 501(e)) should not complete Schedule D.

In order to be entitled to status as a "hospital," an organization must have, as its principal purpose or function, the providing of medical or hospital care or medical education or research. "Medical care" includes the treatment of any physical or mental disability or condition, the cost of which may be taken as a deduction under section 213, whether the treatment is performed on an inpatient or outpatient basis. Thus, a rehabilitation institution, outpatient clinic, or community mental health or drug treatment center may be a hospital if its principal function is providing the above described services. On the other hand, a convalescent home or a home for children or the aged would not be a hospital. Similarly, an institution whose principal purpose or function is to train handicapped individuals to pursue some vocation would not be a hospital. Moreover, a medical education or medical research institution is not a hospital, unless it is also actively engaged in providing medical or hospital care to patients on its premises or in its facilities on an inpatient or outpatient basis.

To qualify as a medical research organization, the principal function of the organization must be the direct, continuous and active conduct of medical research in conjunction with a hospital which is described in section 501(c)(3), a Federal hospital, or an instrumentality of a governmental unit referred to in section 170(c)(1). For purposes of section 170(b)(1)(A)(iii) only, the organization must be set up to use the funds it receives in the active conduct of medical research by January 1 of the fifth calendar year after receipt. The arrangement it has with donors to assure use of the funds within the five-year period must be legally enforceable. As used here, "medical research" means investigations, experiments and studies to discover, develop, or verify knowledge relating to the causes, diagnosis, treatment, prevention, or control of the physical or mental diseases and impairments of man. For further information, see regulations section 1.170A-9(c)(2).

Page 6

Figure 4.1. *(Continued).*

It is suggested that a "No Ruling" letter may be avoided by indicating the name of the person to be contacted and his or her telephone number, along with a statement to the effect that if additional information is needed to complete the consideration of the application, he or she should be contacted by phone.

Every exempt organization is required to have an Employer Identification Number, *whether or not it has any employees.* If your organization does not have an Employer Identification Number, your application for recognition of exemption should be accompanied by a completed Form SS-4, "Application for Employer Identification Number."

If your organization expects to be represented by agents or attorneys, it must file a power of attorney authorizing them to represent it. Form 2848, "Power of Attorney," and Form 2848-D, "Authorization and Declaration," may be used for this purpose.

It is important to note that when the exemption application is submitted, the organization must attach certain important documents pertaining to the organization, some of which must be "conformed copies." A *conformed copy* is one that

Make sure your application is complete.
Please remember . . .

1. **Complete all parts of the application that apply to the organization. If the application is incomplete, we will send it back to you without taking any action on it.**

2. **Show your employer identification number:**
   a. If you have one, write it in the space provided.
   b. If you are a newly formed organization, and don't have an employer identification number, attach a completed Form SS-4 if you haven't already applied for one.

3. **Enclose financial statements** (see Specific Instructions, Part V).
   a. Current year (must include period up to within 60 days of the date the application is filed) and 3 preceding years.
   b. Detailed breakdown of support, revenue, and expenses—no lump sums.
   c. If the organization has been in existence less than one year, **you must also submit proposed budgets** for 2 years showing the amounts and types of receipts and expenditures anticipated.

4. **Include a conformed copy of the complete organizing instrument.**
   a. An organizing instrument means:
      1. Articles of Incorporation
         (a) Signed by the directors and
         (b) Accepted by an appropriate government official (see Specific Instructions, Part II), or
      2. Constitution or Articles of Association (signed), or
      3. Trust Instrument (signed).
   b. If the organization is a corporation (or an unincorporated organization with bylaws), you **must** also include a copy of the bylaws.
   c. A **conformed copy** is one that agrees with the original and all amendments to it.
   d. Your organizing instrument, either expressly or by operation of State law, must limit your activities to those permitted under section 501(c)(3) and must provide for a proper distribution of your net assets upon dissolution. (See Specific Instructions for Part II and Publication 557.)

5. **If you answer "Yes," to question 8 of Part I, be sure to specify the form number of each return filed, the year covered by the return, and the place where filed.**

6. **If the organization is applying as a school, you must also submit:**
   a. A statement of a racially non-discriminatory policy as to students, and
   b. Proof that the statement was published in a newspaper of general circulation, and
   c. Proof that the policy has been **adopted** by your organization.

7. **Have the application signed by one of the following:**
   a. An officer who is authorized to sign, or
   b. A person authorized by power of attorney (submit the power of attorney, too).

8. **Give us the name and telephone number of someone we can call during business hours if we need additional information.**

   Note: You may be contacted by one or more IRS employees regarding your application. If you do not complete all applicable parts of the application or do not provide all required attachments, we will return the incomplete application to you for resubmission with the missing information or attachments. During the technical review of a completed application by the Employee Plans/Exempt Organizations Division in the key district or by the Exempt Organizations Technical Division in the National Office, it may also be necessary to contact you for more specific or additional information.

Figure 4.1. (*Continued*).

agrees with the document it purports to copy. This copy should either be signed by an authorized officer, certifying that the document is a complete and accurate copy of the original. These documents include:[5]

Certificate of Incorporation*

Constitution*

Articles of Association*

Trust Indenture, or other enabling instrument*

*Conformed copies must be attached.

Activity Code Numbers of Exempt Organizations (select up to three codes which best describe or most accurately identify your purposes, activities, operations or type of organization and enter in block 7, page 1, of the application. Enter first the code which most accurately identifies you.)

Code

Religious Activities

001 Church, synagogue, etc.
002 Association or convention of churches
003 Religious order
004 Church auxiliary
005 Mission
006 Missionary activities
007 Evangelism
008 Religious publishing activities
.... Book store (use 918)
.... Genealogical activities (use 094)
029 Other religious activities

Schools, Colleges and Related Activities

030 School, college, trade school, etc.
031 Special school for the blind, handicapped, etc.
032 Nursery school
.... Day care center (use 574)
033 Faculty group
034 Alumni association or group
035 Parent or parent-teachers association
036 Fraternity or sorority
.... Key club (use 323)
037 Other student society or group
038 School or college athletic association
039 Scholarships for children of employees
040 Scholarships (other)
041 Student loans
042 Student housing activities
043 Other student aid
044 Student exchange with foreign country
045 Student operated business
.... Financial support of schools, colleges, etc. (use 602)
.... Achievement prizes or awards (use 914)
.... Student book store (use 918)
.... Student travel (use 299)
.... Scientific research (see Scientific Research Activities)
046 Private school
059 Other school related activities

Cultural, Historical or Other Educational Activities

060 Musuem, zoo, planetarium, etc.
061 Library
062 Historical site, records or reenactment
063 Monument
064 Commemorative event (centennial, festival, pageant, etc.)
065 Fair
088 Community theatrical group
089 Singing society or group
090 Cultural performances
091 Art exhibit
092 Literary activities
093 Cultural exchanges with foreign country
094 Genealogical activities
.... Achievement prizes or awards (use 914)
.... Gifts or grants to individuals (use 561)
.... Financial support of cultural organizations (use 602)
119 Other cultural or historical activities

Other Instruction and Training Activities

120 Publishing activities
121 Radio or television broadcasting
122 Producing films
123 Discussion groups, forums, panels, lectures, etc.
124 Study and research (non-scientific)
125 Giving information or opinion (see also Advocacy)
126 Apprentice training
.... Travel tours (use 299)
149 Other instruction and training

Health Services and Related Activities

150 Hospital
151 Hospital auxiliary
152 Nursing or convalescent home
153 Care and housing for the aged (see also 382)
154 Health clinic
155 Rural medical facility
156 Blood bank
157 Cooperative hospital service organization
158 Rescue and emergency service
159 Nurses' register or bureau
160 Aid to the handicapped (see also 031)
161 Scientific research (diseases)
162 Other medical research
163 Health insurance (medical, dental, optical, etc.)
164 Prepared group health plan
165 Community health planning
166 Mental health care
167 Group medical practice association
168 In-faculty group practice association
169 Hospital pharmacy, parking facility, food services, etc.
179 Other health services

Code

Scientific Research Activities

180 Contract or sponsored scientific research for industry
181 Scientific research for government
.... Scientific research (diseases) (use 161)
199 Other scientific research activities

Business and Professional Organizations

200 Business promotion (chamber of commerce, business league, etc.)
201 Real estate association
202 Board of trade
203 Regulating business
204 Better Business Bureau
205 Professional association
206 Professional association auxiliary
207 Industry trade shows
208 Convention displays
.... Testing products for public safety (use 905)
209 Research, development and testing
210 Professional athletic league
.... Attracting new industry (use 403)
.... Publishing activities (use 120)
.... Insurance or other benefits for members (see Employee or Membership Benefit Organizations)
211 Underwriting municipal insurance
212 Assigned risk insurance activities
213 Tourist bureau
229 Other business or professional group

Farming and Related Activities

230 Farming
231 Farm bureau
232 Agricultural group
233 Horticultural group
234 Farmers' cooperative marketing or purchasing
235 Financing crop operations
.... FFA, FHA, 4-H club, etc. (use 322)
.... Fair (use 065)
236 Dairy herd improvement association
237 Breeders association
249 Other farming and related activities

Mutual Organizations

250 Mutual ditch, irrigation, telephone, electric company or like organization
251 Credit union
252 Reserve funds or insurance for domestic building and loan association, cooperative bank, or mutual savings bank
253 Mutual insurance company
254 Corporation organized under an Act of Congress (see also 904)
.... Farmers' cooperative marketing or purchasing (use 234)
.... Cooperative hospital service organization (use 157)
259 Other mutual organization

Employee or Membership Benefit Organizations

260 Fraternal beneficiary society, order, or association
261 Improvement of conditions of workers
262 Association of municipal employees
263 Association of employees
264 Employee or member welfare association
265 Sick, accident, death, or similar benefits
266 Strike benefits
267 Unemployment benefits
268 Pension or retirement benefits
269 Vacation benefits
279 Other services or benefits to members or employees

Sports, Athletic, Recreational and Social Activities

280 Country club
281 Hobby club
282 Dinner club
283 Variety club
284 Dog club
285 Women's club
.... Garden club (use 356)
286 Hunting or fishing club
287 Swimming or tennis club
288 Other sports club
.... Boys Club, Little League, etc. (use 321)
296 Community center
297 Community recreational facilities (park, playground, etc.)
298 Training in sports
299 Travel tours
300 Amateur athletic association
.... School or college athletic association (use 038)
301 Fund raising athletic or sports event
317 Other sports or athletic activities
318 Other recreational activities
319 Other social activities

Code

Youth Activities

320 Boy Scouts, Girl Scouts, etc.
321 Boys Club, Little League, etc.
322 FFA, FHA, 4-H club, etc.
323 Key club
324 YMCA, YWCA, YMHA, etc.
325 Camp
326 Care and housing of children (orphanage, etc.)
327 Prevention of cruelty to children
328 Combat juvenile delinquency
349 Other youth organization or activities

Conservation, Environmental and Beautification Activities

350 Preservation of natural resources (conservation)
351 Combatting or preventing pollution (air, water, etc.)
352 Land acquisition for preservation
353 Soil or water conservation
354 Preservation of scenic beauty
.... Litigation (see Litigation and Legal Aid Activities)
.... Combat community deterioration (use 402)
355 Wildlife sanctuary or refuge
356 Garden club
379 Other conservation, environmental or beautification activities

Housing Activities

380 Low-income housing
381 Low and moderate income housing
382 Housing for the aged (see also 153)
.... Nursing or convalescent home (use 152)
.... Student housing (use 042)
.... Orphanage (use 326)
398 Instruction and guidance on housing
399 Other housing activities

Inner City or Community Activities

400 Area development, re-development or renewal
.... Housing (see Housing Activities)
401 Homeowners association
402 Other activity aimed at combatting community deterioration
403 Attracting new industry or retaining industry in an area
404 Community promotion
.... Community recreational facility (use 297)
.... Community center (use 296)
405 Loans or grants for minority businesses
.... Job training, counseling, or assistance (use 566)
.... Day care center (use 574)
.... Referral service (social agencies) (use 569)
.... Legal aid to indigents (use 462)
406 Crime prevention
407 Voluntary firemen's organization or auxiliary
.... Rescue squad (use 158)
408 Community service organization
429 Other inner city or community benefit activities

Civil Rights Activities

430 Defense of human and civil rights
431 Elimination of prejudice and discrimination (race, religion, sex, national origin, etc.)
432 Lessen neighborhood tensions
449 Other civil rights activities

Litigation and Legal Aid Activities

460 Public interest litigation activities
461 Other litigation or support of litigation
462 Legal aid to indigents
463 Providing bail
465 Plan under IRC section 120

Legislative and Political Activities

480 Propose, support, or oppose legislation
481 Voter information on issues or candidates
482 Voter education (mechanics of registering, voting, etc.)
483 Support, oppose, or rate political candidates
484 Provide facilities or services for political campaign activities
509 Other legislative and political activities

Advocacy

Attempt to influence public opinion concerning:
510 Firearms control
511 Selective Service System

Code

512 National defense policy
513 Weapons systems
514 Government spending
515 Taxes or tax exemption
516 Separation of church and state
517 Government aid to parochial schools
518 U.S. foreign policy
519 U.S. military involvement
520 Pacifism and peace
521 Economic-political system of U.S.
522 Anti-communism
523 Right to work
524 Zoning or rezoning
525 Location of highway or transportation system
526 Rights of criminal defendants
527 Capital punishment
528 Stricter law enforcement
529 Ecology or conservation
530 Protection of consumer interests
531 Medical care service
532 Welfare system
533 Urban renewal
534 Busing students to achieve racial balance
535 Racial integration
536 Use of intoxicating beverage
537 Use of drugs or narcotics
538 Use of tobacco
539 Prohibition of erotica
540 Sex education in public schools
541 Population control
542 Birth control methods
543 Legalized abortion
559 Other matters

Other Activities Directed to Individuals

560 Supplying money, goods or services to the poor
561 Gifts or grants to individuals (other than scholarships)
.... Scholarships for children of employees (use 039)
.... Scholarships (other) (use 040)
.... Student loans (use 041)
562 Other loans to individuals
563 Marriage counseling
564 Family planning
565 Credit counseling and assistance
566 Job training, counseling, or assistance
567 Draft counseling
568 Vocational counseling
569 Referral service (social agencies)
572 Rehabilitating convicts or ex-convicts
573 Rehabilitating alcoholics, drug abusers, compulsive gamblers, etc.
574 Day care center
575 Services for the aged (see also 153 and 382)
.... Training of or aid to the handicapped (see 031 and 160)

Activities Directed to Other Organizations

600 Community Chest, United Way, etc.
601 Booster club
602 Gifts, grants, or loans to other organizations
603 Non-financial services or facilities to other organizations

Other Purposes and Activities

900 Cemetery or burial activities
901 Perpetual care fund (cemetery, columbarium, etc.)
902 Emergency or disaster aid fund
903 Community trust or component
904 Government instrumentality or agency (see also 254)
905 Testing products for public safety
906 Consumer interest group
907 Veterans activities
908 Patriotic activities
909 4947(a)(1) trust
910 Domestic organization with activities outside U.S.
911 Foreign organization
912 Title holding corporation
913 Prevention of cruelty to animals
914 Achievement prizes or awards
915 Erection or maintenance of public building or works
916 Cafeteria, restaurant, snack bar, food services, etc.
917 Thrift shop, retail outlet, etc.
918 Book, gift or supply store
919 Advertising
921 Loans or credit reporting
922 Endowment fund or financial services
923 Indians (tribes, cultures, etc.)
924 Traffic or tariff bureau
927 Fundraising
928 4947(a)(2) trust
930 Prepaid legal services plan exempt under IRC section 501(c)(20)
990 Section 501(k) child care organization

☆ U.S. Government Printing Office: 1986—153-054/50004

Figure 4.1. *(Continued).*

By-laws or other similar code of regulations, signed by a principal officer and showing date adopted

Classified statement of receipts and expenditures

Balance sheet for the current year and the three immediate prior years (or the years the organization was in existence, if less)

Statement of proposed activities if the application form requires it

Any amendments to the above documents or instruments (e.g., official changes of the organization's name)*

Neither bank statements nor ledger sheets will be acceptable for these purposes, because they are not classified. Profit-and-loss or other similar operating statements are not acceptable, because they do not show all receipts and expenditures.

For prompt action on your application for recognition of exemption, you should be certain that all the statements, instruments, and other material previously described have been submitted in every particular with your organization's application form. Be sure that *every* statement required by the application form is attached. Unless *all* the required documents have been provided with your application, you may have to resubmit it or otherwise encounter a delay in obtaining recognition of exemption.

To ensure that an extended advance ruling will be granted, Form 872-C, "Consent Fixing Period of Limitation upon Assessment of Tax under Section 4940 of the Internal Revenue Code of 1954" must be executed. (See Revenue Ruling 77-115 IRB 1977-16, dated 4/18/77.)

Any information submitted in the application or in support of it that relates to any trade secret, patent, process, style of work, or apparatus, may, upon request, be withheld from public inspection if the commissioner determines that the disclosure of such information would adversely affect the organization. Your request must:

1. Identify the material to be withheld (the document, page, paragraph, and line) by clearly marking it "Not Subject to Public Inspection"

2. Include the reasons for your organization's position that the information is of the type that may be withheld from public inspection

3. Be filed with the documents in which the material to be withheld is contained

An application may be withdrawn at any time prior to the issuance of a ruling or determination letter upon the written request of a principal officer of your organization. However, the withdrawal will not prevent the information contained inthe application from being used by the IRS in any subsequent audit or examination of your organization's returns. The information forwarded in an application will *not* be returned to your organization.

Foreign Organizations[6]

Foreign organizations are treated in the same manner as domestic organizations unless they receive substantially all (90 percent) of their support (exclusive of investment income) from foreign sources. Foreign organizations should send their Form 1023 to the Baltimore, Maryland, Key District, addressed as follows:

Internal Revenue Service
Technical and Service Staff
EP/EO Division
P.O. Box 538
Baltimore, Maryland 21203

*Conformed copies must be attached.

Community Trusts[7]

Community trusts that have been in existence for less than one taxable year may apply for a determination or ruling that they are publicly supported with the key district in which their principal office or place of business is located.

Group Exemption Letter[8]

A central organization with affiliated subordinates under its control may apply for a group exemption letter. The ruling grants exemption to the central organization and its subordinates. The central organization should submit the following information:

1. A letter signed by a principal officer of the central organization setting forth or including as attachments:
   a. Information verifying that the subordinates to be included in the group exemption letter are affiliated with the central organization; are subject to its general supervision or control; are eligible to qualify for exemption under the same paragraph of Section 501(c) of the Code, though not necessarily the paragraph under which the central organization is exempt; are not private foundations, if the application for a group exemption letter involves section 501(c)(3); are all on the same accounting period as the central organization if they are to be included in group returns; and are organizations that have been formed within the 15-month period prior to date of submission of the group exemption application, if they are claiming section 501(c)(3) status and are subject to the requirements of section 508(a), and wish to be recognized as exempt from their dates of creation (a group exemption letter may be issued covering subordinates, one or more of which have not been organized within the 15-month period prior to the date of submission, if all subordinates are willing to be recognized as exempt only from the date of application)
   b. A description of the principal purposes and activities of the subordinates
   c. A sample copy of a uniform governing instrument (such as charter or articles of association) or, in its absence, copies of representative instruments
   d. An affirmation to the effect that, to the best of the principal officer's knowledge, the subordinates are operating in accordance with the stated purposes
   e. A statement that each subordinate to be included in the group exemption letter has furnished written authorization to the central organization
   f. A list of subordinates to be included in the group exemption letter to which the Service had already issued an outstanding ruling or determination letter relating to exemption
   g. If the application for a group exemption letter involves Section 501(c)(3) of the Code, an affirmation to the effect that, to the best of the principal officer's knowledge and belief, no subordinate to be included in the group exemption letter is a private foundation as defined in Section 509(a) of the code
   h. For each subordinate that is a school claiming exemption under Section 501(c)(3) the information required by Revenue Ruling 71-447 and Revenue Procedure 75-50
   i. For any school affiliated with a church, the information to show that the provisions of Revenue Ruling 75-231 have been met
2. A list of names, mailing addresses, and employer identification numbers of subordinates to be included in the group exemption letter

Separate Fund, Contributions to Which Are Deductible

An organization that is exempt from federal income tax other than as an organization described in Section 501(c)(3) of the Internal Revenue Code may, if it desires, establish a fund, separate and apart from its other funds, exclusively for religious, charitable, scientific, literary, or educational purposes or for the prevention of cruelty to children or animals.

If the fund is organized and operated exclusively for such purposes, it may qualify for exemption as an organization described in Section 501(c)(3) of the Internal Revenue Code, and contributions made to it will be deductible as provided by Section 170 of the Code. A fund of this character must be organized in such a manner as to prohibit the use of its funds upon dissolution, or otherwise, for the general purposes of the organization creating it.

Significance of "Organized"

In view of the 15-month requirement for filing, it is important to determine what is considered to be the date an organization is organized. The following is pertinent:

1. A corporation is organized on the date created under the state law in which it is incorporated, that is, on the date its articles of incorporation are filed by the state official in the appropriate state office.[9]
2. An *inter vivos* trust is organized the earliest time that either grantor or any person is treated as owner of the entire trust.
3. A testamentary trust is organized as of the date of death of the testator.
4. A Section 4947(a)(1) nonexempt trust is organized the date it becomes a Section 4947(a)(1) trust.

Exemption from Notice

The following organizations are excused from filing for exemption:

1. Churches, their integrated auxiliaries and conventions or associations of churches.[10]
2. Nonprivate foundations,[11] if gross receipts in each taxable year are normally not more than $5000. By "normally" is meant gross receipts:
    a. During its first tax year are $7500 or less
    b. During its first 2 years are $12,000 or less
    c. for the first 3 years are $15,000 or less
3. Subordinate organizations covered by a group ruling, none of which is a private foundation.[12]
4. Any other class the commissioner of Internal Revenue excludes from filing under the provisions of Section 508(a).[13]
5. Section 4947(a)(1) nonexempt trusts, unless they wish to avoid private foundation status.[14]

Frequently, organizations not required to file for exempt status do so voluntarily so that their exempt status becomes a matter of public record when prospective contributors ask for a written approval citing the section of the Code under which the organization is exempt.[15]

Governing Instrument

If an organization files for exemption under Section 501(c)(3) as a private foundation, it will be denied exemption unless its governing instrument includes provisions that

1. Require that distributions be made so as not to subject the foundation to the tax under Section 4942 of the Internal Revenue Code (Failure to Distribute Income).

2. Prohibit the foundation from engaging in activities as set forth in Section 4941(d) (Self-dealing), Section 4943(c) (Excess Business Holdings), Section 4944 (Investments Which Jeopardize Exempt Status), and Section 4945(d) (Taxable Expenditures).[16] Many states have enacted legislation to conform to the requirements of Section 508(e), thus avoiding the necessity of amending the governing instrument. Familiarity with state law in the private foundation area is an absolute requisite.

Public Charity versus Private Foundation Status

At this point, it is important to know the differences between "public charity" and "private foundation" status.

Organizations exempt under Section 509(a)(1), 509(a)(2), or 509(a)(3) are public charities. They escape the private foundation taint because they are statutorily excluded from the definition of "private foundation." As a result, they are not subject to the restrictions of Sections 4941 through 4945 and the payment of the tax on investment income of Section 4940. Moreover, they are eligible for the full 50 percent of adjusted gross income contribution deduction and favorable appreciated property contribution provisions under Section 170. Grants to public charities are qualifying distributions under Section 4942(g) and need not be disbursed by them in the following year. The managers of these organizations are not required to file the annual report dictated by Section 6056, and they are not required to publish notification in the newspaper.

"Public charity" requirements are not the same for each type of organization. Consequently, each Section 501(c)(3) organization that is applying for exemption as a public charity or that is presently exempt must know the operational needs of each category. As an illustration, Sections 509(a)(1) and (a)(2) both require that public support be more than 33⅓ percent of the total support. However, Section 509(a)(1) also permits an organization to qualify if its public support is as low as 10 percent of the total support. In such case, the 501(c)(3) organization should also fulfill one or more of the following specifications:

1. Be organized and operated to attract new and additional public or governmental support

2. Have a representative governing body

3. Make its facilities or services available to the general public

Thus, an organization that includes in its governing body a broad cross section of community leaders and persons having special knowledge could meet the test of the second item. An organization that is a museum open to the public or a symphony orchestra that gives public performances could meet the test of the third requirement.

The 10 percent floor is not applicable to a Section 509(a)(2) organization. Not only must the public support fraction be more than 33⅓ percent, but it must receive not more than 33⅓ percent of total support from gross investment income sources. Thus, an organization that receives 60 percent of its total support from the general public and 40 percent from investment income cannot qualify under Section 509(a)(2). It may, however, qualify under Section 509(a)(1).

A Section 509(a)(3) organization is a public charity through its support of Section 509(a)(1) or (a)(2) organizations. It must be

1. Organized, and at all times thereafter operated exclusively for the benefit of, perform the functions of, or carry out the purposes of Section 509(a)(1) or (a)(2) organizations

2. Operated, supervised, or controlled by or in connection with Section 509(a)(1) or (a)(2) organizations

3. An organization not controlled directly or indirectly by one or more disqualified persons as set forth in Section 4946, other than foundation managers and other than Section 509(a)(1) or (2) organizations

Going back to Section 509(a)(1) and (2), we see that the nature of the sources of support is essential to determine exempt category. Thus, we must look to support fractions, the denominator reflecting total support with the numerator known as public support. As stated previously, for both Sections 509(a)(1) and (a)(2), public support (numerator) must be more than one-third of total support for each to be considered for public charity status. Section 509(a)(2) requires, in addition, that less than one-third of total support come from gross investment income. We have also stated previously that a Section 509(a)(1) organization may need only 10 percent of public support if additional factors are present. Consequently, the importance of proper classification of receipts cannot be overemphasized.

Classification of Receipts

1. *Exempt function income.*   This refers to income coming from the sale of products or services that result from the performance of exempt functions and does not constitute income from the conduct of an unrelated business. Receipts from admissions to a performance of a 501(c)(3) symphony orchestra is an example.

2. *Services performed for a Section 170(c)(1) organization; benefit of payor.*   This refers to services performed for a unit functioning at the operating level of government and is normally descriptive of a subdivision of a department of government. An example is N, an organization that is a nonprofit educational institution exempt under Section 501(c)(3) whose principal activity is to operate institutions to train employees of various industries in the principles of management and administration. Government Y pays N to train government employees. The particular services rendered serve the direct and immediate needs of the payor, the government. The money received represents gross receipts and is related or exempt function income.

3. *Gifts, grants, contributions, and membership fees, including services performed for the public benefit.*   "Gifts" and "contributions" are payments of money or transfers of property without adequate consideration. The term "grants," as used here, describes payments made to encourage the grantee organization to carry on certain programs in furtherance of its exempt purposes with the public being the primary

beneficiary. An example is organization P, which is an educational organization exempt under Section 501(c)(3). It carries on studies and seminars to assist institutions of higher learning. It receives funds from the government to research and develop a black studies program. The performance of such service benefits the general public. Receipts, therefore, are "grants" as distinguished from "gross receipts." This differs from (2).

4. *Net income from unrelated trade or business.* This refers to income received by an organization for activities unrelated to the purposes for which it received its exemption. As an example, U is an organization exempt under Section 501(c)(3) for scientific purposes. It exploits its reputation in the field of biological research by selling endorsements of laboratory equipment. Since such endorsements do not contribute importantly to the organization's exempt purpose, income is from an unrelated trade or business (and is not considered public support).

5. *Gross investment income.* Gross investment income includes interest, dividends, rents, and royalties to the extent that the income is not subject to the tax on unrelated business income. It is important to distinguish such income from gross receipts that have the same support impact as related or exempt function income. Receipt of more than 33⅓ percent of total support from gross investment income will exclude an organization from Section 509(a)(2), which is public charity status.

6. *Value of services or facilities furnished by governmental units without charge.* A 509(a)(1) organization that has receipts primarily from its exempt function income will not qualify under Section 509(a)(1).[17] On the other hand, a 509(a)(2) organization may have very substantial receipts from its exempt function income with no adverse effect upon its exempt status. Thus, it is important to know whether a receipt is a contribution or exempt function income.

To assist in determining support, Table 4.1 is set forth for guidance.

Note that for Section 509(a)(1) purposes exempt function income (related income) is eliminated from both numerator and denominator. Also, where a Section 501(c)(3) organization receives a substantial or very large grant from a person or another organization, it serves to distort the support fraction and can adversely affect the status of Section 509(a)(1) or (a)(2) charities. If the grant is from an unrelated person or organization, then you should advise the Internal Revenue Service that this is an unusual grant that should be eliminated from both numerator and denominator in accordance with Section 1.170A-9(e)(6)(ii). When a Section 509(a)(2) organization is involved, the receipt of a large grant can be fatal since the support fraction has so much less play because of the requirement that public support must exceed one-third of total support. The reader should be familiar with Section 4946 relating to disqualified persons and Section 507(d)(2), which describes the "substantial contributor" who is a disqualified person.

Determining Eligibility

To determine eligibility under Sections 509(a)(1) and (a)(2), refer to the foregoing. To understand how the chart works, assume the following facts.

Illustration 1

The Reiner Charity, Inc., is exempt as a Section 501(c)(3) organization and claims that it is not a private foundation because it is publicly supported. For the past 4 years, it had receipts from the following sources:

Table 4.1. Comparison of Support Fractions

Item	Section 509(a)(1)	Section 509(a)(2)
Total Support—Denominator		
1. Exempt function income	Excluded	Included
2. Services performed for Section 170(c)(1) organizations benefit of payor	Excluded	Included
3. Gifts, grants, contributions, and membership fees including services performed for Section 170(c)(1) organizations for benefit of public	Included	Included
4. Net income from unrelated trade or business	Included	Included
5. Gross investment income (capital gains excluded)	Included	Included
6. Value of services received from government units without charge	Included	Included
Total support	_____	_____
Public Support—Numerator		
1. Contributions—disqualified persons [Sections 4946, 507(d)(2)]	Included to extent of 2% of total support from any one person	Excluded entirely
2. Direct and indirect contributions from public	Included to extent of 2% total support from any one person	Included in full, except for contributions from disqualified persons
3. Exempt function income	Excluded	Included to extent of $5,000 or 1% of total support from any one person, whichever greater
4. Net income from unrelated trade or business	Excluded	Excluded
5. Services performed for Section 170(c)(1) organizations payor benefited	Excluded	Included to extent of (3) above
6. Contributions from Section 170(b)(1)(A)(vi) and 170(c)(1) organizations—public benefit, including value of services or facilities furnished without charge [Note difference from (2) above]	Included in full	Included in full
Total public support	_____	_____

Total support:

Grant from Private Foundation Y	$ 65,000
Grant from City C (payor benefit)	15,000
Community Chest (public support)	5,000
Interest and dividends	15,000
Total	$100,000

To compute support for Section 509(a)(1) purposes, we must eliminate the $15,000 grant from City C (exempt function income) from both numerator and denominator. The public support computation is based on total support of $85,000.

Public Support:	
Grant from Y Private Foundation	$1,700
(2% × $85,000)	
Community Chest	5,000
Total Public Support	$6,700

Since this is less than 10 percent minimum public support, the organization cannot be exempt under Section 509(a)(1). However, Reiner Charity, Inc., may qualify under Section 509(a)(1) if the grant from Private Foundation Y were eliminated as an unusual grant, since, in that case, it would have public support of $5000 and total support of $20,000 (Community Chest of $5000 plus $15,000 interest and dividends), or 25 percent, which is well above the 10 percent minimum public support required.

For Section 509(a)(2) purposes, we have the following:

Total support:	$100,000
Public support:	
Private Foundation Y is a disqualified person (eliminate)	$ 0
Grant from City C (1% of total support or $5000, whichever is greater)	5,000
Community Chest	5,000
Total public support	$ 10,000
Percent of public support	10%

The organization cannot qualify because it cannot meet the more than 33⅓ percent public support test.

Reiner Charity, Inc., also cannot meet the 33⅓ percent support test of Section 509(a)(2) even if the grant from Y Private Foundation is considered to be an unusual grant and is eliminated from numerator and denominator.

The support computation would then be as follows:

Total support:	
Grant from City C	$15,000
Community Chest	5,000
Interest and dividends	15,000
Total support	$35,000

Public support:	
Grant from City C (1% or $5000, which ever is greater)	$ 5,000
Community Chest	5,000
Total public support	$10,000

$10,000 is less than 33⅓% of $35,000;

$15,000 gross investment income is more than 33⅓% of $35,000.

Illustration 2

Organization O has receipts from the following sources over the last 4 years: dividends and interest, $20,000; City X for nonpublic services rendered, $20,000; City Y for nonpublic services rendered, $30,000; contributions from a substantial contributor, $10,000; sales of educational publications, $10,000; and contributions from the general public (none over 2 percent), $10,000.

Computation for Section 509(a)(1) Purposes

Total support:

1. Dividends and interest		$ 20,000
2. Government Unit X		20,000
3. Government Unit Y		30,000
4. Contributions—substantial contributor		10,000
5. Sales of educational publications		10,000
6. Contributions from general public (none over 2%)		10,000
Total		$100,000

Less: exempt function income

2. Government Unit X	$20,000	
3. Government Unit Y	30,000	
5. Sales of educational publications	10,000	60,000
Net total support		$ 40,000

Public support:

4. Contributions—substantial contributor, 2% × $40,000		$ 800
6. Contributions—general public		10,000
Total public support		$ 10,800
Percent of public support		27%

Organization O does not meet the 33⅓ percent support test, but may meet the 10 percent facts and circumstances test if the organization can show that contributions from nondisqualified persons are attracted by reason of the publicly supported nature of the organization.

Computation for Section 509(a)(2) Purposes

Total support:

1. Dividends and interest	$ 20,000
2. Government Unit X—services rendered	20,000
3. Government Unit Y—services rendered	30,000
4. Contributions—substantial contributor	10,000

Total support:

5. Sales of educational publication (exempt function income)	10,000
6. Contributions from public (none over 2%)	10,000
Total support	$100,000

Public support:

2.	Government Unit X—greater of 1% of total support or $5,000	$ 5,000
3.	Government Unit Y—as above	5,000
5.	Sales of educational publications— exempt function income	10,000
6.	Contributions from public	10,000
	Total public support	$30,000

Organization O cannot meet the 33⅓ percent support test for Section 509(a)(2) purposes even though it meets the 33⅓ percent gross investment income test.

Illustration 3

Organization Z is exempt under Section 501(c)(3) and has receipts from the following sources:

Total support:

1.	Sales of educational material (none exceeding $5000 per person)	$ 60,000
2.	Grant from City M—payor benefit	15,000
3.	Dividends and interest	20,000
4.	Contributions from Contributor C	5,000
	Total receipts	$100,000

Computation for Section 509(a)(1):

Total support = $100,000 less (1) and (2) above	$ 25,000
Public support = Grant from Contributor C (2% × $25,000)	$ 500

Organization Z cannot meet the support tests under Section 509(a)(1). However, here is the computation for Section 509(a)(2) purposes:

Total support:	$100,000

Public support:

1.	Sales of educational material (none greater than $100 per person)	$60,000
2.	Grant from City M	5,000
3.	Grant from Contributor C	5,000
	Total public support	$70,000

Contributor C is not a substantial contributor within the meaning of Section 507(d)(2) because he did not contribute more than $5000, even though $5000 is more than 2 percent of total support. City M's grant, however, must be limited to $5000 in the public support computation since it is a governmental unit (509(a)(2)(A)(ii)). In any case, both the 33⅓ percent public support and 33⅓ percent gross investment tests are met since the sales of educational material are qualified as public support in full under 509(a)(2)(A)(ii).

There is another difference between Sections 509(a)(1) and 509(a)(2) organizations. Upon termination of a private foundation under Section 507(b)(1)(A), only a 509(a)(1) organization may be the recipient of the net assets.[18] A private foundation that turns over its net assets to a 509(a)(2) organization has not made a termination and will continue to be treated as a private foundation for all purposes.[19] Thus, the transferor private foundation must retain sufficient income or assets to pay the Section 4940 investment income tax for that portion of its taxable year prior to such transfer.

An organization that terminates its private foundation status under Section 507(b)(1)(A) is not required to comply with Section 6104(d) (public inspection of its annual reports) in the tax year in which such termination occurs.[20]

Private Foundation

An organization exempt under Section 501(c)(3) of the Internal Revenue Code that does not meet the provisions of either Section 509(a)(1), (a)(2), or (a)(3) and is not described in Section 509(a)(4) is a private foundation and is subject to the 2 percent tax on investment income (Section 4940) and the penalty provisions of Sections 4941 through 4945.

Private Operating Foundation

A "private operating foundation" is a private foundation that spends 85 percent or more of its income directly for the active conduct of the educational, religious, or other purposes for which it is organized and operated and in addition meets one of these tests:

1. *Assets test.* At least 65 percent of the assets of the organization must be devoted directly to the active conduct of organization's Section 501(c)(3) purposes.

2. *Support test.* At least 85 percent of the organization's support (other than gross investment income) comes from five or more exempt organizations and from the general public, with no more than 25 percent of the exempt organization's support coming from one organization and not more than one-half of total support from gross investment income.

3. *Endowment test.* The organization is required to make qualifying distributions of more than two-thirds of its minimum investment return directly for the active conduct of activities constituting its exempt Section 501(c)(3) purposes. For years beginning after December 31, 1975, the mandatory payout is 5 percent.

A private operating foundation is subject to the 4 percent tax [2 percent for years beginning after fiscal year (FY) 9/30/77] on investment income but is not required to distribute its net income. Thus, it is not subject to the penalty provisions of Section 4942.

Section 4947(a)(1) Trusts

A Section 4947(a)(1) trust is a nonexempt trust in which all of the unexpired interests are devoted to one or more purposes described in Section 170(c)(2)(B) of the Code, and for which a charitable deduction was taken. This type of trust is subject to the private foundation provisions.[21] Because of the tremendous numbers of such trusts and the considerable tax impact, a special Revenue Procedure was issued.[22] The Revenue Procedure provides for two types of requests for determination of Section 509(a)(3) status, thus avoiding the private foundation stigma, which could have an adverse tax impact.

The first relates to the transitional rule set forth in Regulations Section 1.509(a) 4(e)(4). The trustees file the request with the district director where the trustee filing the trust's income tax return has his or her legal residence or principal place of business. The request for a determination should include the following information:

1. The name of the trust, its address, and employer identification number

2. A statement as to whether it has received any contributions since November 20, 1970

3. The name, address, and employer identification number of the beneficiary organizations, together with a statement that each such beneficiary organization is described in Section 509(a)(1) or (2) of the Code

4. If a beneficiary organization is not designated in the trust instrument, a copy of the court order or other evidence establishing that such organization possesses an equitable interest in the trust

5. A list of all of the trustees that have served on or after November 20, 1970, together with a statement stating whether such trustees were disqualified persons within the meaning of Section 4946(a) of the Code (other than as foundation managers)

6. A copy of the trust instrument in effect on November 20, 1970, and all amendments adopted thereafter

7. A statement indicating what provision has been made to provide the beneficiaries with the annual reports required by Section 1.509(a)-4(i)(4) of the regulations

The second request, the nontransitional rule, attempts to show that the trust is a supporting organization as described in Section 509(a)(3) of the Code. The request should contain the following:

1. The name of the trust, its address, and employer identification number

2. The name, address, and employer identification number of the beneficiary organizations, together with a statement that each such beneficiary organization is described in Section 509(a)(1) or (2) of the Code

3. A list of all of the trustees that have served on or after October 9, 1969, together with a statement setting forth whether such trustees were disqualified persons within the meaning of Section 4946(a) of the Code (other than as foundation managers)

4. A copy of the trust instrument in effect on October 9, 1969, and all amendments adopted thereafter

5. Sufficient information to otherwise establish that the trust meets the requirements of Section 509(a)(3) of the Code as provided for in Section 1.509(a)-(4) of the regulations [other than Section 1.509(a)-4(i)(4)]

The Revenue Procedure notes that district directors are authorized to issue determination letters with respect to Section 509. In case of an adverse decision at the district, the procedure set forth in Revenue Procedure 72-2, 1972-1 C.B. 695 will be followed. For organizations receiving adverse determinations after September 27, 1976, see Revenue Procedure 76-33.

It is emphasized that Section 4947(a)(1) nonexempt trusts are different from charitable trusts, which file for exemption under Section 501(c)(3) and Section 509 on Form 1023. Such a trust files either Form 990 or Form 990-PF (depending on whether it is a public charity or a private foundation); whereas a Section 4947(a)(1) trust files Form 5227, if a private foundation, or Form 990, if considered to be a Section 509(a)(3) public charity.

Organizations Exempt Prior to July 13, 1970[23]

An organization that was exempt under Section 501(c)(3) of the IRC prior to July 13, 1970, was required to file notice of exempt status on Form 4653 (similar to page 6 of Form 1023) indicating whether it was a private foundation or had either a private operating foundation or some kind of public charity status. If it thought itself to be a public charity, it was required to designate the paragraph of Section 509 under which it was exempt and provide support for such an assumption. If the Internal Revenue Service did not reply or reject it within 30 days of filing, the organization was not a private foundation until a future examination by the Internal Revenue Service decided otherwise. If, subsequently, the organization was found to be a private foundation, it was given prospective treatment.

If the organization did not file Form 4653, which represented notice to the Service, then the organization was presumed to be a private foundation. Such organizations must look to Section 507(b)(1)(B), relating to termination of a private foundation, to achieve public charity status.

Movement of Form 1023 Through the Internal Revenue Service

Key District Office

Within each key district is an exempt organization group charged with the responsibility of passing on Applications for Recognition of Tax Exemption, Forms 1023 and 1024. Form 1024 deals with organizations other than Section 501(c)(3) of the IRC. We are here discussing Form 1023.

An exemption application will usually be processed within 60 days from the date it is received. If the application is incomplete, it may be returned without any further action. As previously stated, a request by the filer that any questions should be directed to him or her by phone might avoid the delay caused by the return of the application. Make certain that the application is filed when required, that is, before the end of the fifteenth month after organization. If the 15-month period is in jeopardy, ask for an extension of time in writing. By so doing, you will protect those who have made contributions within the 15-month period.

No determination letter will be issued if an issue involving the organization's exempt status is pending in litigation before the appellate division.

Referral to the Regional Office

Assume that Form 1023 has been filed with the key district and an adverse determination letter or a letter proposing revocation or modification of exempt status has been issued. The key district will issue a 30-day letter. The organization must file a timely protest and state whether it wishes a regional office conference.[24]

If the key district maintains its position, it forwards the case file to the office of the assistant regional commissioner (Employee Plans and Exempt Organizations). If the key district is sustained, the regional office, in writing, will so advise the organization, giving it 30 days in which to answer and ask for a conference in the national office. After providing supporting arguments to the regional office and indicating that it wishes a national office conference, the organization must wait for national office consideration. If the national office decides that the case will be accepted and an adverse decision is indicated, the organization will be granted one conference. If the national office decides not to accept the case, the case file will be returned through the regional office to the key district director for issuance of a final determination letter. This procedure became effective September 27, 1976.

Note that any determination letter issued on the basis of national office technical advice may not be appealed to the regional or national offices with regard to those issues that were the subject of technical advice.

Where the regional office disagrees with the key district director's determination, it will so advise the taxpayer and return the case to the key district director for appropriate action.

A national office ruling may disagree with an adverse determination considered by the key district office. It will issue a ruling to the organization indicating why it overrode the determination. A copy of the ruling will be sent to the key district office.

Assume further that an organization that has filed for public charity status is held to be a private foundation. All adverse determinations issued by key district directors [including foundation status under Section 509(a) of nonexempt charitable trusts described in Section 4947(a)(1)] are subject to the protest and conference procedures set forth in Revenue Procedure 76-33 above. For information relating to circumstances under which an organization presumed to be a private foundation under Section 508(b) of the Code may request a determination of its status as other than private foundation, see Revenue Ruling 73-504, 1973-2 C.B. 190.

Judicial Review of Adverse Determinations

Assuming further that the organization is held to be a private foundation and that the organization wishes to protest the national office ruling, the organization should file a Form 990-PF and pay the tax on investment income. It should then file a claim for refund. The claim will be processed similarly to income, estate, and gift tax cases. The case goes the conference-appellate division and tax court route. The organization can petition the district court or an action can be brought in the court of claims (but only if there has been no prior court review on the particular action).[25] The organization may decide to wait 6 months after the claim is filed and go directly to the court of claims or the district court.

There are times when the initial filing of Form 1023 presents questions of an unusual nature or that are not specifically covered by statute. The district will transfer such a case to the national office. The national office will issue the favorable ruling letter and send a copy to the district involved should it conclude that exemption is merited. If it concludes that no exemption should be granted or that private foundation status is warranted, it will send a Preliminary Adverse Ruling. If you do not agree with the decision, you will be granted one conference. If no relief is granted, then you will be issued an unfavorable ruling and a copy will be sent to the district. If you do not agree, follow the procedure set forth above.

Note that TD 7567, Part III, establishes a single level of administrative appeal.

This applies to conferences held after September 30, 1978. The description of amended procedure is set forth in IRB 78-45, dated November 6, 1978, page 11. The amendments establish a new provision, Paragraph 601(n)(9), which sets forth the technical advice procedures applicable to exempt organization cases, whether considered by a key district office or in the office of the regional director of appeals, referred as the appeals office. The procedures relating to movement of disagreed cases is similar to that described in Revenue Procedures 76-33 and 76-34. In addition, in certain exempt organization cases, requesting technical advice by the key

Organization Reference Chart

Section of 1954 Code	Description of organization	General nature of activities	Application Form No.	Annual return required to be filed	Contributions allowable
501(c)(1)	Corporations Organized Under Act of Congress (including Federal Credit Unions)	Instrumentalities of the United States	No Form	None	Yes, if made for exclusively public purposes
501(c)(2)	Title Holding Corporation For Exempt Organization	Holding title to property of an exempt organization	1024	990[1]	No[2]
501(c)(3)	Religious, Educational, Charitable, Scientific, Literary, Testing for Public Safety, to Foster National or International Amateur Sports Competition, or Prevention of Cruelty to Children or Animals Organizations	Activities of nature implied by description of class of organization	1023	990 or 990-PF[1]	Generally, Yes
501(c)(4)	Civic Leagues, Social Welfare Organizations, and Local Associations of Employees	Promotion of community welfare; charitable, educational or recreational	1024	990[1]	Generally, No[2,3]
501(c)(5)	Labor, Agricultural, and Horticultural Organizations	Educational or instructive, the purpose being to improve conditions of work, and to improve products and efficiency	1024	990[1]	No[2]
501(c)(6)	Business Leagues, Chambers of Commerce, Real Estate Boards, Etc.	Improvement of business conditions of one or more lines of business	1024	990[1]	No[2]
501(c)(7)	Social and Recreation Clubs	Pleasure, recreation, social activities	1024	990[1]	No[2]
501(c)(8)	Fraternal Beneficiary Societies and Associations	Lodge providing for payment of life, sickness, accident, or other benefits to members	1024	990[1]	Yes, if for certain Sec. 501(c)(3) purposes
501(c)(9)	Voluntary Employees' Beneficiary Associations	Providing for payment of life, sickness, accident or other benefits to members	1024	990[1]	No[2]
501(c)(10)	Domestic Fraternal Societies and Associations	Lodge devoting its net earnings to charitable, fraternal, and other specified purposes. No life, sickness, or accident benefits to members	1024	990[1]	Yes, if for certain Sec. 501(c)(3) purposes
501(c)(11)	Teachers' Retirement Fund Associations	Teachers' association for payment of retirement benefits	No Form[7]	990[1]	No[2]
501(c)(12)	Benevolent Life Insurance Associations, Mutual Ditch or Irrigation Companies, Mutual or Cooperative Telephone Companies, Etc.	Activities of a mutually beneficial nature similar to those implied by the description of class of organization	1024	990[1]	No[2]
501(c)(13)	Cemetery Companies	Burials and incidental activities	1024	990[1]	Generally, Yes
501(c)(14)	State Chartered Credit Unions, Mutual Reserve Funds	Loans to members	No Form[7]	990[1]	No[2]
501(c)(15)	Mutual Insurance Companies or Associations	Providing insurance to members substantially at cost	1024	990[1]	No[2]
501(c)(16)	Cooperative Organizations to Finance Crop Operations	Financing crop operations in conjunction with activities of a marketing or purchasing association	No Form[7]	990[1]	No[2]
501(c)(17)	Supplemental Unemployment Benefit Trusts	Provides for payment of supplemental unemployment compensation benefits	1024	990[1]	No[2]
501(c)(18)	Employee Funded Pension Trust (created before June 25, 1959)	Payment of benefits under a pension plan funded by employees	No Form[7]	990[1]	No[2]
501(c)(19)	Post or Organization of Past or Present Members of the Armed Forces	Activities implied by nature of organization	1024	990[1]	Generally, No[4]
501(c)(20)	Group Legal Services Plan Organizations	Legal services provided exclusively to employees	1024	990[1]	No[4]
501(c)(21)	Black Lung Benefit Trusts	Funded by coal mine operators to satisfy their liability for disability or death due to black lung diseases	No Form[7]	990-BL	No[5]
501(c)(22)	Withdrawal Liability Payment Fund	To provide funds to meet the liability of employers withdrawing from a multi-employer pension fund	No Form[7]	990	No[5]
501(c)(23)	Veterans Organization (created before 1880)	To provide insurance and other benefits to veterans	No Form[7]	990	Generally, No[4]
501(d)	Religious and Apostolic Associations	Regular business activities. Communal religious community	No Form	1065	No[2]
501(e)	Cooperative Hospital Service Organizations	Performs cooperative services for hospitals	1023	990[1]	Yes
501(f)	Cooperative Service Organizations of Operating Educational Organizations	Performs collective investment services for educational organizations	1023	990[1]	Yes
521(a)	Farmers' Cooperative Associations	Cooperative marketing and purchasing for agricultural producers	1028	990-C	No

[1] For exceptions to the filing requirement, see Chapter 2 and the Form instructions.
[2] An organization exempt under a Subsection of Code Sec. 501 other than (c)(3), may establish a charitable fund, contributions to which are deductible. Such a fund must itself meet the requirements of section 501(c)(3) and the related notice requirements of section 508(a).
[3] Contributions to volunteer fire companies and similar organizations are deductible, but only if made for exclusively public purposes.

[4] May qualify as a deductible business expense.
[5] Deductible as a business expense to the extent allowed by Code section 192
[6] Deductible as a business expense to the extent allowed by Code section 194A.
[7] Application is by letter to the key District Director. A copy of the organizing document should be attached and the letter should be signed by an officer.
[8] Contributions to these organizations are deductible only if 90% or more of the organization's members are war veterans.

Figure 4.2

district director or appeals office is mandatory rather than discretionary if the issue is not covered by published precedent or if nonconformity may exist.

Form 1024—"Application of Recognition of Exemption"

Organizations described in sections other than Section 501(c)(3), more specifically, those exempt under Sections 501(c)(2), (4), (5), (6), (7), (8), (9), (10), (12), (13), (15), (17), and (19) of the Internal Revenue Code of 1954, are required to file Form 1024. The reference chart in Figure 4.2 sets forth a description of the organization, the nature of its activities, and the section under which payments to it are deductible. These organizations, when exemption is obtained, file Form 990 annually.

Notes

1. Reg. Sec. 1.508-1(a)(2)(i).
2. Reg. Sec. 1.508-1(a)(2)(ii).
3. Reg. Sec. 1.508-1(a)(4)(b).
4. Rev. Proc. 72-4, 1972-1 C.B. 706.
5. Rev. Proc. 68-4, 1968-1 C.B. 768.
6. Reg. Sec. 1.508-1(a)(2)(VI).
7. Reg. Sec. 1.170A-9(e).
8. Rev. Proc. 72-41, 1972-2 C.B. 820. Superseding Rev. Proc. 68-13, 1968-1 C.B. 764.
9. Rev. Rul. 75-290 I.R.B. 1975-2, 17.
10. Reg. Sec. 1.508-1(a)(3)(a).
11. Announcement 77.62, IRB 1977-17, pg. 22, dated 4/24/77.
12. Reg. Sec. 1.508-1(a)(3)(i)(c).
13. Reg. Sec. 1.508-1(a)(3)(i)(e).
14. Reg. Sec. 1.508-1(b)(7)(IV).
15. Reg. Sec. 1.508-1(b)(8).
16. Reg. Sec. 1.508-3(a)(1) and (2).
17. Reg. 1.170A9(e)(7)(ii).
18. Reg. 1.507-2(a)(1).
19. Reg. 1.507-1(b)(7).
20. Reg. 1.507-2(a)(6)(ii).
21. Reg. Sec. 1.508-1(a)(3)(d).
22. Rev. Proc. 72-50, 1972-2 C.B. 830.
23. Reg. Sec. 1.508-1(b)(2)(ii).
24. Rev. Proc. 76-33 I.R.B. 1976-39, 43. See also, TD 7567, Part III, for conferences held after September 30, 1978.
25. IRC Sec. 7422(g)(2).

5

Nonprofit Organizations in a Technical Perspective

Ken Milani

Ph.D., Arthur Young Faculty Fellow in Taxation, University of Notre Dame

An organization may qualify for exemption from federal income taxes on the basis of both stated purpose and internal structure. As to purpose, the nonprofit entity must have been organized for charitable, religious, educational, scientific, or literary goals, for the enhancement of public safety, for the prevention of cruelty to children or animals, or for the fostering of a national or international amateur sports competition.[1] Further, the goal or goals must be the central focus of the operation of the entity. Structurally, the organization must be a corporation, community chest, fund, foundation, or trust.[2]

Much more than exemption from federal income taxes is at stake for an organization seeking not-for-profit status. If the organization does not meet the criteria established by the Internal Revenue Service (IRS), deductions for charitable contributions will not be allowed to donors who make gifts or bequests to the organization.

This chapter's primary focus is on an entity that is seeking an exemption under Section 501(a) of the Internal Revenue Code (IRC). Specific procedures must be followed if a favorable ruling or determination letter granting an exemption is to be received. Additional areas covered below include protection of an organization's exempt status, operational matters, and other topics.[3]

Types of Exempt Organizations and Significance of Classification

Section 501(a) of the IRC is the basic operative Internal Revenue Code provision granting tax exemption to several broad categories of "exempt activity." An exempt activity can, in some cases, be properly classified in more than one of the general categories prescribed in the law, and the type of exemption claimed by the organization can have a significant impact on its tax attributes. For example,

> Certain social welfare activities normally attributable to civic leagues and other social welfare organizations may be properly classified as charitable (e.g., nature conservancy, arresting physical deterioration of low-income neighborhoods and communities); a charitable exemption under Section 501(c)(3), which is the only category that *automatically* qualifies donors for charitable contribution deductions, should be sought in order to obtain tax-deductible funds.

> The income from certain recreational activities of local homeowners' associations and condominium associations, thought to be exempt as social welfare organizations, may be taxable unless an exemption is obtained for such activities under the subsection covering private social and recreational clubs.

> Since special rules automatically tax nonmember income (e.g., income other than members' dues and receipts such as investment income, rentals, and capital gains) of social clubs and voluntary employees' beneficiary associations only, it may be possible to classify the exempt activity in another area when such outside income is anticipated.

> Where political activities are contemplated (such as lobbying or the writing of publications that are intended to influence federal or local legislation), classification takes on added significance.

> Although no charitable organization can engage in any political campaign, *certain* Section 501(c)(3) public charities are permitted to engage in limited lobbying activities.

> An organization that fails to meet the requirements for charitable exemption because it is a political-action organization may nevertheless qualify for exemption as a social welfare organization under Section 501(c)(4). [It is important to note, however, that a 501(c)(3) organization that *loses* its exempt status because of excessive lobbying is prohibited from future qualification under 501(c)(4).] Like charitable activity, the promotion of social welfare cannot include direct or indirect participation in political campaigns for political office.

> Although other exempt organizations, such as unions and business leagues, have much more latitude in the political arena, the Internal Revenue Service has successfully challenged business deductions for members' dues and assessments deemed relative to such activity.

> Finally, political organizations and newsletter funds may claim tax exemption under Section 527, with very limited tax deductions or credits allowed to individual contributors.

There are many subtle as well as obvious differences among the exempt categories, and proper planning may achieve a more beneficial classification with favorable tax consequences. IRS Publication 557 has a more detailed discussion of exempt classifications, and it should be consulted before applying for tax exemption.

Classification of Various Charitable Organizations

Charitable organizations, described in Section 501(c)(3) of the IRC, are classified into two broad groups—public charities and private foundations. Foundations are further classified into operating foundations under special rules. The significance of being classified as a "public charity" as opposed to a "private foundation" is substantial.

Public charities entitle individual donors to more liberal charitable contribution limitations (e.g., individuals can donate up to 50 percent of their adjusted gross income as opposed to only 20 percent to a private foundation). No carryover is permitted for contributions to private foundations in excess of the limitations. A 5-year carryover is provided in the case of public charities.

Private foundations may automatically treat their grants to public charities as "qualifying" distributions. Grants by private foundations to other private foundations or organizations controlled by the granting foundation may qualify under very limited circumstances, but special follow-up rules must nevertheless be observed. Private foundations are also subject to a host of operating sanctions, penalties, and excise taxes which are described below.

If the private foundation is classified as an operating foundation, donors are entitled to the same liberal charitable contribution rules that apply to public charities. (More information on the private operating foundation is included later in the chapter.)

As indicated above, classification is important and in many cases, a charitable organization can achieve public status while on the surface it would appear to be a private foundation. Proper planning—through the use of facts and circumstances tests permitted by the regulations, and classification as an organization supporting another public charity—can accomplish this. Also, private foundations may convert to public charities under special rules or terminate their status by merging with public charities such as churches, schools, hospitals, and community trusts. (The identity of a legally dissolved foundation may be maintained within a public charity through the use of a separately designated fund.)

Private Foundations

Most exempt organizations are presumed to be private foundations. Notification of the IRS must occur if an organization wishes to be categorized as something other than a private foundation. Although the provisions that apply to private foundations are restrictive, private foundations still offer significant planning opportunities for those in the higher estate, gift, and income tax brackets and should not be overlooked as a family tax planning tool.[4]

A *private foundation (PF)* is defined as any Section 501(c)(3) organization (i.e., an organization operated exclusively for religious, charitable, educational, etc., purposes), *other than*

Churches, schools, nonproprietary hospitals, and medical research organizations

An organization that derives at least *one-third* of its total support directly or indirectly from the general public

Certain organizations with a broad base of public support that normally receive more than one-third of their annual support from persons other than "disqualified persons" and not more than one-third of their support from investment income

An organization that is organized and operated exclusively for the benefit of one or more of the organizations described in the three prior points above, and controlled by, or operated in connection with, such organizations (basically, a support type of organization)

An organization organized and operated exclusively for public safety testing

If the organization cannot assert that it is not a PF, it will be presumed to be a PF and subject to the excise taxes, sanctions, and reporting requirements which are covered below.

Private Operating Foundations

An operating foundation is exempt from the distribution requirements mentioned above, *but is subject to all other rules, penalties, and taxes affecting private foundations.* An *operating foundation (OF)* is an organization that distributes substantially all its adjusted net income (at least 85 percent) *directly* for its intended charitable purposes and that satisfies at least one of three other mechanical tests—the assets test, the support test, or the endowment test. Although the term "directly" is not defined in the Code, the regulations are clear as to the term's import. A PF holding investments and paying out its income to other charities may meet the mechanical tests prescribed, but would not be considered an OF because "directly" contemplates an active charitable operation. For example, it is not sufficient for a PF merely to be engaged in making grants to individuals, even after a screening process. The regulations require that an OF must also have substantial, established, and continuing programs of activities in which the recipients of grants are, or are encouraged to become, involved. Furthermore, significant involvement by the foundation is required in the exempt activities that such grants are intended to support.

Public Charities

Public charities, in general, include organizations which either have wide public support or which actively function in a supporting relationship to such organizations. Also, falling into the category are organizations that do testing for public safety.

Section 509 of the IRC identifies some specific organizations as public charities including

1. A church or a convention or association of churches

2. An educational organization (e.g., school, college)

3. A hospital or medical research organization operated in conjunction with a hospital

4. Organizations operated for the benefit of certain state and municipal colleges and universities

5. A governmental unit

6. A publicly supported organization (e.g., museum, library, American Red Cross)

Rulings and Determination Letters

Exemption from federal income taxes can be requested by filing forms or an application with the IRS. Forms 1023, Application for Recognition of Exemption under Section 501(c)(3) of the Internal Revenue Code, and 1024, Application for Recognition of Exemption under Section 501(a) or for Determination under Section 120, are the prescribed schedules.

Rulings and determination letters will be issued to an organization whose application and accompanying documents support its request and do not raise any issues that might jeopardize the organization's exempt status. The IRS response may be issued before or after the organization has started to function. An advance reaction will be based on a description of the proposed operation, its expected sources of funds and the nature of the expenses contemplated by the entity. Once an organization commences operations, they must apply for recognition of exemption. To avoid difficulties, the application must be filed within 15 months from the end of the month in which they were organized. Meeting the 15-month period will result in a retroactive recognition (i.e., exemption will apply from the date of organization). Failure to file within the 15-month period means that the exemption will be applicable only for the period after the IRS received the application. Denial of the tax-exempt status request can be appealed. The appeal must be made to the applicable district director within 30 days of receiving the "adverse determination letter" by asking for an "appeals office conference."[5]

Some organizations are not required to file for exemption due to their nature, operations, or relationship to another organization. For example, churches and their related organizations are not subject to the filing requirement. Organizations that have annual gross receipts which are $5000 or below will not seek exemption unless they are private foundations. Also, a group exemption letter issued to a central organization can provide exemption to a subordinate organization (e.g., the exemption allowed to a university will cover other components of the school such as an alumni association which has its own corporate status).

Even though the exemption is automatic for the groups mentioned in the last paragraph, it might be prudent to file for exemption anyway. A ruling or determination letter would clearly establish the organization's status while ensuring that all contributions received would be deductible by the donors.

Operational Matters

Several operational considerations are covered in this section. The main thrust of these activities deals with specific actions that pertain to exempt organizations.

Private Foundations

A private foundation is subject to excise taxes, sanctions, and reporting requirements.[6]

Excise Tax on Net Investment Income.   An excise tax on net investment income is imposed on a PF on an annual basis.

Self-dealing.   Acts of "self-dealing" between a PF and a "disqualified person" will result in the imposition of a graduated series of excise taxes on the disqualified person and, under certain circumstances, on the foundation manager participating in the act. "Self-dealing" includes sales, leasing transactions, money lending, compensation arrangements, and transfers of any type. Disqualified persons include substantial contributors, foundation managers and certain family members, related business enterprises, and government officials. There are certain specific exceptions to the imposition of the tax.

Distribution of Income.   A PF is required to distribute an amount equal to its "minimum investment return" or its "adjusted net income"—whichever is greater—reduced by certain taxes. Any amount not distributed by the last day of the next succeeding taxable year is subject to tax. Qualifying distributions include payments to public charities and operating foundations, direct expenditures (including administrative expenses) made for exempt purposes and for the acquisition of assets to be used for exempt purposes, and certain approved set-asides.

Excess Business Holdings.   Limitations are placed on the amount of investment that can be held by a PF in any corporation or other business enterprise. Excess business holdings are subject to excise taxes. Generally, the rules limit to 20 percent (35 percent where the corporation is effectively controlled by others) the combined ownership of a corporation's voting stock that may be held by a PF and all disqualified persons. An exception to this rule is a business enterprise functionally related to the PF's exempt purpose, as well as any trade or business where at least 95 percent of its gross income is derived from passive sources. Furthermore, it should be noted that a *de minimis* rule is provided whereby a foundation may own 2 percent or less of a business enterprise irrespective of the above rules.

Jeopardy Investments.   Excise taxes are imposed against the PF and its managers if an investment is made that would jeopardize the carrying out of the exempt purpose. The regulations indicate that investments in warrants, commodity futures, oil and gas wells, purchases on margin, and short sales are suspect. The determination of whether an investment jeopardizes the carrying out of charitable purposes is to be made as of the time of the investment in accordance with a prudent trustee approach. However, any investments received as donations are not treated as jeopardy investments.

Taxable Expenditures.   Excise taxes are imposed on broadly defined "taxable expenditures." Taxable expenditures include any amounts paid or incurred by a PF:

> To carry on propaganda or otherwise attempt to influence legislation. [The provisions of Section 501(h) that permit limited lobbying activities do not apply to private foundations.]

> To influence the outcome of any specific public election or to carry on any voter registration drive.

> As a grant to an individual for travel, study, or other similar purpose unless an advance ruling on the granting procedure is obtained.

> As a grant to an organization other than a public charity unless the granting foundation assumes certain follow-up responsibilities.

> For any purpose other than religious, charitable, scientific, literary, or educational goals or for the prevention of cruelty to children or animals.

Filing Requirements

Public charities, private foundations, and private operating foundations are required to file returns to the IRS. An annual information return (Form 990 or 990-PF) must be filed by the fifteenth day of the fifth month following the close of the exempt organization's accounting period (e.g., November 15 for an entity with a June 30 year end). Failure to file the information return or an untimely filing can, at best, create some confusion between the IRS and the exempt organization or, at worst, jeopardize the organization's tax-exempt status.[7]

Organizational Changes

An alteration in the legal structure of an exempt organization (e.g., from a trust to a corporation) calls for the filing of a new exemption application. IRS provisions require the new legal entity to establish that it qualifies for exemption. Typically, the application is approved, but the filing should be approached in the same way as an original application.

By-law or articles of organization changes must be communicated to the IRS. This is accomplished by submitting a "conformed copy of these changes to the appropriate key District Director."[8]

Other Matters

This chapter will conclude by addressing several important topics. Administrators of an NPO seeking tax-exempt status will find this information helpful.

Specific Publications

Several IRS publications focus specifically on tax-exempt organizations. They include

No. 557, *Tax-Exempt Status for Your Organization*

No. 578, *Tax Information for Private Foundations and Foundation Managers*

No. 892, *Exempt Organization Appeal Procedure*

Articles of Organization

When seeking a ruling or determination letter, an organization must include a "conformed copy" of its articles of organization. Sample articles are included in Publication 557. Specific conditions (i.e., the "organizational test" details) must be present in the articles of organization. Chapter 3 of Publication 557 provides the guidelines and guidance needed.

Lobbying Expenditures

Denial of an organization's exempt status will be triggered if the organization spends a substantial amount of its time and resources on propaganda activities or in actions which attempt to influence legislation. The exceptions to this general rule are tightly described in Publication 557.

Recent Law Changes

The term "educational" now covers organizations that provide child care for children away from their homes. Substantially all the care must relate to the gainful employment of the parents and the child care must be available to the general public.

Private operating foundations no longer are subject to an excise tax on net investment income. The private operating foundation must be an exempt operating foundation for this recently enacted (i.e., for tax years beginning after 1984) provision to apply.

Notes

1. None of the sports competition activity must pertain to the providing of athletic facilities or equipment.

2. Technically, a trust is a fund or foundation that qualifies for exemption.

3. From this point on, a great deal of the structure and content of this chapter draws on the 1980 effort authored by Joseph J. DioGuardi.

4. Family tax planning is a specialized area where the use of a private foundation may be appropriate. Consultation with competent professionals is advised.

5. The appeals procedure is covered in detail within Publication 557, *Tax-Exempt Status for Your Organization.*

6. The paragraphs in the succeeding sections are designed to provide a brief summary of the private foundation provisions. Publication 578, *Tax Information for Private Foundations and Foundation Managers,* should be used to obtain a better and more detailed description of the provisions.

7. Some organizations do not have to file Form 990. Chapter 2 of Publication 557, *Tax Exempt Status for Your Organization*, details the exceptions.

8. See Publication 557 for the specifics about a "conformed copy."

PART 2
Leadership, Management, and Control

6

Scanning the External Environment

B. J. Hodge

Vice President for Finance and Administration, Professor of Management, The Florida State University, National President, Sigma Iota Epsilon, The Honorary and Professional Management Fraternity

Michael D. Hankin

Assistant to the Vice President, The Florida State University, National Administrator, Sigma Iota Epsilon, The Honorary and Professional Management Fraternity

The Nature and Importance of the External Environment

Nonprofit organizations (NPOs) are not self-sufficient entities that exist in a vacuum. Rather, they exist within an envelope of forces and conditions that affect all facets of their operations. This envelope is the source of an organization's inputs in the form of resources and information as well as the recipient of the organization's outputs in the form of goods and services that satisfy the needs and wants of consumers, members, or clients. This envelope is the nonprofit organization's external environment, i.e., the aggregate of factors and forces that surround the nonprofit organization.

It is essential for nonprofit organization managers to understand the nature of the external environment because the changes that have occurred in the United States, as well as in the world, have greatly accelerated during the past two decades and, moreover, will continue to accelerate. Nonprofit organizations can no longer operate as though they exist in a world that is stable and homogeneous. On the contrary, they exist in a world that is turbulent, volatile, and heterogeneous.

The Concept of Change

Most organizations experience two types of change. The first, *endogeneous* change, originates from the organization itself, for example, through the introduction of new policies and procedures, new products and services, new leadership, etc. In this chapter, we are more concerned with *exogeneous* change, that which originates from sources external to the organization. External, or environmental change, is a concept that organizations must accept in order to adjust. They must understand the source of the change, the reason for the change, its intensity, its implications, and its permanence. Not to have this knowledge can only result in the disruption of the organization's operations.

The Concept of Turbulence

The corollary of change is the concept of turbulence within the external environment. In times of relative environmental calm, an organization can rely on yesterday's plans, policies, procedures, and traditional management methods. However, in times of environmental turbulence, when change tends to be rapid and discontinuous, old methods of managing will not be effective, and if the organization is to survive, it must devise creative and innovative methods for dealing with this turbulence.

To underscore the degree of turbulence in the world and its effect on organizations, a few examples will suffice. Between 1960 and 1982, twenty-eight major laws were passed by Congress dealing with public health and safety, bringing major consequences to every important industry, association, and nonprofit organization in the United States.[1] The Tax Reform Act of 1986, by limiting the deductions that an individual can take for charitable contributions (depending upon income level and itemization procedures), in addition to changing the basic tax rates for all Americans, might very well have a tremendous impact upon those nonprofit organizations that rely heavily upon individual contributions for the accomplishment of their mission. Terrorism has severely disrupted the foreign travel industry, forcing airlines and airports to adopt the most stringent security measures, and has even fostered the creation of new departments within large corporations to combat the menace. Many small colleges and universities, and even larger ones, have been forced to trim some of their operations "to the bone" as our population has shifted from young to old. Indeed, volumes could be written describing how external environmental changes have affected all types of organizations within the 1980s alone.

The purpose of this chapter, therefore, is twofold: (1) to describe the major components of the external environment and cite some examples of recent changes within each component and their effect on organizations and (2) to discuss the environmental scanning process, a method of environmental information gathering that is utilized by organizations in order to prepare for likely environmental changes.

The Components of the External Environment[2]

For our purposes, we have divided the organization's external environment into seven major components: (1) culture, (2) the political system, (3) the economic system, (4) competition, (5) technology, (6) the skill mix of the population, and (7) client groups. Table 6.1 presents a summary of our subsequent discussion.

Culture

Every society develops its own set of values, norms, artifacts, and accepted behavior patterns—in short, culture. Moreover, culture is an important device for defining both what a society is and the role of the nonprofit organization within that society.

For example, the charitableness of the average citizen is determined, to a large extent, by the values that society at large deems important. Think how this affects such organizations as the United Way, the Salvation Army (particularly during the Christmas Season), the Muscular Dystrophy Association, etc. To the extent that society's values change, so must the organization. The case of industrial pollution and its place in American society provides a classic example. Once society determined that there must be a reduction in the amount of pollutants in the physical environment, manufacturers began to make changes in the techniques, processes, and materials that went into their products. Many nonprofit organizations, such as Ducks Unlimited, the Sierra Club, and the Cousteau Society, were either formed, or their activities greatly expanded, as a direct result of society's changing attitude toward pollution and related topics.

Society's norms are the standards that mold the behavior, attitudes, and values of the members who constitute that society, and they originate from religion, law, and common practice. They are "standards" because people take them into account in their decisions and behavior. Dress, speech, taste, and a general understanding of the difference between right and wrong are all affected by norms.

Table 6.1. Components of the External Environment

Major component	Subcomponent
Culture	Societal values, norms, beliefs, artifacts, accepted behavior patterns, institutions
Political system	National, state, and local laws, regulations and ordinances, governmental services, political parties and processes
Economic system	Resource availability and distribution, market structure, price mechanisms, economic regulations
Competition	Nonbusiness competition, substitutability, exit and entry of competitors, demands on members' time and services
Technology	Techniques and science of production and distribution, machinery/automation, work flows and processing, research and development
Skill mix of the population	Labor availability by skill and geographic area, mobility, training and development
Client groups	Expectations (time, place, quality, and quantity), needs, wants, perceptions

SOURCE: Adapted from B.J. Hodge and William P. Anthony, *Organization Theory*, 2d ed., Allyn and Bacon, Boston, 1984, p. 98.

Let us examine some specific cultural changes that have occurred in society which can affect a nonprofit organization. John Naisbitt, author of *Megatrends,* notes that during times of turbulence in our nation, there is often tremendous growth in interest in religion, as Americans search for structure in their lives. The effects of this cultural variable in the external environment are evidenced by the 1300 radio stations and dozens of television stations that devote a large part, if not all, of their programming to religion. In addition, Naisbitt notes that evangelical publishers account for one-third of total U.S. domestic book sales.[3] Therefore, for large, religious nonprofit organizations, with actual or potential telecommunications and publishing capabilities, the revitalization of religion in American culture is an important point to consider. If a nonprofit organization's management takes cultural changes into account in its decisions, it is better able to provide those services which society at large deems most desirable.

Conversely, almost every institution in a society is capable of transfusing some of its values, norms, and behavior patterns into its external environment. Schools and churches, for instance, are responsible to a great extent for the kinds of behavior and values that make up society's culture, as mentioned above. Thus, one must conclude that the cultural component of the external environment is a powerful force with which to reckon.

The Political System

All organizations are affected to varying degrees by the political system, i.e., governmental and political processes. To function—further, even to exist—organizations must comply with a myriad of legal requirements at the federal, state, and local levels. Profit-making organizations, for example, must be aware of government laws regarding such items as antitrust limitations, taxes, depreciations, protection of the physical environment, etc. Similarly, the nonprofit organization must be cognizant of such governmental actions as tax exemption, fund-raising, grants-in-aid, and cooperative agreements.

Managers need to be aware of this component of the external environment because every facet of their operations is affected by legal considerations. Just considering the various personnel functions in organizations, one becomes aware of the many different laws regulating wages, hiring practices, mandatory workers' compensation, and retirement benefits. In fact, many nonprofit organizations are the recipients of government goods and services that are absolutely necessary for the accomplishment of their mission, e.g., halfway houses for newly released convicts.

Concerning recent environmental developments in this area, organizations must recognize and adapt to recent trends indicating that national political power is shifting from the federal government to the states. According to Naisbitt, the states have become "structurally and procedurally stronger, more accountable, more assertive, and perform a major intergovernmental role."[4] In quantitative terms, Naisbitt notes that the states passed an average of 1000 laws apiece between 1980 and 1982, whereas Congress passed only 500 during that same period.[5] In addition, one cannot ignore the potential effect that federal budget cuts will have on state and local operations. As federal sources of monies wither, state and local governments will have to pick up the slack by providing many services formerly funded and managed by Washington. Therefore, organizations are finding themselves more affected by state and local government decisions than by federal ones.

Nonprofit organization managers, then, not only have the responsibility but also the imperative to become thoroughly familiar with the political system and to adjust to it.

The Economic System

The economic component of the external environment includes resource allocation and the distribution of goods and services. Major considerations in this external environmental component include information on current income, savings, prices, credit availability, changes in economic growth, inflation, interest rates, capital availability, income differences between classes and regions, shifts in demand for goods and services, etc.[6] Perhaps the best example of the impact of the economic component on all types of organizations was the energy crisis of the 1970s. The shock of that crisis firmly established a broad awareness of the effects on all types of organizations of external economic developments.

In the United States, the economy is basically one of private enterprise, i.e., decisions about what and how much to produce are made by owners and managers in response to supply and demand. Of course, the government influences most segments of our economy to varying degrees, and in fact governments themselves are producers, distributors, and recipients of goods and services.

One recent trend in our economic system that merits discussion is the changing demographic variables of sex and age. As the average age of our population increases and undergoes a sex-ratio change, concomitant changes are found in consumer tastes and aggregate social services levels. As life expectancy increases, unprecedented demands are placed on social security, medical services, and on those nonprofit organizations serving the needs of the elderly. In addition, demographic changes such as the population shift to the sunbelt states are factors to consider.

Finally, the economy is becoming more global and less national in scope. We drive to work in Japanese cars, work in buildings made from Korean steel, and wear Brazilian-made shoes. In turn, West German firms use computers manufactured in the United States, and Soviet citizens eat bread made from American wheat. Some scholars—such as Botkin, Dimanescu, and State—maintain that we must shift our thinking from a domestic economy based on resource availability to one based on information and knowledge-based resources.[7] This shift mandates a more "global view" by Third Sector leaders to ensure that we focus and coordinate the human, technical, and educational resources in the voluntary action sector necessary to effectively meet public service needs in this type of economy.

Competition

Many people mistakenly believe that competition is a phenomenon that exists only between profit-making organizations. On the contrary, the spirit of competition is at the very heart of most of our modern institutions, both profit-making and nonprofit organizations. Colleges and universities, for instance, compete for faculty and students when they recruit. Fraternities and sororities hold "rushes" to gain new members. Hospitals in the same community, or region, must have a sufficient number of patients to justify their existence as well as staff to serve these patients. Philanthropic organizations must, by definition, compete with one another to obtain contributions from a public with finite resources. In addition, consider the demands placed upon an individual who is a valued member of multiple nonprofit organizations and associations. Each nonprofit organization or association, of which this individual is a member, must compete with any others for his or her time and services. Because of its pervasiveness, competition must be considered an important part of the macro-level environment.

In order to cope with competition, an organization must be constantly aware of its "competitive environment" and be responsive to it. For example, the automotive, electronics, and computer industries, among others, keep watchful eyes on the competition, especially from Japan. Nonprofit organizations offering comparable services to clients within a community or region must be aware of what each is doing. Pricing policies, for example, are one function of "what the competition is doing." If a particular nonprofit organization is charging a fee for its services, while similar organizations are not, does that put the former in a more or less advantageous position over similar nonprofit organizations—all other factors being equal?

What are the environmental factors that an organization examines within the competitive component of the external environment? William F. Glueck developed an excellent composite of these factors, including, but not limited to, changes in population, income distribution of the population, age shifts in the population, and product or service life cycles.[8] The organization must also be cognizant of the exit and entry of rival organizations into the "market." What would be the effect on a government-funded nonprofit substance abuse center if a profit-making organization were formed to provide the same services?

The question of substitutability must also be addressed. The availability and quality of less costly substitutes for an organization's products or services are important considerations. For example, profit-making organizations in the sugar industry must be concerned with such products as fructose and corn syrup. Similarly, in the nonprofit sector, is it possible that a social worker with an M.S.W. degree can offer the same level of services as a social worker with a Ph.D.? Can a former convict be just as effective a counselor for youthful offenders in a certain program as is a degreed professional in another?

Competition within the external environment, therefore, must be taken into consideration regardless of the type of organization. There is little doubt that competition, in all its varied forms, is an important external environmental component.

Technology

Technology is concerned with the art and science of production. Every organization employs technology to some extent, be it the word processor used by the local chamber of commerce to send out memos or robotic systems employed by General Motors to assemble automobiles.

To operate successfully, organizations must have access to modern technology. A carpenter using hand tools cannot compete cost effectively against one using power tools. A hospital cannot effectively treat the sick without the most modern medical equipment. A national honor society cannot meet the informational needs of its members without some sort of word-processing capability. Today's organizations must give considerable attention to technology in deciding which products or services they will make and distribute as well as deciding which processes to utilize for day-to-day operations.

Technological decisions also have profound economic impact. Tremendous amounts of capital are necessary to obtain technology for mass production purposes. Even on a smaller scale, technology is expensive in terms of implementation and training.

It can be argued that an important measure of an organization's success is its ability to adjust to and employ technological innovations. Some scholars believe that the industrial revolution began in England and not in other European countries because the English were willing to accept mass-produced goods while others were not. In the United States, our technological capabilities have introduced new products and techniques that have benefitted all types of organizations.

For these reasons, managers have an obligation to be aware of the technological component of the macro-level environment. In fact, technology will not only influence the effectiveness and efficiency of organizational operations, but might very well alter the organization's basic design and operating structures. For example, Ford and Slocum discovered that as routine technology is introduced into the organization, there is a tendency toward increased formalization of operations and reporting relationships as well as centralization of power.[10]

The Skill Mix of the Population

The effectiveness and efficiency of an organization will be determined, to a large extent, by the quality and quantity of various abilities in its labor force. High-tech firms on Route 128 near Boston, for example, must have an available labor reservoir from which to draw highly educated and skilled employees. In fact, without the plethora of colleges and universities in Boston, such a concentration of high-tech industries in the area would not be feasible. Conversely, the need by the high-tech labor pool for more college-level courses creates a stronger educational "market" for Boston-area colleges.

Two recent trends in the external environmental component are worth noting: (1) women entering the work force and (2) the demand for highly competent technical employees. Regarding the former, Naisbitt notes that, by 1982, women made up 40 percent of the work force and, moreover, that by 1990, women getting professional degrees will be eight times the number of women getting these degrees in the 1960s.[11] Certainly, an organization must take into consideration the fact that women are not only entering the labor force in larger numbers, but they are also taking over positions formerly held by men. Thus, organizations will have to formulate new employment practices regarding such items as maternity leave, part-time employment options, pay differential elimination, etc.

Concerning the second trend, modern organizations of all types must be concerned with obtaining labor that has the necessary skills and education for a high-technology information-based economy. Indeed, the mission of many nonprofit organizations is to serve the social and employment-related needs of individuals who have been displaced from their old jobs as "smokestack" industries continue their decline in America.

In short, no organization can operate smoothly, or even accomplish its basic mission, unless it takes into account the skill-mix component of the external environment.

Client Groups

Any organization processes a variety of inputs into outputs, the latter being in the form of goods and services. In order to accomplish this, the organization must be concerned with providing these outputs in a form acceptable to its clients, i.e., the right good or service, at the right time, at the right place, in the right quantity, and at the right price. In order for a profit-making organization to be successful, it must identify the final consumer of a product or service. It must analyze the market to define the group of people it seeks to serve. Should the profit-making organization not have adequate information about potential consumer tastes and desires before opening up a new business, introducing a new product or service, or eliminating old ones, it faces the very probable prospect of failure.

In a similar vein, nonprofit organizations *must* obtain adequate information about client needs before they can successfully offer their services and accomplish their purposes. For example, when a nonprofit organization is formed to serve the needs of the elderly, its management needs information on this "market" to determine what types of services it will offer and in what quantity. Do elderly clients need psychological counseling, medical care, financial assistance, and social activities? If so, in what proportion to one another? In what quantity? Is there a significant elderly population in the nonprofit organization's operating area to warrant the formation of such an organization? Is the average income of the elderly in the proposed impact area so high that many of the organization's programs are not really needed?

Imagine the mission(s) of the various trade and professional associations in the United States. A statewide insurance association, for example, might only be concerned with legislative lobbying, and thus may best serve its membership by focusing its efforts on political activities. A health care association, on the other hand, might be concerned with many activities besides lobbying, e.g., new advances in medical technology, professional training and development, ethics, cost containment, and the provision of statistical data relating to various diseases. Thus, the latter can best serve the needs of its members by paying attention to a wide spectrum of environmental information.

Once the client group is identified and decisions made about the nature of the product or service to be offered, the organization is in a position to define its operations. Its objective is to produce a particular product or service and provide it to the right client group.

An Environmental Perspective

Nonprofit organization management has a responsibility to be aware of external environmental conditions and to implement effective plans for dealing with them. Management scholar, Ludwig von Bertalanffy, in a classic treatise, states that organizations are open systems interacting with their environment.[12] We have determined that this environment is comprised of seven major components: (1) culture, (2) the political system, (3) the economic system, (4) competition, (5) technology, (6) the skill mix of the population, and (7) client groups. Moreover, these components are not static; rather, they are all characterized by change and turbulence. Therefore, the nonprofit organization, if it is to be successful in accomplishing its mission, must devise a means of obtaining environmental information. This must be done *before* strategies and plans can be devised. The method that organizations utilize to obtain environmental information is called "environmental scanning," and is the focus of the rest of this chapter.

Environmental Scanning— An Overview

Because the components of the external environment can have such a dramatic and important impact on the organization's successful operations and even on its continued existence, many organizations now engage in a process known as environmental scanning. Francis Aguilar, one of the first scholars to investigate "environmental scanning," defined it as "the process that seeks information about events and relationships in a company's outside environment, the knowledge of which would assist top management in charting the company's future course of action."[13] Traditionally, organizations focused their information-gathering activities on internal sources because the external environment was perceived to be relatively stable; however, as we have demonstrated in previous sections of this chapter, such an assumption is now fallacious.

Consequently, beginning in the 1960s, managers developed methods and concepts to include more of the external world in long-range planning and decision-making deliberations. These methods and concepts are geared toward obtaining knowledge of environmental realities *before* effective plans are made. Thus, the process of scanning asks and attempts to answer the following questions: (1) What is the current state of affairs? (2) What are the most important events? (3) What is the history of the external environmental component being studied? (4) What are the apparent trends? (5) What dramatic events can occur? (6) What is the potential for surprises?[14]

Scoping the External Environment

It is virtually impossible for any manager or specialized organizational subunit to scan and process *all* the information from a given external environmental component. The environment is an abstract, difficult concept for many managers occupied with day-to-day operations. Managers know their *immediate* environment in terms of specifics, e.g., suppliers, clients, specific regulatory agencies, etc., but they do not know the environment in a *global* sense. There is simply too much to know.

Therefore managers *scope,* or limit, their environment. They make decisions about which part(s) of the environment they plan to link up to and monitor and which they will ignore (for the time being). Of course, in scoping the environment, there is always the danger of ignoring some aspect that is vitally important. For example, how many managers were really prepared for the OPEC-led oil shock of 1973? How many knew that almost one-half of our oil was imported? Although there is the risk of missing some important environmental event through the process of scoping, managers, nevertheless, should focus their scanning activities on those external environmental components that seem to have the most direct bearing on their organization's current operations and future plans. When the process of scoping is applied to a specialized scanning subunit, it is called "selectivity," and we will discuss this further in a subsequent section of this chapter.

Classifications of Scanning Information

Even with effective scoping, information gleaned from scanning must be presented in such a fashion as to provide the best inputs for planning and decision-making purposes. Paulo DeV. Filho has devised a methodology for classifying environmental information inputs into eight categories:

1. *Threat.* An unfavorable situation which tends to affect the performance of the organization. For example, the introduction of a better product, at a lower price, by a competitor.

2. *Restriction.* A situation which limits the operations of the organization. For example, a government regulation limiting the expenditure of grant-in-aid funds.

3. *Problem.* A situation which requires an adequate solution to prevent it from becoming a restriction or threat. For example, a decline in charitable contributions.

4. *Negative symptom.* A situation which allows for the forecasting of a problem, restriction, or threat. For example, forecasting a population shift away from the organization's operating area.

5. *Neutral variables.* A temporary neutral situation, but with the potential of becoming positive or negative. For example, the appointment of a new, hitherto unknown, member to an external governing body that allocates funds to a nonprofit organization.

6. *Positive symptom.* A situation which permits the forecasting of a stimulus or opportunity. For example, information about the discontinuation of a competing organization.

7. *Stimulus.* A favorable situation that can be transformed into an opportunity. For example, the availability of new technology that can lead to operational cost reductions.

8. *Opportunity.* A favorable situation that can positively affect organizational performance. For example, the identification of an unsatisfied demand in the market where the organization operates, and the organization has the resources to meet the demand.[15]

The utilization of this type of classification system helps categorize information into ways that will facilitate management's decision-making processes in a particular way. For instance, a "threat" situation would require immediate action, while a "stimulus" situation would call for the development of plans and time parameters in order to turn the stimulus into an "opportunity."

Scanning in the Large Organization

Because large organizations have more resources with which to conduct their operations, the parameters of their scanning activities are larger than those of smaller organizations. Large organizations will have access to both internally generated and externally generated detailed reports about the environment. Moreover, the information contained in these reports can cover a wide time continuum—past conditions, the current situation, and future environmental prospects. In addition, large organizations—because of available capital, space, technology, and personnel—are better able to design specific organizational structures, or subunits, for scanning purposes. These subunits have the ability to conduct highly formal and complex scanning exercises.

Engledow and Levy recently conducted a longitudinal study that examined the scanning processes of scanning subunits within large organizations. These formal subunits should be organized with specific roles and reporting relationships. This ensures that the activities of such subunits are directed to obtain the right types of information as well as report this information to the right decision center within the organization. Following is a short discussion of the three basic types of scanning subunits identified in their study.

1. *Policy-oriented.* This is a subunit at the corporate, or headquarters level, with direct access to top management. The focus of the subunit is on early detection of broad strategic issues in the external environment, for example, shifts in attitudes, norms, and social roles. The basic purpose of this subunit is to help define (scope)

the relevant environment, sensitize top management, and avoid blindsiding because of major emerging issues.

2. *Strategic planning integrated.*   This type of subunit may exist either at the headquarters or at the operating level of the organization, and is a regular part of the organization's planning staff. Its specific role is to both sensitize top management to environmental changes as well as to inject specific issues into the planning process. In addition, this type of subunit differentiates between strategic (long-term, integrated) environmental issues and business (short-term, operational) environmental issues.

3. *Function-oriented.*   This type of scanning subunit is attached to a particular function within the organization, e.g., marketing, legal, research, and development. The subunit's search and analysis of the environment is closely linked to a particular function's environment. Its basic purpose is to improve the organization's functional performance by providing operationally relevant information.[16]

The reader should be aware of the necessity to fully integrate and coordinate the activities and information flow between these three types of scanning units. This ensures that scanning can have its greatest impact. For example, the legal function-oriented subunit might learn of a new law of such magnitude that it has the potential to radically alter the organization's basic mission. Therefore, this information must be provided to the other two subunits for policy and strategy purposes.

Forecasting Categories and Techniques of the Large Organization

The large organization often scans its environment with the objective of being able to forecast, in as much detail as possible, future conditions within a particular environmental component. Specialists within the organization's planning department usually make four types of forecasts, and we will briefly discuss the nature of each type of forecast and cite some of the techniques that the large organization can utilize for this purpose.

Economic Forecasts.   This type of forecast covers such topics as the gross national product, products, prices, employment, production, etc. Also, the organization might wish to make its own forecast on special types of future economic conditions. For instance, a public utility would desire a very carefully prepared forecast of future demand for electricity, gas, and water in its area of operations. The necessity and importance of this type of forecast are exemplified by what happened within the auto industry in the late 1970s and early 1980s. Detroit completely misjudged the changes taking place in consumer demand for smaller cars with better gasoline mileage. As a result, foreign manufacturers designed, manufactured, and marketed high-quality, highly efficient smaller cars for sale in the American market. Indeed, foreign firms were so successful in recognizing this changing economic trend that they now control 25 percent of the U.S. auto market.

Techniques for conducting economic forecasts include (1) econometric methods that describe economic activity in terms of a system of mathematical equations, (2) leading indicators, measures of the economy moving in the same direction as the current economy, but doing so several months ahead, (3) surveys conducted by such organizations as the U.S. Department of Commerce, the Census Bureau, Dunn and Bradstreet, or the organization itself, (4) trend analysis, which involves the pattern that exists in a set of time-series data, and (5) statistical methods, such as multiple and linear regressions and correlational analyses, that express the relationship between variables.

Technological Forecasts.   For an organization involved with high technology, this type of forecasting is essential. For large nonprofit organizations, such as the American Cancer Society, for example, it is imperative to gain some insight into potential advances in the field of medical technology. Technological forecasts can refer to developments with respect to existing technology, or they can seek to identify new technological developments.

The *Statistical Abstract of the United States* includes data on such items as research and development, patent trademarks, and scientific education and is an excellent source of information for this type of forecasting. The statistical techniques of regression and correlational analyses can also assist organizations in forecasting the expected outputs from research and development efforts.

Political Forecasts.   This type of forecasting is concerned with assessing the impact of future governmental legislation, and is particularly important for nonprofit organizations that are regulated by, funded by, or cooperatively involved with government agencies.

Many quantitative techniques, such as the use of statistics, are available for political forecasting; however, the uncertainty of political information forces the utilization of qualitative techniques. One is the Delphi Technique that involves four basic program steps: (1) the use of experts on the political component of the external environment, (2) the surveying of the experts' opinions and forecasts, (3) the subsequent interviewing of the experts on an individual basis to allow them to change their opinions, and (4) the determination of consensus opinion by the Delphi Technique coordinator.

Brainstorming is a useful method for producing creative ideas for problem solving, and involves presenting a particular subject to a group of experts and allowing them to present their forecasts. The first phase in a brainstorming session asks group members to present their ideas spontaneously on the future of the subject under study. The group members are encouraged to produce a large quantity of ideas, with no criticisms, probing, or questions being allowed by other group members. The second phase reviews the merits of each individual forecast, which in turn can lead to additional alternatives and the elimination of those with little merit.

Social Forecasts.   Social forecasting seeks to understand the nature of our changing society and to predict the potential effect of these changes on the organization. This type of forecasting is extremely complicated because scanners must deal with highly complex and interrelated social systems.

Time-series analysis can be utilized to forecast variables such as age and sex distribution of the population, birth rates, and educational level. The statistical procedures previously discussed can also be used. In addition, the Delphi Technique and brainstorming are also useful social forecasting tools.

Scenarios are often used by large organizations in attempting to forecast societal and political changes. A "scenario" is a written narrative describing the future; it answers two types of questions: (1) What are the precise steps that might cause some hypothetical situation to develop? (2) What alternatives exist for preventing or facilitating the occurrence of the hypothetical event? Experts in specific areas are asked to write these scenarios, which are then used by top management in examining any potential threats or opportunities facing the organization.

For further information on forecasting, the list of suggested readings at the end of the chapter is recommended.

Qualities of the Effective Scanning Subunit

Our discussion of formal scanning within large organizations would be incomplete if we did not mention some of the qualities that would enable such an organizational unit to accomplish its mission in the most effective manner. These qualities include the concepts of selectivity, resilience, and maintenance.

Selectivity.   Selectivity is similar to the concept of scoping. The scanning subunit must facilitate the flow of information from the external environment to the organization and, yet, somehow focus its scanning efforts on those aspects of the external environment that have a direct bearing on the organization's current operations and long-range plans. The scanning subunit needs to be *selective* in that it screens superfluous information. Unless there is a conscious effort on the part of the scanning subunit to determine what is important and what is not, the organization will suffer from information overload.

Resilience.   The resilience of scanning subunits refers to the degree to which they can respond to changes in the organization's objectives and overall mission by changing the focus of the scanning effort. If the mission changes, then so must the type of information that the subunit gleans from the environment. Therefore, it is important for the subunit to keep abreast of the organization's operating and strategic objectives in order to get matching environmental information. However, this presents a dilemma. If we state that the scanning subunit should concentrate its efforts only on those aspects of the external environment that directly relate to current objectives and mission, how are events outside this present scope with potential importance to be recognized? The answer is to be found within the concept of maintenance.

Maintenance.   Scanning subunits need to be managed just as other organizational units need to be managed. Adequate management of these subunits will ensure that they not only have ample contact with the environment but that they also provide information that is not currently relevant to operational and strategic objectives. This is done through *linkage* to the organization's decision-authority centers, i.e., a two-way information flow. The decision-authority center should provide guidelines concerning potentially relevant information to be scanned, and moreover should further provide the scanning unit with information relating to the organization's basic values and philosophy, the latter helping to define broad scanning parameters.

Scanning in the Small Organization

Unlike the large organization, the small one does not have sufficient resources to organize specific scanning subunits nor the ability to perform complex and formal forecasting procedures. Nevertheless, managers of small organizations must have the ability to scan their environment. This is usually done on a personal or informal-group basis. Information can be obtained from a variety of sources, e.g., suppliers, clients, bankers, consultants, peers, subordinates, personal reading and observation, the use of in-house committees, etc.

The *signals* that announce environmental change usually come with ample warning, and in subsequent portions of this chapter we will examine a variety of techniques that the small nonprofit organization can utilize to process and receive these signals.

Internal Activities

Current organizational personnel are key places to start an informal environmental scanning process. A manager should begin by conducting interviews with key leaders in the organization. If the nonprofit organization is an association, then key voluntary leaders should be contacted to determine which issues they believe are of paramount importance. Both personal interviews and structured questionnaires can be used to obtain information from internal sources.

Use of Committees.   Some experts recommend that a scanning committee, composed of ten to twelve individuals, be formed.[17] These committee members should have functional responsibilities within the organization. The concepts of selectivity, resilience, and maintenance would apply to an informal committee as they would to a formal organizational scanning subunit. In addition, to ensure the committee's long-term value, future leaders within the organization should be appointed.

A scanning committee should meet on a regular basis to consider the type of information that members have obtained from the external environment. Members can gain their information from internal sources, e.g., interviews and questionnaires, or through the reading of periodicals, books, and reports. The telecommunications media are also excellent sources of information. Following a discussion of the information, ideas can be generated, with top issues being decided upon by consensus of opinion. Finally, the committee can recommend appropriate responses to critical environmental issues or even the continuation of the scanning process for more information.

Specialized Exercises

Brainstorming, previously discussed, can also be utilized by the small nonprofit organization as well as by the large one. In fact, specialized exercises have been developed for this purpose.

The Implications Wheel.   The Implications Wheel, developed in the 1970s by Professor Jerome Glenn and Consultant Joel Baker, has been used by many small nonprofit organizations, such as the United Way of Essex and West Hudson, New Jersey, and the Industrial Safety Equipment Association of Arlington, Virginia. The Wheel is basically a tool that can help explore the long-term implications of trends, innovations, policy changes, and goals.

The design of a Wheel exercise is begun by gathering a small group of individuals, say, ten to fifteen people. The group should have representatives from different levels of the organization who are concerned with long-range planning. The only other physical necessities are a meeting room, a blackboard, and chalk.

The exercise begins with the introduction of a central issue derived from environmental scanning. The group leader writes the issue on the center of the blackboard and then circles the issue. The central issue can be any significant development in the external environment, e.g., introduction of robotics in the manufacturing process, youth crime, the increased cancer rate among women, ad infinitum. After the central issue has been introduced, the group leader asks members to state some immediate implications. At that point, a variety of implications can be "spun off" the central issue, and even second implications can be spun off from first implications, and third implications from the second. As these implications fill up the space outside the central issue on the blackboard, the picture of the Wheel develops. At a certain point, reached by group consensus, implications will run out, the final spin-off implications representing a future environmental event of potentially serious magnitude. Figure 6.1 represents a real-life Wheel exercise conducted by a United Way organization.[18]

Probability Impact Chart.   After implications from a central issue have been determined from using the Wheel, it is possible to set priorities for action through the use of the Probability Impact Chart. The first step in this exercise involves estimating the probability of an implication occurring during the organization's long-term planning period, e.g., a period of 1 to 10 years. Secondly, those implications having a direct impact upon the organization—were they really to happen—are discussed. Third, the group members, through voting, prioritize those implications having an impact upon the organization in terms of their relative importance. Once the implications have been prioritized, the group is ready to consider appropriate organizational responses.[19] Figure 6.2 represents a Probability

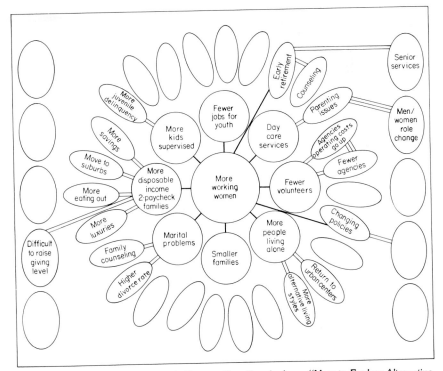

Figure 6.1. The implications wheel. (*Source: Sam Freedenberg, "How to Explore Alternative Futures,"* Association Management, *January 1982, p. 98.*)

Probable Implications	Improbable Implications
Higher divorce rate	Difficult to raise giving level
Family counseling	More luxuries
Move to suburbs	Return to urban centers
More juvenile delinquency	More eating out
Senior services	More savings
Role change: men and women	Fewer agencies
Agency costs go up	Retirement counseling
More pressure on United Way	More alternative living systems
Impact on the United Way	Prioritization
Family counseling	Agency costs go up
More juvenile delinquency	More pressure on United Way
Senior services	Juvenile delinquency
Agency costs go up	Family counseling
More pressure on United Way	Senior services

Figure 6.2. Probability impact chart.

Impact Chart using second- and third-level implications from the Wheel depicted in Figure 6.1.

Concerning the Wheel and Chart, it is essential that openness be encouraged. A group member should not be precluded from expressing unpopular or controversial opinions. In fact, we recommend one of the group members acting as a devil's advocate, expressing the opposite opinion of other group members, so that all implications and their resultant impacts are explored.

External Activities

Nonprofit organization managers have a variety of practices for obtaining environmental information from sources external to the organization. Top management often makes use of personal and professional contacts for this purpose. In fact, many nonprofit organization and association executives sit on multiple boards of directors, and this enables these individuals to obtain important environmental information that might not otherwise be available.

Formal conventions and conferences are also excellent sources for obtaining environmental information. Also, some organizations hold lecture series highlighted by an expert's presentation on a topical environmental event. For example, the Forest Industries Advisory Council regularly hosts such presentations, and noted futurists such as Herman Kahn and Theodore J. Gordon have spoken to the membership on a variety of subjects.

The Media

Perhaps the most practical scanning method utilized by the small organization would be the reading of various media. By reading and analyzing a variety of newspapers, periodicals, and telecommunications broadcasts, management can better recognize those environmental areas today that will impact their organizations tomorrow.

Media scanning can be both passive and active. Passive scanning refers to responding to information that relates to personal interests, goals, values, and professional objectives. This type of media scanning satisfies low-level curiosity and interests, but does not meet the criteria of professional responsibility to know the organization's external environment. Rather, for this purpose, active media scanning is required, i.e., media sources are selected for their known or expected level of information. Active scanning, in turn, is followed by directed media scanning, whereby a specific media source is selected for known items.

If a scanning committee is formed within your organization, members should be instructed to clip or copy pertinent articles to be forwarded to the committee chairman. The chairman, in turn, should identify and classify important items that can supply a central issue or issues for possible utilization in the Wheel and Chart exercises.

Professors John A. Pearce II and Richard D. Robinson, Jr., have compiled an extensive list of media sources for scanning purposes. Figure 6.3 presents excerpts from this exhaustive compendium.[20]

Characteristics of the Effective Scanner

Because so much of the scanning activities of the small organization are conducted by individual managers or by an informal group of managers, one should note those characteristics that facilitate scanning activities. William F. Glueck developed a composite of these characteristics, and following are major excerpts:

1. *Reflectiveness.* The ability to deliberate on an issue and not act impulsively.
2. *Age and experience.* The older and more experienced a manager, the better able he or she is to scan and diagnose the environment.
3. *Conceptualization.* The ability to think abstractly.
4. *Long-range outlook.* The ability to think ahead and the willingness to accept change.
5. *Risk taking.* The willingness to examine the environment and take actions, despite potential danger.
6. *Breadth.* The ability to look at more than one environmental component at a time.
7. *Optimism.* The ability to place the most favorable construction on environmental information.
8. *Delegation.* The ability to assign scanning responsibilities to subordinates.
9. *Time and resources.* The ability to budget the necessary time and other resources; e.g., space, money, personnel, periodicals, etc., to ensure a maximum scanning effort.
10. *Team spirit.* The ability to work with others.[21]

Summary and Conclusions

No organization can exist independent of its environment. For any organization to survive and prosper in the long run, it must be cognizant of the external environ-

Figure 6.3. Media sources for environmental scanning. (*Source: Adapted from John A. Pearce, II, and Richard D. Robinson, Jr.,* Strategic Management: Strategy, Formulation, and Interpretation, *Richard D. Irwin, Homewood, Ill., 1982, pp. 138–140.*)

ECONOMIC AND SKILL MIX

Predicasts

National Bureau of Economic Research

Handbook of Basic Economic Statistics

Statistical Abstract of the U. S.

Various publications by the Department of Commerce

Various publications by The Conference Board

Survey of Buying Power

Kiplinger Newsletter

Business Week

Survey of Buying Power

Business Periodicals Index

Various publications of chambers of commerce

SOCIAL AND CULTURAL

Public opinion polls

Surveys such as *Social Indicators* and *Social Reporting*

Abstract services for sociological journal articles

Various reports from the Brookings Institution and Ford Foundation

Indexes for various newspapers

TECHNOLOGY

Applied Science and Technology Index

Statistical Abstract of the U.S.

Scientific and Technical Information Service

University reports, congressional reports

Trade journals and industrial reports

Annual Report of the National Science Foundation

Research and Development Directory, patent records

COMPETITION

Association Management

Annual reports of nonprofit organizations

Newspapers

Nonprofit organization newsletters

Proceedings from conventions and conferences

POLITICAL

Public Affairs Information Services Bulletin

CIS Index (Congressional Information Index)

Weekly compilation of presidential documents

Monthly Catalog of Government Publications

Various state publications

Figure 6.3. (Continued).

CLIENTS

Statistical Abstract of the U.S.

American Statistics Index

Bureau of Census reports on various subjects

County and City Data Book

Various reports from federal and state social service agencies

---

ment in which it exists. We have determined that the major components of the external environment are culture, the political system, the economic system, competition, technology, the skill mix of the population, and client groups.

Secondly, the organization must have a means of gathering pertinent information from the external environment for both operational and long-range planning purposes. Large organizations have the resources to form specific environmental scanning subunits as well as the ability to perform complex forecasts of the future environment. Small organizations, although limited in resources, have a variety of techniques available to them that permit effective environmental scanning.

The concepts of selectivity (scoping), resilience, and maintenance apply to all scanners, be they individuals, informal groups, or a formal organizational subunit.

Once information is gained from the external environment through scanning, it is pared, diagnosed, and evaluated for planning purposes. The organization is then in a position to make plans and take action based upon this scanning and diagnosis. Finally, the process of "feedback", i.e., the continual integration and coordination of activity and information, is necessary in order to maintain and fine-tune the organization's environmental scanning system. Figure 6.4 diagrams the environmental scanning process as it pertains to organizations.

Unexpected environmental events can have a catastrophic impact upon the organization if managers are blinded to the factors and forces in the external world. We hope that this chapter has not only demonstrated the nature and importance of the external environment but also shown the central role that environmental scanning plays in helping to interpret and prepare for environmental events.

Notes

1. William L. Renfro, "Environmental Scanning Detects Signals of Change," *Association Management,* November 1983, p. 140.

2. The material used in this section has been excerpted from B. J. Hodge and William P. Anthony, *Organization Theory,* 2d ed., Allyn and Bacon, Boston, 1984, pp. 93–111.

3. John Naisbitt, *Megatrends: Ten New Directions for Transforming Our Lives,* Warner, New York, 1982, p. 239.

4. Ibid., p. 104.

5. Ibid.

6. John A. Pearce II and Richard D. Robinson, Jr., *Strategic Management: Strategy, Formulation, and Interpretation,* Richard D. Irwin, Homewood, Ill., 1982, p. 133.

7. James Botkin, Dan Dimanescu, and Roy State, *Ideas from Global Stakes: The Future of High Technology in America,* Ballinger, Cambridge, Mass., 1982.

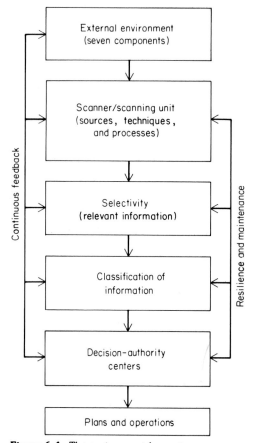

Figure 6.4. The environmental scanning process.

8. William F. Glueck, *Business Policy and Strategic Management,* McGraw-Hill, New York, 1980, pp. 96–99.

9. Refer to Joan Woodward, *Industrial Organizations: Theory and Practice,* Oxford University Press, London, 1965, pp. 68–80, for a treatment of the relationship between technology and success.

10. Jeffrey D. Ford and John W. Slocum, Jr., "Size Technology, Environment, and the Structure of Organizations," *Academy of Management Review,* vol. 2, p. 571, October 1977.

11. Naisbitt, *Megatrends,* pp. 234–237.

12. Ludwig von Bertalanffy, *General Systems Theory,* George Braziller, New York, 1968.

13. Francis J. Aguilar, *Scanning the Business Environment,* Macmillan, New York, 1967, p. 48.

14. Hodge and Anthony, *Organization Theory,* p. 96.

15. Paulo DeV. Filho, "Environmental Analysis for Strategic Planning," *Long-Range Planning,* vol. 33, pp. 28–29, January-February 1984.

16. Jack L. Engledow and R. T. Levy, "Whatever Happened to Environmental Analysis?" *Managerial Planning,* vol. 18, pp. 93–106, April 1985.

17. Renfro, "Environmental Scanning," p. 142.

18. Sam Freedenberg, "How to Explore Alternative Futures," *Association Management,* pp. 97–101, January 1982.

19. Renfro, "Environmental Scanning," p. 143.

20. Pearce and Robinson, *Strategic Management,* pp. 138–140.

21. Glueck, *Business Policy,* pp. 110–112.

Suggested Readings

Journal of Forecasting, Chichester, New York, 1982 to the present.

Armstrong, Jon S., *Long-Range Forecasting: From Crystal Ball to Computer,* Wiley, New York, 1978.

Aschler, William, *Forecasting: An Appraisal for Policy-Makers and Planners,* Wiley, New York, 1978.

—— and William H. Overholt, *Strategic Planning and Forecasting: Political Risk and Economic Opportunity,* Wiley, New York, 1983.

Cleary, James P., *The Professional Forecaster: The Forecasting Process through Data Analysis,* Lifetime Learning Publications, Belmont, Calif., 1982.

Cornish, Edward, *The Study of the Future: An Introduction to the Art and Science of Understanding and Shaping Tomorrow's World,* World Future Society, Washington, 1977.

Granger, Clive W. J., *Forecasting in Business and Economics,* Academic Press, New York, 1980.

Green, Rodney D., *Forecasting with Computer Models,* Praeger, New York, 1985.

Fowles, Jib (Ed.), *Handbook of Futures Research,* Greenwood Press, Westport, Conn., 1978.

Wheelwright, Steven C., *Forecasting Methods for Management,* Wiley, New York, 1980.

7

Management by Objectives

Dale D. McConkey

Professor of Management, University of Wisconsin, Madison

Misnomers and jargon abound in management literature. One of the more popular ones is the term "nonprofit organization." Although some managers of nonprofit organizations may find it repugnant to use the term "profit," this chapter suggests that the term (properly defined and understood) should not be considered pornographic. Any distinction between profits in the profit and nonprofit sectors is primarily one of words used in the organization's charter and the resulting tax treatment.

The profit motive must be present in both profit and nonprofit organizations. A business makes profits depending on the way it manages the resources (assets) entrusted to it. Business profits are enhanced in either or both of two ways:

1. By realizing a *higher* return on the *same* amount of assets
2. By realizing the *same* or better return on a *lesser* amount of assets

Nonprofit organizations have the same mission, as illustrated by the following ways used to realize a higher return on resources:

Increased productivity from present employees

Improved patient care from present staff (in hospitals)

Increased quality and/or quantity of teaching from present staff

Lower overhead costs of fund raising

More effective crime prevention through improved law enforcement techniques

Improved state of defense readiness by replacing troops with electronic or space hardware

Better distribution of relief and disaster funds

Greater results from volunteer workers

Lowering the administrative costs of operating the organization

Reducing wasted effort and/or wastes in the utilization of any assets

Blending together of the efforts of all personnel to achieve an overall effectiveness that is greater than the sum of the individual efforts

Viewed in this light, nonprofit organizations can improve their effectiveness (or profits) in either or both of two ways:

1. By achieving more and better benefits for their constituents on the same amount of funds or resources
2. By realizing the same or better benefits on a reduced level of funding

An Increasing Priority

An increasingly higher priority is being placed on managing nonprofit organizations so as to achieve what Peter Drucker has referred to as being the prime duty of a manager, namely, "to produce economically significant results."

This upgrading of priorities results in large part from the dramatic changes taking place in the mix of organizations comprising our economy. Increasingly, the swing is proportionately away from manufacturing-type organizations to service types—including nonprofit groups. Most informed observers believe, with considerable justification, that we are rapidly approaching a service-oriented economy that will overshadow the manufacturing sector in terms of numbers and impact. Thus, nonprofit organizations now are and will continue to be challenged to adopt more effective approaches for managing their resources.

Another pressure being exerted is the demand for greater accountability on the part of nonprofit organizations. Taxpayers, foundations, corporations, and the public in general are becoming increasingly more critical as to how organizations are utilizing the funds being contributed or allocated to them.

Finally, nonprofit organizations are facing increasing competition for the contribution dollar. The swing to a world becoming more and more oriented to social welfare has brought with it an increase in the number of organizations requesting funding.

The question that plagues most managers, administrators, and executive personnel of nonprofit organizations bent on effective performance is not if they should increase their "profits" but how the improvement can be brought about—what means, methods, or tools are available to them.

One of the means being used with increasing success for improving effectiveness of both the organization and the individuals in these entities, is "management by objectives" (or MBO, or "management by results," as it also is termed). Although MBO developed and has realized its major success in businesses operating for profits, the preponderance of the MBO system is equally applicable and beneficial to the nonprofit organization.

MBO Defined

A simple yet comprehensive definition of the MBO system of managing includes several major provisions:

1. MBO is a systems approach to managing an organization—any organization. It is not a technique, just another program, or a narrow area of the process of managing. Above all, it goes far beyond mere budgeting even though it does encompass budgets in one form or another

2. Those accountable for directing the organization first determine where they want to take the organization or what they want it to achieve during a particular period (establishing the overall objectives and priorities).

3. Requiring, permitting, and encouraging *all* key managerial and administrative personnel to contribute their maximum to achieving the overall objectives.

4. Blending and balancing the planned achievements (results) of all key personnel to promote and realize the greater total results for the organization as a whole.

5. Providing a control mechanism to monitor progress compared to objectives and feed the results back to those accountable at all levels.

Testing for Applicability

In light of the fact that MBO developed in an environment of profit-oriented business organizations, an examination should be made of the system's applicability and value to nonprofit organizations before any decision is made to adopt it. Both writers and practicing managers in nonprofit entities have raised major questions concerning the system's value in the absence of the profit motive.

The subject matter contained in the following questions will serve as an audit checklist for helping to determine the applicability of MBO to nonprofit organizations. The questions cover the major aspects of organizing and managing an operation. Also, they exert the major impact on MBO and, in turn, MBO exerts a major impact on them:

1. Does the organization have a mission to perform? Is there a valid reason for it to exist?
2. Does management have assets (money, people, plant, and equipment) entrusted to it?
3. Is management accountable to some person or authority for a return on the assets?
4. Can priorities be established for accomplishing the mission?
5. Can the operation be planned?
6. Does management believe that it must manage effectively even though the organization is a nonprofit one?
7. Can accountabilities of key personnel be pinpointed?
8. Can the efforts of all key personnel be coordinated into a whole?
9. Can necessary controls and feedback be established?
10. Is it possible to evaluate the performance of key personnel?
11. Is a system of positive and negative rewards possible?
12. Are the main functions of a manager (planning, organizing, directing, etc.) the same regardless of the type of organization?
13. Is management receptive to improved methods of operating?

The applicability and value of MBO to a nonprofit organization is directly correlated to the number of affirmative answers to the above questions. Use of these questions as tests of the wisdom of applying MBO to profit-oriented entities has been well validated by about 30 years of successful practice in every type, size, and category of business entity, both in the United States and abroad. Increasingly the same tests are proving their validity when applied to nonprofit groups.

Naturally, the degree of conviction with which the questions can be answered with a "yes" will vary with any limitations that may be imposed by the nature of the nonprofit organization, especially its locus of authority and its policies or regulations.

MBO as a System

Organizations which realize the greater benefits from management by objectives are those which practice MBO as a *system*—as a total way of managing. The word "system" as used in this context means that application of MBO to all the managerial functions it will serve results in a complete, *interrelated* approach to managing the organization, i.e., MBO serves as the primary basis for

Planning

Organizing

Directing

Controlling

Coordinating

Motivating

Evaluating performance

Rewarding performance

Developing subordinates

Coaching and counseling

Communicating

The importance of the word "interrelated" cannot be overemphasized. For example, some companies follow an MBO approach to planning but fail to integrate the planning with other management functions such as performance evaluation. Other organizations have a performance appraisal plan but do not relate it to planning and rewards. Still others have management development programs which stand by themselves.

When MBO is practiced as a total management system, each function is interrelated with all other functions. Each plays its own role and fulfills its relationship to all other functions.

Planning: First in Managing

Planning must come *first* in the entire process of managing!

Strategic planning must come *first* among the three major components of integrated planning.

These two rather simple truisms will do much to ensure the success of their entities. Those managers who fail to really understand the reasons underlying these two *"firsts"* will do a disservice to their organizations. Each will now be examined in some detail.

The writer has yet to see a list of the major functions of managing in which planning was not listed first among the functions of a manager, and with good reason: Planning is the means by which the whole process of managing is implemented. Without planning there is no basis for setting the other management functions into action.

Planning helps the organization determine *what* it must do. Unless and until the organization has determined what it must do, during a particular time period, the organization has no orderly method of determining *how* it should carry out the other functions of managing. In essence, planning determines the outputs, while the other functions of managing largely determine inputs.

Strategic Planning: First in Planning

The three major components of integrated planning include

Strategic planning

Long-range planning

Short-range planning

Again, note that strategic planning is listed first among the three components of integrated planning. Nowhere is the word "integrated" more important than in the planning context. For example, strategic planning must be completed first to set the broad directions for the organization. Next, and within the strategic plans and decisions, the long-range objectives and plans are developed to carry out the strategic directions. Finally, the short-range ones come into play. Actually, short- and long-range plans must combine to bring reality to the strategies.

Unless the organization first determines the directions in which it must move, it is impossible to establish meaningful long- and short-range objectives and plans. This will be illustrated in later paragraphs.

Contrary to the opinion often voiced by writers and others, strategic planning does not involve itself in any way with the setting of objectives, even long-range ones. Long-range objectives cannot and should not be set until strategic planning has been completed.

Strategic planning concerns itself with establishing the major direction for the organization, e.g., the nature of its purpose or mission, major clients to serve, major programs to pursue, major geographical area, and major delivery approaches. Until these major directions have been carefully thought through and selected, it is foolhardy for the organization to try to determine *what* it is going to do, i.e., its objectives.

To establish objectives prior to strategic planning is tantamount to the driver of a car establishing an objective to drive the distance between Madison, Wisconsin, and Indianapolis in one day without first determining whether the *ultimate* destination is San Francisco, Fort Worth, New York, or Toronto. Yet, the "drivers" of many nonprofit organizations (and many corporations, also) frequently make the same mistake.

Why Does the Organization Exist?

The beginning point for the application of MBO to any organization is first to determine *why* the organization exists—what client group should be served, what are the needs of the client group, and how can the needs be met. Too often, nonprofit organizations (and many corporations too) become extremely busy without first determining what they should be busy at. No matter how efficiently these organizations carry out their activities, they can never become *effective* until they determine what the needs are and how the needs can better be met.

A typical nonprofit organization can identify more needs than it could possibly satisfy. Thus, a "rifle" rather than a "shotgun" approach must be adopted if effectiveness is to be improved.

This rifle approach usually begins with the top managers of the organization agreeing to several premises, which may include the following:

1. The organization cannot be all things to all people (no matter how great the needs).

2. The organization will concentrate its resources (personnel, time, and funds) on a limited number of needs.

3. The organization will develop criteria for determining which major needs to concentrate on, e.g., education, health care, social services.

4. The organization probably cannot address the total problems within the major needs but may have further to delineate specific areas within the major one, e.g., educating the mentally retarded within the major area of education.

Much of the information for determining why the organization exists must come from an effective marketing function. Some organizations have made the mistake of equating marketing with advertising, or promotion, or public relations. While advertising, promotion, and public relations are all part of the "marketing mix," they are only pieces of a bigger picture. They cannot be applied until the organization has identified its market (clients) and its services.

Many colleges and universities, for example, as well as other types of organizations, have become their own best customers. One large midwestern university is located in a metropolitan area whose business executives have long clamored for an evening M.B.A. program. Both the market and the demand are there, but not the evening M.B.A. program. Why? Because the faculty chose not to teach in the evening, thereby ignoring customer demand.

Developing the Criteria

One of the more difficult responsibilities of the manager in a nonprofit organization is to order priorities. However, this must be done if the organization is effectively to utilize its resources. In the final analysis, prioritizing must help the organization determine where it should apply its always-scarce resources to achieve the greater benefits versus needs.

An MBO system contemplates that priorities will be determined by evaluating alternative courses of action against a list of agreed-upon criteria. Therefore, the organization must develop a list of the applicable criteria by which priorities will be ordered.

The administrators of an organization in the continuing education field have agreed upon the following criteria for determining priorities:

1. Number of continuing education hours
2. Contribution to overhead
3. Achievement of stated program objectives
4. Achievement of clientele-perceived needs
5. The degree to which programs are of a high "leverage" or "multiplier" nature
6. The degree to which the program meets the critical needs of the state's economy

A charitable foundation includes the following criteria in its agreed-upon list:

1. Areas relatively underfunded by most other foundations
2. Areas where current efforts—whether public or private—have failed to result in breakthroughs
3. Areas where funding from government or private sources was not available
4. Areas of urgent and growing public concern

Once the organization has agreed to its strategy [its major directions], it is then in a position to determine what specific results it should accomplish and within what period of time—or to formulate the organization's long-range objectives for the next target period.

Formulating the Organization's Objectives

Objectives now become all important as the vehicle by which the efforts of all managers in the organization are brought into focus and lined up to accomplish the desired ends for the total organization. These objectives must provide a common direction and purpose for the organization as a whole.

It is not the purpose of this chapter to delve into the techniques and criteria for writing objectives. This has been abundantly covered elsewhere.[1] However, the following examples illustrate the various objectives that have been formulated in several nonprofit organizations:

1. Achieve average 12 percent penetration in our programs during 1987 (volunteer youth organization)
2. Increase to 6 percent the number of parents reunited with their children in accordance with approved standards (parent services organization)
3. Increase from 84 to 88 percent the number of unwed mothers (planning to keep their babies) completing the infant care course (social services organization)
4. Reduce the dropout rate among high school juniors by 14 percent over last year (educational organization)
5. By July 1, 1989, secure accreditation as a school of nursing (hospital)

Accomplishing the Objectives

Obviously, the organization's objectives will not be achieved just because they have been written down and agreed to. Concerted, coordinated action by every manager in the organization is necessary to facilitate accomplishing the objectives. Thus, each manager in the organization must be delegated and must accept accountability for accomplishing such action as will help accomplish the top objectives of the organization.

A simplified example will illustrate the approach commonly followed at this juncture. Assume that a nonprofit hospital has as one of its top objectives "to secure accreditation" by a certain date. The manager ultimately responsible for this objective is the hospital administrator. However, the objective cannot be accomplished by the administrator alone. The other managers in the hospital must help accomplish it. In this case, it is further assumed that the following people report to the administrator: director of medical staff, director of nursing, director of plant and housekeeping, and the business manager.

Each of these four managers must ask and answer the question: "In order to achieve the accreditation objective, what results must I (and my subordinates) achieve in our departments?" Once this question is answered, the answer is reduced to specific objectives (subobjectives under the top objective) for each of the four managers. All of the objectives of the four department heads—when coordinated together—must at least equal the top objective of securing accreditation.

When the objective setting process has been completed for all levels of management, the completed process resembles a hierarchy of objectives. This can be portrayed as in Figure 7.1.

Lining up the efforts of all managers in the above manner should result in the organization realizing several of the major benefits that MBO is capable of delivering:

1. Accomplishing the real purpose of the organization

2. Better utilization of scarce resources

3. Reduction in wasted effort and "keep busy" activities

4. A better ability to demonstrate the organization's accomplishments

5. An enhanced ability to secure more funding

Conclusion

In essence, MBO is a systematic approach to achieving desired ends. When viewed in this, its true perspective, it appears obvious that it has considerable value when

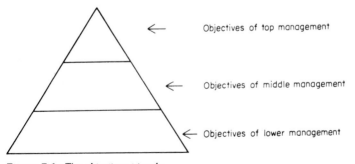

Figure 7.1. The objectives triangle.

applied to nonprofit organizations. Those who would hold otherwise place themselves in the untenable position of advocating that the desired end, e.g., quality education, should be approached by hit-or-miss methods. Nonprofit organizations have no vested right to assume this unique position.

Nonprofit organizations are not unique. They, like all organizations, have an objective to achieve, namely, to provide the highest-quality product or service consistent with the funds available. They have assets entrusted to them—people, capital, and plant and equipment. They serve in a stewardship capacity to those on whom they depend for their continued existence. Managers of these organizations must be held accountable for results.

Highly successful MBO applications have been made in every conceivable type of organization—profit and nonprofit, the private and public sectors, large and small organizations, organizations in the United States, Canada, Europe, Japan, and elsewhere. These include hospitals, schools, police departments, nursing homes, defense departments, municipal government units, and agencies of the federal government.

Over 25 years of MBO experience has demonstrated the value and applicability of MBO to all types of organizations. The nonprofit sector is no exception. This same experience has demonstrated that MBO can be applied to these organizations only if they insist upon and meet the same demands that the system imposes on other categories of organizations and endeavors. As a minimum, these include:

1. The selection of highly competent managers, administrators, and professionals in all key positions

2. In-depth training in the complete MBO system before any attempt is made to apply it

3. Allowing the 3 to 4 years required to make a successful installation

4. Substituting maximum participation from all personnel for the sometimes autocratic and despotic ideas of a few

5. A complete tailoring or adapting of the MBO system to the individual problems or conditions that exist in the individual entity to which it is applied

6. The removal, or diminishing, by legislative or executive action of many of the impediments that act as limitations on the ability of MBO to achieve the full potential of which it is capable—limitations such as emphasizing effort rather than results, provisions that protect the ineffective personnel, practices that stifle individual initiative and permit flexible decision making, and systems that fail to provide recognition and rewards

7. A constant reexamination of the system after installation to improve it and render it responsive to the changing conditions in the environment in which it is being practiced

Note

1. Certain of the material in this chapter is adapted from the author's book, *How to Manage for Results,* 4th ed., AMACOM, New York, 1983.

8

Strategic Planning*

William P. Anthony
Ph.D., Professor of Management, Florida State University

What Is Strategic Planning?

Planning is an essential function for every manager. The old saying "If you don't know where you're going, any road will take you there" underlines the importance of planning. Without planning, it does not really matter what we do; every path is equally valid since we do not know where we are going.

How Does Strategic Planning Differ from Regular Planning?

Few managers would disagree with the importance of planning, although they probably would argue that they do not have enough time to do as much planning as they would like. "Planning" is simply deciding where you want to go and how you want to get there. There are two basic elements to any plan: deciding on a *goal,* or *objective,* and deciding on the best *way* to reach it.

Most managers do *some* planning. However, it is usually day-to-day operational planning. In fact, it might be more appropriately called "scheduling" since the focus is often on a list of activities to be accomplished during a given day or week. The type of planning we mean is very different. Everyday planning is a part of our discussion, but only a small part. Rather, we are concerned with *strategic* planning which differs in importance, scope, resource commitment, time frame, and purpose. Strategic planning involves making strategic decisions about major plans for the organization in the following ways:

- It *recognizes the outside environment* and explicitly incorporates elements of it into the planning process.

*Readers desiring more detailed information on this topic are referred to William P. Anthony, *Practical Strategic Planning: A Guide and Manual for Line Managers*, Quorum Books, Westport, Conn., 1985.

- It has a *long-term time focus,* often 3 to 5 years, but sometimes as many as 10 to 20 years.

- It is conducted at the *top of the organization* and at the top of the organization's major divisions or product groups.

- It involves making decisions that commit *large amounts of organizational resources.*

- It *sets the direction* for the organization by focusing on the organization's identity and its place in a changing environment.

Strategic planning is planning which serves as the ultimate basis for all that the organization does. It provides the criteria for major investment decisions, such as opening a new office, for new product or service development, and for budgetary allocation. It also serves as the basis to evaluate the performance of the organization and its managers.

The basic steps in the strategic planning process are shown in Figure 8.1. Even though other models have been proposed and are in use, I have found this one to be the best in terms of completeness and ease of implementation based on a number of years of consulting with a wide variety of profit and not-for-profit organizations. Let us briefly look at each of the steps in this model.

Environmental Analysis.   The first step in developing a strategic plan is to examine the outside environment surrounding the organization. The idea is to do a

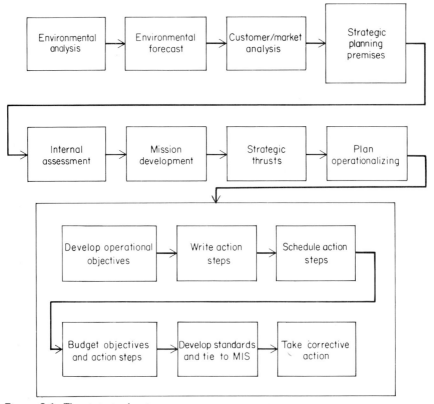

Figure 8.1. The strategic planning process.

point-in-time analysis of significant aspects of the outside environment as they affect the organization.

Environmental Forecast.   After the above step is completed, we now are concerned with predicting how this environment is changing. Trends are explored and new issues of impact are identified. Implications for the future of the organization are explored.

Customer and Market Analysis.   Focus on the reason why the organization exists (i.e., to serve members or a market) is the next step in the planning process. Emphasis is placed on analyzing changes in membership and a member profile of the future is developed.

Strategic Planning Premises.   These reflect key assumptions made about the future. They are based on the forecast and serve as the basis for developing the strategic plan.

Internal Assessment.   We have to establish a planning base and that is the focus here. In this step, we attempt to determine the strengths and weaknesses of the organization as it now exists.

Mission Development.   This step in the planning process outlines the role and mission of the organization in view of the environment it faces and the resources it has or can reasonably expect to obtain. The mission provides the ultimate rationale for the organization's existence. It gives the organization identity.

Strategic Thrusts.   These are three of four major areas where the organization plans to focus its efforts in the next 3 to 5 years. They reflect the mission and the forecast.

Plan Operationalizing.   This implements the strategic plan, from the development of operational objectives through the process of taking corrective action.

Even though we present the strategic planning process in this step-by-step process, the reality is not this neat. Although it is best to try to proceed in the order suggested here, most organizations will revisit previous steps as they move through the process. This is good, and it emphasizes the need to make the planning process *flexible*. Many times a nonprofit organization is reluctant to do strategic planning because it fears that once the plans are typed up, they are cast in concrete. Managers in such an organization fear that their feet will be held to the fire no matter what happens, and so they either refuse to plan or keep their plans vague. This is a mistake, and a flexible planning process will help avoid this syndrome. (This and other barriers to effective strategic planning are discussed elsewhere in this chapter.)

How Does Strategic Planning Compare to MBO?

In a nonprofit organization that operates fully on a comprehensive management by objectives system there may be little difference. However, since several versions of MBO are used today, there can be a substantial difference between strategic planning and MBO. The basic difference deals with the breadth and scope of the planning process. In general, MBO tends to be narrower in scope and to deal with the more operational aspects of planning. Often explicit recognition of the environment never gets fully implemented in the MBO process. Also, MBO tends to focus on a shorter time frame. In our model, MBO is similar to the final step of the strategic planning process—plan operationalizing.

Thus, MBO does have a part to play in strategic planning, and a good strategic plan will use the MBO process to put the plan into operation. Consequently, it is important for managers who engage in strategic planning to know how to use MBO.

How Is Strategic Planning Related to Strategic Decision Making?

When we formulate a strategic plan, we are making strategic decisions about our organization. Sometimes, managers tend to view planning and decision making as two separate activities. However, when we plan, we make decisions about where the organization is going. We choose among alternative courses of action. We allocate resources in order to carry out the plan.

Much of what we consider to be decision making is really problem solving. We see a problem, examine it, review various solutions, choose a solution, implement it, and follow up on it. This is a form of decision making, but tends to be more like operational decision making. It tends to be *curative* in nature rather than *preventative*. It deals with a problem once it exists rather than with trying to prevent a problem from occurring in the first place.

Strategic decision making is preventative in nature. It is integral to the planning process in that, like planning, it is anticipatory in nature. Just as plans deal with the future, so do strategic decisions. The focus is on making major decisions which commit the organization to a direction for some time during the future. These direction setting decisions usually involve a commitment of resources to a course of action at the exclusion of alternative courses of action.

Therefore, a key element for effective strategic planning is a willingness to make the strategic decisions necessary in the planning process. Without this willingness, planning simply becomes a paper exercise. We can play school and write a nice study plan, but the decisions necessary to implement the plan are never made.

How Should Strategic Planning Be Carried Out?

Many nonprofit organizations have participated in strategic planning only to see their efforts fail. One reason strategic planning fails is that the actual planning process was poorly structured and implemented. Unfortunately, in these organizations strategic planning has a bad name even though it was the process used that should be faulted. Therefore, it is very important to the success of the process that it be properly implemented. This is not to imply that there is only one way to implement the process: Actually there are several ways. However, we focus on a procedure that has been used successfully with a wide variety of business, governmental, and nonprofit organizations.

Who Should Be Involved with Strategic Planning?

Strategic planning must start at the top of the organization. In an organization with rather autonomous units, it can start at the top of any unit even though it may not be done at the very top of the organization. However, since the decisions involved in strategic planning are so fundamental to direction setting for the organization, top management (often including the board of directors or a board committee) should be involved at some point.

Beyond top management, the planning process will involve a number of different groups. In general, the process should be kept as participative as possible, given the time constraints present. People are usually more committed to a strategic plan if they have had some input in designing it.

Committees.   Almost all organizations committed to strategic planning use a committee and several subcommittees to facilitate the process. The main committee is usually made up of some board members, top-level executives, a few key staff people, and often one or two operating managers. It is a good idea to keep the size of the committee between ten and twenty people.

The essential elements for a successful committee are as follows:

- Pick those who have an interest and expertise in strategic planning.
- Be sure the committee has a charge that is clearly understood and a date for task accomplishment.
- Be sure the committee has both the authority to request information and to recommend action based on it.

The committee usually acts in an advisory capacity to top management. They usually prepare a draft of the entire plan or specific portions of it for review and action by top management during planning meetings. Seldom does the committee actually adopt the plan for the entire organization; rather it is better to leave final adoption up to top management.

The Role of Commitment.   Making the final approval of the plan a key responsibility of top management (rather than a committee or staff group) is vital to the implementation of the final plan. So often an organization will spend much time and money developing a strategic plan only to fail in implementation. The plan becomes a "nice" document which sits on peoples' shelves and is seldom if ever consulted. One reason for this failure is that top management never really becomes fully committed to the planning process. Rather, the plan is viewed as something being done by "that committee" or by "those staff people." People throughout the organization must *know* that the plan has full and complete commitment from top management if the plan is to have credibility throughout the organization.

How Should Workshops Be Used in Planning?

Very often the focus of the strategic planning process is a series of workshops. It is in these workshops that the plan is developed, discussed, and eventually adopted. The workshops are usually made up of members of the planning committee plus a few others as needed. Once again, caution should be exercised to prevent too large a group from becoming directly involved in the workshop, or the workshop will become unwieldly. Frequently, workshop sessions can be held with subcommittees of the planning committee. A group facilitator can help greatly in conducting a workshop.

If an organization has been involved with strategic planning for some time, it is usually necessary to hold an annual workshop with short review meetings held quarterly. However, if an organization is just starting out with strategic planning, it may need to hold several workshop sessions in formulating the strategic plan. Between-workshop meetings are also usually required.

How Can the Planning Horizon Be Determined?

Frequently a 5-year planning horizon is selected for the strategic plan. Within the overall plan are 1-year operational plans. This time format can vary depending on the nature of the organizational operations and product or service line. For example, an association that faces a 3-year operating cycle based on economic conditions, such as a commercial construction association, may wish to be on a 3-year strategic plan. A governmental agency that faces biennial budgeting may wish to be on a 2-year strategic plan. An organization in a rapidly changing environment, such as environmental law, may wish to be on a 2- or 3-year plan.

Regardless of the planning period selected, the annual review usually involves lopping off the past year and adding the next coming year beyond the existing plan. Thus, if our plan goes through 1991 and our planning horizon were 5 years, at the end of 1987 we would drop that year and add 1992.

Organizations that plan far into the future often develop specific short, intermediate, and long-term plans that integrate with one another. *Short-term plans* are usually defined as 1 year or less in time; *intermediate,* as 2 to 4 years; and *long-term,* as 5 years or more in length. The important point is to make sure that all three plans do tie in with one another.

How Can Plans Be Implemented?

As indicated previously, many factors can hinder the effective implementation of strategic planning. These factors need to be explicitly recognized at the outset if the planning process is to lead to final implementation. Let us look at these planning barriers.

- *No time to plan.* Participants are so caught up in their daily routine that they believe they do not have any time to do planning. They are spending too much post-hoc time and not enough front-end time.

- *Too many crises and changing priorities.* Here people feel that there is no sense in planning since priorities change so quickly that the plan soon becomes meaningless. Usually this is caused by a lack of proper forecasting.

- *Information overload.* Since strategic planning requires a great deal of information, people feel overwhelmed. Keep information down to what is absolutely necessary, and use the computer to help manage it.

- *Too much paperwork.* This is closely related to the above. People feel that all they do on their job is fill out strategic planning forms. Keep these forms to an absolute minimum, and use the computer to store and report planning information.

- *Too much politics.* "Planning is a rational and logical process, and our operation is just too political for it to work." This complaint is common in government organizations, but one also hears it in large companies. Recognize the politics, do not ignore them, but build them into the planning process.

- *Don't play school.* Use the plan. Refer to it in staff meetings. Look at it when decisions are to be made. Tie it into the management performance appraisal process and to evaluation and control.

Planning may fail for other reasons, but these are the more common ones. It is a good idea to specifically address these at some point during the workshop session and ask the group what can be done to prevent, reduce, or eliminate them. One last thought here: No plan will ever get implemented unless the question of who is going to do what and when is answered specifically. The planning process presented in this chapter forces participants to specifically address this question as part of the process.

Environmental Analysis: Status Quo

We are now ready to begin the actual strategic planning process. The first step in the process is to look outside of the organization at the environment that affects it. This action is one key factor that distinguishes strategic planning from regular planning. We do this because we know that many outside forces affect our internal operations. We are particularly interested in identifying environmental opportunities and constraints faced by our organization.

Environmental scanning involves a comprehensive and systematic examination of significant aspects of the outside environment. A judgment is made as to how these aspects affect the organization. Environmental scanning should be a continuous process. Even though every manager is partially responsible for this activity, in large organizations a staff group may help. This scanning is summarized periodically for the planning workshops.

For environmental scanning to be useful, it must be integrated into the planning process. This means that the participants must be willing to look outward before they look inward. Sometimes it is difficult to change this inward orientation since the day-to-day job of line managers fosters a here-and-now job orientation.

One way to break this orientation is to present key information about the environment initially in almost a startling fashion, without all the statistics. Once the attention of the manager is attracted, the statistical information can be added later. For example, among a group of credit unions, the initial discussion of the environment might begin by investigating why Sears is the major competitor in personal banking.[1] Although this probably overstates the case, it would lead to a discussion of how the environment for banking services is changing. This could be followed up with a discussion of the activities not only of Sears, but also of savings and loans, credit unions, and other institutions in traditional banking activities. A discussion of legal, political, and economic factors which made this possible would then be held.

What Are the Key Segments of the Environment?

The importance of the various parts of the environment will vary depending upon the nature of the organization's business. However, the general components of the outside environment are always similar. In this section, we review these components. (Figure 8.2 summarizes all these sectors.)

Economy.   Every organization must be aware of the general state of economic conditions at the national, regional, and local level. Probably no other area of the outside environment so directly affects operations. Some of the data that should be tracked are interest rates, GNP, unemployment rates, leading indicators, and inflation. Also, prices of certain commodities may need to be closely watched. Information on the economy can be obtained by reading business periodicals, such as *The Wall Street Journal* and *Business Week,* by reading the various Federal Reserve bulletins, and by subscribing to services of various economic forecasting firms, such as Chase Econometrics.

It is important to remember that at this stage of the strategic planning process we want only to assess the present state of economic activity. At a later stage we will want to forecast economic information.

Competition.   Even in nonprofit organizations we should be concerned with specifically identifying our competition and how it affect us. We should identify those organizations that both directly and indirectly compete with us. From this we can develop our *competitive advantage* which is how we differ from our competition. We answer the question: why would someone buy our services over our competitor's?

Legal and Political Aspects.   The major laws and political climate as they affect us are examined here. These will include federal, state, local and international law. Laws relating to employment, product safety, pollution control, safety and health, advertising, and contracts are among the areas we would examine. Depending on our industry, other laws may also be pertinent. For example, if we are in the charity industry, there is be a host of federal and state law we would also need to examine. The main objective here is to ensure that we are in compliance with the legislation. Competent legal advice is essential here.

Social Aspects.   We must identify the major social values and norms that are affecting our operations. For example, we may see a trend toward more individual attention and convenience occurring in society. We would need to speculate how that would affect our operations. Good sources for this information are magazines, trade journals, general business periodicals, such as *The Wall Street Journal,* and consultants who specialize in social analysis.

Demographics.   This area deals with statistical information about population. For example, mean age, income, and family size of people in an area are common demographic data. So are net migration figures, population growth, birth and death rates, travel rates, and employment figures. Other demographic data may be important depending on the firm's line of business. For example, an art museum might be interested in the average education level of the local population in order to plan art exhibits. The local chamber of commerce and the U.S. Census Bureau are good sources for this information. Census data are available at most any university library. Also, market research firms will do custom studies for local areas and industries. An excellent

ENVIRONMENTAL SECTOR	KEY INFORMATION	INFORMATION SOURCES
Economy	GNP, unemployment rates, leading indicators, inflation, commodity prices, interest rates	*The Wall Street Journal, Business Week,* Federal Reserve bulletins
Competition	Prices, products, services, technology, competitive edge	Trade shows, trade magazines, general business magazines, own customers
Legal or political	State, federal, local legislation, administrative and court rulings	Newsletters, general business magazines, legal advice
Social	Values, norms, expectations	Trade journals, general business periodicals, consultants
Demographic	Age, sex, income, population growth, net migration, birth and death rates, family size, educational levels	U.S. Bureau of the Census, local chambers of commerce, market research firms
Technology	Technological developments in competition and related areas, technological developments in data processing	Trade shows and trade journals, general business periodicals, electronic data processing journals
Labor market	Unemployment rates, wage rates, skill distribution, labor force participation rates, educational levels, labor force growth	U.S. Bureau of Labor Statistics, local chambers of commerce, state office of business development, union hiring halls
Key physical resources	Commodities, minerals, precious metals, raw materials, semi-finished goods	Suppliers, market newsletters, commodity reports
Suppliers	Past practices and problems, pricing, service, competition	Delivery reports, alternative suppliers, trade shows and journals
Distributors	Past practices and problems, service, information sending, collection and payment	Sales and distribution reports, trade shows and journals, alternative distribution channels
Transportation	Rates, routes, speed, service, safety	Trade journals, transporters
Energy supplies	Availability, delivery, price, alternatives, conservation factors	Energy suppliers, government reports, *Lundburg Letter*
International conditions	International economy, economic trade, exchange rates, tariffs, political conditions	General business journals, trade conferances, *The Economist*

Figure 8.2. Environmental assessment.

magazine in the field is called *American Demographics,* by Dow Jones and Company. (Write *American Demographics,* P.O. Box 68, Ithaca, N.Y., 14580)

Technology.   The technology available for a particular process or operation should be carefully reviewed. Also technologies in related fields should be reviewed to determine the applicability to our operations. The technology used by our competitors should especially be reviewed—this includes any overseas organizations. If the steel industry had reviewed the technology employed by steel producers in Japan during the seventies, it might have avoided the technological obsolescence U.S. producers experienced in the early eighties. Trade journals and trade shows are excellent sources of information on this topic.

Labor Market.   Both the local and national labor market should be reviewed. Unemployment rates, labor force participation rates, wage rates, skill distribution, educational level, and labor market growth are all important here. Data from the local chamber of commerce, U.S. Department of Labor, and the state office of business development are all good sources of information.

Key Physical Resources.   If we are dependent on certain key physical resources, we should assess their availability. For example, if we use rented office space, area rent rates should be carefully monitored. We should thoroughly review our present and possible operations to assess the availability of key resources. Newsletters and commodity reports are good places to find this information.

Suppliers.   We should thoroughly review our relationship with our suppliers. Past problems should be carefully analyzed. Competing suppliers should be reviewed for cost and service comparisons with those suppliers we are now using. Trade shows, trade magazines, brochures, and sales talks with suppliers are all good sources for this information.

Distributors.   A similar review of our distributors should be held. In particular, we should review alternative distribution channels to see if they might be better options for distributing our products and services. Information on distribution channels can be obtained from similar sources as supplier information.

Transportation.   Our transportation network should be reviewed. This is especially important today in view of the deregulation which has occurred in the trucking and airlines industries. Rates and routes are under much more intense competition, and cheaper, more efficient forms of transportation for our products might be available. Trade journals and transportation companies are good sources for information.

Energy Supplies.   An assessment of key energy resources is critical for most firms today. Not only should the availability of present energy resources be reviewed, but also the availability of alternative resources should be reviewed. Energy suppliers as well as special publications on the topic such as the *Lundberg Letter,* should be consulted.

International Conditions.   Depending on the operation, international affairs might have a major bearing on our operations. We should review the present political and economic state of other countries significant to our operations. Special trade conferences and periodicals, such as *The Economist,* are helpful here.

Should Environmental Information Be Classified as an Opportunity or as a Constraint?

At this point, it is possible to feel overwhelmed by environmental information. This feeling would be diminished if we did a good job of narrowing our environment to our relevant environment and domain prior before performing the above scoping exercise. But we also need to do one other activity with this environmental information in order to get a handle on it: We need to categorize the information as to whether we see it as an opportunity or a constraint for us.

"Environmental opportunities" are factors in the environment that provide new markets or advantages for us. "Environmental constraints" are threats in the environment that hinder the performance of our operations or keep us from reaching our objectives. What may be a threat or a constraint for one firm might be an opportunity for another. For example, pollution control laws were viewed as a major constraint by most companies, especially coal burning utilities. However, environmental advocacy groups viewed these laws as a real opportunity. If we are in the business of representing various environmental groups, we would welcome these environmental laws.

In reviewing our environmental assessment, we want to categorize factors that we can identify as either helping us to achieve our objectives and facilitate our operation, or hurting us in our operations. We also must be mindful of any new opportunities our environment presents to us which we are not now taking advantage of. This can be done by making a T chart and by placing opportunities on the left side of the T and constraints on the right. Our plan should take advantage of the opportunities presented to us while overcoming our constraints.

Environmental Forecast

The next step in the planning process is to complete an environmental forecast. An "environmental forecast" is nothing more than an educated guess. Even firms that spend considerable sums of money on building a forecast still are not able to achieve certainty. The idea behind the forecast is to reduce uncertainty, and hence risk, as much as possible. It is pointless to postpone indefinitely the remaining steps in the strategic planning process because we want to reduce uncertainty to near zero. The cost of trying to do this and the added delays are not worth it. We should prepare a careful and thorough analysis and be willing to go with it. To do otherwise is to suffer from "analysis paralysis."

How Is an Environmental Forecast Constructed?

Responsibility for final preparation of the forecast should rest with those doing the strategic planning. These individuals can be aided by a planning staff in larger organizations and by outside sources of information and consultants, regardless of the size of the organization.

The idea behind the environmental forecast is to identify existing trends in various environmental sectors and to speculate as to how these trends will continue during the planning period. Also, emerging trends should be identified.

In identifying trends, we usually look to what has happened in the past and construct either a straight-line trend line or a curvilinear one. This is fine as long as we are fairly confident that the factors causing the trend in the past will continue with the same effect in the future. If this is not so, we will be extending false trend lines into the future. This is a significant problem in high-tech industries where conditions are changing so rapidly.

The best method for constructing an environmental trend for strategic planning is to use a group of educated people who have a good idea of what is going on out in the environment. These people should be well-read, especially on books that deal with the outside environment. Such books as Drucker's *Managing in Turbulant Times,* Naisbett's *Megatrends,* and Toffler's *The Third Wave* are recommended reading. It is at this point that a knowledgeable group facilitator can be very helpful in getting the group to think through their ideas as to what they believe will happen in the various environmental sectors.

Even though the environmental forecast will never be totally accurate, it is important that a sufficient amount of time be spent in constructing the forecast. Among the biggest barriers to effective strategic planning are unforeseen emergencies or surprises that cause us to manage by reaction or crisis. The better the job that we do in forecasting environmental events, the less likely we are to be surprised by them.

How Does an Environmental Forecast Differ from a Scan?   We must use the scan for building the forecast. It is difficult to predict the future if we do not know where we are now. We need a basis for projection, and it is the scan which gives us this basis. This is why it is so important to properly understand our present environment before we begin to speculate what our future environment will be.

Some organizations complete the forecast at the same time they prepare the scan. This is acceptable as long as they realize which statements are statements of what now exists in the environment and which ones are estimations of future events. Keeping the two straight is essential for proper planning. We do not want to confuse what might happen with what *is* happening.

What Areas Should Be Forecasted?   In general, we should prepare a forecast of the same environmental sectors for which we prepared a scan. Certain elements of the environment may be given more detailed analysis than others because of the nature of the business. A hospital, credit union, or trade association might choose to devote more time to forecasting other aspects of the environment deemed more relevant to the particular operation.

In compiling your forecast, you may wish to quantify much of the information. This is fine except that quantification usually takes more time. It can also give the illusion of finiteness and a degree of accuracy not intended. Some people get hung up on the numbers and forget the purpose of an environmental forecast and how it is to be used in the strategic planning process. For this reason, those wishing to use numbers throughout may wish to specify a range and may even wish to specify a confidence level. Thus, for example, data presented in the economic forecast could be presented as follows for prime interest rates: 10 to 12 percent, 75 percent confidence; 20 percent confident above 12 percent, and 5 percent confident below 10 percent. This would convey the message that the forecasters actually believe the 10 rate will be a bit higher than the 12 percent.

Larger organizations often give very sophisticated forecasts. They use probability methods, statistical analysis, and computer software to generate a comprehensive and detailed forecast. This works well since they have the staff to help with this endeavor. The absence of such staff, however, should not keep the organization from forecasting.

The availability of personal computers and databases will enable even the small company to become more sophisticated with environment forecasting in the future. For this reason, you may wish to consider quantifying as many variables as possible when preparing the forecast.

Member, or Customer-Market Analysis

Now we are ready to examine perhaps the most important part of our outside environment: our member, or customer. The customer may go by a different name in your organization, but the intent in this section is to ensure that we explicitly consider the people we intend to serve during the strategic planning process.

In this section, we do not provide a detailed analysis of the market as might be found in a marketing text. Rather, we look at the customer as the basis for developing a strategic plan. It is important that every organization thoroughly understand its customer before it begins formalizing its strategic plan. After all, the customer provides the ultimate justification for the existence of any organization. Any organization that fails to fulfill customer needs will eventually cease to exist.

What Are the Important Customer Characteristics?

Any listing of important customer characteristics to examine for planning purposes will vary depending on the organization. However, most organizations will want to examine two broad categories of data: demographic information and psychological information. Let us look at each of these.

Demographic Information.   Here we are interested in such factors as mean income, age, educational levels, geographic location, family size, and other factors which describe our customer. If our products and services appeal to more than one market segment, then we need to describe each segment. For example, credit unions offer a number of different certificates that are targeted to different market segments.

Psychological Factors.   Here we are interested in the particular needs and wants our services satisfy. Why do people use our service? Usually, a number of different needs are being fulfilled. For example, people buy a new car not only because it provides a means of transportation, but also because it provides prestige and recognition and because it may create an image desired by the patron. In addition to the above needs, services may also satisfy some of the following needs: newness, intelligence, acceptance, innovativeness, practicality, convenience, and economy. This is by no means a complete listing, but rather is illustrative of the type of needs a service can satisfy. The point is that every organization must understand both the demographics and psychological factors of the market if it is to do a good job of strategic planning.

In this analysis, we showed how the customer is changing over time. In strategic planning, we are concerned with satisfying the customer of tomorrow, not the one of today or yesterday. Too often we are offering products and services based on historical information about our market which may be valid for neither the present time nor the future. We want to be sure that we will be able to satisfy the customer we will be serving next year, the year after, the year after that, and so on into the future.

We also need to project the growth of our customer base. What we want to do here is to project a market base that we can target for a sales effort. In doing this, we want to be sure to examine our competitor's market to determine whether we can serve these customers better. The analysis we did previously of our competition should help us here. We also need to consider the effects that population growth and net migration will have on our market. We need to consider any new products or services that we are contemplating adding when we do this growth projection. If our product sales are directly dependent on the sales of another product, we need to forecast the sales of that product. For example, the sales of conference space may be heavily dependent on the sales of memberships in a trade association.

What Is the Role of Consumer and Market Research?

Every organization must be concerned with doing market research. Even cities and counties are conducting resident opinion surveys to determine characteristics of the market. There are many ways to obtain market data: using census data, hiring outside consultants to do the research, in-house staffing of a market research department, initiating consumer panels or focus groups, buying market data through newsletters, and reviewing government studies. Most large organizations use a combination of these methods. Small organizations often do not use any structured method. Organizations that do not regularly monitor their market will have a difficult time surviving in the future.

Organizations which regularly gather market information will be able to complete this step in the planning process rather quickly. Those which have not done much market analysis in the past will find that they will have a considerable amount of work involved here to complete this step in the process.

Based on our analysis up to this point, we are now ready to specify the basic planning premises and key assumptions on which we will build our strategic plan.

Strategic Planning Premises and Assumptions

If we have done a good job of examining our environment and market, we are now ready to make explicit our planning premises and assumptions. Planning premises and assumptions are our estimations about what the future holds. They are based on our environmental forecast.

They help us to determine the implications of forecasted environmental events. They are a way for us to make explicit the impact the environment will likely have on our operations. They also make clear what we see as assumption and what we believe to be fact. We use these strategic premises and key assumptions as the foundation for building our plan. Finally, we use these as a means of building planning scenarios.

What Are Scenarios and How Are They Built?

"Scenarios" are anticipated sequences of events that we believe may happen in the future. They specify a chain of events that will likely occur if something in the environment occurs. For example, if we predict that oil will increase in price by about 20 percent during the next 2 years, a scenario we might build might be as follows: utility costs to run offices, up 20 percent; total costs, up 5 percent; budget deficit, up 10 percent. In doing this, we are trying to trace through the effect of an environmental change on our operations. This serves then as a planning premise.

We might even develop alternative, competing scenarios to the one above. Then we could assign probabilities of occurrence to each scenario. Thus, we would be engaging in *contingency planning* or planning for alternative futures. There is some value to doing this in that it forces us to anticipate what *might* happen, which is different from what we are *actually* planning, and to do something about it before the events actually take place.

This process can become quite complicated, but the use of a personal computer and a software package such as Lotus 1,2,3, or Visicalc 1 or 2 can help with the spreadsheet analysis. We are likely to see more of this type of analysis as computer software becomes more sophisticated.

How Are Specific Planning Premises and Assumptions Formulated?

Usually, planning premises and assumptions are built only for the most significant aspects of the outside environment and for the market. This means that usually only five to ten key premises or assumptions are developed. Of these, only half may have detailed scenarios developed. At some point the costs of planning begin to exceed the benefits. This point is different for each firm but planners must be mindful of reaching this point. (Remember: Avoid analysis paralysis.)

The process of developing these premises and assumptions usually involves a great deal of discussion among the planning group. Frequent reference will be made to the environmental and market analysis. These analyses may even be revised during the discussion. At some point the discussion will need to stop and a final list of premises and assumptions developed, even though everyone might not be happy with them.

Figure 8.3 shows an example list of planning premises for a hospital. Note their straightforwardness and brevity. Several scenarios were built from these premises. The key point to remember when developing these premises is that we are making explicit the assumptions that underlie any planning process. The premises can then be modified during the planning process as new information surfaces. It is important not to get hung up on these but to get something reasonable down and then go on. They can always be revisited later. We are now ready to move to the next step in the process: the internal assessment. We need to know where we are now before we can plan where we want to go.

Internal Assessment

Imagine how difficult it would be to plan a trip if you did not know where your starting point was. Determining where we are now is the purpose of this step in the planning process. Once we know where we are now, it will be easier to plan where we want to go.

An internal assessment is an examination of the status of key areas of the organization. The areas examined usually include personnel, products, services, operations, physical facilities, and so on. This assessment is called variously an organization audit, an operations analysis, a management audit or review, or an

---

PLANNING PREMISES (KEY ASSUMPTIONS)
JACKSON MEMORIAL HOSPITAL

1. The anticipated cost control standards under medicare and medicaid will require us to more closely control our fees and doctor charges. Failure to do so will result in a substantial operating deficit.

2. Increased competition from the new, private for-profit hospital and walk-in emergency facilities will require us to undertake an aggressive marketing effort to keep from losing paying patients at the expense of more indigents.

3. Significant improvements in medical and data processing technology will place an increasing strain on our capital budget.

4. Population growth in the service area will place increasing strain on certain facilities that we have that are not offered by competition (obstetrics, burn treatment center, pediatrics).

5. The nursing shortage will be exacerbated because of competition from other medical facilities driving up salaries by 20 percent during the next 2 years.

6. Energy cost increases will necessitate full implementation of energy cost control program in old wing.

7. Physician shortages in several key specialties will ease.

Figure 8.3.   Planning premises for a municipal hospital.

organizational assessment. Even though each of these terms may have a slightly different focus, the major intent is the same as an internal assessment.

Usually when conducting the assessment, we want to identify the strengths and weaknesses of each of the key internal areas. We do this so that we can build objectives that overcome the weaknesses or problem areas while capitalizing on our strengths. This helps us to prioritize our objectives so that we can get the maximum return for the effort expended.

As we conduct the assessment, recognizing when we have a problem is critical to our analysis. We will discuss some ways of surfacing and describing problems in a later section of this chapter, but one helpful idea to keep in mind throughout this analysis is the use of a desirable *role model.* Here, a role model would be a comparable organization with the qualities we wish to emulate. Pointing to how relevant others do things helps us to determine if we have a problem. This is why the previous analysis of our competition is so important. Thus, we need a basis for comparison if we are to do an adequate assessment.

We also need to examine problems we have been experiencing in a particular area. For example, if we are always having equipment breakdowns, we should gather the data on, e.g., downtime, repair costs, lost production, etc., and include these data in our assessment. Any problem that has been requiring a lot of attention should be included.

What Factors Are Assessed?

Such factors as personnel, products or services, operations, finances, physical facilities, location, management, and research and development are usually evaluated. These factors can vary depending on the particular operations of the organization. Notice that all these factors are *internal* to the organization. We should have already completed an assessment of factors external to the organization. Only a brief judgmental overall assessment of the strengths and weaknesses of each factor need appear. The data and other information to support the evaluation should appear in other reports or in appendices to the planning document.

There are a number of ways to perform the assessment that range from an informal discussion among the planners concerning each area of the organization to quite sophisticated studies of the organization involving outside consultants. However, almost always determination of the strengths and weaknesses occurs through workshops. This occurs even when the organization uses sophisticated studies to gather data and other information for review. A thorough discussion of the strengths and weaknesses of the organization by the planners is important to help crystallize the direction of the strategic plan.

At these workshops, it is important that the participants feel free to honestly express their opinions. Keeping important information hidden for fear of hurting someone's feelings is not appropriate. Any concerns should be raised in a tactful, straightforward manner. One purpose of strategic planning is to surface problems that for one reason or another have not surfaced before even though they have existed for quite some time. The use of an experienced group facilitator can be quite helpful here.

Mission Development

We are now ready to determine the mission of our organization. Notice that we do not formally address this issue until we have looked at the outside environment, the market, and our internal operations. Most likely, as we discussed each of these areas, we would discuss elements of our mission. This is fine; but we should not *formalize* our mission until we have completed a thorough external and internal examination. It is only after we have completed this examination that we are able to accurately align ourselves to our market and environment by capitalizing on our strengths while taking advantage of environmental opportunities. We want to be sure that we are not so wedded to our present mission that we overlook important environmental opportunities. However, we do not want to try to be all things to all people so that we spread ourselves too thin.

A mission statement sets out the overall purpose of the organization. It is an overriding or all-encompassing goal. It is the ultimate rationale for the existence of the organization. Often, the elements of a mission statement can be found in the corporate charter or other important corporate document. If the organization is a government agency, the mission, or elements of it, can be found in legislation creating the agency.

However, even though the elements of a mission statement can be found in an important document, it usually will be incomplete. Therefore, the mission statement should be thoroughly discussed during the strategic planning process.

The mission statement makes explicit the domain of the organization. The domain and domain consensus were discussed earlier when we discussed the environment. However, it is at this point that we really try to pin down what it is that the organization is really about.

What Are the Key Elements of a Mission Statement?

There are nine key elements in a good mission statement. Each of these is discussed below.

Brief.   The mission statement for the organization should be fairly short: no more than a couple of paragraphs in length. Conciseness is important.

All-Encompassing.   Even though brief, it should lay out the key purpose of the organization. Simply stating "to make money" is not enough. Presumably, every business organization has this as its purpose. However, as we see below, money should be addressed someplace in the mission statement.

Commitment to Economic Efficiency.   Even as a not-for-profit organization, we should make a commitment to economic efficiency and effectiveness. We should try not to waste money.

Broad Statement of Products or Services Offered.   Our mission statement should indicate what line of business we are in. It is not necessary to list all products and services, but it is necessary to briefly identify the broad classes of our products and services. It is also important that we understand the industry we are in. For example, the American Cancer Society could define its mission as being in either the "cancer prevention and cure" or in the "medical" industry. The difference is a major one: The cancer industry is much more narrow than the medical industry. Such a narrow approach might very well limit the environmental opportunities for the society.

Market Served.   The geographic market served should be stated. Are we a local, statewide, regional, national, or international organization? What are our major member groups?

Continuing in Nature.   Even though we may want to review our mission statement annually, we should be careful about making major changes in it. The mission statement should have an ongoing nature. It should last for about a 4- or 5-year period without any major changes. Of course, if an opportunity comes along or if other major events occur, the statement may need to be changed. However, this should occur only after very thorough discussion and analysis. This mission statement should serve as an anchoring device.

Unique or Distinctive in Some Way.   The statement ought to tell how the organization is different from other organizations in the industry. This is where the modeling aspects come into play again. With what organizations do we wish to be compared? Do we wish to be viewed as an industry leader or as a follower? How are we different from similar organizations?

Consistent with Unit Missions.   We should be sure that the overall organization mission is consistent with the missions of subordinate units. Generally, the overall mission is set before unit missions are set, but even after unit missions are set, we need to review all mission statements for consistency. It might be that certain facts surfaced during the setting of unit missions that will cause us to modify our overall mission.

Understandable.   This should go without saying but, unfortunately, some mission statements are written in such convoluted English and are so full of buzz words and acronyms that they are virtually impossible to understand. Remember, the mission statement is a key part of the strategic planning process. It should be written to express not to impress.

Strategic thrusts are major goals that set the basic directions of the organization and involve a major commitment of resources of the organization for the planning horizon. Once set, they are not easily changed. They reflect the way in which the organization capitalizes on its internal assets to take advantage of market opportunities. They give added meaning to the mission statement and evolve from that statement. They set the foundation for the development of more specific operational objectives. They are strategic since they reflect a basic strategy that the organization has adopted for carrying out its functions.

For example, a large credit union I once worked with developed a strategic thrust which read as follows:

> To be as convenient for customer use as any other financial institution in the area and to meet or beat the loan and investment rates of any other financial institution in the area

This strategic thrust reflects a strong competitive philosophy which is very different from the traditional philosophy of credit union management. It follows from a mission statement which implied that the credit union wished to be a full financial institution to directly compete with banks and with savings and loan institutions. From this strategic thrust would flow a host of specific objectives and programs in such areas as hours of operation, location of branch offices, staffing of teller windows, drive-in facilities, automated teller machines, toll-free telephone calling, investment programs, loan programs and policies, and cash management. The strategic thrust statements are like arrows which are shot into the future and pull the organization along.

Normally, the organization should write only three to five strategic thrust statements each planning period. During the planning period, as with all elements of the strategic plan, they can be revised as needed. The reason that they are kept to such a small number is to focus priorities. We cannot be all things to all people, and the strategic thrust statements help us to focus our efforts.

Why Are Strategic Thrusts Important?

As indicated above, strategic thrusts help us to set priorities, focus our efforts, and aim our resources at a few very important targets. However, they do more than this. Since they usually deal with new directions or with a refocusing of present programs, they play an important communication role as well. They communicate to others outside the organization what we are all about and where we are going. They also serve an important internal communication function. They help our managers set individual objectives and priorities. They serve as a rallying point for effort. They should reflect major actions that the organization plans or is in the midst of taking. The statements reflect a *proactive* posture with respect to the environment and market. So often, an organization will feel as if it is at the mercy of the market and environment. This is especially true of smaller organizations, or when the environment is uncertain and ambiguous. This reactive posture is not appropriate from a strategic planning perspective. We must understand our environment, not so that we can bow to its pressures, but so that we can take action given the constraints we face. This is really the message of environmental analysis. Unless we come up with clear-cut strategic thrusts, the environmental and market analysis is virtually useless.

However, the development of strategic thrusts is not the entire story. We must make these strategic thrusts operational. That is the subject of the next section.

Developing and Writing Objectives

In order for the strategic plan to become reality, it must be made operational. This means becoming quite specific about elements of the plan by dealing with the three basic questions as follows: *Who? Will do what? By when?*

Answering these questions may not be the province of the strategic planning group; however, seeing that they do get answered is their responsibility. Since strategic planning is to be a participative process, it is at this point that middle- and lower-level managers get involved. The steps involved in operationalizing the strategic are shown in the lower box of Figure 8.1 at the beginning of the chapter.

How Can Operational Objectives Be Developed?

Specific objectives must flow from the strategic thrusts developed in the previous step and must be consistent with the mission of the organization. The manner in which these objectives are actually set can vary from rather autocratic to very participatory techniques, although the literature and research on the subject almost unanimously recommends some form of participation in order to gain commitment from those expected to achieve the objectives. Let us look briefly at some methods which can be used to set these objectives.

Autocratic Announcement.   This is probably the worst way to set objectives since most people resent being told what to do. However, it can buy short-term compliance at the expense of long-term commitment. If time is of the essence or if there is a true crisis, then unilateral setting of specific objectives by a higher-level group is acceptable. Of course true time and emergency constraints must actually exist; some managers cry emergency when none exists as an excuse for unilateral objective setting.

Consultive.   With this method the subordinates at each level in the organization are given the opportunity to have some input to the objectives of their boss and their work group. They do not actually determine the objectives; they simply review those which have been set by their boss and offer suggestions for modification. The boss is free to accept or reject the suggestions. The problem with this approach is that it creates expectations on the part of the subordinate that the opinions offered will at least be considered and accepted. Often they are not.

Participative.   This is the approach most often recommended, because it gets the group involved and enhances the commitment of the group to achieving the final objectives. It has its limitations: It is time-consuming, it requires open discussion, and the participants must want to participate and have the knowledge to participate intelligently. However, most people who have studied the matter believe that the advantages of the approach outweigh the disadvantages.

What Are the Criteria for Good Objectives?

While there is some debate on exactly what a good operational objective should consist of, there is agreement on several important points. These criteria for a good objective are summarized in Figure 8.4.

CRITERIA FOR A GOOD OBJECTIVE
1. Relates directly to a strategic thrust.
2. Relates to mission of the organization.
3. Is clear concise and understandable.
4. Is stated in terms of output or results.
5. Begins with "to" and an action verb. (Examples: to reduce, to increase, to implement, to meet, to develop, to replace, etc.)
6. Specifies a date for accomplishment.
7. Deals with one major subject or outcome.
8. Ties in with upper- and lower-level objectives.
9. Ties in with lateral objectives.
10. Is quantifiable.

Figure 8.4. Criteria for a good objective.

It is important that each operational objective meet each of these criteria in so far as possible. The closer each objective meets these criteria, the easier it will be to track and measure their accomplishment. The tracking and measuring is critical to ensure that the objective usually gets accomplished. Usually the most difficult criterion to meet for a nonprofit organization is quantifiability. A worksheet for use in quantifying a difficult-to-quantify objective is presented in Figure 8.5.

Why Do Objectives Need a Rationale?

A rationale for each objective helps us to better understand why we have the objective in the first place. This rationale should relate to the strategic thrust, an identified problem to be corrected, an expected environmental opportunity or constraint, or a change in mission focus. There is some debate as to whether the specific rationale for each objective should be stated below the objective. Probably the best idea here is to state it only when there is likely to be some confusion on the part of those reading the objective as to why it is needed. If the reason is obvious, then there is little need to state it.

If the rationale is stated, it should be clear and concise. Here is an example:

Objective. To reduce employee turnover from 55 to 25 percent on an annual basis by December 31, 1990.

Rationale. Turnover in our organization has been increasing by about 10 percent per year for the last 3 years. We are now substantially above the 30 percent average rate for our type of organization.

Notice that specific figures are used in the rationale to justify the objective. This is a good idea whenever possible.

What Types of Objectives Should Be Set?

Usually a variety of objectives are listed. Some of these objectives are "improvement objectives": They specify how the organization plans to improve some aspect

---

QUANTIFYING A Hard-to- Quantify Objective

Initial Objective: To improve our organization's image in the community by January 30, 1988.

The above objective, while admirable, is difficult to measure.

Ask these questions:

1. How do we know we need the objective? What tells us we now have a poor community image?

2. How will we know when we have accomplished the objective? What output or performance indicators will tell us when we have a better image in the community?

3. Do we now track or measure any of the above indicators?

4. If not, how difficult would it be to start tracking them?

5. Would the use of a special study (in-house or outside consultant) help us determine some measures?

6. Are there some substitute measures we could use? (Examples: negative press or other media reports, reports from prospective job applicants, employee turnover rates, etc.)

7. What specific factors contribute to a good image? (Examples: location of facility, general appearance of facility and vehicles, receptionist behavior, telephone manners, behavior of sales personnel, reputation of products or services, etc.)

Possible Related Objective: To reduce the number of unfavorable press and media reports by 75 percent by January 30, 1988.

Alternative Restated Objective: To remodel office facility and implement comprehensive landscaping program by January 30, 1988.

(Note: The specific restated objective would depend on the answers to the above questions.)

Figure 8.5. Worksheet for quantifying hand-to-quantify objectives.

of its operations. This is the most common form of objective. However, some of the objectives are "equilibrium objectives." These objectives reflect the fact that the organization is satisfied with some aspect of its operations and intends to continue at the same level. Sometimes it is wise to write equilibrium objectives if the organization is particularly proud of something it is doing or is in the middle of a major project that it wishes to keep visible until it is completed.

The time frame on the objective may vary. Even though operational objectives tend to be short-range, it is not necessary that they be less than 1 year in length. Rather, convenient cutoff points should be used. For example, if a particular phase for a strategic thrust ends at the end of 2 years, then this time frame could be used as the ending date for an operational objective. If, on the other hand, a major phase ends after 2 months, then this date for accomplishment could be used. There is nothing magical about the 1-year period for an operational objective.

The development and communication of operational objectives is critical if the strategic plan is to be implemented. Also critical is the development of action steps and a time frame or schedule for their accomplishment. That is the subject of the next section.

Developing Action Steps and Schedules

This phase of the strategic planning process is concerned with determining the specific steps and timetable required for the accomplishment of each objective. It deals with the how and when of the process. Sometimes this phase is called "action planning," "programming," or "implementing." Whatever the label, it refers to the determination of the major chunks of activities that must be accomplished in order to accomplish the objective and to the scheduling of these activities.

The top-level strategic planning group should not formulate the specific action steps for the operational objectives unless they are actually directly responsible for the accomplishment of the objectives. The general rule to follow here is that the people expected to carry out the objective should be primarily responsible for determining the action steps. Superiors above may wish to review the action steps to ensure consistency and conformity with policy, but they should avoid the temptation of actually writing them. The determination of the action steps by the people responsible for objective accomplishment enhances participation and commitment in the strategic planning process.

When determining action steps, the major chunks of activities that need to be accomplished should be focused on. There is no need to delve into extreme detail in order to determine all the substeps involved. These substeps are important, but they need not be actually determined in the planning sessions. If the person who is going to carry out the action steps is unfamiliar with the steps to be accomplished, he or she could ask for some guidance as to the specifics under each major step. Otherwise, it is best to assume that the person who will carry out the action step knows what to do and will ask for guidance if needed.

The basic question to be asked in determining action steps is: How will we accomplish the objective? In other words, what must be done to ensure successful accomplishment of the objective? In answering this question, we need to be sure we do not leave out a major task that will need to be completed. We also need to be sure that we obtain the cooperation of any other units in the organization that will have some responsibility in helping us to complete an action step.

How Can Action Steps Be Scheduled?

The general rule with scheduling is that the person expected to carry out the action steps should have some say-so as to when it can be accomplished. This does not mean that they should have the *only* say-so but that those involved with establishing and accomplishing the objective should have the major responsibility for determining its date of accomplishment.

Tying the Plan to the Budget

We pointed out that one key difference between normal planning and strategic planning is that strategic planning requires a substantial commitment of resources. Unless these resources are forthcoming, the plan is nothing but a paper exercise; it will not be implemented. Since most resources in the organization are expressed in terms of financial expenditure, the plan ultimately must be tied to the budget.

For an organization just starting out with strategic planning, this tie-in with the budget might not be possible the first year or two of planning. This is acceptable, but at some point the tie-in with the budget should occur. Because of the necessity of this tie-in, the planning cycle should be consistent with the budgeting cycle.

Everything we do in an organization costs us something. This cost can be financial or psychological, or it can be in the form of effort, time, space, or opportunity. When we budget, we explicitly recognize these costs as they relate to specific objectives, and we make a judgment as to whether the benefits derived from the objective are worth the costs. Since we have a limited number of resources—financial, effort, etc.—we want to spend our resources where we can get the greatest return. We can compare the costs and anticipated returns of various objectives, and then focus on those which will give us the greatest return for our expenditures. It is for this reason that our plan should be most flexible at this stage. After we "price-out" our objectives we may wish to modify, add, or delete objectives from our list. Until we actually put our objectives in dollars-and-cents terms, it is easy to be just pie-in-the-sky with our objectives. They sound good on paper, but they are just too expensive and impractical to obtain. The budgeting process forces us to be realistic.

When we budget, we are not suggesting that we hold off on a worthwhile objective simply because we do not have the money for it right now. We might be able to get the money in the future. On the contrary, budgeting involves not only allocating present resources but also future resources that are reasonable and attainable at a reasonable cost.

What Are Some Ways to Budget?

A complete discussion of various budgeting methods is beyond the scope of this book. Rather we briefly outline two basic approaches to budgeting and present a recommendation which has been tested in numerous workshops.

Incremental Budgeting.   This is "add-on" budgeting. The budget for the previous fiscal year is taken as is and a new portion or increment is added to it for the coming fiscal year. This is a very common method of budgeting. The major advantage is its simplicity. We do not have to build an entire budget; we are only concerned with the new funding required.

The increment can be computed several ways. We can simply add an inflation factor to last year's budget. Or we can simply total the cost of new objectives we wish to accomplish this year and add this figure to last year's budget. Or we can total the cost of all modifications we make to last year's objectives and add these to last year's figure. Of course, we can use a combination of all these approaches.

The primary disadvantage to incremental budgeting is that we accept last year's figure as a given. Consequently, we do not review whether the money spent last year should be spent this year. We do not thoroughly review what we have been doing and question whether we should keep doing it. We do not thoroughly examine whether the funds could be better spent on alternative objectives.

Another problem with incremental budgeting is *budget integrity*. We might ask for more money than we really need because we know our request will be cut. In fact, our request is cut because the people who allocate the money suspect that we have asked for more than we need. It becomes a vicious circle that is hard to break. The budgeting process becomes a game of one party trying to outwit the other.

Zero-Based Budgeting.   Because of these problems, an alternative budgeting technique was developed during the decade of the seventies that requires the budget to be built from the ground up, or "zero." This method is also called Program Planning Budgeting Systems (PPBS). This is a more complicated method that requires planners to build the budget around the objectives to be accomplished. Philosophically, it is more in tune with the type of budgeting we envision in the strategic planning model we discuss in this book. Note that the budgeting process does not formally enter our strategic planning process until we have decided what we want to do (objectives), how we are going to do it (action steps), and when we plan to do it (schedule). In other words, our budget is not decided until we have completed our planning.

This method allows us to better justify our budget. It also helps us to set priorities. If our budget request is cut, we can be quite definite as to the specific objectives that will be affected. Some objectives will need to be eliminated or postponed. Others will need to be modified. If we receive additional monies, we can be quite specific as to what we can do to achieve additional objectives.

Let us now turn to systems of tracking and measurement.

Tracking, Measuring, and Standards

The best strategic plan is meaningless unless we have some way of monitoring and measuring how we are doing. Without this, the plan becomes nothing more than a paper exercise: why should we be concerned with performance since we know there is no way to tell how we will do in achieving our objectives? We have already addressed the importance of tracking when we discussed the requirements for an effective objective. At that time we said that the objective should be measurable and verifiable.

What Are the Characteristics of a Good Tracking System?

Most of us are already familiar with the requirements of a good tracking and measuring system, and so the following review will be rather brief.

Timely. The information that we receive ought to be received on a timely basis. We ought to receive fresh information so that we can act on it if necessary *before* things get out of hand.

Accurate. No system provides 100 percent accurate information all the time. However, the system that is used should have a high degree of accuracy so that we are not forced to continually verify figures or to act on faulty information.

Cost-Effective. It ought not to cost us more to gather the information than it is worth. There should be a good reason to obtain the information and this reason should justify the cost of gathering and analyzing the information.

Computer-Based. With today's generation of micros, minis, and mainframe computers there is no reason why a substantial portion of our information handling should not be done by computer. This enhances greatly the ease of access and update and substantially reduces the paperwork and storage space required for information. It also helps us to more quickly and accurately analyze volumes of information.

User Language. The information provided to the strategic planners and other decision makers should be in the language and formats that they desire. This is so very important since sometimes it is the computer experts who dictate language and format. Information needs to be user-based and -friendly. With today's equipment there is no reason why this cannot be so.

Relevant.   The information that we receive ought to pertain to the strategic objectives that we are tracking. Extraneous information should be kept to a minimum so that we do not suffer from information overload caused by wading through reams of unwanted and unnecessary paper. The person who is receiving the information should make the major decision in determining what is relevant.

Appropriate Media.   The information should be delivered via the appropriate media. Sometimes an office conversation or a telephone call is all that is needed. At other times a memo, letter, or report is necessary. On other occasions, a complete report with a computer printout is required. Staff meetings with appropriate visual aids are also helpful to present tracking information. Finally, online access to a database stored in a computer and displayed graphically is a very convenient manner of obtaining the information.

Minimizes Duplication.   Our information systems should not be redundant. We should develop a database that we can use for many purposes in tracking our objectives. We ought not have to go out and create a new database or a series of reports that duplicate what we already have someplace else in the organization.

There is one other key factor in designing a tracking and measuring system: We must anchor it with a set of standards. Anchoring is discussed in the next section.

What Are Standards and How Are They Used in the Planning Process?

Standards are benchmarks of comparison. They give us a frame of reference when making evaluations of our tracking information. There are five basic types of standards: historical, like-group comparison, time, legal, and engineering. Each of these is discussed below.

Historical.   Historical standards compare how we are doing now to how we have done in the past. We develop some measure of past performance and use that as the basis to compare our present performance. If employee turnover had been at a 75 percent annual rate for each of the past 3 years and it is now at 35 percent, then we can point to a substantial improvement in the turnover rate. Most of the historical standards that we develop should come from the assessment phase of the strategic planning process.

Like-Group Comparison.   We should compare our track record with others in our industry. If our membership renewal rate is 60 percent and the rate of similar organizations is 80 percent, we have a problem. We also might want to compare ourselves to organizations in other fields, especially if we are considering diversification. Also, we may want to compare ourselves to organizations of similar size and line of service.

Sometimes we might be in an industry which sets industrywide standards. For example, the telecommunications industry has numerous standards of service dealing with call completion rates, operator assistance time, dial-tone interval, and so on. Professional associations and accreditating associations also set standards for organizations in their industry. For example, hospitals, prisons, and schools all have accreditation standards to meet. Professional groups—such as nurses, lawyers, and architects—also set standards that must be met by members of the profession. All these standards should be considered in developing standards to go along with the strategic plan.

Time.   Time standards are also important. If we wish to decrease employee turnover by 50 percent by June 1, 1988, then we had better set monthly or quarterly standards that we hope to meet as we approach June 1, 1988. For example, if we are starting July 1, 1987, we might set quarterly standards to reduce turnover as follows:

October 1, 1987	20%
January 1, 1988	15%
March 1, 1988	10%
June 1, 1988	5%

These quarterly reductions in the annual turnover rate reflect the fact that it will probably be easier to achieve reductions early in the program and more difficult later in the program. At the end of the period, the turnover rate will be cut by 50 percent if we meet these standards.

To the extent that we can work these standards into the objective or action steps we should do so. Our action steps might relate a specific step to the amount of turnover we think it will cut.

Legal.   There are zoning codes, health codes, occupational safety and health laws, pollution control laws, EEO laws, and numerous other laws and regulations which set standards of performance and operation. For example, many organizations now have a significant list of objectives and standards in both EEO and in safety and health. There are few if any areas in business that surpass these two areas as far as federal law and regulations.

Engineering.   Stress tolerances, chemical composition, metallurgy, time and motion study—all these and more specify manufacturing, construction, mining, and job design standards. These standards must be built into many objectives and action steps.

Thus we see that the effect of standards is that they help us compare our performance and expectations against an established set of criteria or benchmarks. This makes it easier for us to form judgments about how we are doing. Of course, we also consider standards when we originally do the assessment and write the objectives.

We now move to the last step of the strategic planning process. This step involves taking corrective action based on the monitoring and tracking information. It is an attempt to bring out-of-line performance back to desired performance.

Systems for Corrective Action

As the old saying goes, "The best laid plans of mice and men...." Very seldom does actual performance exactly match desired or planned performance. Consequently, every strategic plan needs a system of corrective action. This system must rely on information gathered in the tracking and monitoring phase discussed in the previous chapter. To a large extent, the quality and timeliness of this information will determine the effectiveness of the system for corrective action. Therefore, the first step in the corrective action system is to have an effective monitoring and tracking system for the plan.

What Are Corrective Action Systems?

Corrective action systems attempt to bring out-of-line performance back on line in accordance with the strategic plan. Usually the system addresses one or all of the following factors: performance of people, performance of machines or equipment, or the adequacy of the goals and objectives. Let us look at each of these factors.

Performance of People.   The performance of the people involved in achieving the plan may be deficient for a number of reasons.

1. The people *do not know* what is expected of them. We may not have been explicit as to the meaning of various objectives and actions steps in the plan. We may not have communicated the plan effectively to those who must carry it out.

2. The people may not have *adequate education and training* to carry out their duties under the plan. They may know what they are to do but may not know how they are to do it.

3. The people may not *desire* to carry out objectives. Their level of motivation may be low because either they have a low level of aspiration or because they do not see many incentives and rewards for meeting the plan.

4. *Emergencies* and *crises* may be so frequent that people are deterred from carrying out the plan. Poor forecasting and the development of contingency plans may cause people to completely lose sight of the plan when an emergency or crisis comes about.

5. *Work overload* can keep people from reaching objectives if they are given more work to do under the plan on top of an already full work load.

It is essential that the planning staff anticipate and try to prevent these problems. If they do occur, it is important that action be taken to resolve them quickly before the entire plan is jeopardized. If the problems persist, people will begin to work as if there were no plan at all.

Performance of Machines or Equipment.   We cannot expect people to do an outstanding job in meeting objectives under a plan if they do not have the proper equipment and tools. For example, in the latter half of the decade of the seventies, exhortations to steel workers in the United States to "work harder and faster" to meet Japanese competition were largely fruitless. The obsolete plant and equipment of our steel mills prevented viable competition with the Japanese who rely on much newer and more efficient equipment.

Therefore, if objectives under the plan are not being reached, we need to investigate the role being played by tools, plant, and equipment. If we have done a proper internal assessment and a proper assessment of available technology in the environment prior to developing our plan, we should be better able to determine the impact that tools and equipment will have in helping us to reach our plan. Our plan may need to include major equipment purchases and plant modernization as an integral part.

Adequacy of Goals and Objectives. We may not be meeting our plan as we desire because it is a poor plan. The goals and objectives, which are the heart of the plan, may be poorly set. They may be unrealistically high, ambiguous, and not amenable to measurement, or they may require resources far beyond our capabilities to provide. Furthermore, the plan may not have been properly communicated to those charged with its accomplishment.

What Are the Characteristics of Effective Corrective Action?

Corrective action systems are most effective if they are timely, future-oriented, positive, and preventive. Let us look at each of these.

Timely. A good corrective-action system brings performance back on track before it gets too far out of line. When we let things go hoping that they will correct themselves, we may create the impression that we condone the present state of affairs.

On the other hand, we should not be too quick to correct. Some out-of-line performance will come back on line naturally. If we have conscientious people who are able to handle their own activities, chances are that they will take action and bring out-of-line performance back on line without our having to say anything. This is a fine line that we must walk in balancing the need for timely corrective action with the danger of exercising too-close management control.

Future-Oriented. The corrective action system should concentrate on the future, not the past. We want to study the past only so that we can avoid making the same mistakes in the future. Dwelling on past mistakes by using "shouldas" as in "you shoulda done this" or "we shoulda done that" is counterproductive.

Preventive. If we are future-oriented, our corrective action systems will be concerned not only with correcting the present problem but also with preventing it from happening again in the future.

Positive. We want our corrective action system to bring about positive change not punish past performance. We do not want negative systems. Our systems should be geared to correcting future performance and should stress expected positive performance rather than dwell, in a negative way, on inadequate past performance.

Note

1. For example, see Steve Weiner and Frank Jones, "Sears, a Power in Many Fields Now, Looks into New Ones: Financial Services Businesses Appear Certain to Grow," *The Wall Street Journal,* Feb. 10, 1984, p. 10.

9

Relations between Government and Nonprofit Organizations

Madeleine Wing Adler

Professor of Politics and Vice President for Academic Affairs,
Framingham State College

There are more than 300,000 nonprofit organizations (NPOs) in the United States delivering much of this country's education, health care, and social services.[1] They also provide a host of cultural, civic, and community-based services. Nonprofit organizations are not unique to the United States. However, they do fit neatly into the American political culture. They reflect the pluralist nature of our political system by distributing influence to a vast citizenry and providing the vehicles by which these citizens are able to bring their influence to bear on the political system.

History

The scope of the involvement of government with nonprofit organizations—whether hospitals and social service agencies, arts and culture programs, or colleges and universities—has expanded dramatically over recent decades, but the relationship itself is not new. Since before the colonies united until today, there has been some form of mutual dependency between government and nonprofit (or voluntary) organizations.

Voluntary agencies *predated* governmental concern with social problems. When government began to take responsibility for a variety of social services, it was only natural that it turned to the established voluntary agencies. Rather than set up its own organization, government often subsidized the existing agencies.

It was the viewpoint of decision makers both in and out of government that voluntary agencies were better equipped than government to deliver human services. They were seen as more humane, sensitive, and skilled. It was also thought that voluntary agencies were better able to address the religious and moral needs of the recipients of the service. It fell to government to provide institutional services for the severely handicapped and hopeless, and the nonprofit sector, looked after those less handicapped and more able to benefit from aid.

Among the earliest cooperative efforts were agreements reached between states and nonprofit organizations which served deaf, indigent, and handicapped children. California provided subsidies in the early nineteenth century to private orphanages, institutions which served deaf and blind children and the mentally handicapped.[2] In 1817, the American Asylum for the Education and Instruction of the Deaf and Dumb of Hartford, Connecticut, was established. Created with private funds, the American Asylum later received a land grant from Congress.[3] In a study of American charities completed by Amos Warner in 1894, it was shown that all the agencies serving orphans and the friendless in New York City received two-thirds of their funding from government sources.[4]

By the end of the nineteenth century, subsidies were a predominant means of funding voluntary institutions. Government subsidies to nonprofit organizations continued to be a favored way of delivering social services for the same reasons that they are favored today: (1) The voluntary sector can bring political pressure to bear. (2) The belief continues that voluntary organizations can meet all the needs of the individual recipient including religious and moral needs. (3) A distrust of government as a deliverer of services continues to exist.[5]

Although subsidies were extremely important for the health and survival of the nonprofit sector during the nineteenth and early twentieth centuries, the government's role in affecting the policies and organization of the nonprofit organizations was minimal. Government played an important role, but a subsidiary one. This relationship existed until the 1930s. Ralph M. Kramer argues that the United States lagged behind European countries in developing a national social policy because the nonprofit organizations served as a substitute.[6] However, the great depression changed that. The national government was forced to assume a greater role in social services because state and local governments as well as nonprofit organizations could not adequately cope with the problems brought on by economic collapse.

From the 1930s, government no longer played a subsidiary role vis-à-vis nonprofit organizations in service delivery. A more equal partnership began to develop. Some called this "cooperative federalism."

Since World War II and especially since the 1960s, an explosion of social service activities has occurred, changing fundamentally the nature of the relationship between government and nonprofit organizations. The cooperation of government and nonprofit agencies has become the backbone of the social service delivery system in the United States.[7]

Roles of Nonprofit Organizations

Four basic roles traditionally have been attributed to voluntary agencies:

1. *Pioneering.* Voluntary agencies were considered trailblazers in developing services and in aiding hard-to-reach and difficult-to-serve clientele. These agencies

did not shy away from attempting to serve rare diseases affecting only a few or from setting up programs in geographically remote areas. There is, however, some argument whether NPOs really were the pioneers they are attributed to be. Alvin Schorr suggests that this role is a myth and in fact that most of the innovative efforts since the 1960s in social service areas, such as juvenile delinquency programs, care for the mentally ill, and community action, were the result of government efforts, not the efforts of the nonprofit sector.[8] On the other hand, others argue that nonprofit organizations were innovative, citing such examples as the creation of agencies concerned with providing all types of services to new immigrants.

2. *Promotion of volunteerism.* This role was essential in order to generate funds through individual, corporate, and foundation sources, as well as to provide workers who would assist in service delivery. Nonprofit organizations are labor-intensive. Traditionally the backbone of the staff was largely made up of volunteers.

3. *Advocacy.* Since voluntary agencies were among the first to recognize new needs and identify changing concerns, they frequently have been keen lobbyists for these concerns both before the general public and governmental policymaking bodies.

4. *Provision of services.* Nonprofit organizations developed the expertise and structures to meet social service demands. The interplay of the first three roles increased the ability of NPOs to carry out the fourth role, delivery of services.

Nonprofit organizations, in contrast to the government bureaucracy, tended to have more flexible structures which enabled them to respond quickly to both individual and group concerns and to adapt to changes in demands. These roles, combined with developed expertise in human service delivery fields prior to government's assumption of social responsibility, led to government dependence on the nonprofit sector.

Linkages between Government and Nonprofit Organizations

We can identify five general categories of relations between government and nonprofit organizations which have evolved from these four traditional roles:[9]

1. *Regulatory.* Government regulates nonprofit organizations directly in such areas as fiscal accountability, charitable solicitation, and affirmative action policy.

2. *Advocacy.* A traditional role of nonprofit organizations is that of advocate or lobbyist for a particular cause or interest. NPOs continue to be recognized as expert critics of government's social policies and bureaucracies. By means of coalition lobbying, they have enjoyed great success in promoting social policy interests.

3. *Supporter.* Government often acts in a supportive role by granting nonprofit organizations tax-exempt status and special mailing rates and by allowing both individual and corporate income tax deductions for charitable donations, thus encouraging private funding of NPOs.

4. *Funding.* Perhaps the most important relationship is direct financial support. The federal government's financial support of the nonprofit sector exceeds all private giving combined. In 1981, approximately two-fifths of the income of NPOs came from the federal government.[10] In a study of United Way agencies in New

York City, Hartogs and Weber found that 68 percent of agency budgets came from government funds.[11]

5. *Service delivery.* Most government funding of nonprofit organizations goes to financing human service delivery. Today, the federal government delivers few public services and continues to rely on third parties such as states, cities, counties, and community and social service organizations. By means of grants and contracts, the government continues a centuries-long tradition of subsidizing NPOs and hiring them to provide human services to a wide variety of clientele. As government has assumed a greater responsibility for meeting human needs, it has become more dependent upon NPOs to actually deliver the service.

These five categories are not mutually exclusive, but are parts of an overall pattern of *cooperative dependence.*

Advantages and Disadvantages of Cooperative Dependence

As the partnership of cooperative dependence has grown, advantages as well as disadvantages to each sector have resulted. On the whole, advantages of this linkage outweigh the disadvantages, but there are also some real costs.[12]

Advantages

For government, the advantages are many. The relationship with nonprofit organizations allows the government to use a preexisting human service delivery network, which is more economical than creating parallel institutions. Since NPOs are more flexible and less structured than government agencies, they can be more responsive to changing needs as well as to difficult-to-reach clientele. Government transfers unwanted tasks to the NPOs and, at the same time, gains a supportive constituency. Increased government funding allows NPOs to expand not only the scope of their activities but also the number of clients served. Income is more secure. Status and visibility within the community they serve is enhanced. Amateurs are replaced by professional personnel.

Disadvantages

There are costs to the linkage, however, and the costs are greater for the nonprofit sector than for government. For government, depending on NPOs may lead to fragmented service delivery and perhaps to a less coherent social policy. It has been argued that dependence on NPOs removes some control over costs and allows for an unevenness of service delivery across the country due to variations in the quality of organizations. It also has been suggested that by "contracting out" service delivery, government has trouble maintaining accountability and overall quality of service standards.

The disadvantages to nonprofit organizations of increased reliance on government funds and increased responsibility in service delivery are hotly debated. The primary disadvantage to NPOs is that the tradition of independence and autonomy of voluntary agencies is reduced. The goals of NPOs may be changed to square with what government is funding today. Thus, instead of pioneering new areas of social concern, NPOs may be allowing government to take over and define the goals and concerns of the organization.

A reduction in the promotion of volunteerism may be another disadvantage. As professionalism increases, the need for the amateur or volunteer is reduced. So the original mainstay of voluntary agencies, the volunteer, is no longer as needed. Grassroots contacts are lost in the process. This effects the governance structure as well.[14] Boards of directors no longer play as active a role in directing their agencies when government funding increases. Hartogs and Weber attribute this to the fact that professionalism has replaced board member participation.[15] As NPOs turn more professional attention to acquiring the government contract, there is less urgency in seeking traditional sources of funds: the voluntary gift.

Another disadvantage is the increased trend toward bureaucratization because of the regulations involved in applying for and accounting for government funds. In fact, it has been argued that more staff time is being assigned to these tasks than to the delivery of the service. Paperwork supplants substantive work. As bureaucratization of the nonprofit structure increases, the traditional flexibility which allowed for quick responsiveness declines.[16]

Reimbursement is often slow, causing cash flow problems. Seldom is money given for planning purposes. Smaller agencies with smaller staffs suffer because they cannot begin a new project as fast as larger ones. When government at the federal, state, or local level wishes to initiate a new program, time and money for planning feasibility studies and the like are allocated. On the other hand, government wants nonprofit organizations to be geared up to deliver different kinds of services in different kinds of ways, but without paying for the planning. Finally, a last disadvantage is the danger of co-optation by government and the subsequent loss of the advocacy role.

Government monies have been anxiously sought and gratefully received, but not without costs. These costs have become even more apparent as we have come into the late 1980s.

Nonprofit Organizations in the 1980s

The Reagan Administration held the view that the federal government improperly usurped the roles of both state and local government as well as of nonprofit organizations. In order to "right this wrong" and return functions to their "proper" loci, the federal government has initiated a policy of reduction of monies for social services. Because of the relationship between government and NPOs that has developed over the past decades, these reductions have created enormous disequilibrium for the entire nonprofit sector.

The cuts have affected nonprofit organizations in two major ways: Demand on charitable services is up, and revenues are down. Lester M. Salamon and Alan J. Abramson, of the Urban Institute's Nonprofit Sector Project, have contributed substantial data leading to a better understanding of what the first 5 years of the Reagan Administration's economic policies has meant to the nonprofit sector.

As of fiscal year (FY) 1980, the federal government funded projects relevant to NPOs to the level of $150 billion. This was approximately 25 percent of all federal funding. The largest amount of these monies, 36 percent, went to health-related programs; income assistance, excluding social security, took 25 percent; social welfare, including social services, employment and training, and community development absorbed 19 percent; education and research, 15 percent; and foreign aid, arts, culture and environmental programs, the remaining 5 percent.[17]

While federal spending in health-related activities, especially Medicare, has increased substantially between FY 1982 and FY 1985, federal spending in other areas of concern to the nonprofit sector has declined. The largest drop came between FY 1981 and FY 1982. Depending on what services you include in drawing up the figures, by the end of FY 1985 the drop was anywhere between 10 and 21 percent below the FY 1980 levels. This percentage drop, overall, is approximately $15 billion between FY 1982 and FY 1985. If you eliminate Medicare and Medicaid from the calculations, funding for programs of interest to the nonprofit sector was down by approximately $50 billion in the same time period.[18]

Hardest hit was the social welfare area, primarily because of the elimination of the public service jobs program and the replacement of the Comprehensive Employment and Training Act (CETA) programs. Large reductions in funding of social services also occurred.[19] The current policies of reducing monies to program areas of interest to nonprofit organizations, and in many cases eliminating programs altogether, has swelled the demand for charitable services.

Concurrent with the reduction of monies to areas of interest to nonprofit organizations and the increased demand, NPOs are experiencing shortfalls in revenues because of the direct loss of federal funding to the organizations themselves. Between FY 1982 and FY 1985, federal monies directed to NPOs declined by $17 billion. As would be expected, social welfare agencies were the hardest hit. These organizations lost $9.3 billion during this time, approximately 35 percent of their federal aid. Community development organizations lost approximately 30 percent of their federal government support as well. Arts and culture institutions and higher education were also big losers. Even nonprofit health agencies suffered reductions, especially for outpatient clinics.[20]

Nonprofit organizations whose numbers of services and numbers of clients increased because of the certainty of government support are now confronted with further increased demands with shortfalls in revenues.

NPO Response to Revenue Shortfalls

How have nonprofit organizations attempted to fill the gap created by reduced federal funding? The federal government seemed to expect private charity to fill the gap, but that has not been the case. The amount of giving that would be necessary to fill that gap makes such replacement extremely difficult. Private contributions would have had to increase by 40 percent over the period 1983 to 1985—just to hold revenues constant.[21]

Salamon and Abramson's data indicate that between FY 1980 and FY 1983, private charitable giving did increase, but only by 9 percent, or $4.12 billion. In addition, the impact of the giving was variable. The bulk of the increases went to religious activities and health programs. Social welfare organizations, most hurt by the cuts, gained only $1 billion in charitable support during that time period, and they *lost* $4.1 billion in federal support alone. Therefore, private giving made up for only 25 percent of the cuts. While corporations increased their charity to NPOs most affected by government funding cutbacks, they reduced their contributions to arts and educational programs.[22]

Since private donations from individuals, corporations, and foundations has not made up the gap left by federal support reductions, other sources of income have had to be sought. Many voluntary agencies are increasing fees, charges for services, and dues. These charges also have variable impact. Organizations that service the poor are far less likely to be able to return to these sources of revenue to make up the gap. The move to fees, charges, and dues as a source of income, as well as for-profit ventures, raises the issue of the wisdom of commercializing the nonprofit sector.

The Current Plight of Nonprofit Organizations

Social service needs exist in any society. In the United States, nonprofit agencies, not government, were the first to recognize and respond to the demands that arose from these needs. Eventually, the federal government recognized its responsibility for the delivery of social services and naturally turned to the experts—NPOs. Co-operative dependence evolved. The federal government heavily subsidized the delivery of social services by NPOs.

This partnership resulted in benefits for nonprofit organizations, but there were costs as well. The benefit was the ability to expand services. The costs were the weakening of traditional strengths such as independence, flexibility, and the promotion of volunteerism through voluntary contributions of effort and money. Independence declined because NPOs tended to tailor their goals to the goals of government. Promotion of private charity declined because money was available from government. Promotion of volunteers declined because the NPO became dependent on professionals who could handle government regulations for application and accountability. Now federal funds have diminished; they cannot be counted on as before. Yet, the costs of the partnership are still extant.

What Next?

Generally speaking, the disaster that was forecasted to have occurred has not been fully realized. Evidence suggests that NPOs will survive because they are, somehow, coping. This is not to say that the sector has not suffered some severe buffeting. In fact, the linkage, or partnership, with government that had developed over the last decades has been weakened. In 1981, Kramer suggested that the United States was moving toward a "pragmatic partnership" model of service delivery, one in which the social service system would rely on nonprofit organizations for service delivery and on government for funding.[23] But what NPOs in the United States are experiencing is a step back, perhaps a *leap* back, from that model. The two sectors will continue to coexist, cooperate, and sometimes compete in the world of social service delivery, but in ways that will differ from the past and in a manner not fully understood at this time.

Some benefits should result from the disequilibrium that has been thrust upon the nonprofit sector over the last 5 years. NPOs must take advantage of this opportunity to go back to basics, to restore and rejuvenate their traditional roles and strengths of independence and flexibility, advocacy, pioneering, and promotion of volunteerism. Missions should be rethought; operational structures reexamined; sources of finances diversified and expanded, and reliance on government funding reduced.

In contemplating the future and the place of the nonprofit sector in that future, some suggestions for readjustment come to mind. Nonprofit organizations need to take a short-run as well as a long-run view of their situation. Their primary concern is with survival—not only staying in business but maintaining their ability to meet service demands.

To ensure this survival, NPOs must expand their portfolios of funding. Some steps already have been taken in this direction. Alternative sources of financing, such as dues, fees, and charges have been tapped. However, more ambitious efforts need to be made by NPOs so that they can continue to fulfill their mission.

To reclaim independence and flexibility, attention should be given to redefining the roles of the professional staff and the boards of directors. Boards of directors should be important players in decision making. Their input should be sought on substantive policy as well as financial decisions. In the short run, professional staff should be identified for the task of promoting volunteerism. They should be assigned the responsibility of recruiting and supervising volunteer workers. They should aggressively seek out new constituents and expand the participation of old constituencies as volunteers of time and money.

In the long run, the staff should be assigned to design an economic development strategy as well as a means of using clientele and former clientele as volunteer workers. Finally, in order to free staff members for these activities and not lose the positive benefits of good management, NPOs should work to implement a suggestion made by Nelson Rosenbaum and create an "administrative services consortia" among voluntary organizations to provide the professional services needed to appropriately deal with the requirements for accountability and application for government foundation grants and contracts.[24]

When seeking funds from private sources as well as from government, proposals should be innovative and experimental. In this way, NPOs can attempt to expand the pool of potential contributors and exert independence in establishing their mission. Government should be encouraged to give challenge grants to support efforts to get the profit and nonprofit sectors to collaborate on services delivery programs.[25]

Finally, the advocacy role should become a priority. In the short run, efforts should be directed toward protecting the charitable tax deduction for taxpayers who itemize and for those who do not itemize deductions. In the long run, coalitions should be formed among states, counties, municipalities and nonprofit organizations to lobby the federal government on issues of mutual concern. After all, the NPOs are not alone in their plight.

Conclusion

Nonprofit organizations have an impressive history in the United States. In fact, they serve as a model for European NPOs today. Part of the nonprofit sector's history is its linkage to government. Originally the linkage could be described as "cooperative autonomy": nonprofit organizations delivered services; government provided subsidies. The roles altered, and the relationship became one of "cooperative dependence" with all the advantages and disadvantages that entailed.

Today the relationship continues to be reshaped. The future will see a linkage that may be defined as "cooperative initiative." Nonprofit organizations cannot return to the relative autonomous linkage of the past. However, they should never allow themselves to be as dependent upon government as they once were. By adopting cooperative initiative as its linkage model, the nonprofit sector can distance itself from government, expand its portfolio of funding, rejuvenate its strengths, and become a stronger member of the partnership. Society can only benefit from a strengthened nonprofit sector which defines its mission as the articulation as well as the delivery of the service needs of its people.

Notes

1. John Palmer and Isabel Sawhill (Eds.), *The Reagan Experiment,* The Urban Institute Press, Washington, 1982, p. 13.

2. Ralph M. Kramer, *Voluntary Agencies in the Welfare State,* University of California Press, Berkeley, Calif., 1981, p. 60.

3. Ibid.

4. Lester M. Salamon, "The Results Are Coming in," *Foundation News,* July-August 1984, p. 20.

5. Kramer, *Voluntary Agencies,* pp. 61–62.

6. Ibid., p. 65.

7. Salamon, "The Results Are Coming in," p. 19.

8. Alvin L. Schorr, "The Tasks for Volunteerism in the Next Decade," *Child Welfare,* vol. 49, pp. 431–432, 1970.

9. Frederick S. Lane, "Managing Not-for-Profit Organizations," *Public Administration Review,* September-October 1980.

10. Palmer and Sawhill, *The Reagan Experiment.*

11. Nelly Hartogs and Joseph Weber, *Impact of Government Funding on the Management of Voluntary Agencies,* Greater New York Fund/United Way, New York, 1978.

12. Kramer, *Voluntary Agencies,* pp. 165–166.

13. Nelson Rosenbaum, "Government Funding and the Voluntary Sector: Impacts and Options," in John D. Harman (Ed.), *Volunteerism in the Eighties,* University Press of America, Washington, 1982, p. 253.

14. Ibid.

15. Hartogs and Weber, *Impact of Government Funding,* p. 79.

16. Waldemar A. Nielsen, "The Crisis of the Nonprofits," *Change,* 1980.

17. Lester M. Salamon and Alan J. Abramson, "Nonprofits and the Federal Budget: Deeper Cuts Ahead," *Foundation News,* March-April 1985, p. 49.

18. Ibid.

19. Ibid.

20. Ibid., pp. 52–53.

21. Palmer and Sawhill, *The Reagan Experiment.*

22. Salamon and Abramson, "Nonprofits and the Federal Budget."

23. Kramer, *Voluntary Agencies,* p. 285.

24. Rosenbaum, "Government Funding," p. 257.

25. Ibid., p. 256.

10

The Board of Directors

Tracy D. Connors

Consultant

Why a Board of Directors?

The first and most pragmatic reason for a board of directors is because the law says that you must have one if your organization is incorporated. In this, both profit and nonprofit corporations share many similarities. There are also significant differences, however, between the management of a profit and a nonprofit organization, including the board of directors. Since many directors of nonprofit organizations received their business training and experience in the profit-making business sector, they should not automatically feel that this experience is directly translatable to the nonprofit sector. Further, they also should not feel that the nonprofit organization board is run just like the business board. There is a significant difference in orientation between the profit and the nonprofit organization, a difference in orientation that applies to the board as well.

Experience with boards over the centuries during which standard business practice and law have evolved has provided three general answers to the question: "Why a board of directors?"

1. Complying with the law
2. Fulfilling trusteeship responsibilities for the owners of the business—in the case of nonprofit organizations, the members of the corporation
3. Helping the chief executive officer (CEO) carry out his or her responsibilities

According to *Robert's Rules of Order,* boards of directors are "essentially small deliberative assemblies, subordinate to the body that appoints them, with their duties and authority, and the number of their regular meetings, and their quorums, defined by the parent body, or by its authority." Such boards are usually appointed by organizations that meet rather infrequently, such as annually or quarterly. The

77264

organization therefore delegates to a committee, the board of directors, almost all of its authority, with slight limitations, to be exercised between meetings.

It is common for the board itself (which usually meets monthly), to have the members' authorization (via the by-laws) to appoint from the board an executive committee (EC) of a "specified number who shall have all the power of the board between the meetings of the board, just as the board has all the power of the society between the meetings of the society, except that the subordinate body cannot modify any action taken by its superior." The executive committee often consists of the officers of the organization, plus one or two members at large. A nucleus working EC of some six to eight members is most often the case, since many nonprofit organizations have boards that sometimes number as high as thirty or forty directors. It is important, however, that prior to the appointment of such a committee, the applicable state statute should be consulted with regard to membership qualifications. It is not uncommon for such a statute to require a specified number of trustees to be members of the committee.

Necessary Nuisances?

When a nonprofit corporation begins operations, there is often the feeling among the usually small core of truly involved founding directors that leading members of the community need to be placed on the board to attract funds or to lend political clout for funding or leverage purposes. This practice is often a mixed blessing. Sometimes the directors elected do provide the "services" for which they were selected. In many cases they do not.

There is also the tendency among the inner-circle directors to treat the other directors as necessary nuisances, thus complicating communications and hindering effective action as a board. A much wiser course would be to select directors after reading the following discussion of a director's role and function in a nonprofit organization.

Trustees for Members or Owners

If one word sums up the director's responsibility to the members, clients, or constituency—it is *responsibility*. But does the nature of this trusteeship include considering only the interests of the members, or does it extend to balancing the interests of the members with all other interests—in particular, those of the community at large? There is no clear-cut agreement, and between these two views lies a broad base of opinion. However, it can also be noted that it is relatively easy for the memberships of most nonprofit organizations (NPOs) to communicate with their boards. If the specific membership does not agree with the actions of its board, individual directors and the board are fairly certain to hear about it in short order. This is true, of course, only if the memberships of such organizations ensure the existence of a good internal communications system and insist on a full accounting of actions and activities from the board.

An example of a somewhat restricted view of a nonprofit board's responsibility might include the statement that "the board of directors is, by law, accountable to the members for prudent, effective employment of the members' investment in the corporation."

The board would then meet this obligation to the members by performing all of the following:

1. Electing dedicated, effective officers. (In many NPOs, the members elect the officers as well as the board. If this mode is chosen, it should be provided for either in the articles of incorporation or in the by-laws.)

2. Accepting personal responsibility for an active, involved leadership role as directors, that is, chairing or working on various committees or other action groups.

3. Keeping informed on the organization's performance in all program areas.

4. Selecting a competent chief administrative officer (CAO), often called the executive director. In some categories of nonprofit organizations, however, the practice seems to be on the increase of titling the chief executive officer "the chairperson," and the chief administrative officer "the president." A nonprofit organization can probably benefit from giving the presidential title to its chief administrative officer, particularly if the CAO spends more time in governmental or other important public contacts than does the chief executive officer. As Samuel B. Shapiro points out, "important doors do open more readily to a president than to an executive vice president, executive director, general manager, or executive secretary. The association therefore gains when its executive head is called president.... The term president [has] connotations of power, decision making, and influence not found in the lesser titles....Members may be less likely to regard him as a hired hand."[1] Thus, the reasoning for calling the chief administrative officer the president seems to be to give the CAO a boost in esteem and acceptance by the community as well as greater availability to community leaders. It also seems to provide a title that recognizes the increasing professionalism of full-time staff members of major nonprofit organizations.

5. Delegating to the CEO and/or the executive committee (usually composed of the elected officers) wide latitude and authority for managing the corporation's affairs.

A broader definition of the trusteeship role is noted in this statement that "the board of directors, as trustees for the membership, have the responsibility of maintaining a proper balance among the interests of members, staff, service recipients, and the general public." This interpretation is fast supplanting the former restrictive one.

There seems to be a strong correlation between the narrowness of interpretation of these roles and the type of service provided by the nonprofit organization. NPOs formed to serve the specific interests of a relatively small group of people, such as certain types of artisans or a church, tend to have boards following the more restricted view of board responsibility. NPOs that provide services to a broader public, such as ambulance corps, hospitals, and universities, tend to have boards following the broader definition of trusteeship.

A director of a nonprofit corporation is a representative of the corporation's owners—the members. The director's status is closely related to that of an elected legislator, an agent, or a trustee in a trust of property. The general authority and status of NPO directors is similar to that of directors of other corporations, except that they are more limited in their power to deal with the organization's property—this area usually being decided by the membership with a two-thirds vote, or as otherwise provided in the articles or by-laws.

The board of directors as a whole directs the routine, day-to-day affairs of the organization, usually through the delegation of authority to the prospective officers. It must exercise good judgment and reasonable care in the affairs of the corporation, seeking the advice and information of others when necessary. However, it must use its own judgment when coming to decisions. The directors are the representatives of the membership and their acts are certainly subject to fair criticism and evaluation by the members.

Being the representatives of the members does not include developing a "proprietary" attitude toward the organization—acting as though the organization belonged to the directors. Those organizations having such a board should consider reviewing the by-law that is applicable in such cases. As noted in Oleck's *Nonprofit Corporations, Organizations, and Associations,* high-handed use of managerial status does not go unnoticed by either the members or the courts. "Statutes governing false statement, entries, or reports, of course, are stringent, and misconduct results in personal liability....Public authorities and courts are particularly stern in cases of abuse of powers by trustees or officers of charitable (e.g., religious or educational) organizations."[2] Personal liability of directors may also arise upon an unlawful distribution of assets and in some cases even upon those directors who are present at a meeting which authorized such a distribution and did not vote against the proposal or file a written dissent at such time or within a reasonable time thereafter. Certainly, in this circumstance, silence is not golden.

Boards in Metamorphosis

Many nonprofit boards of directors are undergoing a significant metamorphosis. In the past, the membership of many nonprofit boards came from the community's oldest and most well-established families. Now, board membership tends to be more representative of the total community in which the nonprofit organization operates and which it serves. Two factors are largely accountable for this change:

1. There is an ever-increasing number of cultural, educational, and philanthropic nonprofit organizations competing for support from an ever-smaller pool of "old-line-elite" families.

2. Many environmental factors now encourage boards more directly and proportionately to represent the racial, ethnic, and economic character of the community.

Increasing dependence by nonprofits on federal, state, and local government support means that it is now necessary to ensure that board composition gives evidence that the needs of the total community are being addressed by NPOs. As a direct result, boards are becoming younger and often contain members who serve primarily to represent and involve a particular segment of the community.

Another resulting change is seen in the reasons for selection to board membership. In the past, many individuals were invited to become board members primarily because of their ability to contribute or solicit funds. Increasingly, however, nonprofit board membership is based on representation and on the fact that these individuals have "something to trade on," such as professional skills that may be of use to the new organization or institutions. These skills include legal counsel, accounting, investments, financial, political, or public relations expertise. This is not to say that persons capable of giving or getting large sums of money for the NPO are not still prime candidates for board membership, but only that the rationale for selection is now much broader than in the past.

The number of truly active board members is often about a quarter of the board, the other 75 percent very often being the familiar "dead wood." This is especially true of well-established, "institutional"-type nonprofit boards. A younger organization, on the other hand, will tend to have a more active board, both from the "newness" of appointments and the interest in starting an NPO from scratch.

Younger, more active boards of newer nonprofit organizations are causing problems for the more established boards, however: Unless the established NPO has a very effective professional manager or begins weeding out the nonproductive board members, it is soon caught in the squeeze of growing numbers of NPOs often competing for the same dollar, the same public support and air time, and the same membership.

A growing number of nonprofit organizations are hiring professional managerial staff to administer the affairs of the organization. Not only is this a necessity due to the excessive time such management takes if left solely to the directors, but also since public sources (federal, state, and municipal funds) now account for a growing percentage of the operating budgets of NPOs, professional staff is almost always required to prepare and administer grants from these sources. Further, the auditing and reporting practices of these granting sources have stimulated a concern for sound fiscal and administrative management practices. Such managerial personnel must have a sound knowledge of grant sources and procedures in the nonprofit area in which they operate.

In a growing number of nonprofit organizations, particularly smaller, younger NPOs, the executive director or business manager is practically the total organization in that he or she not only directs the day-to-day operations, but quite often serves in such diverse capacities as development director, fund-raiser, public relations director, artistic director, bookkeeper, grants writer, and administrator. The fact that such managers are expected or required to fulfill so many roles in the NPO further emphasizes the need for skilled management personnel.

In a chapter entitled Board and Staff: Who Does What? (*The Board Member's Book*) Brian O'Connell provides a highly useful discussion of important distinctions in board and staff roles in nonprofit organizations.[3]

Increasingly, too, nonprofit managers are being called upon to develop institutional policy that is initiated at the management level and subsequently brought before the board for its evaluation and ultimate approval. This trend can be very beneficial for the nonprofit organization if the policy initiated is well-founded in good practice, but the practice must be carefully monitored by the board.

Although it is certainly appropriate for boards to receive policy recommendations from professional management, unless the board pays careful attention to the procedures, a trend may develop in which the board may, in effect, slowly abdicate to management its responsibility for policy formulation. And, at every stage, boards must be careful to set policies that serve to reconcile the business and philosophical functions of the nonprofit organization in their charge.

The National Information Bureau notes this example in its *The Volunteer Board Member in Philanthropy* by citing the situation that developed with regard to the Sister Elizabeth Kenny Foundation.

> Newspaper headlines reported gigantic waste of the contributor's dollar and 10-year prison sentences for the Executive Director and certain of the fundraising counsellors of this philanthropic association a few years ago. What went wrong? The Board of Directors, which included many prominent citizens of Minneapolis and one or more movie stars, did not select its staff head with due care and did not supervise the organization adequately thereafter. The commercial firm that did mass fund-raising mailings for the Foundation appears to have corrupted the staff head and absconded with a substantial total of contributed funds. When the Foundation's auditors protested that matters were not properly handled, the Board ignored their report and the auditing firm resigned. It took the District Attorney's announcement to awaken the Board and, before the agency

could be reconstituted effectively under a new name, all of the Board members had to resign.[4]

Boards in being should expedite the metamorphosis discussed above and reconstitute themselves with active members, including those capable of meeting fundraising responsibilities, as well as members who bring to the board a helpful variety of skills and expertise while representing a broad cross section of the community.

There are a number of reasons for cross-representation on public service organization boards of directors, as the Child Welfare League of America notes in its *Guide for Board Organization in Social Agencies:*

> Although boards of directors require the services of persons who bring prestige, influence, affluence, and accessibility to resources, they also need adequate sources of information. In general, it is agreed that boards of directors should be chosen to achieve social heterogeneity and that membership should be drawn from a broad spectrum of the community. The social status from which members are drawn should be sufficiently diverse to lead to the expression of a variety of points of view. There should be a distribution among the membership as to sex, age, race, and representation from professional, labor, business, and other groups, such as potential or former consumers.[5]

New nonprofit organizations being formed should keep these factors in mind, plus another growing problem seen in the expansion of NPOs across the country—multiple board memberships.

Although it is not unusual for an individual to serve on more than one nonprofit board (known perjoratively as "interlocking directorates"), it has often been suggested to this writer by the managers of these NPOs that these board members have divided loyalties. Often, with regard to fund raising and other activities, these members find that they cannot, in good conscience, concentrate their support on any one institution. This not only limits their effectiveness and thereby the effectiveness of the board, it also hampers the programs of all the organizations involved.

It is recommended whenever a member finds his or her effectiveness compromised by serving on multiple boards, that the other members (or, if necessary, the board itself) reconsider whether this person should maintain membership on the board and ask him or her to make a choice between the organizations involved. It must be remembered that as a director or trustee of the organization, a form of fiduciary responsibility attaches and therefore a violation of this relationship could prove detrimental, both financially and professionally, to the director and the organization. Since circumstances will be different in each case, further generalizations would probably not be helpful.

There is, however, one situation that might modify the above consideration and that is when the involved institutions have complementary or mutually dependent programs or objectives. In this case there may be some advantages to a limited number of overlapping memberships. This, however, will need to be examined on a case-by-case basis.

Such overlapping board memberships should certainly be of strong concern when they affect the objectivity of policies developed by one organization that affect other organizations in the same sector. For example, a community arts council was charged with the responsibility of reviewing the funding applications to the city government from all arts organizations in the metropolitan area. Although the process of evaluating the requests was cloaked with the outward appearance of fairness and objectivity, smaller organizations became more and more alarmed when the larger institutions consistently received the funding they requested, whereas the smaller organizations were usually turned down because of "austerity" conditions in the city's budget.

A review of board memberships on the arts council board revealed that almost all the members were members of other boards—all major institutions in the community. At the very least, this situation revealed a board membership that represented only a fraction of its stated constituency (it also refused membership to artists of any discipline or medium and to any professional staff members of area arts institutions or organizations). The situation that was not only unfair but was also unlikely to go unchallenged for very long, with resulting publicity that could be damaging for all involved.

Board Matters and Management Matters

With new nonprofit organizations, one of the first questions is "Who should we have on the board?" With more established NPOs, the question becomes "Who can we *get* to serve on the board?" Instead of beginning with these questions, the "What kind of...What should be...How shall they..." type of inquiry, NPOs should ask themselves the more fundamental question: "What kind of problems will this nonprofit board face?" When similar questions are raised in most successful businesses, the answer is found by defining the duties and responsibilities of the job. Experience has shown repeatedly the validity of simplifying the remaining problems by analyzing the job requirements. It is nearly always followed when choosing the chief administrative officer (CAO) or the staff, and so why not for directors as well?

The job requirements for nonprofit directors basically revolve around the status of the organization itself. Whether or not the organization has established itself to the point where it can afford a professional staff will basically determine whether the board itself will be required to deal in depth with policy matters (the usual area of responsibility for most boards) or whether it will need to set policy *and* to operate the corporation through its officers, thus taking a much more active, individual role as a board in the success or failure of the organization. The qualifications of its board members, individually and collectively, will need to be analyzed in either case.

With a professional staff, many management matters are left up to the CAO working with the chief executive officer (CEO) and the executive committee (EC). With no staff, the CEO and the EC will have the burden of management entirely on their shoulders and will often need frequent assistance from board members in various facets of the operation.

Depending on the staff–no staff status of the organization, the character of the board meetings will also change. Ideally, board matters relate mainly to setting broad directions and goals. Staff and/or the CEO-EC should handle management matters, that is, this month's crises, preferably at separate meetings. The reason for this is that when a single-sitting meeting considers a mixture of agenda items, the urgent matters usually come first. This leaves discussion of the long-range, in-depth policy issues unresolved or only topically discussed—postponed "until the next meeting," where all too often the crises again predominate and the cycle repeats itself. The board is thus caught in a fire-fighting technique of leadership and activity, with little time to function as a policy-making board. This dilemma should be addressed when deciding upon appropriate authority delegation to executive directors or particular officers.

On stating that board meetings should be separate from management-type meetings, we need to answer the question, "What are board matters?"

According to Juran and Louden in *The Corporate Director,*[6] board matters may be classified into nine specific areas, including:

1. Items or areas requiring member (stockholder) approval
2. Course of the business (service) matters
3. Reservation of certain powers of decision making
4. Delegation of powers not reserved by the board
5. Election of the chief executive officer (also normally including the selection of the chief administrative officer if the organization is large enough to have one)
6. Giving advice, counsel, and assistance to the officers
7. Monitoring progress of the corporation and taking appropriate action in the light of this progress
8. Creating adequate organization and machinery for conducting the business of the board and the corporation
9. Providing for creating and maintaining a healthy board

Member Approval Areas

The board must, of course, concern itself directly with those items noted in the articles of incorporation of by-laws as being required to be submitted to the membership for approval and/or consideration. Such vital matters as amendments to the articles, for example, usually need the approval of the majority of the membership. Especially careful attention must be paid to such matters, because the procedure for handling them via the board is usually spelled out in detail in the articles or the by-laws. Deviation from this procedure could bring irate attention from an observant member or even legal action.

Most nonprofit organizations, especially those providing services to a broad-spectrum public, carefully select a variety of directors, each ostensibly representing a certain "public" or faction of the membership. However, their actual legal position is one of trusteeship for all the members. As such, they are held accountable to the same standards of good faith, objectivity, and subordination of personal interests that apply to all trustees, regardless of organization, profit or nonprofit.

Financial Submissions

All nonprofit organizations have budgets, although they may range from the several-hundred-dollar category up into the millions. The formality of developing and approving such budgets varies with the amounts involved. Most major NPOs submit their budgets to the membership for approval, or at very least, publish them in internal newsletters or mailings to members for their information and comment. Usually concurrent with a published budget is the development of an annual plan of operations or activities in support of the corporate purpose(s).

Other types of financial matters that are usually submitted to the membership via the board include:

1. Dissolution of the corporation, obviously the most drastic financial proposal of all. Procedures for this occurrence are always specified in the by-laws and articles of incorporation. The Internal Revenue Service, before issuing a nonprofit determination, will require that the requisite dissolution phraseology be adopted by the membership, inserted in the by-laws and the articles, and filed with the IRS (see Part 2, Chap. 8, for sample by-laws and articles).

2. Major financing programs or fund drives. Most nonprofits depend to a great extent on membership dues and the participation of director and members in fund drives. Directors will want to have the membership solidly behind any such major drive for both legal and success purposes.

3. Broad benefit plans for staff personnel, particularly when such plans or other benefits will project corporate liabilities well into the future.

4. Annual finance reports—usually prepared by the treasurer, reviewed and approved by the board, and submitted to the membership at the annual meeting. Monthly reports are usually required at board meetings, communicated to the membership via the newsletter or available on request.

Other areas submitted by the board to membership include:

1. Reports to members, including the annual report and such other interim reports as are specified or felt necessary. By-laws usually specify that the annual report, usually prepared by the CEO, be submitted to the membership at the annual meeting. NPOs having staff will often require or request that the CAO also submit a report of their activities as well. Interim reports vary in scope and frequency depending on the organization and the board, but NPOs often use the organization's newsletter to effect such monthly or quarterly communications.

2. Annual meetings—the by-laws will usually specify that an annual meeting be held, but leave the exact time, date, and place up to the directors. The by-laws will usually spell out the procedures for the nomination of new directors, notification of members, proxy policy, voting rights, and so on, that constitute an important part of the annual meeting.

3. The procedures for changing the by-laws vary from organization to organization, with some requiring membership approval and others only board approval. Careful attention will need to be given to the procedures for such changes regardless of the specifics in each case. The majority of NPOs seem to favor membership approval before the by-laws are changed and this only after adequate notification of the exact change(s).

Regardless of whether the submission area is spelled out in writing, most effective nonprofit boards realize the morale and communications advantages of keeping the membership as thoroughly informed as possible about the organization and its management. In small NPOs, the submission-to-membership procedure may be quite informal. The net result, however, is the same whether large or small—after-the-fact challenges by members are avoided, legal doubts are resolved in favor of the submission, and the vital element of democratic participation in the nonprofit organization is reinforced.

Powers Retained by the Board

The by-laws phraseology that confers on the board the power to direct the operations and affairs of the corporation varies from organization to organization, but typically takes the following form. Explanatory comments on each power follow the typical wording.

> 1. GENERAL POWERS. The board of directors shall have all the usual powers of a board of directors of a membership corporation and shall govern and direct the affairs of the organization. It shall make all rules and regulations that it deems necessary or proper for the government of the organization and for the due and orderly conduct of its affairs and the management of its property, consistent with its charter and these by-laws.

The board governs the corporation, not the individual acts of the directors. The routine management of the corporation's affairs is in the hands of the board of directors, who may not lawfully abdicate this responsibility to anyone else. The powers of the directors derive from the establishment of the legal entity—the nonprofit corporation—not from the board itself. The directors exercise the powers of the organization. They do not own it in any sense. The power to make fundamental changes in the organization (e.g., articles and by-laws) rests with the membership. In day-to-day matters the board's will prevails, but in extraordinary matters the will of the membership must be sought and followed. The board may not perform acts that amount to changes in fundamental directions, purposes, or methods of the organization, unless expressly permitted to do so in the by-laws.

> 2. NUMBER AND TERM. The number of directors of the organization shall be _____ .

Most states require that there be at least three directors of nonprofit corporations; some require five. Some states have a ceiling of between fifteen and twenty-one on the number of directors of the organization. Check your state statutes for more exact information on this area.

The Child Welfare League of America, in its *Guide for Board Organization in Social Agencies,* says that "as a norm, boards should comprise 15 to 42 members. Boards of less than 15 members are too small to organize a sound board and committee structure or to obtain adequate community representation. Too large boards tend to be run by a small core and thus become undemocratic. Statewide boards are sometimes larger; care must be exercised to make certain that the size does not become unwieldy. Since variation in size is closely related to the factors that influence variation in function, the number of members must be determined by the needs and operations of the individual agency."[7]

> All directors shall serve for _____ years and shall be elected or appointed in the following manner:_____ .

Some states set limits on the director's term of office, but most do not. Most nonprofit corporations now have a system of rotating elections for their boards, thus providing continuity of experienced directors in office. If the elections are not held on time, the old directors continue in office until their successors are duly elected. Express acceptance of the office of director is not necessary, this being presumed unless an individual indicates unwillingness to serve. Once acceptance is given, either expressly or implied, it may not be withdrawn. The director then has to resign to get off the board.

> 3. QUALIFICATIONS. Directors must reside within reasonable distance from [seen in local organization by-laws], allowing regular attendance at meetings that directors are expected to attend. Directors must be members of the organization. No director shall serve for more than _____ terms.

The by-laws of the corporation usually establish the qualifications and the classifications of its directors. The classification phraseology means establishing rotating elections to maintain continuity of experienced directors. Check your state statutes for a determination on age qualifications for directors, residency of state and nation, and organizational membership. Many organizations establish moral and personal-history qualifications for their directors. Aliens may be directors, provided that at least one director is a citizen.

    4. MEETINGS.

      (a). Annual Meeting.   The board of directors shall meet within a reasonable time after the annual meeting of the membership to elect officers for the coming year.

      (b). Regular Meetings.   The board of directors shall meet monthly at a time and place adopted by resolution and announced through either personal or written notice.

      (c). Special Meetings.   Special meetings of the directors may be called by or at the request of the chairperson or any two directors at such place as shall be designated in the call for such meeting.

No specific form is prescribed for calling a meeting of either members or directors, unless the by-laws so specify. Some states do provide official forms for some notification purposes and should be used. Oleck's *Non-Profit Corporations, Organizations, and Associations* should be consulted for its helpful guidance on phraseology relative to forms for calling meetings.[8]

Although most states have few rules concerning meetings of the trustees of nonprofit corporations, a casual gathering of board members is not usually considered a legally binding or effective meeting. It is also not good practice to "arrange" matters via the telephone prior to an official meeting. Although this practice is widespread, it could provide the grounds for a successful challenge to board action by a member of the corporation—an increasing likelihood with the growing scrutiny and demands for accountability now faced by the nonprofit sector.

Meetings must be called at a reasonably convenient place (not necessarily at the organization's home office or headquarters). In general, the directors can meet anywhere or any time (avoid Sundays and holidays), provided that due notice is given and when all consent. Many states allow the meetings themselves to be conducted via telephone. This is especially useful to those NPOs with national membership on the board. Generally, this can be accomplished without much difficulty, but in order for the resolutions to be legally binding, each participant must be able to hear all the conversation regarding each resolution proposed.

It should be clearly stated in the by-laws who has the authority to call meetings of the directors. The chief executive officer is usually held to have such authority, even though it may not be spelled out in the by-laws. The by-laws should provide for the calling of a meeting by a certain number of the directors.

The formality of the director's meeting is usually commensurate with the size of the corporation—the larger it is, the more formal the meeting. Voting is usually a "yes" or "no" to the proposals, with a failure to vote specifically against legally amounting to assent. Opposition to a proposal should be stated clearly and recorded for the record—an action doubly important if any impropriety is felt to be present or if an issue may face a legal challenge.

Minutes should be kept by the secretary and expeditiously distributed to the directors after the meeting. Both approvals and dissents should be recorded.

An agenda should be prepared and followed at the meeting. Many organizations include a general agenda in the by-laws.

A typical order of business would include:

Call to order by the presiding officer

Roll call (names recorded in the minutes)

Note the presence of the quorum in the minutes—announce to those present

Read and consider the minutes of the previous meeting (additions or corrections as necessary)

Approval of corrected minutes

Reports: officers; committee chairpersons

Old business: referrals from previous meetings

Elections (if any)

New business

Appointments (if any)

Set time, date, and place of next meeting

Adjournment

Should your board meetings be open to the public? Reports from across the country indicate that most nonprofit organizations see a growing need to do just that—especially those with individual members. The reasons for this shift in usual practice should be noted:

First is the basic issue of public support for the programs and services of non-profit organizations. Since most depend to a large extent on funding sources in the community, their survival depends on creating and maintaining broad public support. Inviting the press and the public to attend board meetings is a very effective way of gaining awareness of your programs and projects as well as public support (through showing that your organization has nothing to hide). Many NPOs include major press outlets on their mailing lists automatically, including board meeting notices and agendas. Reporting your board's activities will very likely increase with more air time and "column inches" of printed news. This is a result of advance notice on the meeting and its topics of discussion, with a residual benefit that news releases submitted as follow-ups to the media are more often used as they are submitted.

Another reason to open board meetings to the public centers on the growing number of NPOs are using public funds to operate programs or provide services. This, in effect, makes them quasi-public bodies, accountable to tax payers who provided these funds. As the Utah Bar Association said in a questionnaire prepared by the American Society of Association Executives, "As a quasi-public body, in a state with a sunshine law, we would be remiss if we held closed meetings."[9]

Although it may be necessary to go into "executive session" during an otherwise open meeting when discussing disciplinary or personnel matters, in general, the growing practice is to conduct open board meetings. As Charles J. Kickham, Jr., past president of the Massachusetts Bar Association, emphatically states: "The closed meeting concept is outmoded, and its harmful aspects far outweigh the positive good which results from exposing the activities of our organization to the critical scrutiny of the interested public. We should be able to withstand that scrutiny. The days when the business of any organization was conducted in secret are gone, and the organization which clings to that practice is out of step with the times."[10]

> 5. NOTICE.　Notice of any special meeting of the directors shall be given at least 1 week (7 days) previously thereto by written notice delivered personally or sent by mail to each director at his or her address as shown by the records of the organization. The general nature of the business to be transacted at the meeting should be specified in the notice.

Unless the meeting is a regular one, fixed by custom, notice must be given to all the directors—a requirement that also applies to the meetings of any subgroup of the corporation, such as committees, boards, or panels. Such a defect of notice is essentially waived if all the directors attend the meeting and participate without objection.

6. QUORUM. A majority of the directors shall constitute a quorum for the transaction of business at any meeting of same.

Unless stated otherwise in the by-laws, a majority of the directors constitutes a quorum, without which those present cannot act as a board. Less than one-third of the board is usually not considered a quorum. However, a majority of those voting controls the outcome, regardless of how many are present. Any vacancies on the board that reduce it to less than a quorum must be filled before the board can officially act as a board. Likewise, if by early departures from a meeting a quorum of the directors is no longer present, the board can no longer act legally—unless the withdrawals were deliberately intended to create this situation to hinder the board's progress. In this case, the board may continue as though a quorum were present.

7. VACANCIES. Any vacancy occurring on the board and any directorship to be filled by reason of an increase in the number of directors, shall be filled by the membership at either the annual meeting or a special meeting. A director elected to fill a vacancy shall be elected for the unexpired term of his or her predecessor in office.

The owners of the corporation (the members) should fill vacancies in the directorship (unless the members fail to do so in reasonable time, such as 6 months). Vacancies are created by death, resignation, permanent departure from the community, or prolonged neglect or disability. Vacancies are not created automatically by a reduction in the number of directors. In this case, the number drops as terms of office expire.

Directors may resign at any time unless prevented by an overriding contractual obligation or the requirement of acceptance by the board. Even after resigning, however, directors remain liable for acts committed or approved prior to resignation. A resignation may be retracted at any time before it is accepted by the board.

No particular form is prescribed for resignations, even oral resignations or resignations by conduct will suffice, unless proscribed by the by-laws or charter.

8. COMPENSATION. Directors shall not receive any compensation for their services, except for reimbursement for any out-of-pocket expenses incurred on behalf of the organization.

Basic to the nonprofit corporation is the rule that its directors and officers reap no monetary gains from the organization. This does not mean that they cannot be paid a salary or compensated for services, however. It does mean that compensation to officers and directors should only be in accordance with state statutes and corporation rules deliberately adopted. The membership should approve all such rules beforehand. The membership may also approve the granting of fees for directors to attend meetings, usually with fees ranging from $10 to $200 per meeting, depending on the organization.

9. SUSPENSION AND EXPULSION. The board of directors, by a two-thirds vote of the entire board, may suspend or expel any member or director upon evidence of material violation of the by-laws, public laws, or any regulations or practices of the organization. The member or director in question shall be entitled to state his or her case to the board before such action is taken.

Most states now have legal procedures for the removal or suspension of directors or officers, usually based on charges of misconduct, abuse of trust, damages, waste, or improper transfer of corporate funds or assets. If the organization's by-laws also deal with this, they must be in agreement with state statutes. Removal without cause may be effected if the by-laws so provide.

Reasons for removal for cause might include: taking of corporate funds, gross or willful negligence, failure to disclose required information on business matters, refusal to cooperate with or unjustified attacks on the chief executive officer of the corporation. Straightforward disagreement or friction between directors or officers is not adequate grounds for removal for cause. Precise limitations and explanations of procedures on such matters must be included in the by-laws, with the general rule being that those who select should remove when necessary.

The officer or director facing removal must be given a reasonable opportunity to hear and defend against the charges. Such removals have been, and remain, subject to court review. An officer or director improperly removed may obtain reinstatement by the courts.

> 10. ATTENDANCE.   Any director absent from three (3) meetings during a calendar year shall be automatically dropped from the board, unless excused for extenuating circumstances by the board.

> 11. HONORARY DIRECTORS.   Provision is made for "honorary directors," serving in an advisory capacity to the board of directors; such honorary directors shall be elected by the board of directors. The number shall be at the discretion of the board. Honorary directors shall be ex officio, with voice but without vote. (The mayor and/or municipal legislative body chairpersons are often made honorary directors of nonprofit organizations that depend on municipal funding, during their terms of office.)

> 12. INFORMAL ACTION.   Any action required by law to be taken at a meeting of the directors, or any action that may be taken at a meeting of directors, may be taken without a meeting if a consent in writing, setting forth the action so taken shall be signed by *all* the directors.

> 13. PARLIAMENTARY GUIDE.   At all meetings of the board and the membership, *Robert's Rules of Order* (latest edition) shall apply.

The commonly cited rights, powers, and responsibilities of nonprofit corporation boards of directors are listed below.[11] Since practice varies widely among these organizations, the list should be regarded as representative rather than all-inclusive. In practice, of course, each NPO tailors its own board responsibilities to meet its needs.

Communications.   Ensure that regular channels of communication are established, including:

Regularly scheduled and planned conferences between the CAO and the CEO, the CAO and other board members (e.g., officers and committee chairpersons)

Participation of staff members on appropriate committees

Procedures for the timely and effective reporting of staff opinions and recommendations to the board, as well as board opinions and decisions to the staff

Inviting clients, nonboard members, and nonagency or organizational individuals and groups to board or committee meetings or other types of board-sponsored assemblies to explore and develop approaches to common concerns

Membership

Approve by-laws changes.

Approve contracts or other proposals for submission to member meetings.

Approve reports to members.

Approve the agenda for the conduct of the annual meeting.

Financial

Solicit contributions and donations.

Approve the annual budget.

Monitor the financial affairs of the organization, setting policy or taking action to ensure the fiscal integrity of the organization.

Policies, Objectives, and Plans

Approve the annual plan of operations.

Approve policies for the organization.

Develop and approve long-range plan of growth and development for the organization.

Approve specific important projects.

Approve any significant departure from established plans or policy.

Receive and pass on committee or other planning body recommendations.

Ensure that program objectives are assigned to the proper planning or implementing subgroups.

Where applicable, bring other community groups into the planning and decision-making process.

Approve contracts binding on the organization.

Approve major changes in the organization's organization or structure.

Approve broad plans of action.

Management

Provide for the orderly succession to the post of chief executive officer (CEO).

Select the chief administrative officer (CAO).

Define the duties and limits of authority and responsibility for the CEO, CAO, officers, and major committee chairpersons.

Select other counseling personnel to and for the board.

Authorize officers or board agents to enter into contracts or to sign other written instruments and to take financial actions.

Approve the plan, form, and amount of management compensation, that is, salaries, bonuses, vacation, travel, and so on.

Appraise the performance of the management and executive team.

Approve the form and amount of compensation for board or officers.

Approve programs for management development.

Provide advice and consultation to management on matters within the perview of the board's responsibilities.

Employee Relations

Approve contracts with and between any unions involved with the organization.

Approve any employee benefit plans.

Control

Identify types of information needed by the board to analyze effectively the non-profit corporation's directions and objective achievement. Arrange for adequate and timely flow of this information.

Review and assess the organization's performance against objectives, resources, plans, policies, and services rendered.

Inquire into causes of major "shortfalls" in achievement.

Identify obstacles, sense change needs, propose new directions or goals.

Board of Directors

Recruit new members; make nominations for the board.

Ensure, in so far as possible, adequate cross-sectional representation of board membership.

Motivate board members to accept positions of leadership and responsibility.

Remove noncontributors from the board.

Elect the board's agent (usually the CEO).

Appoint, change, or abolish committees of the board.

Define powers and responsibilities of committees of the board.

Appoint, compensate outside auditors or monitors.

Approve contracts, terms for professional services required by and for the board.

Maintain relations with pressure or lobby groups.

Accountability

There is strong concurrence here that accountability is one area that no board can properly delegate. As one organization stated in its director's guide, "The board is not expected to do all the thinking for the organization; however, it must assume responsibility for the final decisions and results."

Although in theory it may be possible for the board to manage and direct all the many phases of corporation business, in practice the board uses its conferred right to delegate much of its power to its "agents" to act in its stead, for instance, officers or committee chairpersons. It must delegate these powers in an orderly, logical way, usually by:

1. Carefully outlining which of its powers it wishes to delegate, to whom, with what reservations and for how long

2. Creating the necessary executive structure and organization to use effectively the delegated powers and to fulfill the responsible posts

What powers do boards actually reserve? This varies from organization to organization, with each board deciding how much to delegate depending on its areas or sector of operations, the size of the board, and the financial state of the organization.

There are certain patterns concerning this area that emerge even from comparing NPOs that are quite dissimilar in outward organization. The nonprofit board is likely to reserve power based on all or some of the following reasons:

1. Statute, charter, or by-laws may forbid delegation in certain areas, such as changes in the by-laws or articles of incorporation
2. Long-range commitments
3. Possible conflict-of-interest situations
4. Structural or organizational changes
5. Contracts or various forms of compensation
6. Changes to basic corporate or organization objectives, goals, or reasons for formation
7. Fiscal integrity of the organization

A chart of the board's delegated corporate powers and responsibility appears in Figure 10.1.

The Good Board

What the "good" board does is the subject of a brief checklist adapted and reprinted by permission of the National Information Bureau from *The Volunteer Board Member in Philanthropy:*[12]

What a Good Board Does

Most board members know the answer, but here is a brief checklist:

1. It *inspires* and *leads.* All three groups—contributors, intended beneficiaries, and the public—need knowledgeable and dedicated leadership.
2. It recognizes that it needs a devoted and energetic staff head as a partner. It formulates with care the job qualifications required and selects the best person

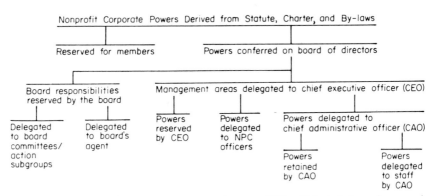

Figure 10.1. Delegated corporate power and responsibility. (*Adapted from Juran and Louden.*)

available. It then calls upon him or her to lead the organization jointly with it and to serve as administrator of its staff and program.

This selection of the staff head is generally the most important decision any board makes. One word of caution: The rapid growth of national philanthropy into big business, with billions of dollars in assets, has attracted not only dedicated staff persons but also promoters more interested in personal gain, prestige, or aggrandizement than in service to society.

Such promoters specialize in maintaining a plausible front of earnest devotion; in taking credit for the achievements of others; in filling their boards with "letterhead" trustees who are prominent but relatively inactive; and in telling the boards only what they want them to hear. Such individuals can demoralize even an excellent organization within a short period of time, while still maintaining a facade of philanthropic respectability to the contributing public.

3. Having employed its staff head, the board *consults* with, *advises,* supervises, encourages, and (when in error) corrects the new appointee. Many an inexperienced staff head has blossomed into a first-class administrative executive under the wise and patient guidance of conscientious board members. If necessary, after careful deliberation, the board terminates the staff head's employment in a fair manner.

4. It identifies *priority needs,* both short-term and long-term goals, and defines what it as a volunteer organization should and should not attempt to do.

5. It ensures that its agency *cooperates* wisely with other groups, governmental and voluntary, that are working toward the same or similar goals. Our society is interdependent; few alert organizations are content to work in an isolated and tightly compartmentalized world of their own.

6. It encourages *experimentation* to find better methods to achieve its goal. Some believe, in fact, that the primary role of voluntary philanthropy should be the use of risk capital for courageous pioneering. Most human institutions, however, including philanthropic ones, have an almost overwhelming tendency toward "hardening of the arteries and organizational senility." A good board avoids this danger.

7. It establishes an orderly procedure for the *selection* of new board members and for their orientation and training. A number of boards establish an automatic rotation system to ensure infusion of "new blood" and the dropping of inactive members. Some agencies provide introductory board member manuals and some communities hold annual institutes to aid new and old board members.

Above all, a good board avoids "letterhead" trustees, that is, prominent individuals who "lend" their names for prestige or fund-raising purposes without undertaking to really serve. Such men and women fly under false colors, betray the public trust, and not infrequently become unwitting fronts for rackets in philanthropy.

8. It searches out and uses *sources of information and guidance* that may help it to improve the discharge of its responsibilities. Local community health and welfare councils or their equivalent may supply vital local information; national associations in almost every field publish materials, hold regional or national conferences, and provide personnel and advisory services; special studies and reports are continuously being issued by voluntary or governmental sources; and accrediting agencies help in the evaluation of an agency's performance.

9. A good board *organizes itself* and its staff for optimum production. To cite a few of the methods:

   a. It selects its officers with care.

   b. Meetings of the board and/or executive committee are regular and total, generally not less than five per year.

c. Meeting agendas are sharply focused.

d. Decisions are made by majority vote, after due deliberation, instead of awaiting 100 percent agreement.

e. The staff head is assigned responsibility for administration under the policy guidance of the board.

f. Subcommittees are appointed, in the case of large agencies, with appropriate subordinate staff assignments.

g. Promotion and fund-raising are supervised.

h. A full and honest report of both successes and failures is made to the public each year.

i. An independent auditor is retained to ensure that financial matters are properly handled and recorded.

j. An annual budget is adopted to translate program plans into financial terms and to provide the board with needed control of expenditures by staff.

Effective Boards of Directors

The Association of Governing Boards of Colleges and Universities lists the characteristics of effective boards to the extent that they possess the following characteristics[13]:

Diversity. The board as a whole contains differences in talents, skills, experience, interests, and social background.

Structure. The board is organized in such a way that individuals and committees assume a proper, active role in its functions.

Member involvement. Members demonstrate a high degree of interest in their role and responsibilities and are genuinely concerned about the agency's problems and prospects.

Knowledge. Members are well informed about the agency's operation and the social forces that are affecting service delivery.

Rapport. Members of the board have mutual respect for each other regardless of differences of opinion, and maintain a productive working relationship with one another.

Sensitivity. The board is representative of, and sensitive to, different constituencies and viewpoints.

Sense of priorities. Board members are concerned with important and long-range issues, not trivial matters.

Direction. The president is respected, and is strong and skilled in making certain that various points of view are expressed and in reaching satisfactory decisions.

Strength. The board is strong enough to achieve effective policy decisions.

Financial support. The board contains a reasonable number of members who obtain financial support for the agency.

Board–executive director relationships. There is a productive working relationship between the executive director and board members.

Accomplishment. The board has a genuine sense of progress and achievement, and members gain satisfaction from their services.

The Board's Organization

The nonprofit organization, its board of directors, and the board's organization all evolve simultaneously. In the beginning, the board meets frequently and in full. Later, as the organization grows, the board begins to subdivide itself into smaller, more specific subgroups to deal with growth functions more efficiently.

The subgroup formed before others most often is the executive committee (EC). Usually composed of the elected board officers, plus one or two board members at large, the EC has the authority to exercise all or most of the board's powers between full meetings of the board. Its chairperson is usually the chief executive officer.

The by-laws phraseology that explains the duties, responsibilities, and authority of the EC will often appear as follows:

> EXECUTIVE COMMITTEE.   The executive committee shall be constituted of the elected officers of the organization, plus a member at large elected by the directors, who will hold office until their successors are duly elected.
>
> The chief executive officer shall serve as chairperson of the executive committee.
>
> The executive committee shall exercise in the intervals between meetings of the board of directors all the powers of the board that may lawfully be delegated in the management of the affairs of the corporation or such lesser powers as may be specified from time to time by vote of the directors.
>
> It shall meet at least monthly and/or at the call of the chairperson.
>
> A majority of the members of the executive committee shall constitute a quorum.
>
> All actions of the executive committee shall be subject to review by the board of directors, and the executive committee shall report all its actions to the board.

There are a number of advantages for having an active executive committee, including:

1. Making it possible for a large board to meet bimonthly or quarterly
2. Allowing for the prompt handling of important decisions that must be made between board meetings
3. Delegating housekeeping matters to the EC, thus cleaning up the agenda for the full board meeting
4. Requiring the EC to "predigest" detailed or cumbersome areas requiring board decisions or actions
5. Requiring the EC to monitor important negotiations, or other important developmental areas, with regular reports to the board followed by its final action

The use of executive committees by nonprofit organizations is very widespread, as a type of subboard of directors, empowered to exercise all of the power of the board between meetings of the body. It executes the policies of the board in *routine* matters between meetings, lacking the power to take extraordinary or drastic action at its own discretion. The executive committee can act validly only within the limits of its intended purpose—interim supervision of the organization between meetings of the board of directors.

The by-laws of the organization should spell out clearly the powers of the executive committee and whether it has the board's approval to take action in such matters as changing officers, amending the by-laws, expelling or changing committee members or chairpersons, or changing the staff of the organization. Any attempts by the executive committee to usurp the control of the board are uniformly condemned by law and standard practice of management. From a legal point of view, any such attempt to engage in activities beyond its enumerate powers would be a nullity. From a practical standpoint, it would be a wasted effort if it is anticipated that anyone would disagree with the action taken.

The executive committee is, in effect, the organization's "cabinet," keeping operations in line with board decisions, handling the week-to-week problems of management and administration, and coordinating the efforts of the organization's leadership—officers, committee chairpersons, and staff. The following practices have evolved relative to the operations of the "cabinet" of the nonprofit organization, the executive committee:

1. All operations of the organization are represented. This does not always mean directly, since a vice president may represent several committees.

2. The cabinet's membership is kept small enough to ensure that operations are effective and responsive to needs.

3. Actions of the cabinet are promptly communicated to all those in the organization who are directly affected.

4. Members of the cabinet *must* attend its meetings.

5. Executive committee members prepare for these meetings in a variety of ways, including: conferences with chairpersons; attendance at committee meetings; reviewing communications; telephoning chairpersons or other representatives.

6. When matters of unusual importance are scheduled for consideration, appropriate committee chairpersons are invited to the meeting. Committee chairpersons may also request a hearing at executive committee meetings, especially if the committee is dissatisfied with some aspect of its endeavor.

7. The executive committee may plan and conduct workshops from time to time during which all the officers and committee chairpersons can see and review the overall workings of the organization. Such workshops should include training in the techniques of management and administration for nonprofit organizations in general, and this one in particular.

Reins on the Executive Committee

To prevent disturbing problems as a result of executive committees overstepping their bounds in relation to the board, a clear understanding of the committee's role and authority, in general or on specific matters, should be made by the board. The board must decide in all cases whether the executive committee's escalating authority in a specific matter is to include

1. Gathering information

2. Preparing recommendations

3. Taking interim action subject to ratification by the board

4. Taking irrevocable action on its own

The safest course is for the board always to require regular reports from the executive committee and to reserve to itself final ratification.

Dealing with Dissidents

At one time or other, every board must deal with members who, for one reason or another, cause disharmony or actual trouble. They may range from the "nitpicker" to the "maverick"—the nitpicker pouncing on the smallest of items to make a point (usually oblivious of the major programs or thrust of the organization) and the maverick being the chronic critic and dissenter.

How does the board deal with dissent? How can occasional negativism be converted to positive results? How can "nitpickers" and "mavericks" be distinguished from "devil's advocates" using such a role to prod a comfortable or complacent board into action? How does the staff determine which approach is operating and how to handle it?

First, we should remember that dissent is not always bad; in fact, a board whose meetings are always placid and where agenda items are unanimous in favor should take a long careful look at itself to ensure that this does not represent trouble of a different nature—a controlled board or one that does not in fact represent all the interests of its constituency. The dissident board member often plays a constructive role by keeping the board from becoming complacent. Such a member may also prompt other directors to examine the basic soundness of their own positions.[14]

It is important, however, to distinguish between compulsive dissidents, whose actions may reflect emotional problems, and the occasional dissidents. The latter use such behavior to needle boards or staff into making what they feel are needed changes.

Another positive role played by occasionally dissident board members is to consolidate the support of other members. This is constructive in itself if it unites a divided board—actually it is a form of the "devil's advocate" role. Not only does this cause other board members to define their personal positions on the issue(s) under discussion, but it keeps chairpersons on their toes—to recognize negativism when confronted with it.

A more destructive role, however, can be played by directors who are using the dissident role for the sake of power alone or to elicit favors or concessions from other board members. Unfortunately, it is often difficult to spot such gamesmanship—at least until a great deal of damage has been done to the organization. One nonprofit organization experienced the following "dissident" game plan to take over the organization.

At the urgent request of the professional staff director, the organization's treasurer was replaced. The officer was a busy corporate executive who had not had time to organize the books to keep pace with the organization's growth and development. Unfortunately, an ambitious director, who used volunteer board memberships as social stepping stones, seized this opportunity to volunteer for the position. During the next year, the new treasurer did indeed improve the bookkeeping—all the while using the position to gather the "power" of the organization around the office of treasurer. Soon, the professional director's hands were tied on fiscal matters because all such matters had to have prior approval of the finance committee, of which the treasurer was chairperson. Because the treasurer was also a member of the executive committee, the individual was able to use this input to begin undermining the position of the professional director—who was soon largely excluded from the meetings.

A constant stream of negative nitpicking about the staff and the way things were being run—all delivered out of the director's hearing—continued to undermine the director's position and respect from the board, and went unchallenged by the board because it was composed almost entirely of good friends, too chummy to ask the penetrating questions needed.

Contrary to basic management practice, the professional director was never advised of the "problems" being heard by other directors. Since the board were all good friends, lived in the same neighborhoods, were members of the same clubs, and had financial ties with one another, to have given the professional director a chance to hear and respond to what were, in effect, charges being made against him would have resulted in the very unpleasant necessity of choosing to believe either a successful professional director or an ambitious, but carping, friend. It was easier to avoid any resolution by simply terminating the professional director's contract.

Puzzled and perplexed at how and why it had become so hard to get anything done, the professional director agreed. At the next board meeting, when discussing a successor to the former executive director, a friend casually suggested the treasurer for the post—"on an interim basis." With a convincing show of modesty, the treasurer thanked the board for its confidence and agreed to "do everything in my power to get this organization on its feet again and moving in the right direction." With smiles all around, the board voted to appoint its treasurer to the post and congratulated itself on having such a selfless, dedicated member.

A period of calm settled over the organization, since the spurious reports of mismanagement had stopped. Unfortunately, although an effective dissident gamesman in board intrigue, the new executive director knew very little about management in general, or about the actual public services the organization was in business to provide. Soon the organization's programs faltered as the evidence mounted that it did not have professional direction from either the board or the new director. Some months later, the executive director resigned "for personal reasons." The organization floundered and went through a lengthy "reevaluation" by its board.

The problems now faced by this organization included the loss of several years of growth and development, many members, and the creation of disillusionment in its member organizations and constituency, which could have been avoided if it had originally constituted itself on a broader base representing the entire community it served, thus eliminating the chummy attitude that prevented board members from asking searching questions on policy matters for fear of offending their friends. Such a board was a pushover for an ambitious, but unprincipled director.

Leaders of nonprofit organizations across the country offer the following as major recommendations on how to cope with board dissidents having negative effects on the organizations:

1. Let them have enough rope, and they will hang themselves.

2. Recognize that many dissidents are hungry for recognition. Give them an assignment or position that will satisfy such an appetite.

3. Bide your time—many rebels eventually become a part of the organization's establishment.

4. If possible, don't let a dissident catch your other board members by surprise. If you see trouble coming, quietly let some of the key members know it in advance of the meeting.

5. Keep your meeting agenda lean—a way of heading off those dissenters who like to agonize over trivial items.[15]

Use the Peer Group

Most senior staff members of nonprofit organizations agree that the most effective means of dealing with the board dissident is to let their peers on the board do the job. One executive said to let the "big guns" on the board deliver a crushing—even humiliating—defeat to the chronic dissidents. However, how you deal with a coalition of big guns who are themselves causing the trouble ("Do it our way or we won't play") is another question—one that is almost impossible to answer with a generalization.

Many mavericks, it will turn out, are self-appointed representatives of small cliques of members. Others rise to the dissident role on the basis of a faction in the membership that feels its opinions are not being given sufficient attention. Those representing "constituencies" obviously pose bigger problems than those speaking solely for themselves.

Those dissidents representing only themselves can often be "disarmed" by giving them other ego satisfactions. Often, after a few board meetings these mavericks will tend to wind down and lose much of their aggressiveness.

Board members with "backers" not on the board should be given time to express their views. Thought should be given to meeting with them and their group separately to try and identify the real reasons for their unhappiness. Perhaps there are actions that the board should take to redress these "wrongs" and smooth the ruffled feathers. At any rate, no matter what the ultimate evaluation, it will certainly help to try and understand what all the furor is about and why the positions are being taken by this group of members.

How should your staff handle the board member(s) they feel "are out to get them?" One senior nonprofit staff director indicated that "Yes, in fact there is a maverick out to get me now." The executive went on to explain the confrontation and the strategy for handling it:

> They (the dissident's clique) are using the same license as a legislator or a court official in that they can say and do virtually anything under the protection of their membership, including half-truths and innuendoes, while I cannot return their attacks.
>
> The only way you can handle this is to judge the effectiveness of the persons and grin and bear it. If it gets to be a potential danger, then you have to call out your own mob. I like to use the method of creating a "credibility gap" around the main person who is out to get me. I try to get to the prime people before he does so that when he comes and starts his story, they have already been prepared and his credibility gap is working against him.
>
> Also, in a situation where I am confronted by him on a face-to-face basis, I use the technique of "Yes, but." I agree with some of the points that he states whenever possible, then I go on to bring out other facts that undercut his arguments.[16]

Some nonprofit organization executives indicate that they face the direct challenge of troublemakers by meeting privately with them to try to reach a livable understanding. Since most boards have sizable memberships, it is the rare dissident who has been able to hound an executive out of a job. As the previous discussion indicates, however, it is possible if the board itself is a clique that is so close it cannot bring itself to question too closely a maverick member. Typically, the nonprofit professional executive manages to command enough respect among the majority of board members to fend off marauding mavericks or at least to neutralize them when their attacks become too personal.

How can professional staff managers improve their relations with their boards, and their effectiveness as hired guides? One of the best and most forceful answers was provided by Ellis E. Meredith, Executive Vice President of the American Apparel Manufacturers Association, Inc.:

"Be candid, do your best, and convince your voluntary leadership that your objectives are the same as theirs, although your contributions are different."[17]

The Ideal Director

The preceding discussion should leave no doubt in your mind as to the importance of selecting the right directors for your organization—usually a duty first undertaken by the nominating committee. Two major reasons for this importance are immediately evident:

1. The board serves as the official policymaker for the organization—and its voice to the community.
2. Every director should be viewed as a potential officer—and chairperson.

The following guidelines were compiled from a variety of sources and personal experience, but many were selected from *Principles of Association Management,* which has an excellent chapter entitled the Role of Board Members and the President.[18] Guidelines for selecting the "ideal director" include:

1. Is the candidate a recognized leader who commands the respect of both colleagues and the public?

2. Is the board candidate interested in more than the honor of being on the board? Selection to the board is not merely a reward for past services, but represents a serious commitment to serve the organization that makes the honor possible.

3. Does the candidate, as a leader, have the time to devote to leading and directing the affairs of the organization? The candidate should be able to arrange his or her own business or personal affairs to allow time to apply to the demanding role of leadership. The nominating committee should secure an advance commitment that the candidate will give the necessary time. Remember, too, the provision in most by-laws that automatically removes a director from the board after missing so many meetings. The average is three unexcused absences.

4. Does the candidate's health permit the investment of energy required to serve as a successful director? Directors must possess a high level of mental and physical energy.

5. Will the candidate be able and willing to assume and carry out important duties for the organization, if called upon to do so?

6. Will the candidate be able to work effectively with the organization's professional executive? The two individuals must be able to communicate effectively and get along with each other. This also applies to the rest of the board.

7. Has the candidate demonstrated his or her ability and loyalty by working on committees or special projects for the organization? What has been the "track record" in such endeavors?

8. Can the individual accept the limelight graciously without becoming pompous or self-centered and tolerate the inevitable criticism in organizations that are changing, growing, or considering new courses of action? Or is popularity more important to the individual than judgment or integrity? How will the candidate handle or override the usual dissident minority, which can immobilize the entire organization if its leaders are not willing to move ahead with what they believe to be best for the entire group?

9. Can the candidate communicate effectively and frequently? A deep thinker or Machiavellian-type personality who cannot or will not communicate is not likely to contribute positively to the role of director.

10. Will or can the candidate subordinate regional, personal, or business biases for the good of the entire organization? The director cannot represent or plead for special interests over the good of the entire organization. This is not to say that past experience may not be reflected in special feelings for a "constituency," only that the interests of the organization must be placed first—before that of any faction or subdivision. There *cannot* be any concern over hidden motives. If there is, such a

director or candidate has not been able to subordinate individual interests to the good of the organization.

11. Does the candidate's personal conduct reflect favorably on the group? Since directors represent the group at times other than meetings, candidates known for unorthodox or even notorious behavior may prove irritating or embarrassing to the organization.

12. If the prospective director is married, will the spouse be helpful or resentful? The opposition of a spouse to a position of leadership and social commitment can render an otherwise effective director almost worthless to the organization.

13. Will the prospective director be willing to step down graciously after the term of office? Does he or she have potential for the organization in the role of "elder sage" for the group following the term of office?

Can we accurately identify the attributes of a perfect board member? The National Information Bureau, in *The Volunteer Board Member in Philanthropy*,[19] says that the question is academic "because all human beings are a combination of strength and of weaknesses." A good board, however, "blends imperfect human beings into an effective working team," and "certain attitudes" can be identified that effective board members maintain. According to the National Information Bureau good board members

1. Are dedicated to helping others and modest in the light of their responsibilities as a board member

2. Approach their responsibilities in the spirit of a trustee on behalf of contributors, their intended beneficiaries, and the public at large

3. Stand up for their convictions, even at the cost of misunderstanding or disapproval in their business or social lives

4. Back up other board members and staff rising to their defense when they are unjustly criticized or attacked

5. Treat staff as partners in a high calling, while maintaining overall supervision and control

6. Avoid being overawed by others on the board, whether they be executive staff; tycoons of business, labor, or society; professionals in social work, education, medicine, and so on

7. Welcome information and the best available advice, but reserve the right to arrive at decisions on the basis of their own judgment

8. Respect the right of other board members and of staff to disagree with them and to have a fair hearing of their points of view

9. Accept as routine that decisions must be made by majority vote and will at times go against them

10. Criticize, when necessary, in a constructive way; if possible suggesting an alternative course

11. Recognize that their time and energy are limited and that overcommitment may prove self-defeating

12. Endeavor to keep disagreements and controversies impersonal and to promote unity

13. Maintain loyalty to their agency, within a higher loyalty to the welfare of the community and humanity as a whole

Notes

1. Samuel B. Shapiro, Why the Chief Paid Executive Should Be Called President, *Association Management,* May 1976, p. 30.

2. Howard L. Oleck, *Nonprofit Corporations, Organizations, and Associations,* Prentice-Hall, Englewood Cliffs, N.J., 1980, p. 596.

3. Brian O'Connell, *The Board Member's Book: Making a Difference in Voluntary Organizations,* The Foundation Center, New York, 1985, p. 43.

4. National Information Bureau, *The Volunteer Board Member in Philanthropy,* New York, 1975, p. 7.

5. Child Welfare League of America, *Guide for Board Organization in Social Agencies,* New York, 1975, p. 7.

6. J. M. Juran and J. Keith Louden, *The Corporate Director,* American Management Association, New York, 1966, passim.

7. Child Welfare League, *Guide for Board Organization,* p. 6.

8. Oleck, *Nonprofit Corporations,* pp. 503–536.

9. Carl A. Modecki, Should Your Board Meetings Be Open to the Public? *Association Management,* June 1976, p. 60.

10. Ibid., p. 61.

11. Adapted from Juran and Louden, *The Corporate Director,* passim.

12. National Information Bureau, *The Volunteer Board Member in Philanthropy,* pp. 8–10.

13. Association of Governing Boards of Colleges and Universities, *AGB Notes,* vol. 2, February 1974.

14. How to Get Along with the Dissidents on Your Board, *Association Management,* December 1973, pp. 35–39.

15. Ibid., p. 37.

16. Ibid., p. 37.

17. Ibid., p. 39.

18. American Society of Association Executives and Chamber of Commerce of the United States, *Principles of Association Management,* 1975, p. 91.

19. National Information Bureau, *The Volunteer Board Member in Philantropy,* pp. 19–20.

Suggested Reading

Child Welfare League of America, *Guide for Board Organization in Social Agencies,* New York, 1975.

Conrad, William, and William Glenn, *The Effective Voluntary Board of Directors,* Swallow Press, Chicago, 1976.

Hanson, Pauline L., and Carolyn T. Marmaduke, *The Board Member: Decision Maker for the Non-Profit Corporation,* Han/Mar Publications, Sacramento, Calif., 1972.

National Information Bureau, *The Volunteer Board Member in Philanthropy,* New York, 1975.

O'Connell, Brian, *The Board Member's Book,* The Foundation Center, New York, 1985.

Oleck, Howard L., *Nonprofit Corporations, Organizations, and Associations,* Prentice-Hall, Englewood Cliffs, N.J., 1980.

11

Officers of the Nonprofit Organization

Tracy D. Connors
Consultant

The performance of duty was very important to the Romans, who used the word "officium" to convey the meaning of a duty or function assigned to or assumed by someone. By extension, it also came to mean the place where these duties were carried out and the administrative personnel working in such a place. One who holds an office of authority or trust in an organization, who is responsible for performing a duty, is also called an "officer."

Some nonprofit organizations tend to assume that all their by-laws need to do regarding their officers is to name them, as the following excerpt indicates:

ARTICLE V: *Officers*

1.. The officers of the organization shall be a president, not more than three vice presidents, recording and corresponding secretaries, and a treasurer, who shall assume their duties upon election by the board of directors from among its members for a term of one year and until their successors are duly elected and qualified.

2.. The duties of the officers shall be such as usually pertain to their respective offices or as are respectively prescribed and assigned to them by the board of directors.

In fact, a good set of by-laws needs to cover the subject in considerably more detail. There are a number of important meanings and considerations applying to the officers of a nonprofit organization that should be understood to minimize problems and to ensure that officers function at their best.

An "office" in a nonprofit corporation is a specific position of special trust and confidence, by which the holder is lawfully and practically invested with some portion of the organization's powers. These powers do not devolve from the board of directors, but from the owners—in this case, the members. Even if the officers of the particular organization are elected by the board, the power to do so originates with the membership. In any case, the officeholder is charged by the appointing group to excercise certain functions and is vested with the authority to do so.

These functions and authority are spelled out in the by-laws, and by accepting the office, the holder must devote such time and attention to the duties as are reasonably required to fulfill them.

An employee, however, is not considered an officer and holds no office. An "employee" is usually considered one who works a specified schedule of days or hours after being retained by an officer who determines the rate of compensation and exercises both control and leadership regarding the activities performed by the employee.

Although officers do have more independence, tenure, and authority than other employees, they are subject to control by both the membership and the board, carrying out the policies formulated by them. Officers *do not* own the corporation's assets, and must exercise good judgment and discretion in this and other areas. The officer is usually elected rather than appointed (or retained by contract), serves for the period fixed in the by-laws, and has a permanence of status (unless removed for cause by the electing or appointing group) not enjoyed by employees.

Most states have few if any statutes regarding the officers of nonprofit organizations, but guidance may be found by consulting the Ohio Revised Code, Section 1702.34, which goes into some detail regarding officers, listing their customary titles, and indicating that

1. Officers need not be trustees or directors.

2. One person may hold two or more offices. (Obviously, this is not good practice even though it is legal in Ohio.)

3. Officers must be elected annually unless otherwise indicated in the by-laws.

4. Their duties and responsibilities are determined by the electing or appointing group.

5. Vacancies in office holders may be filled by the same authority.

Minnesota statutes forbid the same person from holding the offices of president *and* vice president, or president *and* secretary. And, as pointed out by Oleck,[1] it also "allows the articles or by-laws to provide for ex officio membership of officers on the board of directors."

All nonprofit corporations have the power to appoint the officers they need, with the by-laws spelling out how many officers the organization needs, how and when they are selected, their titles, qualifications, terms of office, powers, duties, and compensation (if any). Corporations also have the power to remove these officers, usually for cause, but even without cause in some states. Before removing an officer without cause, an organization should consult state statutes and the by-laws to ensure that it holds this legal right. Otherwise, to do so would make the organization liable for a breach-of-contract suit. In Ohio, for example, an officer may be removed with or without cause by the electing or appointing authority, and an action for breach of contract by the ousted officer will not lie where the "contract" is supposedly grounded upon the general provisions contained in the articles of incorporation, regulations, or by-laws.

Office holders cannot place themselves above the criticism of the members or enact any rules or regulations that would suppress member protests or other action against the officers.

Although there is a tendency to view the president or chief executive officer (CEO) of the nonprofit corporation as the overall manager of the corporation, no one officer, including the CEO, has the authority to act "individually" for the corporation. Officers are the agents of the corporation, acting under the guidance and direction of the board of directors, which is the managing and governing body of the corporation. If an officer acts beyond or without authority, in general, the corporation is not liable for the action(s). However, if the officer who did not reveal the identity of his principal, "the corporation," had the apparent authority to enter into the particular transaction, the corporation (as well as the adventuresome officer) may be held accountable to the injured third party. In addition, if the officer acts in an official way without revealing that he or she is acting as an agent for the corporation, then he or she is personally liable for the consequences. "No officer can commit a corporation to something that its charter does not authorize," Oleck observes, "nor can the corporation ratify such an ultra vires act."[2]

As long as the officers (or the directors) are not guilty of bad faith or fraud, the law, in general, holds them free from liability incurred by the corporation. This will not allow them, however, to act carelessly or with "gross stupidity," to ignore the by-laws, or to fail to take reasonable precautions dictated by common sense, and still remain not liable. And it should be stressed here that a written record of any matter in which this issue may be raised should be carefully prepared and kept. In it, the officer or director should ensure that his or her views and acts indicating good faith and judgment be recorded. Officers having responsibility for monies of the corporation also have increased liability as agents for the corporation. In short, do not take these duties lightly, but carry out the duties of these offices using good practice in the care of and accounting for these funds.

Powers and Duties of Nonprofit Corporation Officers

The by-laws and the charter should spell out precisely the powers and duties of all the officers. Many states also specify certain duties that must be performed by certain officers, for instance, the filing of certain reports or the signing of certain documents. These statutory duties should be outlined so that they are not overlooked by a new group of incoming officers.

The following summary of the duties and responsibilities of the usual officers found in nonprofit organizations was adapted, in part, from the *Model Nonprofit Corporation Act,* prepared by the Committee on Corporate Laws of the American Bar Association.[3]

THE PRESIDENT/CHAIRPERSON. The president shall be the principal executive officer of the corporation and shall in general supervise and control all of the business and affairs of the corporation.

He shall preside at all meetings of the members and of the board of directors.

He may sign, with the secretary or any other proper officer of the corporation authorized by the board of directors, any deeds, mortages, bonds, contracts, or other instruments that the board of directors has authorized to be executed, except in cases where the signing and execution thereof shall be expressly delegated by the board of directors or by these by-laws or by statute to some other officer or agent of the corporation.

In general he shall perform all duties incident to the office of president and such other duties as may be prescribed by the board of directors from time to time.

The president usually has general management powers and may do what is reasonably necessary to fulfill this responsibility. However, these powers do not authorize the borrowing of money or the issuance of notes for the corporation—except as previously authorized by the board of directors. The management powers of the president of a nonprofit corporation are less than those of a president of a profit-making corporation.

THE VICE PRESIDENT(s). In the absence of the president or in event of his inability or refusal to act, the vice president (or in the event there be more than one vice president, the vice presidents in the order of their election) shall perform the duties of the president, and when so acting, shall have all the powers of and be subject to all the restrictions upon the president.

Any vice president shall perform such other duties as from time to time may be assigned to him by the president or by the board of directors.

The vice president(s) rank below the president in order of their number (first vice president, second vice president) or in order of their election at the annual meeting of the members. The senior vice president assumes the functions, duties, and authority of the president, including the power to bind the organization by his acts if the by-laws provide this power for the office of president.

Ordinarily, the office of vice president has no other inherent powers. However, it is common practice to designate the vice presidents with functional titles, such as membership vice president, operations vice president, and so on, depending on the importance attached to these functions by the organization. Some organizations attach the term "executive" to an officer's title to indicate that the individual has general management duties and responsibilities and is paid for these duties, as in executive vice president or executive director.

THE SECRETARY. The secretary shall keep the minutes of the meetings of the members and of the board of directors in one or more books provided for that purpose; see that all notices are duly given in accordance with the provisions of these by-laws or as required by law; be custodian of the corporate records and of the seal of the corporation and see that the seal of the corporation is affixed to all documents, the execution of which on behalf of the corporation under its seal is duly authorized in accordance with the provisions of these by-laws.

The secretary shall keep a register of the post office address of each member, which shall be furnished to the secretary by such member; and in general perform all duties incident to the office of secretary and such other duties as from time to time may be assigned to him by the president and/or the board of directors.

As the above outlines, the secretary has the responsibility for the corporate records, minutes, and seal. In many cases the secretary's job is unglamorous and demanding of time and attention to detail. Yet it is a very important office, not only because proper records and minutes have legal significance, but because most granting organizations or institutions require data supplied by the secretary. If it is in error or evidences a sloppy or unprofessional approach to record keeping, it may cause an otherwise promising grant to be turned down.

A common practice is to divide the secretary's position into its separate functions of recording and corresponding. Another common approach is necessitated when "secretaries" of nonprofit organizations do not have the actual professional skills to perform the technical functions of recording or transcribing that are required. They may then deputize an associate or an employee (often their own secretary) to perform these functions. Regardless, they cannot delegate the responsibilities and duties of the office of secretary and will be held accountable for the performance of these duties whether or not they actually, physically, prepared the minutes or kept the records. In many instances, particularly in larger organizations, the secretary is also the general counsel or attorney for the corporation. The legal significance of the position as related above lends much credence to this choice. A similar approach, discussed in the following, is to elect assistant secretaries or assistant treasurers.

THE TREASURER.   The treasurer shall have charge and custody of and be responsible for all funds and securities of the corporation; receive and give receipts for moneys due and payable to the corporation from any source whatsoever, and deposit all such moneys in the name of the corporation in such banks, trust companies, or other depositaries as shall be selected in accordance with the provisions of Article _____ of these by-laws.

If required by the board of directors, the treasurer shall give a bond for the faithful discharge of his duties in such sum and with such surety or sureties as the board of directors shall determine.

In general, the treasurer shall perform all the duties incident to the office of treasurer and such other duties as from time to time may be assigned to him by the president or by the board of directors.

The treasurer shall report to the board of directors the financial standing of the organization whenever requested to do so and at least monthly, and make a full report to the organization's annual membership at each annual meeting.

The organization's account shall be audited at least annually or upon a change of the individual holding the office, by a nonmember certified public accountant approved by the board of directors.

The retiring treasurer shall within one month after the annual meeting (or a change in the office), deliver to the new treasurer all moneys, vouchers, books, and papers of the organization in his custody, with a supplemental report covering all transactions since the last report to the present.

The treasurer has the responsibility for the corporation's funds, disbursing them as directed by the board of directors or other constituted authority, and maintaining a strict accountability over them. The office has *no* other inherent power, or the power to make other financial transactions such as borrowing, drawing, or issuing funds, notes, checks, or other financial papers, unless it is authorized to do so by the board.

ASSISTANT TREASURERS AND ASSISTANT SECRETARIES.   If required by the board of directors, the assistant treasurer(s) shall give bonds for the faithful discharge of their duties in such sums and with such sureties as the board of directors shall determine.

The assistant treasurers [and/or assistant secretaries] in general, shall perform the following duties: _____ , and such other duties as shall be assigned to them by the treasurer, the secretary, or by the president, or the board of directors.

Many nonprofit corporations now find financial matters so complicated that efficiency and effectiveness dictate that additional, separate offices with distinct functions be created, including such offices as cashier, auditor, comptroller, or assistant treasurers. In each case, the by-laws should spell out exactly the duties, responsibilities, authority, and accountability of the individual position.

PROFESSIONAL MANAGERS.   The executive director/executive secretary shall be the principal administrative officer of the organization, charged with the duties of effectuating the purposes of the organization, carrying out the directives of the board of directors and the members, and performing any and all functions necessary and proper to assure that the policies, objectives, and aims of the organization are carried out.

The board of directors will fix reasonable compensation for the organization's executive and the staff of the organization, including entering into any contractual agreements regarding employment or fringe benefits of same.

The board shall employ an executive director (chief administrative officer) who shall have general charge, subject to the overall control and direction of the board, oversight and direction of the affairs and business of the organization, and shall be its responsible managing head.

The executive director shall have sole responsibility for the employment and discharge of staff.

The executive director shall have the authority to sign on behalf of the organization all necessary papers in connection with the routine administrative or legal matters of the organization, and shall have authority to make contracts and expenditures within the approved program and budget.

The executive director or a delegate shall be an advisory member, with full voting rights, of all committees of the organization. The executive director shall also be liaison between the board and staff and shall ensure that adequate and effective communications exist between them.

A growing number of nonprofit organizations now employ a professional manager, a full-time paid employee who supervises and is responsible for the daily routine business of the organization. Although usually retained on a contractual basis, the by-laws should clearly spell out the manager's duties, functions, and rights—including the procedures to be followed, if the need or desire arises, to replace the manager before the expiration time of the contract.

Many professional areas within the nonprofit sector are establishing high professional qualifications for the executives who manage nonprofit organizations in those areas. In fact, the work of the association executive has become a profession in itself, with its own high code of ethics and standards. For example, the American Society of Association Executives, with headquarters in Washington, D.C., offers many membership benefits and administers a training program leading to certification as a CAE, Certified Association Executive.

Unless the by-laws of the organization are specific to the contrary, the powers of the general manager, or executive director, are just about those of the corporation itself, including the right to hire employees, enter into contracts, obtain legal advice on corporation matters, and represent the organization to the public at large. These powers apply, however, only to routine business or organizational matters, not to major decision areas.

The qualifications of the nonprofit organization's professional manager will vary from category to category of NPO. However, the wise organization will try to spell out the qualifications in the by-laws, to find and compensate the individual with the highest qualifications it can—for in the long run, the professional manager will play a major role in the success or lack of same obtained by the organization.

With great accuracy, the Child Welfare League notes that the executive director "is a catalyst who carries authority," and that "perhaps the most important responsibility of the board is the selection of the executive director. The knowledge, skill, and leadership of the person employed will determine to a significant extent the agency's effectiveness and competence in carrying out its mission.

"The board must establish its expectations for the position, the qualifications, salary, and other benefits. A special committee of the board, composed of several officers and the chairperson of the service and personnel committees, should be appointed to screen and recommend candidates to the Board."[4]

In its *Guide for Board Organization in Social Agencies,* the Child Welfare League of America, Inc., explains that the general responsibilities of the executive director are as follows[5]:

To plan and participate in the formulation of policies and procedures

To organize the services of the agency and coordinate the work of board and staff

Directly or by delegation, to employ, direct, and discharge staff, provide for supervision and training, and give professional leadership in the field of agency service

To prepare budgets and reports and keep the board informed about the agency's operation and program

To represent the agency professionally in the community and to interpret the agency's services

To provide leadership to the board and assist board members in the performance of their roles as board members

The direct correlation between the chief administrative officer (CAO), the board, and the effectiveness of the organization's programs and operations should be recognized. The board has a continuing responsibility after hiring a CAO continually to evaluate the agency's organization and effectiveness under the CAO's leadership. This should include formal and informal procedures. The following approach is used by the Child Welfare League and is a good working model of how such an evaluation can be effectively carried out.[6]

Formal Evaluation

Biennially, the CEO, board committee chairpersons, and the CAO together take stock of the organization's operations, activities, and programs.

Individual committees (with staff participation) are assigned specific aspects of the organization's structure, administration, or programs for review.

Following this review, written reports are presented to the board. The reports include the following evaluations to assist in determining the quality of the organization's services:

Determine if there is compliance with the constitution or by-laws regarding membership, board operations, agency services, and the general responsibilities of the organization's leadership (board, officers, CAO, staff, and committee chairpersons), as noted and explained in the board manual. If not, determine if modifications are necessary to assure compliance and the meeting of responsibilities.

Analyze such board-related areas of operations and administration as:

Regularity of board attendance

Frequency of board and committee meetings

Participation of board and staff in committee work

Relationship of the board to the rest of the organization

Results of committee recommendations to the board

Availability, distribution, and form of minutes of board and committee meetings

Assess fiscal areas for:

Understanding of the board and staff about the financial picture and organization of the agency

The organization's relationship to resources for funding and referral sources

    Soundness of fiscal controls, accounting, cost accounting system

    Adequacy of financial reporting

Study service and program areas for:

    Quality and quantity of services provided

    Whether community trends and needs suggest modification in programs or services

    The people who are served and those who are not

    The adequacy of the statistical reporting system for each service, including its cost effectiveness

    The extent of board members' understanding of the organization's services and community needs

    The community's knowledge and relationships to the organization's programs

    The nature and extent of board and staff participation with public and voluntary groups who share the same goals and objectives or public services

Ensure proper and effective personnel administration by evaluating:

    Descriptions and qualifications for each job with specified salary ranges

    Personnel policies and a manual of the practices

    Examination of high rates of turnover

    Sufficient and skilled staff for its professional services and the management of the organization

    Annual staff review of the organization's objectives and goals

    Ease in communication among the staff and with the board

    An administrative chart that depicts all positions and delineates clear lines of authority

Informal Evaluation

In addition to the above formal evaluation process, there are many ways in which the board can continually evaluate both the agency's effectiveness and the CAO's performance. The ready criteria for such evaluation include:

    The quality and qualifications of the staff

    The CAO's participation in community matters relating to the service(s) provided by the NPO

    The CAO's knowledge of the field and ability to communicate with the board

    The way the agency works with other agencies and organizations in and with the community

    Evidence (or lack of same) of high staff morale and the rate of staff turnover

    Affiliations with the organization's national or state standard-setting organization's in the field or fields in which the organization is providing a public service

    Evaluations by professional consultants in the field

Tenure of the Chief Administrative Officer

As noted previously, the act of identifying and retaining the chief administrative officer is perhaps the most important single process undertaken by the board. In most cases, the process is successful and a well-qualified professional is found to administer the organization. However, even when the detailed and deliberate process outlined above is followed, there are times when a question will arise, prior to the expiration of the CAO's contract, about retaining the CAO. This situation should be given at least as much time and attention as the actual hiring process— and probably more.

Should this situation arise prior to a self-evaluation phase of the organization's annual operations, such a process should be instituted with emphasis on determining the causes of the questions regarding the CAO and their validity. Under these circumstances, the committee selected to secure this information and evaluation is usually the executive committee.

If this committee finds valid reasons for questioning the retention of the CAO, it should meet with the CAO and discuss as objectively as possible the specifics. In most cases, such fact finding and guidance serve to eliminate the problems. It is recommended, however, that the minutes of this meeting be carefully kept, including a detailed report of the findings of the executive committee, the explanations and discussion of the report, and the agreed upon course(s) of action developed during the meeting.

If the executive committee continues to believe, after this course of action, that the facts justify further action on its part, or that corrective measures are ineffectual, it has several courses of action that it may take, including:

Calling in a professional consultant, with the CAO's full knowledge (and, it is hoped, cooperation).

Offering the CAO a stated time (e.g., 3 or 6 months) to improve or correct the situation. Be sure that the guidance provided here is specific enough to allow accurate and objective evaluation as to whether or not the situation has in fact been corrected or improved.

Suggesting that the CAO submit a resignation to the board or agree to the termination of contract provisions prior to expiration of same that are included in the employment agreement

Recommending dismissal to the board. This step should be taken only after obtaining legal counsel regarding acceptable grounds for such action. Consult Oleck for further discussion of this step.[7]

Many NPOs retain their CAO through a contractual arrangement for a period of service (e.g., 3 or 5 years). The contract identifies specific objectives for the organization and details such important specifics as salary (including step or meritorious performance raises); vacation; benefits (medical, dental, travel, retirement plan, etc.); authority and responsibility; and the conditions for termination of the contract prior to its expiration date.

At the end of the contract period, the board reviews the CAO's performance and decides whether or not the contract is to be renewed or dropped. Since it is the board that employs the CAO on behalf of the members, it is the board to whom the CAO is ultimately responsible and which decides whether the CAO is to be retained or not. The CAO does not work for the CEO or the executive committee, but for the board of directors.

In its well-written *Guide for Board Organization in Social Agencies,* the Child Welfare League of America makes the following important observation regarding a precipitous discharge of an executive director:

> Except in instances of malfeasance, mental or physical illness that renders the executive director incapable of competent administration, or flagrant misrepresentation of the agency, precipitous discharge of an executive director is likely to be an indication of a board's failure to carry out its functions responsibly and consistently.[8]

Notes

1. Howard L. Oleck, *Non-Profit Corporations, Organizations, and Associations,* Prentice-Hall, Englewood Cliffs, N.J., 1980, p. 652.

2. Ibid., p. 658.

3. Committee on Corporate Laws of the American Bar Association, *Model Nonprofit Corporation Act,* Philadelphia, 1964, passim.

4. Child Welfare League of America, Inc., *Guide for Board Organization in Social Agencies,* New York, 1975, p. 25.

5. Ibid., p. 24.

6. Ibid., p. 30.

7. Oleck, *Non-Profit Corporations.*

8. Child Welfare League, *Guide for Board Organization,* p. 30.

12

Committees of the Nonprofit Organization

Tracy D. Connors

Consultant

A mutual protection society formed to guarantee that no one person can be held to blame for a botched...job that one man could have performed satisfactorily. RUSSELL BAKER

A group of the unfit, appointed by the unwilling, to do the unnecessary. HENRY COOKE

A cul-de-sac to which ideas are lured and then quietly strangled. JOHN A. LINCOLN

A group which succeeds in getting something done only when it consists of three members, one of whom happens to be sick and another absent. HENDRICK W. VAN LOON

Does any other form of organization take as much abuse and ridicule as the committee? The above are only a few of the broadsides that have been leveled against this "institution" of organization life. Yet fuss and fume as we may, we go right on appointing them in record numbers. The answer seems to be that committees, for all their problems and drawbacks, contribute to the overall health and vitality of our organizations in ways that are irreplaceable. Like them or not, they have been around for thousands of years, and are likely to be with us for a long time to come.

Definition

A committee "is a person or group of persons to whom the consideration, determination, or management of a matter is referred or entrusted. A subcommittee is a division of a committee, charged by the latter with consideration or determination of a part of the latter's functions."[1]

Even though many committees are given executive powers when they are appointed, fundamentally they are administrative bodies created for research and supervision. This distinction is often obscured by the fact that the recommendations, findings, or decisions are usually accepted and acted upon by the organization. It should be noted that when such committees are empowered in management or decision-making areas, they also accept group liability for such management or decisions—in other words, they can be used as an entity.[2]

Far more than with business corporations, the "work" of the nonprofit corporation is carried out through true, mutual cooperation between and with the members of the organization. In most cases, the "work" is performed by a committee, usually composed of volunteers or staff members and volunteers. It takes very little imagination to see that until and unless the committees function effectively, the quantity and quality of the "work" of the nonprofit organization—the public services that form the very basis and rationale for its existence—will achieve far less than could have or should have been achieved, given the trust and confidence placed in them by the public.

Appointing a committee may often seem an easy decision for a board or executive committee to make. The first step is to recognize the problem, the second step is to appoint a committee. Unfortunately, this does not usually solve the problem, and in the process of appointing a committee more damage or waste may occur than would have happened if the committee was never appointed at all. In short, before the knee-jerk reflex of "let's appoint a committee" takes over, consider all the various reasons why *not* to appoint a committee. The following is a concise review of many of the stronger considerations on the negative side regarding committees and their appointment.

1. Committees almost always cost more money or use more resources than having an individual perform the same functions.

2. Only a small percentage of any committee will be active members and provide meaningful leadership.

3. Committee decisions may represent a process that has not fairly examined the various points of view, or be a majority decision that pleases no one.

4. Committees can, and often are, slow-acting in addition to being costly. Unless adequate time is allowed for the committee process to function, it may ruin an important timetable of action for the organization. After everyone has had a say and the group still cannot make up its collective mind, it may decide to appoint subcommittees, a common tactic either to avoid a decision or to kill by neglect certain portions of a committee's mandated responsibility. In any case, the process is quite expensive in labor hours of both volunteers and staff.

5. In the opening rounds of the committee process, a power struggle may develop and need to be resolved as the group settles down into a "pecking order."

6. If committee members differ on the proper solution or course of action, a com-

promise decision may be forced through that does not answer the problems or questions, and indeed, may cause new ones.

Fortunately, there are substantial positive reasons for using the committee system to an organization's advantage. Committees can probably be used effectively when one or more of the following conditions or circumstances exist.[3]

1. If the organization's staff does not have the authority to conduct the actions it believes are necessary. Here the board or a committee appointed by it may provide the necessary input or coordination.

2. When all interests in the problem or situation need to be represented to ensure that a fair and equitable result is obtained.

3. If a variety of information is required before a decision can be reached.

4. When coordination in planning and development is required.

5. In situations where informed and motivated volunteers can be used effectively to implement plans, the education of the group through the committee process will lay a solid foundation for action once the process is completed and a decision(s) is reached.

6. In short, the committee process should be used when there is adequate time for it to function and when the process concerns itself with matters the solutions to which include communication, consolidation, motivation, coordination, representation, and unification. Committees, when properly constituted and led, can provide an organization with an invaluable source of integrated group judgment, increasing participation in the organization's activities, and cooperation in the execution of plans. The committee process also trains members and educates them in the ways and knowledge of the organization and ensures better continuity of thinking and action by the leadership.

Types and Categories of Committees in Nonprofit Organizations[4]

There are two basic kinds of committees used by most nonprofit organizations: special committees and standing committees. The "special committee" (or project or temporary committee) is constituted as the need arises. It has a specific problem or objective in mind and usually disbands following completion of the project or work assigned to it. The "standing committee" performs a continuing function or service and operates almost indefinitely. The standing committees attend to the regular administration or management of the organization's internal affairs and usually include the executive committee, budget committee, membership committee, finance committee, and public relations committee.

Committees serve four major purposes or functions for the nonprofit organization: administrative, liaison, study or problem, and project.

Administrative committees are concerned with the operating and organizational procedures of the organization. They may even include a "committee on committees" to deal with the appointment and rotation of committee members.

Liaison committees promote cooperative relations with other organizations, agencies, or interested groups. The work of these committees is taking on increased importance as the nonprofit sector understands the benefits of mutual cooperation and joint action.

The study or problem committee is appointed to study the feasibility of a new course of action, service, or activity, or to investigate and resolve some problem facing the organization. The value of this approach is in the committee's ability to focus its attention on one area, review the situation thoroughly, reach conclusions, and develop recommendations which are communicated to the group that formed it—and then dissolve, its function completed.

The project committee often picks up where the study committee leaves off, studying and recommending action on a particular organizational program or service—reviewing the problems and needs relative to the organization's program of work.

When a major problem has many facets and cannot be handled successfully by one appointed group, a committee may subdivide itself into several smaller subcommittees. Each subcommittee then deals with a specific aspect of the major problem, reporting back to the full committee (unless it is requested to report for the full committee to the board).

It is a fact that too frequent or indiscriminate use of ad hoc committees may reduce the effectiveness of standing committees, a problem to which boards should be alert. There is a tendency for members of an organization (particularly newer members, not familiar with the structure), when trying to deal with new business in meetings, to offer a motion "that a special committee be appointed" to study the problem or handle the situation. Usually such matters can be handled by one or more existing committees. Presiding officers or chairpersons should be alert to this, note the overlap in such an approach, and suggest that the motion be withdrawn. Unless this is done, more and more special committees erode the usefulness of the organization's standing committees and interfere with the planned and ongoing plans and programs of the organization. The following suggestions are offered to help prevent or overcome this problem:

1. If a member proposes a "special committee," the chairperson, or presiding officer, should suggest to the member that the matter be referred to the executive committee for assignment to the proper committee or other action group.

2. Adopt a policy that all new business must be presented *in writing*. This can be better understood by remembering meetings you have probably attended in which several different concepts of what the item really is are circulating among the attendees. Several more ideas on the solution may also be circulating, further adding to the confusion. Remember the old saying that "a problem well stated is half solved."

3. Most special committees function best when recommending solutions to problems, with the actual work or implementation of the solution going to the standing committee responsible for that area.

4. Dismiss each special or ad hoc committee as soon as the work it was charged to do is completed. Wrap things up with a final report properly prepared and submitted to the appointing person or body, action on the report assigned by that body, and the appropriate expressions of appreciation.

Size of Committees

Although the purpose for which the committee is formed generally determines the size of the appointed group, it should be remembered that the larger the committee, the harder it will be to coordinate, the longer it will usually take to deal with the problems before it, and the easier it will be for it to bog down in irrelevant issues.

Oleck points out that it is good policy to decide in advance the size, composition, type of members, functions, and other important aspects of every committee:

Experienced association and corporation experts affirm that most committees should be small and compact. Practical experience conflicts with the recurrent impulse to assign many members to each committee, in the hope that there will be strength in numbers. Appointing officers sometimes try to assign every member to some committee, in order to give every member something to do. This theory seldom works out successfully in practice.[5]

The average size of the committees serving most nonprofit organizations ranges from three to seven members. Basically, the smaller the committee, the faster the process and the better the product of that process. If you need fast action, appoint a small committee. If you have more time, and need the expression of more viewpoints and opinions and the development of thoughtful recommendations, use a larger committee.

Appointment of Committees

The fundamental power to delegate authority for action in the nonprofit organization rests with the board of directors. Often this power is delegated to the president or other officers, but the power itself remains with the board.

The importance of committees to the success of the organization's program of work dictates that much thought and preparation be invested in their appointment, a process that may, in some cases, have the effect of a contract. It follows, then, that the appointment should be in writing and that it clearly spell out all the important particulars of the committees purpose(s), powers, limitations, and any other directions that would be helpful in keeping it on track and in trying to ensure that it serves the purpose(s) for which it was appointed. Oleck offers these practical warnings on the appointment of committees:

1. Do not form committees merely to distribute titles or flatter members. The glamor soon wears off and skepticism develops.

2. Do not form committees merely for publicity purposes. The members ultimately will resent such deception.

3. Do not form committees merely to muzzle obstreperous members. This only gives them added material and vehicles for blocking action.

4. Do not form committees merely to bury unpleasant issues. Such issues always seem to arise again. It is better to try to solve them at once.[6]

The Chairperson

The key person in every committee operation is the chairperson. The smooth accomplishment of any action group of a nonprofit organization depends on and usually mirrors the chairperson's ability and effort. In most instances, the committees of the organization are instruments for change. This means that the chairperson's job is to help bring about the right change and the right place and at the right time. Seen in this light, the job of being chairperson demands many qualities, with being "convener" and "presider" among the lesser requirements of the position. When your organization is involved in the process of selecting its chairperson, it would be wise to keep in mind the following general responsibilities of chairpersons, which are outlined in *Principles of Association Management* and reprinted with permission.[7]

The chairman's responsibilities and duties can be considered in five general areas.

1. Planning the meetings and the methods by which objectives will be accomplished is the first responsibility of the chairman. Many meetings wander haphazardly because they are poorly planned. The steps of the agenda should lead naturally from one to another.

2. Conducting meetings, of course, is the job of the chairman. He stimulates thinking, bridges gaps, and elicits innovation. This responsibility is seldom overlooked though there is an unfortunate, but common, misconception that being chairman means parliamentarian or some sort of honorary, but passive, role. The chairman must exercise all the great characteristic skills of leadership, yet never draw attention to these skills.

3. Maintaining records and information is a greatly underrated part of the chairman's responsibility. Meeting minutes are generally boring. Nobody gets too excited about motions and reports. It is easy to see this task as busywork. But it only takes one incident for the chairman to see the importance of keeping minutes up to date and accurate and making sure that the written work will communicate accurately the work of the committee.

4. Getting action is up to the chairman. He must ensure that committee members move toward active participation. With overall objectives in mind, he must channel the efforts of multiple individuals into a unified thrust.

5. Evaluation of committee efforts is an important but often overlooked part of the chairman's responsibility. It may be as simple as saying, "We were supposed to do such-and-such and we did it—we succeeded." Whether the evaluation is sophisticated or off-the-cuff, the chairman has not completed his job until the committee has some feeling for its degree of accomplishment.

With these in mind, the board should also try to find a person who has the following qualifications to serve as chairperson:

1. The ability to communicate adequately with all the people and groups within the organization.

2. The ability to create the proper emotional environment and morale to stimulate the group to participate and to accept their share of the responsibility for the task(s) assigned to the committee. The chairperson, of course, should also be willing to accept responsibility for the performance of the committee as a whole.

3. A record of active participation and involvement in the organization's activities and programs. Don't forget to analyze his or her record of follow-through and completion of other projects.

4. The ability to direct and control the motion and direction of the group, but not a desire to dominate. This requires the ability to be a good listener and to direct, but not discourage, the free expression of ideas brought forward during the committee's meetings.

5. The ability to keep the group working and moving toward completion of the tasks assigned to it by the appointing officer or the board. The effective chairperson does not have to be prodded, but takes and holds the initiative.

6. The ability to command attention and to inspire others. This also includes the ability to identify tasks necessary for completion beyond the functioning group and the delegation of them to members capable of fulfilling them. A good chairperson also offers guidance and assistance to those newer members who, though inexperienced, are willing to accept challenging tasks.

7. An understanding of the organizational and power relationships within the organization.

8. The ability to use reports effectively to keep the organization up to date on the

progress of the committee. The chairperson should understand the importance of maintaining good communications with those from whom the committee needs support, cooperation, and coordination.

9. Above accusations of subjectivity—invulnerable to charges or even the appearance of making selfish or self-serving decisions relative to any issue that might be before the committee.

10. Able to accept both praise (with dignity) and criticism (with calm objectivity) for the actions of the group. The chairperson's relations with the "outside" often determine the success or failure of the committee's task.

11. Knowledge in and of the subject area involved. Whatever the subject, the chairperson should carry the prestige and have the respect and support of the committee's members.

12. Knowledge of and practical experience with the accepted techniques of problem solving, discussion, decision making, and group dynamics. The more important the committee and the more complicated the committee's assignment(s), the more helpful these will be.

13. The ability to recognize that the meeting is the proper place for any controversy and the "heat treatment" of ideas and proposals brought forward. This is the place, not in public, where all viewpoints should be expressed and examined constructively.

14. Personal availability to carry out the responsibilities involved. Enough personal time is a prime consideration. If the prospective chairperson does not have the resources it will take to get the job done, he or she should ask for them to ensure that needed record keeping, communication, mailing, and telephoning is accomplished.

15. A clear understanding with the appointing officer or body and the chief administrative officer regarding the position and role of the staff relative to the committee and its chairperson. The chairperson should have the support and assistance of the staff, and be the type of leader who engenders this support in a positive manner.

16. A good working knowledge of parliamentary procedures, particularly for larger, more formal committees. Otherwise, the recommendations of a parliamentarian should be followed on such matters.

Does this list of chairperson's qualifications indicate that it is a position not to be taken lightly—that it requires attention to many details? It should, because being a chairperson means being responsible for the vital "work" of the nonprofit organization, assignments on which the future of the organization depends. It is not an assignment to be handed out as an "ego stroke" or accepted with the idea of chairing a few meetings. On the other hand, such an assignment is an invaluable training ground for volunteers and staff in executiveship. Work? Yes, but also an important opportunity for personal growth and development.

Providing Background for the Chairperson

Prior to the chairperson's participation in the next major activity, that of selecting the committee members, many well-organized groups provide the new chairperson with a kit of information that often includes:

1. A personal letter of thanks from the organization's chief executive officer
2. An up-to-date copy of the organization's by-laws; organization structure; list of other chairpersons and board members with addresses, telephone numbers, and so on; and a copy of the organization's annual program of work
3. All necessary background information and materials, from a record of previous committee and organizational activity in the particular area, to a written outline of the committee's duties, responsibilities, authority, budget, records, and reports
4. A list of previous committee members if the committee has been active before
5. Criteria for the selection of committee members as well as guidelines on the committee's size, representation, background, previous service on the committee, and so on

Unless your organization has printed material of its own on the subject, another suggested enclosure would be a copy of *Highway to Successful Committee Meetings,* published by the Chamber of Commerce of the United States.

Selecting Committee Members

Usually chairpersons of committees select their own members. Often, however, guidance on this important matter is provided by either the board or the appointing officer. Whatever the process followed by your organization, the following considerations should be kept in mind when choosing committee members:

1. Is the committee's area of involvement one in which the members have a personal interest? Have they shown a preference for this assignment? Perhaps even requested to serve on this committee?
2. Do the prospective members have special abilities or technical knowledge needed by the committee?
3. Do the members represent a viewpoint or constituency needed by the committee? Can they nevertheless be objective during the process of problem solving and decision making?
4. Will the members be loyal, cooperative, objective, and interested in the organization's overall good?
5. Do the new members have prior experience or service on this committee? If so, will this contribute to continuity of knowledge, or the establishment of a permanent clique?
6. Will the members work well with the other members as team players, or will they be prima donna types, happy only in the spotlight?
7. Do the members know, understand, and respect the basic responsibilities of all committee members, including:
   a. Acknowledging immediately all communications pertaining to committee work or responsibilities
   b. Informing the chairperson of availability for committee meetings or other related functions
   c. Thoroughly reviewing all pertinent background materials, reports, agenda, and other communications before coming to the meeting
   d. Taking an active, responsible role in all the committee's discussions or deliberations

e. Respecting and trying to understand other ideas presented or conflicting viewpoints brought forward at meetings

f. Dealing with problems and issues impersonally and with balanced objectivity

g. Helping the discussion focus on the subject or problem intended, without digressing

h. Requesting clarification or further explanation of any area not fully understood

i. Accepting and completing assignments

Orienting the Committee

The proper orientation of every committee chairperson is a vital responsibility of the organization's chief executive officer or chief administrative officer. Although the following list of orientation pointers is written for the chairperson, it can also apply just as well to the committee itself, a responsibility of the chairperson.

1. The importance of the chair is emphasized during a full explanation of the chair's duties and responsibilities.

2. The committee's objectives and priorities are reviewed in relation to the organization's objectives and program of work.

3. The committee's bounds of activity, authority, and responsibility are carefully outlined, reviewing the resolution or by-laws provision that established the committee.

4. The organization's policies, practices, and procedures are reviewed, particularly those relating to reporting procedures and those dealing with the receipt, disbursement, and accountability of funds.

5. Copies of the organization's by-laws, constitution, personnel policies, lists of other committees (including their chairpersons and objectives), and names of members of the board of directors should be provided for the chairperson and any committee members who want them.

6. During the review of the committee's program of work, previous committee's activities and accomplishments should be outlined and placed in perspective.

7. Any ongoing projects and programs of relevance to the committee should be reviewed and explained.

8. Any anticipated assignments of individual committee members should be identified and explained.

9. Scheduled meeting dates, times, and places should be outlined and explained.

10. The roster of the previous year's committee membership should be reviewed, in addition to the current listings. The criteria to be used in selecting new members of the committee should be understood and agreed upon by the appointing officer and the chairperson, and understood by the committee.

11. Staff assistance required should be identified and agreed upon by the chairperson, the chief staff executive, and the chief executive officer.

12. The committee should understand how it replaces personnel when someone moves or resigns (important during these days of high mobility).

13. The construction or development of the agenda should be understood. If this is to be handled by the chairperson, do the members contribute items for con-

sideration, and how far ahead of the meeting will the members learn what will be on the agenda?

14. Has the person keeping the official records of the group been selected, and how can members refer to the minutes? Has a procedure been established to ensure that members receive copies of the minutes promptly after each meeting, and will copies be forwarded to officers or board members needing to be kept informed of the work and proceedings of the committee?

15. Stenographic or secretarial support should be identified and explained.

Most of these items as they relate to the committee members can be handled at the first meeting. Obviously, this is an especially important meeting and should be given serious thought and planning. It will help to review the chapter on meetings and to prepare a checklist of items. The members of the new committee (or new members of an existing committee beginning a new year) should come away from the meeting fully understanding the objectives for the group and strongly motivated to participate on the team.

The agenda for committee meetings is somewhat different from that of business meetings since it is built around the need that caused the creation of the group in the first place. Such an agenda would ordinarily include such items as the following:

1. A review of previous meetings, either verbally by the chairperson or via the minutes. The latter, of course, is preferred because it ensures accuracy and completeness.

2. Concise background of facts relative to the problem or problems under discussion.

3. Discussion of the problem(s).

4. Possible decisions or recommendations on the problem(s).

5. Date, time, and place of the next meeting.

In short, the committee's agenda is the framework within which the committee works toward its goals.

Summary of Committee Operating Principles

According to Thomas G. Moore, the typical committee's operating principles can be summarized as follows:

1. Committees expect to be assigned significant work to do on behalf of the organization.

2. Chairpersons and members should be selected on the basis of their competence to complete that work successfully.

3. Committee members should find in their work an environment that encourages personal growth and development through cooperation with others—accomplishing together what none could do alone.

4. Coordination and mediation must be emphasized by committee leadership, ensuring that all points of view are given full representation, making assignments of responsibilities while channeling the group's activities toward effective completion of the tasks assigned to it.

5. A committee should be constituted of only those people who really need to be on it. Others who are needed from time to time for complete representation or technical expertise can be named associate members and invited when needed, minutes being forwarded in the interim to ensure that they are aware of the group's progress.

6. The chairperson of any committee should have the ability to communicate accurately to all involved in the process, the capacity to understand how and where the committee fits into the overall perspective of the organization, the ability to make judgments objectively, and the quality of inspiring sustained group action.

7. "Members of committees should be carefully selected, thoroughly oriented and kept interested by well-planned and operated meetings, a challenging committee program, and an adequate system of keeping them informed on matters relating to the work of their committee."

Duties and Activities of Common Committees

The following review of the duties and activities of the more common committees found in many nonprofit organizations was adapted in large part from a very worthwhile booklet published by the Chamber of Commerce of the United States, entitled *A Look at Association Committees.*[8]

Advertising Committee

1. Study and recommend policy and activities to the board regarding effective advertising and promotion of the organization's services (or products).

2. Study and guide the development of the organization's advertising program. This program should be established to answer a definite need, be long-range in scope and objectives, and be realistic in its projects.

3. Conduct adequate market research before setting up the advertising program.

4. Study and recommend practical and effective methods of financing the advertising program based on the nature of the program and experience of the organization.

5. Ensure that the organization's general budget includes a line item for the advertising program or campaign.

6. Study and recommend the proper media mix to be used in the advertising program—direct mail, newspapers, magazines, films, radio, television, exhibits, billboards, and so on.

7. At least annually, review the organization's advertising program and make appropriate recommendations in light of changing conditions or situations.

Education Committee

1. Study and recommend policy to the board relating to education activities conducted by the organization.

2. Arrange for research to be undertaken and continued pertinent to the devel-

opment and improvement of specific activities within an overall education program.

3. Study and recommend methods of financing the activities of an overall education program.

4. Ensure that the organization's general budget includes a line item for the education program.

5. Arrange for continued review and periodic evaluation of all aspects of the education program.

6. Investigate the development and use of manuals, texts, or other aides for employee and volunteer training purposes.

7. Study and arrange for short courses, clinics, seminars, or institutes to be held for the organization in needed subjects.

8. Investigate and recommend methods of conducting these courses, clinics, and so on, either directly by the organization or in cooperation with schools, colleges, or other organizations in the area providing the same or similar public services.

9. Study and recommend development of continuing education programs for members and staff.

10. Study and recommend establishment of educational training programs in cooperation with local, state, or regional groups within the organization's area of public service operations or emphasis.

11. Study and recommend sponsorship or cooperation with schools or college to establish special training courses for credit. (Many community colleges around the country cooperate with nonprofit organizations to provide training courses for credit in a wide variety of subjects.)

12. Study and recommend the sponsorship of fellowships or scholarships.

13. Study and investigate setting up tours of the organization's facilities for students, teachers, and the general public.

14. Study and arrange for lectures, demonstrations, and so on, aimed at educating the public.

15. Investigate producing and distributing teaching aids.

16. Study and arrange for educational exhibits in conjunction with the annual meeting in cooperation with other organizations and for the general public.

Finance or Budget Committee

1. Control and supervise the finances (funds and assets) of the organization.

2. Prepare, together with the chief administrative officer and treasurer, a recommended budget for the year.

3. Submit a proposed budget to the board for approval.

4. Receive and review monthly or quarterly financial reports on expenditures and income. If necessary, require an accounting of items not consistent with those budgets approved by the board.

5. Review and approve the allocation of funds, payment of bills, and the preparation and control of financial reports.

6. Review and approve the special budgets of other committees when necessary.

7. Review and reevaluate periodically the dues structure and other income-producing activities intended to finance activities and programs of the organization.

8. Review and approve all requests for expenditures by other committees.

9. Prepare and submit to the board a periodic report and analysis of the organization's finances.

10. Study and recommend the investment of surplus funds and advise on the condition of funds in trust.

11. Arrange for and review the results of an annual external audit of the previous year's accounts.

12. Ensure that the bookkeeping and financial records required as a condition of grants received are kept in the manner specified in the grant contract or other guidelines.

Labor Relations—Employer-Employee Relations Committee

1. Study and recommend policy to the board concerning labor relations issues and related matters.

2. Study and develop long-range labor relations and employer-employee relations programs and submit them to the board for approval. Review this program periodically in light of changing conditions and new factors.

3. Study legislative issues in this area and make recommendations to the board concerning legislation to be opposed or supported (ensure that this falls within the allowed limits set by the IRS).

4. Furnish leadership to the organization with respect to government activities in the labor relations field.

5. Study and recommend action by Congress, administrative agencies, or the courts in the labor and employer-employee relations field.

Government Relations Committee

1. Study and recommend policy to the board concerning legislative and government relations matters affecting the sector.

2. Study and inform membership concerning national, state, and local legislation affecting the sector or the organization.

3. Arrange for research and preparation of testimony for presentation before legislative fact-finding committees.

4. Select and arrange for training of organization members to serve as witnesses before legislative fact-finding committees.

5. Study, inform membership, and generate grass-roots support for or opposition to specific legislation.

6. Study and recommend a program aimed at encouraging members to inform their employees, friends, family, or the general public on key legislative issues.

7. Confer with legislators on legislative matters affecting the organization or its area of operations.

8. Encourage organization members to arrange visits with legislators (city or

county council members, state legislators, members of Congress) to become better acquainted and to discuss problems affecting the sector.

9. Prepare and submit to congressional or other legislative bodies written statements on matters affecting the organization or its sector.

10. Study and inform organization members about the voting records of members of Congress and state legislators in areas of importance to the organization.

11. Recommend and arrange for programs on legislative matters to be included at organization meetings, conventions, and so on.

12. Study and arrange for interorganizational cooperation efforts on certain mutually important legislative matters.

13. Study, evaluate, and make recommendations concerning trends that might have future legislative impact on the organization or the sector of public service operations.

14. Study and inform the membership on administrative actions or rulings and court decisions affecting the sector.

15. Study and make recommendations regarding changes in administrative procedures affecting the sector.

16. Confer with government employees on sector or professional matters. Furnish information concerning the sector, and obtain feedback, views, and so on.

17. In some organizations, this committee's scope of overall responsibility, in addition to legislation and government relations, includes activities in the areas of economic education, political education, and advocacy.

Membership Committee

1. Study and recommend policy to the board relating to the building and maintenance of membership in the organization.

2. Study and recommend a long-range plan of membership goals and activities to meet these goals.

3. When appropriate, examine applications for membership and make recommendations to the board.

4. When necessary, reexamine the qualifications of any member for continuance of membership in the organization and make appropriate reports to the board.

5. Explore reasons for each membership cancellation and submit a report on the findings. If applicable, issue a report on any organizational shortcomings responsible for the cancellation.

6. Review periodically, and if necessary make recommendations on current rules and regulations, qualifications, and so on, relating to membership as outlined in the organization's by-laws and constitution.

7. Develop a list of membership prospects with assignments for personal contacts to be made by committee members, other members of the organization, and staff.

8. Assist the staff in acquiring biographies and information about activities of new members for use in the organization's newsletter, journal, and so on.

9. Review regularly with the chief administrative officer the membership recruitment activities carried on by direct mail from the organization's headquarters.

10. Review periodically and make recommendations on methods of selling or increasing memberships, including general approach; specific approach by mail;

personal solicitation; publishing a digest of activities being conducted and their value to members and nonmembers; providing for positions on committees and other participation by members; and field work by the staff.

11. Be familiar with the type and scope of membership activities and programs conducted by other organizations.

Nominating Committee

1. Prepare and submit to the board nominations for officers and board members to be elected that year or for ensuing years. The following points should be considered during the selection of candidates:
   a. Each candidate for the board must have the potential to become an officer of the organization.
   b. All nominees for the board must be members of the organization.
   c. A written statement should be obtained from each nominee in which he or she gives assurances to the board of attending at least 75 percent of the meetings.
   d. Candidates proposed should be reinforced with statements of experience and qualifications for each nominee.
   e. Consent to run should be obtained from each candidate.
   f. Each candidate should have expressed an interest in assuming a leadership role in the organization.
   g. Each candidate should be selected with due consideration as to type of members, geographical or other category of representation, constituency, and so on.
   h. At least one candidate should be nominated for each of the elective offices to be filled.
2. If applicable, arrange to send to all voting members a "nominating ballot" in order that the preference of the members may be expressed to the committee.
3. Prepare and present a formal report (slate of candidates) to the board and the membership at the annual meeting.
4. Meet to nominate candidates for such offices and positions on the board that become vacant during the year (if this is in compliance with the by-laws of the organization).
5. Where applicable, work with the election committee in the actual handling of election proceedings.
6. Provide orientation for the new members of the board.
7. Analyze regularly the attendance of members of the board to ensure that they do not drop below the level specified in the by-laws.
8. Consult with board members who are not attending regularly or who fail to attend the minimum number of meetings.
9. Recommend to the executive committee action regarding inactive members of the board.

Personnel Committee

The personnel committee establishes policies and procedures regarding salaries, fringe benefits, hours, and working conditions so that the organization can employ and retain qualified staff and foster high productivity and quality of service.

Board Personnel Committee

1. Keep informed on the organization's personnel requirements and needs, the physical condition of the office spaces and work areas, equipment, and the organizations' salaries and fringe benefits.

2. Maintain familiarity with any laws or policies that regulate any conditions of employment and plan for their proper and timely implementation.

3. Formulate policy on all matters pertaining to personnel practices and procedures for further recommendation to the board of directors.

4. Establish equitable procedures to hear grievances and to arrange necessary negotiation with any unions involved in the operations of the organization.

Staff Personnel Committee

1. Study all proposals for changes in the manual of personnel policy and practice.

2. Study specific aspects of personnel practices or working conditions while exercising its ongoing responsibility for periodic review and updating of the manual.

3. Provide for further staff review and approval of its recommendations to the board personnel committee.

4. Discuss with the administration any proposals for changes in personnel practices or working conditions.

As the Child Welfare League of America so accurately notes in its *Guide for Board Organization in Social Agencies,*[9] every NPO should have a personnel practices manual that covers

The purpose and functions of the personnel practices committee or committees

The method by which board members are appointed and staff members are elected to serve

The frequency of meetings

The method by which staff suggestions for agenda items reach the committees

The specific procedure, allowing for full staff participation, through which policy is established or changed

Job descriptions; requirements for each position; salary ranges; fringe benefits; basis on which increments are given; agency policy regarding vacations, sick leave and educational leave; and working hours

Provisions for staff attendance at professional meetings and conferences (local and national) that are pertinent to the agency's program

In a public agency the personnel practices are often determined by civil service commissions and legal bodies such as the legislature. The committee, however, should be able to make recommendations for changes when the policies or practices do not serve the best interest of the organization.

Program Planning Committee (also called the Service, Policy, or Case Committee)

1. Determine, through research and study, the needs of the organization and its sector or operations, recommending policy to the board on meeting these needs through the organization's efforts.

2. Review, on a continuing basis, organizational objectives and study problems as well as trends of current growth.

3. Study and recommend plans for directing future organizational growth. Con-

sider priority and scope of new projects, requirements, and the organizational structure of the group.

4. Study and recommend a schedule of goals for organizational growth—immediate, intermediate, and long-range goals.

5. Consider both short-range and long-range planning questions and opportunities and submit policy recommendations to the board.

6. Work with the chief administrative officer and other members of the staff in the study and recommendation of a program of activities.

7. Review the overall organizational program annually with an accompanying report to the board.

8. Work with the chief administrative officer and other members of the staff in the study and recommendation of new activities.

9. Work with the budget or finance committee to determine the amount of income needed to support the organization's program of work or public service.

10. Ensure that adequate preparations are made for future needs, staff, and facilities.

11. Ensure that member service activities expand in proportion to the membership growth.

12. Make direct efforts to ensure that policy decisions will contribute to, and be in harmony with, longer-range objectives of the organization.

Public Relations Committee

1. Study and recommend policy to the board relative to the conduct of an effective and continuing public relations program. Such a program should have as its purpose, to translate into understandable terms the nature of the activities and aims of the organization, and as its goal, to achieve favorable public recognition for the organization, its programs, and its services.

2. Study and arrange for obtaining adequate factual background data through research (use of surveys, etc.) to determine the existence of problems that indicate the need for a public relations programs. Such research can also

   Establish a base from which to measure future progress

   Indicate which aspects or problems should be concentrated on initially

   Identify the public toward which the program should be directed

3. Study and recommend a plan to implement a public relations program taking into account such factors as

   Specific and general public relations objectives

   Means or methods of attaining objectives

   Central themes to be communicated

   Description and analysis of audiences (or publics) to be reached

   Media to be used

   Methods for periodically evaluating the public relations program

4. Study and recommend methods for carrying out a public relations program, considering establishing a program as an organizational staff function; use of

an outside public relations counsel; and use of a combination of staff and outside counsel.

5. Study and recommend methods of financing a public relations program based on the nature of the program and the experience of the organization.

6. Ensure that the organization's general budget includes a line item for the public relations program and campaigns.

7. Study and recommend appropriate media to be used in developing and carrying out a public relations program—newspapers, syndicates and wire services, house organs, magazines, radio, television, films, photographs, organization publications, speeches, exhibits, conventions, and so on.

8. Study and recommend the audiences or publics to be reached—opinion leaders, educators, legislators, civic and community clubs, governmental personnel, allied and other industries, and so on.

9. Keep informed on factors important in implementing a public relations program from within the organization:

   Development of adequate mailing lists

   Review and evaluation of available material on which to base stories or releases

   Development of a photographic file for television or publication use

   Creation and development of news releases, articles, publicity-generating projects, clipsheets, and mats—plus their placement in appropriate media

   Contact with editors and other media personnel

10. Review and coordinate efforts with other organizational committees to achieve maximum impact and success of the public relations program.

11. Study and arrange for progress reports on the impact of the public relations program and inform the board and membership.

12. Periodically review and evaluate the organization's public relations program and make appropriate recommendations in light of changing conditions.

13. When appropriate, and at least annually, submit to the board and membership an overall report on the accomplishments of the public relations program and indicate immediate and future goals.

Research and Evaluation Committee

1. Study and recommend policy to the board regarding the organization's research studies and activities.

2. Study and develop the organization's overall program of research.

3. Study and recommend methods of financing a research program.

4. Ensure that the organization's budget includes a line item for research activities.

5. Review and recommend research findings to be published in scientific journals.

6. Study and recommend those research findings to be made known to the public.

7. Investigate and recommend those discoveries made through organizational research that are to be patented by the organization.

8. Study and recommend research programs to be conducted at laboratories operated by the organization, educational institutions, and research institutions.

Resolutions, or Policy, Committee

1. Prepare recommendations for declarations of the organization's policy for consideration at the annual meeting.

2. Receive and review proposed resolutions. These proposals may originate with members, the board, other committees of the organization, or this committee acting on its own initiative.

3. Ensure that proposed declarations conform to eligibility tests of the organization's by-laws.

4. Prepare and ensure that the text of declarations recommended for adoption at the annual meeting is sent to members for study in advance of the meeting.

Statistics and Information Committee

1. Study and recommend policy to the board regarding the organization's compilation of statistical information, conducting regular and special statistical studies and dissemination of certain data.

2. Study and direct the development of an overall statistical program for the organization.

3. Study and recommend methods of financing a statistical program.

4. Ensure that the organization's general budget includes a line item for statistical activities.

5. Review and recommend the dissemination of data compiled by government agencies, by other outside agencies, or in cooperation with either governmental or other outside agencies.

6. Study and recommend the preparation of long-term and short-term forecasts.

7. Study and arrange for conducting surveys of wages and fringe benefits.

Notes

1. Howard L. Oleck, *Nonprofit Corporations, Organizations, and Associations,* Prentice-Hall, Englewood Cliffs, N.J., 1980, p. 705.

2. Ibid., p. 706.

3. Adapted from American Society of Association Executives and Chamber of Commerce of the United States, *Principles of Association Management,* Washington, 1975, p. 104.

4. Adapted from Chamber of Commerce of the United States, *Association Committees,* Washington, 1976, p. 1.

5. Oleck, *Nonprofit Corporations,* p. 716.

6. Ibid., p. 709.

7. American Society of Association Executives, *Principles of Association Management,* p. 107.

8. Chamber of Commerce of the United States, *A Look at Association Committees,* Washington, p. 43.

9. Child Welfare League of America, Inc., *Guide for Board Organization in Social Agencies,* New York, 1976 p., 17.

13

Managing the Professional Staff of Nonprofit Organizations

Ira M. Berger

Former Associate Dean for Public Affairs, New York Law School

Let us assume that professional staff members are different from other clerical staff. This may or may not be true in the context of the nonprofit organization (NPO) where a pose of professionalism has been adopted by certain types of workers (those with a particular skill, for example, but not necessarily a skill rated as professional in times past) and encouraged by management. Such a pose serves to smooth the path of institutional altruism and to prevent identification with workers of lesser rank. The success of professionalism is aided by the fact that even in the nonprofit world, young ambition prefers to rate itself upward and even to consider itself "lower" or "middle" management.

Whether these workers are in fact professionals in the traditional sense is not the important issue. What is important is that they consider themselves professional. Having abetted this development, management must act in accordance with their self-estimation because perceptions of status and role most often set the tone of management-staff interactions. Where actual work conditions undercut this perception, after a long period of agency instability or wage freeze, for example, the identification with workers of lower status return, and unionization or some other form of group action is often the result.

A word here about a basic dichotomy in NPOs. Management of agencies tends to be hierarchic in organization, whereas work tends to be autonomous or collaborative. Most professional employees can only rarely be told what to do and only in areas of little consequence (the form in which to write their reports, for example). However, the highest productivity occurs where collaboration is obtained. The strictly hierarchic manager as such is at his or her own peril.

We shall discuss the management of professional staff in three divisions: how they are hired; how they are kept or managed; and how, should it happen, they are let go. Because the range of nonprofit organizations and professional staff functions is so broad, an attempt will be made to provide examples from a number of organizations in the sector.

How to Hire Professionals

Internal Conditions

Before one hires professional staff, one should ask: What, in fact, the position is to be and how it relates to the organization as a whole? What style characterizes the organization really, as compared with what the leadership would like it to be? This cannot be overemphasized. Without a clear job description and some absolutely clear awareness of what the organization is really all about, there can be little success for this or any other position.

For example, the decision to hire an accountant rests on the distinction between a bookkeeper, a clerical role, but one that in a smaller NPO might include some accounting functions and therefore an accountant, a position often requiring certification. This choice rests on a careful analysis of fiscal status and level of need. The consequences of a mistake here are not so grave in this situation and would probably involve nothing more than a salary higher than is necessary. However, let us go one step further.

The hiring of a business or financial officer, a position which might involve serious monetary consequences to the organization, rests on an analysis of whether one really is ready for an officer to deal with the management of money or to advise the executive director about structuring the organization financially for planning purposes or for expansion. This is not an accounting function but one that demands an ability to visualize an organization in financial terms.

The decision to hire a development officer, an area of expertise, could also be cited. Frequently, an agency at a certain point in its development, believes that a professional fund-raiser is all that is needed for the organization to reach a new plateau or, sometimes, merely to survive. Yet such an effort is most often a failure. Development officers should most often be facilitators and organizers. A development officer without organized records, clerical support, a sense of organizational focus, the support of the executive director, or a board of directors around whom to organize volunteers, will soon be stymied. There must be at least a minimum of internal structure and agreement on institutional direction. Structure and direction, therefore, might best be handled by a reputable consulting firm rather than by an in-house fund-raiser.

Development officers are not financial magicians. They do not themselves attract money, and they can rarely transfer the commitment of donors from one type of organization to another. Those who purport to do so should be regarded with suspicion. Organizations who seek out such people deserve them.

Once you have a clear idea of what kind of professional staff is needed, how do you meet the need? After a clear job description has been agreed upon, and a concensus of the organization is reached on the need for the position, a number of avenues are open to you.

Executive Recruiters and Placement Agencies

In filling certain, very specialized high-level professional positions, recruiters and agencies often are of value. The cost for these services is high, usually a retainer or a fee, sometimes a percentage of the first year's salary, but the value is that an outside firm participates in the analysis of need and in the development of a job description. Such firms, too, often have a good view of the market and wide connections in the particular fields.

These firms will do initial screening and interviewing. They are generally proactive when they do a search, and they are discreet, an important consideration in searching out higher-placed professionals who would not think of answering an advertisement.

Recruiting firms are dependent, however, on the information that they are given. Their knowledge of agencies and organizations and their own experience with you, aids immeasurably, but the success of a search is dependent on your candor and clarity.

To identify such firms, inquire of other organizations in your area or, at the highest levels, consider such corporate recruiting firms as Korn Ferry International, which have nonprofit expertise as well. Some professional associations and consulting firms, especially in fund-raising, also have recruitment services.

Advertisements

Truth in advertising could never be more important than in seeking professional staff. Successful advertisements must correctly and concisely portray the job and the recruiting organization. One should avoid adjectives and adverbs, although some may be necessary to give a clear picture. "Wonderful arts agency" will not work, but "Growing arts agency," if it is true, is imperative to attract the kind of aggressive person desired. Basic qualifications ("three years experience, B.A. degree, ability to travel") should be stated.

There is some debate as to whether to state salary levels in such an advertisement. On the one hand, to give such information is an indication, aside from the description of the position, of the level of the job and serves to weed out inappropriate applicants. On the other hand, a phrase like "salary open and commensurate with ability" allows for a wider range of applicants in a more flexible situation. You may find someone whose salary history allows for a lower starting salary than you expected to have to pay.

Advertisements should always refer to equal opportunity for two reasons: (1) It should be true. (2) It is the law, and in some rare instance you may be faced with a discrimination suit and have to defend yourself on a charge of bias.

Remember that your own staff will see the advertisement and might also apply for the position. Going public may have internal implications which might be precipitated sooner than expected.

Once the advertisement is written, there are choices for placement. Every area has its own resources insofar as newspapers and journals are concerned. There are some national resources as well, *The New York Times,* for example, but keep in mind what kind of response you want from your ad. Professional organizations,too, have placement services and journals. The *Chronicle of Higher Education* has an extensive focus, and not only for jobs in higher education.

There is also some discussion regarding whether to employ "blind ads"—those which do not identify, except by inference, the searcher (to prevent the application of pressure on the searching organization, for example, or a going around the process by directly contacting the searcher). However, they often serve to uncover dissatisfaction in the organization's own staff when an employee applies for her or his own job in answering such an ad. Blind advertisements also may limit applicants; some professionals simply will not respond to such an ad.

Word of Mouth

Getting the word out is perhaps the most effective method of finding appropriate professional staff. Networks of board members and professional connections are most important here, but beware of the "gift employee." The gift may be a function of an "outplacement service."

Filling the Position

A word on timing. Everything said above or outlined below takes time, frequently more than you think. Certainly you should plan for months, perhaps six or more, and in some cases perhaps a year between the time that a decision is made to seek out a professional staff member and the actual starting date of employment. Do not allow yourself to be rushed into a decision, although one is sometimes forced to take what there is. A certain sense of realism must prevail, sometimes a quality of hopefulness, but never *panic.*

Handling the Résumés

You now, hopefully, have a bundle of résumés from various sources. What will you do with them? First, acknowledge receipt of them in some manner: A card or letter thanking the applicant for showing interest in your firm will do. Aside from being common courtesy, it tells the applicant something about the organization. Then go through the résumés carefully, and sort out any that are clearly inappropriate. Do not be surprised if there are many more inappropriate applicants than you assumed. An extraordinarily high number of inappropriate applicants, however, may indicate that your job description was inadequate, that another search process is more appropriate in that particular field, or that what you wanted was not really clear in your own mind. You may have to run the ad again or in a different medium, or you may have to revise it and start again. You may also want to rethink the job function.

In reading a résumé, look for certain things, aside from the obvious condition of the piece of paper itself. Just as the ad told the candidate about your organization, the résumé should present the candidate honestly and clearly and with some dispatch. Look at the facts of training and employment. Do not overlook errors in presentation or sloppiness. Look askance at overeagerness or self-promotion, except, perhaps, when recruiting a public relations specialist where such qualities are indications of how your own activities will be promoted.

Generally avoid candidates who are eager to take cuts in salary. You should know what the going salaries are in the professional marketplace. If you do not, you will soon find out when the best candidates ask for more than you had expected. However, the person who says that she will take less than she is now earning because your job is so much more exciting and closer to her interests will feel differently after a year.

Do not rule out currently unemployed candidates simply because they are so. In certain fields, unemployment is part of the pattern of employment—in the arts, for example.

The Interview

Once you have culled the best, establish an interview schedule. The person to whom the candidate will report should *always* do the initial interview. Here, too, the matter of time is important, both yours and the candidate's. Some experts say that narrowing the field is best done by seeing candidates in close proximity to one another, but seeing too many can dull the senses. Appointments should be made and kept. Keeping a candidate waiting is read as a sign of administrative style unless it is really unavoidable. Being late weighs against the candidate unless, too, it is unavoidable. Candidates for development positions should never be late. The main point is that once the decision to meet a candidate is made, every aspect of every contact is weighed before the final choice for the position is made.

Managers need to be aware that these initial discussions are perhaps the most important, and potentially the most crucial, of the process. For it is here that the initial, and frequently most vivid, impression is made and conclusions drawn as to the way in which management or professional staff relations are effected. It is not only the characterization of the job and the organization and the candidate's credentials that are important here, but the *way* they are presented.

It is important to mention the "gut reaction"—the immediate sense that the fit is right. Absent other more rational criteria (an appropriate experience, level of training, education, or the like), a positive gut reaction is pleasant but says nothing that is important insofar as the workplace is concerned. On the other hand, no amount of rationalization will serve to replace the immediate feeling that employer and professional employee are *wrong* for each other. If either feels that it is wrong, it probably is.

The professional candidate should be prepared to present samples of his or her work where appropriate, and management should look at them carefully in the light of what needs to be done. Where this is not possible, some other method of objective validation obtains, either through professional certification as a condition of employment (a state license or CPA accreditation, for example), or through the reference process.

Certain special considerations should be observed in the interview. The manager should avoid personal questions. Aside from the fact that they are not professional in terms of style, they are rarely appropriate. Managers may, and perhaps should, draw certain inferences from a discussion, but so should candidates. Since the advantage in the process is with management, management should always present itself in a way that allows the candidate, who often needs a job and is under special pressure, to draw the conclusion that, after all, your organization may not be where she wants to work. Better before employment than after.

Always make certain that more than one person interviews the candidate. Where appropriate, the involvement of key volunteers is important, not necessarily to decide on the candidate (for that would be incorrect insofar as board responsibility is concerned for any position other than the president or executive director) but rather as a reflection of the reality of the job. A development officer who cannot abide the chair of the development committee of the board or a treasurer who has an aversion to the prospective comptroller would be disastrous. A president or executive director who does not recognize this and sees it as board meddling is heading for trouble.

Management should request and check references, and should interpret them carefully. Too frequently, references are inadequate in that candidates give names of people who will give a favorable impression, and these referees often avoid telling you any negative facts for fear of slander suits or some other unpleasantness. As mentioned above, sometimes one has to beware of the gift employee, who comes highly recommended. Some senior administrators pride themselves on their outplacement ability in disposing of troublesome or incompetent employees. (The easiest way to get rid of such employees is to get them another job.) In contrast, some supervisors will provide a poor or equivocal reference because they do not want the employee to leave or because of vindictiveness.

The manager must go beyond the references provided when it is appropriate to do so. At higher levels of employment, where management is attempting to seduce a professional from a like organization, the knowledge that the employee is being seduced might be dangerous to her or him if prematurely advertised. Once it is likely that, all things being equal, an offer is to be made and accepted, everyone, discreetly, if possible, should be approached, recognizing of course that, as head hunters say, no deal is done until it is done. Check, too, the validity of all assertions of degrees and certification. If you have determined that such things are important to begin with, you owe it to yourself to check them out.

Once you and the candidate have decided that you are right for each other, certain procedures should be followed. Management should consider drawing up either a contract or a letter of appointment. This document should state specifically all conditions of employment (salary, responsibility, starting date, and title or level, etc.) or refer the candidate to a standard source for them (an employee handbook or personnel manual, for example). A copy of such a source should be sent to the employee along with the letter of appointment. The language of these documents should be precise and clear. The importance of clarity cannot be overemphasized because the most frequent conflict in management-employee relations comes from misinterpretation of the terms of employment. Nothing should be left to chance, other than the hope that all will turn out well if all the procedures have been followed.

One final step. Once you make your selection, be sure to thank the other candidates. This is not the last search for an employee that you will make in your profession, and you will want to impress the candidates with your own professionalism. You may also want to maintain contact with them; therefore it cannot hurt to have the reputation that your school or agency deals with people humanely.

How to Keep Them

So much emphasis has been placed on the initial contact between management and professional employee because there is general agreement that it is the most crucial stage in management-employee relations determining all that is to come after. What comes next simply builds upon the foundation established here and in the first months of employment.

Let us divide professional employees into two types: those whose professionalism is a reflection of a higher level of expertise in a particular task and those whose professionalism is characterized by a creative approach to the solving of a particular problem in a manner consistent with the profession. Professional employees have two points of reference: the profession against whose standards they define themselves and the organizations for whom they work. It is often a divided loyalty. In some instances, however, what is meant by professionalism is that a certain method of interaction between management and employee develops.

Training

Training should occur in two areas: training to learn how to do the job and training to become familiar with the institution itself. Despite professional status, each organization has its own way of handling clients, materials, and records. The new employee must be trained in the procedures. Further, each organization has its own style of interaction. This, too, must be part of training. All these procedures are taught both formally, through seminars or classes, and, informally, by "learning the ropes." However it is done, management, must "manage" it and not leave it to chance. Such management may even extend to arranging who should lunch with the new employee during the initial period.

The primary point here is that a laissez-faire attitude on the part of management is ill-advised.

Appraisal

There must be a time during which both the employee and the organization are mutually "on approval." Chances are that if the search has been well-handled, the validity of the choice will be proved immediately. Sometimes, however, the fit is wrong, and there must be a process which allows both parties to recognize it. The terms of the process must be clearly stated in the letter of appointment, and the time frame (usually 3 to 6 months) established.

Communication

Management of professional employees in NPOs is a collaborative activity. There is a process of self-selection in seeking such employment, and it can be assumed that such employees are generally in agreement with the aims and goals of the organization. It is also assumed that, as professionals, they know how to achieve a goal. This process sometimes comes into conflict with a hierarchical management in which employees are told what to do and evaluated on objective, often quantifiable criteria. This is seldom the case in NPOs where nothing is manufactured.

In most successful nonprofit organizations, what is crucial is the maintenance of a spirit that implies that all are involved in achieving a particular goal. The management of this spirit most frequently calls for an open, involving style rather than a closed, noninvolving style. Management must be able to articulate the goals of the organization to the professional employee, who in turn must be open to the observations of those who directly interface with the client.

What are the most important considerations of professional employment?

- It is imperative that management recognize the legitimate need of professional employees to know what is going on. There are many vehicles for providing information—newsletters, staff meetings, individual meetings. To privately confide seemingly privileged information to a particular employee may be seen by others as a device to indicate a special importance of the employee. Over the long haul, this is probably a misguided practice that may lead to a reliance on rumor and the reading of tea leaves. Professional employees require valid information openly and freely given to all.

- The promise of advancement is often crucial, but not always in the way one assumes. For some employees, *movement in the profession* is as important as advancement in the organization. Management may not be the only goal for the professional employee.

- *Advancement* is determined by an appraisal of work. Such an appraisal should not be haphazard and must involve the professional employee himself. The setting of annual goals is not unusual.

- *Salary considerations* are critical, but not necessarily in terms of their dollar amount. There seems to be agreement among researchers that what is most important is that the professional employee feel that his salary is equitable, given the job to be done. The development of appropriate salary levels is important and is probably best done by a combination of employees (in comparing job descriptions and grouping similar jobs) and outside consultants (relating the institution to others of its kind). The process is excruciating, but necessary. What is worse is to have a meaningless structure with disgruntled professional employees. After the structure is established, however, some form of merit and cost-of-living increases will usually keep it effective.

    A word, though, about the temptation management frequently succumbs to in asking employees to weather a difficult period by foregoing salary increases. The assumption here is that "we're all in this together" in fighting for (against) abortion, comforting people with AIDS, combating adult illiteracy, and so on. The time limit here seems to be 2 to 3 years. Beyond that, the crisis no longer seems valid, and since it is almost impossible to catch up, management had better have a plan to combat excessive turnover, internal dissensions, or unionization, all of which can affect the ability of the organization to function.

- *Fringe benefits* seem to be important, but not as important as salary, unless they are related (as they perhaps should be) to institutional and professional advancement and are recognized as such.

- *Work conditions* are important, too, but mainly when they are unsatisfactory and play into a sense of crisis. A nice office will not compensate for inadequate compensation.

- In certain areas of professional employment, *creativity* is the key to success. The literature on creativity is extensive, mainly as it relates to technological innovation and science. The manager of creative people should be familiar with this literature because hierarchical structure does not necessarily support creative activity and may in fact be detrimental to it. Jointly establishing deadlines with some adequate room for delay may be more effective than unilaterally applying a rigid, tight deadline or not applying any deadline at all.

- In managing professional staff, the manager should not be assumed to be professionally competent in *all* of the areas he or she manages. For, it is not the task of the manager to *do* all the individual jobs, but to oversee that they are being done. In light of this, I propose that there are only a few areas where the professional task is so complex that the manager is forced to regard it with awe. In most situations, the manager should be comfortable with the application of common sense and be governed by it.

- There is a theory that most professional employees are motivated by a desire for self-actualization. While this may be true for most employees, the possibility of "acting out" in the workplace is not generally beneficial. In some social service agencies, however, where the pressures are extraordinary, where it is difficult to stay afloat financially, and where the employees (because of self-selection) are themselves at risk, managers must give counsel and support to both employees and clients in order that the purpose of the organization be furthered.

If the considerations cited above are realized—shared expectations as to job and outcome, a participatory setting of goals, an equitable salary structure whose bases are open and clear, honest opportunities for advancement honestly perceived, institutional encouragement and recognition of professional improvement—then the conditions for the involuntary leaving of the organization should be obvious and easy for both parties. If they are not realized, then professional staff will voluntarily depart, and there will be a problem of turnover.

It should be noted, however, that in certain professional areas, turnover is an accepted phenomenon, regarded as a reflection of burnout (which can be dealt with institutionally) or of the marketplace and the nature of professionalism itself.

Voluntary Separation

Some experts say that once an employee makes inquiries about other jobs, he or she has already made the decision to leave and will do so sooner or later. With the employee's interests divided, an observant management will be aware of the decision sooner than the employee realizes. There might be a change in work patterns, absences vaguely explained, or an office door kept closed more frequently than before. We should all learn to read signs. But at what point should employees tell their employers that they are considering another offer, and how should management respond?

It should be a given that mutual respect between the professional and management requires the reporting of such information as early as possible, probably at the midpoint of the process. Management, after all, is likely to be a major reference, but is not normally the primary one. How management reacts will reflect general style and may also reflect management's perception of what the employee really wants. Frequently the courting of an offer serves to point up both the employee's value and the institution's need. Therefore, the making of a counteroffer is always an option, and standing on ceremony seldom serves any purpose. The leaving of a key person is never without consequence, even though management must assume that anyone might leave at any time.

Once the quadrille is ended, however, management has two facts to act on. One is that the position needs to be filled; the other is that sooner or later the employee will in fact leave, and management has received fair warning. It is only fair for management to ask an employee who is toying both with another offer and with management's counteroffer to decide in a timely fashion: Uncertainty serves nobody's purpose.

Once an employee has decided to leave, adequate notice must be given. Although 2 weeks is standard in a clerical setting, 1 month should be the minimum for professional staff. Management might even suggest a longer period, but this is very much a matter for negotiation between the parties. Although voluntary separation assumes that the employee will continue to perform on a professional level, the leaving period should not be drawn out. These issues should be dealt with in the personnel manual and should be explicit.

Another kind of voluntary separation relates to stages of professional development. Institutions and employees go through developmental stages, hopefully in tandem. Sometimes, however, a leveling off of performance occurs after long service, and this may occur in the midst of a strong institutional push for greater productivity. To fire such an employee may risk an age discrimination suit and would have a severely demoralizing effect on the rest of the staff. Yet, tenure is a position equally damaging when it demonstrates inequality of application of standards of performance.

What is often surprising to discover is that both management and the employee are in agreement that a particular situation is untenable. Once discovered, some joint action should be undertaken immediately which will result in a new job within the organization, perhaps in an area requiring less creativity, or in a smooth path out.

Involuntary Separation

At times the severance of an employee is contemplated. Such action should not usually be spontaneous, but should come after a long process of growing dissatisfaction or a clear restructuring of the organization.

Where an organization has a policy of periodic appraisals of performance, reasons for dissatisfaction should have appeared over a period of time and should have been documented. Documentation and evidence that the employee knew of the deteriorating quality of her or his work (whether or not she or he accepted management's assessment) is crucial, as is some evidence that the employee was offered the chance to correct performance and did not do so.

It is a reflection of our times that this process should be undertaken from the point of view that it is likely that some outside agency will review the steps and that some consequences may result for the institution. The outside agency may be a union, where procedure for dismissal is part of the contract; a state agency, where sex, race, age, sexual preference, or religious discrimination has been charged; or a court or an arbitrator where the employee alleges to have been harmed by the process because of damage to professional standing, and claims compensation. Where at one time such actions would have been rare, today one must assume that they *will* happen rather than that they *might.*

This should not completely inhibit management's ability to fire staff. It should only point up the fact that the relationship between professional staff and the organization should be a *process* free of caprice and whim. Yet it is significant that the nonprofit area is the only one in which unionization among professionals is increasing, as are employee suits and the cost of liability and director's and officer's insurance. The likelihood is great that the severance of an employee is really the end of one process and the beginning of another which does not end when the employee leaves the premises.

Once fired, the employee should not be required to work an unreasonable length of time. Since nonprofit organizations are *humane,* the Friday afternoon "massacre" should not be necessary. All accrued benefits should have been taken into account and a check prepared. Professional policy should be followed to the letter.

Staff must be allowed the opportunity to express support for the fired employee, as well as for the process. Taking a fired colleague to lunch is not necessarily a subversive activity.

While severance for cause has been emphasized in the above discussion, reorganization can also result in professional employees' being asked to leave. This action, too, should be part of a process in which the employee has been involved; again, there should be no surprises. Management might in this instance, however, consider various outplacement services which might extend over a considerably longer period. In that case, too, other internal options for which retooling or training will be made available, should be considered.

In all of this, resist the temptation to engage in ad hominem discussions or to characterize the employee in any way. In fact, do not initiate any talk about it, and do not answer any questions. Take the high road and allow the facts to speak for themselves. Heat can only damage the perception of the organization and the manager as its representative.

Finally, think, too, about the employees who are left after this process has reached its end. You have dealt with one employee, but the rest of the staff, some of whom have probably seen themselves in his or her place, remain. They have drawn conclusions from the way you handled the situations, and the conclusions had better be ones that put your organization in a positive light.

Main Conclusions

- The management-professional staff relationship must be based on a jointly determined consensus insofar as the purpose of the organization is concerned.

- Management should be participatory and reflect professional competence.

- Procedures should be agreed upon and clearly stated in an accessible place and format, and they should be held to. Part of the procedure, however, should be a mechanism for their revision.

- It is better to deal with problems before they appear than to deal with them after the fact. Management must plan, and the entire professional staff must play a role in that planning process.

- Assume the success of the organization, and build relationships that reflect that assumption. No one delights in success more than professional staff and management.

14

Organizational Analysis and Management Improvement

Frederick S. Lane

Professor of Public Administration, School of Business and Public Administration, Baruch College, City University of New York

The human organizations in which we spend most of our work and volunteer time are fascinating places: often exciting and challenging, sometimes frustrating. This chapter is about organizational analysis, a systematic approach to understanding nonprofit organizations and improving their management.

Organizations are complex for many reasons but principally because they are composed of people, all interacting with one another. Our ability to fully understand, much less predict, human behavior remains quite limited. Moreover, organizations are often ambiguous entities; it is sometimes remarkably difficult to know what is happening in them. Frequently this is because we have insufficient or unclear information or because people are hiding problems or camouflaging their actions.[1]

Nonprofit organizations are particularly difficult to manage. Like business firms, they can and do go out of business. Similar to government agencies, there is no single, broad measure of performance (like profitability in business). Unlike either business or government, however, nonprofit organizations rely significantly on voluntary action—both contributions and volunteers.[2]

Organizational analysis is much like medical diagnosis. When a patient visits a doctor, the doctor sees both symptoms and signs. "Symptoms" are indications of medical problems observed by the patient and reported to the doctor. "Signs" are indicators found by the doctor alone, often with the aid of laboratory tests. The different parts of the body are all related to one another; a disease may move from one area to another, or a disease in one organ might affect the functioning of another. If one part of the body suffers an injury, ranging anywhere from a broken leg to a heart attack, the performance of the entire body can be affected.

Organizational analysis is similar. In applying organizational analysis to a nonprofit organization, we attempt to

- Diagnose the condition of the organization
- Identify the principal strengths and shortcomings of the organization
- Identify areas of the organization which require additional study

Like medical diagnosis, there are both symptoms and signs: circumstances organizational participants reveal and circumstances the analyst discovers after careful assessment. Sometimes a problem is found in just one part of an organization or in one aspect of its operations. Other times a problem is systemic, affecting the entire organization. Problems in one unit of the organization (fund-raising, for example) can indeed affect the entire organization's performance.

Nonprofit management is an art which requires judgment. The goal of organizational analysis is to provide a framework for information gathering and evaluation that promotes informed judgment by nonprofit organization board members, managers and staff.

Uses of Organizational Analysis

There are many opportunities for organizational analysis to be helpful. Inevitably these opportunities focus on management improvement—on the need or desire to better an organization's condition and operations. Productivity improvement, increased organizational effectiveness, organizational renewal—all are widely heard, inherently related terms.

In this chapter, we focus on four principal uses of organizational analysis within nonprofit organizations: problem solving, strategic planning, leadership changes, and periodic assessment. A fifth use is by management consultants hired by an organization.

Perhaps the most typical situation requiring organizational analysis stems from a recognition that there is a problem in some aspect of the organization's functioning. Such a problem could be relatively small, seemingly isolated, and intermittent, or it might be a major organizational disaster that threatens the very existence of the organization. Because even relatively small problems may reverberate throughout the entire organization, a comprehensive approach to analyzing the problem may be preferred by top-management leadership, the board of directors, or others in the organization.

A second common situation calling for organizational analysis is strategic planning. "Strategic planning" stresses setting a mission for an organization and devising a strategy to achieve that mission. It always includes an appraisal of organizational capabilities and resources—hence, the need for organizational analysis.

A third common situation where organizational analysis is employed is when there is new leadership. A new chief executive officer is the most common reason, but significant changes on the board or other changes in key management staff might encourage such an effort. A new chief executive officer is normally highly interested in assessing an organization's condition in a careful and comprehensive way.

The fourth use relates to regular, periodic assessment. Sometimes this is initiated outside the organization; self-study required by an accrediting body or a site visit by an accreditation team are good examples. Other times, organizations periodically analyze themselves, as part of a planning cycle, as part of an organizational transition, or just because it is a healthy organizational practice.

While these four uses of analysis are common *inside* nonprofit organizations, a fifth use is also common—one employed by outsiders. Management consultants regularly seek comprehensive information about an organization, even if they have been called only to solve a specific problem. We have learned, often the hard way, that all parts of an organization affect one another.

Methods in Organizational Analysis

There are two main concerns in approaching the analysis of a nonprofit institution: the process of going about the research and the sources of information to use. These topics are highlighted below.

Implementing Organizational Research

Particularly for organizations without any experience in this, the procedures for organizational analysis can cause concern. The steps require great care, whether the analysis is being carried out by a chief executive officer, a staff team, an outside consultant, or anyone else.

To begin with, objectives for the analysis, the limits on the diagnosis (if any), the staff and resources to be committed, and the time frame for the work should be established and understood. Who actually performs the analysis is an early key question: one person, a small team, one or two people with an advisory committee, or any other option. The announcement that such an analysis is being carried out is critical—to the board, unit heads, key staff, and others.

The process to be used must next be determined. This focuses on the sources of information and data collection methods, which will be discussed below.

Finally, provision must be made to evaluate the accuracy and completeness of the analysis. Consultants, especially, often use feedback as one device. They inform organizational participants about preliminary findings, and both obtain and observe their reactions. The observations are another source of information.

The experience and values of the analysts are important to their understanding and interpretation of the findings, and those conducting such an analysis must be sensitive to this. Even where there is an ongoing office for organizational analysis (management analysis, institutional research, etc.), sometimes this unit becomes isolated and these problems can still occur.

Different information sources sometimes produce different findings. Experienced analysts compare their findings from different sources of information and look for a confluence of data producing the same findings.

The analyst, particularly an outside consultant or someone new to an organization, often finds it useful to give a "sneak preview" of the preliminary results to top administrators individually or as a group, to knowledgeable observers, or to well-informed board members—just to test the findings and to pursue any omissions along the way.

Sources of Information

There are five basic sources of information in organizational analysis. Each has relative strengths and weaknesses in contributing to such a study.

Organizational records are a critical source of information. Organizations maintain much information for their own purposes, and some of this can be very useful. Annual reports, Form 990s, planning documents, organization charts, SOPs (standard operating procedure manuals), budgets, and personnel files are a few examples.[3] Reviewing these records is the least obtrusive to the organization, and is particularly useful in identifying organizational trends.

A second essential research method is interviewing. A great deal of information can be obtained and in depth. This is a flexible device, normally used in combination with others. Interviewing requires a good amount of skill, and some are better than others at gaining the trust of respondents and interpreting their comments. The particularly skilled interviewer may attempt small group interviews in addition to the typical one-to-one format.

A third source of information is the survey. A questionnaire is developed (for example, about the organizational climate); this requires care in wording the questions and including important issues. The analyst needs to understand to whom the questionnaire is being sent, and—through the cover letter, one or more reminders, and other devices—to ensure a significant percentage of responses. Sometimes standard questionnaires or questions can be used; other times, a questionnaire must be customized for a particular group.

A fourth source of information is observation—formally or informally—by experts, by trained personnel, or by the casual observer. Here the emphasis is on what people—staff, board members, volunteers, members, clients, others—actually do rather than on what they think or tell you.

A fifth source of information is grossly underutilized by nonprofit groups. It is comparative analysis, information comparing the condition of one nonprofit organization with other like organizations. Much standard information is available about certain kinds of organizations (schools and hospitals, for example) from government agencies. Form 990s are another standard source of publicly available comparative information. Sometimes "umbrella" agencies—United Ways, religious federations, arts councils, national headquarters—will make certain data available. Occasionally, original data will have to be collected for this purpose. In all this, many types of information could be involved—revenues and expenditures; clients, audiences, or members; government contracts; or staff size. The range is great and depends on the analyst's purpose.

Each of these five sources is potentially valuable in organizational analysis. The sources of information and the conduct of the analysis will greatly influence the findings.

Organizational Analysis: A Comprehensive Approach

Scholars involved in organizational analysis and organizational diagnosis have largely been drawn from the areas of organizational behavior and organizational psychology. Weisbord's excellent work emphasizes organizational goals, structure, behavior, and leadership.[4] A comprehensive approach to organizational analysis, however, requires more information than this. In particular, it must assess both the organization's programs or activities as well as its results or impacts. Accordingly, the approach used here contains nine categories of information or "boxes."[5] These are summarized in Figure 14.1.

This approach to organizational analysis provides a series of key questions for each of the nine categories. In this way, the analyst is encouraged to fill each of the boxes with the necessary information. The nine categories and the key questions in each one are elaborated in this section.

Organizational History

Each organization has its own organizational saga, and it is essential for the analyst to understand the historical development of the nonprofit organization being examined.

- *When and why was the organization founded?* Here we would like to know something about the circumstances, mission, programs, and participants in the foundation period of the organization.

- *What were the major phases in the organization's development?* What changes— gradual or sudden, subtle or dramatic—have taken place in the mission, programs, resources, and participants? Highlight any crises or critical turning points which may have occurred. Sometimes written organizational histories are available to help you with these questions.[6]

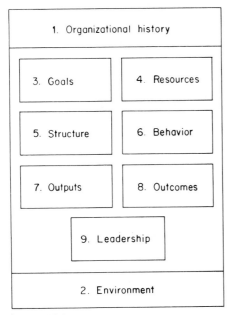

Figure 14.1

Environment

Here we are looking at the external environment in which every organization operates and the "fit" over time between the organization and its setting. Environments present both opportunities and constraints for a nonprofit organization.

- *What is the legal and political context for the organization?* Organizations are closely linked to government through tax exemption, grants and contracts, regulation, and public policy formation. Each of these links should be explored. NPOs, for example, are constrained in their lobbying activities.

- *What is the social and economic environment?* This could be general, in terms of national demographic changes, or quite specific, as in the different socioeconomic mix in the neighborhood near a "Y." The health of the economy, the availability of disposable income, federal tax incentives, and state and local fund-raising regulations (part of the political setting)—all influence the organization's ability to raise funds, for example.

- *What is the physical environment?* The physical or geographic setting for NPOs can be very important. For a community development organization, a few of the items which might be included here are housing stock, vacant property, streets, and parks. Is the locale improving or deteriorating? (The condition of the organization's facilities does not belong under this category, but will be treated later under resources.)

- *What is the market environment?* Most organizations have "competitors," other organizations providing the same, similar, or related services. Is the demand for these services rising or declining? Is your organization's market share increasing or decreasing? What cooperative relations exist with similar organizations—nonprofit, governmental, and for-profit?

- *For organizations which are part of a larger organization, how does this relationship affect the organization being studied?* Many NPOs are affiliated in some way with a larger regional or national organization, and these "umbrella" groups often have a direct impact on an organization. Some examples: The Girl Scouts of the U.S.A. provide materials, program services, and guidance to local Girl Scout Councils. United Ways restricts some of the fund-raising practices of their member agencies, but they are an important source of funds for members. Some national membership organizations restrict eligibility, and some local affiliates have disagreed with these restrictions (as in limiting membership to males).

- *Has the organization's environment changed over time?* Environmental changes often necessitate adaptations by an organization. Has there been much change in recent years? Is the current environment stable or turbulent? What changes are likely to occur?

- *Do society, members (if any), and clients (if any) value the organization's activities and services?* While this general question may be difficult to answer, the answers are critical to the health of any nonprofit organization.

- *How does the organization find out about environmental forces and changes?* Many NPOs now regularly monitor, or "scan," their external environments in order to be more aware of changes. Often this is part of the organization's planning process; sometimes it is done by public relations staff.

- *What efforts does the organization make to influence its environment?* Most nonprofit organizations no longer simply accept environmental changes but also try to influence them. Larger NPOs have organizational divisions which do this full-time: marketing and public relations, governmental relations and lobbying, media relations, and community relations. The activities of these units should be examined as part of any organizational analysis.

Goals

This category focuses on what the nonprofit organization is trying to accomplish and how it determines this.

- *Are the organizational goals specified?* Here we are concerned with whether there is a statement of goals and objectives for the organization. We also want to know how clearly goals are defined.

- *Do some goals conflict with other goals?* In larger, more complex NPOs, goal conflict is frequent, perhaps inevitable. The three basic goals of almost any university are teaching, research, and public service. However, there can often be conflict among these goals. When a professor complains that faculty must either "publish or perish," the comment implies that greater rewards are associated with the research goal than with the teaching goal.

- *How are goals determined? Does the organization have a plan?* A planning process is an essential element in an NPO if there is to be agreement on goals and if goals and organizational activities are to be effectively linked. Here the analyst should examine the planning process and the participation in that process: Is there agreement on goals and commitment to the goals—both at the top and throughout the organization? Are there other—informal or covert—goals prevalent in the organization?

- *Are there societal or community needs which the organization seeks to meet?* Theoretically at least, nonprofit organizations exist to meet human needs. Are there real, demonstrable needs which this organization seeks to fill? Or are many of its activities carried out regardless of need, largely ignoring the fact that other organizations do the same job better?

Resources

The basic issue here is whether a particular nonprofit organization has sufficient resources to accomplish its goals. Resources include

- Finances
- Facilities
- Equipment and supplies
- Employees
- Volunteers

Each of these aspects must be included in responding to the four key questions below.

- *What are the main patterns of resource acquisition?* Here the concern is with how difficult it is for the organization to acquire sufficient resources and with the dependability of the suppliers. This concern would affect all the resources indicated above—revenues and volunteers, for example.

- *Is there a system for allocating resources? What are the main patterns of resource allocation?* Following acquisition, organizational analysis also stresses the internal allocation of resources. When there are new dollars, new computers, or new student volunteers, where do they go? When there are fewer dollars, how are expenditures budgeted? Nonprofit budgeting stresses balancing revenues and expenditures and also allocating available funds. The budget process, the relationship between plans and budgets, and priority setting are all reviewed here.

- *Are resources well-managed?* Normally there is an organizational subsystem for managing each of the resources: financial management, physical plant administration, personnel management (including labor relations), and volunteer administration. Under financial management, for example, bookkeeping, accounting methods, cash management, debt management, endowment management, purchasing, fund-raising and grantsmanship programs, and auditing might all be reviewed.[7]

- *Is there a plan to maintain and improve resources and their utilization?* People resources are improved, for example, by staff training programs, and facilities, by preventive maintenance. Beyond the maintenance of resources, many NPOs seek better resource utilization. This can range from a variety of cost reduction or cost-containment programs, to energy conservation programs, to controlling overtime.

Structure

Structure refers to the formal organizational design—the way the organization is intended to operate. The organization chart, standard operating procedures, and job descriptions are all part of the organizational structure. Structure emphasizes the division of authority and work.

- *How does the organization divide its work?* Here we look for patterns of centralization and decentralization. Every organization of any size has to decentralize in order to accomplish its work. However, organizations also require a certain amount of centralization to coordinate these tasks and to be able to act as a single, unified entity. In decentralization, structures can stress functions, clients, geography, or some mix of these traditional patterns.

- *Is the organization designed to achieve its goals?* Here the relationship between goals and structures is assessed.

- *Do people know what their work group is supposed to do?* If structure distributes the work of the organization, one test is to determine if staff understand the division of labor, at least as it affects their work unit.

- *Are certain important activities not being done?* Sometimes minor items fall between the cracks in organizations. Here, however, we are looking for significant activities not assigned and therefore not being performed.

Behavior

If structure provides the framework for work, behavior asks how the work is actually being accomplished (if at all). The greatest concern here is the fit between individuals and the particular organization being analyzed.

- *Are individuals motivated to perform their best? Are there incentives to perform?*
- *What are the main motivators used in the organization—fear, threats, punishments, rewards, involvement?*

- *Are people treated equitably?*

- *Where is responsibility felt for achieving organizational goals?* Ideally, responsibility is felt throughout the organization—by line managers, professionals, service delivery personnel, volunteers—not just by the chief executive officer, top management and the board.

- *Is there a system for individual goal setting and performance appraisal? Is it effective?*

- *Is organizational communication effective?* Here the concern is with adequate flows of accurate information. Attention should be paid to two-way communication rather than just one-way (top-down) patterns.

- *How much communication focuses on achieving goals?*

- *Are work groups performing effectively?* Many of an organization's tasks are carried out by relatively small, face-to-face groups of individuals. Their performance is critical to overall organizational performance.

- *Do work groups cooperate with one another?* Work groups must coordinate their activities with other groups in the organization. Is this done? If so, is it done harmoniously, or is there conflict?

- *What is the nature of the organizational culture, and does it promote performance?* Every organization has a culture, although some cultures are stronger than others. An organizational culture is a set of basic assumptions and beliefs shared by organizational participants and learned as a part of their organizational experience. The culture exhibits norms for behavior, a philosophy which guides policies toward individuals (employees, or members, or clients), "rules of the game" for operating the organization, and even heroes (Ralph Nader and John Gardner in their nonprofit organizations, for example). Organizational culture shapes the climate in which we all operate and differs widely from one organization to another.[8]

Outputs

"Outputs" are the activities implemented by an organization, whereas "outcomes" are the results or impacts of those activities. In a university, teaching is an output, but learning is an outcome. We often have many ways to measure outputs, but find it far more difficult to measure outcomes. Again in a university, typical measures of teaching outputs include student credit hours taught, cost per credit hour, student-faculty ratio, and average class size.

- *What activities is the organization actually carrying out?.*

- *Does top management know what is being done?.* Here we look for some kind of regular feedback system which allows the organization's outputs to be measured and monitored.

- *Are the outputs (or activities: programs, services, concerts, etc.) consistent with the organizational goals?.*

- *Are the outputs carried out relatively efficiently?.* Most organizations are concerned with the cost per some standard unit of output. Government reimbursement rates for hospitals are based on patients according to various categories of diseases (called DRGs, or diagnostic related groups). Hospitals regularly compare their actual cost for treating a patient suffering from a particular disease with what they are reimbursed for that patient.

- *Is there a plan to improve the outputs?.* A modern definition of productivity improvement would include both outputs and outcomes. Here we ask if any attention is being paid to improving the quantity, quality, or cost of the outputs.

Outcomes

Outcomes are the results, or impacts, of an organization's activities. For the business firm, profitability is the principal outcome sought. Measuring the outcomes of nonprofit organizations is far more difficult, even though there is increasing effort being placed on program evaluation, the term and methodology commonly used in assessing outcomes. In this kind of organizational analysis, original assessment of outcomes is rarely attempted; rather, information is gathered about what the organization already knows about its outcomes.

- *Organizational activities are carried out with what outcomes (results, impacts)?*
- *Does the organization know much about its outcomes?*
- *Do outcomes meet organizational goals?*
- *Are outcomes responsive to demands from the organization's environment?* Here we are particularly concerned with client or consumer satisfaction.
- *Are there unintended consequences?* Especially in the human services, some care must be taken to look for unintended and perhaps undesirable consequences.
- *Is there a plan to improve outcomes?*

Leadership

Leadership here refers to those responsible for orchestrating all the other boxes in a nonprofit organization. In an NPO, the board of directors has full legal authority, but, in reality, shared authority best describes responsibility for central direction and leadership.[9]

- *Who are the most important decision makers in this organization?* In other words, who runs this organization? In addition, what are their sources of power? Formal position, expertise, alliances with others inside the organization, power or prestige outside the organization, problem-solving ability, and/or knowledge about the operations of the organization are all possible sources.
- *Does the board of directors manage itself effectively?* The standards for boards of national nonprofit organizations promulgated by the National Charities Information Bureau (NCIB) call for an active and responsible governing body that holds regular meetings, whose members have no material conflict of interest and serve without compensation.[10] Special attention should be shown to balanced board membership, an active committee structure, and harmonious board-staff relations.[11]
- *Are decisions made which are sound and timely?* Decision making is an important leadership function, and the process of decision making requires attention in organizational analysis.
- *Are decisions made at the appropriate level?*
- *Do subordinates participate in decision-making processes?*
- *Are decisions preceded by appropriate analysis?*
- *Regarding the chief executive officer and top management, is leadership behavior effective?* One related question is whether leadership style is appropriate to the sit-

uation: type of organization, formal authority of the leader, task structure, and leader-member relations?

- *Is confidence shown in subordinates throughout the organization?*
- *Is creativity encouraged?* For example, are new ideas and risk taking encouraged?
- *Is organizational change relatively easy or difficult?* Is there much resistance? Why?

Translating Analysis into Management Improvement

As you are completing an organizational analysis, particularly using the approach outlined here, you should ask yourself: What did I learn? Were there any surprises?

Beyond that, do any boxes in the analysis or units in the organization require additional study? When using this comprehensive approach, one or more areas may stand out as requiring in-depth examination.

One productive type of thinking which grows out of organizational analysis is to consider the linkages between the various boxes: such as environment and goals, outputs and outcomes, resources and outcomes, leadership and both outputs and outcomes.

Recommendations for management improvement almost always flow out of this kind of analysis. However, translating analysis into action requires careful consideration. The need for effective communication, sufficient resources, an appropriate organizational culture, and effective leadership are all central to management improvement efforts.

Management improvement requires a strategy of its own. Both recommended improvements and the strategy for improvement need to be based on the organizational analysis, and once it is finished, it should not be used simply as an excuse to implement a long-held idea unrelated to the analysis. Similarly, the analysis, if it is done carefully and properly, should not be ignored.

Organizational analysis offers the opportunity to improve the management of nonprofit organizations based on systematic study. The comprehensive approach advocated here at least ensures that the right questions be asked. And most organizations, at least healthy ones, view management excellence as an ongoing concern.

Notes

1. Lee G. Bolman and Terrence E. Deal, *Modern Approaches to Understanding and Managing Organizations,* Jossey-Bass, San Francisco, 1985, pp. 10–13.

2. Frederick S. Lane, "Managing Not-for-Profit Organizations," *Public Administration Review,* September-October 1980, pp. 526–530.

3. IRS Form 990 is filed annually by tax-exempt 501(c) organizations. For a complete explanation, see *A Grantmaker's Guide to a New Tool for Philanthropy—Form 990,* National Charities Information Bureau, New York, 1983.

4. Marvin R. Weisbord, *Organizational Diagnosis: A Workbook of Theory and Practice,* Addison-Wesley, Reading, Mass., 1978.

5. Weisbord refers to his approach as a "six-box" model.

6. Marian Neef suggested the questions that were used here in the history category.

7. A variety of guides are available to help in analyzing specific areas dealing with resources. For example, see Robert J. Berendt and J. Richard Taft, *How to Rate Your Development Office,* The Taft Group, Washington, 1983; and *NAEB Purchasing Self Assessment Guide,* National Association of Educational Buyers, Woodbury, N.Y., 1986.

8. Edgar H. Schein, *Organizational Culture and Leadership,* Jossey-Bass, San Francisco, 1986, especially pp. 5–9; Terrence E. Deal and Allan A. Kennedy, *Corporate Cultures: The Rites and Rituals of Corporate Life,* Addison-Wesley, Reading, Mass., 1982.

9. The idea of separating leadership from the behavior category is based on Weisbord's work. Questions related to decision making and leadership are based on Rensis Likert, *The Human Organization,* McGraw-Hill, New York, 1967.

10. *NCIB Standards in Philanthropy,* National Charities Information Bureau, New York, 1982.

11. A variety of assessment guides are available for boards of directors of nonprofit organizations. For example, see William R. Conrad, Jr., *Board of Directors Self-Assessment,* Voluntary Management Press, Downers Grove, Ill., 1983, and *Management Review Program, Department Self Evaluation Series: Hospital Governing Board,* American Hospital Association, Chicago, 1968.

Suggested Reading

The selections in this *Handbook* are a solid starting place for almost every aspect of nonprofit organizational analysis. Beyond these, the reader may want to consult some of the works below.

Babbie, Earl R., *Social Research for Consumers,* Wadsworth, Belmont, Calif., 1982.

Brinckerhoff, Peter C., "The Management Audit: A Task Whose Time Has Come," *Grantsmanship Center News,* spring–summer 1984.

Conrad, William R., Jr., and Hank Rubin, *Management Self Assessment,* Voluntary Management Press, Downers Grove, Ill., 1983.

Elkin, Robert, and Mark Molitor, *Management Indicators in Nonprofit Organizations,* Peat, Marwick, Mitchell, New York, 1984.

Girl Scout Council Self-Evaluation, Girl Scouts of the U.S.A., New York, 1982.

Kopelman, Richard E., *Managing Productivity in Organizations: A Practical, People-Oriented Perspective,* McGraw-Hill, New York, 1986, especially chaps. 2, 13, and 14.

Levinson, Harry, *Organizational Diagnosis,* Harvard University Press, Cambridge, 1972.

Lippincott, Earle, and Elling Aannestad, "Management of Voluntary Welfare Agencies," *Harvard Business Review,* November–December 1964.

Management Systems: A Self-Diagnostic Kit, Resources for Community Alternatives, Santa Fe, N.M., 1978.

Mico, Paul R., *Developing Your Community-Based Organization,* Third Party Publishing, Oakland, Calif., 1981.

Nadler, David A., *Feedback and Organizational Development: Using Data Based Methods,* Addison-Wesley, Reading, Mass., 1977.

—— and Michael L. Tushman, "A Model for Diagnosing Organizational Behavior," *Organizational Dynamics,* autumn 1980.

Newman, Harvey I., William O'Reilly, and Alfons Van Wijk, *Self-Evaluation and Planning for Human Service Organizations,* AMACOM, New York, 1987.

Reigel, Bobette W., *Basic Feedback System: A Self-Assessment Process for Volunteer Programs,* National Information Center on Volunteerism, Boulder, Colo., 1977.

Report of the Pilot Project to Test the Use of Ratio Analysis in Self-Evaluation, Planning, and Reporting of Nonprofit Organizations, National Charities Information Bureau, New York, May 1984.

Standards and Guidelines for the Field of Volunteerism, Association of Volunteer Bureaus, 1978.

Standards of Excellence for Local United Way Organizations, United Way of America, Alexandria, Va., September 1977.

Stone, Eugene, *Research Methods in Organizational Behavior,* Scott, Foresman, Glenview, Ill., 1978.

15

Controlling Instruments of the Nonprofit Organization: By-Laws and the Articles of Incorporation

Tracy D. Connors
Consultant

Robert R. Hart, Jr.
Attorney

Virtually all nonprofit organizations (NPOs) have by-laws, the set of internal rules or laws by which the organization conducts its management. All incorporated "not-for-profit" organizations have prepared and filed with the proper public authorities what amounts to their application for incorporation, called variously "Articles of Incorporation," "Certificates of Incorporation," or "Articles of Association." These documents have much in common in terms of the vital roles they play in controlling and ordering the activities and procedures of the NPO. They also share a problem in that most members are both ignorant of the contents and functions and often are bored by the dry, legalistic phraseology. Yet, effective management of the organization has as its cornerstone the development of a "good" set of by-laws and articles, both of which should be reviewed regularly to ensure that they reflect good internal management practice as well as the will of the membership.

This chapter reviews the basics of formulating a set of by-laws that create the form of internal management you desire for your organization. It also reviews the form and contents of a "typical" set of articles. This discussion can serve only to introduce the subject and to underscore the importance of these documents. Local law and custom differ widely, making it impossible to provide detailed guidance. Leaders of NPOs should consult a knowledgeable local attorney for guidance and recommendations. It is the responsibility of NPO officers, directors, and staff, however, to be familiar with state and local requirements in general and with their own by-laws and articles in particular. For an excellent discussion of by-laws and articles, readers are referred to Oleck's *NonProfit Corporations, Organizations, and Associations.*[1]

By-laws

By-laws are secondary only to the articles in their power to bind and direct the powers of the organization and its members. In any conflict between the by-laws and the articles of incorporation, the articles govern.[2] By-laws are discussed first since not all NPOs are, or will need to be, incorporated, but virtually all will need to create an adequate set of by-laws.

The Model Nonprofit Corporation Act prepared by the American Bar Association notes that " 'by-laws' means the code or codes of rules adopted for the regulation or management of the affairs of the corporation (organization) irrespective of the name or names by which such rules are designated...not inconsistent with law or the articles of incorporation."[3] The extent to which the by-laws are well drafted is the extent to which friction and differences of opinion as to procedures, rights, and powers will be kept to a minimum.

Nonprofit organizations have inherent rights to prepare, adopt, and amend by-laws. Most state statutes on NPO matters assume that by-laws will be adopted. The Internal Revenue Service rarely grants tax exemption to organizations without well-drawn by-laws reflecting effective provisions for the level of internal management adequate to serve the public purpose for which exemption is requested.

Oleck explains that by-laws serve three important purposes:

1. Regulating the internal practices and procedures of the organization.

2. Defining the relations, rights, and duties of the members amongst themselves and in relation to the organization.

3. Defining the powers, duties, and limitations of trustees (directors), officers, and other agents.[4]

In general, the power to prepare, adopt, and amend the by-laws is retained by the general membership. Any move by a group within the organization to alter this basic right should be given strong scrutiny. Granting the general power to change the by-laws to the board of directors does not alter the fact that the basic power over the by-laws rests with the membership and may be withdrawn from the board. Obviously, by-laws should outline an exact procedure for amending the by-laws.[5] Some important points relative to by-laws to keep in mind regarding your NPO:

- Give careful thought to your by-laws and draft them with care.

- Adopt your by-laws soon after organization of the NPO, but do so deliberately, not hastily. Do not attempt to operate your NPO without adopted by-laws.

- Get assistance from a qualified attorney. Avoid letting amateurs draft the by-laws, often simply copying those of another organization—a risky practice, at best.

- Prepare your NPO's by-laws with its specific purposes and objectives in mind.

- In general, it is best to leave the power to adopt and amend the by-laws within the membership, as opposed to the board of directors. Similarly, the board should have only modest amendment powers, hedged with safeguards.

The following Model By-Laws are reprinted by permission of the American Bar Association from its Model Nonprofit Corporation Act, the full text of which is an excellent reference. It may be obtained by writing the American Law Institute, American Bar Association Committee on Continuing Professional Education, 4025 Chestnut Street, Philadelphia, PA 19104.

BY-LAWS[1] OF[*]

. . . .

Article I. Offices

The principal office of the corporation in the State of . . . . shall be located in the City of . . . . , County of . . . . The corporation may have such other offices, either within or without the State of . . . . , as the Board of Directors may determine or as the affairs of the corporation may require from time to time.

The corporation shall have and continuously maintain in the State of . . . . a registered office, and a registered agent whose office is identical with such registered office, as required by the . . . . Non-Profit Corporation Act. The registered office may be, but need not be, identical with the principal office in the State of . . . . , and the address of the registered office may be changed from time to time by the Board of Directors. [§§8 and 9].

Article II. Members

SECTION 1. CLASSES OF MEMBERS.[2] The corporation shall have . . . . class (or classes) of members. The designation of such class (or classes) and the qualifications and rights of the members of such class (or classes) shall be as follows:
. . . . [§11]

SECTION 2. ELECTION OF MEMBERS.[3] Members shall be elected by the Board of Directors. An affirmative vote of two-thirds of the Directors shall be required for election.

SECTION 3. VOTING RIGHTS.[4] Each member shall be entitled to one vote on each matter submitted to a vote of the members [§15].

SECTION 4. TERMINATION OF MEMBERSHIP. The Board of Directors, by affirmative vote of two-thirds of all of the members of the Board, may suspend or expel a member for

---

*Numbers in brackets are references to Sections of the Model Non-Profit Corporation Act. The footnotes are collected at the conclusion of the By-Laws.

Reprinted by permission of the Committee on Corporate Laws of the American Bar Association, "Model Nonprofit Corporation Act," pp. 108–119.

cause after an appropriate hearing, and may, by a majority vote of those present at any regularly constituted meeting, terminate the membership of any member who becomes ineligible for membership, or suspend or expel any member who shall be in default in the payment of dues for the period fixed in Article XI of these by-laws.

SECTION 5. RESIGNATION.   Any member may resign by filing a written resignation with the Secretary, but such resignation shall not relieve the member so resigning of the obligation to pay any dues, assessments or other charges theretofore accrued and unpaid.

SECTION 6. REINSTATEMENT.   Upon written request signed by a former member and filed with the Secretary, the Board of Directors may, by the affirmative vote of two-thirds of the members of the Board, reinstate such former member to membership upon such terms as the Board of Directors may deem appropriate.

SECTION 7. TRANSFER OF MEMBERSHIP.[5]   Membership in this corporation is not transferable or assignable.

ARTICLE III. MEETINGS OF MEMBERS

SECTION 1. ANNUAL MEETING.   An annual meeting of the members shall be held on the . . . . in the month of . . . . in each year, beginning with the year 19 . . . . , at the hour of . . . . o'clock, . . M., for the purpose of electing Directors and for the transaction of such other business as may come before the meeting. If the day fixed for the annual meeting shall be a legal holiday in the State of . . . . , such meeting shall be held on the next succeeding business day. If the election of Directors shall not be held on the day designated herein for any annual meeting, or at any adjournment thereof, the Board of Directors shall cause the election to be held at a special meeting of the members as soon thereafter as conveniently may be. [§13].

SECTION 2. SPECIAL MEETINGS.[6]   Special meetings of the members may be called by the President, the Board of Directors, or not less than one-tenth of the members having voting rights. [§13].

SECTION 3. PLACE OF MEETING.[7]   The Board of Directors may designate any place, either within or without the State of . . . . , as the place of meeting for any annual meeting or for any special meeting called by the Board of Directors. If no designation is made or if a special meeting be otherwise called, the place of meeting shall be the registered office of the corporation in the State of . . . . ; but if all of the members shall meet at any time and place, either within or without the State of . . . . , and consent to the holding of a meeting, such meeting shall be valid without call or notice, and at such meeting any corporate action may be taken. [§13].

SECTION 4. NOTICE OF MEETINGS.[8]   Written notice stating the place, day and hour of any meeting of members shall be delivered, either personally or by mail, to each member entitled to vote at such meeting, not less than ten nor more than fifty days before the date of such meeting, by or at the direction of the President, or the Secretary, or the officers or persons calling the meeting. In case of a special meeting or when required by statute or by these by-laws, the purpose or purposes for which the meeting is called shall be stated in the notice. If mailed, the notice of a meeting shall be deemed to be delivered when deposited in the United States mail addressed to the member at his address as it appears on the records of the corporation, with postage thereon prepaid. [§14].

SECTION 5. INFORMAL ACTION BY MEMBERS.[9]   Any action required by law to be taken at a meeting of the members, or any action which may be taken at a meeting of members, may be taken without a meeting if a consent in writing, setting forth the action so taken, is signed by all of the members entitled to vote with respect to the subject matter thereof. [§95].

SECTION 6. QUORUM.[10] The members holding one- . . . . of the votes which may be cast at any meeting shall constitute a quorum at such meeting. If a quorum is not present at any meeting of members, a majority of the members present may adjourn the meeting from time to time without further notice. [§16].

SECTION 7. PROXIES.[11] At any meeting of members, a member entitled to vote may vote by proxy executed in writing by the member or by his duly authorized attorney-in-fact. No proxy shall be valid after eleven months from the date of its execution, unless otherwise provided in the proxy. [§15].

SECTION 8. MANNER OF ACTING. A majority of the votes entitled to be cast on a matter to be voted upon by the members present or represented by proxy at a meeting at which a quorum is present shall be necessary for the adoption thereof unless a greater proportion is required by law or by these by-laws.

SECTION 9. VOTING BY MAIL. Where Directors or officers are to be elected by members or any class or classes of members, such election may be conducted by mail in such manner as the Board of Directors shall determine. [§15].

ARTICLE IV. BOARD OF DIRECTORS

SECTION 1. GENERAL POWERS. The affairs of the corporation shall be managed by its Board of Directors.[12] Directors need not be residents of the State of . . . . or members of the corporation.[§§2(g)and 17].

SECTION 2. NUMBER, TENURE AND QUALIFICATIONS.[13] The number of Directors shall be . . . . Each Director shall hold office until the next annual meeting of members and until his successor shall have been elected and qualified. [§18].

SECTION 3. REGULAR MEETINGS. A regular annual meeting of the Board of Directors shall be held without other notice than this by-law, immediately after, and at the same place as, the annual meeting of members. The Board of Directors may provide by resolution the time and place, either within or without the State of . . . . , for the holding of additional regular meetings of the Board without other notice than such resolution. [§22].

SECTION 4. SPECIAL MEETINGS. Special meetings of the Board of Directors may be called by or at the request of the President or any two Directors. The person or persons authorized to call special meetings of the Board may fix any place, either within or without the State of . . . . , as the place for holding any special meeting of the Board called by them. [§22].

SECTION 5. NOTICE. Notice of any special meeting of the Board of Directors shall be given at least two days previously thereto by written notice delivered personally or sent by mail or telegram to each Director at his address as shown by the records of the corporation. If mailed, such notice shall be deemed to be delivered when deposited in the United States mail in a sealed envelope so addressed, with postage thereon prepaid. If notice be given by telegram, such notice shall be deemed to be delivered when the telegram is delivered to the telegraph company. Any Director may waive notice of any meeting. The attendance of a Director at any meeting shall constitute a waiver of notice of such meeting, except where a Director attends a meeting for the express purpose of objecting to the transaction of any business because the meeting is not lawfully called or convened. Neither the business to be transacted at, nor the purpose of, any regular or special meeting of the Board need be specified in the notice or waiver of notice of such meeting, unless specifically required by law or by these by-laws. [§22].

SECTION 6. QUORUM.[14] A majority of the Board of Directors shall constitute a quorum for the transaction of business at any meeting of the Board; but if less than a majority of the Directors are present at said meeting, a majority of the Directors present may adjourn the meeting from time to time without further notice. [§20].

SECTION 7. MANNER OF ACTING.   The act of a majority of the Directors present at a meeting at which a quorum is present shall be the act of the Board of Directors, unless the act of a greater number is required by law or by these by-laws. [§20].

SECTION 8. VACANCIES.   Any vacancy occurring in the Board of Directors and any directorship to be filled by reason of an increase in the number of directors may be filled by the affirmative vote of a majority of the remaining directors, though less than a quorum of the Board of Directors. A Director elected to fill a vacancy shall be elected for the unexpired term of his predecessor in office. [§19].

SECTION 9. COMPENSATION.   Directors as such shall not receive any stated salaries for their services, but by resolution of the Board of Directors a fixed sum and expenses of attendance, if any, may be allowed for attendance at each regular or special meeting of the Board; but nothing herein contained shall be construed to preclude any Director from serving the corporation in any other capacity and receiving compensation therefor.

SECTION 10. INFORMAL ACTION BY DIRECTORS.[9]   Any action required by law to be taken at a meeting of directors, or any action which may be taken at a meeting of directors, may be taken without a meeting if a consent in writing, setting forth the action so taken, is signed by all of the Directors. [§95].

ARTICLE V. OFFICERS

SECTION 1. OFFICERS.   The officers of the corporation shall be[15] a President, one or more Vice Presidents (the number thereof to be determined by the Board of Directors), a Secretary, a Treasurer and such other officers as may be elected in accordance with the provisions of this Article. The Board of Directors may elect or appoint such other officers, including one or more Assistant Secretaries and one or more Assistant Treasurers, as it shall deem desirable, such officers to have the authority and perform the duties prescribed, from time to time, by the Board of Directors. Any two or more offices may be held by the same person, except the offices of President and Secretary. [§23].

SECTION 2. ELECTION AND TERM OF OFFICE.[16]   The officers of the corporation shall be elected annually by the Board of Directors at the regular annual meeting of the Board of Directors. If the election of officers shall not be held at such meeting, such election shall be held as soon thereafter as conveniently may be. New offices may be created and filled at any meeting of the Board of Directors. Each officer shall hold office until his successor shall have been duly elected and shall have qualified. [§23].

SECTION 3. REMOVAL.[17]   Any officer elected or appointed by the Board of Directors may be removed by the Board of Directors whenever in its judgment the best interests of the corporation would be served thereby, but such removal shall be without prejudice to the contract rights, if any, of the officer so removed. [§24].

SECTION 4. VACANCIES.   A vacancy in any office because of death, resignation, removal, disqualification or otherwise, may be filled by the Board of Directors for the unexpired portion of the term.

SECTION 5. PRESIDENT.   The President shall be the principal executive officer of the corporation and shall in general supervise and control all of the business and affairs of the corporation. He shall preside at all meetings of the members and of the Board of Directors. He may sign, with the Secretary or any other proper officer of the corporation authorized by the Board of Directors, any deeds, mortgages, bonds, contracts, or other instruments which the Board of Directors has authorized to be executed, except in cases where the signing and execution thereof shall be expressly delegated by the Board of

Directors or by these by-laws or by statute to some other officer or agent of the corporation; and in general he shall perform all duties incident to the office of President and such other duties as may be prescribed by the Board of Directors from time to time.

SECTION 6. VICE PRESIDENT. In the absence of the President or in event of his inability or refusal to act, the Vice President (or in the event there be more than one Vice President, the Vice Presidents in the order of their election) shall perform the duties of the President, and when so acting, shall have all the powers of and be subject to all the restrictions upon the President. Any Vice President shall perform such other duties as from time to time may be assigned to him by the President or by the Board of Directors.

SECTION 7. TREASURER. If required by the Board of Directors, the Treasurer shall give a bond for the faithful discharge of his duties in such sum and with such surety or sureties as the Board of Directors shall determine. He shall have charge and custody of and be responsible for all funds and securities of the corporation; receive and give receipts for moneys due and payable to the corporation from any source whatsoever, and deposit all such moneys in the name of the corporation in such banks, trust companies or other depositaries as shall be selected in accordance with the provisions of Article VII of these by-laws; and in general perform all the duties incident to the office of Treasurer and such other duties as from time to time may be assigned to him by the President or by the Board of Directors.

SECTION 8. SECRETARY. The Secretary shall keep the minutes of the meetings of the members and of the Board of Directors in one or more books provided for that purpose; see that all notices are duly given in accordance with the provisions of these by-laws or as required by law; be custodian of the corporate records and of the seal of the corporation and see that the seal of the corporation is affixed to all documents, the execution of which on behalf of the corporation under its seal is duly authorized in accordance with the provisions of these by-laws; keep a register of the post-office address of each member which shall be furnished to the Secretary by such member; and in general perform all duties incident to the office of Secretary and such other duties as from time to time may be assigned to him by the President or by the Board of Directors.

SECTION 9. ASSISTANT TREASURERS AND ASSISTANT SECRETARIES. If required by the Board of Directors, the Assistant Treasurers shall give bonds for the faithful discharge of their duties in such sums and with such sureties as the Board of Directors shall determine. The Assistant Treasurers and Assistant Secretaries, in general, shall perform such duties as shall be assigned to them by the Treasurer or the Secretary or by the President or the Board of Directors.

ARTICLE VI. COMMITTEES

SECTION 1. COMMITTEES OF DIRECTORS. The Board of Directors, by resolution adopted by a majority of the Directors in office, may designate and appoint one or more committees, each of which shall consist of two or more Directors, which committees, to the extent provided in said resolution, shall have and exercise the authority of the Board of Directors in the management of the corporation, except that no such committee shall have the authority of the Board of Directors in reference to amending, altering or repealing the by-laws; electing, appointing or removing any member of any such committee or any Director or officer of the corporation; amending the articles of incorporation; restating articles of incorporation; adopting a plan of merger or adopting a plan of consolidation with another corporation; authorizing the sale, lease, exchange or mortgage of all or substantially all of the property and assets of the corporation; authorizing the voluntary dissolution of the corporation or revoking proceedings therefor; adopting a plan for the distribution of the assets of the corporation; or amending, altering or repealing any resolution of the Board of Directors which by its terms provides that it shall not be amended, altered or repealed by such committee. The designation and appointment of any such committee and the delegation thereto of authority shall not operate to relieve the Board of Directors, or any individual Director, of any responsibility imposed upon it or him by law. [§21].

SECTION 2. OTHER COMMITTEES   Other committees not having and exercising the authority of the Board of Directors in the management of the corporation may be appointed in such manner as may be designated by a resolution adopted by a majority of the Directors present at a meeting at which a quorum is present. Except as otherwise provided in such resolution, members of each such committee shall be members of the corporation, and the President of the corporation shall appoint the members thereof. Any member thereof may be removed by the person or persons authorized to appoint such member whenever in their judgment the best interests of the corporation shall be served by such removal.

SECTION 3. TERM OF OFFICE.   Each member of a committee shall continue as such until the next annual meeting of the members of the corporation and until his successor is appointed, unless the committee shall be sooner terminated, or unless such member be removed from such committee, or unless such member shall cease to qualify as a member thereof.

SECTION 4. CHAIRMAN.   One member of each committee shall be appointed chairman by the person or persons authorized to appoint the members thereof.

SECTION 5. VACANCIES.   Vacancies in the membership of any committee may be filled by appointments made in the same manner as provided in the case of the original appointments.

SECTION 6. QUORUM.   Unless otherwise provided in the resolution of the Board of Directors designating a committee, a majority of the whole committee shall constitute a quorum and the act of a majority of the members present at the meeting at which a quorum is present shall be the act of the committee.

SECTION 7. RULES.   Each committee may adopt rules for its own government not inconsistent with these by-laws or with rules adopted by the Board of Directors.

ARTICLE VII. CONTRACTS, CHECKS, DEPOSITS AND FUNDS

SECTION 1. CONTRACTS.   The Board of Directors may authorize any officer or officers, agent or agents of the corporation, in addition to the officers so authorized by these by-laws, to enter into any contract or execute and deliver any instrument in the name of and on behalf of the corporation, and such authority may be general or confined to specific instances.

SECTION 2. CHECKS, DRAFTS, ETC.   All checks, drafts or orders for the payment of money, notes or other evidences of indebtedness issued in the name of the corporation, shall be signed by such officer or officers, agent or agents of the corporation and in such manner as shall from time to time be determined by resolution of the Board of Directors. In the absence of such determination by the Board of Directors, such instruments shall be signed by the Treasurer or an Assistant Treasurer and countersigned by the President or a Vice President of the corporation.

SECTION 3. DEPOSITS.   All funds of the corporation shall be deposited from time to time to the credit of the corporation in such banks, trust companies or other depositaries as the Board of Directors may select.

SECTION 4. GIFTS.   The Board of Directors may accept on behalf of the corporation any contribution, gift, bequest or devise for the general purposes or for any special purpose of the corporation.

ARTICLE VIII. CERTIFICATES OF MEMBERSHIP.[18]

SECTION 1. CERTIFICATES OF MEMBERSHIP. The Board of Directors may provide for the issuance of certificates evidencing membership in the corporation, which shall be in such form as may be determined by the Board. Such certificates shall be signed by the President or a Vice President and by the Secretary or an Assistant Secretary and shall be sealed with the seal of the corporation. All certificates evidencing membership of any class shall be consecutively numbered. The name and address of each member and the date of issuance of the certificate shall be entered on the records of the corporation. If any certificate shall become lost, mutilated or destroyed, a new certificate may be issued therefor upon such terms and conditions as the Board of Directors may determine. [§11].

SECTION 2. ISSUANCE OF CERTIFICATES. When a member has been elected to membership and has paid any initiation fee and dues that may then be required, a certificate of membership shall be issued in his name and delivered to him by the Secretary, if the Board of Directors shall have provided for the issuance of certificates of membership under the provisions of Section 1 of this Article VIII.[19]

ARTICLE IX. BOOKS AND RECORDS

The corporation shall keep correct and complete books and records of account and shall also keep minutes of the proceedings of its members, Board of Directors and committees having any of the authority of the Board of Directors, and shall keep at its registered or principal office a record giving the names and addresses of the members entitled to vote. All books and records of the corporation may be inspected by any member, or his agent or attorney, for any proper purpose at any reasonable time. [§25].

ARTICLE X. FISCAL YEAR

The fiscal year of the corporation shall begin on the first day of January and end on the last day of December in each year.

ARTICLE XI. DUES

SECTION 1. ANNUAL DUES.[20] The Board of Directors may determine from time to time the amount of initiation fee, if any, and annual dues payable to the corporation by members of each class.

SECTION 2. PAYMENT OF DUES. Dues shall be payable in advance on the first day of . . . . in each fiscal year. Dues of a new member shall be prorated from the first day of the month in which such new member is elected to membership, for the remainder of the fiscal year of the corporation.

SECTION 3. DEFAULT AND TERMINATION OF MEMBERSHIP. When any member of any class shall be in default in the payment of dues for a period of . . . . months from the beginning of the fiscal year or period for which such dues became payable, his membership may thereupon be terminated by the Board of Directors in the manner provided in Article III of these by-laws.

ARTICLE XII. SEAL

The Board of Directors shall provide a corporate seal, which shall be in the form of a circle and shall have inscribed thereon the name of the corporation and the words "Corporate Seal . . . ." [§5(c)].

ARTICLE XIII. WAIVER OF NOTICE

Whenever any notice is required to be given under the provisions of the . . . . Non-Profit Corporation Act or under the provisions of the articles of incorporation or the by-laws of the corporation, a waiver thereof in writing signed by the person or persons entitled to such notice, whether before or after the time stated therein, shall be deemed equivalent to the giving of such notice. [§94].

ARTICLE XIV. AMENDMENTS TO BY-LAWS

These by-laws may be altered, amended or repealed and new by-laws may be adopted by a majority of the Directors present at any regular meeting or at any special meeting, if at least two days' written notice is given of intention to alter, amend or repeal or to adopt new by-laws at such meeting. [§12].

FOOTNOTES

[1] By definition in the Act, the by-laws are the code of rules adopted for the regulation of the corporate affairs, regardless of the name by which the code is designated. The term is here used because of its prevalence in corporate practice.

The initial by-laws are required by the Act to be adopted by the Directors. They may contain any provision for the regulation and management of the affairs of the corporation not inconsistent with law or the articles of incorporation.

[2] The corporation may have one or more classes of members (such as regular, associate, nonresident, honorary, etc.), or it may have no members. If it has no members, that fact shall be set forth in the articles of incorporation or the by-laws. If it has one or more classes, the designation, qualifications and rights of each class may be set forth either in the articles of incorporation or the by-laws. Even though set forth in the articles of incorporation, the statement may be repeated in the by-laws. The qualifications of a class of members may be described in the following manner:

"Resident Members. Members of the . . . . profession in good standing who reside or have an office within the State of . . . . shall be eligible for resident membership."

[3] Members may be chosen in any manner prescribed in the articles of incorporation or in the by-laws. By way of illustration, Section 2 requires election by the Board of Directors. In the case of social clubs and similar organizations a provision that no member shall be elected over the negative vote of a fixed number of Directors may be preferred. In some types of corporations, applications for membership may be deemed desirable, and for such corporations the following paragraphs may be added to Section 2:

"Except in the initial election of members, all applicants for membership shall file with the Secretary a written application in such form as the Board of Directors shall from time to time determine.

"All applications for membership shall be presented promptly for consideration and investigation to the Board of Directors or to the Admissions Committee, if an Admissions Committee has been appointed by the Board of Directors; and if an Admissions Committee has been appointed it shall report its recommendations promptly to the Board of Directors. A list of applications for membership shall from time to time be posted at the principal office of the corporation or mailed to each member of the corporation.

"Not earlier than . . . . days after a list of applications has been posted or mailed to members, the Board of Directors shall pass upon each application included in said list and either accept or reject it. After an applicant has been rejected, he may not make another application for membership within one year thereafter."

[4] The voting rights of members or any class of members may be limited, enlarged or denied under the Act to the extent specified in the articles of incorporation or the by-laws, but unless so specified each member is entitled to one vote.

The right to cumulative voting for Directors (giving each voting member the right to give one candidate a number of votes equal to his vote multiplied by the number of Directors to be elected, or to distribute such votes on the same principle among as many candidates as he shall desire) may be given by the by-laws.

The following alternative provisions may be used where it is desired to give voting rights to some class or classes of members and not to others:

"Each member of the resident, sustaining and life classes shall have one vote on each matter submitted to a vote of the members. Members of the nonresident and honorary classes shall have no voting rights."

When all members are to be denied voting rights, the following may be substituted:

"No member shall have any voting rights. All voting rights are vested solely in the Directors."

[5] Memberships may or may not be transferable as provided by the by-laws. The following is suggested as an alternative in the event that it is desired to have memberships transferable:

"Any membership in this corporation may be transferred and assigned by a member whose dues are paid in full, to any person who has the requisite qualifications and whose application is approved by the Board of Directors and elected to membership."

[6] In the absence of a provision fixing the number or percentage of members entitled to call a meeting, the Act provides that a meeting may be called by members having one-twentieth of the votes entitled to be cast at such meeting.

[7] The Act provides that in the absence of a provision in the by-laws, all meetings shall be held at the registered office of the corporation.

[8] Unless otherwise provided in the by-laws or articles of incorporation written notice stating the place, day and hour of meetings of members must be sent not less than ten nor more than fifty days prior to the meeting.

[9] The Act expressly confirms the right of members and directors to take action in the manner set forth in this Section.

[10] Unless a different number or percentage is provided by the by-laws, the members holding one-tenth of the votes will constitute a quorum.

[11] Proxy voting by members is authorized unless otherwise provided in the articles of incorporation or the by-laws. Some corporations, such as fraternities, may not wish to have their meetings attended by non-members. In view of the statutory permission to limit voting rights, a by-law providing that a proxy may be given only to another member should be valid when the circumstances make this a reasonable restriction.

[12] The Board of Directors may be designated by other titles (such as Board of Governors, Board of Managers, etc.) as provided in the by-laws. The group vested with the management of the affairs of the corporation, by whatever name designated in the by-laws, constitutes the Board of Directors of the corporation as that term is defined in the Act.

The articles of incorporation or the by-laws may prescribe qualifications for Directors.

[13] The number of Directors may be increased or decreased from time to time by amendment to the by-laws, unless otherwise provided in the articles of incorporation. It shall never be less than three. In the absence of a by-law, the number shall be the same as that stated in the articles of incorporation.

Directors need not be elected by members, but may be elected or appointed in the manner and for the terms provided in the articles of incorporation or the by-laws.

Directors may be divided into classes and the terms of office of the several classes need not be uniform.

The Directors named in the articles of incorporation hold office until the first annual meeting of the members (unless otherwise specified in the articles or by-laws), and there need be no meeting of the members to elect them.

The by-laws may provide that any one or more officers shall be ex-officio members of the Board of Directors. Provision may be made in the by-laws for conducting elections of Directors by mail.

[14] Unless otherwise provided in the by-laws, a majority of the Directors shall constitute a quorum. In no event shall a quorum consist of less than one-third of the whole Board.

[15] Officers may be designated by other titles (such as Grand Master, Recorder, etc.) as may be provided in the by-laws, but shall always include (but need not be limited to) persons who occupy offices corresponding to those of President, Vice President, Secretary and Treasurer.

[16] Officers may be elected or appointed in such manner and for such term, not exceeding three years, as the articles of incorporation or the by-laws provide. In the absence of such provision, officers shall be elected or appointed annually. Where desired, provision may be made in the by-laws for the election of some or all of the officers by the members, and where officers are to be elected by members the by-laws may provide for conducting the election by mail.

[17] Officers elected or appointed by some one other than the Board of Directors can be removed only by the persons authorized to elect or appoint them.

[18] Certificates evidencing membership may be issued but are not necessary. No shares of stock may be issued and no dividends may be paid. If membership certificates are not desired, this Article of the by-laws may be omitted and the subsequent Articles renumbered; but since its phraseology is permissive it may be retained even though membership certificates are not used.

[19] If Article III, Section 7, makes memberships transferable, a section substantially as follows may be added to Article VIII:

"Section 3. Transfers of Certificates of Membership. Transfers of certificates of membership shall be made only on the records of the corporation by a registered member or by his attorney thereunto authorized by power of attorney duly executed and filed with the Secretary of the corporation, and on surrender for cancellation of the certificate evidencing the membership to be transferred."

[20] The amount of dues, if any are to be provided for, may be determined by the members if the by-laws so provide, or may be set forth in the by-laws, or determined in some other manner as may be desired by corporations of various types. This Article of the by-laws may be omitted if dues are not to be required from members.

Articles of Incorporation

At some point in the development of a nonprofit organization, one of its leaders will raise the question of incorporation. Usually this discussion revolves around securing the benefits of tax exemption, which include not only organizational exemption from paying federal income taxes, but also the advantages of deductability of personal donations and lower postal service rates for many categories of NPOs. For a summary review of the various types of nonprofit organizations as defined in the tax codes and whether contributions are allowable, see Part 1, Chapter 6 (Figure 6.2).

The discussion of incorporation and the issue of whether to incorporate should be based on whether the organization needs the powers given to a corporation to accomplish its purposes. Each state invests the corporations authorized to conduct business within its jurisdiction with certain capacities and legal authority to conduct certain types of activity. Although state statutes vary widely with regard to the specific powers and procedures outlined for nonprofit corporations, most specifically grant to or imply the following basic powers:

1. To have perpetual succession by its corporate name unless a limited period of duration is stated in its articles of incorporation.
2. To sue and be sued, complain and defend, in its corporate name.
3. To have a corporate seal which may be altered at pleasure, and to use the same by causing it, or a facsimile thereof, to be impressed or affixed or in any other manner reproduced.
4. To purchase, take, receive, lease, take by gift, devise or bequest, or otherwise

acquire, own, hold, improve, use, and otherwise deal in and with real or personal property, or any interest therein, wherever situated.

5. To sell, convey, mortgage, pledge, lease, exchange, transfer, and otherwise dispose of all or any part of its property and assets.

6. To lend money to its employees other than its officers and directors and otherwise assist its employees, officers, and directors.

7. To purchase, take, receive, subscribe for, or otherwise acquire, own, hold, vote, use, employ, sell, mortgage, lend, pledge, or otherwise dispose of, and otherwise use and deal in and with, shares or other interests in, or obligations of, other domestic or foreign corporations, whether for-profit or not-for-profit, associations, partnerships or individuals, or direct or indirect obligations of the United States, or of any other government, state, territory, governmental district, or municipality or of any instrumentality thereof.

8. To make contracts and incur liabilities, borrow money at such rates of interest as the corporation may determine, issue its notes, bonds, and other obligations, and secure any of its obligations by mortgage or pledge of all or any of its property, franchises, and income.

9. To lend money for its corporate purposes, invest and reinvest its funds, and take and hold real and personal property for the payment of funds so loaned or invested.

10. To conduct its affairs, carry on its operations, and have offices and exercise the powers granted by the state in any state, territory, district, or possession of the United States, or in any foreign country.

11. To elect or appoint officers and agents of the corporation, who may be directors or members, and to define their duties and fix their compensations.

12. To make and alter by-laws, not inconsistent with its articles of incorporation or with the laws of the state in which incorporated, for the administration and regulation of the affairs of the corporation.

13. Unless otherwise provided in the articles of incorporation, to make donations for the public welfare or for charitable, scientific, or educational purposes, and in time of war to make donations in aid of war activities.

14. To indemnify any director or officer (or former director or officer of the corporation) or any person who may have served at its request as a director or officer of another corporation in which it owns shares of capital stock or of which it is a creditor against expenses actually and reasonably incurred by them in connection with the defense of any action, suit, or proceeding, civil or criminal, in which they are made a party by reason of being or having been such director or officer, except in relation to matters as to which they shall be adjudged in such action, suit, or proceeding to be liable for negligence or misconduct in the performance of duty to the corporation; and to make any other indemnification that shall be authorized by the articles of incorporation, by-laws, or resolution adopted after notice by the members entitled to vote.

15. To pay pensions and establish pension plans or pension trusts for any or all of its directors, officers, and employees.

16. To cease its corporate activities and surrender its corporate franchise.

17. To have and exercise all powers necessary or convenient to effect any or all of the purposes for which the corporation is organized.[6]

Most states have followed the Model Act with regard to who can institute legal proceedings with regard to the exercise of these powers. Generally, if the corporation exceeds its authority by engaging in some action not provided for in the articles or by-laws (known as ultra vires), only certain parties may institute legal proceedings to enjoin or correct the action taken. These usually include the state, generally through the attorney general, the corporation itself against the over-reaching trustee, officer, or member, or by a member as such or on behalf of the members in what is referred to as a derivative action against the corporation. The history of ultra vires proceedings is a long and interesting one which unfortunately exceeds the scope of this article.

Many corporations, in those states which allow it, employ the catchall provision that the corporation is formed to engage in all lawful activity for which a corporation may be formed within the state.

To incorporate a nonprofit organization is a cooperative endeavor between the leaders of the NPO and the attorney preparing the articles of incorporation. Although each state sets its own procedures and has specific forms for incorporation (see Figure 16.1 for a specific example), the essential elements are basically the same. Nonprofit organizations preparing to incorporate will save themselves a great deal of trouble and extra expense by familiarizing themselves with the basic contents of the sample articles of incorporation that follow and drafting responses insofar as possible prior to seeking legal counsel. Most articles of incorporation set forth the following.

1. Name of the corporation.
2. Period of incorporation (which may be perpetual).
3. Purpose(s) for which the corporation is organized.
4. Any provisions, not inconsistent with law, which the incorporators elect to set forth in the articles of incorporation for the regulation of the internal affairs of the corporation, including any provision for distribution of assets on dissolution or final liquidation. (Be sure to consult IRS Publication 557 "How to Apply for Recognition of Exemption for an Organization," for recommended phraseology to be incorporated into the articles of incorporation regarding purpose(s), net earnings, lobbying, and dissolution. It may save a great deal of inconvenience to include such wording at the outset, rather than have to amend the articles later during application for exemption.)
5. Address of its initial registered office and the name of its initial registered agent at such address.
6. Number of directors constituting the initial board of directors and the names and addresses of the persons who are to serve as the initial directors.
7. Name and address of each incorporator.
8. Approvals (in some states) of governmental agency (agencies) whose approval is required.

For samples of the Articles of Incorporation—Section 501(c)(3), see Oleck, pp. 332–358.

Notes

1. Howard L. Oleck, *Nonprofit Corporations, Organizations, and Associations,* Prentice-Hall, Englewood Cliffs, N.J., 1980, chaps. 12 and 15.
2. Ibid., p. 399.

3. American Bar Association Committee on Corporate Laws, *Model Nonprofit Corporation Act,* Philadelphia, 1964, p. 9.9.

4. Oleck, *Nonprofit Corporations,* p. 401.

5. Ibid., p. 406.

6. American Bar Association, pp. 2–4.

PART 3

Volunteers: An Indispensable Human Resource in a Democratic Society

16

Trends and Changes Affecting the Volunteer World

Eva Schindler-Rainman

D.S.W., Organization and Community Consultant

Our society is changing. It is moving from industrial to "postindustrial," in transition to a human service economy or society. This is one in which the "people-to-people" services become increasingly important both in quantity and quality, and in which there is a new emphasis on humane, skillful human services. In this changing society a volunteer extends the services of a professional to give clients, patients, members, or consumers more individualized care.

Trends

A number of trends are becoming apparent:

1. *New motivations are emerging.* At one time, people volunteered because they felt altruistic, because their parents had done so before them, or because their churches and schools had taught the values of volunteering. Although many of these motivations are still present, there are some additional ones, including

The desire to help make changes in the organization or society.

The desire to obtain experience that would be useful in exploring the vocational and professional opportunities for paid work.

The desire to advocate and support specific causes, such as cleaning up the environment, helping a political candidate, furthering the work of the church in the inner city, advocating peace, enforcing specific sanctions against terrorists and repressive nations.

The desire to improve one's own quality of life through meeting others; feeling that one is making a difference somehow, somewhere.

The desire to become visible, more influential, or more powerful, and to move in different social circles.

The desire to do preretirement exploration, to see what kind of things one might do in addition to working and later, perhaps, as a major effort after one is no longer employed. This is particularly true for the young retiree or the person who is forced out of work.

The desire to monitor what is going on (this is a rather new motivation arising from people's growing distrust of institutions and their wish to make sure that institutions are doing what they say they will do).

The desire to participate in a worldwide cause or movement: Voluntarism is becoming increasingly international.

2. *More people from a greater variety of lifestyles and backgrounds are volunteering.* All economic, social, racial, religious, and ethnic groups include people who are ready, willing, and able to volunteer. Volunteers come from the ranks of those served, the "clients," as well as from among older people, the disabled, the very young, the unemployed, the underemployed, and the newcomers to this country. Professional men and women are also increasingly offering their services as volunteers when they are not working at their regular jobs. Also, all at-risk handicapped populations are beginning to be valued as making important contributions.

3. *New spaces and places and kinds of jobs for volunteers have become available.* There are opportunities to volunteer in all sectors of the community, including economics, politics, religion, recreation, welfare, education, health (both physical and mental), mass media, culture, and public safety. Opportunities abound in city government, including service in schools, libraries, planning commissions, and assisting international visitors. There are volunteers in prisons, motor vehicle departments, animal shelters, and zoos; and there are volunteers helping the victims of burglaries and other criminal acts. Indeed, volunteers are active in all human service arenas.

4. *The volunteer is demanding new conditions for the relationships between volunteer and agency.* It is not uncommon for volunteers to request some kind of written contract that spells out what the volunteer expects from the agency or organization and what the organization will offer to the volunteer. Items often included in such contracts are conditions relating to space and place, training opportunities, supervision, recognition, chances for upward or lateral mobility, insurance, and enabling funds (e.g., gasoline and meals). Volunteers are also requesting the opportunity to meet with other volunteers on a regular basis, as well as with regular staff. Most volunteers today want an opportunity to do satisfying work, which allows them to learn and grow while volunteering. Many volunteers want to be sure that they will be part of the decision-making and planning processes, particularly those that would affect them. Others want temporary assignments—short-term volunteer jobs. There is a new trend toward staff-volunteer teamwork, which offers closer working relationships.

5. *Pressure is growing for increased collaboration between sectors of the world of voluntarism on international, national, and local levels, and to some extent on the state level.* This is all part of the fact that voluntarism is part of the national and inter-

national agenda. Locally, an increasing number of communities are offering training, recruitment, and placement opportunities through a network of collaborating agencies. Action that may be initiated by only one agency is carried out by many.

Another kind of collaboration that is taking place is between people-helping groups and industry or the corporate world. The Involvement Corps, a privately funded organization, is one example of a national agency that is bringing about this kind of collaboration. ACTION, a government-funded body, is another national group working on getting the private and public sector to collaborate. Corporate volunteer councils bring together administrators of corporate volunteer employee programs.

6. *An increasing number of confrontations are occurring in the volunteer world because of the rapid growth and visibility of voluntarism.* These confrontations came first from the women's movement, which attacked those volunteer jobs for women that made women (according to the women's movement) second-class citizens. This productive confrontation forced all people-helping agencies to take a look at whether they were offering meaningful, growth-producing volunteer jobs that actually made a difference. And, of course, the women's movement itself is a largely voluntary effort. Older Americans as well as persons with special problems are also demanding meaningful roles as volunteers.

Some unions—health, welfare, and educational—have attacked voluntarism because of a fear that volunteers might displace paid personnel. This is a realistic concern, and programs must be examined carefully to ensure that volunteers extend and humanize services, but do not displace or replace paid personnel. There is increasing evidence that some professional groups are worried about the growth of the volunteer movement. Furthermore, underutilized or unhappy volunteers are much more vocal than they used to be. New, cost-cutting legislation bring additional stress and concern to systems with a volunteer component.

7. *Pressure is increasing for new kinds of funding and new methods of accountability.* Several years ago, the United Way of America began to require that human service agencies, when submitting their budgets, do so on a project basis. Pressures for accountability can now be found in both government and private sectors. Moreover, different funding combinations are becoming evident. Some organizations are funded through the private sector, plus private foundations, plus federal and state or local revenue-sharing funds. It is accurate to say that very few organizations are funded purely by private or public sources, and funding changes are occurring constantly in rapid, complex, and unpredictable ways. One of the realities of the day is the increasing number of liability and malpractice suits. Insurance is terribly expensive and puts an additional burden on all human service systems.

8. *Legislative intervention bills are being introduced.* A number of legislative intervention bills are considered by Congress, pointing to the fact that people in the voluntary sector need certain kinds of protection as well as tax deduction allowances for out-of-pocket expenses.

9. *A search for meaning is under way.* Value clarification groups are everywhere—in schools, in the community, and in churches. Individuals have become aware that they can participate in decision making, rather than be the victims of decisions and values held by their predecessors or superiors, or both. There is more mobility among people, both within the communities and between communities, and one may change one's fundamental beliefs if that is found to be necessary. Often a new meaning for life can be found through a volunteer job.

10. *The field of voluntarism is becoming increasingly professionalized.* Graduate courses, seminars, and degrees in volunteer management are now available,

and there are a number of professional organizations, such as the Association for Volunteer Administration, the Association of Voluntary Action Scholars, the Directors of Volunteers in Agencies, and the Corporate Volunteer Councils. Literature in the field has increased greatly: meaningful research as well as professional journals and books are now available that provide a large body of knowledge and resources.

These trends present challenges to all who are involved in the world of volunteering—challenges to utilize available human resources better, to recruit and train new people in new ways, to update and renew the skills of professional people, and to learn about what new funds are available and how to go about getting them.

Changes

What then does the future of the world of the volunteer hold? Here are a few glimpses:

Voluntarism will be taught as an integral part of the curriculum from kindergarten to twelfth grade.

New courses will be offered in community colleges and universities for administrators of volunteer programs as well as for the volunteers themselves.

Credit will be given for volunteer work (agencies will keep records of what volunteers do so that volunteers can include this experience in their résumés). Many civil service systems and corporations are already including volunteer experience as one of the qualifying items in their job specifications.

New funding sources will become available. Business and industry are becoming more and more interested in voluntarism. Local, state, and federal governments as well as foundations, sometimes alone and sometimes in combination, are indicating such interest. Some new funds are already being made available.

Enabling funds for volunteers will become a regular part of agency and organizational budgets.

Insurance coverage will be increasingly needed by decision-making and service volunteers.

Volunteers will be in every sector of the community all over the country, and they will be affecting policymaking as well as policy changes and growth.

Research on values and on the effect of volunteers on the delivery of human services will increase. Indeed, there will be much more research about the world of volunteering, and such research will become readily available to anyone interested.

New collaborative bodies will emerge in order to utilize better the available human and material resources. New, portable, interesting participative training programs for paraprofessionals, professionals, and volunteers will be developed. Voluntarism will continue to become more powerful, and will have increasing visibility, viability, importance and recognition in this country and abroad.

In local, state, and federal situations these changes will be of a formal nature, but there will be increased grass roots recognition of the vital part that voluntarism plays in making our society a democracy in which citizens take an active part in improving the quality of life for themselves and for others.

17

Motivating People to Volunteer Their Services

Eva Schindler-Rainman

D.S.W., Organization and Community Consultant

Successful voluntarism will come about only if individuals feel motivated toward it. "Improvement in the delivery of services" remains an abstract phrase unless more and more individuals become motivated to volunteer their time and energy, to make the commitment, and to achieve the skills needed to help provide these services.

Understanding and supporting the motivation of the individual volunteer are critical. The forces that influence and determine the decision to volunteer one's time and energy are located both inside and outside the individual decider. Common motivating forces include the feelings of "I want to because it sounds as though it's fun, and it interests me." "It's my duty to help," "Something needs to be done," "They want and need me," "Unless I join in and help, they can't be successful," "This organization has to become more relevant, and I want to help it change now," and "I want to explore this field to see if I would like to work in it for pay." Each is a quite separate and distinct force.

Before the decision to volunteer can be faced at all, of course, the opportunity to volunteer must be made available to the individual. Administrators and other professionals have to define activities as needing volunteer help, and they have to decide to recruit volunteers. The forces that determine these decisions of professionals and policymakers are again both internal and external. Again, they vary widely, from the feeling of "I need their help," to "Policy and budget require me to work with volunteers," to "They need me and I need them," to "They are a necessary evil, more bother than help," to "It costs money to administer a good volunteer program."

Let us look at motivational dynamics both within the life space of the volunteer and within the life space and organizational space of the professional who uses volunteers. The following questions will help in exploring the motivation of the volunteer:

1. What are the key forces involved in the individual decision to volunteer or to avoid volunteering? To put a significant proportion of one's discretionary time and energy into volunteer activity or to make only a minor contribution?

2. What forces guide the decision as to the type of volunteer activity to which one will commit oneself?

3. What are the bases of the decision to make a commitment to personal learning, to develop the skills needed to make a high-quality contribution in one's volunteer work?

4. What are the bases of the decision to continue or discontinue volunteer work after a period of service?

In exploring the life space of the users of volunteers we need to try to understand their motivational bases—

1. The decision to perceive and accept the need for volunteers

2. The decisions to define and provide particular volunteer jobs and to recruit particular volunteers for these roles

3. The decision to give priority to the support, training, and growth of volunteers

4. The commitment to learn from and to be influenced by interaction and collaboration with volunteers

To Volunteer or Not to Volunteer

Let us assume for a moment that we are listening in to the thoughts of individuals trying to decide whether to commit their volunteer time and energy to some activity or program. We find that we can organize what they are thinking in several ways. First, we can break down the forces motivating them into two main groups: those pushing toward a "yes" and those pushing toward a "no" decision on volunteering. These two sets of forces are listed in the decision force field in Figure 17.1 which follows the model of Kurt Lewin.[1] Each set is further subdivided into motivational forces that come from inside the self (what Lewin has called "Own Forces"), those that originate outside the self, in the relationship one has with other persons and the membership one has in certain groups ("Interpersonal and Group Member Forces") and those based on characteristics of the total situation of the decision maker: issues of geography, time and space, transportation, economics, and so on ("Situational Forces").

All the forces shown in Figure 17.1 are not operating in any one person facing any one decision, of course. The list is a summary across a number of persons and decisions. Moreover, these forces are not equally strong, and they do not have the same strength for different persons. If we were representing a particular person making a particular decision, only some of the forces would be relevant, and their strength would be quite variable. As you study Figure 17.1, you can, no doubt, make additions to it from your own experience and from that of volunteers you have known.

Saying yes	Saying no or avoiding recruitment
Forces supporting "yes" decisions	Forces inhibiting "yes" decisions and supporting "no" decisions

Forces from
Inside Self
("Own Forces")

It sounds like fun	It sounds like routine "scut" work
I want to be where the action is	Their work isn't as important as it used to be—it's not where the action is
I want to get out of my "box," away from daily routine boredom	I owe my time and energy to my family
What they are doing is very important	I don't feel I have any skill that's needed
They really need and want me	I'm scared of what I might get into
It's a chance to learn new skills	I worked hard to develop my skills —I should be paid
It's a chance to learn things that would help me get ahead	I think I am too old for that
The visibility could help me on my job	It's not clear what kind of help and support I'd get
It could help me with my personal life	The last time I said yes it was a waste of my time
I've gotten a lot of help. Now It's my turn to repay	It might tie me down at times— I'd want to be free to do other things
It's a critical need; I've got to do my part	I need to earn extra money in my spare time
I need something to do	It's unpopular; I'll be involved in conflict
I'll have a chance to really influence what happens	
I'll waste my time if I don't commit it to something	

Figure 17.1. The decision to volunteer or not to volunteer.

*"Forces from Relations
with Others ("Interpersonal
and Group Member Forces")*

Service is a tradition in our family—it's expected	They don't trust volunteers to do the important things
It's one of the things our group memebers do, part of our program	My colleagues would raise their eyebrows at my getting to that
My best friend is asking me	It is too political
He's an important person, I don't feel I can say no	My family would object
She wouldn't ask me if it weren't important	They are paying others for the same thing

"Situational Forces"

It would be a new world, an adventure	I'd have to go too far from where I live; transportation is not easy
We'd have our own office and telephone	There's no place for the volunteers to meet and have a space of their own
They'll fit it to the hours I have free to give	They are too rigid in the time schedule they want
There'll be several of us working at the same place	That area is dangerous
The national leadership has declared it a national priority	
I'd make new friends, and get some recognition	

Figure 17.1.   *(Continued)*

In observing the force field we notice that some volunteers seem to put major motivational emphasis on the *self-actualization possibilities* of an opportunity to volunteer, whereas others put a contrasting emphasis on *service, duty, and the repayment of a "service-received" debt.* The self-actualizers see opportunities for learning, excitement, and personal growth, whereas the servers see opportunities for significant contributions, for the meeting of needs, and for action relevance in the society. No doubt for many volunteers both of these bases of motivation are important, but they certainly have very different priorities for different types of persons and in different decisional situations.

A related contrast in motivational orientations seems to be between what we might call *inner-oriented* and *other-oriented* volunteers. The inner-oriented put more weight on the "Own Forces" in the situation—their own feelings, their own sense of relevance, and their own values—as guidelines for decisions. The other-oriented decision makers are more influenced by the norms of their group, by the potential visibility and status of the volunteer activity, by its potential consequences for their job and social relationships, and by situational factors of risk and support.

A third dimension of difference in motivations we might label the dimension of *action* versus *reflection and policy.* For some volunteers the meaningful opportunity is the one that provides the excitement of direct action with clients and the opportunity to get feedback through interaction and "seeing things happen." Other volunteers feel more comfortable and get more satisfaction in a more reflective and removed type of volunteer activity, such as service on committees and policy-making boards.

Probably closely related is the contrast between potential volunteers who give priority to the opportunities for *power and influence* and those who are interested primarily in the opportunities for *emotional associations* with others. For the former group a key source of motivation is the perceived opportunity to get into a position of influence, decision making, and activity designing. The latter group looks forward to the interaction with other adults or with children, to the chance to "share" themselves and to work on a team with others.

Another important difference seems to be that some volunteers identify with *the larger community and its welfare;* they think in terms of significant community needs to be met through their service. Criteria of social significance and community relevance are important to them in choosing volunteer activities. Other volunteers are oriented primarily to the *interpersonal meanings* and *group membership meanings* of the particular volunteer opportunity. Their decisions to volunteer are determined to a high degree by the image of the people with whom they would be working, the type of interpersonal support they would receive, and the meaning the activity would have for their friends, their family, and the groups to which they belong. Theirs is a very concrete interpersonal world rather than a more abstract social-problem world.

Yet another interesting dimension of difference among potential volunteers can be defined by the three terms *autonomy-oriented, interdependence-oriented* and *dependence-or support-oriented.* As we review the forces listed in Figure 17.1, we see that for autonomy-oriented individuals a very important condition for volunteering is the freedom to "do one's own thing," to get away from routines and boredom, to take some risks and find some new excitement. Interdependence-oriented individuals value peer relationships and opportunities for colleagueship and mutuality of support and working relationships. For these volunteers the human-relations aspect of the peer relationship on the job is a critical factor. Support-oriented individuals want a clearly defined job to do, with clear arrangements for training and on-the-job supervision and help. They want to be sure that what they are being assigned to do is something they will be competent and comfortable in doing. These volunteers place a high value on the guidelines of tradition and well-developed norms and procedures, in contrast to the autonomous volunteers, who prefer new experiences, risk, and freedom from tradition and normative expectations and demands.

As we think about different types of roles and opportunities for volunteers, we begin to sense the importance of finding ways to match the right volunteers to the right opportunities and situations, to take account of individual differences in need for support, and to shift roles and working situations to correct "poor fits."

To Continue or Drop Out

After volunteers agree to serve and have become involved in volunteer activities, they are faced with the questions of whether or not they like the work, whether or not to continue, and whether or not to put more or less energy into the activity. Volunteers, by definition, can change their minds more readily than can professional persons. Also, volunteers must decide how much time and energy to devote to volunteer activities.

Let us once again listen in on a population of decision makers. This time they will be volunteers trying to decide whether to give more or less energy and time to a particular activity, and whether to continue or discontinue their commitment. We shall use the force field in Figure 17.2 as a guide to start us thinking in a systematic way about this area of volunteer motivation. Again we can divide into several clusters the factors that decrease commitment or lead volunteers to discontinue their volunteer work.

One group of volunteers seems to be saying that their major source of disappointment and discontent is the discrepancy between what they have found in their volunteer activity and what they were led by their recruiters to believe it would be like. The *unreal expectations given in recruitment* are a frequent cause of "motivational shock" later on. Discrepancies between expectation and reality may be discovered in the amount of time required for the activity, the type of work, the amount of support from the professionals, the type of clients, the available facilities, and many other areas.

Another important theme is the *lack of appreciative feedback* from staff, clients, and coworkers. This may result in doubt about one's adequacy in doing the volunteer work. Emotional support and appreciation are crucial as part of the "payment" and support for volunteer time and energy.

A related theme is the problem of *relationships with the professionals or supervisory staff.* Some volunteers sense that the professionals are a block to initiative and innovativeness. Others cite a lack of consultative help in critical situations and a lack of the orientation and training they need to do the job well. Perhaps one of the most frequent and serious problems in this area is the feeling that the staff expects full commitment to their particular activity even though the volunteer may have a variety of other legitimate priorities. The staff exerts a kind of "righteous pressure" about the importance of their activity, which makes the volunteer feel disloyal and guilty and which hastens withdrawal from the relationship. Closely related is the volunteer's common feeling that he or she is a second-class citizen involved in the less important kinds of work in the program.

Another group of forces acting to decrease volunteer commitment as seen in Figure 17.2, centers around volunteers' perceptions of *disapproval or devaluation of their commitment by others* whose opinions they value. Such forces might be the spoken or unspoken feelings of family members, the raised eyebrows of coworkers at the office, or the decision of one's service club or group to become involved in a different type of service priority. A related force is volunteers' hesitation to become involved in an activity that may be the subject of public controversy.

Another theme seems to be the *general morale and working conditions* of the volunteer program. If there are persistent rumors that the program is regarded as unimportant and that there are budget cuts in the offing, the volunteer gets the sense of being on a sinking ship. Probably the "Situational Forces" become more of an issue when other and more central psychological factors are already fostering negative attitudes toward one's volunteer work and situation.

Turning to the positive factors pushing toward continued volunteer effort and an increase in personal commitment, we again see several clusters. One very important theme seems to be the *sense of "making a difference,"* of contributing to some

To continue, to increase commitment	*To drop out, of decrease commitment*
Forces toward continuing or increasing commitment	*Forces toward lowering or ceasing commitment*

"Own Forces"

What I'm doing is making a difference	It's not as interesting as I thought it would be
I'm still learning a lot	I want to try something new
This could lead to paid work	It's taking more time than I want to devote to it
They appreciate me	Something more important is attracting me
They've used some of my ideas	I'm feeling too tired
It's helping with my home life, too	I don't feel appreciated
I feel better about myself, more competent	I don't think I am doing my job very well
It's really a chance to do my own thing and be creative	I get no support from people who matter to me

"Interpersonal and Group Member Forces"

I've made a lot of friends and important contacts	Nobody helps me when I need it
I like the "bosses"	My family is feeling neglected
The staff trusts me more and more	The professionals block initiative to try new things
My friends and I have a lot to share about our work	Our group doesn't have its priorities clear
They need me as a member of the team	My colleagues wonder why I spend so much time volunteering
The weekly training sessions are very exciting	The staff acts like I'm disloyal if I don't give all my time

Figure 17.2. The decision to continue, increase commitment, or drop out.

My family feels what I'm doing is important →	← They get "up tight" about confrontation and controversy
I've read several articles about the importance of volunteers →	← Volunteers are second-class citizens

"Situational Forces"

We have a volunteer personnel system →	← The working conditions are terrible—no space or place for us
They've changed to meet my schedule →	← One of my coworkers was robbed
They are paying for transportation now →	← It's too far, I get home too late, it's dangerous
Training plans are being developed with our help →	← I keep hearing they are going to cut the budget for volunteer administration

Figure 17.2.   *(Continued)*

significant service that changes or helps the lives of others or, in the case of a political campaign or other "cause work," the sense of being connected to or even influencing national policy or international events.

Related to the sense of the significance of their work is the volunteers' *feeling that they are appreciated* and influencing their coworkers and the job situation: that their suggestions and ideas are being used, that they are invited to join in planning and policy thinking, and that they are trusted to take on more and more responsibility.

Another important theme is the sense of *self-actualization,* of "doing one's own thing," of feeling more competent and adequate, of learning a lot and being excited about new insights, and even of transferring one's learning and experiences to other parts of one's life situation, such as one's family life.

Another theme is that *volunteers have the support of persons and groups who are important to them.* It may be expressed as being involved in the volunteer work with a friend with whom there is a lot of off-the-job sharing and discussing, as having found new friends, or as finding that one's husband, wife, or teenager is supportive and enthusiastic about the activity. Reading articles in the mass media supporting the importance of one's voluntary effort and having one's company give public recognition to volunteer service by its employees are other important motivating forces toward legitimizing and intensifying one's commitment.

Another group of supportive forces centers around the volunteers' feelings that the organization they are working with is motivated to make *adjustments to fit their schedule* and to support their participation in every way possible—for example, by providing the place and supplies for coworkers to get together for coffee and conversation, by paying registration fees for conferences, and by reimbursing the volunteer for transportation, meals, babysitting, and necessary telephone calls.

Much of the motivation and commitment of volunteers depends on the values, attitudes, and behaviors of their professional supervisors and coordinators, and on the policies and psychological atmosphere of the agency or organization. In turn, the nature of the motivation of the professional, the utilizer of volunteers, becomes a very important topic for our inquiry. What motivates the decision to seek help from volunteers, to provide attractive opportunities for them, and to give them the training and support they need on the job?

Whether to Use Volunteers and How to Use Them

Although there are many trends in society and in the helping professions toward increased use of volunteer personpower, there are also a number of significant forces working against increasing the use of volunteers—in fact, even forces discouraging the use of untrained and inexperienced helpers at all. In Figure 17.3 we have summarized the psychological, interpersonal, and situational forces that motivate professional leadership to make extensive use of volunteers and, on the other hand, the factors that cause some professionals to be very cautious in recruiting volunteers and in giving them responsibility. As with Figures 17.1 and 17.2, we suggest that you check Figure 17.3 against your own experience and make additions to the force field.

A number of themes of motivation emerge from Figure 17.3 as guides to understanding the life space of the professionals and to working with them on the more effective use of volunteers. One important theme is the *rewards and personal satisfactions that come from client feedback.* There is something deeply satisfying about responses of gratitude and growth from those one is attempting to help. Some of this emotional satisfaction is admittedly lost when the professionals "let the volunteers have all the fun" while they, removed from the firing line, act as trainers, supervisors, supporters, and behind-the-scenes administrators and organizers.

A second related theme is *concern about professional standards,* about the quality of service rendered, and about the potential danger to clients from insensitive and unskilled helpers. The idea that volunteers with relatively brief training can be expected to do some of the things the professional spent years getting trained for is a threat and a source of genuine professional concern. Within their own peer group, professionals share anecdotes and attitudes about the irresponsibility or unpredictability of volunteers, their ethical boners in regard to confidentiality, their ignorance of professional standards, the difficulties of training them, their resistance to supervision, and their impulsiveness in ignoring agency policies.

A third source of resistance probably is the fact that some professionals have had *no training in the techniques and skills of recruiting, training, supervising, and supporting volunteers.* They therefore lack a feeling of competence and confidence in this area. Their sense of inadequacy is increased by their awareness that indigenous volunteers have skills and knowhow that the professionals lack, and that many volunteers today have professionally trained skills from their own areas of competence which represent major resources beyond the expertness of the professional.

Another common theme is the *feeling that the need for more personnel can be better met by paraprofessionals* than by volunteers. Many professionals feel more comfortable working with, training, and supervising paid subordinates who fit right into the organizational system and are ready to take supervision as paid staff members. They feel that volunteers are much more difficult to deal with in defined role relationships, and much less predictable in terms of commitment and responsiveness to supervision.

Now it is time to look at the other half of Figure 17.3, at the forces motivating professionals toward increased use of volunteers at higher levels of responsibility. Needs and opportunities for helping services are expanding and will continue to

Decision to use extensively at high level of responsibility	*Decision to make minimal use with limited responsibility*
Forces toward maximal use of volunteers	*Forces toward minimal use of volunteers*

*Forces Inside Professional
Decision Maker ("Own Forces")*

I feel a need to extend service beyond what I can do	I don't want to give up the rewards of direct contact with clients
The volunteers I've worked with have been great and helpful	I am uneasy working with volunteers of different race, class, education, etc.
It is gratifying to train and work with volunteers	I distrust volunteers' ethical sensitivity to the need for confidentiality
They are a key link to clients	Paraprofessionals are easier to train and control
The best delivery of service is by a team of volunteers, professionals, and paraprofessionals	Training, supervising, and supporting them will take too much time
There is great personal satisfaction in seeing volunteers grow as I work with them	The volunteers might be more accepted than I am by clients
I can have more impact by spreading my skills	I don't see what jobs I can give them
More volunteers are available to be recruited	Too much energy is required to recruit and keep them
Volunteers are ready to take on important responsibilities	They resist supervision and often ignore policies
	I don't feel expert enough to supervise new roles and functions
	They just are not dependable

Figure 17.3.   Deciding whether and how to use volunteers.

*"Interpersonal and Group
Member Forces"*

Board says we should give more service with no more professionals	Standards of good service are becoming more professional all the time
The chief executive values extensive use of volunteers	The volunteers are too aggressive in seeking status, power, and independence
The funding agency values our use of volunteers	My colleagues tell me that volunteers are inadequate in many areas
Our agency policy is to use volunteers in many roles	Parents sometimes raise questions about volunteers in the classroom
The trend in the profession and nationally is to want more volunteer participation in delivering services	Volunteers lack commitment to agency policies

"Situational Forces"

Clients can be served better by more volunteers helping	Our budget for volunteer administration has been decreased
Program outreach to new areas is feasible with volunteers	We lack budget for volunteers who need meal, transportation, baby sitting, etc., reimbursement
Having more volunteers will benefit budget allocations	We lack space for volunteer-led programs
Volunteers make it possible to give more individualized service	We can't offer transportation
	We now have paraprofessionals— it's hard to separate their jobs and those of volunteers
	The liability insurance is too high

intensify in the future. The *need for services* will predictably outstrip the training of professional and paraprofessional workers. The economic base will not be available for supporting the training and maintenance of enough staffs of paid workers. For these reasons, more and more agencies and professional workers are seeing the necessity of making much fuller use of volunteers in all areas of service, including some that have previously had no or few volunteer helpers, such as school systems, government offices, health services, cultural centers, food services, prisons, courts, and so on.

A second important source of motivation toward more extensive use of volunteers is the *increasing number and variety of potential volunteers.* More and more persons with highly trained skills, and with great sensitivity and commitment, are available, and often their knowledge and skills complement those of the professional. Organizing, coordinating, and facilitating the use of these volunteer resources are very exciting challenges for professional leadership. Many professionals are discovering that the colleagueship and appreciation of volunteer coworkers can become even more rewarding than their relationships with professional colleagues or with their clients.

Another source of motivation is the realization that *reaching out to serve the populations most in need of help can be effectively accomplished only with volunteers,* because these populations cannot pay for services. Besides, professionals have been discovering that, even if the neediest communities could support fully professional services, these would not be as effective as services by teams of indigenous volunteers, because the *professionals' cultural and economic backgrounds and racial identification often make it difficult for them to connect* with these populations. Many professionals have found a new source of regard and satisfaction in spreading their professionally trained resources to the training and supporting of teams of local volunteers, who are better able to relate to their peers.

As we work toward increased use of volunteers we need to be continuously sensitive to the dilemmas and genuine problems of the professionals and their agencies. We must focus on the problems of their motivation and their future perspectives as well as on those of the volunteer, because the professionals are very much a part of the motivational dynamics of voluntarism in our society.

Generalizations

Let us pause to review some of the major generalizations about motivation that we can derive from this analysis.

Volunteer Motivation

1. A major motivating factor for volunteers is the opportunity to participate in problem solving and significant decision making.

2. The placement of volunteers should include some process for relating the type of work and situation to their particular interests, needs, and motivations.

3. To increase motivation, most volunteer opportunities should provide for both self-actualizing personal development and meaningful service to the needs of others. In other words, the opportunities for volunteer service should be presented both as continuing educational opportunities to learn and grow and as opportunities to contribute one's "tithe" of much-needed social service.

4. The "contract" between the volunteer and the organization should legitimize a feasible level of commitment and allow for personal variations in time, energy, and interest without guilt or tension about divided loyalties and limited energy.

5. The on-the-job experience of the volunteer should include continuing opportunities for reflective study and evaluation and for joint planning and designing of service goals and action. Much of the volunteer's sustaining and renewing motivation comes from seeing clear steps toward the group's goals and from successfully completing them one by one.

6. Needs can be met and motivation sustained more effectively if the work situation also allows for individual advancement through a series of steps leading to higher levels of responsibility, skill, learning, and influence.

7. For many volunteers, motivation will be increased if a record of activities is kept that can become part of a résumé and may lead to paid work.

8. Motivation will be sustained best if there are regular mechanisms for supportive feedback from clients, coworkers, and professional leadership, and for recognition from the agency and community.

9. Participation in meaningful training activities inside and outside the organization (e.g., conferences) is an important source of continuing motivation and growth.

Motivation of the Professional Users of Volunteers

1. The motivation of the professionals to give priority to work with volunteers will be strengthened if the agency policymakers and administrators establish a climate that shows that they value the use of volunteers and encourage the devotion of professional time to recruiting, training, coordinating, and consulting with volunteers.

2. The motivation to use volunteers will be enhanced if professional development opportunities are provided to help promote competence and confidence in the concepts and skills of recruiting, training, administering, and coordinating volunteers. Outside conferences, seminars, consultants, and trainers often provide additional good resources for this training.

3. Opportunities should be provided for the professionals to discuss openly with their peers the importance and techniques of work with volunteers and to develop joint goals, plans, and commitments in this area.

4. The motivation of the professional users of volunteers will be strengthened and sustained if mechanisms for regular feedback are established to provide "appreciation data" from volunteers and from the agency.

5. Designs to get evaluation feedback from clients and client groups about the success of volunteer work will help professionals validate their decisions about the use of volunteers, improve training, and make consultative supervision more effective.

6. Professional motivation to work with volunteers will be strengthened by the establishment of regular procedures for joint study, training, planning, and evaluation by teams comprising professionals, paraprofessionals, and volunteers. These sessions should include sensitivity learning process work on communication, interpersonal feelings, and problems of working relationships.

7. Professionals will be more motivated to work with volunteers if time and money is budgeted for them to be able to do so.

Note

1. Kurt Lewin, Frontiers in Group Dynamics: Concept, Method, and Reality in Social Science; Social Equilibria and Social Change, *Human Relations,* vol. 1, pp. 5–41, June 1947.

18

Recruitment, Orientation, and Retention

Eva Schindler-Rainman

D.S.W., Organization and Community Consultant

Creative use of volunteers is closely related to an effective recruitment and orientation process, linking a person who wants to give time and energy to an organization that needs volunteers in order to operate; linking a need to learn with opportunities for learning; linking a need to be creative with an opportunity to give the most creative service possible. Through this linkage (recruitment) the potential volunteer becomes an actual service and decision-making agent. As the person becomes part of the agency, he or she links the agency to the client and the community. Because the very basis of volunteer service is built at the time the potential volunteer is first recruited, the recruitment process is crucially important.

Preliminary Considerations

The process of recruitment must be thought through and planned very carefully. In locating and attracting "linker-volunteers," an organization should first examine closely its need for volunteers and the special resources, skills, and values they bring. A recruiting organization needs to be very clear about the kinds of jobs and tasks that need doing and about the kinds of volunteers who can do them best. Too often the motivations and needs of the organization are not clearly communicated to the potential volunteer. Also, the organization needs an effective volunteer administrative structure in place, including a competent volunteer administrator.

The second requirement for an organization hoping to link volunteer resources into its service system is to take time to understand what kinds of motivations, needs, and interests each potential volunteer has, so as to match these with the kinds of service opportunities available. Does the potential volunteer feel a need for meaningful involvement in giving service? Or is the motivation a need for self-actualization and for new growth and learning experiences? One volunteer's main interest might be in making good use of special interests or competencies. Another might wish to serve in a particular organization because of the cause it represents. Cause motivation is very important in this day of social revolution. Many volunteers want to be where the action is and where they feel their time and energy will make a difference.

One can also look at volunteers in terms of the kind of service they give. Some give direct service: tutoring, helping patients in a hospital, leading a youth group, working with the mentally retarded, soliciting funds, getting out the vote, training others in a particular skill. Other volunteers do administrative work. Often, these are persons who have had previous experience, although this is not always necessary in order to sit on a board or committee and help the organization make policy and action decisions. Administrative jobs include both those to which volunteers are elected for a certain period of time and those to which they are appointed on an ad hoc basis to complete a particular project, such as revising by-laws.

Where to Find Potential Volunteers

There are, of course, many different kinds of organizations looking for volunteers: private volunteer agencies such as hospitals and scout groups; public agencies such as departments of welfare, mental health, and education; political and cause groups. The easiest and probably the most popular way to recruit new volunteers is through those who are already in a given organization and are having a good experience there. They then act as "referral linkers." Some organizations recruit volunteers through the Volunteer Bureau or Voluntary Action Center in their community. Sometimes potential volunteers present themselves on their own initiative. Newcomers to an area, for example, often volunteer their services in hopes of becoming a part of the community more quickly. People desiring to serve in poverty areas also frequently volunteer on their own initiative. Sometimes there is group motivation: A small number of members of an organization volunteer to serve together to carry out a certain task. Many people, particularly teenagers and senior citizens, feel more secure if they are able to volunteer with at least one friend. Some volunteers can be recruited only through personal contact. Others respond to ads in newspapers, or on radio or television. Because different people can be reached by different recruitment techniques, organizations seeking volunteers should employ the widest possible range of techniques, and try to learn more about when to use which ones. Increasing sensitivity to cultural differences is very important, if a multiethnic volunteer force is to be involved.

Over the years, most of the volunteers recruited by most agencies have been middle- or upper-middle-class white women. Only recently has there been an attempt to draw volunteers from the poorer sectors of the community and from different ethnic communities. This shift has been spearheaded by cause movements, political organizations, and public agencies and by such legislation as the Economic Opportunity Act. The challenge to all agencies, organizations, and movements is to find the important underutilized volunteer resources in areas that have not previously been tapped. It has become necessary to develop new recruiting methods, since new volunteers often cannot be found through the traditional methods. The only people who can be recruited through established agencies, for example, are those who are already connected in some way to these organizations.

To find potential volunteers who are not members of established organizations or groups, recruiters are going to such places as laundromats, bowling alleys, street corner clubs, neighborhood ice cream or hamburger spots, adult education classes, Americanization classes, Job Corps and Head Start centers, post offices, pool halls, and informal neighborhood social groups. Recruiters have also discovered the possibilities of supermarket bulletin boards, merchants associations, labor unions, the neighborhood improvement clubs, and citizen's band radio. The waiting rooms of public health and housing centers, welfare and probation departments, and other public service agencies are particularly good places to recruit previously untapped volunteers. The corporate world is another rich resource for temporary and more permanent volunteers.

"Informants" who can help find volunteers include postal workers, local bartenders, local police (especially those who still walk a beat), adult education teachers, elementary and secondary school teachers and principals, members of the clergy, public health doctors and nurses, owners or managers of neighborhood stores, gas station attendants, bus drivers on regular routes, barbers, beauticians, and older citizens who have lived in the area for a long time. Social workers, community workers, probation and parole officers, directors of public housing and community centers, and many other public service personnel, including volunteers and paraprofessionals, also make good "informants" about potential volunteers.

The main thing to remember is that people know other people who need only to be asked. It has become very clear that most people are eager to participate as volunteers, if they are given the opportunity.

Types of Volunteers

Volunteers can be found with almost every possible combination of age, sex, race, education, religion, experience, and lifestyle. There are the very young (e.g., 9 and 10-year-olds) tutoring the even younger. There are teenage volunteers, such as the Candy Stripers in hospitals. There are the brand new volunteers, who may not even be familiar with the concept of volunteering, and the experienced volunteers whose previous work may or may not be relevant to their new job. (It is important to make no assumptions about how much a potential volunteer knows or has done. The recruiter should ask about previous volunteer work, both what they did and how they felt about it.) There are the native-born and the newcomers, the employed and unemployed, the well, and the disabled.

The history of voluntarism shows that traditionally there have been many more jobs for women than for men. Indeed, there are some stereotypes in the volunteer world: For example, many writers routinely refer to the volunteer as *she.* However, there are just as many interesting opportunities for male volunteers, such as work in museums and as Big Brothers or scout leaders. Moreover, there are now almost as many men as women volunteers active in the United States.

Matching the Recruitment Technique to the Volunteer

Once a potential volunteer has expressed interest in learning more about the opportunities with a particular organization, the recruiter must choose the most appropriate place to meet with the volunteer. Possibilities include the applicant's home or school, the local meeting spot, the recruiting organization's office, or any other place designated by the applicant. If the volunteer must travel a long distance to meet the recruiter, it helps to have the organization reimburse transportation expenses. Often the recruiter can meet the applicant halfway, or even pick her or him up at home. "Car chats" are a great way to begin recruitment and orientation.

The recruiter can meet the prospective volunteer alone or with another recruiter. Pairs of recruiters often give each other the necessary support and courage to do the recruitment job. Other techniques are to bring groups of potential volunteers together or to invite the potential volunteer to participate in some ongoing activity of the organization in order to get a feeling for what it is about.

Offering the Opportunity Effectively

It is important that potential volunteers perceive the opportunity they are being offered as interesting and worthwhile. Following are some techniques that may be especially helpful in this regard:

> In a warm, personal telephone call, make a date to see the applicant at a mutually convenient time and place. (Often it helps to go to potential volunteers' homes rather than ask them to come to an office.)

> Send a handwritten note inviting them to a meeting of potential volunteers or to an appointment with the recruiter.

> Have someone the prospective volunteers know approach them, personally on a one-to-one basis and offer transportation.

> Provide for immediate sign-up after presenting to a group the kinds of volunteer opportunities available, so that the potential volunteers feel that they are really wanted and that there is an organization ready to receive them.

> Have the particular client group needing volunteers recruit directly. For example, teenage groups needing an adult sponsor or resource person often do a better job recruiting their own volunteers than could be done through the general recruiting efforts of the larger agency or organization.

> Seize the right moment, such as a chat at the market where a person shows interest or after a community meeting in which someone has expressed interest.

> Invite potential volunteers to visit the organization's headquarters. Let them meet other volunteers already on the job, perhaps over lunch or coffee, so that they can discuss what they are doing and how they feel about it. Introduce them to some of the professionals on the staff. Here is an opportunity for the potential recruit to get the feel of how the professionals see themselves in relationship to volunteers.

> Use personal follow-up. This may mean telephoning to see how the person feels about the opportunity a week later, or it may mean a warm personal letter, a coffee hour, or a home visit. Whatever the method, follow-up is a crucial factor in attracting the potential volunteer.

> Encourage prospective volunteers to state their needs, interests, and expectations. It is important that people who are about to donate their time to an or-

ganization be given an opportunity to ask all the questions they have and to think over how and when they might best serve and with whom they would like to work.

Use attractive literature to interpret the organization's work. It is better to use one snappy, interesting, clearly written piece than to overwhelm the applicant with packets and packets of materials, most of which make better sense to the already indoctrinated person than to one who knows very little or nothing about the organization's purposes and services. This presentation may need to be in several languages.

Give the volunteer a choice of jobs. Rarely do people fit into jobs; rather, jobs must be molded to the interests and resources of the individual. Job descriptions should be flexible or nonexistent. It is sometimes best for new volunteers to be able to carve out their jobs and then write their job descriptions after several weeks of experience.

Allow for a period of orientation. This gives the volunteers a chance to get used to the job before they commit themselves to long-term service. It also helps to offer short-term possibilities for service, so that volunteers can contribute time and energy without necessarily signing up for a long period of time.

These, then, are some of the ways to attract volunteers—to ensure that potential volunteers will decide to become active volunteers.

Orientation

Orientation really begins with the very first contact between the potential volunteer and a representative of the recruiting organization. Often recruiters are not aware that they are in fact orienting the potential volunteer by means of the very role and behavior they model. Further orientation, of course, comes through more structured training sessions before the new recruit begins work. Orienting new volunteers means making sure that they become acquainted with the new setting and its lifestyles and with the possibilities of their services' making a difference to the total life of the organization as well as to themselves.

Often new, enthusiastic volunteers are the best persons to orient the next wave of new volunteers, because they are still close to what it feels like to be new and yet just enough ahead to be able to tell them a little bit about the opportunities in store for them. There should be a variety of beginning orientation activities, matched to the needs of the volunteer who is young, middle-aged, older, new to volunteering, new to the agency, or experienced in volunteering in other settings. Orientation may continue over the first several weeks or months of service in order to give the new recruit the necessary help and support to do the job.

Retention

It should be clear that how volunteers are recruited and oriented has much to do with the enthusiasm with which they begin their service and the length of time, barring other factors, they remain in the service of a given organization. What are some of the steps an organization can take to build upon successful processes of recruitment and orientation to ensure that new volunteers will have long, happy, and successful periods of service?

1. It is helpful to draw up an individualized plan for the volunteer's on-the-job training, including personal contacts, on-the-job support, and literature that will be particularly relevant.

2. It is becoming increasingly necessary for organizations to provide in their budgets for the reimbursement of volunteers for travel, luncheons, parking, conference registrations, materials and other such items, so that the volunteers who do not have great means will be able to give of their resources, ideas, time, and service.

3. Offering a variety of jobs, opportunities for change and growth in each, and the chance to move from one job to another, or perhaps to have two jobs at once if they are flexible enough, are important factors in keeping volunteers interested and motivated.

4. It is helpful for an organization to have a place for volunteers to meet together socially. This is not to say that staff members cannot go there also, but, if feasible, some kind of volunteer lounge or talk room is highly desirable.

5. Ongoing reciprocal evaluation is very valuable. It is important for volunteers to hear how well they are doing their jobs, to be able to tell the supervisor or consultant how they feel about the service they are giving, and to suggest ways in which they feel the agency could be made a better place in which to work. Identifying needs and wishes of volunteers and finding ways to meet them are helpful in establishing and keeping good volunteer-professional relationships.

6. Finding or creating new areas of service for volunteers can be challenging to volunteers and professionals alike. Often it is the volunteers who come up with the best suggestions for new services or changes in existing procedures or services.

7. Commitments for training and support must be made by both the volunteers and the people with whom they work. Through in-service training, volunteers can learn and grow on the job. Also, the better trained the volunteers are, the more effective the service they can render and the more secure they will feel about the service they are giving.

8. Appropriate ongoing formal and informal recognition is also very important.

Conclusion

We have seen that the world of voluntarism in the United States is experiencing some massive changes. These changes necessitate new techniques and new procedures to find, recruit, select, place, orient, train, and maintain volunteers. A new look must also be taken at in-service training. Mobility of job ladders within an organization or between organizations must be developed. Evaluation, quality control, horizontal referral and linkage, separation, termination or graduation, awards and procedures for recognition—all are functions requiring innovation and creative utilization of the resources that are available. So far, most organizations and agencies do very little to help each other in such areas as the finding of underutilized segments of the population. Little has been done in interagency cooperation to improve volunteer orientation and training. The changing world of voluntarism demands new action in these directions.

19

Training Plans

Eva Schindler-Rainman

D.S.W., Organization and Community Consultant

If organizations are to be viable, they must have an ongoing training plan for self-renewal. Commitment to the self-renewal and agency-renewal ideal implies that plans will be translated into action and that the organization will be flexible enough to change plans when better ones are found and to fit plans to people, rather than the reverse.

An ideal continuous training plan might have five phases, as follows:

1. *Preservice training.* Some orientation or training of a volunteer is needed before beginning work.

2. *Start-up support.* Assistance must be given to the volunteers as they begin their volunteer work. Here the trainer may well be another volunteer who has had some experience in the organization and on the job.

3. *Maintenance-of-effort training.* Throughout the volunteer's period of service, regular times are needed for asking questions and gaining additional job-related knowledge. The volunteer needs to feel that the organization is committed to growth on the job.

4. *Periodic review and feedback.* Frequently in the beginning, probably less often as time goes on, the trainer or administrator and the volunteer need the opportunity, either in a face-to-face conference or in a group meeting, to discuss whether goals are being accomplished, how the volunteer feels about accomplishment and about the organization, how the job and service could be improved, how the trainer feels the volunteer could function more efficiently, and so on.

5. *Transition training.* Volunteers have a need to grow and to assume more responsibility. In order to really enjoy the job, they must take on additional tasks in that job or see that it can lead to additional or alternative avenues of service. This need is too often forgotten. Why, for instance, don't organizations plan explicitly to train potential chairpersons, presidents, and coordinators? If transition training

were given, it would not be nearly so difficult to find new people to take over leadership, because they would have been groomed for that kind of responsibility.

This ideal framework, then, provides, for the self-renewal of the agency, as well as the volunteer.

Preservice Training

Preservice training helps the new volunteer take a look at self and skills, at the job that needs to be done, and at the organization's philosophy and services. It may be given individually or in a group setting, depending of course on the timing, the number of volunteers, and the kinds of resources and facilities available.

Preservice training actually begins with the recruitment process. At the very first contact with an individual or group, some unconscious training usually takes place. It can be made even more effective if the recruiter becomes consciously aware that as the volunteers are being acquainted with the organization's program and philosophy, they are being trained.

One item that should definitely be included in preservice training is a tour of the organization's headquarters or the site of its services. It is important for the potential volunteer to gain an understanding of the operation of the organization through structured observation. If a trainer or guide is not available for the tour, it is possible to use a "taped-tour master" (like those in museums) to guide the volunteer through the site, pointing out the stop points, stop action points, and discussion and observation points and suggesting materials to read in the library. The volunteer might be given a schedule of staff meetings and other meetings to attend, suggesting things to look and listen for during these meetings. Opportunities for informal chats with other volunteers and staff during coffee or lunch hours should also be built into the tour. At its conclusion, there should be time for the volunteer to discuss observations and reactions with some staff members or volunteer trainers who have been assigned to the preservice training process. There might even be a group discussion with staff, board members, potential volunteers, and active volunteers and trainers all participating. At some point in the preservice period, the volunteer should meet, either formally or informally, all the kinds of people involved in the service of the organization, including paraprofessionals and clients.

Another way to conduct preservice training is through "apprenticeship observation." That is, potential volunteers work briefly with staff or experienced volunteers in a variety of jobs around the organization so that they can make a more informed choice of work preferences.

Certainly group meetings are vital in the preservice period. Potential volunteers must be given a chance to talk with one another and to hear each others' questions and ideas, but it is equally important that they receive some conceptual input from someone representing the organization. Most potential volunteers need help in clarifying their future roles or in understanding other people's roles.

They usually also need some anticipatory practice, some role playing to help confront what it means to enter a system as a new person. To ensure a smooth start when they begin their jobs, these role-playing sessions might include practice in such things as how to greet the clients of the organization, how to work with the supervisor, how to use the telephone effectively—whatever is appropriate for the kinds of jobs the volunteers will be assuming.

Preservice training, then, is a vitally important part of the continuous training framework. So often, the beginning steps are either taken too fast or overlooked entirely, and yet this initial training provides the very foundation for later service and contribution by the volunteers, as well as their retention.

Start-up Support

When volunteers, having had some initial training, begin actual work for the organization, they enter a period in which much support is needed. Beginnings are hard for all of us. The period of testing out and getting acquainted, leading toward mutual trust and acceptance, is a very difficult one. But it is also a fruitful period of training, because there is in the new volunteer, as in the child, greater openness to change at the beginning than after patterns have developed.

The start-up is the time when volunteers' repertoire of resources, skills, and alternatives is probably least developed. They often, therefore, find decision making difficult. Volunteers in the start-up period also have a great need to feel recognized and accepted by the people already in the system. Experienced staff members must somehow communicate that they want and need volunteers, that they depend on the resources of volunteers to extend their own services, and that they are really glad to have the volunteers aboard.

How can this kind of start-up support be given? There are a number of ways. One is for a supervisor, trainer, or coworker to have a supportive chat, either in person or on the telephone, with the volunteer after the first day on the job to ask how things went and what kinds of feelings and questions there might be and to share observations about performance, particularly positive and supportive ones. An alternative method is to have each new volunteer paired with a more experienced volunteer or a staff member from the very beginning. The pair goes through the job the first day together and then discusses what each of them observed and experienced. If the number of new volunteers is not too large, it is possible to continue the use of these pairs throughout the start-up period, with the more experienced partner acting as ongoing trainer and consultant, and the new volunteer feeling free to talk either in person or on the telephone at any time. (Good places for these talks that are often overlooked are the car, the airplane, the traveling bus. It is possible to use the time spent going from one place to another, even going from the organization to lunch and back, for productive chats. One might say that we need to develop our "car consultant skills.")

Another way to help at the beginning is to have a short meeting of the new volunteers at which they reflect together on what has happened, on how they feel about it, and on the degree to which they think they have accomplished the tasks set before them. Their administrator should be present to provide answers and feedback. An "open clinic" can also be held at the home of one of the volunteers to discuss their new experience. If there is a large group, discussions and problem clinics can be held weekly throughout the start-up period to give support to all the newcomers together.

A different method sometimes found useful in start-up training is to place volunteers in a variety of spots with experienced people so that, early in their careers, they will understand not only their own jobs but also those of other staff and volunteers. Experienced volunteers often make excellent mentors.

Yet another alternative for start-up training might be for volunteers to tape their own work and then, at the end of the day or the end of several periods of work, to listen to the tape with a helper (a covolunteer, the consultant, a trainer, or the supervisor), and discuss each situation. The focus should be on what went well and on what could be handled differently.

Maintenance-of-Effort Training

The purposes of on-the-job training are to increase the skill of volunteers, to get them out of any ruts they might have fallen into, to answer questions and deal with concerns, and to refine practices. In short, it is the meat of the training once the volunteer has become a part of the system. As good morale does not necessarily come of its own accord, on-the-job training may also be seen as a means of building and maintaining morale. Much of this training is given informally and irregularly by the supervisor or consultant, but there should also be a plan for some formal training sessions—either workshops or individual sessions. The plan should, of course, be flexible and subject to change.

What kinds of maintenance-of-effort training are useful? There can be regular covolunteer meetings at which volunteers interview each other about their jobs and discuss their new knowledge, resources, and questions. Sometimes at these meetings they can be asked to fill out "self-reflection sheets," indicating how they feel about the job they are doing and the people with whom they are working, how they would change the organization if they could, and so forth. These self-reflection sheets can then serve as the basis for group discussion and even for suggestions for new practices within the organization.

Input sessions are another kind of maintenance-of-effort training. In these sessions new plans or procedures or research findings are shared with the volunteers, or additional information about a particular volunteer job or function is given to further their growth. Volunteers can also attend staff meetings as part of their on-the-job training. Such attendance should be carefully planned beforehand, some kind of observation or listening guide should be provided to the volunteers, and there should be full discussion afterward. The content of the staff meetings chosen should, of course, be relevant to the volunteers' jobs and interests.

Another important part of on-the-job training is making time available periodically for the volunteers to read new resource or program material. Most organizations receive and send out many, many materials, such as staff speeches, government pamphlets, films, and so on, but these are rarely available to volunteers. There should also be an opportunity for volunteers to meet new resource people who have entered the system.

Another idea is to give the volunteers a "mini-sabbatical"—perhaps a month off to "travel" in their community to other sites similar to their own to get ideas, or to take a training seminar during the hours in which they would usually be offering service. This kind of renewal has not previously been considered for volunteers, but it is very important if they are to continue to give productive, efficient, and innovative service in a job they have held for any period of time.

Surely the volunteer staff of any organization should be apprised of what is available to them in nearby college, extension, or adult education courses. Often there are relevant courses that an organization could encourage its volunteers to take, perhaps by reimbursing their tuition.

Periodic Review and Feedback

Many types of review sessions for volunteers have been used over the years. One method is to have the volunteer and the consultant each tape-record some of their observations about what they feel is being done well and what could be improved, along with any other comments they wish to make to one another. They then listen to each other's tapes and prepare for a face-to-face discussion of their content.

Another technique is to videotape volunteers' work periodically, encouraging them to look at their own practice and analyze shortcomings. They can then help determine the kind of training they need most. It is also wise to consult the organization's clients in planning training for the volunteers. They can recommend the kind of training they think will get them better service.

Whatever kind of training is used, it is important to plan for implementation of new suggestions and feedback along the way. The implementation plan ought to include some checkpoints or stop-action periods where discussion can be held about how well the implementation is working out and what new problems have come up. Feedback from all sources should be taken into consideration in deciding whether to continue or redesign any training program. Feedback cuts across all phases of training, from preservice to transition training.

Transition Training

A volunteer can be helped to move to levels of greater responsibility, whether in the present job or a new one. Just as when first coming aboard the organization, so in moving to a different job, a volunteer must be prepared for entry and must be helped to look ahead rather than back. If there are new role responsibilities, these need to be delineated through discussion, observation, role playing, interview, or in some other way. It cannot be assumed that because a person has functioned well at one level he or she will necessarily function equally well at the next. Transition training, therefore, whether in individual or group form, should recapitulate the first four phases of the training framework, in a somewhat different manner. That is, there should be pretransition training (a period of referral if the volunteer is going to be working with different people), start-up training in the new job, maintenance-of-effort training, and periodic review and feedback sessions. Thus we have a circle, a framework for continuing training for self-renewal.

Some Assumptions

Listed below are some assumptions about volunteers that have important implications for the training.

1. Volunteers bring with them a wide variation of motivations, experiences, knowledge, and skills. *Implication:* Training methods that build on and use the volunteer's motivation, experience, knowledge, and skills will produce the best and most relevant kind of learning.

2. Volunteers, by and large, will come as self-directed, motivated, interested learners. *Implication:* Volunteers should help plan and conduct their own learning experiences as active participants rather than as passive recipients.

3. Volunteers participate in training events because they want to learn to do their volunteer jobs. *Implication:* The training must be practical and relevant to the learners and must be related to life as they know it.

4. Many volunteers will have been exposed to classroomlike learning situations that were not helpful, relevant, or exciting. *Implication:* The learning activities must take place in an informal, experiential atmosphere.

5. Volunteers have a number of important roles (as parents, workers, students, citizens) that compete for their time. *Implication:* Training should be planned to take into consideration the time available to most volunteers and to accept the legitimacy of their other loyalties.

6. The world of voluntarism has not developed norms or procedures to support and reward participation in ongoing training programs. *Implication:* Training

opportunities and activities must be a rewarding and recognized aspect of organizational functioning.

7. Often the training format and content have been developed over the years and have not been revised or retailored for the particular participants at a particular time. *Implication:* Each training event, if possible, should be planned by trainers and some of the potential participants to meet the current needs of both individuals and the group.

8. Training is often a one-time thing instead of an ongoing support opportunity for volunteers. *Implication:* Ongoing, inservice training is necessary for volunteers, and the importance of follow-up should be communicated at the beginning of the learning experience.

9. Volunteer training is usually seen as an event sponsored by one organization, or for volunteers in one category, such as new, experienced, board, office workers, service personnel, etc. *Implication:* Training should be planned interorganizationally to utilize all the possible resources and to decrease costs.

Training Models

One model for training is the workshop on a particular topic, such as how to communicate better, or how to have more productive committee meetings, or how to keep a board from getting bored. Such workshops might last anywhere from 2 to 6 hours and might be held two or three times a year as a result of determining some special needs. They could be led by a consultant, by an inside-outside change agent, or by trainers and volunteers as a team within the organization. Another model for training is the 1- or 2-day laboratory, where a group of volunteers and some specialized resource people meet for a longer time period and work on a particular series of content items, such as entry into a system, how to cause change to happen in a community, or effective alternatives of conflict utilization.

Still another method of training is to hold "simulation hours," in which participants simulate situations that have occurred or that are anticipated, such as the first confrontation of new youth board members with older, more experienced board members at a board meeting. Another possibility is to use confrontation designs. The confrontation can be either role-played on the spot or watched on film. One national organization developed 45-second to 5-minute filmed confrontations between young and old, white and nonwhite, and other conflicting groups. At the end of each confrontation the trainees were asked to discuss what they would do at that point, sometimes taping their responses and having them evaluated by uncommitted observers, and then trying again until they had developed a repertoire of alternatives for dealing with the confrontation.

Role playing is another method that can be used as part of either a workshop or a total training piece. For instance, teachers were asked to play the role of teenagers, and vice versa, for a period of time. A great deal of learning can come out of such role reversal.

Conferences bringing together organizational staff and volunteers are another training model. Volunteers and professionals from hospital settings, for example, can get together to discuss common problems, ideas, and innovative practices. The results of their meeting can then be disseminated to all those in similar jobs who could not participate in the conference.

The variety of training models is endless. The important factors are that volunteers be involved in the designing of these models and that all alternative possibilities be looked at before a final design is drawn up. So often we rely on models that have worked in the past. By this time, however, they may be dried and true rather than tried and true, or they may not even still be true at all. Each training design should be a package unto itself, designed for a particular group or individual at a particular time for a specified purpose.

20

Administration of Volunteer Programs

Eva Schindler-Rainman
D.S.W., Organization and Community Consultant

Administration of volunteer programs and the role of the administrator has changed over the years. As volunteer programs grow and become a more important part of ongoing services to people, the job of the administrator as well as the scope of the programs will continue to change.

Who Are Today's Volunteers?

This question could be answered in a variety of ways. Three avenues of approach might include groups, organizations, and agencies depending on volunteers to extend their services. These might be divided as follows:

1. Public agencies, that is, governmental tax-based organizations such as public school systems, public welfare systems, community mental health agencies, community hospitals, correctional agencies, public health facilities, cultural facilities, recreational systems, and others.

2. Voluntary agencies and/or organizations such as the YMCA, YWCA, Girl Scouts, Boy Scouts, Camp Fire, Inc., Girls Clubs of America, Boys Clubs of America, Family Service agencies, Voluntary Action Centers, community centers and settlements, and many others.

3. The private business sector—particularly those businesses and industries that encourage their personnel to get involved in volunteer efforts in the community.

This is an important and an increasing source for volunteers and support of volunteer programs. Support may include in-kind service, technology transfer, and sometimes financial gifts, as well as employee volunteers.

4. Cause efforts, including grass-roots, action-orientated cause organizations such as student protest groups, neighborhood and community improvement groups, self-help groups, legal counseling groups, child and family advocacy groups, draft-counselling groups, and other local and national action groups that may be either temporary or permanent. Characteristics of these groups are that the persons involved in them have a commitment to a particular cause and often special abilities and resources to help in the forwarding of that cause. Many of the new cause organizations are more informal in their procedures and able to change as they need to. Many are totally administered by volunteers.

Volunteers in all these groups work in a variety of ways and take on different roles depending on their abilities and interests. They may be on policy and decision-making bodies such as boards of directors, or they may give direct service such as tutoring; they may be involved in direct action–implementing policies and decisions made by the decision makers. Some volunteers also see their roles as catalysts and change agents, either to help bring about change within the organization in which they serve or as a means of using the organization as an impetus for change in the community. Some volunteers are temporary, and some more permanent.

Another way to look at the volunteer world is to divide it by the functions of the community. In each of the functions there are volunteers serving often together with professionals to extend services. They include:

1. The recreation and leisure time community (public and private recreation and leisure time efforts as well as commercial and business recreation)
2. The cultural community (both public and private cultural efforts including the arts, dance, music, writing, drama, and museums)
3. The educational community (public, private, and parochial schools, both formal and informal adult education)
4. The economic community, including private businesses and industry
5. The political community, including governmental functions as well as political organizations
6. The welfare community (private and public welfare efforts and some union efforts in relation to the welfare of workers)
7. The religious community, including volunteer opportunities such as teaching Sunday school and the provision of a variety of programs and educational activities for younger and older people in church settings
8. The health community, including both physical and mental health programs, financed by public, private, and business sources
9. The public safety community, including probation, parole, the court, the police, and other correctional efforts and activities
10. The mass communication community, including television, newspapers, radio, and other kinds of mass communication on both small and large scales
11. The physical, geographic, or ecological community, including opportunities for volunteers to serve as planning aides, newcomer welcomers, statistical documenters, researchers, and so on
12. The unions, including professional organizations

A third way to classify the volunteer world is to divide it into categories of volunteer personpower, including the unemployed, the underutilized, the potential volunteer, as opposed to the more utilized, more fully tapped volunteer. There is great variation as far as the utilization of some of these people is concerned. We seem to be moving from, for example, avoiding elders to a great emphasis on tapping the senior volunteer, so that some of these categories are certainly in an era of transition. However they still include the following:

- *Nonjoiners or unaffiliated persons.* Most recruitment efforts are aimed at people who already belong to some group, such as a known organization or church, and therefore can be motivated through that organization. Traditionally very little has been done to recruit, select, and place the person who is not already in an organizational group.
- *Men, especially single men.* The middle-aged, married white businessman may be found on many boards, but generally there are fewer men than women working as volunteers. Yet the primary need of many organizations is for male volunteers of all ages.
- *Minority-group members.* People of all races, ethnic groups, and religious groups, depending on the community, may find themselves in minority groups that are largely ignored in the recruitment of volunteers. These may include Buddhists, Moslems, Native Americans, blacks, Latinos, Pacific Asians, both those born in the United States and newcomers.
- *Persons lacking formal education.* The person who has not had at least a high school education is often looked down upon by the professional recruiter. As yet, many of the application blanks for volunteer workers ask that the volunteer indicate level of education. However, it has been found that formal education has very little to do with the ability and commitment of volunteers.
- *Persons in rural areas.* Agricultural extension agents and other professional workers say that it is difficult to recruit rural people who may live far from one another, but here is a most likely source if transportation problems can be worked out.
- *The Young.* Even though recently encouraged to tutor, to work in hospitals, and to work with the elderly, the young still find volunteer opportunities difficult to come by.
- *Physically, socially, and mentally handicapped persons* are often not sought as volunteers. This is beginning to change as a result of some of the self-help movements, where, for example, a former drug user becomes a volunteer counselor to a present drug user, and someone who has been through a cancer operation counsels persons about to have such surgery.
- *Institutionalized persons,* whether in prison, forestry camps, mental hospitals, foster homes, or other institutions, have rarely been recruited as volunteers.
- *Blue-collar workers* in some areas have not been recruited at all.
- *Labor union members* have also been underutilized so far, being tapped for their expertise and to help recruit union members as volunteers.
- *Elders.* The older segment of our population has been overlooked as potential volunteers until very recently. It is true that in some parts of the country there is a shift of emphasis to recruiting seniors as volunteers, and they have been found to be both available and able.

Clusters of more highly utilized volunteers include:

Middle-aged, white, married women

Middle-aged, white, middle- and upper-middle-class business and professional men

Persons with religious affiliations and motivations

Educated, high-status minority men and women

Visible, experienced volunteers, that is, volunteers who are so active that everybody in the community knows and wants them, even if in name only

Members of certain organizations and social groups

Professional persons

Having looked at who the volunteers are today, let us now turn to the changing role of the volunteer administrator.

The Changing Role of the Volunteer Administrator

It is clear that a new profession is emerging in the volunteer world. It is the volunteer administrator, director, or coordinator, who oversees and supervises a volunteer program. We can see this emergence not only because so many more paid volunteer director opportunities are available, but also because many community colleges and universities offer courses and degrees in the field of volunteer administration. The volunteer administrator may be the executive director of an agency or organization utilizing a large number of volunteers in order to carry out its services. Or the volunteer director may be a middle-management person within an organization in charge of the volunteer program. Some examples of the latter would include volunteer directors or coordinators who manage school volunteer programs, volunteers in probation programs, docent programs in museums and zoos, hospitals, mental health centers, and business organizations, where they are often known either as director of volunteers or director of community relations, and in many other settings. Most directors of volunteer jobs are full-time, paid positions, but some are as yet part time or staffed by a volunteer who does not get paid for his or her services.

One of the more recent developments in this field is the emergence in more than thirty states in the United States of volunteer coordinators at the state level who are directly responsible to the governor of that state. These administrators are usually responsible for initiating or continuing volunteer programs in state-financed and -run departments and institutions. This is a powerful, able group of professional men and women who are making great impact in their states in recruiting and maintaining volunteers to serve in state services.

Many cities also have hired volunteer coordinators or directors who are directly responsible to the mayor or governing officer of that city. Here the volunteer administrator is responsible for helping initiate volunteer programs in city departments and services, including such departments as city planning, the library, recreation services, police services, tourist bureaus, and others.

The volunteer administrators in all these situations and roles find, besides *new courses* at institutions of higher learning, other *new supports available.* These include the many new professional organizations that have sprung up to organize and support persons who administer volunteer programs. These include the Association of Volunteer Administrators, Association of Voluntary Action Scholars, and the International Association of Volunteer Effort. Many of these organizations have national officers and headquarters with regular national and regional meetings. The common purpose is to provide educational, support and networking opportunities, as well as up-to-date information to the members.

Another support organization is Volunteer, which has related services including a national clearinghouse where information on a vast variety of activities in the volunteer world is readily available, and a journal that gives information on current activities, workshops, people, books in the field.

It is clear that the *role of the volunteer administrator* is more than just administration. It is indeed a new multifaceted, challenging, and versatile role. It includes the following kinds of "hats": the administrative hat, the public relations or community relations hat, consultant hat both within the organization and to organizations in the community, and a training hat, which includes the training of relevant and appropriate staff and volunteers. The latter functions require for most people additional educational help and support to learn consulting and training skills. Both learning and reading opportunities aimed specifically at the administrator of voluntary systems are available.

New Confrontations and Opportunities

Certainly the massive changes going on in the world, in our country, and in the volunteer world bring with them new opportunities as well as new confrontations. These include more *demanding volunteers,* that is, volunteers who are more conscious of their rights, their wishes, the way their services are utilized, and who in many cases demand good training, good placement, and a contract that spells out what they expect of the agency and what the agency expects from them. Human service teams are developing also. These include interdisciplinary teams of which volunteers may be one or two members, for example, the principal, teacher, paid instructional aide, and volunteer in a school; or the doctor, nurse, social worker, and volunteer in a hospital. Another kind of team is the team that may not be interdisciplinary but one in which each person brings different resources. This is the team that includes a professional, a paid paraprofessional, and a volunteer. The implications of this development are that the administrator needs to be able to help human service teams form and function together.

The *women's movement* has brought to the surface many concerns about the second-class citizenship roles women sometimes take when they become volunteers. Criticism has been aimed mainly at the service volunteer, because it is believed that volunteers are needed to help cause social change to happen. These criticisms have certainly been direct and in many cases are helping organizations and agencies to evaluate whether they are giving the best kind of opportunity to the volunteer to serve in meaningful ways, both to the volunteer and to the agency. Also the women's movement, and particularly the National Organization for Women, is concerned about appropriate contracts for volunteers that include adequate insurance coverage. The volunteer administrator needs to handle these confrontations and criticisms and to be able to interpret clearly what volunteers are doing and how both the needs of the volunteer and the needs of the clients of the agencies are being met through volunteer services.

A number of *unions* are concerned about the increasing size of the volunteer movement. Their concern centers largely around the fact that they want to be sure that all the possible persons eligible to be employed are employed. Their criticism of volunteer programs is aimed mainly at making sure that volunteers do not replace paid employees or that they are placed in positions where paid persons belong and that volunteers are not used as an excuse to cut budgets, particularly personnel budgets, in any way. Most persons in the volunteer world would heartily agree that volunteers not be recruited to replace paid personnel but rather to extend professional services to clients.

There is a *raised consciousness about budgets* that confronts the administrator. This has to do both with fewer funds being available in many places, as well as the better utilization of the funds that are granted. Evaluation and accountability are important aspects of good human service administrations, and volunteer administrators need to know or to learn how to make and defend realistic budgets. Further than that, they are now often required to know how to frame and write proposals for funds that may be available for their program, and to be able to evaluate these programs. Creative funding know-how is of utmost importance.

Ambivalent top administrators may be another source of confrontation. There are many administrators who know that a volunteer program will help extend their services. However, some are not really convinced of the wisdom of having volunteers as part of their agency operations. Many of these administrators need to be included in the planning and decision making of the volunteer program so that they can become more knowledgeable about it.

New educational and *renewal opportunities* are much more available and will certainly be helpful to volunteer directors, coordinators, and administrators in meeting some of these confrontations, and encouraging them to handle these challenges in more flexible and effective ways. These opportunities are also important to decrease and prevent burnout.

The Volunteer Program as Part of the Total Organization

Often in the past the volunteer program has been seen as a rather low-status part of the total agency organization. Often the volunteer administration was seen as a weak link in the chain or as heading a department into which could be pushed all those services that did not seem to belong anywhere else. However, this is changing rapidly, with volunteer programs and departments taking on new and added importance as their value as a part of human service organizations is being proved. Also, the professional training and certification of directors makes them more able to be visible, effective, initiative-taking, and heard in their organizations. Volunteer departments are rising in status and becoming more pervasive in their activities throughout most organizations. This changes the relationship of the administrator to the top executive as well as to those staff persons employed within the organization. This also means additional relationships to peer management persons within the organization. Administrators may also relate to boards or to advisory committees of the total organization, as well as to the specific group that helps formulate policy for the volunteer program.

Some characteristics of good volunteer administrative practices include the following:

1. *Clear, communicated, constantly evaluated goals.* It is important for volunteer programs to develop "do-able," understood, broadly decided upon goals. As the program matures, goals are often redefined, refined, and changed.

2. *Involvement of a "vertical slice" of persons in planning, problem solving, and decision making.* It is imperative to include persons to be affected by planning, problem solving, and decision making in the processes.

3. *The actual administration of the program benefits by involving volunteers and staff on an ongoing basis.* It seems self-evident that systems in which many volunteers work should practice what they preach. However, many volunteer systems do not encourage volunteers to act as teammates with paid staff. Together, they can keep an office open, get materials out, train newcomers, solve problems, and consult. It is the unique resources of the volunteers and staff combined that make for the richness of the program.

4. *Regular feedback and staff-volunteer meetings.* Planning, evaluating, and replanning takes place best when people have a regular chance to get together. As they do so, trust and open communication get built.

5. *Short- and long-term spaces and places for volunteers.* They must be included in modern volunteer programs. Mobility and temporariness are an integral part of our society. Therefore, our programs need to have shorter- and longer-term volunteer jobs available, so that persons who cannot commit themselves for long periods will not be lost as a human resource for the program.

6. *Opportunities for orientation, training, and competence improvement and growth.* These are essential for both volunteer and staff. Persons serve for many reasons. Motivations vary widely, including needs to become more competent and successful. It is, therefore, important to offer developmental opportunities before and on the job. Often experienced volunteers as well as staff members can be the leaders of such activities.

7. *Flexible ground rules are needed.* Modern organizations tend to write their rules as they need them. They also keep them to a minimum. They should not be cast in concrete; it may be necessary to change them in this fast-changing world.

8. *Keep connection with similar programs.* In this way, practices can be exchanged; perspective rather than provincialism is encouraged; and strength is gained through joint efforts.

9. *Collaboration* with other agencies, organizations, and causes in the community is essential for a healthy program. To the extent that the program is connected to and intertwined with the larger community, more and more human and material resources become known and available to be tapped.

10. *Recognition* of the importance of *all* contributors to the program at various times makes a program more humane. This may include regular recognition events, but even more important are the "we missed you yesterday," "that is a great idea, thank you," and "it's great to see you today!" At the elbow training (available where and when needed), individual conferences, and volunteer-staff team meetings are also ways to recognize persons' contributions and importance.

Voluntarism Goes Interagency, Communitywide, Statewide, and Worldwide

Another important change to notice in this time of transition is that there are now communities in which there is collaboration between agencies centered in volunteer activities. This collaboration may include communitywide board training for new board members, or it may be that one agency recruits and refers volunteers for several organizations and agencies needing such volunteers. Other collaboration may be built around development of communitywide activity calendars and directories, community information and referral services, and communitywide workshops planned by a collaborative group of organizations to look at better recruitment and utilization of volunteers have already occurred in the United States.

The first International Conference on voluntarism was held in the United States in October 1971. An organization known as the International Association of Volunteer Effort is in touch with volunteers and volunteer movements around the world. Many of its members have traveled to countries and cities abroad to learn about volunteer programs that have developed or are emerging. Also, there have been conferences both in the Philippines and in France in which a variety of international countries and groups participated. In 1974, at the 18th International Conference on Social Welfare in Nairobi, Kenya, another international group was convened to talk about volunteer developments, and as part of the United States Bicentennial there was an International Conference of Volunteers held in 1976 in San Francisco. Since then, there have been additional conferences in England, Switzerland, Colombia, and Australia. It can be said that voluntarism and volunteering have gone international. This means both new relationships and opportunities for volunteers and volunteer administrators as well, and a developing worldwide volunteer network.

This is probably the most exciting time in the history of the United States to be active in the volunteer world. These times offer a tremendous opportunity for volunteers to make important contributions to the quality of life and to human services in their communities. It is clear that the volunteer administrator is a key person in translating the motivation, interest, resources, and skills of volunteers into human services to the clients of our people-helping agencies and organizations.

Suggested Reading

Allen, Louis A., Beyond Theory Y, *Personnel Journal,* December 1973.

Bolder, Eugenie, Take It out of My Salary: Volunteers on the Prestige Circuit, *Ms. Magazine,* February 1975.

Borst, Diane, and Patrick Montana (Eds.), *Managing Nonprofit Organizations,* AMACOM, a Division of American Management Association, New York, 1977.

Cleveland, Harlan, The Decision Makers, *The Center Magazine,* vol. VI, no. 5, September–October 1973.

Drucker, Peter, *Management: Tasks, Responsibilities, Practices,* Harper & Row, New York, 1973.

Famularo, Joseph L., *Handbook of Modern Personnel Administration,* McGraw-Hill, New York, 1972.

Fenn, Dan H., Jr., Executives as Community Volunteers, *Harvard Business Review,* March–April 1971, pp. 4–16, 156–159.

Gappert, Gary, Post Affluence: The Turbulent Transition to a Post Industrial Society, *The Futurist,* vol. VIII, no. 5, October 1974.

Hanson, Pauline L., and Carolyn T. Marmaduke, *The Board Member: Decision Maker for the Non Profit Corporation,* Citizen Participation Skills, Sacramento, Calif., Han/Mar Publications, 1972.

Hersey, Paul, and Kenneth H. Blanchard, *Management of Organizational Behavior,* Prentice-Hall, Englewood Cliffs, N.J., 1972.

Ingalls, John D., *A Trainer's Guide to Andragogy,* Superintendent of Documents, U.S. Government Printing Office, Washington.

Levin, Stanley, *Volunteers in Rehabilitation,* Goodwill Industries, Washington, 1973.

Lippitt, Ronald, and Eva Schindler-Rainman, *Team Training for Community Change: Concepts, Goals, Strategies and Skills,* University Extension, University of California, Riverside, Development Publications, Bethesda, Md., 1972.

Loeser, Herta, *Women, Work and Volunteering,* Beacon Press, Boston, 1974.

Louden, J. Keith, and Jack Zusman, *The Effective Director in Action,* AMACOM, a Division of American Management Association, New York, 1975.

Naylor, Harriet H., *Volunteers Today: Finding, Training and Working with Them,* Dryden, New York, 1973.

Principles of Association Management, American Society of Association Executives and Chamber of Commerce of the United States, Washington, 1975.

Sanborn, Margaret A., and Caroline Bird, The Big Giveaway, What Volunteer Work Is Worth, *Ms. Magazine,* February 1975.

Scheier, Ivan, *Frontier 11: Orienting Staff to Volunteers,* National Information Center on Volunteerism, Boulder, Colo., 1972.

Schindler-Rainman, Eva, Are Volunteers Here to Stay? *Mental Hygiene,* vol. 55, no. 4, October 1971.

_____ , Opportunity—An Answer to NOW, *Voluntary Action News,* National Center for Voluntary Action, Washington, December 1971.

_____ , The Potentials of Volunteers in Urban Planning in L. K. Northwood (Ed.), *Next Steps in Strengthening Social Components of Urban Planning,* Wiley, New York, 1970.

_____ , Toward Humane Management of School Volunteer Programs, *The Volunteer,* Columbus Public Schools, vol. 1, no. 4, spring 1975.

_____ , *Transitioning: Strategies for the Volunteer World,* Val Adolph (Ed.), Vancouver Volunteer Centre, Vancouver, B.C., 1981.

_____ , Volunteer Administration: New Roles for the Profession to "Make a Difference," *The Journal of Volunteer Administration,* Association for Volunteer Administration, Boulder, Colo., winter 1986–1987.

_____ , *The Creative Volunteer Community, a Collection of Writings,* Vancouver Volunteer Centre, Vancouver, B.C., 1987.

_____ , and Ronald Lippitt, *Developing Your Volunteer Community,* XICOM, Inc., New York, 1975. A multimedia package.

_____ , and _____ , Hopes and Prospects in Adult Education: Working with People Whom We Forgot, *Interpersonal Development,* Karger, Basel, Switzerland, vol. 4, pp. 107–119, 1973.

_____ , and _____ , The Shape of the Future Is Already Here, *The Girl Scout Leader Magazine,* January–February 1974.

_____ , and _____ , *The Volunteer Community: Creative Use of Human Resources,* 2nd. ed., Yellowfire Press, Boulder, Colo., 1975.

Smith, David Horton (Ed.), *Voluntary Action Research: 1974,* Lexington Books, Lexington, Mass., 1974.

Smith, David Horton, *Voluntary Sector Policy Research Needs,* Center for a Voluntary Society, Washington, 1974.

Smith, David Horton, Jack Ross, Richard D. Reddy, and Burt R. Baldwin, *Voluntary Action Research Annotated Bibliography,* Greenwood Press, Westport, Conn., 1978.

Smith, David Horton, Marge Schultz, Barbara Marsh, and Cathy Orme, *General Voluntarism: Annotated Bibliography,* Center for a Voluntary Society, Washington, 1973.

Spiegel, Hans B. C. (Ed.), Decentralization, in *Citizens Participation in Urban Development,* vol. III, NTL/Learning Resources Corp., La Jolla, Calif., 1974.

Stenzel, Anne K., and Helen M. Feeney, *Volunteer Training and Development: A Manual for Community Groups,* rev. ed., Seabury Press, New York, 1976.

Training Volunteer Leaders: A Handbook to Train Volunteers and Other Leaders of Program Groups, YMCA, New York, 1974.

Voluntarism: Confrontation and Opportunity, YMCA, New York, 1975.

Volunteer Recognition, Publication of the National Center for Voluntary Action, Washington, 1973.

Walker, J. Malcolm, and David Horton Smith, Higher Education Programs for Administrators of Volunteers, *Volunteer Administration,* vol. X, no. 3, fall 1977.

Wilson, Marlene, *Effective Management of Volunteer Programs,* Volunteer Management Associates, Boulder, Colo., 1976.

21
Membership

Tracy D. Connors
Consultant

"Member (L., *membrum*): A distinct part or element of a whole, a person belonging to some association, society, or other such organization." Relating this definition to the nonprofit organization is deceptively simple. A member is someone who has made a contribution to your organization in the form of membership dues. Therefore, they "belong" to your organization. In fact, collectively the organization belongs to them, something we should never fail to remember.

Your organization belongs to its members instead of to stockholders. Not only is this true in the corporate sense, but in the sense that most nonprofit organizations (NPOs) live or die on the basis of this membership. Ultimately, the elements of a membership program in the NPO—prospecting, recruiting, orienting, training, involving—will determine the success or failure of any nonprofit organization. Most NPOs, however, give only lip service to membership per se. Of course, they have a membership committee, but even then most people get behind its efforts only when memberships are not coming in as expected and dues money is needed to balance the budget.

The following discussion focuses on the four major problem areas pertaining to membership: participation or involvement; members' needs; dues; and recruitment. Much of the material is drawn from the excellent American Society of Association Executives (ASAE) publication, *Membership Promotion Manual,*[1] and other articles on this subject that have appeared in the ASAE journal, *Association Management.* More than any other national organization serving the nonprofit sector, ASAE has provided extensive materials on membership and its importance to the NPO.

Since the great majority of readers will already have a membership, let us first discuss the question of how to retain those members and to take advantage of their talents by involving them more fully in the activities and programs of the organization.

Membership Involvement

In the military, the old saying, "Don't ever volunteer," made some sense, since volunteers were often recruited with promises of cushy duty, only to find a heavy wheelbarrow or shovel waiting for them in the hot sun. But does this axiom hold true for your organization as well? Do your members hold back when there is work to be done? Do they realize that they "volunteered" when they joined your organization—that they have a responsibility to be active—to be a part of things? Are they fond of asking, "What is the organization doing for me?"

As John S. Jenness points out in *Association Management,*[2] the "challenge comes down to this: How can you get your membership to recognize and appreciate the benefits which accrue from volunteering to play an active role?" He calls for a continuous, two-part educational process that involves developing a philosophy and creating a state of mind in the organization.

"First of all, you have the responsibility to educate your members not to expect something for nothing nor to expect everything in return merely for the payment of dues," he says. "It is the responsibility of the association executive to educate each member to realize that there is no such thing as a free lunch, that when a member pays his dues he incurs an obligation to contribute, by his efforts, to the good of all—and that the more he puts into the association, the more he gets out of it." I would broaden the responsibility to include the entire leadership of the organization. The chief administrative officer will not have the clout needed to create and maintain this vital attitude if the leadership does not share it and support his or her efforts.

The second major point that Jenness makes is the importance of impressing "upon your members the fact that...the association (organization) does make needed help of all sorts available to the member who knows how to go about getting that help—and to warrant it." Another danger he notes is that as an organization grows in size, it becomes very easy for a member to become a "phantom" member—a name on the roster, but never seen or heard from. Although such members may feel that they are getting all they need from the organization, in fact, they are shortchanging themselves and the rest of the membership by not being involved, active, and constructive members.

The following list of questions should stimulate your thinking as to ways you can illustrate to members the value of their membership—and the importance to them of volunteering to take a more active role in the programs and services of the organization. It is adapted by permission from *Association Management* (December 1973, p. 44).

1. When your members have a problem, do they
   a. Call other members of the organization for suggestions on how to solve it?
   b. Check through back issues of your publication for articles relating to the problem?
   c. Check with a staff member for suggestions on either the problem itself or for names of others that might help?
   d. Talk about the problem at the next meeting?
2. Before your members go to one of your meetings, do they
   a. Plan in advance to talk about specific professional topics?
   b. Make a date to talk with someone before, at, or after the meeting?
   c. Plan how they can apply the speaker's topic to solving their problem or otherwise use it to their advantage?
   d. Anticipate questions that others there may ask so they can make a real contribution?

    e. Consider how the meeting will add to their self-development?
    f. Plan to volunteer for an assignment helpful to one or more committees?
    g. Look forward to seeing friends and associates who are working as they are, toward providing important public services or solving vital community needs?

3. When members telephone other members with questions or problems, do they
    a. Forget to call back—or cut them off short?
    b. Remember that other members volunteered to take time to help them solve their problems?

4. When one of your officers asks members to serve on a program or on a committee, do they
    a. Automatically turn it down because they are too busy?
    b. Evaluate the amount of time involved and reluctantly ask to be considered next year because they really are too busy this year?
    c. Recognize the opportunities for individual growth different from those open within other organizations?
    d. Know that although the job will be a challenge, they will have the support and participation of the staff and membership to do an effective job?

5. When your members feel out of touch because of lack of personal contact or because they have missed a number of meetings, or because the membership chairperson has not called them, what will be done about it?
    a. Will the executive committee expect and receive the necessary personal follow-up from the membership chairperson?
    b. Is an effective system of personal contact with members in effect?
    c. Are meetings held regularly and attendance noted so that personal follow-up can be started when members miss more than several meetings?

6. In short, since your organization belongs to its members, where does it fit into their individual goals and growth plans?
    a. Does the organization really play a positive role in their self-development?
    b. Do your members fully understand the many benefits, direct and indirect, that they receive for their membership?
    c. Have they had impressed on them what greater benefits they could obtain from that membership by taking a more active role in the programs and services of the organization?

Membership Arithmetic: Divide to Multiply

"Divide the work to multiply the benefits" was the theme of a series of chapter-improvement meetings held by the Institute of Internal Auditors and reported by Arch McGhee.[3] The objective of the meetings was to help the chapters and members derive greater returns on their membership in the organization. The lessons learned are just as valid today.

If your organization has a number of chapters or other subgroups, you might consider doing as the Institute did and plan a series of meetings to explore ways of stimulating member involvement in organizational programs and services. Although somewhat time-consuming, the meetings in themselves provided a vehicle of involvement while offering firm solutions to the problem.

The first axiom stressed by McGhee is that "interest in any voluntary effort varies in direct proportion to one's involvement and participation in achieving the aims of the group. It is true of associations, of church endeavors, community drives, and a host of similar efforts. The majority of voluntary members join such a group with the expectation of participating in the work. The real problem, therefore, is that of utilizing their talents in the best way."

The progressive leadership of any nonprofit organization is a formidable task, requiring far more work than any one person can accomplish. It is absolutely vital, therefore, that others become involved. And, the more widespread the coordinated involvement becomes, the greater the benefits—to the organization and to the member. As a result, the Institute stressed delegation—with follow-up controls.

The organizational leaders who, consciously or unconsciously, believe that they alone are able to do all or most of the work of the organization, refusing to delegate, are not only committing a disservice to the organization, but could well be threatening its very survival. Not only do they deny the benefits of participation to others, but they make the survival of the organization dependent on their continued involvement and participation—a shaky situation at best, since no one can go on at maximum effort forever. Despite Herculean efforts, these leaders usually create regression rather than progress toward their goals. The most effective and beneficial leader of the nonprofit organization is the delegator—one who helps the organization reach its goals through the efforts of other people.

McGhee says that "spreading the work enables each participant to carry a load sufficient to demand some extra effort on his part, but is not so burdensome as to make accomplishment impossible. Psychologically, it is important that a volunteer member achieve the feeling and the satisfaction that comes with successful accomplishment of his...task. The positive reinforcement that comes with successive achievements eventually creates leaders."

Although widespread involvement of organizational members may tend to dilute the quality of performance, "progress was not born in an atmosphere of absolute certainty," he says. Progress is made by those willing to take a risk, he notes, to "make a mistake and to profit from that mistake."

Risk can be minimized, however, through effective management of the delegation process. McGhee cites the following examples used by the Institute of Internal Auditors[4] with great effectiveness:

1. Select assignments that fit the talents and personality of the member. Members will do best those things which they like to do.

2. Make assignments definite. Whenever a member is given an assignment, he should know just what he is supposed to do. Sometimes this may mean consultation to determine the requirements and the limits of the job. Indefinite assignments put the member on the spot—he can feel neither quite sure of what he is to do nor when he is finished.

3. Set completion dates where specific projects are involved.

4. Do not be afraid to ask. A member is complimented, not insulted, by being asked to undertake an assignment. The very worst that can happen is a refusal.

5. Never ask for volunteers. This is usually an evasion of administrative responsibility—by asking the volunteer to select himself instead of being selected. Those who volunteer may not be those best suited for the project at hand.

6. Make sure that each assignment calls for a worthwhile contribution from the member. A member who is given a trivial assignment or is put on a committee with nothing definite to do will not be interested because of his participation—in fact, the contrary, disinterest, is apt to be the result.

7. Never divide responsibility between committees or members. What if everybody's job turns out to be nobody's job.

Another important way of involving members is pointed out by Dennis L. Hilner in his *Association Management* article, "How to Increase Member Involvement,"[5] in which he suggests using the meetings of the board of directors as a source of motivation.

He explains that two members are given special invitations to attend each board meeting. If it is a dinner or luncheon meeting, they are guests of the board. After hearing the discussion of organizational matters for about half of the meeting, the members are asked for their questions and comments, which he reports have been found "to be very constructive."

"Also, as a direct result of their attendance at the board meeting, many have been happy to serve on special committees and really get involved in trying to help solve some of the industry's problems." Many of these "were members who had previously been completely uninvolved" in organizational activities.

Another benefit is that these members become more understanding and empathetic toward the board of directors. They see firsthand the problems that face the organization and have more understanding of the sometimes unpopular decisions the board must make from time to time.

Such a program should strengthen the organization and make the average member much more aware of the challenges facing the organization and how hard it is working to meet them. "This is often the very thing that motivates him to become involved himself," Hilner points out, "he sees the real need for active participation."

It should be noted here that members attending a confidential session of the meeting should have this pointed out. They should be clearly instructed as to what may and may not be said to others in the organization. Meetings where controversial personnel matters may be discussed may not be the best occasion on which to use this technique of member involvement.

Analyzing Member Needs

Ascertaining members' needs is relatively easy when the organization is small or provides a well-defined public service to a specific category of citizen. For these organizations, regular membership meetings and "shoulder-rubbing" participation at organization functions will usually provide enough feedback to alert the organization's leadership to any developing trouble spots in this area.

For organizations established to meet certain specific needs of the collective membership, however, the process of responding to members' needs and maintaining a relevant "services package" is much more difficult. Toffler, in *Future Shock*,[6] says that change is moving so rapidly that he refers to it as a "firestorm." Since this pace also affects the service organization sector, it does not take long for an organization to become out of date or for members to begin questioning the value of the organization itself. Frequent indications are declining membership rates, corresponding decreases in dues revenue, lack of interest in current programs, and growing challenges from dissident members.

Other indicators of stagnation in the member needs area include the centralization of authority and responsibility for the organization at the national level (if it has a national structure); local chapters beginning to feel powerless; continuation of outdated services or programs; busy, but ineffectual committee work; and an organizational bureaucracy that grows but does not produce a commensurate rise in services to either the membership or the public.

Reorganization

When an organization reaches this stage, its leadership often recommends a major reorganization, new services, or a significant infusion of new programs—anything, in fact, that may halt the decline and revitalize the organization, regaining member confidence and support. The problem, however, is deciding where to start the reorganization, what types of new services the organization should inaugurate, what kind of new programs should be begun, how to assign new priorities and develop new objectives—in short, on what database the organization depends to save the day. Perhaps the most obvious answer is to let your members tell you the answers. That is what the American Society for Medical Technology[7] did when it found that its membership was decreasing.

The primary objective in such a program is for the organization to focus on discovering what its members are really seeking, rather than what the organization wants to give them. The technique is basically that of market research based on four principles:

1. A basic philosophy that an organization of this type will prosper only if it effectively services an appropriate and relatively homogeneous market.

2. The organization's leadership is willing to make a policy decision as to who constitutes that market.

3. Determining the needs that this market feels can best be served by an organized group.

4. A willingness of the nuclear organization to restructure or revamp any obsolete policies that are not meeting current needs—the primary function of the organization being to meet today's needs.

Gelb and Friedheim note that the society "carefully considered the types and variety of input available. As a result, we surveyed not only current members, but also members who had dropped out."[8] A questionnaire was critical to the success of the survey and was developed following in-depth interviews with members of the board and key staff.

The data collected through the survey was converted into specific concepts that were considered by the board in finding answers to members' needs. The data also revealed the priorities that members attached to important areas and programs. Simply having the members participate in setting the priorities had a beneficial effect "on the organization's attitude about itself. Members have reflected on their involvement and have a keener feeling of their value as a member."[9] As a result of the survey and the subsequent actions taken by the Society's leadership, membership rose by 31 percent.

The use of marketing research to develop plans for an organization's future, they report, "means taking a deep, probing look at the health of the association itself. It should not be taken lightly nor superficially....It is our belief that the solutions to an association's problems, especially those involving member support, lie within the organization itself. Once the members' interests have been intelligently discerned, then the association can develop and administer programs."[10] The American Society for Medical Technology no longer has to worry about "what our members want."

Another factor to consider is the organization's "culture," its amalgamation of member's attitudes, clearly distinct from its mission, technologies, reward systems, policies, job descriptions, etc. Many nonprofit organizations are not in control of their cultures, as Kilmann notes. Instead, the hidden culture is running the show. "Often, organizations are fighting their pasts, their traditions, their no-longer-relevant assumptions of the environment. They are wearing social blinders, unable to change directions, to see new ways of doing things, or to meet the current needs of their constituencies."[11]

Dues

For most nonprofit organizations, two basic questions must be faced each year regarding dues:

1. What do members get for their dues money?
2. Is our dues structure equitable?

If clear and positive answers are available for these questions, and if they are communicated to your membership, then the problem of collecting dues money almost solves itself.

Emphasizing Membership Benefits. Nonprofit organizations have several different sources of revenue, but virtually all have some form of dues structure. For many NPOs, dues form the major source of operating revenue. In fact, for many NPOs, dues are the only thing that keeps them in business. Yet all too often these NPOs not only do not know what the true value of membership is to a member, but the benefits of membership are rarely communicated to the membership. The danger in this omission is pointed out by C. Wayne Rice, in a recent *Association Management* article.[12]

"An association which serves its members fully and well," he notes, "but which fails to communicate the value of its services to them is no more secure in the long run than the association which fails to serve its members altogether."

It is an easy situation to drift into, what with major problems and challenges facing most NPOs on a daily basis. Certainly it was true for the Greater Cleveland Hospital Association. "Since our membership kept growing and since practically nobody dropped out, we assumed that everyone knew what a bargain we were delivering for the dues. We know now that you can't assume things like that," he said.

After a board member of a member institution questioned membership in the association, its staff began to search for answers, only to find that "knowing the facts was not enough. We had to be able to express them as well." Following an intensive assessment of both the tangible and intangible benefits of membership, the association's leadership "could go to our members with a good explanation of the association's value, because we had a better idea of our value."

Next, they planned the communications process that would deliver the story to the members. Foregoing expensive printing and graphics, they decided on a simple, businesslike, and readable piece on standard $8\frac{1}{2} \times 11$ sheets—"not an appeal but a clear piece of information...very readable." In addition to dealing with the general advantages of working together and other important intangibles, the message stressed the dollar values that most NPOs can place on the services they render to members: "We listed some of the things we do, and affixed dollar signs wherever appropriate. Attached was a pie-chart breakdown of the organization's budget, a credible statement of what it costs to run the organization. In effect, the piece not only stressed what the organization was worth to its members, but what it costs to provide the services."

The process of assessing value of membership and the actual breakdown of costs to deliver X amount of services was a project that brought "comprehensive answers to inquiries about the allocation of dues money." The organization had always placed high on its list of accomplishments its ability to get the most out of the dues dollar, and now it had the means to prove it. The response was prompt, positive, and appreciative.

As Rice summed it up: "Our members are better informed than they used to be about the dollars-and-cents value of their membership to them and, equally important, so is our staff. And most important of all is the fact that our association is in a more secure position than it formerly was."

Establishing the Dues Structure.   How an NPO establishes its dues structure depends in large part on what percentage of the organization's budget is represented by dues. A nonprofit organization that has several sources of revenue in addition to dues money is likely to take one of several approaches to dues money, including

1. Setting dues rates in line with what other organizations in the area that deliver similar public services are charging—the "do as others do" approach
2. Trying to estimate just the costs of administering the membership program (i.e., printing, mailing, staff) and then setting dues at a "reasonable" figure

The more that the organization depends on dues money for operating revenues, however, the more important it becomes that serious and constructive thought be given to the dues structure.

Since each organization will need to approach the area of setting dues based on its own experience and situation, definitive guidelines cannot be offered. However, it seems clear that satisfaction with any dues structure depends on several factors, the first being that the members feel that the particular structure in operation or planned is acceptable. All members need to feel that they are getting their money's worth from the organization in a combination of tangible and intangible benefits. Staff satisfaction and acceptance is another important objective, since ease of administration is important to both members and administrators.

Another important, if not vital, factor is the flexibility of the dues structure. In short, this means that the system should be capable of being easily changed to adapt to new conditions or situations within the organization. For example, if members back more services or new programs, or if inflation or other pressures cause the cost of present services or programs to rise, the dues structure should be capable of handling these very normal situations without overhauling the entire system at great expense in time and money. Of course, there are limits as to how flexible a system can be, but the goal should be flexibility to the extent that conditions permit.

One potential problem in this area that can be avoided is that of including dues-structure guidelines in the organization's by-laws. Some NPOs have done this only to find that when circumstances forced changes in the dues structure, the process was drawn out considerably by having to do so following the usual restrictions to changing by-laws. There does not seem to be any strong support for including the organization's dues structure in the by-laws based on any legal reasoning. Lacking that, to do so may only cause problems later if time is a factor when it becomes necessary to change structure.

There are a number of approaches to establishing acceptable and flexible dues structures. The following are among the most often used, each varying according to the organization employing this approach:

1. *Flat fee.*   Can be the same for all members or varied for each type or category of member as decided upon.
2. *Sliding scale.*   Varied by agreed upon amounts according to one or more criteria, including
    a. Different types or levels of activity
    b. Varying sizes of organizational members, by annual budget, membership, chapters, etc.
    c. Level of service(s) provided for that member

Membership Development

Membership development is vital to the success and growth of most nonprofit organizations, yet few take the time to build a continuous membership development program. Most get around to doing something about membership only when membership levels begin to drop and dues money starts to dry up. Although most professional leadership in the nonprofit sector tries to develop an ongoing membership development program, the annual membership campaign can also be valuable—usually in direct proportion to the amount of planning that has gone into it.

Before devoting detailed attention to the two major areas of membership development—planning the program and then conducting it—the following article by Sheila Moore Campbell, "14 Keys to Boosting Membership,"* is offered as a very practical introduction to the subject of boosting membership.

Like the times, membership development seems to be getting harder.

The truth is—regardless of economic conditions—the more successful you become at membership development the more difficult it becomes to get more new members.

It stands to reason. For a professional society, for example, once you have persuaded a majority of people in the field to join the association, you've got the cream of the crop. It's naturally going to be harder to sign up those who have been holding out. The same is true with a trade group.

Nevertheless, membership development is an essential and continuing function. The astute association executive is constantly seeking breakthroughs in improving results.

Here are 14 starting points:

1. Figure out how much a member is really worth to you. You can't promote new memberships in a vacuum. *You've got to know in dollars and cents what a new member is worth to your association during the first year and what a second-year member is worth.* You've got to know that before you know how much you can afford to spend to get a new member.

Do you know how long a person is likely to remain a member? Exactly how much it costs to service a member? How much revenue a new member will generate in a year on extras: books, seminars, and meetings?

You'll probably find members are worth a lot more than you expected, and that you could be investing more in campaigns to bring them in.

Once you know what a member means to you in total dollars, you can determine what you can afford to spend to attract new members. You may also find that certain groups of members are worth more to the association than others. Can you make a special effort to attract them?

2. Set goals. *There's no way you can do a good job of attracting new members if you can't measure what a good job is.* You can't judge solely on rate of response. If you mail out two brochures and get one application, that's a fantastic rate of response, but not much of a growth in membership.

You have to target the number of new members you need. Without goals, you're setting out on a trip with a map and a compass, but no idea of where you want to go. Only after you know where you're heading can you accurately plan how to get there.

3. Keep at it. *Continuity is the key to good membership development programs.* Your association is in business year-round. It's too risky to count on one or two big membership drives. If one fizzles, you're stuck. You need applications coming in regularly.

Don't feel that a membership offer rejected once is rejected forever. Another time or another approach may work. *One mailing may not convince a person to join. It will usually take several contacts.*

*Reprinted by permission from the November 1975 issue of *Association Management*, copyright 1975 by the American Society of Association Executives.

4. Use a selling theme. *Make your membership drive a unified campaign. Develop a strong selling message around a single selling idea. Concentrate on the most powerful proposition likely to attract new members.*

Don't forget in deciding on a theme that you're selling your memberships; *fight the temptation to use a cute or topical theme that says nothing aobut your organization.* A bicentennial theme might intrigue prospective members of a historical association, but leaves business people cold.

Build everything you use—visually and verbally—around your theme. Each time the theme appears, it reinforces all the other uses of it.

5. Simplify. *Get to the essence of your message. Exactly why should anyone join your association? What's the real reason?* Once you've found it, get it across as simply and dramatically as you can. Don't beat around the bush.

Graphically, stick to the same principle of simplification. Make your message a strong one, and make your promotional materials easy to read and understand.

6. Sell the benefits. *Which of your services are the most appealing to prospective members?* Take a close look; they may not be those your members are using most. It may be that one of the most simple services will interest new people.

For example, in hard times a job placement service might be your biggest draw even though most members never use the service.

Remember that prospective members will be asking, ''What's in it for me?'' The answer to that question can make or break your campaign.

7. Don't bore people to death. We're living in an age of instant communication. *People don't have time to spend pouring over a brochure trying to find out what it's all about. They want to know now, and if they can't find out now, they don't want to bother with it at all.* You'd better catch their attention at once, or you've lost it for good.

Don't use 10,000 words telling people things they don't care about. Show them if you can. *A photograph or an illustration can make all the difference*—let graphic design show your message.

And don't forget that, old as they are, captions under pictures are still more likely to be read than anything except the headline. *So don't bury your message in body copy when you could put it under a photo.*

Visualize your organization and its services as much as possible. Make it look exciting and essential.

This emphasis on graphics doesn't mean people won't read long copy. *They will, but only if it's full of lively facts and information they can use.* Don't automatically turn to a list of services in the interest of brevity. A long list without interesting explanations can be deadly dull.

8. Use a letter with your membership package. *Study after study has proven that people are more likely to read a brochure and act if there's a letter with it.*

The letter can be the most vital part of your campaign. It's a personal (even when it's printed) form of communication. Next to a face-to-face visit or a telephone call, it's the most personal form. Use it to talk in a friendly, personal way about the benefits of joining your association. Make the story interesting; be specific.

9. Develop a memorable graphic identity. *We live in a visual society,* and it's becoming more so every day. The TV babies are now reaching their 30's. The people weaned on television are the decision-makers of today and tomorrow, and they're graphically sophisticated.

Your membership material is often the first thing a prospective member sees. It's the clothes your organization wears. *You can't afford a drab, outdated image.* If your package looks like it was printed in 1956, you'll look like you're caught in 1950's thinking too.

Your graphic image extends to everything with your name on it. Does your logo reflect the kind of people you really represent? Are the colors you use vibrant and exciting, or do they merely tell your age?

Good design costs no more than bad. Sometimes all it takes is a fresh viewpoint. Take a look at your materials objectively. If you can't be objective, find someone to help you who is.

10. Try new media. *Don't limit your membership campaign to one brochure and a direct mail letter. Think about new ways of reaching your audience.* Are there places you can use posters or take-one boxes? Can you put up an exhibit people are likely to notice?

Don't forget to use your own publications, too. You can run house ads in your periodicals, or ads on the inside back covers of publications. There may be other publications in which you can advertise. If you print paperback books, can you bind in a membership reply card?

Trade shows and conventions can be an excellent place to tell your story to an audience that's already interested. *Don't overlook any opportunity to sell.* Use printed messages on the back of your envelopes, or use a postage meter message. Even telephone calls can give you a chance to make a good impression for your organization.

11. Make it easy to join. *Some membership applications look like aptitude tests.* A prospective member has to be firmly committed before even wading into one.

Make your application simple to fill out. Don't force your prospect to fit the information into keypunch coded blocks; that's an internal function. Check the paper your application is printed on to be sure it isn't so slick it repels all efforts to write on it. Put the application on the back of a business reply card, and let your new member elect to have you bill him later. Or include a postage-paid reply envelope.

Check your internal policies on membership promotion. Are you unconsciously weeding out prospective members with old procedures or attitudes? Don't be a slave to old thinking.

12. Don't be afraid to make mistakes. *You learn from your failures, not your successes.* When you do something wrong, you almost always know what caused it to go wrong. When you do something right, it's just about impossible to figure out exactly which element made it work.

Experiment. Try new approaches. You won't be on target every time, but when you do hit it's going to bring in many more members. But don't send out a mistake and think you can call it innovation. Innovation takes even more careful planning than your regular membership solicitation.

13. Be keenly opportunistic. Are you convinced that membership development problems are, in fact, membership development opportunities? Every problem has a solution, whether you work it out or someone else does. Focus on the solutions.

Keep your eyes open for the slightest hint of an opportunity to tell someone about membership; new ways of doing the job. You'll never know if you have a diamond mine or an empty shaft until you've gotten into it.

14. Use your members. *If you're doing a good job of servicing your members, they should be the best sales people for your association.*

A member-get-a-member campaign works—and it is the cheapest, most cost-effective way to build membership. You can make it work.

If you've tried it before and fallen flat on your face, try a different approach. There are scores of ways to persuade your members to cooperate. Keep trying until you find the one that works for them.

Don't sit around and speculate on what might happen. Go out and ask your members for help now. You may be very pleasantly surprised at the result.

Planning NPO Membership Drives

Shortly after the annual meeting and after the new officers have been elected for the coming year, most organizations have at least one eager soul who rises at the next meeting to extol the virtues of new members and to call for a membership campaign. Although new members are badly needed in well-organized, well-led NPOs, they can become a real problem in many respects to organizations that John O'Rourke calls "moribund, outdated, lethargic or poorly managed...." The first task in any membership promotion effort "is to make certain that the association has something to offer the prospective—and current members." The second task,

O'Rourke says, is "to prepare or review existing presentations of the association's concepts, policies, programs and goals in familiar terms which will encourage prospects to want to identify themselves with the associations."[13]

The following discussion identifies the major areas of planning and decision making needed during the formative stages of a membership campaign.

Identification of Membership Benefits.   Every organization has a number of benefits that accrue to its members—benefits that most members seek when they join. In addition, there are very likely many secondary benefits and advantages to membership that may not be as obvious, but that may for many prospects be even more important reasons for joining than the basic membership services package.

Every NPO will have a different combination of these benefits, but whatever the list, it must answer the first question in the membership prospect's mind: "Why should I join this organization?" The membership promotion plan must be based on two fundamentals: the development of honest, compelling reasons why belonging to the organization brings personal benefits in one form or another; and the preparation and dissemination of a convincing body of materials explaining these benefits.

"Membership cannot be sold unless the organization has value to its members" is how *Principles of Association Management* makes this point. "A member obtained through empty promises is unlikely to be retained. An inactive, do-little organization will never get and keep a large membership regardless of the emphasis it places on membership solicitation."[14]

Generally, people join nonprofit organizations not to feel better about themselves or to remedy some social ill but to obtain one or more member benefits provided or offered by the organization. When developing these membership benefits, managers and leaders of NPOs should try to ensure that they[15]

- Offer different levels of memberships, varying the levels of benefits of each
- Examine the costs of benefits offered, ensuring that the revenues generated exceed the costs of providing the benefit
- Do not confuse membership development with annual giving

The most frequently used NPO membership benefits include

- Access to social events, receptions, parties, and so on
- Information of interest to members, e.g., educational materials, courses, videotapes, special reports, and so on
- Special educational or entertainment programs
- Services or free admissions
- Discounts
- Publications
- Volunteer opportunities
- Reciprocal agreements for services provided by other organizations

Determining the Scope of the Membership Promotion or Program

The scope of any membership development effort will depend on the resources available with which to conduct the program; anticipated costs will have to be weighed against anticipated revenues from the program. If this is not done with some accuracy, the organization may very easily find itself in the position of losing money while gaining members.

O'Rourke's "breakeven chart" (Figure 21.1) will help realistically weigh costs against revenues for membership dues. For the purposes of illustration, O'Rourke assumes a large member association

with a low dues income per member of $25 and a prospect list of 10,000 names. The average member longevity with the association is six years. A budget is set which will allow the association staff to "soften up" the prospects by contacting them ten times by direct mail. The theoretical associaion will thus have an additional $250,000 of income if all the prospects join. The prospect list costs 50¢ per name to build, for a total cost of $5,000. A mass-produced letter campaign will cost the association 20¢ per letter, creating a cost of $2,000 per mailing or a total of $20,000 for all ten mailings.

The $5,000 cost for the prospect list and the $20,000 cost for ten mailings at $2,000 each gives a total budget estimate of $25,000. This represents a large outlay for any association. Rather than blindly proceeding, it is essential that the association leadership stop and plan at this point. How many prospects must the association sell to retrieve its investment?

Studying the breakeven chart...will help answer this and other questions. Such a chart will test the membership campaign or program. The money is plotted on the vertical axis—both income and outlay. The number of prospects won into membership by the campaign is plotted along the horizontal axis at the bottom of the chart.

The chart illustrates the computation of the breakeven point based upon making one of the proposed mailings for the hypothetical association. The solid horizontal line indicates the fixed cost for the first mailing, $2,500. How was this determined? Assuming the prospect list cost $5,000 to build and the association plans to use it for ten mailings, then one mailing actually represents a $500 use of this list, or one-tenth. It was also assumed that the cost of each mailing would be $2,000. This gives the $2,500 total which has been charted.

The membership dues received at $25 each are indicated by the sloping solid line. The intersection of the solid lines indicates where income amortizes the cost of the mailing. Thus, the broken line dropped from this point of intersection to the horizontal axis

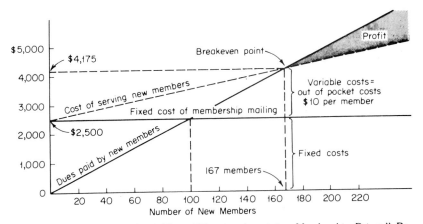

Figure 21.1. Breakeven chart. (From "Planning Association Membership Drives." Reprinted by permission from the November 1969 issue of *Association Management.* Copyright 1969 by the American Society of Association Executives.)

shows that 100 new members are needed at $25 each to cover the fixed costs of the $2,500 mailing.

What about the variable cost? The cost of serving the new members must be considered. This is represented in the chart by the sloping broken line. This variable cost is shown at $10 per member for the hypothetical association.

O'Rourke notes that the $10 figure is used for ease of computation. Very few nonprofit organizations could service a member for $10. It is an "out-of-pocket" expense to the organization, and "the breakeven point occurs at the intersection of the solid and broken lines—the point where the association has signed up 167 new members, with an income of $4,175.

Several important points should be stressed when using the breakeven chart while planning your membership programs:

1. Do you in fact know the longevity of your members?
2. Can your organization afford to wait to amortize the costs of the mailing, or are you in a tight money situation and must have all funds invested in the project returned in new member dues?
3. Once these questions are answered and the proper figures "plugged" into the chart, it should yield important data for planning purposes—certainly more accurate than simply "winging it"—a dangerous practice in any case.
4. The example chart indicates that in this case when the hypothetical organization passes the 167 new members mark, it breaks even on both fixed and variable costs. New members over this figure net the organization a clear profit of $15 each—and, as long as the organization gains more than 167 new members *per mailing,* it will more than break even.

But what happens if the organization needs all the dues income to cover the costs of servicing the new members? The only solution O'Rourke points out "is to establish a 'joining fee,' for if total serving costs equal dues, then it is obviously impossible to get enough members to pay the cost of promotion."[16] In this case the organization would use the joining fee to amortize the fixed costs and the dues to offset the variable costs. The chart would be modified accordingly by extending the number of members needed to reach the breakeven point.

Nonprofits need constituents as much as any politician, but the money they spend to build that constituency can become a source of controversy from both a public relations and a regulatory agency point of view, notes Robert Blum. Some activities currently considered fund-raising are really basic program operations costs, he points out. Generating public support may be as vital to the nonprofit organization's program as any services it provides. However, fund-raising costs have only recently come to be considered as operating costs.

NPO managers should separate new member recruitment costs and revenues from subsequent solicitation, and also separate membership dues from additional donations from that same person within that same fiscal year, Blum recommends. NPO management should think of member acquisition as part of their program and budget for it as a separate entity. Currently, federal grant regulators, the IRS, and many state legislatures do not recognize this distinction, but a trend in this direction seems evident. Meanwhile, budgeting and planning for constituency development will be improved by remembering the importance of the above and the fact that "every nonprofit would be aided by having a constituency of members."[17]

Identifying Prospects

No membership development program goes very far without a good prospect list—it is basic to all such campaigns. In fact, the prospect list should be built and maintained in a regular and continuous process, with costs charged to the membership function.

Every NPO will have a widely varying number of prospective members, and so its methods of developing and maintaining the list will vary accordingly. The smaller the "pool" of prospective members, the more detailed the information you are likely to need about them and vice versa, because in this situation you are increasingly playing a "numbers" game. Although it will be stressed later, the value of personal contact of prospects following the "softening up" process of direct mail or telephone calls cannot be overemphasized. In fact, the success of your membership development effort will probably be in direct proportion to the amount and extent of personal involvement by your members. Some of the major sources of new members include

1. Past members—hard to reinterest but worth the effort since a former member who quit because of poor service or dissatisfaction is a walking testimonial against your NPO. The membership committee should have a very active program component in determining why members drop out—with vigorous efforts directed to correcting the problem and reinstating the member. If the member is beyond the point of being reinstated, try to use whatever conciliatory gestures are appropriate to minimize hard feelings and negative comments.

2. Friends and associates of current members.

3. Lists developed of individuals with demonstrated interests in public service that parallel the service goals of your organization.

4. Technical directories, telephone books, newspapers, public records, trade or technical publications, and rosters of other organizations with similar public service orientation.

Once developed, the list must be maintained—a process that requires constant attention and the allocation of the necessary funds to do so. The investment in this area will depend on the anticipated return per member. Low return equals low investment. Few prospects plus greater potential return equals greater investment. A system must be established to purge the dead wood from the list. After a certain number of contacts (duly recorded on the prospect's file card), the name should be dropped. It is a fact that time and repetition are needed to maximize the benefits of a membership campaign. As many as seven to ten mailings may be required before it may be wise to remove the name from the list. The ratio of mailings required will go down and the number of new members will go up in direct ratio to the extent that personal contacts are employed for the final "sales" effort.

The Budget

Budgeting for a membership campaign will depend on many more variables than can be adequately considered here, however, among the factors which bear on itare the amount the NPO is willing to invest in building new membership; categories and kinds of prospects; type of campaign considered (e.g., direct mail, personal solicitation, telephone); extent of volunteer involvement; and so forth. Obviously, the best budget is the one that brings the greatest net return on new members for the amount spent. Here the breakeven chart can be an invaluable help.

It also helps set the proper goals or quotas for a membership campaign. These are very important from a psychological as well as a fiscal viewpoint. The important point is to set a realistic goal—and the breakeven chart will provide a very realistic and rational way to set the quotas for your membership campaign.

Membership Committee

Most NPOs have a membership committee described in their by-laws. Many have a vice president for membership who chairs the membership committee. Regardless of how the actual function is established within the organization, the success of any membership development program will depend on the selection, organization, motivation, and direction of an effective membership committee. The duties and responsibilities of the membership committee are described in more detail in Part 2, Chapter 12.

The selection of the right chairperson is especially important. O'Rourke suggests that "one of the association's most prestigious members should be selected to head the membership drive." This is undoubtedly true for association membership drives and should correlate highly to most other NPOs. However, even a not so prestigious "name" chairperson can do a very effective job for the organization if he or she has "the active support of a capable committee—which represents all segments of the association—and dependable staff assistance in handling correspondence, mailings and follow-up."[18]

Basic Techniques for Selling New Members

Direct Mail.   Although it is true that direct mail can become very costly and replete with knotty problems if handled incorrectly, it can also be very effective in membership development. An excellent discussion of the basics of a good direct mail membership promotion program is found in the ASAE *Membership Promotion Manual.* This manual and other reference publications on this subject should be reviewed prior to launching a direct mail effort.

Major Elements.   The following overview outlines the eight major elements of any direct mail campaign and are adapted by permission from the ASAE *Manual.*[19]

1. *What is the public-image value of your mailings?*   Any mailing creates either a positive or negative impression on the person who receives it. Every detail of every mailing, then, becomes very important and should be given serious consideration—stock, layout, color, format, illustrations, and copy.

2. *How often should the prospect be contacted?*   There are no hard-and-fast rules here, but if a prospect is really worth having as a member, don't stop after several mailings. As the *Manual* notes, "there's nothing scientific about this, of course, but *seven* seems to be the magic number for direct mail, especially when it is the primary medium used."[20] Time mailings to arrive every 4 to 6 weeks and thereby achieve a seven-piece campaign over the project year. Be persistent.

3. *What appeal should be used in the campaign?*   A variety of appeals should be used—in fact, use every "hook" you can think of as a membership value and appeal. Use more of a target appeal approach than a shotgun approach. For example, don't try to crowd all your appeals into every mailing—space them out, emphasizing one in particular in a particular mailing piece.

4. *How do you get the recipient to open the envelope?* There's no better way than to make it look like a personal letter and/or to make it look important. Some organizations hand-address such appeals and mail them first class with stamps...a process that is both costly and time-consuming. Perhaps a better compromise with less cost in stamps and less time to prepare is to type the envelopes and run them through your postage meter with a bulk-rate slug and appropriate postage. Metered mail is much less obvious than printing your bulk-rate permit number on the envelope. For an additional slight expense a catchy slogan can be obtained from the postage meter company and added to the meter stamp.

Don't forget that the outside of the envelope is your first opportunity to get and hold the attention of the direct mail prospect. And don't forget the *back* of the envelope. Many organizations have used this usually blank area to great advantage by having catchy slogans or artwork printed on the reverse of the envelope.

5. *How do you build in "pulling power"?* Start with the membership benefits package which was developed early in the campaign, the list of what the organization offers its members—then tell them to the prospects. Address prospects through the letter as individuals—friends—and "talk" to them face to face. Your material should be cordial and personal—written simply and directly. If your campaign time frame will allow (or if the size of your budget dictates), test mail a representative sample to evaluators who will be candid with their comments and criticisms.

The ASAE *Manual* points out the final questions you should ask yourself when preparing a direct mail letter:

   a. To whom am I writing?

   b. What truly are his needs in relation to this organization?

   c. Why am I writing him?

   d. How long has he been a prospect?

   e. Does he have any special interests?

   f. Specifically, how can the organization help him?

6. *How do you ensure that your letter will be read?* "Doctor" up your letter—not enough to make it obvious that it is a form letter, but enough to indicate important paragraphs and to add a "personal" note in the margin. Many do this with a felt-tipped pen and then reproduce the letter with the text in black ink and the arrows and "note" in red.

7. *How do you add interest with enclosures?* Successful enclosures have been both simple and elaborate. The ASAE *Manual* lists among them such things as:

   A piece of string to tie on a finger as a reminder to join the organization

   A feather, representing "a feather in your cap" for joining

   An oversized telegram for "really big news"

   A penny pasted to the letter—a "penny for your thoughts"

By using your ingenuity, your organization can come up with better ideas by following some sound ground rules:

   a. Relate the enclosure and the cover letter to each other.

   b. Highlight the sales points that have meaning and importance to the prospect, keeping in mind that different categories of prospects have different interests and needs to be satisfied by membership.

   c. Ensure that the enclosure matches the dignity and image of your organization.

8. *How do you make it easy for the prospect to act?*   Make it as easy as possible for the prospect to send in the application for membership—right then. The letter should "stand on its own feet" as a promotion and sales document and include a membership application form or something on which the prospect can say "yes" and can mail back to you. Make the form easy to fill out. If your membership records need more detailed information, by all means try to gain that information *after* you have asked for and received their membership check.

   Basic Questions.   Any NPO planning a direct mail membership campaign should be prepared to answer the following questions posed by Herbert Auer in an *Association Management* article entitled "Basic Tools Sell Membership."[21]

1. How successful can an organization hope to be that mails out a membership sales folder and an application form without some complementary effort, such as a follow-up personal phone call, a person-to-person contact, or a second mailing of a different nature?

2. Should an organization with a small staff spend the money to prepare an effective membership folder without utilizing a publications consultant or a communications expert, as it would use a legal counsel in legal situations?

3. Should an organization ever decide to print and send out a membership folder on a wide scale without first testing it on a small scale?

4. Can some machinery be set up so that the professional artwork of one organization can be used by a different organization seeking members in a different field?

5. Recognizing that the decision of the prospective member to join or not to join is influenced by the attitudes of others, have you ever determined the attitudes of your members and nonmembers toward your organization and its efforts to serve them and the public?

6. Would your next membership mailing be more productive if you first surveyed your members as to what they consider the major benefits of membership? Their replies might be different from your own views.

7. If you are depending primarily on the printed word to recruit new members, have you ever studied the results of research on "why adults read?"

8. Should an organization ever mail out a membership folder without trying to build into it some scientific method to measure the effectiveness of the message? How important is feedback?

Telephone Solicitation.   Next to a personal contact or visit, the telephone call is probably the most effective means of reaching either new prospects or delinquent members. A program of personal visits will allow only about seven to ten visits per day, while using the telephone will allow up to fifty contacts per day per person.

   For a telephone membership development program to be reasonably successful, however, a number of planning steps must be followed, including:

1. Prepare an articulate but brief message to use in the solicitation. This can either be read by the person using the telephone, or prepared as a taped message from a prominent member of your organization which can be played over the telephone (via an adapter) for prospects.

2. Membership advantages must be not only available to those making the tele-

phone solicitations, but literally on the tip of the tongue for immediate answers to questions presented during the conversation.

3. Send a personal letter to the prospect letting him or her know that he or she will be contacted in several days regarding membership in your organization. Of course, membership literature should be included in the mailing. No more than 3 or 4 days should elapse between the time of the receipt of the letter and the telephone call. Stagger your mailings if necessary to achieve this interval.

4. Use the telephone contact as a two-way street in communications to find out either why the member did not renew membership, or, if a new prospect, what else the organization can do in addition to those advantages outlined in the literature.

5. If the prospect is planning to join, don't forget to ask at the conclusion of the call for additional prospects for membership. Add them to your list.

6. Complete the entire "selling" transaction during the call. There is no need to schedule a personal visit unless it is requested. Ask the prospect to forward the application and check in the return envelope that was part of the package sent announcing the call.

7. Look into renting a WATS (Wide Area Toll Service) line from the telephone company if your prospects are outside your no-toll area.

8. For additional information on the many good techniques of using the telephone for membership solicitation, contact your telephone company. Numerous pamphlets are available on the subject, free for the asking.

Personal Contact. "Personal contact is the most effective single method of acquiring new members," O'Rourke states flatly. For this reason he says that organization members "should be constantly reminded and encouraged to contact their qualified...friends who may be prospective members."[22]

Many other NPOs conduct regular membership programs that focus on contacting and recruiting prospects using the organization's current members. Two recent articles in *Association Management* outline the successful techniques used by the Institute of Internal Auditors and B'nai B'rith to involve their members in bringing in new members.

"We made it a point to get a good early start in planning and developing our membership campaign," notes Kathy Fedell in "How to Get Your Members to Bring in New Members,"[23] "We found it was wise to give ourselves a couple of months to prepare the needed materials and literature. It is a mistake to wait until the last minute and then try to do it all at once."

The Institute first decided on the nature of the campaign, which was to get each member to bring in one new member. The key to this is motivation, which they achieved by adopting a good working slogan for the campaign—GAIN 1—Get Auditor Involvement Now. GAIN 1 buttons and stickers were designed and distributed everywhere, including on the organization's stationery (and even the in and out baskets in the office). A self-audit of membership advantages and services was conducted. The data obtained was included in a colorful, concise brochure explaining membership advantages and qualifications.

A membership recruitment guide was prepared, working "on the assumption that the recruiter would need all the help and information we could give him," Fedell reports. Not only did it list the advantages of membership, but it also listed the major objections to joining that they anticipated hearing from prospects, including: "too many organizations," "no time," "dues too high," "not interested," and so on.

The guide and its associated materials were designed to be carried by the recruiter on personal calls or used over the telephone if soliciting in that fashion.

Joan Millen reports, in "How to Change Membership Losses into Gains," that B'nai B'rith found the secret "was to involve our present members, to go out to the grass roots where they are, and to train them and motivate them to recruit new members."[24] The new approach centered on going into the local communities with a team—pairing a volunteer and a professional—and working with present membership, organizing and equipping them to go out and recruit new members.

The following checklist for personal membership drives is adapted by permission from these two articles in *Association Management.*

1. Prepare a "self-audit" on the membership services and advantages of your organization. Add on, modify, or subtract services or benefits to give your membership package its greatest appeal.

2. Develop an agreed-upon set of goals for the members involved in the campaign. Otherwise, confusion and disappointment will result. Be sure that the goals are realistic and attainable.

3. Develop a relevant and professional theme for the campaign.

4. Following completion of plan (including budget), get the board's approval and promises of support.

5. Prepare all promotional materials.

6. Announce the campaign and explain it thoroughly to the membership—get them enthusiastically involved. Do not ask the individual campaign worker to do more than she or he is capable of doing. Divide the responsibilities so that each worker has a work load. Provide members with all the information and materials they will need.

7. Package the campaign in manageable pieces. This helps sustain enthusiasm and helps members see their contributions.

8. Implement the public relations or publicity aspects of the plan (consult the chapters on public relations for ideas).

9. Monitor progress using the feedback and follow-up features of your plan. Don't let deadlines pass before learning that the campaign is behind schedule. Use the monitoring process to stay in touch with workers and to give them both administrative and psychological support for their efforts.

10. Check constantly to see that goals are being met. Review both successes and failures to see if corrective features need to be built into the plan.

11. Praise and appreciation should be given publicly to the volunteers. Staff efforts should be remembered in such ways as letter of commendation for their personnel files, salary increases when possible and appropriate, and publicity in both house organ and professional publications.

Notes

1. Portions reprinted by permission from the *Membership Promotion Manual for Trade and Professional Associations,* copyright 1972 by the American Society of Association Executives.

2. John S. Jenness, How to Motivate Your Members to Serve Their Association Better, *Association Management,* December 1973, p. 44.

3. Arch McGhee, Why Members Volunteer...and...Work Harder, *Association Management,* August 1971, p. 85.

4. Reprinted by permission from the August 1971 issue of *Association Management,* copyright 1971 by the American Society of Association Executives.

5. Dennis L. Hilner, How to Increase Member Involvement, *Association Management,* February 1973, p. 83.

6. Alvin Toffler, *Future Shock,* Random House, New York, 1970.

7. Gabriel Gelb and Stephen B. Friedham, Using Market Research to Analyze Members' Needs, *Association Management,* April 1976, p. 64.

8. Ibid., p. 65.

9. Ibid., p. 66.

10. Ibid., p. 66.

11. Ralph H. Kilmann, Managing Your Organization's Culture, *The Nonprofit World Report,* March–April 1985, p. 12.

12. C. Wayne Rice, What to Say When Your Members Ask: "What Do We Get for Our Dues?" *Association Management,* June 1976, p. 73.

13. John O'Rourke, Planning Association Membership Drives, *Association Manager,* November 1969, p. 56.

14. *Principles of Association Management,* American Society of Association Executives and Chamber of Commerce of the United States, 1975, p. 130.

15. Richard P. Trenbeth, Members May Make Your Future, *Taft Nonprofit Executive,* November 1986, p. 4.

16. O'Rourke, Planning Association Membership Drives, p. 58.

17. Robert Blum, Constituency Building As A Direct Program Expense, *The Nonprofit Executive,* October 1984, p. 3.

18. O'Rourke, Planning Association Membership Drives, p. 57.

19. *Membership Promotion Manual for Trade and Professional Associations,* copyright 1972 by the American Society of Association Executives.

20. Ibid., p. 25.

21. Herbert Auer, Basic Tools Sell Membership, *Association Management,* August 1972, p. 83.

22. O'Rourke, Planning Association Membership Drives, p. 58.

23. Kathy Fedell, How to Get Your Members to Bring in New Members, *Association Management,* May 1976, p. 65.

24. Joan W. Millen, How to Change Membership Losses into Gains, *Association Management,* February 1974, p. 72.

PART 4

Sources of Revenue for the Nonprofit Organization

22

An Overview of Fund-Raising

Henry A. Rosso
CFRE

The process of fund-raising at the beginning of our national experience was simple in structure: A person with a cause asked a person of concern to respond to a human or social need. Fund-raising, essentially, was a one-on-one experience. There was no "corporate social responsibility" ethic, no foundations to research, no direct mail appeals to process, no complicated computer procedures, no complex planned-giving structure of controls, investments, and regulations to challenge the human mind.

Funding in today's fast-changing environment is ever more complex. Harrassed nonprofit executives strain to match inadequate income to expanding budget requirements. The frantic search continues for a magical fund-raising idea that will produce an abundance of gifts to meet budget requirements with a minimum investment of time, talent, or energy.

But, fund-raising is not easy, and no magic formula has ever been devised to transform a fervent, even desperate, wish into instant results. Fund-raising is demanding, enervating, and challenging to even the most disciplined leaders.

Fund-raising, as an effective instrument for annual renewal, is a management process that must move in an orderly progression from fact-finding to planning, to program execution, to thoughtful analysis and control.

Almost every nonprofit organization has the capacity and the potential to put together a sound, sensible fund-raising plan as well as the means to carry it through to conclusion with reasonable expectations of success. All that is required is for the principals to understand that there is an order to fund-raising based on rules that have been tested over the decades. A successful gift-seeking process respects this order and abides by the rules.

There is a sequence to gift development: progressing in logical order from preparation to planning, program execution to control. This repetitive sequence of orderliness can be depicted as a continuum usually referred to as the "cycle of fund-raising."

Nonprofit organizations must be as concerned about their knowledge of marketing techniques and their ability to prepare wise marketing plans as any profit-making corporation. The nonprofit, or social service, organization must look critically at itself to value its worth, examine its mission, determine whether its statement of mission is being interpreted properly through measurable objectives and meaningful programs, and evaluate its overall impact on the "market" it serves.

The concept of the fund-raising cycle can serve as an effective instrument to help executives of nonprofit agencies understand the relationships of fund-raising elements to one another. It can help them visualize and understand the sequence to follow in moving from initial preparation (or definition of case) through to the solicitation and annual renewal of gifts.

Fund-raising cannot be any haphazard or impulsive action improvised at the last moment to respond to a crisis situation. Fund-raising is an exercise in discipline. Important checkpoints during each cycle are discussed below.

Case Statement Preparation

Every nonprofit entity has come into being as a response to a human or social need. This is the "cause" to which the organization addresses itself. Effectiveness in serving this cause is the organization's case, the sum total of all the arguments as to why anyone should provide gift support.

The necessary first step in preparing for fund-raising is to be able to define the case and express it to any individual or before any group in a position to provide financial support.

This seems basic, certainly, and yet so many eager operators launch a well-intentioned fund-raising project without preparing a case statement, without organizing convincing arguments for support, and without ascertaining whether individuals in the power center of the organization can verbalize the case intelligently and convincingly.

Therefore, the first checkpoint in the cycle demands preparation of a case statement answering these questions:

1. What problem or social need is central to your organization's concern? What justifies your existence?
2. What special service(s) or programs are offered by your organization to meet these human needs?
3. Who should support your organization?
4. Why should any individual or agency offer gift support?
5. What benefits accrue to the contributor for such support? In other words, how can you respond to the real, and serious, question, "What's in it for me?"

Define Objectives

The case starts with a statement of the mission that defines the overall need. This, then, becomes the focus of the organization's concern. The mission statement is then expanded into a set of definitive objectives, expressed in clear, concise terms. They are the basis on which the donor makes yes or no decisions as to contributions. Clearly stated objectives help raise the proportion of yes decisions. The objectives must state the root problem or need and explain how effective programs can resolve the problem.

The objectives must be defined in measurable terms, free from ambiguities and meaningless phrases. They must be clearly stated since they help the potential donor determine whether they can be accomplished.

For example, "elimination of hunger in the world" can be accepted as a philosophical goal or as a statement of mission. Providing hot meals to one, or ten, or one-hundred children every day for a week, a month, or a year can serve as a more practical, quantifiable (not to mention, reasonable) objective. A donor would be hard put to evaluate the agency's ability to eliminate hunger in the world, but the donor can decide quite readily whether the agency has been able to feed a prescribed number of children within a specific period.

To some, flowery phrases have a poetic quality, but to a donor they lack the punch of clearly stated objectives that specify why the organization exists, what it intends to accomplish, how it will go about accomplishing these objectives, who will benefit from this accomplishment, and why anyone should contribute to seeing that it gets done.

The natural progression in establishing the hierarchy of objectives is to move from the more general goal, in this example, "hunger," to specific objectives, such as feeding a specific number of children within a defined period, thus establishing a natural link to program budgeting, cost of programs, and identification of program needs that provide the rationale for all fund-raising activities.

Prepare Needs Statement

The next function in the cycle is the design of the program needed to fulfill the promises of the objectives' assignment. A program is an objective being addressed through a series of action steps. Plans must be developed which express what the objective action will be for this year, for next year, and ideally, for the next 5 years.

These program plans, once developed, are expressed in financial terms—a budget—for annual operating purposes, for capital development in the form of building construction, equipment, or land acquisition, or for endowment to ensure continuing security. These financial needs, scrutinized and validated by key voluntary leadership, constitute the organization's fund-raising objectives in the future.

Analyze Market Requirements

All the case work and program planning in the world can be wasted if the organization, staff, and lay leadership are not sensitive to what the market around it needs or wants.

For example, a youth program in a retirement center would have little more than nostalgic value, whereas a youth program in a suburban community can have real purpose. Organizations that base their programs on meeting societal needs justify their existence and strengthen their case for continuing support.

The case must be acknowledged by a supportive constituency; the needs must be verified by informed and responsive segments within the market area. If the market lacks knowledge of the organization and its case, if the market is ignorant of the needs it plans to address, or if it is unsupportive because it considers the needs unimportant, then the possibilities for effective fund-raising are minimal.

Communication channels from the organization to its markets must be kept open to permit maximum feedback on important issues: Is the case sound? Are the programs reasonable, and do they provide a realistic response to market needs? Are the organization's financial needs—annual operating, capital, and endowment—reasonable ones? Are they within the market's capability to finance through gift support?

When the organization has examined market attitudes and when it can verify that response to questions about case, needs, and goals are positive, then it can move on to the next steps of preparing for fund-raising.

Involve Volunteers

Fund-raising is a people business. It is axiomatic that "causes" by themselves do not raise money. People who support causes raise money. Therefore, people involvement with development of financial resources is essential if the process of fund development is to produce significant results.

The primary responsibility for fund-raising must rest with the NPO's board of trustees or directors. It can be delegated to any functioning committee of the board (a fund-raising committee or a development committee), but the authority and responsibility for fund-raising remains with the governing body.

To carry out this function productively, the governing body must join with administrators in defining the mission and objectives of the organization, in interpreting these in program terms, in determining and validating the financial needs, and in continuing the development function to resolve these needs through active, productive fund-raising activity.

Validate the Needs

If key volunteers are to be responsible for successful fund-raising by marketing their own gifts and by asking others to give, they must have a hand in examining the needs, in weighing whether these needs properly reflect program requirements, and in validating these needs to a giving public.

Too often, the staff does all the necessary work and then asks the board to stamp its approval on a needs statement that may involve the expenditure of considerable funds without permitting trustees sufficient time for careful study. Small wonder, then, that members of the governing body, having had little or no role in preparing the needs statement, give only intellectual approval to the plan and withhold their emotional commitment to it. Emotional commitment results directly from program "ownership." Complacent or apathetic trustees can and should be converted into supportive volunteer workers through thoughtful involvement.

Evaluate Gift Markets

Once the needs have been determined, it is important to decide which of the many gift markets are to be approached for financial support. Selection of the appropriate gift markets should not be a haphazard process.

Individual giving continues to represent approximately 90 percent of the giving force in total American philanthropy. This figure includes gifts from living individuals and gifts through bequests. Foundations and corporations make up the remainder of total annual giving, each adding approximately 5 percent. These figures, reported annually by the American Association of Fund Raising Counsel, Inc. (AAFRC), in its publication *Giving USA,* have remained fairly constant in percentages over the past 5 years, reflecting the continuing trend of philanthropy in America.

With this data serving as a backdrop to planning, the fund-raiser must look critically at each market to weigh its potential. Beware of fund-raising myopia. Symptoms of the "disease" can often be seen among fund-raisers who are convinced that financial support can be secured only through government or foundation grants. Broad-spectrum fund-raising is alien to their experience, and yet, it is broad-based fund-raising, revenue generation—seeking gifts and income from diverse sources and developing a funding mix—that promotes good health within the organization, making it more resilient to change, more aware of market requirements, more sensitive to changes within the environment and more responsive to its constituent force.

The wise fund-raiser preparing to put a plan on paper analyzes the total market potential, making judgments on the basis of gift ability within each market segment. Gift market segments are identified as individuals, corporations, foundations, retail businesses, and associations. The question of willingness to give is deferred until later. That question will be answered during the solicitation process.

The fund-raiser's primary concern when testing market potential focuses on the question: "Is there an ability to give, or a history of giving, to organizations with programs similar to ours?" Responses to this question can help the planner come to a decision about the effective allocation of resources (budget, key volunteers, time, and energy) to cultivate and to solicit specific gift markets with reasonable expectations that the effort will be productive.

Select the Fund-Raising Vehicle

Selection of the appropriate fund-raising vehicle(s) during the planning stages is as critical to the preparation process as picking the right market(s).

Fund-raising vehicles include: the annual gift campaign, direct mail, benefits, project funding, gift clubs, capital campaign, planned giving, grantsmanship, and so on. Each has its own function and impact. Direct mail, for example, can be sent to individuals who have no ties with the organization to acquire donors who, in turn, can be cultivated to continue their gifts as regular donors. Called "donor acquisition," this vehicle is used regularly by agencies wishing to build the size and strength of their constituencies. The direct mail process becomes a part of the annual fund only after these donors have been persuaded to repeat their gifts on a regular basis.

When an organization wants to raise annual funds to support program activities and to pay for overhead, it uses annual fund techniques appropriate to each market, including personal solicitation, personal solicitation by mail, gift clubs, telethons, benefits, grant applications, or media advertising. Which of these techniques, or vehicles, will be more effective in each case can be determined only after thoughtful evaluation of the factors affecting each market and of the manner in which each market segment can be expected to respond.

The management process of "analyze, plan, execute, and control" pertains to the annual exercise of formulating a new annual fund plan. The analysis process must involve a thorough review of past experience—studying the 1-year, 3-year, or 5-year performance records according to:

- Gift sources
- Fund-raising techniques—direct mail, special events, personal solicitation, grantsmanship
- Gift purposes

in order to identify strengths, weaknesses, and future potential. The preplanning analysis will help the fund-raiser to examine cost-benefit relationships and to further examine the effectiveness of each fund-raising vehicle in generating results from various gift markets.

It makes sense to find out what organizations with successful programs are doing, to borrow an idea or two, and then to adjust any new ideas to the new organization's specific environment before using. A number of ideas may be tested, and accurate records kept so that results may be studied after each test and then modified where necessary to improve results.

Identify Potential Giving Sources

Within every gift market, there are potential gift candidates. Identification of gift sources, therefore, is a refinement of the market selection process. If the solicitation approach is to be aimed at individuals in the gift markets, then the refinement process must select specific individuals as candidates for solicitation. This is the important "search-and-appraisal" procedure that builds prospect files for the nonprofit organization. Development of this valuable resource through continuing research is a *must* exercise for any NPO that is striving for greater fund-raising effectiveness. Without it, the funds-seeking organization is involved in a futile exercise of seeking mysteriously fading pots of gold at the end of so many rainbows.

It is easy to see just how important prospect building can be to an organization preparing to launch a capital campaign for major funds. In such an intensive effort, concentration must be on the big gift. Thus, the first ten gifts that are sought in a capital campaign must produce between 35 and 45 percent of the funds required by the campaign goal. The next 100 or fewer gifts must generate between 35 and 45 percent of the goal, and all the remaining gifts—whatever the number—must come up with the balance (20 to 30 percent) of the funds required.

For every top-level gift that is to be solicited, sufficient prospective contributors with a capacity to make the larger gift must be identified. At the upper levels of the gift requirements, from four to five gift candidates must be identified for each gift that is to be solicited successfully (e.g., for the top ten gifts required, from forty to fifty prospects must be identified and assigned for solicitation).

At the bottom of the gift requirements, where all the gifts will produce the final 20 to 30 percent of the funds raised, the prospect to gift requirement ratio is 2:1. Thus, if 1000 gifts are required in smaller amounts, then 2000 gift prospects must be identified and listed for solicitation.

This pyramid of giving flattens out somewhat in an annual fund campaign, and the reason for this is simple: Capital campaigns require an annual renewal of gifts, and these gifts tend to be smaller in amounts. Thus, the top 60 percent of an annual fund's dollar production may come from as few as 10 percent of total gifts received, with the next 15 to 25 percent of money received from the next 20 percent of the contributors.

A "search-and-appraisal" committee comprised of knowledgeable individuals, willing to cooperate with prospect research, can be extremely helpful in the development of prospect lists.

Prepare the Fund-Raising Plan

It must be stated and restated that fund-raising is a management process and that it must follow the rules of sound management: gather the facts, prepare the plan, execute the plan, and evaluate and modify where necessary. All functions or phases in the cycle to this point have involved analysis and fact-finding. Only after the hard questions of fund-raising are answered can the fund-raising plan be written. These questions include:

- What is the case for fund-raising?
- Is it sound, and has it been tested in the market areas?
- Are the objectives of the organization expressed in clear, concise terms, and are they measurable?
- Can they be realized?
- Are the needs valid; do they realistically reflect the program?
- Have the needs been examined and validated by the trustees?
- What are the markets for fund-raising?
- Which ones can this organization approach?
- What vehicles are appropriate to respond to our needs?
- How much time and how much of a budget will be required?
- Do we have a strong volunteer force committed to work with us in carrying our needs to the potential gift markets?
- Can we count on our volunteer leaders?
- Who are the potential contributors? What do we know about them?
- What are their linkages to our organization, our volunteer leaders?
- What is the most effective way that we can reach out to these potential contributors to ask them to give?
- What methods of communication will work best?

The cycle has moved from fact gathering to planning in preparation for program implementation. However, there is still a concern.

Prepare the Communications Plan

The case for support has no purpose, no value until it can be communicated in powerful, effective form to individuals in a position to provide that support, either from their own resources or from funds under their jurisdiction.

Effective communication is not to be confused with information, or data, dissemination—the overproduction of paper, print, sound, and facts designed to convince potential donors that the cause is worthy and the gift needed, which fails in its overall mission due to overweight.

The communications plan must be based on a true reaching out via the media, a "becoming one with another," a warm involvement of people in the mission, purpose, accomplishments, and needs of the organization. Understanding is the base for people involvement because this involvement adds impact, effectiveness, and participation, leading to an acceptance of, and a sharing in, the social-purpose organization's mission. This should be the key objective of the communications plan.

Printed materials have their place in the plan, as do slide presentations, "come and see" tours, news releases, speakers' bureaus, and other activities. Central to the plan, however, is the need to reach out through various communications media to touch another person with your message to encourage each individual's emotional involvement with the organization's mission.

Expand the Volunteer Corps

It certainly bears repeating that fund-raising is a people-oriented business and that people give to other people with causes. The most effective fund-raising mechanism ever devised is the direct solicitation of a gift by a person who is committed to the cause, who is willing to contribute, and who wants to involve another person in that commitment.

Expansion of the organization's volunteer corps must be a continuing effort, because each willing volunteer represents a force in the growing advocacy for the work being accomplished.

If it can be accepted that one effective solicitor is needed for every five solicitations to be carried out in a fund-raising effort, then it can be understood that the need to build a strong volunteer corps is a continuing one. For example, if an organization is planning direct solicitation of 200 gift candidates, then it must enlist a task force of 40 volunteers to see the task through. Rarely, can a force of this size be enlisted from among individuals who know little about, who are not involved in, the cause. Recruitment must start early and end late.

Volunteers convinced of the urgency of the need and the importance of the cause, volunteers who themselves will make a gift that can be considered generous by a peer are the strongest advocacy force working for the organization's cause and the strongest communication link to other gift candidates.

Solicit the Gift

All fund-raising preparation, all techniques, and all principles and theories zero in on one critical point: For fund-raising to be effective, someone must ask someone for some money. In the final analysis, that is what fund-raising is all about.

The distance from the beginning steps of examining the case to the activation step of soliciting the gift is a quantum leap. A great deal must be accomplished in preparing for the actual solicitation of the gift. But the moment must come when someone has to ask someone to make a contribution.

The best time to ask for gifts is when the organization needs the money, and for most NPOs in the land, that is *every day*. Unfortunately, there always seems to be a reason why the actual solicitation can be delayed for another day. But, the most compelling reason for asking for the gift now is the fact that the organization needs the gift now, and tomorrow will not make the solicitation any easier.

The wisest technique to use in soliciting gifts is to call on the potential contributor in person and explain why you, the solicitor, believe the cause is worthy of support and why you are willing to contribute from your personal resources to ensure its continuation. Give dignity to the asking and encourage the gift candidate to share with you and others in the advancement of an important, worthwhile cause.

Renew the Gift

So often, the receiving of a gift is considered the end of all action. The solicitor breathes a sigh of relief that the task has been done; the organization dispatches a formlike "thank you" note and then returns to business as usual. The importance of renewing the gift is forgotten, and the opportunity to effect a bond with a new advocate for the cause is overlooked.

A basic concept of sound fund-raising is: Ask for the gift the first time so that the donor can be listed as a supporter of the organization's work; seek a repeat of the gift so that a habit of gift making to the organization can be formed and a linkage developed; then, encourage larger gifts through increased understanding of, and support for, the cause.

Continuing cultivation is vital to hold the donor's interest in the organization. However, there is a deeper obligation involved here, a trust obligation to use the contributed funds wisely and to describe to the donor how the funds were used.

A gift is received with the tacit promise that it will be put to wise use in moving the organization toward the accomplishment of its mission. Proper stewardship requires periodic reports to the donor. Sound business practice endorses the procedure of accountability and disclosure.

The annual renewal of the gift, and thus an annual renewal of the donor's attachment to the cause that is being served, does not complete the cycle but rather moves the process back to the cycle's entry point of "Examine the Case." Just as the gift must be renewed, so must the case be renewed through regular, critical evaluation of the case in order to determine if, indeed, the cause is being responsive to the changing needs of the market.

A gift cannot be taken for granted, and the case for supporting the cause cannot remain static. Annual renewal is imperative if the case for support is to be compelling and if the gift level is to remain adequate to the need.

Fund-raising is not a simple exercise, and it should never be considered as such. Fund-raising is the complex process of seeking to involve people in a cause that is responsive to human needs and that is worthy of gift support. Through people involvement, the organization creates an advocacy force that constitutes the core of its strength and ensures its advancement into the future.

23

Preparation and Requirements for Successful Fund-Raising

William P. Freyd
CFRE, Chairman, IDC

Fund-raising programs can fail. This may appear to be a self-evident truth, but many people appear to believe that every fund-raising program is guaranteed to be successful.

For its success, fund-raising depends on three simple things: (1) common sense, (2) realistic goals, and (3) a detailed plan.

Common Sense

Most people who have not done it before approach fund-raising with the idea that the principles that determine success in any other field are ineffective in fund-raising. Many will say, "Let's write to a few foundations; they are in business to give money away," when common sense should indicate that millions of people all across the country will have the same idea. One foundation executive has said that he receives requests for as much money each day as he can give away each year. Others have said, "Let's let people know that we need money and then we will get some," when common sense would indicate that if fund-raising were that easy, no nonprofit organization would have a tight budget.

The most fundamental error of all is called "fund-raising by multiplication"—that is, when somebody says, "Gee, if we can get a thousand people to give us a hundred dollars, we'll have a hundred thousand dollars!" Except for situations where the size of the group to be solicited or the amount sought is very small, this never works. The reason is that those who could give more do not do so because they are not asked for it, and those who cannot give the requested amount give smaller sums. The net result is a much smaller collection than the constituency could have produced if a proper solicitation had occurred.

Realistic Goals

Setting a proper goal requires a consideration of three important variables: (1) a fund-raising budget, (2) a time frame, and (3) the number of dollars sought. The more time and money you have, the more dollars you can raise. In the final analysis, fund-raising operates according to laws very similar to those that determine the success of a small business. Instead of having a good location, a nonprofit organization needs to meet a recognized need. It needs an investment to get started and a certain amount of time until a profit is shown. Eventual success depends on support by the community and its conviction that the organization is well managed and will deliver the service promised.

Detailed Plan

A specific plan based on sound and proven fund-raising principles usually makes the difference between a successful fund-raising program and one that fails. The first thing that needs to be identified in the development of a well-conceived plan is the need.

Define the Need

A precise definition of the need is not only important information for the organization that seeks to raise funds, it is also vital information for the prospective donor who wants to know how much is required and how his or her gift will be used. Defining the need requires that four questions be answered:

1. Why is the money needed?
2. How much is required in dollars and gifts in kind to meet the need, and how will the money be spent?
3. How long will the money be needed? Will the need change over time?
4. Why should this fund-raising effort be undertaken here and now?

Discuss what benefits will result if the program is successful, who will benefit, and why it is important that they do so.

Identify Strengths and Weaknesses

The next step is to identify your strengths and weaknesses. To do this, you need to investigate four major areas.

1. *The fiscal situation.* Outline on accounting sheets the details of your organization's cash flow. On one sheet, outline the expense items and on another sheet outline the income items. Each sheet should cover a period of one fiscal year. Prospective donors of larger gifts are particularly interested in learning the details on these sheets. You, on the other hand, will be able to plan more effectively when you have this information spread out in front of you.

2. *Community awareness.* Outline on a separate sheet of paper the details of the recognition your organization receives from the community. Such things as how much publicity is received, from what sources, what level of the community knows about your work, what level of the community is served, what level of the community is represented on the governing board, what level of the community is represented in the membership, all need to be outlined.

3. *Actual support.* Those areas of the community that actually support the work need to be listed and the extent of the support noted. A pattern of strengths and weaknesses should start to emerge here.

4. *Potential support.* Identify those areas in your community which you believe could give additional, or new, support and the tentative amounts for each. One major error that most people make when doing this is to indulge in fanciful thinking concerning the likelihood that major foundations or corporations will support their particular project. The only organizations or individuals that are likely to support your program are those which are either affected by the work or which can be reached directly because you, or someone else in your organization, knows them well.

Identify Objectives

Before presenting your story to the public, you must have a very firm grip on the four major requirements for successful fund-raising:

1. *Cause.* You must be able to show that your organization seeks to meet important social needs that are not presently being met. You must be able to state the importance of your cause in a brief and compelling fashion to attract the attention of the giving public.

2. *Case.* This is a word used by fund-raisers to mean the specific steps that will be taken to meet the needs identified in the statement of the cause. Covered here will be the personnel who will be working on the project and their qualifications, the budgets they will have at their disposal, and the time frames in which they will be working. Frequently it is also important to outline your organization's successes or to establish criteria by which its success may be judged.

3. *Constituency.* You must be able to identify clearly the individuals, groups of individuals, or organizations you will ask to support your organization's work. Each element of your constituency may require a different approach and method of solicitation. Small businesses are solicited differently than big businesses, individuals require different approaches than foundations, and so on.

4. *Leadership.* You will need to identify and recruit those individuals who, by their endorsement of your organization, will lead others to support it and who, by their active participation in your organization's affairs and by their own generous giving, will set an example for others to follow.

Conducting an investigation to uncover the information required to answer the foregoing questions is relatively simple. First, draw up a list of your organization's key leaders. Normally, this list will include board members and key administrators.

Only rarely will it include more than twenty individuals. Each person on the list should be visited and asked to answer three questions:

1. What is the basic purpose of the organization?
2. What goals should be established so that the purpose can be achieved?
3. What programs need to be implemented to reach the goals?

If this is done correctly, you should be able to identify a consensus concerning objectives, goals, and programs for your organization. If you cannot identify a consensus, it is vitally important to create one, as no organization can move forward until its leadership can agree on a direction. (Consult this *Handbook's* section on planning.)

The consensus should be written up in a simple, clear statement identifying the basic cause and the case as defined earlier.

Identify Donors

The next step is to draw up a list of donors and prospective donors of large sums. If your organization's situation is normal, you will find that few of these donors will be corporations or foundations. Most will be individuals who are already affiliated in some way with the organization. If the leadership has been properly structured, many of these donors or prospective donors will already be on the board or actively involved with the top levels of the organization.

It may be necessary to visit individuals interviewed in the first phase of the investigation a second time. It is rarely necessary to have a total of more than thirty or forty individuals on the list for the second set of interviews. It is frequently impossible to find more than that.

Each individual visited should be told what the consensus is concerning the organization's basic objectives and steps that should be taken to reach them. Once it has been determined that the individual being interviewed agrees with the basic purposes of the organization, the dollar amounts required to meet the needs must be spelled out. This is frequently done with a proposed budget showing income, expenses, and the amount that must come from voluntary gifts. A gift chart should be prepared showing that at least 70 percent of the required dollars must come from approximately 10 percent of the donors. (This is based on 75 years of fund-raising experience—that's the way it happens.) This is frequently done by showing that the largest gift required is at least 10 percent of the total goal, the two next largest gifts at least 5 percent of the total goal each, and the next four largest gifts at least 2½ percent of the total goal each. Experienced fund-raisers will vary these percentages and the number of required gifts based on their detailed knowledge of the constituency and the anticipated generosity of the most important donors.

The key question this phase of the investigation answers is whether your most important prospective donors believe that gifts to support your cause can be found in the size and number indicated at the top of your gift chart. Experience indicates that if these individuals believe that others will give in the required range, then they would probably be willing to consider giving in that range also. The next question is whether the individual interviewed would be willing to help achieve the objectives and goals of the organization by giving and getting others to give in the required range.

In an investigation of this nature, it is rarely necessary to talk with more than fifty or sixty individuals. This is because most fund-raising programs generate most of their money from a very few gifts solicited by a very few people. The problem is to identify the five or ten individuals who are going to make the big difference for your organization. It normally takes as many as fifty or sixty interviews to do this. If you find that you are seeing more people than this, you are either going about it in the wrong way or you do not have the potential you need to meet your goal.

Meet Administrative Requirements

Any effective fund-raising program has certain minimum administrative and functional requirements. These requirements may be met by a large staff in a major institution, or they may be the responsibility of a part-time employee in a very small organization. In some cases, volunteers can staff a very modest program. However it is done, the following functions must be included:

1. *Publicity.* This is an activity that tells your organization's story to as many people as possible as frequently as possible. Press releases and pamphlets or flyers are used most often in this function.

2. *Public relations.* This is frequently confused with publicity. Actually, publicity is only one component of a public relations program. Although it is difficult to draw a distinction between publicity and public relations, public relations is normally concerned more with individuals than with groups and seeks to involve individuals with the success of your organization. Publicity is more often thought of as simply telling the story.

3. *Publications.* These are the documents that are used in the public relations and publicity activity. Nevertheless, creating and producing a publication is a different kind of activity than either of the preceding two.

4. *Prospect research.* This activity is the one that is most often overlooked by less experienced fund-raisers. You must try to learn as much as you possibly can about every donor and prospective donor. This information is usually kept in a database, compiled on cards, or filed in dossiers. The purpose is to permit you to design and conduct your solicitations as knowledgeably as possible.

5. *Special events.* These are the dances, fashion shows, and other events that are used to draw attention to your organization and, frequently, to raise a little money. Most experienced fund-raisers will tell you that special events are a very inefficient way to raise money but a very efficient way to involve previously uninvolved supporters.

6. *Administration.* Obviously, the entire fund-raising operation must be coordinated not only within itself but with other activities in the organization. Some responsibility must be assigned for this activity.

7. *Fund-raising procedures.* This is, of course, the center of our concern. Too many organizations, however, make the mistake of doing everything *but* soliciting. *Somebody must ask for money,* and the responsibility for ensuring that this takes place must be assigned.

8. *Volunteer motivation.* The individuals who give their time and money to your organization must be told how important their support is. They must be encouraged to bring others to provide the same kind of support. Again, the responsibility for seeing that these things are done must be assigned.

24

Methods for Successful Fund-Raising

William P. Freyd
CFRE, Chairman, IDC

Soliciting techniques may be organized into nine basic groupings:

1. Annual giving programs
2. Capital programs
3. Deferred giving programs
4. Grant solicitation
5. Collections
6. Direct mail
7. Merchandise sales
8. Advertising
9. Fund-raising events

Annual Giving Programs

An annual giving program seeks unrestricted, repeatable gifts.

Purpose, Requirements, and Methods

Proceeds from an annual giving program are normally used to defray normal operating expenses.

The basic requirement for an annual giving program is a support constituency. The organization needs to identify one or more groups of prospective donors who can be sent letters, telephoned, or visited and asked for regular, ongoing support. Normally, support constituencies are individuals who have been, will be, or are affected by the existence of the organization.

Normal methods of soliciting annual gifts are mail, personal visits, and telephone calls. The greatest part of your constituency will be small donors who will be sent one or more letters inviting them to participate, along with some kind of brochure that explains the purpose of your organization and its accomplishments and, very important, a reply envelope. Individuals or organizations thought capable of making unusually large gifts to the annual giving program should be solicited either in person or by telephone. Most organizations will solicit a constituency several times during a year. Some will solicit all those who have not given previously during that year on several occasions, whereas other organizations will solicit every individual in their support constituency as often as monthly or, in the case of some organizations that take up a collection, weekly.

Productivity and Costs

Annual giving is the basic program for any organization. It identifies, cultivates, and solicits constituencies. Most other fund-raising programs cannot succeed in the absence of a well-established annual giving program. Therefore, although an annual giving program can be, and frequently is, quite productive in its own right, it also generates prospective donors for all other gift-solicitation programs that the organization may conduct.

With respect to costs, established annual giving programs operated by known and noncontroversial organizations will normally spend up to 20 or 30 percent of the amount raised on fund-raising costs. Small, new, and/or controversial organizations will spend considerably more than this, and *may even operate at a loss for the first few years of a new program.*

Capital Programs

Capital programs solicit larger gifts, usually paid in several installments over a period of 3 to 5 years, that are used to improve the asset position of an organization.

Purpose, Requirements, and Methods

Capital gifts are usually given for purposes outlined in a list of needs proposed by the soliciting organization. In effect, therefore, use of capital gifts is restricted to the specific capital needs identified when the solicitation occurs.

The single, most important requirement in a successful capital effort is a program chairman who is not only dedicated, but also able to make one of the larger gifts. Solicitation for capital gifts occurs most successfully when one committed donor can invite prospective donors to join him or her in meeting the need. Additional requirements for successful capital programs include a list of qualified and well-researched individuals and organizations thought capable of making large gifts to your cause. A successful annual giving program, will, of course, have identified these individuals for you.

Capital campaign methods rely most on personal solicitations conducted by volunteers who have already made their own financial commitment. To aid the volunteers in presenting the need, a "case statement" is generally prepared that outlines the amounts needed, the gifts required, and the purposes to be achieved.

A "campaign organization" is usually recruited to operate a capital effort. It should be comprised of the organization's top leadership and most important donors. Each individual in the campaign organization should be required to make his or her own financial commitment before seeking that of others.

Productivity and Costs

Productivity of a capital program is normally very high. In fact, it is probably the most productive kind of fund-raising. Primarily, this is because it solicits an established constituency and asks them to make a special effort to support needs to which they are already committed. A word of warning: It is almost impossible to operate a successful capital program with a new and undeveloped constituency. The success of capital programs rests on the fact that other, previous fund-raising programs have prepared the constituency to respond generously to this one big effort.

In effect, much of the cost of operating a successful capital effort has been picked up by previous fund-raising programs. Therefore, the apparent cost of a capital program is usually quite low. Very large capital campaigns ($100 million or more) can operate at a cost of as little as 2 or 3 percent of the amount collected. Small to medium-sized capital programs ($1 million to $50 million) frequently can be conducted for between 5 and 10 percent of the total collected. Again, it should be pointed out that it is usually futile to conduct a capital campaign until your constituency has been thoroughly cultivated and habituated to support your organization by appropriate annual giving programs.

Deferred Giving Programs

The proceeds from deferred giving programs are normally used to build endowment. Most of the important charitable endowments in the United States have been developed through the receipt of deferred gifts over many years.

Purpose, Requirements, and Methods

A deferred gift solicitation seeks sums that will come to the institution after the death of a donor. The simplest of these is, of course, a bequest that conveys a charitable gift from the estate of a decedent. More sophisticated programs seek more sophisticated gifts, which usually revolve around the concept of a trust that will pay an income to the donor and/or one or more beneficiaries for life. When the last of the trust beneficiaries dies, the sum in the trust then passes to the charity. Because of the complexity of some of these trust arrangements, the phrase "planned giving" has replaced the phrase "deferred giving" in the lexicon of most fund-raisers.

The primary requirement for a successful deferred-giving program is a constituency that has been thoroughly cultivated by an annual giving program and that receives regular information indicating that it is possible to make deferred gifts to the organization seeking them. Deferred gifts generally have had such profoundly beneficial tax consequences for the donor that it is frequently necessary to explain them both authoritatively and in detail. Accordingly, it is usually necessary to have access to legal advice from an individual who is conversant with the laws governing deferred gifts.

The basic method of soliciting deferred gifts is to circulate a newsletter or other literature, on at least a quarterly basis, to that element of your constituency which you believe most capable of making deferred gifts. These newsletters should encourage interested prospective donors to request further information from your institution. The request should be answered by a booklet outlining the advantages of deferred giving and followed up by a personal visit to discuss ways of actually making a deferred gift.

Productivity and Costs

The productivity of a deferred giving program is extremely high. Although it usually takes about 36 months for the first deferred gift to be banked by the recipient, the size of the gift that can be generated by this kind of program is usually large enough that the income from it increases dramatically over the first few years. Even a few gifts in the $10,000-to-$100,000 range received each year can make a major impact on the budget of most organizations.

The cost of adding a deferred giving program to an established fund-raising effort is usually minimal. Nevertheless, you should not expect your deferred giving program to start to pay back the investment your organization makes in it for at least 36 months. As soon as gifts start coming in, you can expect that the cost of operating your deferred giving program will drop to an insignificant percentage of total revenue produced. It is usually quite difficult, however, to cite a specific percentage, as one or two especially large gifts more or less each year can have a substantial impact on the totals received. Costs of operating the program, on the other hand, tend to remain fixed. Therefore, the cost per dollar received can vary quite widely from one year to the next in most deferred giving programs.

Grant Solicitation

Grants are normally used to support specific projects. They underwrite some, or all, of the costs of an activity that probably would not take place if the grant had not been awarded. Thus, with a grant, a performing arts company might launch a new production that could not otherwise be mounted. Similarly, a hospital might conduct a research program that would not otherwise be conducted if the grant had not been received.

Purpose, Requirements, and Methods

The purpose of a grant-solicitation program is to seek sums from foundations, government units, corporations, and other grant-making organizations.

The basic requirements for a grant solicitation program are three: (1) a cause and case that are likely to generate support from grants, (2) a prospect research program that has identified a grant-making organization that is likely to be interested in that cause and case, and (3) individuals connected with the cause and case who have access to the leadership of the organizations that can make the grant.

Once research has identified an organization that might be willing to consider making a grant to support an activity at your charity, it is necessary to create or identify a contact within the grant-making organization. Once the contact has been established, a meeting is requested where the possibility of seeking a grant is explored and the guidance of the grant-making organization is sought concerning the most appropriate way to go about it. Following that, the advice of the grant-making organization should be followed closely, in the hope that the amount requested will be granted.

Productivity and Costs

The productivity of a grant-solicitation program can vary widely. Most small, unknown organizations should not contemplate starting a grant-solicitation program. The amount of effort that must go into a thoughtfully implemented grant-solicitation program is very great. Effort, of course, has a high price. Unless there is a better-than-average chance that you can compete effectively with all of the other organizations that seek grants, forget it.

Initiating a grant-solicitation program is very costly. Normally, at least one full-time person has to be assigned to researching grant-making organizations, making or following up on contacts, writing grant proposals (which can sometimes call for the accumulation and organization of tremendous amounts of data), and doing whatever follow-up the submission of grant proposals may require. Normally, you cannot count on a volunteer to undertake this kind of responsibility. Therefore, a salary must be paid to a staff person, a travel budget allocated, and other expenses—such as telephone, stationery, postage, etc.—must be anticipated.

Collections

Collections are often used when very small sums are sought from many people who are not particularly close to, or aware of, your organization.

Purpose, Requirements, and Methods

Their purpose is to raise operating money when no other solicitation method may be effective in reaching the constituency to be solicited.

The requirements for a successful collection include some way to attract the attention of those individuals whose gifts are sought and some way to encourage them to make a gift. There are three methods for conducting a collection: (1) setting canisters out, usually by cash registers in restaurants and retail shops, (2) passing the basket at church or other functions where there is a captive audience, (3) finding a large group of volunteers who are willing to go house to house, usually on one day accompanied by suitable publicity.

Productivity and Costs

Although some large national collections generate substantial sums, the productivity of a collection figured on an average gift per donor basis is usually very, very small. Unless you are able to reach tremendous numbers of people, the results of a collection will not have a noticeable impact on your budget.

On the other hand, the costs of a collection tend to be fairly low. This is because very small organizations can conduct a collection with volunteer help, and no investment need be made in elaborate literature or other "sales" materials. When a large national collection is being conducted, the relative cost still tends to be very low because of the tremendous amount of volunteer help that is usually a part of taking a collection. The only caveat here is that no organization should contemplate a large national collection until it knows that it can field tens of thousands of volunteers who will solicit more than a million individuals. If this warning is not heeded, substantial sums of money can be spent preparing for collections that cannot possibly pay off.

Direct Mail

Direct mail is used to solicit large groups of prospective donors who could not otherwise be reached. When an organization has an appeal that it believes could be attractive to many, but does not have the volunteers or the volunteer leadership that can effectively carry the message to donors, direct mail may be the most effective way to initiate a fund-raising program.

Purpose, Requirements, and Methods

Gifts received from a direct mail solicitation normally underwrite operating expenses. Another important purpose of direct mail solicitation is to create a donor base—a large number of donors—that can subsequently be cultivated and solicited for other kinds of support, both time and money.

The initiation of a direct mail program requires a substantial investment. Many experts in the field find that a "war chest" of $50,000 is needed to ensure that the most effective direct mail solicitation is designed and implemented. Other requirements include experienced copywriters, solicitation package designers, and list compilers. The basic direct mail package has four components: a mailing envelope, a solicitation letter, a brochure, and a business reply envelope.

After an adequate budget has been secured, the next most important element in the creation of a direct mail program is the selection of lists of prospective donors that are thought likely to respond to the organization's appeal. Commonly, list brokers are consulted and their recommendations compared. Other list sources include known friends of the organization, beneficiaries of the organization's services, published lists of donors to other causes in the community, membership lists of organizations in the community, and friends of board members and key administrators of the organization. Once the lists have been compiled, it will be necessary to design the solicitation package so that it will be likely to move recipients to respond with gifts. Direct mail fund-raising is not normally thought to be a game for amateurs.

Productivity and Costs

There are four basic stages to a direct mail program: (1) donor acquisition, (2) donor renewal, (3) donor upgrading, and (4) renewal of lapsed donors.

Donor Acquisition. A solicitation package is sent to lists of prospective donors. The key objective of this phase is to add names to the "house list"—the list of known donors. Most experts believe that if you can get back as much money as you have spent in a donor-acquisition program, you are doing very well indeed.

Most donor-acquisition programs operate at a financial loss. The profit in donor acquisition comes from the sums that new donors will give over the years to come.

Donor Renewal. The next objective is to get a new donor to give a second, even a third time. If 50 to 60 percent of new donors can be moved to give once or twice more, your program would be regarded as successful.

Donor Upgrading. Once your new donor has given two or three times, your next objective is to increase the gift size. Accordingly, donors are sent solicitations that emphasize the importance of giving at higher levels. Many charities solicit their house list several times a year as part of their donor-upgrading program. If you can get 25 percent or more of your active donors to increase their gift size in any one year, you will be doing well.

Lapsed Donor Renewal. When previously active donors on your house list have not made a gift for a period of time—normally 36 months—they are regarded as "inactive" and are moved to the lapsed donor file. Lapsed donors are sent solicitation packages encouraging them to renew their interest in your organization. These solicitations usually are based on a message to the lapsed donor explaining that your organization does not like "to lose a friend" and inviting the inactive donor to respond with a statement explaining why interest in your organization has dissipated.

Although responses to lapsed donor solicitations can vary widely, it is generally held that activating 10 percent or more of your lapsed donor file is a good result. Factors that can influence the effectiveness of lapsed donor renewal solicitations include your organizations's reputation and whether or not the giving public feels that your organization is effectively meeting current and urgent needs.

Direct mail is costly; unless a direct mail program is thoughtfully conceived and executed, you can lose your shirt. Most knowledgeable direct mail practitioners are more concerned with the dollars generated by their programs, and the dollars spent to operate them, than they are by the number of responses that the programs generate. This is because there is an inverse relationship between the gift size sought and the percentage of those solicited who will respond. Thus, the larger the gift sought in the solicitation package, the lower the percentage of response will be. Experienced direct mail practitioners weigh the effect of these two factors and use their judgment to set a suggested giving level that they believe will generate the most dollars from the solicitation, not the most responses. Because of high start-up costs, new direct mail programs can frequently operate at a loss for the first few years. Established direct mail programs operated by well-known and highly regarded organizations can generate sums at a relatively low cost per dollar solicited. Some major direct mail programs report costs of as little as 10 or 20 percent, but this is an unusually low percentage. Small, new programs will have considerably higher costs.

Among the factors that influence the costs of direct mail fund raising are the following:

1. *Average gift size.* The smaller the average gift, the higher the cost.

2. *Age.* The newer the programs, the higher the cost.

3. *Reputation.* Little-known organizations will tend to have much higher fund-raising costs than well-known ones.

4. *Controversy.* Controversial causes tend to have higher fund-raising costs than noncontroversial causes.

Merchandise Sales

Merchandise sales are used largely by small organizations with limited appeal that do not have high-level volunteer leadership.

Purpose, Requirements, and Methods

The very small sums that commonly are generated by merchandise sales are normally used to underwrite operating expenses.

The basic requirements for a merchandise sales effort are a product that has a ready market and volunteers who are willing to peddle it. There are two basic methods: (1) Set up a place of business for the sale of second-hand items or Christmas trees, or whatever; (2) recruit volunteers who will go from door to door selling cookies or light bulbs, or whatever. Both methods require a group of dedicated volunteers who will agree to commit themselves to spending time, according to a rigid schedule, at the business of selling merchandise. The product must be selected, an inventory acquired, a price established, and detailed schedules for volunteer workers developed, posted, and followed.

Productivity and Costs

Most fund-raisers feel that merchandise sales are the least productive of all fund-raising procedures. This is because most of the money goes to the manufacturer of the product sold. If the same amount of energy and dedication that is invested in merchandise sales were to be spent on an outright solicitation of gifts, the organization would receive a great many more dollars under most circumstances.

The real problem is related to what it is possible to get volunteers to do. Many individuals who are not comfortable soliciting gifts will happily spend time selling merchandise. If this is the only fund-raising avenue that your organization finds open, then by all means pursue it.

The real costs of a merchandise sales program are quite high because the manufacturer gets most of the money. There is, however, one saving grace: If your organization retains the right to return unsold merchandise, it is almost impossible to lose money on a merchandise sales fund-raising scheme. Thus, although costs tend to be very high and productivity tends to be very low, this is the only form of fund-raising where total failure, in the sense that money is lost rather than gained, is almost impossible.

Advertising

Advertising is used to reach a great many people quickly with a message. It is most effective when you have an appeal that is both urgent and emotional—such as helping children who have been suddenly orphaned by a major natural disaster.

Purpose, Requirements, and Methods

Gifts received through the medium of advertising should be spent on the special purposes for which they were solicited.

Successful advertising solicitations require a cause that is usually quite emotional and very urgent as well. In addition, you need to place your advertisements in publications that are likely to reach individuals who can be expected to respond to your appeal. Finally, you should expect to ask for an unusually large gift in an advertisement (such as $15 a month for the next 12 months) to help defray the costs of placing an advertisement and to compensate for the fact that specific follow-up is not possible until the prospective donor has actually given.

The methods used for solicitation by advertising are generally identical to the methods used for any kind of advertisement that seeks a consumer response. Usually, you need some compelling graphics and/or photographs, a message that details a specific need and asks for a specific response, a relatively high suggested gift and—don't overlook it—a coupon that can be filled in and sent to the advertising charity.

Productivity and Costs

Costs of advertising are high. For most causes, advertising cannot pay. It takes a very special appeal, usually in a special situation, to make advertising for gift dollars effective. If you must advertise, look upon it as a way to encourage people to respond more favorably to your other kinds of solicitations. Unless you have a very unusual situation, you probably will not receive enough from running an advertisement to cover the cost of placing it.

Fund-Raising Events

"Special events," as they are more commonly called, are generally used to attract the attention of individuals and other organizations (primarily corporations) that would not otherwise give to your organization. These organizations and individuals are normally moved to support a special event because of their high regard for an individual, or individuals, who will be honored by the event and because somebody they respect has asked them to subscribe to it.

Purpose, Requirements, and Methods

Funds secured through special-event fund-raising are normally used to defray general operating expenses. Sometimes, however, special events are operated for the purpose of giving money to a specific need. In that case, of course, the net sum received should be invested in meeting the need as announced.

The basic requirements for a special event are a large group of dedicated volunteers who will sell tickets and/or do the other things that must be done to make money for the event, along with some way to make the event seem glamorous or significant or both. Normally, this is done by having the special event—as in the case of a dinner—organized to honor some well-known person who commands so much affection and respect that a large group of volunteers will turn out to sell, and buy, the tickets. Special-event fund-raising also requires a great deal of careful and detailed planning and execution.

The standard format for organizing a special event is to start your planning at least 1 year in advance of the time you expect to hold the event. The second step is to find an "honoree" who will agree to be the guest of honor and make a talk. The third step is to recruit a large group of volunteers who will form committees to cover the major functional responsibilities such as arrangements, tickets, publicity, hospitality, and so on. After you have found the place where the event will be held, completed your plan of action, and organized the volunteers, you should have approximately 6 months left in which to tie up all the loose ends. You will probably find that most major hotels, restaurants, and other catering facilities require reservations for events of up to a year in advance or more.

Productivity and Costs

Sometimes an organization's special event can become one of the community's most socially significant occasions. When that happens, the event is a guaranteed success. Normally, special-event fund-raising is not as productive as more straightforward kinds of solicitation, and it requires tremendous inputs of energy and time from volunteers and staff. The main advantage of special events, however, is that they secure income from a wide range of donors who would not normally respond to the appeal of the sponsoring organization. Furthermore, many volunteers who are happy to work in special-event fund-raising would feel uncomfortable in more straightforward solicitation procedures. Therefore, special-event fund-raising can be thought of as being very productive in the sense that it generates income that would not otherwise be available.

Regarding costs, many special-event experts feel that an event that costs no more than 50 percent of the total amount raised to operate it is functioning within reasonable limits. Of course, well-established events that are planned very thoroughly and operated effectively can achieve lower costs. On the other hand, new events operated for new, unknown, or controversial organizations can operate at a much higher cost ratio and, conceivably, lose money.

Fund-Raising Costs

Although costs were discussed for each soliciting technique, a final thought should deal with the area of fund-raising costs in general. There can be no such thing as a "proper" fund-raising cost expressed as a percentage of the total amount raised. Some programs will fail and costs will exceed income. In other cases, costs will be dependent on the kind of solicitation procedure selected, how effectively it is executed, how old the program and the organization are, how big the total receipts are, how controversial or accepted the organization is, the size of the average gift, the quality of the volunteer leadership, and the amount of experienced or professional assistance that the solicitation receives (professional fund-raising advice tends to increase the total amount received and to decrease the cost of fund-raising expressed as a percentage of the total received).

Thus, it would probably be unreasonable for a well-conceived multimillion-dollar capital campaign operated to benefit a widely known organization to have total costs that exceeded 5 or 10 percent of the amount collected. This would be true even though such a program spent more than it raised during the initial year or two.

On the other hand, an organization that was initiating a new fund-raising program could also quite reasonably spend more on it than it raised during its first few years and a relatively high percentage of the amount raised for many years thereafter. Many small organizations seeking vigorously to increase their total gift receipts can expect to run relatively high fund-raising costs because of the expense of the programs which will eventually lead to the desired increases.

In summary, expect to spend money to raise money. In the long run, it will pay off if your programs have been thoughtfully conceived and carefully executed.

25

The Board of Directors

William P. Freyd

CFRE, Chairman, IDC

Boards of Nonprofit Organizations

All fund-raising starts with a governing board. Where fund-raising must be done, governing boards are largely responsible for the soliciting and for the prudent use of the funds raised. One incorrect view widely held by less sophisticated governing board members is that they "give their time" whereas others give their money. It can be emphatically stated here that, with one exception, governing boards must lead the way to raising the funds that their organizations need. The one exception relates to very large, well-established organizations that have successful and ongoing fund-raising programs. Included in this group of organizations would be certain major health agencies and a very limited number of other leading institutions. Still, even these organizations would have markedly improved fund-raising results if the governing boards became directly and personally involved in the fund-raising. More importantly, it is clear that the governing boards were involved with the initiation of the fund-raising program in each case. Furthermore, it can be observed that there is a direct relationship between the success of an organization and the involvement of its governing board with its fund-raising programs. As governing boards become less involved with their organization's fund-raising, the organization's fund-raising tends to become less effective. The "bottom line" is that a board's most important function is to both provide and manage the resources that are required to move the organization toward its goals—usually, if not always, the goals set by the governing board itself.

There are many different kinds of governing boards because there are many different kinds of organizations, each with unique needs. Very large organizations, such as medical centers and universities, frequently attract nationally known figures to sit on their boards and often use the services of leading experts in a variety of fields. Very small organizations, on the other hand, find it useful to attract board members who will, in many cases, become quasi-staff for the organization because it does not have the resources to hire an extensive staff of its own. Still other organizations will be in transition, moving from one kind of circumstance to another. Some organizations are required to seat certain kinds of people on their boards. Such organizations are usually created by other organizations (such as governments), which oblige the created organization to seat certain individuals ex officio on the governing board.

There will be certain skills and talents that many boards will feel should be represented among their members. Thus, an arts organization may feel it necessary to have working artists on its board. Many hospitals have physicians or surgeons on the board, and so on. Then, of course, there are the fund-raising requirements. If an organization wants to raise funds, its board must be intimately involved in the fund-raising operation. Consequently, every member of the board must be selected with this aspect of the board's responsibilities in mind.

Lastly, several kinds of boards may be associated with any one organization. For example, some institutions have one board which reviews policy, another board which is responsible for operations, and a third which is primarily involved with fund-raising. Another example might be a medical center that has a board for the hospital, another for the medical college, and a third—often comprised of members of the other two boards—which is the governing board for the foundation, or fund-raising organization for the medical center. Many colleges and universities have a board for the main institution, advisory boards for the component schools, and separate governing boards for the alumni organization and athletic support programs.

Usually these multiple board situations are cumbersome and reduce the effectiveness of the parent institution by creating a number of kingdoms, the kings of which then insist upon their divine right to do whatever they choose. Usually the existence of multiple boards indicates that there was some reluctance, unwillingness, or inability to deal with the simple reality of institutional progress that the most effective and efficient way to operate is to have *one central source of authority* and repository for responsibility. Multiple boards frequently indicate that at one time a group of leaders wanted to retain authority but hoped to pass off responsibility for the achievement of goals.

One definition of a "governing board" of a nonprofit organization is that it is a "group of individuals organized to hold in trust a charitable, educational, scientific, cultural, or health care institution for public good." This definition is the reason that governing boards of nonprofit organizations are frequently called "boards of trustees" as opposed to "boards of directors."

In fully developing a consequence of this widely accepted definition, one must further define the public good as perceived by the organization and to enunciate it as being the primary cause of the charitable enterprise. From that, then, will flow the organizational or institutional goods that must be achieved and delivered, because they will be determined by the public good, as seen and sought by the organization. Clearly, it will then be good for the staff of the organization to help achieve these goods so that consumers or other beneficiaries of the services provided by the organization will benefit. If the public good, as perceived by the organization, is, indeed, a real good, it will then provide something good for posterity and of course for the governing board that has guided the institution.

It is clear, however, that the entire raison d'être for a charitable enterprise flows from its concept of the public good. If that concept is invalid or its pursuit is ineffective, the enterprise will not prosper. There would not, in that case, be any reason to permit the governing board to continue to hold in trust for a public good which was not being delivered. In this event, such organizations tend to fail because their governing boards are not using their resources for valid or effective purposes.

The functions of the governing board and the organization itself follow clearly from the definitions above. There must be an ongoing concern for the public good. Some individual, or group of individuals, within the organization must regularly determine that the public good to be delivered by the organization is still needed and is in fact being delivered. Too many organizations that were created for very valid reasons tend to become largely concerned with their own survival and to lose sight completely of the important reasons for which they were originally created.

Once it has been determined that the intended public good is needed and is being (or can be) delivered, the next step for the governing board is to make plans and take action based on those plans that will enable the organization to deliver or continue to deliver the public good needed. This usually means that a staff must be hired and that conditions for the efficient and effective operation of that staff must be provided along with a clearly defined set of tasks that the staff will be expected to perform in order to reach clearly defined goals.

Obviously, the tasks and goals set for the staff and organization, as defined by the governing board, must be to meet the specific needs of certain consumers of the services provided by the organization or other beneficiaries of the organization's services. The "public good" for a charity boils down to the delivering of specific services to specific entities. If the goals, plans, tasks, and services are all valid and are pursued effectively, there will be a beneficial impact on posterity, as well as on the present. This, perhaps, is the most important reason for a charitable organization to exist: it will provide a brighter and better future for all. If the entire package is assembled properly and activated correctly, then exemplary results will be achieved expeditiously. It is in this fashion that the governing boards win their own recognition for a job well done. Again, it should be emphasized that the central responsibility of a governing board is to acquire and prudently use resources for the benefit of the organization it governs and for the publics the organization seeks to serve.

Principal Responsibilities

The first responsibility of a governing board is to define institutional goals and make and/or approve major policy decisions. While suggestions for policy direction and goals may come from any source, it is only the board that can make the final decisions in these areas. The first step toward organizational vitality is the making of good policy. *Valid* goals do not necessarily ensure an organization's success, because other resources are needed to pursue the goals and implement the policies. Bad policy and *invalid* goals, however, will ensure an organization's failure regardless of any other resources that might be available.

The next responsibility of a governing board is to select the organization's chief executive officer (CEO) (sometimes, in the case of a very small organization, members of the board will actually operate as the CEO) and to assist the CEO in the selection of other key administrative leaders. Obviously, these people must be capable of implementing the board's policies and pursuing the board's goals. Their qualifications and track records must have been thoroughly verified as well as their commitment to the policies and goals established by the board.

Once the board has set the goals, made the policies and selected the administrative leaders, its ongoing principal responsibility will be to monitor the performance of its staff to make sure that the resources required by the staff to perform the tasks set by the board are provided.

Generally, income from nonprofit organizations comes from two sources: earned income and gift income. While the board's policies and other decisions will have an impact on earned income, it is usually a staff responsibility to carry out the tasks associated with generating earned income. The production of gift income, fund-raising, is a basic responsibility of the governing board. Indeed, many boards of successful organizations have implemented and rigorously follow the rule of the "3 G's": *give, get,* or *get off.*

Many inexperienced board members feel that if they simply serve on the board, others can provide the necessary resources. The point that is missed in this argument is that if board members, who know the organization and its policies, goals, and needs best, cannot or will not provide gift income, then why should anyone else be so inclined? If the arguments are not compelling enough to move the board to give, the arguments certainly will not be compelling enough to move any other individual or organization to provide support.

Less sophisticated and experienced board members who will not provide gift support for the organization they govern attempt to rationalize their positions using different arguments. With the exception of those arguments advanced by individuals who have become members of religious communities and taken vows of poverty, all these arguments are false. Among the more common are:

1. *"I give time instead of money."*   In the first place, time is something that can best be provided by staff. Furthermore, staff usually has great expertise and a more intimate working knowledge of organizational details. Sometimes this argument is given by board members of extremely small organizations who point out that their charity does not have the budget to hire staff. Clearly, if the board were providing adequate financial support, the budget would be big enough to hire staff. Finally, if a board member's time is so valuable that it should be taken instead of money, perhaps that board member should seek gainful employment during the time that would otherwise be donated to the charity. Then, the wages earned could be donated to the charity, and the charity would have the resources it needed to do a better job.

2. *"My name on the letterhead gives prestige to the organization."*   Although this gift of prestige may impress an outsider who looks at an organization and sees the list of names associated with its leadership, any individual on the board who does not work normally has an adverse impact on the morale of other leaders, no matter how prestigious that individual is.

It must be emphasized that the majority of support for most organizations comes from the individuals who are most intimately associated with it, not from people who have little or no association with the organization. Therefore, it is the impact on other leaders and the most committed workers that must be weighed most carefully, not the impact of a prestigious board member on those outside the organization's inner circle. Typically, other leaders and workers become less committed when they learn that some board members feel that they are so important that they do not have to provide gift support.

3. *"My job is to make the decisions."*   This is perhaps the weakest argument of all. It is relatively easy to make decisions when there is no responsibility for carrying them out. When board members assume authority while rejecting responsibility, they almost always ensure the ultimate failure of the organization they govern. This is because qualified staff and volunteer workers will not remain long associated with a situation where they have responsibility, but no authority. For them, it is a "no-win" situation. Those who make the decisions must, if an organization is to be successful, accept the responsibility for carrying them out.

4. *"We'll get someone to let us use their name."*   This argument assumes that there is some magical way to raise funds. That is to say, because of the name, sig-

nificant impact and momentum is generated for your cause, so much so that you may have to stand back from your mailbox to avoid being buried by the money pouring in. Actually, if fund-raising were this easy, no organization would have a short budget. This argument, is of course, very similar to the prestige argument above. Its weakness is the same. Most of the gift income received from any organization comes from a small number of large gifts. Prospective donors of larger gifts will not be impressed by the mere use of a well-known name. Prospective donors of larger gifts will want to meet and talk with the individuals listed as being among the organization's leaders. They will want to know that those individuals are committed to the organization and concerned about the prudent use of the resources entrusted to it. When they find "figureheads," they will typically become concerned that other aspects of the organization may be equally insubstantial.

5. *"Let's have an honorary board of governors that will raise money for us."* This procedure rarely works because of the "responsibility/authority" argument made earlier. There is no reason why an honorary board should accept the responsibility for raising money when it does not have the authority to ensure donors that their money will be used prudently. In the final analysis, there is no valid reason why one group of individuals should spend a lot of time and energy raising funds for another group to spend. If they are capable of raising the funds they probably have charitable goals of their own they would like to see reached.

6. *"Let's have a separate fund-raising committee."* This does not work for exactly the same reasons that were cited concerning the honorary board of governors, except that the reasons would be more emphatically true if the group were merely a committee.

7. *"Let's invite a few people to sit on the board who will be sure to give money."* This procedure normally does not work because such individuals rapidly come to understand their limited role. Usually, they will resign or insist upon a leadership role. Here again is the "authority-responsibility" argument. Normally people who can raise money do not want responsibility for maintaining the organization unless they also have the authority to determine its destiny.

As a final thought, it is important to point out that many boards, when faced with a deficit, will decide to cut budget rather than to intensify their own fund-raising efforts. Such a cut, of course, is disastrous for the organization and will probably lead to its eventual demise. This is because the board is reversing the priorities it should have and is doing things that are the most comfortable for the board rather than those things that are best for the organization. By cutting budget, the burden is shifted to the staff and the beneficiaries of the organization's services. The board has the authority but is not accepting the responsibility. The net result is that staff effectiveness and service delivery decline, often to the point where there is no reason for the organization to continue.

Clearly, the answer should be the raising of additional funds which would call for a redoubled commitment from the board. It is difficult (many would say impossible) for a board to justify its existence when it makes decisions which place the burden on others. Such a board accepts no responsibility for the implementation of these decisions which may lead to the curtailment, and perhaps elimination, of an organization's needed services.

Board Structure

Profit-making organizations have evolved over time from a concentration on production, through a concern with finance, to the current emphasis on marketing.

Today, most well-managed profit-making organizations recognize that these three areas—production, finance, and marketing—are equally important concerns in the management mix.

Nonprofit organizations (NPOs) have three other areas that are strongly analogous to the production, finance, and marketing areas of a profit-making organization. For NPOs they are program, business, and development. Interestingly, the evolution of nonprofit organizations has been analogous to the evolution of the profit-making organizations. That is to say, there was an original emphasis on program (production), which evolved into a concern with finance (business), and is now, in the case of the most successful nonprofit organizations, focused on marketing (development).

In a nonprofit organization, development should be concerned with all external relations including fund-raising, public relations, publications, and so on. Board and administrative structures should be designed to accommodate the importance of each of these three major areas along with any others that may be required by the charity.

For greatest effectiveness, boards frequently have seven standing committees. They are

1. *The executive committee.* The executive committee is most often composed of all the officers and frequently includes nonofficers, as well. Examples of nonofficers would include chairpersons of major committees who are not also officers. The function and responsibility of the executive committee is to act on behalf of the full board between regularly scheduled board meetings.

2. *The development and public relations committee.* Sometimes, this committee is referred to as resources, fund-raising, or planning. By any name, however, its responsibility is to organize and conduct the most effective fund-raising effort possible. Because all fund-raising requires public relations, public relations and publicity are frequently subordinated to the fund-raising committee. In larger organizations, this committee often works with and through a support staff and/or fund-raising counsel.

3. *The program committee.* While this committee will have many different names depending upon the nature of the organization, its responsibility is to oversee the delivery of the services that the organization provides. Thus, an educational institution might have a curriculum committee or a hospital might have a joint conference committee, but each is really responsible for the basic service of the institution.

4. *The facilities committee.* This committee is often called a building and grounds committee, but is named more broadly here because the facilities are not always limited to, or may not even include, buildings and grounds. Nevertheless, there should be a board committee which should be concerned with the physical resources, leased or owned, that are utilized by the organization.

5. *Finance committee.* Obviously, this committee is concerned with the financial resources of the organization and the control and prudent management of cash flow and investments. This committee very often works with and through paid staff.

6. *The nominating committee.* Experience has shown that the nominating committee should be a standing committee which meets regularly and has the ongoing responsibility for identifying, cultivating, and recruiting qualified members of the governing board. Many organizations make the mistake of creating a nominating committee shortly before the annual election meeting which requires that committee to compile a list of qualified nominees within a very brief period of time.

This procedure often breaks down into a frantic effort to find any individuals who are available to fill the vacancies.

It is much more effective for a nominating committee to meet regularly and to consider lists of nominees and to recruit year-round those who are most appropriate to the needs of the governing board.

7. *The by-laws committee.* Again, experience has shown that this should be a standing committee that meets regularly. Far too often, organizations will create an ad hoc by-laws committee at intervals of several years only when situations occur that require immediate attention. It is far better to have a standing by-laws committee which is constantly alert to the need for changes in the by-laws which govern the operation of the organization. Whenever needed, changes can be thought through on a timely basis and proposed for deliberate consideration by all parties.

For a complete discussion of the duties and responsibilities of nonprofit committees, see the chapter on committees of the nonprofit organization.

Each standing and ad hoc committee should meet at a time separate from the regular board meeting to conduct its own business. The reports and recommendations, then, of each committee should be presented to the board at a regularly scheduled meeting for its information and action. Too often, smaller, less experienced organizations will have governing boards that consider the business of every committee in detail as it arises. That is to say, the board becomes, de facto, a committee of the whole as the report from each committee is being read. This practice tends to lead to extremely long, dull, and ineffective meetings where the attention of most board members tends to wander a great deal. Therefore, it is extremely important to make sure that the board understands that its role is to accept, reject, or send back to committee reports by a committee, but not normally to debate each committee report extensively. The real work of an effective board is done within committees.

Individual board members should be asked to serve on one or more committees which would be of the greatest interest to them and appropriate to the expertise of the board member. Those committees, properly constituted, will then be repositories of the governing board's expertise to address the issues brought forward. If, then, the best talent available to the board has thoroughly considered the issues brought to the committees, it becomes redundant and inane for the governing board as a whole to debate once again all those issues. Board meetings should be relatively short and consist largely of hearing reports on the organization's activities and making decisions concerning the organization's future. Do not lose sight, however, of the extreme importance of requiring all board members to support fund-raising in addition to whatever else they are doing on the governing board.

Special Concerns

In the organization and management of a governing board, several important points ought to be covered and policies established before problems arise. These include

1. *Rotation.* Unless a board has a "rotation-off" provision in its by-laws, "dead wood" tends to accumulate over time and the effective functioning of that board is eventually blocked. This is because, as Gresham might have said, bad board members drive out the good ones. On the other hand, a rotation-off provision may be responsible for obliging the board to part company with one of its most effective

members. The traditional answer to this dilemma is to provide for rotation off (usually permitting a term of service of 6 years with the provision that any board member may be eligible for reelection after 1 year has elapsed since their last service on the board) but to exempt certain positions (such as some, or all, of the officers, or some, or all, of the chairpersons of the standing committees) from the rotation-off provision. This way the most valuable members of the board can be put in exempt positions and kept on the board as long as they are willing to serve. The less valuable members, of course, will be rotated off and vacancies created for new and, hopefully, more valuable members on the governing board.

2. *Board orientation.*   The governing board must be seen as the most important group of volunteer workers associated with the organization. Too often, members of the governing board are seen exclusively as a source of power and authority. That they are. But one should never lose sight of the fact that they are also, perhaps more importantly, volunteer workers and leaders. This means that every procedure one would normally use to cultivate and involve the volunteers should be applied to members of the governing board. Every new board member should receive a complete orientation, sometimes in several phases, that covers the operation of the organization, its finances, and the relationship of the governing board to the operation. Similarly, every committee should be given a complete orientation on an annual basis which outlines its goals, its responsibilities, and the tasks it must perform to meet them.

Clearly, a committee should be given comprehensive details which cover its responsibilities and the authority it has to achieve them. Attendance should be kept, and published, for all board meetings and any component of it. Finally, every committee (and the board itself) should use a loose-leaf notebook to record its most important documents (such as minutes, responsibilities, tasks, budgets, membership, leadership, and so on). This notebook should be available for easy, quick reference and should be brought to every meeting of the component group for which it is being kept. The purpose of the notebook is, of course, to keep track of the goals, tasks, and progress of the particular committee.

3. *Size.*   Experience has shown that it is extremely difficult to work effectively with more than 20 or 25 people on the governing board. On the other hand, a number smaller than 12 or 15 frequently is not large enough to permit the work to be done. Therefore, the ideal size of a working governing board is probably between 15 and 25 members. Nevertheless, some organizations have legally constituted governing boards which run up to 100 members or more. In such cases, it is usually necessary to create a smaller group which becomes the de facto governing board, regardless of the name by which it is known (usually, the executive committee).

The advantage of a large board is that a labor pool of some consequence is created. The disadvantage of a large board is that it can become quite cumbersome: It can become difficult to involve each member in the operation of the governing board and will eventually alienate those not involved. The advantage of a smaller board is that it frequently can move and decide quickly and effectively. The disadvantage is that it may not provide a large-enough pool of talent and labor to do all the tasks that may be required of that governing board. Clearly, the answer to the question of size will be different for each organization.

4. *Frequency of meetings.*   Many boards find it necessary to meet monthly. Experience would indicate, however, that this often is unnecessary and is an indication of poor board management. The much more effective model is for the committees of the board to meet as often as necessary and to report their decisions, recommendations, and actions to the full governing board at meetings that may

occur as infrequently as every 3 or 4 months. If appropriate, authority is delegated to the board committees; this latter method tends to be more flexible and more effective.

5. *A well-run board.*   A board is not a debating society. Poorly run boards tend to debate every issue that is placed before them. Well-run boards, on the other hand, make decisions about the committee recommendations and actions that are placed before them. An important objective of board management should be to have as much work done in committee as possible and to have as little done by the board sitting-as-a-whole as possible. Otherwise, board meetings will be both interminable and dull, and less effective action will be taken.

6. *Involve every member.*   One of the key objectives of good board management should be to develop leadership for the future. The only way to do this is to involve new members of the board quickly in board operations. Obviously, their progress, effectiveness, and commitment can then be monitored from the outset. Accordingly, every member of the board should be assigned to at least one, and preferably two or three, committee(s). Each should be assigned responsibilities and tasks not only so that work gets done, but also to encourage involvement by each member of the governing board to give him or her some "ownership" in it.

7. *Staff attendance.*   It is probably important to have certain key members of the staff attend every board meeting with the expectation that they will express themselves freely, but not have a vote. Among those who should attend the meetings are the chief executive officer, the chief financial officer, the chief fund-raiser, and probably the chief program officer. Some smaller organizations may have situations where one person has two or more of these responsibilities, but the principle will still hold: They should attend the board meetings.

The reasons are clear. The chief executive officer reports to the board and should do so at every meeting. The chief financial officer has important information for the board and may receive important instructions from it at every meeting. The chief program officer, of course, is in charge of the activity which follows from the basic reasons the organization exists, and should be at every board meeting to give information to the board and receive instructions from it. As one of the board's most important responsibilities is fund-raising, the chief fund-raising officer should attend every board meeting so that the board's performance in this regard can be reviewed and encouraged. Frequently, in larger organizations, there will be some need for other staff members to attend the board meetings, either regularly or from time to time. Decisions can be made in each case about frequency and duration (some staff members will attend for only that part of the board meeting which is most concerned with their activities whereas others may stay for the entire session).

As a final thought, it should be noted that the board is the source and the repository of the character and goals of the organization it governs. In the final analysis, it is ultimately responsible for everything—good or bad—that happens to that organization. If an organization succeeds, its success will reflect credit on the members of the board. If an organization declines or fails, its diminishment will also reflect on the board's ability to do its job. This is why the most important concern in any organization is the creation, organization, cultivation, utilization, and management of its governing board.

26

Fund-Raising and Professional Counsel

Robert C. Connor

*President and Chief Executive Officer,
Community Service Bureau, Inc.*

The Beginning

In fund-raising today, the experts are aware of the essentiality of all of the following: a committed and influential leadership, a case that is bigger than the institution, trained and involved volunteers, potential donors who before being asked to give have been carefully cultivated through a sound communications program, and what is often characterized as campaign dynamics—a feasible goal, an organized campaign committee, facilities for research, a backup staff, and a set time schedule with specific goals and objectives.

The evolution toward these essentials began 70 to 80 years ago. Fund-raising, as we know it today, is a twentieth-century development. Philanthropy in America's first three centuries was carried along on a small scale, and was largely financed by the wealthy few in response to personal begging appeals.

The campaign method originated in the Young Men's Christian Association (YMCA) during the last years of the nineteenth century. Two YMCA secretaries, Charles Sumner Ward and Lyman L. Pierce pioneered the "whirlwind campaign" approach. With Ward leading the way, the YMCA, using tightly organized methods, raised $60 million in capital funds from 1905 to 1906. Today's professionals, two generations later, are dealing with the same basic elements and are using the same techniques.

Society has changed, as have institutional priorities and needs, but fund-raising is and always was "a people business." Ninety percent of all gifts come from individuals and bequests, and the concerns that motivated our grandparents move us as well.

The Professional and the Nonprofit Organization

It would be nice if all nonprofit organizations (NPOs) could have a full staff of experts on their payrolls who were experienced and knowledgeable in every possible field the organization might need. Yet this is neither possible nor economically feasible, even in the profit-oriented business world.

The most practical and economical solution for executives and administrators of NPOs who need to expand or supplement their own internal managerial resources is to employ the services of an outside, professional fund-raising firm. The cost considerations are important, yet they should be weighed alongside several other factors to get a true picture of what is received for the money. The cheapest way often winds up to be the most expensive way in the long run. Consider the following facts:

1. The amount of money that is expended by philanthropic organizations in employing people with limited or no experience in fund-raising is appalling. The practice of giving such people between 2 and 5 years to produce tangible results is a most costly, yet a generally common, procedure. Professional fund-raising firms are results- and goal-oriented to produce the maximum results in a minimum, but reasonable, period of time.

2. With the professional firm, the nonprofit organization has budgetary control over the program or project. Reputable fund-raising firms do business only on a specified fee basis, never on the unprofessional basis of a percentage of or commission on the amount of funds raised. The fee is based on doing a specific task over a specific period of time. In this way, the NPO knows exactly what it will cost and how long it will take to complete the program. There is no guesswork.

3. By using a professional firm, the NPO gains the experience and knowledge of an entire "team" of fund-raising professionals with expertise in all phases of management relating to the field, without physically having to hire them and then trying to figure out what to do with them after the program is over. The NPO also gains from the fact that the professional already has considerable data and research compiled for program use that otherwise would represent another sizable investment in time and money to acquire.

4. There are many other less direct and tangible benefits inherent in using professional management, which would require too much space to discuss fully; however, two essential benefits should not be overlooked. First, the professional management service permits the NPO's internal staff to continue to function, uninterrupted, in doing its daily, routine work; yet it assures the organization that its project is receiving full-time, undivided attention from competent people. Second, the professional manager brings a fresh, objective viewpoint into play along with the broader perspective that comes only from years of experience in diverse programs for different types of organizations.

Management Services

Most established and reputable professional fund-raising firms offer a variety of management services to the nonprofit organization. These services may be contracted for, in part or in total, to expand the capabilities of an existing staff and provide them with the knowledge and experience to be gained from a full-scale, professionally directed fund-raising program or to provide full management of a program where no staff or expertise exists. These services include, but are not limited to, the following areas of service:

1. *Precampaign counseling and feasibility studies.* When contemplating fund-raising, the first step should be an in-depth analysis or study to determine the feasibility of the program goals. During the precampaign study processes, the past and present constituency, planning, and organizational "image" is thoroughly examined in order to assess leadership and financial potential and to test the "case" and climate for a successful program and its timing. Many other facts, attitudes, and concepts are revealed by the study, which will enable the organization to proceed from a position of strength with its program while avoiding serious errors that otherwise might cripple the effort.

2. *Full-time management services.* Once proved feasible by the in-depth analysis or study, the plan for future program action is established, from the sequence of events and actions to an estimated time schedule when each should occur. The professional program director assumes all responsibilities in establishing the program mechanism, coordinating all elements, and directing the program to a successful conclusion.

3. *Short-term management services.* In some cases, a nonprofit organization needs professional help to accomplish a specific task of a short-term nature, such as raising funds for an annual fund drive, approaching governmental agencies and foundations for grants, establishing ongoing development offices, program planning, assessment or updating assistance, or many other tasks too numerous to mention. The professional fund-raising firm has personnel who are experienced, knowledgeable, and capable of performing any phase of project development and fund-raising, and most reputable firms will provide short-term management and counsel to the NPO on an "as-needed" basis.

4. *Planned giving programs.* NPOs many times have no planned giving program to cover giving situations such as trusts, bequests, and legacies. Through such a program, the NPO can offer key prospects a more practical and sophisticated approach to giving. A professionally designed planned giving format is a proven means of establishing a continuing effort to raise funds for the NPO.

5. *Public relations services.* Development and fund-raising public relations seeks to project the program case to the constituency in the most favorable light. Professional direction ensures proper continuity throughout the program, and close contact with the NPO's staff is always maintained to ensure a consistent "image" with that of the NPO. A successful program's public relations effort will enhance the NPO's position with local media for years to come.

Under the broad areas of management services provided by the professional fund-raising firm, there are numerous specific services that require specialized knowledge and experience. These specific services normally are part of a basic service as outlined previously and are not contracted separately since they would be meaningless if not coordinated with, and related to, other elements of service. Some of these services include

1. The definition and delineation of the case, which is the statement that impels potential donors to give to a program

2. The formulation of the detailed plan of action and time schedule, which en-

compasses leadership enlistment, program publicity, program organization and administration, periodic reporting of funds, and other special events

3. Guidance and assistance in selecting and recruiting leadership and volunteer workers

4. The development of information and educational literature for orientation and cultivation of workers and prospects

5. Providing thorough training and orientation programs as well as continuing assistance to all volunteer workers

6. Prospect list development and evaluation assistance covering all potential sources of giving, including foundations, corporations, and individuals

7. Constantly advising, counseling, and assisting program leaders and volunteer workers and efficiently coordinating their efforts to maintain their enthusiasm and make maximum use of their available time

8. Establishing development office procedures, hiring and training personnel, developing internal forms for program use, and equipping program offices to handle projected work loads at at a minimum of expense, yet with maximum efficiency

9. Establishing collection systems for follow-up to keep pledge payments up to date after the close of the program

The Importance of the Feasibility Study

As stated earlier, when the nonprofit organization is ready to consider a major fund development program, professional counsel almost always will recommend beginning with a precampaign study, often called a "feasibility study." This is an evaluation of the potential leadership involvement and financial support for the NPO which must be sufficient if a program is to prove feasible.

The function of the professional firm is not to raise the money, but to help the organization raise it. This is where the feasibility study comes in. It helps to set priorities, to pinpoint the most important needs, to help volunteer leadership understand what their responsibilities are in the program, and to get the administrative staff and all others concerned with the organization geared up and ready to go before the rest of the world is made aware of what is going to happen.

Since it is a given that a firm does not guarantee results or promise to raise unattainable funds, the feasibility study sets the pattern for both the work of the professional and for the NPO. Professional counsel brings to bear an outside point of view and an accumulated experience on problems that always seem to occur in any major program. The knowledge of professional counsel is based on many diverse campaigns and is not restricted to one-time experiences or solutions. Usually, the individual director assigned to the NPO's program will consult with a supervisor and a group of officers within the professional consulting firm to arrive at a solution based on collective experience.

In some cases, the precampaign study process, which usually includes personal interviews, may be combined with specific action essential to a successful campaign. These include enlistment of key campaign leadership and identification of major gifts and matching grants. In any case, the professional's judgment as to the type of study and elements to be included should be relied upon.

The extent of the possible philanthropic market for the NPO must be assessed along with the capabilities of those who will be selling the product, the volunteers and leadership.

The study is accomplished by first interviewing the key individuals who represent these markets or who are in a position to give an objective judgment of the relationship of the organization to its peer groups. Depending on the scope of the task, anywhere from 25 to 100 key individuals will be interviewed, each on a personal and confidential basis. They will include trustees, parents, alumni, foundation executives whose foundations have a record of interest in programs of similar organizations, business leaders, leaders of the community where the organization or institution is located, and individuals in leadership roles with related or competitive organizations.

These are the kinds of questions normally asked:

1. What is the general stage setting against which a case for this particular organization must be viewed? With a college, for example, this is a review of the entire field represented by the school—whether it be liberal arts or technology-oriented, private or state-supported, small or large.

2. To what extent can the organization claim that its services are serving its constituencies?

3. What do the volunteer leaders really feel and think about the organization? What do community leaders or staff have to say under the protective cloak of confidentiality? When such people are given the opportunity to speak frankly, what do they see as the real strengths and the real weaknesses of the organization?

4. What efforts have gone on in the past to assess the case? Are the problems really recognized? Do the leaders face up to the inevitable shortcomings of the organization? In past performance, have key individuals supported the organization to the extent they should?

5. What is the fund-raising track record of the organization?

6. What is the state of the development office? Will it be an asset in a major campaign, or will it be a liability?

Relationships of the organization to the community are examined. Troubled areas are identified. These must be clearly defined. The study helps do this. Volunteer leadership must be identified, and evidence has to be shown that potential leaders will, in fact, commit themselves to the program.

The principal sources of funds must be charted, and, most important, the potential leadership gifts have to be identified. Without pace-setting contributions, no major effort has a chance. Also assessed are any specific changes in trustee posture, community attitudes, or administrative qualifications that should be addressed before a major campaign is made known to the public.

This study process takes at least several weeks, but from it comes the real parameters as to the feasibility of the institution's goals and needs.

Synthesizing the interviews, the key officers of the professional, fund-raising consulting firm then plan the development program. Included are such essentials as the goal, the time needed to raise the money, the phases of the campaign (often set up for 1-year, 2-year or 3-year periods), the type of staff needed within the institution, the budget (professional counsel is very experienced at estimating the cost of such an effort and staying within the bounds of the agreed-upon budget), the role of the trustees (a very important statement to get on the record as once the trustees accept the findings and the recommendations of a feasibility study, they also, by definition, agree to do their share in implementing the plan), the role of the key administrators, and, finally, the role of professional counsel.

Conducting a feasibility study is a very specific service which does not imply a future obligation or relationship with a client. Most, but not all firms who are members of the American Association of Fund-Raising Counsel, Inc. (AAFRC), offer this service as a separate service.

More often than one would believe, the study is performed and the trustees decide not to go ahead either with the campaign or the employment of the professional counseling firm that performed the study. Sometimes they engage another firm to implement the findings, although understandably the second firm is going to want to do additional reviews on its own. Surprisingly, a number of times the feasibility study shows that the institution is not ready to go into a major program, and the recommendation will be not to attempt a major program until certain improvements are made within the organization or in its activities.

Sometimes the trustees do not accept the professional's findings. Bear in mind, however, that if an established, professional consulting firm makes a recommendation not to go into a development program, the client should listen to this message attentively. An unprofessional consulting firm may tell a client that the organization can raise the kind of money it wishes to raise just to obtain the organization as an ongoing client.

Selection of a Professional Firm

In selecting a professional fund-raising firm, one should deal only with firms that work for a specified fee—never one that works on the unprofessional basis of a percentage or a commission of the money raised. Established, reputable firms afford the NPO with back-up capabilities so that a program is not dependent on any one person.

The major fund-raising firms operate under rigid ethical codes and can show proven performance records over extended periods of time. The American Association of Fund-Raising Counsel, Inc. (AAFRC), headquartered in New York, is recognized as the leading association in the fund-raising field today. Founded in 1935 as the pioneer in its field, the AAFRC annually publishes an authoritative report on the facts and trends in American Philanthropy called *Giving USA*. Through this association, the NPO can secure a considerable amount of information on fund-raising in general and on particular member firms.

In selecting a professional fund-raising firm, the NPO should follow the same good business practices that it would in selecting an accountant, lawyer, architect, or any other professional. Some of these considerations would include the following:

1. Consider carefully the experience of the firm. Look for quality and not quantity alone in past programs and clients. Examine the firm's management and staff. The firm may no longer have the personnel that helped establish its solid reputation.

2. Ask for references on recent programs, not only from administrators and staff members but also from volunteer program leaders. Check these references by phone or a personal visit. Ask if they would employ the firm again on a similar program.

3. Make sure the firm has a permanent headquarters for conducting its business, not just a box number or phone number.

4. Ask for advance approval of personnel to be assigned to your program, and be sure they are experienced in directing programs in your field of interest.

5. Ask for a general plan of service in writing. Be sure it includes an outline of services to be performed and an estimate of the time period of service.

6. Discuss your conclusions with the firms you are considering before making

your final selection. In some cases, a simple explanation may remove an obstacle in the way of retaining the services of the firm you otherwise would prefer.

For a number of reasons, it is recommended that you talk to three or four professional consulting firms. Discussing your program and plans with them helps bring into focus both your needs and the feasibility of the program you are planning. This is a "people" business, and you might prefer one company over another for many different reasons. These interviews will in no way obligate you. Just as reputable firms serve only worthy projects which in their professional judgment offer the prospect of fund-raising success, so from the client's vantage point, the one way to be sure a professional firm can achieve fund-raising success is to look into its track record and be satisfied that it conducts its business in a professional way.

Finally, regardless of which side any of us may be on, whether as an employee of the development staff of a college or university or as a development manager of a professional consulting firm, as fellow professionals we should always remember how much of a people business this really is.

Our most precious commodity is the amount of volunteer human hours we can secure from our volunteers and our leaders. As professionals we must assume a positive stance and be the motivators for action. Sometimes this can be an uphill battle. A volunteer does not have the attraction of a paycheck and is often turned off because things are moving too slowly or because outside factors assume dimensions that are overwhelming.

Cost of Professional Management

It has been widely demonstrated that professionally directed fund-raising programs generally cost less, per dollar raised, than homemade campaigns. Experienced management does not "cost"; it saves money and produces results in a minimum period of time.

A large number of firms, and even more individuals, are engaged in the business of fund-raising today. The ways of remuneration for services are countless. Yet, firms worth hiring are paid only on a specified fee basis, never on the basis of a percentage or commission.

Fees are calculated based on the number of personnel assigned, the length of service, and the out-of-pocket expenses involved. Often, the fees for exploration and initial planning may be figured separately, particularly if certain elements of doubt exist at the outset of a program or project. A portion of the program cost, it should be pointed out, will be an expense to the NPO; however, it will not be included in the management fee of many professional fund-raising consulting firms. Reputable firms break this out as a separate item and refer to it as the program or campaign "incidental expense budget." In this portion will be found such expenses as clerical help, office expenses, printing, publicity, meetings, travel, telephone, and the many other out-of-pocket expenses related to the program or project. Long experience enables the professional manager to estimate accurately in projecting such expenses. Throughout the program, the fund-raising firm should be expected to account for all expenditures on a periodic and consistent basis.

Conclusions

The nonprofit organization in need of money definitely should examine the possibilities of securing all, or at least part, of its needed money through fund-raising.

Chances are that this will be the least costly way of financing the program or project. Talk to a professional firm early in the planning stages. There is usually no fee for asking questions, and you could avoid some serious errors or problems unforeseen at the outset.

Once you have decided to go with a professional fund-raising firm, be cautious. Always keep in mind that nothing is free, and you usually get what you pay for. Cheap help more often than not is the most expensive help you can buy. Your best investment, almost at any price, is an investment in top people—people with integrity, experience, and common sense; people who are loyal and stable, and have proven records of successful performance.

Should you employ outside professional managers, do not expect them or their firm physically to go out and raise money for you. No one can transfer influence to another person, and the right person asking for the right size of gift at the right time is the most important element in a successful fund-raising program. Professional managers are there to provide the vast knowledge and experience of their "team"—their firm—in showing you how to raise funds. They serve as planners, administrators, and coordinators and have as their sole responsibility the function of directing and guiding your program and project to a successful completion.

Suggested Reading

First the Facts/The Logical Approach to Fund-Raising, American Association of Fund-Raising Counsel, New York.

Fund-Raising . . . Cost or Investment? American Association of Fund-Raising Counsel, New York.

Giving USA, American Association of Fund-Raising Counsel, New York.

How to Select Fund-Raising Counsel, American Association of Fund-Raising Counsel, New York.

Rowland, A. W. (Ed.), *Handbook of Institutional Advancement,* Jossey-Bass, San Francisco, 1977.

Seymour, Harold J., *Designs for Fund-Raising,* McGraw-Hill, New York, 1966.

Thinking of a Fund-Raising Program? American Association of Fund-Raising Counsel, New York.

27

Marketing

Arthur Sturm
President, The Sturm Communications Group, Inc.

Marketing is a nebulous word. Students and practitioners of marketing cannot seem to agree on a universal definition of just what it is they are studying and doing. In attempting to converse on the subject, I have encountered executives who warned, "Don't talk to me about advertising." I assured them that I did not intend to. "We already have good public relations," a busy hospital CEO told me. I assured her that marketing is more than public relations. Each of these individuals—quite competent managers, I might add—thought that marketing comprises only those elements. It is, as you will see, a much more intricate process.

What Marketing Is All About

Marketing is not a new idea for nonprofit organizations. You have been doing it, consciously or not, from the first day your organization opened its doors. And you continue to do it every time management makes a policy decision, offers a new service, eliminates or adds a program, changes prices, or publishes a brochure.

In its most straightforward sense, marketing means to make an exchange. You have what I want: a service or product, and I have what you want; usually, money. We trade, or make a market. The marketing process helps maximize one's ability to function and succeed in a competitive environment, to identify existing needs and assess new opportunities.

Two other definitions may also assist in grasping the role and functions of marketing in and for the nonprofit organization:

> Marketing includes the various processes used in selling goods and services, and the knowledge by the seller of how to employ them effectively to achieve a gainful exchange.[1]

> Expressed in its most basic terms, marketing is the performance of business activities that *direct* the flow of goods and services from producer to consumer (or user) in order to satisfy customers and accomplish the organization's objectives. The marketing con-

cept is the recognition on the part of management that all business decisions of an organization must be made in the light of customer needs and wants.[2]

Development of NPO Marketing

Marketing is currently capturing the covers of professional journals and causing major changes in our country's nonprofit organizations. Historically, the nonprofit organization has had a relatively easy time of things. Until recently, it was a foregone conclusion in our society that people need medical attention, an education, and other services generally provided by not-for-profit organizations. There was a natural market, one in which demand for the services of nonprofit institutions *did not need stimulation.* In fact, demand often exceeded supply—students could not find a college; patients, a hospital. Competition for consumers among nonprofit agencies was minimal, at least on the surface. When business was "good" and funding was "flush," nonprofit staffs seldom gave more than lip service to public needs when charting the direction of their programs.

Everything was going along fine, until several significant events occurred. Rather than go into detail, suffice it to say that the age of our population shifted from young to old, the number of nonprofit agencies proliferated at a time when demand was falling, the economy went downhill, and a large number of institutions lost their credibility.

As we entered the 1980s, our nation suddenly found itself with approximately 250,000 more hospital beds than it needed. Our colleges and universities were competing for a college-age population that had dropped by one-third. And an evening of exposure to the arts cost three to five times more than it had just a few years before—without dinner.

From a marketing standpoint, the nonprofit sector has entered an environment long familiar to for-profit organizations. We have discovered that while demand for many of our services is finite, a seemingly infinite supply of agencies exists to meet it. There is a limited supply of consumer dollars to spend in the nonprofit sector. Furthermore, the consumer is now highly selective. Once consumers had to qualify for acceptance by colleges and hospitals; now institutions must qualify for consumers. In short, changes in consumer behavior, fluctuations in the economy, and the proliferation of nonprofit providers are forcing the nonprofit institution to become more aggressive and precise in the ways it relates services and messages to the community. Life for the nonprofit organization is changing drastically. But, in the long run, both the institutions and the consumer will benefit... if they act now.

Marketing: Panacea, Promise, Perils

Marketing is an attempt to meet consumer needs with a particular product. It is matching what your organization does with what consumers need or at least with what they think they need. More logically, marketing is finding out what the consumer wants and then designing a service to meet those wants. If marketing is the tool for-profit business uses to sustain growth and maintain a competitive edge, there is no sound business reason that marketing principles should not be applied to influence the ways in which people seek health services, education, cultural programs, social assistance, and other products of the nonprofit sector.

Marketing assumes there is demand for goods and services or that a demand can be created or directed. Marketing also assumes there will be competition. As much as nonprofit agencies attempt to deny competition among themselves, they have, in fact, gone out of their way to aggravate it. Hospitals are tripping over each other to get the latest technology. Why? So they can get more physicians and more patient-days. That is competition. Colleges are vying for students and faculty with financial incentives such as scholarships and research grants. Theaters are offering discounts and special rates on tickets to draw new audiences.

The fact that competition exists, it should be noted, does not mean that institutions must become enemies. Competition simply acknowledges that today's consumer has options that did not exist before. Further, increased consumer control over the purchase decision is why nonprofit organizations must pay attention to marketing. In marketing, a major objective is to influence the consumer to select your product.

Identifying the NPO Market

This argument may be sound for sellers of consumer goods, but what can a nonprofit organization expect from marketing? Insight, for one thing. Marketing is a process that forces an organization to define itself in terms of consumer needs and wants. More specifically, marketing can identify your constituents, help you design and promote services for those constituents, and give you a consistent image.

The marketing process is logical. First, you must identify what it is you wish to take to market. There is more to this than saying "we provide health care (or undergraduate education)"; the marketing process should refine those generalities. You should examine the strengths and weaknesses of your institution, isolating those elements that make it truly unique or different from all other agencies. The proliferation of nonprofit organizations and institutions has given us thousands of colleges and universities that offer "a good undergraduate education"; an equal number of hospitals that give "warm, personalized attention"; and countless symphonies that have the "finest music heard anywhere." These are not marketable commodities.

What distinguishes an institution or organization?

Size

Affiliation

Types of programs

Location

Staff

Price (a distinction of growing importance these days)

Current users

These are just a few of the characteristics that may separate your institution from the pack. But, once you learn *who* you are, what next?

It is important to find out, first, what consumers *think* they need, and second, how they perceive your services. This is done through research—taking a scientific sampling of individuals or families from your service area or constituency and asking them in quantifiable or qualitative terms what they believe, what they think, how they behave and what they want in relation to your product. For example, can the consumer identify your principal services? How does he or she perceive the quality of the programs you offer? Are consumers satisfied with your product?

Research is going to tell you who your constituency is...or should be. In a changing market, affinities and allegiances can change without an institution's knowledge. At the same time, new constituencies are continually arising, but are often unidentified. Market research can keep you abreast of changing attitudes and identify new audiences.

For example, an educational institution in the east was disappointed in enrollment for its evening continuing education programs. Market research showed that interest in evening programs was highest among women age 35 and older who were looking for self-improvement programs. Furthermore, these women were willing to spend money to get what they wanted. By adding and promoting programs to meet the needs of this newly targeted audience, the college increased enrollment significantly, and the evening program became an important source of added income.

Research recently told us that patients at a community hospital in the midwest had a need for spiritual counseling during their stay. Yet the hospital had no chaplaincy program. By adding one, the hospital hopes to increase patient satisfaction in a highly competitive market for health care services. True, a chaplaincy program may seem tangential to health care, but it is critical to consumer satisfaction. And satisfaction affects repeat utilization.

Although research can tell you what you are doing right, as well as what you are doing wrong, it is not an end in itself. America has compiled enough statistics to keep researchers busy for years. Herein lies one of the perils of marketing: subscribing to part of the theory, but not all. I have talked to a number of institutions who say they have done research and no more. Perhaps the research told those institutions some things they did not want to hear, and so they rejected or ignored the results. Remember that research *done properly* does indeed provide an accurate picture of the manner in which you are perceived by your constituent groups. Be assured that if you do research, you *are* going to hear some things about yourselves you are not going to like. Force yourself to listen. If the data tells you that people do not perceive you as you perceive yourself, then something in the communication process is in need of improvement or correction. Find the problem and address it.

Research must be interpreted in a larger context to be valuable as a basis for decision making. For example, if you are a community-based hospital, and your research shows that only 17 percent of the households in your service area know you have a 24-hour physician-staffed emergency room, do you panic? Perhaps not. It could be that high utilization, often a function of visibility, is not a goal for your hospital. In fact, 17 percent may be *too high,* and you ought to be focusing your efforts on discouraging demand for emergency services, without drying up demand entirely or damaging public support.

The Marketing Plan

Once your research is complete, the next phase of activity is the development of a marketing plan (see chapter Appendix). The marketing plan states the goals of your marketing activity and outlines the way in which you will achieve them. The plan is a comprehensive, detailed review of where the organization is in the marketplace, the strengths and weaknesses of the organization, and a calculated projection of where the organization should be in the future, given its strengths and weaknesses.

In some ways, I think you could consider the marketing plan as a behavior book. A good plan tells you:

- What it is you want to have happen
- What it is you are taking to the marketplace

- Why people would want to buy your products (as opposed to your competition's)
- What to say to get consumers to act
- When to say it
- How much it will cost to get your plan to reach its objective

Begin your marketing plan by setting some measurable goals for the institution. Note the word *measurable.* Say that you want to increase enrollment by 10 percent, or your number of patient days by 2 percent, or raise your visibility among high-income groups by 7 percent. Each of these goals can be measured. The more general you make your goals, the more difficult it is to measure your success and the more frustrating your overall planning becomes. Imagine trying to design a plan in response to the goal: We want more people to like us. How could you possibly ever know if you had succeeded?

When you develop a marketing plan, take a hard look at the way your service matches consumer preferences or needs. Recall here our example of the college looking to increase enrollment in its continuing education program. You must also evaluate

- What legislation (federal, state, and local) exists or is pending that could have an impact on your institution, organization, or program
- How current trends in the economy affect consumer-user attitudes toward your service(s)
- Your target audience and what you know about them as revealed by the research
- How price relates to what you are offering the consumer

The Positioning Statement

An equally important part of the marketing plan is the development of communications strategies and recommendations. Here too, there is a lot of confusion about what constitutes marketing activity. One of your most important tasks in developing a marketing plan will be the creation of a positioning statement—that is, a concise statement of what makes you different from your competitors that shows the consumer the benefit of using your product or service. In effect, *your positioning statement is your promise to the consumer.* It is your demonstration of how you will meet a specific need.

An effective positioning statement puts your institution in a place *not* held by the competition. In the eyes of the consumer, your positioning statement is what separates you from the pack. While McDonald's was telling us that "You deserve a break today," Wendy's responded with "Where's the beef?" How would you compete with "Weekends are made for Michelob" if you were marketing a competing beer?

Positioning must be accurate. A bank on the east coast said, through its advertising, that it wanted to offer loans to as many people as possible. In practice, the bank's loan policy discriminated against middle- and lower-income groups. A restaurant in Florida advertised itself as a "great place to visit anytime." But, in fact, the place was dirty, and at 3 a.m., you risked getting mugged in the parking lot. Therefore, you must be sure that the organization will be able to deliver what it promises. Better yet, *promise something no one else is offering.*

Positioning statements for nonprofit organizations are more complex than they are for commercial products. After all, we can hardly say that "Weekends are made for open heart surgery." But NPOs *can* draw on what they do best to create an effective positioning statement.

For an alcohol and chemical dependency program, our firm positioned a client as a "low-cost, family centered treatment program"—because no one else was talking about price. And, with another health service, we simply identified the hospital as the sole source for important health information in a particular category: "We'll tell you everything we know about cancer." *If you do nothing else well in the planning process, develop an effective positioning statement.*

A Good Marketing Plan

To be successful, marketing uses a variety of methods for reaching consumers. Marketing is not advertising per se; it is not public relations; it is not just changing the design of a service or getting a new logo. Marketing is a mixture of activities that maximizes your potential to influence the consumer's decision to purchase a product—your product.

Marketing does not always require megabucks and armies of experts. It can be a very personalized effort. The marketing plan explores all the options the institution has for motivating and influencing consumers and makes cogent recommendations on how each of those resources can be used most effectively.

Finally, a good marketing plan is going to give you a method by which you can evaluate your efforts. If you have started with measurable goals, then the task of evaluation is clear. But in other situations, such as those problems that deal with changes in attitudes, a different methodology may be required. Each organizational or institutional situation will dictate a different method of evaluation.

To Market, to Market

Given a well-thought-out plan, you should be ready to market. Some organizations can market their own services; others must rely on assistance from consultants, advertising agencies, or free-lance talent. With a fully endorsed plan, decisions on implementation should be self-evident. The plan has told you what to do. Now you simply have to act.

While it is important to understand the marketing process, we should also pay some attention to who is going to do the marketing within the institution. Quite simply, everyone should. Since marketing is a direct experience between a program and the consumer, each person in the organization—staff, officers, board, and corps of volunteers—is an integral part of the marketing effort. Just as hospitals have developed cost-containment programs that involve every department in the organization, all NPOs can benefit by developing broad internal awareness of marketing activity.

This is not to say that *everyone* should participate in the development of the marketing strategy or plan. However, people who are directly affected by the marketing plan should have an opportunity to contribute before it is finalized. Both staff and volunteer leadership must be aware of their impact on consumers and users, they must understand how the organization perceives itself in the marketplace, and they must share in and support the institution's plans for future programs and activities. Marketing is as much an internal motivational tool as it is an external influence on consumer behavior.

Development as a Marketing Function

Philanthropy is a classic marketing model of exchange, and philanthropy succeeds because nonprofit organizations meet the needs of consumers on two levels. First, the organization provides a service to a consuming public and makes an exchange. Second, through its philanthropic activities, NPOs fulfill the needs of the donor to support a worthwhile social goal. There are few business enterprises that have the same amount of marketing potential with the same product as does the nonprofit organization.

Independent research conducted among upper-income households in Chicago identified giving patterns, preferences, and motivation. The first group of questions dealt with giving patterns: *"Please tell me the kinds of organizations your household is most likely to support financially."* The answers were:

Church/synagogue (or their affiliates)	54%
Specific health organization (ACS, Heart, etc.)	43%
Private college or university	29%
Performing arts organizations	25%
Crusade of Mercy	20%
Community association	19%
Hospitals (private)	17%
Museums	15%
United Jewish Appeal	14%
Hospitals (public or community)	7%
Catholic Charities	5%
Environmental groups	5%

In reviewing interviewer and respondent comments on this question, we noted the following:

- Health-related organizations, not hospitals, made a particularly strong showing. The American Cancer Society and the Heart Association were the most frequently mentioned organizations.
- A large percentage of our sample appeared to be Jewish and gave along religious lines.
- There is some evidence that the religious affiliation of a private school is important.
- Donors appear to be parochial. While they give to major organizations or institutions, they also support a large number of small community organizations, such as the garden club or community associations.
- Public television received a particularly strong number of mentions.

Respondents were then asked to identify their reasons for making a gift: *"In general, what personal reasons for financial giving would you say is the most important to you?"*

Help less fortunate	24%
Personal affiliation with the organization	24%

Help society	18%
Makes me feel good	11%
Use their services (museum, etc.)	10%
Private giving is important	9%
Memorialize a loved one	2%

The data confirm what many of you already suspect: giving is still an emotional issue. To help the needy is considered a "noble gesture," but equally important, donors told us that the institution must somehow have "touched their lives," either through a direct experience as a student or patient, or indirectly, through a family member's involvement.

Only 4 percent cited tax savings as a reason for giving. However, a Gallop poll indicated that Americans who itemize their personal deductions actually *give more than three times as much* as those who take the standard deduction. This was among the many significant findings of the survey, cosponsored by the Coalition of National Voluntary Organizations (CONVO), whose data lend considerable support to the argument that tax incentives are an important determinant of the *levels* of charitable giving.

All respondents in the survey were asked the amount of charitable donations they gave to organizations or institutions in each of five categories:

- Church and religious organizations
- Educational groups
- Hospitals and medical centers
- Other health organizations
- All other donations

Sixteen percent reported that they made *no* charitable donations that year. About one-third (34 percent) reported that they gave between $1 and $100; 14 percent made donations of $101 to $200; 17 percent gave $201 to $500; and 19 percent donated more than $500. The mean average total donation was $358.

A substantially larger proportion reported having made a donation to a church organization (69 percent) or other health organizations (66 percent) than made donations to educational groups (27 percent), hospitals (23 percent), or all other organizations (49 percent). Similarly, the mean average donation reported for church organizations ($239) is considerably larger than the mean average amount donated to educational groups ($35), hospitals ($16), other health organizations ($35), or all other charities ($25).

More than four out of five reported that they made a charitable donation, 91 percent of those itemizing, 83 percent of those taking standard deductions. However, the *mean average total donation was considerably higher among those who itemized than among those who took the standard deduction*—$652 compared with $210.

The response to the next question says something important to all nonprofit leaders and managers during the 1980s: *"In general, is the quality of management at an organization important to you in your decision to donate funds?"*

Yes	80%
No	20%

The response was strong enough to tell us that the requesting organizations had better have their organizational act together if they expect to impress major donors. Probing the respondents, two organizational issues struck us as important—the caliber of the person making the request for money and the perceived need for or contribution of the organization. Results of the survey are available to boards of trustees upon request to Campbell & Company, Chicago.

From a marketing standpoint, this information tells us how we should base our appeal. We should talk to donors on an emotional level and try to relate what our client does to the life of the individual donor. If there is no existing experience between the donor and the institution, we had better start one *soon*.

Additional Benefits of Marketing

If you are a leader or manager of a nonprofit organization, marketing can make your life a little simpler and your yield a lot higher. Marketing can help the public recognize your organization's specific contributions in contrast to other organizations in your area. Marketing lays the groundwork for your organization's revenue-generating programs. It gives you an identity among various constituents in the community. Specifically, marketing can identify opportunities to direct key messages about your organization to community and corporate leaders—the people who make philanthropy happen. For example, research could tell you that corporate leaders do not have a clear understanding of how a hospital controls its costs. Good cultivation of prospects could begin by designing a health costs education program, especially for business executives.

In addition, if marketing is introducing you to constituent groups, it is also providing you with valuable insights into their needs and perceptions. Marketing can help identify the chief concerns of constituent groups, and allow your organization to target messages to them and influence the perceptions they form. Marketing can be a key force in creating a "climate for giving." And, since marketing has helped your institution design services that more clearly meet the needs of the community, development officers, in particular, will be much better able to articulate the case for supporting your goals.

Marketing Case Histories

Theory certainly serves as the cornerstone for all important programs. But let us look at some actual case histories to see how nonprofits have used marketing and how they fared.

A prime example is the March of Dimes organization. The group was chartered to secure funds to combat polio through research. Thankfully, they were quite successful in their efforts—so successful that they eliminated a need for polio research.

With fine volunteers and staff in place, it seemed appropriate to continue activities, even if for another cause. Through marketing, the agency discovered a field of clinical research that was in need of additional support and had appeal to potential donors. Thus, the March of Dimes moved from an organization concerned with polio to one that now concentrates its efforts on combatting birth defects. It literally found a new market for itself. The needs of society are being met; and a fine organization continues to raise needed funds. A for-profit parallel to that experience is the baby food industry, which risked losing its market when confronted with a declining birth rate. To combat this threat, many companies diversified and are now introducing products for society's older citizens.

To cite another example, a community hospital in the midwest was concerned about poor utilization of its emergency room by local ambulances. Although the hospital was the newest in town, it was unable to capture a significant share of the market for emergency medical services. Research, including interviews with ambulance drivers, uncovered a simple explanation. The architect who designed the building emphasized aesthetics over practical considerations and created an emergency room entrance that required ambulances to back into the loading area.

The problem was exacerbated, according to the paramedics, by physicians who chose to park illegally along the narrow drive. Though ambulance drivers preferred the hospital's staffing and facilities, the competition's drive-through portal made life a lot easier for the paramedics and a lot more profitable for the competition.

Here, I think, we have a fine example of how consumers behave. The decision to make a purchase—in this case to use a hospital emergency room—was influenced more by convenience than by the perceived quality of the product. How could an institution recognize and respond to such a problem without research?

Resistance to Marketing

While we can see from these examples that marketing has a definite role to play in the administration and management of nonprofit organizations, it, unfortunately, has run into some resistance from management. Many believe that marketing will influence the organization to engage in some sort of hucksterism that will undermine credibility with the public.

Perhaps that danger does exist. But every marketing program with which I have been involved has had the implicit guidance and approval of top-level management. The institutions themselves are the purveyors of their idealism and the guardians of their integrity. They are their own censors, their own watchdogs. Advertising agencies cannot act unless the client approves. You *can* control the aggressiveness of your marketing program with the same care and caution used to establish institutional goals and objectives.

Perils

I should also mention here some of the perils of marketing. Cost is something the NPO must be aware of. Marketing, especially in the early stages, can be costly. It is possible to buy cheap research, but frequently bargains in research reap unreliable data. Whatever your marketing costs, they will have to be passed on to your consumers as higher prices or user fees. Be acutely aware of the financial dominos before you begin the marketing process. Set some limits on your spending, but do not budget yourself into a catatonic state. With some serious thought, you can make your marketing dollar work effectively for your institution.

The marketing tool, unlike many others, is by nature manipulative. And manipulation can be an awesome responsibility, since it is the nonprofit sector that sustains health, instills values, and imparts knowledge. If individuals elect to employ chicanery in moving audiences to use those services, then the nonprofit sector has lost its most important characteristic, its integrity.

Promise of Marketing

What can we say, therefore, about the promise of marketing the nonprofit organization? Marketing has the potential to clarify the image of the institution. It can point to new opportunities for serving communities and constituents. It can help institutions and agencies deliver a more exacting level of service to a receptive audience.

Marketing is a logical, organized system that can help you respond to the needs of the communities that gave your initial charters. Use it wisely, and you will do much to improve the quality of life for all of us.

Notes

1. Tracy D. Connors, *Dictionary of Mass Media and Communication,* Longman, New York, 1982.
2. Patrick J. Montana, *Marketing in Nonprofit Organizations,* AMACOM, New York, 1978, p. xi.

Appendix

Mount Sinai Hospital/Minneapolis Marketing Plan Outline

INTRODUCTION

A statement of the purpose and goal of the plan

THE SITUATION ANALYSIS: DIABETES IN MINNEAPOLIS

An overview of the health problem including any major changes expected in diabetes care; an overview of statistics on the frequency of the disease and approximate size of the market; a summary and/or profile of diabetes care in Minneapolis; attempt to isolate needs of the patient (in general)

THE MOUNT SINAI DIABETES PROGRAM

Review of the design of service including pricing structure and reimbursement policies; review current utilization statistics; comparison with other programs in Minneapolis; advantages and disadvantages of Mount Sinai program; accessibility of program to patients and physicians; perceptions of program by patients and physicians

THE ROLE OF MARKET RESEARCH OR FINDINGS (OPTIONAL)

Factors that affect selection; the purchase decision

LEGISLATION AFFECTING DIABETES PROGRAMS

STATEMENT OF MARKETING GOALS AND OBJECTIVES

Measurable goals; communications objectives

IDENTIFICATION OF TARGET AUDIENCES AND MARKETS

Primary:
  Physicians
  Patients
  Families of patients
Secondary:
  Staff
  Referral sources
  Review any relevant geographic considerations of target audiences

RECOMMENDED MARKETING STRATEGIES

Considerations:

- Design of service
- Pricing
- Location of services
- Programs for physicians
- Referrals
- Shared services
- Other

COMMUNICATIONS RECOMMENDATIONS

Development of a positioning statement Communications programs

- Advertising
- Direct mail
- Events
- Collateral material
- Merchandising
- Other

METHOD OF EVALUATION

BUDGET OF PROPOSED ACTIVITIES

TIMETABLE OF PROPOSED ACTIVITIES

SUMMARY

APPENDIX/EXHIBITS

28

Telemarketing

Diane M. Carlson

CFRE, President; IDC

Every day, the multiplicity of human need seems to increase. Our mail becomes more laden with fund appeals. The technology associated with the solicitation process becomes more sophisticated. A key aspect of the competition for the charitable dollar involves the increasing necessity to get personal.

Most fund-raisers would agree that *personalization* provides the competitive edge. The more personal the approach, the higher the response rate and the larger the gift. Clearly, the face-to-face appeal is the best solicitation approach. However, for large groups of donors or prospects about whom little is known—people on a rented list, for instance—the face-to-face solicitation process is out of the question. Here, direct mail may be the most viable, cost-effective option. But what other choices are available? Consider small to medium previous donors or persons with a known affinity for your cause or organization. How do we reach this "mass" market in the most effective and most personal way possible? More and more often, the answer to that question is "by phone."

In recent years, the phone has proved to be one of the most profitable tools of fund-raising. However, the methods by which the phone is used in the overall appeal process are almost as varied as the institutions and causes using it. For new and senior fund-raisers alike, the options can be mind-boggling. What exactly are the alternatives and under what circumstances might we select one over another?

The Phonathon

By definition, phonathons are fund-raising efforts in which volunteers solicit gifts or pledges by telephone. They are relatively inexpensive and uncomplicated, and they permit personal contact with a large number of people over a short period of time. Based on direct response techniques, they are used most frequently to make advance calls on special gift club prospects, to wrap up annual appeal efforts, or to conclude a capital or other special campaign. The phonathons also offer a way to generate goodwill about the institution from coast to coast. They have proved to be a successful form of fund-raising, capable of outdoing traditional mass solicitation techniques, such as direct mail, by as much as one hundred to one.

There is no question that the phonathon is an especially effective solicitation method when the caller knows the prospect or shares some association in common.

Generally staffed by volunteer callers, phonathons lend themselves particularly well to the educational setting where an in-house base of callers is found. Alumni and parents already know about the school or college and are often pleased to receive a call enabling them to ask specific questions and renew warm feelings of association with the institution. When student volunteers are used, the phonathon offers a wonderful opportunity to groom a cadre of enthusiastic and giving-conscious alumni. Any other type of nonprofit organization can also give the volunteer caller an opportunity to serve.

While phonathons are still among the least advanced methods of personalizing the appeal process, success does depend in some measure on careful planning, monitoring, and follow-up. The key ingredients for a successful phonathon include

1. *Planning and preparation.*   This means researching phone numbers, preparing prospect cards and report forms, designing and printing the follow-up mailing pieces.

2. *Location.*   A place, preferably free of charge, with ample office space and phones. The type of phone service available will help in making decisions about the wisdom and cost effectiveness of long-distance calling. In some instances, it may be advisable to arrange phonathons on a regional basis.

3. *Solicitors.*   A dependable group of capable and enthusiastic callers. These people may be volunteers or, in some instances, paid participants.

4. *Follow-up.*   A prompt follow-up mailing should be sent within a day of the phone call.

Volumes have been written on the how-to's of phonathons, and samples of prospect cards, mailing packages, report forms, scripts, and so forth abound. Any and all of this material is worth examining by those planning a phonathon. But what are the factors that might suggest the wisdom of a phonathon in the first place?

If the following circumstances apply, a phonathon is probably worth your consideration:

1. You are interested in reaching a constituency who already has some knowledge about your cause or institution and a sense of loyalty to it.

2. You are raising funds for a purpose with which the prospects are already familiar, or one which can be explained in a brief introductory statement on the phone.

3. You have a willing group of volunteers.

4. You do not wish to commit yourself to more than a month of weekday evening calls. Or, the number of people you really want to reach by phone is small enough to be contacted within that amount of time.

In conducting a phonathon, a major investment of time and energy is demanded of staff members in planning, recruiting volunteers, and administering the program. Working full days and running phonathons at night is a practical impossibility over any extended period of time.

In summary, the successful phonathon strengthens relationships with members of your organization's "family"; it enables you to reach a lot of people in a short amount of time; it is financially productive, and the out-of-pocket costs are relatively low; and, most important, it's *personal.*

Telemarketing

Phonathons, in actuality, are a form of telemarketing. However, as technology has become more sophisticated, so has terminology. Today, telemarketing generally implies a serious focus on the marketing aspects of the task. It means combining professional marketing and communication techniques in a variety of ways to sell products or services or even to raise funds. It is a sophisticated communications tool, and can be used by professionals representing of all kinds of nonprofit organizations to gain support.

Telemarketing is, however, often described as a "sales tool," and with good reason. In the case of direct mail, there is no real way of knowing whether the customer is interested in the product in the first place, and customer feedback is limited to returning a reply card (and check). Mail which arrives at a person's home and sits passively on the desk does nothing to press a response, elicit concerns or objections, or communicate personally in any way with the recipient. A phone call, on the other hand, as sales companies across the country will assure you, commands attention. It is far more difficult to ignore. A phone call is more personal and enables the caller to make the pitch, answer questions, and counter objections—in short, to make the "sale."

The five key steps in conducting a telemarketing campaign are

1. Establish the objective.
2. Conduct a market test.
3. Select and prepare personnel.
4. Decide on the quota for each caller (usually the number of calls to be made within a particular time period).
5. Determine a means of evaluating the success of the program

Telemarketing is more expensive than direct mail and usually more expensive than the phonathon. However, the rate of return can be rewarding, and it can be used successfully in concert with other fund-raising techniques.

Telemarketing can be used to test a market group much faster than direct mail. It can raise money, find new subscribers, sell tickets, and build a personal bridge between the organization and the prospect or donor.

Today, a wide variety of institutions and agencies use telemarketing techniques with enormous success. Educational institutions use it to raise money for everything from annual campaigns to capital campaigns to creating endowment funds; hospitals use it to solicit funds for new wings and new services and to promote special events; arts and cultural organizations use it to raise money, find new subscribers, and sell tickets. Significantly, telemarketing is used much more effectively than phonathons to find new donors for NPOs of all kinds.

The boldest organizations are using telemarketing for large donor acquisition campaigns. Because of the magnitude of the task, it is generally impossible to use volunteer callers. Thus a paid staff must be recruited. Because this staff may have little familiarity with the cause, training is vital and adherence to a script may be a necessity. The nature of the job requires cheerfulness and enthusiasm. It is also repetitive. Most workers cannot be expected to be effective for more than 4 hours a day. When using hired workers, not related in any way to the cause, some organizations have found that a taped message is a great way to carry the burden of the sales pitch. The caller, upon reaching the prospect, asks whether he is willing to listen to a short, recorded message from the president or other respected representative of the cause. When the tape ends, the caller returns to the line to conclude the "sale."

How do you decide whether to conduct a telemarketing campaign? Some of the factors that would influence that decision would be the following: (1) You need to reach a *lot* of people, (2) You have a large number of LYBUNTs (people who gave Last Year But Not This year) and SYBUNTs (people who gave Some Years But Not This year), (3) You need to find many new subscribers or donors, and there is a reasonably natural constituency from which they may be found, (4) Your primary objective is donor *acquisition*. An intense cultivation effort is not the priority.

The Telephone-Mail Campaign

The object of any appeal program is to elicit a response. The more letters that are mailed, the more phone calls that are made, the bigger and better the response is likely to be. Therefore as fund-raising professionals examine the components of a successful telemarketing effort, they ask themselves tougher and tougher questions about just what it is that will produce the most positive results. What kind of process goes beyond a massive telephone sales effort?

The answer to this question is the "telephone-mail campaign"—a fund-raising technique created by IDC, a fund-raising consulting firm. Unlike direct response techniques which has been the focus of this chapter so far, this process is aimed at truly *cultivating* donors and constituent prospects for long-term support.

One of the most creative innovations in the development field, the telephone-mail campaign is more than merely a combination of mailings and telephone solicitation. It is based on and employs face-to-face solicitation techniques. It is a highly specialized process which makes it possible to appeal on an extremely personal level to donors and never-givers who often once heard from the organization only by mail. Just how are face-to-face solicitation methods employed?

To answer this question, we must look at precisely what the steps are in the face-to-face solicitation process. The first step is to identify the prospects. The second is to evaluate them and decide how much to request them to give. Third is to develop and implement a plan for soliciting them, a plan which includes a cultivation process. The final step is to make an appointment, present the case, and then follow up until the prospect reaches a decision.

The telephone-mail campaign can do all this through a highly orchestrated effort involving serious prospect research and evaluation, a series of well-prepared letters, and timely phone calls. First communications are by mail, with a very brief note over the signature of the organization's chief executive officer, to get the prospect's attention. This is followed by *a long letter* that states the case, relates the experience of the prospect to the institution's needs, and involves the prospect in the solicitation process.

The call comes within a week from a highly trained, paid caller who ideally has an identifiable relationship with the calling institution. This phone conversation is not simply a "pitch"—it is a dialogue based around questions that cannot be answered with a yes or a no. The questions elicit feelings and attitudes. The purpose of the call is not just to make contact with the prospect, but to seek a *decision* from him.

The results of this program have proved remarkable. Never-givers give. Small donors increase their gifts. Lapsed donors renew. Some small donors become major donors. It must be pointed out, however, that to be successful over the long haul, a highly effective system of pledge-payment reminders must be in place.

Under what conditions might a sophisticated telephone-mail campaign such as this be considered? (1) You wish to reach a large number of prospective donors who have a known relationship with the soliciting organization (this program is generally not cost-effective for cold acquisition). (2) You wish to give the needs of the prospect major consideration. (3) You are not interested simply in reaching the largest possible number of prospects within a given period of time; you are interested in cultivating prospects. (4) You are prepared to hire paid callers and probably enlist the services of an outside firm to prepare for and manage the campaign. (5) You are capable of or are willing to invest in the components which are required in this technically advanced process. (6) You are committed to the concept of employing face-to-face solicitation techniques to reach a mass market. You truly want that very important prospective donor to know just how important she or he really is.

In Summary

Short of face-to-face solicitation, *nothing* is more effective in fund-raising than using the telephone, especially when you combine it with the *right* mailings. The keys to success are (1) setting your goals and objectives, (2) deciding on a strategy to achieve them, (3) carefully *planning* every step, and (4) following up meticulously.

Use to full advantage the competitive edge that this degree of personalization affords and do not diminish it by making common errors: Do not use high-pressure, coercive sales tactics. Avoid calling at inconsiderate hours. Do your homework and know as much as possible about your prospect. Listen carefully to what your prospect has to say. Above all, remember that the person on the other end of the line is a *person* whose feelings, privacy, and time command respect. Using the phone wisely, you have every possible chance to gain that prospect's involvement and commitment. Why? Because, short of face-to-face solicitation, a phone call is as *personal* as you can get!

29

Annual Giving Programs

James L. Maxwell

Director, Development & Public Relations Houston Metropolitan Ministries

Purpose

The annual giving campaign is the "life blood" of most nonprofit organizations (NPOs). It serves not only to produce needed revenue but also can involve the volunteer and donor in a manner which ensures their continued interest and involvement. If properly managed, the annual campaign ensures a regular base of support with growth potential from the donors. Effective publicity and special events can create a climate for annual support and can also bring a greater understanding of the purpose of the organization to the general public.

The annual operating campaign shares many basic organizational principles with endowment and capital campaigns: a need for planning, organization, effective use of volunteers, a clearly defined sense of purpose and goals (a "case statement"), a timetable, community understanding, volunteer commitment, and trained professional staff.

Planning

Probably no ingredient is as essential for a successful operating campaign as planning. Job descriptions for staff and volunteers, a timetable, and goals should be expressed in writing.

A campaign plan contains objectives, timetables, and an assignment of responsibilities. The plan will ensure that volunteers and staff have a total understanding of their respective assignments. The timetable will ensure that the campaign stays on schedule. An abbreviated planning guide would look something like the following:

Week ending 3/1
Responsibility: *Director of Development*

Present recommended goal to development committee.

Week ending 3/8   Meet with potential campaign chair.
Responsibility: *President*

Week ending 3/15   Begin expanding lists for direct mail cam-
Responsibility: *Development staff*   paign; work on campaign brochure with
                                         printer.

Organization

The organization of an annual fund campaign varies depending on the sophistication of previous campaigns and the nature, scope, and staffing of the institution. A
national organization may depend primarily on direct mail for its annual income.
A communitywide campaign may include every known aspect of fund-raising
from direct mail to in-person solicitation of major prospects, special events, corporate solicitation, proposals to foundations, and door-to-door appeals.

An ideal annual operating fund organization begins with a carefully selected
board of directors—a volunteer governing group which reflects the diversity of the
community and the special requirements of the organization's objectives. The
board should have a standing committee entrusted with the institutional funding
which oversees the agency's development operation. A major function of the committee is the recommendation of (and assistance in securing) an annual operating
fund chairperson. Usually the committee proposes the choice, and the president
does the appointing with the approval of the board. The development committee
also recommends the goal for the campaign to the board for approval.

The campaign chairperson recruits and appoints the required campaign leadership. Ideally there would be a leader for each prospect category: major gifts, corporate gifts, foundations, special events, service organizations, and so on. Other
often desirable positions include publicity chairperson, campaign treasurer, and a
vice chair.

Good organization mandates a job description for each key leader. Such a description proves valuable in the recruitment of the volunteer. A good job description will include a timetable for each responsibility, as indicated below:

By January 2   Appoint major corporate chair
By January 15   Appoint individuals chair
By February 1   Meeting of all key chairpersons for planning session

Each individual chairperson is given a job description by the general chair that
outlines the number of committee members to be recruited, the committee's goal,
and a calendar for completing each assignment.

The number of committee members required can be determined by the number
of prospects in the category for which the committee is responsible. If fifty businesses have been targeted for solicitation, and the volunteers will accept as many
as ten prospects each for solicitation, then five or more committee members will be
needed. Previous experience and the level of commitment of the volunteers will
guide one in assessing the number of committee members.

Once the committee is organized, members should be allowed to choose their
assignments based upon their personal relationships or ability to influence a contributor. By knowing the prospect personally, the solicitor will understand the
most effective means of solicitation, i.e., a presentation at lunch, a personal visit, a
letter, or a call. Each prospective donor is unique; therefore personal relationships
between solicitor and prospect will indicate in most cases the most effective manner for the solicitation.

Campaign Growth and Development

The campaign for annual operating funds may begin with as simple an organization as a few volunteers agreeing to solicit their acquaintances for institutional support. As volunteer involvement increases, the campaign may be divided into major individual prospects and major corporate prospects. This division can be expanded by dividing individuals into major and lesser prospects, with emphasis given to the major potential donors. The business community can be divided into major corporations and businesses. Campaigns can also be divided into geographical areas with separate individual and business committees for each area. The organizational objective is to secure as personal a solicitation as possible on a priority prospect basis.

Components of the Annual Giving Campaign

Direct Mail

Prospecting by direct mail is a highly effective means of identifying new donors. Professional direct mail firms and consultants offer a variety of services to the nonprofit organization. For those who are willing to invest in prospecting, numbers of new donors can be secured. However, it should be noted that this is often an investment that produces results over a period of time and requires an initial investment of resources. A more limited form of prospecting is the acquisition of lists of donors from similar organizations in one's community, with form letters sent over the signature of the campaign chair or agency president. Although the section of this chapter concerned with prospect solicitation stresses a very personal approach, all donors and prospects should be solicited annually at least, and this can be effected by a letter of appeal should the volunteer force be too small for a planned, personal approach.

Memorial and "In Honor of..." Gifts

Annual contributions can be secured through the effective marketing of a memorial and "in honor of..." program. In the simplest terms, this means that the organization lets its public know that memorial and "in honor of..." gifts are welcomed and acknowledged appropriately. Listing of such gifts in the agency's newsletter or other publication further communicates the importance of these kinds of gifts. Continued emphasis on these programs will mean increased awareness and increased giving with limited expenses and minimal volunteer or organizational requirements.

Special Events

A fund-raising event can be the "icing on the cake" of the annual campaign. It should be planned to follow the personal solicitation of all prospects so that general annual giving will not be substituted for paid attendance at galas, auctions, balls, etc. Events should be tailored with so much appeal that in addition to the annual gift, a donor will elect to support the organization further by participating in the special event. Special events are important means of securing an additional gift from regular contributors, but they are also an opportunity to appeal to a wider audience, including those who would not necessarily support the organization's other appeals. An agency can have a number of special events annually if they are carefully planned as to timing and for their appeal to diverse groups. That is, a group can host a black-tie ball, a walkathon, and a designer's show house and ostensibly reach a varying group of prospects.

Memberships and Membership Program Group

Annual giving can also be promoted through an every-year membership. Often the membership offers specific tangible benefits such as free admittance to a museum. Other more peripheral offerings are newsletter subscriptions, annual reports and annual dinner (meeting) invitations, discounts on tickets to performing arts presentations, and similar enticements. Not to be overlooked is the "membership card," which promotes a feeling of belonging and which is often a special motivator to the prospect.

Special membership or donor program groups are highly successful entities for sustained annual giving. These include associate programs, where a specific fee is required for membership and the member receives very special benefits for belonging, such as programs tailored to the group's interests and available only through membership. Memberships are renewed each year through billing, and the members are considered prospects for special project gifts and levels of support higher than and in addition to the program dues.

Membership Campaign Budgets and Costs

It is axiomatic that it takes money to make (or raise) money. A qualified development professional or counsel is a wise investment for any nonprofit organization. Professional expertise in development can often result in the savings of more dollars than the compensation of the staff. The effective fund-raising executive is an institutional development specialist. The development officer will not only recommend policies and procedures that will benefit the institution's long-range growth but also will make possible through organizational expertise and skills the most productive volunteer employment. It is important that all campaign budgets be prepared and approved in advance for such items as publications, postage, extra clerical support, telephones, and counsel. Special events should have a separate budget. The budget will vary depending upon a range of factors, including length of the campaign, history of the organization's fund-raising (start-up campaign costs are often much higher than ongoing campaign expenses), geographical area to be covered, nature of the appeal, and so on. It cannot be stressed too strongly that the campaign budget is part of the blueprint for building annual support and therefore should be carefully planned.

Campaign Communications

Good communications, both internal and external, are as important to a campaign's success as any other component. Written job descriptions, a carefully planned and written campaign calendar, and timely progress reports are essential. In addition to written reports from the chairperson, campaign progress can be communicated through the institutional newsletter, a special campaign newsletter, and news items to the media. Campaign report functions can also be effective. A kickoff for the campaign can produce a *team spirit* and be a focus for media publicity. Regular report luncheons or meetings serve to keep the key volunteers informed and also stimulate peer group interaction and stimulus. These sessions often uncover problem areas which can be addressed, thereby ensuring that the campaign stays on target.

Records and Reporting

Good records of donors and prospects are the backbone of successful annual campaigns. Almost any information about a donor or prospect can be beneficial in developing the support sought. Potential support and possible levels of giving can be assessed through such valuable data as personal hobbies, clubs and memberships, schools, religious affiliation, corporate relations, and support of other organizations.

The very basic requirement of record keeping is to note the donor's gift amount, date made, and solicitor. The organization's staffing and capabilities together with information required will dictate how extensive additional information is recorded. Computerization is highly desirable where possible.

At a minimum, the solicitor should receive reports which indicate the results of their efforts. Preferably progress reports will be sent at intervals to provide information for follow-up. Records and reporting are facets of careful communication needed for good campaign management.

Final Note

All campaigns are people-oriented; therefore, no two campaigns are alike. Common sense, experience, and, most of all, a genuine respect and appreciation for the donor and the volunteer participant are more important than any other factor.

30

Capital Fund Appeals

James L. Richardson, Jr.

Executive Vice President, Community Service Bureau, Inc.

Introduction

In early America, people gave their money and donated their time and labor to build public structures like churches, schools, and meeting halls. Americans still show their generosity today, but with a multiplicity of financing options and needs which seem to support fund-raising as literally being built around the capital fund appeal.

The sheer number of private institutions in the country which have arisen as a result of this uniquely American philanthropy continue to validate a capital fund appeal, simply stated, as a campaign to acquire and utilize private funds to

1. Build structures
2. Improve structures
3. Purchase furnishings and equipment
4. Provide a permanent endowment fund to enrich programs

In higher education, there is a new generation of fund appeals which are somewhat different from traditional capital fund appeals of the past. These "major campaigns" or "major development programs" have become complex, all-inclusive events taking place every decade (or more frequently) at many American colleges and universities. They encompass scholarships, fellowships, and other endowment needs, planned giving, and even annual operating needs in some instances—programs which seemingly have been designed to offer everyone a way and a reason to give. Even in such a nontraditional appeal, "capital" funding continues to be the basis for the integrity of the overall program thrust.

In almost all other types of nonprofit institutions and organizations, such as hospitals and medical centers, the arts, social welfare organizations, and others which improve the "quality of life" in cities throughout this country, the straightforward, if infrequent, capital fund appeal remains the dominant fund-raising mechanism. There is no reason to expect any sudden change in this trend as long as there continues to be a significant number of potentially large givers who relate to capital giving, which is directed toward the purchase or creation of something tangible and on which a donor's name can be placed for posterity.

A successful capital or major gifts appeal occurs at a time in which demand for resources has accumulated to the point where it is appropriate to focus on those needs. It occurs in consonance with all other giving efforts both annual and planned. A capital appeal requires sharpness, organization, and a tightly held schedule in order to maintain the level of leadership interest necessary to attract gifts required to meet the goals.

Benefits

The undertaking of the capital development program every 10 years or so is considered by most financial and fund development professionals to be of major importance. It helps to ensure the continued health and viability of the nonprofit organization or institution. It also provides the unique opportunity to take a fresh and creative look at all aspects of the nonprofit organization's operations in the early stages of planning. The considerable amount of self-analysis and self-evaluation that must be done in determining needs, priorities, and institutional readiness for a major, capital fund-raising effort provides many benefits including:

1. Creating greater awareness, understanding and knowledge about the organization and its services throughout the area it serves, establishing the real value of the organization to its constituency or community

2. Establishing patterns that raise the levels of all giving

3. Broadening of the base of support as it seeks and encourages financial support from various constituents—businesses, foundations, and individuals—who may have never before supported the organization

4. Attracting and involving many new business and civic leaders in the organization's programs and activities, many of whom will continue to support the organization long after their leadership and financial commitments to the capital development program have been concluded

5. Maximizing the amount of dollars to be provided through a fund-raising goal larger in size than several annual operating fund campaign goals

6. Establishing schedules and deadlines so essential in motivating volunteers

7. Establishing, if directed properly, a base for immediate as well as long-range planned gifts

8. Helping, in practically every instance, to increase the flow of annual and other financial support.

The many benefits to be derived from a capital development program are simply too important for any nonprofit organization or institution to overlook if it wishes to ensure a healthy future and continued standing in its community.

The Planning Stage

The timing of a capital development program is a function of institutional or organizational vitality, readiness, and the existence of a favorable fund-raising climate. Simple need is incidental since it is safe to assume that capital needs always exist to some degree. The greater the urgency and degree, of course, the greater the case for a capital fund development program.

A thorough, internal self-analysis is vital because a capital fund development program starts from within. In developing a strong case, key persons in the organization or institution must become involved in identifying challenging needs and any contacts or connections that result in potential donors. The organization's key people include:

1. *Universities and colleges.* Members of the board or trustees, administration, faculty and staff, alumni, and close friends

2. *Hospitals.* Trustees or board members, medical staff, administration, and employees

3. *Other organizations or institutions.* The management, volunteer leaders, and the membership

These are people who must also be challenged to give commensurate with their ability to do so. Because the pattern of giving always starts from within, lay leaders must realize that if new patterns of giving are necessary to reach the goal, it must start with them.

Today, almost all nonprofit organizations undertake long-range planning to ensure continued viability. Most plans are for 5, 10, or 15 years; however, a few of the more ambitious organizations will project 20 to 25 years into the future. It is important to remember some of the factors which must be considered in formulating a long-range plan:

1. An analysis of the geographic and socioeconomic characteristics within the area of service for the previous 10 to 15 years and ahead for the period covered by the plan

2. An analysis of the organization's services and programs over the same periods to determine what, if any, impact the changes in characteristics may have had or can be projected to have

3. An analysis of all available data from local and area chambers of commerce and from city, county, state, and federal planning agencies to help project future geographic and socioeconomic changes within the area of service

4. A self-analysis and self-evaluation of current programs and services to combine with the findings and conclusions from earlier analyses in forming the basis for projecting program needs and priorities over the next 5 or, preferably, 10 years

The long-range plan establishes

1. The programs and services necessary to fulfill the organization's mission in future years

2. The priorities of these in order to arrive at a chronology for initiation and completion

3. The volunteers and staff to support these services and programs

4. The capital equipment and structures needed to provide the optimum-size program of service

5. An estimate of the cost of capital improvements, new construction, and of new

and replacement equipment through the final year of the long-range plan. This is a definite must because when you build only to meet immediate needs, your physical facilities may be out of date and inadequate by the time they are completed. By providing for future capital needs at the outset, certain cost savings will be realized over the build-as-needed concept. Adequate estimates of potential increases in cost are essential because of the payout inherent in pledges.

A capital development program, to be successful, must encompass long-range planning. The better developed the long-range plan, the better the "case" for the capital development program. For this reason, long-range plans should constantly be updated and never be allowed to go longer than 18 months without review and modification.

Translating the long-range plan into a capital fund appeal requires the skill of a unique professional, one with broad and diversified experience in fund-raising, yet one with specialized skills and knowledge in project or program development for a specific nonprofit field. While many nonprofit fields have planning consultants who specialize in long-range planning, few of them can translate capital needs into a fund-raising effort. The programmatically mature nonprofit organization recognizes the need to secure the services of a professional fund development firm on a consulting arrangement to provide early advice and counsel to the board and administrative management, and to begin laying the groundwork for a successful capital development program.

Institutional vitality is the first quality required of a nonprofit organization hoping to undertake a successful capital development program. It is expressed by

1. A lively sense of mission and purpose, understood and subscribed to inside and outside the organization

2. Services and programs that clearly support the mission

3. Committed volunteer leadership of the highest caliber

4. A talented, enthusiastic staff to provide services and operate the programs

5. A market made of people needing and willing to subscribe to these services and programs

Once institutional vitality is confirmed, the long-range plan is interpreted into the form of a capital development program by a fund development specialist, knowledgeable and attuned to the development of facts and figures which authenticate the urgency of the stated capital needs of the long-range plan. Counsel's services will ensure that the strongest and most salable "case" will be developed and that every reason which might impel someone to give has been considered.

In its simplest terms, the case statement is the "logical" statement of purpose of a cause and the reasons for contributing to that cause. It is not sufficient to indicate that the institution *needs* dollars; the need is presumed in developing the leadership and prospects. It can be further presumed that the leadership and the prospects are aware of *many* circumstances which need support. The institution should be addressing problems that relate to a human concern that is bigger and more significant than the ability of the institution to resolve without major support. This promises the most basic benefit, a benefit to people, and the best of both worlds, a benefit to the donor and to the institution.

1. What is it for which the institution is seeking financial support?

2. Why the institution deserves support, and what would it accomplish with that support?

3. To whom will the benefits of the support accrue?

4. What difference will it make if the institution does or does not get the funds and therefore does or does not undertake its programs?

In addition, practical questions must be addressed, such as

1. How much money must be raised, and is this amount feasible?
2. Is it *enough* money?
3. When does the program begin and end?
4. What will be the outcome, and how will it be demonstrated, measured, and quantified?
5. What is the cost-benefit ratio?

Finally, the question has to be addressed as to what is in it for the prospect if he or she, or the corporation or foundation, becomes a donor. Certainly, the answer is not an income tax deduction which simply is a vehicle by which the donor, other than the foundation, can express interest and support. There has to be a *quid pro quo,* some exchange that will make the proposal one that has a good chance of being accepted and funded. Such exchanges may include any of the following:

1. The donor sees something accomplished that he or she wants accomplished.
2. The donor's interests, whatever they may be, are advanced.
3. Perhaps because of the donor's support the community addressed by the proposal turns out to be a better community.
4. Recognition.
5. Joining with others who are both important and supportive.
6. Satisfaction of being a solver of problems.
7. Significance accrues to the donor by his or her support.

Recognizing that the case statement only ultimately is transposed into a written proposal or brochure will assist in determining that the case statement addresses

1. Problems for which the institution is concerned and a proposed solution
2. The important dimensions of the human element to be supported
3. The needs, problems, conditions, and other factors surrounding the community to be served
4. Some comparison with other similar institutions to provide potential donors with a measure
5. The individually priced components of the case
6. Measurability followed closely by evaluation
7. The difference to be made by the success of the program
8. The competency of those who will undertake the program—given the funding—and why the particular institution should be the one
9. How all the above relates to the problems which are the institution's overriding concern
10. What is available to the donor

This last question makes it imperative to know who the donors *will* be and *could* be with little thought given to who they *should* be. (Who they should be is often a value judgment that does *not* translate into support.) This is a perfect opportunity for broadening the constituency of support beyond a small, but closely related group of supporters. If the need is strong enough and can be successfully stated, then the campaign has some expectation of success.

However the case statement ultimately is defined, it becomes both an inside and outside document available for use by the leadership of the campaign and by the institution, and is ultimately articulated to the broader giving community. It is at this point that it is translated not only into campaign brochures but into virtually all the literature and communications undertaken by the institution.

The Feasibility Study

If the elements of the capital development program have been defined, the initial case has been developed to document the need, the institutional vitality has been confirmed, and the amount of funds required from all sources of financing has been estimated; then, it is time to "test" the market for a capital fund appeal.

The primary tests involve

1. Whether a favorable fund-raising climate exists or whether it can be developed
2. Institutional readiness for launching a capital fund appeal
3. The establishment of the most ambitious, yet still realistic, goal for a capital development program to fulfill the maximum needs of the long-range plan

In order to accomplish these tests, the nonprofit organization should have a development program study done by a competent outside professional. An independent external source is able to operate on higher levels than an internal staff and can achieve greater candor during interviews. Such a study process will be more objective and its conclusions less biased. The development study, although similar to a marketing feasibility study for a commercial product or service, is more comprehensive, and, more importantly, it literally is the selling phase of the program under study. Each interview, when conducted by persons trained in this technique, becomes an important public relations event for the client organization involved.

When properly conducted, the development study will

1. Identify the amount of money which can be raised; thereby indicating what is feasible and reasonable for a program goal
2. Identify potential program leaders as well as classify them into potential levels of leadership
3. Lay the initial groundwork for recruiting the strongest leadership from those identified
4. Pinpoint potential sources of funds
5. Confirm both the strong and weak points of the initial case and indicate alternatives which would serve to strengthen the appeal
6. Establish a general blueprint for the program, including time and cost requirements
7. Appropriately condition those most closely associated with the organization to their special responsibility in helping to create a favorable climate for the program by setting a strong early pattern of support

The development study provides the best single vehicle from which to assess the potential for a successful capital development program on the basis of the strength of the organization and its case, its leadership, and its constituency. The time required to do the study will vary depending on the type of organization or institution involved, the area served, the size and location of the constituency, the type of service provided, and so on. When the future is at stake, one thing should be kept in mind at all times: The proper amount of time must be allocated to do the job right.

Once the climate has been deemed favorable for a capital development program through a study, the organization is ready to enter into the final stages of readiness.

The Organizational Stage

Once the development study is accepted by the client organization and they are ready to launch the program, the first and most important step is to prepare a plan. The plan includes schedules of events, meetings, and deadlines—all of which are important in motivating volunteers. The "case statement" is the basic source document from which all future program material and information will be developed.

There then are two primary things which must be in a state of readiness prior to launching a capital development program. They are

1. *Processes.* The mechanical aspects of the program from which prospects evolve and which carry through to the final stage of receipt and acknowledgment of the individual gift. These systems must be proven and must be functioning at the start of the program to avoid any possible errors or delays which could cause a loss of momentum or otherwise severly cripple the fund-raising effort.

2. *People.* The most important element in any program. The program's volunteer and staff leadership must be able and willing, and they must be provided with experienced direction and advice by a professional in fund development. A lack of readiness here will mean that the organization might not be able to sustain a major campaign, regardless of the strength and vitality of the nonprofit organization or institution.

Let us look at some of the steps in organizing a program to the point of being ready to go. There are, of course, other steps and a considerable amount of detail omitted from the following list; however, the main steps include

1. Recruiting the top program leader, using the findings from the development program study and the influence from among the organization's board and administration. As it is very important that this person must represent top influential leadership among the constituency or the community, it goes without saying that you do not *elect* people to the top positions of leadership in a capital fund program: They must be carefully handpicked!
2. Selecting a location for the program office which is convenient to the program chairperson.
3. Beginning the processes of research to build a prospect list and develop the proper mechanisms for the most effective solicitation of the prospects. Whether there is already an identified constituency, the size of the community or the service area, the availability of records, the amount of updating necessary, and innumerable other factors will dictate the amount of time required in this stage. And, it cannot be stressed too strongly the fact that time must be taken to develop the mechanisms and the list right in order to reduce the risk of serious errors which are commonly inherent in rushed projects. The misspelling or wrong arrangement of a name can cost the program potential gifts. There is a

sanctity to the proper spelling of a name. The rule is, "check, double-check, and when you are absolutely positive, recheck once again."

4. While developing the prospect list, the influence of the leadership and the program chairperson, and of the organization's board, are used to recruit a sizable *development council* or *board of development* composed of the top business and civic leaders within the area of service of the organization. The size of this group will vary, depending upon the size and economic composition of the community or area of service. Often, the number will range from about 100 up to as many as 250 or 300. By agreeing to serve, these people have made a commitment to work and support the program.

5. At this point, the various levels of solicitation for the program are structured. There are three main factors to consider in determining the number of levels to be established for a program: (1) the sizes of individual gifts needed for success, (2) the number needed of each size, and (3) the most effective combination of the two to achieve certain rule-of-thumb percentage factors used by professional development counselors in dividing the campaign into manageable "sections" or "divisions." The function of each is more important than its name. Below is a listing of what the typical rationale might be on an average capital development program in a medium-size city in the heartland of the United States:

   a. As a rule of thumb, expect that 80 to 90 percent of the goal will come from 10 to 20 percent of the prospects. This group of prospects will become our "lead" division and will be the first launched. Of course, percentages and numbers may vary with the depth of prospecting.

   b. On most major capital efforts, active prospects are limited to those capable of giving gifts of $500 or more, and all others will be solicited last through a "clean-up" effort such as direct mail or telephone solicitation.

   c. In the depth of our example, the number of prospects might be 1000 to 1500. Therefore, it would not be unusual to expect in the range of 100 prospects for large, key gifts to set the pace for the effort. These key prospects will be composed of individuals, businesses, and foundations; therefore, an additional breakdown could be effective.

   d. As for the remaining 80 to 90 percent of the prospects from which the rest of the goal will come, this can be broken into two divisions: a "middle" range of givers who would receive a more personalized asking approach and a "lower" range. The larger number of remaining prospects will fall into the last category. The last division is optional, and like many other factors, can only be decided as it is approached, since each community and fund appeal are distinctively different.

   e. Since we touched on the aspects of leadership, let me say here that the leaders of these divisions (or of any to be formed later) should be picked from those in the "power" structure in much the same manner as was the program chairperson, and as each is enlisted, each one becomes part of the leadership "group" who selects and recruits the next. The source of these leaders might be the "council" or "board" formed earlier.

   f. In working prospects within the divisions, I like to use what I call, "the rule of fives" (yet, I know of others who opt for "tens" or other numbers in between). Use whatever is comfortable and manageable, but I strongly recommend no more than ten. Example: Assume a base of 250 prospects. Using the rule of fives, I would enlist 2 division chairpersons, each of whom would enlist 5 team captains; each team captain would then enlist 5 workers, making a total of 50 workers to cover the 250 prospects. Again, the situation dictates the need and form.

6. While structuring and organizing the various divisions in a program, do a prospect "evaluation," or "rating." This evaluation is a must in providing volunteer

workers with a definite amount to ask of prospects. It is also a basic prerequisite before calling on prospects and must be done with care to ensure that ratings are made on "peer levels" within the leadership structure. Temporary rating committees, composed of previously rated volunteer leaders, can be most effective in rating those on their peer level. When a division's organization is completed, so will be the ratings of all prospects in that division.

7. From the time the doors of the program office are opened, all the necessary forms and procedures to attract, receive, and confirm gifts have been developed and finalized. These are the "mechanisms," and they contribute to putting the "processes" for the program in readiness. The case for the program has been honed, fine-tuned, and finalized. It has been "packaged" into various printed and other visual forms for use in orientation of leadership and volunteer workers and in cultivation of prospects.

8. Finally, it is time to blend people with processes. At this stage, the leaders and workers have become more than dedicated advocates of the organization's cause. They are indoctrinated into the reasons and needs for the program at hand, thereby becoming informed advocates. They must be provided with all the support material and information necessary to help them do their jobs in the most effective manner. Once this stage of readiness is complete, the capital development program is on *go.*

Motivating Labor Resources

Major capital development programs are goal-and deadline-oriented. These are most effective devices in motivating program leaders and volunteer workers.

Too many internal development people, and even a few veteran professionals, minimize the need for consistent, periodic campaign meetings. Most of the time, the underlying reason for this is an unwillingness to put forth the effort; however, some simply have never grasped the dynamics of meetings and planned events. You need a series of serious deadlines to convince your leadership of the importance of the appeal and to present an appropriately businesslike approach which they can respect—dates against which you can (1) press for action, (2) set intermediate goals, and (3) aim for fresh targets just ahead. Meetings also gain sustained program visibility through their publicity activities.

Planned events, which are things other than program meetings, are important as they keep the *good talk* and *good thoughts* flowing about the organization while the program is under way, helping to create and to maintain a favorable fund-raising climate.

There should be a continuous flow of written information about the program and its progress going to the leaders and volunteer workers. Summaries of meetings to those who could not attend; notices of forthcoming meetings and events; memos advising of the progress of program, division, or section or just urging the volunteer workers on—all can be important in the motivation of human resources.

Two main elements are involved in motivating program leaders and workers:

1. Interest

2. Enthusiasm

A high degree of both is necessary to sustain the momentum of a program. People have learned to deal with accident and disaster; yet they have found no easy cure for indifference and apathy. Momentum means keeping alive the feeling that the cause is relevant, important, and urgent. Of course, a sense of urgency brings on the feeling of pressure, which some people deplore; however, nothing worthwhile ever gets done without it.

The basic reasons people are motivated to support a nonprofit organization initially include

1. *Religion.*   For the fulfillment of spiritual and moral needs

2. *Education.*   To help the individual attain maximum potential and to help develop the brainpower and technology needed to run our businesses, industries, and government, driving our country ever forward

3. *Hospitals and health care.*   To protect our most valued possessions—good health and long life

4. *Civic and cultural.*   To enhance and enrich those things which add to the quality of our lives

5. *Human resources and welfare.*   As an expression of responsible citizenship and out of true humanitarian concerns

Some of the basic traits of human nature that motivate people, not only for financial support but also to provide volunteer service for fund development programs, include

1. Pride of association

2. Confidence in leadership

3. Desire for praiseworthy attainment

4. Personal recognition

5. Inner satisfaction

There are other traits of lesser importance, but these seem to be the most impelling when it comes to giving or raising philanthropic funds.

Strategy at Different Levels

As inflation continues to create real needs for additional capital to permit growth and ensure future viability, the competition for the private dollar gets keener. The nonprofit organizations and institutions which garner the greater share of philanthropic giving will be the ones which are the most aggressive and which develop the more sophisticated strategies and alternatives to identify and reach prospects and maximize giving.

Two very simple strategies are employed in securing the maximum gift from an interested qualified donor.

1. A pledge extended over a number of taxable years (3 to 5 years in most cases—more if needed from very substantial sources)

2. A planned giving committee consisting of persons who serve as financial advisors (trust officers of banks, CPAs, attorneys, insurance agents involved in estate planning, investment bankers or brokers and realtors) and who can provide guidelines for a better approach for immediate gifts in the form of appreciated properties, as well as gifts in the form of trusts, annuities, insurance, and bequests

Both means may give donors certain attractive tax advantages and permit them to give more money at less actual cost than could be done through a single, one-time gift.

Many other strategies can be employed in seeking gifts throughout the various strata of the program's organization; however, they are more specialized and apply only to specific groups or segments. When it comes to soliciting a prospect for a lofty or special portion of a capital fund appeal, experience dictates that some special type of presentation is needed. Foundations today almost always seem to require this type of approach, and many corporations and individuals are increasingly receptive only to this method of asking. The format should include

1. The problem

2. The proposal

3. The cost

4. The opportunity

Arthur Packard, when he was philanthropic secretary for John D. Rockefeller, Jr., was quoted as saying that "to escape the trivial image, the special presentation should be at least ten pages long; yet to avoid the risk of tedium, it should not go much beyond fifteen." Personally, I prefer a simple presentation in double-spaced copy, typed with adequate margins on a soft-colored paper and "packaged" in a simple, refined special cover or "jacket" rather than one in an avant-garde or elaborately formal layout or one that is so long that it seems to weigh importance by the pound. The special presentation should be delivered personally by the "right" person wherever possible with a cover letter of about one and one-half pages from someone involved in the program who could have some influence on the person or entity to which the presentation is directed.

In the campaign organization itself, there must be a definite order of asking. This might be called a strategy; the organization should think of it as standard operating procedure. The procedure is as follows:

1. Divisions should be launched and completed in a definite progression to ensure maximum impact and influence on level-to-level giving. Internal giving should be completed prior to going to external constituents or to the general public in order to show internal unity and belief in the capital campaign.

2. Volunteers at all levels should be already committed financially prior to asking others for their gifts. Our knowledge of human nature tells us that it is much easier and much more forceful to ask someone you know for a sizable gift if you yourself have already made one of the same size or larger.

Even in the capital funding effort, there is a place for direct mail appeals (which are discussed in another section). It would be inappropriate to try to reach every single person in the community or constituency through the capital campaign structure, yet among those who remain after removing "active" prospects to be solicited on a one-on-one basis, there is a significant amount of potential giving that might otherwise be lost unless some form of asking is presented to them. These people may be in this category for such reasons as distant geographical location, too small a rating, no previous expression of support, or any number of others.

Consider a theory evolved from the findings of two top psychiatrists which were discussed in *Designs for Fund-Raising*. It indicates there are two main things people want most:

1. To be sought

2. To be a worthwhile member of a worthwhile group

Accepting these to be truths, it is clear to see that a direct mail approach is a viable alternative as a cleanup technique at, or near, the end of the public appeal for funds. There is an art to this type of approach as you will note in other sections;

however, I would like to stress a few things here that should always be contained in a direct mail appeal:

1. Be brief and to the point: Explain the program quickly in letter form, not editorial form.
2. Personalize the asking in every way possible.
3. Ask for a specific gift.
4. Stress the urgency of the program.
5. Set forth a reasonable deadline.
6. Ask for immediate action and provide forms, return envelopes, or any other items that might make remitting a gift more convenient for the donor.
7. Send at least one follow-up letter containing news about the program's progress where a gift has not been received by the deadline stated in the initial letter. Later action or activities could spark interest not shown at the time of the first asking for funds. Experience proves that the third letter helps to obtain the maximum results from mail appeals.

Along with these techniques, I would say the most dominant element to consider at all levels is simply human psychology. It also helps to have knowledge in the dynamics of peer pressure.

Conclusions and Comments

In conclusion, let me say I still see capital fund appeals as the best, least expensive alternatives in financing capital equipment purchases, new construction, or capital improvements for nonprofit organizations and institutions. I do feel, however, that the capital fund appeal—especially in the field of higher education—will become an integral and prominent part of a unified "major" development program which will simultaneously seek capital gifts, annual gifts, and planned gifts. I also see these "new generation" fund appeals becoming states of a continuing development program, with each stage starting upon completion of the previous one, and with each having a new volunteer leadership team, a new set of objectives, and a new goal and closing deadline. I do see dollar goals becoming more realistic in view of the shortened stages demanded by the continuous development program and by the necessity to conclude each stage successfully so that the following stage can be launched under a favorable fund-raising climate.

Competition for private, philanthropic funds will continue to increase. It will be those nonprofit organizations which can prove their real value to their constituencies and communities and which maintain aggressive programs to attract philanthropic support that will garner the larger share of these funds in the future. As an example of this increased competition, both public and private colleges and universities today are deeply involved in seeking philanthropic support. Despite the merits of the liberal arts education, we find that many small liberal arts colleges are struggling for existence or have simply faded from the scene because they lack the aggressiveness to counter this keener competition. The leaders of business and industry are looking more and more toward our private and public institutions who produce the brainpower, technology, and technological skills needed to keep our society moving forward. Community colleges and junior colleges are rapidly growing more attractive to business and industry since these schools provide the technical and vocational education needed within a specific region or community and they are more actively seeking and getting increased philanthropic support. By the same token, as competition increases in the field of higher education, other nonprofit organizations—hospitals, medical centers, religious organizations, secondary schools, civic and cultural organizations, and a multitude of character-building, social, and welfare organizations—will have to take a more aggressive position in attracting philanthropic funds.

I also feel that the need for the professional fund-raising firm will increase because of the growing complexities and broader scope of fund-raising in the non-profit field. The combined talent and knowledge of an entire team of professionals can provide the nonprofit organization and institution with a more diversified, broader range of experience in fund development than could ever be amassed by a single organization, even if the exorbitant cost of such an internal staff could be justified. Such expertise and counsel can greatly enhance the work of an existing staff, as well as provide trustees and other key leaders with an assured objective view of the capital fund program. The many advantages of professional counsel are discussed in detail in other sections of this handbook.

A professional in the fund development and fund-raising field, such as myself, quickly develops a personal philosophy that serves as a guide in making decisions. I would like to share the personal philosophy, "The Reluctance to Ask," of the late J. O. Newberry, founder of Community Service Bureau, with the readers of this book in the hope that they may gain, as I have, from his experience:

> *I believe* that one of the greatest deterrents in our way of life is the reluctance to ask—to ask for what we need in terms of people, leadership and manpower, as well as money.
>
> *I believe* that equally obstructive is the tendency to say only those things that we think will please people, rather than saying the realistic things that need to be said.
>
> *I believe* that we must constantly improve our techniques to help make volunteers better salesmen of philanthropy, and we must constantly strive to help them conquer timidity and the reluctance to ask.
>
> *I believe* we can effectively prepare a volunteer up to the point of entering a prospect's door, but how he performs from that point depends on how proficient we have been in orientation and in training him to overcome the basic traits of human nature such as the reluctance to ask or to say what needs to be said.
>
> *I believe* that, in this more sophisticated society, we must be more knowledgeable and aggressive in accompanying volunteers in negotiations with prospects to help answer questions and offer guidelines on the various aspects of giving today.
>
> *I believe* that thorough research, orientation and cultivation is vital to attract the proper degree of involvement in any project, and that taking time to do a job right, rather than in a hurry, is a most essential ingredient in a successful development program.
>
> *I believe* that we must constantly foster the true meaning of Trusteeship and the acceptance of the privileges and responsibilities of citizenship.
>
> *I believe* that no one has to apologize for Philanthropy today as it is of a very positive nature, and it is a very important part of the American way of life.

Suggested Reading

Seymour, Harold J., *Designs for Fund-Raising: Principles, Patterns, Techniques,* McGraw-Hill, New York, 1966.
Netzel, Paul A., *YMCA Capital Development,* YMCA of Metropolitan Los Angeles, 1977.

31

Special Events Fund-Raising

Eileen R. Lentz

President, Events Management, Inc., an affiliated service of IDC

What Are Special Events?

Special events are something truly out of the ordinary, not just "business as usual." They can be real *happenings* in the sense of *making* things happen in the organization as well as being a *happening* on the day of the actual special event.

Special event fund-raising is a growing dimension in the development of non-profit organizations. The special event, in and of itself, increases organizational visibility and broadens the financial base of the organization. It also heightens enthusiasm and builds support through *people energy*.

The special event also offers new opportunities in fund-raising, providing an amplification of the fund-raising process and new ways to approach potential donors "one on one." In addition to their fund-raising aspects—and sometimes more importantly—special events create an atmosphere in which participants can have an enjoyable time, share in the success of an organization, catch the spirit of the group, and expand their circle of coworkers.

Why Have Special Events?

Organizations conduct special events for many reasons:

- *To have fun.* The single most important goal for any event
- *To honor.* Corporate, celebrity, volunteer, supporter, major contributor, community leader, etc.
- *To award.* Achiever, winner

- *To thank.*   Staff, sponsors, contributors, volunteers, etc.
- *To entertain.*   Creates visability, even though very expensive
- *To promote.*   Gains recognition for your organization
- *To raise money.*   Should not be the prime objective
- *To broaden giver lists.*   Membership, sponsors, volunteers, donors

Frequently, special events are planned to honor someone. This may be at the corporate level, perhaps a celebrity, a volunteer (one of your own organization), a supporter, a major financial contributor, or a community or political leader.

The presentation of awards is another reason to create a special event. It could be an achievement award, one recognizing outstanding support or commending the attainment of a particular goal.

The hoopla of a special event can be a great way to say thank you, to your staff, volunteers, the capital campaign chairperson, or a community leader or local press who have stepped forward on behalf of your cause.

Major entertainment events are important and costly to organize. Celebrity entertainers are expensive. Even if they donate their time, you are usually required to pay for travel and lodging not only for them, but for their entourage—and it's all *first class.* On the other hand, celebrities increase your organization's visability and offer numerous public relations and publicity opportunities. In order to raise money, you need to plan on sponsorship or underwriting dollars to cover event costs.

Many of these special events can raise money for nonprofit organizations, whether or not raising money was their initial objective. The fund-raising potential is at the bottom of the list because special events *are indeed special,* and very different from familiar fund-raising areas, such as capital campaigns, direct mail, phone-mail programs, and annual giving or membership drives. Those are very specific programs that are laid out strictly to raise money. Special events should never be confused with that: They are really geared to promote or extend your image to others, to show people what you are all about. If you happen to make money because of it, terrific! Now it may indeed be your goal to raise money, but you must realize that it usually takes 30 to 50 cents to make a dollar, and sometimes more.

Last but not least, particularly in the fund-raising area, special events are an outstanding vehicle to broaden your giver lists! This is true, also, for those of you who are looking for new members, for in the special event you attract many new people. The event will provide you with lists of names of people who can be invited to become part of your program. You do not have to spend a lot of money on special events to get maximum attention.

Now that you understand all the reasons why you should promote a special event, you need to remember that your primary purpose in spending time, money, and boundless energy is to promote good public relations for your organization. By creating this positive image through special events, you will open the doors for other fund-raising opportunities.

Special Events: The Love/Hate Relationship

Why Do NPOs Hate Doing Special Events?

Most nonprofit organizations do not have special events expertise on their staff. Further, they do not have a separate staff member or consultant whose full-time responsibility is to coordinate special events. Any major event is generally too great a commitment for an executive director or a staff member to do well. Special events take valuable time away from a staff member's job, which is—and must continue to be—top priority. Consequently, the special event may fall short of its goal and, more importantly, may not be handled with professional quality.

Special events, while really a full-time job, very often do not generate enough funds through the event itself, to justify hiring a full-time staff. Special events staff or consultant expenses should be compared to that of advertising and public relations, which all organizations need to some degree. NPOs that hate coordinating events lose sight of the fact that the primary purpose of special events is to increase visibility and improve public relations, rather than simply to raise money.

Why Do Others Love Them?

Some nonprofit organizations have full-time staff, as well as full-time (or practically full-time) volunteers, and professional counsel to coordinate their special events. These are the NPOs that like special events. They also understand that the financial rewards will come later when they are able to tap their new resources through their normal fund-raising activities. Many NPOs look upon special events positively for the following reasons:

- Because of the event, the organization becomes more well known. Furthermore, because of the public relations for the event, the organization is usually able to get more publicity throughout the entire year.

- The NPO usually raises a lot of money, not always through the event, but *because* of the event. For example, the president of a corporation, who had not been on any major funding lists, attended an organization's gala and showed great interest in becoming involved with the organization. He was approached after the event and gave close to $100,000 in support. His comment was, "Keep asking; I'll let you know when it hurts." That support would never have surfaced without the special event.

- Publicity and public relations impact is also tremendously effective in building support for the organization's "old" givers by keeping them enthusiastic and alive.

- Special events often increase the number of new volunteers and major contributors by 10 to 20 percent per year.

Getting Started

Setting Goals

The main objective of a special event is to have fun. This is the single most important goal for any event, and it should be paramount in your planning. This is not a frivolous goal—far from it—for if you cannot plan an event that is fun, it will be neither special nor successful. By having fun, I mean that when people leave an event, they can say "That was absolutely fabulous; I can't wait to do it again" or "If this organization does something again, I want to be sure that I'm involved with it."

Goals should be set for the entire year, before any individual events are coordinated. Take a look at what's been done in the past, at what has been successful and at what has not. Review your plans for the short term, take a look long-range, then consider what you want to be doing in the way of special events for your organization to help achieve those goals.

You must understand what your needs are, who your audience might be, and whether you need events primarily to raise money or whether you need them merely as public relations tools. This is also a good time, if you are uncertain of your direction, to call in outside counsel to help evaluate your organization's position and set appropriate goals. Once you have a clear picture of what your goals are for the year, you can move forward to put the strategies in place to achieve those goals.

For example, a museum may coordinate over 1000 events in a year. These could include

Art opening previews

Educational seminars or classes

Art movies

Children's parties

Foreign, domestic, or day tours

Galas

New members' picnic on the museum lawn

Special VIP receptions for annual givers of $5000 or more

Special recognition luncheon for major corporate donors

The list goes on and on.

Planning

When you think about coordinating a special event, you must first define your specific goals for that specific event. Precisely what is it you want to achieve? What volunteers and support staff are available to you for the project? What funding is necessary? What is your budget? Discover who you can get to underwrite your project or whether the money must all come from the organization's pocketbook. How much time do you have to plan this event?

You must know how to control the event. It must *not* control you. There are many questions, not the least of which is how to begin? (See Figure 31.1.)

Committee and Honoree Selection

After you have set your goal for the year and chosen a special event to work on, the very first thing you must do is choose your event committee. Prepare written job descriptions. While people are usually very willing to give their time, they do not like to have their time wasted. Nor do they like to discover they've accepted a job they either do not like or are not capable of doing. Unless you have written job descriptions, you may have several unhappy committee members and will face more difficulty switching them out of that job and into something else. Be prepared to make those changes, if necessary, with members in charge of other committee tasks or volunteer jobs.

The Committee.   The committee is usually composed of three parts:

1. *Working committee.* Made up of board members or members of the organization; they set the goals and the concept for the event.

2. *Executive committee.* Chosen by the chairperson. These should be corporate or community leaders who have a lot of clout and are willing to support the event through their friends or corporations.

3. *Volunteer committee.* Especially important if the event is being done without the assistance of a professional. You need a cadre of 5 to 100 volunteers, depending on the event.

Working Committee. Five to six people (no more than eight) which should also include the chairperson and/or a representative of the chair. This committee is the decision-making body that determines who the honored guests—guest speaker, master or mistress of ceremonies, entertainers, and so on—will be. This committee also assists in getting commitments for attendance from those special guests.

Once you have selected a goal and have decided how the event will be funded and how much time you have to coordinate the event, you proceed to

I. Choose an event committee—be sure there is a written job description for each member.
  A. Chairperson (there are two kinds); a "working chairperson" or a "name chairperson"—the latter usually sends a representative to meetings.
  B. Five or six (no more than eight) additional members who will coordinate the following:
    1. Volunteers
    2. Program
    3. Public relations
    4. Invitations/reservations
    5. Contracts/agreements
      a. Facility
      b. Catering
      c. Decorations
      d. Printing (work with program and invitation persons)
      e. Favors
      f. Entertainment, etc.
II. *With committee,* plan your event from beginning to end. Be sure to have enough meetings early on so that everyone understands their responsibilities and is excited about the event. Make committee replacements early if a member's commitment cannot be fulfilled.
III. Prepare guest lists—this is often the most important and crucial task. They may need reviewing eight or nine times to be sure that there are no duplications or errors. That means *no* errors—in names, titles, addresses, etc.
IV. Notify committee members by written memo of meetings (at least 5 days in advance of the meeting.) It's best to have an agenda with the memo. Meetings should start on time, be well run by you or the chairperson, and never run longer than 1 hour.
V. Present a budget to the committee (after working out the costs with the appropriate members) for their approval.
VI. Personally follow up with each committee member to see that the task is done, and done properly. If you have a "working chairperson," be sure to be in touch with that person weekly, or daily if necessary.
VII. Give constant support to your committee and let *them* do the work.
VIII. Good luck and have fun!

Figure 33.1. How to begin your special event.

Executive ("Blue Ribbon") Committee.   Should be as large as possible, consisting of leaders willing to make personal phone calls to boost attendance and for fund-raising. They should be asked to do as little as possible, attend no more than one or two meetings, and make no more than ten phone calls.

Volunteer Committee.   From five to a hundred, depending on size of the project. Volunteers are special people. They are willing to give generously of their time and talent. However, if there is a major crisis in their lives, very often they will desert you. You must always be aware that if something happens to one of your volunteers, you need to find a replacement or to do the job yourself.

The Chairperson.   Every event needs a chairperson. The best one possible. It may be you, or it may be someone you choose outside the organization, or perhaps someone from the organization itself. There are, however, two kinds of chairpersons: working chair and chair "in name only." The chairperson is responsible for generating financial support, allowing his or her signature to be used on any necessary mailings and his or her name on all event materials. The chairperson also coordinates an executive committee if one is needed. Be sure to choose the kind of chairperson that is right for your needs.

The chairperson in name only may be some very prestigious person in your area or field of interest, whose name alone will induce people to attend your event. These chairpersons, however, do not have time to actually do the work for the event and are often represented by another member of their organization, such as a public relations or community relations executive. They must then be provided with a top-notch "lieutenant" or working chairperson who will actually pull the event together. These are vital decisions because it is critical to have a good chairperson for an event of any size.

The selection of a chairperson will dictate the success of the event itself. If everyone in town likes and respects the chairperson, people will respond. If the chairperson is a celebrity that everyone knows and would like to meet, people will respond. In any case, it is vital that the chairperson be enthusiastic and extremely supportive not only of the event itself, but of the goals of the organization.

The Honorees.   Choice of honorees—if the event has honorees—should be done with the approval of the chairperson, and must have his or her complete endorsement. Sometimes, the honoree has already been chosen, and choice of a chairperson will follow, whether it be a special friend of the honoree or someone who represents a logical choice.

The honoree should be chosen *before* the rest of the committee so that the committee selected will be the strongest possible in support of the honoree and, therefore, of the event itself.

Selection of Date, Time, and Place

A decision of the working committee. This follows the selection of the blue-ribbon committee, so that you will know where your audience is geographically situated—whether close to the city, in the suburbs, or near a key transportation hub.

The most creative and interesting facility is the best choice—not always the one everybody uses or the one that is the easiest to get to. The possibilities include an unused train terminal, shopping mall, corporate headquarters, and so forth.

If an event must take place outside, it should—if a large event—have "rain insurance." For example, a recently held polo match and art show had rain insurance, which netted them $30,000 when it did rain, to cover their losses for expenses that day. They were able to hold the event the following week and able to realize a profit.

Budget and Timeline

The most crucial step in organizing an event is producing an *accurate* budget and timeline—and sticking to them. A budget should not be "beefed up" to take care of things you forget. That kind of error causes the ticket price or sponsorship request to be too high, and you may lose attendees or be unable to find sponsor underwriting. A budget that is too low "in order to get board approval" will become a major disaster later when you report back to them with red ink. Do your homework and come as close as you can to actual costs. (See Figures 31.2 and 31.3.)

EXECUTIVE WOMEN OF NEW JERSEY
DRAFT BUDGET

"SALUTE TO THE POLICY MAKERS" AWARDS DINNER
APRIL 8, 1986

Postage	$ 400
Telephone	700
Photocopying	100
Letter service ($1.00 per letter, includes 39¢ postage)	700
Awards ($70 per honoree)	4,060
Flowers/decorations ($30 per table + dais, etc.)	1,700
Printing	4,000
PR Expenses (folders, postage for mailing, photocopies, mailing envelopes, etc.)	3,000
Follow-up letter (after the dinner)	2,000
Professional fee	15,000
Out-of-pocket expenses	500
Miscellaneous (research staff, captains' tips, coat check, etc.)	1,000
	33,160
Food covers, $46	27,600
Total anticipated expenses	$60,760

Income profit projections

Benefactors	3 × $5000		$ 15,000
Patrons	3 × 3500		10,500
Tables	35 × 2000		70,000
$1000 tables	6.5 × 1000		6,500
Contributions			1,000
Underwriting*			7,000
Total income			$110,000
	Anticipated net profit		$49,240

*Underwriting confirmed, $7000 for printing and PR costs.

Figure 31.2

Increasing Support through Special Events

Sponsorship/Underwriting

Sponsorship packages have become increasingly popular as a way of generating contributions of many different sorts and providing visibility for various donors. Early in the planning of the event, sponsor "opportunities" should be focused upon, to defray costs, increase net profit, provide additional sponsor publicity, add in-kind donor opportunities, and attract new sources of contribution. These include everything from printing, postage and mailing, graphics, flowers, decorations, music, awards, public relations, photography, sound systems, transportation, and press table costs.

These need not necessarily be donated outright by the sponsor, but can be "contributed" in one of several forms:

EXECUTIVE WOMEN OF NEW JERSEY, AWARDS DINNER TIMELINE

"SALUTE TO THE POLICY MAKERS"
AWARDS DINNER
APRIL 8, 1986
TIMELINE

12/2–12/9	Research on women members of boards of directors
12/16	Begin work on invitation/letterhead art work package.
1/6	Letters to honorees (on chairman's letterhead)
1/10–1/20	Telephone confirmation of honorees
1/6	Letters to chairmen of honorees' boards for executive committee
1/20	Budget
1/22–1/28	Executive Dinner Committee telephone confirmation Concept for awards
1/23	Letterhead package to printer
1/29	Vice chairmen letters mailed
2/16	Telephoning for vice chairmen confirmation
2/20	Vice chairmen list to printer
2/25	All corporate letters and social invitations go out
3/17	Telephone follow-up begins for: Dais confirmation Reservations (beginning with the Honorary Dinner Committee and vice chairmen)
3/21	Deadline for program to printer
4/8	Dinner
5/6	Final report

Figure 31.3

1. A company actually doing the work itself—a printer, for example, or a florist.

2. A corporation, offering the services of their in-house printer or graphics specialists (this, however, can mean delays).

3. Services underwritten or paid for by a donor individual or corporation.

4. Benefactor or Patron packages are arranged, which support the general expenses of the event. These usually range from $500 to $10,000. These levels of sponsorships can be called whatever you want—gold, silver, or bronze givers (with appropriate program recognition on gold, silver, or bronze paper). More fun, however, is to "tailor" those titles to the event itself. For a race, for example, you could have: marathon sponsor, 10-K sponsor, fun-run sponsor, "victory" givers, "challenge" donors, etc.

All these forms of sponsorship should be explored to increase funds for an event. Most often, a combination of several sponsorship opportunities will work best.

List of Invitees, Possible Sponsors, Donors, Suppliers, etc.

Key to the success of your event is broad, accurate, and updated lists of potential attendees, donors, and friends of the organization. Names come from all sources—executive committee, working committee, honoree, chairperson, vice chairperson, volunteers. If you are going to invite people to serve as vice chairpersons (for use of their names only with no obligations), hoping that they will generate support from others as well as themselves and their companies, then the *formulation of the vice chairperson list itself is a key function of both the executive and working committees.* This is an important task, and attention should be given to choosing appropriate people according to honoree, occasion, industry served, etc.

All lists need to be computerized and printed out by company, or if only a social list, alphabetically by last name. Lists should be checked and rechecked many times by committee (in a working session specifically to go over lists) as well as individually. They must be revised to be sure there are no duplications and that other mistakes or breaches of etiquette have not been made, such as inviting the chairperson and the plant manager (or low-echelon official) to both serve as vice chairpersons or attend the function together. It sometimes takes seven or eight reviews and adjustments to get the list right.

People do not look favorably on receiving two or three invitations to the same event, especially if it is a fund-raiser, because it indicates lack of professionalism and waste of money on postage. Be sure there are *no* duplications. It is permissible, however, if you are sending corporate letters and social invitations (to the organization's members), that the chief executive officer also receive an invitation at home as his or her spouse may be a member or supporter of the organization coordinating the event.

Event Arrangements

Site surveys and contracts. Check out the facility thoroughly. If for a dinner, make sure dining room is large enough, but not too large (10 square feet per person, more if there will be a large dais: a 9000 square-foot room holds 700 including a two-tier dais of 80). If you have a dais, be sure to allow at least 2 feet per dais guest. Be sure that appropriate lighting is available; if not, arrange with the facility for additional dais lighting—hopefully, the facility will pick up the cost. Arrange for separate rooms for VIP reception and for the general reception.

If you are planning a large event, make sure nothing else is scheduled at the facility at the same time that could cause logistical or space problems with your event. (Never try to squeeze your event into the place you have selected—no matter how nice the facility—under crowded circumstances.) You may suddenly need an extra room for an unexpected celebrity appearance and press interviews. If the facility is filled, you could be confronted with an embarrassing situation. Also, if someone else earlier in the day is using a room that you need and stays beyond the scheduled time, you could lose valuable setup time, not to mention jeopardizing the entire event itself.

Another reason to check on what is happening earlier in the day is to be able to get in early to set up at your convenience.

Be sure that valet parking and coat checking are available near your event. See whether the restrooms are nearby, and check that the facilities are large enough to provide for your guests. (A ladies room with two stalls will *not* adequately service an event of 500.)

Press room. If the event is to be heavily covered by the press, see that there is a press room conveniently located, with bar and buffet. If a press conference is to be held, be sure that the room accommodates electronic media, that it has chairs and a lectern, and that it is situated away from kitchen noise and reception traffic.

Cocktails. If the dinner ticket price is expensive, there should be an open bar, not a cash bar. After dinner, there should be a bar, as well as coffee, available to provide a place for people to congregate and extend the evening if they wish.

Wine. Both red and white wines should be offered at dinner, poured from the bottle, and bottles *not* left on the table. If certain wines have been specified, check to be sure you are getting the wines you have paid for.

Food. When deciding on the menu, linens, and wines, meet with the caterer of the facility and tell them how much you want to spend and what you would like in return—then go from there. You will get much more for your money with this approach than by asking the caterer "How much will it cost for a filet mignon dinner for 200 people?" Be sure that the linens and gratuities are included. Take the time to actually sample menu selections before the event.

Discover how the meal is to be served, i.e., French service, White Glove service, and which dishes (if any) are preset (salad; rolls and butter). It saves time to have the dinner plates prepared, but this is not preferred and should *only* be done when time is critical.

Flowers and decorations. It is advisable to have these prepared by outside suppliers because when you pay for this service through the facility, there is usually an additional mark up. Also, you lose control of your specific order, and often do not get exactly what you want. Dais flowers should be low, so that honorees can be seen from the audience; avoid tall candelabras.

Music. Decide whether you want background music, a pianist, or strolling strings during the cocktail reception, dais entry, etc. Sometimes, "canned" music from the facility is acceptable, but you must listen to it ahead of time. Be sure you have proper audio equipment; most musicians have their own, or will ask for specifics. When contracting with musicians, be sure you know exactly what the charges are, when they take breaks, what the union regulations are, and, most important (no matter how highly recommended) what they sound like.

Awards. These should be ordered at least 10 or 12 weeks before event. Also allow time for engraving. Choose something relevant or appropriate to the event and to the honorees (such as a music director's baton in a shadow box for symphony awards).

Public relations. If at all possible, work with a separate committee provided by a corporation, or with your own public relations department, if your organization is large enough.

Telephone contact. All executive committee members and vice chairpersons are called to confirm attendance at the event; they are asked whether they will be a sponsor and whether are taking a table or individual seats, etc. Continued follow-up is necessary, not only to seek participation, but to get correct names for the seating list and to verify spelling of additional guests. After the event, follow-up is needed for unpaid reservations.

Printed Materials

Letter and Invitation Composition

If you are seeking to build support for your event through vice chairpersons and corporate involvement, it should be done through a letter, on corporate letterhead, signed by your event chairperson. A printed social invitation may follow to additional lists of individuals. However, the corporate invitation letter, response card, and reply envelope, *not* the social invitation, are sent to all corporate invitees. The letter should be only one page, brief and to the point. The social invitation should be just that, social and very attractive.

Invitations and Mailings

Generally speaking, it is better to use stamps rather than postage-metered invitations. This is because metered mail, particularly that which is sent to someone's home, is likely to go unopened for days.

A stamped envelope, on the other hand, gets opened immediately, whether received at the office or at home.

Never, under any circumstances send other than first-class mail. Not only do you run the risk of delays in receiving responses but also the chance that it may not be received at all. Moreover, a "third-class" indicia on the envelope cheapens the entire affair, and takes away from the special nature of your event.

Be certain to have the return address of the event coordinator on the envelope. This enables immediate updating of the list and the issuing of a new invitation when possible, if mail cannot be delivered.

Note that vice chairpersons are initially invited only to loan their name, and therefore should *not* receive a reservation card in this mailing but will receive a return reply card for their response. This is because you want them to say yes only to participating as a vice chairperson. The cost of attending is not mentioned. Your return letter to them should be geared to their response: whether they said yes or no and whether you want to invite them to be a sponsor or to take a table, etc. Remember, however, that their *name* is what you initially want to secure.

Printed Materials: The Invitation Package

- Vice chairperson response card.
- Committee letterhead. (If a small committee, with prestigious members, titles

and companies should appear at the left; if list is large, names only; if list is small but not prestigious, no titles should be used.)

- Social invitation, if needed.
- Reservation card and envelope (different versions for corporate letters and social invitations).
- If you do not yet have a "committee with clout," send initial letters to vice chairpersons on the chair's personal or corporate letterhead.
- A separate *printed* (not typed) list of vice chairpersons should be enclosed with the invitation letter to corporations, along with the reservation card and reply. [*Note:* The weight of your mailing may require more than a single first-class stamp, especially if you are including a vice chairperson list. Be aware, therefore, of paper weights as you order, but avoid using cheap stock. Be sure to choose good-quality paper of heavy enough weight so that, if printed on both sides (as the vice chairperson list may be) the type does not show through.]

Program

As soon as possible after the chairperson and honorees are selected, contact them for pictures and biographies for the program. The organization needs to prepare an introduction and supply an updated board of trustees list. Some items to be included: accurate executive dinner committee and vice chairperson lists; menu; lists of past honorees and past chairpersons; biographies and pictures of the chairperson, all honorees, and guest speakers; and the program for the event. Layout should be carefully worked out with a graphics specialist; be sure paper is of high quality. Anything in gold or silver generally needs to be varnished, primarily to keep fingerprints from smudging, and at least 5 extra days are usually needed to allow for printing that kind of material.

Since the program is usually the first thing guests see at an event, it should be as attractive and as first class as possible. Avoid advertising journals, as people tend not to read large programs at events, but are more interested in who is there, the program itself, menu, executive committee members and vice chairperson. Further, the use of an advertising journal tends to dilute support for the event. There are, of course, exceptions and very often such a journal can be the fund-raising *tool* for the event.

Tickets

Tickets to special events (other than auditorium or arena-type events with reserved seating) should have the look and feel of an invitation. Separate tickets should also be printed for VIP receptions.

Numbered tickets are not necessary for anything other than reserved seating for auditorium-type events, as long as an accurate seating list is provided. Handwriting or typing each guest's name on the back of each ticket is an excellent idea. It solves the problem of who gets the VIP tickets, and if there is a change in attendees, you are more likely to receive a call from the individual or corporation telling you of the change, if the tickets have already been inscribed with an individual's name.

Tickets are always sent with a letter. Include a reminder of dress requirements for the evening, as well as directions and a map to the facility.

Seating List

This should include dais seating (if there is a dais) and should provide names and table assignments of all companies attending as well as their guests and other attendees. Capitalize the names of all corporations for easy reference. This list can also encompass last-minute sponsors, contributors, or anything of great importance that you were not able to put into the program at the time of printing. In order to be as current as possible, the list should be prepared *no more than 2 days* before the event.

Posters and Fliers

These publicity materials may be needed for greater visibility, especially for events not entirely dependent on corporate support. Weigh the need for these materials carefully, however. Unless you can get some "in-kind" support for the design and printing and unless you have a cadre of volunteers to deliver them to the community, they can be very costly.

Press Releases/Public Relations

Publicity releases and press kits should reflect the same letterhead logo as the stationery, and should be prepared as professionally as possible. They must be sent out well in advance of the event, with telephone follow-up to request press attendance or coverage.

The public relations committee or director should prepare press releases and press packets including information about the organization, arrange for reservations for attending press, and stimulate press attendance. Assign certain members of the committee to specific reporters to coordinate their needs during the event and to arrange for interviews with specific guests, honorees, etc. Send out pre-event publicity, prepare "shot list" for photos, arrange for photographer, and for follow-up publicity as well. This committee is key to getting maximum visibility from the event itself on the day of the event and even many weeks after.

Day-of-the-Event Schedule

Be at the facility with a minimum of two staff members to take care of setting up (depending on size of event and what needs to be done, anywhere from 10 a.m. to 3 p.m. for a 6 p.m. dinner). If assigned seating, be sure that table numbers are in proper order, that lighting and sound systems work, that programs are arranged as you wish (on plate, on seat, standing up, etc.). Ensure that a bar is open for early arrivals; be sure that the facility staff has an exact timeline showing precisely when everything is going to happen.

If you are using a dais, you must set up dais assembly area (usually in, or close to, the room where the VIP reception takes place) by lining up chairs with names written on self-adhering memo notes and attached to chairs in the correct order.Once everyone is in the proper chair, inform them of entrance procedures. Make sure place cards on dais are in the right order. Make sure no tables or seats are obstructed by poles, columns, or lighting and sound equipment.

Constantly check service and delivery of meals. Arrange an unobtrusive spot behind the dais for yourself during the program to assist when necessary—to let speakers know if adjustments are needed with the sound system, to warn them if they are running overtime or if there are any problems with the visual aids, to hand them the honoree awards (so that they don't have to remove them from a box or check inscriptions), etc.

Perhaps the most important thing to remember when overseeing any event is that it should not run too long. (Corporate-supported dinners should end by 9:30 p.m.) All speeches should be very short. A keynote speech should be no more than 15 or 18 minutes. Be sure that all speakers have a copy of the timeline during the event and that they adhere to it.

Bring an organization checkbook to the dinner to pay for the dinner, musicians, and captains' tips. Ask in advance about the customary tipping procedures at the facility. Such an inquiry can ensure outstanding service since, by asking in advance, the captains will know that you intend to tip and will therefore be more conscious of providing the best service.

Make sure all guests are well taken care of, and if there is a special request for something that a guest has a reasonable right to expect, it should be granted. (For example, if a guest who has just arrived requests a drink although the bar has closed, he or she should probably be accommodated.) Most importantly, you must tell the facility what you want them to do under any special circumstances.

Be sure to sample the food during the event, even if you are rushed, to be sure that what is being served is what you had ordered and tasted before the event.

The Event Itself

During the week prior to the event, follow up with all contractual agreements to confirm time, all materials needed, menu, etc. (See Figures 31.4 and 31.5.)

1. *Timeline.*   Prepare a minute-by-minute timeline, taking into account the timing of all speeches, introduction of speakers, content, and time for applause. Send copies to the master of ceremonies, honorees, clergy, guest speakers, etc., so that they have a clear picture of their responsibilities that evening. Be sure that the master of ceremonies has all the information, regarding special guests, needed to tie the entire program together.

2. *Staff Assistance.*   Arrange for staff to assist at event or dinner, (six to eight, with additional greeters, is sufficient for an event of 500 to 800 guests; allow an additional staff person for every 100 guests). One or two people are needed to assist at the reception table. Guests do not necessarily need to check in, but greeters should be on hand at the entrance to offer assistance and to hand out seating lists. Young people—high school juniors and seniors and college students—make the best greeters. Other staff requirements: One or two staff members to assist the press; one dais organizer and one assistant; two "floaters" to handle any problems that may arise. The greeters are also used to move the guests from the reception area into the main-event area.

After the Event

Follow-up

The day following the event, unpaid guests should be called to request their check. If the check does not come in within 7 to 10 days, send a bill. Thank you letters should go out to all guests who attended for whom you have addresses. All executive committee members, vice chairpersons, sponsors, and contributors who did *not* attend should receive a letter updating them on the success of the event and thanking them for their support.

All statements for any expenses incurred for the event should be sent directly to you, approved by you, and paid promptly.

1985 Tri-County Scholarship Fund Dinner
Timeline

6:00	Receptions begin VIP—The Gallery (overlooking the hotel lobby on the 2nd floor) Main—The Atrium (to the left of the ballroom, through the doors)
6:45	Students begin ushering guests into the Grand Ballroom for dinner VIP Dais guests prepared to enter dais (room just off the Gallery)
6:50	VIP spouses escorted to their tables in the Grand Ballroom
7:00	VIPs escorted to dais (no formal introduction—there will be about 80) Bill Kearns asks guests to greet the VIPs as they enter Bill Kearns then introduces (after dais is in place and seated):

Bob Mulcahy	President of TCSF
Bishop Rodimer	Bishop of Paterson
Don Criqui	Master of Ceremonies
William R. Hartman	Leadership Award Honoree
Henry Taub	Hall of Fame Award Honoree

Special Guests:
The Honorable William E. Simon
Senator Frank R. Lautenberg
Bill Kearns welcomes guests & dais, and introduces Don Criqui as MC

7:12	Don Criqui introduces Reverend Monsignor Stephan J. Patch
7:15	Invocation—Msgr. Patch
7:17	Dinner begins
7:28	Entree is served
7:48 to 7:58	Plates cleared, dessert is served
8:12	All plates cleared
8:25	Bob Mulcahy—Remarks and introduces Don Criqui (Benefactor presentation)
8:30	Don Criqui—Remarks and introduces Bishop Rodimer
8:35	Bishop Rodimer presents award to Bill Hartman
8:40	Hartman acceptance
8:44	Bishop introduces Senator Frank R. Lautenberg
8:46	Senator Lautenberg presents award to Henry Taub
8:50	Henry Taub acceptance
8:57	Criqui acknowledges student ushers and introduces Paul Hildim, student speaker
9:02	Hildum remarks
9:12	Criqui, few words, then turns over to Bishop for closing
9:18	Bishop—remarks and introduces Rabbi David H. Panitz
9:26	Rabbi Panitz—Benediction
9:28	Closing—Bill Kearns

Figure 31.4

PROGRAM COMMENTS
TRI-COUNTY SCHOLARSHIP FUND
AWARD DINNER
OCTOBER 9, 1985

Note: These times include applause, getting up and sitting down time.

Bill Kearns (12 minutes)	Welcome Announcement of dais entry Introduction of special guests: Escorted by students (use timeline for list) Introduction of Don Criqui, delighted that he is joining us for the fourth year.
Don Criqui (3 minutes)	Opening comments: mention size of dais (approx. 80) Introduction of Reverend Monsignor Stephen J. Patch for invocation Pastor, Corpus Christi Church, Chatham
Msgr. Patch (2 minutes)	Two-minute invocation
Bob Mulcahy (5 minutes)	(*after dinner*) Comments on the Tri-County Scholarship Fund, acknowledge the Executive Committee, and ask benefactors to stand, present the benefactor award to Bill Kearns, turn over to Don Criqui
Don Criqui (5 minutes)	Comment on the benefactors (there are 26 benefactor tables) Introduction of Bishop Frank J. Rodimer
Bishop Rodimer (5 minutes)	Leadership award—Bill Hartman
Bill Hartman (4 minutes)	Acceptance
Bishop Rodimer (2 minutes)	Introduces Senator Frank R. Lautenberg
Senator Frank Lautenberg (4 minutes)	Introduces Henry Taub—Comment specifically on his association with the Business Employment Foundation in Paterson
Henry Taub (7 minutes)	Acceptance
Don Criqui (5 minutes)	Some references to Hartman's and Taub's remarks Introduction of student ushers—back table of eight seniors from Paterson Catholic. Ask them to stand at their table Introduce student speaker Paul Hildum, 1985 Graduate of Paterson Catholic High School; Freshman at Rutgers University in New Brunswick, majoring in English. He was a National Merit Scholarship finalist
Paul Hildum (10 minutes)	Comments
Don Criqui (5 minutes)	Remarks—note that Hildum and the eight students from Paterson Catholic are here tonight not so much to represent but to remind us of the 23,000 students enrolled in diocesan schools this year Introduction of Bishop Rodimer for remarks

Figure 31.5

Bishop Rodimer (8 minutes)	Remarks (special thanks to Bill Kearns, the Executive Committee, the benefactors, and especially to Don Criqui) and introduces Rabbi David H. Panitz, Temple Emmanuel
Rabbi Panitz (2 minutes)	Benediction
Bill Kearns (3 minutes)	Immediately following benediction: Thank people for coming—hope to see you next year Thank Don Criqui for once again serving as Master of Ceremonies

Figure 31.5. *(Continued)*

Final Report and Evaluation

The final report should be completed *no later* than 1 month after the event. (See Figure 31.6.) By that time, all bills should be paid and all receipts collected. This report should include an evaluation, as concise as possible, of the strengths and weaknesses of the event, a complete financial report, and recommendations as to how to improve the event in subsequent years.

If there is to be any individualized follow-up solicitation of event attendees, you should work closely with the committee organizing that project. Input from the event coordinators will maximize the information about each and every individual on the list, their level of support for the event, guests he or she sponsored, in-kind contributions made, etc.

After the event, the organization may become increasingly visible, and you may then be able to generate additional dollars for smaller events through corporate support.

Feedback is all-important. It reveals what's good and what's bad; what you want to change and what should stay the same. After the event is over, you must ask yourself, Was it worth it? Have your goals been met and were you within budget? How long did your guests stay after the event? If they lingered a long time afterward, they probably had a great time. If not, perhaps the event was not quite so successful. What was lacking that should be corrected before your next special event?

How Many Times Should You Repeat an Event?

If the event is a success, you will probably want to try it again. The biggest problem is that an organization often repeats an event for 10 years without making many changes, and after the third year it usually is not quite the shining success that it was the first year.

It is important to try new gimmicks in the form of speakers, facilities, format, etc., to attract the attention of your desired audience. That does not mean that if you have something especially attractive about your event that you must change it for the sake of change. There is an old saying, "If it ain't broke, don't fix it." But if the kudos sound a bit weak, start looking for new ideas. Producing special events is one of the most creative and challenging activities; it should be approached with great energy and imagination.

FINAL REPORT
4TH ANNUAL TRI-COUNTY SCHOLARSHIP FUND AWARDS DINNER
DECEMBER 3, 1985
FINANCIAL REPORT

		Budget	Actual
Fixed Expenses			
Postage		$ 400.00	$ 218.64
Telephone		600.00	119.68
Photocopying		100.00	77.10
Letter service		1,200.00	928.00
Awards			
Honorees — $1,354.50			
Benefactors — 1,445.50		3,000.00	2,799.00
Music		800.00	750.00
Flowers		2,000.00	2,517.25
Professional fee		17,500.00	17,500.00
Follow-up letter		2,500.00	2,500.00
Out-of-pocket		500.00	276.26
Miscellaneous	1,000.00	1,450.00	
Coat check $ 50.00			
Captains tips 400.00			
Dais lighting 500.00			
Additional dais 500.00			
Total fixed expenses		$ 29,600.00	$ 29,136.83
Variable expenses			
Dinner covers 635 × $55			$ 34,925.00
Total Expenses			$ 64,061.83
Income			
Tickets and contributions			$253,600.00
Expenses			64,061.83
Total net income			$189,538.17*

*Total net income was originally $191,038—with Mutual Benefit contribution of $1,500. Please see attached copy of letter received.

	1982	1983	1984	1985
Guest	632	609	591	635
Tables	41	42	42	50
Individual seats (including dais)	188	122	80	135
Contributions	$13,300	$13,150	$ 30,650	$ 44,350
Net profit	$70,000	$72,000	$104,379	$189,538

Figure 31.6

Professional Help

There is a tremendous need in special event coordination for professional guidance because most people who have special event responsibilities have very little experience in the field. It is a hard, detailed time-consuming job. Consulting can often lead you in the right direction in the planning process as well as in the complete coordination of the event itself.

Reasons to use a professional include

1. A professionally run event usually *nets* 20 percent more than an in-house event unless staff is hired specifically to run special events.
2. Events run by the professional frees the in-house staff to work on other fund-raising and administrative activities.
3. Professionals very often come with their own lists, but if not, you must know how to generate good lists. Lists, the *right* lists, are the key in making the event special.
4. The professional
   a. Uses telephone follow-up as a key tool
   b. Attends to every detail; professionals are detail people.
   c. Is organized—the better organized, the better the special events coordinator.
5. A major event (concert or sports event) can take as much as 1 to 2 years to coordinate; most events take 5 to 7 months.

Communication Tools

Very often you need to keep your executive committee, honorees, board members, etc., informed, or you need information from them. Figures 31.7 through 31.9 show several tools that may be used to solve the problem. (For the event discussed, 60 honorees were involved, requiring a lot of detail work and good communication.)

EXECUTIVE WOMEN OF NEW JERSEY
1986 "SALUTE TO THE POLICY MAKERS" AWARDS DINNER
Executive Dinner Committee Personal Information Form

Please print or type all information.
Name (for program listing): _____
Name (as it is pronounced): _____
Title (for program listing): _____
Company name (for program listing): _____
Business address (for immediate contact): _____
_____
_____
Business phone (direct contact): _____
Name of contact person in case we cannot reach you directly: _____
_____
Phone number of contact person: _____
  If unable to attend, my substitute will be: _____
  Name: _____
  Title: _____
  Company: _____
  Telephone: _____

Figure 31.7

Trends

Major developments in special events and corporate sponsorship are taking place. Even smaller organizations that come up with a very special idea and that hire professional special event counsel are beginning to build up major support.

Organizations getting visibility through the press and public service announcements—and which attract thousands of people to participate or "spectate"—will find that they can command many more thousands of dollars in support from large contributors, especially corporations.

Sponsors who spend $500,000 can get a good deal more visibility and free publicity by participation in events than if they were to try to reach the same number

---

EXECUTIVE WOMEN OF NEW JERSEY
"SALUTE TO THE POLICY MAKERS" AWARDS DINNER
FACT SHEET

Date: Tuesday, April 8, 1986
Time: Reception   6:00 p.m.
          Dinner   7:00 p.m.
Place: Mayfair Farms, 481 Eagle Rock Avenue, West Orange, New Jersey
Dress: Optional, Business Attire
Ticket price:
  Benefactor $5000 (table for 10, priority seating, special program listing)
  Patron $3500 (table for 10, special program listing)
  Table $2000 (table for 10)
  Seats $200
Dinner Co-chairperson:
  Governor Thomas H. Kean, Governor of New Jersey
  Robert R. Ferguson, Jr., President & CEO, First Fidelity Bancorporation
Honorees:
  Women directors of New Jersey's major corporations and foundations
Executive Dinner Committee:
  The Chairperson, President or CEO of the Honoree's Board
Vice Chairperson:
  Chairpersons & CEOs from New Jersey and New York who respond favorably to loaning their name for the program
Guest Speaker:
  Charles Marshall, Executive Vice President for Administrative and External Affairs, AT&T
Scholarships:
  Funds raised will offer scholarships to women pursuing graduate studies relevant to their fields.
Format:
  Honorees will sit on the dais. Their CEOs will join them on the dais and will serve as their presenter. There will be *no* presentation or acceptance speeches, only introductions by the EWNJ Dinner Committee Chairperson. Chuck Marshall will speak before the award presentations. The evening will conclude by 10:00 PM.
Committee Headquarters: Special EWNJ Phone #:
  Events Management, Inc.   (201)762-2984
  111 Dunnell Road   P.O. Box 1072
  Maplewood, NJ 07040

Figure 31.8

of people with the same number of dollars through advertising or promotion. However, the pursuit of these high-level financial sponsors can cost a great deal of money, time, and effort. Nevertheless NPOs should be sure to hire the right professionals in marketing and special event coordination, who will assist in getting those sponsorship dollars.

Indeed, many hundreds of thousands—even millions—of dollars can be raised. Sponsors are constantly looking for new business, new events, new ideas. Most NPOs are afraid of this, but if they commit to enough up-front money to work with an event organizer and a marketing consultant, they will net tremendous financial rewards.

Event Concepts

Many of these concepts have come from brainstorming sessions during special events seminars. Figure 31.10 lists tools that can aid you in your own special events creativity.

PLEASE RETURN IMMEDIATELY IN THE ENCLOSED ENVELOPE
EXECUTIVE WOMEN OF NEW JERSEY
1986 "SALUTE TO THE POLICY MAKERS" AWARDS DINNER
HONOREE PERSONAL INFORMATION FORM

Please print or type all information.
Name (as it should appear in the program): _____
Name (as it is pronounced): _____
Company name of directorship (as it should appear in the dinner program): _____
_____

I will attend on April 8   Yes _____   Uncertain _____   No _____
Your initials as you would like them used for engraving purposes:
* * * * * * * * * * * * *

Current Professional Affiliation
Company: _____
Title: _____
Business address (for immediate contact): _____
_____

Business phone (for immediate contact): _____
Home address (for immediate contact): _____

Home phone number (for emergency contact): _____
Name of contact person and their phone number in case we cannot reach you directly:
Name _____ *Phone* ( ) _____
If you have not yet sent us your biography and photo, please give us the following background information to be used for immediate press release:
Educational background: _____
Directorships: _____
Committee or organization affiliations: _____

Figure 31.9

Archery vs. golf tournament
Art & animals—"Zoo do"
Art sales
Auction of dinners at people's houses or restaurants
Balloon race
Balloon ride and raffle
Balloon sculpture
Bar-B-Q
Beautiful eyes contest
Bed race
Birthday party for organization
Black-tie tailgate
Book sales
Bowl-a-thon
Breakfast at night
Car races, road rallies
Carnival
Casino night
Celebrity waitress or waiter night
Chili cook-off
Come as your favorite artist or painting
Consignment sale (shop)
"Construction" or hard-hat party
Cookbook
Cooking demonstrations
Crafts sales
Dance, skate, aerobic, etc., marathon
Dance—formal to casual
Dinner w/special group in town (Navy, etc.)
Dog show
English country fair
Evening of intrigue
Fair
Fashion show
Flea market
Free car wash
Gallery dinner—different course or dish per gallery
Golf tournament: winter, in the snow
"Guiness"-type records
Gymkhana
Haunted house at Halloween

Holiday trees auction
Horse show
Kids art show
Kiss the pig
Logo building contest
Mardi Gras
Mystery weekend (clue)
National progressive dinner
No-show ball
Nonevent: First ask for money
Paint-your-own-picture party
Panda (bear) party
Phantom dinners, vanishing parties
Phone-a-thon
Pick-out-the-fakes party
Progressive dinner
Races: bicycle, running, etc.; "a-thons"
Raft race
Regatta and boat races
Renaissance fair
Rodeo
Scavenger hunt
Slumber party in the museum
Sneak preview "sneaker party"
Sock hop
Softball tournament
Sports event
Street carnival
Suitcase party
Summer sports in winter
Sunrise party: "Shed New Light on Sculpture"
Tennis tournament
Theater party
Tin Lizzie auction (cars)
Treasure hunt
Trivial pursuit tournament
Underground party (grafitti)
Used record/music sale
Victorian croquet tournament and kite flying tea
Walks: nature, historic
White elephant bingo
Wine tasting

Figure 31.10. Fund-raising event concepts.

32

Constituency Development

Donald A. Campbell, Jr.

President, Donald A. Campbell and Company, Inc.

Introduction

An organization *is* its constituency—not its buildings or its by-laws, not its programs or its staff. The constituents—that is to say, the components of the organization, are the people who comprise the organization, whose ends it serves. It is no contradiction to state that the first principle of constituency development is that constituents do not exist to be cultivated for the organization; they *are* the organization, and the organization must be developed to serve their needs.

Viewed according to this principle, "constituency development" is scarcely different from institutional development. To justify its existence, an organization—whether it is a hospital or a museum, a university or a social service agency—must serve its public. To do that, it must know itself: that is, it must know its constituents. It must identify them, define their needs, discover how they perceive and relate to the institution, and respond to them appropriately and effectively through its mission and its activities.

Identifying Constituents

In order to develop its constituency, your organization—any organization—must first identify who and where its constituency is. That takes thought, a bit of creativity, a lot of talking to people and asking them to talk to other people. But to begin with, you need to know, generically, *who* your constituents are.

The task is less obvious than it seems. Some of those with the greatest stake in your organization have yet to identify themselves as your constituents. Some may not even be aware of your organization, though their needs and interests are compatible with your own. They are, nevertheless, a potentially very valuable part of your constituency; let us call them "the unacquainted."

More commonly identified as a constituent is what we might call "the consumer"—anyone who uses the services or facilities of your organization. They might be the students at a college, the patients in a hospital, the members of a church or a professional association, the patrons of a theater or museum, or the recipients of a foundation grant or of aid from a social service agency. These are the constituents whose needs the organization meets as an institutional objective.

Another kind of constituent—who may also be a consumer—is "the friend." Friends of organizations, like our own friends, run the gamut of involvement. Some are merely favorably but passively disposed toward the organization. For example, the man who drops loose change in the Salvation Army's kettle at Christmas time; the woman who agrees with the aims and programs of N.O.W. but has not become a member; the parent of a child well cared for during a hospital stay who now regards the hospital in a more favorable light.

Given the opportunity, such friends may become "advocates," speaking positively of the organization and recommending it to others. If they are community leaders and if they understand the organization and its importance, such advocacy can be of significant value.

With the proper development, friends and advocates can become volunteers. "Volunteers" are an organization's most active constituents, but they are not merely those who participate in phonathons or wheel library carts through hospital corridors. We are using the term broadly, to encompass many different types of involvement. The most obvious, of course, is the administrative or program volunteer, who offers service as an unpaid staff member. Hospitals depend heavily on program volunteers, as do many community groups and social organizations.

"Donors," too, are volunteers—those who willingly support an organization through financial contributions. Fund-raising volunteers, who often are and ought to be donors as well, contribute their time and their influence in soliciting funds for the organization. And governance volunteers serve as directors or trustees, planners and policy makers who assume responsibility and leadership in the organization.

Overlapping with these are "special interest groups." These are groups defined by their active interests, their membership in a formal group, or simply by their distinguishing characteristics. For example, members of a special task force or advisory board are likely to share an active interest focusing on a specific issue. A committee that is exploring the feasibility of setting up a halfway house for a mental health agency may draw its members from many sources: the agency's staff, outside experts, residents of the neighborhood where the house will be located. All, however, are concerned with the placement and success of the halfway house. Members of a symphony orchestra's woman's board or junior league, on the other hand, may be united only by their sex or age group. Some may have an intense interest in music, others in charitable work, and still others in social contact; it is important for the organization to recognize and respond to these differences within the common cause.

Special interest groups *outside* the organization may also form part of its constituency. Some of these will be formally organized groups with related interests and concerns. A government watchdog group, a peace organization, and an environmental club may, for example, find themselves equally concerned, if for somewhat different reasons, with the construction of a nuclear power plant. Each may well consider the others part of its broad or potential constituency, and could reasonably expect to find other shared interests as well. Similarly, an organization can look for constituents among special interest groups that are not organized, but defined only by a shared characteristic or concern. For example, an agency conducting research into AIDS might broadly consider all homosexuals its legitimate constituency.

Determining the Needs of Constituents

Once you have identified who your constituents are, you must accurately identify their needs. Their needs are not what *you think* they want and not what *you want* to give them, but what they themselves believe they want. And while there are many techniques for discovering these needs, they all depend on one underlying principle: You cannot know unless you ask.

The principle is obvious, but often ignored. Many nonprofit organizations have never conducted research, formal or informal, into their constituents' knowledge, attitudes, or behavior. They have never asked what the members want of their professional association, what volunteers know about their hospital, or why donors give to the historical society instead of the art museum. They rely instead on intuition, casual impressions, and stereotypes. The trouble is they are often wrong. As eminent an authority as Peter F. Drucker has noted that what people inside an institution think they know about the consumer (read the word "constituent") and the market (read "constituency") is more likely to be wrong than right. Consumers, for their part, rarely "buy" what the institution thinks it is selling them.

No amount of thought, reasoning, and consultation *within the walls of your organization* will tell you what your constituents want, think, and need; how they perceive your organization; why they chose it over another; how satisfied they are with its programs and services. Only research can do that. But research can take many forms. The forms you choose depend on the resources of your organization—both financial and human—and on the nature of your constituency and what you need to know. We can give only a few examples here.

Most people, when they think of market research or constituency analysis, think first of the large-scale market survey. While it is both a highly developed art and a technically sophisticated science, the survey also has its less formal embodiments, such as the patient questionnaires frequently used by hospitals or the mass-mailed surveys sent out by social action groups.

When is a formal market analysis truly necessary for an organization to know and understand its constituents? One good example would be a national political organization, a group that needs to simultaneously define its positions and its constituency from a broad and heterogeneous set of possibilities. Another might be a professional association, a group whose constituency is well-defined, but with varying levels of involvement. Such an organization could use a large-scale survey with the aim of instituting or strengthening those activities that would get *more* members *more* involved. Such an approach would, on the other hand, be virtually meaningless for a small choral society with a very specialized and limited purpose and constituency.

In-depth interviews are another popular tool for market or constituency analysis. A university planning a capital campaign, for example, might begin developing major donors and campaign leadership this way. One-on-one, in-depth interviews with selected constituents, representing a variety of constituencies, would allow them to determine much of what they need to know for a successful campaign—which projects would be looked on most favorably, where other major prospects can be found, how much support they can expect and from what quarters, and where to set campaign goals.

The person-to-person interview also has important uses outside of immediate campaign goals. Where an organization's leadership and its most influential constituency are closely allied, or where a few major, well-defined issues are of paramount importance, informal meetings between equals can help each understand and appreciate the other's concerns. We have seen this technique work well for hospital leadership in dealing with the city's key business and opinion leaders over health care costs. Such an undertaking would be much more difficult, on the other hand, for a large and locally segmented organization like the Girl Scouts or the American Red Cross.

One other approach we will mention here is the focus group, a technique only recently borrowed from the profit sector but fast gaining popularity with nonprofit organizations. Such discussions can stimulate thinking and uncover significant issues that a predetermined survey or a one-on-one interview might miss, simply because no one in the organization knew to ask. Questions generated this way can then be tested on a larger scale.

One final point must be made on the issue of determining constituent needs. This is not a one-shot effort, but a continuing program of research and communication. Constituencies change; social contexts and other circumstances change; needs change as a result; and organizations themselves change in response. Remember that you are analyzing your constituents in order to institute or enhance programs and activities to meet their needs; it is essential that you monitor these changes and the reactions of your constituents to your efforts. Complacency has been the downfall of more than one overconfident institution.

Raising Interest Levels

Let us assume that your organization has identified its constituents, thoroughly researched their needs, and continued to adapt itself to those needs. Still, your constituents, the ungrateful wretches, are not falling all over themselves to support you. Why not?

The key may be public relations. While public relations itself raises no money, it is the window through which the world views your organization and forms its interpretation of your fund-raising message. It can determine the success not only of your constituency development, but of all your development efforts.

Public relations can raise the interest level of a constituent from consumer to friend, from advocate to donor, but to generate this kind of increasing involvement, you must set goals and create opportunities at each level for constituents to become

Informed. Of the organization's existence, its purposes, and its methods of achieving these purposes

Educated. About the institution's history, the people it serves, the problems it is designed to solve, its impact on society, the rationale behind its current programs, and its aspirations for the future

Involved. With the organization in action, its staff and volunteers as well as consumers; to become a volunteer or consumer, with access to the organization and a voice in its workings

Committed. To the organization; that is, to cross the subtle line between intimate acquaintance and emotional involvement

Helping the constituent advance from one level to the next can be a formidable task. There are barriers to overcome at every step: fierce competition for the person's time and attention, fear of one's own disillusionment or the disapproval of others, and so on. It is up to the organization to surmount these barriers. You must generate a conviction that your organization and its programs are important and useful, that they reflect well on those involved with them, and that the constituent's own involvement is important, even indispensable, in helping the organization accomplish its goals.

Public relations lays the groundwork for these efforts. Its objective is to decrease the distance—intellectual and emotional—between your organization and its constituents. There are many kinds of public relations activities, however, reaching different percentages or different sectors of your constituency. Notice, in the following brief list, how a wider coverage also implies a wider distance between organization and audience, whereas those activities reaching smaller numbers also involve them more intensely. For example:

Media coverage.   Whether national or local, reaches the largest number of possible constituents, but does so most impersonally.

Institutional newsletters, brochures, and annual reports.   Somewhat more involving, since they are mailed to specific people, known to the organization by name.

Films and speakers, or special events and tours.   These are more effective, involving active, on-the-scene participation between representatives of the organization and groups of constituents.

Person-to-person advocacy.   Including interviews with staff and leadership; this is the most intense and personal of public relations activities.

Research by our firm has indicated, not surprisingly, that constituents must know not only the institution but at least one member of its leadership, either staff or volunteer, before they will extend consistent, significant support. The principle can be applied to every level of increasing interest: A constituent will cross barriers more readily if someone he or she identifies with and respects acts as a guide.

Developing Constituencies

There are many time-tested methods for developing constituencies. Here we shall look at a few of the most common.

Membership Programs

Membership programs should be viewed not as an end in themselves, but as another means of expanding and developing constituencies, a step on an ascending ladder of involvement. While they may not be appropriate to every organization, the creative use of membership programs is not out of order in, say, a social service agency or medical research institution.

The key is to design a package of benefits sufficient to justify the cost to members. Access to special facilities, activities, and special events is the norm for cultural organizations, whereas professional associations may offer a range of benefits from insurance and educational opportunities to legislative advocacy and marketing programs. In some cases, such as environmental groups, consumer advocates, and government watchdogs, a belief in the organization's goals and a visible association with it may give sufficient membership benefits.

Your organization must also decide whether membership itself will be used to raise funds for the organization (as is usually the case) or whether membership is to serve as a springboard to greater involvement and can therefore be offered at cost. (Subscriptions to alumni magazines might fall into the latter category.) Such a decision weighs the risks involved in accepting a smaller degree of support when a larger gift might be had with further cultivation.

Volunteer Programs

The success of a volunteer program—whether we are speaking of fund-raising, governance, or program volunteers—depends on the same rules of sound personnel management you would apply to paid staff. The program must take into account the volunteer's needs and talents, as well as those of the organization.

The first step, then, is to determine the roles volunteers can play in your organization and to classify and organize those roles in a hierarchical structure. Volunteers must have clear job descriptions, and must be able to advance toward leadership positions along a well-defined chain of command. The next step is to develop training programs and materials. Remember, the volunteer must be educated not only in the job he or she is expected to perform—what you expect the volunteer to do, when, and how—but also in the history, mission, goals, accomplishments, and future of the organization. Only then can recruitment begin.

You may recruit through any of the public relations methods listed in the previous section: through print coupons or spots in the media, with direct mail appeals, by carrying your message in presentations to clubs and churches, and so on. Whatever method you choose, though, remember that it is the first impression that counts. Staff members involved in recruitment must *sell* your organization, and to do that they must not only articulate the benefits of association with it but must convey the impression of an organization that is competent, sure of its course, and confident in the future. The staff must be backed by a CEO who is very visible and who is of rather distinguished bearing, for it is to this individual that prospective donors and volunteers will ultimately look in assessing your organization.

Finally, keep in mind that recruitment must be tempered by sensitivity and selectivity in making job assignments for volunteers. Time spent in careful interviewing is just as important as it is with paid staff. Remember that a dissatisfied volunteer can, in the long run, be more costly than a defection by a paid employee.

Recognition

No matter what their level of participation—whether through contributions of time or talent or money—constituents must be recognized. They must be told, in whatever way may be appropriate, that they are helping to advance the mission of the organization and that the organization appreciates their support. If you ignore this most basic of rules you need not worry about your constituencies. There won't be any. Recognition, moreover, should be more than just a payoff, a favor or reward *bought* by the donor or volunteer. Rather, it is a way of telling constituents that they are one of you, a *part* of the organization and not an adjunct to it.

You can use recognition programs to advance your constituents' levels of involvement by offering different forms of recognition at different levels, the most desirable being the most publicly visible and the most difficult to attain. "Giving clubs," the listing of names in annual reports and other publications, volunteer award ceremonies, named gifts and plaques are all variations on this theme, and each can itself encompass a variety of levels of recognition. Their value depends entirely on public awareness of their significance.

Never Forget...

We began this chapter by telling you never to forget that your organization *is* its constituency. We have tried to show you that constituency development is more than collecting people into an institutional corral. Viewed at its highest level, it is both insurance for the well-being of your organization, and an embodiment of the philanthropic approach to improving the world in which we live.

By serving your constituents well, you are doing much more than fund-raising. You are advancing your institution, carrying out its mission, and fulfilling its highest goals.

33

Grants Preparation and Management

Stephen R. Wise

Ed.D., Florida Community College at Jacksonville

All too often the board members of a nonprofit organization (NPO) think that the organization's financial troubles will be over once a grant has been received. Even before seeking federal support, however, a nonprofit tax-exempt organization should assess its needs, mission, potential for expansion, organizational structure, and cash reserves. It is certainly possible for a nonprofit tax-exempt organization to receive federal and, even, foundation support, but often the strings that are attached to such support may strangle the organization. In many cases, the NPO must spend its own money first and submit vouchers to the granting agency prior to receiving funds. If the granting agency has a heavy load or if reported expenditures are disallowed for any number of reasons, the NPO will receive less money than it spent, thus becoming strapped for operational funds.

If the NPO's mission is such that seeking federal funds will enhance its operational objectives and supplement presently offered services, then by all means it should make a concerted effort to put together the necessary documentation to obtain a federal grant or contract. The competition is keen, and a proposal developed without adequate thought, time, and effort is easily spotted by the governmental or foundation program directors.

Grantsmanship

Grantsmanship is not a mysterious science that takes years to learn. It is simply salesmanship. James J. Kilpatrick, a syndicated columnist, wrote the following about the "Great Game of Grantsmanship."

> The General Accounting Office provided some fresh insights last month into the fastest growing and riches sport in America. This is not tennis as you might surmise. It is grantsmanship.
>
> The role of the grantsman is, of course, to get grants. But that states the matter too simply. The essence of the competitive sport is to wrangle a grant at the last possible moment from the least possible source, under the most flexible terms. This may seem easy, but considering the obstacles, it is fearfully hard.
>
> To the connoisseur of political affairs, grantsmanship is more than a mere game. It is an art, a science, a profession. The true grantsman must have the eyes of an eagle, the speed of a quarterhorse, the tenacity of a bulldog, and the greed of a hungry hog.

The Federal Office of Management and Budget publishes the *Catalog of Federal Domestic Assistance*. There are other reference books which can be obtained in the public libraries or in a local college development office.

Strategy

Strategy is a plan for making something happen successfully. Strategy in grantsmanship means first to identify a fundable project, then to find a funding source for that project, and finally to promote the project, the people in the project, and the benefits of the project. Here, then, is a strategy.

Investigate Funding Sources

First you need information: Where are the funding sources? The more you know about the potential for funding projects in general, the more likely you will find a funding source for your specific project.

However, knowing where the funding sources are is not enough. You also need to know what types of projects the funding sources are actually looking for and the priorities the funding sources have assigned to various types of projects. Rather than accept written guidelines at face value, try to learn what the guidelines, regulations, and various publications do *not* say. Contact a reliable source, the agency's personnel, to determine the real priorities. Every funding source states priorities but does not necessarily state which priorities are more important. Call the agency and ask for information. (The *Catalog of Federal Domestic Assistance* lists telephone numbers.) Basic questions to ask include:

1. What is the deadline date?
2. How much money has been appropriated?
3. How much money is available for this funding period?
4. Can an organization like ours submit a grant?
5. How many grants were funded last year?
6. Can you send me a list of last year's grants and the project director's names?
7. How many grants will be funded during this funding period?
8. What are the program priorities this year?
9. Do you want a preliminary proposal?
10. Can you send the program guidelines today?
11. How many proposals were submitted last year?

To judge your chances of securing funding, look further into the funding source: Determine what problems it encounters in meeting stated priorities, what projects it funded in the past, and at what dollar level funds were distributed on a geographical basis. Federal funding sources, for example, may be required to distribute at least one grant to every state.

Learn as much about the funding source as possible. Keep in mind that the funding agency must have a good grant track record in order to obtain appropriations from Congress.

Prepare a Needs Analysis Study

Never go to a funding source with an abstract idea stated in general terms. First prepare what is called a "needs analysis study," detailing *what is* as opposed to *what should be.* You should know what the present situation is and how the present situation should be changed to meet certain needs or to meet the criteria of the funding agency. The only way you can make a clear problem statement or needs statement is to make a needs analysis.

There are many techniques for assessing needs. One method is to administer an opinionnaire to a group of faculty members or community leaders to determine their attitudes toward a possible problem and get their opinions on what should be done to solve it. Use of the Delphi technique includes distributing a questionnaire, analyzing the results, refining the results into a new opinionnaire, evaluating the second questionnaire, and using this second or even a third refinement in forming the needs statement.

If there is a requirement for getting community information, such as a community impact study showing how well the organization serves the community, a more extensive model may have to be developed. In any event, there are guidelines for doing studies, and the data from the assessment is needed to substantiate the problem statement.

State Objectives

After completing the needs analysis, develop a statement on how to meet the needs, determine the initial objectives, and outline the most significant activities needed to meet the objectives.

Objectives should be written in the proper frame of reference, such as competency-based objectives or performance-type objectives. Now you are halfway home in anticipating how you will propose to evaluate the project. Such evaluations are becoming more and more critical to successful grantsmanship. Proposal writers show clear designs of how they expect to know when objectives have been met, granting agencies are not going to support their projects.

After conceptualizing an idea, a prospectus might be developed. A prospectus can be used to determine the possible interest of a grantor. From the prospectus, you will be able to discuss the idea with an agency's program personnel, show the needs analysis results, specify who the beneficiaries of the product or service will be and the approximate cost of the proposed project. Make an appointment to meet the agency's program personnel to ascertain if your idea is in the right direction.

You will also want to make certain that funding agency personnel know you are trying to understand their objectives, their problems, and their pressures. You should assure the agency that you accept their guidance. Your objective is to complete a proposal that will be a credit to your organization and to the funding agency.

Each governmental agency has a review and an evaluation process. If possible, obtain the criteria and rating sheets or at least ask the program official to talk to you about how the proposals are evaluated. This is important, because a proposal writer must supply the information on which the proposal reviewers base their evaluation.

Always show your appreciation for any assistance. A letter of appreciation is an excellent means of saying thanks for the assistance received.

If encouragement is obtained, a full proposal must now be written.

Developing a Full Proposal

The development of a full proposal is both demanding and costly in terms of personnel time. The motto of many NPO's seems to be, "We never have time to do it right, but we always have time to do it over." It is important to read the guidelines and supplementary materials before any actual writing takes place and to follow the agency's specific proposal format. The following mechanics of a proposal should also be kept in mind while preparing the final document:

1. Use the first page of a proposal as the title page; keep the title short.
2. Include a table of contents, showing the same headings as in the guidelines.
3. Put charts and long tables in an appendix.
4. Number the pages in the same place on each page. Be sure that pages are in chronological order, and that there are no blank pages. All pages should face the same way—the only exceptions are those pages typed lengthwise. Paper should be standard $8\frac{1}{2} \times 11$ inch sheets.
5. Avoid unexplained acronyms and abbreviations.
6. Staple pages in the upper left-hand corner on the diagonal so that readers can read the entire page.
7. Avoid fancy bindings.
8. Do not put each page in plastic.
9. Be sure that figures, statistics, and percentages are accurate. Be sure to use percentages and not whole numbers where requested, and vice versa.
10. Avoid over-documentation.
11. Eliminate unnecessary words. Brevity is important.

In developing a proposal, the guidelines that are furnished by the agency are essential and should be followed without exception. If no particular format is required by the agency, the following sequence of components should be considered:

1. Abstract or summary
2. Agency data
3. Statement of the problem
4. Objectives to be accomplished
5. Procedures to accomplish stated objectives

6. Evaluation procedure
7. Staff job descriptions
8. Organizational chart
9. Facilities to be used
10. Budget building
11. Budget narrative
12. Future funding

Abstract or Summary.   The summary is a very important part of the proposal. The summary should be written upon the completion of the proposal and should be clear, concise, and specific, using not more than 300 words. The reviewer usually reads the summary first, and first impressions are extremely important.

Agency Data.   The agency data section is used to brag about your organization and to build credibility in the eyes of the funding source. More often than not, proposals are funded on the basis of the reputation and past experiences of the organization.

In developing the narrative on your agency, keep in mind what you think "turns on" the funding sources program personnel and what they are interested in knowing about your agency that will encourage them to "buy" your proposal over similar ideas from other nonprofit, tax-exempt organizations. You should use this section to reinforce the connection between your interests and those of the funding source. Below is a list of the kinds of things that might be developed in this section.

1. How old your organization is and how you got started.
2. How many people you served last year and for what purpose.
3. Exactly where your organization is located, and anything that makes you unique, such as being the first, or only, such organization in your geographical area. What you have done in the past.
4. What your major mission is.
5. What your present operational budget is.
6. What support you have previously received from other organizations, foundations, and so on.

Statement of the Problem.   In requesting support from any agency, the problem to be addressed should be identified and narrowed to a scope that can be logically accomplished within a reasonable time frame with a reasonable amount of money. Needless to say, the problem and the potential solution to the problem must be within the purview of the funding agency.

The problem should be carefully documented. A needs assessment should be performed to justify the problem. Be quantitative, and identify the sources that provided the data. Do not just assume that everyone knows that this is a problem. You are trying to document the fact that your agency is cognizant of the problem. Utilize some key statistics, but do not fill the proposal with excessive amounts of tables or charts.

What has been done in the past to solve the identified problem? What does the latest literature say about the problem and potential solutions to the problem? It is your job to convince the funding source that there is a real need to solve the problem and that your organization can reduce the problem within a reasonable time frame and with a reasonable amount of money.

The Grantsmanship Center News, in an article by Norton J. Kirtz, Executive Director of the Grantsmanship Center, successfully outlines "The Characteristics of a Good Problem or Needs Statement."

Present Documentation.   A well-prepared problem statement presents documentation of the existence and extent of the problem. Where statistics are not available, authoritative statements describing the problem may be cited. For example, if you are dealing with drug abuse in an area where statistics have not been collected (e.g., in a particular school in your community), statements of the problem could be obtained from the school nurse, school administrators, local public health officials, and other agencies that might have contact with the student population.

The problem must be documented through statistics or authoritative statements. The assumption should never be made that you or your funding source clearly understands the nature of the problem and, therefore, that documentation is not necessary.

Understand Your Statistics.   Statistical support of your problem statement is extremely valuable. Understand, however, what your statistics say, and use them sparingly. A few well-chosen, valid, and documented statistics are far more powerful than pages of tables, charts, and graphs. A ream of statistics, thrust into the body of your proposal, will most likely intimidate, bore, or otherwise turn off the reader. If you feel compelled to use very extensive statistics, save them for an appendix.

Make sure that you know what your well-chosen statistics say. In a great many proposals the statistical presentation of the problem fails to support the thesis of the writer. The statistics may illustrate another point, deny an argument, or in some other way fail to support the proposal.

Use Comparative Statistics.   Whenever possible, use comparative statistics to make your point. What does it mean if 15 percent of the population of a community is elderly? The figure by itself tells nothing. However, if 10 percent of the surrounding communities is elderly, you can indicate that the population of elderly in your community is 50 percent higher than that in communities around you. In addition, what are the comparable statistics for the county, state, and nation? If you know these statistics, you can determine whether your community has a relatively high concentration of elderly, or whether it does not. It will help you put the problem in perspective.

Limit Your Scope.   Avoid overwhelming the reader with your problems or needs! Many planners or proposal writers overkill in their problem statements. They are so concerned about the nature and extent of problems that exist in their community that they attempt to "sell" the funding source primarily on the basis of needs. This results in proposals that describe all the ills in a low-income community—lack of jobs, school dropouts, malnutrition, juvenile delinquency, drug and alcohol problems, and so on—and then ask for $25,000, presumably to deal with all these problems. In this instance you have such a broad problem statement that you cannot possibly deal with it. The alternative is to narrow your scope to those problems with which you can deal considering your existing resources and those you are asking of the funding source, within the time frame of the proposed program.

Understand the Problem.   A drug rehabilitation center, concerned with the inability of its graduates to obtain jobs, proposed a major, in-house aircraft mechanics training school. The center had a good record in rehabilitating drug users, but knew that staying clean was more likely if the graduate had a job to go to after graduation. Two aircraft companies were located near the center and each had openings for mechanics, as well as their own training programs. The drug center proposed that an in-house training program (costing $500,000) could prepare its graduates for employment with these two companies. But they had not researched the problem adequately!

There had not been sufficient discussion with these two potential employers to determine *why* their graduates were not gaining entrance to the existing training programs at the two companies. The attitudes of the potential employers toward drug offenders might have been a critical factor. If the companies did not want to employ former offenders or former drug abusers, then all the training in the world would not have secured additional jobs at these two companies. On the other hand, a much more modest program, geared toward changing the attitudes of the employers, might bring about the desired results without the need for creating a new training program. With changed attitudes, the graduates might well be placed in the existing training programs of these two companies. *The moral of this is to keep your focus on identifying and solving the problem, not on creating new programs.*

Do Not Fall in Love with Your Program.   In other words, do not become so committed to your program, your methodology, or your solution that you lose sight of the problems or needs of your constituents. Focusing on problem identification and then setting objectives that relate to the problem allows you to explore all possible alternative for solving the problem. If your commitment is to your methodology, your proposal may well end up as an attempt to rationalize—to justify your program. If your commitment is to solving problems and meeting needs, then you just might do it.

Avoid the Circular Program Statement.   One kind of often-seen problem statement declares that the problem is the lack of a specific program in a particular geographic area. This is an excellent example of circular reasoning. For instance: "The problem in this community is that there is no effective tutoring program available, and therefore we propose to establish one." This statement says that the problem is the lack of what we have to offer. Avoid this kind of statement. The problem is underachievement in school. Your proposed *solution* is some specific tutoring program. There could be many reasons for the lack of a tutoring program in your area. Maybe it is not a very good idea. Maybe it has been tried and has failed many times in the past several years. Just because something is not there does not establish a need for it.

Objective to Be Accomplished.   The problem has been defined and stated in the previous section. An "objective" is a statement of a precisely measurable outcome to be accomplished by a project within the time allotted and the funds requested. This is the most important section of the written proposal because the objectives structure the selection of appropriate procedures, evaluation design, dissemination, personnel, facilities, and budget. The quality and care taken to specify program objectives can be measured in the quality of the program section of the proposal. The objectives should use action-oriented or measurable verbs. Examples of these and other words are shown at the end of the chapter.

An objective should have a particular outcome, a particular time frame, and a minimum level of acceptability. The logical flow from the objectives will be into procedures to accomplish the measurable objectives.

Procedures to Accomplish Stated Objectives.   In developing procedures, the more detailed they are, the easier it will be to put the plan of action into force once the project is funded. Develop a procedure for each objective. In developing procedures, some of the questions that might be addressed include

1. What is the project's time frame? (Show a starting and ending date.)
2. What is the population to be served?
3. How many people will be served?
4. How will the participants be selected?
5. Who will perform the tasks?
6. Where will the tasks be performed?
7. What will be the role of the advisory board?
8. How will the services or products be disseminated?

The tasks should be described and placed in sequential order. A Program Evaluation Review Technique (PERT) chart, or some other type of pictorial chart, can be developed. If you cannot draw a picture, you probably do not understand what you are trying to accomplish. The process will assist in describing the activities and placing the tasks in sequential order. The process will also assist in describing who will perform the tasks, where the tasks will be performed, and how long it will take to accomplish them.

Evaluation Procedure.   The evaluation design is an outgrowth of the objectives and need not be sophisticated or complicated. Evaluation is any systematic process designed to reduce uncertainty about the effectiveness of a particular program or program component. Evaluating a project should be continuous and not an after-the-fact activity. The evaluation process can be used as a tool to provide information necessary to make appropriate changes and adjustments in a program as it proceeds.

There should be at least one measurement for each objective, and more for critical objectives. In reality, an evaluation process will assist the reviewer in determining whether the stated objectives have been met. In many instances it will be necessary to utilize outside evaluators to effect changes in a program if the program is not meeting the stated objectives. The reason for not meeting the objectives may be such that the project manager does not have necessary influence or tools to cause the changes.

In developing a proposal, it is sometimes necessary to ask an outside agency to develop a method or procedure for evaluating the project within both a time frame and an estimated cost schedule. When the project is funded, a contract can be awarded to that outside agency. This procedure may not only guarantee a more objective evaluation, but it may also add to the creditability of the total application. Whether an outside independent evaluator is used or an in-house evaluation is developed, the procedures for answering the following questions need to be included in designing the evaluation section of the proposal:

1. Did the program accomplish its objective?
2. Did the program operate as it was designed to operate?
3. What kinds of decisions can be supported by the evaluation findings?
4. Is the project worth continuing, and from what source(s) can additional funds be derived?

The evaluation component of most proposals leaves much to be desired. If a well-structured evaluation procedure is developed, the proposal reviewer will probably be convinced that the organization that developed the proposal is thorough and systematic and that it can accomplish the stated objectives if properly funded.

Staff Job Description and Organizational Chart.   A project is only as good as the staff selected to carry out the stated objectives and procedures as outlined in the proposal. Grants programs should not be the place to shelve personnel who cannot do anything else or to reassign personnel who have had problems at other positions within the organization. Careful selection is necessary, and the first step in this process is to develop a detailed job description for each position and the minimum acceptable qualifications for that position.

The staff must report to someone on the organization chart; this should be clearly spelled out. An organization chart should be included in the attachments or appendix to the proposal, and job descriptions should be included and referenced in the proposal narrative. If personnel are already employed, résumés should be included to ensure that the proposal reviewers is aware of the staffs' qualifications, accomplishments, and previous activities.

Facilities to Be Used.   If the use of facilities is important in the accomplishment of the program objectives, then a statement should be made as to suitability, ownership, costs, and so on. Facilities and space can be used as in-kind match in many instances, but documentation is necessary in order to build a case as to cost. The location of the facilities often will be significant to the project's objectives. The proposal writer should make value judgments as to whether to include a section pertaining to facilities, locations, and related costs.

Budget Building.   The budget, which is always included in a proposal, is one of the most important aspects of the proposal. It presents the proposal's ideas in a financial sense. The budget indicates such things as who will be doing the job; anticipated travel expenses; what supplies will be needed; and what the organization's commitment is to the grant request from the standpoints of both cash and in-kind services. The budget must be derived from the objectives, tasks, and activities as expressed in the proposal.

A proposal budget consists of two major parts: financial figures (reporting costs), and a budget narrative (explaining how the costs were derived). The financial figures are the compilation and computation of the estimated costs of accomplishing the tasks described within the proposal. The budget narrative or written justification thoroughly explains how the financial figures were obtained for each category within the estimated budget.

The budget can be divided and subdivided into any number of categories and classifications. However, for most organizational proposals the program budget sheet (Figure 33.1) can be readily adapted.

The format is shown as a model with the express purpose of ensuring that the proposal writer will be cognizant of the many and varied budget items.

The budget is divided into ten major cost areas:

1.0   Personnel

2.0   Consultants

3.0   Travel

Program Budget Sheet

	Federal	Cash Match	In-Kind Match	Total
1.0 Personnel				
1.1 Administrative				
1.2 Clerical				
1.21 Part-time				
1.22 Full-time				
1.3 Fringe benefits				
Personnel subtotal				
2.0 Consultants				
2.1 Per-day honorarium				
2.2 Contract services				
3.0 Travel				
3.1 Local travel (car)				
3.2 Air fare				
3.3 Per diem				
3.4 Taxis — ground trans.				
4.0 Office supplies				
4.1 General office supplies				
4.2 Nonconsumable supplies				
5.0 Telephone/postage/utilities				
5.1 Long distance				
5.2 Monthly service				
5.3 Installation				
5.4 WATS line				
5.5 Postage				
5.6 Utilities				
6.0 Rental				
6.1 Equipment				
6.2 Office space				
6.3 Other				
7.0 Reproduction services				
8.0 Education materials/supplies				
9.0 Misc. items				
Subtotal				
10.0 Indirect costs				
11.0 Federal request — total				
12.0 Cash match — total				
13.0 In-kind match — total				
14.0 Total of 11.0, 12.0, 13.0				

Figure 33.1

	Federal	Cash Match	In-Kind Match	Total
1.0　Personnel				
1.1　Administrative				
1.2　Clerical				
1.21　Part-time				
1.22　Full-time				
1.3　Fringe benefits				
Personnel subtotal				

Figure 33.2

4.0　Office supplies

5.0　Telephone, postage, utilities

6.0　Rental

7.0　Reproduction services

8.0　Educational materials and supplies

9.0　Miscellaneous items

10.0　Indirect costs

A closer look at the program budget sheet (Figure 33.1) section by section, will illustrate areas of concern that need to be addressed in many proposals or as a selling point within the proposing organization.

1.0 Personnel. This subsection is the most important. (See Figure 33.2.) If the proposed plan is to be successful, the personnel associated with the program will be the key to success.

1.1 Administrative personnel. Administrators can be hired on either a full- or part-time capacity.

1.2 Clerical. Part-time or full-time clerical personnel may be used on a project. All personnel would be hired on a duration-of-contract basis.

1.3 Fringe benefits. If appropriate, fringe benefits should be calculated on all employees, both federal and cash match. Items that might be considered include social security, medical insurance, dental insurance, life insurance, workers compensation, and retirement plans.

2.0 Consultants. Consultants (See Figure 33.3) can be paid on a per-day basis or as a contract service. On a contract basis, the rate is for a specific set of tasks or objectives and usually covers travel, per diem, secretarial services, and all other services incurred in the agreement.

	Federal	Cash Match	In-Kind Match	Total
2.0　Consultants				
2.1　Per-day honorarium				
2.2　Contract services				

Figure 33.3

	Federal	Cash Match	In-Kind Match	Total
3.0 Travel				
3.1 Local travel (car)				
3.2 Air fare				
3.3 Per diem				
3.4 Taxis — ground trans.				

Figure 33.4

3.0 Travel.   (See Figure 33.4.)

3.1 Local travel.   Local travel is calculated at the government rate, institutional rate, or the rate that is the least. Local parking fees and tolls are included in this category.

3.2 Air fare.   Air fare should always be calculated at coach rate.

3.3 Per diem.   Per diem is calculated at the institutional rate or the governmental rate, whichever is lower. Always calculate for trips over 700 miles, via air, 1-day travel time.

3.4 Taxis and other ground transportation.   Upon arrival at a site via plane, it is usually necessary either to rent a car or to take a taxi to get to the designated destination. Gas and parking fees for the rental car should be calculated in this category.

4.0 Office supplies.   When a new project is started, an office must be established, and consumable and nonconsumable supplies must be obtained. (See Figure 33.5.)

5.0 Telephone, Postage, Utilities.   (See Figure 33.6.)

5.1 Long distance.   An estimate of the cost of long-distance telephone calls should be calculated. If the project is local in nature, then long-distance calls will not be a large item. A telephone credit card should be obtained for the project.

5.2 Monthly telephone service charge.   A monthly telephone service charge should be calculated into the telephone costs. The number of lines and telephones will determine the costs.

5.3 Installation.   Installation charges must be calculated.

5.4 WATS line.   Some organizations have access to a WATS line, and therefore a project can be charged a specific percentage of the yearly costs.

5.5 Postage.   If the project requires substantial mailings, this may be a very costly item, especially with the increased postage rates. Consideration might be given to using bulk rate, book rate, third-class mail, and so on.

5.6 Utilities.   A percentage of the utilities cost might be calculated, if not in-

	Federal	Cash Match	In-Kind Match	Total
4.0 Office supplies				
4.1 General office supplies				
4.2 Nonconsumable supplies				

Figure 33.5

	Federal	Cash Match	In-Kind Match	Total
5.0 Telephone/postage/utilities				
5.1 Long distance				
5.2 Monthly service				
5.3 Installation				
5.4 WATS line				
5.5 Postage				
5.6 Utilities				

Figure 33.6

cluded, in the indirect cost rate. If a separate office is used away from the institution, this item should be budgeted.

6.0 Rental.   (See Figure 33.7.)

	Federal	Cash Match	In-Kind Match	Total
6.0 Rental				
6.1 Equipment				
6.2 Office space				
6.3 Other				

Figure 33.7

6.1 Equipment.   Rental or lease of equipment such as typewriters, calculators, desks, and chairs is a necessity in many projects. Many times the purchase of equipment is not allowable in a project. However, an organization may purchase the equipment and lease it back to the project at the same rate that a commercial firm would enter into a rental agreement for the use of the equipment.

6.2 Office space.   Many times it will be necessary to secure office space at a site other than at the institution.

7.0 Reproduction Services.   (See Figure 33.8.) Every project has reproduc-

	Federal	Cash Match	In-Kind Match	Total
7.0 Reproduction services				

Figure 33.8

tion, photocopying, and offset press requirements. With the cost of paper and the demand for these services continuously increasing, this item should be considered very closely.

8.0 Education Materials and Supplies.   (See Figure 33.9.) Many projects include materials and supplies that will be used for instruction or by the clients. A method of calculating might be on a per-client basis.

	Federal	Cash Match	In–Kind Match	Total
8.0 Education materials/supplies				

Figure 33.9

9.0 Miscellaneous Items. (See Figure 33.10.) Anything that does not fit in the other eight categories should be included. A subtotal must be calculated for each of the categories.

	Federal	Cash Match	In–Kind Match	Total
9.0 Miscellaneous				

Figure 33.10

10.0 Indirect Costs. (See Figure 33.11.) Indirect cost can in most instances be calculated on the federal and cash match share, at a predetermined rate, as allowed by either the project or a negotiated rate with granting agency. The totals are then calculated and entered in the correct box (See Figure 33.12.)

Budget Narrative. A budget narrative must be written to justify each of the items shown on the program budget. This is done as the project writer determines what is needed to complete the tasks assigned and as the writer mentally estimates the costs of the project. The writer is justifying to the proposal reader/evaluator, in writing, how the figures were derived. The following are pitfalls to avoid:

1. *Loose or exaggerated items.* Request what is needed; do not work on the assumption that the program officer at the agency will cut the budget automatically.

2. *Salaries too low.* Salaries should reflect the costs of hiring competent personnel to complete the project. A low salary scale alerts the agency to the possibility that the project may flounder because of the inadequacy of the personnel involved. Always include job descriptions for all positions.

3. *Inconsistent budget and written proposals.* Make certain that the budget does not contain categories of items not covered in the proposal.

4. *Incorrect totals.* Double-check the arithmetic in order to ensure that all columns are added correctly.

Future Funding

This is the last section in the proposal narrative, but by no means the least important. It is important that if the program is a success and generates the desired re-

	Federal	Cash Match	In–Kind Match	Total
Subtotal				
10.0 Indirect costs				

Figure 33.11

	Federal	Cash Match	In-Kind Match	Total
11.0 Federal request — total				
12.0 Cash match — total				
13.0 In-kind match — total				
14.0 Total of 11.0, 12.0, 13.0				

Figure 33.12

sults, some or all the components can be continued either by the organization submitting the proposal or by other organizations within the community. Many times a program has not been present within the community because of the potential risk involved, but through seed money from the grant, the idea will be accepted. A "try it, you'll like it" attitude may be generated.

A plan to generate funds through the project itself—such as fees for service that will build up over a year or two, subscriptions to publications, and so on—is an excellent plan. The best plan is a plan that does not require outside grant support.

Appendix and Attachments

Appendix or attachments are necessary in almost any proposal. Within the program narrative, references can be made to a report; an article in a newspaper, journal, or other publication; job description, résumé; organizational chart; and letters of support, to name a few. The body of the program narrative should not be cluttered with extra information that can better be placed in a separate section. The appendix or attachments can be used to verify facts cited in the narrative and provide creditability to the rationale and needs section of the proposal.

Self-Evaluation of the Proposal

Now that the proposal is completed and in draft form, a self-evaluation should be attempted.

1. To what extent does this project meet the mission of the organization?

2. Has the proposal adequately identified and documented the need for the project?

3. To what extent has this proposal shown an awareness of similar programs, research findings, or the knowledge or recognized experts?

4. Are the objectives derived from the needs statement? Are they measurable?

5. Are the terms used in the proposal defined? Will others apply the same meaning to the key words in the proposal?

6. Is the evaluation technically sound? Is it appropriate in relation to the objectives and presented in a complete and detailed manner?

7. How adequate is the staff? Are there job descriptions and résumés?

8. Is the proposal paged in sequential order at the bottom of the page?

9. Is the budget adequate and not over cost? Is the "fat" out? Is there a budget justification section?

10. Are there proper organizational signatures on the project?

Proposal-Writing Terminology

A jargon has developed that explicitly describes certain procedures, processes, and documents with which all proposal writers should be acquainted. Presented below is a list of the primary technical terms used by government employees that is rapidly becoming a part of the grants writer's lexicon.

1. *Authorization.* A specific sum of money legislated by Congress in support of a public law. The amount authorized by congress is usually more than that which is usually appropriate.

2. *Appropriation.* The actual amount of money legislated by Congress (as suggested by the Office of Management and Budget) to be spent in support of a public law.

3. *Proposal document.* A communication instrument used to convey to the granting agency a set of prescribed activities for a stated sum of money. The document, when properly negotiated, becomes a legal, binding agreement between the applicant and the granting agency.

4. *Grant.* A sum of money offered by a granting agency to support an activity described in a proposal to that agency. A grant does not require the delivery of a product, but the grantee obligates itself to make a reasonable attempt to meet the grant conditions.

5. *Contract.* A legal, binding agreement between an agency and an organization for that organization to perform specific services desired by the agency.

6. *Direct costs.* Direct costs include the money specified in the budget of a proposal allocated in direct support of the project. It includes such items as personnel, employee benefits, travel, supplies and materials, office supplies, services, and special equipment.

7. *Indirect costs.* Known as "overhead," indirect costs include the peripheral services, facilities, and salaries of nonproject personnel that are required of an organization in support of the project. Generally, the basis on which the overhead percentage is computed has to be supplied.

8. *Cash match.* Commonly called the "matching funds provision," refers to the local financial contribution that the organization or institution expects to contribute to the project. For some grants and contracts it is required, whereas in others it is encouraged. Cost sharing is considered by federal agencies to be an indication of local interest and commitment in the project.

9. *In-kind match.* The money an organization puts into services, such as cost of building rent or rental of space, utilities, sometimes salary match.

10. *"Fixed-cost" grant or contract.* A grant or contract in which it is specified that an activity will be conducted for a fixed amount of money as described in line items of the budget. The total amount of money expended may not exceed the total amount budgeted, but generally, when authorized, a line item may vary by plus or minus 10 percent.

11. *Negotiation.* Process by which a legal and mutually satisfactory agreement

is reached between the funding agency and the grantee. The resulting grant or contract instrument states the conditions under which the award is made by the funding agency.

12. *Letter of intent.* Indicates your interest in applying for grant(s).

13. *Planning grant.* You are requesting money from a funding agency for planning the development of a program. The main budgetary items here are personnel, supplies, and travel.

14. *Prospectus.* Many government agencies are requesting a prospectus in place of a full-blown proposal. The prospectus is simply a method of stating your proposal in a two- or three-page statement, including all the components but not necessarily in the form of a proposal. The prospectus allows the reviewer to determine whether or not the proposed program is supportable without reading through a complete proposal. Ordinarily the reviewer will critique a prospectus and inform the organization of how the proposed program might best be strengthened.

Proposal-Writing Words

Action Verbs

Throw	Place	Depict	Deflect
Pitch	Run	Illustrate	Descend
Catch	Manipulate	Locate	Ascend
Type	Salvage	Label	Propel
Sing	Put	Justify	Carry
Strum	Tell	Rectify	Transport
Play	Call	Bring	Fly
Blow	Listen	Steer	Change
Strike	Cross	Characterize	Magnify
Reproduce	Dramatize	Render	Enlarge
Dissect	Jump	Decide	Disguise
Slide	Act	Detect	Circumscribe
Conjugate	Multiply	Start	Paint
Rotate	Erase	Turn	Shade
Alternate	Operate	Twist	Mold
Interchange	Infiltrate	Rebound	Tint
Generate	Confiscate	Activate	Maneuver
Evolve	Segregate	Instigate	Destroy
Interrelate	Integrate	Recuperate	Ignite
Punctuate	Assemble	Graph	Answer
Subtract	Dissemble	Draft	Alphabetize

Evaluation Words

Segregate	Preclude	Declare	Rescind
Assimilate	Review	Affirm	Abstain
Accumulate	Expedite	Establish	Stipulate
Rectify	Arbitrate	Categorize	Resolve
Justify	Insure	Clarify	Generate
Incorporate	Assure	Capitalize	Stimulate
Eliminate	Account	Disseminate	Facilitate
Modify	Delineate	Confirm	Reiterate
Mediate	Derive	Revise	Comply
Conciliate	Devise	Recycle	Promote
Respond	Mitigate	Alleviate	Reduce
Conclude	Interact	Secure	

Proposal-Writing Words (*continued*)

Other Words

Initiate	Measure	Institutionalize	Enforce
Develop	Assimilate	Duplicate	Empathize
Propose	Disseminate	Replicate	Deny
Institute	Evaluate	Require	Allow
Establish	Inculcate	Mandate	Systematize
Demonstrate	Validate	Deduce	Delineate
Innovate	Postulate	Teach	Inform
Modify	Reorganize	Veto	Abstract
Change	Posit	Fund	Substitute
Exemplify	Expend	Charge	Justify
Design	Submit	Reduce	Translate
Encourage	Approve	Monitor	Indoctrinate
Facilitate	Reject	Recycle	Maintain
Stimulate	Amend	Chart	Project
Integrate	Delete	Model	Improve
Unify	Reassess	Compute	Habilitate
Diversify	Conceptualize	Determine	Rehabilitate
Motivate	Internalize	Regulate	

34

Private Foundation Grants

Candace Kuhta
Consultant

In the latest available year of record (1985) there were 24,859 private grant-making foundations in the United States, and their giving totaled approximately $5.7 billion.[1] They gave this sum of money because they are public trusts, although their assets are derived from private sources, established to aid educational, social, charitable, or other activities serving the common welfare primarily by making grants to nonprofit organizations (NPOs). They are required by law to pay out a minimum of 5 percent of their assets at market value each year in grants. NPOs are often urged to establish a broad base of financial support, to consider all possible sources of funding and not to rely on one alone. Given the nature of private foundation activity, this source of funding should be investigated. A more complete understanding of the character and role of private foundations and a realistic assessment of foundation funding as compared to funding from other sources will help an organization decide whether to spend time seeking this type of support.

Types of Foundations

The type of foundations of interest to grant-seeking nonprofit organizations are *active* grant-making foundations, public or private. Three types of private foundations make grants: the independent, the company-sponsored, and, to a limited extent, the operating foundation. Community foundations, classified as publicly supported organizations, are also significant grant makers in their localities.

The independent foundations are the largest category of private foundations, and are usually established with an endowment from an individual or family with grants awarded from investment income. Grants from some, particularly smaller, independent foundations may be made with funds contributed periodically by a living donor, with an endowment often established after the donor's death. Family members or people designated by the family administer the funds for either general or special purposes permitted by the foundation's charter. The designation "independent" indicates a foundation of the size usually found in *The Foundation Directory,* with such varied names as The Edna McConnell Clark Foundation, the Carnegie Corporation of New York, King Ranch Family Trust, H.H. Kohl Charities, Inc., and Egenton Home, as well as smaller foundations such as the Edward A. Thornhill Foundation, Information for the Partially Sighted, and the Vera Hollen Memorial Scholarship Trust.

The company-sponsored foundation is established with an endowment and annual contributions from a profit-making corporation, but is a separate legal entity. It is governed by a board mainly of corporate officers but sometimes includes outside board members. Company employees often approve grants for charitable purposes that usually benefit communities in which the company carries out its business. The names of company-sponsored foundations often include the name of the donor company, such as the Gulf & Western Foundation, Inc., and the General Motors Foundation, while others do not. Table 34.1 lists the largest company-sponsored foundations by total giving.

An operating foundation conducts programs of its own, and only occasionally makes grants to other organizations. Only 107 of the 2184 currently active operating foundations are included in *The Foundation Directory* based on outside grant-making activity and asset size (see Table 34.2). Operating foundation activities in-

Table 34.1. The Largest Company-Sponsored Foundations by Total Giving

(All dollar figures expressed in thousands)

Name	State	Total giving	Gifts received	Assets	Fiscal date
AT&T Foundation	NY	$29,789	$ 456	$125,000	12/31/86
General Motors Foundation	MI	28,019	61,000	169,915	12/31/85
Amoco Foundation	IL	23,825	0	78,619	12/31/86
Exxon Education Foundation	NJ	21,363	26,933	67,909	12/31/86
General Electric Foundation	CT	18,395	8,200	57,581	12/31/86
Shell Companies Foundation	TX	17,437	9,967	25,496	12/31/86
ARCO Foundation	CA	15,238	14,000	6,126	12/31/86
Dayton Hudson Foundation	MN	14,540	13,043	12,758	1/31/86
Burlington Northern Foundation	WA	14,532	13,550	25,600	12/31/85
Mobil Foundation	NY	13,747	13,186	15,202	12/31/86
Procter & Gamble Fund	OH	12,710	13,000	15,027	6/30/86
Ford Motor Company Fund	MI	12,296	70,010	124,109	12/31/86
Southwestern Bell Foundation	MO	11,929	24,691	28,056	12/31/86
GTE Foundation	CT	11,184	11,022	15,004	12/31/85
Alcoa Foundation	PA	10,507	0	198,593	12/31/86
Brunswick Foundation	IL	10,499	11,836	5,035	12/31/85
Prudential Foundation	NJ	10,494	35,000	117,410	12/31/86

SOURCE: *The Foundation Directory,* 11th ed.

Table 34.2. Directory Operating Foundations by Asset Categories

(All dollar figures expressed in thousands)

Asset category	No. of foundations	Percent	Total assets	Percent	Total giving	Percent	Program amount	Other giving
$100 million or more	8	7.5	$5,023,347	79.7	$210,018	79.2	$194,861	$15,157
$50 million—under $100 million	5	4.7	415,437	6.6	14,133	5.3	12,473	1,660
$25 million—under $50 million	9	8.4	358,175	5.7	7,262	2.7	4,413	2,849
$10 million—under $25 million	19	17.7	292,085	4.6	10,618	4.0	6,495	4,123
$5 million—under $10 million	14	13.1	101,122	1.6	8,596	3.3	6,512	2,084
$1 million—under $5 million	38	35.5	106,117	1.7	9,297	3.5	5,215	4,082
Under $1 million	14	13.1	4,625	0.1	5,299	2.0	1,531	3,768
Total	107	100.0	$6,300,908	100.0	$265,223	100.0	$213,500	$33,723

SOURCE: *The Foundation Directory*, 11th ed.

clude the operation of museums, such as those of the Norton Simon Foundation and the J. Paul Getty Trust; and the sponsoring of research in science, social science, and medicine, such as the work of the Charles F. Kettering Foundation, the Russell Sage Foundation, and the Research Corporation.[2]

The community foundation is a publicly funded organization, with contributions received from many donors, in some cases from private foundations. It is classified by the Internal Revenue Service as a public charity, and makes grants in a particular community or region (see Table 34.3). The governing body which distributes the grants is composed of people representative of a community's interests.

Foundation Giving in Perspective

The *Giving USA* Annual Report for 1986[3] describes private foundation giving (excluding company-sponsored foundations which it includes in its corporate category) as comprising only 5.9 percent of the total of private giving. Giving by individuals represents 82.2 percent of the total, bequests 6.7 percent, and gifts from corporations 5.2 percent. These figures indicate that an individual who benefits from an organization's activities is the most likely private entity to support that organization. The total of private foundation grants is small when compared to other sources, and yet foundations have the potential for responding quickly to society's needs, for funding new responses to problems, and for taking risks. One would think that it would be difficult for corporate and government funding

Table 34.3. The Twenty Largest Community Foundations by Assets

(All dollar figures expressed in thousands)

Name	State	Assets	Total giving	Fiscal date
New York Community Trust	NY	$527,360	$42,006	12/31/86
Marin Community Foundation	CA	430,000	15,207*	6/30/87
Cleveland Foundation	OH	415,000	18,674	12/31/86
Chicago Community Trust	IL	237,400	23,397	9/30/86
San Francisco Foundation	CA	177,000	12,800	6/30/87
Boston Foundation	MA	167,202	12,163	6/30/86
Communities Foundation of Texas	TX	124,975	16,614	6/30/86
Hartford Foundation for Public Giving	CT	112,946	6,013	9/30/86
Columbus Foundation	OH	104,000	6,371	12/31/86
Saint Paul Foundation	MN	100,008	4,664	12/31/86
Pittsburgh Foundation	PA	87,541	4,335	12/31/85
New Haven Foundation	CT	73,674	3,567	12/31/86
Metropolitan Atlanta Community Foundation	GA	62,851	12,767	6/30/86
Philadephia Foundation	PA	56,000	3,824	4/30/86
Rhode Island Foundation	RI	54,000	2,816	12/31/86
California Community Foundation	CA	53,302	5,925	6/30/86
Kalamazoo Foundation	MI	52,688	4,273	12/31/85
Milwaukee Foundation	WI	48,475	3,146	12/31/85
Minneapolis Foundation	MN	45,576	4,667	3/31/86
Indianapolis Foundation	IN	40,623	1,334	12/31/86

* Estimated grants for 6 month period January 1 to June 30, 1987, including grant commitments made by The San Francisco Foundation, renewal of expiring grants, emergency and technical assistance, and new projects.

SOURCE: *The Foundation Directory*, 11th ed.

sources to take risks with taxpayers' and shareholders' money. In reality, however, many foundations choose to fund well-established, traditional organizations and projects, while some corporations and government agencies fund very *innovative* programs.

It has been established so far that several types of grant-making foundations have a large amount of money to give to nonprofit organizations each year, although perhaps not as much as individuals or the government. Some private foundations may be more willing to support innovative projects than other funders. If an organization should decide to pursue foundation funding, additional research will be required to identify which individual foundations might be interested in funding its work.

The Foundation Center

The Foundation Center provides information that can assist a nonprofit organization in its search for foundation support. Libraries provide access to information collected by the center about foundations and their grant-making activities and offer reference services and seminars to instruct in the use of this information, while the publications contain facts derived from foundations reporting directly to the center and to the Internal Revenue Service. The Foundation Center has been serving the nonprofit community, grant makers and grant seekers alike, for 30 years, since its chartering in 1956. During that time it has developed and improved its methods of data gathering and display and research instruction to give the grant-seeking public varied and thorough access to potential sources of funding, and the grant-making institutions improved knowledge of activity in their field.

The libraries operated by The Foundation Center in New York, Washington, Cleveland, and San Francisco are open and free of charge to the general public during a full schedule of hours. The self-guided research format in these libraries is augmented by the availability of professional reference assistance and free seminars which introduce The Foundation Center's publications and services, describe foundations' similar and disparate characteristics, and instruct in the research process required to identify the most appropriate source of funding for an organization. Although telephone reference service is not available to the general public, an organization may subscribe to the center's Associates Program and have toll-free or local phone access to the reference expertise of the staff in the New York and Washington libraries. Research materials are made available in the rest of the country and in several international locations through the center's Cooperating Collection Network, composed of over 165 public and university libraries, foundation and grant-makers' association offices, and other organizations. These sites maintain a core collection of Foundation Center publications and, when possible, acquire additional reference materials and give seminars in foundation research. Questions about holdings and service availability should be directed to each collection. The most recent list of Foundation Center collections and a description of complete services for Associates Program subscribers are available from:

The Foundation Center
79 Fifth Avenue
New York, N.Y. 10003

The Foundation Center's Gladys Brooks Library in New York serves 15,000 visitors each year. It is responsible for acquiring, arranging, and distributing varied resource materials about philanthropy to the other libraries. It provides information about the center to nearly 10,000 people each year who make inquiry through the mail and issues program brochures to several hundred conferences, seminars, and other programs.

Materials acquired by the library include the center's basic resource, the IRS 990-PF Information Return in microfiche format available for every one of the 24,859 private foundations in the United States. This form is a public record, and must be filed by private foundations each year. It provides facts about a foundation's assets, gifts received, total grants awarded, officers and trustees, investments, and descriptions of individual grants, including name of the recipient, location, amount of grant received, and a brief description of the project that received the grant. In the case of the smaller foundations, this form may be the only source of information about them.

The library also acquires books about individual foundations, philanthropists and philanthropy in general, recent studies, magazines, newspapers and newsletters, conference proceedings, and it maintains foundation files of clippings, news releases, factual updates, foundation publications, and historical materials. The center attempts to collect everything that might help an organization determine whether a particular foundation is its most appropriate source of funding.

The editorial division of The Foundation Center enters the information it collects from foundations and additional sources—such as foundation publications and the 990-PF Information Return—into its three databases, *The Foundation Directory* database, *The Foundation Grants Index* database, and the National Foundations database. Recently the structure and the procedures for entering data into *The Foundation Directory* and *The Foundation Grants Index* databases have been revised to eliminate redundancy and to provide a more integrated, useful entry in the databases' various published products. The information in the databases is available online through DIALOG Information Services in Palo Alto, Calif.[4]

The Foundation Center's publications include indexes, directories, and guides to the grant-making interests and activities of foundations and are used together to provide accurate information about prospective funders. The uses of the major publications will be described in the following discussion of the research process.

The Foundation Research Process

Throughout its years of working with foundations and the grant-seeking public, The Foundation Center has developed and taught a research method designed to identify all prospects with related, but broad, areas of interest in common with the interests of the grant seeker and then to narrow this list—by studying the limitations on a foundation's giving, the specific grants it has made, and all available facts about a foundation's methods of operation—to those few foundation names which seem to be the most likely to fund a specific need. The specific need must be very clear to the requesting organization as well. Before deciding to pursue grants of any kind, an organization should analyze its capabilities, its plans, and its role in the community. It must have a thorough knowledge of any other groups doing the same sort of work, and should have investigated the possibility for joint efforts. This analysis will give the grant-seeking organization a strong sense of purpose, one that will be transmitted to the foundation in the grant proposal and in any personal contact with foundation staff. It is through a mutual respect on the part of foundations and grant-seeking organizations for each other's purposes and through honest open communication that the most successful partnerships will be formed.

Foundations do not usually announce the availability of their grants, therefore it is the responsibility of the grant seeker to determine a foundation's interests and patterns of giving through the study of grants that have already been made by that foundation. In 1986 over 40,000 grants of $5000 or more—more than $2.2 billion—were reported to The Foundation Center by 459 large foundations, including the 100 largest, for entry into *The Foundation Grants Index* database. Table 34.4 shows the distribution of these grants by foundation type. The printed indexes which are the products of this database include *The Foundation Grants Index* annual, the *COMSEARCH* series of broad and narrow subject indexes, and *The Foundation Grants Index Bimonthly,* a service providing updates on grants, addresses, trustees, and foundation publications. These publications are used in the initial stage of research to identify prospects, those funders who have already made grants for projects or to organizations similar to your own. Access is provided to the grants listings by state location of the foundation, through subject and recipient name or category. Each book is arranged by state, then alphabetically by the foundations in each state, with a statement of any limitations on a foundation's giving program.

Once a list of prospects has been compiled, the nonprofit organization must find out as much as possible about the foundations on that list using every available source. It must identify foundations that will make grants of the desired size in its geographic area for the type of support it needs. It must learn all the application requirements of the prospects, and the name of the person to contact at the foundation when making inquiries and appointments, and when submitting a proposal.

The Foundation Directory, 11th edition, will provide much of this information for the 5148 largest foundations, which represent $89.9 billion in assets and $5.3 billion in annual giving. This group comprises only 20 percent of all active grant-making foundations, but represents approximately 97 percent of the total assets and 92 percent of the total grant dollars distributed in 1985. In order for a foundation to be included in the directory, it must have assets of $1 million or more or give $100,000 or more in the latest year of record. *The Foundation Directory* is published every other year from *The Foundation Directory* database, alternating with *The Foundation Directory Supplement* which provides updates received during the year. It is arranged alphabetically by state, then by the foundations within each state, with access provided through the Index of Donors, Officers and Trustees, the Geographic Index, Types of Support Index, Subject Index, and the Foundation Name Index.

Source Book Profiles is a quarterly publication that provides more detailed information for the 1000 largest foundations in the country based on total giving. It is compiled within a 2-year publishing cycle, profiling 500 foundations each year with continuous updating of the foundations profiled in the previous year. A special feature of each is the Grants Analysis, a statistical and analytical profile which highlights the key characteristics of each foundation's program. The indexes provided are Types of Support, Subjects, Geographic, and Foundations.

More information about a foundation's history, personnel, program, and plans may be included in a printed annual report when it is available. Approximately 742 foundations of the size of those listed in *The Foundation Directory* now publish annual reports, and more are being encouraged to do so through the efforts of The Council on Foundations and its annual awards for the best annual reports in various categories and through other organizations that urge philanthropy to be more responsive. The 990-PF Information Return mentioned earlier is available for every foundation, and a study of the grants lists on several years' returns may indicate certain patterns of giving.

To research smaller foundations, those 19,711 which do not appear in *The Foundation Directory,* one must search by geographic area. Smaller foundations may or may not have specific program areas of interest, but will usually make grants to organizations in the community with which the foundation is concerned. To identify those foundations which are located in your area, use the *National Data Book* as

Table 34.4. Distribution of Reported Grants by Foundation Type*

Foundation type	Number of foundations		Dollar value of grants		Number of grants	
	No.	%	Amount	%	No.	%
Independent foundations	319	69.5	$1,732,528	78.2	22,006	54.3
Company-sponsored foundations	78	17.0	336,948	15.2	14,964	36.9
Community foundations	56	12.2	138,727	6.3	3,454	8.5
Operating foundations	6	1.3	8,445	0.4	122	0.3
Total	459	100.0	$2,216,647	100.0	40,546	100.00

* Dollar figures expressed in thousands; due to rounding, figures may not add up.

SOURCE: *The Foundation Directory*, 11th ed.

the first step. It is the only complete listing of all private foundations in the country, regardless of size. The primary source of data for this publication and its corresponding database is the IRS transaction tape from the annual information returns filed in that year. The staff at the center verifies data and updates names and addresses to reflect the most current information available. The main volume is arranged alphabetically by state and then by foundations in decreasing order of grants awarded. Each entry includes the name and address of the foundation, principal officer, assets, grants paid, gifts received, and an indication of whether the foundation publishes an annual report. This volume is accompanied by an alphabetical index. The *National Data Book* includes a bibliography of directories of state and local grant makers, which are additional sources of information about smaller foundations in specific areas. These directories are published by a wide range of organizations and vary in size and quality, but they may give facts that are unavailable elsewhere.

Once you have identified private foundations in your area, you can look at the 990-PF Information Return for more details. Community foundations are included in a separate section of the *National Data Book,* providing information about this important source of local funding.

Approaching the Foundation

When your list of prospects has been reduced to a small group of well-researched foundations that seem most likely to be interested in receiving a proposal from you, make your initial contact in exactly the manner requested by those foundations in one or more of the resources mentioned above. Some foundations prefer to receive a letter which briefly describes your organization, its project, and its needs. On the basis of this description, a foundation can then decide whether it wants to pursue the project and request a full proposal. Some foundations require a complete proposal at the outset, whereas others will accept an initial telephone call. When possible, speak with someone at the foundation and make an appointment to make a presentation about your organization and its program at some stage in the application process. Most foundations do not have sufficient staff to accommodate all such requests, but when it is possible, it is to your advantage to make a contact with someone who will then have a voice, a face, and a personal presentation in mind each time your organization's name comes up. When a full proposal is requested, include all information requested by the foundation. Consult, for example, such guides to foundation proposal writing as *Program Planning and Proposal Writing,* a booklet developed and distributed by The Grantsmanship Center, a for-profit organization which provides training in fund-raising and proposal writing across the country.[5]

If your request for funds is rejected (even though you have submitted what you are convinced is a well-researched, accurately targeted proposal for a project that is new and necessary in your community), try to benefit from the reasons for rejection that you are given. There may be any number of reasons why a proposal is rejected, and even in the absence of error on your part, foundations receive many more appropriate requests than they can possibly fund. If you are successful, thank the foundation, and whether you are asked for periodic reports or not, provide them. Tell the people at the foundation how your work is progressing, and if you run into trouble, discuss the problem with them. Once you have obtained foundation funding, don't lose it through carelessness.

Notes

1. *The Foundation Directory,* 11th ed., The Foundation Center, New York, 1987, Introduction.

2. Joseph Foote, Service Unlimited, *Foundation News,* vol. 26:4, July/August 1985, pp. 10–19.

3. AAFRC Trust for Philanthropy, *Giving USA: Estimates of Philanthropic Giving in 1986 and the Trends They Show,* 32d Annual Issue, New York, 1987, p. 11.

4. Further information about DIALOG searching is available from DIALOG Information Services, Inc., Marketing Dept., 3460 Hillview Ave., Palo Alto, Calif. 94304.

5. The Grantsmanship Center is located at 1031 S. Grand Avenue, Los Angeles, Calif. 90015.

35

Seeking Revenue
or Support
from Corporations*

Tracy D. Connors
Consultant

Stephan R. Wise
Ed.D., Florida Community College at Jacksonville

Corporate giving, or "corporate social responsibility," is well on its way to becoming the new "darling" of funding sources for nonprofit organizations (NPOs)—or, so one might believe by reading headlines in some publications. While that is obviously going too far, nevertheless, the extent and variety of relationships between business and NPOs is convincingly on the rise. We can get a better perspective on what is happening in this area by considering the following:

- Only 20 years ago, corporate giving to philanthropy amounted to a mere $350 to $400 million annually.

- Today, it totals over $4.3 billion annually (out of over $80 billion given to philanthropy by all sources—individuals, bequests, corporations, and foundations).

Even though corporate giving is on the increase, effective corporate fund-raising depends on the professionalism of those seeking corporate support. An increase in corporate support can be expected, but it will not be automatic. It will come about for individual institutions and organizations as a direct result of their research and the application of the operative principles at work in the business-philanthropic symbiosis. It is encouraging, however, that national leaders have begun to come out strongly in favor of increased corporate giving. The following summary of representative quotes by national business and philanthropic leaders illustrates the

*Adapted in part and with permission from the author's Introduction to *Taft Corporate Directory*, 1982.

importance that these leaders place on the relationship between business and philanthropy and offers a great deal of insight into how they view the future of that relationship. Obviously, these insights should be kept in mind during the formulation of any corporate giving program:

> Those of us who are regularly solicited by nonprofit organizations have heard the same familiar litany of needs and priorities, no matter what the organization. Each area—the arts, education, health, you name it—each thinks it is more critical, more essential, more deserving. Everyone, in other words, is fighting for a bigger and bigger "slice of the pie." But, the trouble is, it's a diminishing pie....It makes good sense. The fastest way to increase giving to any one segment is to increase total giving to the entire sector.... Concentrating on "pie size" rather than "slice size" is simply a more profitable way for each of us to be using our energies.... And, I submit, the fastest way to increase our "pie size" is to join forces and press for a major—and measurable—increase in corporate philanthropy.
>
> From my vantage point, America's corporations and America's voluntary sector are natural allies.... The public is displeased with our [business] priorities and the way we conduct our businesses.... So, I firmly believe, business must be pushed to take steps now to redeem itself in the public's eyes.... One very effective way to do that, I submit, is for Corporate America to enact a positive program of community philanthropy on a scale that will assure America [that] the business of business is more than just making money. The business of business really is serving society.—Kenneth N. Dayton, Chairman, Dayton Hudson Corporation.

> Business cannot survive and prosper unless the society in which it operates is healthy and vibrant. It is, therefore, in business' own self interest, on behalf of its stockholders, employees, and various other constituencies, to engage in philanthropic activities which serve to strengthen the fabric of society.—Clifton C. Garvin, Jr., chairman, Exxon Corporation and The Business Roundtable.

> Business can no longer sit back and tell itself, as some economists advocate, that social progress is not the business of business. It is a question of whether business will have the vision and good sense to work with its partners in the public and volunteer sectors to help shape the nature of that change.... In the balance of this decade, we as a nation are facing problems of such magnitude that we cannot any longer afford the luxury of permitting the three major sectors of our society to be adversaries. We must work together to create a new era in which the public, private, and volunteer sectors work cooperatively to stimulate and direct positive change.—Robert V. Van Fossan, chairman and chief executive officer, Mutual Benefit Life, in *The Christian Science Monitor.*

Trends in Corporate Giving

You can expect corporate giving to steadily increase, bearing in mind that corporate giving correlates very strongly with the overall profits picture. When corporations make money, more of it can be allocated to social responsibility efforts. However, because of their dependence on before-tax profits, which may be volatile in coming years, corporate contributions are likely to be a fluctuating source of annual funding. Although an erratic annual performance in this sector is likely, the total estimated growth rate suggests to experts that corporate contributions will be on the increase in coming years, even after accounting for the forecast rate of inflation.

Expect corporations to adjust their giving programs to economic conditions: When profits go up, gifts go up; when profits are down, gifts are reduced accordingly. A balanced fund-raising program is essential, one that aggressively seeks corporate support, but which maintains a balanced base of components for individual, foundation, and planned giving as well. Bear in mind that a corporation's social responsibility efforts and strategies are increasingly linked to its overall business operations and activities.

The majority of major, national U.S. corporations are aiming for a corporate giving level of between 1 and 3 percent of pretax net income (PTNI). This is growing awareness by corporate leaders that a giving level of lower than 1 percent of PTNI is not responsible. The rise in corporate giving to NPOs will continue as the U.S. business community rapidly becomes more educated, enthusiastic, vocal, and supportive of its support for philanthropy.

Most major U.S. corporations now have professionals to organize and manage their philanthropic activities. The application, review, selection and management processes that corporations use for their philanthropic grants can be expected to become more structured and formalized. Corporate giving programs will be carefully planned to get something in return—credibility, exposure, image, goodwill, etc. Accordingly, local efforts will be very important to locally based corporations as well as to national firms with major operations in your particular geographic area.

Nonprofit organizations can be expected also to push corporations to disclose publicly their giving patterns, habits, and amounts—even though they are not legally required to do so. Activists continue to push corporations to give such a public accounting through brochures or inclusion in their annual reports and to note such giving as a percentage of pretax net income.

One of the most significant signs of the move toward increased corporate contributions to NPOs was the issuance of a strong position paper on corporate philanthropy by The Business Roundtable. Before reviewing the major points emphasized by the Roundtable, we should note that the organization's policy committee included, in addition to Mr. Garvin, such national leaders of American business as Theodore F. Brophy, William M. Agee, A. W. Clausen, Justin Dart, William A. Klopman, Archie R. McCardell, Thomas A. Murphy, Donald T. Regan, Irving S. Shapiro, Richard R. Shinn, George P. Schultz, and Rawleigh Warner, Jr.

The Roundtable paper pointed out that the ability to make contributions tends to rise and fall with the course of the economy, and thus runs counter to times of greater or lesser social need. It urged businesses to "make an effort to maintain support of their most important philanthropic programs even during economic downturns." The principal alternative to private philanthropy is government funding, the Roundtable noted, and the sources of government funds, it must be emphasized, are tax-paying individuals and business enterprise. It is in everyone's self-interest to support society through private social investments rather than through the complex and costly redistribution of tax dollars by government.

In its assessment of corporate giving, the Roundtable included not only financial contributions, but also a broad range of business activities including loans of personnel, donations or loans of equipment and space, volunteer programs, and dollar investments in economic redevelopment efforts. It said that corporate philanthropy should be recognized "as good business and as an obligation."

NPOs can expect the Roundtable's positions on corporate philanthropy will be adopted in large part in coming years by the majority of America's larger corporations, certainly those wishing to have any credibility with the communities they serve and with philanthropic organizations in general. The following highlights of the Roundtable's positions should be kept in mind during the formulation of your corporate support programs and, perhaps, used wherever appropriate as additional justification for corporate support:

- Corporate philanthropy, primarily through contributions, is an integral part of corporate social responsibility.

- All business entities should recognize philanthropy both as good business and as an obligation if they are to be considered responsible corporate citizens of the national and local communities in which they operate.

- All businesses should establish appropriate programs to handle philanthropy in a businesslike manner.

- Although financial contributions to not-for-profit organizations are an essential element in business philanthropy, participation also encompasses a broader range of activities than has been traditionally accepted or defined by the Internal Revenue Service. For example, corporations frequently assist not-for-profit institutions through loans of employees, donations or loans of equipment and space, volunteer programs, and direct dollar investments in economic redevelopment efforts—all of which may be accounted for as business expenses.

- Government funding is considered to be inherently less efficient in the distribution and control of funds for philanthropy than direct contributions. It is, therefore, in everyone's self-interest to support society through private social investments rather than through the complex and costly redistribution of tax dollars by government. If business is serious in seeking to stem overdependence on government and still allow the private not-for-profit sector to make the same contribution to society that it has in the past, business must itself increase its level of commitment.

- It has become increasingly evident that business cannot survive and prosper unless society continues to improve and develop. Businesses, on behalf of their stockholders, employees, and various other constituencies, have a self-interest in philanthropic activities which serve to strengthen the fabric of society. However, there is evidence that the business community has not fully recognized the value of corporate philanthropy.

- Each business firm has a responsibility to manage its philanthropic activities according to the same standards it uses to manage the other parts of its business. These standards apply not only to the quality of the individuals managing these functions, but also the personal involvement of top corporate officers in the management of these activities.

- Decisions about the amount and distribution of corporate resources allocated to voluntary organizations and projects must and should be left up to individual companies. Accordingly, the philanthropic programs of businesses will differ depending, for example, on the needs of the communities in which they operate. It is most important that all businesses develop an effective means of assessing these needs and regularly review their support programs to determine the appropriate level of support for not-for-profit organizations.

- The extent of philanthropy by a given business enterprise in a particular year is dependent upon a large number of factors including profitability, investment requirements, and capital structure as well as the nature of the business. For this reason, the ability to make contributions is often countercyclical to the needs of society, and businesses should make an effort to maintain support of their most important philanthropic programs even during economic downturns.

- All companies should make public, in a manner they deem appropriate, information on their corporate philanthropic programs. Whatever form is chosen, public dissemination of this information would serve as one means of increasing public awareness of the involvement of business in improving the quality of life.

Points to Remember When Planning Corporate Giving Programs

Based on assets, U.S. corporations give on the average about 0.05 percent of domestic assets. Per employee, it is about $60 per employee.

On the average, corporate giving programs allocate nearly 40 percent of their contributions to local programs. National and headquarters city programs account for the remaining 60 percent, divided about equally between them.

Local programs take about 40 percent of direct giving budgets. The remaining 60 percent is divided about equally between national and headquarters city programs.

Perhaps as much as 75 percent of a company's direct-giving budget is composed of items that give the contributions office little or no flexibility in reallocation. Capital support pledges, federated campaign support, donations to higher education (particularly to colleges and universities from which employees are recruited or corporate-related research conducted) are usually substantive in nature and agreed upon by a committee of high senior corporate officials. Changes in this area require adequate lead time (usually many months) and approval from very high up in the corporate structure. Of course, when they can be arranged, such changes can represent very substantial amounts.

Cooperative funding by several companies of important projects is a growing trend, particularly in support of cultural and urban development projects.

Direct Giving and Foundation Giving

Direct corporate contributions accounted for about 60 percent of total corporate giving in recent years, whereas grants by company foundations made up the remaining 40 percent. The majority of the country's larger corporations have a direct-giving program, whether or not they also have a corporate foundation. Corporations having a foundation, however, augment its support program with direct giving as well.

A corporate foundation is a separate legal entity created and funded by a business corporation under the nonprofit corporation laws of the state for the purpose of making grants and otherwise contributing to one or more educational, scientific, religious, or other charitable purposes. Following incorporation under state statutes, application is made on IRS Form 1023 to the federal Internal Revenue Service for designation as an organization exempt from federal income taxes and to which gifts are deductible by the corporate contributor of up to 10 percent of its pretax income.

Reasons for creating a corporate foundation were outlined in a "Memorandum on Corporate Giving," prepared by the Council on Foundations in Washington, including

- Leveling of the flow on contributions which a company foundation makes possible. By building a reserve or "cushion" of assets in the foundation during years when the parent company has high earnings, a relatively level flow of contributions from the foundation is maintained even when the parent company's earnings are off. This cushioning effect permits the company to reduce its taxes in good years when it may have other pressing needs for its cash flow. The foundation can dip into its reserves at a time when operating charities are likely to be suffering cutbacks in individual giving and are particularly in need of constant sources of support.

- Most company foundations function with relatively small endowments. They receive annual contributions from the parent company and pay out similar amounts in grants.

- A charitable tax shelter is available to companies. They can deduct contributions to the foundations, including principal amounts that are not paid out but are added to endowment. Such additions to endowment can be attractive to a corporation for another reason. The immediate deductibility of gifts to the foundation means that in good years a corporation can "endow" its foundation, and, as the earnings of that endowment build up, use those earnings to supplement the grants made possible by the corporation's annual contribution to the foundation. Thus, what might be termed an "inflation hedge" is created. The earnings on the foundation's endowment make possible an increase in annual giving, even though the corporation's annual contribution to the foundation remains unchanged.

- Corporate foundations provide other advantages to the parent company. Senior corporate officers are visible targets for fund-raisers, and are frequently importuned by those seeking corporate contributions. The company foundation serves as a buffer, and makes possible better organized and more selective giving than is usual when the senior officer's only intermediary is a contributions committee of the board. Fund seekers assume, often incorrectly, that such a committee is controlled by the chief executive officer and that decisions about grants are governed by this CEO's personal power and discretion. A company foundation, however, particularly if it has adopted and published guidelines for its giving, is much more likely to be seen by grant seekers as independent and as acting according to regular procedures when reviewing grant requests.

- The process of establishing the corporate foundation frequently provides an opportunity for a useful reappraisal of the corporation's philanthropic objectives and the upgrading of the giving function within the corporation. Such steps often bring about a more effective use of the charitable dollar and justify any added administrative expenses involved.

Corporate foundation management requires sharp attention to the Tax Reform Act rules restricting self-dealing between the donor and the foundation and the threat of various penalty taxes which may be incurred by the foundation and its managers, even for inadvertent missteps.

Types of Corporate Support

Corporations have a lot more to offer philanthropic organizations than money. For example, in the area of in-kind contributions and gifts, corporations can be more creative than in any other area of support. Six basic areas of support from corporations should be considered:

1. *Gifts and grants.* (*a*) Outright check to cover small gift, e.g., tickets, Girl Scout cookies, etc., (*b*) general support contribution given primarily to an agency

as a token of its public image, good work, or respect, (*c*) programmatic grant for a specific project that addresses a defined philanthropic objective supported or endorsed by the corporation, and (*d*) corporate-sponsored programs initiated by the company itself.

2. *Employee matching gifts.* Traditionally, more often done for educational organizations, but now being done more frequently for health-related, arts, and public media organizations. Companies with such programs agree to match with corporate funds the collective contributions of its employees. Some companies match dollar for dollar, whereas others match on a 3:1 basis. This type of corporate giving is expected to increase since companies see it both as an employee benefit and as an escape from the pressure on the corporation itself to contribute.

3. *Volunteer or released corporate staff time.* The concept of "giving people" in addition to money has grown in attractiveness to many corporations. Three versions of the released-time approach are currently in use, including (*a*) company support for organizations in which employees volunteer, (*b*) loaned executive programs in which an employee is released on full pay and benefits to work for a specified period of time for an approved nonprofit, philanthropic organization. This program has high publicity value for the corporation and provides a tremendous service for the nonprofit organization, and (*c*) corporate-wide volunteer program focusing volunteer efforts on a particular agency or program area. Advantages to this approach include that of having employees understand and participate in the corporation's overall philanthropic programs, plus providing for the employees a sanctioned reason for being away from the office.

4. *Gifts in kind.* For those companies which donate product merchandise, this approach may be helpful for those NPOs needing the products (not for resale) in support of their exempt purpose.

5. *Program-related investments.* A loan or purchase of bonds or stocks in a somewhat financially risky organization, whose goals are similar to the philanthropic or social responsibility priorities of the corporation. If the agency or organization fails, it is considered a grant; if it repays the amount, it is considered an investment.

6. *United Way.* While it may be argued that the United Way is more a type of recipient than a type of corporate support, it is included here as a way of pointing out the enormous importance of this type of corporate support to NPOs. Approximately half of all corporate financial support goes to local United Way chapters. Corporate support of these campaigns through executive time, accounting, payroll deduction, flyers, posters, and rallies is enormous.

Evaluation

Increasingly, cost effectiveness of program support is a major factor in evaluating a proposal from an NPO. "Best investment" is either a spoken or an unspoken criteria for program evaluation.

The great majority of companies conduct some form of evaluation or assessment of the support they offer. The sophistication of this process is likely to increase as companies become more professional in the administration of their social responsibility programs.

Both the qualitative and quantitative impact of support on recipient organizations and their proposed programs are increasingly a part of the evaluation process of corporate giving programs.

Grants

For most companies, it is rare that they publicize grants either within the company or to the general public. This situation will no doubt change over the coming years, but for now it is the norm.

Increasingly, attention is being paid to the management of the entire social responsibility program to create a balanced "mix" of grants as to their high risk-high payoff or low risk-low payoff potential.

Guidelines

Most U.S. companies with social responsibility programs have established formal guidelines and qualification standards for NPOs requesting support.

The successful approach for corporate support is the one which meets both the needs of the nonprofit organization and that of the corporation. A *must* here is knowing the company's guidelines, qualifications, and internal and external corporate needs.

Management

About 60 percent of corporate contributions are made through giving committees. The remaining 40 percent is contributed through corporate foundations.

Companies with a developed internal structure for corporate social responsibility programs are more likely to assume leadership roles in funding innovative programs proposed by NPOs.

Increasingly, company social responsibility programs and efforts are being managed as legitimate, important activities included in the mainstream of company management. This is reflected in the increasingly professional caliber of program administration and evaluation.

About one-third of the corporations having a direct-giving program located it in the public affairs department, whereas about 20 percent leave the administration of such programs in the office of the company's CEO. The larger the company, the more likely that this department will handle direct giving by that corporation.

The Council on Foundations in Washington reports that the search for personnel to staff the grant functions of corporations has

> broadened not only geographically, but in the range of background training and skills that are sought in such individuals. The range and complexity of the nonprofit, philanthropic sector and the issues that such personnel must confront command, today, different skills than seemed to be needed in the first several decades of corporate philanthropic activity. Indeed, to get the range of staff skills that are required, an increasing number of corporations now combine grantmaking and other social responsibility activities in multi-staffed departments, a long step ahead of staffing in earlier decades, with the part time service of a member of the office of the corporate secretary or the legal or other department of the corporation

according to its "Memorandum on Corporate Giving." Most companies give greater priority to support requests from organizations in communities in which the company is a "major presence" or has located major offices.

The majority of major diversified corporations have separate budgets designated for charitable giving. Direct giving authority is usually delegated to regional or field offices, subsidiaries, and affiliated companies or divisions.

Approaching Business for Support

Successfully approaching business for support involves the consideration of a number of factors and the development of a basic *strategy,* even if it never reaches a written form. Obviously, it is impossible to specify exactly which approach to use—all companies are different. As corporate social responsibility programs assume a general character and structure however, basic generalities do apply. The following summary of considerations to be kept in mind as you evolve an approach strategy was adapted from materials prepared by the Business Committee for the Arts in New York, a very active NPO in the area of corporate support for its constituency and a very successful one, as recent data on the percentage of corporate support for the arts reveals. The advice it offers is that of businessmen and businesswomen who are responsible for granting funds and pledging support to nonprofit organizations.

Fund-Raising Theory

- Corporate giving differs from personal giving. The individual gives from the heart, the corporation from its mind. A nonprofit organization facing bankruptcy does not stand a better chance of gaining support. Corporate philanthropy is induced by evidence of its value to the corporation, its employees, and the community at large of the particular public service provided by the applying philanthropic organization.

- Try to get the prospective donor to attend a function sponsored or conducted by your organization prior to approaching the company for assistance. Corporate involvement in the activities and services of the NPO is very important. Involvement or participation of a top executive on the NPO's board or in its activities is vital.

- Appeals to corporations should always be positive.

- Fund-raising should be recognized as a permanent and year-round function, as important as paid admissions and any other source of income. When NPOs fail, frequently it is because their fund-raising was conducted on a *crisis* basis.

- One person should have overall responsibility for fund-raising. That person should participate in preparation of budget projections, balancing total essential expenses against probable earned income and a realistic projection of funds that can be raised.

- If possible, all fund-raising should be done for the succeeding year's budget. Be sure to differentiate between capital funds and operating funds.

- Be careful of how you use the word "deficit." Clear explanations should be given when it is used. For example, "operating deficit," should be explained as total expenses less earned income; "net deficit" as total expenses less earned and contributed income, and "carryover deficit," as deficit not made up in any way.

Documentation

Most potential donors prefer a short, concise introductory letter containing basic information on the organization. The letter should be tailored to the company you are approaching. It should be on organization stationery, which should include a list of the persons officially connected with the organization and the return address and telephone number. The addressee should be the executive determined as the best person to approach (see below, Whom You Should Approach).

The letter should include

- A brief statement of the proposal
- Reason for approaching the corporation (the "bridge")
- Total sum needed for the project, including a breakdown of the percentages anticipated from other funding sources, e.g., business, government, foundations, and individuals
- List of established corporate sponsors
- Suggested contribution
- Organization's background
- Concluding statement asking for an appointment with either the addressee or an executive he or she might designate

Attachments and enclosures to the letter should include

- Summary statement of the organization's main activities, its value to the community, its constituency and potential constituencies, its work with other institutions, and, if appropriate, how it benefits and serves the corporation's employees
- Budget for the preceding, current, and succeeding years, together with audited financial statements, if available
- Copies of the IRS forms indicating tax-exempt status and stating whether the organization is a public or private foundation

Whom Should You Approach

- The best prospects are large local corporations and large national corporations with local operations. With the latter, the first step is to "sell" local management on the value of your organization. The decision to grant funds is usually made in the local office when it regards local organizations. Even if the decision is made at corporate headquarters, it will almost surely need the favorable recommendation of the right executives as the local unit or subsidiary.
- Research the relationship of the corporation to the community, the corporation's patterns of giving and the public service interests of local corporate leaders and their families. Ideally, the local manager or corporate executive to approach would be a personal friend of the fund-raiser or a member of the NPO's board.

The Visit

You should be on time for your visit to the prospective corporate contributor. Be informative, but keep your remarks brief. Have confidence in your project and your organization. Be well-informed about its value to the corporation. If you have permission, mention companies which have already contributed to your organization. Do not imply that possible contributions are firm commitments.

Begin your presentation with the strongest, most positive aspects of your proposal. Try to use questions to get your story across, and listen as much as you talk.

Remember that business people are impressed by a good sales presentation. You are, in effect, "selling" the benefits of your organization's public service, the benefits it provides for everyone involved, and particularly the corporation whose support you are seeking.

Follow-up

Follow-up your visit with a letter thanking the prospective donor for his or her time and interest and inviting them to visit your organization for a tour, exhibit, or performance. *This is very important.* The invitation should be for a specific time and date.

Avoid using the visit as an occasion for hard-sell fund-raising. Let the prospective donors see for themselves the value of what is around them. Invite them "backstage" to talk to staff, volunteers, and board members to see how the organization actually works.

Do not be discouraged if you are turned down or receive a smaller grant than expected. Continue to develop contacts during the time between fund-raising campaigns. Often the tone of the turndown letter will reveal that a subsequent appeal might bring most positive results. Perhaps the timing of the application was wrong, coming after the succeeding year's contributions budget was prepared, for example. Find out when the next budget will be prepared and begin the next approach accordingly.

Many corporate foundations have fiscal years different from their corporation's, and their grants are almost invariably made in the current year for the following year. Often, less time is required to be considered for grants from companies without foundations.

A small grant should not be discouraging. Any corporate gift is an indication the company has researched your organization and found it worthy of support.

To help small grants lead to large ones, immediately thank the donor in a personal letter and later report precisely how the grant was used. Keeping the donor informed is one of the best ways to ensure future consideration.

Do not assume that another grant will come automatically. The initial grant is merely an indication that continued efforts toward this corporation may prove worthwhile. Remember, fund-raising is a permanent, year-round effort.

Qualities of Applicant Organizations

The question is often raised: "What are corporations looking for in nonprofit organizations as they evaluate grants or support requests?" Again, there is no set answer since corporate social responsibility is anything but standardized across the country. However, a good example of what a company is looking for can be found in the following excerpt from guidelines provided by the American Telephone and Telegraph Company for NPOs seeking its support:

AT&T looks for financial accountability in applicant organizations, as evidenced by

- Ready availability of reliable information on all financial activities and conditions, including annual audited financial statements.
- Sound financial principles and practices, resulting in reasonable fund-raising and administrative expenses.
- Well-planned funding strategies that demonstrate a need for the company's contributions in support of its services but that avoid developing undesirable depen-

dence on any single source of assistance. The company also takes into consideration evidence that organizations have clear purposes and that they are efficiently organized and dedicated. It looks for (1) clearly stated objectives, (2) long-range planning, (3) active participation by the governing board, (4) competent leadership and efficient administration, (5) qualified professional staff in place and effective use of volunteers, and (6) accountability for its actions through regular self-evaluation and public reporting.

In evaluating the services performed by applicant organizations, AT&T considers it important that these services

- Generate information and increase public awareness and support for the organization's objectives
- Promote citizen participation and voluntarism
- Develop skilled leadership
- Promote communication and cooperation among organizations and individuals in all segments of the community
- Be considered particularly beneficial to the constituencies important to the company's operations, including minorities, women, youth, senior citizens, and the physically challenged

AT&T (and most other major corporations) *excludes* the following:

- Individuals
- Organizations not eligible for tax-deductible support
- Organizations that discriminate by race, color, creed, or national origin
- Political organizations or campaigns
- Organizations whose prime purpose is to influence legislation
- Religious organizations when denominational or sectarian in purpose
- Special occasion goodwill advertising
- Operating expenses of organizations supported by the United Way, other than through United Way
- National health organizations, other than through United Way

Ways Business Can Support the Public Service Organization (PSO)

The following suggestions were adapted by permission from the Business Committee for the Arts publication, "126 Ways to Support the Arts."

Space and Facilities

Exhibit employees' art or other public service organization (PSO) product on company premises.

Make a gift of used equipment to a local PSO.

Provide publicity for special events on company bulletin boards.

Exhibit community artists' work on company premises.

Devote window space to the promotion of community service organization activities.

Make a company facility a community center by regularly scheduling PSO events on the premises. Contribute unused facilities to a PSO for long-term use.

Sell tickets for PSO events on company premises.

Lend office equipment—typewriters, reproduction machines, calculators—to PSO managers.

Provide work space on company premises for PSO volunteers.

Permit local PSOs to solicit contributions on company premises.

Products and Services

Publicize PSO activities in house organs.

Donate a company product to a fund-raising auction for a PSO.

Provide corporate products appropriate to the needs of the PSO—materials, paper, bandages, etc.

Provide promotional materials on tape, film, or slides for a local PSO.

Subsidize a PSO art, crafts, or other project for work with new materials, especially the company's own products.

Encourage employees to work with PSOs by providing compensatory time off.

Assist a PSO with expert staff advice.

Contribute advertising and promotional staffs to create materials publicizing PSO activities.

Provide labor, tools, and supervision for the construction or rehabilitation of space for PSOs needing same.

Encourage lawyers, accountants, and physicians to give professional counseling *gratis* to PSOs.

Employee Benefits

Exhibit employees' art work or materials used or made by them for PSOs on company premises.

Buy tickets to local performances for distribution free or at a discount to employees and their friends.

Invite a local arts group to give a performance or a local PSO to give a demonstration for employees on company premises.

Reward outstanding employees with a piece of contemporary sculpture created by a recommended artist and commissioned by the company.

Arrange payroll deduction plans for employee contributions to PSOs.

Community Participation

Provide space on company premises for a community PSO exhibition of products or services.

Sponsor an exhibit or presentation in a ghetto or shopping center to celebrate the company's anniversary or other special occasion.

Give a high school student an award in recognition of public service achievement.

Sponsor a public service class for the community.

Offer new customers a pair of tickets to a PSO event.

Donate an art object to the community or state.

Donate portions of company advertising contracts to publicity for PSOs.

Make a company facility a cultural and public service center by regularly scheduling art and PSO events on the premises.

Invite a local PSO to give a performance or demonstration for employees on company premises.

Help initiate local historical or environmental preservation projects.

Hold annual stockholder meetings in a PSO facility.

Organize a PSO committee within the local chamber of commerce, Rotary Club, or other service club.

Encourage the local development group to emphasize the community's PSOs as an attraction to new business.

Through business associations, encourage local zoning variances that would benefit realtors who help PSOs move to the business district.

Bring PSO practitioners together in a symposium for creativity and the exchange of experiences.

Provide scholarships for school children to attend a summer art camp or other PSO summer program.

Arrange for interviews and regular news announcements about PSOs on local radio programs.

Combine with two or three other companies to sponsor a PSO activity.

Invite a PSO volunteer or professional to discuss their work or programs at a business meeting or service club luncheon.

Employ community young people to sell tickets to PSO events.

Sponsor an arts and crafts show by prison inmates or other isolated segments of society.

Arrange special Saturday morning workshops to bring young people in contact with local PSO volunteers and professionals.

Underwrite a small conference to determine means of creating broader community involvement in public service activities.

Make a gift of a painting or sculpture to a local educational or other public service institution.

Contract with an artist to prepare a coloring book publicizing local PSOs.

Sponsor production of a teacher's manual on some aspect of local PSOs for use with the youth of your community.

Help establish an inexpensive storefront museum or PSO display-demonstration center in a ghetto or shopping center.

Provide a grant for a special performing arts presentation for disadvantaged children.

Underwrite a special performance or demonstration by PSOs.

Provide advertising space in newspapers, magazines, radio, or television for the promotion of PSO activities and programs.

Finance community education programs in public service by bringing lecturers and groups to the area.

Commission an artist to produce a work for civic display.

Sponsor a traveling art show, creative workshop, or public service display for school children.

Provide "Jazzmobile" concerts for a ghetto or suburban area.

Sponsor a summer movies series in a park.

Print calendars of PSO events and distribute them to stockholders, customers, and other company publics.

Pay for a management consultant firm to train PSO volunteers or professionals in dealing with the public or in some other special skill or technique.

Restructure the company's aid-to-education program to include PSO programs.

Arrange local television programs for interviews, critical reviews, and news about PSOs.

Sponsor a series of radio broadcasts of performing arts productions.

Establish a summer theater school for elementary and secondary school students.

Contribute to research projects that investigate possible solutions to the financial problems of PSOs.

Sponsor an auction, ball, or fashion show to raise funds for PSOs.

Develop a program of admission-free performing arts events designed to serve suburban communities with programs of meaningful quality.

Establish a museum depicting the development of items connected with the company's products.

Create a public service development program aimed at broadening the base of local PSO activities over a given period.

Sponsor a summer series of outdoor performing arts presentations, and donate all or a portion of the receipts to scholarships for talented young people with demonstrated abilities in public service.

Donate a building to serve as a PSO center.

Underwrite renovation of a movie theater or other hall for use by arts organizations or other PSOs.

Sponsor the use of outstanding architects to design new buildings that help improve the appearance of the municipality.

Buy three or four art treasures and place them on permanent exhibit at the local museum.

Sponsor a festival featuring outstanding local artists.

Lobby for federal, state, and municipal legislation providing adequate funding for PSOs.

Support legislation to encourage tax-free gifts to PSOs.

Support zoning legislation to stop destruction of landmark sites.

Support legislation to give power to city commissions to prevent ugly construction and the despoiling of park, recreation, or environmentally important areas.

Initiate and support development of public service education courses, seminars, and conferences at area institutions of higher learning.

Regional or National Involvement

Expand the company's gift-matching program to include PSOs.

Join with national PSOs in sharing a matching grant to a local PSO.

Restructure the company's aid-to-education program to include PSO education programs, particularly those whose goal is more effective management and administration.

Contribute to research projects that investigate possible solutions to the financial problems of the public service sector.

Subsidize the publication of a work by a promising author, artist, or by a PSO on a topic of importance to the public service sector.

Share in the sponsorship of a network television program designed to advance the level of awareness on an important public service issue or the importance of the sector as a whole to the nation.

Sponsor a speaking or performing tour by representatives of a national PSO.

Provide advertising space in newspapers or magazines, or on radio or television, for the promotion of PSO activities or programs.

Publish calendars of PSO events, and distribute them to stockholders, customers, and other company publics.

Provide for a "public service mobile" to introduce or provide services to communities in rural areas.

Guarantee a performance of national performing arts organization in your area against loss.

Sponsor a series of radio or television broadcasts about PSOs.

Circulate a display of some of your area's art treasures or successful PSO projects to other areas or states.

Circulate a company art collection or PSO display to colleges from which the company recruits employees.

Develop a program of admission-free performing arts events or PSO-oriented programs designed to serve suburban communities with programs of meaningful quality and information.

Circulate abroad a display of America's art treasures or public service achievements.

Send a touring cast of performing artists to selected foreign countries.

Conduct a national competition to select talented young people with public service achievements.

Help fund recordings of contemporary composers for sale and general distribution.

Sponsor the cinematic recording of outstanding arts performances.

Sponsor network television specials to advance the nation's public service awareness and level of information.

Underwrite the creation of a major exhibition of art, crafts, or products by PSOs for extensive showing nationally or internationally.

Produce a major motion picture for national distribution, showing the value and meaning of public service to the nation.

Lobby for federal, state, and municipal legislation giving support to the public service sector.

Sponsor a national student competition to develop new public service approaches and involvement by young people.

Other Ways to Help

Contract with an author to prepare a special brochure for the company emphasizing public service involvement.

Provide a scholarship for an outstanding public service education student.

Employ a performing individual or group to visit colleges and to help the company's image and recruitment potential.

Commission an American composer to write a new work for a special occasion with a focus on public service.

36

Foundation Funding

Tracy Connors

Consultant

*"Dear Applicant: Thank you for submitting your
proposal. We regret that it does not suit our
present needs. If it ever does, we're in trouble."*
CHARLES SCHULTZ
Peanuts

The Grant-Seeking Proposal

After preliminary research among the sources cited in the previous chapter or similar references, most foundation grant seekers prepare a "proposal outline," usually following the generally accepted format suggested by the Grantsmanship Center, including the following major sections:

- Proposal summary
- Introduction
- Problem statement or assessment of need
- Program objectives
- Methods
- Evaluation
- Future funding
- Budget

The Mott Foundation, as an example of a major U.S. foundation, favors a five-part proposal, very similar to the above model, including

1. Cover letter by authorizing officer of the organization, indications of the commitment of the organization to the project, and a summary of the project (purpose, cost, inclusive dates of the project)
2. Program description covering:
    a. Problem statements: Why project is needed and whom it will affect
    b. Background and state of the art
    c. Concise goal and measurable objectives
    d. Work plan (including leadership)
    e. Future of the project or program
3. Evaluation, dissemination, and longer-term benefits
4. Line item budget, including notation of any matching funds
5. Organizational background
    a. Tax-exempt status
    b. Governance
    c. Track record
    d. Statement of how any organizational impediments will be overcome

Preparation of the proposal outline becomes an important (many say, vital) planning and evaluation process in and of itself. In addition to helping clarify all elements of the concept being developed, it forces the NPO manager to focus the idea and to consider those things of concern to foundation officials reviewing the eventual final proposal. The following list of considerations kept in mind by foundation program officers reviewing proposals is not all inclusive. However, it is offered to help you understand the issues and questions that will need to be answered or covered in a final grant application to a private foundation:

- Does it fit with the aims of the foundation? For example, does the proposal fit the common denominator of the foundation to which it will be submitted, e.g., "improving the quality of life in community settings."

- What, precisely, is the problem being addressed, including background and dimensions of the problem?

- What is the key purpose of the program or project?

- Does it have the full commitment of the organization or institution and its leadership? Foundations receive many programming ideas, but relatively few qualified, dedicated, committed people to implement them.

- To what extent do the trustees or directors take part in policy formulation and program dedication?

- Who are the staff personnel involved and what are their professional qualifications?

- Will any additional staff be required? If so, what will be their qualifications? Who will direct and manage their efforts?

- Is the project a priority of the institution and of its public philanthropic purpose? Or, is it an "add-on" for money?

- Has the community or constituency affected by the project been involved in the planning, or is this another "do unto the community" proposal?

- Is the idea really new? Is it creative? Is it well thought out? Will it make a difference? Or, is it the "same old stuff" that program officers receive almost every day?

- How serious is the need being addressed, and how is this quantified, if at all?

- How long will the project take to complete or to show major results?

- Is what is known about other similar projects shown in the proposal?

- What evidence is there of knowledge of the foundation's prior work in this particular grant field?
- Why should this proposal receive more serious review, attention and funding than other, similar projects? Why does it deserve more consideration than its competition?
- What is the target "market" or group addressed or help by the proposal?
- What results (translate that as "benefits"), short- and long-term, are expected?
- What is the methodology planned for the project's implementation?
- What is the price tag? A detailed, line item budget is expected, one that gives evidence of coming at the conclusion of a corporate planning process, i.e., it specifies the money needed to achieve or accomplish defined, quantifiable objectives through action steps.
- Is the budget large enough, or too large? How does the budget compare with the project results? How about salaries, are they in line with comparable positions elsewhere?
- What is the budget for the applying organization?
- What is the source of the funding mix, including institutional or other matching funds?
- Will the project be audited? If so, by whom and when?
- Does the proposal include an explanation of other funding or self-sufficiency at a given point in its development? Or, will it self-destruct when the foundation providing the funding is consumed or withdrawn?
- Is funding being sought for this project from other funding sources? If so, for how much and from whom is it being sought?
- What reporting period and process is proposed?
- What provisions are being made for progress reports and a final report?
- How will an objective evaluation be made of the actual results obtained? Who will make the evaluation and what technique(s) will they use?

Although these questions relate most directly to major projects or programs, even if a proposal is for a special gift, all the above elements may need to be considered in so far as they relate to the particular need or request. They are particularly pertinent to the foundation grant seeker since most foundations prefer supporting projects, as opposed to providing general operating support or a capital gift.

A significant factor in a successful private foundation grant request is the background and track record of the organization requesting the support, and in particular, the achievements of those who will manage the project. Most foundations regard good people as the key to success in a funded program. For this reason, as J. Richard Taft, chairman of the Taft Corporation points out, "If you asked foundation people about the most important element in this long list, I think you would find that they would respond by saying that the background and track record of the person and the institution submitting the request would rank highest."

After Preparing the Proposal

Once the proposal or a heavy concept outline is prepared which represents a basic management plan for the project, what next? Does the process of identifying prospective foundations using the references noted earlier continue until all possible prospects are identified? No, say experts like Taft: Once about ten solid foundation prospects are selected using the various indexes of major foundation references, it is time to proceed with the next step—the solicitation process.

A strategy, however formal or informal, is needed at this point for each foundation you plan to contact. The strategy will help you to contact the foundation initially in one of the following ways:

- Seek an introduction through a colleague to the program officer or other foundation official.
- Telephone to ask for a meeting while in the vicinity of the foundation office.
- Send for an application form.
- Send a concept paper to a specific contact person.
- Forward a full proposal.
- Write a letter.

The final strategy you select for each foundation will depend on what you feel will be the best approach following your thorough review of the information contained in the foundation directories and references. Once you have selected your strategy, then it is time to move forward, keeping in mind that what you are working with is basically a *marketing process.* There is no *one* best way to get in the door to convince the program officer of the merits of your proposal. Although the best advice is probably to follow the procedures outlined by the foundation, proposals have been funded by foundations as a result of many different approaches (most not being mentioned in the directories), including

- Appointments obtained stressing the need for the program officer's advice and guidance
- Appeals to the egos of foundation personnel—program officer, trustee, or even the corporate ego of the foundation itself because of the appeal of being "first" to do a certain type of philanthropic work.
- Intercession by trustees on behalf of a favored project
- Letters followed by telephone calls

The list is endless, but the bottom line is creativity, imagination, and, for most, persistence.

According to the experts, some procedures that do not work or that turn off foundation officers are

- Badly written or lengthy letters. The Mott Foundation annually receives over 1500 letters of inquiry. Ineffective letters full of "bull roar" and jargon waste their valuable time and are rejected almost immediately.
- Funding requests based on campaigns or anniversaries.
- The warning of a dire emergency facing your agency or organization. In fact, foundations would view most appeals of this type as evidence of organization mismanagement.

Once you have contacted the foundation, you will either be (1) turned down by the foundation citing the reason (some have over 20 different types of denial letters), or (2) asked to move on to the next step, which may be a visit by you to the foundation or by the foundation to you, or a request for the submission of a full proposal.

If you are turned down, should you consider that the end, the finis, to all the efforts you have made? Certainly not. First, remember that you have other proposals under consideration by other foundations. Most importantly, however, remember that you are not just looking for funding from the foundation. You are seeking *financial resources* from them by which to do something important: to help people in a way encouraged and supported by that foundation. Your first contact should not be seen as a one-shot approach, but rather as the opportunity to build a *relationship* between you and your organization and the foundation. Eventually, if you persist in the process of refining and improving your proposal, you will stand an ever-better chance of being funded. After all, a proposal is not an appeal for funding. It is a management plan outlining how a needed project with quantifiable objectives is to be conducted. Its budget, of which foundation funding is probably only a portion, represents necessary allocations of money (financial resources) necessary to accomplish the objectives.

With this in mind, when and if you are turned down, you next must find out *why*. Where did your proposal miss the mark? Is it possible to redraft or reorganize and to submit again next year? When is the next deadline? Keep in touch with the program office about the project.

The other possibility is that the foundation will want more information. What if they ask for an appointment? What should you keep in mind as you prepare to defend and explain your proposal in person? The following suggestions may prove helpful, including:

1. Take with you the person who will be directing or managing the project.

2. If the project will benefit the entire organization, bring with you a senior officer or trustee of the institution representing the organization as whole.

3. Know as much as you can about the foundation: its programs, policies, and personnel. Go back to the directories and other sources for this information.

4. Tell the program officer what he or she wishes to know. Resist the temptation to launch into an impassioned, lengthy monologue about your project or your organization.

5. Involve the program officer in the discussion, drawing out their knowledge and expertise.

6. Unless you have already submitted a full proposal, make your objective that of having the foundation representative ask you for a full proposal. Although it will be work for you, it represents the next step of commitment to your project by the foundation.

7. Follow up with correspondence indicating what you learned and what you are doing to follow up and complete action items identified during the meeting. Letters from others attending the meeting or from the leadership of your organization are also helpful.

8. Stay in touch following up until you are certain that you have done everything possible to provide the information needed by the foundation to make its decision about your project. If, after this process, the proposal is turned down, start over with the steps mentioned above that should be taken in the event of a turndown.

When they request your proposal, try to keep the following format points in mind as you prepare your final draft for mailing:

- *Clarity.* Be straight and "up front," avoid jargon unless it is necessary for technical reasons, then translate.
- *Brevity.* Only 10 or 15 pages are preferable. Some program officers admit to a correlation between length of proposals and denials.
- *Packaging.* Loose-leaf binders are preferred by many foundations, not spiral notebooks. No gimmicks (no peanuts from Georgia), please. Delete supporting letters: The object is not to overwhelm.
- *Thoroughness.* Mail the complete proposal.

Once the proposal is ready, proofread it thoroughly and check for completeness. Mail your copies to the foundations you have targeted. Sit back and wait for the foundations to respond (or move forward to start the process over again with other foundations your research has indicated might be interested). Resist the temptation to call or visit at this point.

When the proposal is received by the foundation it may start through a process like this:

- Received and dated by the foundation.
- Referred to a reader who denies (50%?) or decides to write a "precis," a brief description of the project as seen by the foundation.
- Referred to a program review committee where it is either denied (50%?) or forwarded to a program officer for further review and analysis.
- Read by the program officer who denies most of the rest (some exceeding 95%), and contacts the remaining grant requestees.
- Once the proposal is approved by the program officer, it is usually started through a multisignature (large foundations may have over 30) process before it arrives at a meeting of the foundation's trustees which is held periodically throughout the year (often, quarterly). A project can be denied at any point in this process.
- Denials usually clear the foundation quickly, in a few months.
- Good ideas—ones which may eventually be funded—can take much longer, many months or even a year or more.

37

Investment Strategies for Nonprofit Organizations

Frank L. Stanley
Portfolio Director, Phoenix Mutual Life Insurance Company

Scott Van Battenburg
Vice President, Connecticut National Bank

The direct relationship between good financial management and the overall well-being of a nonprofit institution (NPO) is widely recognized. *Intensive* management of financial assets, however, offers a unique, new revenue source. Financial assets—cash and endowment funds—seldom receive the close attention they deserve. Although the efforts of trustees and staff must be primarily directed to the management of programs, the subsidiary concern of financial asset management should not be neglected. Specifically, to increase income demands a formal cash management system and more flexible and accountable endowment management. The strength and excellence of America's cultural, educational, and philanthropic institutions fundamentally depend upon the income and stability created through intensive financial asset management. Unless conscious counteraction is taken, the financial stresses that are increasingly overwhelming most nonprofit institutions will diminish their strength and dilute their programs.

This chapter outlines the elements of a sound cash management system and the management approach required to exact full performance from an endowment fund. External sources of new funds have been vigorously cultivated. Fund-raising programs are conducted with almost clinical precision. Earned income from tuitions and fees have been rapidly increased. Although these external revenue sources capture the spotlight, however, other golden opportunities—intensive cash and investment management—remain hidden in the wings. Neither a business manager working alone to augment and invest cash balances nor an endowment committee refining investment policies and reviewing a manager's performance offer quick fixes. The long-term nature of most NPOs and their inherent resistance to change demands continuous, patient management improvements.

How to Profit from an Intensive Cash Management System

In today's economic environment it is essential for nonprofit organizations to take full advantage of cash flow. Cash management is rapidly becoming a standard business office function. From an income-producing perspective, the more cash a nonprofit institution can amass and invest, the better. Intensive cash management means accelerating the receipt and processing of payments; concentrating these funds into a single, easily managed account; delaying disbursements until the last possible moment while staying within accepted billing terms; and, as fully as possible, investing cash balances.

Do you have a sound cash management system? Have you made an effort to

- Accelerate cash collections?
- Lower deposit balances?
- Reduce the number of checking and savings accounts?
- Pool short-term assets?
- Batch disbursements?
- Improve cash information and control?

The result of these improvements will be clear: increased investment income.

Accelerating the Receipt and Processing of Cash

Techniques used to accelerate the receipt and processing of payments start in the business office. Systematic billing and accounts receivable management can go a long way toward ensuring a solid and predictable cash flow. Accelerating remittances can be accomplished through bank processing of checks, commonly called "lockbox services," and direct bank collection of payments through preauthorized payments. A nonprofit institution that uses a lockbox service will have all its payments sent directly to a bank for processing. Using a lockbox can shorten by many days the processing and clearing of checks, thus increasing cash balances. In some cases, a bank can also provide information on the sources of these revenues.

Lockbox Services

A lockbox service allows a nonprofit organization to direct all payments to be sent to a post office box. An authorized bank courier collects these mail remittances several times a day. The bank opens the envelopes, removes the contents, endorses and deposits any checks, and prepares bookkeeping records. From a bank's perspective, lockbox receipts are either manually processed or are subject to partial automation. Automated processing requires a standardized "turnaround" or remittance advice document containing payment information. This document must be machine-readable. The bank uses this document as the key element in an automated lockbox service. The data contained on the document, plus the actual payment amount, is captured and stored in a file on a magnetic tape or other electronic storage medium, and information on payments received is systematically added to that file. This file is then transmitted either physically or by electronic transmission to the NPO's business office. A fully automated lockbox system reduces remittance processing costs, speeds check deposit, improves audit control, and isolates accounts receivable data collection and subsequent accounting update. All billing documents are physically transmitted to the NPO's business office once the lockbox service has been completed.

Many utility and charge card billing systems employ the use of automated lockboxes. In the nonprofit sector, lockboxes are most commonly used by educational institutions for tuition payments and by health institutions to receive third-party reimbursements.

Lockboxes can also be used to collect contributions in a fund-raising program. NPOs located in urban areas frequently turn to a lockbox service simply as a device to ensure the security of receipts. A high likelihood of employee fraud and other difficult security conditions encourage the use of a lockbox.

To determine the dollar value of the lower processing costs and float reduction (more rapid conversion of check remittances into investable funds) inherent in a lockbox service, the following calculations can be used:

1. *Current processing cost.* Number of checks received per year multiplied by in-house processing cost per check equals dollar cost per year without lockbox

2. *Value of float reduction.* Marginal cost of capital multiplied by average daily receipts equals the average daily float reduction benefit multiplied by estimated float reduction in terms of number of days equals the value of float reduction

3. *Cost benefit.* Value of float reduction minus lockbox costs less current processing costs equals dollar value of lockbox service

In deciding whether to use a lockbox, the estimated dollar value is seldom the sole deciding factor. Improved accounts receivable control, enhanced remittance security, and less daily in-house processing pressure are often heavily weighted factors as well.

Preauthorized Payments

The use of preauthorized checks (known as PACs) and their companion, preauthorized electronic payments (PAPs), offers another technique to accelerate the receipt and processing of cash.

The nonprofit institution which pioneered preauthorized payments was Boston College. In the early 1970s, Boston College approached New England Merchants Bank, which had a number of the college's alumni on its board of directors, about trying a system in which Boston College graduates would automatically contribute to the college's annual giving campaign on a monthly basis, with each contribution debited from a bank account which the donor would specify.

Although preauthorized payment systems are still in their infancy as fund-raising tools, preauthorized checking has long been used by the insurance industry for monthly installment payments of insurance premiums. The 80 percent participation rate enjoyed by some insurance companies has recommended preauthorized checking to utility companies, which are now using this service increasingly. How does it work?

As a first step, the organization that is engaged in fund-raising markets the service to its universe of regular donors. Those contributors who opt for the preauthorized mode of contributing must sign an authorization form, specifying the amount of the monthly debit. They include with their authorization form a voided personal check which gives all the information (in magnetic ink characters) necessary for electronic processing.

The bank serving the fund-raising institution (the originating bank) prepares a master file on the contributors and then sends a notification to each contributor's bank, indicating that the fund-raising institution will be debiting its customer's account, on his or her instructions. Each month, the contributor is notified of the contribution, either through a notation on the monthly statement, or by a draft enclosed with the cancelled checks. The fund-raising institution receiving the contribution has the total amount of all its preauthorized payments credited to its account and is able either to use the funds immediately or to invest them.

When the preauthorized mode has been used on an appropriate scale, the results have been rewarding for the fund-raising institution in several ways. One charitable organization with a donor universe of approximately 33,000 was implementing an office automation plan. Part of this plan included offering on an active marketing basis the preauthorized payment option. After 6 months of marketing, 3600 donors had opted for the PAC system. This increased to 4900 a year later and further grew to 10,000 after 5 years. At present, about 25 percent of this organization's donors use the PAC service. These donors' contributions average $20 monthly, or $240 a year. Thus, the not inconsiderable sum of about $2.4 million is collected by using preauthorized checks. A Canadian affiliate of the same organization has a payment universe of approximately 37,000 persons, of whom more than 30 percent use preauthorized checks as their donation mode.

There are six major advantages of automatic collection services:

1. Improved donor retention
2. Timely information on pledges payable
3. Timely information on changes in donor status
4. Reduced payment processing cost
5. Reduced bookkeeping costs associated with pledge payment ledgers, pledge billings, and receipt notices
6. Greater investment earnings through payment acceleration

From Boston College's pioneering step in 1972, the concept of preauthorized payments has gained increasing acceptance, and refinements are regularly being introduced. One is an inflation provision as part of the initial pledge: an automatic annual increase of 8 or 10 percent, or any specific percentage amount. Another improvement allows conversions from PAC to PAP entries automatically as more banks become part of the automated clearing houses.

Automatic payment services are not for every fund-raising institution. Moreover, not every bank can establish a program employing them. The size of donor universe and annual contribution levels are factors for each NPO to consider in an assessment of this collection technique. If the dimensions are correct, the cost savings can be significant, and the aggregate level of contributions will be substantially increased.

Single-Account Management

Regardless of what method of receipt and processing of payments—manual, lockbox, or electronic—is employed, a bank can establish a single cash account to receive a nonprofit organization's cash balances. Separate accounts are often unnecessary and reflect an inappropriate equivalence of funds accounting and bank accounting. Reducing the number of bank accounts can markedly improve cash management.

Concentrating cash requires understanding and acceptance of the principle that a single bank or trust account can contain funds which are reflected on an NPO's bookkeeping records as separate accounts or funds. Separate bank or trust accounts may be maintained for bookkeeping simplicity, but this will hamper effective cash management. Through the use of simple account coding, a single deposit or disbursement can be charged or credited to separate fund accounts. Any income earned can likewise be logically allocated to any fund participating in the investment in proportion to its share of the fund.

By pooling or concentrating cash in a single account, investments can be made in larger denominations, and that will directly translate into higher rates of return. Pooling, by definition, permits a maximum level of investment of an NPO's "separate" funds. The principles of funds accounting are in no way constrained through the use of a pooled investment fund. From an accounting point of view, the concentration account is merely a bookkeeping aid. It is not a financial statement fund. Prior to statement preparation, this account is closed out to the major fund accounts.

Analysis of the short-term investments of many nonprofit institutions reveals a patchwork quilt of investment and savings investments representing separate funds and carrying yields far below those which intensive cash management would generate.

Controlling Disbursements

Since all cash is by its technical definition awaiting a disbursement and therefore being temporarily warehoused, controlling disbursements offers yet another cash management avenue to be explored. Control techniques include comprehensive disbursement float analysis reports and automatic balance controls. For a small nonprofit institution, as a first step, internal payment schedules can be easily developed to ensure that payments are not made early. For example, tax withholdings are often prepaid thus reducing cash available for investments. Controlling disbursements generally offers an excellent opportunity to increase the pool of cash.

Taking cash discounts has always made good business sense. However, given fluctuating and often lofty money market rates lately available, a review of the cost benefit of taking all cash discounts might be warranted. A cash discount of "½% in 10 days" is not always as attractive as "net, 30 days" which can be stretched to 45 days. However, if 30-day billing terms must be strictly adhered to, the investment yield earned by delaying payment for only 20 days will usually not be enough to offset the loss of the ½ percent discount.

Prepayment of bills is without question a nonproductive use of funds. Prepayment does not improve an institution's credit record. Indiscriminate bill paying is a common affliction of most business offices. The simplest remedy is to adopt a batched disbursement system for "normal-size" payments and a discrete disbursements program for "large-size" payments. Under this approach, normal bills are paid once or twice a month while large payments are made as late as is feasible. Paying a $10,000 bill with terms of net/60 within 15 days would "cost" a nonprofit institution an extra $150 by foregoing investing the $10,000 at 12 percent. For those NPOs with heavy cash flows, such as hospitals and universities, more sophisticated disbursement services might be employed. Comprehensive disbursement float analysis reporting, automated balance controls, and check-draft systems all can assist in achieving pinpoint disbursement accuracy.

Determining Your Investable Balance

After employing techniques to increase cash balances—accelerating the receipt and processing of payments, concentrating cash in a single bank account, and delaying disbursements—two additional tasks remain before cash can be put to work; analyzing cash flow patterns and determining the balance, if any, required by the bank to handle your checking accounts.

Analyzing cash flow patterns relies on historical data. A year's record of daily deposit and disbursement information is ideal. This will identify those periods when either revenues or disbursements are concentrated. Focusing on the extremes in your cash flow patterns can help identify what short-term investment program best matches your organization's financial operations. A comparison of this daily information with bank checkbook records will highlight how long it takes your disbursement checks to clear the bank. You will usually discover that the average bank balance is higher than the average balance on your books. This is due to the time lag, called "float," between the date of check issuance and the date of final payment by your bank, that is, when your account is debited. Figures 37.1 and 37.2 illustrate the difference between your checkbook balance and the bank balance. As the example illustrates, almost $20,000 more was in your bank account than your checkbook balance indicated.

Collecting daily deposit, disbursement, and final payment data will give you basic information needed to forecast your future cash flow patterns and to identify what short-term investment program is most suitable. The opportunities to invest cash balances, although continuous throughout each year, may be greater at certain times. This is especially true for NPOs such as colleges, trade associations, and those receiving grants or actively undertaking fund-raising programs.

Cost of Bank Services

The portion of your average cash balance which can be invested in short-term or money-market instruments depends upon the balances required by your bank to provide your organization basic checking account services. Banks allow customers to pay for bank services by maintaining a certain minimum or average balance in their checking accounts. All funds on deposit can count toward meeting the required balances. It is therefore important that all your checking accounts be combined in a bank's reporting system in order that full credit be given for all your funds. Some banks will also include savings accounts on the combined analysis. Your bank should be able to provide your organization on a regular basis with an analysis of your accounts containing the earnings credit given your balances, your ledger and collected (i.e., investable) balances, volume and cost of services given, and required compensating balance. Figure 37.3 presents a simplified version of an account analysis. The analysis identifies an opportunity to invest excess funds in the month covered of $236,120.

Date	Deposits	Disbursements	Balance
	CHECKBOOK BALANCE MONTH: JANUARY		
1	$100,000	—	$100,000
2	—	—	100,000
3	1,000	—	101,000
4	—	—	101,000
5	125	$25,000	76,125
6	—	—	76,125
7	—	—	76,125
8	—	—	76,125
9	—	—	76,125
10	6,000	—	82,125
11	—	—	82,125
12	—	—	82,125
13	—	—	82,125
14	—	—	82,125
15	400	45,000	37,525
16	—	—	37,525
17	—	—	37,525
18	—	—	37,525
19	—	600	36,925
20	—	—	36,925
21	—	—	36,925
22	25,000	—	61,925
23	—	—	61,925
24	—	—	61,925
25	4,500	—	66,425
26	—	—	66,425
27	—	—	66,425
28	—	—	66,425
29	—	—	66,425
30	900	—	67,325
31			67,325
Totals	$137,925	$70,600	
Final balance			$ 67,325.00
Average balance			$ 67,957.26

Figure 37.1. Checkbook balance.

Short-Term Investment Management

Accelerating receivables, concentrating cash balances, and controlling disbursements are all designed to increase cash balances. However, if these balances, net of the bank's required compensating balances, remain uninvested, no real advantage is created for the nonprofit institution. A short-term asset management program will ensure that these excess cash balances are creating income for the organization. For many NPOs, such a program begins with a negotiable order of withdrawal (NOW Account) checking account. These accounts were begun as an experiment in New England in the early 1970s and were recently expanded nationally. Most banks providing these accounts treat them as normal checking

BANK BALANCE MONTH: JANUARY			
Date	Deposits	Disbursements	Balance
1	$100,000(good funds)	—	$100,000
2	—	—	100,000
3	500	—	100,500
4	500	—	101,000
5	125	—	101,125
6	—	—	101,125
7	—	—	101,125
8	—	3,000	98,125
9	—	2,000	96,125
10	5,000	—	101,125
11	1,000	1,000	101,125
12	—	—	101,125
13	—	—	101,125
14	—	—	101,125
15	—	19,000	82,125
16	—	—	82,525
17	—	—	82,525
18	—	—	82,525
19	—	5,000	77,525
20	—	—	77,525
21	—	—	77,525
22	20,000	10,000	87,525
23	5,000	—	92,525
24	—	—	92,525
25	—	30,000	62,525
26	4,500	—	67,025
27	—	—	67,025
28	—	—	67,025
29	—	—	67,025
30	—	—	67,025
31	900	600	67,325
Totals	$137,925	$70,600	
Final balance			$ 67,325.00
Average balance			$ 87,244.35

Figure 37.2. Bank balance.

accounts with the important exception that the balances earn interest at the current annual rate of 5¼ percent. Most nonprofit institutions are eligible to establish NOW Accounts and could benefit from the NOW Account service.

Organizations that have average checking account balances of $25,000 or more should evaluate the use of other short-term asset management services, particularly pooled investment funds offering overnight liquidity and money market rates. The yields on these funds usually vary daily and have recently ranged between 6 and 18 percent. Naturally, the use of such investment vehicles requires a correspondingly higher level of financial sophistication on the part of the nonprofit institution. Unfortunately, many NPO officers and board members are frequently not well-versed in financial management. Many nonprofit institutions have embarked upon sophisticated investment management programs employing investment ve-

NATIONAL BANK AND TRUST COMPANY
CUSTOMER ANALYSIS STATEMENT
ACCOUNT #111111
OCTOBER 1–OCTOBER 31, 19—
TRINITY HOSPITAL
CENTERVILLE, U.S.A.

Balances Provided

Average ledger balance	$730,900	
Less uncollected funds	158,300	
Total average collected balance		572,600
Less 14.70% legal reserve on demand deposits		84,172
Total available funds		488,428

Loan Support

Less 10.0 balance to support commitment	100,000	100,000
Less 0.0 balance to support loan	0	0
Total balance available for services		388,428

Service Support

Less balance needed to support services at 13.67% earnings credit	152,308
Net balance available for administrative and advisory services	236,120

Services Provided

Services	Total Units	Cost/Unit	Balance/Equivalent Price/Month
Account reconciliation	7,996	.04	28,077
ARC photo/retrieval	1	2.00	176
ARC stop payments	6	3.60	1,931
ARC-special statement	1	10.00	878
Automatic balance control	3	5.00	1,317
Automatic balance control	1	25.00	2,195
Automatic balance depositing	21	3.00	5,530
Coin/currency set-up	8	3.00	2,107
C savings bonds	36	1.39	4,389
DDA account maintenance	9	5.00	3,951
DDA checks paid	7,996	.10	70,192
DDA deposited items	4,753	.03	12,517
NOW acct-interest paid	4	49.25	17,293
Returned items	20	1.00	1,755
			$152,308

Figure 37.3

hicles with market and credit risks not well understood by either the institution's financial officers or by those board members involved in financial decision making. The financial assets of an NPO require the utmost in prudent management.

Short-term investment opportunities are drawn from the money market. The term "money market" does not apply to any single market but rather to a group of markets. In common usage, the "money market" refers to the markets for short-term credit instruments such as U.S. Treasury bills, commercial paper, banker's acceptances, negotiable certificates of deposit, repurchase agreements and pooled short-term funds ("money funds") made up of these individual instruments. As a general rule, money market instruments are issued by obligors (borrowers) which receive the highest credit ratings on the instruments they issue. Such instruments offer a very high degree of safety of principal. A pooled money fund combining these same instruments offers the further advantages of diversification and overnight availability. Maturities of pooled fund investments are normally 90 days but may extend on occasion to as long as 1 year. The money market is broad, large and efficient. Ease of access and almost instantaneous transactions are characteristic. Trading can be made in almost any volume and at low cost. The money market is essentially a "telephone market" and can be "plugged into" throughout the United States. No NPO is located in too provincial an area to restrict access to the wide variety of short-term investment offerings.

Although money market instruments are close substitutes, there are significant differences in risk, minimum purchase amount, maturities, and marketability. Table 37.1 highlights the salient differences among these instruments.

While different market instruments possess individual characteristics, the rates of return on the various investments tend to be similar and fluctuate closely together in a tight rate band. On occasion, the yield on a specific investment may diverge from the others. Such variations are always temporary since sophisticated investors will quickly adjust their portfolios, thus restoring a normal relationship among the various rates of return.

Determining an Adequate Amount of Short-Term Assets

How large a short-term asset position should a nonprofit organization have? Determination of the optimum amount of short-term assets—cash and short-term investments—as a percent of total annual revenues depends upon two basic factors: seasonality of cash flow and cash flow timing. The task is to balance both factors against the risk of technical insolvency: an inability to meet cash obligations.

There is generally some seasonality in the cash flow of most NPOs. Educational institutions offer a textbook example with tuition and other fee payments displaying a bimodal or trimodal receipt pattern. Other nonprofit institutions, particularly those which rely upon fund-raising for a significant portion of revenues, will also have seasonality built in through the fund-raising process. The cash flow patterns of the Easter Seal Society and the Salvation Army offer classic examples of seasonality. Cash flow timing is another complicating factor. Timing differences between receipt of revenues and associated disbursements are commonplace. Government grants are illustrative. The receipt of government funds seems inevitably to lag behind the first disbursements for the project or program.

Bearing in mind the seasonality and timing patterns of an NPO's cash flow, one basic way of approaching the task of determining the required short-term asset position is through the use of the basic defensive interval. This accounting technique developed in 1960 by George Sorter and George Benston gauges the amount of short-term assets needed as a cushion to avoid technical insolvency.

Table 37.1

Short-term investment instrument	Obligation	Usual minimum purchase	Usual maturities	Marketability
United States Treasury bills	Direct obligations of the U.S. government. May be purchased at weekly and monthly auctions or in secondary market.	$10,000	Up to 1 year	Excellent secondary market
Federal agency issues	Obligations of agencies created by Congress and closely supervised by U.S. government.	$1000 to $10,000 depending on issue	6 months to 30 years	Excellent secondary market
Negotiable time certificates of deposit (CDs)	Negotiable time deposit issued by large commercial banks.	$100,000	14 days minimum; traditionally 1 year maximum	Good secondary market
Prime banker's acceptances	Time draft drawn upon and accepted by a banking institution, which in effect substitutes its credit for that of the importer or holder of merchandise. Issued by large commercial banks.	$100,000	30 to 270 Days	Good secondary market
Prime sales finance Commercial paper	Unsecured promissory notes of finance companies placed directly with investor.	$100,000 $25,000	1 to 29 days 30 to 270 days	None
Repurchase agreement (Repo) Reverse repurchase agreement	Sale or purchase of U.S. Treasury or agency obligations with the agreement to repurchase or resell at a future date.	$100,000	Overnight to 90 days	None
Money market funds	Specified in the prospectus, usually U.S. Treasury bills, federal agency issues, CDs, prime banker's acceptances, prime commercial paper, and repos.	$5000	Overnight	None.

Basic Defensive Interval

The basic defensive interval (BDI) measures the period of time a nonprofit organization can operate on existing short-term assets without having to resort either to delaying disbursements beyond normal patterns, borrowing, or dipping into endowment or other long-term funds.

The basic defensive interval is calculated as follows:

$$\frac{\text{Total defensive assets}}{\text{Projected daily operating expenditures}}$$

Projected daily operating expenditures are found by dividing total annual expenditures by the number of days in a year (365). Defensive assets consist of cash, short-term investments, and some percentage of receivables. Do not include prepaid expenses. The percentage of receivables to be included depends upon the certainty that they will be received and the timing of the receipt of payment. The percentage chosen is judgmental and requires factoring in the cash flow seasonality and timing factors discussed earlier.

An Example.   The use of the BDI is shown below:

I   *Total defensive assets:*

Cash	$42,000
Accounts receivable, adjusted (adjusted to 50% of accounts receivable)	7,500
Short-term investments (savings account)	10,000
Total defensive assets	$59,500

II. *Projected daily operating expenses:*

$$\frac{\text{Total annual expenses } \$187,000}{365 \text{ days}} = \$512 \text{ per day}$$

III. *BDI:*

$$\frac{\$59,500}{512} = 116 \text{ days}$$

At first glance this NPO seems to have only modest short-term assets totaling $59,500. However, since annual operating expenses are only $187,000 the BDI is 116 days. Interpreting the basic defensive interval requires regular monitoring of changes in this ratio over time and comparison to the ratio of other similar nonprofit institutions. A BDI of less than 90 days for most NPOs would probably be unusually low and trigger a review of that institution's short-term asset management.

The importance of determining the required short-term investment position becomes clear given the commonplace confusion which exists in defining the boundary between short-term and long-term assets. Many NPOs believe they have long-term, or endowment, funds, but really have only working capital instead. A belief that funds required in day-to-day operations are really permanent, income-producing assets will lead to mismanagement of financial assets, a false sense of fiscal stability and well-being, and regular cash flow squeezes. All nonprofit organizations face the need to manage intensively their cash; whereas only a fortunate minority of the almost 1 million NPOs in the United States need to be concerned about intensively managing permanent funds.

Intensive Management of Cash: Conclusion

An intensive cash management program will increase the amount of investable cash. However, if cash remains uninvested, no real advantage is created for an NPO. The use of special checking accounts and pooled investment funds can put cash to work creating income. The short-term asset position that NPO should strive to maintain involves balancing cash flow seasonality and timing against the risk of technical insolvency: an inability to meet cash obligations. One technique which can be easily employed to help in determining the required amount of short-term assets is the basic defensive interval. This guide, which links an NPOs balance sheet assets to its operating expenses, can gauge the amount of short-term assets required to allow an NPO to function efficiently.

How to Profit from Intensive Management of Long-Term Assets

As pressures increase for delivery of services by nonprofit institutions, greater attention is being paid to endowment funds. Few institutions find themselves to be endowed adequately, and even those who believed themselves to be so blessed in the past have found themselves "suddenly short," as their costs and obligations have increased faster than the pace of donations and portfolio appreciation.

Similarly, institutions which have traditionally relied on annual infusions of funds from individuals, government and other sources have come to the realization that prudence, if not necessity, dictates augmentation and intensive management of their own endowment funds.

In any case, whether an institution is one of the few with an adequate endowment or one striving to create a viable long-term fund, intensive investment management can pay off handsomely. Often the institution is its own worst enemy. For instance, there may be a lack of understanding as to the maximum level of income an endowment fund might be able to generate prudently. On the other hand, the potential for capital growth may be improperly understood during budgetary or long-range planning processes. The result can be unrealistic short-sighted demands, most often for high current income. Another not uncommon problem occurs when investment policies are changed in midstream, not because of fundamental adjustments required by the institution's circumstances, but rather because of changes in investment committee personnel, temporary equity or debt market conditions, or investment management personnel. In such cases, the purpose of the endowment fund is forgotten. New departures are undertaken with vague expectations of "better results."

Unlike intensive cash management which applies techniques to everyday business operations, the intensive management of long-term assets increasingly relies upon the management of individuals who in turn exercise their financial judgment on an institution's behalf. What follows is a primer on how to manage the individuals who collectively manage your endowment.

First of all, until your endowment fund is quite impressive, reconcile yourself to the fact that you will be restricted to investment in conventional marketable securities: stocks, bonds, and the various short-term instruments also used in a cash management program. Writing options against your fund or lending securities may be possible income enhancers for a moderately sized fund. However, such refinements should not be attempted unless you are satisfied with the basic investment results and the manager producing them. In other words, do not be distracted by the marginal increment if you should first be paying closer heed to the corpus itself. On another front, "lockup," or high-risk, investments, no matter what the vehicle, are only for those who can afford the risk; to put it bluntly, for those who can afford to lose the particular investment entirely. We all know of the success of Haloid Xerox, but we never hear about the inventor in the garage down the street who developed a "superior" widget and pleaded with individuals and institutions for financial backing, only to find that the widget would not work. As a general rule, stick to marketable securities. Save real estate, venture capital, timberland, oil production, and other exotica for the day when your fund is larger than you need and the risks inherent in these investments can be prudently borne.

As to how best to organize for intensive investment management, the alpha and omega is: "Get yourself a good committee." At one time, NPOs routinely turned their investments over to a "grand old man" who figuratively kept the portfolio in his desk drawer and managed it without check or control. Occasionally you will find such a situation today, but the newer generation of "grand old men" tend to be professionals both male and female doing the job for pay and affiliated with a management organization. Further, if you were to operate in the old-time way, and your solo performer were to hit a series of sour notes, your constituents—and maybe even the courts—would not be very tolerant of your adherence to tradition. Form a committee to oversee your financial affairs and have them seek out a responsible investment management organization.

This committee—which, by the way, should for obvious reasons be of an odd number—has five basic responsibilities:

1. Determining an investment policy

2. Selecting investment manager(s)

3. Ensuring consistent application of its investment policy

4. Assisting in budget preparation and long-range financial planning

5. Planning for continuity and rejuvenation of membership

The key responsibility is the employment of a professional investment manager. Whether you already have one or are searching for one, you should test your investment policy (if you have one!) by asking the manager to evaluate its suitability for your institution and for your resources. Almost any institution would gladly spend all the current income an endowment fund could generate. However, when a financial squeeze is being felt, one of the first questions is bound to be "How much more can we get out of the endowment?" The committee must be the body to determine how much income the endowment fund can safely earn. It should therefore work with the investment manager to determine a reasonable policy regarding asset allocation and income generation.

A "reasonable policy" identifies that allocation of assets between equities and debt, or short-term securities, which will produce satisfactory income with due consideration to the long-term well-being of the fund's capital. The generation of higher income pulls you toward debt. The prospect of increasing income through dividend growth and appreciation leads you toward equities. This determination of the asset mix that is best-suited to meet defined needs is your basic task. You must define what you expect and set down explicit policy guidelines, in terms of asset mix, income generation, and long-term capital growth. The result can be a short paragraph; getting there can be an education.

Some of the issues that should be specifically addressed in developing a formal investment policy include

- Minimum current income required

- Minimum total return expected
- Asset mix as a ratio between equities and fixed-income securities
- Liquidity needs
- Minimum size of companies in portfolio
- Minimum quality rating for bonds
- Average maturity of bonds
- Amount invested in any one industry
- Amount invested in any one company
- Maximum portfolio turnover
- Amounts, if any, to be invested in nontraditional investments
- Voting of proxies on public interest issues
- Restrictions on investment in industries or companies for public interest reasons

Having set a policy, stay with it. If you decide to seek long-term growth through emphasis on equities at the expense of lesser current income, do not switch to debt because the stock market falls. By and large, if you have defined your needs and capabilities well and if there are no truly significant changes in your institution's basic financial condition, your original decisions probably will be valid for an indefinite period. Most successful endowment funds are intensively managed under policies and guidelines which were defined by people no longer on the committee.

Arrival at this happy point depends, of course, on *who* is on your odd-numbered committee. It is hard to make specific rules, but here are a few hints. Seek people with practical knowledge of business. One of the better areas to be represented is retail trade or the production of consumer goods. Observations of such individuals concerning consumer behavior can be most helpful, both to the manager and other committee members, in reviewing the specific current portfolio composition. Seek people with unbiased knowledge and insights into political and social matters. As a general rule, a person who is professionally involved in investment management may not be a good committee member. This prejudice arises from the discomfort which can be felt when a professional not managing the fund sits on a committee which is not completely satisfied with the current manager. Professional courtesy and the appearance of a conflict of interest can get in the way. Ask people at other institutions to identify good investment committee members. Do not try to woo them away to your committee, but perhaps they would take on another assignment. At least, they in turn might recommend good candidates. Be sure your members will support a common decision once reached, suggesting alternatives only after (not before) that decision *begins* to look as though it might have been a poor one. It is most unhelpful to have a committee member constantly bringing up a discarded policy or tactic. Once voted down, let it rest until the conditions which led to that vote have changed, or, as mentioned, until an error is suspected. By the same token, avoid anyone who either has a pet theory of investment or is an extremist ("I never own bonds and stocks, or either," "Buy gold," "Sell everything"). The committee should listen, ask, and judge. It must be open-minded and fair, and it must not dictate! Perhaps most important is that committee members be devoted to the nonprofit institution and work courteously and cooperatively with one another.

After having set your policy and ensuring that your manager is in tune with it (preferably through the process of arriving at the policy with the manager's help), you then should manage by review. A quarterly written report and semiannual meetings are satisfactory communication; monthly reports and quarterly meetings are better, if you can afford it. (Remember, even the "grand old man" would charge for his time these days.) Reports should include portfolio reviews, summaries of transactions, a commentary on the endowment fund, and such performance data as may be appropriate. Your manager should have full discretion; he or she is the professional. Intensive management requires this flexibility.

At your meetings, ask why specific actions were or were not taken. Be sure the manager complies with your policy. If there are significant deviations, try to find out why and whether corrective action is being, or should be, taken. Obviously, objective performance standards are needed, and you should work out such criteria with your manager. The ideal is to compare your endowment fund's performance to a peer group of institutions with resources and needs similar to yours. Such comparative data is not easy to obtain. If such comparisons can be made, a goal of being in the top half of the equity and debt portion of those peer funds in terms of results is a good one. This goal is tougher than it would seem, for the composition of the top half is constantly changing. Achievement of the goal of consistently outperforming one-half of your peer group will create truly exemplary results. In the absence of such a peer group, comparison either against a group of mutual funds with generally similar investment policies and asset mix or against general equity and debt indices can be adequate. However, "performance" in the sense of measuring capital value changes or measuring total return [(i.e., combined percentage change of asset value (appreciation or depreciation) plus current income)] may well not be the most suitable standard. Rather, examine the level of income alone and prospects for increases (if costs go up, so should income). Consistency and increase in income may be at least as important as increasing asset value.

The final and very important duty of the committee is to work with the NPO's staff, budget, and long-range planning committees to agree upon a reasonable level of income to be generated by the endowment fund. Ever-increasing demands for current income will bring you to, as one leading investment manager has put it, "the yield to liquidation." In order to increase levels of current income from a portfolio which is not growing through contributions, one must move more and more into debt issues. As this happens, the prospect of increasing income through the grinding process of dividend increases and appreciation will fade, since equities constitute less of the portfolio. Then, as costs go up, more income is needed, and a further shift is made to higher-yielding fixed-income investments. Finally one is left with a 100 percent fixed-income portfolio, and a zero percent chance of increasing income. Saying *no* is always a difficult job when a worthy institution says it needs more income, *now*. But doing so, may well be the most important contribution a committee can make.

Conclusion

The management agenda for contemporary nonprofit institutions covers an impressive range of seemingly critical issues, most of which impinge on "finances." Professional staff and trustees can achieve striking successes in intensively managing cash and long-term assets. These two largely unnoticed assets offer NPOs a new revenue source. Increasing tendencies to push out institutional limits is creating a set of forces requiring these greater financial resources.

Capitalizing on these revenue opportunities requires conscious deliberate efforts to put cash balances to work and to exact greater performance from endowment funds. Reemploying existing assets to better advantage offers significant financial rewards for those institutions willing to take the initiative.

38

Tax Implications of Charitable Giving

Ken Milani

Ph.D., Arthur Young Faculty Fellow in Taxation, University of Notre Dame

James L. Wittenbach

Professor, University of Notre Dame

Support of NPOs is manifested in many ways. Some backers provide their time, whereas others give of their talent to the NPO. This chapter focuses on those who donate all or a part of their "treasure" (i.e., cash, assets, and other property) to an NPO. Further, the tax benefits of charitable contributions to the donor are discussed in depth. Later in the chapter a sampling of tax planning opportunities available to a donor is presented.

It is hoped that this chapter will be useful to NPO administrators who deal with donors and who are often asked questions about the tax implications of specific giving patterns. The provisions explained here reflect the recent changes brought on by the Tax Reform Act of 1986.

Character of the Recipient Organization

Organizations that receive donations that are deductible by the donor fall into two broad categories. Federal income tax laws make a distinction between a public charity and a private nonoperating organization. Public charities receive substantial support from the general public and include both national organizations (e.g., CARE, the American Cancer Society) and local organizations (e.g., churches, schools, museums).

Private nonoperating organizations receive much of their support from only a few sources. In other words, the private nonoperating organization does not receive substantial support from the public at large. The family foundation is an excellent example of a private nonoperating organization.

Two special types of organizations, the private operating organization and the private foundation, are treated similarly to public charities for tax purposes if their major emphasis in serving the public involves the distribution of their funds to public charities.

The distinction between "public" and "private nonoperating" is important because it may affect the total contribution a donor can deduct in arriving at taxable income. The tax treatment applicable to the public charity is generally more favorable than that afforded the private nonoperating foundation. *For the remainder of this chapter, it is assumed that the recipient organization is a public charity.*

Individual Donors

Charitable contributions can be classified in several ways. One dichotomy looks at current contributions (completed immediately) and deferred contributions (incomplete gifts consummated sometime in the future).

Current contributions of property—such as cash, stock, or real estate—create tax benefits for the donor from both income tax and estate tax provisions. Income tax benefits will be emphasized below. However, the savings in estate tax that results from eliminating the gifted property from the donor's taxable estate can be substantial.

An individual who donates to a public charity will be allowed to list all or a part of the contribution as an itemized deduction on his or her tax return.[1] The type of property donated and the taxpayer's adjusted gross income (AGI) play an important part in determining how much will be included on the taxpayer's 1040.

Other considerations to be dealt with below include timing of the contribution, tax planning strategies, and certain technical issues that both the donor and the recipient organization must be aware of if they are to adhere to the tax laws governing contributions.

Type of Property Donated

Cash is one type of property that can be contributed. Two other general categories also exist: long-term capital gain (LTCG) property and ordinary income property. The latter category includes short-term capital gain (STCG) property. The tax provisions that apply to each type are examined below.

Cash. A payment of cash to a charitable organization is a common type of contribution. There are no valuation problems and the only substantiation requirements are either a cancelled check or a receipt from the donee (or other reliable written evidence). It is becoming increasingly popular for charitable organizations to accept payment of contributions by credit card. The IRS has taken the position that a donor who uses a bank credit card to make a charitable contribution is entitled to a deduction in the year the charge is made. Concerning payment by check, the regulations provide that the "unconditional delivery or mailing of a check which subsequently clears in due course will constitute an effective contribution on the date of delivery or mailing."[2] Payment made to a charitable organization for a ticket to a benefit performance is deductible only to the extent the cost of the ticket exceeds its fair market value (FMV). However, the cost of raffle or lottery tickets is generally nondeductible. The maximum deduction allowed in any one year for the contribution of cash to a public charity is limited to 50 percent of the donor's adjusted gross income (AGI). Any contribution in excess of this amount may be carried forward for 5 years.

Long-Term Capital Gain (LTCG) Property.   This category includes all assets which if sold at a profit would generate long-term capital gains (e.g., stock and other property held for a period deemed to be long-term for tax purposes). As of January 1, 1988, the long-term holding period is more than 12 months.[3] In a contribution made to a public charity, consideration must first be given to the type of LTCG property donated. If it represents intangible property (securities), real property, or tangible personal property related to the charity's tax-exempt function, the donor is allowed to elect one of two alternatives:

1. Under the *regular* method, the qualifying contribution is the fair market value of the property reduced by the amount of applicable depreciation recapture.[4] A ceiling, 30 percent of AGI, may create an excess which can be carried forward for 5 years.

2. Under an *elective* method, the qualifying contribution is determined by the fair market value decreased by the difference, if any, between FMV and adjusted basis (i.e., the foregone LTCG). The elective method's ceiling is 50 percent of AGI, and any excess may be carried forward over 5 years.

> *Example 1.*   Data processing equipment used in a sole proprietorship, Flo's Finest Flowers, is donated to a local college for use in its computer lab. The equipment which has a fair market value of $13,000 carries an adjusted basis of $4900 (i.e., acquisition cost $12,000 reduced by depreciation of $7100). Flo Frey, the sole proprietor, reports an AGI of $30,000.
>
> Using the two methods available, the charitable contribution may be either $5900 (regular method) or $4900 (elective method). Both are well within the AGI limitations of $9000 and $15,000, respectively.

	Regular	Elective
FMV	$13,000	$13,000
Less: Depreciation recapture	(7,100)	
Foregone LTCG		(8,100)
Charitable contribution	$ 5,900	$ 4,900

In certain situations, use of the elective method can be beneficial to the donor. Factors to be weighed include the following: (1) the amount of the unrealized appreciation in the property, (2) the donor's current versus future marginal income tax bracket, (3) the life expectancy of the donor since carryovers are unavailable to the estate, and (4) the donor's future contribution plans.

However, if the LTCG property is tangible personal property that is unrelated to the organization's tax-exempt function, the deduction is limited to the fair market value of the property reduced by the applicable amount of depreciation recapture less all of the foregone LTCG, if any. Again, the 50 percent of AGI ceiling applies. A work of art is a common item used to illustrate whether tangible personal property is related to the charity's tax-exempt function. For example, a painting donated to a hospital is usually unrelated to the hospital's tax-exempt function.

However, the same painting donated to an art museum for display would be related to its tax-exempt function. A donor must have documentation from the donee organization which states that the use of the donated property will be related to the organization's tax-exempt purpose.

Example 2. Marvin Irish's only donation in the current year was a painting with a FMV of $5000 to the city art museum. Marvin, who is retired, paid $4200 for the painting in 1980. Marvin's AGI for the year is $16,000. Assuming that the museum will display the painting, the donation represents a type of LTCG property which is related to the charity's tax-exempt function. Therefore, Marvin's deduction is limited to 30 percent of AGI or $4800, which is lower than the property's FMV of $5000. The excess of $200 is carried forward over 5 years. As an alternative, Marvin may deduct $4200, which is equal to the property's FMV of $5000 minus the $800 appreciation.

Example 3. Assume in the preceding example that Marvin Irish donated the painting to a local hospital for sale at an auction. Although the LTCG property is donated to a public charity, it is unrelated to the charity's tax-exempt function. Therefore, the deduction is $4200 which is the painting's FMV of $5000 less the $800 appreciation in value over cost. No carryover is available.

Ordinary Income Property.   This includes all assets which, if sold, would generate ordinary income. Examples include merchandise inventory, investments in securities held (as of 1/1/88) for a period of 12 months or less, a work of art created by the donor, a manuscript prepared by the donor, and letters and memoranda.

The deduction allowed for a contribution of ordinary income property to a public charity is limited to the lesser of the property's fair market value or its adjusted basis in the hands of the donor. Since the 50 percent ceiling continues to apply, any excess is carried forward 5 years.

Example 4. Bradley Belding owns a sporting goods store. In August of the current year, Belding donated football equipment to the local high school. The equipment cost $500 and the retail price amounted to $800. No other charitable contributions were made by Belding during the year. Assuming Belding's AGI amounted to $18,000, his deduction is equal to the adjusted basis of the property, or $500, which is far below the 50 percent of AGI (i.e., $9000) ceiling.

Other Matters.   To complete this portion of the chapter dealing with the type of property donated, two unrelated topics will be touched upon—the limitation rules and deferred contributions.

In applying the limitation rules, contributions subject to the 30 percent limitation (i.e., LTCG property contributed to a public charity) are considered last. An example illustrates this provision.

Example 5. Dan Byrne has AGI for the current year of $25,000. During the year he contributes cash of $9000 to the YMCA and stock with an FMV of $11,000 to the Boy Scouts of America. Dan paid $4000 for the stock in 1980. Because the stock represents LTCG property that is contributed to a public charity, it is subject to the special deduction ceiling of 30 percent of AGI or $7500 ($25,000 × 30 percent). However, the sum of the two contributions ($9000 in cash + $11,000 FMV of stock) equals $20,000 which exceeds 50 percent of Dan's AGI (i.e., $12,500). Consequently, because the cash donation is considered first, Dan's deduction is limited to $9000 in cash and $3500 in stock. The remaining portion of the stock (i.e., $11,000 − $3500 = $7500) can be carried forward to subsequent years.

Excess contributions which are carried forward for 5 years are used up on a first-in, first-out (FIFO) basis.

Deferred giving involves a charitable contribution of the remainder interest in property. Any full property interest may be segmented into an income interest, the right to receive the income that the property generates, and the remainder interest, the portion left following the severance of the income interest. In general, no current deduction is allowed for the contribution of a remainder interest. The two major exceptions to this treatment—use of a qualified charitable trust and the donation of the remaining interest in a personal residence or farm—are complex and beyond the scope of this effort.

Tax Planning Strategies

A donor can give property to an NPO in several different ways. Understanding the possible tax outcomes can be useful as an NPO approaches a donor or responds to donor queries.

Bargain Sales

A bargain sale is a sale (or exchange) of property to a charitable organization for an amount less than its FMV. Consequently, the transaction is partly a charitable contribution and partly a sale. The charitable contribution portion is determined by subtracting the selling price from the property's FMV.

A typical bargain sale finds the donor selling appreciated property to a charitable organization at a price equal to the property's adjusted basis. The end result is that the donor recovers his or her investment in the property and receives a charitable contribution deduction equal to the property's appreciation. To determine the donor's gain on a bargain sale, you must allocate the property's basis between the part sold and the part contributed. The formula to compute the adjusted basis of the property sold is as follows:

$$\frac{\text{Sales price}}{\text{Fair market value}} \times \text{property's basis} = \text{basis of property sold}$$

Example 6. Assume that Donna Domer, who is in the 28 percent tax bracket, owns land (held for investment) which she purchased in 1970 for $8000. The land has a current FMV of $20,000. Donna desires to donate $12,000 to her church and therefore she sells the land to the church for her tax basis of $8000. The gain recognized and the cash flow generated are shown below:

	Taxable gain	Cash flow
Computation of selling price of land	$ 8,000	$ 8,000
Allocation of basis:		
$\frac{\$8,000}{\$20,000} \times \$8,000$	3,200	
Taxable gain on part sold	4,800	(1,344)*
Deduction for part contributed ($20,000 − $8,000)	$12,000	3,360†
Net cash flow to Donna Domer		$10,016

*$4800 × 28% = $1344.
†$12,000 × 28% = 3,360.

A bargain sale usually generates more cash flow to a donor than an outright sale of appreciated property for its fair market value followed by a contribution of cash to a charitable organization in an amount equal to the recognized gain (i.e., appreciation). Furthermore, a bargain sale will usually result in more cash flow to the donor than a direct gift of the appreciated property to a charitable organization. For instance in the above example, a sale of the property for $20,000 followed by a donation of the recognized gain would have generated a maximum cash flow of $8000 for Donna Domer (i.e., proceeds of $20,000 reduced by the $12,000 donated). The $12,000 provides a tax savings of $3,360 which equals the tax on the $12,000 gain. A direct gift would trigger a positive cash flow of $5,600 (i.e., 28 percent of the $20,000 allowed as a charitable contribution).

Care should be exercised when the donated property is subject to a mortgage. The IRS position is that the bargain sale provisions are applicable to such a contribution. Furthermore, the fact that the charitable organization does not agree to assume the mortgage or pay it off is of no consequence. One way of avoiding this problem is to retire the mortgage before the transfer.

Property that Has Increased in Value

As a general rule, it is to an individual's advantage to donate appreciated LTCG property directly to a public charity rather than to sell the property and donate the proceeds to the organization. This rule applies regardless of the donor's marginal tax bracket. For example, assume that Bill Jordon is married and has taxable income for the current year of $200,000 before recognizing any gain from the sale of property or deducting contributions to charitable organizations. He is interested in donating $60,000 to his alma mater, Ferdley College. Bill owns stock which he purchased 5 years ago for $20,000 and has a current FMV of $60,000.

Two courses of action for Bill to consider assuming a bargain sale is not possible include: (1) contributing the stock directly to the college or (2) selling the stock first and contributing the proceeds to the college. As the information in Table 38.1 illustrates, Bill would lower his taxable income contributing the stock directly to his alma mater.

Property that Has Declined in Value

As explained above, no gain is recognized when appreciated property is contributed directly to a charitable organization. Likewise, no loss is recognized when

Table 38.1

	Donate stock directly to college	Sell stock and donate proceeds to college
Taxable income prior to sale of stock or charitable donation	$200,000	$200,000
Reduction of taxable income due to donation of stock to college or sale of stock and donation of proceeds to college	(60,000)	(60,000)
LTCG from sale of stock		40,000
Taxable income	$140,000	$180,000

property which has declined in value (below its original cost) is donated to a charitable organization. Consequently, it is usually wiser for the donor to sell property which has lost value in order to realize the loss (to offset other income) and then donate the cash proceeds to charity. This strategy applies whether the property is long-term or short-term.

Other Types of Contributions

Several other possibilities are available to an individual donor. For example, a qualified trust or a charitable lead trust could be established. A life insurance policy can be an excellent form of charitable gift. Another approach involves a charitable gift annuity which finds the donor selling property to the charity and receiving a lifetime annuity from the charity. All these approaches plus others (e.g., deferred gift of a personal residence or farm, annuity trusts, contributions of undivided interests) carry both income tax and estate tax implications which cannot be covered in detail here. When such situations are encountered, it would be prudent to seek the advise and counsel of a trained tax professional such as a certified public accountant or an attorney who is well-versed in tax matters.

Other Provisions

The tax laws include provisions applicable to appraisal requirements, donee information returns, and penalties for overvaluations.

Appraisal Requirements. In the past, donors were not required to obtain an appraisal in order to document the FMV of property gifted to charitable organizations. However, procedures for property contributions made after 1984 by individuals (as well as certain closely held corporations and personal service corporations) are now in place. Qualified appraisals must be obtained for each item or a set of similar items donated to one or more donees with a claimed value in excess of $5000 ($10,000 for nonpublicly traded stock). Publicly traded securities are exempt from this provision.

The appraisal must (1) be prepared by an independent appraiser who is qualified to appraise the type of property donated; (2) contain specific information such as a description of the property, the method of valuation, the FMV of the property on the date of the contribution, a statement that the appraisal was prepared for income tax purposes, the appraiser's qualifications, and the signature and taxpayer information number (TIN) of the appraiser; and (3) be included, in summary format in the donor's tax return for the year of the contribution along with the appraiser's signature (and TIN) and the donee's acknowledgment. Furthermore, the appraisal summary must include the acquisition date of the donated property and its cost.

Valuation Overstatements. At one time the income tax law provided for a graduated penalty structure for income tax valuation overstatements. The penalty ranged from 10 to 30 percent based on the extent of the overvaluation. Property that had been held by the donor for more than 5 years was exempt from the penalty.

For tax returns filed after 1984, the graduated penalty for overvaluations of charitable contributions is a flat 30 percent. However, the graduated penalty continues to apply with respect to overvaluations of property other than donated property. The 30 percent flat rate, which does not apply to donations of publicly traded stock, may be imposed on individuals, closely held corporations, and personal service corporations. The new penalty tax is triggered when the donor's claimed valuation is 150 percent or more of the correct value, and the result is an underpayment of income tax of $1000 or more. The amount of the penalty tax is determined by multiplying the resulting tax underpayment by 30 percent. The 5-year exception is not available. Thus, the penalty tax will apply regardless of how long the property was held by the taxpayer.

If the IRS determines (1) that the claimed value of the property was based on a qualified appraisal made by a qualified appraiser and (2) that the taxpayer made a good faith investigation of the value of the contributed property, it can waive the 30 percent penalty.

Donee Information Return.   If the recipient charitable institution sells, exchanges, or otherwise disposes of donated property which was subject to the appraisal requirements discussed above within 2 years of receipt, it must file with the IRS an information return (with a copy of the return to the donor) containing the following information: (1) the donor's name, address, and TIN, (2) a description of the property, (3) the date of contribution, (4) the amount received on disposition, and (5) the date of the disposition. Dispositions of publicly traded stock are again exempt from this reporting requirement.

A $50-per-failure penalty will be assessed each time the donee fails to file the necessary information return with the IRS or fails to furnish the donor a copy of the required report to the IRS. Both penalties will, however, be excused if the failure was due to reasonable cause.

Corporate Donors

Three components must be considered when dealing with contributions from corporations: (1) the type of recipient organization, (2) the accounting method used by the donating corporation, and (3) the type of property donated. The first component was covered earlier in the chapter and will not be addressed further. Nonetheless, we reiterate our assumption that all contributions discussed are received by public charities.

Accounting Method

For purposes of the contribution deduction, the corporation is either a cash-basis or an accrual-basis taxpayer. Generally, contributions qualify for deduction in the year they are completed. This treatment applies to both cash-basis and accrual-basis corporate donors.

However, the accrual-basis corporation's qualifying contributions will include cash contributions authorized in a tax year and paid within 2½ months following that tax year. Thus, a cash donation authorized by an accrual-basis corporation during the current calendar year will qualify for deduction on the current calendar-year return if it is completed on or before March 15 of next year.

The term "qualifying contribution" as used in this section recognizes the validity of the donation prior to application of a 10 percent ceiling that is in place for the corporate donor. The ceiling which is based on 10 percent of corporate taxable income after certain adjustments creates the possibility of deferring all or a part of the contribution deduction to a later tax year.

Type of Property Donated

Cash is one type of property that can be contributed. Two other general categories also exist, LTCG property and ordinary income property. The latter category includes STCG property.

Cash. The rules which apply to cash contributions were touched upon above. The qualifying contribution is measured by actual cash contributions and those made within the 2½ month period described earlier for accrual-basis donors.

> *Example 7.* Patriot Enterprises, a corporation, reports the following cash payments during 19Y2 and 19Y3:
>
> 3/1/Y2—$3000 to a charity. This completes a 19Y1 pledge made by the Patriot board of directors.
>
> 6/30/Y2—$40,000 to various charities per approval of the board of directors.
>
> 12/31/Y2—$26,000 which represents the first half of an authorized donation to a local church, St. Robert's.
>
> 2/15/Y3—$26,000 is disbursed to complete the authorized contribution to St. Robert's.
>
> Based on the above data, Patriot Enterprises would include the $3000 in its 19Y1 tax return. Patriot Enterprises' 19Y2 tax return would include $92,000 of qualifying contributions (i.e., $40,000 + $26,000 + $26,000) prior to considering the 10 percent of taxable income annual limit.

LTCG Property. LTCG property includes all assets which, when sold at a profit, generate long-term capital gains (e.g., investments in stock, Section 1231 assets held for more than 12 months). This is probably the most complex portion of the law dealing with the qualifying contribution.[5]

When LTCG property is donated to a public charity, the FMV of the property qualifies for deduction if the LTCG property is (1) intangible, (2) real, or (3) tangible personal property intended for use in the charity's tax-exempt function. For example, the FMV of the following corporate contributions to a local Red Cross chapter would qualify for deduction:

Description of Property	*Type of Property*
Investment securities	Intangible LTCG property
A parcel of land	Real LTCG property
Equipment used to measure blood pressure	Tangible LTCG personal property intended for use in the charity's tax-exempt function

When LTCG tangible personal property not intended for use in the public charity's tax-exempt function is contributed, the amount of qualifying contribution is the lower of the FMV of the property or the adjusted basis of the property.

Ordinary Income Property. Ordinary income property includes all assets which if sold would generate ordinary income. Merchandise inventory, investments in securities held for 12 months or less and Section 1231 assets (i.e., machinery and equipment) held for 12 months or less are examples of this type of property.

Corporate contributions of ordinary income property to a public charity (with some exceptions) involve comparing (1) the property's FMV with (2) the property's adjusted basis. The lower of these figures qualifies for the corporate charitable contribution. Thus, a corporation which donates merchandise inventory (FMV of $400 and an adjusted basis of $600) plus investment securities held for 5 months (FMV of $2400 and an adjusted basis of $1600) would generate a qualifying contribution of $2000 ($400 plus $1600).

An exception to the above rule with respect to certain types of ordinary income property pertains to inventory and other ordinary income property contributed to a public charity for use in the care of infants and/or sick and/or needy individuals. This charitable activity generates a qualifying contribution equal to the basis of the donated property plus 50 percent of the difference between its FMV and its basis. The deduction is limited to the donor's basis times two and it cannot be used by S Corporations. For example, assuming Manilow Corporation, a wholesaler of surgical supplies and not an S Corporation, donated dressings and bandages (cost basis of $5000 and a FMV of $7200) to orphanages, nursing homes, and health care centers operated for indigent elderly people, its qualifying contribution would amount to $6100 ($5000 plus $1100).

To encourage corporations (other than S Corporations) to gift ordinary income scientific property to colleges and universities for use in research endeavors, the law allows a corporate taxpayer to deduct its basis in the property contributed plus 50 percent of the unrealized appreciation. However, the deduction cannot exceed twice the basis of the property donated. Specific conditions that must be met to qualify for the equipment donation deduction include

1. The contribution must be made to an institution of higher education.

2. The property must be constructed by the taxpayer.

3. The contribution must be made not later than 2 years after the date of the construction of the property is substantially completed.

4. The original use of the property is by the donee.

5. The property must be scientific equipment or apparatus substantially all of which will be used by the donee (i.e., at least 80 percent) for research or experimentation or for research training in the United States in physical or biological sciences.

6. The property must not be transferred by the donee in exchange for money, other property, or services.

7. The donor must receive from the donee a written statement representing that the use and disposition of the property will be in accordance with conditions 5 and 6 above.

As an example, assume that Hoosier State University receives a piece of scientific equipment from Granger, Inc., during the current year. On the date of the gift the equipment, which was manufactured by Granger, Inc., at a cost of $4000 had a FMV of $16,000. Assuming that the seven conditions outlined above are met, Granger, Inc., is entitled to a charitable deduction of $8000. The general rule of cost (i.e., $4000) plus 50 percent of the appreciation (i.e., $6000) cannot be utilized because the resulting figure of $10,000 is greater than twice the basis of the property donated (i.e., $8000).

Tax Planning

As indicated above, there are many types of qualifying corporate charitable contributions. In any given tax year one or more of these types of donations may be made. When these contributions are summarized, the corporate taxpayer faces an overall limitation on the allowable deduction. Under current law, the annual ceiling is 10 percent of corporate taxable income computed without (1) deductions for charitable contributions, (2) the dividends-received deduction, (3) any net operating loss deduction carryback to the tax year, and/or (4) any capital loss carryback to the tax year. If the total qualifying corporate charitable contributions are equal to or less than 10 percent of the adjusted taxable income figure, the total is fully deductible on the corporate tax return. In cases where the total exceeds the 10 percent figure, the deduction is limited to the 10 percent figure, with the excess being carried forward for a period not to exceed 5 years.

Conclusion

It is a rare NPO that operates "in the black." For example, tuition only covers a portion of the cost of running a high school, college, or university. Support from contributors is an important resource. This chapter has looked at both individuals and corporations as donors. The stance adopted was one of being able to assist donors who would be seeking guidance about the federal tax implications of their contribution.

A word of warning will conclude this chapter. The tax laws are complex and constantly changing. The coverage above focused on the more traditional types of giving. An administrator of an NPO should have an understanding of the tax provisions. However, the details and intricacies should be handled by competent tax professionals.

Notes

1. Charitable contributions may be deducted by taxpayers who itemize deductions in a manner and in an amount that exceeds the standard deduction.

2. Section 162(b) Regulations.

3. The long-term holding period was altered by the Tax Reform Act of 1986. Since this is a volatile area, it would be wise to periodically verify the length of time required for long-term treatment.

4. Depreciation recapture is based on the amount of depreciation recorded on the asset prior to its contribution, the type of asset donated, and the length of time the depreciable asset was held by the donor. When confronting a situation where depreciation recapture is likely, a person well-versed in depreciation provisions should be consulted.

5. Section 1231 asset (e.g., machinery and equipment) provisions plus the depreciation recapture rules combine to make this a very rigorous type of contribution to address from a deduction point of view.

39

Fund-Raising Administration

Henry A. Rosso

*CFRE; Director, The Fund Raising School, Indiana University
Center on Philanthropy*

Effective fund-raising involves planning, goal setting, marketing, preparing, re-search, prospect development, communications, cultivation, solicitation, management of resources, action by group endeavor, and efficient administration of the myriad details that comprise the total.

Management Responsibilities

The wise fund-raising practitioner seeks support for this activity as a function of management in that the authority for fund-raising must be anchored within the governing board of the organization, and responsibility for implementation must rest with the chief executive officer. The chief executive can delegate the task for planning and execution to the staff fund-raiser while retaining responsibility for spurring the program to success.

Fund-raising is a function of management. It is also a process of management which emphasizes basic disciplines of analysis, planning, execution, and control, giving form and order to the development program. Within a management stance, the chief executive and the governing board, with the involvement of responsible staff, defines the organization's mission, delineates this mission in terms of goals and objectives, and refines goals and objectives into a statement of priority needs—operating budget, special project, capital, and endowment needs. To fulfill these needs, the fund-raising manager designs a functional program with a focus of working with and through people, of working with things and the tools of the trade to convert ideas into action to ensure gift production.

The Manager

The fund-raising manager is pivotal in the management structure, working closely with the chief executive, with key staff, with trustees, and with other key volunteers to promote acceptance of the gift development concept and to create a form by which this concept can be activated. As a strategically important member of the management team, the staff fund-raiser reflects the organization's mission, its policies, and its value system to the constituency. The fund-raiser reaches out to clarify and to interpret the mission while seeking market input for ideas, opinions, expressions of attitude, prejudices to ensure an empathetic environmental match. In this capacity, the fund-raiser serves as a link between the organization that has services to offer and the market area that has needs related to these services.

Essentially, the experienced fund-raiser utilizes a full array of skills to perform effectively in this sensitive position: *technical skills* to make effective use of the mechanical, routine tools of the profession; *human relations skills* to influence, involve, motivate people to act; and *conceptual skills* to perceive the totality of the organization within its environment, to understand interrelating forces that may impinge on its ability to raise money and to grasp the extensiveness of the gift support needs.

Conceptual thinking is critical analysis and planning. It is the creative management process that demands a thoughtful ordering of facts, ideas, and opinion before the plan can be drafted and the action determined.

Analysis provokes questions: What are the needs? Are they immediately urgent? Are they short term or long range in nature? How can these needs be met through fund-raising? Which of the different fund-raising vehicles can be employed? Which gift markets can be addressed? What volunteer human resources, staff resources, time resources, dollar resources must be allocated to meet the task requirements? What represents top priority in the plan?

For ideas to come to life, action is required. Action, for effectiveness, must depend upon orderly organization and administration of details that are the essential elements in the program.

Hard answers to searching questions will suggest planning format and, consequently, the program, staff, logistical and budget requirements, and guidelines for administrative procedures. In logical order, the fund-raiser moves from identifying needs, to defining program, to organizing staff, to prescribing procedures, to directing and controlling the action that will produce the required gifts. Thus, the plan is formed, the goals determined, and the action set. Conceptualization has been transformed into motion by the experienced fund-raiser; ideas and things have been ordered within the proper context. The principal supporting element that can help the plan to succeed or can sidetrack it into chaotic disorder is the fund-raising office and the people who staff that office—the staff support for the fund-raising plan.

The Fund-Raising Office

The fund-raising office exists solely to provide support for the fund-raising program. It can be as simple in its structure as a single-person staff operation with manually processed prospect and donor records and mass-produced letters and communications, or it can be as complex as a multifaceted, multiple-staffed development plan would require it to be with sophisticated data processing and word processing equipment and procedures.

Program needs and not prevailing fads should determine the operation and purpose of the fund-raising office. The basic requirement of the office staff is to gather and store information and to provide for quick, easy, and complete retrieval of information essential to the fund-raising process. The staff must serve in a support relationship to the professional staff and to the volunteer corps that should devote its talents and energies to gift production.

This office is the nerve center for the development program. Gifts are received, recorded for accountability purposes, acknowledged, reported to appropriate individuals to encourage their involvement, and catalogued to provide an historical profile of gifts for analysis and planning reasons.

Sensitive information of intelligence value is checked for accuracy and relevance, recorded, stored in hand-kept records to be available when required for planning, for strategic decision making, or for reporting. This information can take many forms: prospect data, gift data, case materials, statistical data, program information, and corporate and foundation research files for grant application preparation. Orderly filing for ready accessibility is essential.

Once the plan is accepted and varied fund-raising programs set into action, the fund-raising manager's energies must be directed to and utilized fully in strategic decision making, in motivating volunteers, in orchestrating lay solicitations, and in pressing fund-raising targets to deadline conclusions. Administration of office affairs, orderly processing and maintenance of all data, gift receiving, recording, and acknowledging should be procedurally routine, demanding minimum portions of the manager's time for review and control purposes on a periodic basis. The manager administers by influencing others to attend to the details.

Support services—the essence of fund-raising administration—can be delineated in four major categories: space, equipment, personnel; records; office management; and financial control.

Space, Equipment, Personnel

The relative place of fund-raising in the priority hierarchy and in the management philosophy of nonprofit organizations can be determined by the physical location and the adequacy of the furnishings of the fund-raising office. If the office is close to the chief executive's office and if it is adequately furnished, this is partial evidence that fund-raising shares a primary concern with program development and financial management. If, conversely, fund-raising space is inadequate and makeshift, distant from the chief executive's office, and incidental in its equipment, the process of volunteer involvement and gift procurement is obviously incidental and low on the organization's priority scale.

Fund-raising must demand a dignity of its own, reflective of its acceptance as a forceful, and yet sensitive, instrument for institutional advancement and program enrichment. Trappings in themselves are not symbols of dignity, and the reference here is not made to the overdecorated, richly appointed, overequipped office. The fund-raising office should be strategically located, suitably equipped and appropriately furnished to give testimony to staff, to trustees, to key volunteers, and to donors and prospective donors that fund-raising is accepted within the organization as a major program, as an expression of advocacy and as evidence of constituency support.

Adequate space for the fund-raising manager's personal office and conferences with voluntary fund-raising leadership should allow for quiet planning, for staff meetings, and for those rare opportunities for quiet deliberation. But this is wishful thinking! Such space allocation in too many instances would be construed as a luxury rather than a much-needed allowance for creative thought through analysis and planning or for productive evaluation and strategy development with the well-disciplined mind of a volunteer leader.

Certain basic equipment and basic furnishings are required such as adequate desks, typing chairs, steel files in which confidential files can be stored and locked, and support elements. During the year, fund-raising staff members becomes privy to extensive personal information that must be protected from any prying, curious people. Facilities should be provided to store this information for immediate availability when needed and yet protected from unwarranted examination by casual observers.

If computers are used for storage of vital information, the office is organized around data processing requirements. In the early planning stages, the fund-raising manager should make the important decision to utilize data processing to its optimum value in accepting and feeding back vital information beyond the name, address, and zip code donors. The data bank should include such data as size, frequency and nature of gifts, donor gift history, interests, affiliations, and so forth.

If a manual system of information storage is employed, appropriate filing procedures should be defined in a standard operating procedures manual available to every person in the fund-raising office. This manual becomes the guiding document for the department with written procedures for every activity, each assigned responsibility, within the fund-raising office.

Files of critical information tend to be extensive: prospective donors, individuals, families, corporations, professions, commerce, associations, churches or church groups, foundations, coordinating agencies, government. Alphabetical master control system and subsidiary category files are mandatory if the office is to function in an orderly manner and if information retrieval is to be simple with information organized in a way to serve the needs of the fund-raising officer.

If the fund-raising office is to serve as a nerve center or central informational base for the fund-raising function, then those who populate that office must be competent and sensitive people, capable of working with the stresses, the demands, the requirements for attention to details, the constant and compelling need for accuracy in all record keeping, and the inviolable rule that all things great and small that seem provocative enough for outside conversation must be kept confidential and cannot be discussed beyond the boundaries of assigned office space.

The fund-raising office secretary must be a highly trained individual who can function as an administrator with the ability to give attention to tedious detail and the managerial skill to oversee people, ideas, objects, and procedures to accomplish a specific goal. The secretary is the determining agent as to whether the fund-raising manager's talents and energies can be directed to strategic decision making and goal attainment or to de-energizing attention to time-consuming, unavailing administrative detail.

Records

Records are at the core of fund-raising office procedures. Records of prospective, current, and past givers; records of unpaid pledges and past gifts; records of potential big givers and potential givers; and records of local, regional, and national foundations and a profile of their grants making. Records for many purposes—all so important to the fund-raising effort. The process would have no meaning without them. The process would be mired in the mud of chaos if the records were to be mixed up or if a careless clerk typist or record keeper were to post the wrong information or spell the names incorrectly.

An orderly procedure for list development and list maintenance should be described in detail in the standard operating manual for office procedures. Without this careful definition of procedures and responsibilities, the function of the fund-raising manager would be confined to records sorting and file repairs rather than to the important task of gift production. At that juncture, it must be said that the fund-raising manager is judged more by an ability to raise much-needed money than by the ability to prepare and file prospect cards.

The combined judgment of a competent staff and an experienced fund-raising manager will facilitate decision making about computerizing fund-raising records. The shift from manual operations to data processing is complex, warranting many more words than can be allotted in this space. Let it be said that extensive preparation for the shift is required and that when the shift is contemplated, the process of transferring information should be so organized as to provide for effective feedback about donors, prospective donors, voluntary leadership, gift capabilities, gift history, gift patterns and all the strategic data so vital to critical analysis and thoughtful planning.

Data processing of fund-raising records is more than storage of names, addresses, and zip codes. Data processing can, and should, provide for storage and easy retrieval of extensive information to help the fund-raising manager and staff keep track of gifts, contributors, potential contributors, potential large givers, potential volunteer leaders, and other salient information for analysis, planning, and reporting purposes.

Managing the fund-raising function means management of sensitive data. The computer is the most efficient, most complex, mechanism devised to provide for data management.

Office Management

It has been said before that the primary function of fund-raising is to raise money. If this is to be accomplished, then the fund-raising manager's job is to promote gift solicitation. Undue preoccupation with routine office procedures will detract from gift solicitation because it will keep the manager chained to tedious, unproductive tasks of office management. The wise manager will see to the preparation of a procedures manual, will prepare or will require the preparation of job descriptions, and will make job assignments to move the office efficiently through normal operations.

The jobs are identified and defined, tasks assigned, and the fund-raiser can devote energies and talents to the primary concern of raising money with only periodic procedures and job reviews with staff. Card shuffling can become addictive, particularly if the process can justify itself as a distraction to the somewhat more challenging, more demanding, and somewhat more onerous assignment of soliciting gifts.

Gift receiving, processing, and acknowledging should be the responsibility of a single person, preferably a gift records clerk who can be induced to make a religion of accuracy in spelling, in identifying and listing names, in posting gifts to ledgers, and so forth. The attention of one person to this procedure can help to regularize it, reducing to a minimum chances for errors and oversights.

Preparation, maintenance and control of mailing lists may be a shared duty, but the principal responsibility must rest with one individual who will see to it that all pertinent data—full name, business address, residence address, city, state and zip code—are checked for completeness and accuracy before this data is entered on the organization's records.

Training of the entire staff is a vital necessity. This training should not be limited to the more mechanical aspects of the fund-raising program. Each staff member should be helped to understand the principles and techniques of fund-raising and should be encouraged to develop a working familiarity with management terms.

As far as feasible, staff members should be able to verbalize the organization's case and to speak intelligently about its needs. Be prepared—a fund-raising maxim—for the day when a philanthropist will call to seek assistance in the transfer of a handsome gift, and the only person available to offer counsel is an untrained, inarticulate clerk.

Training has an upward, lateral, downward flow: upward to involve the chief executive, trustees, and volunteers in understanding fund-raising; laterally to promote understanding of the function among organizational staff people, and downward within the fund-raising office to hone staff skills to a cutting edge. The fund-raiser who seeks to move from beginner to statesperson within the profession must shoulder the responsibility to inculcate staff members with the values of professional advancement and growth.

Financial Controls

The American Institute of Certified Public Accountants (AICPA) has prepared a set of guides which will be mandatory upon CPAs in their audit of nonprofit entities. The purpose of these guides is to encourage uniformity in accounting procedures so that nonprofit financial records can be understood readily and can reflect the financial status of all organizations. It is incumbent upon all administrators to organize their records and financial reporting systems to coincide with the recommended AICPA form.

Sound public accounting procedures within the fund-raising office fulfill these basic functions: stewardship in the receiving of, and accountability for, all gifts; reporting to the institution, to affiliated agencies, to the executive director, and to the governing board at regular intervals; organization of records to facilitate reporting to regulatory agencies when required, or to provide for a review of fund-raising costs to city, state, or federal agencies when necessary.

The gift trail moves through the institution with the receipt of the gift, followed by posting in ledgers, on gift cards, on accounts receivable forms (in the event of pledges), on receipts that are sent to donors, on reports prepared for internal dissemination or those for distribution to external audiences (donors, prospective donors, advisory boards, broader markets, etc.); or listing in annual reports, designation on plaques or other recognition devices, special involvement in minimum gift clubs, or for specific restrictions in accordance with the donor's wishes.

The reasons for efficient gift accountability might be: (1) receiving, recording, and honoring the gift; (2) transmitting the funds in orderly fashion for deposit to designated or undesignated accounts; (3) preparing and distributing receipts to donors and to organizational records; (4) summarizing and distributing information to use in measuring progress and determining continuing action; (5) reporting to involved constituencies; and (6) maintaining an accounts receivable system for the collection of unpaid pledges.

Budget Preparation

The fund-raising budget is an expression in dollar values of program activities that will be undertaken to accomplish the stated objectives for the fund-raising program. Program budgeting and budget planning are interrelated. A budget properly drawn should accomplish more than to predict expenditures. It should reflect the scope and the potential of the program it intends to support and should allocate resources accordingly.

Program elements for the organization's development program can be staff, office supplies, public information, general expense and nondollar values such as staff time and volunteer time attributed to fund-raising activities. Program activities that would necessitate these supporting program elements can be annual giving campaigns, gift clubs, special events, big gifts, capital gifts, planned gifts, grantsmanship, public information, training, and so forth.

The fund-raising manager, in preparing the budget, will move through three distinct steps, from preplanning, to planning, and to prescribing program elements.

1. *Preplanning, or fact gathering.* Economic evaluation; analysis of past fund-raising performances; examination of anticipated need for the next year, or possibly 3 years, ahead; objectives and policies, preparation of operating plans to accomplish objectives.

2. *Planning, definition of program.* Definitive statement of needs, objectives, policies, preparation of specific plans to accomplish objectives.

3. *Prescribing the program elements.* What specific program elements will be required to meet stated objectives through the annual giving fund (memorials, direct mail, benefits, gift clubs, phon-a-thons, business solicitation, grants, etc.); big gifts (research, cultivation, solicitation); planned gifts (training, travel, promotion, technical assistance); foundations (research, The Foundation Center Associates membership, preparation of applications, etc.); capital campaign (professional counsel, extra staff, campaign office, special electronic equipment, printing, meetings); public information (printing, publications, special events, meetings, etc.); all office and staff activity required to support program execution.

The fund-raising manager prepares the budget, seeks approval for it, accepts full responsibility to control it effectively through regular reviews and through an established procedure for reporting to staff superiors, to a development committee and through the committee to the governing board as warranted.

A good system of budgeting is a two-sided affair that provides:

1. Planning to establish an overall development goal commensurate with the organization's needs and to define department objectives within that goal

2. Control of reports and of procedures that will enable management to make sure that such reasonable objectives become accomplished results

Summary

The fund-raising manager uses efficient management as a principle to promote the accomplishment of stated objectives.

The experienced fund-raising manager uses efficient administration—the nuts and bolts of management—as an effective tool to break free from unnecessary, time-consuming preoccupation with office details so that maximum time, energy, and talent can be directed to those activities that can be of maximum effectiveness in producing gift dollars.

The fund-raiser must be administrator, counsel, educator, trainer, public speaker, writer, motivator, activator, organizer, trouble shooter, persuader, financier, tax authority, salesperson, planner, bookkeeper, knowledge bank, diplomat, researcher, institutional representative, businessperson, and poet.

What it all comes down to in the crunch is the fact that the fund-raiser must be primarily a *fund-raiser* because when all things are measured, it is the volume of gift dollars produced each year that counts.

PART 5
Public Relations

40

Planning the Public Relations Program

Tracy D. Connors

Consultant

"Planning is more crucial in public relations than other fields." notes David Finn, partner, Ruder, Finn & Rotman, Inc., of New York. Reason: "Public relations effectiveness is amorphous, ephemeral, difficult to measure."[1]

A successful communications and public relations program, Lucille Maddalena points out, "is one very important element of a marketing plan. To design a successful program, you must understand the needs of your audience, who you are, what you have to offer, who you want to reach, what message you want to send, and what results you would like to achieve from your efforts."[2]

There are two basic types of public relations programs: remedial and planned. These two types have sometimes been dubbed the "fire-fighting" program and the "fire-prevention" program.

In the fire-fighting program (if it can actually be called a program), the organization's public relations people spend the majority of their time and effort putting out all the little and big "fires" of noncommunication or damaging communication that happen when no effective program of public relations has been planned. Inevitably, this approach to public relations is far more costly and less effective than its opposite—the planned or fire preventive approach.

A planned, or preventive, program is based on facts relative to the situation and essential for effectiveness, has objectives developed to avoid the obvious problems, is directed to achieve the desired objectives, and is flexible enough to be modified or changed when necessary to adapt to the shifting climate of the organization's publics.

An organized approach to public relations solves many potential problems before they obstruct progress. Problems that do arise can usually be headed off early, before they reach crisis proportions.

The Planning Process

The basic planning process for effective public relations involves four steps: (1) fact finding, (2) planning, (3) communicating, and (4) evaluating. Finn adds that major elements[3] in a public relations plan should include: (1) gaining consensus as to what the major goals should be, (2) developing written recommendations for the year's public relations activities, (3) providing a budget, an estimate of staff support needed, and a timetable, and (4) merchandising results in regular progress reports.

Facts are the basic elements of any plan, and the public relations planner should begin with a systematic search for them. Two categories of facts are needed: facts about the organization itself and facts about the public with whom it is trying to communicate. Many organizations use these facts intuitively, but whether they are formally written down in an official planning document of some kind or simply considered during other stages of the planning process, they are very important.

The first step in the planning phase is to establish objectives. Whenever possible these should, of course, parallel the overall objectives of the organization's annual or master plan. Any public relations objective that does not relate to the annual plan should be carefully and critically reviewed.

In selecting the organization's public relations objectives, the planner(s) should consider the public relations needs of the organization as revealed by the fact finding about the organization and its publics.

Facts needed about the organization include more than just its history, programs, membership, and budget; they include the facts needed concerning the attitudes about the organization held by both the general public and the organization's members. Research is the way these facts are gathered, whether it consists of a modest questionnaire or survey, or an in-depth professional analysis.

Contrary to much current practice, communications begins with listening—in many forms. Whatever its form, research provides "much-needed emphasis on the listening phase of public relations and gives substance to the two-way street concept," explain Cutlip and Center. They also note that research "provides the objective look required to know thyself...reveals festering trouble spots before they inject a large body of public opinion...increases the effectiveness of outbound communication...and provides useful intelligence...."[4]

Other fact-finding vehicles useful in developing information helpful for public relations planning include such informal methods as panels, juries, advisory committees, mail analysis, media and field reports, plus more formal (and usually more expensive) methods as cross-section surveys, in-depth interviews, news media content analysis, mail questionnaires, and professional opinion research. Whatever the vehicle, fact-finding and research are invaluable in helping an organization assess attitudes important to an effective public relations plan.

In addition to considering the public relations needs of the organization, the planner(s) should consider such important factors as the following:

1. The particular service or public benefit provided for the public by the organization

2. The resources available in the form of money, time, personnel, talents, and facilities

3. Remembering to give a planning voice to the personnel who will later be called upon to implement the public relations plans

As noted in *Principles of Association Management,* the public relations plan should include the following elements:[5]

1. A summary of the facts revealed by the research efforts
2. A statement of the problems and goals of the program, based on research findings
3. A statement of the planning phases
4. Analysis of competitive factors affecting the program
5. A statement of priorities, timetables, and media for carrying out the program
6. A description and analysis of the publics
7. A description of the methods of program implementation
8. An outline of the organization and personnel requirements needed to carry the program into effect
9. A list of examples of subject matter (articles, news releases, etc.)
10. A prepared budget adequate to effect the plan

Additional considerations that may be helpful in the planning stage of a public relations program, include the following:

1. Making up a checklist of audiences, communications with whom are considered to be important if the organization's objectives are to be achieved. Keep track of how often each one is reached to help determine during a subsequent review if your program has achieved balance in reaching them.

2. Preparing a calendar of news stories or "breaks" throughout the year to help your public relations people space newsworthy stories evenly and to allow adequate planning and preparation time for each story. A calendar will help prevent duplication and overlaps in coverage, as when two separate committees or units of the same organization attempt to place stories with the same media outlet. "Slow" news periods such as holidays and summer vacation periods, and seasonal news items, can be utilized to great advantage with such a calendar.

3. "Coattailing" your organization's events or activities to coincide with local events if there is some enhancing relationship between your event and a local news angle.

4. Selecting key leaders, influential people, and opinion makers from your target publics and considering the development of special communications efforts for this group, such as direct mail distribution of position papers, leaflets, brochures, or resolutions.

In planning a public relations program to advance organizational goals, note Cutlip and Center, "it is important that the content be devised so that it tells, over a period of time, the institution's history, ideals, and achievements, publicizes its people, its policies, and its products or services, and projects its plans for a better tomorrow. Unless such yardsticks are used periodically, emphasis is apt to become disjointed under exigencies of the moment. To touch all bases, program content must be planned and devised....By following a checklist, each press release or special event will bring progress toward the broad goals of good repute and wide recognition for public service."[6]

Communication is the third step in the four-step public relations cycle. Public relations personnel demonstrate skill during this phase in three important ways.

First, they are selective in identifying and selecting the key publics that must be reached and the type of information that needs to be transmitted to the organization's internal publics. This avoids the dead-end situation that results from thinking that public understanding and support will result simply from transmitting large amounts of information.

Second, they have a good working knowledge of the mass news media available for the transmission of information about the organization, and use this knowledge to advantage when selecting the major media best suited for the message.

Third, they have the skills needed to provide lateral, upward, and downward internal communications within the organization itself, which are necessary to implement any public relations program successfully.

Cutlip and Center conclude their discussion of this phase with what they call "The 7 C's of Communication":[7]

1. *Credibility.* Communication starts with a climate of belief. This is built by performance on the part of the source. The performance reflects an earnest desire to serve the receiver. The receiver must have confidence in the sender. He or she must have a high regard for the source's competence on the subject.

2. *Context.* A communications program must square with the realities of its environment. Mechanical media are only supplementary to the words and deeds that take place in daily living. The context must provide for participation and playback. The context must confirm, not contradict, the message.

3. *Content.* The message must have meaning for the receiver and it must be compatible with his or her value system. It must have relevance to him or her. In general, people select those items of information that promise them greatest rewards. The content determines the audience.

4. *Clarity.* The message must be put in simple terms. Words must mean the same thing to the receiver as they do to the sender. Complex issues must be compressed into themes, slogans, or stereotypes that have simplicity and clarity. The farther a message has to travel, the simpler it must be. An institution must speak with one voice, not many voices.

5. *Continuity and consistency.* Communication is an unending process. It requires repetition to achieve penetration. Repetition—with variation—contributes to both factual and attitude learning. The story must be consistent.

6. *Channels.* Established channels of communication should be used—channels the receiver uses and respects. Creating new ones is difficult. Different channels have different effects and serve in different stages of the diffusion process.

7. *Capability of audience.* Communication must take into account the capability of the audience. Communications are most effective when they require the least effort on the part of the recipient. This includes factors of availability, habit, reading ability, and receiver's knowledge.

The fourth and final stage in the communications cycle is the evaluation or, "How did we do?" step. To retain its effectiveness and focus, a public relations program must include procedures and funds for the proper feedback and evaluation of the organization's communications efforts.

A formal evaluation might include a "lessons learned" analysis of each step taken in the specific program. For those organizations that have the necessary funds, such evaluation techniques might include formal opinion polls, newspaper clipping services, depth interviews with key members of the public, or a comparison of the organization before and after implementation of the program.

Informal (and less expensive) evaluation techniques might include simply asking (and carefully listening to) the opinions of other members of the staff and organization on the effectiveness of the program. Trends in complaints, amount of coverage, and status of relationships in the community are also informal indications of the success of the public relations program. Evaluation, once complete, should be put back into the planning process and the cycle begun anew.

Financing the Public Relations Program

Although there is no standard pattern for financing a public relations program, it is obvious that without adequate financing, the entire program will quickly come to a halt. A great deal depends, of course, on the nature and composition of the organization preparing the plan. The plan and the budget will usually reflect its service and financial posture in the community. A comprehensive and adequate budget must be a part of any public relations plan if it is to be given any reasonable chance of success in achieving its objectives.

The method of financing the public relations program of a public service organization depends largely on whether the organization itself is a single entity in the community, a local chapter or unit of a regional or national organization, or an association of member organizations each with its own separate budget.

Autonomous organizations will include the public relations budget as a portion of their operating budget. A local chapter or unit of a larger public service organization will probably have its own operating budget, a portion of which will likely include funds for public relations. In addition, it will have the added advantage of being able to obtain and use the public relations materials supplied by the national organization and to capitalize on its national public relations program.

According to the Chamber of Commerce of the United States, public service associations finance their public relations programs in four ways: (1) financing from a regular income, and as a part of the present dues structure; (2) increasing dues, or levying a special assessment on the membership (if the program is for a definite, short-range objective; (3) establishing a subscription system separate from the dues structure; (4) seeking voluntary contributions, or charging members on the basis of services rendered.[8]

Notes

1. David Finn, Planning Is Key to Public Relations Efforts, *The Nonprofit Executive,* January 1984, p. 3.

2. Lucille A. Maddalena, *A Communications Manual for Nonprofit Organizations,* AMACOM, New York, 1981, p. 4.

3. David Finn, p. 3.

4. Scot M. Cutlip and Allen H. Center, *Effective Public Relations,* Prentice-Hall, Englewood Cliffs, N.J., pp. 111–114.

5. *Principles of Association Management.* American Society of Association Executives and the Chamber of Commerce of the United States, Washington, 1975, p. 204.

6. Cutlip and Center, *Effective Public Relations,* p. 135.

7. Ibid., pp. 166–167.

8. *Association Public Relations Guide,* Chamber of Commerce of the United States, Washington, 1968, p. 27.

41

Public Information*

Tracy D. Connors

Consultant

Public information includes the preparation and dissemination of information and other material to the mass news media. When the public relations people for your organization consider your PR objectives, they think in terms of how to use these various media—the press, radio, and television—to best advantage. To obtain the greatest effectiveness, they must analyze the available media to determine how best to present the story and to ensure that the information prepared is in usable format for the media to which it is directed.

There are many mass news media communications vehicles open to your PR personnel, including:

Printed news releases, mailed or delivered to reporters

Answers to queries

Interviews

News conferences (in essence an interview with more than one reporter present)

Tape recordings

Photos released with captions, with or without accompanying story

35-mm slides—most often as public service announcements

Motion picture film or videotape, with or without sound

It is important to note that regardless of the method chosen to release information to the public, the PR person must maintain a record of what was released or said to the press. This is not necessarily a legal "must," but the result of overwhelming common sense and past experience. If a written release is prepared, the problem of maintaining a record is satisfied simply by retaining a file copy. How-

---

*Adapted in part by permission from the *Applied Journalism Handbook,* Defense Information School, Fort Benjamin Harrison, Indiana.

ever, when a reporter calls or visits your office seeking information, a record in the form of a "query sheet" should be maintained.

The query sheet should include the name of the caller, the organization he or she represents, the phone number, the question, and—very important—your answer. If it is necessary to obtain the answer from one or more members of the staff, a notation should be made on the query sheet regarding the source of the information.

About the News Media

The chance of any individual selecting any given news item from the mass media's output is fairly small, although the average American devotes about 4 to 5 hours a day to the disgorgements of the mass communications media. A vast array of media products surround us in our daily lives. Morning, evening, and weekly newspapers await reading, any one of which would take several hours to read in its entirety. Readership therefore falls off sharply after the first few paragraphs, so that the latter part of a long newspaper story is unlikely to be read at all.

Radio pours forth around-the-clock broadcasts of fare, ranging from classical music to virtual noise. Most areas have many television channels from which to choose a wide variety of programs. A bewildering variety of magazines, books, and other printed materials flood bookshops and newsstands. Motion pictures use methods ranging from sensate techniques to enhance perception to depiction of sensual subjects to attract audiences. And even after a choice is made from this competing array of media, the level of attention is often rather low, as when several media receptions are combined, for example, listening to music while reading, playing cards or eating while watching television—or even watching several television sets at once, à la former President Lyndon Johnson.

Thus it is important to stress once more the problems faced by the public relations team in getting your message(s) across to the public. Even though the odds are against you in many respects, a carefully planned and executed public relations program can greatly increase these odds by knowing and fulfilling the individual requirements of each medium available to you.

In terms of your public relations program, the news media should be thought of as the tools by which and through which you tell your story to the public. As an ambulance corps would use different techniques to rescue various victims, or a symphony different interpretations when playing the music of various composers, different media and approaches to them are needed to solve each public relations problem. Each has unique requirements and unique potentials to offer in implementing your public relations program.

The following is a brief analysis of the major news media as a guide to their use for public relations.

Newspapers

Newspapers are the oldest medium of mass communication and still the bedrock of in-depth news coverage. Although newspapers have lost considerable ground to television and radio, aggregate newspaper circulation of all daily papers is increasing. Characteristics of newspapers relative to their role in public relations include the following:

Newspapers have regular readers, many of whom have confidence and trust in the paper.

Newspapers cover a story in greater depth than broadcast or pictorial media under normal circumstances.

The style of organization and presentation of newspapers permits readers to gain summary or superficial knowledge simply by reading the headlines and lead paragraphs. Very few people read an entire page.

Newspapers provide timely coverage of news events in comparison to magazines and books.

Newspapers provide information and entertainment helping to shape public opinion.

Newspapers have little lasting value, but are still more permanent than the ephemeral messages from electronic media or oral communications.

The essential differences between metropolitan dailies, suburban dailies, and weekly newspapers should be kept in mind.

The "product," news, spoils very rapidly. Editors want news in their hands as soon as possible, preferably before the event that generates it.

Radio

Radio is a newcomer compared to newspapers; its virtues include immediacy, variety, mobility, and appeal to its listening audience, which, in the aggregate, includes nearly everyone in this country. It can reach people whether they are at home, in a car, at the beach, or wherever. Radio's characteristics include the following:

It is friendly, informal, intimate, and timely.

It has an almost instantaneous reaction time to fast-breaking news stories—a boon for your "good" news and a real problem when the news (as far as your organization is concerned) is bad.

It is limited in depth of treatment.

News items are written in clear, concise, conversational style, including the *who, what, when, where, why, and how* of a news story.

Entire news stories are usually covered in anywhere from 15 seconds to 1 minute of broadcast time.

Television

Television is the newest of the mass communications media. More Americans have television sets than have either telephones or bathtubs. Television combines the features of sight and sound.

Television's principal value to NPOs is as an audiovisual medium to relay news and public service announcements (PSAs) to key publics.

There is no common standard in preparing television news or feature material.

This should be determined by liaison with individual television program and news directors for station requirements for format, length, features, photographs, and slides.

Broadcasting in General

The following tips were provided by the National Association of Broadcasters[1] and should be kept in mind as you plan and implement the broadcast-media portions of your organization's public relations program.

> Broadcasting is under no obligation to grant time to any specific group. No law says that a station must devote a fixed amount of time to community organizations, although most stations pride themselves on their alertness to community needs and their record of public service.
>
> Since time and available facilities vary widely from station to station, a call on the station and its news and program directors (first arrange for an appointment) is strongly advised.
>
> Success in dealing with the broadcasting media is improved if you know your stations and their programs—taking time to listen to or watch local shows first so you will be familiar with their format and know what you are talking about before you approach them for public service or news time.
>
> If your public service appeal is to be effective, you must know the following before you contact the station:
>
> *What* your message is and the basic idea you want to convey
>
> *Who* is the intended receiver of the message and can it be tailored to those you want most to reach
>
> *How* that message can best be put across
>
> Public service announcements must be carried on radio and television *only* on behalf of bona fide nonprofit organizations. A successful application to the IRS for designation as an exempt organization is a prerequisite for public service time in the broadcasting media. (See Part 1, Chapter 4.)
>
> Broadcasters face an enormous demand for free public service air time—not all appeals can be honored.
>
> Preplanning and adequate station lead time are very important, because a station's "product" is its air time, and air time cannot be expanded (like newspaper space) if some extra material turns up.
>
> Remember that you and your organization are competing with many other fine groups that believe just as strongly (if not more so) that their own projects and programs deserve attention and coverage. Empathize with station personnel and don't get "bent out of shape" if your event or program does not get the coverage you feel it should. An understanding attitude this time will ensure a receptive welcome on your next visit to the station.

News Services

More often referred to as wire services, the news services provide coverage to news media that they could not afford to get by other means. Two news services predominate in the United States: Associated Press and United Press International.

The Associated Press (AP) is a nonprofit service owned by its members, which include more than 1700 publications and 2000 radio and television stations. They feed information into the system while taking it off the wires for themselves. AP files about one-half million words per day, plus offering features, photos, and technical advice to members. Its major news services include the following:

1. *Broadcast wire.* Around-the-clock coverage, providing 22 daily news summaries of 5 and 10 minutes air time, immediate bulletins, and regional news. It is written in broadcast style for immediate use with national and international news, plus sports, women's, weather, and market news.

2. *"A" circuit.* Around-the-clock national and international news.

3. *"Single circuit."* Used most often by smaller morning and afternoon papers.

United Press International (UPI) is a profit-making service selling news and feature material to mass media. It offers virtually the same services as AP, including features and wire-photo service. It tends to be less conservative and more colorful than AP.

Wire service representatives should always be considered and invited to participate in any significant news event you sponsor or coordinate. Members of local media are often employed by the wire services as "stringers."

Magazines

Magazines are generally grouped as news, entertainment, or special-interest publications.

Magazines have wide circulation, although they are published less frequently than newspapers.

Magazines provide better interpretation, with clearer meaning often given to items published piecemeal by other media.

Magazines provide more background material as a result of having more time to dig into a story.

Magazines show greater selectivity in the material they print.

Magazines are more permanent than newspapers, staying in homes and offices for longer periods, and are often reread.

Entertainment magazines appeal to the wide variety of subjects in which the general public is interested. Stories here need not be as timely as in news magazines or newspapers.

Few magazine editors want or will accept handouts of news material except as possible leads for internal, staff-written stories. Editors provided with individually prepared feature material suitable for their publication (don't forget good photographs) will either politely refuse the material (unless requested by them), adapt the material as a filler, or follow through with a staff-written article.

Magazines permit greater opportunities for creative and imaginative writing.

Magazines are not condensed newsletters or even newspapers, but have a format of their own requiring more planning, editing, and imagination in such important areas as layout.

A magazine has an almost unlimited appetite for photographs, illustrations, and other artwork. This is an important consideration in planning an approach to a magazine editor.

Books

More than 10,000 new book titles are published annually. With increased readership in the nonfiction area, this presents a growing market and potential for public service organizations wishing to have their programs or services mentioned or even described fully in a book.

Producing a high-quality useful book is no small job. A growing number of public service organizations, however, do have the internal resources from staff or volunteers to produce such a work. There are three basic ways to go, according to an excellent article in *Association Management* on this subject.[2]

1. Following copy preparation by staff or members of the organization, the book can be published by the organization itself, a route that provides for maximum control and monetary benefits. With total freedom in selection and control, however, comes total responsibility for such important and tricky decision areas as copy, layout, design, printing, binding, illustrations, artwork, photos, dust jacket, promotion, advertising, and sampling, in which a mistake can be costly in time and money. Unless you are experienced in the intricacies of dealing with printers, much grief and money will be saved if you obtain and consult a valuable reference on this subject entitled *Printing Trade Customs*. Adopted by the Printing Industries of America (PIA), the booklet is available through your printer, the PIA, or the American Society of Association Executives.

2. Another approach is closely related to the above, differing in the relationship with the author. Following arrangements with the author regarding payment for services, the author then accepts full responsibility for writing corrections and for the authenticity of the manuscript.

3. The third approach is to contract with a respected publisher for the publication. Although this may reduce the potential for income from the publication, it also minimizes the risk associated with total responsibility for publication. The publisher assumes all responsibility for the publication, from design to size, selling price to promotion—all these decisions are made by the editor assigned by the publisher to this publication. If you plan to use this approach, the best policy is to contact the prospective publisher early in the development of the publication, before it is too far advanced. Expertise offered and accepted at this time can be most valuable in saving time and money, plus result in a superior product for your organization.

How to Release News

News releases are the most common, the most efficient, and usually the most economical method of disseminating news to the media. As much as 50 percent of what is reported in the printed and electronic news media originates outside the city rooms and news desks of the media, saving them millions of dollars annually. The ever-increasing flood of news releases clogs desks and in-baskets, however, causing resentment by editors toward "handouts" in general. To get the space or air time you want for your organization, your releases must be worthy of the time and attention of the editor or news director. Consideration of the following "Dos and Don'ts" will help your chances for getting into print.

Do remember that the editor or news director is looking for news. Make it easy for them to find it.

Do get news releases to the editor or news director as soon as possible—for the broadcast media, a week in advance, if possible. Be meticulous about time. If you promise an editor a story at a certain time, have it on the desk on or before the appointed day and hour.

Do use a clean ribbon for legible copy. Photocopies are recommended over carbons, which can become smudged.

Do use common sense and good taste in your news stories and in your relationships with news media representatives.

Do follow up on your news release a few days after you have mailed it to the editor. "Ask if they received it, if the format was acceptable, and when they will be printing it. Thank them for their help and cooperation. A courteous follow-up can often make the difference between a release published on time and one published too early, too late, or not at all."[3]

Do provide the editor with any additional information he or she may require as promptly and as accurately as you can obtain it.

Do make sure that your story contains information of real interest to readers with enough substantial information to make it meaningful—no disguised advertising.

Do ensure that the information is completely accurate and does not duplicate an earlier release.

Don't "leak" the story to other media or editors if you have promised an "exclusive" to an editor.

Don't be too upset if the editor doesn't use your story in its entirety or at all. Time and space limitations can intervene over the best intentions of all concerned. Be patient, take a raincheck, thank him or her anyway, and begin planning the next release.

Don't play favorites—make sure each newspaper receives the same story at the same time.

Don't ask an editor for coverage as a favor to you or your organization.

Don't try to use free newspaper space to promote the merits or value of any commercial product. Some papers object to using or listing the corporate affiliations of your officers or directors. Check local usage.

Don't omit essential information. Check your copy to be certain that it does in fact tell who, what, why, when, and where—and possibly, how.

Don't ask an editor to send you a copy or tearsheet of the printed article. You are expected (with your organization) to *buy* copies and help increase circulation.

Don't use staples to attach the pages of your story. A paper clip is preferred because it can be removed easily.

Don't mention the name of your president or chairperson in every release no matter how significantly he or she may be involved in the news event.

Don't use jargon when it is not essential to the story or even understandable to a "civilian" audience.

Don't send out a news release every time the organization does anything. This has the effect of crying "wolf" to the editor of a metropolitan daily.

Don't write the release in a style inappropriate to a particular medium, or send the same style release to all media.

Somehow, despite all their shortcomings, news releases do get into print. They can be mailed, hand carried, or telephoned (only *very* important news), depending on the circumstances. But once it is there, it must speak for itself.

The comments made by one city editor to a PR chairperson emphasize this point beyond any doubt: "Please, if that's a news release or handout, just hand it to me. If we can use it, I'll have a reporter rewrite it in our style and in the space we have for this edition. If we can't use it, I'll throw it away. Please don't hold it under my nose and read it to me with your finger tracing every line. I can read. And don't suggest that we have a talk about it. I haven't got the time for any conferences. No...please don't bother to wait. I've got calls waiting and deadlines to meet."

Oral release of information can be made in person or by telephone. Caution: When phoning information to any media, the release should always be read from a prepared text.

A reply to an oral query from a media representative is another form of oral release. Here, a "query sheet" should be used, containing the following items of information in its format: date and time; name and organization of caller; telephone number of the caller; question asked; reply; source of information and co-ordination; name of the person handling the query (especially important in a large office or diverse organization).

Using a "query sheet" is very helpful for nonroutine questions, but it is vital when handling oral releases of sensitive information that, depending on the service performed by the organization, can range from sex offenses, embezzlements or other crimes, to medical information, to child abuse.

Press interviews on subjects not covered by fact sheets or background data in a printed form are fairly common. It cannot be overstated that such interviews should be conducted by those in your organization most familiar with its policies and operations. They should use the utmost caution in answering questions, which will probably be considered the official position of the organization.

It is very helpful if an experienced public relations person first discusses the interview with the reporter and then with the leader being interviewed. It helps them prepare their thinking for the particular line of questioning and to organize their responses.

Magazine and book writers often use the interview to obtain first-hand information about a particular subject or person.

News conferences are essentially interviews with several news representatives simultaneously. A rule of thumb: Never call a news conference unless you are asked to by the news media concerned, or there is simply no other way to present the news. A news conference *must* be worth the time of those concerned. Suggestions for preparing and conducting a good news conference include the following.

Since attendance at press conference depends on what other news events are happening that day that may compete for the reporters' time, it is better not to hold one if sparse attendance would embarrass your organization or its leaders.

Timing of the conference is a most important consideration. Choose a time that is convenient for the reporters, keeping their deadlines in mind. Obviously, a time that is convenient for the morning papers will be inconvenient for the afternoon papers and vice versa. One possible compromise is to alternate times so that one conference is set for the morning whereas the next is planned for the afternoon. Don't schedule the conference for odd hours, however, or over weekends when most media operate with skeleton staff. A few informal queries among the press representatives in your area should help you find the right time to schedule such conferences.

Unless the reason for calling the news conference includes emergency or crisis elements, send invitations to the press by letter or telegram a week to 10 days before the scheduled conference. The invitation should provide enough information so that the editor can decide whether your event should be covered. If you will provide possibilities for photographs, indicate this and tell them whether you will have a photographer on hand. Follow up the invitation with a telephone call a day or so before the conference, and try to learn who the news outlet will send to cover it. The follow-up call will also help you plan for the number of representatives who will attend to ensure that enough chairs, and so on, will be on hand. For safety's sake, however, use a room that will allow for expansion of seating in case more people show than you expected.

As reporters arrive, give them a copy of the spokesperson's statement, a press release summarizing its key points, biographical data about the spokesperson, background information about the organization and its services, photographs—in short, anything pertinent and appropriate that will help them get their story.

Provide a "sign-in" book—obtaining the names, affiliations, and addresses of those in attendance. This list can be helpful later in exploring the possibilities of follow-up coverage.

A typical format for a news conference might be as follows:

1. Introduce the spokesperson, giving background and "credentials."

2. The spokesperson delivers a brief statement summarizing the news story that is the reason for the conference.

3. While this is being done, ensure that a copy of the statement is in the hands of all reporters and that they are prepared to underscore important points.

4. Conduct a question-and-answer session.

The spokesperson must be knowledgeable and articulate. Coach him or her on what to expect. Try to anticipate the questions likely to be asked—make sure the spokesperson has an adequate and responsive answer. If your choice will shy at the prospect of a vigorous verbal give-and-take, get a new spokesperson. Remember that just a few "no comments" can kill your press conference, not to mention giving your organization a "black eye."

Have other "experts" on hand to help the spokesperson if the questioning is likely to cover more areas than he or she can answer effectively—but try to decide in advance what areas each will cover.

Begin and end the news conference on time. Try to keep it moving or reporters may begin to "drift" away, with the conference simply winding down to a vague end. End it with some appropriate wrap-up or closing remarks.

Consider having the conference taped. This is not only a help in preventing finger pointing if things do not go as planned, but the tape will help your team assess how the conference went and how to better the next one.

If both print and electronic media are covering the conference, try to hold the conference for the print media first because the broadcast media have a time advantage over the print media. In addition, the equipment necessary for the electronic media to cover such an event disrupts many conferences and tends to rob many print media reporters of a relatively quiet atmosphere in which they can ask meaningful questions and get meaty answers.

Don't forget the technical needs of the electronic media, including electrical power, lights, and communications amplifiers if the room is large. Telephones and a suitable background for still photographers should also to be considered.

Have your organization's public relations team on hand at the conference, before and after, to talk to reporters. Not only can they answer any background questions, but in this way they will often uncover opportunities for future feature stories or follow-up interviews.

After the conference is over, forward copies of the statement(s), releases, and other information to those media outlets not represented. Many will use the material even if they were not able to send representatives. Even if they do not use it, they will appreciate the gesture and the professionalism shown by your organization.

Be sure to write letters of appreciation, offering to furnish additional information, to those media representatives who attended.

How Not to Be Misquoted

These guidelines for communicating with the press can help you, your officers, and your board members get accurate news coverage. They were prepared by Peter C. Goulding and appeared in *Association Management* magazine.[4]

No reporter will deliberately misquote a person. You must begin with that assumption. The reporter may misunderstand your point, he may shift the emphasis improperly, but what he does, he does with the belief that he is being accurate.

How do you help him achieve accuracy?

1. You may generally make the following assumptions:
   a. The reporter usually is general assignment, that is, he may be covering a women's club one day, supermarket opening the next day.
   b. He probably is basically uninformed about your industry or profession (organization or service).
   c. He will return to his paper with some kind of a story.
   d. He is more likely today to use some judgment in interpreting the fact, rather than simply reporting them.
2. Have a written, prepared statement or a news release.
3. Ask the reporter to read the statement or news release before he begins the questions. If it is a press conference, you should read it.
4. Take your time in answering. If the reporter interrupts, ask him to wait just a moment and finish giving your answer. Don't let him hurry you into hasty responses.
5. State your main points simply and in short sentences. Don't philosophize. Stay as close to facts as possible.
6. Restate the salient points, once or even twice, until you are sure the reporter understands what you are trying to say.
7. A reporter will generally make notes, or underline parts of the news release, on those points which he considers most important. If he is not making notes on what you consider are the salient points, feel free to say, "I want to emphasize that our essential position is..." and restate it.
8. Don't rush the interview. Give the reporter as much time as he needs to do his job.
9. Don't start chatting with the reporter about the weather or sports in the middle of the interview. Stick with the subject matter.
10. Keep in mind that the reporter has no control over the headline or over a picture caption. If they are misleading, it is not his fault.

Media Relations

Public support in many different but vital ways for the nonprofit sector depends on how effectively we convey our messages of public service to the general public. Informing the public takes place through a wide variety of communications media. Answering a letter or a telephone call from a private citizen is a public information activity. From speeches before civic organizations to a cover story in the weekly news magazine, appearing on a "talk" show to testifying before your city council—your leadership can and should have many opportunities to bring your message to the public that sustains and benefits your organization.

The public is interested not only in what you do, but they have an increasing right to know since a growing number of nonprofit organizations are receiving public funding in one form or another and thus voluntarily subjecting themselves to public scrutiny and accountability. The interest varies, of course. Obviously, the announcement of a fund-raising activity is not of such general interest as the quality of emergency medical care provided by a volunteer ambulance corps.

Dealing with news media representatives is an important part of any NPO's communications program and will have far-reaching effects on the organization. As with any other aspect of human relations, there is no set formula to ensure positive feelings by all concerned, or that they will always take your point of view. Journalists, like all of us, come in all sizes, shapes, outlooks, motivation, intelligence, and nearly everything else. Common traits would likely include: they have an important job to do, they want to do it, and they know how to do it. If you and your public relations personnel understand their problems, you can help them get their story—and probably, on the average, fair much better in both coverage and favorable story attitudes.

The following "Dos and Don'ts" regarding media relations represent many hard lessons learned by experienced public relations professionals:

Do be available whenever news is needed—at all hours if necessary.

Do tell the truth. If you cannot comment because of the confidentiality of the information requested, say so. If you do not know the answer, say so, and then find out and get back to them—pronto.

Do get the facts, get them right, and get them out.

Do know the people who work in the media...their audience...and the time or space limitations they must deal with.

Don't, above all, lie—even halfway—or hedge or evade the issue.

Don't snow the editors with unimportant or unusable releases.

Don't be partial in dealings with news representatives for any reason.

Don't ask them to slant their copy, withhold information, or do unwarranted favors.

In short, respect their professionalism, just as you expect them to respect yours.

Preparing a Release for Distribution

Editors, like the rest of us, tend to give more credence and attention to materials prepared in a professional manner and reproduced in a format which indicates that the organization knows something about professional communications. In short, if you follow established techniques and accepted patterns of preparation, you are likely to get more space and air time than if you do not. The following guidelines are not difficult to follow and do not require a degree in journalism to give your organization a news release that really looks like a professional prepared it.

Stationery. Use standard 8 ½ × 11 white paper; odd sizes make the editor's job more difficult. Use a good-quality paper that can stand repeated handling and shuffling without tearing. Do not use onion skin, tissue paper, or erasable bond.

Identification. Either use your organization's letterhead stationery (if it meets the above criteria) for the first page, or type the name of your organization at the top left. Either here or at the conclusion of the article, type the name and telephone number of the writer or another responsible individual who is qualified to provide the editor or rewrite person with additional information about your release. Select a person who will *be there* if the call comes through.

Time of release. Space down four lines and then show your release date/time in one of three ways:

FOR RELEASE ON JANUARY 1

FOR RELEASE ON OR AFTER JANUARY 1

FOR IMMEDIATE RELEASE (insert date here)

If at all possible, stipulate "For Immediate Release." This allows the editor to use the material at once or whenever it fits into the schedule. When you ask for a specific release date or time you are complicating the editor's task. A busy editor might well head your release for the circular file if it is a low-priority item and your release date indicates that it must be held for several days.

Headline.   In the final article as it appears in publication, the headline functions to announce today's news, interest the reader with essential facts, advertise the most important stories by their placement on the page, dress up the page with typography, and summarize the story with a super-lead. The "headline" in your release, however, is most often of the summary head variety—an all-caps summary of *the* most important news in the story. It allows the editor to determine in a glance or two the general nature of the news that is contained in the release and to begin planning how, or whether, to use the release.

In this area of your release you will also need to leave enough writing space for the editor to write the final head for the story and to give other instructions to the composing room. If you choose not to provide a summary head, then start typing your copy one-third of the way down the first page. This should provide enough room for the editor's needs.

Body of the release.   Keep these points in mind:

Type double-spaced or even triple-spaced on only one side of the paper.

Indent each paragraph at least five spaces.

Leave ample margins—1 to 1½ inches.

If the story runs more than one page, type "more" at the bottom of *each* page except the last.

Always end each page with a complete sentence and paragraph.

Minimize hyphenations (particularly in radio/TV copy)

When the release runs more than one page, type your organization's name at the top left of *each* succeeding page. Then drop down about 1 inch and continue your copy.

Number each page—the upper right-hand corner of the page is usually most convenient.

Type several **# # #** under the final paragraph of the news release. (The 30-30-30 tradition is no longer in general use.)

Other general preparation and distribution guidelines include the following:

- Be sure to keep a copy of every release you send out.

- Never send carbon copies. These smear easily, leading to errors in spelling. They also get the editor's hands dirty. If you need numerous copies for a wide distribution, either mimeograph them or get photocopies made. Not only is this much less messy, but it also alerts the editor that others are also getting this release. You can then expect a rewrite for individuality. Newspapers do not want to run the same release everyone else is running or using.

- Staples should not be used to hold the pages of your story. Instead, use a paper clip, which can easily be removed. If it becomes detached and shuffled, the identification in the upper-left-hand corner of pages 2+ will make for quick relocation.

- If you are mailing your release, fold it with the top third of the first page visible.

Notes

1. *If You Want Air Time,* National Association of Broadcasters, Washington, 1974, passim.
2. W. L. Robinson, How to Publish a Book, *Association Management,* November 1971.
3. Cornelius M. Pietzner, Getting Your Story into Print, *Nonprofit World,* vol. 4, no. 4, July–August 1986, p. 22.
4. Peter C. Goulding, How Not to Be Misquoted, *Association Management,* July 1971, p. 33.

Suggested Reading

Maddalena, Lucille A., *A Communications Manual for Nonprofit Organizations,* New York, AMACOM, 1981.
Maloney, Martin, and Paul M. Rubenstein, *Writing for the Media,* Englewood Cliffs, N.J., Prentice-Hall, 1980.
Reuss, Carol, and Donn E. Silvis, *Inside Organizational Communication,* New York, Longman, 1981.

42

Involving Community Leadership

George W. Corrick

University of North Florida

Every nonprofit organization—however rational, compelling, or seemingly apparent its value—must recognize the absolute necessity for winning and retaining community support. The price paid in the past for failure to win this support has been all too high.

This chapter stresses the vital role of community leadership in building community support. It describes both formal and informal community leadership and outlines proven techniques for identifying, communicating with, and involving community leaders.

No single chapter can, however, substitute for a constant sensitivity and awareness of the special nature of community leadership and support in the field situation. No formula exists or is likely to be found that ensures success in gaining community support. No writer or researcher in the broad field of community action can claim to have laid down scientific principles to ensure success. Lacking such absolutes, the problem remains and must be dealt with through the knowledge and experience available.

Community Leadership: Two Views

Broadly defined, leadership is the process by which a relatively small number of individuals behave in such a way that they effect (or prevent) a significant change in the attitudes or actions of relatively large numbers of others. The process is easier to define than to pinpoint the actors in it.

Until fairly recently community leadership was thought of only in terms of the formal system. It was assumed that, by definition, the hierarchy of government was the hierarchy of community influence. The mayor, city manager, or other top community official was clearly the most influential and the ultimate community decision maker.

While not discounting the importance of this formal and readily apparent system, broader and somewhat conflicting views are now recognized and well-documented by research. Current views generally recognize a second pyramid of community leadership. This leadership is seen as composed of nonelected and informal leaders who wield influence from power bases that are economic, social, cultural and that are often rooted in longevity and community involvement. These newer views of community leadership and influence recognize an informal community leadership pyramid variously called a "power structure," or "power elite."

Floyd Hunter first described such an informal community leadership pyramid by documenting that a handful of nonelected leaders virtually ran a city of more than 500,000 people.[1] (References at the end of this chapter include several research efforts of this type for readers interested in more detailed analysis of informal community power structures.)

Most current community research and theory is, however, a synthesis of the formal, or "convential wisdom," point of view and the conflicting power structure, informal system viewpoint. Academic theories aside, practical evidence in most communities speaks strongly in support of the view that community decisions are shaped by both formal and informal leaders. Mayors, legislators, council members, and other elected officials are sensitive and alert to the views of business leaders, financial leaders, old families, and civic activists. Decisions made within the formal governmental system are not made without reference to such informal leaders. Officials know that such views, pro or con, must be taken into account, however unofficial or informal the influence such spokespersons may wield. NPO leaders must take into account both leadership structures in seeking support.

Identifying Leadership in the Formal System

The structure of government, however it may vary from place to place, is more easily discerned among the top leadership groups. Thus, this formal structure can be simply traced by visits to the courthouse, city hall, or other government headquarters. An understanding of the structure of local government should be high on the list of early priorities in establishing community support for the NPO. Most officials are reasonably available by appointment, and most are flattered when sought out for assistance. Particular attention should be devoted to ensuring early communication with those officials actually representing the geographic district, precinct, town, or city council in which a program is begun.

The nature of applicable local licensing, zoning, and similar regulatory matters will also dictate early contact with a variety of lesser officials within the local governmental units. Few relatively obscure officials wield more real power than those in such regulatory positions. Early assurance that full compliance in all such areas is accomplished can avoid major problems later. Beyond compliance, visits to get acquainted and convey personal assurance of cooperation and concern for such often neglected matters builds goodwill in areas of government whose work is usually ignored or criticized. In fact, approaching all local officials with a "bread upon the waters" posture of cooperation and goodwill is wise and prudent.

No guide to the relative importance of government figures can be accurate everywhere. But in times when public officials face daily distrust and criticism, few efforts are more productive of goodwill and potential support than those devoted to understanding the roles of local officials and to meeting and becoming acquainted with as many as possible.

Identifying Leadership in the Informal System

The matter of identifying community leaders in the informal system is immensely more complex than in the formal one. Here no chart or table of organization is available. Obviously, the larger and more complex the community, the more difficult this job. Occasionally, it may be possible to obtain studies done by university or college researchers. Such community power studies are frequently conducted by political science, public administration, or education departments and colleges. Although the likelihood that such studies exist for the area of concern is slight, the potential of such a find makes inquiry worthwhile. Unfortunately, even when available and current, such studies frequently mask leaders' names to protect the researchers.

Many pitfalls exist in attempting to identify community leadership. Perhaps the most frequent is the temptation to jump to conclusions. Self-acclaimed leaders abound in all communities. Upward mobiles, without particular influence but with a great thirst for it, are easily visible everywhere. Less astute community residents are frequently deceived by those whose high visibility and eagerness for the public spotlight lends a glow of importance and significance to their words and actions. Many—if not most—of the high-ranking influentials identified in the research-based power studies scrupulously avoid such visibility. Similarly, many utilize such visible power aspirants as representatives or "fronts" for their interests and concerns.

The following is a series of steps by which may be conducted a relatively systematic effort aimed at identifying the informal leadership of any community. Using these guidelines, it is recommended that a personal notebook or card file be established for this purpose. Such a file should ultimately contain names, business or professional associations of the leaders, sources of the names, organizations in which they are active, their major interests, close friends, and any seemingly relevant material obtained.

Ask People in the "Know"

"Who are the real leaders in this city, town, or community?" Although the answer of any one person may not have much validity, cumulative answers will bring growing validity. Within limits, perceived power is real power; people who others believe have influence do tend to have and gain influence. Asking such a question—if done casually—is not an unnatural or suspicious act. Be selective about who is asked, keep track of who names whom, keep score on the frequency of those named, and the beginnings of a list will unfold.

Who Fits the Assumptions?

Who holds the top positions in the largest, wealthiest, or strongest business concerns? Who has the top law or accounting practice? Whose support do political figures seek? Whose advice is sought by others? Who responds to whom? Who sits on several major corporate or bank boards? (Few lists are so revealing as a cross-match of major bank boards.) Who holds multiple board memberships in major public service nonprofit organizations in the community? Who owns major real estate holdings? Economic power, is always significant and a key to community influence on every dimension. Again, no single answer to these questions can be accepted as proof of leadership or influence. But names that are proper answers to all or most of these questions should be treated as very likely candidates for informal community leader status.

Studying Major Past Issues

Who supported, opposed, initiated? This is a fertile field. Answers can be obtained from inquiries of community friends and review of community studies and newspaper files. The more important the issue—a major bond issue, a hotly contested major election, a referendum on annexation or tax matters—the more likely that most informal community leaders played a decisive part. Top leaders can and frequently do conserve their influence by avoiding involvement in lesser issues, but almost without exception become active—though not always visible—in issues of major proportion, particularly those of economic import.

It is important to recognize that these recommended steps are guidelines and not a formula. List building should be done slowly and cautiously. Again, the most visible names may not be the most important. But careful use of each of these guidelines, and cross-checking the names developed in each step will produce a relatively sound list of the informal community power structure.

Some Cautions

The smallest communities frequently reveal a clear and fairly apparent influence pyramid with one leader widely accepted as the most influential, most powerful, most important citizen of the town. Where such a clearly dominant and accepted leader exists, all other community leaders can frequently be viewed as having influence in a subordinate relationship.

As a general rule, this simple power pyramid will be less likely or less apparent in larger communities. More frequently, larger and more complex communities will have multiple power structures, camped around different leaders and frequently divided by issue positions, political parties, or simply as oldtimers versus newcomers, eastsiders versus westsiders, and so on. Where such multiple influence groups are found, no single dominant leader is likely to exist, although the emergence of one is always possible.

Despite the American commitment to being a "melting pot," it should be recognized that community leadership does not often mirror a balance of race, religion, or national origin. Racial and ethnic minorities are not yet reflected proportionately in community power pyramids. Most often such minority groups are represented through separate power or leader pyramids. Communication and accommodation usually exist between such groups and the dominant community leadership. But leaders of minority segments most often are not perceived as full members of overall community leader structures.

Often it will be necessary to conduct the leadership identification exercise as a separate study where ethnic or racial subcultures are a significant part of a community. In a rapidly changing society, it is difficult to assess the importance of such groups to community action. Clearly their influence has grown. And any program committed to serving a total community must seek minority support however great or small its total community influence.

Informal Leaders—Their Interests and Behavior

Before discussing techniques of communication and influence with community leaders, a general word should be said about their interests and behavior. Although generalizations here are risky, it is fair to observe that "major" community leaders are interested and involved primarily in what they perceive as "major" community matters. This is true in part because—like top executives—they must ration their time, energy, and power. Such priorities also grow from their recognition that others—leader aspirants, emerging leaders, upward mobiles, etc.—are ready and willing to devote their energies to "lesser" matters. Top community leaders can reason that important matters will rise to their attention or that they alone can perceive accurately and deal effectively with such matters.

What qualifies in this context as a "major" community concern? What matters are likely to be of interest to top community leadership? Much remains to be learned in this area. But some general observations can be made. Most informal community power figures are linked by a body of similar beliefs, often unspoken ones. These common beliefs are frequently rooted in a common cultural heritage, similar educational background, common social experiences, related and interwoven financial and economic interests, political affiliations, and even family ties. They hold a large common body of operational beliefs about the "right" or "wrong" functions of government, about the nature and proper direction of society, about the values of local ways of life, about the value of work, about "what is happening to this country," about what is "good" and "bad" about education, and a whole host of deep-seated, strongly held, frequently unspoken but ingrained common beliefs.

These operational beliefs among informal community power leaders are the "glue" that binds community leader groups together. Major or important issues, they perceive, are those matters that advance these operational views, or conversely, those that threaten or modify them. Taken together, these operational beliefs are their framework for deciding the best interests of the community. Implicitly or explicitly, all matters are judged against these beliefs.

It is within this framework of existing operational beliefs that any new program must be presented for community acceptance and support. To the degree that new activities can be seen or interpreted as consistent with these dominant views, they can be easily accepted and supported by such leaders. Obviously, not all programs will fit easily within such existing norms. The real measure of the communication and influence task to be accomplished is in first assessing the nature and pattern of these leadership norms and interpreting the values of any new programs in light of them.

Communicating and Influencing

Two all-important principles should guide efforts to communicate with community leaders:

1. Whenever possible, such communication should be personal.

2. Communication should be selective.

There are no adequate or effective substitutes for personal face-to-face communication when seeking to get a message through to top community leaders. The more important the leaders (or the more important they believe they are), the more their actions, opinions, positions, attitudes, and beliefs grow from personal, direct communication. The national and international scene mirrors this daily. Lesser figures correspond and pave the way, relay preliminary positions and views, but top leaders, governors, senators, presidents, heads of state, and people of influence see and talk to people. The same model is apparent in the corporate world, and again in politics, professional organizations, and labor unions. Such leader perception of the way to communicate appears to be universal, a part of the operational methodology of leadership.

Similarly, such personal communication is most effective when devoted only to matters the leaders perceive as significant. Such leaders are likely to judge the message and its communicator by their perception of the necessity and appropriateness of the communication. "Did I really need to hear this," they think, "Does this need my attention?" Or, "Why bother me with this?" Both a negative reaction regarding the message and a negative view of its conveyer can result from poorly chosen communication. Conversely, messages perceived as important by the leaders and brought to their attention are ones that serve to recognize their leader role and reflect positively upon the conveyor's understanding of that role. Such messages are most likely to be well received and seen as worthy of support.

How can such communication be personally conveyed and properly chosen? First there is the matter of personal communication. A soundly developed card file of community leaders will contain information on who relates with whom, who associates most closely with given leaders. These names tell likewise who can assist in communicating with community leaders. The newcomer must recognize that relationships with community leaders take time, patience, and tolerance of the norms and traditions of the community. Merely proving that one can get in to see community leaders is not a productive objective. Reaching them in the right setting, with the right message, through or with persons whom they respect and trust is a more fruitful goal.

Involvement Techniques

One major mechanism available to most activities are advisory groups, panels, boards, and other citizen bodies, lay or professional. These provide opportunities in which personal communication can be structured. Involvement remains the most important dimension of winning support. People will support and advocate those activities where they have an opportunity for input, where they "invest" themselves, financially or psychologically. Such mechanisms provide natural ways to bring citizen leaders close to a new activity, preferably in the planning or earliest stages. They give opportunities to explain first-hand the mission, purpose, and benefits to the community of a program. Equally important, they provide feedback and idea-testing opportunities where some signals about possible community acceptance and response can be heard and evaluated.

Whatever the nature of a nonprofit program, it can benefit from such an advisory body. When carefully chosen and utilized, such a group provides a proven means for winning community leadership support. Although major community leaders may not themselves be willing to serve, representative members can be chosen with a view to their access to such leaders. They can provide viewpoints that can be assumed to be relatively consistent with those of such leaders and means of determining in advance potential acceptance or opposition from top leaders.

Building Social and Cultural Access.   Ease of access to the same social and cultural circles with top community leaders varies immensely with community size and openness. Most communities grant such status to newcomers almost exclusively in terms of their immediately visible status. In smaller towns a new high school principal or coach, the newly appointed manager of a major factory, a new hospital director, community college president, or other newcomer moving into a recognized high-status position may receive immediate, though tentative, access to such circles. Such acceptance will take the form of early invitations to top civic clubs, social clubs and organizations, and similar closed groups. In larger communities, only the very highest status and most visible newcomers can expect such early acceptance.

These social and civic circles offer the most productive environment for the kind of communication, trust, and confidence winning needed to gain community leader support. Where such early acceptance is granted to the newcomer, it provides a major advantage. But most often this access is not quickly available. Again, the importance of gaining interest and involvement from those who already have such access is apparent. The knowledge and positive impressions gained by advisory group members or others provided opportunity for direct involvement may be the most useful and realistic access to such leaders' circles. Many a public service program has risen or fallen on little more than a casual social encounter between community leaders that began, "Hey, let me tell you what I heard today about this new...."

Communication Tools

But just as community leader identification is a systematic process, communication too should be approached in that fashion and not left to chance cocktail party remarks.

Beyond the advisory board or panel, several useful means can be utilized. VIP visits or tours offer one means. The flattery of being personally invited to have an "inside" look is appealing, and when successful it provides unparalleled opportunities to tell the program's story and its community importance to leaders, formal and informal. Even here, however, the chances of getting an invitation accepted may be enhanced by extending it through someone—a friend or advisory panel member—who can communicate more successfully and effectively with the identified leader. Such visits should be carefully planned. They should be long enough to ensure adequate understanding but brief enough to reflect the value of the important visitor's time.

Special events, such as open house, groundbreaking, dedications, special topical speakers, panels, and so on, offer additional communications vehicles. Such events, carefully planned, can operate on two or more levels: (1) by providing the larger public opportunities to become acquainted with a program through tours, speakers, and other presentations, and (2) by building within the event more personalized opportunities where leaders may receive special invitations, a chance for more in-depth looks, opportunities to meet key staff, and other activities aimed at giving them a "special guest" feeling.

Although newsletters and other mass communication are aimed primarily at broader public audiences, a program of "rifleshot" written communication can be effective with leaders. Many organizations make a practice of sending advance copies of important news releases or announcements of major events to a small list of top influentials. Such communication should be covered with a short but personal note indicating that it was felt the recipient would want to know about this before public announcement. Such advance notice gives the leader a feeling of being an insider, important to and included in your organization or program. Such insider communication should be initiated only after a personal level of communication has been established with an individual. And done to excess, such a program can appear false and hollow, resulting in negative reactions.

These suggestions are by no means an exhaustive list of involvement-communication techniques for community leadership. They represent merely some proven examples of effective means to accomplish leader understanding and support. Those who understand the importance of such efforts can create new and equally effective techniques. In this area, as in most others, there are few really new ideas. Most are borrowed from other successful programs or are modifications of the effective efforts of similar programs. Whatever variations are adopted, the central element of personal face-to-face communication should be the key ingredient.

Selective Content

The second principle for effective communication and influence with community leaders has been identified as selective content. Community leaders have been previously characterized as concerned with "major" community matters. Further, it has been stated that they hold a relatively consistent set of operational beliefs about what is "right" and "good" for the community. Thus, messages should be chosen and conveyed with these premises in mind.

Put simply, such messages must significantly relate to the leader's present view of what the community needs. Such messages must convey the worth of a new program in terms of what tangible good it will bring to the community; in terms of how the program will serve recognized needs (or help the leader recognize new needs, then present solutions); in terms of how the program advances aims already held by the community; or how it prevents damage of existing values and norms. Ideally, such communication should:

Be based factually in recognized community needs or assist in identifying, documenting, and clarifying previously unrecognized needs

Avoid presentation as "we think you should..."

Include recognition for past community efforts in related areas

Stress payoffs in tangible terms, whether human or economic

Build upon and stress the involvement and need for input of local citizens and leaders

Convey the program's goals as an extension of the community's (e.g., *his/her*) past efforts

The Other Half—Listening

And communication, accurately defined, is a two-way process. Telling is half, listening the other half. Effective communicators must be sincerely willing to listen, not just so as to rebut, but because they cannot afford to ignore or make light of the views and opinions of local leaders. In part, the price that must be paid for community support is a willingness to listen—not to sell out or back away from new or conflicting positions, but to recognize that such new or different views must be shown to be needed and beneficial to the community. Ultimately, new ideas must become a part of the community's own sense of what is "good" and "right" if they are to succeed. Community leadership holds the key to this process.

Summary

In summary, the attention to community leadership and its importance revolves around three major understandings that this chapter has outlined.

First, it must be recognized from the outset that no new program can be expected to succeed on its self-evident rationality and worth. Community support is critical to such success and must be sought and won. Attention to winning community support is not a peripheral concern. It is not an area to which attention can be devoted when time allows, but a vital, central ingredient of the whole effort, and a key responsibility of the management of that effort.

Second, total community leadership is not readily apparent and obvious to all. It is a complex matter involving formal system leaders and an at least equally important network of informal community leaders. Only a willingness patiently and systematically to identify such community leadership can yield the understandings necessary to comprehension of it.

Finally, communication with such leadership must be primarily personal and selective in nature. And such communication with leaders must be conducted in forms that recognize their existing beliefs and norms and must interpret the new program in ways that recognize, build upon, and complement these existing beliefs.

Notes

1. Floyd Hunter, *Community Power Structure,* The University of North Carolina Press, Chapel Hill, N.C., 1953.

Suggested Reading

Aiken, Michael, and Paul E. Mott (eds.), *The Structure of Community Power,* Random, New York, 1970.
Dahl, Robert, *Who Governs?* Yale University Press, New Haven, Conn., 1961.
Hunter, Floyd, *Community Power Succession,* The University of North Carolina Press, Chapel Hill, N.C., 1980.
Kimbrough, Ralph B., *Political Power and Educational Decision-Making,* Rand McNally, Skokie, Ill., 1964.

43

Utilizing the Electronic Media*

Tracy D. Connors
Consultant

Kenneth A. Jarvis
Executive Director, West Virginia Public Broadcasting

The Communications Act of 1934 created the Federal Communications Commission (FCC) integrating under the FCC regulation of broadcasting, telephone, telegraph, and later, satellite communications. It also contained several other important provisions that are important to any public service organization seeking to use radio or television in its communications program.

Section 304 of the 1934 Act decrees that a licensee must sign a waiver disclaiming the permanent ownership or possession of an assigned frequency. This provision reaffirms the principle first stated in the 1927 Radio Act that the airwaves are owned by *the public* and not by the stations using them.

Section 307 of the 1934 Act gives the FCC the authority to issue licenses "if public convenience, interest, or necessity will be served...." Other sections of the Act empower the FCC to assign frequencies, transmitter power, and hours of operation. It should also be noted that Section 326 of the act warns that "Nothing in this Act shall be understood...to give the Commission the power of censorship over the radio communications or signals transmitted by any radio station, and no reg-

---

*Adapted in part and with permission from the *Radio and Television Handbook,* Defense Information School, Fort Benjamin Harrison, Indiana.

ulation or condition shall be promulgated or fixed by the Commission which shall interfere with the right of free speech by means of radio communications."

The act does not provide a specific definition of "public convenience, interest, or necessity," even though this is the very basis for the issuance of broadcast licenses. However, interpretation of these phrases has developed over the years through the federal court system. For many years the FCC required stations to state precisely how much time they would devote to commercial (sponsored) time and to non-commercial (sustaining) time. This requirement has been relaxed. It continues, however, to expect commercial broadcasters to provide programming that is responsive to important issues in the communities they serve. This may be accomplished by whatever program mix they believe appropriate. Such programming would probably include public service announcements (PSAs), public affairs programs, community bulletin boards, religious programs, and editorials.

It is important for your planning to remember that the individual station has (and exercises) the freedom to decide (1) how much of its total schedule will be devoted to issue-oriented programming, (2) what type of material will be broadcast and from which organizations, and (3) when these programs will be scheduled. (You will find little or no public service programming or announcements during "prime time." Instead, most stations schedule them during time periods when fewer people will be watching, hence time that has far less commercial value and can be "donated" to the public interest at less cost to the station in lost revenues from commercial sponsors.)

Another standard that should be mentioned is that which the broadcasting industry itself developed to stress the broadcaster's responsibility to the community. The National Association of Broadcasters' (NAB) Radio and Television Codes establish general guidelines for education, culture, decorum and decency, acceptability of program material, treatment of news, public events, and controversial issues, presentation and amount of advertising, and production practices. The provisions of the Codes can be summarized as *accuracy, propriety, and good taste.* Stations may or may not subscribe to the Codes. They are not compelled to do so by the NAB, which has no legal authority to enforce its codes. Any station violating a provision of the Codes is subject only to the penalty of losing the right to display the NAB's "Seal of Good Practice."

Station Relations and Management

In most commercial broadcasting stations, there are four or five departments, including:

Sales (sometimes called advertising).

Program (sometimes called operations).

Engineering.

Administration.

News—In a few stations, the news department is a part of the program department.

Stations vary in size, including personnel and staffing roles. In smaller stations one person will fill several job functions, including appearances on the air.

The programming department is responsible for selecting and scheduling programs. Although a network affiliate has much of this done by the network staff, there is still a tremendous burden on the program manager to deliver the largest possible audience to the advertisers.

The engineering department is responsible for the technical quality of the transmitted program. The chief engineer, as a department head, reports to the general manager regarding maintaining transmission production and other electronic equipment within accepted standards.

The sales department is the backbone of the commercial broadcasting station. It generates the revenue that supports the station. This department sells the "time" that is the commodity of the commercial broadcaster.

The news department is responsible for the gathering, editing, writing, and presentation of the news—including wire service input and locally generated news.

It may be simplistic to stress here that it is imperative that your organization maintain good relations with the broadcast stations in your area. Without good relations your efforts to communicate with the general public will be impaired or negated. Your efforts to establish good relations will be paid back with interest from the broadcaster.

It helps to remember and understand the motives of commercial broadcasters. They are in business to provide a service. Only by making a profit can they stay in business. Profits in this business depend on the broadcasters' ability to attract and hold a mass audience to whom the station's commercial sponsors direct their messages—for a fee. Although it is true that the station must serve the public interest, it must also interest the public—and that is where your objectives and those of the station can coincide to your mutual benefit. When you provide the type of information that is of interest to their audiences, you are helping them both serve the public and hold their mass audience—a commercial asset.

Public broadcasting is structured a bit differently from commercial broadcasting. These stations operate as not-for-profit organizations attached to universities, local school districts, state or local governments, or other private nonprofit corporations.

The sales department found in commercial stations is replaced by a development department. Its role is to generate operating funds, which it does through a variety of methods. Two of the most common include (1) underwriting (the solicitation of funds from businesses to defray programming costs in return for a brief on-air mention) and (2) on-air pledging (the direct solicitation of funds from individual viewers).

The program department plays a major role in public broadcasting. Not only does it have more flexibility in scheduling than that in a commercial station, but it generally produces a greater variety of local programs.

Very few public television stations have news departments although many public radio stations do. If a public broadcasting station does not have a news department it will usually have a public affairs department. Since most public stations were created to meet local educational and public affairs needs, you will find them generally very responsive to your needs. The following suggestions for improving your organization's relations with broadcast stations were provided by the National Association of Broadcasters and the Defense Information School:

1. Analyze the station's audience and adapt your material to the needs and interests of this audience.

2. Prepare your material to fit the station's format.

3. Approach the station with something concrete and of high quality. Be prepared to submit specific facts—workable ideas. Avoid wasting the station's time on a fishing expedition with vague generalities.

4. Provide the station with releases or other material that it can use with a minimum expenditure of time. Provide the material in a timely manner on orga-

nizational letterhead. Last-minute requests are an embarrassment to an organization. If it has to rewrite your release, you may never hear it on the air
because it ended up in the wastebasket.

5. Accept suggestions. Remember, you are working with experts in their field—
   probably a field that is alien to you.

6. Know your limitations and theirs. For example, time is at an absolute premium. Instead of a 30-minute interview, spot announcements are not only more
   feasible but, when well done, much more effective than a long program inad-
   equately prepared.

7. Planning an appeal for funds or support? Check with the station first. Many
   have a policy against this type of program or broadcast. Also check your local
   statutes for the legal requirements for fund-raising. Many require that your organization be licensed before beginning a fund drive.

8. Treat all stations fairly and equally. Do not favor one station, even if the others
   do not favor you.

9. Respond cheerfully and completely to any station's request for information,
   advice, or assistance.

10. Comply with the station's policies or format to the maximum degree possible.
    Do not expect them to change their formats or habits just to suit you or your
    organization no matter how much good you are doing or how prominent the
    citizens involved in your activities.

11. Keep a file of the "hot line" number for each station—a number that is to be
    used for providing news and giving telephone "beeper" reports. A beeper is
    so-called because of the beep sound required on all recorded telephone mes-
    sages, including recordings made over the telephone for later replay over the
    air.

12. The best people for you to know at radio or television stations are the public
    service director, the program director or manager, and the news director.
    Whether you are trying to get time for a program, spot announcement, or
    hard news or feature story, the backing and support of the station manager is
    invaluable. The program director (or public service director), in turn, is ulti-
    mately responsible for finding a place in the broadcast day for such programs
    or announcements. Accept the fact that no matter how important your chair-
    person or board thinks a particular story is, it must stand on its own merits—
    being newsworthy to the audience the station services—and that decision rests
    with the news director.

In summary, your chances of getting public service broadcasting time will be
much improved if your message is important and of widespread interest and if it is
presented in the best possible form.

Radio

Radio Program Types

Over the years, ten program types have become standardized in radio, including
musical, news, interview, feature, sports, drama, special event, audience participation, discussion, and variety.

Musical. Although most nonprofit organizations will not have programming opportunities in this area, since music sells, spot announcements on such programs provide very valuable opportunities through which to disseminate public information.

News. Without newscasts, radio would not be the influential medium of mass communications that it is today. Many stations either have unsponsored newscasts that carry public service announcements or will be happy to include them as "news adjacencies," particularly if the material is itself news. The industry classifies newscasts in categories such as bulletins, items, summaries, newscasts, analyses, and commentaries. The news item is the quickest and easiest way for your public relations person to handle the news of your organization. Individual items can be easily written in radio style and released almost immediately to the radio stations in your area.

Interviews. Since people are interested in other people, interviews serve to satisfy their natural curiosity about the thoughts and opinions of others. There is no need to get a celebrity; the continuing popularity of the "ordinary average person" type of program indicates that people are interested in almost anyone from any walk of life. Interviews make it possible to explore a subject of importance to your organization or to feature pertinent questions followed by intelligent, enlightening answers. Always plan the interview in advance. This does not mean that you must have all necessary materials in writing, since most participants on this basis will sound as though they are reading the material and will turn off most audiences. However, a detailed outline of the topic and the important points you wish to cover is certainly a big help in using the interview program format to your best advantage.

Features. Another highly popular form of programming is human interest and information features. These are very similar to newspapers' human-interest feature stories. The "truth-is-stranger-than-fiction" theme is one that many radio newscasters seem to thrive on—a fact that you will want to keep in mind if your organization can generate such items—and if they can be used to advance your communications program toward its objectives.

1. *Human-interest feature.* This format highlights subjects that are close to people or the qualities we share as humans. Broadcasters are always looking for such material to perk up or brighten newscasts, especially if the story has an amusing or odd twist. Consider the potential in goodwill or increasing public awareness via a touch of humor about your organization. A caution here would be the potential danger in putting your organization in a bad light—exposing it to ridicule if the story is handled in the wrong way. If in doubt, it is safer to let this particular opportunity pass by.

2. *Informational feature.* A subject of importance to your organization can be given feature treatment to great advantage—with proper planning. Plan a story that highlights the meaning or the content of an interesting topic, then approach the program director.

Sports. This is probably not an area of programming that offers a great deal of potential to nonprofit organizations as a whole. Since such broadcasts are quite popular, however, a public service announcement (PSA) adjacent to a sports program will reach a large audience.

Drama. During the "golden age of radio," programs such as "The Lone Ranger," "The Shadow," and "Inner Sanctum" thrilled millions. The advent of television ended radio drama as a popular program category. Dealing with an event of major community importance, or with a historical event, is a type of programming that may have some value to your organization. Any documentary will need careful planning and preparation if it is to be successful (the only kind of result with which you should be satisfied). Contact the program director far in advance of the date of such events or activities to gain his or her interest and the station's participation.

Special Events. The value of this type of program is its ability to travel outside the studio to capture the immediacy and the "it's-happening-right-now-right-here" atmosphere of an important event. Many nonprofit organizations have events or activities tailor-made for such a program. You may find a somewhat surprising eagerness on the part of the program director to schedule such a program. Remember several things, however:

1. Most radio stations will not know of the important coming event unless you inform them as far in advance as possible, and invite them to cover the event.

2. Remote broadcasting costs additional money and requires thoroughly trained personnel to be successful. You will need to provide additional assistance and support for such efforts, but you will also reap the benefits of the communications "adrenalin" such coverage will give to your public awareness.

Audience Participation. This type of programming will probably not provide too much potential for your public information program. Perhaps the announcer can work in a "plug" for your organization or its activities.

Discussions. With careful judgment and common sense, this type of programming can provide many new and important opportunities to spread the word about your organization. Audiences enjoy arguments, controversies, and the presentation of opinions by "experts" on such programs. The "danger" of such program formats is the vulnerability of the participants to "zinger"-type questions that may embarrass your organization more than they enlighten. If your organization deals with one or more controversial subjects or services, you should anticipate such questions before participating on such programs. A "devil's advocate" brainstorming session with your staff or leadership can usually identify such potential questions before they are asked, and your participant can be prepared to answer them in the best manner possible. Properly handled and answered, such questions can help your public image and awareness. Improperly handled, they can do great damage.

Variety. Any show that contains more than one type of entertainment can be called a "variety" show—from such famous radio variety programs as "The Jack Benny Show" (which passed with the coming of television) to the variety format used by some local radio stations. A "variety" program of news, interviews, features, or other program types might well capture and hold audience interest in your area. If such a program does not exist, you might explore the potential with the leaders of your organization or other similar organizations in the community, and then see if you can "sell" the idea to a program director of an area radio station.

Radio News

The news plays a vital role in keeping Americans informed and aware of the events and activities that shape and influence our world. By supplying information about the public service missions of the nonprofit sector, you help make the public aware of its heavy responsibilities and duties, and in particular, of the special role played by your organization. Because it can deliver the news in a capsule form more rapidly and with a minimum of delay, radio is the most responsive medium in terms of time.

At one time, the newspaper industry believed radio to be a threat to its share of the communications market. Experience has shown, however, that one frequently complements the other. Each has specific functions in the mass communications process, and only together do they give the American public a timely and complete (not to mention colorful) treatment of the news that neither could provide alone.

Most of the principles of press news handling can be applied to radio. Other similarities include the following:

They are guided by the same set of rules and ethics.

They stress the principle of accurate, factual reporting without bias.

They are governed by the laws of the land.

Constitutional safeguards of freedom of the press and freedom of speech protect both media.

They share the same responsibilities and liabilities under the law. The same warning against libel applies to radio and press alike. A story must be reported as it is, objectively, with no bias, and no more.

Radio News Style. Radio's need for getting and holding the attention of an audience also dictates to a great degree its style of reporting the news. The most important style features of radio news writing include the following:

Factual clarity. The principal quality for radio writing of any kind is factual clarity. To avoid the easy possibility of a story being misunderstood, it must be written in perfectly clear language. Once it passes the radio's speaker, the story is gone, and there is no opportunity for the listener to ask the announcer to repeat it or check back for a better understanding.

Sentence brevity. Another must for radio newswriting is sentence brevity, since radio news is spoken and not read. Long sentences with many details, modifying clauses, and esoteric words are difficult to announce and tend to confuse the listener (not to mention the announcer). Long experience has shown that normal radio speech sounds and is understood best when sentences average about seventeen words in length. Of course, to avoid monotony this rule must be flexible. But, as a rule, radio script sentences should be short and undetailed. Communicating the main thought—concisely, clearly, and completely—is the prime objective in radio news writing.

Word utility. This is important because of sentence brevity. On the average, announcers have a speech delivery rate of about 125 to 150 words per minute. Although words must be carefully selected to convey the most meaning with the smallest number, they must also be chosen wisely for their descriptive color and precise meaning. In addition, the words of everyday speech are preferred over longer, multisyllabic words.

Conversational facility. Also known as "flow," conversational facility is very important to radio news style. Since the newscaster is not talking down to the listeners, but *to* them, only unstilted and informal language is acceptable. On the other hand, one should not go to extremes and prepare copy that will insult the listeners' intelligence. Try to have a mental image in mind when you write for "Mr. and Ms. Average Listener." Since this will vary considerably across the country, you will have to be the best judge of this concept for your area.

Aural simplicity. This summarizes these characteristics of radio news style. The whole idea is to make the news so clear, easy to read, brief, and focused on one point that it will be immediately understood by the listeners the moment the words come over the receiver. Before sending your copy off to the station, re-read it aloud with these characteristics in mind. Does it seem to measure up to these standards? Can you eliminate any flaws or deviations in style that your copy may contain?

Radio News versus Newspaper News. The inverted pyramid structure characterizes the structure of most newspaper stories; that is, the summary appears in the first (lead) paragraph. After providing the who, what, when, where, why, and how of the event or activity, the reporter arranges the story facts in descending order of importance.

Conversely, in a radio news item, the lead sentence describes the central news fact or facts. Since the average length of the radio news story is 30 seconds of air time, nonessential details are edited from the copy. To gain the attention of listeners and to orient them to the facts that will follow, the lead sentence of the radio news story tells the listener *what happened.* From there, the body of the story can be developed in any one of three ways, or combinations of these ways:

1. *Chronologically.* The story narrated from the beginning to the conclusion
2. *Expanding the W's.* Further amplifying the "what happened" by specifically identifying the who, when, where, and so on
3. *Descending importance.* Placing the facts in order of descending importance

Radio Spot Announcements. Whether it is a name, an idea, an opportunity, a product, or your organization, the specific purpose of the spot announcement is either to provide information or to sell. Radio spot writing is highly specialized. Professional writers use countless gimmicks and angles. You and your public relations team can also prepare professional-quality copy if you are familiar with and follow the basic techniques and principles that have been developed through the years. None guarantees "surefire" success, but the following techniques and principles are effective and do bring results.

The primary consideration in preparing a public service spot is the message itself. Michael J. McCurdy, in an *Association Management* article, notes that "the public service message carries an extra social responsibility because we are trying to reach people in situations that reflect life as it is; situations that the public must be able to identify with and recognize as affecting them personally.

"Your message should provide valuable information to the general public that is not coming from any other source. There is always advice or a call-to-action in a public service message, and if the presentation is not credible, the message is lost."

Because the maximum length of a public service announcement is usually 60 seconds, the message must be condensed to its least complex form and communicated within this short time frame. The effectiveness of the full message hinges on the opening "attention getter," which should be unique, but should not overwhelm the audience.

"Selecting the message," McCurdy says, "determines most other factors concerned with the public service announcement. For the association producing a public service spot, the message should be an extension of its overall public relations programs, both on a community level and a national level."[1]

There are two types of spot announcements useful to the nonprofit organization: the selling spot and the informational spot. Both are usually short—60 seconds or less.

Changing attitudes or taking action are the purposes of the selling spot. Examples include messages such as "Be there"; "Do it now"; "Join the _____ today."

The informational spot informs. You try to get across some important (but brief) message about your organization and the service(s) it provides for the public. "Thanks to you it's working," "When need is great, help is near," and "Arts change lives" are some examples of the informational spots used by nonprofit organizations.

Spot Writing Techniques. In writing either type of spot announcement, keeping the following techniques in mind will pay big dividends in giving you the quality (and the draw) you are seeking.

1. Plot the pitch. Remember the nature of the audience you are trying to reach or that is likely to be tuned to the station to which you are supplying the spot. What is likely to be a productive theme for one audience may not be for another. Consider the differences in audiences likely to be found listening to an "arts and information" station versus the audience of a "rock 'n' roll" station. Your approach or angle must consider the special needs and wants of the prospective audience.

2. Be alert to consider the "new" audiences that might respond to one of your appeals. Many nonprofit organizations sponsor or produce special events—from open houses to demonstrations—that probably appeal to many more types of people than you realize. Direct your spot to their needs.

3. Try to arrive at a direct and personal approach to your writing. Your message will reach thousands, but each person listening should feel as though the message was just for him or her. Use terms like "you," "you've," and "your" in your copy, which should project the warmth and friendship of your organization.

4. Your copy should speak to listeners in the language they know—conversationally, but avoiding slang. Use the active voice and verbs that are positive and colorful, such as go, see, take, get, visit, join, give, support. Avoid using terms or abbreviations that the listener is not familiar with, such as "The E-M-T Class will practice E-C-P-R on the H-L-R followed by a refresher course on defibrillation techniques."

Structure of the Selling Spot. Although there are countless ways of structuring your selling spot, one of the most successful is the one that approaches the copy from the standpoint of *attention, appeal,* and *action.*

Leads that draw the listener into your message are usually those that are slanted toward emotional or motivating drives. Copy that is directed toward your listener's desires, aspirations, dreams, and ambitions is copy that is far more likely to bypass natural resistance or apathy and get attention.

In the *appeal* portion of your spot, the selling material—the message you are trying to get across to the audience—is presented. One caution at this point: Keep your message simple, and stay with a particular subject. Too many points crammed into a short announcement will reduce its effectiveness. Needless to say, don't promise the impossible—a sincere and honest message is one that will be believed and acted upon by most people.

The *action* step gives the listener a definite course to follow or instructions to satisfy the emotion or drive that you have reminded him or her of in the lead. Here you should combine forcefulness (not too pushy), with a compelling invitation to move the listener toward a positive action on your behalf. The *action* step should motivate the listener to join, buy, contribute, write, support, or take some other action that you have determined is important to the organization. Your success is measured not only by the listener's actual response to the product advertised, but in a more intangible way by public awareness about your organization—an important "product" in itself. Following is an example of a selling spot announcement read by an announcer:

> Even if you have a full-time job...but no college degree...there's not a better time to get that diploma than right now. Fairfield Community College has a variety of evening and correspondence courses for those of you who need that important college degree...and the training that goes with it. Learn about receiving credits in a wide variety of courses...call Fairfield Community College today at...633-2950-...Conveniently located at Interstate 10 and Peabody Road.

The Information Spot

The information spot differs from the selling spot because your purpose is to convey as much interesting information as possible, and not necessarily to produce a response from the audience. Therefore no *action* step is provided, only the *attention* step followed by the *appeal*. Following is an example of an information spot announcement read by an announcer:

> S-A-C doesn't spell anything...but it does mean something...Stamford Ambulance Corps—S-A-C...a group of dedicated men and women on duty around the clock to provide you with quality emergency medical service. The volunteers of S-A-C are ready to assist Stamford area residents with the latest emergency medical technology and modern methods of patient care. You'll know them by their emblem...which says a lot about S-A-C..."when the need is great, help is near."

Spot Preparation.   Your spots will be given more air time and will be more effective if you keep the following points in mind during preparation:

1. Follow the station's style guide. Otherwise the station manager may not use your PSA but another organization's which fits in more closely with the format used by the station.

2. Don't expect the station to retype or reproduce your spot for you. Submit clean copy with no corrections. Know how many copies of the announcement they want—then provide them.

3. Meet any deadlines imposed by the station. If you are asked to have the spot at the station by a particular time, have it there. You've wasted a lot of time and effort if it is received too late.

4. Remember that the station is under no obligation to use your material. You and your organization are competing not only with commercial interests, but increasingly with other organizations that also provide important public services. Significantly, some of these nonprofit organizations have chosen to pay the going commercial rate for air time to ensure the best position for their spot. Because of

this, some broadcasters may be reluctant to accept your PSAs unless you agree to pay for part of the time. The number of nonprofit organizations across the country is steadily increasing. Each one feels strongly that the service it provides is of great value to the community.

When these organizations approach broadcast stations for free air time, what is the station manager to do? Only so much of the free material can go on the air before profits begin to show the effects. The usual result is a steady winnowing out of material submitted by organizations that might have been accepted in previous years. Now, many organizations have public relations committees composed of members who either have experience in the field or who have done their homework and are working hard to provide the station with the type of stories and other copy it needs, within its particular format and meeting its deadlines. If you were the station manager, wouldn't you tend to use the material from these organizations more often than that brought in 15 minutes after deadline and typed on an antique typewriter using four carbons complete with strikeovers? Of course you would.

More Effective Messages

The effects of your message will go up proportionate to the sum of the following conditions you are able to fulfill in your writing for radio:

1. If your appeal fulfills existing personality needs and drives, it will be more likely to influence the audience.

2. A message that is in harmony with, or supported by, existing group norms and beliefs is more readily accepted.

3. The source of the message should be considered by the audience to be trustworthy, friendly, expert, or as having high prestige.

4. Results will be improved if the initial appeal is reinforced by a face-to-face appeal.

5. The audience should be given a specific program for action or a specific course to follow.

6. The effectiveness of a message meeting opposing appeals will be lessened, or even negated. Note: With unfortunate regularity, nonprofit organizations with similar services will plan and launch an important appeal for assistance, members, or support, only to find that another nonprofit organization with a similar mission has done the same. Neither thinks to contact the other to prevent such overlapping, which reduces the appeal of each by a significant degree. A few minutes spent on the telephone before launching an appeal will be well worth the effort. Better yet, why not form an association of nonprofit organizations in your area with similar missions or purposes among whose goals would be to work together to solve problems like this one?

7. Modify the message slightly while repeating it as often as possible to provide the audience with maximum and cumulative exposure.

8. Since many people get or reinforce their opinions from "thought leaders" or "opinion makers" whom they respect, try to reach these leaders (or include them in your appeal or message to begin with) to accept or approve your message first.

9. Concentrate on modifying the audience's attitudes rather than completely changing their values or attitudes—it is much more economical in time and ef-

fort to swing opinion or support in your favor using smaller increments from a previous course, rather than try for a whole new course on a very different heading.

Public service time opportunities are wide open for the organization that learns how to prepare them because the time allocated for PSAs by commercial broadcast stations is not normally fully utilized, and because such stations are being pressured to provide more public service air time on a regular basis.

But, as McCurdy points out, "television public service directors complain that current available public service programs are below their standards or have too narrow an audience appeal. In either case, there are opportunities for an association to contribute to the well-being of the community, individual, or family through public service programs."[2]

Radio Interviews

Radio interviews are highly effective ways of getting your message or other important information across to the public, but their success depends on what preparations you have made before you approach the microphone.

The *personality interview* and the *informative interview* are the two types of interviews most commonly used. The former features Mr./Mrs./Ms./ Personality, an individual of interest to the audience because of some event in which he or she is participating or because of the position held with the organization.

In an informative interview, the information being offered is more important than the person making the statements. The interviewer is talking to the person about an event, activity, or happening of interest to the listening audience. For example, the interviewer may talk to the person in charge of the floats for an upcoming parade. The interview in this case is not primarily about the person, but informs the listeners concerning the floats and the parade.

Interviewing Techniques.   Techniques used in an interview include: the ad lib method, the fully scripted method, and the semi–ad lib method. In planning for an interview, you should keep the following pluses and minuses in mind:

1. Although the ad lib approach requires little preparation, it catches both the interviewer and interviewee off guard—resulting all too often in an interview that sounds hesitant and awkward, definitely not well organized. Since you never know what the interviewer might ask, this format is one you might well avoid.

2. The fully scripted method is the extreme opposite—all questions and all answers are completely written out before hand. One advantage here is the close control that can be maintained over the content and direction of the interview. The major disadvantage of course, is that the interview usually *sounds* prepared and stilted, with the result that listeners may lose interest. If you use this approach, remember to prepare your copy using a conversational style, not a literary style, to help overcome the inherent stiffness in this interview technique.

In the semi–ad lib method the opening and closing of the interview are scripted in advance, but only the questions are prepared in advance and discussed with the interviewee, not the answers. By discussing the questions with the participant before the interview, without writing down the answers, the on-the-air discussion sounds much more natural and relaxed. Troublesome questions can be amended or replaced before the broadcast. This approach is probably the best type to use in your communications program. In spite of the fact that this may be to your advantage, most broadcasters will insist that they develop the questions themselves. By providing them with background information, however, you can greatly influence the type of questions you are likely to be asked.

The Interviewer.   The interviewer represents Every Person, the listener, who cannot see or talk directly to the interviewee. Therefore, the interviewer must do a number of things during an interview, many of them simultaneously, including

1. Asking the questions the audience has in mind

2. Developing the questions in a logical order to lead all parties to the right conclusion

3. Making the opening interesting and keeping the body of the interview informative—without letting it drag or become bogged down in too much detail for the average listener

4. Selecting only the very best points of interest to the audience, on this station, during this time period—and wrapping them into a neat, interesting package

   The interviewer will be considering a number of important factors before, during, and after the interview. By knowing these in advance, you can come prepared to satisfy many of them and help ensure that your efforts generate maximum effects for your organization's communications program. These considerations include the following:

1. What is the "news peg" for the interview? Does the listener really want to hear this information?

2. What time frame is operative in this case? Will the interview be outdated by the time it gets on the air? Is it a feature type or a hard news type? In other words, can it air any time, or must it go out right away? If it is the latter, what other programming needs must be met—is there time?

3. Will the answers and questions of the interview stay within the dictates of common sense, courtesy, and decency?

4. Will the facts quoted or mentioned during the interview be accurate?

5. Should the interview be taped or live? Which is more important, the immediacy and extemporaneousness of the live program, or the lack of opportunity to edit the program for accuracy, propriety, or good taste, or the safety found in the taped program?

The Interview.   More often these days your organization may be able to obtain air time for a program of your own, or to air a tape that you developed "in house," perhaps through the efforts of your public relations team. In many of these cases, the "interviewer" will be one of your own—an officer or staff member.

   The following comments about the structure of the radio interview and some "do's and don'ts" for the interviewer are included to help you prepare for the interview, either following the station's guidance, or that of your own personnel.

   The interviewer should use a relatively brief period of time to identify himself, the locale (if pertinent), and the interviewee. Keep the introduction short, but prepare the listener to follow the line of questions and answers.

   Since the interviewer represents the listener, he should occasionally ask opinion-type questions to draw out the interviewee and to feature what the interviewee has to say. Remember that questions which can be answered with a simple "yes" or "no" usually are answered that way resulting in a stilted, one-sided interview.

The interview should be closed with a brief thanks to the interviewee, with reidentification of the person and the organization (for those who tuned in late), and then a final identification of the interviewer.

Questions should be arranged in a logical sequence so that one leads to another. Don't lose track of where you are in the sequence. Keep listening to the speaker, however, and be alert to any opportunity to ask follow-up questions based on the preceding answer.

Always have more than enough questions on hand. Don't be caught short with time to "fill." On a live show this can be disastrous. On a taped show, obvious filling is both embarrassing to the interviewer and a pain to the engineer who must go back to edit out the bumbles and long periods of either deadly silence or rambling dialogue. "Do's" and "don'ts" in this department include the following:

1. The guest should be able to speak as an expert on the particular topic under discussion. If not a complete "expert" on the subject, then certainly he or she should have the ability to speak with a certain degree of authority.

2. The opening, questions, and closing of the interview should be written out before air time and discussed with those participating.

3. Questions should be asked that require comment and interpretation.

4. Rehearse carefully, of course. Don't lose spontaneity in the process, however, or let the interviewee memorize the answers.

5. If the interview is taking place outside the studio, consider ways of making background noise an integral part of the audio "setting" for the interview. Such sounds can be highly effective in adding authenticity to the program.

6. The subject matter will tend to set the mood for the interview—exciting, solemn, adventurous, light, and so on.

7. Explain all slang, abbreviation, jargon, or other specialized terms used during the interview. The listener will probably not be familiar with them. Don't talk down to the audience; just explain the terms concisely in passing. Don't let the explanation detract, distract, or sidetrack the interview.

Television Production

As a medium of communication, television offers visual immediacy as an outstanding asset to your communications program. This includes your internal public as well as the general public. Richard D. Pirozzolo, in an *Association Management* article, "Ways to Get Your Association's Story on Television,"[3] notes that "associations involved in the public sector, such as those in the fields of mental health, teaching, and life insurance, have an obvious need to reach a general audience on a regular basis. But many…organizations that exist mainly for the benefit of their members often lose sight of the need to reach the public through television. These… could safely ignore the general public only if they could be sure of never being involved in public controversy."

Organizations that do not have a direct link to the general public often devote their attention to internal communications programs. What they tend to forget is that their members are also part of the public, and also watch television. As Pirozzolo points out, "when the association appears on television the value of membership is further demonstrated. Constituents learn that, in addition to serving their needs, their association also serves the public."[4]

Television production, however, is a highly complicated and costly process requiring many people and split-second timing to ensure that each activity occurs as planned. If your organization is to take full advantage of television's assets, your staff and leadership, those most likely to be appearing on television on your behalf, should understand the basics of television production and some of the language used. Knowing these, television will not seem so foreign to them, allowing them to concentrate on and relate naturally the message they want to convey.

The control of any television show is in the hands of the director. Using an intercom system connecting the control room and the studio floor, the director talks to the camera crew, floor manager, and engineers. Everyone acts on the director's instructions. While the camera crew sets up shots called by the director, the floor manager (the director's representative on the studio floor) relays cues from the director to the talent, newscaster, or announcer by means of hand and arm signals.

A well-run television show in production is an intensely subtle performing and visual art—behind as well as in front of the cameras. While camera crew quietly jockey for positions giving them proper angles and framing, the director orchestrates a finely tuned team of technicians. Some of the directions given to camera crew include the following.[5]

1. DOLLY IN (SLOW, FAST, ETC.): Move camera toward the action or subject.

2. DOLLY BACK (SLOW, FAST, ETC.): Move camera back from the action or subject.

3. PAN RIGHT (OR LEFT): Pivot camera horizontally.

4. TRUCK RIGHT (OR LEFT): Move camera parallel to the action.

5. TILT UP (OR DOWN): Pivot camera vertically.

6. FRAME: Center the subject or action in the viewfinder.

7. BREAK TO...: Move camera to another location in the studio.

8. FOCUS: Bring the subject into focus by turning the appropriate knob on the camera.

The director also calls for different types of camera shots:

1. COVER SHOT: Establishes a scene in the opening shot. Used to help viewers see the entire scene in an overview situation.

2. LONG SHOT: Closer to the action than a cover shot. Here a group of people could be seen and their physical relationship to each in space established.

3. MEDIUM SHOT: Closer to the subject or action than a long shot. In the medium shot, the subject's waist is about at the level of the lower edge of the television screen.

4. MEDIUM CLOSE-UP SHOT: Closer than the medium shot—from the chest up.

5. CLOSE UP: Closer than preceding shot—head and shoulders.

6. EXTREME CLOSE UP: Shows just the face, or a portion of it.

7. 2-SHOT: Camera frames two people.

8. 3-SHOT: Camera frames three people.

9. OVER-THE-SHOULDER SHOT: Over the shoulder of one person and into the face of another.

10. LOOSEN: Camera moves back slightly to show more area around the action or the subject.

11. TIGHTEN: Camera moves in slightly to show less area than that now showing.

Television shots are classified in four ways:

1. MOVEMENT: Dolly shot, pan shot, tilt shot, zoom shot, etc.

2. ANGLE: High, low, head on, over-the-shoulder, etc.

3. CONTENT: 1-shot, 2-shot, 3-shot, etc., or waist shot, shoulder shot, chest shot, etc.

4. FIELD OF VIEW: LS—long shot; ELS—extreme long shot; MS—medium shot; MCU—medium close up; CU—close up; ECU—extreme close up.

Every television program requires complete coordination and cooperation by the talent (including your representatives) and the technical crew (camera crew, audio engineer, video engineer, switcher, etc.). This coordination of people and highly specialized equipment has led to the evolution of certain standard commands and language required to bring certain actions or responses.

The "switcher" or technical director is the member of the production team who operates the control board called a "switcher." In some stations the director and the switcher are the same person. At the director's command, the switcher punches a button or moves a lever that electronically selects one or more pictures for transmission. Commands are normally given in two stages to prevent premature reaction. The first command will be a "ready" cue and the second will be the command of execution. Here are some examples to familiarize you with both the terminology and the various elements that go into even the most routine of television productions:

"Ready to take two...take two."

"Ready to dissolve to one...dissolve to one."

"Ready to fade to black...fade to black."

"Ready to super one and two...super."

"Ready to fade in one...fade in one."

"Ready to change slide...change."

Commands to the audio control person might include:

"Ready music"—stand by.

"Hit music"—start music.

"Music under"—reduce music volume.

"Booth"—open the microphone in the announcer's booth.

"Music up"—increase music volume.

"Sneak music under and out"—fade out music slowly.

"Fade out sound and picture"—simultaneous visual fade to black and audio fade out.

As mentioned earlier, the stage manager is the director's representative on the studio floor, relaying the director's instructions to the on-camera performers. In some cases, one of the camera crew acts as the stage manager, giving cues from behind the camera. Each of the director's commands calls for an action by the stage manager and a responding understanding or action by the performers, in this case, members of your organization. Generally, the signal or cue can be relayed by a hand or arm signal. The following commands are those that your stage manager is likely to hear over the earphones from the director and relay to those in the studio either verbally or through hand/arm signals:

Command	Meaning and Description
Places	Meaning: See that all personnel participating in the production are in place, ready to begin; that the audience (if any) is settled and ready Description: Call out "places, please."
Stand by	Meaning: Alert the people in the studio that the program or rehearsal is about to begin Description: Call out "stand by, please."
Ready to cue him (her, them)	Meaning: Alert the performer(s) that the camera is about to be switched on, and that on the cue, he should begin.
Cue	Meaning: Signal the performer to begin Description: Point at the performer using the whole arm.
Cut	Meaning: We shall stop at this point. Signal the performer to stop. Description: Draw the index finger across the throat.
Ready to move to 1, 2, etc.	Meaning: We are about to switch camera. Alert the performer(s) so he (she, they) will be ready to transition smoothly into facing the other camera. Description: Elbows straight, point with both hands to the camera that is *on* the air.
Move her (him) to 1, 2, etc.	Meaning: I am now switching cameras. Indicate this to the performer. Description: Using a pendulumlike motion, swing both arms from the camera previously on the air to the one just switched on.
Ready to show her (him) (15, 10, 5, 4, etc.)	Meaning: The performer will have this number of minutes *remaining* in his/her portion of the production/program. Description: Pick up the time card with the proper numbers on it, but do not show it to the performer.
Show her (him) (15, 10, 5, 4, etc.)	Meaning: The performer has this number of minutes of remaining time. Description: Hold the card near the lens of the on-the-air camera or wherever the performercan see it. The card is held until the floor manager is sure that it has been seen. Note: The performer(s) are *not* expected to acknowledge it in any way.

Stretch him (her)	Meaning: We are approaching the end of the material for this program but we have time remaining. Signal the performer that he (she) must slow down or ad lib to fill the time. Description: With arms extended forward, slowly draw the hands apart as if stretching a rubber band.
Move them together	Meaning: Indicate to the performers that they are standing too far apart. They must move closer together. Description: Bring hands together, palms in.
Move them apart	Meaning: The performers are standing too close together and must move apart. Description: Push hands apart, palms out.
Move him (her) closer	Meaning: The performer is too far from the camera and must move slightly toward it. Description: Move hands toward face from performer with palms facing you.
Speed him (her) up	Meaning: We are running out of time and the performer is not far enough through the material. Indicate to him (her) that he must hurry through or delete some portions. Description: Make large, rapid, circular motions with fingers and hand in front of body.
Show him (her) a cut	Meaning: Indicate to the performer that he (she) must conclude remarks. Description: Draw one finger across the throat.

Tips for Television Participants

1. Assume that the camera is on you and "live" every moment; although it may not be at that instant, it is far better to assume this and be poised and in control all the time rather than to be caught off guard "picking your nails" on occasion.

2. The microphone is only inches away—there is no need to project your voice.

3. Act and speak naturally—television is an intimate medium.

4. Pay attention to and work closely with the stage manager—the director's representative in the studio.

5. Ask the stage manager to demonstrate the signals to be used and explain the meaning of each so that you will have no trouble recognizing and understanding them while on camera.

6. When you move, move slowly and in the ways planned with or by the director.

7. Give consideration to the style and type of clothes that should be worn. Check ahead of time and dress appropriately.

8. Carefully organize and rehearse your materials.

9. As with radio, try not to read from a prepared script. If this is necessary, use cue cards or a teleprompter—it helps you come across with more spontaneity.

10. When you are addressing the camera, talk right to the "taking lens."

Television News

Those of you involved in television news production or in providing such material for your organization have two sides to consider: audio (sound) and video (sight). Audio carries the facts or details of a story, supplemented by the video, which adds impact and interest without coloring the facts. You have to remember that sound and picture compete with each other for the viewer's attention. The viewer's attention tends to wander when the words and the picture don't coincide. The writer of such material must produce copy that matches the mood and content of the video image of that time period. This is a challenge when you remember that in seconds the images may switch from film or video tape, to graphics, to the announcer, and the copy for each must mesh smoothly.

Film or videotape captures the sounds, sights, and movements of fast-breaking news events with immediacy and no visual detail omitted. The viewer becomes an eyewitness to these events.

Graphics and "visuals" add amplification, clarity, and interest to the news. Such materials include still photographs, slides, maps, charts, graphs, cartoons, and diagrams. Graphics should be properly contrasted and simple enough in content to be instantly understood. Remember to keep their proportion within the television aspect ratio of four units in width to three in height.

Writing Techniques. In television news writing, story leads serve two basic purposes: to arrest attention and to prepare the audience to receive the facts that will follow. The lead, therefore, should give the story's central news facts, or the general "what happened."

Long quotes should be avoided in television news. All too often leads are too difficult or involved for the audience to comprehend quickly. If a quote is used, identify the source (who) before stating what was said. The viewer gauges the authority of the statement by the measure of the person quoted.

Incorrect example: A blue-ribbon committee has been appointed to determine the cause of the accident, the Mayor said today.

Correct example: Mayor John Sampson says that a blue-ribbon committee has been appointed to determine the cause of the accident.

Remember that if a person is not widely known, his or her title or other brief identification should be given before the name is mentioned. This usually has more meaning for the listening audience.

Example: Belltown Volunteer Fire Chief William Smith said today....

Television News Script. In television, directions must be given to both the audio and video teams. Over the years the industry has evolved a script page divided into two columns—one side for video directions, the other for audio. A portion of a television news script is reproduced (Figure 43.1) to familiarize you with the format.

Television Interviews

Television interviews evolved from their radio predecessors and have most things in common with radio, except that the listener becomes the viewer. Video material

```
PAGE _____A1_____

SLUG _____MAYOR_____

WRITER __HWK_____

TIME _____:15_____
```

(JOHN/CK: City Hall)

JACKSONVILLE MAYOR HANS
TANZLER TOLD HIS DEPARTMENT CHIEFS
TODAY THAT HE HAS EVERY INTENTION
OF INCREASING THE NUMBER OF WOMEN
IN GOVERNMENT.

TANZLER TOOK THE POSITION
THAT IF HE DOESN'T MAKE AN EARNEST
EFFORT TO HIRE MORE WOMEN, THE
CITY COULD LOSE A LOT OF FEDERAL
REVENUE SHARING MONEY. OFFICIALS
IN WASHINGTON HAVE ALREADY HINTED
AT THAT PROSPECT.

THE MAYOR ORDERED HIS
DEPARTMENT HEADS TO GET TO WORK
IMMEDIATELY DRAFTING SPECIAL
HIRING PLANS. TANZLER SAID HE
WANTS TO SEE THOSE PLANS ON HIS
DESK ONE WEEK FROM TODAY.

#

"12 ACTION NEWS WTLV Jacksonville, Fla.

Figure 43.1

plays an important role in the planning that goes into such a production. Compared to a dramatic or documentary program, the television interview is easily produced and ranges in length from the short segments seen on television news up to a complete program.

The audio portion of a television interview is about the same as a radio interview, except that demonstrations or other visual material can be used or referred to during the program. Here again, the semi–ad lib format, in which the interviewer is well prepared and the interviewee provides "off-the-cuff" answers to questions known beforehand, is the best approach to use.

Video, in this case, is even more important because the viewer is not likely to concentrate for long on just a head-and-shoulders shot of the interviewee in a staged setting. Careful thought to the video potentialities in this case will pay off in more interesting interviews. Consider taping or filming at your organization's offices, headquarters, or service facilities. If the interview extends beyond several minutes, consider what kind of visual material, such as maps, photos, and demonstrations, could be incorporated into the interview.

The success of the television interview will largely depend on the interviewer and the preparations he or she has made for the program. You should carefully choose your interviewer if at all possible. (Of course, this should be done with a great deal of tact. You just can't say to the program director, "Could our organization's representative be interviewed by Bill S——, instead of Jim L——. We don't want our public image messed up by an amateurish interview by a new station employee, fresh out of IOU's College of Journalism.")

Regardless of whether your interviewer is an old hand at the business or not, another important factor in the success of the program is the preparation he or she has made for the interview. Here you can be of great assistance. Be prepared to provide the interviewer with much (if not all) of the background material or other support materials he or she will need for the show. Even if you must nearly do the show yourself, it will help ensure that the message about your organization comes out and goes over the way you want it to.

Some of the thinking, planning, and preparation areas that should be considered before a program of this type include the following:

1. Determine the point of interest that needs to be brought out. Refer to your organization's overall public relations or communications plan for the year. If it has been properly prepared, such a plan will be very helpful about the general and specific points of information that should be emphasized during the program.
2. Compare the points that need to be brought out on behalf of your organization with those that your analysis indicates the audience would like to hear—on this show, at this time, in this way, from this person.
3. Arrange the points that have emerged via your twofold analysis process in a logical sequence that will permit an orderly development of the interview. The idea flow might proceed as follows:
    a. Title, name, field of guest.
    b. Guest's position in the field, that is, why does he or she have the right, authority or interest to talk in or about this field?
    c. Bring out aspects of the guest's personality establishing him or her in the minds of the viewers in a humanistic as well as "expert" light.
    d. Explain what is to be discussed and why this subject is important and newsworthy.
    e. Move into developmental questions evoking facts, opinions, and comments.
    f. Leave time for peak or climax questions (next to last) and consider where and how they should be placed in the sequence to achieve the planned impact.
    g. Leave time for a wrap-up or summary period at the conclusion of the interview. This should consist of the major points of information you wish to leave with the viewing audience.

There are many ways to structure an interview besides this particular approach, but it is the one perhaps most often used. Other modifications or orientations to the television interview include the chronological approach (past, present, future), the geographical approach (north, midwest, west coast, south, etc.), or sociological considerations of the audience (men, women, children, young, old, wealthy, poor, employed, unemployed, etc.). The list is virtually endless. What is important is advance planning and preparation with the station personnel who will be producing the program. Decide together on the best approach to produce the best possible program on behalf of your organization and the viewing audience. You and your organization's public relations team can do a great deal to ensure a better product all the way around by understanding the basic mechanics of such programming and working with station personnel to provide whatever they may need.

There is an important fringe benefit to all of this. The station will not forget the professionalism demonstrated by your organization. And the next time you approach them for air time, they will probably be even more receptive to working another program into their schedule. By making their job easier, you will always be welcome at that station.

Feature Programs

A feature program explores, explains, or demonstrates a noteworthy subject in an imaginative and colorful way. The emphasis is on the "factual," not the "editorial." Since they are most effective when used this way, features tend to emphasize or focus on events of current need or interest—ideal potential for telling your story.

If you are considering using the feature program approach, the potential for development is almost endless. It leads itself to virtually any type of information program format. Certain basic elements should guide your plans and the writing you put into the script.

Usually, the basic objective or focal point of a feature is the creation of a behavioral response, for example, "wanting" to be a better "anything," or a desire to achieve something of importance to the listener. The emphasis is on people being interested in other people—especially the unusual experiences of others. Your subject and your treatment of it should stay on the "people" aspect and not wander too far afield, or the focus of the feature program will be lost.

Both figurative and literal color should be injected into the program. Words heighten interest and intensify the response you are aiming for. Vivid, precise language is a major ingredient of "color," with verbs in the active voice. Word "pictures" can be painted, whether the program is intended for radio or television. Don't forget to call attention to the central idea at several points in the script.

As far as structure of the feature program, the inverted pyramid format commonly used in journalism generally does not work well. The development here is usually logical, flowing easily from what is outlined during the opening and developed throughout the body of the program. The opening is usually of the "attention-getting" variety—quotations, statistics, questions, imagery. The body of the program involves some form of orderly or logical development, which the writer should clearly spell out early in the program. The conclusion follows naturally from the form being used in the body. A "circular development" format, however, does help give the impression of unity and logical development while reinforcing the basic idea. This is done by having the end of the program repeat the central idea introduced at the beginning.

The information objective of the feature program must be kept in mind at all times. Everything written into the program must relate to the objective. Extensive research followed by a written outline helps a great deal in this respect.

If You Want Air Time: Do's and Don'ts

The following distillation of good advice on increasing the air time donated to your organization by radio and television stations was provided in large part by the

Public Relations Service of the National Association of Broadcasters in Washington, D.C.

Do submit all program copy to the program director as far in advance as possible. Ten days would not be too soon.

Do get news releases to the news director as early as you can—a week in advance, if possible. Then follow up with a phone call.

Do typewrite all copy *triple-spaced* on 8 ½ × 11 paper, using one side only. Start one-third of the way down the first page. Leave ample margins.

Do use a clean ribbon for legible copy. Provide extra copies as requested.

Do put the name of your organization, and your own name, address, and telephone number, at the top of each item.

Do give all the facts—the what, when, where, who, and why of your event. Be sure to give specific starting and ending dates, such as: "Use between July 4 and July 7," not "Monday through Thursday."

Do write all copy for the voice—a bit more informal in style than copy written only for the eye. If you normally use "don't" in oral conversation, write it that way in your script. Use "let's" instead of "let us." A good rule: Be informal, but don't be breezy.

Do provide a biographical sketch of any person to be interviewed, along with six or eight points to be covered. If the name is difficult to pronounce, give the phonetic spelling. Include a black-and-white photo for them to release to print media if your representative is a newsmaker.

For Radio

Do time spot announcements to run 10 seconds (25 words), 20 seconds (50 words), or 60 seconds (150 words).

Do use simple, descriptive words that form pictures, give dimension and color. Radio reaches only the ear, and the listener must be able to sketch in his or her own mind the picture you are trying to create.

Do submit several copies of all material, and make sure that the last one is as legible as the first.

For Television

Do check with the program or news director about slides, films, photographs, and videotapes that can be used to illustrate your message.

Do make sure that copy written to accompany such visual aids matches the slide, film, or photo shown.

Do time your copy at a slightly slower pace than for radio. Standard announcements for television run 10 seconds (about 12 words), 20 seconds (35 words), and 60 seconds (125 words).

Do provide one slide or photograph for each 10-second spot; two for a 20-second spot, and so on.

Do keep in mind that slides are preferable in most cases to photographs. They can be made professionally at minimum cost. When photographs are used, matte or dull-surfaced prints are preferable since glossy prints reflect studio lights.

Do request return of your visual material if you want to preserve it. Otherwise, it may be thrown away.

Do provide prepared film announcements only in segments of 60, 30, 20, and 10 seconds each. These should be totally self-contained, requiring no live copy or insertion of live material such as slides or a live announcer. Your film *must* contain the name of the sponsoring organization. The same applies for videotape—use color, high-band videotapes.

Do make sure that the 35-mm *color* slides you submit are in a horizontal format. Such slides should have ample open space along all four sides, approximately the outer 10 percent of the slide. Your slide *must* contain the name of the sponsoring organization and minimal information, since too much cannot be absorbed by the viewer. Each slide will require live or prerecorded copy of exactly 10 seconds in length. Obviously, slides that tell the story at a glance are more likely to get this additional valuable exposure.

Don't ask for public service time to publicize or promote bingo parties or lotteries.

Don't try to use free air time to extol the advantages of any commercial product.

Don't plead, beg, or threaten in an attempt to get time. A good presentation in the public interest will stand on its own merits.

Don't submit copy scribbled on scratch paper or on a postcard. Writing in longhand invites errors.

Don't omit essential information. Check over your copy to be sure that it tells who, what, why, when, and where, and includes your name, address, and phone number.

Don't get carried away by trivialities, superlatives, and overenthusiasm. Omit adjectives and avoid nicknames.

Don't abbreviate telephone numbers. "FE" might be FEderal or it might be FEntworth. Never abbreviate or hyphenate any words in a script.

Don't use onion skin paper for on-the-air copy—it rattles.

When You Are About to Go on the Air

The station will want you to sound and look your best. Whether your appearance is live or recorded, you will be given helpful suggestions to that end, and your cooperation will be appreciated. For example:

On Radio

You will receive instructions as to:

The proper distance from the microphone

How to handle your copy or script with the least possible noise

Ways to avoid extraneous noise, such as removing dangling bracelets, etc.

You will be asked to caution friends who may come with you to a broadcast or recording session to be as quiet as possible.

On Television

Personal appearance will be of vital importance to the success of your presentation.

Wear suits or dresses of soft, medium colors or pastels. Avoid sharply contrasting patterns and colors, especially white.

Keep jewelry simple and uncluttered. Pearls and dull-finished metals reflect less light than sparkling or highly polished jewelry.

Men may require a little powder on a bald head, or if the skin is exceptionally oily. Pancake makeup is advisable for a heavy beard or shadows around the eyes.

Women should avoid heavy makeup and overuse of lipstick.

Don't worry about eyeglasses. If your eyes are used to glasses, they will react unnaturally if you try to appear without them. The studio crew will arrange lighting to avoid any glare.

Cooperate with the director and floor managers during your appearance. They may find it necessary to give you hand signals during the show to guide the speed of your presentation.

A Word of Thanks

After your presentation has been made, you should send letters of thanks to station personnel in appreciation of the help they have given you. Such expressions strengthen relationships and enhance your chances of getting public service time in the future. Also let the station know of any reactions you receive. The station is vitally interested in the response to your program.

Sample: Public Service Announcement for Radio

From:

Frank W. Edwards
Publicity Chairman
Woonsocket Teachers Association
Randolph Mason High School
Woonsocket, Rhode Island
387-1234

AMERICAN EDUCATION WEEK— RHODE ISLAND

For use Monday, February 21, through Friday, February 25

AMERICAN EDUCATION WEEK IN RHODE ISLAND
February 21–February 28

TIME: 30 seconds

WORDS: 74

ANNCR: Drive by a school. Watch the faces of the hundreds of students as they come and go. These are the faces of the men and women who one day will govern this nation.

During American Education Week, the teachers of Rhode Island invite you to watch this vital form of freedom in action. Visit your local school and observe techniques of instruction that help prepare our children for tomorrow. This is American Education Week.

Sample: The Same Announcement for Television

From:

Frank W. Edwards
Publicity Chairman
Woonsocket Teachers Association
Randolph Mason High School
Woonsocket, Rhode Island
387-1234

AMERICAN EDUCATION WEEK—
RHODE ISLAND

For use Monday, February 21, through
Friday, February 25.

AMERICAN EDUCATION WEEK IN RHODE ISLAND
February 21–February 28

TIME: 30 seconds
WORDS: 66

Video	Audio
Slide No:...(School with many students walking alongside it)	ANNCR: Our nation's schools are home to millions of our children for 17 years of their lives.
Slide No:...(Lincoln Memorial with two children looking at statue)	America looks to these future citizens for the maintenance of the free world, and these students look to the great men of the world
Slide No:...(American Education Week. Visit Your Schools)	During American Education Week, visit your local school. Rhode Island teachers urge all of you to participate in this observance.

(Note: The blank following "Slide No:" is for the station to insert its own identifying number of your slide.)

Sample: Public Service Announcement for Radio

From:

North Florida Council
Girl Scouts of the U.S.A.
Ms. Dorothy Smoothly
Publicity Chairman
5001 Primrose Lane
Jacksonville, Florida
388-7105

GIRL SCOUT WEEK

Starting Date: 3/6
Ending Date: 3/12

GIRL SCOUT WEEK
March 6 to March 12

TIME: 20 seconds

WORDS: 47

ANNCE: This is Girl Scout Week. It's a very special week. The Girl Scouts celebrate their 60th birthday. Throughout the years, Girl Scouting has helped prepare young girls to be useful and active citizens in their home and world communities. Join in supporting the Girl Scouts. Help them BE PREPARED!

Sample: The Same Announcement for Television

From: GIRL SCOUT WEEK

North Florida Council   Starting Date: 3/6
Girl Scouts of the U.S.A   Ending Date: 3/12
Ms. Dorothy Smoothly
Publicity Chairman
5001 Primrose Lane
Jacksonville, Florida
388-7105

GIRL SCOUT WEEK
March 6 to March 12

TIME: 20 seconds

WORDS: 36

Video	Audio
Slide No:...(Girl Scout badge)	ANNCR: This is Girl Scout Week. And it's really special. The Girl Scouts are celebrating their birthday—their 60th birthday!
Slide No:...(Group of Girl Scouts)	Girl Scouting has helped prepare girls to be active and useful citizens. Support the Girl Scouts. Help Them BE PREPARED!

Sample: News Release for Radio or Television

From: For release:

Handley Music Club   Thursday, January 20th
W. A. Mozart
Publicity Chairman
1357 Lydian Street
Handley, California
229-3227

Seventeen-year-old Theresa Ann Blankenship (BLANK'-IN-SHIP) is the winner of the five-hundred dollar first-prize scholarship award in the Handley Music Club Essay Contest. Her entry was the judges' top choice in the 19th annual competition.

Miss Blankenship is a junior at Handley High School.

Runners up were 15-year-old Edwin R. Newman of Handley, and 16-year-old Patricia Neff of Freemont. Each received a two-hundred-dollar scholarship.

All of the students were required to write essays on "America Needs Music."

The awards were presented last night by club president Joan Saints during ceremonies at the Wellington Hotel.

Sample: News Release for Radio or Television

From: For release:

The Rotary Club   Thursday, January 20th
John C. Corbet
Publicity Chairman
1632 Warren Street
Monmouth, Missouri
245-7787

Arthur C. Best is the new president of the Rotary Club of Monmouth.

Best has been active in Rotary for the past six years. His election came at a luncheon meeting today. Best, who takes office on Friday, succeeds George W. Miles, whose term has expired.

Henry P. Castle was elected vice-president, a post Best held for two years.

Other officers are secretary, Gordon H. Changel, and treasurer, Robert J. Lapham.

Notes

1. Michael J. McCurdy, Guidelines for Planning Public Service Programs, *Association Management,* May 1976, pp. 41–42.

2. Ibid., p. 43.

3. Richard D. Pirozzolo, Ways to Get Your Association's Story on Television, *Association Management,* May 1976, p. 36.

4. Ibid.

5. Adapted in part from *Dictionary of Mass Media and Communication,* Longman, New York, 1982.

44

Telling Your Story to a Legislative Body*

John Jay Daly

President, Daly Associates, Inc., Washington, D.C.

When it comes to influencing legislation on behalf of your organization, it is wise to remember: Giving effective testimony before any legislative body—whether Congress, state governments, or your local city council—is not easy. You have to plan for it—and you need to be smart.

Although this chapter focuses on the important "do's and don'ts" of congressional testimony, it also applies in large measure to appearances before other governmental bodies—state, local, or any agency or department of the federal government. The principal point to remember when preparing to face any of these bodies is that there are as many pitfalls as there are paradoxes in the process. Yet if one remains aware of them—every step of the way—the result can often redound to your organization's strength. Even if the issue is resolved contrary to the position you had taken, by following the principles outlined, your organization will be respected for its professionalism—another benefit that can be used at a later date—and there almost always is another date.

Similarly, lack of awareness or weak preparation can court disaster with any legislative body. Giving legislative testimony is no job for amateurs—unless you are prepared in advance to concede the issue to the opposition.

*Adapted and reprinted by permission from the January 1974 issue of *Association Management.* Copyright 1974 by the American Society of Association Executives. This article won the author a coveted ASAE award as the best member-written article of the year.

The Role of Public Hearings

Hearings before congressional committees are commonplace in the capital. Thousands of sessions are held each year, resulting in tons of testimony. Until national television showed the public that part of the complex legislative process, relatively few Americans ever saw first-hand how their national legislators expose important facts. Now, with House debate available—and the Senate following suit—the process is becoming more revealing.

Public hearings to elicit pertinent points have long been with us and will continue to be. Thus, it behooves all progressive organization executives to be aware that they too, might be called on to enter the congressional arena. If so, they and their witnesses would be well advised to be aware of the nuances to make the most of it.

Although presenting open testimony is but one part of the legislative labyrinth, it is important that nonprofit organization (NPO) executives, their elected officials, and supporting staff know as much as possible about how to handle it.

Here, then, are some pointers about the paradoxes and pitfalls gathered after more than a dozen years preparing and delivering testimony for large and varied national associations. Of course, not all apply to every situation—no one can prepare a witness for every contingency—but these should generally see you through. They reflect comments from other NPO executives in Washington as well as viewpoints from the other side of the witness table—from senators, members of Congress, and their staffs.

The basic problem is that all too often there is not enough time to touch properly all the bases and do all the things that one should do to come away with an extremely effective job. However, since that situation applies to so many areas that NPO executives find themselves in, just knowing the road may be helpful. The purpose here is to advise what you should do before, during, and after the testimony. As more than one ill-prepared or careless witness has learned to his later sorrow, congressional appearances can be fraught with danger.

Yet NPO spokespersons should not be so overcome with stage fright or concerned about the clout of Congress that they shy from presenting testimony on issues important to their members' best interests.

Where the Real Work Is Done

Although televised hearings sometimes show the committee process to millions of Americans, experienced NPO executives have long known that it is in the *committees* and *subcommittees* of Congress where the real work is done—most of which is not televised or broadcast. In general, this is true of all legislative bodies.

Actually, the most effective role in shaping legislation is to know about the proposed legislation while it is being drafted. Much of this work is usually confined to knowledgeable and trusted lobbyists who are able to talk with influential subcommittee members and key staff aids who help frame legislation.

Remember, however, that proper presentation of testimony before Congress is important not only for industry, but also for the country, since it is a citizen's duty to present expert viewpoints and opinions about the possible effects of proposed legislation on individual businesses or industries. In addition, where possible, it would be valuable to comment on the social or economic aspects of not passing legislation.

Statements for the Record

Understandably, it is usually a policy decision when an organization decides to testify before Congress or any legislative body. For many, the decision is easily arrived at because the interests are so intense. For others, the relationship might be remote or even casual. In the latter case, not testifying, but submitting statements for the record could suffice.

Naturally, however, a written statement simply cannot be as effective as that which is personally and forcefully delivered before an attentive lawmaking body by an articulate, knowledgeable witness. Under the best circumstances, even oral testimony does not have all of the impact or effect that the witness might wish.

Importance of Being Concise

It is a simple fact of life that, since there are only 100 U.S. senators and 435 representatives, each is an extremely busy person. With the foreshortened congressional hearing week—often Tuesday through Thursday when the Congress is really heated up—most members have several subcommittees that they must keep up with simultaneously, plus one or two major committees (as well as other demands).

It is not at all unusual for several of these groups to meet within a 2-hour period, thus requiring the member either to divide attention by physically covering all the meetings or have his or her mind wander while listening to a witness.

Therefore, it is extremely important for witnesses before committees to be as concise as possible—yet tell a complete story that gets essence of their point across.

One point the witness should never forget is that, however lofty their position, legislators and their staff aides are human. Generally speaking, they make a particular point of being polite to the witness and, within the realms of practicality, pay attention to what is said. However, being human, they also tend to forget key points that witnesses make unless something is done to dramatize the key points.

Some of the basic rules for public appearances, then, still prevail.

The Value of Case Histories

It is within reason for witnesses to illustrate their remarks dramatically or forcefully. Analogies and case histories, if brief and colorful, can often bring home a point or augment an argument far better than stacks of statistics.

Thus, although knowledge of all ramifications of the legislation is important, a key to effective testimony is proper selection of a knowledgeable, articulate witness—one who can sense the mood of the hearing and quickly and properly adapt to it.

Presenting the testimony in a dull monotone, stuffing testimony with dry statistics that tell of huge industry problems—whether in thousands or millions or billions of dollars—seem to make relatively little impact on Congress.

Such data might be needed as background to support testimony, but talking in terms that an average member of Congress can see or grasp is much better. If possible, take a tip from the way *The Wall Street Journal* handles many page-one features: Put human interest into the story.

If organizations have several live witnesses—particularly from the committee member's district—describe how they or their businesses will be affected by proposed legislation, so much the better.

A Good Choice for Spokesperson

While it is preferable to have someone from the member's district, if the spokesperson who would be chosen would also make a poor presence—either due to latent hostility or the simple truth that the witness is dull—select someone else. After all, it is the overall impression that counts, not the single vote-getting aspect.

One compromise solution is to have a member from the chairperson's district or state introduce the principal witness. Some groups like to have a fellow member of Congress make the introduction. Often, however, the extra trouble this causes (before or after) is not necessarily worth the effort.

Although it is logistically more difficult to arrange for out-of-town witnesses and school them in the ways of Washington, the effort helps build understanding and thus rapport between members and their association.

The benefit for the legislators is that they can hear firsthand from live, articulate witnesses just what the proposal might do to individual businesses and livelihoods. In some cases, of course, the results against an industry are so harsh or inevitable that even sobbing case histories of potential disasters will not do any good.

How Many Witnesses Should Appear?

Unless you are counting on a smash star, the number of witnesses should depend on the circumstances, but certainly less than half a dozen, perhaps only three or even just one.

One pitfall to guard against is overly long testimony. Keeping witnesses on for just a few minutes will suffice even though many hours might be spent in persuading them to come, coaching them, and helping edit or write testimony.

Another point to remember is that if the witnesses are well known to the committee, they will be more effective because they can develop a rapport that is unequaled in getting your story across. This is particularly true if you happen to have access to a witness who is very well known.

Write Out Your Testimony

Unless the witness is extremely confident, capable, and articulate, it usually is not wise to ad lib. This naturally means a double preparation, but results should be worth it. Perhaps it could be done in outline form or, if fully written, in a conversational style.

After the documents have been studied, written testimony has been prepared, drafted, circulated for policy viewpoints, facts, and so forth, it is wise to have rehearsals with perhaps one or two knowledgeable staff members playing the role of devil's advocate to ask questions and simply to listen to the testimony itself to make sure it flows smoothly and makes total sense.

Critical listeners should pay particular attention to how the presentation flows: Is there a logical order to it? Within the tight time constraints, does it completely answer the questions that are asked or that earlier portions of the testimony may have raised? Does the presentation hit major points solidly?

Can the witness easily and correctly pronounce every word and combination of words? If not, change the words—or change the witness.

Tell Where You Stand on Issues

Often it is useful after the introduction simply to state the position and outline the testimony. As in speech writing, it is wise to let your audience know where you are going and what stops you will be making along the way. For instance, after the introductory part you simply note that you are testifying in complete favor of, or in complete opposition to, or with a modified position to the proposed legislation. If you enumerate the reasons for the support or opposition, this might be a good place to do so. You then can elaborate on them.

During the elaboration, avoid the common mistake that John Yeck, one of America's great copy writers, terms the "sin of CIPU." CIPU is defined as "clear if previously understood." How often have you seen or heard examples of CIPU? It seems particularly prevalent when expert witnesses come in from industry—any industry—and quickly lapse into the technical jargon or easy parlance of their trade, which is not generally understood by anyone else.

Many times, those who help with the testimony do not notice that the "sin of CIPU" is being committed, for they understand the terms being used. But think of the members of Congress or their staff aides. They often do not know precisely what the witness is talking about. Yet, because time is precious, they will not take the time to stop the babble in midsentence to ask: "By the way, what do you mean when you say...?"

The Tactic of Summarizing

An important point, small perhaps, but useful: If different witnesses, despite best efforts to coordinate testimony in advance, do find that they are inadvertently duplicating and become repetitive, the wise witness will simply refer to previous remarks or will quickly shorten or summarize his or her remarks and leave more time for questions. Because sitting through variations of a basic theme cause busy members of Congress mentally—if not physically—to wander from the hearing room, it is best to be alert to this tactic of quickly summarizing.

Another tip to save precious time is simply to identify the witness in the beginning by name and affiliation. Later, document capabilities, experience, and formal education, and so forth. These data can be provided as attachments to the written testimony rather than elaborated on directly.

The Use of Exhibits

What about charts and diagrams? They often will make testimony come alive. Remember, though, that many times the peculiar positioning of the formal hearing rooms on Capitol Hill and the window lighting conditions mitigate against effective audiovisuals. Even though we now live in an audiovisual age, showing films and slides often becomes more difficult in Congress than they would be in other settings.

Supplemental charts, when reproduced for the legislators and their staff to look at individually during the presentation, add to the effectiveness of the audiovisuals. It is also useful to present charts or particular quotations and dramatize statistics by analogy.

Opposing Points of View

Remember that, in addition to hearing your story, all members of Congress are subject to a wide variety of pressures and influences from many sources—lobbyists for the opposing viewpoints, other members of Congress, pressures of their own district, business, staff, and family distractions. Be specific in your testimony. If possible, it is best to try to aim at one and at most no more than three major points that you would like to convey.

Many times, in social conversations with staffers or committee members immediately following a routine session, I have simply asked them what they might be able to recount about the various witnesses who had just appeared. Not surprisingly, those witnesses who were clear and concise and articulate—with perhaps a dash of color—were the most remembered.

During the long and often heated hearings on postal reform legislation, I remember particularly that a representative of a nursery association attracted pleasant attention by bringing along samples of his products and leaving some blooms and plants for later enjoyment by staffers, secretaries, and representatives. By the simple technique of bringing into the drab hearing room the plants and flowers, which had to be specially packed to survive the rigors of mail handling, he not only made his remarks come alive, but effectively dramatized the need for better postal handling procedures.

Dramatize Your Point

The same thing happened for occupant mailers. To show the many steps that such mailers' own sorting eliminated, one experienced witness set up a conventional carrier's sorting case in the hearing room. He only used it for a 2- or 3-minute session, but in that short space of time he graphically demonstrated the problems clerks have in sorting properly—which occupant mailers bypass by their procedures.

His basic point was to dramatize tremendous savings that presorting and other steps allow. This quick, live demonstration—while difficult to arrange for such a brief period—made a memorable impression on many members of Congress.

Another approach to "dramatizing" a point before a legislative body was proposed by the author as a "sound" idea to the Recording Industry Association of America (RIAA). The objective was to impress upon congressional committees holding hearings on a revised postal reform measure that "sound recordings inherently belong among items included in the special fourth-class rate."

Nearly a dozen groups were to testify on that particular day. All were allowed only 10 minutes of presentation time apiece. If we were to be successful we knew we would have to be dramatic (1) to attract attention and (2) to sustain interest.

A written statement was prepared that covered in detail all the major points we wished to make. The oral statement simply enumerated in rapid form the points that were spelled out in detail in the written statement. These are standard approaches, of course; the really important portion of the plan involved a dramatic use of "our" medium. Although simple, it was time-consuming to execute.

Following a brief reference to the written statement, the RIAA spokesman noted that in a world of paper and print the Congress was wise in recognizing the priceless heritage of sound recordings. Just before pushing the button of an excellent tape cassette player, the speaker summarized the importance of sound recording with: "If one picture is worth a thousand words, then conjure how many pictures and memories come to mind as we present this too-brief montage from one hundred years of recorded sound."

The 7-minute recording that held the hearing room spellbound was a carefully produced sound montage entitled "The Loveliest Miracle" and narrated by the late Francis Robinson of the Metropolitan Opera, which captured the high points of sound and of America's history. Of course, extra cassettes of the *entire* statement and recording were made available to committee staffers for rehearings, and many requested those copies for it truly was of interest, far more than any photocopied testimony might have been.

Be Ready for Questions

Besides being articulate, witnesses should also be well prepared for all sorts of questions. It goes without saying that questions should be answered crisply and succinctly. Most important, if a witness—even one billed as an expert—is not certain or does not know a particular answer, it is always possible (and more acceptable) to ask if the answer could be supplied later for the record. Note: Be particularly sure the answer is supplied in time to make the record. Failure to do so could be considered not only unprofessional, but perhaps as a dodge; worse, the staff might call attention in the record itself to the fact that, though promised, the answer was never supplied.

Keep asking yourself, "If I were a busy member of Congress, who only half heard this testimony just once, what would I get out of it?" It's a tough question to pose, but it's valid. How often have you heard someone rave about a speaker, or praise a sermon, yet be deflated with a vague answer when you asked: "Oh, that's interesting. But what did he say?"

Highlights of Your Testimony

The same thing is true for effective testimony. After your witnesses are excused, each member of the committee—no matter how distracted he or she might have been during the presentation—should be able to summarize highlights in a few words. It is no easy trick, but it is essential. Of course, the backup material—charts, documents, statistics, etc., which give credence and heft to the testimony—must be available, but no matter how complex, the thrust of the testimony should be so clear that the gist of it can be gotten across in a few sentences.

Because of the time limits which guide crowded committee hearings—many are held only between 10 a.m. and noon in midweek, thus challenging the free time of all elected officials—several groups are often scheduled consecutively. Even large groups are seldom granted more than an hour to present their viewpoints. Best way to solve this is to

1. Carefully prepare written testimony in complete detail with backup charts, statistical tables, or other data that will document the point.

2. Confine that which is presented orally to a highlight summary that is easily graspable and conveys important essence of message.

Be Thoroughly Knowledgeable

Another obvious but often overlooked point: Be thoroughly familiar with the legislation and related bills. Someone should attend the hearings and report what questions are being asked since some come up regularly. If you can, gather views of both sides.

Another clue: Rare is the legislation that springs full-blown and is passed in one session. The legislative history of futile tries reveals vital data to whoever is charged with drafting the reply.

Opening statements follow a set ritual that briefly identifies the witnesses, their affiliations, and for whom they are testifying. It is also best to state forcefully and clearly the bill or bills that are being commented on, and, if possible, to give a short opening statement as to the general or specific position of the association regarding them.

If it is possible to state at the outset the rationale for the position, this sets everything straight and makes the comments that follow easier to comprehend.

You would be surprised how many witnesses do not follow this technique. Sometimes they are halfway through—or worse yet, all the way through—and the careful listener still does not know what the position is.

Make sure your witness knows the background of committee members, especially senior ones, so that he or she can address them by name and make reference to their state. Alert your witnesses that they can expect sharp and often hostile questions. Especially warn them that they can get those barbs right in the middle of prepared remarks. Sometimes, because of congressional exigencies that no one can predict, even the most friendly of chairpersons will ask witnesses to "file their remarks" for the record and go into questions from a battery of committee members sometimes more interested in getting to the floor for a vote than in getting an answer to a question they posed.

How Experience Pays Off

When the time comes for questions, experienced witnesses shine. Not only are they well prepared for the expected questions, they also are deft at dodging or returning the tough and often unexpected ones. If one expects a verbal tweak, one is better prepared to cope. Sometimes the criticism will come not because of anything said or unsaid in the testimony but because of a late development in the field the spokesperson represents. That is why it is wise—despite the time pressures of preparing testimony—to keep current with events so as to be rehearsed with proper answers, particularly if a political business angle is involved.

Particularly apropos is the view of John Gabusi, knowledgeable former special assistant to Rep. Morris K. Udall (D-Ariz.), who has served in the House since 1962:

> The one characteristic that keeps coming up is that of absolute candor. It really is irritating to have a question asked and then to have it skipped and slid around. Most members would really prefer a straight answer which might include such things as "I don't know," or "I'll have to check it out and give you an answer." When a witness attempts to obfuscate and throw out a welter of words in the hope that that will suffice, irritation really sets in on our side of the witness table.
>
> The other main factor is keeping your verbal comments as short as possible. Most members really want to ask questions and are not interested in hearing a twenty-page statement on any subject. If they need more information, they'll ask for it or they'll read the prepared statement which is inserted into the record.

Anticipate Questions

If an answer cannot be supplied because the question is not precise, politely asking for clarification of the question or phrasing it another way is quite permissible. If you do not agree with premise do not accept it at outset.

Generally speaking, it is wise for the witness to have a rehearsal. Knowledgeable NPO staff members should ask questions that might arise. Having testified dozens of times and sat through hundreds of hearings, it is sometimes easy to anticipate questions, particularly from certain members.

From the Senate side of the Hill, South Carolina Democrat Ernest F. Hollings has definite views of what makes an outstanding witness. Senator Hollings lists half a dozen points, among them: "Know what the committee is interested in so the statement will be responsive. Be straightforward and pragmatic. Consider discussing your interests with staff members prior to going before the committee." Senator Hollings' advice is well-taken and reinforced in different ways by others to whom I have talked about effective presentations.

Because sticky situations can and do develop, it is also helpful to have friendly members present during the questioning; they often can ease the climate without appearing too biased. Experienced lobbyists make various efforts to get busy members to attend. Letters far ahead of time, phone calls to appointment secretaries the afternoon before—and sometimes early on the morning of the hearing—all serve as gentle reminders of the importance of this particular testimony.

Yet, if your witness is not warned about that sure-fire question, it is quite possible that he or she will flub it, causing some on the committee to dismiss the credibility of the prepared statement. That is why rehearsals with your witness are essential.

How to Answer Questions Well

Another point about answering questions: Do not give more information than is requested. To avoid this, unless you are absolutely sure, rephrase the question to ensure that you do understand it but do not make this a habit.

Often, a friendly member will pose a question that is not recognized or perceived as helpful. This can be worse than not answering, and so witnesses should be briefed about the lineup of the committee. That is why it is a good idea to sit in on earlier sessions of the same hearing. Not only can you quickly pick up the mood of the committee but, more important, you can determine who is actually asking what kind of question. Often the questions of elected officials center around problems peculiar to their district, and so if references in the prepared testimony can be easily worked up to show how things affect different states or congressional districts, testimony becomes much more pertinent and alive.

A good example of this occurred some years ago when the then-Postmaster General, Larry O'Brien, was arguing for changes in parcel post zone rates. All citations and references he made were between states and cities that not so coincidentally were represented by members of the Post Office Committee. Because it involved geography, he was able to tie together in specific ways all the cities covered by the committee members.

That might have seemed like an obvious ploy, but it is one that all too often witnesses simply ignore. Again, it is the simple technique that brings things home to the audience.

Another technique, again an obvious one, is to address representatives or senators by their names when responding to questions. This might require some work on the part of the NPO executive or staff, but it does pay off.

If time permits, it is also highly useful for witnesses to meet with the members of the committee before testifying. Sometimes this can only be accomplished in a brief coffee or quick handshake immediately before testimony—but even this is better than cold confrontation without any prior meeting.

Come to Town Early

Sitting through a session can also be useful to help a witness become more comfortable in strange surroundings, even though it means coming to town a bit early. It is similar to the advantage home teams have when they are on their own turf.

A basic point to remember about answering questions is not to be argumentative. Be firm. Be forceful. Be positive. Be witty. But *never* argue. You are not at home or at your office. Even if you are right, you just will not win. Although other members of the committee may actually agree with you, they seldom will do so in public, and congressional courtesy will compel them to defend a fellow member, especially if that member is with the same political party.

Another tip: Keep track of your witness. Know his or her itinerary. Not all congressional hearings come off as scheduled. Sometimes, because of other witnesses' problems yours might be asked, as a favor, to go on earlier than planned. If you are ready, and the chairperson is grateful for your adaptability, you can win points. Similarly, if the session is suddenly cancelled, it is important to know your witnesses' whereabouts (including flight numbers in case you have to stop them at a distant airport) to advise the revised plans.

The best position for a witness is usually to be in the leadoff spot, although this is usually reserved for cabinet members and administration spokespersons. Worst is to be last witness on an afternoon—a Friday afternoon. In that case it might be better to mail in your statement.

PR Value of Pictures

Many NPO executives fail to recognize fully the public relations value—inside and outside of the organization—that can be derived from appearances before congressional committees. Have photographs taken of your witness, if possible. Although some committees are lax in enforcing them, the Rules of the House forbid photographs during the hearings themselves. The best time is just before they open or during a break. The Senate is much more relaxed in this regard, consequently more pictures are made.

Retaining a photographer to take the pictures can pay off in good relations on many scores. I have found it useful to have group pictures taken of witnesses chatting with the chairperson or with key members of the committee. These can be used in organization bulletins and sometimes in local news publications. In addition, it is good member relations to send copies to the witnesses themselves. If further publicity is desired, send copies to smaller dailies and weekly publications in each witness's hometown. This can add a public relations plus.

Although it may be a little more effort, it is worth the work to ask the member of Congress to autograph a print and to have this sent to the witness. I have visited many organization members' homes and have found autographed pictures occupying prominent places. To judge from the number of requests for extra prints from witnesses I've worked with, it is really worth the investment.

Getting Out Press Releases

Testimony also can serve as the basis for news releases to the nonprofit sector publications, sometimes for the witnesses' major hometown dailies, and occasionally for the broadcast networks or major wire services.

Unless there is an unusual flare-up in the committee room—and this is not advised since this is not the arena to conduct an argument—most coverage will be slight, even if it is a light news day. In fact, most hearings are largely ignored except by the industry trade press.

One way to hype the possibility of media coverage is to make it easier for reporters to handle the story. This is where preparation can help. It is wise to have the public relations staff in on the testimony from the beginning; their wise counsel every step of the way can play an important part in eventual success.

Another tip you might find useful is to turn over the nearly complete testimony to an experienced news writer; if there is none on the staff, retain a writer for just these occasions. Ask him or her to look over the draft text and seek a compelling lead for the harried wire service reporter. The reporter probably can, but usually will find the going difficult under pressure. The answer might lie in letting this trained reporter recast a few phrases to punch them up and make them more colorful. These, even if buried midway in the testimony, will be what the reporters ferret out when they try to summarize your organization's remarks in two or three paragraphs. Having gone this far, it is best to prepare your own news release to accompany the statement. We do this regularly for retainer and ad hoc clients.

Don't Get Carried Away

Caution: Do not overdo the zingy line and get carried away, but a well-turned phrase, one that is catchy and timely, can make a dull statement come alive. I grant that it is not easy to come by, and the PR pro, either on staff or retained, should not be fired if he or she cannot produce one every time—though it should be sought.

A point that not all experienced witnesses agree on concerns summary statements. Some argue that providing a summary at the end of the text only encourages committee members to skip quickly to it and then prepare questions based on compressed statements, not on those carefully constructed words with all the squishy adjectives. My rebuttal: It all depends. If the basic statement is less than a dozen pages, there probably is no need for a summary. If it is more, a summary will be helpful. It certainly does make it easier for the witness who is suddenly forced to summarize his or her statement. It also can be useful for staffers when reviewing the testimony of several dozen witnesses.

In any case, if you decide to use the summary, be sure to state the points in order of importance and give close attention to the precise wording since the summary becomes an official document or statement of position. Just because it is done last does not mean that it should be done in such a hurry that it is not done carefully!

Depending on the committee, 50 to 75 copies of the testimony should be prepared in advance to conform to rules. And not only does committee staff need additional copies for perusal in advance, each member of the committee requires one and, in addition, the Senate and House press galleries regularly send messengers to each committee room to fetch extra copies of texts. In reality, you may often need 200 to 500 copies of the text, particularly if you want key industry members to be aware of what was told to the legislators.

Press Release Distribution

If the situation warrants, extra copies of the testimony could be sent or placed in the press rack at the National Press Club for distribution to correspondents and others unable to attend the hearings in person.

There are also commercial services in Washington that, for a modest fee, will send your release and statement by messenger to some 500 news outlets—thus giving you the broadest possible coverage. There are also some good commercial services that will distribute the essence electronically.

With all those steps to follow, you might ask how long the process takes. Sometimes it is months, but you often may have weeks or sometimes only days or hours—hardly enough time to complete all the steps in the circuit. For emergency hearings, the only solution is to bring the testimony team or key witnesses into the capital so that all can meet together. The matter of producing timely testimony in proper shape is one that requires considerable scheduling skill—and often a lot of overtime.

Having quick writers on call who are knowledgeable of the subject and of the organization's nuances is a necessity. A battery of typists and access to quick duplicating services is another must. I have been in situations where witnesses ahead of *our* witness's appearance or an unexpected line of questioning caused us to rewrite huge hunks of our testimony. Getting group approval of new approaches has sometimes meant polishing the final phrases late at night or early in the morning.

Fresh Crew of Typists

Since the hearings usually begin at 10 o'clock, we have found it most effective to have a fresh crew of typists ready to come in one or two nights before to begin the all-important work of preparing the final text and of duplicating and collating sufficient copies for presentation the next day. It is best, of course, to anticipate all possible exigencies and do this work well ahead, but this is not always possible, and so contingency planning is often required. Word processors and high-speed duplicating machines have helped considerably with this chore.

Once the testimony has been delivered, it can also serve as material for speeches and can even be reproduced as a booklet to send to members of the legislative committees, your board of directors, and so on. In short, if the witness truly says something important and memorable, the good NPO executive should ensure that the seeds that are cast do not fall on rocky soil.

The Need for Extra Copies

The point is, the life of testimony before Congress can easily be extended with a little forethought and planning. Although many PR people first think of newspaper and broadcast coverage, consider the value of well-prepared testimony as the basis for a major article, even in a popular magazine. It certain can serve as the thesis for a major piece in an important industry trade publication.

Finally, because researchers and reporters and others need backup documents months and sometimes years after the testimony has been given, it is useful to have additional file copies handy as basic reference material to illustrate the tone and the mood of the industry at that point.

Once it is all done, there is nothing like a personal, warm letter of thanks to the chairperson and any staffers—individually, please—who have been particularly helpful. Despite the reams of written materials NPO's produce, you might be surprised how often even experienced NPO executives forget this simple courtesy. But make sure it's personalized!

Be sure, of course, not to make the thank you too routine. Relate it to the witness, his or her feelings and reactions. This also can be a good time to send along additional material requested, but it is not advisable to send along additional viewpoints unless they are truly gems. You had your time in court.

In short—the few minutes spent testifying in the hearing room are but the beginning of a long chain of events. That is why it is so important to take extreme care at all stages in preparing for an appearance before Congress or any legislative or regulatory body.

You may spend only a few minutes giving testimony. But you can influence legislation that helps or hurts the members of your organization for a long time to come.

There really is no way you can avoid the time spent in thorough preparation. What you do to get your witnesses ready for their appearance, how you prepare them—these are the elements of success.

Tips on Writing to Congress

1. Keep your letters as brief and to the point as possible.

2. Write on your business or personal letterhead, if possible, and sign your name over your *typed* signature at the end of your message.

3. Identify your subject clearly. State the name of the legislation about which you are writing. Give the House or Senate bill number, if you know it or the short abbreviation or nickname of the bill.

4. State your reason for writing. Your own personal or professional experience is your best supporting evidence. Explain how the issue would affect you, or your family, business, or profession—or what effect it could have on your state or community.

5. Do not "cry wolf." Not every governmental action is going to put you out of business, and members of Congress give little credence to that claim *unless* you can prove it conclusively. And even then it is a relatively common argument.

6. Avoid being argumentative. Make your points as succinctly as possible, but remember that you are not engaged in a debate—presumably you are trying to "convince."

7. Be careful in the way you categorize those who disagree with you. Name calling distracts attention from the point you want to make.

8. If you have met the member of Congress personally or have some connection over and above that of a constituent, draw attention to it in your letter if you feel it is necessary.

9. Ask your legislator to state his or her position on the issue in replying. As a constituent, you are entitled to know. Read what they reply carefully, for sometimes they send enigmatic answers.

10. Do not be discouraged if you get what appears to be a "form" letter in return. Many congressional offices are swamped with mail and are forced to wait some time before drafting personal responses. Depending on the issue, size of the staff, etc., you may not receive a personal response to your letter.

11. Consider the factor of timing. Try to write your position on a bill while it is in committee or subcommittee or if it soon will be. Your senators and representatives can usually be more responsive to your appeal at that time than later when the bill has already been approved by a committee. Of course, this is not

always so. Sometimes legislators reserve judgment—and their votes—until the sentiment of their constituencies has crystallized.

12. Do not write to your legislators only when you have a complaint. Let them know when they have voted in a way that pleases you or have taken another action you like.

13. In other words, be sure to congratulate members of Congress when they do something you approve of. All too often, constituents forget this important point; thus, the majority of congressional mail tends toward "the complaint side" rather than the "congratulatory side." Praise is more likely to be remembered.

14. Write only when other forms of personal communication are not realistically available. When you can, attempt to talk to your representatives when they are home in your district; they are more likely to listen and respond then. When you are in Washington, drop by and try to talk to your senators and representatives. Since they are *busy* people, do not feel put down if you talk to a staff aide.

15. Never threaten political or other consequences if the legislator refuses to see it your way. Although few respond to blatant power plays, this does not mean that you or your colleagues should be totally subservient.

16. Think twice, even three times, before sending local newspapers the text of your letter. It puts the legislator on the spot and will not help long-term relationships. You may, however, wish to write print media a special brief explanation about an issue in public mind.

17. Avoid pattern phrases and sentences that give the appearance of "form" letters. They tend to identify your message as part of an organized pressure campaign—and produce little or no impact, unless received in huge quantities—and I mean huge.

18. Send your Washington public affairs counsel informational copies of your correspondence and significant responses you may receive.

The following are suggested addresses and salutations:

Honorable John Doe	Honorable John Doe
United States Senate	House of Representatives
Washington, D.C. 20510	Washington, D.C. 20515
Dear Senator Doe:	Dear Mr. Doe:

You might close with Sincerely yours,.

If you know the senator or representative on a personal basis, you may address her or him by first name, and the complimentary close can be as warm a greeting as you care to use.

Note: To obtain copies of bills, you can ask your representative or senator to send them to you, or for faster service, you can obtain up to three free by sending a self-addressed label and a note asking for the bill by number to:

Document Room	Document Room
U.S. House of Representatives	U.S. Senate
Washington, D.C. 20515	Washington, D.C. 20510

Daly's "Dozen Tips for Long-Term Success in Government Affairs"[*]

1. The old values—"integrity," "trust," and "knowledge"—still count.

2. People still make the difference; know well as many as possible. Keep in reasonable contact.

3. Keep abreast of current developments; anticipate important social trends, new lifestyles, and consumerist needs.

4. Keep figuring out what the "real" problem is, but remain ever alert to hidden dangers.

5. Embrace (rather than resist) change; understand how it can be beneficial. Timing can be everything.

6. There are not just two sides (but several) to every question; try to figure out most of them.

7. Understand governmental processes well; know *how* the machinery operates (and who operates it).

8. Learn to think like a government bureaucrat—but also *not* to *act* like one!

9. Since the political or emotional elements in an equation are almost always more important than the logical ones, be aware of their impact. Can you harness them to work for you?

10. Find where changing levers and buttons of power are; learn how to "push" or "pull"—and when to *ignore* them.

11. When needed, utilize the ricochet technique to *really* get a power broker's *attention.* Who does he or she truly heed?

12. Structure your strategy for the long haul; do not fail to keep *everlastingly* at it!

---

[*]A free catalog describing 70+ tipsheets about this subject and related communications topics is available by contacting the author at: 702 World Center Building, Washington, D.C. 20006.

PART 6

Financial Management and Administration

45
Nonprofit Accounting and Financial Reporting

Barron H. Harvey

Ph.D., C.P.A., Howard University

Horton L. Sorkin

Ph.D., Howard University

Historical Overview

Inadequacies in Financial Reports

Until recent years, financial reporting by nonprofit organizations (NPOs) has been of relatively little interest to nonmanagement board members and the general public. An attitude of permissiveness, which focused on good works and a desire to minimize administrative costs, has permitted the issuance of financial statements that were often incomplete and misleading. Fund-raisers, in an effort to build a climate responsive to their appeal, have tended to influence reporting in a way that emphasizes financial need. The accounting profession has either ignored the area entirely or has made excuses for inadequate reporting, often specifically excluding NPOs when accounting principles were promulgated.

Expansion of State Regulation

Some recognition that this state of affairs was not in the public interest developed in the late 1950s. At that time, one particularly well publicized charity fraud led to the expanded requirement in several states that specified financial data be filed annually with a branch of state government. This has since expanded to the point where more than forty states now impose some type of reporting.

Health and Welfare Standards

Since voluntary health and welfare organizations were among the most vulnerable to the adverse public reaction resulting from public charges of incomplete, inconsistent, and misleading financial reports, this sector of the nonprofit field reacted. A broadly representative committee was formed under the sponsorship of the National Health Council and the National Social Welfare Assembly to attempt to develop industry standards. The result was publication in 1964 of *Standards of Accounting and Financial Reporting for Voluntary Health and Welfare Organizations.*[1]

This book, for the first time, attempted to deal with the broad range of accounting principles applicable to these organizations and to illustrate financial presentations that might serve as standards. The member agencies of the National Health Council, including most of the nation's largest voluntary health and welfare organizations, agreed to follow voluntarily the recommendations of the *Standards.*

Hospital Developments

During the 1960s the hospital sector, spurred in part by the growth of third parties as the principal providers of hospital revenues, recognized the need for more consistent and improved financial reports. The American Hospital Association issued a number of publications[2] designed to move the hospital industry toward such uniformity.

University Guidelines

Similarly, the nation's colleges developed accounting guidelines. Industry groups working with the American Council on Education issued a number of publications over the years, including, in 1968, the second edition of *College and University Business Administration.*[3] This provided significant guidance in a number of business and related areas, including financial reporting.

Other Developments

By comparison, almost nothing was happening to deal with the problems of the thousands of other organizations. However, among the more significant of the industry-type efforts, the Catholic Bishops did issue *Diocesan Accounting and Financial Reporting*[4] in 1971; the Club Managers Association of America updated *Uniform System of Accounts for Clubs*[5] in 1967; the National Association of Independent Schools published *Accounting for Independent Schools*[6] in 1969 and updated it in 1977; and the Association of Science-Technology Centers developed *Museum Accounting Guidelines*[7] in 1976.

Lack of Accounting Profession Involvement

Notably absent in these activities was the American Institute of Certified Public Accountants (AICPA). Although accounting principles may become "generally accepted" by usage, they normally are not binding unless officially sanctioned by the accounting profession. The Accounting Principles Committee and later the Accounting Principles Board of the AICPA almost entirely ignored the needs of nonprofit organizations.

Initial Audit Guides

Nevertheless, the AICPA did begin to move haltingly in the mid-1960s to provide limited direction through the issuance of "audit guides." These booklets, although not carrying the weight of official pronouncements, do represent the best thought of the profession, and practitioners may be called upon to justify departures.

The first of these was issued in 1967 and dealt with voluntary health and welfare organizations.[8] Although it provided useful information regarding approaches to auditing, the guide did little to narrow the wide range of alternative accounting principles being followed.

Thus, for all practical purposes, the nonprofit sector entered the 1970s with no official guidance from the accounting profession. In fact, what little guidance did exist could be interpreted to say that nonprofit organizations were not covered by generally accepted accounting principles and that their financial statements could be viewed as "special-purpose reports."

Pressure for Improvement

However, the pressures had been building during the 1960s for more meaningful financial reports from the nonprofit sector. Government was spending an ever-increasing amount for health, education, and welfare services being delivered by these organizations. Government was also having difficulty in later determining from the financial reports how the funds had been used. The general public was becoming considerably more sophisticated and concerned about both the cost and the quality of services being delivered. Probably of greatest importance, however, was the fact that members sitting on the boards of exempt organizations no longer were satisfied to ignore their fiscal responsibilities. These developments, coupled with ever-increasing calls for action from within the accounting profession, finally moved the AICPA to take action.

Authoritative Literature

Early in the 1970s, several AICPA committees began work on definitive audit guides. As might be expected, the areas to receive first attention were those where the industry had already initiated its own efforts. The first result of this work was the publication in 1972 of the *Hospital Audit Guide.*[9] Next was *Audits of Colleges and Universities*[10] in 1973, and finally, *Audits of Voluntary Health and Welfare Organizations*[11] in 1974. In each of these projects, the AICPA committees consulted extensively with industry representatives. However, certain differences in basic accounting principles between the AICPA guides and the existing industry literature developed. These and other needs for modification resulted in the issuance in 1974 of a revised edition of *College and University Business Administration*[12] and an AICPA *Statement of Position* to amend the 1973 university audit guide.[13] In addition, a 1974 revision of *Standards of Accounting and Financial Reporting for Voluntary Health and Welfare Organizations*[14] was issued. At the same time, United Way of America published its *Accounting and Financial Reporting—A Guide for United Ways and Not-for-Profit Human Service Organizations.*[15]

Filer Commission Study

These audit guides were significant in helping to standardize accounting and financial reporting, at least for the types of organizations specifically covered. Unfortunately, a broad spectrum of nonprofit organizations was still left to its own devices in selecting accounting principles and reporting formats. This was clearly illustrated in the *Accounting Advisory Committee Report to the Commission on Private Philanthropy and Public Needs*[16] (Filer Commission) in 1974.

This survey of then-current nonprofit accounting practices demonstrated the existing chaos in financial reporting both among and within segments of the industry. In addition, it pointed out the seemingly illogical differences in accounting for certain transactions and in recommended reporting principles among the three audit guides.

Nonprofit Accounting Statement

Partially in response to the interest generated by the report of the Accounting Advisory Committee, the AICPA Accounting Standards Executive Committee (AcSEC) formed a Subcommittee on Accounting for Nonprofit Organizations in 1975. This group was charged with the task of developing a statement of position on nonprofit accounting principles for organizations *not* covered by existing AICPA literature. Early in 1977, the subcommittee issued a discussion draft for public comment containing a tentative set of accounting principles and reporting practices. This draft generated considerable response, with a wide divergence of opinion in several areas. The subcommittee reviewed the results of the public exposure in the latter part of 1977 and issued a final draft statement of position for public comment in 1978. After approval by AcSEC, the statement[17] was presented to the Financial Accounting Standards Board (FASB).

Financial Accounting Standards Board

In 1977 the Financial Accounting Standards Board (FASB), the official rule-making body of the profession, commissioned an exploratory research study of the conceptual issues relating to financial accounting in nonbusiness organizations. The results of this research, *Financial Accounting In Nonbusiness Organizations*,[18] was published in May 1978 and identified basic issues and the principal matters to consider in their resolution. A discussion memorandum entitled *An Analysis of Issues Related to Conceptual Framework for Financial Accounting and Reporting: Objectives of Financial Reporting by Nonbusiness Organizations*[19] was issued in June 1978, requesting public comment. In December 1980, FASB issued Concepts Statement No. 420 (SFAC 4), entitled "Objectives of Financial Reporting by Nonbusiness Organizations."[20] A "concept statement" does not contain sufficient detail to provide how-to information for the actual preparation of financial statements. The statement describes "concepts and relations that will underlie future financial accounting standards and practices and in due course serve as a basis for evaluating existing standards and practices." As was expected, SFAC 4 has had only negligible impact on current practice up to now. FASB stated that itself would "likely be the most direct beneficiary" because the statement "will guide the Board in developing accounting and reporting standards." SFAC 4 therefore is of interest to the practitioner primarily as a framework for anticipating changes in the permissible methods of generating and presenting financial information for NPOs.

Future Reconciliation

With the completion of the nonprofit statement, the AICPA now has four guides for nongovernmental nonprofit organizations. As previously noted, the existing guides differ with respect to certain basic issues (e.g., health and welfare organizations and hospitals record depreciation; colleges and universities do not). The new statement differs in some ways from each of the other three. Accordingly, it is anticipated that one final effort will be made by an ongoing AICPA committee to reconcile the differences so that the underlying logic and accounting principles will be both sound and consistent. This potentially could result in modifications to the guides.

Focus on the Real Purposes

Although the record has not been good, it is clear that both the motivation and skills needed to provide the nonprofit sector with adequate techniques for reporting on its financial affairs are now in place. Although the outcome of the individual issues may be debated, it is universally recognized that the nonprofit sector cannot survive without fiscal credibility. The ability to report the financial record in a clear and understandable way will permit the development of fund-raising appeals based on financial facts. It will also permit the first steps in qualitative cost-benefit determinations which may be critical to the long-term survival of nonprofit organizations as a viable "third-sector" alternative to government and business in our society.

Key Accounting Concepts

Purpose of Financial Reports

Underlying any decisions regarding the techniques to be employed in preparation of an organization's financial statements is the need to focus on the purposes for which they are prepared. Normally, the management and active board members have access to detailed financial data needed to measure progress against stated goals. However, others outside of this group also have a legitimate interest in the affairs of the entity. It is for this latter group—contributors, third-party payers, members, beneficiaries, regulators, the general public—as well as for board members, that generally accepted accounting principles are needed to permit preparation of comparable and understandable annual financial statements.

Income Recognition

Earnings Concept. The development of nonprofit financial reports is significantly impacted by the view taken of the process of income recognition. One approach considers that all receipts, with the exception of unrestricted contributions, must be "earned" in order to be retained. This concept most parallels that of commercial enterprises and provides a rationale for matching of income and expense as well as for considering certain contributions to have been made directly to the "capital" of the entity. Under this approach, which is essentially followed by hospitals and by universities, restricted expendable contributions are not reflected in the operating statement until spent.

Proponents of this concept note that since the operating statement most parallels that of a commercial business entity, it is more readily understood by business executives and the public generally. Critics point out the difficulty of relating fund-raising costs to results, since restricted contributions are not shown in the operating statement until spent. Dispute also exists regarding the bypassing of the operating statement entirely for property and endowment gifts, which are reported directly in fund balances.

Stewardship Concept. An alternative approach followed by voluntary health and welfare organizations focuses on the stewardship responsibility of the entity. Under this approach, the operating statement is designed to reflect the changes in assets made available to the organization to conduct its programs. Although certain revenues under this concept are matched with related costs (such as ticket sales and special event expenses), public support, whether restricted or not, is reported when available to the organization. Program and supporting service costs are reflected in the period incurred. This technique also requires that *all* support, including property and endowment gifts, be included in the determination of the net change in stewardship responsibility for the year.

Proponents of this approach point out the ability of the reader of the financial statements to focus on the entire activity of the entity in the operating statement, rather than on selected transactions. They believe that contributions are not "earned." Accordingly, restricted contributions and costs of operation are related only in that total contributions limit the scope of programs that may be conducted. Critics focus on the possible misunderstanding that may result by reporting an excess for the year, however labeled, which includes amounts that must be retained for permanent investment, property additions, or specified restricted purposes.

Compromise Revenue Concept. The 1978 AICPA statement of nonprofit accounting principles suggests a third alternative. It would require reporting property and endowment gifts in the determination of the net change in stewardship for the year with appropriate segregation and disclosure of the "capital" nature of these gifts. However, gifts restricted for operating purposes by contributors would be reflected as deferred liabilities until spent, at which time "support" in amounts equal to the restricted activity expenses would be reported in the operating statement. A related and highly significant rule would necessitate that donor restrictions be considered to have been met whenever *any* costs are incurred that would legally satisfy the restriction. Thus, management would lose some flexibility in this area.

Those who favor this approach consider it to be a best representation of the economic facts, since it is possible that restricted gifts might be returned to the contributors if not spent. In addition, the requirement that restricted gifts be considered to have been spent whenever any costs are incurred that fall within the parameters of the restriction helps avoid possible "window dressing." This might be considered to have occurred when an organization would elect to charge unrestricted funds with all operating costs, even to the point of creating a deficit, while restricted funds are retained that might have been used for these purposes.

Critics maintain that the board of directors has the legal obligation to determine the proper uses for the funds entrusted to it and that this accounting rule may infringe on the ability to do so. Some would also argue that a concept of "capital" is as valid for a nonprofit entity as it is for a commercial one. Accordingly, at least property and endowment gifts are the equivalent of contributions of capital to a corporation by its stockholders, thereby justifying reporting of the receipt of these amounts directly in fund balances.

Need for Resolution. The ultimate resolution of this issue is critical to the development of an underlying conceptual framework that will provide a basis for consistent financial presentation of the same facts by different types of nonprofit organizations. In the meantime, it is particularly important that the footnotes to the financial statements adequately disclose which principles have been employed.

Fund Accounting

To help assure that restrictions imposed by contributors are met, nonprofit organizations have traditionally employed fund accounting. This is a bookkeeping technique whereby separate self-balancing sets of asset, liability, income, expense, and fund balance accounts are maintained for each restricted gift or type of restriction. In addition, to help track compliance with self-imposed restrictions established by boards of directors, additional funds have often been set up or, in some cases, board-designated assets have been added to donor-restricted funds.

Reporting of Funds in Financial Statements.
Depending on the view taken of the nature of funds, as well as the purposes of financial reporting, nonprofit organizations have prepared financial statements with varying degrees of fund detail. Prior to the development of industry guidelines, some universities issued financial statements reporting on the activity in all funds—well over 100 in some cases. Although factual and informative, at least in a technical sense, such forms of financial reporting defied comprehension in terms of the overall activities and status of the organization.

With the development of accounting principles for at least some portion of the nonprofit sector, it has been acknowledged that grouping of funds with similar restrictions is essential for financial statement purposes. However, there continue to be differences regarding the propriety of presenting combined fund data as well as in the degree to which it is appropriate to combine third-party and internally restricted assets. However, agreement does exist with respect to the basic fund groupings.

Unrestricted funds. Those available for use at the full discretion of the board

Restricted funds. Those over which third-party restrictions exist, but which are available for expenditure when the restricted activity is conducted

Property funds. Those which are restricted for or already invested in fixed assets

Endowment funds. Those which by third-party restriction must be invested for a specified period or in perpetuity to generate income for general or specific purposes

Annuity funds. Those required to be maintained with amounts contributed for this purpose to provide income to a beneficiary and ultimately make a remainder available for the organization

Loan funds. Those required by agreement to be maintained on a revolving basis for loan to others

Custodial funds. Those for which bookkeeping and custodial services are provided for another entity which controls the use of the funds

Combined Fund Reporting.
The form of financial reporting presently followed by universities treats the separate funds as entities in themselves. Accordingly, total data for all funds are not shown, and it is somewhat difficult to determine the overall status and operating results, particularly since certain interfund transfers are reported with support and expenses in the respective funds.

Hospitals generally report on a basis whereby a single-column operating statement is used (restricted contributions are included in this statement only when spent). However, fully separate balance sheets and statements of changes in fund balances for each fund group are illustrated in the industry audit guide.

Voluntary health and welfare organizations typically use columnar operating statements, which show the activity for each fund as well as a total column. Either layered (fully separate) or columnar balance sheets are used.

The nonprofit accounting statement indicates a strong preference for total all-funds data. In addition, illustrative financial statements include examples that reflect combined expendable and combined nonexpendable data.

Impact on Contributors.   The current controversy regarding the best technique for reporting information regarding respective funds is fueled by a perception that simplistic overviews may be misleading. In order for NPOs to survive, they must look to parties outside the organization for support. These sources must understand that although endowment and fixed assets may create large fund balances, the organization may nevertheless be legitimately in need of current operating support. At the same time, adequate understanding requires that the data be presented in a way in which the overall operation and status are clear. To some extent this issue involves many of the same considerations involved in the development of techniques for reporting consolidated financial statements for business entities. The trend appears to be toward statements that will provide an overview as well as disclosure of restrictions imposed by third parties.

Combined Entity Reporting

Of probably even greater significance to many nonprofit organizations is the issue of combined financial reporting with related entities. Often control over these entities is clear and complete. However, unlike commercial organizations for which relationships may be more readily determined by stock ownership, many NPOs maintain loose affiliations or are serviced by auxiliaries over which they exercise little control. Nevertheless, these relationships must be probed in order to determine if an organization's financial statements are complete without including those of the affiliate. To date, the accounting profession has provided little guidance with respect to this issue.

Hospital Foundations.   Hospitals are particularly concerned with this issue. Developments in this industry over the last 10 years have shifted hospital revenue sources from private patients to third parties. Government, through Medicare and Medicaid programs, and insurance, through Blue Cross and other plans, have increasingly established hospital operating costs as the basis for reimbursement. Due to the significant escalation in health care costs caused by inflation, upgrading of compensation levels to attract and retain competent personnel, and technological advances, the third parties have also increasingly attempted to limit increases in reimbursement. For example, Medicare regulations require that the first possible qualifying costs be charged to funds restricted by contributors for specific operating purposes, so that the remaining cost pool to be reimbursed will be lower. Effectively, this has the result of using contributors' gifts to underwrite governmental programs rather than to enhance the quality of health care.

In view of this erosion of the giving base and the more significant threat to require offset of all gifts in the future, some hospitals have established foundations to solicit contributions on their behalf. Similarly, university foundations are often established to solicit and hold funds for ultimate use by state-owned universities. In these instances also, direct contributions to the institutions might simply result in reduced governmental appropriations.

Criteria for Combination.   The nonprofit accounting statement proposes criteria along the following lines as an aid in determining when financial statements of significant affiliates should be combined for fair presentation. They should be when the "parent" organization controls the affiliate; i.e., the parent has the ability, directly or indirectly, to cause the direction of the management and policies of the affiliate, whether through ownership or by contract or otherwise, and one of the following circumstances exists:

1. The affiliate raises funds in the name of the parent and substantially all proceeds are transferred to or used at the discretion of the parent.

2. The parent transfers some of its resources to a separate entity whose resources are held for the benefit of the parent.

3. The parent assigns functions to an affiliate whose funding is primarily derived from sources other than public contributions.

This requirement would have the effect of presenting financial statements that include all assets ultimately available to the organization and would eliminate misleading reporting. For example, a case of abuse in this area was cited in a recent congressional investigation of charitable activities. In this instance, an organization in one state incurred high fund-raising costs as compared with amounts collected. The organization avoided the problem by obtaining a contribution from a related organization in another state, which resulted in an overall favorable relationship between total reported contributions and total fund-raising costs. Combined financial statements would have eliminated this opportunity for abuse and presented a fairer picture of the activities of the entity as a whole.

Probable Solution.   Establishing separate legal entities to house a portion of the assets will in the long run not stand the test of fair financial presentation. It is also not likely that such action will effectively shield these funds from third-party consideration. The underlying issue regarding financing of services must be dealt with on its merits rather than through the presentation of incomplete financial data. Similarly, agencies that use a common name to appeal for funds through a series of entities must face the issue of presenting combined data. The ultimate use of amounts transferred internally must be adequately reported, and the costs of fund-raising at all levels must be shown in a way that permits a determination of the results of the combined effort. Accordingly, it is likely that the accounting profession will move to require combined financial reporting in those circumstances where the control criteria noted above exist, whether exercised or not.

Property Accounting

Accounting for fixed assets has historically been one of the most controversial areas of nonprofit accounting. Extensive and conflicting hypotheses have been developed to relate the flow of capital in a nonprofit entity to funding and replacement concepts that differ from commercial entities. As a result, every possible combination of accounting techniques is presently in use by one NPO or another.

Capitalization of Assets.   Some organizations have capitalized fixed assets at their acquisition cost (or fair market value if received as a gift). Others have consistently charged all fixed assets to expense when acquired. Clearly, the trend is in favor of capitalization—the audit guides for hospitals, universities, and voluntary health and welfare organizations as well as the nonprofit accounting statement all provide for this accounting. Omission of the cost of significant fixed assets from the balance sheet understates stewardship responsibility and misstates financial position.

Depreciation. The theories regarding the propriety of depreciating fixed assets are many and varied. Some hold that a depreciation charge is appropriate only if an actual cash replacement fund is established in a like amount. Others indicate that since contributors paid for the assets to begin with, reporting of depreciation would somehow constitute a double "charge" to the contributor. Still others focus on the problems caused by inflation and the inadequacies of a cost-based accounting process, thereby concluding that depreciation for such entities may be unnecessary and impractical.

Present Practice. The motivation to give recognition to depreciation increases when the organization is reimbursed for these costs. Accordingly, with the advent of Medicare in the 1960s, hospitals readily accepted and adopted depreciation accounting. Voluntary health and welfare organizations also have adopted depreciation accounting. However, their focus was more on the accounting concepts involved than the immediate promise of additional funding. Essentially, this concept focuses on the need to report all costs associated with the conduct of the exempt activity and identifies the use of fixed assets as one of these costs. Fully expensing the cost of fixed assets in the year of acquisition overstates the costs of that period, understates those of succeeding periods, and never reports how the assets are used to accomplish the exempt purpose. Capitalization without depreciation understates the costs of operation, as illustrated by statements of organizations that differ only in that one owns its building while the other rents. University financial statements would differ from one another in this way since depreciation is not presently required, although as a practical matter, almost all own their property.

Trends. Depreciation accounting is proposed by the nonprofit accounting statement. Again the trend seems clear. It is relevant to determine the cost of providing services as an essential part of reporting on the stewardship process. Whenever fixed assets are significant in amount, their cost should be allocated in a systematic and rational manner over their useful lives. This is neither a process of funding or replacement, which are budgeting and financing issues, but simply a matter of associating the costs of facilities and equipment with the programs for which they are used.

Investments

To some extent, nonprofit organizations have been ahead of the business sector in developing meaningful techniques for reporting investment activity. Traditional, generally accepted accounting principles have been based on an underlying rule learned by all accountants in their first week of basic accounting study, that is, "anticipate no profits and provide for all losses." Accordingly, commercial accounting requires carrying investments at values no higher than cost and writing them down to market in certain instances. This accounting gives no recognition to the fact that a decision to hold a security is as much an investment decision as is a decision to buy or sell. Thus, at least in the case of readily marketable securities, a better measure of stewardship is attained by relating investment income to the market value of the portfolio rather than to its original cost.

Cost-or-Market Alternative.   Present accounting for universities, for voluntary health and welfare organizations, and that proposed by the nonprofit accounting statement, permits carrying investments at cost or at market, provided only that the option chosen is followed consistently. The hospital audit guide provides only for traditional cost-based accounting.

Clarification Needed.   Although the use of market as a basis for reporting investments should provide a better measure of management effectiveness and of the current financial status of the organization, the fact that cost may also be elected results in inconsistency and confusion. Again, organizations with exactly the same financial situation might report vastly different status and results due solely to the basis used for reporting investments.

Receivables

Since the accrual basis of accounting has been or will shortly be the only acceptable basis of accounting for nonprofit organizations, income should be recorded when earned, even if not yet received. Accordingly, receivables must be recorded, some of which, such as legacies, pledges, and grants, are unique to these types of entities.

Legacies.   Problems are often encountered in determining the time at which recognition should be given in the financial statements to legacies and bequests. Although income from this source is often significant, uncertainties exist regarding possible other claims against the estate as well as potential market value changes while the assets are under control of the executor. As a result, it has been generally acknowledged that legacies receivable should be recorded at the time that an unassailable right has been established in favor of the organization and the proceeds are measurable in amount. Normally, this is late in the legal process. Prior to this time, the organization should disclose in a footnote the existence of such contingent assets.

Pledges.   Pledges of future support are solicited by many organizations, ranging from local United Way campaigns to university building-fund drives. However, guidance from the AICPA regarding accounting for this source of income is also conflicting at present. Universities are permitted the option of recording such pledges or of simply disclosing their existence in a footnote. Hospitals and health and welfare organizations are required to recognize written pledges as assets, subject to normal evaluation procedures needed to provide for estimated uncollected amounts. Since the nonprofit accounting statement also would require recording pledges, it appears clear that this technique will ultimately prevail.

A related issue involves the time at which recorded pledges receivable should be recognized as income. The nonprofit accounting statement would permit deferral in the liability section of the balance sheet of pledges containing a payment schedule until each scheduled payment date arrives. This gives recognition to the effective restriction imposed by the contributor in establishing the payment schedule; that is, in the absence of language to the contrary, the support is restricted for future use.

Grants.   Grants receivable are simply a type of pledge receivable, although the term is normally associated with institutions, foundations, and government agencies rather than individual givers. The *University Audit Guide* takes the position that grants not yet funded should not be recorded until services are provided. However, the nonprofit accounting statement provides that grants which are the equivalent of contributions should be recorded at the time the recipient receives notification. Income should be recognized during the periods to which the grant applies. If silent, the payment schedule will determine the proper period.

Some grants, however, take the form of contracts requiring performance on the part of the recipient before entitlement to the grant is established. In these cases, percentage of completion accounting is normally appropriate.

Grants Payable

The nonprofit accounting statement provides that recognition should be given to the liability for grants awarded to others at the time that written notification is sent to the recipient. Even though the grant may contain a payment schedule, the liability of the granting organization is established at this point and expense should be recorded for the full amount. The fact that the recipient organization may consider future scheduled payments to be an effective restriction and therefore treat such amounts as a deferred liability does *not* impact the accounting on the part of the granting entity. If the liability is fixed, subject only to the passage of time, the granting entity should give full and immediate recognition to the grant.

Contributed Services

In order to report adequately on the full scope of operations of a nonprofit entity, the financial statements should reflect accountability for all gifts received, regardless of their nature. This includes gifts of money, securities, inventory, fixed assets, use of facilities, professional or other services. Practical problems are encountered, however, in assigning values to less liquid assets, and questions are raised regarding the purpose and benefit of attempting to value volunteer services. The existing authoritative literature requires that contributions in forms other than money be recorded at their market value at date of gift. In certain cases, this requires that independent appraisals be obtained, that professionals be requested to advise the organization of the contribution element in their services, or that the rental value of comparable facilities be determined.

Criteria for Recognition.   Valuing contributed services involves unique problems due both to the assignment of monetary values and to the determination that productive services have been received. Accordingly, the practical application of this concept has evolved to the point where the value of such services should be recorded only if it can be clearly demonstrated that all three of the following exist.

1. The organization exercises employeelike control over the volunteer. This involves determining what work shall be done, who shall do it, how, when, and where.

2. The work is within the mainstream of the organization's program or supporting service activities. This means that peripheral but unnecessary volunteer effort would not qualify for recording. In addition, a determination must be made that the organization would hire someone to do the work if the funds were available and the volunteer was not.

3. There is a clearly measurable basis for assigning values. This requires that a reasonably objective technique exist for determining how much would have to be paid in the local community to employ someone with the skills needed to perform the required tasks. This also requires that a record be maintained of hours worked by the volunteer.

The services of nuns as nurses in a hospital operated by a religious order would normally clearly qualify under these criteria, and the value of services provided in excess of stipends paid would be recorded as a contribution. The services of volunteer fund-raisers in a door-to-door fund-raising effort would normally not qualify for recording because of the lack of the employer-employee type of relationship required under the first criterion. In those instances where volunteer services are significant but do not qualify for recording, footnote disclosure should be made of this fact together with commentary regarding the scope and impact of the unrecorded volunteer effort.

Functional Expense Reporting

Unlike for-profit entities, whose "bottom line" provides some indication of success in the goal of accumulation of wealth, exempt organizations may be most successful when they use their income promptly and effectively. Accordingly, although it is important to determine whether more has been spent than received during a particular period, the real measure of success must be found in the degree to which the organization accomplishes its stated objectives. An important step in this evaluation process should be a determination of the costs of each program. As a result, increasing requirements have evolved for reporting of expenses in "functional" categories. This is most highly developed in the voluntary health and welfare field, where expenses are allocated into three basic categories, as follows:

1. *Program services.* The costs of carrying out the activities that accomplish the organization's goals. Normally expenses are reported in several program categories covering each major area of effort.

2. *Management and general.* The costs associated with the basic stewardship and management effort needed to have the corporate vehicle to deliver the program services. These costs include bookkeeping, auditing, overall direction, general board activities, and similar necessary expenses which provide an overall general benefit.

3. *Fund-raising.* Costs associated with obtaining the resources needed to conduct the program. Grant solicitations, contract proposals, and membership development fall in this general area of effort, although normally identified separately from public fund-raising, if significant.

Both hospitals and universities employ techniques that provide for partial allocation of costs into functional categories. The nonprofit accounting statement proposes expense reporting employing the health and welfare approach if public support is significant. The trend in this area appears to be in the direction of functional-type reporting which seeks to determine not simply the amounts paid for salaries, rent, and so on, but how the employees utilized their time and available facilities. Ultimately, related statistical data useful in determining unit cost where applicable, as well as measures of quality of effort, must be developed to fully accomplish this objective.

Generally Accepted Accounting Principles

As indicated previously, the accounting profession has often specified that accounting principles applicable to commercial entities do not apply to nonprofit organizations. The hospital audit guide dealt with this issue unequivocally by indicating that such principles do apply unless they are inapplicable. Although a number of differences remain, the evolution is in the direction of acceptance of existing commercial accounting principles for all applicable issues and the adoption of an underlying set of concepts applicable to those areas that are unique to nonprofit organizations.

Other Issues

This review of key accounting and reporting concepts has been limited to those issues that have broadest applicability and greatest impact on the form and content of financial reports. Other issues exist and must be resolved, particularly as they relate to individual types of nonprofit entities. For example, with few exceptions, museums issue financial statements that do not report the collection as an asset. Although arguments are strong in support of this practice, a basic question exists as to whether this technique deals adequately with the organization's full stewardship responsibility.

Form of Financial Statements

The form of financial reporting employed by an organization significantly impacts the effectiveness of communication of its financial message. As previously noted, current practice varies widely. Even the financial statement illustrations included in the AICPA audit guides differ significantly from each other in several important respects. Nevertheless, they illustrate acceptable ways of complying with the recommended accounting principles for the types of organizations involved. The nonprofit accounting statement illustrates several possible ways of preparing financial statements; each would be acceptable in appropriate circumstances.

As an aid to those who are preparing financial statements, the illustrations included in the hospital, university, and voluntary health and welfare audit guides are reproduced herein.

The Future

The elements needed to resolve the long-standing problems associated with nonprofit financial reporting are now in place. Although much has been done, a great deal remains. In addition to guidance for accountants, both in and out of public practice, education is needed for financial statement users, both in and out of the organizations themselves. Readers must be in a position to understand the data presented, and to make comparisons with other organizations. They also must understand the inherent limitations that exist in communicating goals accomplishment as well as the needs for continued support. This is a challenging and exciting opportunity. The degree to which it is accomplished will significantly shape the future role of this third sector of our society.

Notes

1. National Health Council and National Social Welfare Assembly, *Standards of Accounting and Financial Reporting for Voluntary Health and Welfare Organizations,* New York, 1975.

2. American Hospital Association, *Accounting Manual for Long-Term Care Institutions,* Chicago, 1968; *Chart of Accounts for Hospitals,* Chicago, 1983; *Uniform Hospital Definitions,* Chicago, 1960.

3. American Council on Education, *College and University Business Administration*, 4th ed., Washington, D.C., 1982.

4. National Conference of Catholic Bishops, *Diocesan Accounting and Financial Reporting*, Washington, D.C., 1971.

5. Club Managers Association of America, *Uniform System of Accounts for Clubs*, 2d ed., Washington, D.C., 1967.

6. National Association of Independent Schools, *Accounting for Independent Schools*, 2d ed., Boston, 1977.

7. Association of Science-Technology Centers, *Museum Accounting Guidelines*, Washington, D.C., 1976.

8. American Institute of Certified Public Accountants, *Audits of Voluntary Health and Welfare Organizations*, New York, 1974.

9. American Institute of Certified Public Accountants, *Hospital Audit Guide*, 3d ed., New York, 1980.

10. American Institute of Certified Public Accountants, *Audits of Colleges and Universities*, New York, 1973.

11. American Institute of Certified Public Accountants, *Audits of Voluntary Health and Welfare Organizations*, New York, 1974.

12. National Association of College and University Business Officers, *College and University Business Administration*, 4th ed., Washington, D.C., 1982.

13. American Institute of Certified Public Accountants, *Statement of Position 74-8 on Financial Accounting and Reporting by Colleges and Universities*, New York, 1974.

14. National Health Council, Inc., National Assembly of National Voluntary Health and Social Welfare Organizations, Inc., and United Way of America, *Standards of Accounting and Financial Reporting for Voluntary Health and Welfare Organizations*, rev. ed., New York, 1974.

15. United Way of America, *Accounting and Financial Reporting—A Guide for United Ways and Not-for-Profit Human Service Organizations*, Alexandria, Va., 1974.

16. Commission on Private Philanthropy and Public Needs, *Accounting Advisory Committee Report to the Commission on Private Philanthropy and Public Needs*, Washington, D.C., 1974.

17. American Institute of Certified Public Accountants, *Statement of Position 78-10 on Accounting Principles and Reporting Practices for Certain Nonprofit Organizations*, New York, 1979.

18. Financial Accounting Standards Board, *Financial Accounting in Nonbusiness Organizations*, Stamford, Conn., 1978.

19. Financial Accounting Standards Board, *FASB Discussion Memorandum—An Analysis of Issues Related to Conceptual Framework for Financial Accounting and Reporting: Objectives of Financial Reporting by Nonbusiness Organizations*, Stamford, Conn., 1978.

20. Financial Accounting Standards Board, *Accounting Standards, Original Pronouncements, July 1973–June 1, 1985*, 1985–1986 ed., McGraw-Hill, New York, 1985.

Illustrative Financial Statements

The following illustrative financial statements are consistent through current editions and are reprinted with permission of the American Institute of Certified Public Accountants from:

Hospital Audit Guide, copyright © 1972.

Exhibit A
Sample Hospital
Balance Sheet
December 31, 19___
With Comparative Figures for 19___

Unrestricted Funds

Assets	Current year	Prior year
Current:		
Cash	$ 133,000	$ 33,000
Receivables (Note 3)	1,382,000	1,269,000
Less—Estimated uncollectibles and allowances	(160,000)	(105,000)
	1,222,000	1,164,000
Due from restricted funds	215,000	—
Inventories (if material, state basis)	176,000	183,000
Prepaid expenses	68,000	73,000
Total current assets	1,814,000	1,453,000
Other:		
Cash (Note 2)	143,000	40,000
Investments (Notes 1 and 2)	1,427,000	1,740,000
Property, plant, and equipment (Notes 4 and 5)	11,028,000	10,375,000
Less—Accumulated depreciation	(3,885,000)	(3,600,000)
Net property, plant, and equipment	7,143,000	6,775,000
Total (Note 2)	$10,527,000	$10,008,000

Liabilities and fund balances	Current year	Prior year
Current:		
Notes payable to banks	$ 227,000	$ 300,000
Current installments of long-term debt (Note 5)	90,000	90,000
Accounts payable	450,000	463,000
Accrued expenses	150,000	147,000
Advances from third-party payors	300,000	200,000
Deferred revenue	10,000	10,000
Total current liabilities	1,227,000	1,210,000
Deferred revenue—third-party reimbursement (Note 4)	200,000	90,000
Long-term debt (Note 5):		
Housing bonds	500,000	520,000
Mortgage note	1,200,000	1,270,000
Total long-term debt	1,700,000	1,790,000
Fund balance*	7,400,000	6,918,000
Total	$10,527,000	$10,008,000

Exhibit A (Continued)

Restricted Funds

Assets	Current year	Prior year	Liabilities and fund balances	Current year	Prior year
Specific purpose funds:			*Specific purpose funds:*		
Cash	$ 1,260	$ 1,000	Due to unrestricted funds	$ 215,000	$ —
Investments (Note 1)	200,000	70,000	Fund balances:		
Grants receivable	90,000	—	Research grants	15,000	30,000
			Other	61,260	41,000
				76,260	71,000
Total specific purpose funds	$ 291,260	$ 71,000	Total specific purpose funds	$ 291,260	$ 71,000
Plant replacement and expansion funds:			*Plant replacement and expansion funds:*		
Cash	$ 10,000	$ 450,000	*Fund balances:*		
Investments (Note 1)	800,000	290,000	Restricted by third-party payors	$ 380,000	$ 150,000
Pledges receivable, net of estimated uncollectible	20,000	360,000	Other	450,000	950,000
Total plant replacement and expansion funds	$ 830,000	$ 1,100,000	Total plant replacement and expansion funds	$ 830,000	$ 1,100,000
Endowment funds:			*Endowment funds:*		
Cash	$ 50,000	$ 33,000	*Fund balances:*		
Investments (Note 1)	6,100,000	3,942,000	Permanent endowment	$ 4,850,000	$ 2,675,000
			Term endowment	1,300,000	1,300,000
Total endowment funds	$ 6,150,000	$ 3,975,000	Total endowment funds	$ 6,150,000	$ 3,975,000

See accompanying Notes to Financial Statements.
*Composition of the fund balance may be shown here, on the Statement of Changes in Fund Balance (such as illustrated in Exhibit D), or in a footnote.

Exhibit B

Sample Hospital
Statement of Revenues and Expenses

Year Ended December 31, 19__
With Comparative Figures for 19__

	Current year	Prior year
Patient service revenue	$8,500,000	$8,000,000
Allowances and uncollectible accounts (after deduction of related gifts, grants, subsidies, and other income—$55,000 and $40,000) (Notes 3 and 4)	(1,777,000)	(1,700,000)
Net patient service revenue	6,723,000	6,300,000
Other operating revenue (including $100,000 and $80,000 from specific purpose funds)	184,000	173,000
Total operating revenue	6,907,000	6,473,000
Operating expenses:		
Nursing services	2,200,000	2,000,000
Other professional services	1,900,000	1,700,000
General services	2,100,000	2,000,000
Fiscal services	375,000	360,000
Administrative services (including interest expense of $50,000 and $40,000)	400,000	375,000
Provision for depreciation	300,000	250,000
Total operating expenses	7,275,000	6,685,000
Loss from operations	(368,000)	(212,000)
Nonoperating revenue:		
Unrestricted gifts and bequests	228,000	205,000
Unrestricted income from endowment funds	170,000	80,000
Income and gains from board-designated funds	54,000	41,000
Total nonoperating revenue	452,000	326,000
Excess of revenues over expenses	$ 84,000	$ 114,000

See accompanying Notes to Financial Statements.

Exhibit C
Sample Hospital
Statement of Changes in Fund Balances
Year Ended December 31, 19__
With Comparative Figures for 19__

	Current year	Prior year
Unrestricted Funds		
Balance at beginning of year	$6,918,000	$6,242,000
Excess of revenues over expenses	84,000	114,000
Transferred from plant replacement and expansion funds to finance property, plant, and equipment expenditures	628,000	762,000
Transferred to plant replacement and expansion funds to reflect third-party payor revenue restricted to property, plant, and equipment replacement	(230,000)	(200,000)
Balance at end of year	$7,400,000*	$6,918,000
Restricted Funds		
Specific purpose funds:		
Balance at beginning of year	$ 71,000	$ 50,000
Restricted gifts and bequests	35,000	20,000
Research grants	35,000	45,000
Income from investments	35,260	39,000
Gain on sale of investments	8,000	—
Transferred to:		
Other operating revenue	(100,000)	(80,000)
Allowances and uncollectible accounts	(8,000)	(3,000)
Balance at end of year	$ 76,260	$ 71,000
Plant replacement and expansion funds:		
Balance at beginning of year	$1,100,000	$1,494,000
Restricted gifts and bequests	113,000	150,000
Income from investments	15,000	18,000
Transferred to unrestricted funds (described above)	(628,000)	(762,000)
Transferred from unrestricted funds (described above)	230,000	200,000
Balance at end of year	$ 830,000	$1,100,000
Endowment funds:		
Balance at beginning of year	$3,975,000	$2,875,000
Restricted gifts and bequests	2,000,000	1,000,000
Net gain on sale of investments	175,000	100,000
Balance at end of year	$6,150,000	$3,975,000

See accompanying Notes to Financial Statements.
* Composition of the balance may be shown here, on the balance sheet, or in a footnote.

Exhibit D

Sample Hospital

Statement of Revenues and Expenses and Changes in Unrestricted Fund Balance (Alternative Presentation)

Year Ended December 31, 19___
With Comparative Figures for 19___

| | Current year | | | | Prior year |
	Operations	Other	Plant	Total	Total
Patient service revenue	$8,500,000	—	—	$8,500,000	$8,000,000
Allowances and uncollectible accounts (after deduction of related gifts, grants, subsidies, and other income—$55,000 and $40,000) (Notes 3 and 4)	(1,777,000)	—	—	(1,777,000)	(1,700,000)
Net patient service revenue	6,723,000	—	—	6,723,000	6,300,000
Other operating revenue (including $100,000 and $80,000 from specific purpose funds)	184,000	—	—	184,000	173,000
Total operating revenue	6,907,000	—	—	6,907,000	6,473,000
Operating expenses:					
Nursing services	2,200,000			2,200,000	
Other professional services	1,900,000			1,900,000	
General services	2,100,000			2,100,000	
Fiscal services	375,000			375,000	
Administrative services (including interest expense of $50,000 and $40,000)	400,000			400,000	
Provision for depreciation	300,000			300,000	
Total operating expenses	7,275,000			7,275,000	
Loss from operations	(368,000)	—	—	(368,000)	(212,000)

45.23

Exhibit D (*Continued*)

	Current year				Prior year
	Operations	Other	Plant	Total	Total
Nonoperating revenue:					
Unrestricted gifts and bequests	—	$ 228,000	—	228,000	205,000
Unrestricted income from endowment funds	—	170,000	—	170,000	80,000
Income and gains from board-designated funds	—	24,000	$ 30,000	54,000	41,000
Excess of revenues over expenses	(368,000)	422,000	30,000	84,000	114,000
Fund balance at beginning of year	153,000	1,780,000	4,985,000	6,918,000	6,242,000
Transferred from restricted funds	—	—	628,000	628,000	762,000
Transferred to restricted funds	(230,000)	—	—	(230,000)	(200,000)
Intrafund transfers	832,000	(632,000)	(200,000)	-0-	-0-
Fund balance at end of year	$ 387,000	$1,570,000	$5,443,000	$7,400,000	$6,918,000

See accompanying Notes to Financial Statements.
Note: If the alternative format above is presented, the total column must be included to present fairly the information presented therein

Exhibit E
Sample Hospital
Statement of Changes in Financial Position of Unrestricted Fund
With Comparative Figures for 19___
Year Ended December 31, 19___

	Current year	Prior year
Funds provided:		
Loss from operations	$ (368,000)	$ (212,000)
Deduct (add) items included in operations not requiring (providing) funds:		
Provision for depreciation	300,000	250,000
Increase in deferred third-party reimbursement	110,000	90,000
Revenue restricted to property, plant, and equipment replacement transferred to plant replacement and expansion fund	(230,000)	(200,000)
Funds required for operations	(188,000)	(72,000)
Nonoperating revenue	452,000	326,000
Funds derived from operations and nonoperating revenues	264,000	254,000
Decrease in board-designated funds	210,000	—
Property, plant, and equipment expenditures financed by plant replacement and expansion funds	628,000	762,000
Decrease in working capital	—	46,000
	$1,102,000	$1,062,000

	Current year	Prior year
Funds applied:		
Additions to property, plant, and equipment	$ 668,000	$ 762,000
Reduction of long-term debt	90,000	90,000
Increase in board-designated funds	—	210,000
Increase in working capital	344,000	—
	$1,102,000	$1,062,000
Changes in working capital:		
Increase (decrease) in current assets:		
Cash	$ 100,000	$ (50,000)
Receivables	58,000	75,000
Due from restricted funds	215,000	(100,000)
Inventories	(7,000)	16,000
Prepaid expenses	(5,000)	1,000
	361,000	(58,000)
Increase (decrease) in current liabilities:		
Note payable to banks	(73,000)	50,000
Accounts payable	(13,000)	10,000
Accrued expenses	3,000	2,000
Advances from third-party payors	100,000	40,000
Deferred revenue	—	2,000
	17,000	104,000
Increase (decrease) in working capital	$ 344,000	$ (46,000)

See accompanying Notes to Financial Statements.

Sample Hospital
Notes to Financial Statements
December 31, 19___

Note 1.　Investments are stated in the financial statements at cost. Cost and quoted market values at December 31, 19___ are summarized as follows:

	Cost	Quoted market
Board-designated funds	$1,427,000	$1,430,000
Specific-purpose funds	200,000	210,000
Plant replacement and expansion funds	800,000	838,000
Endowment funds	6,100,000	8,200,000

Note 2.　Of total unrestricted assets of $10,527,000, $10,570,000 has been designated for expansion of outpatient facilities; these assets are shown as other assets because they are not expected to be expended during 19___.

Note 3.　Revenues received under cost reimbursement agreements totaling $4,000,000 for the current year and $3,000,000 for the prior year are subject to audit and retroactive adjustment by third-party payors. Provisions for estimated retroactive adjustments under these agreements have been provided.

Note 4.　Property, plant, and equipment is stated at cost. A summary of the accounts and the related accumulated depreciation follows:

	Cost	Accumulated depreciation
Land	$ 300,000	$ -0-
Land improvements	140,000	100,000
Buildings	7,088,000	2,885,000
Fixed equipment	2,000,000	800,000
Movable equipment	1,500,000	100,000
	$11,028,000	$3,885,000

Depreciation is determined on a straight-line basis for financial statement purposes. The hospital uses accelerated depreciation to determine reimbursable costs under certain third-party reimbursement agreements. Cost reimbursement revenue in the amount of $110,000 resulting from the difference in depreciation methods is deferred in the current year and will be taken into income in future years.

Note 5.　The 3 percent housing bonds are payable in varying annual amounts to 19___ and are collateralized by a mortgage on a nurses' residence carried at $800,000.

The mortgage note is payable in quarterly installments of $17,500 with interest at 4 percent through 19___, and is collateralized by land and buildings carried at $2,800,000.

Note 6.　The hospital has a noncontributory pension plan covering substantially all employees. Total pension expense for the year was $48,000, which includes amortization of prior service cost over a period of 20 years. The hospital's policy is to fund pension costs accrued. The actuarially computed value of vested benefits as of December 31, 19___ exceeds net assets of the pension fund and balance sheet accruals by approximately $156,000.

Exhibit 1
Sample Educational Institution
Balance Sheet
June 30, 19___
With Comparative Figures at June 30, 19___

Assets

Current funds	Current year	Prior year
Unrestricted:		
Cash	$ 210,000	$ 110,000
Investments	450,000	360,000
Accounts receivable, less allowance of $18,000 both years	228,000	175,000
Inventories, at lower of cost (first-in, first-out basis) or market	90,000	80,000
Prepaid expenses and deferred charges	28,000	20,000
Total unrestricted	1,006,000	745,000
Restricted:		
Cash	145,000	101,000
Investments	175,000	165,000
Accounts receivable, less allowance of $8,000 both years	68,000	160,000
Unbilled charges	72,000	—
Total restricted	460,000	426,000
Total current funds	$ 1,466,000	$ 1,171,000

Liabilities and fund balances

Current funds	Current year	Prior year
Unrestricted:		
Accounts payable	$ 125,000	$ 100,000
Accrued liabilities	20,000	15,000
Students' deposits	30,000	35,000
Due to other funds	158,000	120,000
Deferred credits	30,000	20,000
Fund balance	643,000	455,000
Total unrestricted	1,006,000	745,000
Restricted:		
Accounts payable	14,000	5,000
Fund balances	446,000	421,000
Total restricted	460,000	426,000
Total current funds	$ 1,466,000	$ 1,171,000

Exhibit 1 (Continued)

Loan Funds

Assets	Current year	Prior year	Liabilities and fund balances	Current year	Prior year
Cash	$ 30,000	$ 20,000	Fund balances		
Investments	100,000	100,000	U.S. government grants refundable	$ 50,000	$ 33,000
Loans to students, faculty, and staff, less allowance of $10,000 current year and $9,000 prior year	550,000	382,000	University funds		
			Restricted	483,000	369,000
Due from unrestricted funds	3,000	—	Unrestricted	150,000	100,000
Total loan funds	$ 683,000	$ 502,000	Total loan funds	$ 683,000	$ 502,000

Endowment and Similar Funds

Assets	Current year	Prior year	Liabilities and fund balances	Current year	Prior year
Cash	$ 100,000	$ 101,000	Fund balances		
Investments	13,900,000	11,800,000	Endowment	$ 7,800,000	$ 6,740,000
			Term endowment	3,840,000	3,420,000
			Quasi-endowment—unrestricted	1,000,000	800,000
			Quasi-endowment—restricted	1,360,000	941,000
Total endowment and similar funds	$14,000,000	$11,901,000	Total endowment and similar funds	$14,000,000	$11,901,000

Annuity and Life Income Funds

Assets	Current year	Prior year	Liabilities and fund balances	Current year	Prior year
Annuity funds			Annuity funds		
Cash	$ 55,000	$ 45,000	Annuities payable	$ 2,150,000	$ 2,300,000
Investments	3,260,000	3,010,000	Fund balances	1,165,000	755,000
Total annuity funds	3,315,000	3,055,000	Total annuity funds	3,315,000	3,055,000
Life income funds			Life income funds		
Cash	15,000	15,000	Income payable	5,000	5,000
Investments	2,045,000	1,740,000	Fund balances	2,055,000	1,750,000
Total life income funds	2,060,000	1,755,000	Total life income funds	2,060,000	1,755,000
Total annuity and life income funds	$ 5,375,000	$ 4,810,000	Total annuity and life income funds	$ 5,375,000	$ 4,810,000

Assets

Unexpended:		
Cash	$ 275,000	$ 410,000
Investments	1,285,000	1,590,000
Due from unrestricted current funds	150,000	120,000
Total unexpended	1,710,000	2,120,000
Renewals and replacements:		
Cash	5,000	4,000
Investments	150,000	286,000
Deposits with trustees	100,000	90,000
Due from unrestricted current funds	5,000	—
Total renewals and replacements	260,000	380,000
Retirement of indebtedness:		
Cash	50,000	40,000
Deposits with trustees	250,000	253,000
Total retirement of indebtedness	300,000	293,000
Investment in plant:		
Land	500,000	500,000
Land improvements	1,000,000	1,110,000
Buildings	25,000,000	24,060,000
Equipment	15,000,000	14,200,000
Library books	100,000	80,000
Total investment in plant	41,600,000	39,950,000
Total plant funds	$43,870,000	$42,743,000

Agency Funds

Cash	$ 50,000	$ 70,000
Investments	60,000	20,000
Total agency funds	$ 110,000	$ 90,000

Liabilities and Fund Balances

Unexpended:		
Accounts payable	$ 10,000	—
Notes payable	100,000	—
Bonds payable	400,000	—
Fund balances:		
Restricted	1,000,000	$ 1,860,000
Unrestricted	200,000	260,000
Total unexpended	1,710,000	2,120,000
Renewals and replacements:		
Fund balances		
Restricted	25,000	180,000
Unrestricted	235,000	200,000
Total renewals and replacement	260,000	380,000
Retirement of indebtedness:		
Fund balances		
Restricted	185,000	125,000
Unrestricted	115,000	168,000
Total retirement of indebtedness	300,000	293,000
Investment in plant:		
Notes payable	790,000	810,000
Bonds payable	2,200,000	2,400,000
Mortgages payable	400,000	200,000
Net investment in plant	38,210,000	36,540,000
Total investment in plant	41,600,000	39,950,000
Total plant funds	$43,870,000	$42,743,000

Agency Funds

Deposits held in custody for others	$ 110,000	$ 90,000
Total agency funds	$ 110,000	$ 90,000

See accompanying Summary of Significant Accounting Policies and Notes to Financial Statements.

Exhibit 2

Sample Educational Institution Statement of Changes in Fund Balances

Year Ended June 30, 19___

	Current funds		Loan funds	Endowment and similar funds	Annuity and life income funds	Plant funds			
	Unrestricted	Restricted				Unexpended	Renewals and replacements	Retirement of indebtedness	Investment in plant
Revenues and Other Additions									
Unrestricted current fund revenues	$7,540,000								
Expired term endowment—restricted						$ 50,000			
State appropriations—restricted						$500,000			
Federal grants and contracts—restricted		$ 500,000							
Private gifts, grants, and contracts—restricted		370,000	$100,000	$1,500,000	$800,000	115,000		$65,000	$ 15,000
Investment income—restricted		224,000	12,000	10,000		5,000	$ 5,000	5,000	
Realized gains on investments—unrestricted				109,000					
Realized gains on investments—restricted			4,000	50,000		10,000	5,000	5,000	
Interest on loans receivable			7,000						
U.S. government advances			18,000						
Expended for plant facilities (including $100,000 charged to current funds expenditures)									1,550,000
Retirement of indebtedness									220,000
Accrued interest on sale of bonds								3,000	
Matured annuity and life income restricted to endowment				10,000					
Total revenues and other additions	7,540,000	1,094,000	141,000	1,679,000	800,000	230,000	10,000	78,000	1,785,000

Expenditures and Other Deductions

	Current Unrestricted	Current Restricted	Loan	Endowment	Annuity and Life Income	Plant: Unexpended	Plant: Renewals and Replacements	Plant: Retirement of Indebtedness	Plant: Investment in Plant
Educational and general expenditures	$4,400,000	$1,014,000							
Auxiliary enterprises expenditures	1,830,000								
Indirect costs recovered		35,000							
Refunded to grantors		20,000	$10,000						
Loan cancellations and write-offs			1,000						
Administrative and collection costs			1,000						
Adjustment of actuarial liability for annuities payable					$75,000				
Expended for plant facilities (including noncapitalized expenditures of $50,000)						$1,200,000	$300,000	$ 1,000	
Retirement of indebtedness								220,000	
Interest on indebtedness								190,000	
Disposal of plant facilities									$115,000
Expired term endowments ($40,000 unrestricted, $50,000 restricted to plant)				$ 90,000					
Matured annuity and life income funds restricted to endowment					10,000				
Total expenditures and other deductions	6,230,000	1,069,000	12,000	90,000	85,000	1,200,000	300,000	411,000	115,000

Transfers Among Funds—Additions/(Deductions)

	Current Unrestricted	Current Restricted	Loan	Endowment	Annuity and Life Income	Plant: Unexpended	Plant: Renewals and Replacements	Plant: Retirement of Indebtedness	Plant: Investment in Plant
Mandatory:									
Principal and interest	$ (340,000)							$340,000	
Renewals and replacements	$ (170,000)						$170,000		
Loan fund matching grant	(2,000)		$ 2,000						
Unrestricted gifts allocated	(650,000)		50,000	$550,000	$ 50,000				

45.31

Exhibit 2 (Continued)

	Current funds		Loan funds	Endowment and similar funds	Annuity and life income funds	Plant funds			
	Unrestricted	Restricted				Unexpended	Renewals and replacements	Retirement of indebtedness	Investment in plant
			Transfer Among Funds—Additions/(Deductions)						
Portion of unrestricted quasi-endowment funds investment gains appropriated	40,000			(40,000)					
Total transfers	(1,122,000)		52,000	510,000		50,000	170,000	$340,000	
Net increase/(decrease) for the year	188,000	$ 25,000	181,000	2,099,000	$ 715,000	(920,000)	(120,000)	7,000	$ 1,670,000
Fund balance at beginning of year	455,000	421,000	502,000	11,901,000	2,505,000	2,120,000	380,000	293,000	36,540,000
Fund balance at end of year	$ 643,000	$ 446,000	$683,000	$14,000,000	$3,220,000	$1,200,000	$260,000	$300,000	$38,210,000

See accompanying Summary of Significant Accounting Policies and Notes to Financial Statements.

Exhibit 3

Sample Educational Institution
Statement of Current Funds Revenues, Expenditures, and Other Changes
Year Ended June 30, 19___

	Current year			Prior year total
	Unrestricted	Restricted	Total	
Revenue				
Tuition and fees	$ 2,600,000		$2,600,000	$2,300,000
Federal appropriations	500,000		500,000	500,000
State appropriations	700,000		700,000	700,000
Local appropriations	100,000		100,000	100,000
Federal grants and contracts	20,000	$ 375,000	395,000	350,000
State grants and contracts	10,000	25,000	35,000	200,000
Local grants and contracts	5,000	25,000	30,000	45,000
Private gifts, grants, and contracts	850,000	380,000	1,230,000	1,190,000
Endowment income	325,000	209,000	534,000	500,000
Sales and services of educational departments	190,000		190,000	195,000
Sales and services of auxiliary enterprises	2,200,000		2,200,000	2,100,000
Expired term endowment	40,000		40,000	
Other sources (if any)				
Total current revenues	7,540,000	1,014,000	8,554,000	8,180,000

Expenditures and Mandatory Transfers

	Unrestricted	Restricted	Total	Prior year total
Educational and general:				
Instruction	$ 2,960,000	$ 489,000	$3,449,000	$3,300,000
Research	100,000	400,000	500,000	650,000
Public service	130,000	25,000	155,000	175,000
Academic support	250,000		250,000	225,000
Student services	200,000		200,000	195,000

45.34

Exhibit 3 (*Continued*)

	Current year			Prior year total
	Unrestricted	Restricted	Total	
Expenditures and Mandatory Transfers				
Institutional support	450,000		450,000	445,000
Operation and maintenance of plant	220,000		220,000	200,000
Scholarships and fellowships	90,000	100,000	190,000	180,000
Educational and general expenditures	4,400,000	1,014,000	5,414,000	5,370,000
Mandatory transfers for:				
Principal and interest	90,000		90,000	50,000
Renewals and replacements	100,000		100,000	80,000
Loan fund matching grant	2,000		2,000	
Total educational and general	4,592,000	1,014,000	5,606,000	5,500,000
Auxiliary enterprises:				
Expenditures	1,830,000		1,830,000	1,730,000
Mandatory transfers for:				
Principal and interest	250,000		250,000	250,000
Renewals and replacements	70,000		70,000	70,000
Total auxiliary enterprises	2,150,000		2,150,000	2,050,000
Total expenditures and mandatory transfers	6,742,000	1,014,000	7,756,000	7,550,000
Other Transfers and Additions/(Deductions)				
Excess of restricted receipts over transfers to revenues		$ 45,000	$ 45,000	$ 40,000
Refunded to grantors		(20,000)	(20,000)	
Unrestricted gifts allocated to other funds	$ (650,000)		(650,000)	(510,000)
Portion of quasi-endowment gains appropriated	40,000		40,000	
Net increase in fund balances	$ 188,000	$ 25,000	$ 213,000	$ 160,000

See accompanying Summary of Significant Accounting Policies and Notes to Financial Statements.

Sample Educational Institution
Summary of Significant Accounting Policies
June 30, 19__

The significant accounting policies followed by Sample Educational Institution are described below to enhance the usefulness of the financial statements to the reader:

Accrual Basis. The financial statements of Sample Educational Institution have been prepared on the accrual basis except for depreciation accounting as explained in Notes 1 and 2 to the financial statements. The statement of current funds revenues, expenditures, and other changes is a statement of financial activities of current funds related to the current reporting period. It does not purport to present the results of operations or the net income or loss for the period as would a statement of income or a statement of revenues and expenses.

To the extent that current funds are used to finance plant assets, the amounts so provided are accounted for as: (1) expenditures, in the case of normal replacement of movable equipment and library books; (2) mandatory transfers, in the case of required provisions for debt amortization and interest and equipment renewal and replacement; and (3) transfers of a nonmandatory nature for all other cases.

Fund Accounting. In order to ensure observance of limitations and restrictions placed on the use of the resources available to the institution, the accounts of the institution are maintained in accordance with the principles of "fund accounting." This is the procedure by which resources for various purposes are classified for accounting and reporting purposes into funds that are in accordance with activities or objectives specified. Separate accounts are maintained for each fund; however, in the accompanying financial statements, funds that have similar characteristics have been combined into fund groups. Accordingly, all financial transactions have been recorded and reported by fund group.

Within each fund group, fund balances restricted by outside sources are so indicated and are distinguished from unrestricted funds allocated to specific purposes by action of the governing board. Externally restricted funds may only be utilized in accordance with the purposes established by the source of such funds and are in contrast with unrestricted funds over which the governing board retains full control to use in achieving any of its institutional purposes.

Endowment funds are subject to the restrictions of gift instruments requiring in perpetuity that the principal be invested and the income only be utilized. Term endowment funds are similar to endowment funds except that upon the passage of a stated period of time or the occurrence of a particular event, all or part of the principal may be expended. While quasi-endowment funds have been established by the governing board for the same purposes as endowment funds, any portion of quasi-endowment funds may be expended.

All gains and losses arising from the sale, collection, or other disposition of investments and other noncash assets are accounted for in the fund which owned such assets. Ordinary income derived from investments, receivables, and the like is accounted for in the fund owning such assets, except for income derived from investments of endowment and similar funds, which income is accounted for in the fund to which it is restricted or, if unrestricted, as revenues in unrestricted current funds.

All other unrestricted revenue is accounted for in the unrestricted current fund. Restricted gifts, grants, appropriations, endowment income, and other restricted resources are accounted for in the appropriate restricted funds. Restricted current funds are reported as revenues and expenditures when expended for current operating purposes.

Other Significant Accounting Policies. Other significant accounting policies are set forth in the financial statements and the notes thereto.

Sample Educational Institution
Notes to Financial Statements
June 30, 19__

1. Investments exclusive of physical plant are recorded at cost; investments received by gift are carried at market value at the date of acquisition. Quoted market values of investments (all marketable securities) of the funds indicated were as follows:

	Current year	Prior year
Unrestricted current funds	$ 510,000	$ 390,000
Restricted current funds	180,000	165,000
Loan funds	105,000	105,000
Unexpended plant funds	1,287,000	1,600,000
Renewal and replacement funds	145,000	285,000
Agency funds	60,000	20,000

Investments of endowment and similar funds and annuity and life income funds are composed of the following:

	Carrying value	
	Current year	Prior year
Endowment and similar funds:		
Corporate stocks and bonds (approximate market, current year $15,000,000, prior year $10,900,000)	$ 13,000000	$10,901,000
Rental properties—less accumulated depreciation, current year $500,000, prior year $400,000	900,000	899,000
	$13,900,000	$11,800,000
Annuity funds:		
U.S. bonds (approximate market, current year $200,000, prior year $100,000)	$ 200,000	$ 110,000
Corporate stocks and bonds (approximate market, current year $3,070,000 prior year $2,905,000)	3,060,000	2,900,000
	$ 3,260,000	$ 3,010,000
Life income funds:		
Municipal bonds (approximate market, current year $1,400,000, prior year $1,340,000)	$ 1,500,000	$ 1,300,000
Corporate stocks and bonds (approximate market, current year $650,000, prior year $400,000)	545,000	440,000
	$ 2,045,000	$ 1,740,000

Assets of endowment funds, except nonmarketable investments of term endowment having a book value of $200,000 and quasi-endowment having a book value of $800,000, are pooled on a market value basis, with each individual fund subscribing to or disposing of units on the basis of the value per unit at market value at the beginning of the calendar quarter within which the transaction takes place. Of the total units each having a market value of $15.00, 600,000 units were owned by endowment, 280,000 units by term endowment, and 120,000 units by quasi-endowment at June 30, 19___.

The following tabulation summarizes changes in relationships between cost and market values of the pooled assets:

| | Pooled assets | | Net gains (losses) | Market value per unit |
	Market	Cost		
End of year	$15,000,000	$13,000,000	$2,000,000	$15.00
Beginning of year	10,900,000	10,901,000	(1,000)	12.70
Unrealized net gains for year			2,001,000	
Realized net gains for year			159,000	
Total net gains for year			$2,160,000	$ 2.30

The average annual earnings per unit, exclusive of net gains, were $0.56 for the year.

2. Physical plant and equipment are stated at cost at date of acquisition or fair value at date of donation in the case of gifts, except land acquired prior to 1940, which is valued at appraisal value in 1940 at $300,000. Depreciation on physical plant and equipment is not recorded.

3. Long-term debt includes: bonds payable due in annual installments varying from $45,000 to $55,000 with interest at 5⅞ percent, the final installment being due in 19___, collateralized by trust indenture covering land, buildings, and equipment known as Smith dormitory carried in the accounts at $2,500,000, and pledged net revenue from the operations of said dormitory; and mortgages payable due in varying amounts to 19___ with interest at 6 percent, collateralized by property carried in the accounts at $800,000 and pledged revenue of the Student Union amounting to approximately $65,000 per year.

4. The institution has certain contributory pension plans for academic and nonacademic personnel. Total pension expense for the year was $350,000, which includes amortization of prior service cost over a period of 20 years. The institution's policy is to fund pension costs accrued, including periodic funding of prior years' accruals not previously funded. The actuarially computed value of vested benefits as of June 30, 19___ exceeded net assets of the pension fund by approximately $300,000.

5. Contracts have been let for the construction of additional classroom buildings in the amount of $3,000,000. Construction and equipment are estimated to aggregate $5,000,000, which will be financed by available resources and an issue of bonds payable over a period of 40 years amounting to $4,000,000.

6. All interfund borrowings have been made from unrestricted funds. The amounts due to plant funds from current unrestricted funds are payable within one year without interest. The amount due to loan funds from current unrestricted funds is payabie currently.

7. Pledges totaling $260,000, restricted to plant fund uses, are due to be collected over the next three fiscal years in the amounts of $120,000, $80,000, and $60,000, respectively. It is not practicable to estimate the net realizable value of such pledges.

Exhibit A

Voluntary Health and Welfare Service

Statement of Support, Revenue, and Expenses and Changes in Fund Balances

Year Ended December 31, 19X2
With Comparative Totals for 19X1

	19X2				Total all funds	
	Current funds		Land, building and equip-ment fund	Endowment fund	19X2	19X1
	Unrestricted	Restricted				
Public support and revenue:						
Public support:						
Contributions (net of estimated uncollectible pledges of $195,000 in 19X2 and $150,000 in 19X1)	$3,764,000	$162,000	$ —	$ 2,000	$3,928,000	$3,976,000
Contributions to building fund	—		72,000	—	72,000	150,000
Special events (net of direct costs of $181,000 in 19X2 and $163,000 in 19X1)	104,000	—	—	—	104,000	92,000
Legacies and bequests	92,000	—	—	4,000	96,000	129,000
Received from federated and nonfederated campaigns (which incurred related fund-raising expenses of $38,000 in 19X2 and $29,000 in 19X1)	275,000	—	—	—	275,000	308,000
Total public support	4,235,000	162,000	72,000	6,000	4,475,000	4,655,000
Revenue:						
Membership dues	17,000	—	—	—	17,000	12,000
Investment income	98,000	10,000	—	—	108,000	94,000
Realized gain on investment transactions	200,000	—	—	25,000	225,000	275,000
Miscellaneous	42,000	—	—	—	42,000	47,000
Total revenue	357,000	10,000	—	25,000	392,000	428,000
Total support and revenue	4,592,000	172,000	72,000	31,000	$4,867,000	$5,083,000

Expenses:

Program services:						
Research	1,257,000	155,000	2,000	—	$1,414,000	$1,365,000
Public health education	539,000	—	5,000	—	544,000	485,000
Professional education and training	612,000	—	6,000	—	618,000	516,000
Community services	568,000	—	10,000	—	578,000	486,000
Total program services	2,976,000	155,000	23,000	—	3,154,000	2,852,000
Supporting services:						
Management and general	567,000	—	7,000	—	574,000	638,000
Fund-raising	642,000	—	12,000	—	654,000	546,000
Total supporting services	1,209,000	—	19,000	—	1,228,000	1,184,000
Total expenses	4,185,000	155,000	42,000	—	$4,382,000	$4,036,000
Excess (deficiency) of public support and revenue over expenses	407,000	17,000	30,000	31,000		
Other changes in fund balances:						
Property and equipment acquisitions from unrestricted funds	(17,000)	—	17,000	—		
Transfer of realized endowment fund appreciation	100,000	—	—	(100,000)		
Returned to donor	—	(8,000)	—	—		
Fund balances, beginning of year	5,361,000	123,000	649,000	2,017,000		
Fund balances, end of year	$5,851,000	$132,000	$696,000	$1,948,000		

See accompanying Notes to Financial Statements.

Exhibit B
Voluntary Health and Welfare Service
Statement of Functional Expenses

Year Ended December 31, 19X2
with Comparative Totals for 19X1

	19X2									
	Program services					Supporting services			Total expenses	
	Research	Public health education	Professional education and training	Community services	Total	Management and general	Fund raising	Total	19X2	19X1
Salaries	$45,000	$291,000	$251,000	$269,000	$856,000	$331,000	$368,000	$699,000	$1,555,000	$1,433,000
Employee health and retirement benefits	4,000	14,000	14,000	14,000	46,000	22,000	15,000	37,000	83,000	75,000
Payroll taxes, etc.	2,000	16,000	13,000	14,000	45,000	18,000	18,000	36,000	81,000	75,000
Total salaries and related expenses	51,000	321,000	278,000	297,000	947,000	371,000	401,000	772,000	1,719,000	1,583,000
Professional fees and contract service payments	1,000	10,000	3,000	8,000	22,000	26,000	8,000	34,000	56,000	53,000
Supplies	2,000	13,000	13,000	13,000	41,000	18,000	17,000	35,000	76,000	71,000
Telephone and telegraph	2,000	13,000	10,000	11,000	36,000	15,000	23,000	38,000	74,000	68,000
Postage and shipping	2,000	17,000	13,000	9,000	41,000	13,000	30,000	43,000	84,000	80,000
Occupancy	5,000	26,000	22,000	25,000	78,000	30,000	27,000	57,000	135,000	126,000
Rental of equipment	1,000	24,000	14,000	4,000	43,000	3,000	16,000	19,000	62,000	58,000
Local transportation	3,000	22,000	20,000	22,000	67,000	23,000	30,000	53,000	120,000	113,000
Conferences, conventions, meetings	8,000	19,000	71,000	20,000	118,000	38,000	13,000	51,000	169,000	156,000
Printing and publications	4,000	56,000	43,000	11,000	114,000	14,000	64,000	78,000	192,000	184,000

Awards and grants	1,332,000	14,000	119,000	144,000	1,609,000	—	—	—	1,609,000	1,448,000
Miscellaneous	1,000	4,000	6,000	4,000	15,000	16,000	21,000	37,000	52,000	64,000
Total expenses before depreciation	1,412,000	539,000	612,000	568,000	3,131,000	567,000	650,000	1,217,000	4,348,000	4,004,000
Depreciation of buildings and equipment	2,000	5,000	6,000	10,000	23,000	7,000	4,000	11,000	34,000	32,000
Total expenses	$1,414,000	$544,000	$618,000	$578,000	$3,154,000	$574,000	$654,000	$1,228,000	$4,382,000	$4,036,000

See accompanying Notes to Financial Statements.

45.41

Exhibit C

Voluntary Health and Welfare Service

Balance Sheets
December 31, 19X2 and 19X1

Assets	19X2	19X1	Liabilities and fund balances	19X2	19X1
			Current funds unrestricted		
Cash	$2,207,000	$2,530,000	Accounts payable	$ 148,000	$ 139,000
Investments (Note 2):			Research grants payable	596,000	616,000
For long-term purposes	2,727,000	2,245,000	Contributions designated for future		
Other	1,075,000	950,000	periods	245,000	219,000
Pledges receivable less allowance for			Total liabilities and deferred reve-		
uncollectibles of $105,000 and			nues	989,000	974,000
$92,000	475,000	363,000	Fund balances:		
Inventories of educational materials,			Designated by the governing board for:		
at cost	70,000	61,000	Long-term investments	2,800,000	2,300,000
Accrued interest, other receivables,			Purchases of new equipment	100,000	—
and prepaid expenses	286,000	186,000	Research purposes (Note 3)	1,152,000	1,748,000
			Undesignated, available for general		
			activities (Note 4)	1,799,000	1,313,000
			Total fund balance	5,851,000	5,361,000
Total	$6,840,000	6,335,000	Total	$6,840,000	$6,335,000
			Restricted		
Cash	$3,000	$5,000	Fund balances:		
Investments (Note 2)	71,000	72,000	Professional education	$ 84,000	$ —
Grants receivable	58,000	46,000	Research grants	48,000	123,000
Total	$ 132,000	$ 123,000	Total	$ 132,000	$ 123,000

Land, Building and Equipment Fund

Cash	$3,000	$2,000	Mortgage payable, 8% due 19XX	$32,000	$36,000
Investments (Note 2)	177,000	145,000	Fund balances:		
Pledges receivable less allowance for uncollectibles of $7,500 and $5,000	32,000	25,000	Expended	484,000	477,000
Land, buildings and equipment, at cost less accumulated depreciation of $296,000 and $262,000 (Note 5)	516,000	513,000	Unexpended—restricted	212,000	172,000
			Total fund balance	696,000	649,000
Total	$728,000	$685,000	Total	$728,000	$685,000

Endowment Funds

Cash	$4,000	$10,000	Fund balance	$1,948,000	$2,017,000
Investments (Note 2)	1,944,000	2,007,000			
Total	$1,948,000	$2,017,000	Total	$1,948,000	$2,017,000

See accompanying Notes to Financial Statements.

Voluntary Health and Welfare Service
Notes to Financial Statements
December 31, 19X2

1. *Summary of significant accounting policies.* The financial statements include the accounts of the service and its affiliated chapters. The service follows the practice of capitalizing all expenditures for land, buildings, and equipment in excess of $100; the fair value of donated fixed assets is similarly capitalized. Depreciation is provided over the estimated useful lives of the assets. Investments are stated at cost. All contributions are considered available for unrestricted use unless specifically restricted by donor. Pledges for contributions are recorded as received and allowances are provided for amounts estimated to be uncollectible. Policies concerning donated material and services are described in Note 6.

2. *Investments.* Market values and unrealized appreciation (depreciation) at December 31, 19X2 and 19X1, are summarized as follows:

	(Thousands of Dollars)			
	December 31, 19X2		December 31, 19X1	
	Quoted Market Value	Unrealized Appreciation	Quoted Market Value	Unrealized Appreciation (Depreciation)
Current unrestricted fund:				
For long-term purposes	$2,735	$8	$2,230	$(15)
Other	1,100	25	941	(9)
Current restricted funds	73	2	73	1
Endowment funds	2,125	181	2,183	176
Land, building and equipment fund	184	7	153	8

Interfund transfers include $100,000 for 19X2, which represents the portion of the realized appreciation ($25,000 realized in the current year and $75,000 realized in prior years) in endowment funds that, under the laws of (a state), were designated by the governing board for unrestricted operations. At December 31, 19X2, $200,000 of realized appreciation was available in endowment funds, which the governing board may, if it deems prudent, also transfer to the unrestricted fund.

If the organization accounts for its investment on the market value basis, the first part of the above note might be worded as follows: Cost and unrealized appreciation (depreciation) at December 31, 19X2 and 19X1, are summarized as follows:

	(Thousands of dollars)			
	December 31, 19X2		December 31, 19X1	
	Cost	Unrealized appreciation	Cost	Unrealized appreciation (depreciation)
Current unrestricted fund:				
For long-term purposes	$2,727	$ 8	$2,245	$(15)
Other	1,075	25	950	(9)
Current restricted funds	71	2	72	1
Endowment funds	1,944	181	2,007	176
Land, building and equipment fund	177	7	45	8

3. *Research grants.* The service's awards for research grants-in-aid generally cover a period of one to three years, subject to annual renewals at the option of the governing board. At December 31, 19X2, $1,748,000 had been designated by the board for research grants, of which $596,000 had been awarded for research to be carried out within the next year.

4. *Proposed research center.* The XYZ Foundation has contributed $50,000 to the service with the stipulations that it be used for the construction of a research center and that construction of the facilities begin within four years. The service is considering the construction of a research center, the cost of which would approximate $2,000,000. If the governing board approves the construction of these facilities, it is contemplated that its cost would be financed by a special fund drive.

5. *Land, buildings and equipment, and depreciation.* Depreciation of buildings and equipment is provided on a straight-line basis over the estimated useful lives of the assets. At December 31, 19X2 and 19X1, the costs of such assets were as follows:

	19X2	19X1
Land	$ 76,000	$ 76,000
Buildings	324,000	324,000
Medical research equipment	336,000	312,000
Office furniture and equipment	43,000	33,000
Automobiles and trucks	33,000	30,000
Total cost	812,000	775,000
Less accumulated depreciation	296,000	262,000
Net	$516,000	$513,000

6. *Donated materials and services.* Donated materials and equipment are reflected as contributions in the accompanying statements at their estimated values at date of receipt. No amounts have been reflected in the statements for donated services inasmuch as no objective basis is available to measure the value of such services; however, a substantial number of volunteers have donated significant amounts of their time in the organization's program services and in its fund-raising campaigns.

7. *Pension plans.* The organization has a non-contributory pension and retirement plan covering substantially all of its employees. Pension expense for the current year and the prior year was $__ and $__, respectively, which includes amortization of prior service cost over __year period. The service's policy is to fund pension cost accrued. At December 31, 19X2, the actuarially computed value of the vested benefits in the plan exceeded the fund balance of the plan by approximately $__.

8. *Leased facilities.* Most of the buildings used by the organization for its community services programs are leased on a year-to-year basis. At December 31, 19X2, fifteen such buildings were being leased for an annual cost of approximately $12,000.

46

Overview of the 1986 Tax Reform Act

Barron Harvey

Ph.D., C.P.A., Howard University Washington, D.C.

Horton L. Sorkin

Ph.D., Howard University Washington, D.C.

The Tax Reform Act of 1986, although initially touted during development as being a simplification of the tax code, is considered by most experts as being the most complex code ever. Moreover, the implications of changes in the tax code for non-profit organizations (NPOs) are many, and not all are desirable. The act is anticipated to have an effect on charitable giving and other revenue sources. In addition, substantial changes in the code concern employee benefits, with especially large changes affecting retirement plans. Overall allowable expenses have been limited and redefined.

The complexity is further increased by two factors. First, the numerous provisions of the act have varying effective dates. Therefore, the issue and the opportunity of advantageous timing of economic transactions requires attention during the phasing in of the Tax Reform Act of 1986. Second, experts generally agree that the Tax Reform Act of 1986 will, in the near future, be substantially changed for any of the following four possible reasons:

1. The Tax Reform Act may not be revenue-neutral as designed. The sweeping changes contained in the act have made the estimation of expected governmental revenues as much of an art as a science.

2. The size of the current and future governmental deficits may lead to legislation to increase tax inflows.

3. There may be a political backlash to aspects of the bill similar to the requirement for auto record keeping enacted in 1984.

4. An economic recession could lead to enactment of specific tax preferences to stimulate the economy.

At this point in time, guidelines have not been issued concerning all aspects of the act. However, two conclusions in terms of its effect on nonprofit organizations are inescapable. NPOs will require more professional tax guidance than in the past, and that guidance will be required for at least the next 3 years.

Background

The United States tax code throughout much of its almost 75-year history has, to a large extent, been used to enhance social, industrial, and fiscal policy. The legislators have sought to encourage certain behaviors, for instance, by allowing tax preferences for charitable deductions, rapid amortization of pollution control equipment, deductions for professional dues, and home mortgage interest payments. The Tax Reform Act of 1986 is intended by Congress to reverse that trend and mitigate the effects of the tax code as a motivating factor in personal and business decision making.

Conceptually, the primary goal of the act is to implement a *flat tax rate* that should be applied to the broadest base of income. The immediate implications of this concept is to broaden the taxable income by eliminating deductions and credits. A secondary goal is to make the act revenue-neutral in relation to prior total tax payments received by the federal government. Thus the flat tax rate is lower than prior rates to compensate for the individual's increase in the amount of taxable income resulting from the fewer deductions and credits.

Political and social considerations resulted in the act containing some modifications of the goals stated above. Congress did not fully remove all major incentives from the tax code. Tax preferences for certain items, such as charitable contributions and home mortgage interest, are retained. There is still some rate progressivity. The overall tax burden is designed to include a shift from the individual to the corporate taxpayer. The Tax Reform Act of 1986 thus contains features that can be construed as being motivating factors in personal and business decision making.

As a result of the inclusion of preferences, framers of the act anticipated that not all taxpayers with "real economic" income would pay an appropriate amount of taxes. Therefore, the framers decided that it was necessary to include very stiff alternative minimum taxes on individuals and corporations to compensate for instances in which preference items would result in an inappropriately low tax liability.

Effect on Charitable Giving

The experts are not in agreement as to the overall effect on charitable giving as a consequence of the Tax Reform Act of 1986. The effects of the 1981 tax cuts were projected at that time to result in a decrease in donations. However, giving has increased over 50 percent since 1981. The issue is complex. There is the question as to the degree of charitable giving that is tax motivated. In addition, a decrease in the tax savings associated with donations to NPOs is mixed with the impact of changes in disposal income resulting from the Tax Reform Act of 1986.

Loss of Nonitemizer's Deduction

Taxpayers who do not itemize their deductions cannot deduct charitable contributions after 1986. Taxpayers for whom itemized deductions exceed the new standard deduction amount must report those deductions separately as under the prior law. However, fewer taxpayers are anticipated to file itemized tax returns as a result of larger standard deduction amounts, the availability of fewer deductions, and increased limitations on those deductions that are available.

Perhaps of extreme importance to certain NPOs is the fact that professional dues now may not be deducted when the conditions stated above apply. In addition, as unreimbursed business expenses, the total of such expenses are permitted as deductions only to the extent that they exceed 2 percent of the individual's adjusted gross income. This may be enough of a threshold to motivate certain individuals to decrease the extent that they maintain active membership status from the standpoint of both payment of dues and, consequently, donations of time.

Increase in After-Tax Cost of Giving

The decreased tax rates, for most itemizers, will result in lower tax savings from donations with respect to the federal burden. Of course, the overall effect must take into consideration state and local tax impacts on the individual. The following table illustrates simplistically the effect of tax savings associated with a $5000 charitable gift under the current law, the transition year of 1987, and the full effect of the new law after 1987.

Effect of New Law and Cost of Giving

Year	Gift amount	Tax rate	Tax savings	Cost after tax
1986	$5000	0.500	$2500	$2500
1987	$5000	0.385	$1925	$3075
1988	$5000	0.280	$1400	$3600

In this simplistic setting, the net effect of a $5000 gift will cost the donor 23 percent more in 1987 and 44 percent more than the same gift would have cost in 1986.

Many individual and corporate taxpayers will be subject to an alternative minimum tax (AMT). As stated previously, the purpose is to prevent taxpayers with a large amount of tax preferences from escaping from a predefined tax burden. The individual and corporation must pay the greater of the regular or the AMT tax liability. Some reasons why individuals will be subject to the AMT under the Tax Reform Act of 1986 include the smaller difference between the regular and the minimum tax rate. The taxpayer needs only a relatively small amount of tax preferences to have the tax burden higher under the AMT.

Charitable contributions of appreciated property are now considered preference items in the Tax Reform Act of 1986. For example, a gift of a $100,000 with a basis of $20,000 will now result in an increased tax individual liability of $16,800

($80,000 times AMT rate of 21 percent) if the AMT would now apply to that individual. Taxpayers living in high tax states may be pushed into AMT by the fact alone that state income taxes are not deductible when the AMT is calculated.

Opportunities for Increased Revenues

The Tax Reform Act of 1986 provides for the exemption from unrelated business income tax the following for nonprofit organizations:

1. Monies received from other exempt organizations from the rental or exchange of lists of members or donors
2. Monies from the distribution of certain low-cost items incident to a solicitation
3. Transfers of prizes and awards for certain achievements by individuals who are no longer allowed to exclude the prizes and awards from income unless they are assigned to a tax-exempt charitable organization
4. Deductions for the donation of newly manufactured scientific equipment is now extended from colleges to certain tax-exempt scientific organizations
5. State and local governments can issue bonds with tax-exempt interest payments providing the bonds are used, with certain limitations, to finance activities of tax-exempt organizations such as hospitals, and other organizations that are religious, charitable, or educational
6. Income from qualifying trade shows under expanded definitions

Although not part of the Tax Reform Act of 1986, the final regulations regarding conservation donations were published in early 1986. Fundamentally, these donations by a taxpayer are the development rights of environmentally significant or historically important property to a qualifying charitable organization. The interests that may be donated include (1) a fee interest, with the right of the donor to extract subsurface minerals; (2) a remainder interest in the property; and (3) an easement. This type of donation has a unique complexity due to the need to consider all the relevant real property legislation. Expert tax and legal counsel should be utilized by the involved nonprofit organization.

The anticipated overall increase in the size of adjusted (taxable) income indicates that a tax windfall will initially be provided to state and local governments. This is true for those tax bodies which base their tax receivables on adjusted income and which do not reduce their tax rates. The political process of these bodies may produce additional transfer payments or additional considerations for certain nonprofits.

Effects on Employees of NPOs

Under the Tax Reform Act of 1986, only 80 percent of business meal and entertainment expenses are deductible including the cost of meals furnished by an employer on premises. The actual increased burden of meal and entertainment expenses will either have to be shared or will have to be borne by the NPO or the employee. The benefits associated with health, insurance, and retirement plans have been restricted to an extent by the new law. The appropriateness of any benefit scenario is among the most complex area of the tax law, and the NPO should utilize experts to resolve the benefit issue.

Caveats

Two disturbing events have recently occurred. These events have implications for the extent that nonprofit organizations might undertake certain revenue schemata. The American Bar Endowment (and its insurance programs) and the American College of Physicians (and advertising revenues) cases imply that a more conservative environment may exist concerning limits on NPO behavior. By a like notion, the removal of the exempt status of Blue Cross under the Tax Reform Act of 1986 also indicates more questioning of NPOs by society.

A tax-exempt organization that owns more than 5 percent of the outstanding stock of a corporation is now subject to unrelated business income taxes on received dividends.

The new law is a fact. The stability of the new code through time is conjecture. Good news and bad news coexist for NPOs in the Tax Reform Act of 1986. The bottom line effect cannot be determined at this time. The authors can safely assert, however, that the environment is definitely "different."

47

Financial Management and Budgeting*

Ken Milani

Arthur Young Faculty Fellow in Taxation, University of Notre Dame

Introduction

In a world where unlimited needs for human services are pitted against very limited resources, financial management is an essential activity for managers and administrators of nonprofit organizations (NPOs). More specifically, budgeting is an important exercise. The budget's main role in the NPO is to guide the allocation of financial resources (i.e., to act as a navigational instrument).

The "budget," "annual financial plan," or "financial resource report" (it has many names) is not a neutral instrument. Indeed, in most organizations, the budget generates a variety of responses including exhilaration, anger, and bewilderment—but seldom apathy.

This chapter examines the budgeting process. Initially, the focus will be on the three basic phases of the process: preparation, comparison, and reaction. Then budgeting and decision making will be discussed since, like death and taxes, budgeting and decision making are the inevitables that confront the administrator of any nonprofit organization. Various budgets will be described, and, finally, use of the budget as a control tool will be covered.

*This chapter has used (with permission) the information and concepts included in chapters 1 through 8 of *Financial Management For Nonprofit Organizations,* Amacom Book Division, American Management Association, New York, 1982. The contribution of Professor James F. Gaertner of the University of Texas in San Antonio is gratefully acknowledged.

Budgeting's Basic Phases

Budgeting is done in three phases: preparation of the budget, comparison of the budget to actual results, and reaction to differences between budgeted outcomes and actual outcomes.

Budget Preparation.   A budget cannot be prepared until the NPO's policies, priorities, and plans have been clarified. Without clearly stated goals and quantifiable objectives, the NPO cannot make worthwhile projections of the future. Moreover, the NPO cannot expect budgeting to substitute for planning. Policies, priorities, and plans—both long-range and short-range—must be in place before budget preparation can commence.

In the long run, the NPO must examine its unique contribution to society and determine whether the need for this effort will still be present in 5 or 10 years. (Several hospitals, for example, shifted to other and new forms of service as a reflection of society's changing demands in the early part of the 1980s.) Part 2 of this book which deals with leadership, management, and control is a valuable look at this often-neglected aspect of NPO administration.

On a short-term basis, the NPO must establish basic policies in such areas as wage and salary changes, level of employment, level and type of service, and capital expenditures. The budget expresses these elements in objective financial terms. For example, a 9 percent salary hike plus two additional staff members might add $65,000 to a given organization's operating costs for the upcoming budgetary period.

The budget must be approved by the NPO governing body (that is, the board of trustees or directors or the administrative committee) in a manner that involves questioning and analysis, not just a rubber stamp. Approval of the budget should be regarded as a commitment on the part of the governing body and the NPO administrators to carry out the policies, respect the priorities, and support the plans that are communicated in dollar terms by the budget.

Proper preparation of the budget will be a time-consuming and challenging task. The method of budget preparation described later encourages some time for reflection as the budget is being prepared. This time will usually be fruitful since the process of active and then of passive involvement in preparation usually produces a more effective budget.

Budget Comparison.   The second phase of budgeting involves comparing the actual with the anticipated results. Both monthly and year-to-date comparisons are recommended since fluctuations on a monthly basis tend to level out over the course of a year. This contrasting of actual revenues and expenses to those budgeted must occur in a timely fashion or the budgeting process will not serve its function as a control tool. Unfortunately, many organizations do not make the comparisons at all, or they delay them until the comparison phase is meaningless.

Budgeting has been referred to as a planning and controlling activity for NPO administrators and managers. Budget preparation concludes the planning phase, and budget comparison is the start of the controlling activity. A difference (or variance) between budgeted and actual figures leads to the reaction phase, as described below. The final section of this chapter focuses more directly on the generation, analysis, and interpretation of variances.

Reaction to Variances.   If the budget is to be a meaningful control tool, there must be several possible responses to variances between the actual and anticipated results. One response involves a continuation of original strategies, policies, and activities. Other responses involve some type of change in procedure, approach, or another element of the NPO. Later on this chapter will provide a more detailed look at the range of reactions available to the NPO administrator.

Budgeting and Decision Making

Throughout the budgeting process, there are points at which decisions must be made. There are two sets of factors that will probably influence decision making in the NPO: external factors and internal factors.

External Factors. Perhaps the most dominant external factor that influences decision making during the budgetary process is the state of the economies—local and national—within which the NPO operates. On the national level, inflation is a primary factor that cannot be ignored during the budget preparation, comparison, or reaction phases. Local economic conditions such as unemployment, rising utility rates, and special assessments must likewise be programmed into the budgeting process.

A second external factor, which many NPOs overlook, is competition. NPOs are vying for increasingly scarce resources of time, talent, and "treasure" (i.e., money), and this fact must be taken into account in budgeting. It may mean allocating funds for special promotional activities. Or it could lead to the pursuit of a subsidy or grant that would enable the NPO to charge lower fees or enhance its services.

Other external factors such as changing attitudes or shifts in client population should also be considered. The budgeting process must consider the influence and effect of these external factors.

Internal Factors. Several internal factors affect the budget and its implementation. In most cases, the most substantial internal factor is the statement of goals and objectives developed explicitly or implicitly by the NPO. This statement creates certain organizational obligations and develops or reinforces the organization's character. It can also generate dysfunctional pressure within the organization if goals are unrealistic. For example, an NPO whose objective is to serve the elderly in the inner city may have to consider cutbacks in service because of rising costs, a physically deteriorating facility, or other goals that are being promoted by benefactors, employees, or other interested parties.

A multiplicity of internal factors can influence the budget as it is prepared, and the comparison and reaction phases can also bring several internal factors to the surface. The administrators of the NPO must recognize and respond to these internal factors as decisions are made.

Revenue Budget

Part 4 of this book focuses on sources of revenue with a particular emphasis on fund-raising. Herein, a broader concept of revenue will be examined. For example, school revenue would include tuition, fees, and receipts from vending machines whereas hospital revenue would primarily involve patient billings and similar items. Many NPOs receive the largest share of their revenue from contributions. Dividends and interest on investments must also be considered.

A revenue budget is a summary statement of revenue plans for a given period expressed in quantitative terms. It is typically prepared annually, with subdivisions of the budget prepared monthly or quarterly for comparison purposes. Long-range revenue budgets of from 3 to 5 years are often developed as well.

In many NPOs, the revenue budget may be the starting point on which many of the other items in the organization's budget depend. Often, without a realistic and reasonable revenue budget, several other elements of the NPO budget cannot be accurately established or estimated. In such situations the revenue budget of an NPO acts as the foundation for periodic planning because several other plans are built on it. For example, if the primary source of cash for an NPO is operating revenue, then the projections of expenses, additions, labor requirements, and other vital operational aspects of an institution are contingent on the amount of revenue to be received in a given period of time.

Often, however, the revenue budget is not the starting point in the budgeting activity of an NPO. In many NPOs the expenses are budgeted and then revenues are obtained through grants, donations, and other sources in an effort to achieve a break-even point. This is an entirely logical approach to budgeting for many NPOs because in many situations revenues cannot be readily determined in advance. More importantly, in many situations the revenues that an NPO receives are contingent on the expenses that those revenues are to cover. However, there are definite weaknesses with this approach.

First, the incentive to improve may diminish. If expenses are budgeted with the expectation that revenues will be received to cover those expenses, in some cases the incentives to hold down expenses may be lessened.

Second, the budgeting process is often done incrementally. If expenses are budgeted and then if the revenues are not sufficient to cover those expenses, the expenses must be budgeted again. This incremental process of budgeting is not as likely to be necessary if the organization budgets revenues first and then budgets expenses.

It should be pointed out that the revenue of some NPOs is relatively fixed and consequently does not require much budgeting effort. This is the case when a donor organization such as United Way provides the majority of revenue for an NPO.

Forecasting Revenues

In a typical business situation, revenue planning might be initiated by the top marketing executive, who would analyze previous trends in terms of product lines, territories, and personnel. The executive might ask all salespeople to submit sales estimates (entered order forecasts) for the coming year, compare those projections with his or her own, and make appropriate adjustments. The sales budget would then be provided to top management for final approval. This approach has the advantage of allowing each person an opportunity to help establish the budget. This sometimes results in enhancing employees' attitudes toward the budget, the job, and the organization.

In an NPO, previous revenue activity is often used in the preparation of revenue budgets. The NPO administrator or manager examines previous revenue trends and prepares projections based on factors considered important to the future of the organization. For example, the number of students, patients, or client contact hours are estimated and converted into revenue dollars.

The external and internal factors described above can have significant influence on these revenue projections. External factors such as drop in the birthrate will have a substantial effect on enrollments in the lower grades of an elementary school, whereas shifting population patterns could create a rise in upper-grade enrollments. Also, an internal factor such as a hospital's decision to provide a cardiac care unit may increase the total number of patients by attracting those who need cardiac care.

Statistical tools such as regression analysis, trend and cycle projection, and correlation analysis are widely used in revenue forecasting. These rather elaborate statistical techniques are beyond the scope of this chapter.

Other Considerations.   The pattern or timing of revenues is extremely important in budgeting revenues. Within a typical annual budgetary period there can be three basic revenue patterns: regular, seasonal, and random. A regular revenue pattern follows the normal trend of NPO activities. In other words, revenues are anticipated to be received on a regular basis, such as monthly, weekly, or quarterly. Examples of this include collections in a church, patient billings in a hospital, quarterly interest receipts, or any type of revenue that is usually received on a somewhat regular basis. The second typical revenue pattern is seasonal. Tuition revenue received twice a year at a private school, the concession receipts from sporting events, or summer rental income would be seasonal sources of revenue. The random pattern of revenue receipts would include all other types of revenue within a typical annual budgetary period, such as the windfall charitable contributions an NPO receives, special bequests, and grants.

Several other considerations should be recognized when budgeting revenues for a year. If the institution has decided to provide a new service, this new decision could affect the revenues of the entire institution. For example, the addition of a pastoral counselor at a retreat house will not only generate additional consultation fees, it could also affect rental, meals, and donation revenue. The pricing of services might have an effect on the demand for them. Lowering normal tuition rates for county residents could generate additional revenue as local students are attracted to a private university, and increasing the daily rate at a day care center could cause a drop in the enrollment.

The capacity of the institution must be taken into account. This is particularly true in the health care industry, where regardless of the demand for the service, capacity constraints of the institution can have a significant impact on revenue. Finally, economic conditions—both in general and especially in the immediate area—should be considered. A strike or layoff can cause a loss of enrollment in a private school, collection difficulties for a hospital, and other dysfunctions within other NPOs. On the other hand, a period of economic growth can cause a marked increase in number of potential clients, so that the capacity constraint plays an important role in revenue budgeting.

Other Comments.   Budgeting of revenues is the starting point in the budgeting process for many NPOs. The revenue budget is a summary statement of the revenue plans expressed quantitatively, and it is often based on previous revenue trends. However, the past is not always a good reflection for the future. New services, changing economic conditions, and other factors will also affect the revenue budget. Participative budgeting, where many people at various levels of the organization become involved in the budgetary process, is recommended because it improves people's attitudes toward the budget and the organization.

It would be easy to treat the revenue budget in a somewhat mechanical fashion, such as simply multiplying the number of expected client contact hours times the fees generated per hour from the client and from a government subsidy program. This strictly mechanical approach, however, will not provide an effective planning and controlling mechanism. Creativity, a challenging attitude, and sensitivity to both external and internal factors must be part of the administrator's stance toward the revenue budget.

Expense Budgets

"Where does the money go?" That question is asked in living rooms as well as corporate board rooms throughout the world. The preparation of the expense budget of a nonprofit organization (NPO) partially shows where the money should go by focusing on operating, administrative, and other expenses.

The people involved in budgeting must identify the expenses or costs to be incurred and analyze how these costs will behave within a relevant range of activity. The relevant range is an anticipated level of service or activity for the budgetary period. (For example, a day care center might expect to have only between 90 and 120 students, whereas an alcohol abuse counseling center might expect to maintain or establish contact with as many as 3000 to 3600 clients.)

Cost Behavior

In this section cost behavior will be identified and discussed using five categories: variable expenses, nonvariable (fixed) expenses, semivariable (mixed) expenses, step expenses, and other expenses. Since each organization is unique, these categories should be of greater general benefit to NPO administrators than line-item analysis. Once the behavior of a cost or expense has been identified, the amount to be budgeted can be determined.

Variable Expenses.   A cost labeled as variable will move in direct response to a certain activity. In other words, if the activity increases, the cost will increase, and vice versa. There are several examples of this type of cost behavior in the NPO sector. For example, the wages paid to part-time hourly employees will move up or down as the number of hours worked fluctuates. Certain types of supplies will be consumed in proportion to the number of pupils, patients, or clients that an NPO serves. Finally, if the NPO operates a gift shop or cafeteria, there will be movement in cost of goods sold based on total dollar sales or total unit sales.

Variable expenses are diagnosed in Figure 47.1. In some cases the slope of the line AB will be determined by a policy of the organization, such as a policy of selling gift shop items at 120 percent of their wholesale cost. In other situations, the slope is based on a required level of service mandated by external requirements. (For example, a minimum wage must be paid to certain employees.)

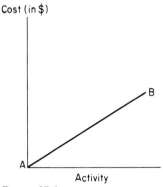

Figure 47.1

Nonvariable (Fixed) Expenses.   At the other end of the NPO cost spectrum are expenses that will not be influenced by changes in activity. These costs (typically called "fixed," or "nonvariable") arise from the possession of plant, property, and equipment as well as from the basic organization structure of an NPO.

Figure 47.2 illustrates a level of cost (line *CD*) that does not respond to alterations in activity. Plant, property, and equipment will generate this behavior since insurance on these items, property taxes levied on them, or rent paid for their use will not be influenced by the level of activity. Basic organization structure contributes significant nonvariable expenses in the form of administrative salaries.

These nonvariable expenses can be the easiest to budget and control but the most difficult to reduce or eliminate. The discussion below on step costs will focus on nonvariable costs that can be changed by shifts in policy and other considerations.

Semivariable (Mixed) Expenses.   There are costs that are a combination of the variable and the nonvariable expenses described above. These costs have a nonvariable component, which is not influenced by activity, and a variable element, which will move in response to activity changes. Two examples of the semivariable pattern are utility costs and repair and maintenance expenses.

Utility costs, especially electricity, typically include a fixed demand charge as well as a minimum charge for usage, regardless of activity level. Additional cost then varies with usage beyond a certain level. In Figure 47.3, one can portray the fixed amount by line *EF* (that is, the demand charge plus minimum electricity needed for security, safety, and equipment operation) and the variable amount by line *EG*. An analysis of repair and maintenance costs would reflect a similar semivariable pattern.

Line *EG* will not really be a straight line, since pure variability of the variable element will probably not be found in practice. Electricity rates, for example, reflect a drop in the charge per kilowatthour as more and more power is consumed. Repairs and maintenance also do not vary at a constant rate with activity.

Step Expenses.   Step costs are nonvariable costs that can be changed by administrative decisions. Perhaps the purest example of a step cost is the on-or-off nature of some situations. In such instances, the NPO administrator can decide that the cost is *off* (there will be no resources allocated to a specific use) or *on* (a certain level of spending will occur). An example of this type of decision within an NPO would be whether to seek the assistance of an outside consultant. The NPO

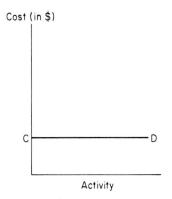

Figure 47.2

Cost (in $)

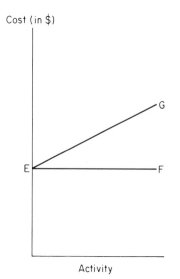

Activity

Figure 47.3

either says no and incurs a zero dollar cost, or says yes and agrees to a specific level of service.

Also falling into the category of the step cost are the nonvariable expenses that can be changed, though not eliminated, by an administrative decision. For example, an NPO may decide that it is underinsured and may increase its level of coverage (line *HI* in Figure 47.4), thus stepping up to a new level of premium cost (line *JK*). Or a full-time staff member is dismissed with no replacement planned, creating a step down to an altered level of professional salaries (from line *LM* to line *NO* in Figure 47.4).

Other Expenses.   Several important expenses do not fit into the first four categories described above. Since these costs display a variety of behaviors, we lump them into a catch-all category labeled "other."

Federal and State Payroll Taxes.   Two types of federal payroll taxes can be incurred by NPOs: the employer's share of Social Security (FICA), and the unemployment tax. For the majority of NPO employers the FICA cost, or expense, will be the present FICA rate multiplied by the wage or salary paid to the employees. However, since there are maximums established, this cost must be regarded as neither variable nor fixed. Unemployment tax at the federal level works with a current rate, a maximum amount of earnings, and a credit for unemployment taxes paid to the state. Again, a separate and specific calculation is involved. State unemployment tax rates vary, and in many states certain experience factors may increase or decrease the amount of state tax levied on an NPO employer. Obviously, estimating these expenses will not be a straight mathematical function.

Federal Income Taxes.   An NPO may find itself engaged in specific types of activities that will have federal income tax implications. Chapter 3 of Part 1 covers this aspect of an NPO operation. If an NPO determines that it is liable for federal income tax, the budget should reflect this cost.

Fringe Benefits.   Because of the wide variety of fringe benefit packages now available, it is quite possible that an NPO will have several alternative plans. (For example, a university's fringe benefit coverage could be divided four ways: faculty,

Cost (in $)

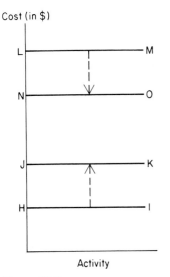

Activity

Figure 47.4

professional staff, support staff, and other.) The budgeting of this cost would focus on each group of employees and the specific fringe package that applies.

Cost Estimation

After classifying behavior of costs, the NPO administrator can estimate costs for the upcoming budgetary period. Several elements will affect this activity, but the most important are organization policies, logic and knowledge of the organization's operations, and statistical analysis.

All three of these elements will affect budgeting in most NPOs. In addition, there will be costs that occur on a random basis. Effective budgeting will allow for such random occurrences as an unexpected breakdown in machinery or the need for special equipment on a short-term basis and will allocate resources for these situations.

Organization Policies. Several kinds of expenses will be based on policies established by the NPO. For example, if all salaries are to be increased by 9 percent with $60,000 allocated to merit increases, the salary and related payroll tax budgets can be computed. However, a great deal of "blood, sweat, and tears" will be required before a policy and budget for the future period can be clearly established.

Policies established by the NPO will be sensitive to the external and internal environments discussed above. Because of their convenient locations, hospital gift shops or university bookstores usually have higher prices on their goods than other retail outlets. Nevertheless, customers at these special outlets would resist efforts to establish excessive prices. The NPOs involved must therefore be aware of their competition's prices—an external factor. On the other hand, a fringe benefit established for union members in an NPO labor force will normally be included in the nonunion employees' fringe benefit package because of the morale problems—an internal factor—that could surface if such an action were not taken.

Logic and Knowledge of Operations.   Common sense, experience, and hard facts will form the basis for several expense budget items. If an NPO operates in a changing climate, the costs of heating or cooling the physical plant will be based on data from the past plus information about the future provided by a supplier of the energy source used to operate the heating or cooling system. Material and supply budgets will also reflect past, present, and future data from the NPO administrators' information bank.

In essence, the people who establish the budget identify an informal relationship between independent and dependent variables. That is, the expense being estimated (the dependent variable) is based on logic or knowledge about some particular aspect of the operation (the independent variable). Although this part of the process seems to be downplayed in most descriptions of budgeting, it is a very important aspect of expense budgeting in an NPO.

Statistical Analysis.   Estimating expenses based strictly on a statistical analysis does not occur frequently in NPOs since most NPOs do not have direct material and direct labor standards that are characteristic of manufacturing organizations. (These kinds of expenses lend themselves well to statistical analysis.) Nonetheless, statistical approaches like account analysis, high-low analysis, visual fit, and regression analysis all have their place. In some instances, the statistical analysis can provide information that will lead to the establishment of an organization policy concerning the specific cost. For instance, a retreat house could determine that it will spend $8 a day per resident for food. More likely, the statistical analysis will provide an NPO administrator with information that would not otherwise be available, such as the fact that it costs $80 a month plus 25 cents a mile to operate a van used for a variety of purposes by the organization.

The use of statistical analysis must always be tempered by common sense and logic, since statistical tools can be misused or used in a misleading way. However, it would not be wise to completely dismiss or ignore statistical analysis since it has many applications in NPO expense budget preparation.

Preparing an Expense Budget

A time for reflection while preparing the expense was mentioned above. We shall now take a look at three stages of establishing the expense budget: the preliminary budget, the revised budget, and the final budget.

Each of these three stages is necessary to create a realistic budget that will serve as an effective management tool. The time separating the stages must be long enough to allow those involved in establishing the budget to gather additional information and, more importantly, to reflect on possible alterations in the operation or organization of the NPO that could affect certain budget items.

Preliminary Budget.   The first stage involves a preliminary budget where several hopes, expectations, and "dream sheet" items are encouraged. Notice in Table 47.1 that the preliminary budget is established from a perspective that includes last year's actual spending plus the current year's budget and estimated actual spending. In practice, more columns of actual information could be added to provide a longer range for comparison purposes.

Table 47.1 has abstracted four specific items to illustrate the three stages involved in expense budget preparation for a specific department, function, or project. These items (salaries, supplies, equipment rental, and telephone) are affected by both the external and internal environments discussed earlier. Also, they are capable of being altered by organization policy. Finally, their behavior within an organization can be influenced somewhat by activity within the organization. That is, the more students, clients, or patients served, the higher the expense for supplies or telephone.

Note that the comment section of the budget format could be used for all the expense categories. Since salary information that supports budget requests is often sensitive, its details usually are not shown on the budget preparation sheet.

It is imperative that the organization's department heads, coordinators, and supervisors be allowed to contribute ideas to the preliminary budget. The comment section will be significant to these lower-level managers since they will be primarily responsible both for creating the preliminary budget and for reacting to any changes that may be made by middle and higher management.

Revised Budget. The preparation of a preliminary budget will provide the NPO with a projected surplus or deficit if all elements of the preliminary budget are approved and actually occur. Of course, it would be a rare situation that found middle and upper levels of NPO management agreeing to all factors proposed or predicted in the first draft.

Time between drafting the preliminary budget and completing the revised budget should be used to gather more information, discuss alternatives proposed by lower-level management, reach firm decisions on policy matters such as salary increases and new positions that were contingent on the projected financial situation, and investigate other matters—such as new suppliers—that will affect the budget.

The comment section of the budget preparation sheet should be used here to explain changes and indicate alterations in another budget or line item. This portion could also act as a sounding board for any manager who disagrees with budget revisions. Since the input of lower-level managers was sought, it is imperative that their reactions to revisions be sought and formally recorded. Also, the climate of the NPO must be open and frank so that subordinates can express their disagreement with budgetary revisions without feeling that they have jeopardized their positions within the NPO.

Final Budget. The final budget is not the product of a haphazard game of trial and error. Rather, it has already received a great deal of care, concern, and managerial commitment from people who have sought to improve it at every step

Table 47.1. Budget-Setting Format

Expense category	Last year actual	Current year budget	Current year estimated actual	Preliminary budget	Revised budget	Final budget
Salaries	$160,000	$182,000	$186,000	$228,000		
Supplies	15,000	16,500	18,000	22,200*		
Equipment rental	4,000	4,500	6,000	6,480†		
Telephone	8,000	8,700	9,600	7,500‡		

Comments: *Based upon a 10% increase in costs ($1,800) plus additional usage ($2,400) created by adding one person to the professional staff. $22,200 = $18,000 + $1,800 + $2,400.
†An increase in the rental rate of 8%.
‡Monthly service charge for limited WATS service of $525, plus estimated $100 a month in long distance and toll charges.

along the way. The final budget will serve as the guidepost for the coming year. In the best tradition of Harry Truman: "The buck stops here"—for the final budget communicates to everyone in the organization the priorities, plans, problems, and potential of the NPO. Of course, since this signal is strictly financial, it must be supplemented by other modes of communication that are more applicable in certain situations.

The final budget is created after further reflections and discussions and the gathering of more information. Throughout, the lines of communication between top, middle and lower levels of management must be maintained. Failure to do so will create a feeling of pseudoparticipation among middle- and lower-strata personnel, and this alienation could create severe managerial problems when the budget is implemented. Communication should lead to commitment and eventually to control in its best sense—that is, to the budget being used as a guide, benchmark, and standard.

The process described above of classifying cost behavior, estimating costs, and preparing the budget in three stages is neither easy nor quick. However, the effort involved is worthwhile if the product is an expense budget that provides the NPO with a reasonable and realistic financial game plan for the upcoming period.

Cash Budget

Administrators of a nonprofit organization have three responsibilities relating to cash: to have sufficient cash, to have very little cash idle, and to safeguard adequately the cash on hand.

The need for having enough cash is obvious: Even a temporary cash shortage can have very serious implications for the credibility and the credit rating of the organization. It is important also not to have an overabundance of cash on hand at any one time: Any organization that keeps large amounts of undeposited cash on hand is certainly risking the safety of that cash. Additionally, keeping bank checking accounts stocked with many times more cash than necessary loses potential interest income. It is important, therefore, to have adequate money on hand to meet short-term needs but to deposit funds promptly and to invest excess cash reserves when practical.

Many organizations have assets that are more valuable than the cash they control, such as buildings and land. However, because cash is an easily negotiable asset, special safeguards should be taken to ensure that proper controls exist in managing cash.

In the area of safeguarding cash, several fundamental rules should be followed. These rules, generally referred to as internal control procedures over cash, include the following:

Timely deposits. It is important that each day's cash receipts be deposited daily and intact. The daily deposit of cash received reduces the amount of cash on hand and possible loss from theft.

All disbursements by prenumbered check. Although disbursements made by cash can be simpler and less expensive than disbursements made by check, the advantages of disbursing by check far outweigh the additional cost and effort. Any employee can reach into the cash drawer and make a "withdrawal," but only authorized persons whose signatures are on file at the bank can make disbursements by check. As an extra precaution, many organizations require two signatures on each check issued.

A complete record of every disbursement is available when the paid checks are returned by the bank. It is important that checks be prenumbered and that the

NPO carefully accounts for all numbers. Checks that have been voided should be kept on file.

Separation of duties. Implicit in any system of internal control over cash and other assets is the concept that no one person should have control over all aspects of a given transaction from beginning to end. For example, if one person is allowed to order supplies, sign the receipt, pay for supplies, and balance and reconcile the checkbook, there would be virtually no protection against either accidental errors or fraud. In organizations with only a few employees, it may not be possible to arrange for an extensive subdivision of duties. However, separating duties as much as possible is a valuable tool in the internal control procedures of an organization.

More cash control procedures are discussed in the next chapter. Although it is natural for managers to try to develop a foolproof system of internal control over cash, no such system exists. Moreover, as the intricacies of a system increase, the costs of that system also rise. In the final analysis, the cost of a system of internal control must be balanced against the perceived benefit derived from the prevention of errors and losses.

Sources of Cash

Once an administrator is convinced that cash is adequately safeguarded, the process of budgeting cash receipts and disbursements may begin. The process of budgeting sources and uses of cash is as much an exercise in common sense as in accounting techniques. Systematizing the process is the key to success in budgeting cash.

Probably the most likely place to begin a systematic analysis of the sources of cash is with the revenue budget. This budget can be used to identify the major kinds of cash input such as fees, tuitions, donations, and investment income.

Financing activities are another source of cash for many organizations. For example, institutions with an excellent credit reputation may establish a line of credit with a bank. The line of credit makes it possible to borrow up to a predetermined amount of money with very little prior notice required. Consequently, in the budgeting of cash for a given period it would be possible to plan on the availability of cash if it becomes necessary to borrow.

The sale of securities or the sale of physical assets may provide additional sources of cash for an institution.

Uses of Cash

A systematic analysis of the uses of cash for a cash budget should begin with the expense budgets which identify the major cash needs of the organization. Typically these expenses would include salaries, utilities, supplies, and other items.

It should be noted that in an accrual accounting system (in which expenses are costs incurred but not necessarily cash spent), some expenses may not coincide with cash spent on that item. Supplies expense provides an example of this, since in an accrual accounting system supplies expense reflects the cost of supplies used during a period of time. This might differ substantially from the amount of cash spent on supplies during the same period. For example, assume that the beginning balance of supplies is $1000, that supplies totaling $2500 are purchased during a year, and that the ending balance of supplies on hand is $1650. The supplies expense for that period would be calculated as follows:

Supplies—beginning inventory	$1000
Add: Purchases	+2500
Supplies	3500
Less: Supplies—ending inventory	−1650
Supplies expense	$1850

The supplies expense or supplies used in this case amounts to $1850, which obviously does not coincide with the cash spent on supplies of $2500.

Items like supplies can be converted from an accrual expense item to a cash budget item by making the following simple calculation:

Ending inventory + anticipated requirements − beginning inventory
= planned purchases

For example, if we assume the same amounts in the illustration above and assume that these are projections, we can use the formula to arrive at the following:

$1650 + $1850 − $1000 = $2500

Therefore, by stating that the ending inventory requirement was $1650, that the anticipated usage was to be $1850, and that the beginning inventory was anticipated to be $1000, we discovered it would be necessary to purchase $2500 to meet the requirements. The $2500 would be the "cash budget amount."

Additionally, in an accrual accounting system some expenses listed in the expense budget do not reflect an outlay of cash. The best example of this is depreciation. Depreciation expense is a systematic allocation, over a period of time, of dollars already spent on depreciable assets. Consequently, in a given period an organization might report a substantial amount of depreciation expense. However, this would represent the allocation of initial cash previously spent, not an outlay of cash in the present period. Depreciation expense, then, is a noncash item and should be treated as such in the cash budgeting process.

In the systematic analysis of anticipated uses of cash, another important reference is the capital expenditure budget. In addition to determining whether specific major expenditures are advisable, a capital budgeting system can be designed to provide details about committed payments for major acquisitions. These items are not ongoing expenses and therefore would not appear in an expense budget. They are, however, typically very large and significant, and must be incorporated into the cash plans of the organization. (The capital expenditures budget will be discussed in a later section of this chapter.)

Finally, in the systematic analysis of probable uses of cash, it is important to consider debt retirement information. In the repayment of a debt, only the interest amount is considered an expense, and the repayment of the principal would not appear in the expense budget. This repayment of principal is a clear use of cash, and must be incorporated into the cash budget.

Other Considerations

Cash budgets can be prepared for any period of time that fits the needs of the organization. Often operational cash budgets are prepared monthly, quarterly, semiannually, or annually. Strategic cash budgets must be prepared for periods of 3 to 5 years.

To prepare a cash budget, you must have an estimate of the organization's beginning cash balance and the required or desired cash balance at the end of each month in the budget period. Seasonal fluctuations of revenues and expenses (such as revenues and expenditures associated with seasonal activities in a school) must be taken into consideration as well.

The specific format to be used in a cash budget is certainly up to the person preparing the budget. A typical format that should meet the needs of many NPOs is shown in Figure 47.5.

Cash budgeting is a projection of anticipated cash receipts and cash disbursements for a given period of time. For a cash budget to be successful, cash receipts and disbursements must be projected systematically and accurately.

A careful analysis of projected cash receipts should begin with the revenue budget. Other cash receipts might include donations, financing activities, and the sale of securities or other assets. An estimate of projected cash expenditures should be based on the expense budget, capital expenditures, debt service, and depreciation expense. From these estimates it should be possible to calculate how much cash the organization will have on hand each month, whether it will need to borrow additional funds, and whether it will have excess cash to invest.

Other Budgets

A variety of other budgets may be prepared by a nonprofit organization. Some may be prepared for external parties. For example, budgets often are included in grant requests. Or a specialized budget format may be used when seeking assistance from present and/or potential donors.

For internal purposes, a capital expenditures budget is established. The process of creating a capital expenditures budget calls for the evaluation of various proposals and the funding of specific additions to the asset base of an NPO. Evaluation techniques used may be rather straightforward (e.g., the payback method) or rigorously analytical (e.g., the net present value method). Treatment of these techniques in detail is beyond the scope of this book. When completed, the capital expenditures budget will detail the spending approved by the NPO administrators.

Special projects budgets are also part of the planning process in an NPO. These budgets focus on a specific event (e.g., anniversary celebration, dedication ceremony, homecoming) where an established level of spending has been approved and certain outcomes are sought. Although the special projects do not involve as much money as capital expenditures, some form of administrative authority is im-

	First Quarter	Second Quarter	Third Quarter	Fourth Quarter
Beginning cash balance	$			
Add: Cash receipts				
Total cash available				
Less: Cash disbursements				
Prefinancing cash balance	$			
Financing activity:				
Borrow				
Repay				
Invest	$			
Ending cash balance				

Figure 47.5

portant. A budget establishes a clear signal about how much money will be spent and how it will be expended.

Budget as a Control Tool

Earlier in this chapter, budgeting was described as a three-phase process of preparation, comparison, and reaction. This section of the chapter concentrates on the final two phases. Administrators must compare the anticipated activity to what actually happens before they can react to it and restrict or reward certain types of performance.

The budget's use as a control tool is very similar to using a road map for guidance. There may be some unexpected detours and shortcuts along the way, but a specific destination is the ultimate objective. The main objective of budgeting is to see that the NPO's limited resources are utilized and managed in a manner that achieves in so far as possible, the objectives outlined in the organization's strategic plan, thereby satisfying the greatest possible number of needs.

Flexible Budgets

A budget is typically based on an estimated level of activity or service. Since the actual level will undoubtedly be somewhat different from the estimate and since managers want to understand the impact of certain external and internal factors on their organization, the original budget must be supplemented by a flexible budget. The flexible budget accomplishes two things: First, it reflects the anticipated behavior of elements that are sensitive to levels of activity, such as revenue and variable costs. Second, it reflects the seasonal nature of particular components that have been identified as such by NPO administrators, such as dividend income and repair and maintenance expenses.

Use of the flexible budget concept enables the accounting system to generate more meaningful signals to management. This is especially true when there has been an alteration in anticipated patterns of revenues or expenses. The flexible budget also provides data that can be used to better understand differences or variances between actual and anticipated financial figures.

Behavior of Sensitive Elements. A school budget based on an enrollment of 500 students cannot be meaningfully compared to actual figures generated by an enrollment of 580 students. Revenue from tuition and fees will be higher, but some revenue may be lost due to a breakdown in collection procedures. Some expenses will rise, but efficiency may increase in some areas as more services are being rendered. Examine, for example, the following situation:

Golden Dome Academy (GDA) prepared the following budgets based on a projected enrollment of 500 students who are served lunch daily while attending GDA: Tuition and fees revenue, $520,000 ($1040 per student × 500); cost of meals, $150,000 ($300 per student × 500).

During the year, 580 students enrolled at GDA. The actual results (which will be shown later) must be compared to the original budget, but a flexible budget will allow a more meaningful comparison and provide for analysis that will be useful to GDA's administrators as they react to variances. Flexing the budget to reflect the new enrollment figure of 580 students provides these figures:

Tuition and fees revenue	$603,200 ($1040 × 580)
Cost of meals	$174,000 ($300 × 580)

Seasonal Elements. The revenue and expense items presented above were sensitive to changes in enrollment at GDA. What about elements that do not respond to enrollment or other activity but are tied to the passage of time or climatic conditions? Can budgets for these items be flexible? Overall, the answer would be no. During the year, however, flexing must occur or an erroneous signal will be generated by the accounting system. For example, assume that GDA had established the following budgets:

Endowment fund dividend income	$80,000
Repairs and maintenance	$54,000

At the time the budgets are set, the GDA administrators know that $65,000 of the dividend income will be reported in the second quarter of the fiscal year. The details of the repairs budget include $3000 per month plus an $18,000 tuck-pointing project scheduled for the fourth quarter of the fiscal year. If the budget is not flexed based on this knowledge of operations, the first-quarter budget report would record the following:

	Actual	Budget	Variance
Endowment fund dividend income	$5,000	$20,000	$(15,000)
Repairs and maintenance	$9,000	$13,500	$ 4,500

The large unfavorable revenue variance showing that actual revenue is less than anticipated revenue is not an accurate figure. With the budget not flexed, the above report could generate some uneasy moments for an NPO manager who was called upon to explain first-quarter operations to a board of trustees or to a present or potential creditor. Similarly, the favorable expense variance showing that actual expense is less than anticipated expense is not a meaningful indication of spending on building repair and maintenance, since the large tuck-pointing project is not scheduled until the latter portion of the year.

A more meaningful treatment of the situation would have flexed the quarterly budget to take the known seasonal factors into account. The report would be a more effective management tool and would be less likely to generate feelings either of unnecessary panic or of false security. A flexible budget would have reported the following:

	Actual	Budget	Variance
Endowment fund dividend income	$5000	$5000	$-0-
Repairs and maintenance	$9000	$9000	$-0-

Needless to say, the NPO's information system must be capable of applying the proper flex to the original budget. This is the initial step in the comparing phase. Now let us look at variances.

Variance Isolation and Analysis

The term "variance" is consistently used to mean a difference between actual and budgeted revenues or expenses, either favorable or unfavorable. These designations indicate a relationship between actual and budgeted outcomes and are not indicative of effective or poor performance.

A favorable revenue variance occurs when actual revenue exceeds budgeted revenue. Conversely, a favorable expense variance occurs when actual expenses are lower than budgeted expenses. Remember, the label "favorable" does not necessarily indicate effective administration in either case. For example, actual spending falling below anticipated spending in an area such as employee development may be created by mismanagement if money is allocated for employee development but no time is scheduled for the development activity, or it may be caused by shortsightedness if the allocation is made but management feels that enhancement of employee skills is not warranted at this time.

Unfavorable revenue variances occur when actual revenue is lower than the anticipated revenue. On the expense side, unfavorable variances result from actual expenses exceeding the budgeted expenses. It is a natural tendency to view unfavorable variances as a manifestation of poor or ineffective management. However, there could be external factors that contribute to the drop in revenue, such as a long strike or a layoff that leads to unemployment, which in turn decreases enrollment or clients. Spending in excess of budget might be a direct result of climatic or other conditions that are out of an administrator's control, such as severe weather conditions that contribute to excessive auto maintenance expense.

Fortunately, there are techniques available for analyzing variances and breaking them down so that it is easier to tell whether they are caused by external or internal factors. Let us look at these techniques.

Revenue Variances. To isolate a revenue variance, we compare actual revenue with the original budget revenue. Analyzing this variance involves the flexed budget and concentrates on two components: volume of activity, and rate or price. Using the Golden Dome Academy example, assume that the actual revenue from tuition and fees for the year was $580,000. Thus the variance to be analyzed is $60,000, and it is *favorable* since actual revenue ($580,000) is greater than the budgeted revenue ($520,000). The flexed budget for the actual enrollment of 580 students was determined above to be $603,200 (that is, 580 × $1040). Analysis of the $60,000 variance follows this pattern:

Volume component		Rate component	
Flexed budget	$ 603,200	Actual revenue	$ 580,000
Original budget	−502,000	Flexed budget	−603,200
Favorable volume variance	$ 83,200	Unfavorable rate variance	$ 23,200

The analysis can be checked since an enrollment increase of 80 students at an average tuition of $1040 would generate $83,200 in additional tuition and fees. On the other hand, the average tuition and fee charge collected dropped to $1000. Thus a decrease of $40 per student for 580 students would result in a revenue drop of $23,200 when compared to the anticipated tuition and fee revenue for an enrollment of 580.

The volume and rate analysis of the revenue variance is not the last step in the process. The GDA administrators, in our case, must now interpret the data. Although we will discuss variance interpretation in more detail later in the chapter, let us develop some possible interpretations of these variances. One possibility was that the introduction of new programs attracted more students to GDA. However, these new programs did not have the same fee structure as other courses, and thus the average tuition and fee charge dropped from $1040 to $1000 per student. Also, if GDA was a cash-basis organization, the actual revenue recorded was determined by actual cash collected. The $40 drop in tuition and fees might indicate that the sharp rise in enrollment placed an unanticipated strain on GDA's ability to bill and collect tuition and fees, with a resulting decrease in actual cash received. This could alert GDA's administration that a new or improved system for billing and collection should be investigated and implemented.

Expense Variances. Like a revenue variance, an expense variance is isolated by comparing actual expense with the original budgeted expense. The flexed budget information can then be used to break down the expense variance into two components, usage and cost.

Once again the Golden Dome Academy example will be used to illustrate this concept. If the actual cost of the luncheon meals served was $191,400, the expense variance to be analyzed would be $41,400, and is considered *unfavorable* since the original budget was $150,000. Flexing the cost of meals budget to reflect the increase to 580 students established a budgetary level of $174,000. Thus, the analysis of the variance would indicate the following:

Usage component		Cost component	
Flexed budget	$ 174,000	Actual revenue	$ 191,400
Original budget	−150,000	Flexed budget	−174,000
Unfavorable usage variance	$ 24,000	Unfavorable cost variance	$ 17,400

Accuracy of this analysis of the overall variance can be tested since meals for the 80 extra students, at $300 per student, would cost $24,000 over and above the original budget. This much is strictly a volume variance, but the actual spending per student, $330, was $30 over the $300 figure used in establishing the original budget. Applying the $30 to 580 students would establish an unfavorable cost component of $17,400, and the $24,000 and $17,400 figures would add up to the total variance of $41,400.

As in the case of the revenue variance analysis, an interpretation of the expense variance components must occur. The volume component is obviously tied to the rise in enrollment. However, the cost component warrants further investigation, since the increase in actual cost of $30 per student represents 10 percent of the original budget of $300 per student. An external factor such as an unexpected rise in food costs might be the culprit. However, there could also be an internal problem like waste, pilferage, or diminishing returns. Clearly, the administrators of GDA would have to examine these explanations and others in order to see what can be done about a situation that appears to be somewhat out of control.

Variance Interpretation

As indicated earlier, variance isolation and analysis is not the ultimate answer to management's information needs. Variances must be interpreted, since variances raise questions instead of providing ready answers to complex situations. Additionally, the variances provide information that may be helpful to NPO managers as they react to the present set of events and establish a foundation for budgeting in future years. Thus, variance interpretation is an important aspect of budgeting's third phase.

Forecasting.   Any variance could be the by-product of a poorly prepared forecast, one that is outdated, incomplete, or flawed in some other way. For example, an NPO that establishes a budget based on last year's budget with no adjustment for inflation or activity level changes will undoubtedly report several variances.

Interpreting variances can improve the methods of forecasting for the next budgetary period. Management may feel the need for training or expert assistance in forecasting. This is not an unusual situation in a budgeting system. The cost of training or assistance is an effective use of resources since it should have beneficial long-term effects.

Prediction Methods.   The prediction methods used by an NPO will have a strong influence on its forecasting. For example, a common prediction method is to assume that last year's annual revenues and expenses will serve as a good measure for predicting what is going to happen in the upcoming budget period. When the NPO experiences sizable pressures caused by dynamic external and internal environments, this prediction technique is not very useful.

Predictions must be based on empirical data about the past, expectations about the future, and an elusive but real "gut feeling" about where the NPO will be directed during the upcoming year.

Future Budget Input.   Existence of a chronic unfavorable variance or a continuing favorable variance provides management with information that can be used in setting future budgets. Where an unfavorable variance has consistently surfaced, it is wise to budget the item in a manner that reflects what has happened in the past and takes into account whether current trends are likely to continue. For instance, a heating budget based on a fuel oil price of $1.00 a gallon would be inappropriate if the last price paid for fuel oil was $1.10 a gallon and an oil supply depot mailing has indicated that the price will probably be $1.20 a gallon in the coming year. Painful as it may be, management must "tell it like it is" and establish a budget using the $1.20 cost.

Favorable variances usually do not bring wrinkles to the brow of an NPO administrator, but they should lead to an adjustment in the budgetary process. If an NPO is consistently budgeting for a 5 percent level of uncollected fees even though the actual pattern is perennially 2 percent, the budget should be adjusted to reflect this information. Of course, changes in the external or internal environment should also be allowed to influence the budgetary estimate.

Variance Trade-off.   It is not uncommon to restrict spending in one area during a given budgetary period in order to offset overspending in another area. This is referred to as "trading-off variances," and is an appropriate part of the reaction phase in budgeting. However, the person responsible for managing the physical, financial, and human resources of the NPO must move with great care and concern when deciding on going ahead with one of these trade-offs. Frequently, organizations shelve important activities such as maintenance or employee development and promise to restore the original level of spending in a later budgetary period. Unfortunately, the cuts are rarely replenished, and a depressed level of actual spending becomes characteristic. The short-term solution seems painless, but the long-range impact can be severe: Equipment is likely to malfunction more frequently when not adequately maintained, and poor employee morale has an enormous long-range—if not immediately obvious—effect on the organization.

Conclusion

This chapter concentrated on the budgeting process. Operating budgets, cash budgets, and other budgets have been described, discussed, and demonstrated.

Before a budget can serve as an effective management tool, two resources—time and talent—must be effectively applied to the preparation, comparison, and reaction phases of budgeting. In addition, management must fully understand and support the budgetary effort. Lines of communication must be kept open, especially during the preparation phase. Finally, emphasis must be placed on the budget as a benchmark or guideline, because the budget must not be regarded as some type of idol to be worshiped and followed regardless of the consequences.

All in all, budgeting is worth the effort. The typical NPO approaches its students, patients, or clients with a desire to be of true assistance. Budgeting provides management with an opportunity to see that resources are used effectively and that the NPO can be of the greatest possible service.

48

Accounting Procedures for Nonprofit Organizations

James F. Gaertner

C.P.A., University of Texas at San Antonio

The Uses of Accounting

Whether in the business world or in the nonprofit sector of our economy, "accounting" refers to a method of communicating information about enterprises to interested parties. Just as there is an insatiable demand for information of all kinds in the modern world, there is a strong demand on the part of those interested in the operations of profit-oriented and nonprofit enterprises for information bearing on the past successes and failures and future prospects of those organizations. It is the function of accounting to identify, measure, record, and report information (mostly financial in nature) about the activities of the societal entity. An organization, whether profit-making or nonprofit, has financial activities and a responsibility to report these activities to interested and responsible parties.

Good financial reporting should recount the activities and results of the past primarily as a basis for future action. It is particularly important that reporting be unbiased, inclusive of all significant happenings, and thorough in its analysis of the meaning of the reported data. Thus, accounting involves a system of putting data together in a meaningful way, ensuring its propriety and completeness, and reporting the resulting information to interested parties. Unfortunately, like most devices fashioned by human beings, accounting systems are not perfect, and elements of bias and errors of omission and commission do exist. In order to evaluate the adequacy of accounting information, one must take into consideration the needs of the users of accounting data and the general economic climate, as well as the accounting procedures relating to the recording, verification, and reporting of the financial information.

It is the responsibility of the accountant in the nonprofit entity to ensure the reliability of financial information. This information is valuable for both financial reporting and budget planning, and is also vital as a tool for daily decision making. The understanding of accounting and the information it provides is essential to the discharge of this responsibility. This chapter presents an overview of accounting. Because of space limitations and the general orientation of the book, it does not delve into the details of bookkeeping. The objective of this chapter is to provide the reader with a general description of accounting for a nonprofit organization.

Fund Accounting

In the business area of our economy, accounting practices are based on "generally accepted accounting principles" (GAAP). The pronouncements of the Financial Accounting Standards Board (FASB) and its predecessor organizations are the major sources of such accounting principles. In the nonbusiness area, however, the source of accounting principles is not nearly so well defined. This is largely because of the diverse nature of nonbusiness organizations, which include governmental units, hospitals, churches, colleges and universities, health and welfare organizations, professional associations, and many others.

Ordinarily, the accounting and reporting systems of nonprofit organizations are maintained on a fund basis, with their financial information systems being divided (segmented) into separate financial and accounting entities (funds) corresponding to their diverse nonprofit objectives and to various restrictions upon their operations and resources. Accounting principles have been developed to provide standards of accounting and reporting for particular types of nonprofit organizations. These include *Governmental Accounting, Auditing, and Financial Reporting*, published by the Municipal Finance Officers Association (for state and local governmental units); *Chart of Accounts for Hospitals*, published by the American Hospital Association (for hospitals), *College and University Business Administration*, published by the American Council on Education (for colleges and universities), and a series of Industry Audit Guides prepared by committees of the AICPA for state and local governmental units, hospitals, colleges and universities, and voluntary health and welfare organizations. Because of the absence of accounting principles for numerous other types of nonprofit organizations, in 1978 the AICPA issued a statement of position (SOP), entitled *Accounting Principles and Reporting Practices of Certain Nonprofit Organizations*. This SOP provides guidance in preparing financial statements for nonprofit organizations not covered by other authoritative pronouncements.

For many years, the National Council on Governmental Accounting (NCGA) was the official body charged with the responsibility of issuing pronouncements on governmental accounting. A serious problem with the NCGA as a standard-setting organization was that it was composed of only part-time members. Therefore, in 1984, the five-member Governmental Accounting Standards Board (GASB) was established to assume the responsibility of issuing official pronouncements relating to governmental accounting practices. One of its first actions was to issue Statement I, giving authoritative status to NCGA pronouncements. It also placed three issues on its working agenda, including basis of accounting, financial reporting, and pension accounting. Currently accepted practice calls for use of the modified accrual basis. Thus, it can be seen that accounting principles for nonprofit organizations come from many diverse sources and carry varying degrees of authoritative support.

Basis

The first concept to understand is the basis for an accounting system. The two bases that accountants cite are *cash* and *accrual.* Cash systems differ from accrual systems in both recording and reporting financial activity or position. Although a cash system is easier to maintain, an accrual system is more comprehensive. Regardless of the system chosen, and "unqualified opinion" from an auditor (see the section on audits) requires that financial statements be presented on the accrual basis. This is a requirement of the most recent nonprofit audit guide being prepared by the American Institute of Certified Public Accountants (AICPA).

Cash

A cash system is easier, since it records changes in cash when actually received or disbursed. In its simplest form, the system can be maintained by adding deposits to and subtracting checks from your previous cash balance. This system does not comprehend the wear and tear on organization resources. For example, if your group owns and uses a van for program activities, the van cannot be depreciated using a cash system. Yet, a van is continually wearing out through use. Another drawback is that a cash system reflects neither outstanding bills nor pledges or grants receivable.

Accrual

An accrual system generally presents a more accurate picture of the activity and position of an organization. The trade-off is a more complex system requiring more records and transfers of data between records. Care must be exercised when using accrual accounting, since its complexity increases the possibility for error.

An accrual system is necessary where unpaid bills (payables) and uncollected resources (receivables) are substantial. Moreover, if you have resources with long useful lives (e.g., automobiles and buildings), it is necessary to depreciate them. This involves recording their wear and tear each reporting period. The van noted above is a good example. Let us assume the straight-line depreciation method. First, determine the vehicle's useful life. Next, subtract its estimated trade-in value (salvage value) from its original cost, and then divide the remainder by the useful life:

Example

1. Useful life:	5 years
2. Cost:	$6450.00
Estimated trade-in value:	450.00
Depreciable value:	$6000.00

3. Dividing the depreciable value by 5 yields a yearly depreciation of $1200 ($6000÷5), or a monthly depreciation of $100 ($1200 ÷ 12).

This $100 of depreciation affects the monthly financial records when maintained on the accrual basis. It is an expense in the same way that rent or utility bills are expenses. When a system keeps track of payables, receivables, and depreciation, an enterprise is able to present a comprehensive picture of accounting data. Only when accrual accounting is used is information truly useful for budgeting, controlling, and planning.

Objectives and Concepts, or Principles

Accounting has as its basis certain fundamental concepts, or principles, which have slowly evolved over many years of accounting practice and regulatory effort. A logical starting point in the establishment of these principles is considered to be the *objectives* of financial reporting. In other words, if the objectives of accounting and financial reporting can be delineated, then certain principles that will result in those objectives can be presented. These basic objectives are presented below.

Objectives

Understandability.   Sometimes we tend to forget that accounting is, in the final analysis, a system of communication. The basic key to this process of communication is the concept of understandability. If the readers of financial statements are unable to understand the message being communicated, they will either disregard the data and seek other sources of information or they will be misled by the data and a poor economic decision may result. In either case, the financial statements will have failed to serve their basic purpose. This is why the starting point in any delineation of the qualities that should be contained in financial statements is *understandability.*

Usefulness.   In addition to being understandable, the information transmitted by the accountant must be useful. Accountants must therefore maintain a continuing awareness of the kinds of economic decisions being made. In determining whether information is useful with respect to decisions, accountants generally consider two other qualitative characteristics of accounting information: relevance and reliability.

"Relevance" is defined as the capacity of the information to make a difference in a decision by helping users to form predictions about the outcomes of certain events. To be relevant, the information presented must be timely and must enable users to confirm or correct prior expectations.

"Reliability" is defined as the quality that ensures that the information is reasonably free of error and bias. To be reliable, the information must be neutral, verifiable, and representationally faithful (or valid).

"Comparability" is defined as the quality of information that enables users to identify similarities in and differences between two sets of economic phenomena. To go along with the idea of comparability, financial statements presented should be consistent. "Consistency" is defined as conformity from period to period with unchanging policies and procedures.

Materiality.   Even if the information presented in the financial statements is reliable, timely, and so on, that information would be useless unless it is material. Information is considered "material" when its inclusion or deletion would probably change the judgment of a reasonable person. The exact amount of money that constitutes materialty is *relative,* however. For example, the omission of a note payable for $10,000 from the personal financial statement of most individuals in the United States would probably be material. However, the same $10,000 note payable would certainly have no impact on the way a person might evaluate the financial statements of a major corporation. In the case of General Motors or Exxon, for example, the inclusion or omission of a $1 million amount would probably not be material. It is difficult to imagine, but the inclusion or omission of a $1 billion amount would probably not be material for the United States government. In other words, the inclusion or omission of $1 billion would probably not change the judgment of a reasonable person concerning the financial condition of the United States government.

As the foregoing examples illustrate, it is impossible to establish an arbitrary dollar amount as the level at which transactions become material. Instead, each transaction must be considered individually. It is very important to emphasize that in this area (and many others), accountants must use their professional judgment in determining the materiality of a given event.

Basic Principles, or Concepts

Now that we have discussed the method by which accounting principles are established and the basic objectives of financial reporting, we shall take a look at some basic accounting principles, or concepts, that govern the accounting process.

The Entity Principle.   One of the most basic concepts of accounting is concerned with the unit for which economic information is compiled and presented. An accounting entity is any economic unit which controls resources and is actively engaged in economic activities. Governmental agencies are economic entities as are other nonprofit organizations, as well as corporations and other profit-oriented businesses. Under this separate entity concept, all financial reports are developed from the viewpoint of the particular entity. This provides a clear-cut distinction in analyzing transactions between the enterprise and its owners. For example, a building owned by a church which also owns an unincorporated business is not considered an asset for the business to report, although the building and the business have a common owner.

The Cost Principle.   Under the cost principle, all goods and services acquired are recorded at cost, irrespective of what the item is actually "worth." At the time that an item is originally acquired, cost normally represents the "fair market value" of the goods or services acquired. However, with the passage of time, the fair value of many assets (such as land and buildings) may change dramatically from their original cost. These changes in the fair market value of assets are generally excluded from the accounting records, and the assets are continually presented in the financial statements at historical cost (less the portion of cost that has been allocated to depreciation expense).

It is important to note that the primary reason given in support of the cost principle is objectivity. In most cases, the historical cost of an item is readily available and can be measured with complete objectivity (from a cancelled check or invoice). However, evidence concerning the current fair market value of assets is usually less readily available. It is important that the users of financial statements have confidence in those statements, and many believe that this confidence might be eroded if a less-objective measure than historical cost was employed in the preparation of financial statements.

The Going-Concern Principle. The going-concern (or continuity) principle asserts that an accounting entity will continue indefinitely unless there is evidence to the contrary. We can prove that we believe in this principle by many of the things we do in accounting practice. For example, entities typically depreciate some assets over an extended period of time because we assume that the entity will continue in existence for a period of time sufficient to carry out the planned depreciation schedule. On the other hand, if we assumed that the entity is likely to terminate in the future, it would be forced to depreciate long-lived assets over the anticipated remaining life of the entity, not the remaining life of the asset.

The Time-Period Principle. Although every economic entity has a beginning and an end, in accounting we assume an indefinite existence for most entities. Accountants are not, however, allowed the luxury of waiting until the end of an entity's life to prepare the only and "final" financial report. Users of financial information require periodic measurements for decision making. Therefore, it is commonly necessary to break up the real life of an entity into several artificial time segments and to report financial activity for those periods. These time periods are typically referred to as "fiscal years." Many economic events that occur throughout the life of an entity affect many different fiscal years; therefore, because accountants are forced to report by artificial time segments, numerous estimates and assumptions are required. Because of these estimates it is obvious that the period measurement of net income and financial position are only reasonable approximations. This tentative nature of periodic measurements should be understood by those who rely on periodic accounting information.

The Monetary Principle. In the United States, accounting transactions are measured in terms of dollars. In this context, the dollar is a unit of measure, like the inch, the acre, or the gallon. However, unlike the inch, the acre, or the gallon, the relative value of the dollar changes in the general price level. To illustrate the impact of this changing value of the dollar, assume that an enterprise reports two $100,000 buildings on its balance sheet. One of the buildings was purchased in 1962 and the other 25 years later in 1987. It is obvious that although the dollars will be the same for both buildings, it is very unlikely that the two buildings will be anywhere near comparable in value.

Therefore, although most units of measure are stable (remain unchanged over time), the unit of measure used in accounting is not stable in that the purchasing power of the dollar changes over time. The dollar remains, however, as the basic unit of measure in accounting.

Basic Equation

Once the basis of your accounting system is understood, you can begin analyzing its results. There are two equations that accountants use in breaking down accounting data. The first states that the value of the resources (assets) available to your organization at one point in time can be divided between what you own ("fund balance") and what you owe ("liabilities"). Generally presented, assets equal liabilities plus fund balance or

$$A = L + FB$$

To illustrate this equation, apply it to one resource (e.g., an automobile). Assume that on May 31 you purchased a car for $12,000 by putting $1000 down and promising to pay $11,000. (Disregard depreciation or interest changes.) The equation as applied to this example would be

$$\frac{\text{Asset (car)}}{\$12,000} = \frac{\text{liability (loan)}}{\$11,000} + \frac{\text{fund balance}}{\$1000}$$

The second equation states that the change in fund balance between two points in time is the difference between the actual and accrued resources that enter your organization ("revenues") and those actual and accrued resources that leave your organization ("expenses"). In other words, revenues less expenses equals a change in the fund balance, or

$$R - E = \Delta FB$$

The two equations tie together. The first equation analyzes the financial position *at a specific point in time.* The second equation analyzes the financial activity *between two points in time.* In other words, the monetary difference between two points in time is explained by the financial activity occurring between those two points. To continue our example, let us look at another point in time, June 30.

Assume the same conditions as above. Assume that during June you spent $20 maintaining the car while collecting membership dues totaling $100. On June 30, you take the remaining $80 and make your first car payment against the promise to pay.

The equations would present the example, as shown in Figure 48.1.

Notice how the activity equation ties the position equations together. The difference between the position equations of May 31 and June 30 is $80. This increase in the fund balance is explained by the activity equation for the period between May 31 and June 30.

By using these two equations we are able to analyze this example or any others to determine where we stand and how we got there. Unfortunately, understanding

A = L + FB May 31			
Assets:		*Liabilities:*	
		Notes payable	$11,000
Automobile	$12,000	*Fund balance:*	
		Ownership	1,000
Total	$12,000	Total	$12,000

R − E = ΔFB June Activity			
Revenue	$ 100	Dues collected	
Less expenses	20	Auto maintenance	
Excess of revenues over expenses	$ 80	Change in fund balance	

A = L + FB June 30			
Assets:		*Liabilities:*	
		Notes payable	$11,920
Automobile	$12,000	*Fund balance:*	
		Ownership	1,080
Total	$12,000	Total	$12,000

Figure 48.1

accounting and the relationship between these two equations is not simply a matter of change in fund balance. In accrual accounting, to the extent that you have outstanding bills, you have less ownership. If after subtracting expenses from revenues you have a $1000 favorable change in your fund balance, you must subtract from that any of the expenses that remain outstanding.

To illustrate, let us use the same example. Assume that during July you improve (on credit) the van at a cost of $75. During July, you neither generate revenues nor incur other expenses. At July 31, the $75 bill for van improvement is still owing (see Figure 48.2). The more resources your organization uses, the more debt you assume; and the more financially active you are, the more useful these equations are.

Statements

The two equations provide the basic framework for the two most commonly used financial statements in accounting. The first equation (A = L + FB) determines the format of the *balance sheet,* and the second equation (R − E = ΔFB) defines the format of the *statement of revenue, expenses, and changes in fund balance.* Figures 48.3 and 48.4 are suggested formats for these statements.

Internal Control

No discussion of the accounting procedures for a nonprofit organization would be complete without some elaboration on internal control.

Internal control can be defined as "the plan of organization...adopted to (1) safeguard the assets, (2) check the accuracy and reliability of accounting data, (3) promote operational efficiency and (4) encourage adherence to managerial policies."[1]

Internal controls are classified as either accounting or administrative. "Accounting controls" are those which deal with matters that have a direct impact on the organization's financial statements. They are the ones that (1) safeguard the assets, (2) ensure reliable accounting data, and (3) enable the management of the organization to ascertain that expenditures are properly authorized and made in accordance with appropriate laws and regulations. Specific accounting controls will be discussed later in this chapter.

	A = L + FB July 31		
Assets:		*Liabilities*:	
Automobile	$12,075	Bills payable	$ 75
($75 represents		Notes payable	11,920
increased value			11,995
in resources)			
		Fund balance:	
		Ownership	1,080
Total	$12,075	Total	$12,075

Figure 48.2

"Administrative controls" are those which deal with matters that have an indirect impact on the financial statements. They are the ones that (1) promote operational efficiency and (2) encourage adherence to prescribed managerial policies. Specific operational controls include time-and-motion studies, energy usage controls, statistical analyses, quality controls, employee training programs, and operational audits.

Internal controls are basically preventative measures that an organization puts in place in order to *prevent* bad management and theft, *not* to catch bad managers or thieves. A good system of internal controls can serve as a deterent to poor management and even defalcation, by removing much of the temptation to steal or engage in lax business practices.

To be effective, a system of internal control must possess the following elements:

1. Reliable personnel and rotation of duties

2. A clearly defined organization plan

3. Separation of duties

4. Physical control over assets

5. Cash controls

6. An independent check

City of Pleasantville General Fund Balance Sheet as of June 30, 19X2		
Assets		
Cash and cash equivalents	$ 22,500	
Investments	26,048	
Property taxes receivable	10,602	
Other accounts receivable, net	10,351	
Due from other governments	39,954	
Due from other funds	12,436	
Current portion of notes and mortgages		
receivable, net	2,434	
Inventories, at cost	13,726	
Other current assets	10,064	
Notes and mortgages receivable, net	110,500	
Other assets	12,020	
Total assets		$270,635
Liabilities and Fund Equity		
Liabilities:		
Accounts payable and accrued liabilities	$ 73,560	
Property taxes payable—state	1,721	
Deposits subject to refund	6,391	
Deferred revenue	25,673	
Total liabilities		107,345
Fund balance:		163,290
Total liabilities and fund balance		$270,635

Figure 48.3

City of Pleasantville
General Fund
Statement of Revenues, Expenditures, and
Changes in Fund Balance
for the Year Ended June 30, 19X2

Revenues:

Taxes—local	$720,874	
Taxes—state-shared	15,836	
Licenses and permits	14,370	
Fines and forfeits	12,870	
Interest and other investment income	39,971	
Federal grants	30,000	
State grants	396,111	
Other grants	10,000	
Charges for current services	30,602	
Miscellaneous revenues	13,481	
Total revenue		$1,284,115

Expenditures:

General government	$129,577	
Public safety and regulation	299,499	
Corrections	34,111	
Conservation of health	130,047	
Social services	2,872	
Education	488,121	
Public library	17,444	
Recreation and culture	42,005	
Highways	1,612	
Sanitation and waste removal	38,741	
Public service	10,555	
Economic development	22,188	
Total expenditures		1,216,772
Excess of revenues over expenditures		$ 67,343
Beginning fund balance (July 1, 19X1)		95,947
End fund balance (June 30, 19X2)		$ 163,290

Figure 48.4

Reliable Personnel

Obviously, the success of any operation relies to a significant extent on the people who are chosen to perform the duties assigned. This basic fact applies as much to nonprofit enterprises as it does to other segments of our society.

Internal control in this area begins before the hiring process. Before they are hired, prospective employees should be carefully screened to make certain that they are qualified for the position being filled and that they have no previous record of questionable activities. In addition, all employees should be promoted or given greater responsibilities on the basis of performance, rather than exclusively on the basis of seniority or length of service.

Employees performing accounting functions and any other employees who handle cash or other readily salable assets should normally be bonded. Bonding not only protects the organization from loss but acts as a psychological deterrent to potential thieves because, even though the organization might not prosecute them, the bonding companies will. In addition, the bonding companies often perform a screening function for their client organizations because they generally make thorough background checks of any employees they bond.

After employees have been hired, they should be trained not only for the position that they will fill immediately, but also for other positions into which they may move. This procedure not only broadens the employee's knowledge of the entire operation (and often enhances job satisfaction) but also enables the organization to enforce a system of job rotation. Employees should be rotated periodically to new duties, and they should be forced to take annual vacations while their duties are handled by others in the organization.

It is not an uncommon occurrence in the nonprofit world to have a particularly loyal employee who is performing a function (normally accounting-related) that no one else in the organization wishes to perform. Often, such an employee becomes embedded in the position and never even takes a vacation. Others in the firm simply leave the person alone to perform a function that no one else understands or honestly wishes to understand. At some point in time the inevitable happens: the person dies or otherwise becomes incapacitated and cannot continue to perform the function. No one knows what to do. At that point, it is often very expensive to bring in outside experts, such as certified public accountants, to sort through the system and train someone new for the job. Such confusion can be avoided by simply requiring that jobs be rotated periodically and requiring that employees take regular vacations.

Obviously, vacations also have the effect of "recharging" employees, and job rotation reduces the monotony of routine tasks. Job rotation also allows various employees to become familiar with several different aspects of the organization's operation.

A Clearly Defined Organization Plan

A formal, clearly defined organization plan is essential for a system of good internal control. Such a plan must include definite lines of responsibility and should specify who is responsible for each activity. It must also provide for the delegation of tasks and responsibilities throughout the organization while making clear where the ultimate responsibility for each activity lies.

Every organization should maintain an up-to-date, carefully prepared organization chart. Each position listed on this chart should report directly to a higher position. In addition, the tasks should be arranged in such a manner as to provide for the separation of operating, custodial, and accounting responsibilities. Specific individuals should be assigned the responsibility for particular assets and for the performance of each task.

By reference to the chart, each employee should know to whom he or she reports, and who reports to him or her. In addition, employees should be provided with a job description of their own position and of the positions of others in the organization with whom they work.

Separation of Duties

A proper allocation of responsibilities is essential to a good plan of internal control. In general, no *one* individual should be responsible for handling all phases of a transaction. Such a division of responsibility provides for certain efficiencies derived from specialization, and makes possible a system of cross-checking that helps ensure the accuracy of the accounting data.

Specifically, controls which fall under the general category of separation of duties include the following:

1. One person should not handle a transaction from its inception to its final recording.

2. The accounting system should be structured in a manner that provides independent cross-checking of each employee's work.

3. Custody of assets should be separated from the record keeping for those assets.

4. Operational responsibilities should be separated from record-keeping responsibilities.

5. Responsibility for the authorization of transactions should be separated from record keeping and, in the case of purchases, custodial responsibility.

6. Mail should be opened by someone other than the cashier or bookkeeper.

7. The purchasing function should be separated from the receiving function.

When accounting systems are computerized, the problem becomes one of separating the programming, operating, and data storage functions. The person who programs the computer should not prepare the input data or operate the machine. Similarly, the person who maintains the transaction and data files should not perform programming or operating functions. In addition, the computer's output should be reviewed and reconciled with its input by an independent party, and the computer should be "off limits" to unauthorized personnel.

Obviously, it would be very difficult for the small nonprofit organization to achieve a completely satisfactory system of separation of duties. In such organizations, it may be necessary for nonaccountants to occasionally perform a traditionally accounting function. For example, a private school dean may make bank deposits, a secretary may collect cash from tuition, and another person—who has no other cash handling functions—may prepare the bank reconciliation. On the other hand, small organizations often have less need to rely on a tight system of internal controls for adequate information and control. The limited scope of operations and the number of employees ordinarily make it possible for the overall administrator to have personal contact with every phase of the operations.

Finally, although a good system of separation of duties is an essential element to a good overall system of internal control, it can be overcome by two or more dishonest persons working in collusion. Nevertheless, it can go far in the prevention of fraud and errors.

Physical Control over Assets

Physical controls over assets include the safeguards which are incorporated to help ensure that certain assets do not disappear or are not misused. Some of these controls include

1. Keeping cancelled checks and other similar documents in a safe, fireproof place for a sufficient length of time.

2. Taking a periodic inventory of physical assets and comparing the results of this inventory with the accounting records. In keeping with the separation-of-duties doctrine, the inventory should be taken by someone other than the custodian of the assets or the person who maintains the asset records.

3. The use of check protector machines which stamp dollar amounts on checks in a manner that is difficult to duplicate or change. These machines should be locked away when not in use.

4. The use of cancellation machines which print the word "paid" or "void" on

documents making it virtually impossible to accidentally reuse documents such as invoices, purchase orders, and the like.

5. The use of fireproof safes and locked fireproof file cabinets.

6. Depositing cash receipts intact on a regular (usually daily) basis. Allowing cash to accumulate leads to temptations to use such cash to make certain payments, not to mention the temptation which can lead to theft. Again, in keeping with separation of duties, the deposit should be made by someone other than the person who physically collects the cash or who keeps the accounting records concerning it.

Cash Controls

Although cash is usually not a significantly large item in a nonprofit organization's financial statement, it is an item which moves in and out of the organization regularly, and is readily negotiable. Therefore, it is particularly subject to defalcation. Special procedures are therefore normally adopted in the accounting for cash, which are often more stringent than for other (often larger) assets.

These procedures include the following:

1. All disbursements except small ones made from petty cash should be made by check.

2. Cash receipts should be prelisted, by someone other than their custodian or the person who accounts for them, before being deposited in the bank; and the deposit slip should be compared with the prelisting, as soon as it is returned, by someone other than the person recording the receipts.

3. Subsidiary and control accounts should be used whenever possible for cash, (and receivables, payables, and other items requiring many transactions). The subsidiary records should periodically be reconciled with the control accounts by a person not responsible for recording transactions, and the differences should be investigated and resolved.

4. Prenumbered documents, especially checks and receipts, should be used. Numbers should be assigned in a specific sequence and an accounting made for all missing or voided documents.

5. A bank reconciliation should be prepared, at least once a month, by someone not responsible for collecting cash or recording cash transactions. The monthly bank statements and cancelled checks should be received, unopened, by this person.

6. Checks should not be signed without proper supporting documentation. Those for large amounts should require two signatures. Advance signing of checks should be forbidden.

7. Payroll disbursements should be backed up by employee time cards or time sheets in order to avoid erroneous payments or payments to persons not on the payroll. A separate bank account should be used for payrolls.

Independent Check

Large commercial businesses are normally required to submit to an audit by a firm of certified public accountants. This audit, or independent check, is to ensure the general accuracy of the financial statements being prepared by the business.

Although such an audit of the financial records is generally not mandatory for an NPO a procedure referred to as an operational audit is often done. Operational auditors are more concerned with the managerial practices employed by nonprofit organizations. They focus on such things as the efficient use of resources and the reasonableness and adherence to management procedures. Audits of the financial records are often done when required because of large bank loans, or when theft or embezzlement is suspected.

Cost-Benefit Considerations

Often administrators of NPOs begin to implement internal control procedures without due regard for the cost of such systems. Although certain very elementary control procedures (such as prenumbered checks and timely deposits) are inexpensive and readily available to every organization, others (such as fireproof vaults) are sometimes very expensive.

It is very important that a cost-benefit analysis be performed before each control is installed. A cost-benefit analysis means that the cost of each control should be commensurate with the perceived benefit of that control. This, obviously, often requires a large degree of judgment on the part of the manager in a nonprofit organization.

Note

1. Committee on Auditing Procedure, *Internal Control—Elements of a Coordinated System and Its Importance to Management and the Independent Public Accountant*, AICPA, New York, 1949, p. 6.

49

Bookkeeping Procedures for the Nonprofit Organization

Barron H. Harvey

Ph.D., C.P.A., Howard University

Horton L. Sorkin

Ph.D., Howard University

The purpose of bookkeeping is to compile financial data in an organized fashion. This mechanism provides the framework for eventual preparation of any and all financial statements to be used by nonprofit administrators and trustees, funders, governments, and others who request data concerning financial position or financial activity. As mentioned in the chapter on financial analysis, this information is most useful when it is current.

In preparing financial statements, the bookkeeper regularly and systematically summarizes and compares categories of like financial events. These categories are called "accounts" and the financial events are called "transactions." Transactions represent *any* events that affect the accounts of the organization. Like pieces in a puzzle, transactions take on meaning only when placed together.

Presenting financial position is simply a matter of listing recorded amounts of all resources available to your organization (assets), the amounts representing what you owe for the resources (liabilities), and the amount representing what you own (equity) (Figure 49.1). Presenting the financial activity of an organization involves comparing the resources flowing into the organization (income or revenue) against the resources flowing out (expenditures and expenses); see Figure 49.2.

```
┌──────────────────┬──────────────┐
│ All the resources│ YOU OWE      │
│ available to the │              │
│ organization     │  ─────       │
│                  │              │
│                  │ YOU OWN      │
│                  │              │
│                  │  ─────       │
│      ─────       │  ─────       │
└──────────────────┴──────────────┘
```

Figure 49.1

The resulting excess or deficiency is then added to or subtracted from the previous balance sheet (specifically, that section representing ownership) in determining current financial position. This is done periodically, generally by month or quarter, but at least once a year (see sections on equations and reports).

Depending on the needs of the organization, this financial report will be prepared monthly, quarterly, and/or annually. In order to prepare periodic financial reports, the bookkeeper is required to record and track transactions within predetermined time periods. To accomplish this, your bookkeeper maintains various records that comprise the "books." This tracking process makes up the bookkeeper's day-to-day activity. The bookkeeping system serves to facilitate basic bookkeeping steps:

1. Recording transactions

2. Summarizing transactions

3. Preparing financial statements

Recording of transactions is very important in the bookkeeping system and is generally completed as transactions occur. Depending on the type of system employed and the extent of the system needed, transactions are recorded in a journal, receipt, and disbursement record or in the checkbook stub of the organization's bank checking account. The summarizing step in the bookkeeping system requires that similar or like transactions be grouped together.

This summarization may be completed using a ledger of accounts or a worksheet. The summarizing step is important because it provides the information needed for the third step: preparing financial statements. There are three basic financial statements that are recommended by the American Institute of Certified Public Accountants. They are (1) statement of financial position (balance sheet); (2) statement of activity or statement of support, revenue, and expenses; and (3)

```
┌───────────────────────────────────┐
│ (Revenue or Income)               │
│ Resources flowing in    ───────   │
│                                   │
│ MINUS                             │
│ (Expenses)                        │
│ Resources flowing out   ───────   │
│                                   │
│ EQUALS                            │
│ Excess or deficiency    ───────   │
└───────────────────────────────────┘
```

Figure 49.2

statement of changes in fund balances. In addition, the statement of changes in financial position, (an important and required financial statement for *for-profit* organizations) may be included in the financial statements prepared by a nonprofit organization (NPO).

The Basic Accounting Equation and Double-Entry System

The basic framework for any bookkeeping and accounting system is the basic accounting equation:

Assets = liabilities + fund balance (owner's equity)

This fundamental equation, which is reflected in the statement of financial position, must remain in balance after each transaction. Each transaction has at least two sides and represents an exchange. Generally, the organization is either giving something it owns to receive goods or services or it incurs debt (a liability) in order to receive goods or services. In any event, each transaction has at least two sides. Examples may more clearly explain the two sides of a transaction and its impact on the basic accounting equation. Examine the following:

Purchase of an automobile on credit. Asset is increased and a liability is increased.

Purchase of office supplies for cash. One asset is increased—supplies, and another is decreased—cash.

Payment of a debt. An asset is decreased—cash, and a liability is decreased—debt. Cash received from membership (dues)—an asset is increased—cash and revenue or income is increased.

Underneath each of these examples, the two sides of a transaction are reflected. After each transaction the basic accounting equation will remain in balance (if the transaction is recorded correctly). It is also important to note that every transaction affects at least two accounts.

Debts and Credits in a Bookkeeping System

In accounting or bookkeeping, the terms "debit" and "credit" are terms which refer to the two sides of a transaction. These terms are used to describe the left side of an account and the right side of the account, respectively. An account can be visualized in the form of a T, with the top having the name of the account, the left side representing debits, and the right side representing credits (see Figure 49.3). Asset and expense accounts generally have debit balances and liability, and revenue accounts generally have credit balances. Thus, to increase an asset or expense account, you would add the amounts to the left side of the account, the *debit* side; and to increase a liability or revenue you would add the amount to the right side of the account, the *credit* side. Table 49.1 shows the effects of debits and credits on the various types of accounts.

		Cash		
1/1	$ 5,000		1/5	$1,000
1/15	15,000		1/16	7,000
1/25	8,000		1/27	5,000
Balance	11,000			

	Title of Account	
Left side		Right side
(debit)		(credit)

Figure 49.3

Cash Basis System

In a cash basis system, only transactions involving cash are recorded. This is a relatively simple system but one which uses the three basic stepsof a bookkeeping system.

Recording Transactions

The recording of transactions must be done in systematic manner when they occur. To assist in recording the cash transaction, a cash basis system would employ a cash receipts journal, cash disbursements journal, and a general journal. Journals are called "books of original entry" because this is how the transaction enters the system.

The "cash receipts journal" is used to record the inflow of cash from any source. As illustrated in Figure 49.4, the cash receipts journal has a number of columns with the date column being first. The second column, the description column, is used to state the source of the funds. The subsequent column titles will depend very much on the activities of the organization. Note that the cash receipts journal

Table 49.1

Type of account	Debit	Credit
Assets. Resources available to the organization, i.e., cash, furniture, land	Increase	Decrease
Liabilities. Amounts the organization owes for resources and other services, i.e., mortgage, accounts payable, notes payable, etc.	Decrease	Increase
Revenue, or income. Resources flowing into the organization from its activities, i.e., sales, contributions, membership dues	Decrease	Increase
Expenses. Resources consumed in the activities of the organization, i.e., rent, salaries, supplies	Increase	Decrease.

			ABC NONPROFIT ORGANIZATION Cash Receipts Journal				Page 1
Date	Account Credited	Explanation	Misc. Accounts Cr	Contributions Cr	Dues Cr	Fees Cr	Cash Dr
4/5		Monthly Dues			$1,200		$1,200
4/10		Fees				$1,400	$1,400
4/11	Interest Rev.		$100				100
4/15		Community Fund		$3,000		1,400	1,400
4/25		Fees	$100	$3,000	$1,200	$2,800	$7,100

Figure 49.4

has a miscellaneous column for funds received that do not fit in the labeled columns.

The "cash disbursements journal" is used to record all transactions involving the outflow of funds. Usually the disbursement of cash is completed using a check.Thus a column for check number, as illustrated in Figure 49.5, is added to the group of column titles. The cash disbursements journal is very similar to the cash receipts journal.

A few transactions in a cash basis system require the use of a general journal. Transactions recorded in the "general journal" for a cash basis system involve corrections or adjustments and "closing" transactions. Figure 49.6 shows the general journal and a transaction recorded. The general journal has a date column, account column, and debit and credit columns. The transaction illustrated is a correction of an entry in the cash receipts journal. The entry begins with the date, followed by the recording of the account(s). The amounts to be credited are recorded next, with the account(s) to be credited indented to distinguish it from the debit. Following each transaction recorded, a brief explanation is given to describe the transaction. Please note that for all the journals used, after each transaction, debts and credits must equal.

			XYZ CLUB CASH DISBURSEMENTS JOURNAL				Page
Date	Check No.	Account Debited	Misc. Accounts Dr	Salary Expense Dr	Rent Expense Dr	Supplies Dr	Cash Cr
4/2					$ 500		$ 500
4/5				$1,000			1,000
4/10		Interest Exp.	$150				150
4/15						1,000	1,000
4/29				1,000			1,000
			150	2,000	500	1,000	3,650

Figure 49.5

	DATE		DESCRIPTION	POST. REF.	DEBIT	CREDIT	
1	1986 May	1	Cash		1 8 2 2 25		1
2			Sales			1 8 2 2 25	2
3			Cash sales for the day				3
4							4

JOURNAL   PAGE

Figure 49.6

Summarizing Transactions

The general ledger is a book of all accounts of the organization, and each account is used to gather like transactions together. The general ledger will have a separate page for each: assets, liability, revenue, and expense accounts. In addition, an equity account will be represented, which shows the net worth of the organization. Transactions are posted to the general ledger from the cash receipts journal, cash disbursements journal, and the general journal. An illustration of a general ledger account is shown in Figure 49.7. The process of transferring transactions from the journals to the general ledger is called "posting." The posting is completed periodically as opposed to the daily recording of transactions in the various journals.

At the end of the month after the posting process is complete but before the preparation of financial statements, a trial balance should be taken. The trial balance is simply recording the balance of each general ledger account, reflecting debit and credit balances. The primary purpose of the trial balance is to ensure that debits and credits equal one another. Figure 49.8 illustrates a trial balance. Once the trial balance has been prepared and proved (i.e., debits equal credits) the bookkeeper is ready to prepare financial statements.

A somewhat complicated element of the summarization step is the "closing of

ACCOUNT Cash   ACCOUNT NO. 11

DATE		ITEM	POST. REF.	DEBIT	CREDIT	BALANCE DEBIT	BALANCE CREDIT
1986 June	1		1	80 0 0 0 00		80 0 0 0 00	
	2		1		3 6 0 0 00	76 4 0 0 00	
	8		1		6 0 0 00	75 8 0 0 00	
	10		1		1 5 0 0 00	74 3 0 0 00	
	14		1		6 0 0 00	73 7 0 0 00	
	15		1	8 0 0 0 00		81 7 0 0 00	
	15		1		29 4 0 0 00	52 3 0 0 00	
	25		1	6 9 3 0 00		59 2 3 0 00	
	28		1		1 4 0 0 00	57 8 3 0 00	
	30		2		3 8 0 00	57 4 5 0 00	
	30		2		6 0 0 00	56 8 5 0 00	
	30		2	11 0 0 0 00		67 8 5 0 00	

Figure 49.7

ABC Organization Trial Balance April 30, 19xx		
	Debits	Credits
Cash	$ 2,872	
Supplies	187	
Equipment	5,608	
Land	5,000	
Building	42,500	
Furniture	12,817	
Accounts payable*		$ 1,307
Notes payable*		1,000
Fund balance		65,169
Revenue		9,208
Salary expense	3,700	
Utilities expense	850	
Depreciation expense*	2,250	
Interest expense	900	
Total	$76,684	$76,684

* Accounts *not* appearing in cash basis financial statements

Figure 49.8

the books." This process is usually done at the end of the year. Closing involves the revenue or income accounts, expense accounts, and the equity or fund balance. The object of the closing process is to transfer revenue and expenses amounts (net income or net loss) to the fund balance account. To transfer the debit balance of an expense account, a credit is entered into the account for the balance thus reducing the account balances to zero. This is done for every expense account. The process is the same for income accounts, but the accounts are reduced to zero by entering a debit for the account balance to the account. The difference between the debits and credits in this process represents the net income (or net loss) for the organization and will be credited (income accounts totaled more than expense accounts) to the fund balance account. Figure 49.9 illustrates the closing entry which would be recorded in the general journal and then posted on the ledger accounts. At the end of the posting, all revenue or income accounts and all expense accounts will be reduced to zero.

Preparation of Financial Statements

Various groups and individuals are interested in the financial statements of a nonprofit organization. They include donors, client groups, the NPO's board of directors, management, employees, members, governmental agencies, creditors, potential donors, and potential creditors. Financial statements should be designed with the user in mind. The primary purpose of a financial statement is to communicate information. The information conveyed should help the reader assess the organization's activities and financial health. There are three basic financial statements:

Closing Entry	
December 31, 19xx	
Debit:	
Dues	$155,000
Fees	78,000
Contributions	50,000
In-kind contributions	10,000
Other	3,000
Credit:	
Rent	$ 50,000
Utilities	20,000
Salaries	86,000
Insurance	10,000
Supplies	12,000
Interest	9,600
Taxes	12,000
Program expenses	35,000
Other expenses	13,000
Fund balance (excess of revenue	
over expenses)	48,000

Figure 49.9

PRH Club		
Statement of Revenue, Expenses, and Changes in Fund Balances		
for the Year Ended December 31, 19xx		
Revenue:		
Dues	$155,000	
Service fees	78,000	
Contributions	50,000	
In-kind contributions	10,000	
Other	3,000	
Total revenue		$296,000
Expenses:		
Rent	$ 50,000	
Utilities	20,000	
Salaries	86,000	
Insurance	10,000	
Supplies	12,000	
Interest	9,600	
Taxes	12,000	
Program expenses	35,000	
Depreciation	10,000	
Other	3,000	
Total expenses		$247,600
Excess (deficiency) of revenue over expenses		$ 48,400
Fund balance, beginning of year		173,000
Fund balance, end of year		221,400

Figure 49.10

(1) statement of revenues and expenses and of change in fund balance, (2) statement of financial position (balance sheet), and (3) statement of changes in financial position. The trial balance provides the information necessary for preparing financial statements.

The statement of revenues and expenses reflects this classic equation:

Revenue − expenses = income

Thus revenue, expense, and the fund balance is presented on this statement (see Figure 49.10).

The statement of financial position (balance sheet) presents the balances for assets, liabilities, and net worth (cumulative fund balance) and reflects the basic accounting equation:

Assets = liabilities + fund balance

(See Figure 49.11.) The statement of changes in financial position shows the resources that were available to the organization during the period and how those resources were used. This statement reflects the financing and investing activities of the organization (see Figure 49.12).

Accrual Basis System

Although a cash basis system is simple to implement, many organizations employ an accrual basis system. The accrual system provides more information than the cash basis system. In addition to the cash transactions, the accrual basis system records transactions that do not involve cash, for example, unpaid bills, unpaid salaries, and uncollected income.

The basic steps under the accrual basis system are the same as those for any basic bookkeeping system: recording transactions, summarizing transactions, and preparing financial statements.

Recording Transactions

The required journals under the accrual basis system are the same as those outlined under the cash basis system. In addition, a chart of accounts as illustrated may be used with the accrual basis system. A chart of accounts is a listing of all the accounts used by the NPO. The chart of accounts usually has assigned account numbers which are used in the general ledger (see Figure 49.13).

In the accrual basis system there are monthly accrual entries necessary for a complete and accurate set of books. The monthly accrual entries are for unpaid bills, unpaid salaries, uncollected income, expired prepaid expenses, and depreciation. They are recorded in the general journal at the end of the month. Examples of these monthly accrual entries are shown in Figure 49.14.

Summarizing Transactions and Preparing Financial Statements

Under the accrual basis system the summarization and preparation steps are similar to that shown for the cash basis system. The only difference is the additional accounts for the accruals.

Payroll

Employer Responsibilities

The employer responsibilities and liabilities described in this section apply to those persons who may legally be characterized as your employees. They are generally applicable regardless of the nonprofit or tax-exempt status of your organization or the terms you may use to describe or disguise an employment relationship.

```
                    ASC Nonprofit Organization
                    Statement of Financial Position
                    for Year Ended December 31, 19xx

                              Assets
Current assets:
  Cash                                      $ 14,431
  Investments                                 15,142
  Accounts receivable*                         3,643
  Prepaid expenses                             2,943
                                            --------
    Total current assets                                  $ 36,159

Fixed assets:
  Land                                      $ 25,000
  Building                                   145,000
  Furniture and fixtures                      28,133
  Equipment                                   15,482
  Automobiles                                 22,870
Less accumulated depreciation*                43,178
    Net fixed assets                                      $193,307
                                                          --------
    Total assets                                           229,466
                                                          ========

                 Liabilities and Fund Balance
Current liabilities:
  Accounts payable and accrued expenses*    $  9,674
  Deposits*                                    3,204
  Taxes                                        1,212
                                            --------
    Total current liabilities                             $ 14,090

Long-term liabilities:
  Mortgage note payable*                    $ 75,000
  Note payable*                               10,000
    Total long-term liabilities                           $ 85,000
                                                          --------
    Total liabilities                                       99,090

Fund balance:
  Fund balance (Jan 1, 19xx)                $ 93,104
  Excess of revenue over expenses             37,272
    Total fund balance                                    $130,376
                                                          --------
    Total liabilities and fund balance                     229,466
                                                          ========

* Accounts not appearing in cash basis statements
```

Figure 49.11

Ash Inc.
Statement of Changes in Financial Position*
for Year Ended March 31, 19xx

Sources of working capital:

Excess of revenue over expenses	$ 62,000
Capital additions	14,000

Add (deduct) items not using (providing) working capital:

Depreciation	8,000
Sale of investment	10,000
Total sources	94,000

Uses of working capital:

Purchases of equipment	25,000
Purchase of land	32,000
Purchase of investment	15,000
Total uses	72,000
Increase in working capital	$ 22,000

Changes in the components of working capital:

Cash	+4,000
Accounts receivable	+10,000
Investments	+5,000
Inventory	+18,000
Accounts payable and accrued expenses	−10,000
Notes payable (current)	−5,000
Increase in working capital	$ 22,000

AME Church
Statement of Changes in Financial Position
for Year Ended December 31, 19xx

Source of cash:

Excess of revenue over expenses	$ 86,726

Add deductions not decreasing cash:

Depreciation	12,000
Increases in accounts payable and accrued expenses	2,200
Total sources of cash	$103,926

Uses of Cash:

Purchase of equipment	$ 45,000
Reduction in mortgage note payable	36,700
Purchase of supplies	1,850
Increase in prepaid expenses	2,000
Increase in accounts receivable	10,000
Total uses of cash	85,550
Increases in cash	18,376
Cash, beginning balance	5,732
Cash, ending balance	$ 24,108

Figure 49.12

AP Inc.
Charts of Accounts

Assets (1–20)
1. Cash in bank
2. Petty cash
3. Investments
4. Accounts receivable
5. Prepaid expenses
6. Land
7. Building
8. Furniture and fixtures
9. Automobiles
10. Equipment
11. Accumulated depreciation—building
12. Accumulated depreciation—building
13. Accumulated depreciation—automobiles
14. Accumulated depreciation—equipment

Liabilities (21–30)
21. Accounts payable
22. Accrued salaries payable
23. Taxes payable

24. Mortgage payable
25. Notes payable

Fund balance (31–40)

Revenue (41–50)
41. Dues
42. Fees
43. Contributions
44. Other

Expenses (51–70)
51. Salaries
52. Payroll taxes
53. Repair and Maintenance
54. Insurance expense
55. Depreciation
56. Interest
57. Supplies
58. Other

Figure 49.13

Date	General Journal Description	Debit	Credit
	To record unpaid gas bill:		
	Debit: Utilities expense	xxx	
	Credit: Accounts payable		xxx
	To record unpaid salaries:		
	Debit: Salaries	xxx	
	Credit: Accrued salaries payable		xxx
	To record uncollected income:		
	Debit: Accounts receivable	xxx	
	Credit: Fees		xxx
	To record expired prepaid expenses:		
	Debit: Insurance expense	xxx	
	Credit: Prepaid insurance		xxx
	To record depreciation of office equipment:		
	Debit: Depreciation expenses—office equipment	xxx	
	Credit: Accumulated depreciation—office equipment		xxx

Figure 49.14

Who Is an Employee?   Under the "common law test," an individual is an "employee" when performs services for you and you have the right to control and direct his or her work. You must also be able to dictate the means employed to accomplish the task and have discretion over the results or end products themselves.

Generally, payments to a plumber for fixing a broken pipe or to an attorney for incorporating your organization will not create a common law employee-employer relationship. However, if the plumber is hired as a maintenance person, and the organization directs this person to fix the broken pipe during a pay period, he or she will be an employee even though the task and payment may be identical.

The same could be true for the attorney, if hired for general staff purposes and then directed to do specific tasks.

It is the right to control and direct the work of an individual that determines employee status. The use of legal terms such as "independent contractor," "consultant," or "professional service" to describe a relationship as other than an employment relationship is unlikely to succeed if, in fact, the organization paying for the services has the right to exercise control and direction over the details and manner of accomplishing the tasks.

Although employer's responsibilities should not be taken lightly, you should not allow them to intimidate you from hiring needed employees. They can be managed quite efficiently when supported by adequate payroll accounting.

Finally, in addition to gaining other benefits of employee status, individuals generally prefer that their employers make their withholdings, and so on, so that they will not have to lose sleep over estimated tax returns and the like.

Income Tax Withholdings—Federal

Nearly all employers are required to withhold an estimated federal income tax from the wages or salaries of their employees. They are liable to the government for the amounts that are required to be withheld even if they fail to withhold anything.

The amounts withheld should be accounted for carefully and deposited regularly. From the time you write a check for wages, the amount required to be subtracted as withholdings belongs to the government and not to you. You, the employer, only hold it in trust for the government.

Although accounting for and depositing these amounts is not very difficult, failure to do so will inevitably result in burdensome tax problems that will threaten the survival of your organization. Treat these responsibilities with respect.

Employers (even if exempt from taxes themselves) are responsible for withholding federal income taxes from nearly all wages paid to common law employees. If your organization is doubtful about whether or not an individual is an employee, you can obtain an IRS ruling on the question by filing Form SS-8, which should be available at your local IRS office.

Registering as an Employer.   If your organization plans to hire employees, or if it needs a federal Employer's Identification Number for other reporting purposes, you should register with the IRS, by filing Form SS-4. It is a very simple form, which asks for the name and address of the organization, some basic identifying information such as the organization's type (nonprofit corporation, etc.) and purpose (charitable—combatting community deterioration, etc.), and when if ever the organization anticipates hiring employees. If you say that the organization plans to hire employees, the IRS will mail you the information (Circular E) and the forms

(W-4s, 501s, and 941s) that your organization will need for making federal withholdings.

The amount you are responsible (and liable) for withholdings from wages depends on the amount of pay classified as gross wages, the marital status, and the number of exemptions (or withholding allowances) claimed by employees. The IRS's Employer's Tax Guide (Circular E) has tables in which you can easily find the amounts to be withheld from weekly, biweekly, semimonthly, or monthly wages.

In making the withholding computations, you must rely on information from your employees concerning their marital status and withholding allowances. The tax laws make employers liable for the highest rate of withholdings (single with zero withholding allowances) unless the employees have completed valid Form W-4, "Employee's Withholding Allowance Certificate."

A certificate is not valid if it is not signed or if the employee tells the employer that it is false.

Reporting and Paying Withholdings.   As an employer you are required to make quarterly reports of the amounts of wages and other compensation paid and the amounts of federal income taxes withheld on IRS Form 941 or 941E. These reports are due on the last day of the month following the end of each calendar quarter.

Form 941 is to be accompanied by a check for any withholdings that were not deposited during the quarter. Deposits are made to a local bank (a member of the Federal Reserve System) at intervals that vary with the amounts being withheld. At the end of each calendar year (by January 31), employers are required to complete an annual Wage and Tax Statement, Form W-2, for each employee with copies being distributed to employees and the IRS.

Form 941 or 941E: Employer's Quarterly Federal Tax Return.   Completing Form 941 is relatively simple if you have an adequate payroll accounting system. If the system is inadequate, Form 941 and all other payroll reporting will be a nightmare.

To be adequate, the payroll account or card of *each* employee must show both the cumulative total of wages paid him or her during the quarter and the taxes withheld. On the 941 or 941E quarterly reports you will aggregate these figures for all employees, but you will have to have the information for each individual employee for the annual reports.

Form 941E is to be used by those employers (1) who are not required to pay, *and* (2) who have also elected not to pay Social Security (FICA). [Organizations that have or are applying for 501(c) (3) tax-exempt status may qualify for the election not to pay FICA, along with state and local governments; see the discussions about FICA below.] The deadlines for filing either form are the same (see Table 49.2).

The forms differ only in that Form 941E does not provide space for reporting

Table 49.2. Filing Deadlines for Forms 941 and 941E

Quarter	Quarter ending	Due date
January–February–March	Mar. 31	Apr. 30
April–May–June	June 30	July 31
July–August–September	Sept. 30	Oct. 31
October–November–December	Dec. 31	Jan. 31

Social Security (FICA) payments. A sample Form 941 with instructions can be obtained from a local IRS office.

On Form 941 you simply report the total wages paid, the total federal income tax withheld for all employees, and the amounts deposited during the quarter. If the deposits were insufficient to cover the amounts withheld from wages, you must include payment for the difference. File Form 941 with the appropriate regional Internal Revenue Service Center (see Table 49.3).

Deposits: Form 501. Employers are currently required to make deposits prior to filing their quarterly 941's when their total withholdings *and* Social Security (FICA) owing for a quarter exceeds $500. The frequency of these deposits depends on the amount of taxes owing. The deposit rules are summarized in Table 49-4. Although these rules will probably not change frequently, updated rules can be found in Circular E or on the back of Form 941.

The IRS will give you Form 501, computer deposit cards, with your name and Employer's Identification Number typed on them. To make a deposit you merely write the amount of the deposit on the appropriate card and on a check, and sub-

Table 49.3. Filing Addresses

Regions	Center addresses
New Jersey, New York City and counties of Nassau, Rockland, Suffolk, and Westchester	Internal Revenue Service Center 1040 Waverly Avenue Holtsville, N.Y. 00501
New York (all other counties), Connecticut, Maine, Massachusetts, New Hampshire, Rhode Island, Vermont	Internal Revenue Service Center 310 Lowell Street Andover, Mass. 05501
District of Columbia, Delaware, Maryland, Pennsylvania	Internal Revenue Service Center 11601 Roosevelt Boulevard Philadelphia, Pa. 19155
Alabama, Florida, Georgia, Mississippi, South Carolina	Internal Revenue Service Center 4800 Buford Highway Chamblee, Ga. 30006
Michigan, Ohio	Internal Revenue Service Center Cincinnati, Ohio 45298
Arkansas, Kansas, Louisiana, New Mexico, Oklahoma, Texas	Internal Revenue Service Center 3651 S. Interregional Highway Austin, Tex. 78740
Alaska, Arizona, Colorado, Idaho, Minnesota, Montana, Nebraska, Nevada, North Dakota, Oregon, South Dakota, Utah, Washington, Wyoming	Internal Revenue Service Center 1160 West 1200 South Street Ogden, Utah 84201
Illinois, Iowa, Missouri, Wisconsin	Internal Revenue Service Center 2306 E. Bannister Road Kansas City, Mo. 64170
California, Hawaii	Internal Revenue Service Center 5045 East Butler Avenue Fresno, Calif. 93888
Indiana, Kentucky, North Carolina, Tennessee, Virginia, West Virginia	Internal Revenue Service Center 3131 Democrat Road Memphis, Tenn. 38110

Table 49.4. Summary of Deposit Rules

Deposit rule	Deposit due
1. If at the end of a quarter the total undeposited taxes are less than $500	Payment is due at the end of the next month
2. If at the end of any month (except the last month of a quarter), cumulative undeposited taxes for the quarter are $500 or more, but less than $3000	Within 15 days after end of month
3. If the combined withheld taxes and employer-employee Social Security taxes are $3000 or more for an eighth-monthly period (that means one-eighth of a month)	Within 3 banking days after the quarter-monthly period ends

mit it to an authorized local bank. Any Federal Reserve Bank and many commercial banks are authorized to accept deposits.

If the IRS did not send you a Form 501 upon your registration or specific request, you must nonetheless make deposits by the applicable deadlines. Mail these deposits to the regional service center to which you will send your Form 941.

Make the check payable to the Internal Revenue Service and note the employer's name, employer identification number, address, and the tax and period covered by the deposit. If deposits are insufficient, interest penalties may be charged. If the deposits exceed the amount due, the excess can be claimed as a credit on the Form 941 report filed at the end of the quarter.

Forms W-2 and W-3: Annual Wage and Tax Statements. The W-2 forms are, of course, the small duplicate certificates that employees must attach to their personal income tax returns to claim a credit for the amounts withheld by their employers. The W-2 forms simply report the total wages and other compensation paid to each employee along with the amounts withheld for Social Security and federal, state, and city income taxes. (If you have state and local taxes, be sure that your forms include enough copies for employees to file with each return.)

If your payroll accounting system is adequate, this cumulative annual data will be readily available for each employee. (See Circular E for specific instructions.)

As the employer, you will keep Copy A of the W-2 forms. The other copies must be given to the employees by January 31. Then, you must complete Form W-3, A Transmittal of Income and Tax Statements. This is basically a summary of your annual payroll data. It and Copy A of the W-2 of each employee must be sent to the IRS Center where you file your Form 941s by February 28.

Income Tax Withholdings—State and City. If the state or city in which your organization hires employees has a personal income tax, the organization is probably required to make payroll withholdings for these taxes. You should check with your accountant or with the Income Tax Division or Treasury Department of your city or state to determine your responsibilities.

Forms for registration and reporting are usually similar to the federal forms. In fact, they may even have similar numbers. You can obtain these forms and employer's withholding tables, and so on, by calling or writing the appropriate governmental department.

Read the explanatory materials that you obtain to be sure you are meeting all the requirements, such as having employees complete extra W-4 forms for each taxing government. These explanatory materials should be included in a loose-leaf notebook with your federal Circular E, and so on. If your organization cannot afford an accounting manual, this notebook can provide similar guidance.

Since these local withholdings are generally computed and reported in a manner parallel to that required for the federal forms, they will not be burdensome if you are generating the required data through your payroll accounting system.

Government-Required Benefits

Government-required benefits, unlike the income taxes in the previous sections, may provide specific and individualized benefits to your employees. Also, Workmen's Compensation, unemployment taxes, and part of Social Security are employer taxes. As such, they are payroll costs that must be added to gross salaries and should be considered in developing program budgets.

Social Security

Social Security (or FICA) is another payroll tax that employees and employers are generally required to pay. FICA rates were 7.15 percent for both the employer and the employee, or a total of 14.3 percent, and were taxed on the first $42,000 of wages per employee in 1986. These will be adjusted upward each year to reflect economic changes. Be sure to consult the IRS Employer's Tax Guide, Circular E, for current information on FICA rates and taxable wages.

Reporting and Depositing Social Security Contributions.
If your organization must or elects to make Social Security contributions, you will report the amounts due and make deposits at the same times and on the same forms as you will be using for federal income tax withholdings. The organization will have to withhold 7.15 percent of each employee's wages and contribute a matching 7.15 percent on the taxable FICA wages. In 1986, taxable FICA wages were the first $42,000 of wages received by each employee. The IRS Employer's Tax Guide, Circular E, provides current wages taxable for FICA. Employee payroll records or cards should include a year-to-date column for wages so that you will know to stop deducting FICA when the maximum amount of wages taxable by FICA have been paid.

FICA information must be reported on the Employer's Quarterly Federal Tax Return, Form 941 (rather than 941E) with your federal income tax withholding information. A good payroll accounting system is important since it will easily generate the total taxable FICA wages paid each employee during each quarter. Similar information on an annual basis will be required for the W-2 forms. See the previous discussion on reports and deposits for federal income tax withholdings for explanations of the reporting deadlines and the frequency of deposits. (Also see Circular E.) For determining the frequency of deposits, you must aggregate both the FICA owed and the federal income tax withheld.

Unemployment Taxes

Unemployment taxes are levied to provide the funds from which employees who have been laid off (and so on) draw unemployment benefits. These taxes are paid by the employer and are not withheld from the wages of employees. There are both federal and state unemployment taxes.

In 1986, federal unemployment taxes (FUTA) were levied on the first $7000 of wages paid each employee at a rate of 3.5 percent. The tax is applicable to wages paid common law employees receiving more than $50 per quarter. However, groups qualifying for 501(c)(3) tax-exempt status are exempt from this federal tax. This exemption does not usually apply to state unemployment taxes.

If not exempt, your group should file IRS Form 940, Employer's Annual Federal Unemployment Tax Return, by February 2. Payments made for state unemployment taxes are generally deducted (as credits) from the federal tax owed. The tax should be computed quarterly and deposited with a Form 508 card at a federal depository bank within the month following the quarter if the amount owed exceeds $100. For further details see the instructions on Form 940.

Although employers with 501(c)(3) tax-exempt status have not always been held liable for state unemployment taxes, they generally are now. Currently, most states allow 501(c)(3) tax-exempt organizations to meet their liabilities on either a contributing or reimbursing basis. Under "contributing" basis liability, the employer pays a tax (about 3.5 percent on the first $7000 of wages) and the state unemployment fund agrees to pay benefits to cover employees who may become unemployed. Under "reimbursing" basis liability, the employer makes reports but pays no tax contributions.

If employees become unemployed, they may claim benefits from the state; however, after paying the benefits the state will require the employer to reimburse the amount of the benefits paid. Although the reimbursing basis will be cheaper in the short term, your organization will be faced with a liability should it have to lay off employees. Consider the reimbursing method only if you know that your budget and unemployment bases are very stable.

Again, your payroll accounting system should have wages paid year-to-date for each employee so that you will know when to stop making unemployment tax payments for each one.

Workmen's Compensation (Worker's Disability)

State laws generally require Worker's Disability coverage for all employees. Worker's Disability pays for damages and injuries to employees injured in connection with their work. Employers generally meet this obligation through the purchase of insurance from a private insurance agent. The premiums for this insurance are usually set by the state. Rates vary from about 0.25 percent of wages to nearly 3.5 percent, depending on the organization, the region, and the type of workers.

This responsibility should be taken seriously, since injuries to employees can result in substantial liability. Further, states frequently impose personal liability on the members of the board of corporate employers that fail to procure acceptable worker's compensation insurance for injuries.

Payroll Accounting

If your organization has paid employees, it will be helpful to incorporate the use of another specialized journal into your bookkeeping system along with your cash receipts and cash disbursements journals. This specialized payroll journal resembles the other two in format (i.e., date section, record section, and summary section). The only difference lies in the account titles and classifications used in the recording section.

As pointed out in the section on employee responsibilities, employers are required to withhold income taxes and Social Security taxes from their employees' wages. The purpose of the payroll journal is to record the *amounts of these withholdings* and the employee's *gross* wages *at the same time* that the employee's *net* wages (the actual amount of the paycheck) are recorded and the paycheck is written. Recording all payroll information in one specialized journal assists you in maintaining current information regarding your payroll responsibilities so that required deposits of withheld taxes can be made accurately and on a timely basis.

Several accounts are affected with each payroll transaction—the specific number of accounts depends on the number of payroll deductions. Generally, there are four major deductions:

1. Withholdings for FICA taxes (Social Security)

2. Federal income tax withholdings (FWT)

3. State income tax withholdings (SWT)

4. City income tax withholdings (CWT)

Your own payroll system may require more deductions (if employees pay part of their own health insurance or have money taken from their pay for union dues) or fewer deductions (if your organization has elected not to pay FICA, or if your city does not impose an income tax). For illustrative purposes let us use the standard four.

All payroll deductions for these four taxes must, at some time, be paid to the governmental unit imposing the tax—either the IRS or your state or local government. Hence they are considered *liabilities* of the organization. Since these liabilities increase each time a paycheck is written, the various accounts (FICA, FWT, SWT, and CWT) must be *credited* for the amount withheld from the employee's salary.

Only two other accounts are affected when preparing a payroll journal. The first is cash, which is decreased (credited) for the amount of the paycheck. The second is salary or wage expense, which is increased (debited) for the amount of *gross* salary or wage. In our example, then, each payroll transaction would affect six accounts and the payroll register would be designed to capture the information relating to each of these accounts each time a paycheck is written (see Table 49.5).

Gross payroll (particularly for hourly wage employees) must be based on the time records of each employee and should be approved by the director or employer supervisor in order to ensure an accurate payroll. Amounts to be deducted for various taxes are based on the employee's gross wages, marital status, and number of exemptions (see the section on employer responsibilities for further discussion).

For internal control purposes, someone other than the bookkeeper should approve the payroll journal before checks are written and also compare the checks to the approved payroll journal before signing them.

The summary totals for each account are then posted to their respective ledger cards and new cumulative balances drawn. By examining the balances in the FWT and FICA accounts, one can determine the required amount of the deposit. According to IRS regulations, the deposit must include all federal income tax withheld as well as *both the employees' and employer's* share of FICA taxes.

To determine the amount of the deposit, simply double the total in the FICA account (this will represent both the employees' and employer's contribution) and

Table 49.5. XYZ Nonprofit Organization Payroll Register

Pay Period Ending 6/30/198X

Transaction	Cash credit	FICA credit	FWT credit	SWT credit	CWT credit	Salary expense debit
			Accounts			
John Jones; ½ mo. Salary	$ 747.50	$ 70.00	$127.00	$ 35.30	$20.00	$ 1000.00
Mary Smith: ½ mo. Salary	695.00	70.00	173.00	42.00	20.00	1000.00
Tom Burke: 40 hrs. @ $4	272.70	22.40	9.00	9.50	6.40	320.00
Jane Doe: 40 hrs. @ $4	239.90	23.40	35.80	15.50	6.40	320.00
Julie Thomas; 40 hrs. @ $3	200.44	16.80	11.96	6.00	4.80	240.00
Totals	$2,155.54	$201.60	$356.76	$108.50	$57.60	$2,880.00

As with the cash receipts and cash disbursements journal, accuracy can be checked by ensuring that the total of all credits equals the total of all debits.

add the total from the FWT account. In our example, the required amount of the deposit would be $759.96 (2 × 201.60 = 403.20 + 356.76 = $759.96).

It is in the area of payroll that the importance of keeping your records current becomes most apparent.

According to the IRS deposit rules, if your required deposit calculated by this method exceeded $3000, you would have to make your deposit within *three banking days!* Penalties and interest are charged by the IRS for failure to deposit these taxes when due. You, as managers, should pay strict attention to these liabilities. It is foolish to take a chance on being hit with tax penalties (and they can be quite costly) for the sake of the few minutes it takes to calculate your deposit liability.

When a check is written to make the deposit, the transaction is recorded in the cash disbursement journal, as is every transaction that decreases cash. Four accounts are affected: (1) cash (decrease or credit), (2) FWT withholdings (decrease or debit), (3) FICA withholdings (decrease or debit), and (4) Employer's FICA expense (increase or debit).

Your bookkeeper is also required to maintain individual earnings cards for each of your employees. The earnings card resembles the payroll register itself with an additional column entitled Salaries or Wages Year-to-Date. This column represents the cumulative total of gross wages paid to the individual employee as the year progresses. As mentioned in the section on employer responsibilities, this year-to-date column becomes important in determining when to stop deducting FICA taxes and paying unemployment taxes (i.e., when the maximum amount of taxable wages has been paid).

Employee earnings cards also help to facilitate the preparation of quarterly and annual unemployment tax reports and annual W-2 forms (employee earnings statement). Total wages and withholdings paid for each employee are easily transferred from the earnings card to the individual W-2 and other payroll reports requiring similar information, such as that requested in Forms 941 and 941E. Figure 49.15 shows a payroll flowchart.

Audits

For any number of reasons, it may be desirable to have an audit of your financial records and statements. The board of directors may wish a review of the financial statement to be sure that they fairly represent the activity of your group.

Funding sources, governmental agencies, and others may require you to submit reports on your activities and to provide them with a statement from an independent third-person expert that the figures you are presenting are fair.

Certified Public Accountant

The best way to satisfy the requirements of all these groups is to retain a certified public accountant (CPA). A person who is a CPA is an expert in auditing with a reputation for professionalism that "certifies" your statements as fair, uniform, and consistent.

The audit is a set of procedures that tests the transactions and internal controls, which leads to an opinion, by the auditor, of the accuracy of the financial statements. Let us break that down and study it in more detail.

"The audit is a set of procedures"—an organized, tested, and approved system.

"Which test"—with random sampling techniques that call for the examinations

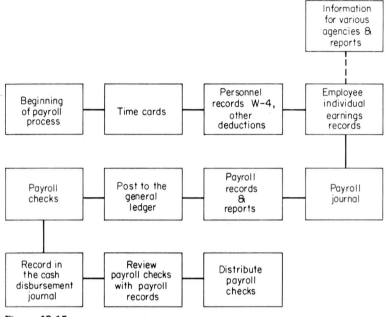

Figure 49.15

of not every, but selected transactions that lead with high probability to a comprehensive evaluation.

"Transactions and internal controls"—the way you document and manage what happens and how you protect the assets of the organization.

"Which leads to an opinion"—not a guarantee of truth but rather the opinion of an expert that you are keeping your records in an approved way.

"By the auditor"—a person with special training and experience.

We recommend certified public accountants because they are generally the best-trained of the people who do auditing. Since they are held to be the best, their opinion carries the most weight. They are, therefore, the best for public relation reasons as well.

Further, funders and governmental agencies often require that your statements be "certified." Only a CPA can do that.

Because of the comprehensiveness of the certified public audit, the auditor is also an excellent source for advice on taxes, internal operations and controls, filing responsibilities, and the adequacy of your present system.

You should also be aware that although certified public accountants are the best available, they are also the most expensive. Generally, however, you get what you pay for.

Public Accountants

Another professional accountant that is available (in many states) is the public auditor. As the name implies, this auditor is not certified and may not be eligible to "certify" your statements. Generally, the fees of the public accountant are less expensive. Depending on your needs, the public accountant may be perfect for your organization.

Others

If you do not need the certification and especially if the audit is for internal purposes, several other options are available to you.

You need only have an audit by a professional accountant who knows how to audit. Since you are concerned with the fairness of the statements, ask someone who can confirm that for you.

If you are a small organization, there is an excellent chance that someone (a CPA or other professional accountant) will look at your system without charging you. Such a person may not issue a statement, but at least you will be reassured that your accounts are probably in order. Ask a managerial accountant, an accounting teacher, a banker, or the past treasurer of your board to provide the "independent" review of your system.

You may also have access to a nonprofit public interest accounting organization or management support organization. These are organizations formed by accountants and other business professionals to provide free or at-cost services to nonprofit groups like yours. Ask your funders and supporters if there is such an organization in your area.

Appendix 1
IRS Form 990
and Instructions

1986

**Department of the Treasury
Internal Revenue Service**

Instructions for Form 990

Return of Organization Exempt From Income Tax

Under section 501(c) (except black lung benefit trust or private foundation) of the Internal Revenue Code or section 4947(a)(1) trust
(Section references are to the Internal Revenue Code, unless otherwise indicated.)

General Instructions

Paperwork Reduction Act Notice.—We ask for this information to carry out the Internal Revenue laws of the United States. We need it to ensure that you are complying with these laws. You are required to give us this information.

Purpose of Form.—Form 990 is used by tax exempt organizations and nonexempt charitable trusts to provide the IRS with the information required by section 6033(a)(1). An organization's completed Form 990 (except for the list of contributors) is available for public inspection as required by section 6104(b). The procedures for inspecting or obtaining completed Forms 990 are outlined in instruction M, below.

A. Who Must File Form 990.—Except for those types of organizations listed in instruction B, an annual return on Form 990 is required from every organization exempt from tax under section 501(a), including foreign organizations and cooperative service organizations described in sections 501(e) and (f), and child care organizations described in section 501(k).

Any nonexempt charitable trust (described in section 4947(a)(1)) not treated as a private foundation is also required to file Form 990 if its gross receipts are normally more than $25,000. See instruction C10 for information about possible relief from filing Form 1041.

If your application for exemption is pending, check the "Application Pending" block at the top of page 1 of the return and complete the return in the normal manner.

If you are not required to file Form 990 because your gross receipts are normally not more than $25,000 (see instruction B11 below), we ask that you file anyway if we sent you a Form 990 Package with a preaddressed mailing label. Attach the label to the name and address space on the return, check box H in the area above Part I to indicate that your gross receipts are below the $25,000 filing minimum, sign the return, and send it to the Service Center for your area. You do not have to complete Parts I through VII. This will help us update our records, and we will not have to contact you later asking why no return was filed. If you file a return in the above manner, you will not be mailed a Form 990 Package in later years and need not file Form 990 again until your gross receipts normally exceed the $25,000 minimum or you terminate or undergo a substantial contraction as described in the instructions for line 79.

Organizations which are eligible to receive tax deductible contributions are listed in Publication 78, Cumulative List of Organizations Described in Section 170(c) of the Internal Revenue Code of 1954. An organization may be removed from this listing if our records show that it is required to file Form 990, but it does not file a return or advise us that it is no longer required to file. However, contributions to such an organization may

continue to be deductible by the general public until the IRS publishes a notice to the contrary in the Internal Revenue Bulletin.

B. Organizations Not Required To File Form 990.—For state filing purposes, see instruction D. The following types of organizations exempt from tax under section 501(a) do not have to file Form 990 with IRS:

1. A church, an interchurch organization of local units of a church, a convention or association of churches, an integrated auxiliary of a church (such as a men's or women's organization, religious school, mission society, or youth group), or an internally supported, church-controlled organization (described in Rev. Proc. 86-23, 1986-20 I.R.B. 17).

2. A school below college level affiliated with a church or operated by a religious order.

3. A mission society sponsored by or affiliated with one or more churches or church denominations, if more than one-half of the society's activities are conducted in, or directed at persons in, foreign countries.

4. An exclusively religious activity of any religious order.

5. A state institution whose income is excluded from gross income under section 115.

6. An organization described in section 501(c)(1). Section 501(c)(1) organizations are corporations organized under an Act of Congress that are:

(a) Instrumentalities of the United States, and

(b) Exempt from Federal income taxes under such Acts as amended and supplemented.

7. A private foundation exempt under section 501(c)(3) and described in section 509(a). (Required to file **Form 990-PF**, Return of Private Foundation.)

8. A black lung benefit trust described in section 501(c)(21). (Required to file **Form 990-BL**, Information and Initial Excise Tax Return for Black Lung Benefit Trusts and Certain Related Persons.)

9. A stock bonus, pension, or profit-sharing trust which qualifies under section 401. (See **Form 5500**, Annual Return/Report of Employee Benefit Plan.)

10. A religious or apostolic organization described in section 501(d). (Required to file **Form 1065**, U.S. Partnership Return of Income.)

11. An organization whose gross receipts are normally $25,000 or less; but see instruction A, paragraph 4. Gross receipts are the sum of lines 1d, 2, 3, 4, 5, 6a, 7, 8a (both columns), 9a, 10a, and 11 of Part I. The organization's gross receipts are the total amount it received from all sources during its annual accounting period, without subtracting any costs or expenses.

However, if a local chapter of a section 501(c)(8) fraternal organization collects insurance premiums for its parent lodge and merely sends those premiums to the parent

without asserting any right to use the funds or otherwise deriving any benefit from collecting them, the local chapter should not include the premiums in its gross receipts. The parent lodge should report them instead. The same rationale applies to other situations in which one organization collects funds merely as an agent for another.

An organization's gross receipts are considered to be $25,000 or less if the organization is:

(a) Up to a year old and has received, or donors have pledged to give, $37,500 or less during its first tax year;

(b) Between 1 and 3 years old and averaged $30,000 or less in gross receipts during each of its first 2 tax years; or

(c) 3 years old or more and averaged $25,000 or less in gross receipts for the immediately preceding 3 tax years (including the year for which the return would be filed). If your gross receipts are normally $25,000 or less, see the fourth paragraph of instruction A, above.

C. Other Forms You May Need To File.—

1. **Schedule A (Form 990).**—Filed with Form 990 for a section 501(c)(3) organization that is not a private foundation (including an organization described in section 501(e), 501(f) or 501(k)). Also filed with Form 990 for a section 4947(a)(1) trust not treated as a private foundation. An organization is not required to file Schedule A if its gross receipts are normally $25,000 or less (see instruction B11).

2. **Form 990-T.**—Exempt Organization Business Income Tax Return. Filed separately for organizations with gross income of $1,000 or more from business unrelated to the organization's exempt purpose. For details, see the instructions for Form 990-T or Publication 598, Tax on Unrelated Business Income of Exempt Organizations. Publication 598 is available free from IRS.

3. **Forms W-2 and W-3.**—Wage and Tax Statement, and Transmittal of Income and Tax Statements.

4. **Form W-2P.**—Statement for Recipients of Annuities, Pensions, Retired Pay, or IRA Payments.

5. **Form 1096.**—Annual Summary and Transmittal of U.S. Information Returns.

6. **Form 1099 Series.**—Information returns for reporting payments such as dividends, interest, miscellaneous income (including medical and health care payments and nonemployee compensation), original issue discount, patronage dividends, acquisition or abandonment of secured property, and lump-sum distributions from profit-sharing and retirement plans.

7. **Form 940.**—Employer's Annual Federal Unemployment (FUTA) Tax Return. Used to report unemployment tax paid by an employer.

8. **Form 941.**—Employer's Quarterly Federal Tax Return. Used to report social security and income taxes withheld by an employer and social security tax paid by an employer.

9. **Form 5500, 5500-C, or 5500-R.—** Used to report on employee benefit plans.

Employers who maintain pension, profit-sharing, or other funded deferred compensation plans are generally required to file one of the 5500 series forms specified in the following paragraph. This requirement applies whether or not the plan is qualified under the Internal Revenue Code and whether or not the deduction is claimed for the current tax year. The Employee Retirement Income Security Act of 1974 imposes a penalty for late filing of these forms.

The forms required to be filed are:
Form 5500.—For each plan with 100 or more participants.
Form 5500-C or 5500-R.—For each plan with fewer than 100 participants.

10. **Form 1041.**—U.S. Fiduciary Income Tax Return. Required of section 4947(a)(1) trusts that also file Form 990. However, any such trust may use the filing of Form 990 to satisfy its Form 1041 filing requirement under section 6012 if the trust has zero taxable income under subtitle A of the Code. If this condition is met, check box C on page 1 of Form 990 and do not file Form 1041, but complete Form 990 in the normal manner. A section 4947(a)(1) trust that normally has gross receipts of not more than $25,000 (see instruction B11) and has zero taxable income under subtitle A must complete only the following items on Form 990: name; address; employer identification number; box C; the section 4947(a)(1) block in box D; box H in the area above Part I; and the signature block on page 4.

11. **Form 8282.**—Donee Information Return. Required of the donee of "charitable deduction property" who sells, exchanges, or otherwise disposes of the property within 2 years after the date of receipt of the property.

D. Use of Form 990 To Satisfy State Reporting Requirements.—Some states and local government units will accept a copy of Form 990 and Schedule A (Form 990) in place of all or part of their own financial report forms. At this time, the substitution applies primarily to section 501(c)(3) organizations, but some of the other types of section 501(c) organizations are also affected.

If you intend to use Form 990 to satisfy state or local filing requirements, such as those arising under state charitable solicitation acts, note the following:

1. You should consult the appropriate officials of all states and other jurisdictions in which you do business to determine their specific filing requirements. "Doing business" in a jurisdiction may include any of the following: (a) soliciting contributions or grants by mail or otherwise from individuals, businesses, or other charitable organizations; (b) conducting programs; (c) having employees within that jurisdiction; (d) maintaining a checking account; or (e) owning or renting property therein.

2. Some or all of the dollar limitations applicable to Form 990 when filed with IRS may not apply when using Form 990 in place of state or local report forms. Examples of IRS dollar limitations that do not meet some state requirements are the $25,000 gross receipts minimum that gives rise to an obligation to file with IRS (see instruction B11), the short reporting format explained in instruction I for organizations that report total revenue of $25,000 or less on line 12, and the $30,000 minimum for listing professional fees in Part II of Schedule A (Form 990).

3. State or local filing requirements may require you to complete additional lines and columns of Form 990 and to attach to Form 990 one or more of the following: (a) additional financial statements, such as a complete analysis of functional expenses or a statement of changes in financial position; (b) notes to financial statements; (c) additional financial schedules; (d) a report on the financial statements by an independent accountant; and (e) answers to additional questions and other information. Each jurisdiction may require the additional material to be presented on forms they provide. The additional information does not have to be submitted with the Form 990 filed with IRS.

Page 2

4. Even if the Form 990 you file with IRS is accepted by IRS as complete, a copy of the same return filed with a state will not fully satisfy that state's filing requirement if required information is not provided, including any of the additional information discussed above, or the state determines that the form was not completed in accordance with the applicable Form 990 instructions or supplemental state instructions. In that event, you may be asked to provide the missing information or to submit an amended return.

5. To ensure that all organizations report similar transactions uniformly, many states require that contributions, gifts and grants on lines 1a through 1d in Part I and functional expenses on lines 13, 14, and 15 and in Part II be reported in accordance with the AICPA industry audit guide, Audits of Voluntary Health and Welfare Organizations, as supplemented by Standards of Accounting for Voluntary Health and Welfare Organizations (Revised 1974) and by Accounting and Financial Reporting—A Guide for United Ways and Not-for-Profit Human Service Organizations. However, a significant exception applies in the case of donated services and facilities. Although reporting such services and facilities as items of support and expense is called for in certain circumstances by the three publications named above, many states and IRS do not permit the inclusion of those amounts in Parts I and II of Form 990. The instructions for line 82 discuss the optional reporting of donated services and facilities in Parts III and VII.

6. If you submit supplemental information or file an amended Form 990 with IRS, you must also furnish a copy of the information or amended return to any state with which you filed a copy of Form 990 originally to meet that state's filing requirement.

7. If a state requires you to file an amended Form 990 to correct conflicts with Form 990 instructions, you must also file an amended return with IRS.

8. Most states require that all amounts be reported based on the accrual method of accounting.

9. The time for filing Form 990 with IRS differs from the time for filing reports with some states.

10. The Form 990 information made available for public inspection by IRS may differ from that made available by the states. See the cautionary note to the specific instructions for line 1d.

State Registration Number.—Insert the applicable state or local jurisdiction registration or identification number in box B (in the heading on page 1) for each jurisdiction in which you file Form 990 in place of the state or local form. When filing in several jurisdictions, prepare as many copies as needed with box B blank. Then enter the applicable registration number on the copy to be filed with each jurisdiction.

E. Other Forms as Partial Substitutes for Form 990.—Except as provided below, the Service will not accept any form as a substitute for one or more parts of Form 990. A labor organization that files Form LM-2, Labor Organization Annual Report, or the shorter Form LM-3 with the U.S. Department of Labor (DOL) can attach a copy of the completed DOL form to provide some of the information required for Form 990. This substitution is not permitted if the organization files a DOL report that consolidates its financial statements with those of one or more separate subsidiary organizations.

An employee benefit plan may be able to substitute Form 5500, Annual Return/Report of Employee Benefit Plan, or Form 5500-C for

part of Form 990. The substitution can be made if the organization filing Form 990 and the plan filing Form 5500 or 5500-C meet all the following tests:

(a) the Form 990 filer is organized under section 501(c)(9), (17), (18), or (20);

(b) the Form 990 filer and Form 5500 filer are identical for financial reporting purposes and have identical receipts, disbursements, assets, liabilities, and equity accounts;

(c) the employee benefit plan does not include more than one section 501(c) organization, and the section 501(c) organization is not a part of more than one employee benefit plan, and

(d) the organization's accounting year and the employee plan year are the same. If they are not, you may want to change the organization's accounting year, as explained in instruction F, so it will coincide with the plan year.

Whether you file Form 990 for a labor organization or for an employee plan, the areas of Form 990 for which other forms can be substituted are the same. These areas are:

Part I, lines 13-15 (but complete lines 16 through 21);

Part II, and

Part V (but complete lines 59, 66, and 74).

If you substitute Form LM-2 or LM-3 for any items on Form 990, you will need to attach a statement to reconcile the disbursements shown on the DOL forms and the total expenses on line 17 of Form 990. The reconciliation is necessary because the cash disbursements section of the DOL forms includes non-expense items. If you use Form LM-2, be sure to complete its separate schedules of expenses.

F. Accounting Period Covered.—Base your return on your annual accounting period (fiscal year) if one is established. If not, base the return on the calendar year.

Your fiscal year should normally be selected to coincide with the natural operating cycle of your organization; it is not necessary that your fiscal year end on December 31 or June 30.

The 1986 Form 990 should be used to report on a calendar year 1986 accounting period or a fiscal year beginning in 1986.

For a group return, see instruction J.

To change your accounting period, file Form 990 for the short accounting period resulting from the change and indicate at the top of the form that a change of accounting period is being made. If you changed your accounting period within the 10-calendar-year period that includes the start of the short period, and you had a Form 990 filing requirement at any time during that 10-year period, you must also attach a Form 1128, Application for Change in Accounting Period, to the short period return. See Rev. Proc. 85-58, 1985-2 C.B. 740.

G. When and Where To File.—File Form 990 by the 15th day of the 5th month after your accounting period ends.

If the organization is liquidated, dissolved, or terminated, file the return by the 15th day of the 5th month after the change.

If your principal office is located in—	Send your return to the Internal Revenue Service Center below—
Alabama, Arkansas, Florida, Georgia, Louisiana, Mississippi, North Carolina, South Carolina, or Tennessee	Atlanta, GA 31101
Arizona, Colorado, Kansas, New Mexico, Oklahoma, Texas, Utah, or Wyoming	Austin, TX 73301
Indiana, Kentucky, Michigan, Ohio, or West Virginia	Cincinnati, OH 45999
Alaska, California, Hawaii, Idaho, Nevada, Oregon, or Washington	Fresno, CA 93888

Connecticut, Delaware, Maine, Massachusetts, New Hampshire, New Jersey, New York, Pennsylvania (ZIP codes beginning with 169-171 and 173-196 only), Rhode Island, or Vermont	Holtsville, NY 00501
Illinois, Iowa, Minnesota, Missouri, Montana, Nebraska, North Dakota, South Dakota, or Wisconsin	Kansas City, MO 64999
Maryland, Pennsylvania (ZIP codes beginning with 150-168 and 172 only), Virginia, District of Columbia, any U.S. possession, or foreign country	Philadelphia, PA 19255

Extension of Time To File.—To request an extension of time to file, send in **Form 2758**, Application for Extension of Time To File.

H. Penalties.—*Against the organization.*—Under section 6652(c), a penalty of $10 a day, up to a total of $5,000, may be charged when a return is filed late, unless you can show that the late filing was due to reasonable cause. The penalty begins on the due date for filing the Form 990. The penalty may also be charged if an incomplete return is filed, since filing such a return does not satisfy an organization's filing requirement. To avoid having to respond to requests for missing information, please be sure to complete all applicable line items; to answer "Yes," "No," or "N/A" (not applicable) to each question on the return; to make an entry (including a "-0-" when appropriate) on all total lines; and to enter "None" or "N/A" if an entire part does not apply.

Against responsible person(s).—If a complete return is not filed, IRS may write to give you a fixed time for filing. After that period expires, the person failing to file the return will be charged a penalty of $10 a day, not to exceed $5,000, unless he or she shows that not filing was due to reasonable cause. If more than one person is responsible, they are jointly and individually liable for the penalty (section 6652(c)).

There also are penalties—fines and imprisonment—for willfully not filing returns and for filing fraudulent returns and statements with IRS (sections 7203, 7206, and 7207). States may impose additional penalties for failure to meet their separate filing requirements.

I. Short Format for Small Organizations.—If your total revenue on line 12, Part I, is $25,000 or less and your gross receipts are normally more than $25,000, you need not complete all items on the Form 990 you file with IRS. (Gross receipts are explained in instruction B11.) In that case, you are not required to complete lines 13, 14, and 15 of Part I and columns (B), (C), and (D) of Part II. Be sure to check box I in the area above Part I to indicate that you did not have to complete all items.

Also, organizations that report total revenue of $25,000 or less on line 12 and total assets of $25,000 or less in column (B) of line 59, Part V, are required to complete only lines 59, 66, 74, and 75 of the beginning and end-of-year balance sheets in Part V.

J. Group Return.—A central, parent, or "like" organization can file a group return on Form 990 for two or more local organizations that are:

1. Affiliated with the central organization at the time its annual accounting period ends;

2. Subject to the central organization's general supervision or control;

3. Tax exempt under a group exemption letter that is still in effect; and

4. Have the same accounting period as the central organization.

If the parent organization is required to file a return itself (see instruction B for a list of organizations not required to file), it must file a

separate return and may not be included in the group return.

Every year, each local organization must authorize the central organization in writing to include it in the group return and must declare, under penalty of perjury, that the authorization and the information it submits to be included in the group return are true and complete.

If you prepare a group Form 990, attach schedules showing (1) the total number of local organizations included and the name, address, and employer identification number of each one; and (2) the same information for those not included. When you prepare the return, be sure not to confuse the four-digit group exemption number (GEN) in box G, page 1, with the nine-digit employer identification number in box A. If none of the local organizations covered by the group return has more than $25,000 in total revenue (line 12, Part I), you may use the short format described in instruction I. If each local organization included in the group return also has $25,000 or less of total assets, the short format instructions for completing the balance sheets in Part V also apply to the group return.

K. Organizations in Foreign Countries and U.S. Possessions.—Report amounts in U.S. dollars and state what conversion rate you use. Combine amounts from within and outside the United States, and report the total for each item. All information must be given in the English language.

L. Completing Form 990.—

1. Label—Name, Address, and Employer Identification Number.—If we mailed you a 990 Package with a preaddressed mailing label, please attach it in the name and address space on your return. Your using the label helps us avoid errors in processing your return. If any information on the label is wrong, draw a line through that part and correct it.

You should have only one Federal employer identification number. If you have more than one and have not been advised which to use, notify the Service Center for your area (from the list in instruction G). Tell them what numbers you have, the name and address to which each number was assigned, and the address of your principal office. IRS will advise you which number to use.

2. Accounting Method.—In box C box D line 1 indicate the method of accounting used in preparing this return. Unless the specific instructions say otherwise, you should generally use the same accounting method on the return to figure support, revenue, and expenses that you regularly use to keep the organization's books and records. To be acceptable for Form 990 reporting purposes, however, the method of accounting used must clearly reflect income.

If you prepare a Form 990 for state reporting purposes, you may file an identical return with IRS even though it does not agree with your books of account, unless the manner of reporting one or more items on the state return conflicts with the instructions for preparing Form 990 for filing with IRS. For example, if you maintain your books on the cash receipts and disbursements method of accounting but prepare a state return based on the accrual method, that return could be used for reporting to IRS. As another example, if a state reporting requirement requires you to report certain support, revenue, expense or balance sheet items differently from the manner in which you normally account for them on your books, a Form 990 prepared for that state would be acceptable for IRS reporting purposes if the state reporting requirement does not conflict with the Form

990 instructions. Your records should contain a reconciliation of any differences between your books of account and the Form 990 you file.

Most states that accept Form 990 in place of their own forms require that all amounts be reported based on the accrual method of accounting. See instruction D.

3. Legible Form 990 for Public Inspection.—All information you report on or with your Form 990, including attachments, will be available for public inspection, except the list of contributors required for line 1(d), Part I. Please make sure your forms and attachments are clear enough to photocopy legibly.

4. Signature.—In order to make the return complete, an officer authorized to sign it must sign in the space provided. For a corporation, this officer will be the president, vice president, treasurer, assistant treasurer, chief accounting officer, or other corporate officer, such as a tax officer. A receiver, trustee, or assignee must sign any return he or she files for a corporation. For a trust, the authorized trustee(s) must sign.

If the return was prepared by an individual, firm, or corporation paid for preparing it, the paid preparer's space must also be signed. For a paid firm or corporation, sign in the firm's or corporation's name. If you checked block C on page 1 (section 4947(a)(1) trust filing Form 990 in lieu of Form 1041), you must also enter the paid preparer's social security number or employer identification number in the margin next to the paid preparer's space. Leave the paid preparer's space blank if the return was prepared by a regular employee of the filing organization.

M. Public Inspection of Completed Exempt Organization Returns and Approved Exemption Applications.—Form 990, Form 990-PF, and certain other completed exempt organization returns are available for public inspection and copying upon request. Approved applications for exemption from Federal income tax are also available. IRS, however, is not permitted to disclose portions of certain otherwise disclosable returns and attachments, including the list of contributors required by Form 990.

A request for inspection must be in writing and must include the name and address (city and state) of the organization that filed the return or application. A request to inspect a return should indicate the type (number) of the return and the year(s) involved. The request should be sent to the District Director (Attention: Disclosure Officer) of the district in which the requester desires to inspect the return or application. If inspection at the IRS National Office is desired, the request should be sent to the Commissioner of Internal Revenue, Attention: Freedom of Information Reading Room, 1111 Constitution Avenue, N.W., Washington, DC 20224.

For more information, call any IRS office or see **Publication 910,** Taxpayer's Guide to IRS Information, Assistance and Publications, which is available free at IRS offices.

Specific Instructions

In General.—You may show money items as whole-dollar amounts. Drop any amount less than 50 cents, and increase any amount from 50 through 99 cents to the next higher dollar.

Unless you are permitted to use certain DOL forms or Form 5500 series returns as partial substitutes for Form 990 (see instruction E), do not leave blank any applicable lines or attach any other forms or schedules instead of entering the required information on the appropriate line on Form 990.

Attachments.—Use the schedules on the official form unless you need more space. If you use attachments, they must:

(1) Show the form number and tax year;

(2) Show the organization's name and employer identification number;

(3) Include the information required by the form;

(4) Follow the format and line sequence of the form; and

(5) Be on the same size paper as the form.

Part I—Statement of Support, Revenue, and Expenses and Changes in Fund Balances.—

All organizations filing Form 990 with IRS or any state must complete column (A) and the items to the left of it. Columns (B) and (C) are optional for reporting to IRS, although some states that accept Form 990 in place of their own forms may require these columns to be completed on the Form 990 filed with them. (See instruction D.)

Columns (B) and (C).—The following instructions apply if you use columns (B) and (C). In preparing a Form 990 to be filed with IRS, you may complete what items you choose in columns (B) and (C), rather than all applicable lines in these two columns.

Columns (B) and (C) are to let you indicate any externally imposed restrictions on how and when certain funds can be used. The amounts are a breakdown of the information you must report in column (A) and the items to the left of it. The combined column (B) and (C) amounts for any line should equal the amount on the left.

If you use columns (B) and (C), cross out the inapplicable words in the headings to show whether you are reporting unrestricted and restricted amounts or expendable and nonexpendable funds.

Use the *Restricted* column to reflect any externally imposed restrictions on the use of contributions, gifts, grants, endowment income, and other amounts the organization received in the current year. Also use that column to summarize the use of restricted funds received in the current year or any earlier year. The term "externally imposed restrictions" primarily refers to those imposed by donors and grantors for use of their separate contributions and grants. In the case of endowment gifts, restrictions on the use of the income earned by those funds may also be imposed by the donor. The term also applies to restrictions imposed by any applicable state or Federal statute or to regulations issued by an administrative agency of a state or the Federal government. For example, the laws of some states permit noncharitable organizations to conduct certain types of special fundraising events only if the proceeds are used for charitable or other specified purposes. An appropriation of funds made at the discretion of the organization's governing body is not an externally imposed restriction. A donor-imposed restriction can specify either how the funds are to be used (for scholarships, for example) or when they are to be used (for example, a fixed term endowment). In the case of noncash contributions particularly, the donor may designate that the organization may not dispose of the property and use the proceeds for a certain period of time.

When an externally imposed restriction on the use of funds lapses, use line 20, Part I, to report the transfer to an unrestricted fund if

Page 4

the amount being transferred was recorded as support or revenue of a restricted fund when received. Enter a decrease in the amount involved in the *Restricted* column and a corresponding increase in the *Unrestricted* column. The offsetting entries would result in a "-0-" entry on line 20 of column (A). Also reflect the change on lines 67–70 in the fund balance section in Part V of the return. Do not show the transfer as an item of support or revenue on lines 1–12 of Part I, since those lines are for reporting the initial receipt or accrual of restricted and unrestricted amounts. Any portion of the funds utilized by the unrestricted fund in the current year would be reported as a current year expense in the normal manner.

These instructions also apply to expendable and nonexpendable funds. Expendable funds include both unrestricted and donor-restricted amounts that may be spent for current activities. For example, if a donor earmarks a contribution to be used for scholarships, that contribution (although restricted as to a specific use) would be expendable. If the donor indicates that the contribution should become part of the permanent endowment, that contribution would be nonexpendable. This is true whether or not the donor designated a specific program to be supported ultimately by the contribution or by the income earned on those funds. That income itself would be treated separately as expendable or nonexpendable, depending upon whether the donor specified when the organization could use the income.

Contributions, Gifts, Grants, and Similar Amounts Received.—On lines 1a through 1c, report amounts received as voluntary contributions; that is, payments, or the part of any payment, for which the payer (donor) does not receive full consideration from the recipient (donee) organization. (For grants, see "Grants equivalent to contributions.") Report all expenses of raising contributions in column (D), Part II, and on line 15 of Part I.

On line 9, report income from special fundraising events and activities such as dinners, door-to-door sales of merchandise, carnivals, and bingo games. However, when the buyer pays more for such goods or services than their value, report the excess on line 1a as a contribution representing direct public support. This usually occurs when organizations seek support from the public through solicitation programs that are in part special fundraising events or activities and in part a solicitation for contributions. For example, an organization announces that anyone who "contributes" at least $40 can choose a book worth $16 retail. Those who pay $40 and choose to receive the book would be both buying the book and making a contribution. Each such buyer's contribution reported on line 1a would be $24, the amount by which the buyer's payment is more than the merchandise's fair market value. (Rev. Rul. 67-246, 1967-2 C.B. 104, explains this principle in detail.) A buyer who paid more than $40 would pay the same amount for the book, but would have made a larger contribution. The primary purpose of such solicitations is not to sell the merchandise at its fair market value (even though this might produce a profit), but to receive the contributions. Therefore, all the expenses incurred, except those attributable to the merchandise furnished the buyer, should be reported as an expense of raising contributions (fundraising expense) in column (D), Part II. The revenue ($16 per book) and the expenses relating to the sale of the merchandise would be reported on line 9 as revenue and expenses of a special fundraising event.

If the organization provides merchandise of only nominal value, report the entire receipts on line 1a as contributions (direct public support) and report all the related expenses in column (D), Part II.

The differentiation between revenue and contributions derived from special fundraising events is particularly important for any section 501(c)(3) organization that claims to qualify as a publicly supported organization described in section 170(b)(1)(A)(vi) or 509(a)(2). In the public support computations under these two sections, the revenue portion may be excluded entirely, treated as public support, or, if it represents unrelated trade or business income, treated as nonpublic support. Section 501(c)(3) organizations must compute the amounts of revenue and contributions from fundraising events in accordance with the above instructions in preparing the Support Schedule in Part IV of Schedule A (Form 990). The Support Schedule generally includes only the 4 preceding years, but includes the current year as well if there have been material changes in the organization's sources of support in that year.

See the line 3 instructions for information about membership dues that should be treated as contributions.

Section 501(c)(9), (17), (18), and (20) organizations provide life, sick, accident, welfare, unemployment, pension, group legal services, or similar benefits, or a combination of these benefits to participants. When such an organization receives payments from participants or their employers to provide these benefits, report the payments on line 2 as program service revenue, rather than on line 1 as contributions.

In Part I, do not include the value of services donated to the organization, or items such as the free use of materials, equipment or facilities, among the contributions received. See the instructions for Part III and for Part VII, line 82, for the optional reporting of such amounts in Parts III and VII under certain circumstances.

Grants equivalent to contributions.—On line 1, report grants to the organization that are equivalent to contributions. Such grants are normally made to encourage the grantee organization to carry on programs or activities that further its exempt purposes. The grantor may set conditions to ensure that the grantee's programs conform to the grantor's own policies. The grantor may specify which of the recipient's activities the grant may be used for, such as a voter registration drive or restoring a historic building.

A grant is still equivalent to a contribution if the grantee performs a service or produces a work product that benefits the grantor only incidentally. (See examples in line 1c instructions.) However, if the terms of a grant require that a specific service, facility, or product be provided the grantor—the purpose of which is to serve the direct and immediate needs of that grantor rather than primarily to confer a direct benefit upon the general public or that segment of the public served by the organization—that grant does not represent a contribution, but a payment for services. In general, any payments made primarily to enable the payer to realize or receive some economic or physical benefit as a result of the service, facility, or product obtained should not be treated as contributions.

For example, a public interest organization described in section 501(c)(4) makes a grant to another organization to conduct a nationwide survey using a scientific sampling method. The survey is to determine voter attitudes on issues in which the grantor has an interest. The grantor plans to use the results in planning its program for the next 3 years. Under these circumstances, the grant to the organization making the survey is not a contribution, since conducting the survey and furnishing the report primarily serve the grantor's direct needs and benefit the grantor more than incidentally. When the grantee reports the grant as income, it should be treated as either program service revenue (line 2) or other revenue (line 11), not as a contribution.

If research is done to develop products for the payer's use or benefit, treat it as serving the payer directly. Basic research or studies in the physical or social sciences generally should not be treated as serving the payer's needs.

See Regulations section 1.509(a)-3(g) for information about determining whether a grant represents a contribution reportable on line 1 or a revenue item reportable elsewhere on Form 990.

Noncash contributions.—To report contributions received in a form other than cash, use the market value as of the date of the contribution. For marketable securities registered and listed on a recognized securities exchange, measure market value by the average of the highest and lowest quoted selling prices (or the average between the bona fide bid and asked prices) on the contribution date. (See section 20.2031-1 of the Estate Tax Regulations for this general rule, exceptions, and special rules that may be applied to determine the value of contributed stocks and bonds.) When market value cannot be readily determined, use an appraised value.

To determine the amount of any noncash contribution that has an outstanding debt attached, subtract the debt from the property's fair market value. Record the asset at its full value; record the debt as a liability in the books of account. See the *Note* in the instructions for line 1d.

Line 1a—Direct public support.—Enter the total contributions, gifts, grants, and bequests that the organization received directly from the public. Include amounts received from individuals, trusts, corporations, estates, and foundations. Also include contributions and grants from public charities and other exempt organizations that are neither fundraising organizations nor affiliates of the filing organization. (See instructions for line 1b.) Report membership dues and assessments on line 1a to the extent they represent contributions from the public rather than payments for benefits received (see the instructions for line 3) or payments from affiliated organizations. Report government grants on line 1c if they represent contributions, or on line 2 or 11 if they represent fees for services.

Amounts contributed by a commercial co-venture should be reported on line 1a as a contribution received directly from the public. These are amounts due the donee organization for letting an outside organization or individual use its name in a sales promotion campaign in which the donor advertises that it will contribute a certain dollar amount to the named donee organization for each unit of a particular product or service sold or for each occurrence of a specified type.

Contributions received through special fundraising events should be reported on line 1a.

Line 1b—Indirect public support.—Enter the total contributions received indirectly from the public through solicitation campaigns conducted by federated fundraising agencies and similar fundraising organizations (such as

a United Way organization and certain sectarian federations). These organizations normally conduct fundraising campaigns within a single metropolitan area or some part of a particular state, and allocate part of the net proceeds to each participating organization on the basis of individual donors' designations and other factors.

Also include on line 1b amounts contributed by other organizations closely associated with the reporting organization. This would include contributions received from a parent organizaton, subordinate, or another organization having the same parent. National organizations that share in fundraising campaigns conducted by their local affiliates should report the amount they receive on line 1b.

Line 1c—Government grants.—The instructions on page 4 under the heading "Grants equivalent to contributions," apply to this item in particular. A grant or other payment from a governmental unit represents a contribution if its primary purpose is to enable the donee to provide a service to, or maintain a facility for, the direct benefit of the public rather than to serve the direct and immediate needs of the grantor (even if the public pays part of the expense of providing the service or facility).

Following are examples of governmental grants and other payments that represent contributions:

1. Payments by a governmental unit for the construction or maintenance of library or hospital facilities open to the public;

2. Payments under government programs to nursing homes or homes for the aged in order to provide health care or other services to their residents;

3. Payments to child placement or child guidance organizations under government programs serving children in the community. The general public gets the primary and direct benefit from these payments and any benefit to the governmental unit itself would be indirect and insubstantial as compared to the public benefit.

Line 1d—Total contributions, etc.—Enter the total of amounts reported on lines 1a through c.

Schedule of contributors (not open to public inspection. **Caution:** *See Note below).*— Attach a schedule listing contributors during the year who gave the organization, directly or indirectly, money, securities, or other property worth at least $5,000. Show each person's name and address, the total amount received, and the date received. "Person" means an individual, fiduciary, partnership, corporation, association, trust, or exempt organization.

In determining whether a contributor gave at least $5,000, total that person's gifts of $1,000 or more. Do not include smaller gifts. If the contribution consists of property whose fair market value can be determined readily (such as market quotations for securities), describe the property and list its fair market value. Otherwise, estimate the property's value.

Note: *For contributions to you of property (other than publicly traded securities) whose fair market value is greater than $5,000, you should usually receive from the contributor a partially completed* **Form 8283,** *Noncash Charitable Contributions. You should complete the appropriate information on Form 8283, sign it, and return it to the donor. Retain a copy for your records. Also see General Instruction C11.*

If an employer withholds contributions from employees' pay and periodically gives them to the organization, report only the employer's

name and address and the total amount given unless you know that a particular employee gave enough to be listed separately.

If the organization meets the terms of either of the following exceptions, some information in your schedule will vary from that described above. If no one contributed the reportable minimum, you do not need to attach a schedule.

Exception 1: *Organization described in section 501(c)(3) that meets the 33⅓% support test of the Regulations under section 170(b)(1)(A)(vi) (whether or not the organization is otherwise described in section 170(b)(1)(A)).*

In your schedule, give the information described above only for contributors whose gifts of $5,000 or over are more than 2% of the total gifts (reported on line 1d) the organization received during the year.

Exception 2: *Organization described in section 501(c)(7), (8), (10), or (19) that received contributions or bequests to be used only as described in sections 170(c)(4), 2055(a)(3), or 2522(a)(3).*

The schedule should list each person whose gifts total $1,000 or more during the year. Give the donor's name, the amount given, the gift's specific purpose, and the specific use to which it was put. If an amount is set aside for a purpose described in sections 170(c)(4), 2055(a)(3), or 2522(a)(3), explain how the amount is held (for instance, whether it is mingled with amounts held for other purposes). If the organization transferred the gift to another organization, name and describe the recipient and explain the relationship between the two organizations. Also show the total gifts that were $1,000 or less and were for a purpose described in sections 170(c)(4), 2055(a)(3), or 2522(a)(3).

Note: *If you file a copy of Form 990 and attachments with any state, do not include the list of contributors discussed above unless the list is specifically required by the state with which you are filing the return. States that do not require the information might nevertheless make it available for public inspection along with the rest of the return.*

Line 2—Program service revenue.—Enter the total program service revenue from Part IV, line f. Program services are primarily those that form the basis of an organization's exemption from tax. (See the instructions for Part II, column (B).) For example, a hospital would report on line 2 all of its charges for medical services (whether to be paid directly by the patients or through Medicare, Medicaid, or other third-party reimbursement), hospital parking lot fees, room charges, laboratory fees for hospital patients, and related charges for services.

Other examples of program service revenue are tuition received by a school, revenue from admissions to a concert or other performing arts event or to a museum, royalties received as author of an educational publication distributed by a commercial publisher, interest income on loans a credit union makes to its members, payments received by a section 501(c)(9) organization from participants or employers of participants for health and welfare benefits coverage, insurance premiums received by a fraternal beneficiary society, and registration fees received in connection with a meeting or convention.

Program service revenue also includes income from program-related investments, which are investments made for the primary purpose of accomplishing an exempt purpose consistent with the investing organization's

Page 5

exempt status, rather than to produce income. Examples are scholarship loans and low interest loans to charitable organizations, indigents, or victims of a disaster.

Unrelated trade or business activities (not including any special fundraising events or activities) that generate fees for services may also be program service activities. A social club, for example, should report as program service revenue the fees it charges both members and nonmembers for the use of its tennis courts and golf course.

Books and records maintained in accordance with generally accepted accounting principles for hospitals, colleges, and universities are more specialized than books and records maintained in accordance with generally accepted accounting principles for other types of organizations that are required to file Form 990. In view of this circumstance, hospitals, colleges, and universities may report as program service revenue on line 2 sales of inventory items otherwise reportable on line 10a. In that event, the applicable cost of goods sold would be shown as program service expense on line 13 of Part I and in column (B) of Part II. All other organizations should not report sales of inventory items on line 2.

Line 3—Membership dues and assessments.—Enter members' and affiliates' dues and assessments that are not contributions. Regardless of whether membership benefits are used, dues to a charitable organization are a contribution to the extent they are more than the monetary value of these membership benefits to the dues payer. (See Rev. Ruls. 54-565, 1954-2 C.B. 95, and 68-432, 1968-2 C.B. 104.)

Examples of such benefits include subscriptions to publications, newsletters (other than one about the organization's activities only), free or reduced-rate admissions to events the organization sponsors, the use of its facilities, and discounts on articles or services that both members and nonmembers can buy. In figuring the value of membership benefits, disregard other intangible benefits, such as the right to attend meetings, vote or hold office in the organization, and the distinction of being a member of the organization.

When a member pays dues primarily to support the organization's activities, rather than to derive benefits of more than nominal monetary value, that dues payment represents a contribution. The availability of benefits worth more than a nominal amount shows that the intent in paying the dues was to receive those benefits and not to make a contribution.

For membership organizations other than those described in section 501(c)(3), members generally receive benefits or consideration in return for dues; therefore, dues in that situation are not contributions and should be reported on line 3. This is particularly true of organizations described in sections 501(c)(5), 501(c)(6), or 501(c)(7), although benefits to members may be indirect.

Line 4—Interest on savings and temporary cash investments.—Enter the amount of interest income from savings and temporary cash investments reportable on line 46. So-called dividends or earnings received from mutual savings banks, etc., are really interest and should be entered on line 4.

Line 5—Dividends and interest from securities.—Enter the amount of dividend and interest income from debt and equity securities (stocks and bonds) of the type reportable on line 54. Include amounts

received from payments on securities loans, as defined in section 512(a)(5). Do not include any capital gains dividends reportable on line 8. See the instructions for line 2 for reporting income from program-related investments.

Line 6a—Gross rents.—Enter the gross rental income for the year from investment property reportable on line 55. Do not include amounts that represent income from an exempt function (program service) which should be reported on line 2 (and the related expenses which should be reported in column (B) of Part II). For example, an organization whose exempt purpose is to provide low rental housing to persons with low income would receive exempt function income from such rentals. Renting office space or other facilities or equipment to unaffiliated exempt organizations is not income from an exempt function (and should be reported on line 6a) unless the charge is well below the fair rental value of the property, and the lessor's purpose in charging less than the fair rental value was to help the lessee carry out its exempt purpose. Only for purposes of completing Form 990, treat income from renting property to affiliated exempt organizations as exempt function income (program service revenue) and report it on line 2.

Line 6b—Rental expenses.—Enter the expenses paid or incurred for the income reported on line 6a. Include depreciation if it is recorded in the organization's books and records.

Line 6c—Net rental income (loss).—Subtract line 6b from line 6a. Show any loss in parentheses.

Line 7—Other investment income.—Enter the amount of investment income not reportable on lines 4 through 6 and describe the type of income in the space provided or in an attachment. The income should be the gross amount derived from investments reportable on line 56. Include, for example, royalty income from mineral interests owned by the organization. However, do not include income from program-related investments (see instructions for line 2). Also exclude unrealized gains and losses on investments carried at market value (see instructions for line 20).

Lines 8a-c—Capital gains.—Attach a schedule listing each asset (other than inventory items) sold or exchanged. Show for each one: (a) date acquired, how acquired, date sold; and to whom sold; (b) gross sales price; (c) cost, other basis, or if donated, value at time acquired (state which); (d) expense of sale and cost of improvements made after acquired, and (e) if depreciable property, depreciation since acquired. The schedule should show security transactions separately from the sale of other assets.

Publicly traded securities.—For sales of publicly traded securities through a broker, you may total the gross sales price, the cost or other basis, and the expenses of sale on all such securities sold, and report lump-sum figures in place of the detailed reporting required in the paragraph above. For this return, publicly traded securities include common and preferred stocks, bonds (including governmental obligations), and mutual fund shares that are listed and regularly traded in an over-the-counter market or on an established exchange and for which market quotations are published or otherwise readily available. You may use average cost basis to figure the organization's gain or loss from sales of securities to be reported on Form 990. For this purpose, when securities are sold, you may figure gain or loss by comparing the sales price with the average cost basis of the particular

security. Do not use average cost basis to figure gain or loss from security sales reportable on Form 990-T.

Report all sales of securities on lines 8a-c in the column with that heading. Use the "Other" column to report sales of all other types of investments (such as real estate, royalty interests, or partnership interests) and all other capital assets (such as program-related investments and fixed assets used by the organization in its regular activities).

For each column, enter the total gross sales price of all involved assets on line 8a, Part I. Total the cost or other basis (less depreciation), and selling expenses and enter the result on line 8b. Enter the total net gain or loss on line 8c. On lines 8a and c report capital gains dividends, the organization's share of capital gains and losses from a partnership, and capital gains distributions from trusts. Indicate the source on the schedule described above.

Add the gain and/or loss figures reported in the "Securities" column and the "Other" column on line 8c and report that total on line 8c in the "Total" column. Do not include any unrealized gains or losses on securities carried at market value in the books of account. See the instructions for line 20.

Lines 9a-c—Special fundraising events and activities.—On the appropriate line enter the gross revenue, expenses, and net income from all special fundraising events and activities, such as dinners, dances, carnivals, raffles, bingo games, and door-to-door sales of merchandise. In themselves, these activities only incidentally accomplish an exempt purpose. Their sole or primary purpose is to raise funds (other than contributions) to finance the organization's exempt activities. This is done by offering goods or services of more than nominal value (compared to the price charged) in return for a payment higher than the direct cost of the goods or services provided. If the goods or services have only nominal value, report all of the receipts as contributions on line 1 and all of the related expenses as fundraising expenses on line 15 and in column (D) of Part II.

An activity which generates only contributions, such as a solicitation campaign by mail, is not a special fundraising event and should not be reported on line 9.

The proceeds of solicitation campaigns in which the names of contributors and other respondents are entered in a drawing for the awarding of prizes (so-called "sweepstakes" or "lotteries") are contributions and the related expenses are fundraising expenses reportable in column D of Part II. However, raffles and lotteries in which a payment of at least a specified minimum amount is required for each entry are special fundraising events unless the prizes awarded have only nominal value. Characterizing any required payment as a "donation" or "contribution" on tickets or on advertising or solicitation materials does not affect how such payments should be reported on Form 990. As discussed above, the amount of the contribution is the excess of the amount paid over the value received by the payor.

Special fundraising events sometimes generate both contributions and revenue. When a buyer pays more than the value of the goods or services furnished, report that excess on line 1 as a contribution and report the value of the goods or services on line 9a as gross revenue. Report on line 9b only the direct expenses attributable to the goods or services the buyer receives. See "Contributions, Gifts, Grants, and Similar Amounts Received" on page 4 of these instructions.

Attach a schedule listing the three largest special events conducted, as measured by gross receipts. Describe each of these events and indicate for each event the gross receipts, the amount of contributions included in gross receipts (see instructions above), the gross revenue (gross receipts less contributions), the direct expenses, and the net income (gross revenue less direct expenses). Furnish the same information in total figures for all other special events held that are not among the three largest. Indicate the type and number of the events not listed individually (for example, three dances and two raffles).

If the above schedule is prepared in columnar format, the total of the gross revenue column will be the amount reportable in the column on line 9a; the totals of the direct expense column and the net income column will be the amounts reportable on lines 9b and 9c, respectively; and the total of the contributions will be the amount that should be entered in the parentheses outside the column on line 9a. The latter amount should also be combined with all other direct public support and reported on line 1a.

If you include an expense on line 9b, do not report it on line 10b or in Part II.

Lines 10a–c—Gross profit on sales of inventory.—Enter the gross sales (minus returns and allowances), cost of goods sold, and gross profit (or loss) from the sale of all inventory items, other than those sold in special fundraising events and activities reported on line 9. These inventory items are ones the organization either makes to sell to others or buys for resale. The latter does not include investments on which the organization expected to profit by appreciation and sale. Report sales of investments on line 8. On line 10, report sales revenue and the related cost of goods sold, whether the sale of the merchandise involved is an exempt function or an unrelated trade or business.

Hospitals, colleges, and universities should refer to the instructions for line 2 for an optional method of reporting sales of inventory items that would otherwise be reportable on line 10.

Line 11—Other revenue.—Enter the amount from Part IV, line g. This figure represents the total income from all sources not covered by lines 1 through 10. Each of these revenue-producing activities must be listed in Part IV. Income reportable on line 11 would include interest on notes receivable not held as investments; interest on loans to officers, directors, trustees, key employees and other employees; and royalties that do not constitute investment income or program service revenue

Line 12—Total revenue.—Enter the total of lines 1d through 11. If the amount is $25,000 or less, see instruction I about the short format for small organizations.

Lines 13 through 15—Program services, management and general, and fundraising expenses.—*4947(a)(1) trusts and section 501(c)(3) and (c)(4) organizations.*—If you report more than $25,000 of total revenue on line 12 you should complete Part II and then come back to lines 13 through 15. Enter the appropriate amount from the column (B), (C), and (D) totals reported on line 44, Part II.

If line 12 is $25,000 or less, you do not have to enter an amount on lines 13, 14, or 15 of the Form 990 you file with IRS, and should skip to line 16. However, see instruction D if you use a copy of Form 990 for state reporting purposes.

All other organizations.—You are not required to complete lines 13 through 15 regardless of your total revenue.

Line 16—Payments to affiliates.—This expense classification is used to report certain types of payments to organizations "affiliated

with" (closely related to) a reporting agency. Predetermined quota support and dues payments (excluding membership dues of the type described below) by local agencies to their state or national organizations for unspecified purposes, i.e., general use of funds for the national's own program and support services, are to be reported on this line. Purchases of goods or services from affiliates are not reported here but as expenses in the usual manner.

In addition to payments made directly to affiliated organizations, expenses incurred in providing goods or services to affiliates may be reported on line 16 if: (1) the goods or services provided are not related to the program services conducted by the organization furnishing them (for example, when a local organization incurs expenses in the production of a solicitation film for the state or national organization); and (2) the costs involved are not connected with the management and general or fundraising functions of the reporting organization (for example, when a local organization furnishes a copy of its mailing list to the state or national organization, the expense of preparing the copy provided may be reported on line 16, but not expenses of preparing and maintaining the local organization's master list).

Federated fundraising agencies (see the instructions for line 1b) should include in their own report the full amount of contributions received in connection with a solicitation campaign they conduct, even though donors designate specific agencies to receive part or all of their individual contributions. These fundraising organizations should report the allocations to participating agencies as awards and grants (line 22) and quota support payments to their state or national organization as payments to affiliates (line 16).

Voluntary awards or grants made by the reporting agency to its state or national organization for specified purposes should not be reported here but on line 22, grants and allocations.

Membership dues that represent amounts paid to procure general membership benefits, such as regular services, publications, and materials, from other organizations should be reported as "other expenses" on line 43. This would be the case, for example, if a charitable organization pays dues to a trade association comprised of otherwise unrelated members, all of which solicit contributions by mail or telephone. Dues payments by the local charity to its affiliated state or national (parent) organization would usually be reportable on line 16.

Attach a schedule listing the name and address of each affiliate that received payments reported on line 16. Specify the amount and purpose of the payments to each affiliate.

Note: *Properly distinguishing between payments to affiliates and awards and grants is especially important if you use Form 990 for state reporting purposes, as discussed in instruction D. If you use Form 990 only for reporting to IRS, payments to affiliated state or national organizations that do not represent membership dues reportable on line 43 (see instructions above) may be reported either on line 16 or on line 22 and explained in the required attachment.*

Line 17—Total expenses.—Organizations reporting $25,000 or less on line 12 should complete column (A) of Part II and then enter the total of line 16 and line 44, column (A). Organizations using Form 5500, 5500-C, or an approved DOL form as a partial substitute

for Form 990 (see instruction E) enter the total expense figure from Form 5500 or 5500-C, or from the required reconciliation schedule if Form LM-2 or LM-3 is used. Other organizations enter the total of lines 13 through 16.

Line 18—Excess (deficit) for the year.—Enter the difference between lines 12 and 17 If line 17 is more than line 12, enter the difference in parentheses.

Line 19—Fund balances or net worth, beginning of year.—Enter the amount from column (A) of line 74 (or from Form 5500, 5500-C, or an approved DOL form if instruction E applies).

Line 20—Other changes in fund balances or net worth.—Attach a schedule explaining any changes in fund balances or net worth between the beginning and end of the year that are not accounted for by the amount on line 18. Amounts to report here include adjustments of earlier years' activity and unrealized gains and losses on investments carried at market value. If you use the *Unrestricted* and *Restricted* columns, show transfers between unrestricted and restricted funds. The net effect of such transfers would be "-0-" in the Total column.

Line 21—Fund balances or net worth, end of year.—Enter the total of lines 18, 19, and 20. The figure in the Total column must equal the amount reported in column (B) of line 74

Part II—Statement of Functional Expenses.—

All organizations must complete column (A) unless they are using an approved DOL form or Form 5500 or 5500-C as a partial substitute for Form 990 in accordance with instruction E. Columns (B), (C), and (D) are optional for all organizations other than section 4947(a)(1) trusts and section 501(c)(3) and (c)(4) organizations. Section 4947(a)(1) trusts and section 501(c)(3) and (c)(4) organizations must complete columns (B), (C), and (D) if total revenue (line 12 of Part I) is more than $25,000. They need not complete these three columns if total revenue is $25,000 or less. (See instruction I.) Those organizations, however, may be required to complete all of the columns in Part II for a Form 990 filed with one or more states (see instruction D).

Part II reflects the organization's expenses by object classification (salaries, legal fees, supplies, etc.) allocated into three functions: program services (column (B)); management and general (column (C)); and fundraising (column (D)). These functions are explained below in the instructions for the columns. Do not include in Part II any expense items you must report on lines 6b, 8b, 9b, 10b, or 16 in Part I.

For reporting to IRS only, use the organization's normal accounting method to report total expenses in column (A) and to segregate them into functions under columns (B), (C), and (D) (but see instructions L2 and D). If the accounting system does not provide for this type of segregation, a reasonable method of allocation may be used. The amounts reported should be accurate and the method of allocation documented in the organization's records.

Expenses which are directly attributable to a particular functional category must be reported in the appropriate column. Expenses which relate to more than one functional category generally should be allocated. For example, allocate employees' salaries on the basis of each employee's time. For some shared expenses such as occupancy, supplies, and depreciation of office equipment, use an appropriate basis for each kind of cost. However, you should report some other shared expenses in column (C) only. The column instructions below discuss allocating expenses.

Column (A)—Total.—Column (A) is the total of columns (B), (C), and (D) for each line item in Part II. Except for expenses you report on lines 6b, 8b, 9b, 10b, or 16 of Part I, you should use column (A) to report all expenses the organization paid or incurred.

Column (B)—Program services.—Program services are mainly those activities which the reporting organization was created to conduct and which, along with any activities commenced subsequently, form the basis of the organization's current exemption from tax. They may be self-funded or funded out of contributions, accumulated income, investment income, or any other source.

Program services can also include the organization's unrelated trade or business activities. For example, publishing a magazine is a program service even though it contains both editorials and articles that further the organization's exempt purpose and advertising, the income from which is taxable as unrelated business income.

If an organization receives a grant to do research, produce an item, or perform a service, either to meet the grantor's specific needs or to benefit the public directly, the costs incurred represent program service expenses. Do not treat these costs as fundraising expenses, even if you report the grant on line 1 as a contribution.

Column (C)—Management and general.—Use column (C) to report the organization's expenses for overall management and functioning, rather than for its direct conduct of fundraising activities or program services. Overall management usually includes the salaries and expenses of the chief officer of the organization and that officer's staff. If part of their time is spent directly supervising program services and fundraising activities, their salaries and expenses should be allocated among those functions. Other expenses to report in column (C) include those for meetings of the board of directors or similar group; committee and staff meetings (unless held in connection with specific program services or fundraising activities); general legal services; accounting, auditing, personnel, and other centralized services; investment expenses (except those relating to rental income and program-related income—report rental expenses on line 6b and program-related expenses in column (B)); general liability insurance; preparation, publication, and distribution of an annual report; and office management.

However, you should report only general expenses in column (C). Do not use it to report costs of special meetings or other activities that relate to fundraising or specific program services.

Column (D)—Fundraising.—Fundraising expenses represent the total expenses incurred in soliciting contributions, gifts, grants, etc. Report as fundraising expenses all expenses, including allocable overhead costs, incurred in: (a) publicizing and conducting fundraising campaigns; (b) soliciting bequests, grants from foundations or other organizations, or government grants reportable on line 1c; (c) participating in federated fundraising campaigns; (d) preparing and distributing fundraising manuals, instructions, and other materials; and (e) conducting special fundraising events that generate contributions

Page 8

reportable on line 1a in addition to revenue reportable on line 9a, but any expenses attributable to revenue on line 9a (that is, the direct expenses incurred in furnishing the goods or services sold) should be reported on line 9b.

Allocating indirect expenses.—Colleges, universities, hospitals, and other organizations that accumulate indirect expenses in various cost centers (such as the expenses of operating and maintaining the physical plant) that are reallocated to the program services and other functional areas of the organization in a single step or in multiple steps may find it easier to report these expenses in the following optional manner:

First, the expenses of these indirect cost centers may be reported on lines 25 through 43 of the management and general expense column in Part II, along with the expenses properly reportable in that column.

Second, allocate the total expenses for each cost center among program services, management and general, and fundraising as a separate item entry on line 43, Other expenses. Enter the name of the cost center on line 43. If any of the cost center's expenses are to be allocated to the expenses listed in Part I (such as the expenses attributable to special fundraising events and activities), enter these expenses as a negative figure in columns (A) and (C). This prevents reporting the same expense on both Parts I and II. If part of the total cost center expenses are to be allocated to columns (B), Program services, and (D), Fundraising, enter these expenses as positive amounts in these columns and as single negative amounts in column (C). Do not make any entries in column (A), Total, for these offsetting entries.

The above instructions can be illustrated by the following example. An organization reports $50,000 of actual management and general expenses and $100,000 of expenses of an indirect cost center that are to be allocated in part to other functions. The total of lines 25 through 43 of column (C) would be $150,000 before the allocations were made. Assume that $10,000 (of the $100,000 total expenses of the cost center) was allocable to fundraising, $70,000 to various program services, $15,000 to management and general functions, and $5,000 to special fundraising events and activities. To report this in Part II under this alternate method:

(1) Indicate the cost center, the expenses of which are being allocated, on line 43, "Allocation of (specify) expenses";

(2) Enter a decrease of $5,000 on the same line in the Total column, representing the special fundraising event expenses already reported on line 9b in Part I;

(3) Enter $70,000 on the same line in the Program services column;

(4) Enter $10,000 on the same line in the Fundraising column; and

(5) Enter a decrease of $85,000 on the same line in the Management and general column, representing the allocations to functional areas other than management and general.

After these allocations were made, the column (C) total (line 44, column (C)) would be $65,000, consisting of the $50,000 aggregate amount and the $15,000 allocation of the aggregate cost center expenses to management and general.

The above is an example of a simple one-step allocation that was used to show how to report the allocation in Part II. This reporting method would actually be needed more in the case of multiple step allocations in which two or more cost centers are involved. The total

expenses of the first would be allocated to the other functions, including an allocation of part of these expenses to the second cost center. The expenses of the second cost center would then be allocated to other functions and any remaining cost centers to be allocated, and so on. The greater the number of these cost centers which are allocated out, the more difficult it would be to preserve the identity of the object classification (salaries, interest, supplies, etc.) of the expenses of each cost center. The reporting method described above avoids this problem.

Note: *The above instructions are intended only to facilitate the reporting of indirect expenses by both object classification and function. They do not in any way sanction the allocation to other functions of expenses properly reportable as management and general expenses.*

Line 22—Grants and allocations.—Enter the amount of awards and grants to individuals and organizations selected by the filing organization. United Way and similar fundraising organizations should include allocations to member agencies. Voluntary awards and grants to affiliated organizations for specific (restricted) purposes or projects also should be reported on line 22, but not required payments to affiliates reportable on line 16.

Scholarship, fellowship, and research grants to individuals should be reported on line 22. Certain other payments to or for the benefit of individuals may be reportable on line 23 instead. See the instructions for line 23 for specific information.

Only the amount of actual grants and awards should be reported on line 22. Expenses incurred in selecting recipients or monitoring compliance with the terms of a grant or award should be reported on lines 25 through 43.

Attach a schedule of amounts reported on line 22. Show: (a) each class of activity; (b) donee's name and address and the amount given; and (c) (in the case of grants to individuals) relationship of donee if related by blood, marriage, adoption, or employment (including employees' children) to any person or corporation with an interest in the organization, such as a creator, donor, director, trustee, officer, etc.

On the schedule, classify activities in more detail than in such broad terms as charitable, educational, religious, or scientific. For example, identify payments for nursing services, laboratory construction, or fellowships.

If the property's fair market value when the organization gave it is the measure of the award or grant, also show on the schedule: a description of the property; its book value; how the book value was determined; how the fair market value was determined; and the date of the gift. Any difference between fair market value and book value should be recorded in the organization's books of account.

Line 23—Specific assistance to individuals.—Enter the amount of payments to or for the benefit of particular clients or patients, including assistance rendered by others at the expense of the filing organization. Do not include grants to other organizations that select the person or persons to receive the assistance available through the use of grant funds. For example, a payment to a hospital to cover the medical expenses of a particular individual should be reported on line 23, but not a contribution to a hospital to provide some service to the general public or to unspecified charity patients. Also, do not include scholarship, fellowship, or research grants to individuals even though selected by the grantor organization. Report these grants on line 22 instead.

Attach a schedule showing the total payments for each particular class of activity, such as food, shelter, and clothing for indigents or disaster victims; medical, dental, and hospital fees and charges; and direct cash assistance to indigents. For payments to indigent families, do not identify the individuals.

Line 24—Benefits paid to or for members.—For an organization giving benefits to members or dependents (such as organizations exempt under section 501(c)(8), (9), or (17)), attach a schedule. Show amounts of: (a) death, sickness, hospitalization, or disability benefits; (b) unemployment compensation benefits (state their nature). Do not report on this line the cost of employment-related benefits the organization gives its officers and employees. Report those expenses on lines 27 and 28.

Line 25—Compensation of officers, directors, etc.—Enter the total compensation paid to officers, directors, and trustees for the year. In Part VI list each one's name and compensation (if any), along with the other information requested.

Each person you list should report this compensation on his or her income tax return, unless the Code specifically excludes any of the payments from income tax. Publication 525, Taxable and Nontaxable Income, may be helpful and is available free from IRS.

You must file Form 941 to report income tax withholding and social security taxes, and you must also file Form 940 to report Federal unemployment taxes, unless the organization's exemption letter states that it is not subject to these taxes.

Line 26—Other salaries and wages.—Enter the total of employees' salaries not reported on line 25.

Line 27—Pension plan contributions.—Enter the employer's share of contributions that the organization paid to qualified and nonqualified pension plans for the year. Complete Form 5500, 5500-C, or 5500-R, as appropriate, for your plan and file as a separate return. If you have more than one plan, complete the appropriate form for each plan. File the form by the last day of the 7th month after the plan year ends. See instruction C9 on page 1.

Line 28—Other employee benefits.—Enter the amount of your contributions to employee benefit programs (such as insurance, health, and welfare programs) that are not an incidental part of a pension plan included on line 27. Also see instruction C9 on page 1 and the instructions for Form 5500.

Line 29—Payroll taxes.—Enter the amount of Federal, state, and local payroll taxes for the year, but only those taxes that are imposed on the organization as an employer. This would include the employer's share of FICA taxes, the FUTA tax, state unemployment compensation taxes, and other state and local payroll taxes. Do not include taxes withheld from employees' salaries and paid over to the various governmental units (such as Federal and state income taxes and the employees' shares of FICA tax).

Line 30—Professional fundraising fees.—Enter the organization's fees to outside fundraisers for solicitation campaigns they conducted, or for providing consulting services in connection with a solicitation of contributions by the organization itself.

Line 31—Accounting fees.—Enter the total accounting and auditing fees charged by outside firms and individuals who are not employees of the reporting organization.

Line 32—Legal fees.—Enter the total legal fees charged by outside firms and individuals who are not employees of the reporting organization. Do not include any penalties, fines, or judgments imposed against the organization as a result of legal proceedings. Report those expenses on line 43, Other expenses.

Line 33—Supplies.—Enter the total for office, classroom, medical, and other supplies used during the year, as determined by the organization's normal method of accounting for supplies.

Line 34—Telephone.—Enter the total telephone, telegram, and similar expenses for the year.

Line 35—Postage and shipping.—Enter the total amount of postage, parcel delivery, trucking, and other delivery expenses, including the cost of shipping materials.

Line 36—Occupancy.—Enter the total amount paid or incurred for the use of office space or other facilities, heat, light, power, and other utilities (other than those reported on line 34), outside janitorial services, mortgage interest, real estate taxes, and similar expenses. Do not include depreciation (reportable on line 42) or any salaries of your own employees (reportable on line 26).

Line 37—Equipment rental and maintenance.—Enter the cost of renting and maintaining office equipment and other equipment, except for automobile and truck expenses reportable on lines 35 and 39.

Line 38—Printing and publications.—Enter the printing and related costs of producing the reporting organization's own newsletters, leaflets, films, and other informational materials. (However, do not include any expenses, such as salaries or postage, for which a separate line is provided in Part II.) Also include the cost of any purchased publications.

Line 39—Travel.—Enter the total travel expenses, including transportation costs (fares, mileage allowances, and automobile expenses), meals and lodging, and per diem payments.

Line 40—Conferences, conventions, and meetings.—Enter the total expenses incurred by the organization in conducting meetings relating to its activities. Include such expenses as the rental of facilities, speakers' fees and expenses, and printed materials, but not the salaries and travel expenses of the reporting organization's own officers, directors, trustees, and employees who participate. Also include the registration fees (but not travel expenses) paid for sending any of the organization's staff to conferences, meetings, or conventions conducted by other organizations.

Line 41—Interest.—Enter the total interest expense for the year, excluding any interest attributable to rental property (reported on line 6b) or any mortgage interest treated as occupancy expense on line 36.

Line 42—Depreciation, depletion, etc.—If your organization records depreciation, depletion, and similar expenses, enter the total for the year. Include any depreciation (amortization) of leasehold improvements. You are not required to use the Accelerated Cost Recovery System (ACRS) to compute the depreciation you report on Form 990. If you record depreciation using ACRS, attach **Form 4562**, Depreciation, or a schedule showing

the same information required by Form 4562. If you do not use ACRS, attach a schedule showing how you computed depreciation.

You should use the same method of computing depreciation on line 42 that you use for the balance sheet, Part V of this Form 990.

If you claim a deduction for depletion, attach a schedule explaining the deduction.

Line 43—Other expenses.—Indicate the type and amount of each significant expense for which a separate line is not provided. Report all other miscellaneous expenses as a single total. Expenses that might be reported here include: investment counselling and other professional fees not reportable on lines 30 through 32; penalties, fines, and judgments; unrelated business income taxes; and real estate taxes not attributable to rental property or reported as occupancy expenses. Attach a schedule if more space is needed.

Some states that accept Form 990 in satisfaction of their filing requirements may require that certain types of miscellaneous expenses be itemized regardless of amount. See instruction D.

Line 44—Total functional expenses.—Add lines 22 through 43 and enter the totals in columns (A), (B), (C), and (D). Report the column (B) total on line 13 of Part I, the column (C) total on line 14, and the column (D) total on line 15. If you reported $25,000 or less on line 12, add the column (A) total to the amount on line 16 and enter the sum on line 17.

Part III—Statement of Program Services Rendered.

Provide the information specified in the instructions above line a of Part III for each of the organization's four largest program services (as measured by total expenses incurred) or for each program service if the organization engaged in four or fewer of such activities. If part of the total expenses of any program service consists of grants and allocations reported on line 22, indicate the amount of the grants and allocations in the space provided.

Attach a schedule that lists the organization's other program services and the total expenses incurred in connection with each. The detailed information required in Part III for the four largest services is not required for the services listed on the attached schedule.

If the organization reports on line 82 the value of any donated services or use of materials, equipment, or facilities it received, it can also indicate in Part III the amount received and utilized in connection with specific program services. However, the applicable amounts should be disclosed only on the lines for the narrative description of the appropriate program services and must not be included in the expense column in Part III.

A program service is a major, usually ongoing objective of an organization, such as adoptions, recreation for the elderly, rehabilitation, or publication of journals or newsletters. Service outputs or products are measures of a program service, such as clients served, days of care, therapy sessions, or publications issued. Quantity is the number of outputs or products rendered, such as 4,080 counseling contacts.

If it is inappropriate to measure a quantity of output, as in a research activity, describe the objective of the activity for this time period as well as the overall longer-term goal.

You may furnish reasonable estimates for the statistical information (number of clients, patients, etc.) called for by Part III if exact figures are not readily available from the records you normally maintain. In that event, please indicate that the information provided is an estimate.

Listing expenses optional for certain organizations.—If your organization was not required to complete column (B) of Part II (see the instructions to Part II), you need not list the expenses of the program services you report in Part III or the attached schedule described above.

Part IV—Program Service Revenue and Other Revenue.—

List each revenue-producing program service activity and each "other" activity as described in the instructions for lines 2 and 11. Enter the gross revenue (that is, without subtracting any related expenses) from each such activity in the proper column. Line a is to be used only for reporting fees from government agencies that do not constitute grants reportable on line 1c of Part I. Report the total of each column on lines f and g of Part IV and on lines 2 and 11 of Part I.

Part V—Balance Sheets.—

All organizations except those that meet one of the exceptions in instruction E above, must complete all of the required lines of columns (A) and (B) of Part V of the return and may not submit a substitute balance sheet. Failure to complete Part V may result in penalties for filing an incomplete return. See instruction H. Smaller organizations filing Form 990 with IRS are not required to complete all line items in those two columns, as explained by instruction I and the information in the Part V heading on page 3 of the return.

Columns (C) and (D) are optional for reporting to IRS, although some states that accept Form 990 in place of their own forms may require that those columns be completed on the Form 990 filed with them. Some states may also require smaller organizations to complete the entire balance sheet instead of only those lines specified in instruction I. See instruction D for more information about completing a Form 990 to be filed with any state or local government agency.

When any line item in Part V calls for a schedule to be attached, a schedule is required only for the end of year balance sheet figure reported in column (B). Similarly, when space is provided to the left of column (A) for reporting any receivables or depreciable assets and the related allowance for doubtful accounts or accumulated depreciation, enter the end of year figures. (We do not need this information for beginning of year figures in column (A).)

Line 45—Cash—non-interest bearing.— Enter the total of non-interest bearing cash in checking accounts, deposits in transit, change funds, petty cash funds, or any other non-interest bearing account. Do not include advances to employees or officers or refundable deposits paid to suppliers or others.

Line 46—Savings and temporary cash investments.—Enter the total of interest bearing cash in checking accounts, savings and temporary cash investments, such as money market funds, commercial paper, certificates of deposit, and U.S. Treasury bills or other governmental obligations that mature in less than 1 year. Report the income from these investments on line 4.

Page 10

Line 47—Accounts receivable.—Enter the total accounts receivable (reduced by the corresponding allowance for doubtful accounts) that arose from the sale of goods and/or the performance of services. Claims against vendors or refundable deposits with suppliers or others may be reported here if not significant in amount. (Otherwise, report them on line 58, Other assets.) Any receivables due from officers, directors, trustees, or key employees must be reported on line 50. Receivables (including loans and advances) due from other employees should be reported on line 58.

Line 48—Pledges receivable.—Enter the total pledges receivable recorded as of the beginning and end of the year, reduced by the amount of pledges estimated to be uncollectible.

Line 49—Grants receivable.—Enter the total grants receivable from governmental agencies, foundations, and other organizations as of the beginning and end of the year.

Line 50—Receivables due from officers, directors, trustees, and key employees.— All receivables due from officers, directors, trustees, and key employees and all secured and unsecured loans to such persons must be reported on line 50 and in an attached schedule described below. The term "key employees" refers to the chief administrative officers of an organization (such as an executive director or chancellor), but does not include the heads of separate departments or smaller units within an organization.

In the required schedule, report each loan separately, even if more than one loan was made to the same person, or the same terms apply to all loans made.

Receivables that are subject to the same terms and conditions (including credit limits and rate of interest) as receivables due from the general public and that arose during the normal course of the organization's operations may be reported as a single total for all the officers, directors, trustees, and key employees. Travel advances made in connection with official business of the organization may also be reported as a single total.

However, salary advances and other advances for the personal use and benefit of the recipient, and receivables subject to special terms or arising from nontypical transactions, must be reported as separate loans for each officer, director, etc.

Attach a schedule that shows the following information (preferably in columnar form) for each loan or other receivable outstanding at the end of the year that must be reported separately in accordance with the above instructions:

(a) Borrower's name and title;
(b) Original amount;
(c) Balance due;
(d) Date of note;
(e) Maturity date;
(f) Repayment terms;
(g) Interest rate;
(h) Security provided by the borrower;
(i) Purpose of the loan; and
(j) Description and fair market value of the consideration furnished by the borrower (for example, cash—$1,000; or 100 shares of XYZ, Inc. common stock—$9,000).

The above detail is not required for receivables or travel advances that may be combined and reported in total (see above instructions); but report and identify those totals separately in the attachment.

Line 51—Other notes and loans receivable.—Enter the combined total of notes receivable and net loans receivable.

Notes receivable.—Enter the amount of all notes receivable not listed on line 50 and not acquired as investments. Attach a schedule similar to that called for in the instructions for line 50. The schedule should also identify the relationship of the borrower to any officer, director, trustee, or key employee of the organization.

Notes receivable from loans by a credit union to its members and scholarship loans by a section 501(c)(3) organization do not have to be itemized. These loans should merely be identified as such on a schedule and the total amount of such loans outstanding indicated.

For a note receivable from another organization exempt under the same paragraph of section 501(c) as the filing organization, list only the name of the borrower and the balance due. For example, a section 501(c)(3) organization would have to provide the full details of a loan to a section 501(c)(4) organization, but would have to provide only the name of the borrower and the balance due on a note arising from a loan to another section 501(c)(3) organization.

Loans receivable.—Enter the gross amount of loans receivable, less the allowance for doubtful accounts, arising from the normal activities of the filing organization (such as loans by a credit union to its members or scholarship loans by a section 501(c)(3) organization). A schedule of these loans is not required.

Loans to officers, directors, trustees, and key employees must be reported on line 50. Loans to other employees should be reported on line 58.

Line 52—Inventories for sale or use.— Enter the amount of materials, goods, and supplies purchased or manufactured by the organization and held to be sold or used in some future period.

Line 53—Prepaid expenses and deferred charges.—Enter the amount of short-term and long-term prepayments of expenses attributable to one or more future accounting periods. Examples include prepayments of rent, insurance, and pension costs, and expenses incurred in connection with a solicitation campaign to be conducted in a future accounting period.

Line 54—Investments—securities.— Enter the book value (which may be market value) of securities held as investments, and attach a schedule that lists the securities held at the end of the year, and indicate whether the securities are listed at cost (including the value recorded at the time of receipt in the case of donated securities) or end of year market value. Debt securities of the U.S., state, and municipal governments, corporate stocks and bonds, and other publicly traded securities (defined in the instructions for line 8) do not have to be listed individually, except for stock holdings that represent 5% or more of the outstanding shares of stock of the same class. However, show separate totals for each type of security (U.S. government obligations, corporate stocks, etc.). Do not include amounts reported on line 46.

Line 55—Investments—land, buildings, and equipment.—Enter the book value (cost or other basis less accumulated depreciation) of all land, buildings, and equipment held for investment purposes, such as rental properties. Attach a schedule listing these investment fixed assets held at the end of the year and showing for each item or category listed, the cost or other basis, accumulated depreciation, and book value. Report the income from these assets on line 6a.

Line 56—Investments—other.—Enter the amount of all other investment holdings not reported on line 54 or 55. Attach a schedule listing and describing each of these investments held at the end of the year. Show the book value for each and indicate whether the investment is listed at cost or end of year market value. Report the income from these assets on line 7. Do not include program-related investments (see instructions for line 58).

Line 57—Land, buildings, and equipment.—Enter the book value (cost or other basis less accumulated depreciation) of all land, buildings, and equipment owned by the organization and not held for investment. This would include any property, plant, and equipment owned and used by the organization in conducting its exempt activities. Attach a schedule listing these fixed assets held at the end of the year and showing, for each item or category listed, the cost or other basis, accumulated depreciation, and book value.

Line 58—Other assets.—List and show the book value of each category of assets not reportable on lines 45 through 57. Attach a separate schedule if more space is needed.

One type of asset reportable on line 58 would be program-related investments, which are investments made primarily to accomplish some exempt purpose of the filing organization rather than to produce income.

Line 59—Total assets.—Enter the total of lines 45 through 58.

Line 60—Accounts payable and accrued expenses.—Enter the total of accounts payable to suppliers and others and accrued expenses, such as salaries payable, accrued payroll taxes, and interest payable.

Line 61—Grants payable.—Enter the unpaid portion of grants and awards that the organization has made a commitment to pay other organizations or individuals, whether or not the commitments have been communicated to the grantees.

Line 62—Support and revenue designated for future periods.—Enter the amount of contributions, governmental fees or grants, grants from foundations or other organizations, and other fees and support that contributors or grantors have designated as payable for or applicable to one or more future years, either by the terms of the gift or by the terms of the contract or other arrangement. Do not include any amounts restricted for future use by the filing organization's own governing board. Attach a schedule that describes each contribution or grant designated for one or more future periods and indicates the total amount of each item and the amount applicable to each future period.

Line 63—Loans from officers, directors, trustees, and key employees.—Enter the unpaid balance of loans received from officers, directors, trustees, and key employees (see the instructions for line 50 for definition). For loans outstanding at the end of the year, attach a schedule that provides (for each loan) the name and title of the lender and the information listed in items (b) through (j) of the instructions for line 50.

Line 64—Mortgages and other notes payable.—Enter the amount of mortgages and other notes payable at the beginning and end of the year. Attach a schedule showing, as of the end of the year, the total amount of all mortgages payable and, for each nonmortgage note payable, the name of the lender and the other information specified in items (b) through (j) of the instructions for line 50. The schedule

should also identify the relationship of the lender to any officer, director, trustee, or key employee of the organization.

Line 65—Other liabilities.—List and show the amount of each liability not reportable on lines 60 through 64. Attach a separate schedule if more space is needed.

Line 66—Total liabilities.—Enter the total of lines 60 through 65.

Lines 67 through 74—Fund Balances or Net Worth.—

Organizations using fund accounting.—If the organization uses fund accounting, check the box above line 67 and complete lines 67 through 70 to report the various fund balances. Also complete line 74 to report the sum of the fund balances and line 75 to report the sum of the total liabilities and fund balances.

Organizations not using fund accounting, see the instructions under that heading (below) for completing the net worth section. Under fund accounting, an organization segregates its assets, liabilities, and net worth into separate funds according to externally imposed restrictions on the use of certain assets, similar designations by the organization's governing board, and other amounts that are unrestricted as to use. Each fund is like a separate entity in that it has a self-balancing set of accounts showing assets, liabilities, equity (fund balance) "income," and expenses. Since these funds are actually part of a single entity, they are all included in that organization's own financial statements. Similar accounts in the various funds may or may not be consolidated in those statements according to the organization's preference and practice. Parts I, II, and V of this form, however, require such consolidation. Recognition of the separate funds and the net changes within the various funds during the year is accomplished by the fund balances section (lines 67 through 70) of the balance sheet.

Some states that accept Form 990 as their basic report form may require a separate statement of changes in fund balances. See instruction D.

Lines 67a and 67b—Current funds.—Enter the fund balances per books of the current unrestricted fund and the current restricted fund.

Line 68—Land, building, and equipment fund.—Enter the fund balances per books for the land, building, and equipment fund (plant fund).

Line 69—Endowment fund.—Enter the total of the fund balances for the permanent endowment fund and any term endowment funds. Annuity and life income fund balances may be reported here if not significant in amount, or on line 70. Do not include the fund balances of any quasi-endowment funds (funds functioning as endowment) or other internally designated funds.

Line 70—Other funds.—Enter the total of the fund balances for all funds not reported on lines 67 through 69. Indicate the type of fund in the space provided or on an attachment if more than one fund is involved. On the attachment, show the beginning and end of year fund balance for each fund listed.

Organizations not using fund accounting.—If the organization does not use fund accounting, check the box above line 71 and report net worth account balances on lines 71 through 74. Also complete line 75 to report the sum of the total liabilities and net worth.

Line 71—Capital stock or trust principal.—For corporations, enter the balance per books for capital stock accounts. Show par or stated value (or for stock with no par or stated value, total amount received upon issuance) of all classes of stock issued and, as yet, uncancelled. For trusts, enter the amount in the trust principal or corpus account.

Line 72—Paid-in or capital surplus.—Enter the balance per books for all paid-in capital in excess of par or stated value for all stock issued and, as yet, uncancelled. If stockholders or others gave donations that the organization records as paid-in capital, include them here. Any current year donations you include on line 72 should be reported in Part I, line 1.

Line 73—Retained earnings or accumulated income.—For a corporation, enter the balance in the retained earnings or similar account, minus the cost of any corporate treasury stock. For trusts, enter the balance per books in the accumulated income or similar account.

Line 74—Total fund balances or net worth.—For organizations that use fund accounting, enter the total of lines 67 through 70. For all other organizations, enter the total of lines 71 through 73. The beginning of the year figure in column (A) should be carried over to the Total column in Part I, line 19. The end of year figure in column (B) should agree with the figure on line 21 of the Total column in Part I.

Line 75—Total liabilities and fund balances/net worth.—Enter the total of lines 66 and 74. That figure must equal the figure for total assets reported on line 59 for both the beginning and end of the year.

Part VI—List of Officers, Directors, and Trustees.—

List each of the organization's officers, directors, trustees, and other persons having responsibilities or powers similar to those of officers, directors, or trustees. List all of these persons even if they did not receive any compensation from the organization. Show the compensation, if any, the organization paid each one during the period covered by the return.

Column (C).—Enter each officer's or director's compensation in the space provided. DO NOT aggregate all of the officers' and directors' compensation into a combined total.

Column (E).—Enter amounts that the recipients must report as income on their separate income tax returns. Examples include amounts for which the recipient did not account to the organization, or allowances that were more than the payee spent on serving the organization.

Part VII—Other Information.—

Line 76—Change in activities.—Attach a statement explaining any significant changes in the kind of activities the organization conducts to further its exempt purpose. These new or modified activities would be those not listed as current or planned in your application for recognition of exemption; or those not already made known to IRS by a letter to your key district director or by an attachment to your return for any earlier year. Besides describing new activities or changes to current ones, also describe any major program activities that are being discontinued.

Line 77—Changes in organizing or governing documents.—Attach a conformed copy of any changes to the articles of incorporation, constitution, trust instrument, or other organizing document, or to the bylaws or other governing document.

A "conformed" copy is one that agrees with the original document, and all amendments to it. If the copies are not signed, they must be accompanied by a written declaration signed by an officer authorized to sign for the organization, certifying that they are complete and accurate copies of the original documents.

Photocopies of articles of incorporation showing the certification of an appropriate state official need not be accompanied by such a declaration. See Rev. Proc. 68-14, 1968-1 C.B. 768, for more information.

When a number of changes are made, send a copy of the entire revised organizing instrument or governing document.

Line 78—Unrelated business income.— Check "Yes" on line 78a if the organization's total gross income from all of its unrelated trades and businesses is $1,000 or more for the year. Gross income is gross receipts less the cost of goods sold and/or operations. See General Instruction C2 for a description of unrelated business income and the Form 990-T filing requirements for section 501(c), 501(e), 501(f), and 501(k) organizations having such income. Form 990-T is not a substitute for Form 990. Items of income and expense reported on Form 990-T must also be reported on Form 990 when the organization is required to file both forms. For purposes of line 78c, the term "business activities" includes any income-generating activity involving the sale of goods or services or income from investments.

Note: *For tax years beginning after December 31, 1986, all tax exempt organizations must pay estimated tax with respect to their unrelated business income.*

Line 79—Liquidation, dissolution, termination, or substantial contraction.—If there was a liquidation, dissolution, termination, or substantial contraction, attach a statement explaining which took place.

For a complete liquidation of a corporation or termination of a trust, write **"Final Return"** at the top of the organization's Form 990. On the statement you attach, show whether the assets have been distributed and the date. Also attach a certified copy of any resolution, or plan of liquidation or termination, etc., with all amendments or supplements not already filed. In addition, attach a schedule listing: the names and addresses of all persons who received the assets distributed in liquidation or termination; the kinds of assets distributed to each one, and each asset's fair market value.

A *substantial contraction* is a partial liquidation or other major disposition of assets, except transfers for full consideration or distributions from current income.

A *major distribution of assets* means any disposition for the tax year that is:

(a) At least 25% of the fair market value of the organization's net assets when the tax year began; or

(b) One of a series of related dispositions begun in earlier years that, together, add up to at least 25% of the net assets the organization had at the beginning of the tax year when the first disposition in the series was made. Whether a major disposition of assets took place through a series of related dispositions is determined by the facts in each case.

See Regulations section 1.6043-3 for special rules and exceptions.

Line 80—Relation to other organizations.— Answer "Yes" if most of the organization's governing body, officers, trustees, or membership are also officers, directors, trustees, or members of any other organization.

Disregard a coincidental overlap of membership with another organization (that is, when membership in one organization is not a condition of membership with another organization). For example, assume that a majority of the members of a section

501(c)(4) civic organization also belong to a local chamber of commerce described in section 501(c)(6). The civic organization should answer "No" on line 80 if it does not require its members to belong to the chamber of commerce.

Also disregard affiliation with any statewide or nationwide organization. Thus, the civic organization in the above example would still answer "No" on line 80 even if it belonged to a state or national federation of similar organizations. A local labor union whose members are also members of a national labor organization would answer "No" on line 80.

Line 81—Expenditures for political purposes.—A political expenditure is one intended to influence the selection, nomination, election, or appointment of anyone to a Federal, state, or local public office, or office in a political organization, or the election of Presidential or Vice Presidential electors. Whether the attempt succeeds does not matter.

An expenditure includes a payment, distribution, loan, advance, deposit, or gift of money, or anything of value. It also includes a contract, promise, or agreement to make an expenditure, whether or not legally enforceable.

Section 501(c) organizations must file Form 1120-POL if their political expenditures and their net investment income both exceed $100 for the year.

Section 501(c) organizations that maintained separate segregated funds described in section 527(f)(3) should refer to the instructions for Form 1120-POL for filing requirements.

Line 82—Donated services or facilities.— Since Form 990 is open to public inspection, you may want the return to show contributions the organization received in the form of donated services or the use of materials, equipment, or facilities at less than fair rental value. If so, and if the organization's records either show the amount and value of such items or give a clearly objective basis for an estimate, you may enter the information on line 82. IRS does not require any organization to keep such records. Do NOT include the value of such items in Part I or II or in the expense column in Part III. However, you may indicate the value of donated services or use of materials, equipment, or facilities in Part III in the narrative description of program services rendered. See the instructions for Part III.

Line 83—Section 501(c)(5) or (6) organizations.—Attempts to influence the opinion of the general public, or any segment of the general public, on legislative matters or referendums constitute grassroots lobbying. Such lobbying may be explicit, as in an advertisement that urges the public to contact legislators for the purpose of proposing, supporting, or opposing legislation. Grassroots lobbying may also be implicit in any advertisement or other communication directed at the public if the communication is an attempt to mold public opinion on a legislative matter or referendum. Any lobbying directed at the members of the organization is not grassroots lobbying. Lobbying directed at "potential" members, employees of members, or stockholders of members would be grassroots lobbying. See Regulations section 1.162-20(c) for a discussion of grassroots lobbying.

Line 84—Section 501(c)(7) organizations.— A section 501(c)(7) organization may receive up to 35% of its gross receipts, including investment income,

from sources outside its membership and remain tax exempt. Part of the 35% (up to 15% of gross receipts) may be derived from public use of a social club's facilities.

For this purpose, "gross receipts" are the club's income from its usual activities. The term includes charges, admissions, membership fees, dues, assessments, investment income (such as dividends, rents, and similar receipts), and normal recurring capital gains on investments. Gross receipts do not include capital contributions (as defined in the Regulations under section 118), initiation fees, or unusual amounts of income such as from the club's selling its clubhouse. Although gross receipts usually do not include initiation fees, these should be included for college fraternities or sororities or other organizations that charge membership initiation fees, but no annual dues.

If the 35% and 15% limits do not affect the club's exempt status, include the income from line 84b on the club's Form 990-T.

Section 501(i) provides that a section 501(c)(7) organization cannot be exempt from income tax if any written policy statement, including the governing instrument and bylaws, provides for discrimination on the basis of race, color, or religion. However, section 501(i) allows social clubs to retain their exemption under section 501(c)(7) even though their membership is limited (in writing) to members of a particular religion if: (1) the social club is an auxiliary of a fraternal beneficiary society that is exempt under section 501(c)(8) and limits its membership to the members of a particular religion; or (2) the social club's membership limitation is a good faith attempt to further the teachings or principles of that religion, and the limitation is not intended to exclude individuals of a particular race or color.

Line 85—Section 501(c)(12) organizations.—One of the requirements that an organization must meet to qualify under section 501(c)(12) is that at least 85 percent of its gross income consists of amounts collected from members for the sole purpose of meeting losses and expenses. For purposes of section 501(c)(12), the term "gross income" means gross receipts minus cost of goods sold.

For a mutual or cooperative electric or telephone company, "gross income" does not include amounts received or accrued as "qualified pole rentals" as defined in section 501(c)(12)(D).

For a mutual or cooperative telephone company, "gross income" also does not include amounts received or accrued either from another telephone company for completing long distance calls to or from or between the telephone company's members, or from the sale of display listings in a directory furnished to the telephone company's members.

Line 86—Public interest law firms.—A public interest law firm exempt under section 501(c)(3) or 501(c)(4) must attach a statement that lists the cases in litigation, or that have been litigated during the year. For each case, describe the matter in dispute and explain how the litigation will benefit the public generally. See Rev. Proc. 71-39, 1971-2 C.B. 575. Also attach a report of all fees sought and recovered. See Rev. Proc. 75-13, 1975-1 C.B. 662, about acceptance of attorney's fees.

Line 87—List of states.—List each state with which you are filing a copy of this return in full or partial satisfaction of state filing requirements.

19**86**

🦅 **Department of the Treasury
Internal Revenue Service**

Instructions for Schedule A (Form 990)

(Section references are to the Internal Revenue Code, unless otherwise noted.)

Paperwork Reduction Act Notice.—We ask for this information to carry out the Internal Revenue laws of the United States. We need it to ensure that taxpayers are complying with these laws and to allow us to figure and collect the right amount of tax. You are required to give us this information.

Purpose of Form.—Schedule A (Form 990) is used by section 501(c)(3), 501(e), 501(f), and 501(k) organizations and section 4947(a)(1) trusts to furnish additional information not required of other types of organizations that file **Form 990,** Return of Organization Exempt From Income Tax. If you are not required to file Form 990, you need not file Schedule A. Do not use Schedule A if you file for a private foundation. (Private foundations file **Form 990-PF,** Return of Private Foundation, instead of Form 990.)

For purposes of these instructions, the term *section 501(c)(3)* includes organizations exempt under sections 501(e), 501(f), and 501(k).

General Information

A. Who Must File.—If you file Form 990 for an organization described in section 501(c)(3), or a nonexempt charitable trust described in section 4947(a)(1), you will need to complete and attach Schedule A. If you are not required to file Form 990, you need not file Schedule A. Do not use Schedule A if you file for a private foundation. (Private foundations file **Form 990-PF,** Return of Private Foundation, instead of Form 990.)

B. Period Covered.—Your Schedule A should cover the same period as the Form 990 with which you file it.

C. Penalties.—Schedule A (Form 990) is an integral part of Form 990 for section 501(c)(3) organizations and section 4947(a)(1) trusts required to file that form. Therefore, any such organization that does not submit a completed Schedule A with its Form 990 does not satisfy its filing requirement and may be charged a $10 a day penalty. See General Instruction H of the Form 990 instructions for more information about this and other penalties.

To avoid having to respond to requests for missing information, please be sure to complete all applicable line items; to answer "Yes" or "No" to each question on the return; to make an entry (including a "-0-" when appropriate) on all total lines; and to enter "None" or "N/A" if an entire part does not apply.

Specific Instructions

If you need more space for any part or line item, attach separate sheets on which you follow the same format and sequence as on the printed form. Show totals on the printed form. Be sure to put the organization's name and employer identification number on separate sheets and identify the part or line that the attachments support.

You may show money items as whole dollar amounts. To do so, drop any amount less than 50 cents, and increase any amount from 50 through 99 cents to the next higher dollar.

Part I.—Complete for the five employees with the highest annual compensation over $30,000. Do not include employees listed in Part VI of Form 990 (List of Officers, Directors, and

Trustees). Also enter in Part I the number of other employees with annual compensation over $30,000 *who are not listed in Part I.*

Part II.—Complete for the five highest paid independent contractors who performed personal services of a professional nature for the organization and, in return, received over $30,000 for the year from the organization. Examples of such contractors include attorneys, accountants, and doctors, whether these people perform the services as individuals or as employees of a professional service corporation. Also show the number of other independent contractors who received more than $30,000 for the year for performing such services and are not listed in Part II.

Part III.—

Line 1.—For a definition of *attempting to influence legislation,* see the instructions for Part VI.

Line 2d.—If the only compensation or repayment relates to amounts you reported in Part VI of Form 990, check "Yes" and write "See Part VI, Form 990" on the dotted line to the left of the entry space. For transactions between the organization and another section 501(c)(3) organization (other than a private foundation), write "N/A."

Line 4.—In the statement, do not include payments for materials or services the organization receives.

Qualify means that organizations or individuals will use the funds you provide for charitable purposes described in sections 170(c)(1) and 170(c)(2).

Qualify also means that individual recipients belong to a charitable class, and the payments are to aid them. Examples include help to the aged poor, training of teachers and social workers from underdeveloped countries, and awards such as scholarships to individuals.

Part IV.—

Definitions.—The following terms are used in more than one item in Part IV. The definitions below generally apply.

Support (boxes 10, 11, 12, Support Schedule), with certain exceptions described below, means all forms of support including (but not limited to) contributions, investment income (such as interest, rents, royalties, and dividends), and net income from unrelated business activities whether or not such activities are carried on regularly as a trade or business.

(a) *Support* does not include—

(1) Any amounts the organization receives from exercising or performing its charitable, educational, or other similar purpose or function. In general, these amounts include those from any activity which is substantially related to the furtherance of such charitable, etc., purpose or function (other than through the production of income). **Exception:** Section 509(a)(2) organizations that check box 12 do include these amounts as part of their support.

(2) Any gain on the sale or exchange of property which would be considered under any section of the Code as gain from the sale or exchange of a capital asset.

(3) Contributions of services for which a deduction is not allowable.

(b) *Support from a governmental unit,* with certain exceptions described below, includes—

(1) Any amounts received from a governmental unit, including donations or contributions and amounts received in connection with a contract entered into with a governmental unit for the performance of services or in connection with a government research grant, provided these amounts are not excluded from the term *support* as amounts received from exercising or performing the organization's charitable purpose or function. An amount paid by a governmental unit to an organization is not treated as received from exercising or performing its charitable, etc., purpose or function if the payment is to enable the organization to provide a service to, or maintain a facility for, the direct benefit of the public, as for example, to maintain library facilities which are open to the public.

(2) Tax revenues levied for the organization's benefit and either paid to or expended on its behalf.

(3) The value of services or facilities (exclusive of services or facilities generally furnished, without charge, to the public) furnished by a governmental unit to the organization without charge; for example, a city pays the salaries of personnel to guard a museum, art gallery, etc., or provides the use of a building rent free. However, the term does not include the value of any exemption from Federal, state, or local tax or any similar benefit.

Indirect contributions from the general public are what the organization receives from other organizations that receive a substantial part of their support from general public contributions. An example is the organization's share of the proceeds from an annual community chest drive (such as the United Way or United Fund).

A disqualified person is:

(1) A *substantial contributor,* who is any person who gave an aggregate amount of more than $5,000, if that amount is more than 2% of the total contributions the foundation or organization received from its inception up through the end of the year in which that person's contributions were received. Gifts from the contributor's spouse are treated as gifts from the contributor. Gifts are generally valued at fair market value as of the date the organization received them. Special rules apply for contributions made on or before October 9, 1969. (See section 1.507-6 of the regulations.) In the case of a trust, the creator of the trust is considered a substantial contributor without regard to the amount of contributions received by the trust from the creator and other persons. Any person who is a substantial contributor at any time generally remains a substantial contributor for all future periods even if later contributions by others push that person's contributions below the 2% figure discussed above.

(2) An officer, director, or trustee of the organization or any individual having powers or responsibilities similar to those of officers, directors, or trustees.

(3) An owner of more than 20% of: the voting power of a corporation, profits interest of a partnership, or beneficial interest of a trust or an unincorporated enterprise that is a substantial contributor to the organization.

(4) A family member of an individual in the first three categories. A family member includes only a person's spouse, ancestors, lineal descendants, and spouses of lineal descendants.

(5) A corporation, partnership, trust, or estate in which persons described in (1), (2), (3), or (4) own more than 35% of the voting power, profits interest, or beneficial interest. See section 4946(a)(1).

An organization is considered *normally* to satisfy the public support test (boxes 10, 11, and 12) for its current tax year and the tax year immediately following its current tax year if the organization satisfies the applicable support test for the 4 tax years immediately before the current tax year. If the organization has a material change (other than from unusual grants—see instructions for line 28 on page 3) in its sources of support during the current tax year, the data ordinarily required in the Support Schedule covering the years 1982 through 1985 must be submitted for the years 1982 through 1986. You must prepare and attach a 5-year schedule using the same format as provided in the Support Schedule for lines 15 through 28.

Boxes 5 through 14.—Check one box to indicate why the organization is not a private foundation. The organization's exemption letter states the reason, or your local IRS office can tell you.

Box 6.—Check box 6 for a school whose primary function is the presentation of formal instruction, and which regularly has a faculty, a curriculum, an enrolled body of students, and a place where educational activities are regularly conducted.

A private school, in addition, must have a racially nondiscriminatory policy toward its students. For more information about these requirements, see the instructions for Part V.

Box 7.—Check for an organization whose main purpose is to provide hospital or medical care. A rehabilitation institution or an outpatient clinic may qualify as a hospital, but the term does not include: medical schools, medical research organizations, convalescent homes, homes for the aged, or vocational training institutions for the handicapped. Also check box 7 for a cooperative hospital service organization described in section 501(e).

Box 9.—Check for a medical research organization operated in connection with or in conjunction with a hospital. The hospital must be described in section 501(c)(3) or operated by the Federal government, a State or its political subdivision, a U.S. possession or its political subdivision, or the District of Columbia.

Medical research means studies and experiments done to increase or verify information about physical or mental diseases and disabilities: their causes, diagnosis, prevention, treatment, or control. The organization must conduct the research directly and continuously. If it primarily gives funds to other organizations (or grants and scholarships to individuals) for them to do the research, the organization is not a medical research organization.

The organization need not be an affiliate of the hospital but there must be an understanding that they will cooperate closely and continuously in doing medical research as a joint effort.

An organization qualifies as a medical research organization if its principal purpose is medical research and it devotes more than half its assets, or spends at least 3.5% of the fair market value of its endowment, in directly conducting medical research. Either test may be met based on a computation period consisting of the immediately preceding tax year or the immediately preceding 4 tax years. If an organization does not satisfy either the assets test or the expenditure test, it may still qualify as a medical research organization based on the circumstances involved. These are discussed in Regulations section 1.170A-9(c)(2)(v) and (vi). Value the organization's assets as of any day in your tax year, but use the same day every year. Value the endowment at fair market value, using commonly accepted valuation methods. (See Regulations section 20.2031.)

Box 10.—Check box 10 and complete the Support Schedule (lines 15 through 28) if your organization receives and manages property for, and expends funds to or for the benefit of, a college or university that is owned or operated by one or more states or their political subdivisions. The school must be as described in the first paragraph of the instructions for box 6.

Expending funds to or for the benefit of a college or university includes acquiring and maintaining the campus, its buildings, and its equipment, granting scholarships and student loans, and making any other payments in connection with the normal functions of colleges and universities.

The organization must meet essentially the same public support test described below for box 11. See Rev. Rul. 82-132, 1982-2 C.B. 107.

Box 11.—Check this box and complete the Support Schedule for an organization that normally receives at least 33⅓% of its support (excluding income received in exercising its charitable, etc., function) from a governmental unit or from direct or indirect contributions from the general public.

To determine whether the 33⅓ percent-of-support test is met, donor contributions are considered support from direct or indirect contributions from the general public only to the extent that their total amount during the 4-tax-year period is 2% or less of the organization's total support for those 4 tax years as described below:

Denominator.—Any contribution by one individual will be included in full in the total support denominator of the fraction determining the 33⅓ percent-of-support or the 10 percent-of-support limitation.

Numerator.—**Only** the portion of each donor's contribution that is 2% or less of the total support denominator will be included in the numerator. In applying the 2% limitation, all contributions by any person(s) related to the donor as described in section 4946(a)(1)(C) through (G) (and related regulations) will be treated as if made by the donor. The 2% limitation does not apply to support from governmental units referred to in section 170(c)(1), or to contributions from publicly supported organizations (section 170(b)(1)(A)(vi)), that check box 11.

Example: For the years 1982 through 1985, the X organization received $600,000 in support from the following sources:

Investment income	$300,000
Y City (government source)	40,000
United Fund (indirect contributions from general public)	40,000
Direct contributions	220,000
Total support	$600,000

Six donors each gave more than 2% of the total support (which is $12,000). While the donors' full contributions are counted in X organization's total support, only $12,000 from each of these six donors is included in the organization's public support. The public support is figured as follows:

Government support (Y City)	$40,000
Indirect contributions from the general public (United Fund)	40,000
Contributions from various donors, none of whom gave over 2% of the organization's total support	50,000
6 contributions limited to 2% of the organization's total support (6 x $12,000)	72,000
Public support	$202,000

One-third of X organization's total support is $200,000 for 1982 through 1985. Since the organization received more than one-third of its total support for the period from public sources, it qualifies as a publicly supported organization.

An organization which does not qualify as publicly supported under the test described

above may be publicly supported on the basis of the facts in its case if it receives at least 10% of its support from the general public. If you believe you are publicly supported according to applicable regulations, attach a detailed statement of the facts upon which you base your conclusion.

Box 12.—Check box 12 and complete the Support Schedule (lines 15 through 28) for an organization that meets both of the following support tests (section 509(a)(2)):

(A) normally receives more than one-third of its support in each tax year from any combination of—

(i) gifts, grants, contributions, or membership fees, and

(ii) gross receipts from admissions, sales of merchandise, performance of services, or furnishing of facilities in an activity which is not an unrelated trade or business (within the meaning of section 513), not including such receipts from any person, or from any bureau or similar agency of a government unit (as described in section 170(c)(1)), in any tax year to the extent such receipts exceed the greater of $5,000 or 1% of the organization's support in such tax year, from persons other than disqualified persons (see Definitions, above) with respect to the organization, from governmental units described in section 170(c)(1), or from organizations described in section 170(b)(1)(A) (other than in clauses (vii) and (viii)), and

(B) normally receives not more than one-third of its support in each tax year from the sum of—

(i) gross investment income (as defined in section 509(e)), and

(ii) the excess (if any) of the amount of the unrelated business taxable income (as defined in section 512) over the amount of the tax imposed by section 511.

For purposes of section 509(a)(2), determine your support solely on the cash receipts and disbursements method of accounting. For examples, see Regulations section 1.509(a)-3(k).

Retained character of gross investment income.—To determine whether an organization meets the gross investment income test set forth in section 509(a)(2)(B), amounts it receives from:

(a) an organization which claims to be described in section 509(a)(3) because it supports a 509(a)(2) organization; or

(b) a charitable trust, corporation, fund, or association described in section 501(c)(3) (including a charitable trust described in section 4947(a)(1)), or a split-interest trust described in section 4947(a)(2), which is required by its governing instrument or otherwise to distribute, or which normally distributes, at least 25% of its adjusted net income (within the meaning of section 4942(f)) to a 509(a)(2) organization, and that distribution normally comprises at least 5% of the distributee organization's adjusted net income, will retain the character of gross investment income (rather than gifts or contributions) to the extent that such amounts are characterized as gross investment income in the possession of the distributing organizations described in (a) and (b) of this paragraph or, if the distributing organization is a split-interest trust described in section 4947(a)(2), to the extent that such amounts would be characterized as gross investment income attributable to transfers in trust after May 26, 1969, if the trust was a private foundation.

All income characterized as gross investment income in the possession of the distributing organization is considered to be distributed first by the organization and keeps its character as such in the possession of the recipient.

For further details see Regulations section 1.509(a)-5, covering special rules of attribution.

If your organization received any amounts from either kind of organization above, attach a statement. Show each amount received from each organization, including amounts, such as gifts, that are not investment income.

Box 13.—Check box 13 and complete items a and b for a supporting organization operated only for the benefit of and in connection with organizations listed in boxes 5 through 12, or with organizations described in section 501(c) (4), (5), or (6) that meet the tests of section 509(a)(2) (described in box 12). General principles governing supporting organizations are described in Regulations section 1.509(a)-4.

Under item 13b, "Box number from above," identify the organization supported if it is included in the list of boxes 5 through 12. For example, if your organization supported a hospital, enter "7" in item 13b.

Box 14.—Check box 14 only if the organization has received a ruling from the IRS that it is organized and operated primarily to test for public safety.

Support Schedule for Organizations Described in Sections 170(b)(1)(A)(iv) or (vi) and 509(a)(2).—Complete the Support Schedule if you checked box 10, 11, or 12.

If the organization has not existed during the whole period the schedule covers, fill in the information for the years that apply. If the organization's status is based on years not shown in the Support Schedule, attach an additional schedule for the other years.

Lines 15, 16, 17, 26, and 27.—Refer to Regulations section 1.509(a)-3:

(1) To distinguish gross receipts from gifts and contributions, grants, and gross investment income; and

(2) For the definition of membership fees and a bureau or similar agency of a governmental unit.

Line 17.—In addition to income the organization receives from performing its charitable, etc., functions, include on line 17 gross receipts from section 513(a)(1), (2), or (3) activities. These are activities in which substantially all the work is performed without compensation, or carried on by the organization primarily for the convenience of its members, or which consists of the selling of merchandise, substantially all of which has been received by the organization as gifts or contributions.

Line 28.—Unusual grants generally are substantial contributions and bequests from disinterested persons and:

(1) Are attracted because of the organization's public support,

(2) Are unusual and unexpected because of the amount, and

(3) Are large enough that they would endanger the organization's status as normally meeting the support test described in the instructions for box 10, 11, or 12.

A grant that meets these terms may be treated as an unusual grant (that is disregarded entirely in the public support computation) even if the organization receives the funds over a period of years. In your list of unusual grants, show only what the organization received during the year.

Do not treat gross investment income items as unusual grants. Instead, include all investment income in support.

See Regulations sections 1.170A-9(e)(6)(ii) and 1.509(a)-(3)(c)(3) and (4) for more information about unusual grants.

Part V.—All schools that checked box 6, Part IV, must complete Part V. Rev. Proc. 75-50, 1975-2 C.B. 587, gives guidelines and recordkeeping requirements for determining whether private schools that are presently recognized as exempt from tax have racially nondiscriminatory policies as to students.

Section 4.01 of the Rev. Proc. requires a school to include a statement in its charter, bylaws, or other governing instrument, or in a resolution of its governing body, that it has a racially nondiscriminatory policy as to students.

Section 4.02 requires every school to include a statement of its racially nondiscriminatory policy as to students in all its brochures and catalogues dealing with student admissions, programs, and scholarships. Further, every school must include a reference to its racially nondiscriminatory policy in other written advertising that it uses as a means of informing prospective students of its programs.

Section 4.03 requires a school to publicize its racially nondiscriminatory policy at least once annually during the period of its solicitation for students, or, in the absence of a solicitation program, during its registration period, unless it meets the criteria set out in section 4.03-2 of the Rev. Proc. See section 4.03-1 for examples of acceptable methods of publicizing the policy, including the use of newspapers and broadcast media. Whatever method is used, it must make the school's policy known to all segments of the general community it serves.

Section 4.03 further requires a school to be prepared to demonstrate that it has publicly denied or withdrawn any statements claimed to have been made on its behalf that are contrary to its publicity of a racially nondiscriminatory policy as to students, to the extent that the school or its principal officials were aware of such statements.

Section 4.04 requires a school to be able to show that all of its programs and facilities are operated in a racially nondiscriminatory manner.

Section 4.05 generally requires that all scholarships or other comparable benefits at any school be offered on a racially nondiscriminatory basis. However, a financial assistance program favoring members of one or more racial groups will not adversely affect exempt status if it does not significantly detract from a racially nondiscriminatory policy as to students.

Section 4.06 requires an individual authorized to take official action on behalf of a school that claims to be racially nondiscriminatory as to students to certify annually, under penalties of perjury, that to the best of his or her knowledge and belief the school has satisfied the applicable requirements of sections 4.01 through 4.05 of the Rev. Proc. This certification is line 35 in Part V.

Part VI.—Complete Part VI only for an eligible organization that filed **Form 5768**, Election/Revocation of Election by an Eligible Section 501(c)(3) Organization to Make Expenditures to Influence Legislation, to elect to be subject to the lobbying expenditure limitations of section 501(h) and the election was in effect for its tax year beginning in 1986. For lines 36 through 44, complete column (b) for any organization using Part VI, but complete column (a) only for affiliated groups, defined on page 4.

An organization that makes the election can have nontaxable lobbying expenses within certain dollar limits. It will be subject to an excise tax under section 4911 if its lobbying expenses exceed these limits in a particular year. Lines 36-44 are used to determine whether any of the organization's current year lobbying expenditures are subject to tax. File **Form 4720**, Return of Certain Excise Taxes on Charities and Other Persons Under Chapters 41 and 42 of the Internal Revenue Code, if you need to report and pay the excise tax.

If, over a 4-year averaging period, the organization's average annual lobbying or grassroots lobbying expenses are more than 150% of its dollar limits, its exempt status may be jeopardized. Lines 45-50 are used to determine if the organization exceeded these limits during the 4-year averaging period.

Definitions.—The following terms are used throughout Part VI. The definitions below generally apply.

Exempt purpose expenses are:

(1) The total amounts paid or incurred for religious, charitable, scientific, literary, or educational purposes, or to foster national or international amateur sports competition (not including (except for qualified amateur sports organizations described in section 501(j)(2)) the providing of athletic facilities or equipment), or for the prevention of cruelty to children or animals.

(2) Administrative expenses paid or incurred for the purposes above.

(3) Amounts paid or incurred to try to influence legislation, whether or not for the purposes described in (1) above.

Exempt purpose expenses do not include amounts paid or incurred to or for either the organization's separate fundraising unit or other organizations, if the amounts are primarily for fundraising.

Lobbying expenses are spent in an attempt to influence legislation by:

(1) Affecting any segment of the general public opinion (grassroots lobbying expenses), or

(2) Communicating with any member or employee of a legislative body, or with any government official or employee who may help form legislation.

Influencing legislation does not include any of the following:

(1) Making available the results of nonpartisan analysis or research.

(2) Providing technical advice or help (that would otherwise be influencing legislation) to a government body, committee, or other subdivision in response to a written request by that group.

(3) Appearing before, or communicating with, a legislative body about its possible decision that might affect the organization's existence, powers, duties, tax-exempt status, or the deduction of contributions to the organization.

(4) Communicating with a government official or employee who is not a member or employee of a legislative body, unless the main purpose of the communication is to influence legislation.

(5) Communications between the organization and its members about legislation or proposed legislation that directly interests the organization and its members. However,

influencing legislation does include requests from the organization to its members that they.

(1) try to influence legislation by communicating with anyone who helps form it; or

(2) encourage nonmembers to try to influence legislation, either by grassroots lobbying or by communicating with anyone who helps form the legislation.

Legislation includes action with respect to acts, bills, resolutions, or similar items by the Congress, any State legislature, any local council, or similar governing body or by the public in a referendum, initiative, constitutional amendment, or similar procedure.

The term *action* in the preceding sentence is limited to the introduction, amendment, enactment, defeat, or repeal of acts, bills, resolutions, or similar items.

Figuring lobbying expenses. —When an expense is incurred partly in connection with exempt purposes and partly in connection with any other type of activity, allocate the expense between the two activities on a reasonable basis. For example, if a person spends half the time on lobbying activities and half the time on investment activities, allocate that person's salary expense equally between the two activities. The same rule applies to other operating expenses, such as telephones or printing, and to overhead or fixed expenses, such as rent, insurance, or depreciation. Figure depreciation on the straight-line basis. Do not include capital expenses, such as improvements to an office, when figuring lobbying expenses.

Affiliated groups. —Two organizations are affiliated if one is bound by the other's decisions on legislative issues (control) or if enough representatives of one belong to the other's governing board to cause or prevent action on legislative issues (interlocking directorate). If you do not know whether your group is affiliated, ask IRS for a ruling letter. Send the request to: Assistant Commissioner (Employee Plans and Exempt Organizations), Exempt Organizations Technical Division, OP:E:EO, 1111 Constitution Ave., NW, Washington, D.C. 20224.

If the electing organization belongs to an affiliated group, complete lines 36 through 44 of column (a), Part VI, for the affiliated group as a whole, and complete column (b) for the electing member of the group. The electing member must also attach a schedule showing each group member's name, address, employer identification number, and expenses. Use the format of Part VI, and show which members elected and which did not.

If the group has no excess amounts on either line 43 or 44, column (a), each electing member will be treated as not having excess amounts. If the group has excess amounts on line 43 or 44, column (a), each electing member will be treated as having excess amounts, and each must file Form 4720 and pay the tax on its proportionate share of the group's excess lobbying expenses. To find a member's proportionate share, multiply the affiliated group's total lobbying expenses (on lines 43, 44, or both) by a fraction. The numerator is the electing member's total lobbying expenses (line 38, column (b)), and the denominator is the total lobbying expenses of all electing members of the affiliated group. Enter the proportionate share in column (b) of line 43,

line 44, or both. Include each electing member's share of the excess lobbying expenses on the schedule you attach. Any nonelecting members would not owe tax, but would remain subject to the existing rule, which provides that no substantial part of their activities may consist of carrying on propaganda or otherwise trying to influence legislation.

Limited control —If two organizations are affiliated because their governing instruments provide that the decisions of one will control the other only on national legislation, apply expenses as follows:

(1) Charge the controlling organization with its own lobbying expenses and with the national legislation expenses of the affiliated organizations. Do not charge the controlling organization with other lobbying expenses (or other exempt-purpose expenses) that the affiliated organizations may have.

(2) Treat each local organization as though it were not a member of an affiliated group. That is, the local organization should account for its own expenses only. It would not include any national legislation expenses deemed to have been incurred by the controlling organization under (1) above.

When this type of limited control is present, each member of the affiliated group should complete column (b) only.

Group returns. —Although membership in a group affiliated for lobbying does not establish eligibility to file a group return, a group return can sometimes meet the filing requirements of more than one member of an affiliated group. (See General Instruction J of Form 990 to see who may file a group return.) If a central or parent organization files a group return on behalf of two or more members of the group, complete lines 36 through 44 of column (a) of Part VI for the affiliated group as a whole. Include the central, electing, and non-electing members. In column (b), except on lines 43 and 44, include the amounts that apply to all electing members of the group if they are included in the group return. Also attach the schedule described above under "Affiliated groups," and show what amounts apply to each group member.

If the group return includes organizations that belong to more than one affiliated group, show the totals for all such groups in column (a). In the schedule you attach, show the amounts that apply to each affiliated group and to each group member.

If the parent organization has made the lobbying expense election, its separate return must also show in column (a) the amounts that apply to the affiliated group as a whole and, in column (b), the amounts that apply to the parent organization only. Similarly, a subordinate organization not included in the group return would also complete column (a) for the affiliated group as a whole, and column (b) for itself only.

However, if "limited control" (defined above) exists, complete only column (b) in Part VI of the group return for the electing members in the group. Attach a schedule to show the amounts that apply to each electing member. In the separate returns filed by the parent and by any subordinate organizations not included in the group return, complete only column (b).

Lines 45-50. —Any organization for which a lobbying expense election under section 501(h) was in effect for its tax year beginning in 1986 must complete columns (a) through (e) of lines 45 through 50 except in the following situations:

(1) An organization first treated as a section 501(c)(3) organization in its tax year beginning in 1986 does not have to complete any part of lines 45 through 50.

(2) An organization does not have to complete lines 45 through 50 for any period before it is first treated as a section 501(c)(3) organization.

(3) If 1986 is the first year for which an organization's first section 501(h) election is effective, that organization is required to complete only the column for 1986 and enter the same amounts in column (e) if the amount in column (a), line 47, is less than the amount in column (a), line 46, and the amount in column (a), line 50, is less than the amount reported in column (a), line 49. If the organization does not satisfy both tests (that is, if its total lobbying expenses or its grassroots lobbying expenses exceed the applicable ceiling amount), complete all five columns unless exception (1) or (2) above applies.

(4) If 1986 is the second or third tax year for which the organization's first section 501(h) election is in effect, that organization is required to complete only the columns for the years in which the election has been in effect and enter the totals for those years in column (e) if, for those 2 or 3 years, the amount entered in column (e), line 47, is less than the amount in column (e), line 46, and the amount in column (e), line 50, is less than the amount reported in column (e), line 49. If the organization does not satisfy both tests (that is, if its total lobbying expenses or its grassroots lobbying expenses exceed the applicable ceiling amount), complete all five columns unless exception (1) or (2) above applies.

If your organization is not required to complete all five columns, attach a statement explaining why. In the statement, also indicate the ending date of the tax year in which the organization made its first section 501(h) election and state whether or not that first election was revoked before the start of the organization's tax year that began in 1986.

If your organization belongs to an affiliated group, you should enter the appropriate affiliated group totals from column (a) when completing lines 45, 47, 48 and 50.

Line 45. —Lobbying nontaxable amount. —For 1984–86, enter the amount from line 41 of the Schedule A (Form 990) filed for each year. For 1983, enter the amounts from line 42 of the Schedule A (Form 990) you filed for that year.

Line 47. —Total lobbying expenses. —For 1984–86, enter the amount from line 38 of the Schedule A (Form 990) filed for each year. For 1983, enter the amounts from line 39 of the Schedule A (Form 990) you filed for that year.

Line 48. —Grassroots nontaxable amount. —For 1984–86, enter the amount from line 42 of the Schedule A (Form 990) filed for each year. For 1983, enter the amounts from line 43 of the Schedule A (Form 990) you filed for that year.

Line 50. —Grassroots lobbying expenses. —For 1984–86, enter the amount from line 36 of the Schedule A (Form 990) filed for each year. For 1983, enter the amounts from line 37 of the Schedule A (Form 990) you filed for that year.

Form **990**

Department of the Treasury
Internal Revenue Service

Return of Organization Exempt From Income Tax

Under section 501(c) (except black lung benefit trust or private foundation)
of the Internal Revenue Code or section 4947(a)(1) trust

Note: You may be required to use a copy of this return to satisfy state reporting requirements. See instruction D.

OMB No. 1545-0047

1986

For the calendar year 1986, or fiscal year beginning _____ , 1986, and ending _____ , 19 ___

Use IRS label. Other-wise, please print or type.	Name of organization	**A** Employer identification number (see instruction L)
	Address (number and street)	**B** State registration number (see instruction D)
	City or town, state, and ZIP code	**C** Section 4947(a)(1) trusts filing this form in lieu of Form 1041: check here ▶ ☐ (see instruction C10)

D Check type of organization—Exempt under section ▶ ☐ 501(c) ( ) (insert number), OR ▶ ☐ section 4947(a)(1) trust
E Accounting method. ☐ Cash ☐ Accrual ☐ Other (specify) ▶

Check here if application for exemption is pending . . ▶ ☐

F Is this a group return (see instruction J) filed for affiliates? . . . . . ☐ Yes ☐ No
If "Yes," enter the number of affiliates for which this return is filed ____
Is this a separate return filed by a group affiliate? . . . . ☐ Yes ☐ No

G If "Yes" to either, give four-digit group exemption number (GEN) ▶

H ☐ Check here if your gross receipts are normally not more than $25,000 (see instruction B11). You do not have to file a completed return with IRS but should file a return without financial data if you were mailed a Form 990 Package (see instruction A). Some states may require a completed return.

I ☐ Check here if gross receipts are normally more than $25,000 and line 12 is $25,000 or less. Complete Parts I (except lines 13-15), III, IV, VI, and VII and only the indicated items in Parts II and V (see instruction I). If line 12 is more than $25,000, complete the entire return.

501(c)(3) organizations and 4947(a)(1) trusts must also complete and attach Schedule A (Form 990). (See instructions.)

Part I Statement of Support, Revenue, and Expenses and Changes in Fund Balances

These columns are optional—see instructions

			(A) Total	**(B)** Unrestricted / Expendable	**(C)** Restricted/ Nonexpendable
	1	Contributions, gifts, grants, and similar amounts received:			
	a	Direct public support			
	b	Indirect public support			
	c	Government grants			
	d	Total (add lines 1a through 1c) (attach schedule—see instructions)			
	2	Program service revenue (from Part IV, line f)			
	3	Membership dues and assessments			
	4	Interest on savings and temporary cash investments			
	5	Dividends and interest from securities			
	6a	Gross rents			
	b	Minus: rental expenses			
	c	Net rental income (loss)			
	7	Other investment income (Describe ▶)			
	8a	Gross amount from sale of assets other than inventory [Securities] [Other]			
	b	Minus: cost or other basis and sales expenses			
	c	Gain (loss) (attach schedule)			
	9	Special fundraising events and activities (**attach schedule**—see instructions):			
	a	Gross revenue (not including $_____ of contributions reported on line 1a)			
	b	Minus: direct expenses			
	c	Net income (line 9a minus line 9b)			
	10a	Gross sales minus returns and allowances			
	b	Minus: cost of goods sold (attach schedule)			
	c	Gross profit (loss)			
	11	Other revenue (from Part IV, line g)			
	12	Total revenue (add lines 1d, 2, 3, 4, 5, 6c, 7, 8c, 9c, 10c, and 11)			
	13	Program services (from line 44, column (B)) (see instructions)			
	14	Management and general (from line 44, column (C)) (see instructions)			
	15	Fundraising (from line 44, column (D)) (see instructions)			
	16	Payments to affiliates (attach schedule—see instructions)			
	17	Total expenses (add lines 16 and 44, column (A))			
	18	Excess (deficit) for the year (subtract line 17 from line 12)			
	19	Fund balances or net worth at beginning of year (from line 74, column (A))			
	20	Other changes in fund balances or net worth (attach explanation)			
	21	Fund balances or net worth at end of year (add lines 18, 19, and 20)			

(Left margin labels: Support and Revenue / Expenses / Fund Balances)

For Paperwork Reduction Act Notice, see page 1 of the instructions.

Form **990** (1986)

Appendix

A.19

Form 990 (1986)   Page **2**

Part II — Statement of Functional Expenses

All organizations must complete column (A). Columns (B), (C), and (D) are required for most sections 501(c)(3) and (c)(4) organizations and 4947(a)(1) trusts but optional for others. (See instructions.)

Do not include amounts reported on lines 6b, 8b, 9b, 10b, or 16 of Part I.	(A) Total	(B) Program services	(C) Management and general	(D) Fundraising
22 Grants and allocations (attach schedule)			/////	/////
23 Specific assistance to individuals			/////	/////
24 Benefits paid to or for members			/////	/////
25 Compensation of officers, directors, etc.				
26 Other salaries and wages				
27 Pension plan contributions				
28 Other employee benefits				
29 Payroll taxes				
30 Professional fundraising fees		/////	/////	
31 Accounting fees				
32 Legal fees				
33 Supplies				
34 Telephone				
35 Postage and shipping				
36 Occupancy				
37 Equipment rental and maintenance				
38 Printing and publications				
39 Travel				
40 Conferences, conventions, and meetings				
41 Interest				
42 Depreciation, depletion, etc. (attach schedule)				
43 Other expenses (itemize): a				
b				
c				
d				
e				
f				
44 Total functional expenses (add lines 22 through 43) Organizations completing columns B-D, carry these totals to lines 13-15.				

Part III — Statement of Program Services Rendered

List each program service title on lines a through d; for each, identify the service output(s) or product(s), and report the quantity provided. Enter the total expenses attributable to each program service and the amount of grants and allocations included in that total. (See instructions for Part III.)

Expenses (Optional for some organizations—see instructions)

a _____
_____
_____
_____
(Grants and allocations $)

b _____
_____
_____
_____
(Grants and allocations $)

c _____
_____
_____
_____
(Grants and allocations $)

d _____
_____
_____
_____
(Grants and allocations $)

e Other program service activities (attach schedule)   (Grants and allocations $)

f Total (add lines a through e) (should equal line 44, column (B))

Part IV	Program Service Revenue and Other Revenue (State Nature)	Program service revenue	Other revenue
a	Fees from government agencies		
b	. . . .		
c	. . . .		
d	. . . .		
e	. . . .		
f	Total program service revenue (enter here and on line 2)		
g	Total other revenue (enter here and on line 11)		

Part V   **Balance Sheets**   If line 12 or Column (B) of line 59 is more than $25,000, complete the entire balance sheet. If line 12, Part I, and Column (B) of line 59 are $25,000 or less, you may complete only lines 59, 66, 74, and 75. See instructions.

	Note: **Columns (C) and (D) are optional.** *Columns (A) and (B) must be completed to the extent applicable. Where required, attached schedules should be for end-of-year amounts only.*	(A) Beginning of year	End of year		
			(B) Total	(C) Unrestricted/ Expendable	(D) Restricted/ Nonexpendable
	Assets				
45	Cash—non-interest bearing				
46	Savings and temporary cash investments				
47	Accounts receivable ▶ _____				
	minus allowance for doubtful accounts ▶_____ .				
48	Pledges receivable ▶ _____				
	minus allowance for doubtful accounts ▶_____ .				
49	Grants receivable				
50	Receivables due from officers, directors, trustees, and key employees (attach schedule)				
51	Other notes and loans receivable ▶ _____				
	minus allowance for doubtful accounts ▶_____ .				
52	Inventories for sale or use				
53	Prepaid expenses and deferred charges				
54	Investments—securities (attach schedule)				
55	Investments—land, buildings and equipment: basis ▶ _____				
	minus accumulated depreciation ▶ _____ (attach schedule) .				
56	Investments—other (attach schedule)				
57	Land, buildings and equipment: basis ▶ _____				
	minus accumulated depreciation ▶ _____ (attach schedule) .				
58	Other assets ▶ _____ .				
59	Total assets (add lines 45 through 58)				
	Liabilities				
60	Accounts payable and accrued expenses				
61	Grants payable				
62	Support and revenue designated for future periods (attach schedule) .				
63	Loans from officers, directors, trustees, and key employees (attach schedule)				
64	Mortgages and other notes payable (attach schedule) . . .				
65	Other liabilities ▶_____				
66	Total liabilities (add lines 60 through 65)				
	Fund Balances or Net Worth				
	Organizations that use fund accounting, check here ▶ ☐ and complete lines 67 through 70 and lines 74 and 75.				
67a	Current unrestricted fund				
b	Current restricted fund				
68	Land, buildings and equipment fund				
69	Endowment fund				
70	Other funds (Describe ▶ _____) .				
	Organizations that do not use fund accounting, check here ▶ ☐ and complete lines 71 through 75.				
71	Capital stock or trust principal				
72	Paid-in or capital surplus				
73	Retained earnings or accumulated income				
74	Total fund balances or net worth (see instructions)				
75	Total liabilities and fund balances/net worth (see instructions) . . .				

Form 990 (1986)   Page **4**

| **Part VI** | List of Officers, Directors, and Trustees (List each officer, director, and trustee whether compensated or not.) (See instructions.) |

(A) Name and address	(B) Title and average hours per week devoted to position	(C) Compensation (if any)	(D) Contributions to employee benefit plans	(E) Expense account and other allowances

Part VII	Other Information		Yes	No

76   Has the organization engaged in any activities not previously reported to the Internal Revenue Service?
    If "Yes," attach a detailed description of the activities.

77   Have any changes been made in the organizing or governing documents, but not reported to IRS?
    If "Yes," attach a conformed copy of the changes.

78 a   Did the organization have unrelated business gross income of $1,000 or more during the year covered by this return?

   b   If "Yes," have you filed a tax return on Form 990-T, Exempt Organization Business Income Tax Return, for this year?

   c   If the organization has gross sales or receipts from business activities not reported on Form 990-T, attach a statement explaining your reason for not reporting them on Form 990-T.

79   Was there a liquidation, dissolution, termination, or substantial contraction during the year? (See instructions.)
    If "Yes," attach a statement as described in the instructions.

80   Is the organization related (other than by association with a statewide or nationwide organization) through common membership, governing bodies, trustees, officers, etc., to any other exempt or nonexempt organization? (See instructions.)
    If "Yes," enter the name of the organization ▶ _____
    _____ and check whether it is   ☐ exempt **OR**   ☐ nonexempt.

81 a   Enter amount of political expenditures, direct or indirect, as described in the instructions

   b   Did you file Form 1120-POL, U.S. Income Tax Return for Certain Political Organizations, for this year?

82   Did your organization receive donated services or the use of materials, equipment, or facilities at no charge or at substantially less than fair rental value?
    If "Yes," you may indicate the value of these items here. Do not include this amount as support in Part I or as an expense in Part II. See instructions for reporting in Part III   ▶

83   *Section 501(c)(5) or (6) organizations.* —Did the organization spend any amounts in attempts to influence public opinion about legislative matters or referendums? (See instructions and Regulations section 1.162-20(c).)
    If "Yes," enter the total amount spent for this purpose

84   *Section 501(c)(7) organizations.* —Enter amount of:

   a   Initiation fees and capital contributions included on line 12

   b   Gross receipts, included in line 12, for public use of club facilities (see instructions)

   c   Does the club's governing instrument or any written policy statement provide for discrimination against any person because of race, color, or religion? (See instructions.)

85   *Section 501(c)(12) organizations.* —Enter amount of:

   a   Gross income received from members or shareholders

   b   Gross income received from other sources (do not net amounts due or paid to other sources against amounts due or received from them)

86   *Public interest law firms.* —Attach information described in the instructions.

87   List the states with which a copy of this return is filed ▶ _____

88   During this tax year did you maintain any part of your accounting/tax records on a computerized system?

89   The books are in care of ▶ _____ Telephone no. ▶ _____
    Located at ▶

Please Sign Here	Under penalties of perjury, I declare that I have examined this return, including accompanying schedules and statements, and to the best of my knowledge and belief, it is true, correct, and complete. Declaration of preparer (other than officer) is based on all information of which preparer has any knowledge.

▶ _____ _____   ▶ _____
     Signature of officer   Date   Title

Paid Preparer's Use Only	Preparer's signature ▶		Date	Check if self-employed ▶ ☐
	Firm's name (or yours, if self-employed) and address ▶		ZIP code	

SCHEDULE A (Form 990) Department of the Treasury Internal Revenue Service	**Organization Exempt Under 501(c)(3)** (Except Private Foundation), 501(e), 501(f), 501(k), or Section 4947(a)(1) Trust Supplementary Information ▶ **Attach to Form 990.**	OMB No. 1545-0047 1986

Name	Employer identification number

Part I   **Compensation of Five Highest Paid Employees Other Than Officers, Directors, and Trustees (See specific instructions)**

Name and address of employees paid more than $30,000	Title and average hours per week devoted to position	Compensation	Contributions to employee benefit plans	Expense account and other allowances
- -				
- -				
- -				
- -				
- -				
Total number of other employees paid over $30,000 . . . . ▶				

Part II   **Compensation of Five Highest Paid Persons for Professional Services (See specific instructions)**

Name and address of persons paid more than $30,000	Type of service	Compensation
- -		
- -		
- -		
- -		
- -		
Total number of others receiving over $30,000 for professional services . . . . ▶		

Part III   **Statements About Activities**

		Yes (1)	No (2)
1	During the year, have you attempted to influence national, state, or local legislation, including any attempt to influence public opinion on a legislative matter or referendum? . . . . If "Yes," enter the total expenses paid or incurred in connection with the legislative activities $ _____ Complete Part VI of this form for organizations that made an election under section 501(h) on Form 5768 or other statement. For other organizations checking "Yes," attach a statement giving a detailed description of the legislative activities and a classified schedule of the expenses paid or incurred.	**1**	
2	During the year, have you, either directly or indirectly, engaged in any of the following acts with a trustee, director, principal officer or creator of your organization, or any organization or corporation with which such person is affiliated as an officer, director, trustee, majority owner, or principal beneficiary:		
a	Sale, exchange, or leasing of property?	**2a**	
b	Lending of money or other extension of credit?	**2b**	
c	Furnishing of goods, services, or facilities?	**2c**	
d	Payment of compensation (or payment or reimbursement of expenses if more than $1,000)?	**2d**	
e	Transfer of any part of your income or assets?	**2e**	
	If the answer to any question is "Yes," attach a detailed statement explaining the transactions.		
3	Do you make grants for scholarships, fellowships, student loans, etc.?	**3**	
4	Attach a statement explaining how you determine that individuals or organizations receiving disbursements from you in furtherance of your charitable programs qualify to receive payments. (See specific instructions)		

For Paperwork Reduction Act Notice, see page 1 of the separate instructions to this form.   Schedule A (Form 990) 1986

Schedule A (Form 990) 1986   Page **2**

Part IV   Reason for Non-Private Foundation Status (See instructions for definitions)

The organization is not a private foundation because it is (check applicable box; please check only **ONE** box):

5   ☐ ¹ A church, convention of churches, or association of churches. Section 170(b)(1)(A)(i).

6   ☐ ² A school. Section 170(b)(1)(A)(ii). (Also complete Part V, page 3.)

7   ☐ ³ A hospital or a cooperative hospital service organization. Section 170(b)(1)(A)(iii).

8   ☐ ⁴ A Federal, state or local government or governmental unit. Section 170(b)(1)(A)(v).

9   ☐ ⁵ A medical research organization operated in conjunction with a hospital. Section 170(b)(1)(A)(iii). **Enter name, city, and state of hospital** ▶ ....

10 ☐ ⁶ An organization operated for the benefit of a college or university owned or operated by a governmental unit. Section 170(b)(1)(A)(iv). (Also complete Support Schedule.)

11 ☐ ⁷ An organization that normally receives a substantial part of its support from a governmental unit or from the general public. Section 170(b)(1)(A)(vi). (Also complete Support Schedule.)

12 ☐ ⁸ An organization that normally receives: (a) no more than 1/3 of its support from gross investment income and unrelated business taxable income (less section 511 tax) from businesses acquired by the organization after June 30, 1975, and (b) more than 1/3 of its support from contributions, membership fees, and gross receipts from activities related to its charitable, etc., functions—subject to certain exceptions. See section 509(a)(2). (Also complete Support Schedule.)

13 ☐ ⁹ An organization that is not controlled by any disqualified persons (other than foundation managers) and supports organizations described in (1) boxes 5 through 12 above or (2) section 501(c)(4), (5), or (6) if they meet the test of section 509(a)(2). See section 509(a)(3).

Provide the following information about the supported organizations. (See instructions for Part IV, box 13.)

(a) Name of supported organizations	**(b)** Box number from above

14 ☐ ⁰ An organization organized and operated to test for public safety. Section 509(a)(4). (See specific instructions)

Support Schedule (Complete only if you checked box 10, 11, or 12 above) Use cash method of accounting.					
Calendar year (or fiscal year beginning in) ▶	**(a)** 1985	**(b)** 1984	**(c)** 1983	**(d)** 1982	**(e)** Total
15 Gifts, grants, and contributions received. (Do not include unusual grants. See line 28.)					
16 Membership fees received					
17 Gross receipts from admissions, merchandise sold or services performed, or furnishing of facilities in any activity that is not a business unrelated to the organization's charitable, etc., purpose					
18 Gross income from interest, dividends, amounts received from payments on securities loans (section 512(a)(5)), rents, royalties, and unrelated business taxable income (less section 511 taxes) from businesses acquired by the organization after June 30, 1975					
19 Net income from unrelated business activities not included in line 18					
20 Tax revenues levied for your benefit and either paid to you or expended on your behalf					
21 The value of services or facilities furnished to you by a governmental unit without charge. Do not include the value of services or facilities generally furnished to the public without charge					
22 Other income. Attach schedule. Do not include gain (or loss) from sale of capital assets					
23 Total of lines 15 through 22					
24 Line 23 minus line 17					
25 Enter 1% of line 23					//////////

26 Organizations described in box 10 or 11:
  a Enter 2% of amount in column (e), line 24.
  b Attach a list (not open to public inspection) showing the name of and amount contributed by each person (other than a governmental unit or publicly supported organization) whose total gifts for 1982 through 1985 exceeded the amount shown in 26a. Enter the sum of all excess amounts here					

(Continued on page 3)

A.24

Appendix

Schedule A (Form 990) 1986

Page **3**

Part IV Support Schedule (continued)(Complete only if you checked box 10, 11, or 12 on page 2)

27 Organizations described in box 12, page 2:

a Attach a list for amounts shown on lines 15, 16, and 17, showing the name of, and total amounts received in each year from, each "disqualified person," and enter the sum of such amounts for each year:

(1985) .... (1984) .... (1983) .... (1982) ....

b Attach a list showing, for 1982 through 1985, the name and amount included in line 17 for each person (other than "disqualified persons") from whom the organization received more, during that year, than the larger of: the amount on line 25 for the year or $5,000. Include organizations described in boxes 5 through 11 as well as individuals. Enter the sum of these excess amounts for each year:

(1985) .... (1984) .... (1983) .... (1982) ....

28 For an organization described in box 10, 11, or 12, page 2, that received any unusual grants during 1982 through 1985, attach a list (not open to public inspection) for each year showing the name of the contributor, the date and amount of the grant, and a brief description of the nature of the grant. Do not include these grants in line 15 above. (See specific instructions)

Part V Private School Questionnaire
To Be Completed ONLY by Schools That Checked Box 6 in Part IV

		Yes (1)	No (2)
29 Do you have a racially nondiscriminatory policy toward students by statement in your charter, bylaws, other governing instrument, or in a resolution of your governing body?	29		
30 Do you include a statement of your racially nondiscriminatory policy toward students in all your brochures, catalogues, and other written communications with the public dealing with student admissions, programs, and scholarships?	30		
31 Have you publicized your racially nondiscriminatory policy by newspaper or broadcast media during the period of solicitation for students or during the registration period if you have no solicitation program, in a way that makes the policy known to all parts of the general community you serve?	31		
If "Yes," please describe; if "No," please explain. (If you need more space, attach a separate statement.)			
32 Do you maintain the following:			
a Records indicating the racial composition of the student body, faculty, and administrative staff?	32a		
b Records documenting that scholarships and other financial assistance are awarded on a racially nondiscriminatory basis?	32b		
c Copies of all catalogues, brochures, announcements, and other written communications to the public dealing with student admissions, programs, and scholarships?	32c		
d Copies of all material used by you or on your behalf to solicit contributions?	32d		
If you answered "No" to any of the above, please explain. (If you need more space, attach a separate statement.)			
33 Do you discriminate by race in any way with respect to:			
a Students' rights or privileges?	33a		
b Admissions policies?	33b		
c Employment of faculty or administrative staff?	33c		
d Scholarships or other financial assistance? (See instructions)	33d		
e Educational policies?	33e		
f Use of facilities?	33f		
g Athletic programs?	33g		
h Other extracurricular activities?	33h		
If you answered "Yes" to any of the above, please explain. (If you need more space, attach a separate statement.)			
34a Do you receive any financial aid or assistance from a governmental agency?	34a		
b Has your right to such aid ever been revoked or suspended?	34b		
If you answered "Yes" to either 34a or b, please explain using an attached separate statement.			
35 Do you certify that you have complied with the applicable requirements of sections 4.01 through 4.05 of Rev. Proc. 75-50, 1975-2 C.B. 587, covering racial nondiscrimination? If "No," attach an explanation. (See instructions for Part V)	35		

Schedule A (Form 990) 1986   Page **4**

Part VI Lobbying Expenditures by Public Charities (See instructions)
(To be completed ONLY by an eligible organization that filed Form 5768)

Check here ▶ **a** ☐ If the organization belongs to an affiliated group. (See instructions)
Check here ▶ **b** ☐ If you checked **a** and "limited control" provisions apply. (See instructions)

Limits on Lobbying Expenses	(a) Affiliated group totals	(b) To be completed for ALL electing organizations
36 Total (grassroots) lobbying expenses to influence public opinion		
37 Total lobbying expenses to influence a legislative body		
38 Total lobbying expenses (add lines 36 and 37)		
39 Other exempt purpose expenses (See Part VI instructions)		
40 Total exempt purpose expenses (add lines 38 and 39) (See instructions)		
41 Lobbying nontaxable amount. Enter the smaller of $1,000,000 or the amount determined under the following table—		

If the amount on line 40 is—	The lobbying nontaxable amount is—
Not over $500,000	20% of the amount on line 40.
Over $500,000 but not over $1,000,000	$100,000 plus 15% of the excess over $500,000
Over $1,000,000 but not over $1,500,000	$175,000 plus 10% of the excess over $1,000,000
Over $1,500,000	$225,000 plus 5% of the excess over $1,500,000

42 Grassroots nontaxable amount (enter 25% of line 41)		
(Complete lines 43 and 44. File Form 4720 if either line 36 exceeds line 42 or line 38 exceeds line 41.)		
43 Excess of line 36 over line 42		
44 Excess of line 38 over line 41		

4-Year Averaging Period Under Section 501(h).
(Some organizations that made a section 501(h) election do not have to complete all of the five columns below. See the instructions for lines 45-50 for details.)

Lobbying Expenses During 4-Year Averaging Period

Calendar year (or fiscal year beginning in) ▶	(a) 1986	(b) 1985	(c) 1984	(d) 1983	(e) Total
45 Lobbying nontaxable amount (See instructions)					
46 Lobbying ceiling amount (150% of line 45(e))					
47 Total lobbying expenses (See instructions)					
48 Grassroots nontaxable amount (See instructions)					
49 Grassroots ceiling amount (150% of line 48(e))					
50 Grassroots lobbying expenses (See instructions)					

Index

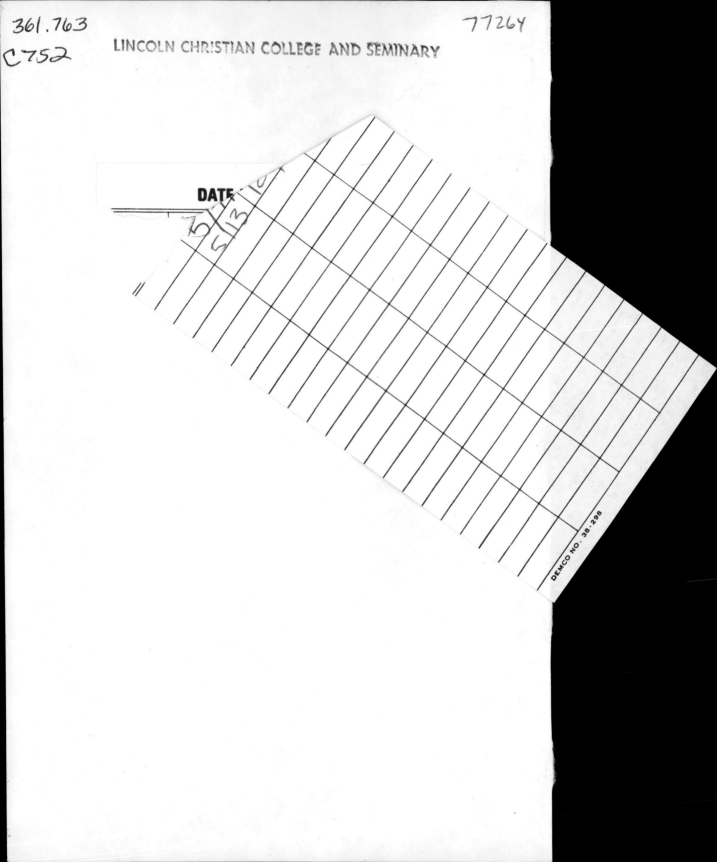

MAVERICKS
Big Sky Brides

The legend of the Brennan family holds that their women only marry for love. So when marriages of convenience are proposed for Suzanna and Diana, will they discover the wedded bliss their great-great-grandmother Isabelle knew?

Suzanna Brennan: With a baby on the way, it seemed kind of foolish of Suzanna to wish for her hasty groom-to-be's heart. But once she's sharing her bed with her cowboy husband, she can't help hankering for more....

Diana Brennan: Diana wasn't as sentimental about love as her baby sister, Suzanna. So there didn't seem to be any harm in her tying the knot with the brooding single dad she had once loved from afar. Or so she thought....

Isabelle Brennan: Though this nineteenth-century society woman knew better than to take the name of a half-breed rancher, sassy Isabelle was ready to take on the challenge of being Kyle "Running Horse" Brennan's wife to save her family ranch. And if her marriage is the match she hopes it will be, Isabelle will show future generations of Brennan brides just what it takes to turn a marriage of convenience into a forever kind of love!

CHRISTINE RIMMER

"Famed for her deliciously different characters,
Ms. Rimmer keeps the...love sizzling hot."
—*Romantic Times Magazine*

A reader favorite whose books consistently appear on the
Waldenbooks and *USA Today* bestseller lists, Christine Rimmer
has written over thirty novels for Silhouette Books. Her stories
have been nominated for numerous awards, including the
Romance Writers of America's RITA Award and the *Romantic
Times Magazine*'s Series Storyteller of the Year Award.

JENNIFER GREENE

"...The fabulous Jennifer Greene is one of the romance genre's
greatest gifts to the world of popular fiction."
—*Romantic Times Magazine*

Jennifer Greene has been married to her hero for over twenty-
five years, which is why she's such an exuberant believer in love
stories. Known for her warm characters and real-life humor,
Jennifer has won numerous honors, ranging from RWA's Hall
of Fame Award to *Romantic Times Magazine*'s Lifetime and
Career Achievement Awards. She loves kids, dogs, cats, antiques
and—of course—books.

CHERYL ST.JOHN

"...a style reminiscent of LaVyrle Spencer's earliest books."
—*New York Times* bestselling author Linda Howard

Cheryl's first book, *Rain Shadow*, a Harlequin Historicals
novel, was nominated for the Romance Writers of America's
RITA Award, and her Silhouette Intimate Moments title,
The Truth About Toby, won a reader award from the Wisconsin
RWA. Cheryl is a married mother of four and a grandmother
several times over. Please write to her, sending a SASE, to:
P.O. Box 12142, Florence Station, Omaha, NE 68112-0142.

MONTANA MAVERICKS

Big Sky Brides

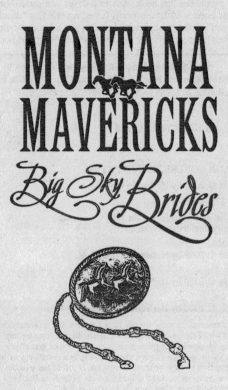

Silhouette Books

Published by Silhouette Books

America's Publisher of Contemporary Romance

Special thanks and acknowledgment are given to
Christine Rimmer, Jennifer Greene and Cheryl St.John for their
contribution to MONTANA MAVERICKS: BIG SKY BRIDES.

 SILHOUETTE BOOKS

MONTANA MAVERICKS: BIG SKY BRIDES

Copyright © 2000 by Harlequin Books S.A.

ISBN 0-373-48381-3

The publisher acknowledges the copyright holders
of the individual works as follows:

SUZANNA
Copyright © 2000 by Harlequin Books S.A.

DIANA
Copyright © 2000 by Harlequin Books S.A.

ISABELLE
Copyright © 2000 by Harlequin Books S.A.

CONTENTS

Dear Reader,

Looks like there are gonna be more weddings under the Big Sky as Silhouette brings you *MONTANA MAVERICKS: Big Sky Brides,* an anthology with three brand-new stories by reader favorites Christine Rimmer, Jennifer Greene and Cheryl St.John, and featuring an exciting new family. The Brennans are ranchin' folk who go way back. In fact, this anthology brings you the contemporary marriage-of-convenience stories of Suzanna and Diana Brennan, as well as a historical romantic tale featuring great-great-grandmother Isabelle Brennan.

MONTANA MAVERICKS: Big Sky Brides is just the first of the brand-new MONTANA MAVERICKS stories we have in store for you in the coming months. In May 2000, Silhouette Special Edition presents a sexy new story by Jackie Merritt, which introduces the other half of the exciting Kincaid clan. Then, starting in June 2000, the lives and loves of the Kincaid heirs will be told over twelve books, one available each month, when the newest continuity series, MONTANA MAVERICKS: WED IN WHITEHORN, begins!

We at Silhouette hope you enjoy this anthology, as well as the upcoming books in MONTANA MAVERICKS: WED IN WHITEHORN, where more of your favorite authors will take you back to the town where legends live on...and love lasts forever!

Happy reading!

The Editors at Silhouette Books

SUZANNA

Christine Rimmer

For Tom and Ed

Prologue

Trailing satin ribbons, Sierra Conroy McLaine's wedding bouquet of white Derringer roses sailed through air. All the single girls reached up eager hands.

"It's mine!"

"I've got it!"

The bouquet found its highest point. Excited, happy cries followed it down.

"Oh, look! Here it comes...."

Suzanna Brennan closed her eyes. She didn't need to look. She *knew*.

And she was right. The roses dropped right into her outstretched arms.

"Suzanna!" one of the girls cried. "Suzanna's got it!"

There was more laughter—and a few rueful sighs.

Suzanna opened her eyes and looked down at her prize. So beautiful, those velvety, snowy-white blooms. And it was so *right* that she should be the one to catch it. After all, according to local superstition, any girl who caught a bridal bouquet of roses from the Derringer garden would marry soon and happily.

Her engagement diamond sparkling on her hand, Suzanna brought the flowers close for an intoxicating whiff. A little hint of heaven, the smell of those roses.

Lucky me, she thought. Lucky me, I've got it all. In five months, on March twenty-fourth, *I'll* be the one tossing the bouquet....

Chapter 1

"Those eggs are not going to eat themselves."

Suzanna stopped pushing the food around on her plate and looked across the breakfast table into blue eyes much like her own. Say it, she silently commanded herself. Just open your mouth and tell him. You swore that you would. This very morning, you swore it.

And yesterday morning.

And the morning before that.

It had gotten to be a habit, for the past month or so. Every morning Suzanna got up and threw up—and then promised her own grim image in the bathroom mirror that this was the day she would tell her father about the baby.

So far, every day, she had broken that promise. And today was turning out the same as all the other ones. She just couldn't make herself do it.

"I guess I'm not too hungry," she muttered, as she silently called herself a yellow-bellied coward.

"A body needs fuel," Frank Brennan coaxed.

So Suzanna made herself spear up a bite of the eggs. She stuck it into her mouth and chewed, fighting an unnerving feeling of queasiness. Over the past few weeks, she had discovered that she didn't much care for eggs anymore. She didn't much care for food, period, of late. Pregnancy and guilt had conspired to ruin her appetite.

To her surprise, the eggs went down all right.

Her father was still watching her. She could see in those eyes that he was worried about her. Wondering what was wrong with her. And waiting for her to tell him. But she just couldn't. Not today.

Tomorrow. Yes. Tomorrow, she would do it.

Tomorrow...

Doggedly, Suzanna ate more eggs, washing them down with milk. Concentrating on her breakfast had a definite advantage—it gave her an excuse to stop looking into her father's eyes.

"The new man's due today," he said.

She looked up again, frowning, her mind still stuck on that important promise she never managed to keep.

"Nash Morgan," her father reminded her. "The new horse trainer." A teasing light pushed the worry from his eyes a little. "I think I mentioned him once or twice."

They shared a smile. "Yes," Suzanna said. "I believe you did." Sometimes it seemed that Nash Morgan was all her father talked about since he'd met the man and hired him a few weeks back at the Yellowstone Quarter Horse Show.

On the Big Sky, the ranch that had been in Suzanna's family for several generations now, they raised horses, quarter horses known for their stamina, good looks, steady dispositions and plain cow sense. The Big Sky had a well-deserved reputation for producing fine, well-trained stock. And Frank Brennan was always on the lookout for a certain kind of trainer, for a man who had "the touch," as he called it, a man who knew how to "think like a horse." Such men were rarities, Suzanna's father always said. And Frank Brennan believed that Nash Morgan was just such a man.

Suzanna's father had had to do some fancy talking and pay a very high salary to get this paragon to come and work for him. Nash Morgan, apparently, was in the market for his own horse ranch now. But Frank had a plan. If the man worked out the way Frank thought he would, he hoped to talk the trainer into investing his talents, his capital—and his future—in the Big Sky.

"If he gets here before lunch, you can show him around," her father suggested. "See he gets settled in, tell him where to park his rig—and put him in

the cabin.'' Her father referred to the separate cot-
tage several hundred feet behind the main house,
where business guests always stayed. ''I don't want
him in the bunkhouse with the rest of the men. I
want him to feel comfortable and I want him to—''

''Dad, the cabin's all ready for him. I promise,
I'll make him feel welcome.'' That, at least, was a
vow she knew she could keep.

Her father left to join the other men at the corrals
a few minutes later. Suzanna cleaned up the kitchen
and got the stew meat simmering for lunch. Then
she went to the office off the living room and
worked for a couple of hours, paying bills and
checking on feed orders.

Suzanna had a business degree, and she'd been
putting it to use, handling all the bookkeeping for
the Big Sky, since her final return home from college out in Sacramento last January. She'd met
Bryan Cummings there, in Sacramento. But Bryan
was long gone now. He'd joined the Peace Corps
three months ago, back in March—on the day they
were supposed to have been married, as a matter of
fact.

So much for the luck of the Derringer roses.

At least she had her education, she kept telling
herself. She wouldn't have to worry about that *and*
about trying to raise a baby on her own.

As a rule, taking care of the books always soothed
her. Suzanna enjoyed the orderliness of numbers, the
way there was always a right answer and all a person

had to do was find it. But today, the columns of figures on her computer screen couldn't hold her attention. She kept making errors, entering data incorrectly, punching up the wrong commands, blinking back to the present to find herself staring into the enormous stone fireplace opposite the old mahogany desk where she sat. No fire burned there now.

She looked toward the window. A mild, clear June day. Outside, beyond the shadows of the wraparound porch, the endless Montana sky was blue as her father's loving eyes.

Maybe she should get out and ride. She could choose one of the two-year-olds just graduating from the round pen, where every Big Sky colt's real training began. She could give the animal a little break from his lessons—and get her mind off that promise she was going to have to keep one of these days very soon.

With a sigh, Suzanna shut down her computer and left the office. She wandered up the stairs to the second floor. And then, instead of going into her room to trade her sneakers for some heavy socks and the old beat-up boots she used for riding, she found herself standing on the landing at the top of the stairs, looking at the pull-down ladder that led to the attic.

The heavy satin rope that would bring the ladder down was anchored along the wall. Suzanna unhooked the rope and gave a tug, caught the center joint and swung the bottom section of rungs to the floor. Then she started climbing.

Suzanna loved the attic. On a mild day like today, it was toasty warm and smelled rather pleasantly of wood and dust. It was also full of several generations' worth of treasures, things that the Brennans didn't really need anymore yet somehow couldn't bear to throw away. The two small windows at either end let in enough light to see by, but Suzanna pulled the chain on the bare bulb overhead anyway.

Dust motes danced in the air around her as she surveyed the rows of boxes stacked along the eaves, boxes full of Christmas decorations and old clothes, of dishes and linens and toys and board games. In addition to all the boxes, there were floor lamps with their shades missing and chairs with wobbly legs. The two-story dollhouse, which had first belonged to her big sister, Diana, and eventually to Suzanna herself, stood in a corner beside a sagging, faded easy chair.

And to the right of the dollhouse, beneath the east window, sat her great-great-grandmother Isabelle's cedar hope chest. The old boards creaked beneath her sneakers as Suzanna approached the chest. When she reached it, she knelt and took the key from where it hung on a nail beside the window.

"This is too self-indulgent," she whispered aloud to the silent stacks of boxes and the broken-down furniture. "I shouldn't...."

But she did. She stuck the key in the tarnished brass lock, gave it a turn and lifted the lid.

A wistful smile curved Suzanna's lips at the mingled scents that wafted up to her, lemon and lavender, oranges and cloves. Over the years, the women of her family had taken care of the trunk and its contents. The satins and laces had been lovingly cleaned and mended whenever necessary. And a variety of sachets kept everything smelling sweet.

Right there on top was the dress, Great-Great-Grandmother Isabelle's wedding gown of silk and Irish lace. Like the trunk's lining, the gown had mellowed to ivory over the years.

"Almost..." Suzanna whispered.

Almost, she had worn this dress. Almost, she had lived the dream she'd cherished since she'd been a little girl playing with the dollhouse inherited from her sister—to walk down the aisle in the wedding gown her great-great-grandmother had worn on the day she'd married Kyle Running Horse Brennan, over a century ago.

Now, *that* had been a scandal: the pretty, Eastern-educated Cooper girl's marriage to the handsome but penniless half-breed who worked as foreman on her father's ranch. But Isabelle had bravely defied the disapproval of her neighbors. She had married for love and never regretted it.

There had been a string of happy Brennan marriages down the years since then. Suzanna had thought hers would be the next one. She'd had a

dream of a Brennan-style wedding, of a Brennan-
style lifetime of love.

And when that dream had slipped away from her,
she had gone just a little…well, there was only one
word for it.

Crazy.

Yes. She'd gone a little crazy, thinking that even
the Derringer roses hadn't been powerful enough to
make her wish come true. Thinking of how she'd
saved herself for her wedding night with Bryan. And
now the wedding night was here, and Bryan wasn't.

Crazy. That was how she'd felt. Crazy enough to
go and have herself a wedding night anyway.

With some footloose cowboy.

Some cowboy whose real name she didn't even
know.

She'd been twenty-two on the day Bryan left her
at the altar. She was *still* twenty-two, but she felt a
lot older now. Years older. And sadder. And wiser.
And *guiltier*…

"Fool," she whispered to the ivory lace. "Silly,
dreamy-eyed, *reckless* fool…" She let out a small
moan of self-disgust.

And downstairs, the doorbell rang.

Suzanna glanced over her shoulder toward the
ladder to the second floor.

It must be her father's new horse trainer.

She lowered the lid of the chest and was about to
turn the key when she spotted the tiny bit of lace

sticking out. She raised the lid again and swiftly folded the lace out of the way.

That was when she noticed that a section of the trunk's lining, right near the lock, had come loose from the wood. She'd have to come up later and figure out the best way to repair the damage. She slipped her finger into the gap between satin and wood—and felt something wedged between the lining and the wall of the trunk.

Suzanna leaned closer to peer into the narrow space. Envelopes. They were yellowed with age like the trunk lining, like her great-great-grandmother's wedding dress.

She had to pull loose more of the lining to get them all out. There were six of them, each one addressed to Mr. Kyle Running Horse Brennan in a flowing, rounded, very feminine hand.

Apparently, she hadn't matured as much in the past few months as she'd thought. That dreamy-eyed fool must still live inside her. Because her heart pounded hard in pure elation.

From Isabelle. The letters were from Isabelle. Suzanna would have known it even if the return address hadn't told her so.

Could it really be possible? Might she actually be holding Isabelle's love letters to Kyle in her hands—love letters hidden away for over a hundred years now?

Downstairs, the doorbell rang again.

Suzanna ordered her heart to a more dignified

rhythm. The love letters would have to wait—if they really *were* love letters. By now, Mr. Nash Morgan must doubt that anybody was home. In a minute, he'd wander off toward the corrals in search of the welcome she wasn't providing. And her father would wonder why she hadn't had the courtesy to answer the door.

Suzanna shut and locked the trunk. She hooked the key on its nail. Then she flew to the light, pulled the string and rushed down the ladder, levering it up so quickly that it clapped hard against the frame.

She didn't even bother with hooking the rope back into its place on the wall. She just left it dangling and raced to her room where she yanked open the bottom drawer of her bureau and tucked the envelopes beneath a stack of heavy winter sweaters.

The doorbell rang for the third time as she pounded down the stairs. "I'm coming, I'm coming," she muttered under her breath. She could see the tall form of a man through the etched and frosted oval of glass in the center of the front door.

"I'm coming!" She called out that time, so he would know she was on her way.

She paused at the bottom of the stairs to smooth her hair and tuck her shirt more neatly into her Wranglers, running her hand nervously over her stomach, thinking that nothing showed yet, thank goodness. Finally, she put on a smile and pulled open the door.

"I'm so sorry, I was—'' The words turned to dust in her throat.

And her heart froze in her chest, just stopped dead—and then began beating triple time.

Oh, sweet Lord. It was *him.* The man she'd met on what should have been her wedding night. The man she'd known only as Slim.

It couldn't be....

But it was.

The father of her unborn child was standing right before her on her own front porch.

Chapter 2

Like someone blinded by a hard burst of piercing light, Suzanna blinked. Maybe she was just imagining—but no. When she dared to look again, he was still there. Still Slim. She would have known those leaf-green eyes anywhere. For an awful moment, she was certain that she would throw up on his worn rawhide boots.

Suzanna swallowed hard, pushing down the urge to be sick, using every ounce of grim determination she possessed. It worked, to a degree. She still felt dangerously unsettled, but the immediate danger of losing her breakfast had passed.

Slim took off his hat. "Nash Morgan, ma'am." His voice was low and soft, with a sort of a purr in it, just the way she remembered. He smiled, a true cowboy's smile, friendly but not forward. A pleased-to-meet-you sort of smile.

He didn't know her! Dear Lord, he'd forgotten.

But that couldn't be, could it? He had, after all, spent a whole night with her. The lights might have been low—in that roadhouse and then later, in that room at the motel. But they hadn't been *that* low. He'd gotten a good look at her. At *all* of her.

And besides, she'd seen that flash of recognition in his eyes when she first opened the door—hadn't she?

He held out his hand. She took it automatically, felt the heat of it, the strength in it, the roughness of calluses along the palms and finger joints. A blush tried to creep up her neck as she recalled the way those hands had felt gliding along her naked skin. She ordered that blush down.

"Mr. Morgan." She smiled at him, a big, fake smile that she prayed he wouldn't recognize as such. "Our new horse trainer."

"That's right."

"Welcome to the Big Sky." Her hand still lay enclosed in his. She pulled it free.

"Frank's daughter, right?"

"Yes. That's right. Suzanna." She was positive now. He didn't remember. She'd been just another warm and willing woman to him. How many must there have been for her to have vanished from his mind after only three short months?

Suzanna decided it would be safer not to ask herself such a dangerous question right now.

Beyond his shoulder, down the stone walk and past the white picket fence that defined the yard, a dark green pickup and a gooseneck trailer waited in the bright late-morning sun.

She gestured toward the vehicle. "There's room in the wagon shed for your rig." She tipped her head toward the structure in question, several hundred feet to her right, near the well and the slowly turning windmill that loomed above it.

He was staring at her so strangely. Did she look as stunned and sick at heart as she felt? She babbled more suggestions. "There's a tack room in the closed-off end. You're welcome to store whatever riding gear you've brought in there. You have horses in that trailer?"

He shrugged. "It's empty."

"Oh. Well. All right, then just put it with the pickup."

"I'll do that." He started to turn away.

"Oh. And…" He stopped. Looked at her again, waiting. She gulped. "When you're done, come on back and I'll take you to your quarters, see that you get settled in."

"Good enough."

She watched him stride down the steps and along the walk, admiring in spite of herself the proud breadth of his shoulders and the way that the sun picked up auburn lights in his thick dark hair.

It didn't take him long to come striding back.

This can't really be happening, Suzanna kept thinking, as she went through the motions of making him welcome.

She led him to the cabin. He looked around and shook his head. "This is real nice. But I'd prefer to stay with the other men."

"But my father thought you'd be more comfortable if you had your own—"

"As long as I'm here, those men will be training your horses by my methods. I want to get to know them. You learn a lot more about a man who bunks next to you."

So she took him to the bunkhouse, gave him a bed and showed him where he could stash his personal belongings. The whole time, images of their night together kept trying to sneak into her mind, stealing her breath and threatening to make her voice crack.

Clear as his tanned face before her now, she could see him—first at that roadhouse outside of Billings where they'd met, bending across the felt-topped pool table to sink a shot, glancing up to give her a teasing smile. And then later, his face above her, those eyes that didn't know her now burning, green fire, into hers in the motel-room bed.

Finally, she led him to the corrals and left him with her father and the other men. She thought as she went to the house that she had never in her life been so glad to walk away from someone.

Her father appeared at twelve-thirty. "So Nash refused to take the cabin." Frank chuckled. "Got himself a narrow cot when he could have had a nice big comfortable bed. Now, there is a man dedicated to his work."

Suzanna chuckled, too, and hoped it sounded more sincere than it felt.

Then her father told her he wanted to invite the men in to share the stew at one. Normally, the men took their meals in the bunkhouse. But this was a special occasion, since it was Nash's first day.

What could she say? Suzanna served up the stew and tried to act as if nothing was bothering her as the men talked horses and wolfed down the food.

She did her best not to look Nash Morgan's way too much. But memories kept grabbing at her.

Memories of the way it had been that night. The way *she* had been, just plain crazy in her mind and heart, after Bryan didn't show up for the wedding.

Diana, who'd taken time off work and come all the way from Chicago to be her maid of honor, had stayed by her side that whole afternoon. Finally, when dark came, Suzanna had told her big sister that she couldn't bear being cooped up in the house a single moment longer. She had to get out and drive. And she needed to be alone for a while.

At first, Diana had tried to dissuade her. But Suzanna wouldn't listen.

Finally, her sister gave in. "Be careful," Diana warned, shaking her head, sounding like the mother she had been to Suzanna after their real mother had died so young. ''Don't do anything crazy....''

''I won't,'' Suzanna promised. ''I just have to get out.''

She'd climbed into the Bronco her father had bought her when she went away to Cal State and she'd hit the road, driving reckless and fast in a hopeless attempt to outrun her humiliation, her anger, the hot pressure of the tears she was not going to let fall.

She considered driving north, toward Whitehorn, the town where she'd gone to school and where many of her friends lived. But she wasn't in the mood to see friends that night, to have them look at her with pity in their eyes. Most of them had been there, for the wedding that didn't happen. And news traveled fast in Whitehorn. Anyone who'd missed the actual event would know the whole story by now.

So she went east on the interstate, exiting the main highway about twenty miles outside of Billings. She drove two-lane blacktop for a while, going nowhere in particular. And then the roadhouse, Fanny Annie's, had loomed up on her right. She'd swung across the centerline, kicking up a high cloud of dust when she pulled into the dirt parking lot.

She knew at a glance that Fanny Annie's was one of those places a woman probably shouldn't enter alone. But she went in anyway. Just strolled through the doors and started drinking long necks and playing eight ball—with Nash Morgan, though she hadn't known his name at the time.

The truth was, she'd never asked for his name. And he'd never asked for hers. He'd called her Deadeye as a joke, because every time she took a shot, those balls never went where she meant for them to go. And she had called him Slim. She'd thought that the name fit him.

Raised on the Big Sky, where the cowboys came and went, Suzanna had known a number of Slims in her life. They had hips that matched their names and they wore faded denim and you could see the shape of lean, hard-worked muscle beneath their worn Western shirts. They had good hearts and a tender way with women and horses. And they never stayed around that long.

She hadn't started out to end up in bed with him. It had just moved on to that, somehow. What with the craziness in her heart and too many long necks and…something about him that felt so consoling. He was a stranger, and a stranger was just what she needed that night, someone who didn't know of her shame and embarrassment. A teasing, handsome stranger—one who somehow reminded her of coming home.

"Suzanna." Her father's voice snapped her back to the here and now. "Pass those biscuits down here. Nash needs more."

Nash laughed. "I wouldn't say I need 'em, but they sure are good."

Suzanna pasted on her most gracious smile and passed the biscuits down the table.

"My baby girl's got a light hand with biscuits and a good head for figures, too," Frank announced proudly. "She's gone and dragged the Big Sky right into the twenty-first century since she came back from college. Got this whole operation on that computer of hers. Anything you need to know about what's on hand or what's on order, you just ask her. Has it all at her fingertips, and that's a fact."

Nash made an admiring, agreeable noise.

"And you better be nice to her," Frank warned. "She's the one who'll be cutting your checks."

"I'll remember that." Nash looked right at her, causing her queasy stomach to lurch and her heart to start banging against her rib cage.

Suzanna kept on smiling, letting everyone know that she was just dandy, just a happy little biscuit maker with good computer skills. By the time the men finally returned to their work at a little after two, her face felt stiff and the muscles around her mouth ached from all that grinning.

She put a casserole together to heat up later, though her head was pounding and her heart felt like a big ball of lead inside her chest. She cleaned up the kitchen. Then, finally, she went upstairs to lie down with a cool, damp rag over her eyes.

Later, over dinner, her father asked her right out if something was bothering her. It was a perfect opportunity to tell him the truth.

She didn't. She said she had a headache. Then she listened, smiling that smile that made her face ache, as her father went on about what a find Nash Morgan was, how he'd had Darcy's Laddy, a spirited three-year-old who'd been giving them trouble, eating out of his hand in the space of an hour.

For the next few days, Suzanna hid out in the house. Immobilized, that was how she felt. Stuck in a low, dark place, with only her own indecision and self-loathing to keep her company. She felt sick to her stomach—and not just because of her pregnancy. The sickness came from dread at the prospect of running into her baby's father again. Being cooped up in the house drove her right up the wainscoted walls, but still, she couldn't bring herself to go out, not until she was ready to face Slim—er, Nash.

And she did know that she would have to face him, to tell him about the baby, even though it appeared that he had forgotten her by the morning after he bedded her. No matter if it turned out, as it most likely would, that he didn't want a thing to do with her or his child. Whatever he ended up thinking or saying when he learned the truth, he *was* the father and he did have a right to know.

So now there were two men who deserved to be informed of the mess she'd gotten herself into. One had raised her and loved her all her life. One had spent a single night in her arms.

But Suzanna said nothing. She was stuck—stuck in that low place where her stomach churned and her head pounded and she couldn't seem to make herself do what had to be done.

More than once, her father tried to get her to tell him what was eating at her. Each time, she brushed off his concern. She was just tired. She had another headache. There was nothing really wrong....

By Thursday morning, Frank Brennan had heard enough lame excuses. And he told his daughter so.

"By God, girl. Something is wrong with you, and I will know what."

"There's nothing."

"Don't lie to me."

"I'm..." *Pregnant,* she thought, pregnant by Nash Morgan, that top-notch horse trainer you hired and won't stop talking about. "Fine. Honestly. It's just a little twenty-four-hour bug, that's all." Ha, she thought. A twenty-four-hour bug? Talk about an understatement. This was a bug she'd carry for six more months. And when she got over it, she'd have herself a child to raise.

"Fine?" Her father, always soft-spoken, raised his voice. "*Fine?* You think I don't have eyes in my head? You've been draggin' around this place for weeks now. And the past few days, it's gotten nothin' but worse. You haven't left the damn house since Monday. I want you to tell me now. What is going on with you?"

"Dad, I—"

"Are you still mooning over that idiot social activist from California who left you flat on your wedding day?" Her father glared down the table at her. "You'd better not be, that's all I've got to say. You're lucky to be shut of that fool, and it's time you got smart and realized as much."

"No, I'm not mooning over Bryan, Dad." That, at least, was the truth. But what she said next was not. "Nothing's the matter. I'm fine."

"Fine," her father repeated again in pure disgust. "You think saying that word is gonna make it true? Something's wrong with you, and if you won't tell me what, I'll take you into Whitehorn today. We'll pay a visit to Doc Winters. Maybe he can figure out what's ailing you."

"I am not sick, Dad. I don't need a doctor."

They stared at each other, a battle of wills.

Frank was the one to lower his gaze first—but he hadn't surrendered the field, only changed tactics. "All right then. If you're not sick, I want to see you out and about. You can take a colt or two out for a nice, quiet ride—and get a little fresh air for yourself at the same time. Nash is completely in charge of the training schedule now. You talk to him this morning. He'll tell you which horses he wants you to ride."

Dear Lord. Nash. He wanted her to talk to Nash. "But, Dad, I—"

"You get out and ride, Suzanna. Or we are payin' a visit to the doc."

* * *

She found Nash at the round pen, where he'd just finished putting Bucky Boy, a fine sorrel two-year-old out of their treasured King broodmare, Chocolate Jessie, through his paces.

When he saw her, he dismounted, then he spent a few seconds talking softly to the animal. Bucky Boy stood very still, as if he really were listening, then he turned his head and seemed to be whispering in Nash's ear. Nash laughed and rubbed the horse's forehead affectionately. Then he led Bucky Boy out of the pen and turned him over to one of the other wranglers.

Finally he came toward her, those long, strong legs of his eating up the ground between them. He touched his hat brim in a sort of salute to her.

"Miss Brennan." He said *miss* the cowboy way, so it sounded like there were z's instead of s's at the end of it, a little like Ms., but softer, longer, more drawn out. "Frank said you'd be riding today."

Suzanna nodded, feeling awful, so awkward and formal, hurt slicing through her all of a sudden that he didn't remember, that they really were strangers in spite of the fact that she'd once lain naked in his arms, even though she carried his baby beneath her heart.

She coughed to clear the sudden obstruction from her throat. "Yes. He said I should check with you before choosing a horse."

He led her to the tack room, where the big training schedule was mounted on one wall, a line for
each colt and filly, the days marked off in squares.
Her father had always kept that chart, but often the
wranglers got lazy about filling in the blanks. Since
Nash had come, though, each blank space was
crammed with notes and instructions for what the
trainers should concentrate on in the next session.

"I like to have a plan," Nash said. He was standing behind her as she looked at the chart. His nearness sang along her nerves. She breathed deeply and
told herself to relax.

He went on. "Every horse is different, and this
way we don't just pick up on the weak points and
drill them to death." He chuckled. The rough, warm
sound sent a naughty thrill coursing up her spine.
"A colt is a lot like a schoolkid, if you think about
it. A colt needs a good teacher. And a good teacher
always works from a lesson plan."

Suzanna made a noise of agreement, which was
all she could manage right at that moment. She
could see him out of the corner of her eye. And she
could smell him. He smelled the same as she remembered, an earthy, warm, healthy sort of scent—
a scent she realized she would have recognized anywhere. A scent that hollowed out her midsection and
made her want to lean back against him.

She stiffened and turned. "I...it looks real good."

A half smile lifted the left side of his mouth, the
mouth that had kissed her, deep and wet and long.

The mouth that had roamed her whole body so that she had moaned and writhed beneath him, begging him not to stop, crying out for more.

She shifted her glance. "Well. If you'll just tell me which of your students could use a little field trip today, I'll get out of your way."

His eyes caught hers again—and wouldn't let go. "Did I say I wanted you out of my way?"

"Well, no. No, of course you didn't. But you know what I mean."

He shrugged and turned to the wall hung with bits and bridles. "Get your gear and we'll get going."

She didn't move. "Uh. *We?*"

He chose two snaffle bits and a pair of cinch straps, each with a flat-sided ring. "I'll ride out with you to see how you do."

"But—"

He turned, snared her with that green glance once more. "But what?"

"It's not necessary. Not necessary at all. I've been riding Big Sky colts since I was knee high to a gnat, for heaven's sake. You just tell me what you want me to watch for on any colt you give me and I'll—"

"You got some major objection to riding with me?" All of a sudden, his eyes were flat as paving stones, all the gleam gone out of them—and they still wouldn't let go of hers.

"No. No, of course I don't mind riding with you."

"Then grab a saddle." He pointed to the row of
lighter-weight cutting-horse saddles, not far from the
wall of bits and bridles. Then he asked with a definite note of challenge in his voice, "You need
someone to haul your saddle for you?"

"I do not."

"All right, then. Let's go."

It was a perfect morning for an easy, quiet ride,
warm but not hot yet, with a nice breeze blowing
off the white-crested Crazy Mountains to the north-
west. The grasses moved, rippling soft and silvery
in the path of the wind. Black-eyed Susans and pur-
ple-headed bull thistles turned their faces to the yellow ball of the sun.

They rode for an hour, hardly speaking, roughly
following the winding path of Bear Tooth Creek, the
ranch's major water source. Suzanna kept thinking
of what she had to tell the stranger on the horse
beside her. She also wondered sourly if he approved
of the way she handled her mount. But then he must,
mustn't he? Or he'd be giving her instructions in
that low, rough-velvet voice of his.

"There's a nice shady spot up ahead," Nash said
eventually. He pointed at a cluster of cottonwoods
along a wide place on the creek. "We'll stop there."
He clucked to his horse and took the lead. Her stomach suddenly churning with foreboding, Suzanna
followed.

In the shade of the trees by the sloping bank of

the creek, Nash dismounted and hobbled his horse. Suzanna did the same. Their horses drank from the creek and then nipped at the low grass along the bank. Suzanna watched them, though they weren't doing anything she hadn't seen a thousand times in her life. But watching them meant she didn't have to look at Nash.

He made small talk. In that soft, gentle voice of his, he remarked on how much he liked her father, how the Big Sky was a fine operation and the other handlers were good men. He talked about the colt and the filly grazing idly along the bank. About how Dingo was still slow to pick up a lead and Baby June tended to laze along rather than walk out as she should.

Somehow, Suzanna managed to make intelligent noises in response. But her mind was a whirlwind.

There *was* something in the way he kept looking at her, something in the knowing curve of that mouth, which had once kissed her with such wild passion. His glances and his half smiles were clues, it seemed to her.

Clues that communicated without his saying as much that he *did* remember, after all. That the way he'd seemed not to know her had been only an act. That she really had seen recognition in his eyes in that first moment on the porch Monday morning.

All of a sudden, he asked, "What's on your mind right now?"

She'd been staring at the horses again. But his

question had her whipping her head around, made
the skin down her arms and at the backs of her knees
go hot and prickly with something that felt very
much like fear. "I…what?"

"What are you thinking?"

"Well, nothing," she baldly lied. "Just…I was
just listening to what you were saying, that's all."

His expression said he didn't buy that for a minute. "You want to know what *I'm* thinking?"

No! her cowardly heart cried. *I don't. I do not
want to know….*

But he told her anyway. "I'm thinking that you're
a much better rider than you are a pool player, Deadeye."

Chapter 3

Deadeye.

Oh, God. He *did* remember.

Suzanna's stomach lurched dangerously. Sweet Lord, she was not going to be able to stop it this time. She was going to be sick....

She sucked in a breath, closed her eyes and bent over, getting ready.

Nash touched her shoulder. "Suzanna..."

She put up a hand, waving him away. Her stomach lurched again—and settled, at least somewhat.

She opened her eyes. She could see Nash's boots planted firmly not two feet to her left.

With a sigh, she let herself sink to a sitting position on the bank.

After a moment, Nash dropped down beside her. She shot him a furtive glance, then quickly looked away.

He asked, "You all right?"

She didn't answer. There was no need. He could see that she was very far from all right.

"Look," he said. "As far as I'm concerned, what happened was between us. If you're worried that I'm a man who likes to talk about things that are nobody else's business—"

"I…no. No, it isn't that."

"Then what?"

It was the moment, the moment to tell him. She looked at him hopelessly. "I…" The words just would not come.

She hung her head.

And he put his arm around her. Strangely enough, it felt utterly natural for him to do that. And so comforting. She let out a hard sigh and buried her face against his shoulder. He pulled her closer, stroked her hair.

A long time passed. Nash held her, and she huddled against him, breathing the wonderful scent of him, glad for his strong arms around her at the same time as she found it impossible to raise her eyes and look at him.

"Come on," he said at last, putting a finger under her chin, making her raise her eyes to meet his. "Come on, it can't be *that* bad.…"

She hitched in a tight breath. "But it is. It really is. You don't understand...."

"Then maybe you'd better tell me."

"I..."

"Come on. Tell me."

Something in his eyes undid her. She blurted out the truth. "I'm pregnant."

Lord, it sounded awful, just to say it like that. She shied away from him a little, and he dropped his arm from its comforting position across her shoulder. For a time, they sat very still, not touching, staring toward the mountains, neither knowing what to say next.

Finally, Nash picked up a pebble and tossed it overhand into the water. Suzanna watched the ripples move out when it dropped through the glassy surface.

She wondered if he was thinking the same thing she was thinking, that it was a pretty bum deal for her to go and get herself pregnant when he'd only made one little slipup the whole night they'd spent together.

He *had* used protection. But there had been that one time, near dawn, when some last, frantic eagerness had taken them both. He had reached for her and she had pressed herself against him—and the necessary precautions had been the furthest thing from their minds.

He asked carefully, "Was there...anyone else besides me?"

She shook her head fiercely.

"Then it's mine."

She nodded, biting her lip to hold back the hopeless little moan that was trying to squeeze itself out of her throat.

"We'll get married," he said.

She looked right at him then. "I don't even *know* you."

"It doesn't matter. It's the right thing to do."

"No," she said firmly, then decided that maybe that sounded a bit harsh. She tried to soften it a little. "I mean, no, thanks. It's...very nice of you to offer, but...I just couldn't marry someone I didn't love."

He gave her a long look, one that made her extremely uncomfortable. Then he said flatly, "Think about it."

She turned her gaze toward the mountains again, to get away from those eyes of his. "No, really. I don't have to think about it. I don't love you and I—"

He stopped her in midsentence, skipping right on to the next order of business. "Frank doesn't know yet, does he?"

"Uh. No. I...I've been meaning to tell him."

"But you haven't."

"Not yet."

"Well, I think we'd better do it tonight, then."

We. He intended to be there with her. To face her father with her. Gratitude washed through her in a warm wave.

She made herself turn to him. His eyes were waiting. "I... You don't have to do that."

He looked at her steadily. "Yeah. Yeah, I do." He touched her shoulder, and she knew that *he* knew exactly how she felt. He understood the dread inside her at the prospect of telling Frank Brennan what they'd done. "You're three months gone," he said. "It can't wait any longer."

"I know." She sighed the words.

"We'd better get it over with then. Tonight, like I said."

What else could she answer? "All right."

"I'll come to the house."

"Okay. Um, come at six, for dinner. We'll tell him after. It will be better that way, not quite so abrupt." It wouldn't be better. Nothing could make such a thing better. But still, if the poor man insisted on standing by her when she broke the news, he ought at least to have a nice dinner first.

Her father came in at five-thirty. Nash had already told him he'd be dropping by for supper.

Frank seemed to think that was a dandy idea. "I'm glad you asked him." Her father winked at her. "And he does like your biscuits."

Suzanna drew a fortifying breath. "Well. I made plenty."

The meal went smoothly enough. Her father and Nash seemed to have a lot to say to each other. They talked business. Frank brought up the two-week trip he'd be taking near the end of the month, first to the annual Wyoming quarter horse show in Gillette, and then on to visit a friend in Colorado.

"I'm real glad you'll be here, Nash," Frank said. "Between you and Suzanna, I'll be leavin' the Big Sky in capable hands."

Suzanna kept her eyes on her plate and wondered if Nash would be around by then. Would her father have so much faith in his new trainer after he heard what they had to say to him? And would Nash want to stay? She did admire him for sticking by her to-night—but she couldn't expect him to want to hang around watching her stomach get bigger and bigger with the baby they'd made. He'd made his obliga-tory offer of marriage, and she had turned him down. Really, it might be better for everyone if he decided to move on down the road.

But then again, the more contact she had with him, the more he seemed like a man who wouldn't walk away from his own child. So maybe they'd have to work something out, arrange things so he could see the baby now and then.

Oh, who could say? The truth was, she didn't know what Nash Morgan would do.

The dinner was over too soon for Suzanna. She cleared the plates and served peach cobbler and made herself eat it as she'd eaten her pot roast and vegetables, forcing the food down to keep her father from looking at her with a worried frown between his brows.

Finally the time came. She sent a swift, questioning glance at Nash. He nodded—and all she wanted to do was leap from the table, grab the empty dessert plates and flee to the kitchen.

She made herself stay put.

And Nash said, "Frank, there is something you need to be told."

Her father pushed his plate away and looked from Nash to his daughter. "Sounds like something serious."

"It is." Nash waited. Suzanna understood that he was giving her a chance to say the words.

"What?" Frank demanded. "You two are makin' me nervous."

Nash cleared his throat.

And somehow Suzanna found her voice. "I'm going to have a baby, Dad."

The silence that followed was downright deafening. Her father's face went dead white, then flushed with hot color. He turned a brutal glare on Suzanna, a look that made her long to slide off her chair and scurry under the table like a naughty child, to curl herself up in a ball under there—and never, ever come out.

And then Frank Brennan swore, a single, very ugly word. "That weaselly little rat bastard," he muttered. "I should have known."

Suzanna gulped in a breath, then found herself echoing in a numb voice, "Weaselly?"

"I didn't trust him. Never. Not for a minute, from

the first day you brought him here. All that talk of
the homeless and hungry. All those big-shot ideas
about changing the world. Charity begins at home,
that's what the Good Book says. And a man who
gets a girl in trouble and then runs off to join the
damn Peace Corps is no man at all in *my* book.''

"Bryan?" Suzanna heard herself murmur dazedly.
"You mean Bryan?"

"Who the hell else would I mean?" asked her
father in utter disgust. Another crude epithet followed. He glowered. "You been in touch with
him?"

"I…no. I don't have any idea *how* to get in touch
with him. And anyway, Dad, it wasn't—"

"Well, okay. Okay, fine. I wouldn't want that
damn fool for a son-in-law anyway, and that is a
plain fact. If he ever sets foot on the Big Sky again,
I'll skin him for the polecat he is and stretch his
sorry pelt on the tack room wall."

"Dad—"

Nash cut her off. "Just a minute," he said quietly.
"Who's Bryan?"

Frank snorted. "Who's Bryan? I'll tell you who
Bryan is. Bryan's her fiancé—her *ex*-fiancé. Left her
flat, the weasel. Three months ago, on their wedding
day, last March the twenty-fourth. Joined the damn
Peace Corps, wouldn't you know?"

Nash cast her a glance. Suzanna read its meaning.
She'd never said a word about Bryan to him—not
during that night three months ago, and not today,

either, when she'd had a clear opportunity to say anything that needed saying.

"March twenty-fourth," Nash said, his soft voice even softer than usual. Too soft, actually. Accusingly soft. "That was supposed to be your *wedding* day?"

Lord. How could she have thought he'd forgotten? It was painfully clear that he remembered everything—including the calendar date of the night he'd spent with her.

She swallowed. "I...I suppose I should have explained."

"Yeah," he said. "I suppose you should. But then, I guess there were a lot of things you didn't explain."

That got her dander up. "Just you wait a half a minute, here, mister. You didn't do a lot of explaining, either, if memory serves. You didn't even—"

"Stop." Frank fisted his hand and hit the edge of the table with it. Plates and flatware jumped and clattered. "Don't you two go getting into it. There is no sense at all in us turnin' on each other—which reminds me." He swung his gaze on his daughter and asked in a tone midway between curiosity and fury, "Suzanna, why the hell did you have to go dragging Nash into this mess?"

Suzanna had that urge again—to crawl under the table and hide. She slid a glance at Nash. Those green eyes were on her, waiting for her to tell her father the truth.

And she knew she must do exactly that.

But how? Where were the right words to say? How could she explain to the conservative man who'd raised her that she'd gone out on what should have been her wedding night and had sex with a stranger?

"I…"

"Speak up, girl. Answer me, now."

"Well, because I…"

"Yeah?"

"Because he, um, well…"

Nash must have grown tired of waiting for her to get the words out. He said wearily, "Because the ex-fiancé is *not* the man at fault. *I* am."

Frank Brennan looked as if he just might keel over from the shock of that news. "You, Nash? You?"

"Yeah, Frank. Me."

"But you don't even *know* each other. You just met this past Monday."

"We met before. The night she was supposed to have married that other guy. At a place called Fanny Annie's, a few miles outside of Billings."

Her father stared from Nash to Suzanna and back again. His face showed disbelief and disappointment and a host of other emotions too painful to contemplate.

"Oh, Dad," Suzanna cried. "Dad, I'm so sorry, I—"

Frank waved a hand at her, as if he couldn't bear

the sound of her voice, of her excuses. Then he sank down in his chair. Slowly, he lifted both big, blunt-fingered hands. He raked them through his thick graying hair. "Oh, Suzanna. This is not like you, to pick up a stranger, in some roadside bar."

"It was...a really bad time for me, Dad. I was feeling so crazy, just out of my mind and I—"

"Never mind." Frank shook his head and let out a deep sigh. "So. What are you gonna do now?"

And Nash said very calmly, "Now, she's going to marry me."

Chapter 4

A slow smile spread across Frank Brennan's tanned, lined face—a relieved, indulgent kind of smile. He sat up straighter in his chair. "Well," he said. "I gotta admit, I feel a lot better hearin' you say that, son. But I guess I should have known. You're not a man to run from his responsibilities."

Frank turned his smile, only slightly dimmed, on Suzanna. "So, I guess everything will work out all right, after all. The fact is, you and Nash will make a great team. I have to admit, the thought that you two might get together has already crossed my mind a time or two. And now, well, things could be a damn sight worse, couldn't they? You'll get married and I can rest easy—and not only because my little girl's baby will have a father, but also because I can be certain the Big Sky will end up in capable hands when it's time for me to pass on the reins.''

Nash said, ''Frank. We're not talking about your ranch, here. We're talking marriage. Period.''

''I know, I know. You're right. I understand. You two will get married. We can worry about the rest as time goes by.''

Suzanna realized she'd better speak up before the two of them planned out her whole life for her. ''Wait just a minute here.''

Both men turned to her. ''What?'' they said at the same time.

She looked from one strong-jawed, masculine face to the other. The men muttered, ''What?'' again, simultaneously as before.

Suzanna's father was frowning at her. She dared to turn to Nash, to look him square in the eye. He stared right back, calm as you please. She demanded, ''How could you do this?''

Nash shrugged. ''Do what?''

''I told you I can't marry you. I told you this afternoon.''

''You *what?*'' Frank bellowed.

Suzanna answered her father, but she kept looking right at Nash. ''I told him I couldn't marry him.''

Her father loosed another expletive. ''Now, why would you go and say a crazy thing like that?''

Suzanna ignored him. ''Look,'' she told Nash.

"We don't love each other. We don't even *know* each other."

"It's a good match," her father said stubbornly. "And you need a husband right now. Love will come later."

She whirled on him. "How can you say that? I'm a Brennan, Dad. And Brennans always marry for love."

Frank grunted. "This is no time for silly sentimentality."

"Sentimentality?" Suzanna echoed the words in outrage. "That's what you call it now? You're the one who told me all the old stories. I learned them sitting on your knee. How Great-Great-Grandmother Isabelle married Kyle Brennan because she loved him with all of her heart, even though—"

"Suzanna, I know the old stories."

"Then how can you suggest that I marry a man I don't love?"

"Because he's the father of your baby. Because he's a damn fine man. Because it's the best thing and it's the *right* thing."

"It is not. It's the *convenient* thing."

"Whatever," her father said gruffly. "It's the best solution to a bad situation."

"No, it is not. It's wrong, that's what it is. And I can understand that you don't think much of my judgment right now. I have made a pretty bad mess of things. But I am still a Brennan, born and raised. And I will marry for love, or I won't marry at all."

Her father's face had flushed deep red again. "You will do as I tell you—in this, at least."

Suzanna held her ground. "I will not."

"You are in trouble, girl. You are having a child. Your baby's father is willing to marry you. Don't be a damn fool about this, on top of everything else."

She squared her shoulders and stuck out her chin. "I am sorry you think I'm a fool, Dad. But I don't love Nash, and I'm not going to marry him. It's not right."

"It *is* right."

"I won't do it. I can raise my baby on my own just fine. If Nash wants to help, well, we can talk about that. But not about marriage."

Frank shoved his chair back and loomed above her. "I have had enough of this moony-eyed foolishness!" He was shouting. "You will marry Nash…or else!"

"No, I won't. I won't, I tell you."

"Wait a minute, here." It was Nash's voice, quiet and low, utterly calm.

Both Suzanna and Frank shut their mouths and turned to him.

He rose to his feet and said to Suzanna, "Thank you for a fine dinner. I'm headed back to the bunkhouse now. You think about my offer and let me know what you decide."

Then he stepped away from his chair, pushed it gently under the table and went out the back way.

Once the door shut behind him, Frank glowered at Suzanna. "You'd *better* do some thinking, girl. Some hard thinking. And when you're through thinking, you'd better come to a reasonable decision."

Suzanna glowered right back at him and didn't say a word.

A stare-down ensued.

In the end, her father tossed his napkin on the table, growled good-night and retired to his room.

Suzanna cleaned up the dishes.

Then, desperately needing emotional support, she picked up the phone on the kitchen wall to call her sister in Chicago.

But she hung up without dialing. Diana, who was five years Suzanna's senior, truly had been like a mother to her through her growing-up years. Diana had bandaged her hurts, nursed her when she got the chicken pox and shared all her secrets.

But it wouldn't be fair to draw her into the middle of this situation. Since Suzanna and her father were totally at odds, confiding in Diana would be tantamount to asking her sister to take sides. And even if Diana held to the middle ground, she would be bound to worry. If she got too concerned, she might just decide she had to drop everything and pay a visit home.

No, bothering Diana with this wouldn't be right.

The time had come for Suzanna to handle her difficulties on her own.

She trudged up the stairs, her feet as heavy as her heart. In her room, she dropped to the edge of the bed and kicked off her shoes.

If only there was someone she could talk to about this. Someone to reassure her, to tell her she was right not to want to marry a stranger, even if that stranger did happen to be the father of her child.

She hung her head and stared at her socks. If only she could...travel across time. Take a little trip to the past. Have a nice, long talk with her great-great-grandmother Isabelle about love and marriage and—

The letters.

Suzanna's head came up. She stared at the bow-fronted bureau across the room, where she'd put the letters on Monday when Nash Morgan had come knocking on the door. She'd yet to read them, had more or less forgotten them in the misery and upheaval of the past few days.

Suzanna rose from the bed and padded across the hooked rug to the bureau. She knelt and pulled open the bottom drawer. With hands that shook just a little, she withdrew the six envelopes.

Then she went to her desk at the window that looked out on the front yard. She switched on the lamp and sat down to read.

An hour later, Suzanna carefully refolded the last yellowed sheet and put it in the envelope from which she'd removed it. She neatly stacked the envelopes in a corner of her desk. Then she put her head on her arms and cried.

She had hoped they would be love letters. And they were. Love letters written a year after Isabelle and Kyle's marriage, while Kyle was away on a trail drive and Isabelle looked after the Big Sky. Isabelle's passion, tenderness and commitment shone forth in every line. She had loved her husband deeply.

Suzanna switched off the lamp and sat back in her chair. She stared blindly out the window, where twilight had brought the bats and swallows out to dip and sail through the darkening sky.

"For love," she whispered to the night as the last lonely tear tracked its way down her cheek. "To marry for love. Is that so much to ask?"

The night gave no answer. After a while, moving very slowly, feeling weary right down into the center of herself, Suzanna rose and got ready for bed. She settled beneath the comforter with a heavy sigh and waited for sleep to steal all her cares.

But in spite of her weariness, sleep wouldn't come.

The next day at breakfast, Suzanna's father hardly spoke to her. He ate his meal in silence, then without a word took his plate to the sink, rinsed it and stuck it in the dishwasher rack.

He headed for the back door, but then couldn't

resist turning and demanding, "You made a decision yet?"

She looked at him pleadingly. She really did hate to have this hostility between them. "Dad, I—"

He grunted. "Never mind. I can see you haven't." He left her there.

She lasted through that whole day and another never-ending, mostly sleepless night. Her father barely spoke to her during the day. And later, as she lay in bed, she thought about Nash, wondered what he was thinking out there in his narrow bunkhouse cot. Did he already regret speaking up and offering marriage? Or did he remain steadfastly determined to do the right thing?

Saturday morning, as she was zipping up her jeans, she finally admitted to herself that they were getting tighter. Soon she'd have to buy herself some pregnant-lady clothes.

It was another pretty morning, clear and cool with the promise of a hot afternoon to come. Suzanna decided she'd drive into Whitehorn later, since the pantry needed filling. But first, before it got too hot, she would go riding. She'd have to face Nash to do it, in order not to disrupt his precious training schedule, but she could manage that. She could manage that just fine.

She put on her boots and grabbed her hat and went out to the corrals, but Nash wasn't there. One of the handlers told her that Nash and her father were in the near pasture, putting a first lead on one of the foals.

It wasn't that far to walk. Five minutes later, she found them. They had a set of pipe panels surrounding the mare and the sweet little chestnut foal. They'd used the mare, who was accustomed to such goings-on, to maneuver the frightened foal into a corner. Then her father, halter in hand, slid between the foal and the back panel, blocking escape on that side. Nash stepped up and wrapped one arm under the foal's neck and the opposite hand firmly around the base of his tail. Frank slipped on the halter.

Watching them, Suzanna thought that they worked together as if they'd been doing it all of their lives. Her father was holding the lead rope, stroking the little fella about the face and neck. Nash was making soothing sounds, talking softly, saying reassuring things. The foal tried to toss his head and cried out for his mama.

The mare gave a low, rough snort, a questioning sound.

Nash said gently, "It's all right, girl. We won't hurt your baby."

The mare snorted again and shook herself. Turning her back on the proceedings, she moved a few steps away.

Really, Nash Morgan was a wonder with a horse.

And Suzanna had to admit that he'd been pretty terrific with her, as well. So tender and passionate on their one night together, he'd made her first time a beautiful thing. There was also the way he had held her so kindly, day before yesterday, down by the creek, when she'd almost lost her breakfast right in front of him. And he hadn't made a single mean wisecrack when she told him the baby was his.

And then he had faced her father with her. A lot of men wouldn't have been willing to do that. He'd stepped right up to accept complete responsibility. He'd offered to marry her—well, *insisted* on marrying her, really.

He *was* a good man.

It occured to Suzanna right then that maybe she needed more than some jeans with elastic in the waist. Maybe she needed to face the fact that love wasn't everything. Once, she'd thought she'd loved Bryan Cummings—and look where that had gotten her.

She wasn't her great-great-grandmother. She was only herself, Suzanna, who had made a few mistakes and now ought to be finding the best way to set things right.

Nash Morgan was a good man. She could do a lot worse than to become his wife.

Chapter 5

Her father looked up and saw her. Nash cast a quick glance her way, all he could manage with the foal in his arms. Frank said something to Nash, and Nash slowly backed away from the nervous foal, leaving Frank holding him by the lead. Right away, the foal whinnied and tried to back up.

Nash said, "You okay?"

"Go on." Frank spared him a wave. "The day I can't handle a haltered foal is the day I need to find myself another line of work." The foal yanked on the lead. "Easy, boy," said Frank. "Take it easy, now..."

Nash moved the panel aside and stepped through the gap. He skimmed off his hat. "Something I can do for you, Suzanna?"

She made herself smile. Her mouth kind of quivered at the edges, but it was the best she could do. "Well, I was wondering if maybe you'd go for a ride with me."

They just naturally seemed to head for that same spot along the creek. And when they dismounted, Suzanna felt almost as nerved up as she had the other day.

But somehow she did it. She told him, "I have considered your offer, and I've decided that I will marry you." Her stomach seemed to drop toward her boots as it occurred to her that he very well might have changed his mind. "Er...that is, if the offer's still open."

"It is."

A slightly frantic laugh escaped her. "Whew. That's good. I mean, okay. I mean..."

The tangle of words died in her throat as he grasped her arm and pulled her toward him.

She landed against his chest with a soft little, "Oh!"

He looked at her, roving her face with that green glance of his. "You want me to let go?"

She felt terribly flustered. "I...no. I don't. Really, it's just..."

"What?"

"I...I'm nervous, I guess." She added silently, *And you feel so warm and big and good. So exactly as I remember you feeling...*

"A man usually kisses a woman, doesn't he? When she says she'll marry him?"

"Well, yes. I mean, that's how I understood it. I mean—"

She wasn't really sure what she meant. But it didn't matter, because he lowered his mouth and started nuzzling hers and she didn't have to say anything more anyway.

She didn't *want* to say anything more. He truly was a wonderful kisser. He kissed the same way he talked to a horse. With complete concentration. And also with respect. He knew never to force the issue. He just made the whole experience so lovely, a woman would have to be a total fool to say no.

He nipped her lower lip, then scraped it softly between his teeth. She sighed, her mouth opened a little and the tip of his tongue went roaming there, at the entrance, teasing her with the idea that he just might come all the way inside.

And then he did come inside. He swept the tender wet surfaces beyond her lips with a tongue that knew exactly what to do when it was inside a woman's mouth.

She sighed some more, pressed herself closer to him, there beneath the cottonwood tree. She felt the ridge of his arousal against her belly and she melted down there, her body knowing what was needed of it, going open and ready. His hands roamed her back as the kiss grew ever deeper.

Oh, yes. She wanted him. As she had wanted him

that very first night when he'd come up to her at the long bar in Fanny Annie's and asked if she was open to a little company.

She'd turned to him and looked in his eyes, and suddenly all her misery and humiliation seemed to have happened to some other woman. Suddenly, she felt good about herself. Good about being there in the smoky, loud bar. Good about everything.

A little wild, maybe. A little too ready to risk what she shouldn't.

But good. Very good.

She slid her tongue around his, moaning at the contact, at the wetness and the heat.

Too soon, he pulled back. "Just a kiss," he said, as if reminding them both that they weren't going any further.

She dragged in a big breath and let it out slowly. "Yes. Just a kiss..."

He had her by the shoulders, his strong fingers digging in a little. "This Bryan guy. He still special to you?"

"No." It was easy to say. After all, it was the truth. "I...I realize now it wasn't love with him. It was just..."

"What?"

"...a dream I had. Love and marriage. Walking down the aisle in my great-great-grandmother's wedding gown."

"You hate him now, for walking out on you?"

"No. I just...don't have that much feeling at all

for him. A little sadness and a whole lot of embarrassment that I made such a bad choice in a man."

He looked...what? Satisfied, maybe. "Good." He was still holding her shoulders.

"What?" she asked, all at once feeling nervous again.

"There were a lot of things you didn't tell me that night. Like your name."

"You didn't tell me yours, either."

"Okay, so we're even on that score. But what about it being your first time? That was a real shocker."

"Well, it didn't seem to stop you."

He had the grace to look abashed. "You didn't tell me to stop. And I didn't want to stop, so..."

"Nash. It's okay. All I'm saying is, you didn't volunteer much information yourself that night. It wasn't a night for talking. We had a lot of fun. And we ended up doing a few things we shouldn't have. And the vital information just never got exchanged."

He smiled a little ruefully, then grew serious again. "You left in the morning, when I was still sleeping."

"It seemed...the best way."

"I wondered if I'd dreamed you or something."

She understood that. Sometimes she'd wondered herself if that night had really happened. At least, at first. But then, when she'd realized she was pregnant, she'd been forced to admit that it had been very, very real.

She glanced at their two sets of boots, so close together, pointing toward each other on the mossy bank. Then she lifted her face to him once more. "You didn't dream me, Nash."

He looked at her for a very long time. Then he shook his head slowly. "No. I reckon I did not."

Her father was waiting when they got back to the home place.

"Well?" he demanded when they rode up.

In a formal tone that plucked at Suzanna's heart-strings, Nash said, "Your daughter has decided that she will be my wife."

That night after dinner, the three of them firmed up the details.

Frank was in an expansive mood. "You'll have that big wedding you always dreamed of after all, Suzanna. Diana will come home and—"

"No, Dad." She cut in before he could get rolling.

Her father drew back in surprise. "Why not? I thought a big wedding was what you always wanted."

"Maybe it was. Once. But I'm through with that kind of foolishness now. And I don't want to drag Diana back here all over again just to see me get married. I think we'd better make it simple. And soon."

Frank looked at Nash, who said nothing for a moment, then shrugged. "I guess Suzanna knows what she wants."

Frank spoke. "A nice honeymoon, then. On me. How's that? Two weeks, wherever you two want to go."

Suzanna and Nash both vetoed that one.

Nash said, "Listen, Frank. Thanks a lot, but I'll pay for my own honeymoon."

And Suzanna added, "I really don't want to make a big deal of this, Dad." She glanced questioningly at her husband-to-be. "Just a few days away, that's what I was thinking."

"Whatever you want."

"Someplace nearby would be nice," Suzanna said. "Since it will only be a short stay."

Nash shrugged again. "I've got a friend who owns a bed-and-breakfast in Buffalo, Wyoming."

Suzanna had been to Buffalo and remembered it as a lovely little town. "Wyoming sounds fine."

"All right, then. Wyoming," Nash said flatly. "We can get the blood tests this week, then get married at the county courthouse next Friday. We'll stay in Buffalo till Tuesday. That'll get us back before Frank leaves for the horse show in Gillette."

"Take your time," her father said. "I can skip the horse show this year."

"There's no need for that," Nash said. "We'll be back on Tuesday." He was still looking at Suzanna. It wasn't a cold look—but it wasn't warm, either.

"All right?" He seemed so distant all of a sudden, not at all like the tender lover who had kissed her at the creek that very afternoon. She wondered if something was bothering him and decided that she'd ask him later.

She said brightly, "Yes. That's fine."

Next, her father announced that he intended to give Nash a share in the Big Sky. The year before, when Suzanna had turned twenty-one, Frank Brennan had seen his lawyer in town. He'd had it fixed so the Big Sky belonged half to him and the other half equally to his two daughters. Now that Nash would join the family, Frank had decided to split his own half with his new son-in-law.

"We'll see the lawyer this week," Frank declared expansively. "We can do it when you two go in for those blood tests and—"

Nash said no before Frank could finish. "I won't lay claim to another man's land—even if I am marryin' his daughter."

"But, son. You'll be part of the family now and—"

"Forget it, Frank. I earn what I own, or I pay for it. If I decide I want a piece of your ranch, then I'll buy in. I won't have you handing it to me as a wedding present."

Her father tried to make him see reason, but Nash wouldn't budge. Suzanna couldn't decide whether to be thrilled at the high level of Nash's integrity— or to start getting worried. She did believe that Nash was an honest man. And an honest man might hesitate to take a chunk of his father-in-law's land if he had doubts about how long his marriage would last.

Frank left them alone a little while later.

They walked out to the front porch together. Suzanna sat on the swing suspended from the porch eaves. Nash hitched a leg up on the railing a few feet away.

Suzanna toed the porch boards, making the swing creak a little on its heavy chain. Far away, a coyote howled at the new moon, which seemed to hang from a star in the indigo sky. In the near pasture, one of the mares let out a high, nervous whinny in response to the sound.

"How old are you, Nash?" she asked.

"Thirty-one. You?"

"Twenty-two." The swing creaked some more. "Strange, isn't it? We're getting married in less than a week, and I just learned how old you are."

He took off his hat and dropped it to the porch boards. "Not so strange, really. Not given the circumstances."

She swallowed. "Yeah. I guess you're right about that. You...ever had the urge to settle down before?"

He didn't answer right away. Her stomach tightened, and she found herself expecting him to say something like, *No, and to tell you the truth, I don't really want to settle down now.*

But he didn't. He replied simply, "I've never been married. Never even been close to it before."

Her lips felt dry. She pressed them together and ran her tongue along the inner seam. "Why not?"

In the light of the porch lamp, his eyes were dark as the bottom of a well. "What are you after here, Suzanna?"

She felt her face pinkening, felt like a person prying into someone else's private business. But he was to be her husband, wasn't he? And didn't that make his private business *her* business, too? "I just...I want to know about you, that's all."

"You want my life story, is that it?" His tone was gentle, as always, but she thought she detected a thread of sarcasm in it.

She answered frankly. "Yes, I want to know everything about you that you're willing to tell me."

Another nerve-racking silence, then he said, "All right."

He began rattling off facts. "I was born in Laramie. My father died when I was seven. I was ten when my mother remarried. My stepfather didn't like me much. He had a mean streak and a big leather belt and he exercised both on me regularly. I never graduated from high school, ran off when I was seventeen, at the beginning of my senior year. That was when my mother died. I didn't see much sense in sticking around there after that.

"I've been on my own since then, working as a ranch hand and then finding I had a certain way with horses. I've called myself a horse trainer for the past eight years and now I'm to the point where I can ask a premium wage for my services. I've got a pickup, two good saddles, an empty gooseneck trailer. And fifty thousand dollars in a bank in Billings against the day that I can buy my own spread.'' He chuckled, a mirthless sound. ''My big dream is to get my own place, which I'm always telling myself I'll do real soon. Fifty thousand doesn't go that far, though. Not in the ranching business. Sometimes, I gotta admit, my big dream seems about as likely to happen as…meeting a pretty virgin college girl in a roadhouse and spending the night with her.''

If Suzanna's cheeks had felt pink before, now they felt bright red. Nash was watching her, his eyes intent.

He asked, ''Why'd you choose me that night, Suzanna?''

She felt embarrassed to tell him—but it was only fair to reveal a few of her own secrets after the things he had just said to her. ''I…looked at you and forgot how unhappy I was. That night, I forgot everything but what it felt like being with you. And, well…''

''Well, what?''

''You made me think of home.''

His eyes were velvet-soft and so was his voice when he said, ''That's not such a bad start, I guess.''

She made a noise of agreement low in her throat,

then dared to ask, "If you want your own place, why didn't you take what my dad offered you?"

His broad shoulders tensed, and the softness left his expression. "I think I made that pretty clear."

Yes, she thought, *you certainly did.* "Because you want to earn what you own. But was that the only reason?"

"It's reason enough."

"It just seemed like something was bothering you when we were talking about the wedding and the honeymoon and...everything."

She waited. He only looked at her, his eyes well-deep once more. She wondered at the way she felt with him. There was a low, constant hum inside her, a waiting, eager kind of feeling, something she'd never experienced with any other man. Arousal would probably be the word for it. Yes. She felt aroused. And utterly at home—yet curiously on edge at the same time. As if she knew him to his soul. As if she didn't know him at all.

It was terribly confusing.

She murmured, "If I said something that offended you while we were talking about the wedding—"

He stood and came toward her. "You said what you wanted, right? What you were willing to do. A plain ceremony, nothing fancy. And a little trip to Wyoming afterward."

She stilled the swing and stared at him. The whole night seemed to hang suspended, between her eyes and his. "I...yes. Nothing fancy. And a trip to Wyoming is great."

"So that's what you'll have." He held out his hand.

She put hers in it and he pulled her up, into his arms.

He kissed her, pressing her against him, so that she forgot everything but the way his body felt along hers. When he let her go, she wanted only to grab him close again.

He stepped back, bent and scooped up his hat. "Good night, Suzanna." He went down the steps and across the lawn, vanishing into the shadows around the side of the house.

She stood there, watching, until he was gone. Then she dropped to the swing again and leaned back in its swaying embrace.

Later, she went into the house and called Diana. She told her big sister the truth. That she'd gotten pregnant the night of the day that Bryan Cummings had left her at the altar. She was marrying the father of her baby—who, as it turned out, was also the new horse trainer their father was so impressed with.

Diana immediately offered to come home. But Suzanna said no. Diana tried to argue. Suzanna remained firm. It was only a simple legal ceremony, after all. Nothing to make a big fuss over. And she and Nash were going away for a few days right after.

"You know I'll come if you need me," Diana said.

And Suzanna answered that yes, of course, she did know. And she was fine. There was no cause for worry.

Suzanna hung up the phone and felt sad. It really would be nice to have Diana there, when she and Nash said their vows. She reached for the phone again.

But she put it back in its cradle before she hit the redial button. After all, Diana had her own life. And Suzanna was a grown-up now. She needed to get beyond silly sentimentality. She'd dragged her sister all the way home to play maid of honor one time already this year. It was enough. This time, the ceremony would be very short. A couple of "I do's," a kiss, and maybe a simple gold band. Not a big deal.

No maid of honor required.

Chapter 6

They were married as they'd agreed, the following Friday morning in a plain civil ceremony. Her father and one of the other horse trainers stood as witnesses. They had lunch afterward at Whitehorn's newest and nicest restaurant, the State Street Grill. Then Suzanna and her husband climbed into his pickup and headed for Wyoming.

Buffalo, Wyoming, was a charming little town. It reminded Suzanna of Whitehorn, with lots of picturesque brick buildings on its wide main street and proud, craggy mountains not far away. Cottonwood fluff blew in the air, just like at home, and the prairie rolled off forever into the distance, the grasses still early-summer green.

Suzanna loved the Clear Creek Inn on sight. It was as old as the house she'd grown up in, with similar dark woodwork, high ceilings and generous-size rooms. Their hostess, Nash's friend, greeted them in the front parlor on their arrival. An attractive red-haired woman who appeared to be in her mid-forties, Emma Marie Lawrence instructed Suzanna to call her Marie and smiled affectionately at Nash—maybe a little too affectionately.

"You two come on now," Marie said. "I'll show you to the room I've saved especially for your honeymoon."

All too aware of the big four-poster lace-canopied bed just a few feet away, Suzanna hovered near the door after Marie left them alone.

"Marie seems…real friendly," she said. Nash set down their suitcases near the mahogany armoire on the far wall and then turned to look at her. She coughed. "So. How do you two know each other?"

He chuckled. "Suzanna. You been listenin' to too many Garth Brooks songs."

She made a face at him. "What is that supposed to mean?"

He'd worn new jeans to marry her in, olive green in color, neatly creased and stacked just right over his tooled dress boots. He hooked his thumb in his watch pocket and slung out a hip, pure cowboy—and purely insolent, she thought.

"Marie's a friend," he said. "And that's all. I worked for her and her husband before he died.

They owned a ranch, ran cattle, about twenty miles out of town.''

Suzanna twisted her wedding band on her finger. It felt so new on her hand—new, but not really strange. She could get used to it very easily.

It struck her again how little she really knew of the man she'd just married. He'd had a hard life— she understood that from what he'd told her the other night. And yet there was that softness about him sometimes, that natural gentleness.

"You...really do like women, don't you?" The question escaped before she realized it wasn't exactly what she meant. She hastened to amend. "I mean, you're good with them...er, *to* them, I mean...."

He chuckled again. "I think that's a compliment you're stumbling all over."

"Yes, it is," she said, relieved he hadn't taken it wrong.

He suggested gently, "Could it be that you're also asking how many there have been?"

She looked at the pretty Oriental-style rug between them. "Well, yes. I suppose that I am."

"More than one." He didn't chuckle that time, but she could hear laughter in his voice. "And less than a hundred. How's that?"

Her head came up. She could feel the color in her cheeks. "It's not very specific, if you want the truth."

Now he looked rather solemn. "I'll tell you this.

I take my promises seriously. Today, I promised to be true to you. And I will.'' He looked at her sideways then. ''You gonna be true to me?''

Though she knew it was a tad unreasonable, she felt vaguely put out with him for even having to ask. ''Of course I will.''

''You sure? After all, I was your first and only...so far. Maybe you'll end up regretting that you didn't try out a few more before ending up with me.''

''Well, I will not. Not the way *you* mean, anyway.''

''And what way do I mean?''

He honestly was beginning to irritate her. ''That's not fair.''

''You started it. And why wouldn't you wonder about other men? You said yourself that you're not in love with me.''

She glanced away from the strange light in his eyes, then made herself face him. ''Why would I want some other man touching me, with the way it was that night between us?''

His smile was slow, the sweetest thing she'd ever seen. ''You liked how it was that night, between us?''

Her belly was hollowing out, and that lovely, shimmery feeling had started moving all through her. ''Yes. I liked it. I liked it very much.''

He cast a glance toward the four-poster. ''That's a nice, big bed.''

She had to cough again. "Yes. I noticed that."

"Got something in your throat?" He started toward her. "Let me have a look."

Opposing urges struck simultaneously—to run forward into his arms or to back up against the door. She gave in to neither and held her ground. "There is nothing in my throat."

"Well, good." He reached her. "And as long as I'm here, I might as well kiss you." He put his finger under her chin and tipped her face up. "Would a kiss be agreeable to you?"

That wasn't hard to answer. "Uh, yes. A kiss would be very nice."

He obliged, settling his mouth so tenderly over hers. She felt his smile against her lips, and she sighed.

He kissed her for a very long time. It felt just wonderful. And it seemed perfectly natural that he would begin undressing her as he kissed her.

Slowly, he undid the front buttons on her dress. Then he peeled the dress open and slid it over her shoulders. It dropped to the floor.

She stepped to the side, free of the dress, and he went with her, his lips still playing over hers, taking her slip straps in those gentle fingers of his and guiding them over her arms. She held her mouth to his eagerly, kissing him back as she shimmied the slip down and over her hips.

Next, she kicked off her shoes, her heart pounding

deep and hard, all of her warm and quivery and hungry for the pleasure she knew he could bring to her.

Being married to someone who knew how to kiss definitely had advantages, she decided, as he took away her bra and then pushed at her panty hose. She had to break the kiss to wiggle out of them.

When she tossed the wad of nylon aside, he was looking at her. She felt just fine, having him look. He had looked at her on *that* night, and it hadn't bothered her at all then, either. Of course, then the room had been swathed in shadow. Now, the sun shone golden and bright beyond the lace-curtained double-hung windows.

But even with the light so bright and unforgiving, she didn't mind. It seemed a natural thing, to be naked with him.

He brushed the back of his index finger over her breast, which she knew was fuller than it had been the last time. The nipple was pebbled up, hard and pouting with her excitement.

He touched her belly. "I can see the roundness now."

She looked at his hand, then laid her own over it, thinking of the baby, so tiny inside her, the hands of both father and mother pressed so close right then. Could he—or she—feel that? Was it possible the baby knew?

She looked at Nash again.

He said, "Your eyes are shining."

"It just hit me. There really is a baby inside me.

And everybody who should know about it does know about it. I don't have to be so…miserable anymore. I don't have to be so worried. I can just…"

He hooked his free hand around her neck, under the waves of her hair. "You can just what?"

"Well, I can get on with living, I guess."

His hand was warm and rough on her neck, massaging, making her sigh a little. "And that's good?"

"Yes. That's wonderful."

He caressed her cheek, ran the side of his finger over her lips. She opened her mouth a little and touched that finger with her tongue. And then, with a low sound, he hauled her close again. He kissed her deeply, then lifted her high and carried her to the bed.

He laid her down carefully, as if she were the most fragile of women. And then he stood back to remove his clothes.

Once he was naked, too, she held up her arms to him. He came down to her, laid his hard, lean-muscled body against hers. He kissed her breasts and her belly, where their baby lay sleeping. And then his mouth went lower. He parted the tender folds and kissed her in her most private place, slow and gentle, then deeper, until she clutched his head and moaned and writhed on the white sheets.

It wasn't long before she hit the peak. Pleasure pulsed and cascaded through her, clear and pure as water from some deep mountain spring. He held her hips in his rough hands and continued his endless, intimate kiss until the waves of pleasure faded to a soft, lovely glow.

Then he slid up her body and he filled her.

He rode her slow and sweet at first, putting his big hands on either side of her head, tangling his fingers in her hair. He looked at her as he moved within her, his eyes moss-green, full of color and light.

Again, her climax rolled through her, starting slowly this time and increasing in intensity. Her body bowed toward him. He rode her harder. She wrapped her legs around his lean hips and clutched him to her heart, hitting the peak a second time as she felt his completion taking him. They cried out together as fulfillment sang through both of them at once.

I love you. I love you, Nash. The words came into her mind and echoed there, insistent, unwilling to fade.

But of course, she didn't say them. She was not the foolish, romantic child she had once been. She desired him. She loved making love with him. They were going to have a baby. And he had married her to do the right thing.

Love was something else again. Love took time to build. After what had happened with Bryan, she'd learned her lesson. A woman could fool herself too easily when it came to loving a man.

A while later, they bathed and got dressed and took a long walk along Clear Creek Trail, which wound its way through the heart of the town. Box elders and willows shaded their progress, and they picked out patches of wild roses, yellow monkey flowers and the little five-petaled faces of blue flax along the way.

Blackbirds and magpies chattering at them as they went, Nash talked of the future. He told her that he and her father were making plans to improve on the already solid reputation of the Big Sky. They were going to make some changes to the breeding program, become even more selective as to which mares they used for breeding stock. And they planned to buy a few more top-quality stallions. With Nash around to supervise the training, Frank hoped to enter more of their horses in quarter horse shows and rodeo competitions.

"We want to build ourselves a reputation for raising more than just solid working horses," Nash said. "We want to be known as the best quarter horse outfit around."

Suzanna listened and encouraged him and thought that maybe all her fears had been groundless, after all. Until now, he might have been the kind of man who'd spent most of his life moving from one ranch job to the next. But right then, he sounded like a man who liked where he was and had no intention of leaving. Her heart felt lighter the longer he talked.

They ate at a nice place on Main Street, and they talked money. How much it would cost to buy those stallions they needed. How much they had—and how much they'd need to borrow. Since she handled the books, Suzanna had a pretty good idea of what it was going to require.

Her heart soared when he teased that he knew where they could get fifty thousand easy. It wasn't near enough, he said, but it would help, wouldn't it?

"It certainly would," she agreed with alacrity, thinking that his willingness to invest his life savings was just more proof that he truly did intend to settle down for good—on the Big Sky, with her and their child.

They lingered over dessert. He talked of some of the outfits he'd worked for over the years and asked her how she'd liked college out in California.

"I'll tell you this," she replied. "I always knew I'd come home."

He looked at her quizzically.

She leaned toward him across the table. "What does that look mean?"

He shrugged. "We're having such a good time. I don't want to ruin it by asking the wrong thing."

"Go on, say it," she told him. "I can take it, whatever it is."

He looked doubtful, but he did confess. "I was just wondering what that fiancé of yours knew about horse ranching."

"You were, huh?" She wrinkled her nose at him. "Yeah. I was."

"Well, then, I'll tell you. Bryan Cummings didn't

know a thing about horse ranching—and he didn't *want* to know a thing about it, either.''

"Then why did *you* want to marry him?''

She fiddled with her teaspoon, stirring the tea the waitress had brought her, though by that time it was too cold to drink. "To be embarrassingly honest, I hadn't thought a lot further than the wedding and the honeymoon. Bryan had a job lined up in San Francisco, working for an organization called the People's Antipoverty Brigade. I was going to move there with him. But in my heart, I knew that somehow, eventually, I would convince him to give all that up and move to Montana with me." She tapped the teaspoon on the side of the cup and set it carefully in her saucer. "Pretty foolish, wasn't I?''

Nash said nothing, only watched her with a bemused expression on his rugged face.

She added, "The fact is, the best thing Bryan Cummings ever did for me was to run off and join the Peace Corps on our wedding day.''

A smile was flirting with the corners of Nash's mouth. "But you didn't think so at the time.''

She lifted her chin. "No, I did not. At the time, I went a little wild.''

"I guess you did." He reached across the table and took her hand. "Wild enough to pick up some no-account cowboy and spend the night with him.''

"I beg your pardon." She captured his thumb inside her fingers and gave it a squeeze. "That cowboy was not a no-account. That cowboy was my future husband.''

They laughed together, and Suzanna knew with absolute certainty that everything was going to work out just fine. She was happy at that moment, holding Nash's hand across the table, happy in a way she hadn't been in a long, long time.

Maybe, she thought, she'd never been quite this happy. Never known this lovely, *fulfilled* kind of feeling, with her baby lying peacefully under her heart and her husband's hand surrounding hers and their shared laughter in her ears.

They returned to the Clear Creek Inn at a little after ten. Suzanna had barely shut the door behind them when Nash reached for her and started kissing her and taking off her clothes.

She kissed him back and unbuttoned his shirt for him, laughing a little at her eagerness to do again what they'd already done just a few hours ago.

He barely got his jeans and boots off before he was lifting her, guiding her legs around him and sliding inside her. Her body gave him not the slightest resistance. She was wet, primed for him.

She held his broad shoulders and let her head fall back, moaning. He put his mouth at her neck, licking and sucking, walking backward until he got to the bed.

Once there, he sat down, with her in his lap, her legs wrapped tight around his hips. It felt so wonderful, she couldn't help but cry out. Maybe she cried a little too loud, because he put his hand over her mouth as those waves of fulfillment cascaded through her again.

Then he finished, too, and she returned the favor, kissing him to keep him from shouting the house down. Finally, they collapsed across the bed, snickering together like a pair of very naughty kids.

They fell asleep sometime after midnight, dropping off with their arms and legs twined together, so that Suzanna's last thought before sleep claimed her was that it was hard to tell where she ended and he began.

It seemed to Suzanna that the three days that followed were a little bit of heaven on earth. They explored the wilderness area outside town together, visited the huge, spring-fed tree-shaded public pool—the largest in Wyoming, everyone said. They studied the contents of the glass display cases in the Jim Gatchell Museum, then walked the narrow halls of the historic Occidental Hotel, where the Virginian finally got his man.

They talked and they laughed. They made love at every opportunity. And they slept close together.

Oh, how Suzanna loved that, dropping off with Nash all wrapped around her—and then maybe coming half-awake a little before dawn, with his arm across her waist, his broad chest warm and solid at her back. She felt so *close* to him then. As if they'd been sleeping that way for years and years. Just an old married couple, close and safe and intimate in the big canopy bed. She would drift back to sleep with a smile curving her lips.

Monday night, the last night of their brief honeymoon, they stayed awake very late, making love and then whispering together about nothing in particular, then making love again. When they finally fell asleep, it was after two.

Suzanna woke sometime later to a feeling of…absence.

Nash had left their bed.

She opened her eyes and dragged herself up against the headboard.

He was standing at the lace-curtained window, looking out at the night.

"Nash? What's wrong?"

He dropped the edge of the lace panel and turned to her, the muscles of his powerful shoulders gleaming silver, limned in starlight.

"Nothing." His voice was flat, lacking emotion, the way it had been that night they planned their marriage, when she had sensed that something was bothering him, though he'd later told her it wasn't so. She peered at him through the darkness, seeking…what?

She couldn't say exactly. And she couldn't see his eyes. The only light came from outside, behind him. He seemed a stranger all over again at that moment, a stranger in her bedroom in the dark. She could have switched on the lamp, but something held her back from that, some feeling that he wanted the darkness and too much light would only make him turn away from her.

She waited, longing for him to come to her. When he just stood there, she couldn't bear it and held out her hand.

He did come then, the shape of him so perfect and male and beautiful to her, lean and economical, all hardness and ready power. He took her hand and sat on the bed beside her, leaning his body across hers, bracing his other hand on the mattress near her hip.

At last, she could see his eyes. He looked at her probingly. "It's good," he said. "This thing between us."

Much better than good, she thought. But all she said, very softly, was, "Yes."

"You really think it's going to last?" He tried to sound offhand, yet there was such intensity in his eyes.

She took time before she answered. It seemed very important that she give him a thoughtful reply, not just toss something off.

He spoke again before she could come up with the words she sought. "In my experience, nothing lasts all that long. Look at us, that first night. It was good then, wasn't it?"

She nodded.

He finished. "And then, in the morning, you were gone."

She licked her lips, swallowed. "Nash. I thought you understood how confused I was that night."

"I do understand. I'm not blaming you. I'm just saying that you did leave."

"I'm not going anywhere now. We're married now."

He looked so sad. "A marriage is a promise. And sometimes, even when people have the best intentions in the world, promises get broken. When my real father died, I remember my mother trying to get me not to worry. She promised she'd take care of me. And I believed her. I knew she loved me a lot and she'd never have done anything to hurt me. But in the end, she married my stepfather, and she didn't take such good care of me, after all. She broke her promise, even though she never meant to. He was so damn mean. She never could stand against him, even for my sake."

"Oh, Nash. I'm so sorry." She put her hand on his shoulder, a touch meant to soothe. He still bore very faint, pale welts there, fine lines of scar tissue, where the cruel belt had struck. She could feel them, just barely, beneath the pads of her fingers.

Carefully, he shrugged out from under her touch, a gentle but firm rejection of her sympathy. She let go of his shoulder—but not of his hand. That she held tighter than before.

She told him steadily, "I won't break my promise

to you, Nash. And I know we can make it last. If we stick together, if we work hard to stay open to each other, to build a good, honest life.''

He looked at their twined hands. ''A good, honest life.'' He glanced up. ''Sounds real solid.''

''I think it could be. I think we could make it that way.''

''You think what we have is solid?''

''I said, I think it could be solid.''

''You're only twenty-two. You've got a college education and you come from a good family. If I hadn't slipped up and forgotten to wear a condom that one time, you would never have—''

''Nash.'' She reached out, brushed his dark hair off his forehead.

''What?''

I love you. There were those words again.

But wouldn't that be too easy, just to say those three words?

She needed time to make sure the words were true. To *earn* the right to say them to him, the same way Nash wanted to earn what he owned.

''We're married,'' she said, instead of *I love you.* ''And I want to make it work. I honestly do.''

He squeezed her hand, and his eyes seemed to lighten a little. ''All right.'' He looked at her for a long moment, then he leaned forward and kissed her, a kiss that started out sweet and quickly turned hungry.

Soon, neither of them felt much like talking anymore. He slid under the covers with her and he loved her again.

And later, when she wondered what had gone wrong, she couldn't help thinking that whatever it was, it had started right then, when she'd awakened to find him at the window and hadn't known what to say to ease the doubts in his mind.

Chapter 7

They drove home after lunch the next day. Nash was quiet during the drive, but then Suzanna didn't feel much like talking herself. They'd been up so late the night before. She was tired—and a little sad, as well. Their honeymoon had been lovely. Too bad it had to be over so soon. She wouldn't have minded a little more time just for the two of them, time to get past the doubts that had troubled him last night.

At home, the ranch would make its demands on them. They'd have their nights together. But long, leisurely hours in each other's company would be harder to come by. She was jealous of that, she realized with some surprise. Jealous of the hours they couldn't be together.

Which was silly and childish and extremely self-indulgent. They had a horse ranch to run, for heaven's sake. Life was not a honeymoon—darn it, anyway.

She must have sighed or done something to betray her melancholy mood, because Nash turned to her with a worried frown. "You all right?"

She sent him a wan smile. "Fine. A little tired, I guess."

His frown deepened. "Maybe you'd better call Doc Winters when we get to the ranch."

Now she was frowning, too. "What for? You know I saw him just last week. He said everything was fine." Nash had gone with her for her first pre-natal visit, on the day they got their blood tests.

"But if you're feeling sick—"

"Nash, I'm not sick. I've been feeling just fine for days, as a matter of fact." And she had. The morning sickness that had dogged her for over a month had faded the past week or so. "I'm just a little tired." *And our honeymoon is over and I wish that it wasn't.* "I need a nap, not a visit to the doctor."

"I still think you should—"

"I said I am fine." She hadn't meant to snap at him. It just came out that way, impatient and angry-sounding.

He turned back to the road.

"I'm sorry," she said softly.

"For what?"

"Sounding so mean."

He shrugged and said it was okay, but he didn't say another word the rest of the way.

When they got home, he insisted that she go upstairs and take the nap she needed.

She didn't argue with him. She thought a nap was an excellent idea. An idea that would be even more excellent if her husband agreed to take a nap, too.

She gave him a look from under her lashes. "I will, if you'll come with me."

He shook his head. "I'd probably better go on out and find Frank. I'll let him know we're home, see what needs doing around here and get after it."

She knew he was right, of course. Besides the breeding and training of horses, there were always fences that needed mending and ditches that required burning. Not to mention hay fields to tend and cattle to look after. The herd they kept was small but necessary. You couldn't train a good cow horse without cattle for the animal to practice on.

Suzanna made a sour face. "Oh, all right. Go on and get back to work." She thought of their room at the Clear Creek Inn and had to suppress more sighing as she wished they were still there.

Nash went upstairs with her briefly, to their new room, the one in the southwest corner that had once been Diana's. It was a little larger than Suzanna's old room, and it had its own bathroom, too. Last week, before the wedding, Nash and Frank had moved Suzanna's queen-size bed in there, along with her bow-fronted bureau and an extra dresser for Nash.

Suzanna kicked off her shoes, stretched out on the bed and watched her husband change into work clothes. He came close and bent down to kiss her on the forehead before he left.

"You could at least give me a real kiss, since you insist on leaving me here alone," she muttered grumpily.

He chuckled. Was that the first time she'd seen him smile all day? "A real kiss, huh?"

"Uh-huh. On the lips. Like you mean it."

He did just that. Then he stood tall above her. "Rest now," he commanded.

"Oh, all right." She sat up, punched at her pillow, then flopped down again.

"Don't worry about dinner," he said before he went out. "Frank and I can rustle up something."

"No way will I be on my back at dinnertime. I'll cook. And you'll eat it."

He really was grinning now. "Yes, ma'am." And then he left.

Suzanna closed her eyes.

When she opened them again, it was after five and she felt rejuvenated. She got up and went downstairs and pulled some cube steaks from the freezer.

Nash and her father came in at a little after six, both covered in mud acquired while hauling a stubborn bull out of the pond in the south pasture. Suzanna sent them upstairs to get cleaned up and had the dinner on the table when they came down.

Frank asked how his daughter and his son-in-law had enjoyed their stay in Buffalo. Suzanna told him all about the beauty of the northeastern Wyoming countryside, about how homey and comfortable they'd found the Clear Creek Inn.

Her father's smile was knowing. "Sounds like you two had yourselves a real good time."

Suzanna felt the warmth in her cheeks. Why, she was blushing like some silly fool. She shot a glance at Nash, who said calmly, "Yes. A real good time."

"Well, I'm glad to hear it," her father replied, his tone grave, his eyes gleaming.

Suzanna picked up her fork and paid attention to her cube steak. Soon enough, as always, the talk turned to horses.

After they'd eaten, Nash and Frank went out to look over the training schedule together. Nash needed filling in on how the colts had performed in his absence.

Suzanna didn't know what time her father came in, but Nash didn't appear till after eleven.

Suzanna was already in bed. She sat up and turned on the lamp when she heard the bedroom door creak slowly open. Her husband stood in the doorway, his boots in his hand, squinting against the sudden burst of light.

"Er, sorry. Thought you'd be asleep...."

She knew immediately what he'd been up to. "Having a few belts with the boys, huh?"

He shoved the door shut and set his boots down. "They had to have a li'l toast, to the new bridegroom."

She shook her head. "Looks to me like it turned out to be more than one toast."

His mouth flattened out. "You mad?"

She smiled. "No." And she wasn't. She'd been irritated earlier, when he hadn't come in by eight or by nine. But then she'd given herself a stern talking-to. They weren't at the Clear Creek Inn anymore. He had his work to do, and he had a right to a little free time of his own, as well.

Besides, she'd reasoned, harping at him wasn't going to help lure him to her side. She had better ways to do that. Like wearing her prettiest little shorty nightgown, the pink one with the matching pink lace panties, which Nash had told her made a man think only of getting to what was underneath.

She lifted the covers and held them open for him. "Come on to bed."

Something happened in his face. Something almost too painful to witness. She dropped the covers and leaned toward him. "Nash. What's wrong?"

He cut his eyes away. "Nothing. I think I'll brush my teeth first."

"Are you sure you're—?"

He didn't even let her finish her sentence. "I said

there's nothing." His voice was rock-hard. "Turn off the light. I'll be there in a minute."

She obeyed him, rather numbly, wondering what she had done to make him look at her that way, as if she'd cut him to the quick somehow. She'd only smiled at him, held open the covers, sweetly suggested that he come on to bed.

She heard his feet whispering across the floor. The bathroom door opened and then clicked shut. There were the sounds of water running, of the toilet flushing.

Finally, the door opened again. A wedge of light fell briefly across the bed, then winked out. He came to stand over her in the dark. She heard the rustle of his clothing as he undressed.

Then he slid in next to her.

They lay there in silence.

Strangers, she thought. Strangers all over again...

Right then, their honeymoon closeness seemed like no more than a dream. A wishful fantasy of her yearning heart. The same as their first night had sometimes seemed to her, far away, unreal, something magical and wild that had happened to someone else.

"Nash," she whispered into the darkness. "Something *is* wrong. Just tell me. Just—"

He lifted up and canted over her so suddenly that she gasped. "I told you. Nothing." She smelled whiskey and toothpaste and that arousing scent that was only him. The three-quarter moon shone in the front window, its silvery light catching in his eyes. Feral and dark, those eyes. The eyes of a stranger.

But then he breathed her name. "Suzanna." He looked at her mouth.

A small, lost cry escaped her.

He took that cry, lowering his lips to hers and drinking the sound as if it were liquid, her need, her confusion, her desire to share again what they had so briefly known.

Together.

His rough-tender hand found her thigh and trailed under the short hem of her gown. He traced the elastic of her lace panties with a finger, then hooked that finger under them. She lifted herself, her mouth still locked with his, so that he could pull them down.

Then he raked the gown upward, the lace abrading her skin in the most erotic way. He found her breast, his hand closing over that fullness with heat and undeniable possession. She surged toward his touch—and he let go, only to take that burning touch lower. He found the female heart of her, found it ready, open, weeping for him.

He swallowed another of her lost, hungry cries as he slid on top of her, positioned himself and, with a quick pulse of his hips, came into her.

She cried again, the sound muffled, as her other cries had been, by his consuming kiss. He pushed into her, pulled back—and waited. She whimpered. Still, he held himself just slightly away.

She could not bear that, the feel of him inside,

but not fully. Hers but not completely. And he went on kissing her, driving her wild with his lips and his tongue, while down there he kept himself just a little away.

With a low sound of pure need, she shoved her hands under his arms, swiftly, forcefully, so that he had no time to stop her. She grasped his hard hips and pulled him sharply in to fill her again.

He moaned into her mouth then. She surged up, tighter, closer still.

And at last, he gave in to her. He moved with her, rocking into her, rocking back, rolling to the side, so that she was on top, then rolling again, to end up above her.

She rolled with him, clutching him close, wild and needful, alive to each separate, delicious thrust. She kissed him as he kissed her, in a never-ending, liquid pulse of purest sensation. The sensation spread out, a ripple in a pond of light, traveling wider and wider in a bright, burning circle, until it encompassed the room, the night, the moon and all the stars in the dark Montana sky.

Finally, he pushed in so deep, deeper than any of the thrusts that had gone before. She held him, felt his satisfaction taking him in a long, hard shudder. She shuddered in kind.

He said her name again on a low, endless groan.

And then it was over, leaving her limp, her body fulfilled, her mind and heart sad and just a little bit empty.

"Nash?"

He slid to the side and gathered her close, the way he'd done each of the four wonderful nights in Wyoming, so that her back was against his chest, his legs cradling hers.

"Sh. Go to sleep now." He brushed her hair aside, kissed her nape.

"But, Nash—"

"Go to sleep, Suzanna."

Almost, she tried again. Almost, she softly pleaded, *Please. Talk to me....*

But no.

Not tonight. She'd tried over and over again already tonight, and each time he'd rebuffed her. He'd made it so painfully clear that he wasn't in a talking mood.

Let it go for tonight, she thought. There will be time. Soon, very soon, I'll get him to talk to me, to tell me what's wrong.

Suzanna closed her eyes. She concentrated on relaxing, on how good and right it felt to have her husband's arms around her. Eventually, she managed to drop off to sleep.

Chapter 8

Frank left for Gillette on Thursday. From the horse show there, he'd go on to visit an old school friend in Colorado. He'd decided to stay in Colorado a bit longer than he'd originally planned. For three weeks, Nash and Suzanna would have the house to themselves.

Surely, Suzanna told herself, the privacy would be good for them. The intimacy they'd known at the Clear Creek Inn would be theirs again.

She tried, in the mornings before Nash left the house and in the evenings when they sat alone at the table, to reach out to him. At first, by asking what was bothering him.

When she saw that her questions only made him

close up tighter against her, she tried to talk of safer things. Of his plans for the breeding program, of which shows he wanted to see their horses enter in the months to come.

He would answer her questions, but he never really volunteered anything. More and more she felt that their conversations were like strained interviews. She asked, he answered—and then there was silence unless she asked something more.

For a few too-brief and shining days, she had thought she was coming to know him. Now she wondered if what they'd shared in Buffalo was all she would ever really have of him. A memory of closeness slipping further and further off into the past.

In the first few days after Frank left, when her work in the office was done and the house in order, she would get out Isabelle's letters and read them again and again. She was seeking some clue, some sign from her ancestor, something that would tell her what she needed to do to make her husband open his mind and heart to her again.

Isabelle wrote of an amulet given to her on her wedding day by Kyle's Cheyenne aunt, Mae, an amulet that Mae had promised would secure Kyle's love for all time.

Was that what Suzanna needed? An amulet to charm him? Unfortunately, no distant Cheyenne relative had appeared to provide one.

Suzanna racked her brain for new ways to reach

him. She went to the corrals every day, ready to ride any horse he would put her on, being helpful and hoping that he might ride with her.

He always had some reason he couldn't accompany her right then. He would tell her which colt to choose and what to watch for in the animal's behavior, and then he would leave her to ride out alone.

She tried enlisting his aid in fixing up her old room for the baby. On the last Thursday in June, when her father had been gone exactly a week, she drove all the way to Billings to get wallpaper books and fabric samples to share with Nash. He barely glanced at them.

"Whatever you want to do," he said, "that's fine with me."

Every night he went out after dinner and didn't come in until very late. She would lie in their bed alone and listen for the sound of his pickup leaving.

But he never went anywhere—except out to the bunkhouse with the other men. Suzanna knew what went on out there, and it was nothing to worry about, really. They played cards, watched TV, drank a few beers.

She kept telling herself that as long as he only went to the bunkhouse, it didn't really mean anything. He'd spent half the nights of his life in a bunkhouse, after all. He was used to hanging out with the boys. He felt at home there.

Now that was depressing. Her husband felt more

at home in the bunkhouse than with her. And depressing wasn't the only word for it.

It was scary, too. It made her fear that her original doubts about him ever truly settling down had been valid. That the real Nash Morgan was the cowboy she'd called Slim, good to horses and to women but not someone likely to stick around for too long.

Some night, and some night soon, he wouldn't just visit the bunkhouse. He'd get in his pickup and he'd head for a place like the one where she'd met him. He'd stay out all night and he'd come home smelling of whiskey and some other woman's perfume.

Maybe she'd forgive him. The first time.

But eventually, she'd run out of forgiveness.

And he would run out of patience with staying in one place.

He would leave her, with his name and his baby to remember him by.

Lord, it made her sad to think that.

Or at least, it made her sad at first.

But soon enough, as the days went by, she stopped being quite so sad.

She started to get mad.

She stopped trying to reach out to him, to get him to talk to her, to coax him to show an interest in the baby's room or to share with her his plans and dreams. She fed him his meals and she spoke to him only when necessary, and at night, when he came in late, she turned on her side away from him and pretended to be asleep.

On the first Thursday in July, when Frank had been gone for two weeks, Suzanna woke to the awareness that she did not intend to keep on like this.

She rolled over, toward the still form of her husband. He slept on his side, with his back to her. They both slept like that now, hugging their separate sides of the big bed, like strangers on a large, soft raft, floating in a vast sea of words not spoken.

Strangers.

Yes. Strangers so careful of intruding on each other's space.

It had to stop. She didn't care anymore if it drove him away for good. She was going to confront him. And, one way or another, she would make him listen to what she had to say—whatever it *was* that she had to say. She wasn't really sure yet what that should be. But she would find the words somehow.

As she glared at his back, he stirred.

Without turning her way, he pushed aside the covers and left the bed.

"Nash?"

For a determined woman with real anger in her heart, her voice sure did come out soft—barely a whisper, really.

Either he didn't hear it or he didn't want to hear it. He went into the bathroom and closed the door.

He got away from her at breakfast, too, slipping out while her back was turned as she went to clear the table. And then he didn't show up for lunch.

But he did come in at dinner. He went upstairs to clean up. She waited until he'd had time to get into the shower before she followed him.

When he emerged from the bathroom, he found her sitting on the bed. He gave her a quick glance, then ignored her as he swiftly dressed in clean clothes.

He'd sat in the corner chair to pull his boots on when she said in a clear, concise tone, "Nash, I don't know what I have done to make you turn away from me, but I want you to give me a chance to understand. I want you to tell me what it is that's been eating at you for the past two weeks." She stopped, breathed, swallowed and added, "Please."

He pulled on his right boot and then the left. Then he planted both boots firmly on the floor and looked at her.

He looked for a long time, his gaze running over her face. She had no clue what he might be thinking. Was he studying her to gauge how much she could take? Or *memorizing* her? That was what it felt like. As if he were storing her face in his memory.

But why would he need to do that? Unless…

No, she would not think that. She wouldn't. He was not planning to leave her. He couldn't be….

At last, he stood and told her gently, "Suzanna.

You haven't done anything. There's nothing wrong.''

She gaped at him. And then she couldn't help it. She let a growling sound rise up from her throat and she said, "You are a liar, Nash Morgan. A damn liar, and you know it."

He sighed. He had the nerve to stand there in front of her and to *sigh*. "Suzanna…"

She fisted her hands, though what she really wanted to do was grab something and throw it at him. "You have been strange since the last night we were in Buffalo. I don't like it. I want it to stop. I want you to tell me—"

He raised a hand. "I'm going out."

She jumped to her feet. "No. No, you are not going out. You are going to stay here and—"

But he was already at the door to the hall. "Don't wait up."

"Nash!"

He didn't stop. He just kept on going, into the hall and down the stairs. She heard the front door shut.

She rushed to the window and watched him walk out the front gate. He left her line of vision as he headed in the direction of the wagon shed.

She knew what was coming.

And she was right.

Moments later, she heard the roar of an engine. His pickup appeared, swinging into the drive. He sped off, leaving a high trail of dust in his wake.

Chapter 9

Suzanna's righteous anger failed her as she watched Nash race away from her. She stood at the window for a long time, until all the dust of his leaving had settled. Until the shadows began to lengthen and the bats came out.

Then, at last, she went downstairs, cleared the clean dishes off the table and put the untouched dinner away in the refrigerator. That accomplished, she climbed the stairs, took off her clothes and soaked in the bathtub for an hour and a half.

Then she put on another shorty nightgown—the blue one this time—and she got into bed.

The hours crawled past. She did try to sleep, but sleep wouldn't come and relieve her of her misery.

So she just lay there, staring at the ceiling, rolling over, hitting her pillow to try to fluff it up a little, lying down, staring at the wall.

It was after two when she heard his pickup again. She threw back the covers and raced to the window. He stopped in the turnaround outside the picket fence. She watched him emerge from the driver's side, slam the door and approach the gate. He strode up the walk and then disappeared beneath the overhang of the front porch.

She was standing by the window, in the dark, when he came in the room. He paused in the doorway.

"Mind if I turn on the light?"

"Go ahead."

She blinked at the brightness when he flicked the switch. When she opened her eyes again, he was striding to the closet.

He got out his big, battered canvas duffel, carried it to a chair by his dresser and started pulling his clothes from the drawers.

Apparently, he was leaving her.

Her worst fear coming true.

She asked softly, "Have you been with some other woman tonight?"

He froze, turned to her. His eyes looked dead. "No."

She believed him. But it didn't make her feel any better.

"Where are you going?"

"Into town, for the night at least."

"And then?"

He paused in the act of pulling open a drawer. "Suzanna. Face it. It's time I moved on."

"Moved on?" She echoed his words as if their meaning eluded her. Then she cast about frantically for all the reasons he couldn't leave. "But...what about the Big Sky? What about all your plans? What about my dad? My dad *depends* on you."

He started piling socks and underwear into the duffel. "The Big Sky and your dad were getting along just fine before I showed up."

"But he—we...we *need* you."

"No, you don't. You needed my name. So our baby wouldn't be a bastard. And you've got it. For as long as you want it."

"No. No, that's not so. It's not just your *marrying* me. It isn't. I need *you,* Nash. I need you as my husband. Our baby needs you."

He shook his head. He didn't even glance at her. He only went on loading up that duffel bag.

Her legs didn't feel all that steady. She made them carry her to the end of the bed and then let herself sink down onto it.

He left the duffel. She watched him stride across the hooked rug and disappear into the bathroom. She stared at the open bathroom door, wishing, *yearning,* for the right words to come to her, the words that would make him change his mind and stay.

A few minutes later, he returned with his shaving gear. He put it in the bag with everything else.

She sucked in a tight breath and made herself speak with excruciating civility. "Would you mind, now that you're going, just telling me why?"

He froze—and he turned and looked at her. "Why?" he said. She wasn't certain what he meant. Maybe, *Why do you want to know?* Or just, *Why?* all by itself, just repeating her own question back at her.

She licked her dry lips and smoothed the lace of her skimpy nightie over her thighs. Her throat felt as if someone was squeezing it. She had to work to suck in a deep breath, but she managed it. Then she attempted to explain herself.

"It seemed, at first, that we were doing so well. I just don't understand, that's all. Where did it go wrong?"

"It doesn't matter." His voice held no inflection. But there was something in his eyes, something that told her it mattered very much.

"I think it does." She got the words out in a whisper. "I think it does matter, and for some reason, it's…terribly hard for you to say it. Harder than just picking up and leaving me."

He seemed to have forgotten the duffel and all the clothes he'd stuffed into it. He stood there, arms limp at his sides, staring at her.

She pulled in more air through her constricted throat and suggested quite reasonably, "After all, you've had a lot of practice at leaving. But telling your wife what she's done to...hurt you. Well, I'm pretty sure you have never tried that before.''

"It's not your fault." His voice was harsh—yet somehow tender at the same time.

"But there is something?"

A muscle worked in his jaw. "Nothing you can do anything about."

"Well. That may be so. But if you told me, it would...help me." She felt a smile quiver across her mouth as she added, "Men keep leaving me, have you noticed? And it would be nice if someone would tell me why."

"Suzanna..." He took a step toward her, then seemed to catch himself and stayed where he was. "I haven't got a clue why that fool you were going to marry before joined the Peace Corps."

"Well, okay. But you. Why are *you* leaving?"

His mouth worked. She really thought he was going to tell her the truth. Then he loosed a crude oath and muttered, "Just...leave a man a little pride, won't you?"

"What? I don't—"

"Just let it be!" He shouted the words.

She ordered strength into her legs and made herself stand. "No, Nash. I can't. I really can't do that. I want you to tell me. I *need* you to tell me. Why are you leaving me? What have I done?"

He swore again, and his expression was thunderous. "All right. All right, since you just have to know." She waited, not even realizing she was holding her breath until he said, "I love you. All right? Damn it, I love you."

Chapter 10

Suzanna let the air out of her lungs in a rush and sank to the edge of the bed. "You...I...what?"

"I love you." He said it again, like he was rubbing it in. "I love you, and damn it, I *hate* loving you. It's nothing but a stone heartache for me."

All she could do was sputter. "B-but, if you love me, then why—"

He sliced the air with a hand. "You want to hear it? You want to hear *all* of it? Is that what you want?"

"I...yes. I do. I really do."

"You want to hear how, after that first night, I couldn't forget you? How all I did was think about you, think about the way you were that night...so sweet and so wild?"

"The way I was that first night? Since that first night, you—"

"—couldn't forget. That's right. Like some messed-up, lovesick kid, I couldn't forget. I told myself for weeks that it was only the whole idea that I was the first one for you. That I was just getting old enough that I needed someone to yearn for, needed the one that got away to dream about while I lived my life in other men's bunkhouses and wondered if I'd ever really get my own place."

"You...thought about me? All the time?"

His mouth curled into something she could only have called a snarl. "Yeah. I thought about you. I was pining for you." He gestured widely, a move that seemed to take in the room and the big, generations-old house, the acres and acres that made up the Big Sky. "And this job I took here? You want to know the real reason I took it?"

"Yes. I do. I—"

"I took it because good old Frank pulled a picture out of his wallet, a picture of his younger daughter on Chocolate Jessie, that King broodmare of yours." Nash let out a pained laugh. "Poor Frank. He thought I was impressed by the look of that horse. Well, it wasn't the damn mare that made me sit up and take notice. I came to the Big Sky with my stupid heart in my throat, just for a chance to see Deadeye again."

He shook his head as if he couldn't believe the extent of his own foolishness. Then he started across the room in the direction of the closet, muttering over his shoulder as he went. "And you...you denied me right from the start. You pretended not to know me that first day."

She couldn't let that pass. "But, Nash, you acted like you didn't recognize me, either."

He stopped in the middle of the room and turned to her. "What the hell was I supposed to do? You looked sick to your stomach at the sight of me."

"Well, Nash. I'm pregnant. I *did* feel kind of sick."

He swore some more. "Come on. You didn't *want* me to know you. So I let you off the hook—for a while, anyway. Then you wouldn't even admit to your father that the baby was mine."

"I was trying to admit it. I was doing my best to tell him and I—"

"You would have hemmed and hawed until hell froze over. I had to tell Frank. And then you went on and on about how you wouldn't marry me, wouldn't get yourself hooked up with a stranger, a man you didn't love. And when you finally did agree to be my wife, you refused a *real* wedding with me. For me, you wouldn't wear your grandmother's dress, you wouldn't call your big sister to come stand up beside you. You were eager enough for a big wedding with that college boy who walked out on you. But a big wedding just to marry me? Hell, no."

She said, rather cautiously, "I thought you said you didn't *blame* me."

"I don't. I'm just telling you, telling you how it was."

"But I was trying to be more *mature* this time. I was trying to—"

"Whatever." His broad shoulders rose and fell in a shrug that dismissed her arguments before she could even phrase them. "I realized it that last night in Buffalo. It came crystal clear to me then that every day we were together, I only loved you more. And you...you don't love me. You like what I can do to you in bed. And you want to do the right thing, because of the baby, to be a good wife to me."

"Is that...so awful?"

"Hell, no. It's not awful. It's just...not enough. It's not love. You don't have the same feeling for me that I do for you. You never would have married me if it hadn't been for the baby. But I jumped at the chance to make you my wife."

She tried to speak. But he spoke first. "I jumped too damn fast, I realize that now. All my grown life, I've had sense enough to keep my heart to myself. And I know why. Because it hurts. It hurts like hell. To love someone who doesn't love me back, that's just no good for me. It steals my peace of mind. It leaves me thinkin' all the time that you've got five extra years of education on me. Leaves me thinkin' that we live in your father's house and I work your father's horses, that I haven't given you much of anything but a plain gold wedding band and a baby to tie you down."

That made her mad. "What are you talking

about? I *want* our baby.'' She held up her left hand and shook it at him fiercely. ''And I am proud to wear this ring.''

He wouldn't believe her. ''This was all a giant-size mistake, trying to make a marriage work between us. You can do better than a man like me, and we both know it. And the best thing I can do for both of us is to head on down the trail.'' He turned and strode the rest of the way to the closet. She watched him in misery, wanting to shout at his back that she loved him, too—but certain in her heart that he would never believe her.

She should have told him, that last night in Buffalo, that night when he'd tried to reveal all this to her, that night when she'd been so careful, so *reasonable,* so *mature.*

From the closet, he collected his dress boots and his winter jacket and his few good Western shirts. Then he shut the closet door and started across the room.

''Nash,'' she began, and then said no more.

He wasn't listening. He hooked his shirts and jacket on the back of the chair as he tucked the boots into the duffel. Then he zipped it up and grabbed the handle, scooped up the shirts and jacket and slung them over his shoulder. ''I'll drop by tomorrow to pick up my saddles and my trailer. And after that, I'll keep you posted as to my whereabouts. You'll get regular checks from me. Put them in a college fund for the kid or something. And once the

baby's born, you can send me the divorce papers.
I'll sign them and ship them right on back."

Oh, Lord. He was leaving her. Really leaving her.
"Nash. Please..."

But he turned his back on her. He strode away
from her and disappeared through the door.

Suzanna sat on the bed and listened to his boots
echoing down the hall. It was the sound of him leaving her—this time for good.

She felt poleaxed. Hit square between the eyes
with a big, heavy club.

Nash *loved* her? He loved her and that was why
he'd kept himself from getting close to her?

The more she considered that thought, the more
dazed she felt. So she went on sitting there, on the
end of their bed, turning her thin gold wedding band
around and around on her finger, utterly confused
by the emotions churning inside her.

Shock. And worry. And anger. Why didn't he tell
her all this before?

And...joy. Yes. Joy.

Because...well, because, after all, she did love
him, too.

Down in front, she heard his pickup start up.

That crazy fool. What did he think driving off
would prove? Nothing. Absolutely nothing. He had
another think coming if he thought he could get
away from her!

She jumped to her feet and sprinted across the
floor, flying down the hall, taking the stairs two at
a time. He was turning the pickup around when she

flung back the front door and raced down the porch steps, the lacy hem of her little blue nightie floating high on her thighs.

"Nash! Nash, come back here!"

He swung the truck around, started heading away from her.

She ran faster, her hair flying out behind her, bare feet slapping the paving stones, down the front walk, through the white gate.

"Nash! Nash, you get back here!" Her feet pounded the dirt drive. And she was breathing kind of hard. She had no air left to waste on shouting. She ran for all she was worth, her heart seeming to pound his name through her blood.

Nash. Nash. Nash. Nash...

Thirty yards down the drive, he must have glanced in his rearview mirror and seen her.

The pickup slowed to a stop. She ran faster, right up to his open side window.

He leaned out at her, scowling. "What the hell has gotten into you, woman?" he growled.

So she told him. "*You,* Nash Morgan. You've gotten into me good. I love you, and if you leave me now, I will hunt you down in every roadside bar from here to New York City."

He blinked. "You're crazy."

And she nodded, gasping for breath, clutching the ledge of the window, thinking she'd hold him there with her bare hands if he dared to try driving off again.

"I am," she said, panting. "Crazy in love with

you. I'm gone. There's no hope for me. And I'm calling my dad, Nash. Calling him in Colorado. I'm going to do it right now, at two-thirty in the morning, as soon as you come inside with me. I'm telling my dad that he was right, that you were just the man for me. That I love you. That I went crazy on what was supposed to be my wedding day—and while I was being crazy, I found you.''

She paused, gulped in air, pressed one hand against her racing heart. "And I'm also telling him that I want that big wedding, after all. That I'm marrying you all over again. A real, honest-to-goodness wedding this time. I'll be carryin' Derringer roses...."

She stopped, panted some more, frowned at him. "You know about Derringer roses? White roses from the garden of the Derringer ranch?"

"Damn it, Suzanna, you're out here half-naked."

She shrugged. "It's important. Those roses. They bring good luck."

"Suzanna—"

"And I'll wear my great-great-grandmother's wedding dress. Somehow. If I can just fit into it, with my stomach the way it's getting. And..." All of a sudden, tears were filling her eyes. She dashed them away. "Please. Oh, please, Nash. Believe me. You really are the best thing that ever happened to me, and I don't want to lose you. I *need* you. Our baby needs you. And the Big Sky needs you, too."

He said, "Move back, Suzanna."

Her heart stopped. "Why? No. I won't. I won't let you go!"

He smiled. He actually smiled. That tender smile of his. She understood now it was a smile of pure love. "Suzanna. I only want to get out of the truck."

She stared. "I...oh. Oh, all right." She let go of the door and stepped back.

He got out.

And then he took her in his arms and kissed her. Far away somewhere, a coyote howled.

She whispered, "Marry me, Nash."

And he said, "I believe that I will."

A month later, on the first Saturday in August, Nash and Suzanna had their big wedding, right there in the house that had been in her family for so many years.

Suzanna wore Isabelle's dress—altered temporarily to accommodate her growing stomach with delicate lace panels Suzanna had found in the old trunk upstairs. She carried a bouquet of very special white roses. With a satisfied smile on his craggy face and a tear in his eye, her father gave her away.

Diana was there, too. She'd come home to be her baby sister's maid of honor for the second time.

Late in the day, after the cake had been served and an endless series of toasts raised to the new bride and groom, Suzanna and Nash climbed hand in hand to the top of the stairs. Below them, in the front hall, Diana had gathered all of the single girls and guys.

Nash leaned toward his bride and whispered in her ear. "Garter first, right?"

She turned her head just enough that their lips briefly met. "Right."

Everyone applauded as he knelt before her. Taking her time about it, looking into her husband's beautiful green eyes, Suzanna lifted the delicate lace. Nash's teasing hand glided up the inside of her thigh. She suppressed a sigh of pleasure as she felt him unhook the garter and slowly slide it down.

He stood. Below them, a sea of familiar faces gazed up expectantly. Nash tossed the garter over the banister.

The scrap of blue silk and white lace sailed out—and dropped into the plump, outstretched hand of a blue-eyed, dark-haired child.

"Molly," someone shouted. "Molly Derringer's caught it!"

Nash chuckled. "Blew that one."

But then the little girl turned to the tall man standing next to her. "Here, Daddy. You take this."

Trey Derringer, a handsome widower, held out his hand.

Everyone laughed and applauded and then started calling encouragements.

"The bouquet, Suzanna!"

"Throw it!"

"Throw it now!"

Suzanna, bemused, stared at her sister—who just happened to be looking at Molly Derringer's dad.

"Diana!" Suzanna shouted.

Her sister jerked her glance upward—just in time to see the bouquet coming at her. She caught it, but only to keep it from hitting her in the face.

"Cheater!" someone called out, but good-naturedly.

There was more laughter, more happy cheers.

Nash bent close again and murmured for her ears alone, "You did cheat. You didn't give any of those other girls a chance."

"No," she said proudly. "I certainly did not."

"It was a good shot," he allowed.

"Just call me Deadeye," she said, and lifted her mouth for his tender kiss.

* * * * *

Look for

THE MILLIONAIRE SHE MARRIED.

*The last installment in
Christine Rimmer's popular miniseries,*

CONVENIENTLY YOURS,

available May 2000
from Silhouette Special Edition.

DIANA

Jennifer Greene

Chapter 1

Diana Brennan pushed open the school door and stepped outside. For a second she closed her eyes and breathed in the crisp Montana morning.

It was hard to believe that just weeks ago she'd been a sane, practical, unshakably responsible kind of woman. She'd loved her third-grade teaching job in Chicago. She'd paid her bills, came early to work, ate healthy, was seeing a couple of decent guys.

Now *phfft*. Here she was, in Whitehorn, Montana, on September first, her whole sane life down the tubes. Did a rational woman quit a job she absolutely loved? No. Would an intelligent woman come home for a family wedding and abruptly shuck everything—her job, her income, her apartment, her guys—just because she discovered she was home-sick? Of course not.

It wasn't a pleasant thing, discovering at the young age of twenty-seven that one was suffering from lunacy. At fourteen, sure, she'd been a love-sick, mortifying, romantic dreamer—but what adolescent wasn't a lunatic? She'd grown up. Matured. Competently and capably taken charge of her life. Only, at the moment, she seemed to be standing on the school steps, having applied for substitute teaching work that at best was going to cover her car payments, sniffing the air as if she didn't have a care in the world.

Worse yet, she felt like whistling.

Off to the west, the Crazy Mountains were bathed in sunlight, the sky a spectacular ice blue, the air so fresh it stung the lungs on an inhale. Her dad would be working the horses by now. Hay would be cut today, alfalfa harvested, every live body on the ranch stretched to the work limit at this time of year, and her dad did the training in the morning, the most rambunctious horses first while he had the most patience. She couldn't smell the fresh-cut hay from here, couldn't hear cows bawling just outside of town, couldn't see or smell the long, rolling sweep of meadow and western larch on the road to the Brennans' Big Sky ranch...but it was all there in her mind's eye.

She should never have come home for her sister Suzanna's wedding. There'd been no threat of lunacy before that. She hadn't been a harebrained romantic dreamer, not since her mom died years ago, and for ages she'd talked herself into believing that she loved the excitement of big-city life. Possibly there were a few teensy signs that she was fibbing to herself. She never tried applying her rent money toward a down payment on something she owned. The nice guys came and went; she shied from anything too settled with them, too. But as much as she loved her dad, there was just nothing she really wanted to do on the ranch. She *loved* teaching. She'd been so positive she was happy in Chicago.

Only every single day since Suzanna's wedding, she'd gotten up in the morning and inhaled that Montana air. All this time, she didn't know how fiercely she'd yearned for it, how addictive the smells and tastes and scents of home would be. Surely this problem of lunacy would pass soon. She just had to get her head together and decide what to do next. She'd get practical again. She'd get serious. But right now being home felt *right,* as if her heart recognized all along that it had unfinished business in Whitehorn before she could ever really try settling anywhere else.

Suddenly she heard a child's high-pitched shriek.

Something about the little girl's shrill soprano was familiar but that wasn't why Diana swiftly spun around, her eyes snapping open. She knew children. Which meant she knew children's shrieks. There was a mountain of difference between an earsplit-

ting, Mom-I'm-sick-of-shopping shriek and a cry of
pain or a whine of fear.

This was a shriek of outrage—but Diana also
heard an underlying real fear in the child's cry,
which was why she instinctively responded. Fast.
Her boots charged down the steps, aiming right toward the source of those shrieks, her blue-eyed gaze
darting around the playground.

The school was divided into two wings. The administration wing where Diana had just applied for
substitute teaching work also held the preschoolers,
who were separated from the elementary-age kids
for the obvious reason. The urchins hurtling around
this section of fenced yard were all bitsy size, the
swings and slides smaller and safer for the squirt
set. She saw braids and freckles and runny noses
and apple cheeks and way-cool big jeans and flop-
ping shoelaces.

Her gaze swiveled past the swing sets, then back
again, honing swiftly on the mean-eyed boy in the
red plaid shirt. He was the problem. The little girl
with the head full of bouncy dark curls on the swing
set was his prey. Diana saw him yank on the girl's
hair. Yank hard. So hard that the little girl screamed
again and instinctively reached to try and free her
hair from the bully's clutches—but that unfortunately meant that she had to loosen her grip on the
swing handles.

Diana galloped faster. There was no hope of preventing the little girl from taking a backward tum-

ble. Thankfully the preschool swings were set low to the ground, so the child shouldn't be hurt too badly, but it was still going to be a good fall. The bully was already pumping in the other direction, but from the corner of her eye, Diana caught sight of a long denim skirt—the preschool teacher, who was finally catching on to the problem.

"I'll get her!" she called. When the teacher spun around, Diana motioned toward the bully to identify the culprit and direct the teacher's attention, so she could concentrate solely on the girl.

She reached her in seconds, but the little brunette moppet had already crashed in the dust by then. Diana saw big blue eyes drowning in a whole lake of tears, saw skirts splash up and show off frilly underpants. The head full of magnolia-brown ringlets was sprinkled with good old Montana dust, and the cherry-bud mouth let out a boisterous screech of pain worthy of an Academy Award for sound effects. Diana dove in fast. The swing was waving and weaving like a drunken sailor—ready to slap back and hit the little one again.

"There, there. You're going to be okay, Molly."

She used one hand to steady the swing and scooped the child into her lap with the other. The warm body promptly snuggled to Diana's—although she was still wailing as if a murderer were torturing her. Diana almost smiled. Some kids were born victims. Not this one. This child was never going to take even the slightest injustice without letting the whole world know she was ticked—and yes, Diana recognized her almost instantly. She was Molly.

Trey Derringer's daughter.

Diana had never met Molly before her sister's wedding, but all it took was one look for her to feel a kindred-spirit connection to the child. Remeeting Molly's dad, though, had been a lot more emotionally complicated. Trey was the mortifying crush she'd had when she was fourteen. He'd been her white knight, her Rambo, her dream boat, her prince, her leather-clad biker bad boy—and every other darn fool fantasy an idiotic adolescent girl could think up. That was back in the days when she'd been a full-time romantic lunatic.

Everyone had some embarrassing growing-up moments. Trey had just been her worst—yet a single glance had still brought all those stupid, lustful, yearning feelings back. Maybe there was something lethal in the fresh Montana air. She'd been sane in Chicago. She'd been doing fine all these years. Come home, and in a matter of hours her life had started turning into shambles—she was even drooling after an old crush again, for Pete's sake.

But at that instant, her only concern was Molly. "Remember me, Mol? I'm Diana Brennan. We met in the bathroom at the wedding for my sister, Suzanna, just a couple weeks ago? You had cake in your hair? And you were thinking about murdering the ring bearer who was teasing you. There, there, you're going to be fine, honest. Just let me see...."

But Molly was wrapped around Diana tighter than peanut butter clung to jelly, and she wasn't finished with the boisterous, heartrending sobs. "I hate all boys!"

"Believe me, I understand."

"I hated that Jimmy Rae who put cake in my hair. And I hate Walter Tucker even worse. All boys should drown in a bathtub with grape Kool-Aid and Vicks VapoRub thrown in. I hate you! You're so ugly! My daddy'll get you!" she shrieked to said hateful, ugly bully, after which she turned much more delicate tears on Diana. "You saw what he did? Pulled my hair and made me fall?"

"I sure did."

"Would you kill him for me?"

"Um, I'll make sure your teacher knows that he pulled your hair on purpose." The tears weren't flowing quite so exuberantly. Diana could feel the little one looking her over, remembering, measuring her. And she was still checking for damages and trying to do repairs. She brushed the grit from those piles of soft, springy curls. Tugged down the dress. Fell in love.

Oh, man, Molly was impossible *not* to fall in love with. All the other preschoolers wore jeans or play pants. Miss Priss was dressed like a duchess, with flounces underneath, flounces on top, pink rosebuds on her socks and pink bows in her hair. Her daddy wasn't going to have to worry about this one following any crowd. But she was so pure girl that

Diana would be checking out convents and chastity belts if she were her mom. Four years old, and the boys were already chasing her.

"I'm gonna get that Walter Tucker," she informed Diana with most unladylike zeal. "He's gonna be sorry he was ever born. He's gonna eat dirt. He's gonna... Hey, now I remember. You were talking to my daddy at the wedding, weren't you? You told him how Jimmy Rae put cake in my hair?"

"Yes." Diana hadn't found any injuries beyond a scuffed stocking, dirt and skinned pride, but she heard two more dramatic half-sobs. Molly seemed to be losing interest in the dramatic expression of pain, though, because she was suddenly studying her with shrewd old-woman eyes.

"Did you think my daddy was cute?"

"Um, yes." Diana sensed the trick question, but she still had to lie for the child's sake. No woman was going to label Trey Derringer *cute*. Trey was a panther, cut and dried, with hair black as jet, dark searing eyes and a long, sleek, athletic build. If life were fair, he'd have a pooch by now, but no. He'd looked sexy enough in a navy blue suit to make every woman at the wedding drool—except for the bride. Just then, though, Diana understood perfectly well that she was dealing with his daughter's biased opinion—and she'd have said anything to make the tyke stop crying, besides.

"Did you know that my mommy died?" Molly asked her.

"Yes, I heard." Suzanna had told her that Trey's wealthy young wife, Victoria, had died in a car crash two years ago. Undoubtedly that was why Diana had felt such an instant kinship for the child. "I'm sorry, honey."

"Why would you be sorry?"

Diana didn't miss a beat. She knew how blunt four year olds could be. "Because I lost my mom when I was a little girl, too. So I know how hard it is, sweetie."

"You don't have a mom, either?"

"Nope. I was fourteen when my mom died. And my sister, Suzanna, was around nine." Diana reached for the shoulder bag she'd dropped and started foraging for a brush and tissue. "Thankfully, just like you, though, we had a wonderful dad to help us through that rough time—"

"Yeah. My daddy's the best in the whole world. But I still need a mom, and I'm really tired of waiting. Are you married?"

"Um, no—"

"Are you 'gaged?"

"Engaged? No—"

"Well, do you like dolls? And telling stories?" The interrogation was curtailed for a few seconds. Molly first blew into the tissue Diana pressed to her nose, then lifted her face for some mopping up with a handkerchief.

"Sure."

"You're pretty." Molly announced this, then avidly scrutinized her head to toe, from her long denim dress and boots to her mink-brown short hair. "In fact, you're more than pretty. You're prac'lly gorgeous. You're not a digger, are you?"

The conversation had gone far enough, Diana mused wryly. Still she couldn't resist asking, "A digger?"

"Yeah. Like for money. Simpson keeps saying that women keep chasing my daddy because he has a bunch of money. We don't want diggers. We want someone who likes to sing songs and tell stories and wants to love us."

"Ah." Diana had no idea who Simpson was, but it was a pretty good guess that *digger* was a reference to gold digger. And she felt helplessly touched by the child's matter-of-fact seeking someone to love them. She stuffed the tissues in her shoulder bag and grabbed a brush. A little brushing and fussing and the little one looked almost back to normal—except for that rabid look in her huge, innocent blue eyes. Diana wondered if Trey realized his daughter was scouting women for him, and suspected yes. Molly wasn't a child to leave an adult doubting what her opinion was about anything. "Well, Mol, I'm a teacher—so naturally I like to sing songs and tell stories. Just like I'll bet your preschool teacher does, too. And right now, I think your recess is over and she's going to start missing you if you don't head inside."

"No, she won't. Ms. Hawthorne saw me with

you. And I'd rather talk to you, okay? Let's talk about sex.''

The little devil paused, obviously anticipating a shocked look from the nearest adult. When Diana failed to look embarrassed, Molly tried out a lofty look.

"It's okay. I know all about it. Everybody always starts whispering when that word comes up. Like they think I'm stupid and couldn't figure it out.'' Molly rolled her big blue eyes in clear disgust. "It's something dads and moms like to do together. Everybody knows that. So. If you don't like to do it, say now, okay?''

"Well, you know, lovebug, we can talk about sex any old time…but right now, you really are going to be late unless you hightail it back to class. Come on, I'll take you in.''

Minutes later, Diana was winging toward home, having safely pawned off Molly into her teacher's care—but she was still chuckling at some of the child's precocious, manipulative antics. That one could keep two adults running without half trying, she mused. And she was so young to have lost her mother.

The dazzling noon sunlight almost blinded her as she turned onto Brennan land. The yearlings were kicking up their heels in the west pasture, a tractor leaving a wake of dust in the far east alfalfa field. All the sounds and smells were familiar from her childhood—and so were the memories of losing her own mom. At fourteen, she had thought she'd die from the grief.

She'd grown up that summer. She'd had to. Her dad had been lost, and so had her younger sister. She had no more time for a crush on Trey Derringer, no time for romantic daydreams of any kind. Overnight she'd turned into a realist—which she needed to do—but losing a mom was still the most heart-tearing pain she'd ever experienced. Really, it was impossible *not* to feel a special compatibility with little Molly. Maybe she'd never gone mom hunting quite like Mol—but she'd missed her mother so fiercely and so long that she could still taste that old pain.

She wondered if Trey realized how dedicated his daughter was to the mom-hunting cause—and thought, of course he must. And a shiver teased up her spine at the thought of running into him again. Best not. Making a fool of herself mooning after him as a young teenager was understandable—the stuff one could laugh at as a grown-up. But it wouldn't be funny to make a fool of herself for the same man a second time.

Not that she was even remotely afraid that could happen.

"Diana! Telephone for you!"

"Thanks, Dad, I'll get it." She was hugging and puffing, her arms precariously loaded with bedding and pillows as she charged downstairs, but moving would wait. All evening she'd been expecting a return call from some old Chicago teacher friends. Jogging swiftly, she dumped the armload on the cracked leather couch in her dad's library and then, breathless, grabbed the receiver on his desk. "Hello?"

"Diana...it's Trey Derringer. Did I catch you at a bad time?"

Well, shoot. Weakly Diana sank into the ancient desk chair, thinking that a sniper's bullet couldn't have caught her more unprepared. Trey didn't have to bother identifying himself any more than he'd needed to at her sister's wedding. She'd have known that lethally low, sexy baritone anywhere, any time. Unfortunately, even the sound of his voice was enough to make an adolescent girl's crush roll through her memory with the subtlety of a Mack truck. He could still do it to her. Invoke that feeling of lunacy.

Of course, she was mature enough to hide her feelings these days. Or die trying. "You didn't catch me at a bad time at all—actually, you saved me from a fate worse than death. I was moving."

"You're leaving Whitehorn again?"

"Oh, no, I'm staying home. At least for a while—I'm not sure about jobs right now. But I've been trying to move my things from the big house over to a cabin we have on the property. It's empty, no reason I can't use it, but the family's been giving me a hard time about it all day." She could hear her sister and new brother-in-law in the kitchen. "They all keep saying there's plenty of room here—which is true. But I don't want to be underfoot with Suzanna and Nash—"

"I wouldn't want to intrude on newlyweds, either."

"And it's different for Dad. He's off in his own wing. Also, when he and Nash start talking horse breeding... Well, let's just say they're both as happy as two pearls in the same clam. Anyway—I didn't mean to run on, but I can promise, you're not interrupting anything but a bunch of work I'm happy to take a break from. You had a reason for calling?"

"Yes. I just wondered if you realized that the two of us were wildly in love and engaged to be married."

She almost choked—but of course she realized this had to be some kind of joke and tried to keep her voice deadpan to play along. "Why, no, I had no idea. Thanks for letting me in on that news. Have we, um, set a date?"

"I don't know. I forgot to ask my daughter. Molly's the one who has all the details."

"Somehow I suspected that," Diana said with a chuckle. And then heard a sigh, heavy with relief and pure male.

"Thank God you're laughing. I should have remembered you had a great sense of humor. I almost didn't call," he admitted, "but I was afraid you'd hear all about our wedding plans and exotic love affair in town and wonder what on earth was going on. In fact, that's exactly how I heard. *Not* from my daughter. But when I got into town this morning, I started hearing details at the gas station, the school, the post office. And the Hip-Hop Café, naturally, was buzzing with anything resembling new town gossip.''

''Where else would news travel faster than the speed of light in Whitehorn? And yikes. It sounds like you've been taking quite a razzing.'' She propped her stockinged feet—with hole—on her dad's desk. Her gaze wandered around the library shelves, filled with books on horse breeding, vet medicine, ranch journals—but no fiction, and for sure no romance novels. The room smelled of pipe smoke and a soot-stained chimney and those old dusty books. The way a ranch library was supposed to smell. A little leathery, tough, hearty, no-nonsense sensible. The way she tried so hard to be.

''Well, I'm used to the problem. You're not. And I'm afraid you're going to hear about this love affair of ours sooner or later—''

''It's okay. I've met your daughter twice now, Trey. And I adored her both times.''

''Well, I do, too. But not when I'm inclined to kill her. When Molly lies…it's like she's in church. Everyone believes her. Those big blue eyes. The sincerity. Even as those whoppers are spilling out of her mouth. I don't understand where she got this inventing streak—''

"She's four, Trey. Nobody lies as well as a four year old. Even a con artist behind bars could take lessons. You didn't really think I'd take offense, did you? She's obviously auditioning women for a mom. I assume she's done it to you before."

"Actually, no. She hasn't." A sudden silence. "I just...thanks for being so understanding. And good luck with your move."

He'd obviously said all he wanted to and was about to end the call, which in principle Diana thought was a fantastic idea. Even the lighthearted conversation gave her heart a kick—as if they were friends, had a relationship, could easily talk together. Only her pulse was suddenly galloping like a runaway colt. She never had, never could think of Trey as a plain old pal. As quickly as she wanted to hang up, though, suddenly she hesitated. "Wait a minute—"

"You're busy, Diana. I don't want to interrupt—"

"But there's something else, isn't there?" She heard that something in his voice. "Something related to Molly that you didn't want to say? I'm touched that she likes me, Trey. Honestly, don't waste a second worrying that I would be offended or take news of our, um, wedding plans in the wrong way."

"I wasn't that worried. I remember you as a kid. You always did have the warmest heart in Montana."

Her heart started racing faster than a loony clock. For Pete's sake, he'd only offered her a small compliment. She decided it had to be best to take the practical bull by the horns. "You remember I had a crush on you, huh?" she asked dryly.

"I was honored."

"I'll bet. Every high school senior loves a fourteen year old following him around like a puppy dog, but it was partly your own fault. You were so kind. You never made me feel bad about it." She kept her voice light, and to her surprise, discovered her mood was becoming light, as well. It *was* a good idea to get this said. Partly so Trey knew she was mature enough to face an old embarrassment, and just maybe to convince herself of that, too. "I never had a chance to tell you. I'm sorry about your losing your wife, Trey."

"Thanks." Again, an odd silence, with the flavor of something troubling in his voice. "Actually, there is one other thing I'd like to bring up. I hate to ask you for a favor, but I would appreciate if you'd be...careful...about any comments you made about this imaginary engagement of ours."

"Well, sure. But I don't understand."

"It's just... Molly's my life, Diana. But since Victoria died, her parents have been trying to fight me for custody. That's no secret. If you're in Whitehorn long, you're bound to hear something about it."

Diana wasn't sure what to say. He was obviously

trying to be honest with her, but there was pain in his voice. Pain that was an unexpected intimacy to share with someone he barely knew—like her. And she suddenly didn't care about that old stupid crush. The sound of his pain touched her. "Are you afraid the Kingstons could win custody?"

"No, not really. No one could doubt that I can provide financially for Molly. And I'm her dad. There has to be a reason for the court to take a child away from a parent, and there is no reason. They've looked for all the obvious kinds of dirt—that I'd expose Molly to drinking or drugs or inappropriate behavior with a woman. But there's nothing like that and never will be."

She read between the lines. "But it could be troublesome, if Molly suddenly started telling stories of a woman in your life. Like me."

"There's no problem with an adult female being in my life, but there's a difference between that and Molly implying that she's been exposed to intimate behavior." He sighed, again clearly embarrassed. "I'm just asking that if someone teases you...if you'd be aware that anything you say could get back to the Kingstons. And could be taken in a very serious light."

"Good grief, Trey. That's terrible. Having to worry all the time what someone could say. Or that a friendship could be taken wrong."

"It's not your problem. And I sure didn't mean

to make it sound as if it were. I just had to ask you, to be careful—''

''I will be. Please don't worry.'' She hesitated, thinking that it was past time they both hung up. Neither could possibly have anything else to say. Yet somehow she just couldn't let the conversation go without opening her mouth one more time. ''Look. Is there any chance it would help if I talked to Molly?''

Chapter 2

Two nights later, Diana pulled into the Derringer driveway, feeling mad enough to kick herself. Where was her head when she agreed to do this? Inside a cuckoo clock?

She had no business offering to help Trey with his daughter. None. That whole telephone conversation had simply been flustering. She'd been startled to discover that she was the only woman Molly had glommed onto for a potential mom. Somehow that made her feel responsible. And she hadn't realized Trey's in-laws were fighting him for custody. And she naturally felt a kinship for a little girl who'd lost her mother, because she had, too. And somehow it just bubbled out. That offer to help.

Offering to help wasn't a bad thing. Volunteering

to spend more time around Trey was the bad thing. Did a dieter expose herself to crème brûlée? Did a drinker deliberately walk by bars? Did a broke woman go to a sale?

No, of course not. Anyone with a brain would avoid the dangerous substance. Yet here she was, gamboling like a carefree, nitwit yearling toward trouble.

And Diana's first glance at Trey's house only made her feel more morose. Reluctantly she turned the key in her dad's red pickup and stepped out. She'd dressed in a long khaki skirt with a vest and shirt, casual clothes that seemed appropriate for a dinner centered around a four-year-old child.

The casual clothes seemed all wrong. She kept forgetting that Trey had a ton of money now, because he'd grown up on the poor side of the Derringer family, and that's when she'd known him before. He'd worked every job on the ranch he could get as a kid—which had always been part of his allure for her. Growing up, she was always around horse ranches, which meant she was always catching sight of his bronzed, hot, sweaty muscles—mucking out stalls, working horses, pitching hay. It wasn't *just* his muscles that she'd drooled over, but his whole hunklike, heroic character. Not a spoiled bone in him. He'd made his own way, on his own brawn and brains, from the time he was a young squirt.

Only now he'd made it—made it so high that Diana felt even more awkward being around him. She hiked toward the front door, trying not to gawk at the view, but the structure was less a house than a Western palace. The place was built of stone, with cool glass walls overlooking the mountains and a balcony with a hot tub jutting out of the second floor. Investments. She'd never been positive exactly what that meant—but Trey made piles of money doing it, that's all everyone kept saying. Back when, he'd aced a scholarship to some Ivy League school—broke her heart when he left Whitehorn— then landed some pricey-dicey job in an East Coast investment firm, then presto, four years later, came back home to start up his own. At thirty-two, he was still practically a kid, for Pete's sake. And already hauling in zillions.

Coming here was dumb. Dumb, dumb, dumb, her agreeing to this dinner.

Yet the front door opened before she could back out and skedaddle for the truck like the coward she wanted to be. The unfamiliar man suddenly framed in the doorway looked like the scary ogre in the Beanstalk fairy tale. His height pushed past six and a half feet, and he had to be carrying more than three hundred pounds. His thinning long hair was shagged back in a ponytail. He had a built-in inner tube around his middle and tattoos running down his bare arms. "Hey," he greeted her.

Hey? And this dude worked in a millionaire's house? "Hi," she returned.

He offered her a beefy hand and a thousand-watt grin at the same time. "I'm Simpson. Molly's nanny, Trey's mechanic, the cook...hell, I don't know what my formal job title is. I just live here. Come on in, we'll get you a drink— Oops, I guess that drink'll wait two seconds.''

Molly suddenly erupted from behind Simpson and catapulted toward her. ''Ms. *Brennan!* I'm *so* glad you're here! Simpson, isn't she beautiful just like I told you?''

''Yup, she is.''

Diana returned the exuberant grin, feeling like she was melting from the inside out. Okay. So this was dumb. But she was so crazy about Molly that there was absolutely nothing dumb or wrong about wanting to help the little one. And then Mol grabbed her hand and tugged. ''You just come on in and talk to my daddy. I'm gonna be so good and so quiet you won't believe it. And Simpson made us a *great* dinner, just for company—''

''I did,'' Simpson confirmed as he shut the front door. ''Meat loaf and mashed potatoes. And no, the peas won't be touching the meat loaf. Not on my dinner plates. Hot fudge sundaes for those who finish their suppers.'' His voice dropped two octaves. ''Just for the record, I had no vote in this particular menu—''

''But I did!'' Molly said happily. ''We had to have something specially good for you, Ms. Brennan!''

''And I'm so grateful. They sound like my most favorite foods of all times, munchkin.'' She could hardly take her eyes off the living room. She'd half expected a notably expensive feminine decor, be-

cause Victoria Kingston had been quite a socialite,
yet it was obvious Trey had beat to his own masculine drummer. Everything was giant size. The fireplace was made of sandblasted granite with a spectacular bronze mantel. Huge couches and chairs
were square in shape and terra-cotta in color, heaped
with cushions big enough for Molly to curl up and
nap on. The plank chestnut floor was softened with
Turkish rugs. Red stone doorways and oak ceiling
beams made the window view of the Crazy Mountains seem a natural part of the inside.

Trying to walk through the living room almost
took a map. Diana couldn't help but be charmed.
Not by the cool-guy decor, but by the nonstop
messes. Some kind of marble board game was in
midprogress, taking up the entire coffee table. A
Barbie Vet Center blocked an aisle. A computer was
blinking a game with basic-reader words on it.
Spread liberally everywhere were coloring books
and baby doll carriages, naked dolls and tea sets.

It was easy to see who ruled this place—and the
only tyrant wielding any power around here was significantly shorter than four feet tall.

And then Trey suddenly stepped in from the ter-
race, his hand stretched out to greet her, striding
through the debris as if he were an old pro at walking the gauntlet. Oh, dear. Oh, dear. Her brain
picked up the chant and kept repeating the refrain.
He was wearing jeans and a comfortable chamois
shirt, his dark hair wind-brushed and his carved face
ruddy from the brisk air. He was good-looking. That

wasn't news. That wasn't the reason her pulse felt
stunned. Truth to tell, she'd never cared that he was
handsome in that dark panther kind of way. Good
looks in themselves would never have made her
blood pound.

But his smile did. Always had, and tarnation,
maybe always would. And for some unknown reason, he smiled at her as if she mattered. As if he
wanted to see her. As if he liked her looks, liked her
program, was enjoying the visual stroll from her
head to her toe and wanted her to know it. That
slow, lazy crack of a smile was so darned intimate
that Diana could almost believe he was attracted to
her—but she'd have to be a total lunatic to believe
that.

And she'd accepted having a problem with lunacy
since she came home, but she refused to believe that
she couldn't shake this idiocy with some guts and
determination.

With his feet up and his stomach full, Trey took
a sip of cappuccino, watching Diana with his daughter, trying to remember the last time he'd been this
attracted to a woman.

Never, he decided. Which was a considerable period of time.

That Molly had chosen Diana for him especially
struck his funny bone, because Mol had been a pis-
tol and a half any time he'd had a woman over since
her mother died—even if the sole reason for the visit
was business. His family told him that the issue was

jealousy. Molly'd had her daddy to herself all this time and she liked it that way. The surprise of Mol's taking to Diana so completely had naturally motivated him to take a look at her, too.

Truth to tell, he hadn't looked at a woman in an intimate way since Victoria died. But he was now.

A small fire lapped the logs in the stone hearth. This early in September, the evenings were usually still mild, yet this night there was a sting in the air, a hint of white on the mountaintops. Trey could already feel the chill of another lonely winter coming on, coming soon.

Backlit by the fire, Molly was scrunched on Diana's lap in one of the oversize chairs, a book of Shel Silverstein poems open between them, the two heads nestled together, both giggling. Trey had no prejudice about his daughter. With her shiny mahogany curls against that porcelain skin, she was the most beautiful child ever born—that was Trey's story and he was sticking to it. But for once, it was another female who'd snared his attention.

Diana's clothes were very nice—particularly if she were interviewing for a job as a nun. The khaki skirt concealed everything from waist to ankles. A loose, thick shirt revealed nothing of her upstairs figure, and the vest further hid the shape of her breasts, as well as advertised she was a homebody children lover. Everything she wore could have had a don't-touch-me-fella sign.

He got the message. But everything about her appearance—including her clothes—inspired him to know her better, and specifically to touch her. Preferably nonstop, and he hoped soon.

Her hair was a short, silky pelt brown. It framed her face, with a wave tucking under her chin. Her eyes were brown, too, only a deeper, richer, sultry brown, and that mouth of hers was just as sexy. She wore no gloss or lipstick. No makeup at all to call attention to herself. Yet her skin had a natural sun-kissed glow, a rise of color riding the delicate line of cheekbone, and when she smiled, the spirit and warmth in her eyes easily sent a man's heart slamming. Beneath all those figure-concealing clothes were long coltish legs, a long and low-waisted figure and a body that moved with her. There was no coyness to her walk, just grace. And so unlike Victoria, there was absolutely no look-at-me in Diana's appearance. Instead she radiated a natural feminine sensuality that tripped his nerves faster than a hair trigger.

He could have participated with the girls, but sitting back and watching the two of them was doing a good job of pulling at his heart. The amazing thing was that Trey hadn't been aware he had a heart to pull—except for his daughter. And after Di finished reading Molly the Silverstein poems, she gently, deliberately led Mol into a discussion. Belatedly he remembered that this discussion was the excuse he'd had for inviting her—which somehow he'd completely forgotten about.

"You know what telling the truth means, punkin wunkin?"

"Sure." Molly cuddled closer on Diana's lap.

"Okay. When you see a movie, and someone on the movie screen gets hurt, is that true? Is the actor really hurt?"

"No, that's pretend."

"You're so smart." Diana touched a fingertip to his daughter's precious nose. "And you're so right. That's pretend. Do you like the Cinderella story?"

"Oh, yeah."

"I do, too. But can you tell me if that story is real or pretend?"

"Pretend."

"Holy mackerel. You're right again. And when you told some people that your daddy was engaged to be married, was that true or pretend?"

Molly tried the big-innocent-eyes routine on Diana. God knows the kid knew it worked on him every time. "Listen," Molly said charmingly. "You could love my daddy so easy. He's wunnerful. I love him more than everything in the whole world. And then you could live here and read me stories every night, just like tonight. Wouldn't that be great?"

His daughter was talking about him as if he wasn't in the same room. Trey considered being embarrassed, but the thing was, Diana didn't seem to be. She just nodded.

"I hear you, punkin, but that didn't answer my question. When you told people your dad was engaged to be married, was that real or pretend?"

"It was pretend. I *know* I was making it up. But

it *could* be real. Is it the sex thing? You can do the sex thing, can't you?''

Trey's coffee mug dropped from his fingers to the carpet. Behind the chair, Diana made a hand gesture that Molly couldn't see, as if to privately communicate to him that everything was hunky-dory, stay cool.

''We're not talking about me, Mol. And we're not talking about sex right now, either. We're talking about you telling the truth, and first I want to be sure you know the difference.''

Molly hunched up her knees more seriously. ''Are you mad at me?''

''Nope. But there is a problem, Molly. The thing is, we're just getting to know each other. And I like you so much. But if I'm going to like you even more, it would help if I could trust you. And I can't trust you if you tell fibs.''

The princess tried arguing with her—Molly did have a teensy tendency to try arguing her way out of trouble—but Diana didn't let up, just kept gently teasing her into seeing what was right in terms a four year old could grasp. Trey marveled. Twenty minutes later, when Simpson poked his head in, naturally Molly didn't want to leave Diana's lap— much less go to bed. Eventually, though, she was conned. Simpson promising her a piggyback ride all the way upstairs was always an effective bribe. But the instant those two left the room, Diana leaped to her feet.

"Dinner was wonderful. I really enjoyed it, but now I should go," she said swiftly.

"No way," he said in his best slow, take-it-easy voice—but he was fascinated. As far as he could tell, Diana had nerves of steel. Hell, she could handle a four year old's questions about sex without even blinking, yet suddenly—now they were alone—nerves showed in her eyes and she was edgily bolting for the door. "You have to stay at least long enough for me to give you a brandy—or pay you in solid gold for a thank-you. I really appreciate how great you were with Mol."

The smile was a little flustered, but at least she stopped that mad flight for the nearest exit. "Not great. I'm just used to being around kids. You know I'm a teacher—"

"Uh-huh. But I'm her dad, and she can still run rings around me. In fact, I think I'm going to be an old man before she reaches her fifth birthday. I almost had a stroke when she suddenly brought sex into the conversation. How come you weren't mortified? I was." Simpson had brought in a tray of cognac and glasses earlier, but neither of them had touched any while Molly was around. Now, though, coaxing her to stay a few more minutes was simply a matter of pouring a few sips in a snifter—not so much it could possibly affect her driving later—and handing her the glass.

She didn't turn it down. She chuckled at his confession about being mortified, although she rolled her eyes as if she didn't believe him. "I think it's too late for me to be embarrassed by anything kids do. Besides, when little squirts use a word like sex, it's almost always because they figured out it has a shock effect for adults. It doesn't really mean anything more than that, Trey. Nothing to worry about.''

"I'm not worried. But I have to admit, my in-laws could well have a stroke if they heard Mol talking about sex or come out with any other suggestive words. I know they'd blame me.''

He watched her hesitate. She obviously didn't want to pry, yet she didn't want to cut off the conversation about his daughter, either. Finally she said, "I never really knew your wife, Victoria, because you two were that far ahead of me in school. But I did kind of know the Kingstons, because they went to our church. They were never unkind, but they just seemed, um, stiff.''

He set down his glass, but his gaze never left her face. "They are stiff. But that really isn't the reason that Molly's grandparents and I are at odds. And I hate making you uncomfortable by talking about this, Di, but I do feel it'd be easier in the long run if I just cleared the air and was frank with you. You'll hear it in town if I don't say it anyway. The Kingstons blame me for their daughter's death.''

Her lips parted in surprise. "But how could they? I understand your wife died in a car accident. And she was the only one in the car, I was told.''

He nodded. "Yes. She was alone in a car, coming home from a party. She'd been drinking. Skidded on an ice slick and crashed into a tree.'' He shook his head. ''The Kingstons blame me for Victoria being unhappy. They see it as my fault that she was drinking. My fault she went to that party alone. My fault she died.''

''I can understand their mourning their daughter. But not their blaming you,'' Diana said gently.

''Well, reality is that Victoria and I weren't happy, which her parents were well aware of. And when they started this custody fight, their primary argument was that I neglected my wife because I spent all my time making money, and I would neglect my daughter the same way. And they're right about their daughter. But not about mine.''

Diana opened her mouth as if to argue with him— the polite thing—yet instead she cocked her head and simply listened.

Trey never found it easy to talk about this. But there was no possibility of his developing any kind of trust relationship with Diana unless he were honest with her. ''I never meant to neglect Victoria in any way. But I grew up poor, where she grew up with wealth. I wanted money and everything money could buy, where she wanted to take things from her parents, have the two of us just live off them. I couldn't. It wasn't in me to live off someone else. But when I was working long hours, she went off with her own crowd, partying, drinking and so on— Diana, my daughter doesn't know any of this. Even if it would help me with this custody problem with her grandparents, I really don't want to down-talk

Victoria to Molly. Mol thinks that her mom was an angel. I want her to have that positive impression.''

"I understand.''

"And so far, the Kingstons—Regina and Ralph—have worried the hell out of me, but there doesn't seem to be a real threat. The court's backed me. There never was a question about my financially supporting Molly. It was about whether I was too busy to provide attention and a loving home—the way two full-time grandparents claim they could. But Mol's my life, Diana. Yeah, I work, but—''

"Trey.'' Diana motioned to the mountains of toys and child entertainments strewn through the living room. "You don't have to tell me that you adore your daughter. And more to the point, I can see the way she is. Happy, secure, sure of herself.''

"Spoiled rotten.'' He filled in another blank.

"Yeah, that, too.'' She grinned. "I imagine what you don't manage to give Molly, Simpson does.''

Trey washed a hand over his face. "Yeah, well, Simpson's another one of the Kingstons' complaints. And I know how he looks with the tattoos, the long hair and all—hardly your typical nanny. I also realize that Mol needs a woman's influence, but it isn't that simple. Simpson is as crazy about Molly as she is about him. I can't see hiring a stranger just because of gender when he worships the ground she walks on.''

"For heaven's sake, Trey. All anyone should have to do is look at Molly to be sure what you're doing for her is great, including Simpson. She's

adorable. Full of herself, high on life and everything
in it. What's to worry?'' Impulsively she reached
over and touched his hand, the gesture clearly meant
to express affection and sympathy, nothing more.
But she seemed to notice her pale white hand against
his sun-ruddy skin, and suddenly she was surging to
her feet again. "Good grief, it really is late now. I
never meant to take up your whole evening, and I
need to get home."

Because he could see that she was serious about
leaving this time, he walked her outside. The tem-
perature had plummeted at sunset. The sky was a
chilled-down navy blue, peppered with icy stars, and
Diana had brought no jacket. She clutched her arms
as she walked next to him to her father's red pickup
with the Big Sky logo on the door.

"Diana, I want to apologize—"

"Apologize? For the wonderful dinner or the
good company?" she teased him. "I fell in love
with your daughter at my sister's wedding, if you
didn't notice. She's a total darling."

"Good. But I'm still apologizing for airing all our
family linen. I never wanted to make you feel awkward...but I did want to be honest ahead of time.
Because I'd like to ask you over again. To see you
again. At least, if the total picture didn't scare you
off."

"You want to see me again?"

She dug in her shoulder bag for the truck keys,
and when she found them and tilted her face toward

his, her expression reflected both surprise and confusion.

She didn't get it, he mused. All evening he could feel the combustible chemistry between them, could see her eyes shying from his, then darting back, could see her cheeks flushing, had felt her pulse startle when his hand accidentally brushed hers. And yes, more than a dozen years ago, he remembered a coltish young girl who'd followed him around as faithfully as a puppy. She'd been so sweet, so painfully yearning. He wasn't a particularly sensitive teenager, but still he'd have shot himself before hurting her feelings, and hoped he never had. For sure he'd never let on that he was aware of her crush to avoid embarrassing her.

But that was then.

And this was now.

Her dark eyes looked like liquid chocolate in the moonlight, her smile alluring and luring both. Just looking at her, his gut tightened and his pulse started tripping like an ungainly teenager's. He couldn't help but be aware how different she was from Victoria.

He'd married once for practicality, because he thought it was time to be married, time to settle down. Truthfully, Victoria had picked him and done the chasing more than the other way around, but her country-club taste and blond perfection had been everything he had ever dreamed of. He expected to be a good husband. Expected to give one hundred percent. And he'd revered the ground she walked on in the beginning.

But it wasn't and never had been a marriage of love, and Trey would never make that mistake again. Both of them had been in hell before Victoria died. Neither, really, at fault. He'd never stopped trying, and if Victoria had, well, he'd blamed himself for that as long as he was going to. She'd wanted him, but she hadn't loved him, either. Ever. And he'd withered on the inside for a long time, feeling more and more alone, feeling wanted only for his money and what he could do, never for himself. Long before she'd died, he'd felt a chasm of silence from dying on the inside himself.

In the past couple years, he'd occasionally gone out, but not often. He carried a lot of problems that it wasn't fair to ask someone to share, he'd felt, but more than that, there hadn't been anyone he cared enough about to even try. Trey never wanted to make the same mistake. If he ever fell, he wanted nothing unless he could have it all. He wanted the flame, the magic, the power. He wanted a woman who made his knees shake with wanting. He wanted to feel crazy in love—and for her to feel the same— or he didn't want to waste time even stepping foot in the ballpark. And truth to tell, he never expected to find any such thing. He wasn't positive that kind of love existed—at least for him.

But damned if, for the first time in his life, he hadn't found a woman who finally did it. Made his knees shake. Her hair like a simple cap, skin so smooth she wore no makeup, no artifice to her, all bundled up in those figure-concealing clothes, making it so obvious that she hadn't come over for dinner with any intention of alluring him...yet she was alluring. That smile. Those eyes. The scent she wore, a tickle of flowers and a hint of a soft, summer wind and then something sexy right behind it, like a punch.

He could taste risk, just being in the same room with her. The kind of risk he'd never dared in his life before. The kind of risk he really hadn't known was out there.

Of course, he hadn't tested this amazingly fascinating problem with a kiss yet.

But that was next.

Chapter 3

"I just can't believe how chilly the night suddenly turned, and after such a warm day," Diana said with a nervous laugh. "I don't know if I mentioned that I drove up to the Laughing Horse Reservation this morning. My great-great-gramps, Kyle Brennan, was half Cheyenne...."

Diana wanted to give herself a morose kick in the keester. Why was she telling Trey all this? Why should he care? *Just shut up, Diana. Just get in the truck and say good-night and quit babbling like a nervous brook.*

But the problem was Trey, standing right in front of the driver's door. He'd always induced a white-hot sexual awareness in her, and this close was too close. Moonlight silhouetted his broad shoulders and rumpled dark hair and that slow, lazy smile of his. She could smell late-season roses and the ghost-clear night and her own nerves. Out spilled more babble.

"Anyway, I've been picking up some substitute teaching work, but not enough to make a living. And truthfully, what I'd really love to do is teach on the reservation, so I drove up there to see if there was any chance I could catch someone to talk one-on-one. In Chicago, I taught the high-risk kids. The little ones who were having trouble reading right from the start. And I doubt folks would normally think inner city and Native American country kids would have anything in common, but the problems that can make a child a high academic risk can be exactly the same. I had a great talk with the principal. She was on the same bandwagon with me right off. Unfortunately, there's just no funding for the kind of special-ed program I'd really love to put together."

She had to stop babbling long enough to take a breath. Her lungs hauled in a big chug of oxygen, but not enough to quell the light-headed, white-hot feeling.

The thing was, her specific problem had gotten worse. Trey was no longer just blocking the driver's door. He'd started moving. He lifted his arms as if he were reaching toward her. If Diana hadn't had a recent problem with lunacy, she'd have thought the man was going to kiss her...a thought that inspired her common sense to snap awake. For Pete's sake, catering to this lunacy thing had gone far enough. Old crushes didn't come back. Fantasy lovers didn't suddenly turn into the real thing. Sure, a woman could waste a few rag tail minutes daydreaming about Daniel Day-Lewis or Brad Pitt. What was the harm? You knew nothing was going to happen.

Only Trey suddenly bent down.

And he seemed to be studying her, staring at her face, looking at her in a strangely intimate way that made no sense at all.

And then his arms swept around her.

And the kiss that only a lunatic woman would believe could happen...was happening.

Holy hokum. Holy hooch. Her knees seemed to turn into dribbling noodles. Her toes and fingertips iced up. All the wonderful IQ points that had always handily glued her mind together suddenly flew out her ears into that big Montana sky.

His hands slid around her shoulders, scooped her back. His mouth tilted, then swooped. A butterfly kiss whispered down on her lips, soft, gentle, more a tease of sensation than the real thing...but that was followed by a hot stamp of a kiss that could melt a blizzard. No sound intruded on the still silence of the night, no cars, no birds, no humans. She heard nothing but the sound of his groan against her soft mouth, and her gulping in air. Or trying to.

Okay, okay, so she'd always been crazy about

him, but she'd only agreed to this dinner for Molly's sake. She adored his daughter. There was no reason to deny that. And after hearing about Molly's losing her mom, Diana felt even more drawn to the urchin. Mol had a fabulous dad. So had Diana. And Molly was so wonderful, so fearless, so pure girl, the kind of spoiled kid Diana had once been, too. Mol was loved and lucky and blessed. Diana had that same kind of background—yet all her life she'd ached for her mom. A daughter who lost her mother too young had a hollow spot that never went away. Diana knew exactly how the little one felt.

And right now, she kept trying, fiercely, to think about Molly.

Yet Trey suddenly lifted his head and smiled at her in the darkness. Not a nice smile. Not a friendly smile. More of a *Damn! I hoped you'd be this much trouble* smile, and then he nuzzled down for another kiss, spinning her around so he could lean against the truck and splay his legs and pull her right into the lariat of his arms.

Eek. A girl couldn't cook her goose on just a few kisses, could she?

Nothing earth-shattering could happen as long as they both stayed fully clothed out in the open, could it?

Besides, a few kernels of rational common sense finally seeped into her empty brain and started rattling. Obviously she could make herself behave any minute. She always behaved. She was a teacher, for heaven's sake. Respected. Respectable. A kid lover, a believer in families, a wanna-be mom.

The only reason she was having a teensy difficulty getting a grip was from the shock of Trey initiating a kiss, and not just any old peck of a kiss but this kind, the kind that started out sleepy and safe and somehow turned into drumrolls thundering inside her heart. He wanted her. Trey. Wanted. Her.

Really, it was way, way easier owning up to a problem with basic lunacy than admitting how much she was loving this embrace, loving him, loving this moment as if she'd been waiting for him her whole life.

Trey suddenly lifted his head, severing a kiss that had sampled her throat and earlobe and the side of her jaw before any kind of hesitation. His dark eyes were still kissing her, still savoring, but his expression had turned grave.

He didn't pull away. Instead, his arms tightened and he cuddled her in a hug for a moment longer. She could feel his arousal, feel the heat and electric tension pouring off his body, yet somehow that hug managed to communicate affection and comfort, as well. She had the sensation of a panther tired of dark, lonely nights and, instead of pouncing, trying to soothe the lamb in his clutches. A wildly crazy image, Diana realized. Trey wouldn't hurt her. She wasn't physically afraid of him in any way. Yet the instinct that he was dangerous for her was as real as the moonlight.

"You have to go," he murmured.

That should have been her line, her first words. She tried to pull back, and this time he let her. Yet his eyes still chased hers as if willing her to stay with him—when, of course, she couldn't. He said quietly, "It's been easier for me to stay uninvolved since my wife died. Particularly with in-laws watching every breath I take and hoping to find the grounds to judge me. But you know what, Diana?"

"What?"

"I think that you and I are going to get complicated real fast." A smile. A touch on her cheek. And then he watched her drive off.

Weeks later, Diana stood in her cabin window, towel drying her hair, mesmerized by the first snowfall. The snow fell like a hush in big, fat, crystal flakes, filling up the corrals, mounding on the fence posts, shining silver in the windowsills of her dad's house across the yard. Snow clouds hovered low in the witchy black sky. The first of October was early for a serious snow—even in Montana—but all she could think about was how much Molly was going to love waking up to this in the morning.

When a knuckle rapped on her door, she whirled in surprise. Her sister, Suzanna, poked her head inside. "Hey. You busy?"

"As if I were ever too busy for you. Come on in. How's my niece today?"

"Your nephew—" Suzanna pushed off her hat

and jacket, then patted her bulging tummy "—has been kicking me nonstop all day. I swear this boy already has attitude. But Dad and Nash are closed up in the den, talking horse breeding, the two of them happy as two peas in a pod, so I took off." She waddled toward the couch. "I've had a surprise I wanted to show you ever since you came home. Only first you insist on living in this pipsqueak-size cabin instead of in the big house with us, and then you're never here, besides!"

"You don't like the way I've fixed the place up?" From long habit, Diana studied her sister with the practiced skill of an honorary mother—but the glowing cheeks and deep contentment in Suzanna's eyes were ample testimony to how exuberantly happy her sis was. And happier yet when Diana produced a dish brimming with dark chocolate nougats—one of her sister's vices since the start of her pregnancy.

"Oh, God. Oh, God." Her sister spotted the nougats. And pounced. Unfortunately, though, even chocolate couldn't divert her train of thought right then. "You've fixed the place up wonderfully. But that has nothing to do with how little you're home—"

"Well, really, I'm lucky they're calling me so often for substitute teaching."

"I'm not talking about work hours, and you know it. You've been seeing Trey Derringer for weeks now. I want a full report. Skip the details and go right to the X-rated stuff. The more pregnant I get, the best I can do is hear about it vicariously.''

Diana's pulse suddenly climbed in her throat. Suzanna couldn't have any idea how fast and complicated her relationship with Trey had become— nor did she want to tell her. Suzanna was not only a new bride but expecting a baby in a matter of weeks. Diana had seen the two lovers together. No one could doubt they were happy, but something about the relationship had been stormy at the start— they hadn't opted for a big wedding at first, for one thing—yet Suze had been closemouthed about whatever the troubles had been. Diana didn't want to pry. And didn't need to, when she could see for herself that her sister was happy. But all the same, she'd never let her younger sister worry about her before and certainly wasn't about to start now. ''Well, I hate to disappoint you on the lascivious details, but really, I've just been spending time with Molly to help out. I admit I've fallen for his daughter big-time, but we've just been doing girl stuff—shopping and haircuts and that kind of thing—''

''Uh-huh. Sure. Like you expect me to believe a four year old put that new kick-ass swish in the way you walk or those stars in your eyes. Is Derringer serious? Because if he's playing with you, I'm gonna sic Nash on him with a bullwhip. I always did think he was a heap of man, but then there was so much talk. His wife was the fastest thing this town ever saw. And his in-laws are real public about their fighting for custody. And more to the point, you think I didn't know you had a thing for him when we were kids?''

"I sure did," Diana admitted smoothly. "In fact, when I'm around him now, I thank God I've grown up and don't believe in shining knights and wild romantic dreams anymore. You know you can count on me to be practical. Have you ever known me to do one irresponsible thing?" If none of this were precisely true, Diana hoped it would be enough to reassure her sister. Just in case, though, she swiftly crossed the room and opened a drawer. She had another bag of nougats stashed for emergencies just like this. "Didn't you say you had some kind of surprise?"

"Yup. I found a treasure in an old trunk in the attic months ago. Letters. Love letters. From our great-great-grandmother Isabelle to Kyle. And I wanted to tell you right away, but you came home for the wedding first, and then Slim and I took off on the honeymoon, and, well, I just wanted to show these to you when the two of us had a little time alone.''

"You found love letters? Between our legendary Isabelle and Kyle? Sheesh, how'd you ever keep that secret this long? Let's see, let's see." Diana curled up on the couch, immediately becoming immersed in the fragile parchment letters as Suzanna divvied them out.

As young girls, both had always devoured the legend of their great-great-grandmother's love story. Their mom had first told it to Diana, and then Diana had told it to Suzanna a hundred times as a bedtime tale, how the young, gorgeous and pampered Isabelle had come west with her parents, then been stranded when she was nineteen because her mom and dad died. Still, she'd fallen in love with the dashing half-breed, Kyle Brennan. In those days, she'd risked her future and her reputation to marry a man of mixed race, and together they'd built up the Big Sky ranch.

Every time Diana had heard the story from her mother, she'd dreamed of that kind of a love—the kind of man you could trust beyond all rhyme or reason, the kind of love so strong that nothing else mattered. "Mom and Dad loved each other like that, you know," she told Suzanna, as they switched letters yet again. "I don't know how well you remember Mom—"

"Well, not as well as you. But you and Dad both helped keep her alive for me. And Dad still gets a softness in his eyes when he talks about her." Suzanna started carefully folding the finished love notes. "I didn't think love would ever happen like that. Not to me."

Diana's eyes shot up. "What do you mean? You married Nash—"

Her sister nodded, but her gaze was focused on the snowy landscape outside. "At the time I thought it was the right thing to do. For the baby.

For...everyone. And the first time I saw Nash with the horses... Well, I can't explain exactly. I felt I could trust Nash, and that mattered. I just never believed we'd always create sparks together. I remember saying my vows and wanting to cry. I felt like a fake. Not like a bride—at least not the bride our mom and grandmothers were. The thing was—"

When Suzanna hesitated, Diana coaxed her to finish. "What?"

"Well, to be honest, I thought the romantic kind of love that our parents had—that I thought Isabelle and Kyle had way back—was old-fashioned. Corny. Wonderful to weave stories about, but nothing that happens for real today. People get divorced all the time. Nobody stays together. I just thought I should work on making a good relationship, but not count on ever feeling that corny type of being in love, you know?"

Diana felt her heart squeeze in a protective fist. "Suzanna, the way you and Nash look at each other, I just assumed...I hoped—"

"Oh, yeah. I fell in love—hard. And so did he. Loving him is the best thing that ever happened to me...which is partly why I wanted to tell you all this. I'm worried about you, Di—"

"Me? There's no reason for you ever to worry about me!"

"Well, you take care of everyone else. But I never see anyone taking care of you. And I'm just saying, if this Trey's got your heart, go for it. I never expected to love anyone like I feel about Nash, not down deep at the soul level. And I just don't want you to settle for less. You deserve someone who'll love you for who you really are. Oh, God. Am I sounding corny?"

"Um..." Diana felt uncomfortable. Her sister was the baby in the family. It was always Diana who'd done the caretaking and mothering and lecturing. Suzanna had never done it to her. "You're being a sweetheart, sis. But I really don't want you worried about me—"

"Okay, okay. I'm not worried. Or I'll let you off the hook for now, because I still want to talk about the love letters. Come on, Diana, didn't you notice something was odd?"

"Um..." As fascinated as Diana had always been by the old family love story, she hadn't been paying that much attention. She was suddenly remembering Suzanna's wedding, and how her sister had hurled the wedding bouquet right at her chest. Whatever trouble Suzanna had found with Nash, the couple had obviously worked through it and found real love on the other side. Diana only wished she could believe the same thing could happen with her and Trey. She couldn't seem to stop worrying about her building worrisome feelings for him. But she forcibly returned her concentration to the family love letters. "To be honest, I didn't notice anything odd. The tone of the letters was wonderfully romantic and loving, just what we always thought. So what did you think was weird?"

"That there could even *be* any letters. Think about it. She's writing to him. To her lover. And judging from the number of letters, her Kyle was obviously gone for quite a while, right?"

"Yeah, so?"

"So when were they ever separated? All those years—you know the legend—once they met, they were never supposed to be separated. She was in a terrible mess when her parents died and she was left with a horse ranch that she didn't have a clue what to do with. So why would he have left her?"

"You're right," Diana mused. "That doesn't make sense."

"I hate loose ends like that. And Isabelle's so much a part of our family. Every time we've ever talked about love and what family means, it goes back to her and Kyle." Suzanna stood, pressed her knuckles to the aching small of her back, then reached for her jacket and mittens. "I don't like their suddenly being a mystery in the family history when we were always so sure we knew the whole story."

"Well, maybe my niece will unravel all the old genealogy when she comes of age."

"Your nephew, you mean?"

Obviously they were done talking about serious subjects. Sister fashion, they fought over the gender of the baby, then whether Diana was going to walk

Suzanna home. Suzanna said she was pregnant, not ill, and it was dumb for Diana to get all cold when the big house was just across the yard, for Pete's sake. Diana listened to the rant—as she clutched her sister's arm protectively the whole walk. The night was dark and sleety, and her sister could too easily fall—which Nash obviously realized, too, because her new brother-in-law's tall, broad-shouldered figure emerged from the shadows before they were halfway across the yard. He'd come to make sure Suzanna made it safely inside.

"The two of you are a total pain!" Suzanna complained. "My God, I can't even walk a hundred yards without somebody babying me!"

Diana patted Nash's arm sympathetically. "I told you before—you should have married the nice sister instead of Ms. Crab here."

"Aw, she's not crabby. It's just that our daughter's been kicking her so many nights, she's getting short on sleep."

"Our *son.* I've told you guys a zillion times. I'm positive it's a boy."

"Excuse me, Diana," Nash murmured. And kissed his bride—which was the last anyone heard any further cranky complaints. Nash winked a good-night at Diana.

Moments later, still chuckling at the newlyweds' antics, she let herself into the cabin. Abruptly her smile died. Normally the silence and privacy of the cabin were guaranteed to soothe her after a long day.

Heaven knew, she'd fought the family to stay alone here.

Her dad had built the cabin years ago because they had so many people coming and going during the breeding season. There were plenty of spare rooms in the big house, but that wasn't always comfortable for either the strangers or the family.

Her gaze skimmed the cabin as she locked up and started cleaning glasses and turning off lights. The place was set up like a studio apartment, with a corduroy couch and chair clustered in the small space in front of the fireplace. A bar served as dining table, desk and work space, and separated the living from the kitchen area. The kitchen had a hodgepodge of blue enamelware from the main house and cupboards always stocked with enough staples to put together a quick dinner or snack. Hiding behind an old-fashioned fabric screen was the bedroom area— a double bed, side table and storage trunk.

And that was it, Diana mused, but she'd done her best to make the place hers. She'd added the ivory down comforter and crocheted pillows, the nest of gardenia-scented candles, hung an Amish quilt and draped thick rugs to warm up the plank floors. But it was a frustrating lack of space for a woman used to her independence and autonomy all these years. And she felt like she was camping out, in between, not sure what rung on the life ladder she was climbing next.

Her sudden unsettled mood came from talking

with her sister, she knew. Maybe there was a sudden
mystery about Isabelle, but Isabelle still had the
courage to reach for love in spite of very difficult
odds in her time. As had their grandmother and
mom, and now, Diana suspected, her sister, too. The
Brennan women had always found strength in themselves.

And growing up, Diana had understood where
that strength had to come from. When her mom
died, her dad had needed her to be strong. No one
valued a weak woman. A woman stood up for what
was right, took care of family, sacrificed for those
she loved.

She didn't go mooning after wild hairs and moon-
beams...the way she'd done years ago with Trey.

The way she seemed to still be doing with him
now.

The telephone jangled just as she'd finished lock-
ing up and was pulling the sweatshirt over her head.
She sank on the ivory comforter to grab the receiver
on the far side of the bed.

"Am I calling too late?"

Oh, man. It was her own personal wild hair and
moonbeam, and his question struck her as downright
humorous. Was there ever an inconvenient time for
chocolate? Winning the lottery? Being happy? Diana closed her eyes, knowing darn well she was
thrilled to hear Trey's voice no matter what the personal risk to her heart. Just hearing his slow, magnetic baritone invoked memories of the first night

when he'd kissed her and either warned her—or promised—that things could get complicated between them real fast. "No, Trey, the hour's fine. And how's our miniature femme fatale today?"

"Well, I guess she decided to tell the preschool teacher how to run the class. Specifically I think she had in mind revamping the disciplinary system on how little boys with cooties should be handled."

She started chuckling, and Trey recounted more of Molly's antics to make her laugh again. She always loved hearing about Mol, and she'd taken so strongly to Molly—and vice versa—that Trey's encouraging the three of them to spend more and more time together was no surprise. Except that the little one was invariably asleep by eight, and Trey had developed these sneaky, subtle tricks to make her stay just a little longer. Even after weeks, she felt startled when he initiated a kiss or embrace. And more confoundedly stunned at the power of the force field between them.

"You were going to drive up to the reservation today, weren't you?" he asked her.

"Yes." Diana snuggled into the comforter. "I guess that's pretty foolish when I know there's no funding for a full-time job. But the principal's been so enthusiastic about listening to the reading program I'd like to set up. And on days I'm not called to substitute teach, there's really no reason I can't go up there and tutor little ones every day if I wanted to."

"Except that no one wants to pay you." Trey had listened to her on this subject before.

She sighed. "Well, it's not like it's anyone's fault that there's no funding. And I love doing it. The money is a problem. If I'm going to stay in Whitehorn, I need to get serious about finding full-time work. I hate mooching off my dad—and I'm just too darn old to be dependent on family for a living."

"Something tells me your dad is perfectly happy you're there."

"Yeah, he is. And he keeps telling me to relax. Enjoy being home. Think through what I really want to do, and quit being in such a hurry." As she spoke, Diana realized this was exactly one of the things she'd never expected. That Trey would be so easy to talk to. Or that in such a short time, he'd know so much about her.

"You've suddenly gone quiet on me," Trey murmured. "You getting tired?"

"A little," she said, which was a total lie. The same confusion wrapped around her mind every time she talked to Trey. At first, she'd assumed he was being nice because Molly had taken such a liking to her. And after that, she'd assumed the lunacy that affected her in Whitehorn would simply go away if she gave it some time. Only time kept passing.

Enough time that right now, curled under the ivory comforter with the phone tucked to her ear, she could so easily imagine him. Curled under the

blanket with her. Naked. In the dark. Kissing her
like the other night. A good-night kiss that started
in her car and somehow astoundingly ended up in
the cold grass sparkling like diamonds in the moonlight, Trey's laughter sounding low and throaty, both
of them breathing hard.

"Diana, will you be able to come over on Tuesday night? To help me with that costume thing for
Molly's school play?"

There. Some sanity. She swallowed fast. Everything stayed wonderfully easy if they just kept talking about Molly. "No problem. I told you I'd be
glad to."

"You're sure we're not imposing? I'm afraid Mol
would ask for your full-time attention if we didn't
put a lid on it. That doesn't mean I want you to feel
obligated to say yes every time."

"Trey, I love spending time with her. Honestly.
Unless you're worried that she's starting to get too
attached to me—"

His voice caressed her ear like the stroke of velvet. "Oh, I think she is. And I know I am. Are you
going to scare off if I finally come out and admit
that the two of us are wooing you, Diana Brennan?"

Chapter 4

Trey didn't want to marry her. He wasn't wooing her. He couldn't be. It was just that problem with lunacy that had shown up since she'd been home—the one that cropped up every time she was around him. Like now.

Diana managed to look at the daughter rather than the dad, and reminded herself that Brennan women were strong. Strong, self-reliant and steady as rocks. And by God, she was going to shake this problem with lunacy or die trying.

"Do I look bea'ful?"

Diana rocked back on her heels and removed the pins from her mouth so she could answer. "More than beautiful. You look breathtaking, Mol. You're going to be the most beautiful pumpkin in the whole play—although I don't think we'd better let your daddy go shopping alone again."

Said daddy glanced up from where he was hunkered by the fireplace, as if he sensed he was being insulted. "Hey, I took Simpson," he said defensively.

"Yeah, and the two of you came home with how many yards of orange velvet? This is going to be the most expensive pumpkin that ever starred in a preschool play."

Molly tugged at Diana's pale blue sweater. "But I'm worth it, aren't I, Diana?" she asked confidently.

"You're worth more than the sun and the moon," Diana agreed, with absolutely no hesitation. "And okay. You're all done getting fitted. Would you like to practice your lines?"

"Yes! Yes! Daddy! Listen to me! And everybody has to be *quiet!*"

"I'm listening," Trey gravely assured her. "Believe me, none of us would miss any of these rehearsals."

And this, Diana mused, was exactly what she was here for. Molly. Maybe she'd been a romantic, ditsy dreamer as a kid, but when her mom died, she fiercely remembered how much her dad and sister had needed her. Really, it was the reason Molly seemed to need her now. Maybe the household was missing a mom, but Diana was the kind of person a child could depend on, which Molly seemed to sense. She'd always come through for people. It was who she was.

And Molly was loving every minute of the attention. The urchin twirled to the middle of the living room, where she paused dramatically. For this epic preschool play, Diana had padded pillows under the stitched orange velvet to make Molly's figure resemble a pumpkin. The orange tights matched perfectly. And once Molly lifted off the pumpkin-lid hat, dark curls tumbled wildly around her shoulders. "Trick or treat!"

These three words, not surprisingly, were greeted with wild applause from her appreciative audience. Diana stood up, and between whistles, screamed, "Encore, encore!" Trey roared, "Bravo!" And Simpson put a beefy hand over his heart to express respect for Molly's acting ability and fervently hissed, "What a star!"

Eventually Molly was conned into taking her costume off, after which a pre-bed tea party was served with real milk and virtual reality cookies on teensy doll-size dishes. When Trey finally stood up and gently insisted it was *really* time for bed this time, though, Molly threw herself in Diana's arms.

"Are you gonna come see me in the play?"

It was all too easy to snuggle the warm, wriggling body. Diana kissed the top of her head, conscious of her daddy standing barely a kiss away himself. "If it's okay, I'd love to come to your play."

"It's okay. I want you to. But you know what, Diana?"

"What?"

"I think you should be my mom, that's what. Then you could make me costumes every day. And we could play. And I could hide my peas in your napkin like we did at dinner."

Diana stroked the soft, dark curls. "You know what, Mol?"

"What?"

"I can be your friend. And help you with things like costumes. I don't need to be your mom to love you or be part of your life, did you know that?"

"Yeah. I guess. But I still think it'd be better if you were my mom."

"I'm honored that you think that, lovebug."

"All you have to do is marry my daddy, you know. It's easy. We get to get new dresses. Then we go to church and throw flowers. Then we go on a honeymoon. That's it. That's all you have to do—"

The rest of the instructions were muffled by a hand over her mouth, courtesy of her father, who carried the little one upside down to bed—which was the best way to keep her giggling. It took a few minutes before Trey returned, because he never rushed his good-nights with his daughter. But when he ambled in the living room, he threw himself on the couch next to Diana.

"She's a monster," he announced.

Diana chuckled. Simpson had typically disappeared a few minutes after Mol's bedtime, and the room felt entirely different with just the two of them. "Something tells me dads have used that particular descriptive term on their daughters before."

"I got a lecture on how to make you fall in love with me. Her best advice was chocolate ice cream." Trey swiped a hand over his face. "When I was four, I'm pretty sure the only thing on my mind was playing with trucks."

Again, she smiled, but her smile suddenly wavered. "Trey, do you think I'm spending too much time with her? I've been worried for the obvious reason. She really seems to be getting attached to me."

He stretched his arm on the back of the sofa, fingers dropping naturally on her shoulder. "Well, I'll tell you the truth. She's never done anything like this with any other woman. Which is partly why she's always startling me with the stuff that comes out of her mouth—I'm just not expecting it. And maybe I should be feeling more embarrassed, but I keep taking lessons from how you're handling this. She never seems to fluster you, Di."

"She doesn't. Not really." She felt his fingertips on her shoulder. Grazing. Skimming the curve of her neck. Exposing her collarbone to the charge of a couple dozen lightning bolts. "One of the things I love best about kids is their honesty. Obviously we have to teach them some tact and get them civilized sooner or later...but that just comes with some coaching en route.'' A fingertip strayed into her hair, curled around his finger, made her feel shivery. "And sometimes I think if you let them see you're embarrassed, you're giving them the wrong message. That it's okay to be curious about certain things but not others, and that their feelings are wrong."

"Well, I think you're incredible with her." His dark eyes did the same thing. Grazing. Skimming. Exposing her face—her mouth—to the charge of his gaze.

"I think the credit goes to you, Dad, that she has so much confidence and sense of self, especially for a squirt that age." She leaned forward, thinking that she'd dropped her shoes somewhere. She had to get up, go home. One of these times, Trey was going to discover she was having this problem with lunacy—if he hadn't already. "I don't get any credit for anything. I'm just around kids all the time. I'm used to them. But back to my question. Do you think she's getting too attached to me?"

Trey didn't protest when he saw her pushing her toes into loafers. "I don't know what 'too attached' means. I think her relationship with you is fantastic for her. She discovered that another adult woman besides her mom can mean something special. How could that possibly be bad?"

"But if I go away, Trey, she'd have to deal with another loss."

"Are you thinking about going away?"

It was a simple question. If he weren't so close, possibly she could have come up with a simple answer. She'd never realized how homesick she was in Chicago, how badly she wanted to be home…yet maybe going back to the big city was her best choice. In Chicago, everything was so much safer. Nothing there but crime and drive-by shootings and gangs to worry about. Here there were shifting timbers. All the petrifying alligators under the bed she'd feared as a child.

Here there was a strong, compelling man coming toward her, his dark eyes on her face, his mouth already open and tilted to take hers in. And then he did, with a kiss that took her breath. Somehow she never expected those kisses, never expected Trey to make any kind of pass. Even after all these weeks, she couldn't seem to believe he actually wanted her. And like before, by the time his lips connected with hers, it was too late.

Magic whispered in the air. The sough of his breath, the masculine scent of him, the feel of his hand cupping her head, angling her close to him…for her, everything about those moments was suspended in time. Outside, she heard the moan of a lonely wind. Inside, she heard only the soft hiss of fire and the potent shadows of firelight, illuminating his face, glowing on the lines of character and strength and power. It wasn't the boy she'd had

a crush on—but the man who she'd fallen hopelessly, helplessly in love with.

His palm stroked her throat, down to the swell of
her breast. Under her navy angora sweater, her heart
started slamming, louder than a drum, louder than a
wild wind and a blizzard gale both. Through her
sweater, through her bra, she could feel her nipple
tighten. Tauten. Ache. Her whole breast seemed to
swell to the molding fit of his palm, and he made a
sound, of desire, of need, and he suddenly pulled
her closer, cradling her on his lap.

Her whole body was electrified. Blood pooled
low, as if her womb were responding to an empty
ache, a need to be filled. Whisper-soft kisses touched
her cheek, caressed her nose, came back to settle
long and compellingly on her mouth, taking in her
tongue, taking in her last shreds of sanity at the same
time.

Trey needed a mom for his Molly. She knew that.
He appreciated that she was a good feminine influence for his daughter. She knew that, too. Possibly
his in-laws would get off his back if he had a mother
in house—or they'd give up fighting him for
custody. Diana didn't believe for a second that
Trey was being deliberately manipulative. A man
couldn't kiss with that kind of tenderness, that kind
of longing, if there wasn't feeling.

But she'd always understood what drew people to
her. When her mom died, it had become so crystal
clear how useless a romantic dreamer was. Her dad

and sister had needed her to be rock steady, strong.
That's what people always needed from other people. A doer, not a dreamer. Someone who was
strong, not someone weak. Her identity, her whole
self-worth, had long hinged on being the kind of
person that others could rely on—the kind of person
who never let a loved one down. She *liked* the practical, responsible woman she'd turned into.

And she was scared of the blindly impulsive
woman she seemed to become around Trey...but oh,
this lunacy had a magical, exciting side, too. He'd
kissed her before. She knew his taste, his scent, his
textures. She knew his first kisses always seemed
questing. Not tentative, but always asking. Did she
want this? And only when he felt sure of an answer
did he move into deeper, darker kisses, softer kisses,
dangerous kisses. Kisses that dragged moans out of
her and groans out of him. Hands were suddenly
hustling to clutch, to claim. Skin temperatures
soared fever high. Oxygen was sucked from the
atmosphere. Annoyances—a couch arm, lamplight
glaring, a distant telephone—struck her as infuriat-
ing and unreasoning frustrations.

She could feel how much he wanted her, feel how
hard and pulsing he'd become as she twisted closer
in his lap. Her fingers sieving through his hair only
seemed to make his eyes darken with fire. The bones
in his face seemed to tighten and tense, as if suffering pain...yet she caught smiles between his kisses,

and a gurgle of low masculine laughter when her elbow accidentally poked him.

He liked this teasing. And so did she. She knew perfectly well that a grown man wasn't going to be happy volunteering for this kind of frustration forever, but she couldn't seem to think that far ahead. She only knew him when he was kissing her. And when she was with him, it felt like everything in the world could come right with desire this powerful, this fabulous, this silky pull from deep, deep inside her so huge that it obliterated any fears in her head.

"Trey? Diana? I wondered if you two might like a nightcap before— Oh. Hey, I'm sorry, excuse me."

Faster than a hair trigger, Diana's head jerked up at the sound of Simpson's voice. Yet, that swiftly, Simpson was already disappearing from the doorway and pulling the door closed behind him. And though her heart was suddenly hammering with the alarmed guilt of discovery, Trey was still only looking at her. Still only intent on her. He never even glanced up or seemed to notice that Simpson had been in the room.

"Diana," he started to say gently.

"I have to go. It's so late. I can't believe how late it is, I—"

As if she weren't making frantic movements to vault off his lap and stand up, he only looked more calm, more intent. "Why are you afraid of this?"

"Afraid? I'm not afraid."

His eyes searched hers. "I'm not playing around. Is that what you're worried about? That I'm not serious about you? But, Diana, being a single dad with a daughter as old as Molly, I couldn't sleep around even if I wanted to. And I don't have a great history behind me. I have no interest in a relationship with a woman unless I really believe we've got a shot at a real one."

A wave of protectiveness—all right, of love—swept through her. She reached over and kissed him. It was the first time she'd ever initiated physical contact between them, but she reassured herself that this wasn't a kiss of passion, but only one intended to communicate caring. "I know you're not playing, not in any manipulative or careless sense," she said softly. "And I care about you, too, Trey."

Enough to not want him—or Molly—hurt. At least by her. And if that meant keeping a physical distance between her and Trey, then Diana was determined. She simply had to try harder.

"Are we finally ready?" Trey called up the stairs. "Come on, punkin, shake a leg. We need to leave if we're going to get to the school on time."

"Well, I can't go, Daddy. My hair isn't right. The play'll just have to wait."

Trey stared at Simpson. Simpson stared back at him. "Um, can't you just brush it and come down, sweetie?"

"Daddy!"

Both men heard the tone of disgust. Simpson cleared his throat. "I think they come out of the womb this way. Don't argue with her. Go with it."

"Is there anything I could help with?" Trey called.

"No!"

Simpson motioned for him to sit on the third stair up, then plunked his three hundred pounds next to him. "Maybe it's the star temperament. Or stage fright. She couldn't be getting PMS before the age of five, could she?"

"I don't know. Diana would know. But then if Diana were here, we wouldn't be having the problem with hair to begin with."

Simpson smoothed his Mickey Mouse tie over the ample shelf of his stomach. The last time Trey had seen Simpson in a suit was for a funeral. Same suit. Same tie. "I could get us a bracer," Simpson suggested hopefully.

"Nah. The precedent is too scary. Think. If we need a drink before a nursery school play, how are we ever going to cope with the big stuff? Like high school graduation. And a wedding."

"Don't go there." Simpson shuddered. "One crisis at a time. At the moment, a nursery school play seems traumatic enough. Is Diana coming?"

"You already asked me that twice. And yes, she'll be there. But she wanted to drive separately because she was working until almost five on the reservation this afternoon. She was afraid we'd be late if we waited for her.''

"I think you should tell her what you did," Simpson said grumpily.

Trey sighed. They'd already argued about this several times. His friendship with R. L. Simpson went back to the days before Trey had money. Few outsiders understood how two totally unalike men could be close friends, but Simpson had been a wrangler on the Derringer ranch when Trey first knew him. An injury ended his cowboy days, but the injury hadn't stopped Simpson from befriending a green, hungry, dumb kid like himself back then. Maybe R.L. was tough around the edges and lacked formal education, but he'd stand in front of a semi to protect Mol—his loyalty was beyond absolute. Valuing his old friend, though, didn't mean Trey didn't occasionally find him a pain in the keester.

He tried explaining. Again. "If I tell Diana that I funded the program for the high-risk kids on the reservation, then she'll think I did it for her."

"Which you did."

"Yeah. But the point is that Diana's independent. And the reading program she put together for the high-risk Native American kids is really outstanding. She deserves credit. But she won't believe that if she thinks I pulled strings."

"You more than pulled strings. You paid for the whole damn thing."

Trey scowled at Simpson. "But that's the problem. She could feel beholden. Like she owes me. And that's the last thing I want Diana to feel for me.''

''Why? It was a great thing for you to do. Seems to me it shows that you care about her.''

''Simpson—we've had a four year old keep us waiting more than an hour to go to a nursery school play. You think either of us can claim to be an expert on the female mind?''

''Well...no.''

''I'm afraid of making a mistake with her. It matters too much. So just forget about it, okay? I do plan to tell Diana about it some day. Some day when she will understand in her own heart why I did it.''

The princess eventually came flouncing down the stairs. Both men were too smart to say anything about her hair and risk the four year old's wrath all over again, and they were late besides. Ten minutes later they barreled into the parking lot of the nursery school. Diana had parked her dad's red pickup and stepped out.

Just seeing her, his heart arrested and then pumped double time. The sky was all roiled up with snow clouds, heavy and dark in midafternoon, but even against that steel-gray background she looked gorgeous. She was wearing a red wool cape over a long swirling skirt and boots, her face flushed from hustling, her hair whipping in the wind as she charged toward them—swooping to kiss Molly first, then say, ''Hi there, sweetie,'' to Simpson, and when she got good and around to it, she smiled at him.

It was just a smile. And a stingy one. But it was still a personal smile—nothing like she was giving anyone else—and the flare of her color in her cheeks was clearly about awareness. Sexual awareness. The way her eyes met and ducked and then remet his echoed that vibrant, lusty sexual awareness...and so did that little swish in her behind when she took off with Molly, talking girl talk and rehearsal preparations and leaving the men in their wake.

"I'll help her get into the pumpkin costume, but you guys save me a seat, okay?" Diana called over her shoulder.

Anything she did was okay. Trey just kept thinking, *Oh, man, I don't want to make a mistake with her.* She didn't get it, he knew. She just couldn't seem to believe he was wooing her—much less that he loved her. Maybe she believed a single dad with a none-too-happy first marriage was a lousy risk. Maybe his money got in the way. He felt unsure exactly what made her so cautious...only that she lost that caution when he kissed her.

And so did he. His whole life he'd been lonely, and truth to tell that never seemed like all that big a problem—until he met Diana. Kissed Diana. Spent time with the first and only woman who'd ever spun his world the right way. Tonight, Trey mused. Tonight he was determined to escalate their relationship. To show her more of what he felt. To *risk* more of what he felt.

Something had to give. Trey felt like he was standing on a cliff edge, with a killer fall below and a perilous climb in the other direction. One way or another he had to move, because living in this limbo netherworld was untenable.

At the moment, though, the nursery school class was flooding on stage. Amazingly—for a play that only lasted ten minutes—there was standing-room only in the auditorium. One star actor tripped, fell to his knee and cried. One star actress socked the girl next to her. Costumes fell apart en route to center stage. Still, the audience stayed spell-bound...except when individual actors spoke their lines, at which point certain biased folks in the audience leaped to their feet to scream and stomp and shriek approval.

"Do you believe how these grown adults are behaving for a little kids' play?" Trey whispered to Diana.

But when it was his daughter's turn to do her epic line...well, obviously Trey had to whistle and stomp and thunderously applaud louder than the other parents. They had nice kids, but he was clearly the only one with the real prodigy.

"Oh, my God," Diana said to Simpson. "He's pitiful. Even worse than the rest."

"Hey. Did you see her? Was she perfect? Was

she beautiful? Did she put the other kids to shame or what?''

He had a single red rose—thorns removed, of course—waiting for Molly when she came out, cheeks flushed like fever and her curls bouncing. ''Did you see me, Dad? Did you?''

''I did, and you were fabulous.''

''I get the rose? For real?''

''Yup, just for you.''

Simpson and Diana got to give her kisses, but Trey got to give her the piggyback ride to the car and then let her win the con job for ice cream even though it was before dinner. Most days he had panicked moments about what kind of parent he was, whether he was good enough, whether he had anything in him worth the precious charge of his incredible daughter. But some days, like this one, it was just so damn much fun to be her dad that the doubts all slipped under the cracks for a while.

Later, much later, after dinner and when Mol was finally put to bed, he climbed downstairs to find Diana pouring both of them short glasses of wine in the kitchen. ''I have to go home. Really full day tomorrow. But I figured you were exhausted, Dad.''

''Man, I am. This being in a play is hard work.''

She laughed. ''I don't know why you waste your time making money and doing all that silly investment stuff when it's perfectly obvious that you were born to be around kids.''

''Are you kidding? I couldn't survive a classroom

the way you do. Raising one is giving me gray hair...and she isn't even five yet. And we've been so busy, I never had a chance to ask you—how's it going with the new job?''

"Oh, Trey." Her face lit up like diamonds in the sun. "Those kids are so special, you can't imagine. They're just thriving. That's the whole point, you know? I don't believe there's any such thing as a child who can't read. Some just need an innovative and personal approach to get them moving. And the point is, if we don't catch those high-risk kids in the beginning, they start thinking of themselves like failures. Even by sixth grade, it can be too late. They already think of school and tests as their enemies by then...."

He'd heard her rant and rave at length on this subject before.

"So that's the whole thing. Never giving a child the chance to fail. Making sure they're successful from the start. Making sure they *can* read. And then inspiring them to want to get ahead. Kids *want* to learn. All kids. It's their nature. With a child like Molly, who's already so bright..."

He'd heard her rant and rave on that angle of the subject before, too.

"But I'm so worried that it won't be funded for another year. I'm trying to document everything, the progress of every single child who's participating, with as much detail as I can. You know. Really *prove* what a program like this is doing and is capable of doing—''

"I don't know, Di, somehow I just have a feeling that you won't have a problem with funding next year."

"Well, you're more of an optimist than I am. I'm afraid to take any chances. I really am going to document every child's progress with absolute care, no mistakes, no leaving anything out. No fudging it, either. I think people have gotten suspicious about wasted money in educational programs because there's been cheating before. I want to show what these teaching methods can really do, especially for high-risk kids...."

He kissed her. Not because he wanted to shut her up. Not because he'd heard all this before—positively this was her favorite rant-and-rave subject—and he could finish some of her sentences by now. Truth to tell, she lit up so high when she was talking about teaching that he could have listened to her all night.

The kiss, though, it just wouldn't wait. He'd loved watching her with Molly. Loved watching her tease him for being hopelessly biased as a dad. Loved watching her shy, gentle ways of fitting in with his three-person family, never intruding, not even once, not ever, but just seeping into their lives the way a flower bud could bloom even through cracked soil sometimes.

She didn't seem to mind being jumped right in the middle of his kitchen.

Her lips softened under his. Then, slowly, her right hand lifted to his arm. Then, slowly, her left hand lifted to his shoulder. And this soft, slow, woman sound came from her throat. A sigh of need. Of willfulness and pleasure. Maybe nine o'clock in the middle of his kitchen, with ice cream bowls getting stickier on the counter by the minute, was a crazy time and place to kiss her, particularly when she was teaching tomorrow and obviously didn't need to be up late.

But she didn't kiss as if she were thinking about tomorrow's school day.

She didn't kiss like she noticed they were standing in the middle of a kitchen, either.

And Trey thought, *Now. It's now or never.*

Chapter 5

Could a heart actually shake?

His mouth. Oh, my, his mouth. Like silk-satin sex. Warm and wooing. Kisses that plugged straight into her emotions like a direct current to a lightning storm.

Diana didn't know how long she'd been telling herself lies. That she'd been spending all this time with the Derringers solely because she was crazy about Molly. That the kisses she'd shared with Trey before had been accidental, incidental. She'd have to be crazy to believe that a killer hunk of a multi-millionaire would seriously be attracted to your average plain old grade-school teacher.

She'd been trying so hard not to sucker into that kind of lunatic type thinking.

Only damn.

Hearts did shake. And she never wanted this lunacy to end. Possibly she was unsure what Trey felt, but she was absolutely sure about what she did. All her life, she'd dreamed of this. All her adult life, she'd tried to talk herself out of believing in the fairy tale, yet still she'd yearned for the kind of love that would take her under, sweep her away, wasn't just about sensible compatibility but about the one man who made her feel different than every other man ever had. Or could.

It was stupid, believing in anything so unrealistic.

She believed it all. Her hands climbed his arms, wrapped around his neck, hung on. He picked her up, still kissing her, blindly walked out of the kitchen, still kissing her, began a precarious, perilous, stair-climbing journey upstairs, still kissing her. The only thing she knew about his house's upstairs was that Molly's bedroom was to the right.

He aimed in the opposite direction, down a pitch-black hall. His shoulder banged against a wall. He kept going, ducked inside a yawning black room with big, burly shadows. Stopped. Used a boot to close the door—not a slam, but none too quietly. She whispered swiftly, "Molly—"

"—could sleep through an earthquake. Don't worry. But if you plan on going home tonight, Diana, you'd better tell me in the next three seconds."

Within the next three seconds, she framed his face in her hands and kissed him hot and fiercely.

Eventually shadows turned into discernible shapes. She could make out no colors in the room, nor did she need to. Silver shafts of moonlight slanted across a king-size bed. Her spine dropped onto something cool and feather bouncy. That quickly he followed her down, his weight and heat welcomed. Lips sucked at lips. Tongues twisted together. One openmouthed kiss hissed into another, moaned into another.

Clothes were peeled off. His boots first, then her long skirt. If there'd been time, she would have stopped to laugh, because he pulled one arm out of her sweater, then seemed to forget about it...and he got around to unbuttoning the skirt at her waist, skimming it down, but neglected to remember she was still wearing her boots. Both of them were more than half dressed when his hand dove inside silk, cupped her, teased her with a long, slow finger. And still his mouth kept coming with more kisses, each sweeter and more intoxicating than the last.

She ripped at his shirt, tore at his pants, yanked his tie off with strangling speed. That he'd dressed up for his daughter's nursery school play both charmed and frustrated her. There was so much more to take off, soft, ironed linen, trousers that landed with a woosh, too many buttons, too much material of all kinds. And when she finally managed to get him bare, he disappeared on her.

But not far, and not for long. First she sensed him at the side of the bed, hurling pillows, and then she heard his laughter wicked and low from the bed's foot as he yanked off her boots. After that he dove back in bed with her, hauling a comforter with him and draping it over their heads as if making a cocoon. He was already her cocoon. The darn man slept with his window open. The wind had started to howl, a typical Montana night wind talking all about the winter ahead, trying to bring that chill in.

But there was no chill. Not in Trey's bed.

So dark. All she knew were textures. The pleat of crisp hair on his chest. His stubbly cheeks, the muscles rippling under his shoulders, the tautness of his abdomen, and beyond those gruffly masculine textures was the sensual contrast of his mouth. His tongue was soft and warm. Evocative, tender, loving. This was so much more than sex. Maybe she was caught up in that want-to-believe world, but she tasted kisses of tenderness and sharing, kisses fierce with wanting and wooing both, kisses that yearned for far more than just physical release.

She told herself she'd die if he only wanted this one night, but the truth was, she didn't care. At that moment, being with him was everything. She'd loved him for so long. He was the prince in her every dream, the man she heard in every song of love. Tomorrow, she could go back to being sensible and responsible again.

Tonight, she wanted her man. She wanted to be the lover her great-great-grandmother had been—a woman who gave everything for love, who was strong and free enough to risk everything for the one man who mattered to her.

At some point, he clawed away from her and found protection, but that only took moments. Then he was back, feeding the rush and fire that both of them wanted. They'd been teasing for weeks and weeks now. Both of them had had enough. It was impossible to stop an arrow once the bow released it. It simply flew, straight and true. She flew, straight and true, toward the one man who'd started this aching, reckless, exhilarating longing for completion with him...only with him.

As he started a relentless rhythm, pleasure sheared through her, slicing past any fears she'd ever had. She'd never felt alive, not like this, not like with him. She called his name as if lost in a thick woods and desperate to be found...and then he found her, took her with him, out, up, higher than she could ever remember climbing, ever imagine feeling. When they both tipped off the sun, she felt the joyful emotion of belonging to him, with him, part of him. And then they both collapsed, still wrapped tight around each other.

Diana's eyes suddenly shot open as if she had been startled by the bang of a gun. But there was no bang, no noise at all in the quiet house—except for the deep, slow breathing of the man beside her. Trey's arm was tucked under her breast, effectively scooping her into the sheltering spoon of his body.

Warm, evocative memories flooded her mind of their lovemaking, and a lump suddenly filled her throat. Like a crazy woman, she suddenly wanted to cavort on a rooftop singing love songs at the top of her lungs. Instead—thankfully—she spotted the clock on the bedside table.

The luminous dial claimed it was five o'clock. Time for a woman to get sane. Fast. The last Diana knew, it had been midnight. She'd intended to get up and drive home just the minute she caught her breath...only Trey hadn't seemed inclined to let her catch her breath at midnight—or any other time.

Quickly, silent as a cat, she inched away from that warm, evocative male body and stood up. Swiftly she gathered her clothes—everything but her underpants, which were hiding somewhere in the wicked shadows—and tiptoed out the door. Across the hall from the bedroom was a bathroom with a unicorn night-light. Bleary-eyed, she stepped in there—and almost shrieked when she heard a sudden voice.

"Hey, Di." Molly climbed down from the toilet. Hair tumbling in her face, her feet bare, she stumbled toward her bedroom, dragging a two-foot yellow rabbit in her wake.

She'd disappeared from sight before Diana remembered to breathe. Molly had looked and acted so sleepy that she might never remember seeing her...but guilt bells were suddenly clanging in Diana's pulse. This was the exact reason she'd intended to leave earlier, so there was no chance

Molly or Simpson could realize she'd spent the night with Trey. It just wouldn't be right. She yanked on clothes, flew downstairs and grabbed her coat.

Outside, frost rimmed the lawn and dressed the black tree branches with a silvery white coating. The moon had fallen, but the predawn light had a magical moon glow that seemed to put a pearl hush on the whole world. She wanted to savor that precious magic, not charge off like a guilty bandit trying to get away. She still had that magical feeling on the inside from Trey's touch and the emotions he'd shared with her. And yeah, she knew exactly how badly she'd fallen in love with him.

Thick in love. High in love, scary in love. Like she'd rather be with him than eat or sleep. Like she could dance on mountaintops for the sheer joy of it. There'd just never been any other man for her, not like him—and never would be—which Diana figured was about time that she finally faced.

But love didn't make her choices any easier.

She drove home, feeling shaky and edgy, as if every safe mooring she'd always counted on had suddenly turned illusive and uncertain. She hadn't stopped being a romantic dreamer in her youth for nothing. When her mom died, she'd felt ripped apart. Being there for her sister and her dad had held her together. Being needed gave her an identity.

She wasn't afraid of being hurt. But she *did* need to be there for others. And turning into some lunatic wild-eyed dreamer was inexcusable when there was

a child involved—and a man who'd already been
hurt by a troubling relationship. Loving Trey meant
wanting to be the kind of woman he could count on.

But she truly didn't know what he needed in his
life, and that problem was still dominating her mind
Saturday when she kidnapped her sister for lunch at
the Hip-Hop Café in town. Suzanna's baby was due
anytime after Thanksgiving, which meant she was
getting too big to be comfortable doing anything.
Diana figured they both needed a break away from
the ranch and work and real life. She treated her
sister to a manicure and haircut, and then both settled into a booth at the Hip-Hop and ordered heaping
bowls of barley soup.

She'd gotten Suzanna laughing over a steady
round of terrible pregnant-woman jokes when her
sister suddenly stood up, gasping and still chuckling.
"Well, you know where I'm going. Between the
baby and laughing so hard, my kidneys are in real
trouble."

Diana couldn't help but grin as her sis waddled
toward the ladies' room...until her gaze was suddenly drawn to a woman at the back of the café.
There would have been no particular reason to notice her, except that the minute Suzanna disappeared
into the bathroom, the tall, slim older woman stood
up and seemed to be deliberately striding toward
her.

Diana vaguely recognized the face—most faces
were familiar in Whitehorn—but she couldn't im-

mediately place her. Church, she thought. She remembered seeing that patrician profile and swept-up
hair and that pricey, snobby look, the woman talking
to the minister outside church sometimes…and
abruptly her stomach knotted in a fist. She recognized her, all right. It was Molly's grandmother. Regina Kingston.

The Kingstons who'd been fighting Trey for custody of Molly ever since their daughter had died.

Diana's toes suddenly went ice cold with nerves.
She couldn't imagine why Mrs. Kingston would be
interested in talking to her, yet the older woman kept
coming, looking tall, proud, determined…and holding her gloves as she stopped at their booth. "I see
your father in church most Sundays, Diana. But I
haven't seen you in years now."

The Kingstons had always considered themselves
too upper crust to spend much time chatting up the
Brennans. Again, Diana felt needles of worry clench
in her stomach…but hiding from trouble had never
been her way. "Well, I've only been home for a
couple months now. And I especially haven't had
much time since catching a teaching job on the
Laughing Horse Reservation…but I've still been
lucky enough to meet your incredibly wonderful
granddaughter."

Surprise shone in the older woman's gray eyes,
followed by a brief hesitation. "That's why I
stopped to talk. For Molly."

"I adore her," Diana said easily, honestly.

Again she appeared to take the older woman aback, but then Mrs. Kingston started meticulously threading her fingers into kid leather gloves. "Yes, well. Molly's mentioned you. More than once. But yesterday she happened to mention that you'd been to a sleepover at her house."

Diana heard the ice cold disapproval in the older woman's voice and felt terror, hotter than fire, lick at her heart. Oh, God. No court would ever take a child away from her natural father unless there were serious grounds. Grounds like immoral conduct. Her smile dropped faster than a lead ball. She just couldn't let it happen, couldn't do nothing, couldn't be part of a problem for Trey and Molly without trying to fix it. Words slipped out before she could think. "Mrs. Kingston," she said seriously, "I want you to know that I love Molly. And I had hoped that word of our engagement wasn't going to get out—even to Molly—until Trey and I had a chance to—"

"Engagement?" One leather glove fell to the floor.

Words kept bubbling out of her mouth like a babbling brook. "We never meant for Molly to realize I was there, of course. In fact, it was strictly for Molly's sake that Trey and I have chosen to be quiet about our relationship. Neither of us want to hurry Molly into—"

"Engagement?" Mrs. Kingston repeated.

"Believe me, Mrs. Kingston, I realize that no one

could ever take the place of your daughter. I would never try. But actually, I hope I can help Molly always remember her real mom...just by being another female adult in her life who really loves and cares for her. And who she can talk to about her mother whenever she wants to.''

When Suzanna emerged from the bathroom, Mrs. Kingston was gone and Diana was so shaken she could barely lift a teacup without spilling.

Her sister noticed immediately. ''Hey, what's wrong? You're all white—''

''Oh, God. I've just done a terrible thing, Suzanna.''

She never lied. It went against her whole grain. And she called Trey the very instant she got home to confess the mortifying fib she'd told, but Molly was right in the room and he couldn't talk. Rather than risk Molly overhearing the conversation, she asked if he might come over to her place later. Trey didn't hesitate. He kept saying that he didn't know what the trouble was, but to quit worrying about it.

But he didn't know what she'd done.

Trey drove toward the Big Sky, his fingers drumming a rhythm of anticipation on the steering wheel. Diana had sounded upset on the phone. Something was wrong—yet ironically, he felt nothing but relief. Hell, he'd known something was wrong from the night they made love, because she'd been skittering away from him ever since. Whatever put this partic-

ular bee in her bonnet, Trey was grateful. Few problems were unsolvable if people just talked, but until
now, Diana had been so obviously shying away
from any serious talk time with him that he'd been
worried what was wrong.

The headlights of his black Camry illuminated the
Big Sky Ranch sign. Once he turned, the corrals and
barn and wagon stable were off to the left. Something was going on tonight in the horse barn, because the doors were open, yellow light spilling out
in a rectangular pool. The big house was on the
right, white with green shutters, rockers on the wraparound veranda and the yard neatly snugged in with
a white picket fence.

Nothing about the Big Sky setup was as fancy as
the Derringer spread where he'd worked as a boy,
but growing up—even in the years he'd been drawn
to money the way only a poor kid could be—he'd
been drawn to the Brennans. Everything about their
place was built to live in, built to last. His aunt used
to say that the Brennans were good people, long-
distance runners. That's how Diana's family struck
Trey, too, as folks who'd stick it out through the
tough times, tend toward common sense, always
have a coffeepot going on the kitchen stove and no
one minding if you walked in with your boots on.

Diana's place was just beyond the house to the
east, a miniature echo of the big house with the same
white framing and green shutters. Just seeing the
light in her window put a bullet of speed in his

pulse. He cut the engine and bolted toward her door, warning himself to slow down, take it easy, give her space, give her time, just keep his hands to himself until he knew what the problem was.

Something sabotaged his good sense, though, because the instant she opened the door, he hauled her close and plastered a soft one on her mouth. It wasn't his fault. Maybe a saint could have resisted her, but not a man as hopelessly, fiercely in love as he was. She looked so damned tempting besides, with a coral cord shirt jammed into jeans, waist cinched tight, all that flaming nervous color in her cheeks and her hair all over as if she'd brushed it with a tornado wind.

And she didn't seem to really mind being hauled up against him. She met his kiss. More than met it. Her eyelashes fluttered down and then her eyes closed and she clutched his arms for ten seconds— a good ten seconds—before suddenly jerking back and getting that hand-wringing-worry look in her eyes again.

"Okay, you. Now what's so terrible?" He shot in, pushed off his coat and boots, looked around when she offered him a drink. He volunteered to take a beer off her hands if she had one, thinking her place was nice. Too small. Barely camp-out room. But the ivories and candles and silk flowers she had around were distinctly Diana, no doodads and clutter, but the scents and textures all distinctly sensual, like her. She emerged from the little kitchen, handing him a wineglass and motioning him toward the couch.

He considered teasing her about the wine he'd never asked for and instead just took it. To test how distracted she was, though, he pulled a pale scrap of coral fluff with lace from his back jeans pocket. "You left something at my place last Tuesday night." He watched her expressions change until she recognized the underpants. First her eyes flashed to his. Then came the flush. Then the hint of a wicked, shared smile—which he loved…but then her gaze darted swiftly away from him.

She sat down on the couch like her heart was carrying lead. "I can't believe I forgot those. And I'd think it was funny, except…except it isn't." She gulped a breath. "Look, Trey. I did something I shouldn't have. I lied. It was wrong. What happened is that I got shook up and I didn't think. I couldn't be more sorry. But the thing is—the thing that matters is—we can make the problem go away. In fact, it never has to be any kind of problem for you. You just have to dump me."

He was expecting trouble. Not a gushed garble of words that made no sense at all. "Huh?"

"I had lunch today. With my sister. And while I was sitting at the restaurant, Regina Kingston stopped at my table. Your mother-in-law—"

At the mention of his late wife's mother's name, he decided maybe he'd have a sip of wine, after all. A patient sip. "Yeah, I know who she is, and she's

Molly's grandma—but she's no relation to me, not any more.''

"Well, she stopped to talk to me when Suze was in the bathroom. The problem, Trey, is that Molly saw me the other morning when I left so early.''

"So?''

"So she told her grandmother that I was there for a sleepover.'' More words gushed out. "That's why she stopped to talk to me. Because she knew I'd spent the night. And it just came out of my mouth— I said we were engaged. God, I'm sorry—''

"Engaged?''

A vigorously guilty nod. "I never meant to do anything to embarrass you. I was just so afraid that the Kingstons would try to make something of that—make out like we'd done something deliberately illicit in front of Molly—when the truth is, Mol would never have known I was there if she hadn't gotten up in the middle of the night to go potty. But the thing is, I just got rattled because I was afraid the Kingstons would try and cause you trouble—''

"So we're engaged, are we?'' Trey stroked his chin and tried to look suitably grave. That seemed a more mature response than using her mattress for a trampoline and yahooing at the top of his lungs. Privately, though, he thought, *Who'd have thunk it? Sometimes people really do win the lottery.* He said slowly, "Molly will be thrilled.''

Diana didn't seem to catch that. She yanked a guilty hand through her hair. Again. "It'll all be okay, Trey. You just need to wait a little bit and then kind of let it be known in town that you dumped me. I don't think anyone would judge an engaged couple for spending the night together, and there's no reason the Kingstons ever had to know that wasn't the real circumstance. I'm sorry I made the darn lie up. At the time, all I could think of was trying to protect you both from the Kingstons—''

"What if…" Slowly he stroked his chin again. "What if I like the idea?"

"Pardon?"

"You love my daughter. In fact, you're darn well crazy for my daughter."

A bewildered frown. "Well, of course I am. But—"

Be careful, he warned himself. And he'd already realized that he needed to tread more carefully than a mouse in rattlesnake country with Diana. It was easy to see how fast she leaped to do the responsible thing—one of the things he loved about her—but for some unknown reason, she ducked hard and fast anywhere near the subject of love. Still, there was no way he could have the sun this close without trying his best to reach for it. "You understand Mol better than anyone ever has, Diana."

"Not better than you—"

"In a different way than me. Come on, you have to know how fantastic you are with her."

"It's just that I lost a mother, too, Trey. So we have this kindred spirit thing going—"

"Uh-huh. That's what I'm saying. You *do* have a great relationship going. No one could ever be a better mom for Molly than you. And then there's the two of us."

Shock seemed to stun her to silence. Then she said, "The two of us?"

"Maybe you weren't thinking of marriage. Maybe I wasn't, either, at exactly this moment in time," he lied. "But we've gotten along like a house afire ever since we re-met up. The two of us just keep getting better all the time. I suspect we'd have ended up talking seriously about marriage in a matter of time anyway—"

"Trey, I'm not so sure of that. I can't imagine you would—"

"You seem happy to be back in Whitehorn. You also really seem to love your teaching job on the reservation. And I can't believe you've got any questions about Molly—"

"I don't. About Molly. But—"

He hesitated. Then deliberately let out a worried sigh. "Man, I'm surprised I haven't heard from the Kingstons' lawyers already. It would be just like them to jump on any sign that I was less than a fit parent. They hit their lawyer when I had Mol up until ten o'clock for the county fair last year, did I tell you that?"

"No. Oh, good grief, Trey, they sound so vindictive—"

"Well, I don't want you worried about that. It's

my problem, not yours. But think on it, will you? Marriage?''

''I—''

Before she could try saying anything else, he tugged her close and kissed her. It was the same as before. For some confounded reason, Diana just couldn't seem to believe he really cared about her— no matter what he did, no matter what he said. Yet when he kissed her, everything became mirror clear for both of them.

His heart started chugging. So did hers. Warmth heated her skin. Her lips softened, melted, swelled under his. Her body bowed closer. Fingertips touched his face, shivery, trembly, and then wrapped around his head and pulled him down, pulled him deeper into that nice, wicked, wild kiss.

''Just say yes,'' he murmured. And kissed her again. And again. ''Say yes, love.''

''Yes. Yes. Yes.''

Right then, he wasn't positive if she were saying yes to his spending the night or to the marriage proposal. But when a man was on a winning streak, he didn't test fate with questions. He just went with it.

Chapter 6

Diana felt as if she were stuck in the middle of a magic spell. Her childhood bedroom had been turned into a dressing room for the wedding, but the last time she'd spent any time in this room, she'd been an adolescent girl who still believed in fairy tales and white knights. Now she was getting married. Only somehow she couldn't exactly remember saying yes. She had no idea how Trey had arranged everything so fast. And something was terribly frightening—because this was exactly how the fairy tale was supposed to end, with the damsel getting the white knight.

And that would be wonderful instead of frightening—except that everyone knew real life never, never worked out that way.

One of the two females in the bedroom, however, was dancing on air.

"We're going to get married today, aren't we?"

"Uh-huh." Diana pinned the last rosebud in Molly's hair. Her sister had raided the famous Derringer greenhouses for the coral roses, because for damn sure there were none locally blooming on Thanksgiving weekend. Outside the wind was howling itself into a fitful blizzard.

"And then I get to call you Mom, right?"

"Now, lovebug, we already talked about this. You can either keep calling me Diana or call me Mom. Whatever you want is great with me." She studied her darling's face, then reached over to the dresser for her blusher. Molly needed rouge like she needed a hole in the head, but she instantly tilted her face with an ecstatic grin for this grown-up treat.

"Put on *lots*, okay? And after we get married, then I get to be your daughter, right?"

"Right."

"And then we get to go on our honeymoon, right? To Disney World? Simpson and I both get to go, for real?"

"I don't know how we could possibly have a honeymoon without both of you," Diana said gravely.

"And I look beautiful, don't I? In fact, I'm pro'bly the most beautiful girl you've ever seen, right?"

"Without question." Because the little one was still hopefully staring at all the makeup pots on the dresser, Diana spritzed her wrists with a little Shalimar.

"Diana?"

"What, darlin'?"

Molly met her eyes in the dressing table mirror. "You look beautiful, Di. Not as beautiful as me, but still really cool. But I have to tell you, if you'd just asked my daddy, I just know he'd have bought you a new dress. You didn't have to wear an old one. You coulda had a new dress just like me."

Diana chuckled. "As hard as this may be for you to believe, I wanted to wear this old one. This wedding dress belonged to our great-great-grandmother Isabelle. My mom wore it went she got married. And then my sister, Suzanna, wore it for her wedding. The thing is, we think of the dress as lucky, Mol. Every woman who's worn the dress so far has had a loving marriage." And man, she needed any luck today that she could beg, borrow or steal. "You're going to go out and find my sister now, okay? You stand with Suzanna and she'll tell you when to go down the aisle."

"With the rose petals. I get to throw all the rose petals."

"Yup. You've got the most important job of anybody," Diana assured her, and kissed her forehead...which resulted in an exuberant two-way hug, which messed both of them up all over again. Still, once Molly pranced downstairs to find her new aunt Suzanna, Diana had a couple minutes alone.

She pressed a hand to her nervous stomach, staring at herself in the dresser mirror. Wearing her great-great-grandmother's dress was not only tradition, but she'd prayed it would give her courage. The gown was so precious, long-sleeved with a demure scooped neck, the Irish lace faded from stark white to an delicate antique ivory. It was the kind of dress that could make a girl believe in magic and white knights and honorable quests and...

Lunacy.

She squeezed her eyes closed, thinking that her dad was downstairs. Family. Friends. It seemed right to have a wedding in the home where she'd grown up, the house where all the Brennan traditions of happy marriages had begun. Yet her stomach was suddenly rolling in waves of panic.

She'd been making nonstop jokes about becoming a lunatic ever since she came home to Whitehorn, but suddenly she wasn't laughing. Coming home had forced her to face up to what really mattered, and the truth was, she'd never wanted to live in a high-rise apartment and teach in Chicago's inner city. She wanted to live where she had roots. She wanted to teach where she had an investment in the kids and the community. She wanted love. The whole-cabana kind of love. The kind her grandmother had, and her mom. Romantic love. The risk-everything-and-don't-look-back kind of love. She wanted to raise children with a hero of a man, wanted to fight and make up and grow old with him, wanted to deepen the soul of what they both were in a place that mattered to them. Only...

Nobody really got it all. Only a lunatic believed in the fairy tale—and that was the whole problem. She believed the whole kit and kaboodle when she was with Trey.

Abruptly she opened her eyes and scowled fiercely at the pink-cheeked bride in the mirror. *He doesn't love you,* she warned herself. Sure, he cared about her. And the chemistry was fabulous. But he needed a mom for his daughter—a stable mom and wife, not a lunatic. She thought, hoped, that if she kept her head screwed on in a practical, responsible fashion, she could work hard at making a good marriage and love would come. For both of them.

With her hand on her heart, she spun around, inhaling the memories from her childhood bedroom. So many nights, she'd dreamed of princesses and castles and knights on white horses in that tall feather bed. So many nights, she'd cried herself to sleep after her mom died. But finally, that pain had lessened and started healing, when she'd turned a corner on growing up and determined to turn herself into a woman that her mom would be proud of. Her mom, her grandma, her great-great-grandma Isabelle—they were all women Diana fiercely respected and was proud of. And somehow she just couldn't imagine any of those good, strong women holding out because of some fierce, loony desire for a truly romantic love. It was past time she gave up those stupid illusions once and for all.

She glanced at the wall clock, swiftly adjusted her veil one last time and was turning toward the door when there was a knock.

"Come on in," she called, expecting Suzanna or Nash or Dad—anyone but a complete stranger. The ceremony was due to start ten minutes from now.

The woman who stepped in was older, wearing the garb of a traditional Cheyenne medicine woman—which made Diana automatically respond with a respectful smile of greeting. Her skin was as wrinkled as a brown raisin, her long gray hair coiled into a loose bun at her nape, her expression hard to read...yet her bark-brown eyes seemed warm and perceptive as they settled on Diana.

"Diana...do you know who I am?"

"I'm sorry, but no. Your face is somehow familiar, but I'm just not sure—"

The older woman nodded. "It's all right. I didn't expect you to recognize me. But I've watched you for weeks now, coming to teach the little ones on the reservation. For me, it has been like watching a circle being completed, seeds planted decades ago finally breaking through the soil to grow. You've come home. Really come home where you belong."

"I..." Diana felt mystified. There seemed to be both caring and affection in the older woman's expression, yet she had no idea what any of this conversation meant.

"Don't be upset. I know you have little time before the wedding ceremony. And it's not a day when you should be concentrating on a stranger's words. I just came to bring you a present. My name is Aiyana, and we are kin. I'm the great-niece of Kyle Running Horse."

"Kyle? As in Kyle and Isabelle?"

"Yes." From a pouch at her waist, Aiyana withdrew a small package wrapped in paper.

When Diana peeled back the crinkly folds, she discovered an oval-shaped amulet of hammered silver. An engraving of two running horses was carved into the top of the locket. "This is gorgeous," Diana said reverently, and stroked the striking carving with a delicate fingertip. "But, Aiyana, I'd feel guilty accepting anything like this. It looks like a valuable heirloom. Surely you have family closer to you than—"

"Blood kin closer, yes. But this amulet belongs specifically to you, Diana. Again, it is like watching the arc of a circle finally come together. The first woman to wear this was your great-great-grandmother Isabelle, and she wore it on her wedding day."

"She did?" Diana's eyes widened.

"She did. And inside the amulet is a herb that the old wise ones have always said would bring love to a marriage. That was why your great-great-grandmother wore it, because she feared she would never know love, never be loved. She felt unworthy.

Afraid to believe. Afraid to reach for what was in her heart."

Diana frowned, feeling more confused than ever. "Aiyana, could you have me confused with someone else? Because my sister and I have letters between Isabelle and her Kyle. She was never worried about being loved—they were crazy in love for each other."

"I know nothing of letters. But I am very sure of the history of Kyle and Isabelle." The older woman backed toward the door. "The women in your family are strong, of good hearts. You take care of others well and you seek to do the right thing. This is all good. But I think you and your great-great-grandmother were kindred spirits, Diana. She feared being unworthy, thought that no one would need her for herself. Wear the amulet and follow your heart. It will give you luck."

"But I really don't feel that I can accept—" Before Diana could finish the thought, the Cheyenne woman had backed from the room and closed the door.

She was still standing in stunned confusion in the center of the room when knuckles rapped again on the door. "Aiyana," she started to say. But it was her sister poking her head in.

"Oh, man. You look so beautiful! But you're going to be late if we don't get you downstairs." Suzanna walked in, looking beautiful but distinctly ready to pop her baby any second. She set the bride's bouquet of coral roses on the bed and aimed for Diana.

"You goof! You didn't have to climb the stairs— I was coming—"

"Yeah, well, I started to worry when you weren't already down that something could be wrong. And maybe something is." Her sis came over, brushed a strand of hair here, smoothed a fluff of lace there. "You're looking scared."

"I am."

"Yeah, well. That's like saying a rabbi is Jewish or the Pope's Catholic. Brides are supposed to be jittery. It's in the rule book. The question is more, are you sure? Because if you want to call this off, believe me, I'll make sure it happens. We can run off to Poughkeepsie together if we have to. We can—"

Diana started to smile. Her sister made it impossible not to. "I don't think you're going to be *running* anywhere for a little while, Suze. Or that Nash would appreciate my taking off with you."

"Nash loves me. Nash will recover from any darn fool wild hair I come up with, so you can forget Nash. You're the one who matters right now. And you don't have to do anything unless this is what you really want."

Again Diana smiled. She wanted to tell Suzanna all about the mysterious Cheyenne woman and what she'd said—but that would wait. She picked up the bridal bouquet of roses, pausing only long enough to bury her nose in the sweet promising scent for a moment.

"Stop worrying, Suze. I'm sure," she said softly. And she *was* sure that she could be a good mother to Mol. Sure that Trey needed a mother for his daughter. Sure that they'd get along fine when the lights went off, that they liked and respected each other when the lights were on. She was sure that he needed her.

And if she were wildly, painfully in love with him...well, she just wasn't going to worry about whether Trey loved her right now. The old Cheyenne woman seemed to have some family history confused, but Aiyana had still managed to remind her about what really mattered. Her great-great-grandmother's letters had spoken of a passionate love that only grew deeper with time. Isabelle had defied all convention to marry a half-breed in her day, completely ignoring what others believed was important to a good marriage.

Diana could do the same. She would love Trey. They would make a relationship their own way. And maybe in time the kind of love she dreamed of would grow. To give him up—no, there wasn't a chance.

And with that last thought, she clasped the amulet, grabbed her bouquet, hustled Suzanna out and danced down the stairs to find her groom. Guests were congregated in the living room, furniture pushed aside to make room for chairs and create a makeshift aisle. Her dad was waiting at the stair bottom, pacing and staring at his watch. Molly was doing impatient pirouettes that threatened to topple all the rose petals in her basket. Diana saw all of them....

But not really.

She saw the man standing at the fireplace, looking so piratelike and elegant in the black suit and virgin white linen shirt, his dark eyes waiting for her.

He wanted this marriage. She knew from his smile, from the way his hand unconsciously lifted, just the smallest amount, as if automatically wanting to reach for her. They could make anything work, she told herself.

And desperately wanted to believe that.

Chapter 7

F̲ive days later, Trey stood alone on the hotel balcony overlooking a vista of palm trees and aquamarine water and the beginning of a jewel-toned sunset. The magical landscape had no effect on the facts. As honeymoons went, Trey figured theirs qualified for disaster relief funds.

But that was about to change.

He heard the snick of the door lock opening, then a quiet voice. "Trey?"

"I'm here." He turned just in time to see his new bride stumble toward him. Diana had a smile, but no one would guess they'd been in Florida for the last five days. Her face was as pale as if they'd never left Montana's blizzard weather, and her eyes had soft smudges from tiredness. "Oh," she said warily, "you're still dressed for dinner. I'm so sorry, Trey, I couldn't help being so late—"

"I know you couldn't. And I have to believe after this long day that you're too tired to go out to dinner at all, aren't you?"

"I am a little beat," she admitted, "but if you haven't eaten—"

"Not to worry. No reason to change or lift a finger—or go anywhere. I've got a little surprise planned, but all we have to do is walk down one flight."

"A surprise? Well, that sounds like fun."

The words were right, the positive smile was there, but Trey figured Diana was as excited about a surprise as a case of poison ivy. She was trying to be a good sport. The only thing she likely wanted was twelve straight hours in the closest bed—alone. Which he understood. But things couldn't continue the way they had been.

Guiding her toward the door, he asked, "Did you manage to reach your sister?"

"Yes, finally!" No matter how exhausted she was, her face suddenly glowed with enthusiasm. She didn't seem to notice that he was steering her out the door and down the hall. "Oh, Trey, the baby sounds adorable! And they finally settled on the name Travis. Suzanna said both Nash and Dad were just beside themselves—"

"I'll bet."

"Eight pounds, seven ounces, so he's a healthy little slugger already, even if he was a little early. And the labor wasn't so bad. As far as I can tell, all labor is horrible. But at least it only took six hours, which Suzanna was told is really fast for a first baby—"

Trey wondered if that experience was something that ran in families, such that Diana might be more inclined to have a short, not too bad labor if her sister had. But he didn't dare ask. The subject of babies didn't seem to be in their future. Now that they were legal, apparently they were never again going to make love, either.

So far, their marriage seemed headed in a distinctly backward direction. He steered her past Simpson and Mol's suite, past the elevator, down one flight of stairs. It was a measure of how tired Diana was that she never asked where they were going.

Five days ago, he'd innocently believed he had a shot at winning Diana. And yeah, of course, he realized that Di wasn't that positive about being in love with him. It nipped that she thought he needed rescuing from the accusations of his in-laws—as if he couldn't protect and fight for his own daughter without a marriage to hide behind. But at the time Diana said yes, Trey hadn't cared why she'd agreed to the wedding. Gluing that ring on her finger was the only thing on his mind. Making her part of his life. Sealing their vows with time together.

He'd also assumed that loving her—fiercely, strongly, compellingly, night and day—would eventually encourage her to feel the same. One could only fight exposure to an infectious substance for so long before succumbing—he was sure. But then, five days ago, he'd also been sure that getting married was a way of guaranteeing he'd have private time with his bride.

He pushed open an unmarked door on the seventh floor. Diana looked at him with a curious frown. He didn't answer, only gently motioned her through the doorway.

Until this moment, they'd had no private time.

None. Zip. Zero.

The original plan had been to go to Disney World. Maybe it wasn't the most romantic place on the planet, but it happened to be an unbeatable place to keep his daughter busy and happy, and they had a carry-along baby-sitter in the form of Simpson. The disaster began on the afternoon of their wedding, when their flight to Orlando ended up getting plunked down in Denver for an all-nighter in the airport until a raging blizzard cleared.

That was bad enough, but then Simpson got sick when they finally got a Florida flight. Airsickness was unpleasant in itself, but it seemed he had the beginnings of a full-blown flu. Once in the wilds of

Orlando, they stuffed Simpson in a suite with several pounds of medication—Simpson and Molly had
separate bedrooms in their own suite down the hall
from the newlyweds—and Trey and Diana took
Molly off for the next three days to do the Disney
World thing. Molly was ecstatic. She also bunked
in their suite because the adults didn't want her exposed to Simpson's bug. Mol was ecstatic about
sleeping with them, too.

Until she came down with the flu bug herself
forty-eight hours ago. His daughter was the most
precious, perfect girl a father could have—priceless—she could do no wrong in Trey's eyes. But
she was just a *teensy* bit cantankerous when she
didn't feel well. She wanted either him or Di constantly.

Her fever had broken that afternoon, and she was
on the mend.

Simpson was up and around and feeling hot to
party.

It was only the newlyweds who were so exhausted
they could barely make it through *Wheel of Fortune*
before conking out—and so far they hadn't spent a
single night since the wedding without a small body
between them either because she didn't feel good or
because she was scared from being alone or because
his darling daughter was outstanding at conning her
two favorite adults.

"Trey? I don't understand where we are." Diana

had wandered through the doorway where he'd motioned her. "Isn't this room part of the motel spa?"

"Yup. In fact, it's the massage therapy room—which is why you see those sheet-covered stretchers. And just through this door—" he opened it "—is one of the motel's indoor pools. The smaller one."

"But no one else is here," Diana said curiously.

"Exactly. I rented this whole area for the next three hours."

"You mean the pool and spa are ours? They're closed to the rest of the motel?"

"Completely. And by the pool, there are drinks and a seafood buffet waiting for us, where you can put your feet up and indulge until you're full. Then, madame, my plan is to treat you to a full body massage. After which, I believe, you'll likely feel like melted Jell-O and will be in no mood to do anything but be poured into bed. So that's the agenda. Food, because we both need it. Then a massage, because you've been running twenty-four hours a day since we got here, and I know you're overtired. And then sleep. Noninterrupted sleep."

"Sleep," she echoed blankly, as if that word was completely unfamiliar to her.

He almost laughed at that carefully bland look in her eyes. She hadn't had a wedding night yet, and God knew, neither had he. If he didn't get his hands on her soon, he just might lose his sanity. This had to be the longest chaste honeymoon on record.

But that wasn't the point. No matter how much they'd shared, he'd had no chance to woo Diana, much less to win her. He hoped to have a lifetime of making love to his wife. First, though, he had the crazy, old-fashioned idea that it might be a better idea to just plain show her...

Love.

"Come on, you," he coaxed. "It's been hours since lunch. No matter how tired you are, you have to be hungry for something."

"Something? Holy moly, Trey." Her mouth dropped when she saw the feast of trays set out buffet-style by the water. In no time, he'd mounded a plate for her, dripping with crab and lobster, strawberries and iced melon, marinated asparagus and chilled pea salad and exotic dips for all types of breads.

He'd brought her bathing suit down earlier—and his. No one was around, including waiters. The doors were all locked. There were times it paid to have money. This was one of them. He'd known she'd be too tired to go out, but he could tell, he could see, this was what she needed. Time with no interruptions. Time when she could stop being on, when no little voice was calling her name and no one needed her.

Once she started diving into the food, the smudges under her eyes seemed to soften, lighten. Relaxed smiles showed up, then laughter, as they sprawled in loungers like decadent sultans, eating a grape here, a bite of succulent white lobster there.

"I didn't even know I was hungry," she said with disbelief when she suddenly realized her plate was empty.

"We haven't touched the desserts yet. They're still covered up, on ice. I was told there's a decadent chocolate mousse and some Napoleons and some key lime pie and—"

"Are you planning on rolling me back to our rooms?"

"If we have to crawl back to our rooms, who's to know? Don't you think we've earned it? This has been a vacation that should get high-risk pay so far."

"It's not exactly the relaxing week we planned, now, is it?" she admitted humorously. "But really, Trey, things just happen. Especially with kids. It's not like we don't have time to be together after this. It's no one's fault the flu bug caught on. And I think Mol would have been scared if she'd woken up sick and you weren't there."

"You know what I think, Mrs. Derringer?"

Her lips curved at the sound of the new name. "What?"

"I think you thrive on being needed." When she leaned forward to set down her plate, he moved behind her, cupped his hands on the curve of her shoulders and started kneading.

Immediately she turned serious, although her eyes closed at the first touch of his hands. "Actually, I do, Trey. I really like doing for others. It's not like I'm so unselfish or anything like that. But I think it stems back from when I lost my mom. Doing for my dad and sister just made me feel good about myself. Sitting around being taken care of would just never be my way. I'd be miserable."

When her voice trailed off, he had to smile. She was succumbing to a simple back rub as if it were a magic spell. The more he rubbed her shoulders and back, the more she turned into putty, liquid, silky, her breath coming hopelessly slower and easier. She really had been up too many nights. Not because Trey wouldn't take care of his daughter himself, for heaven's sake, but because Di kept volunteering. And Molly soaked up attention from her like a sponge.

But over the last few days, Trey had really come to understand exactly how that need thing worked for Diana. She *did* instinctively fire up when she was needed. In fact, he'd come to believe her saying yes to his marriage proposal had that element at the core. She responded one hundred percent to Molly needing her as a mother, to helping him with his in-laws, to wherever her heart understood she was needed.

And that was terrific, Trey considered, since need was sincerely a part of his love for Diana. He *did* need this woman of his heart. Missing, though, had been any chance to show her exactly what kind of need he felt for her...and that this kind of need had nothing to do with dependency and everything to do with choice.

Her head drooped limply. He heard her sigh, heavy and low. And he continued kneading, kneading, kneading.

Eventually her eyelashes lay silent as shadows on her cheeks. Her heart began a slow pattern of respiration that indicated she was out for the count. Absolutely dead to the world. And, after all these days, finally aiming for the restful sleep Trey knew she needed.

A ribbon of shiny yellow sunlight peeked through the curtains. Diana was aware of that first, then aware that she felt rested, the way she hadn't felt in days. And pampered and treasured, the way she'd never felt...ever. She turned her head to find Trey crashed on his stomach next to her.

They'd been sleeping next to each other for the last six nights, of course, being married and all—but sleep had been the only action going on in the midnight hours.

Last night she'd been so positive would be different.

Last night she'd been positive that Trey had been seducing her, with the feast and the privacy and the long, lazy, sexy back rub.

She'd been well aware that his body was aroused and trigger ready. She'd felt him, intimately, when he'd pulled his arms around her. Yet nothing had happened beyond his carrying her to bed and her—apparently—falling into a coma-like sleep.

Absently she remembered something the mysterious old Indian woman said, about her great-great-grandmother Isabelle feeling unworthy, afraid to believe she was loved. The stranger knew nothing about her, couldn't. Yet Diana's heart kept remembering those words, the thought surfacing over and over in her mind like a bubble trapped underwater.

She'd never really felt worthy. Loved. Lovable. Unless she was doing for someone else. And part of what had drawn her to Trey—reassured her into saying yes—was knowing that he needed her.

Yet last night, he hadn't seemed to need her at all. He'd done nothing for himself. Taken nothing for himself. Only arranged everything about the evening specifically for her sake.

Slowly her palm slid under the crisp white sheet, finding warm, bare, bronze skin. Tentative, she offered a feather caress. Just a gentle, exploring touch, meant to be soothing, not arousing. Comforting, not aggressive. Giving. Not taking.

Yet she rubbed and stroked that skin until it heated under her fingertips. Then, quiet as a thief, she ducked her head under the sheet—carefully leaving no drafty air pockets—and pressed her lips

Diana 245

along the same wandering path, over ridges and val-
leys, shoulder blades and the ridge of his spine and
the hollow at his nape.

She was busy. Extremely busy. Molding his skin.
Learning him. Loving him. Not—honestly—trying
to wake him but only to have her loving feelings
incorporated into his dreams, into the deepness of
his rest.

On that silky, shiny morning, though, she suddenly heard his voice. Something in his husky whisper made her suspicious that he'd been awake for
some time. "Are you looking for trouble, ma'am?"

Her fingertips stilled. "Um...I wasn't looking to
wake you, if you still need sleep."

"I don't need sleep. In fact, I can't imagine ever
wanting to sleep for the next ten years or so. My
mind seems to be dominated by other ideas entirely.
Did anything in particular bring on this, um, back
rub?"

"You love me," she announced.

Abruptly he turned on his back, somehow managing to drag her possessively across his chest at the
same time. His gaze pounced on her face as if he
would memorize every part of her, eyes, lips, nose,
patch of freckles, all savored equally, all loved...the
way she never thought anyone would love her.
"You're just getting around to figuring that out, Di?
Why did you think I asked you to marry me?"

"I don't know. Because you realized how much

I loved Mol. And you and I seem to get on so well.
And the way you described your first marriage, it
sounded painful and awful, and you surely had to
know the two of us could be so much better than…''
She heard herself start chattering and stopped. ''I
really didn't know, Trey.''

A long, slow fingertip stroked her jawline. ''Just
for the record, my first marriage didn't give me low
expectations of what a relationship could be, but the
opposite. I was never planning on getting married
again. But assuming I was so crazy as to fall, I
promised myself I'd never take the risk unless I
loved someone, heart and soul. Diana?''

''What?''

''I love you. Heart of my heart, soul of my soul.''

''Oh, Trey.'' She sank into his arms feeling as if
she were finally coming home. Really home.
''That's how I felt about you. I was just so afraid
of believing in it. It doesn't happen in life, you
know? That your first crush turns out to be your first
love. That your hero turns out to be…well, your
hero.''

''I'm no hero, Di. I've made a lot of mistakes. I
make a lot of mistakes. But I do love you, the way
I never dreamed I'd find love in my life.''

''And I love you,'' she whispered, and kissed
him. A kiss of promise and passion both. For so long
she'd doubted that she had the strength of the Brennan women, yet this man she loved had taught her

otherwise. Love—the right kind of love—was a woman's source of strength like none other.

As their kiss deepened and darkened and caught fire, she wound her arms around him and hung on. They were not only way overdue a honeymoon night, but the sun-filled morning struck her as an ideal time to start their true life together.

* * * * *

Look for YOU BELONG TO ME,
Jennifer Greene's next book in the exciting
MONTANA MAVERICKS
series in August 2000.

ISABELLE

Cheryl St. John

Chapter 1

Glancing at the nearly deserted train station behind him, Kyle Running Horse Brennan squinted into the afternoon sun and impatiently tugged the brim of his hat lower over his eyes. He scanned the horizon for the train that was now half an hour late. He could have sent one of the hands to meet it, but seeing to Isabelle Cooper had become his responsibility, and he wasn't one to shirk duty—even if that duty was to a silly pampered city female.

She didn't belong here. Ranch life wasn't a society ball. And this ranch in particular, Big Sky, was soon going to be his, anyway.

In the distance, the long, low whistle from what his mother's people called the iron horse broke the stillness. The rails hummed, and the ground beneath his scuffed boots shivered. A covey of quail soared skyward in the distance as the train flushed them out of the tall, dry grass along the metal tracks.

Smoke appeared, then the huge black engine, with dried brush stuck in the cowcatcher. In a hiss of steam and squealing brakes, the shiny monstrosity lurched to a halt beside the station.

At a snail's pace, a black-suited conductor lowered himself to the ground and unfolded a set of metal stairs.

On the grate above, a solitary figure came into view. Kyle had caught only glimpses of her during the four years that he'd worked for her father, and he remembered her as a tall, willowy fifteen-year-old with shining auburn hair.

The exquisite young woman in an elegant dove-gray traveling suit and matching hat who gracefully opened a frilly parasol and descended the stairs with her gloved hand in the conductor's made his heart give a crazy little thump. He recognized Isabelle by her unusual height and the expensive clothing, but the fact that she was a fully grown woman—and that he'd responded—caught him off guard.

He spent as little time around whites as possible—and even less around white women. Being staked in the noon sun over an anthill would probably be less irritating than having to convince the spoiled daughter of his late boss to sell out to him and go back to the city.

She turned, and another portly railroad employee attentively handed down a stack of cylindrical boxes fastened together with gold cord, as well as a dome-shaped object covered by an embroidered cloth. The latter she held aloft, grasping it by a metal ring at the top.

She approached Kyle with her odd parcels, the sun glinting from her shiny golden ear bobs and the jeweled brooch at the base of her slender throat. "Mr. Brennan?"

He removed his hat and didn't miss the fact that her perusal included the sweep of his straight black hair that fell to his shoulders. "Miss."

Beneath the jaunty brim of her useless hat with the unnatural-looking flowers, her wide eyes were a stunning blue-gray. He'd never seen them up close before, and focused intently on his face they made him uncomfortable and hitched his breath momentarily.

The conductor helped her stack the boxes at her feet. At her thanks, the man's neck and ears reddened; he tipped his hat and waddled to the rail car.

"The train was late," Kyle said, grateful for the interruption. "We'd better get going."

From the corner of his eye, he noticed two red-faced porters carrying an enormous securely strapped trunk between them. They lowered it not-too-gently to the battered platform.

He frowned at the cumbersome piece of luggage, then at her. "That yours?"

She nodded.

He tested one end by the leather handle. The thing weighed near as much as his horse! He slid it to the edge of the wooden structure, muscled it onto his back and carried it to the waiting wagon. Catching his breath, he turned.

She stood expectantly at the edge of the platform, the cloth-covered dome securely in her grasp. What did she expect him to do? Carry her, too?

Carefully, she set the object down. "While you get the other one, I'll be just a moment."

The other one? He cut his gaze to where they'd been standing. Sure enough, another steamer trunk had been placed on the wooden landing while he'd wrangled the last. "What the hell have you got in these things?"

Her brow wrinkled. "Why, my clothing, of course. A few necessities."

"A *few?*"

Ignoring his displeasure, she brought the stack of round boxes forward. "I'll be right back."

"Where do you think you're taking off to?"

Her cheeks grew pink, but she straightened and spoke without a qualm. "To use the facilities, Mr. Brennan, since you so rudely insist upon hearing me say it."

He looked away and adjusted his hat. "Be quick about it."

He loaded the other trunk, then the boxes, and grabbed the draped parcel, which was surprisingly light. As he swung it into the back of the wagon, a rapid, fluttering racket burst from beneath the cloth, startling him. He released the ring and flung back the fabric. Tiny feathers scattered in the breeze. Kyle stared at the yellow bird frantically battering itself against the sides of the cage. "A bird."

Isabelle's peg-heeled shoes clicked as she neared.

He turned with a puzzled frown and said again, "A bird!"

She ran down the set of stairs and through the billowing dust. "You've frightened the poor darling! Please, place his cover back over him."

"He's scared because he's trapped," Kyle said. "Has he been hurt? Is that why you've caged him?"

"No, he's not injured, unless he's hurt himself just now." She peered at the bird from beneath her hat brim, concern marring her perfect porcelain-skinned features, then lifted an accusingly haughty brow at Kyle.

"Then you should set him free." He reached for the tiny wire door.

Isabelle yelped and grabbed his wrist. "No!"

He stared at her stark white glove against his sun-weathered skin, and his heart fluttered as if another living thing was caged within his chest.

"It's a domestic creature, Mr. Brennan. Canaries are bred as tame pets. He's never been outside his cage and wouldn't know what to do if you set him free. He'd die of hunger and exposure."

She removed her hand and, able to breathe again,

he lowered his to his side. He blinked at the delicate
bird, still feeling Isabelle's pleading touch on his
skin. Only a city woman would place such importance on a bird as inappropriately bred for this land
as she herself was. Silly bird wouldn't make a decent meal for one of the barn cats.

Apparently assured that her pet was safe, she
draped its prison. "Please set the cage down on the
floor of the wagon, so that the wind doesn't reach
him."

With his mouth held firmly in an irritated line,
Kyle did her bidding, then turned to raise a brow as
if asking if the placement of the cage met her frivolous standards.

Moving to stand beside the wagon and wearing a
calculating expression, she studied the distance between the ground and the footboard, then met his
gaze.

"Want a lift?" he asked.

Obviously lacking a better solution, she nodded.
"Yes, thank you."

He spanned her waist with both hands and lifted
her easily into the wagon. She wasn't a delicately
built woman, but beneath his fingers, her body felt
toned as well as feminine. He shouldn't have noticed. He released her as soon as her feet touched
the wood, painfully uncomfortable with the familiarity.

She caught her balance, adjusted her ridiculous
hat and seated herself. Kyle bounded up in one easy

motion, picked up the reins and released the brake handle. The horses responded to his command and pulled them forward.

A quarter of an hour passed before she spoke again. "The mountains are as beautiful as I remembered."

She was studying the climbing acres of lodgepole pines in the distance, the twin peaks of the snow-capped Crazy Mountains above. An awelike expression lit her black-lashed, smoky eyes.

"How long are you staying?"

She turned her head, and those disturbing eyes focused on him. Something behind them changed. "How long am I staying? Not, 'Please accept my condolences on the loss of your father, Miss Cooper.' Not, 'It's a pleasure to see you. How was your trip?' But, 'How soon will I be rid of you?'"

Her words pricked him with a swift twinge of guilt. "I'm sorry about your father. I did what I could to save him."

"I've no doubt you did." Her voice had become throaty, and she spared him only brief glimpses. Several seconds passed. "I'm planning to stay for good. The Big Sky is going to be my home."

Well, that figured. He should have known dealing with her wasn't going to be easy. He would have to change her mind. He would have to show her she didn't want to stay. Isabelle Cooper was going to have to make different plans.

Isabelle breathed the vibrant air and relished the

wide-open blue sky and the land that stretched and rolled in all directions. Her grief for her father conflicted with her newfound and astounding sense of freedom. The only joyful memories she possessed were those of her too-brief childhood visits to Montana. She thought those memories had been well buried—she'd hidden them to escape the hurt and longing they carried. She'd determinedly made the best of the world her father had insisted she live in and prided herself on becoming a modern young woman.

But now that her father wasn't here to prevent her from staying, she could do as she pleased. She was, after all, the new owner of the Big Sky. Blinking away stinging tears, she remembered how he'd always met her at the station. He'd hugged her, and she'd been deliriously happy to see him—even if he hadn't needed her.

Isabelle cast a furtive glance at the intimidating dark-eyed, copper-skinned man who shared the wagon seat. She'd had only quick looks at him in the past, and he was just as unsmiling and gruff as she recalled. He'd been her father's right-hand man for the past four years. Sam Cooper had trusted him, and she had no choice but to trust him, too.

She didn't know the first thing about running a ranch—but she was going to learn.

The ranch house and buildings came into view, and as always, the sight warmed Isabelle with a safe, secure feeling.

Her attention focused on the enormous house her father had built for her mother after he'd bought this land. After his wife's death, he'd sent Isabelle away and had never allowed this to be her home.

The house stood two stories tall, white with green shutters and pitifully empty planter boxes beneath the upstairs windows. She could picture them overflowing with colorful petunias and verbena, just like when her mother had been alive.

Kyle halted the team before the dooryard, and Isabelle eagerly jumped down without waiting for assistance. Her heels clicked on the stone walk that led to the gate in the white picket fence surrounding the house and separating it from the rest of the ranch buildings.

She stepped through the opening and studied the welcoming etched-oval window that graced the front door. A wide porch stretched across the front and the west sides of the house. Rockers and a swing beckoned for a shady afternoon rest.

Her yearning gaze caressed the house, absorbed it with a sad hollowness that made her chest ache, then she turned and stared toward the wagon shed and the enormous rust-red barn beyond. She would never see her father cross the yard again—never have an evening to sit on the porch with him and ask about the horses. Any chance of gaining his love or getting to know him was gone—except whatever she could learn by being here, by finding out who

he'd been and what he'd thought and done all those
years they'd been apart.

A small glimmer of hope flickered in Isabelle's
heart. The fulfillment of her plans and dreams would
eventually crowd the loneliness from her heart, and
she would belong. She was home at last.

Chapter 2

Kyle and two of the hands noisily carried the unwieldy trunks up the stairs.

"First room on the left," she called, daintily slipping her gloves from her hands.

Tott, a wrangler barely out of his teens, and Sidestep, the second-best trainer on the ranch, stared at the primly dressed and coifed young woman. Kyle spotted their enamored gaping and urged their attention to the task.

Kyle's aunt had helped him clean the house and launder the curtains and bedding, but he hadn't seen Isabelle's room until he stepped into it with the dusty ranch hands. The three lowered their cumbersome loads.

Sheer white ruffles adorned sparkling windows and draped a canopy above the mahogany bed. The walls had been covered with rose-trellis paper, and the plush, dawn-tinted carpet sank beneath their boots.

Mouth open, Tott swept his hat from his head, then turned and nearly trampled Sidestep in his eagerness to exit.

Sidestep slugged him on the shoulder and thundered down the stairs behind him.

Kyle followed at a slower pace.

"Will one of you gentlemen help me move this table?" Isabelle's cultured voice called from the dining room beyond the enormous tiled foyer.

Tott and Sidestep stopped midstride, glanced at one another and collided shoulders on their way through the door. Kyle shook his head.

"I'd like it over here in front of these windows, if you please. That way Chipper will get the morning sun."

Chipper? Kyle almost snorted, but cleared his throat instead.

At her direction, the two men hauled an oak table from the corner and set it before the lace-curtained windows. Isabelle draped the table with a daintily crocheted cloth, then placed her birdcage atop it. She removed the embroidered cover with a flourish. Wispy feathers floated on a beam of indirect sunlight. Tott and Sidestep stared at the bird huddled on the floor of the cage.

"Thank you, gentlemen."

They mumbled something incoherent and hot-footed it out of the room. The front door opened and closed.

She had removed her hat, and her lustrous hair shone in the afternoon light filtering through the filmy curtains. Her jacket was gone, too, revealing a wrinkled white shirtwaist tucked into the narrow band of her skirt. Kyle forced his attention to one of the china cabinets that flanked the open glass-paned doors leading to the kitchen.

"What time is dinner?" she asked. "I think I'd like to freshen up and rest."

"Harlan rings the bell at the bunkhouse when he has dinner ready." He spared her a glance.

Her expressive eyes widened with a question. "We always had dinner in here when I was home."

"Your father hired someone from town for your visits," he replied honestly. "He ate with the hands the rest of the time."

Her brow furrowed. "Oh. I see."

He couldn't let the woman starve, but her eating alongside the hands was out of the question. "I'll bring you a plate."

"Will you join me?"

She needed to see what ranch life was really like, but she'd just arrived. Maybe she needed one night to rest from her trip. His gaze drifted to the long, empty table where she'd have to eat alone if he didn't join her, and without considering his reasoning, he replied, "Yes."

She folded her hands and gave him a satisfied smile. "Good. I'll see you then."

She picked up her hat and jacket and swept gracefully from the room. He followed slowly, turning to see her gliding along the upstairs hallway toward her room.

Agreeing to join her for supper was all right. He needed to talk to her, anyway. Ambling into the study that had been her father's, he rearranged the papers on the desk and seated himself to finish reading the ledgers he'd left open that morning.

Already her presence was a distraction and a hindrance. He'd wasted his morning and then called hands in from their chores to unload her things. The woman was a nuisance. The sooner he got her out of here, the better.

He'd asked Tott and Sidestep to help him because they were the two he trusted most around women. Even he knew that an unmarried, attractive female shouldn't be alone on a ranch with a dozen men.

What was he going to do about it? The more he thought of her alone here day after day—night after night—the more he knew he had to do something.

He would ask his aunt's advice this afternoon. He only needed a short-term solution. As soon as Isabelle saw how much painstaking work the ranch took, how all the money went into its operation, she'd be on a train bound for finer living.

He'd been working for years to save up enough to offer to buy out her father. Sam hadn't been willing to sell, even though his poor management had brought him to that point. But he had been ready to go into partnership. They'd come to a verbal agreement just before Sam had been killed leading horses from the burning barn.

Sam's death was a tragedy, and Kyle mourned his senseless passing. But his death was also an opportunity—a chance for Kyle to get the land that had been his father's.

Only here on the land where he'd been born did Kyle belong. No prissy city woman was going to keep him from getting what should have been his.

The clang of the dinner bell woke Isabelle, and she sprang from the bed, surprised that she'd napped so soundly. She cleaned her teeth and brushed her hair into order before hurrying down the stairs to set the dining table with a linen cloth and gold-rimmed china that had been her mother's.

The kitchen door closed, and the tall half-breed appeared in the dining room with cloth-covered plates. He stopped and stared at her table setting. "Already have plates here."

He placed them on the table and peeled back the napkins, revealing meat and vegetables in dark gravy. Several biscuits rested on the edge of each plate.

Isabelle removed the china quickly, arranged the

full plates and seated herself in the chair she'd always used. She couldn't help glancing at her father's empty place at the head of the table.

Kyle left that chair empty, took a seat across from her and pulled his meal toward him.

"Did you make coffee?" he asked, picking up the fork.

She unfolded her napkin and placed it across her lap. "No. I can boil water for tea."

"Can you light a fire in the stove?"

She picked up her fork and looked at the food rather than face his scrutiny. He thought she was helpless, and she didn't want to add to his thinking by admitting her lack of ability.

She didn't reply.

"This afternoon there was warm water for you to wash, because I heated it earlier and left the coals banked. I don't do that every morning. I'll have to show you how."

His words registered. "You've been living here—in the house?"

"I've been staying here since Sam died. Someone had to look over the house and the barns," he replied. "I have my own place—my own land to the east."

"Of course."

"I'll be staying here, though."

She met his dark, unreadable eyes.

"You can't stay here alone."

But with him? She couldn't stay in the house alone with him! The thought was scandalous.

"I'm sending a young woman to keep you company so you won't be alone with me. Her name is Pelipa. She'll be here before dark and she'll stay upstairs with you."

"A chaperone?"

"A paid helper."

"Oh."

He ate his meal without further conversation.

Isabelle dug in and found the stew surprisingly tasty and filling.

"You going to eat those?" He gestured to the two remaining biscuits on the edge of her plate.

"No."

He reached across the table and helped himself.

She watched him dunk them in the gravy on his plate and eat them. She'd never eaten a biscuit without preserves or jam, but her father's hired man seemed to think they were a delicacy.

Glancing at the napkin beside his plate, he picked it up and wiped his fingers and mouth and stood. "I'll show you where the wood is. After we make coffee, we have business to discuss."

He handed her a canvas sling, led her out the back door and across the yard where he pointed to a pile of split wood. She loaded the manageable-sized chunks into the sling and carried the heavy bundle. He followed with a few bigger logs.

He opened the door on the cast-iron stove. "Now you build the fire."

Awkwardly, she poked a few logs inside the charred belly of the stove, discovered matches in a tin on the wall and tried ineffectually to light one of the pieces of wood. Frustrated, she avoided looking at him, not wanting to see his criticism.

"Like this." She moved aside, and he showed her how to prop the wood with dry kindling beneath and light the sticks. His movements were sure and methodical, his hands graceful.

Isabelle caught herself glancing from his long-fingered hands to the sleek ebony hair that fell to his broad shoulders. Beneath the fabric of his well-worn flannel shirt, his muscles corded and bunched with each movement.

He glanced up and caught her staring.

Her cheeks warmed, and she dropped her gaze.

"The water," he said, standing. He moved to open the door and showed her the wooden barrel outside. "Fill buckets from here, but keep this barrel filled from the well."

In the past, there'd been a tub carried in for her, but she wouldn't ask him to do that for her. She'd look for it later. As it was, Isabelle had changed from her grimy traveling suit, but she'd barely had enough water to sponge bathe.

He started the coffee boiling himself, then left her alone.

She found the teapot in a china cupboard,

knocked a dead spider from its depths, rinsed the china pot with boiling water and added tea.

While the tea steeped, she searched until she found a tray for the pot and cups, then poured his coffee and found him in her father's study.

The room still smelled faintly of tobacco, and the scent unleashed a flood of memories that immediately saddened her. A fire burned in the enormous stone fireplace that took up the outside wall.

The man sat in the leather chair, and before him on the desk lay an open ledger. From all appearances, it looked as though he belonged there. "Things are not very good."

Not used to a man remaining seated when she entered the room, Isabelle gathered her wits and sat on an upholstered chair. "What do you mean?"

"Your father had been steadily losing money over the past several years."

She blinked. "That's not possible."

He gave her a disgusted look. "Why not?"

"Because he owned land and horses and this house."

"Your father was a good horseman, but a poor businessman. Three years ago when I brought in new breeding stock and got him a contract with the army, things started to turn around. More than half the horses on the Big Sky are mine."

Fear burst in her chest at his words. He could be lying in order to swindle property that belonged to her. "How can I know that for sure?"

A muscle in his lean jaw jumped. Brusquely, he opened a desk drawer, withdrew an accordion-pleated folder and thumbed through a stack of documents before withdrawing several and shoving them across the desktop.

Isabelle took the legal-looking papers and read them, her heart sinking. Her father's signature was unmistakable.

Kyle Running Horse Brennan owned the horses he'd brought to the ranch, as well as half the offspring bred over the past two and a half years. It seemed he already had more stake in this place than she did—and he knew how to run it. As always, she was the outsider.

Chapter 3

"Sam and I came to an agreement," Kyle continued. "I was going to buy half ownership and have my name added to the land deed."

She stared at him. "Why would Father agree to that?"

"He owed me wages. Still does."

"Well, I'll pay you."

"*He* would have paid me if he'd had the cash. He didn't. And since his death, I've covered the pay for the hands as well as building the barn and buying supplies."

An overwhelming, lost sensation wrapped around Isabelle with frightening intensity. But she wouldn't be pushed away again, not for any reason.

"We lost four mares and their foals in the fire," he added. "That sets us back even more."

"Why, that's awful," she said, thinking of the loss of the beautiful animals.

"I'll buy you out."

She blinked, her mind grasping his words on the top of so much dreadful news. "Pardon me?"

"I've saved enough to pay down. I can send you an agreeable amount each quarter. It would be enough for you to live on until—"

"Wait a moment."

"It's sensible," he insisted.

"I don't intend to—"

"You can go back to the city. You'll be getting enough to live on until you find yourself a husband."

A soft roar built to a crescendo in Isabelle's ears. She leaped to her feet and faced him across the desk. She clenched her fists, knowing she was about to break propriety by raising her voice but unable to stop the rush of emotion. "How dare you tell me what to do! I didn't take a husband when my father wanted me to, and I certainly am not going to marry someone just so I'll be out of *your* way!"

"I didn't mean—"

"Oh, I know what you meant. You laid out all the bleak details so I'd see I had no choice but to hand over my house and my land to you and get back on a train. Just who do you think you are, Mr. Brennan, to sit in my house at my father's desk and think you can plan my life so it suits your tidy little scheme?''

He pushed back his chair and moved to stand. ''I know this is upsetting.''

''Upsetting? I haven't even seen my father's grave yet and you have taken over here. Besides which, I've resigned my position at the academy and moved all my possessions across the country with the idea that I would stay. Now I learn that my father's ranch has met reverses and you are trying to undermine my interests.''

He came to his full height and glared at her. It took all her courage not to show that his height and fierce expression intimidated her. ''There's nothing wrong with my suggestion.'' He bit the words out. ''It's best for both of us.''

Anger started her heart thumping, and his proposed exile brought a sting of tears she refused to allow. ''You don't know what suits me. You don't know anything about me.''

She hated the quiver in her voice and clamped her lips closed determinedly.

''I know enough.''

Insult added to injury. Just like her father thought he'd known what was best for her all those years. And just like her father, this man couldn't wait to be shut of her. Well, he didn't have the power to send her away. She was not under his authority.

At the moment she sensed another presence in the room, he glanced over her shoulder. Isabelle spun to see a young Indian girl in a doeskin dress and moccasins.

"This is Pelipa," Kyle said by way of introduction.

"Didn't she knock?" Isabelle whispered, embarrassed at having her unseemly outburst overheard.

"A white custom," he replied so she alone could hear. He spoke to the girl in their language, and Isabelle understood only her name.

The situation and her life seemed to be spinning out of her control, and Isabelle hated the helpless feeling. She hated not knowing what was being said right in front of her. She faced Kyle again. "I'd like you to leave the house, please."

"What?" He scowled.

"I am going to locate a tub and bathe before I retire for the night." She raised her chin a notch. "We will speak again tomorrow, and another solution will have to be found. I am not leaving the Big Sky no matter how many cruel things you say and no matter how bleak the situation appears."

He looked as though he wanted to oppose her statement, but he held his tongue.

"This is going to be my home whether you like it or not. Whether *you* stay or not."

Nothing showed in his expression. He held her gaze unwaveringly.

She turned to leave, and he stopped her. "One more thing."

She turned hesitantly.

He opened a desk drawer and withdrew a deadly looking revolver.

Isabelle's heart leaped. Unconsciously, she raised a hand to her breast.

He turned the weapon abruptly so that the handle faced her and extended it. "Keep this with you at night."

Isabelle's hand remained where she'd flattened it on her chest. Beneath her fingers, her heart raced. "I—I don't know the first thing about guns."

"You're going to have to learn if you're going to stay, aren't you? All you do is aim it and pull the trigger."

She wouldn't be able to shoot at anyone. "I won't need to use it, will I?"

"I hope not."

The weapon he held toward her was a direct challenge. The concept of keeping a gun by her side went against everything she'd ever learned or experienced, and contradicted all that her shielded education had prepared her for. But if she didn't accept it, he wouldn't take her seriously.

Isabelle took a calming breath and reached for the revolver. He released it, and the weight immediately pulled her arm down. She stared at the deadly weapon, shuddered with the anxious sensation that she held a lit stick of dynamite.

"Tomorrow I'll show you how to use it," he said, his voice a shade kinder but no less firm. Then he spoke to Pelipa in Cheyenne.

Their exchange irritated Isabelle, and she hurried from the room.

After locating the copper tub holding potatoes and onions in the pantry, Isabelle transferred the vegetables to burlap bags. Pelipa watched her haul the basin outdoors to scrub it, then drag it to the semi-private pantry.

"Would you mind giving me a hand with this?" Isabelle asked, huffing. The girl merely blinked.

Isabelle pointed to the other end of the tub and then at Pelipa. "You? Lift that end?"

"Pelipa not help," she said, shaking her head. "Pelipa stay with you only."

Isabelle scowled. "Is that what he told you? He told you not to help me? You are being paid to help me, so please lift that end of the tub."

"Pelipa not help."

Isabelle gave her a scathing look and carried buckets of hot water until her arms ached. The girl watched the procedure with mild interest, then wandered away.

Finally climbing into the steaming water and allowing it to soothe her limbs, Isabelle decided the relaxing bath had been worth the work. Behind her in the kitchen, apparently not doing anything useful, Pelipa hummed, and Isabelle's trembling hurt and anger mellowed into a leaden ball of determination in her belly.

Kyle Brennan had done nothing but add misery

to her already heavyhearted homecoming. The ranch's situation was not his fault, she conceded, but his chafing superiority and this...this *rudeness* were inexcusable.

Isabelle had been only six when her mother had fallen from a horse and died and her father had sent her off to boarding school. Sam had insisted through the years that it was for her own good she live in the East and attend school and travel with her mother's despotic aunt.

She had convinced herself that he was right, that she preferred growing up away from this uncivilized country and the dangers it presented. She'd hoped after she graduated from finishing school that Sam would allow her to come back, but he'd insisted she seek a suitable husband.

She'd taken a position at the academy where she'd grown up and had been writing to her father for months, begging his permission for an extended visit. His replies were terse. Her prospects for an appropriate husband were nonexistent in Montana; she was unsuited for the rugged life and treacherous hazards of the untamed land.

Well, that was his fault, she reasoned. She'd become exactly what he'd insisted she be—a well-bred, well-mannered lady. She could play the pianoforte and embroider and set a table. She knew how to behave in polite company and how to dress for a ball, understood the correct manner in which to call on a friend and the proprieties of walking with a gentleman caller.

And even the things she'd learned to do well she'd never been able to show Sam Cooper.

Tears mingled with the drops of water on her cheeks, and she buried her face in a soft cloth. She'd never been wanted or welcomed here when her father was alive, but this was her land and her house now, and no one was going to send her packing.

Kyle helped Sidestep fork down fresh bedding for the yearlings in the barn and changed a herb poultice on the foreleg of a chestnut mare who'd been snakebitten. Kyle ran his hands soothingly over the horse's neck and flank and spoke softly. Her ears pricked, and she bobbed her regal head in reply.

He brushed her coat, as much for his own peace and harmony as for the mare's. In his mind he saw Isabelle Cooper, her lustrous auburn mane, skin as pure and soft-looking as a rose petal, eyes like a summer storm. Her delicate features and feminine form hid a steely determination and a stubbornness he couldn't help but admire.

He didn't want her here—but he was wise enough to know that nothing he said was going to change her mind. She was right—he had no authority over her. She was the legitimate owner of the ranch. But if Sam Cooper hadn't been able to keep the Big Sky afloat on his own, there was no way this silly girl was going to.

Should he sit back and watch her lose it all? What would that gain him? What would happen to the ranch? He wasn't about to move one foot from the land he believed was rightfully his. Hank Brennan's foolishness had cost Kyle his legacy. Kyle had been seven when his father had run out, and Sam Cooper had acquired the land. Kyle's mother had worked for Sam until her death, and then Kyle had set out on his own.

He'd lived with the Cheyenne for a time, but he didn't fit in among them any more than he did the whites. He learned he had a way with horses and that catching and breeding and breaking them could earn him enough money to buy back the land he wanted.

Kyle had never resented Sam. The man had come by the land fairly enough. He'd earned it and had worked hard, even if he hadn't been good at handling money.

But he did resent Sam's daughter. The girl had done nothing to earn the Big Sky. She was spoiled and unsuited for this life and had a romantic notion of being able to take her father's place.

He patted the mare's rump and hung the curry brush before exiting the stall and blowing out the lanterns.

The moon illuminated the roof of the house; the twinkling stars stretched forever. He studied the other buildings, the corrals and the two-story bunkhouse, where a curl of smoke drifted from the chimney.

A soft light in an upstairs window drew his attention. She meant to stay.

He didn't have to make it easy for her. Nobody got a free ride. Life was hard. Nature could be brutal. A creature was either quick and strong or it was prey for something that was. Same with people. He didn't like what he was doing, but she had to understand the order of things out here. Isabelle would have to learn the hard way.

Chapter 4

Pelipa had taken the room beside hers, but the next morning Isabelle found the tidy space empty when she made her way along the hall toward the stairs.

The icy water in the barrel numbed her hands as she baled a bucketful. The stove wasn't lit, and she fumbled with kindling and a few logs until she had a feeble fire going. It took forever for a pot of water to heat. Her shoulders ached from the buckets she had carried the night before. But, determinedly, she carried water to her room and washed and dressed for breakfast in a traditional flowing morning dress in pale green, a minimum of jewelry, her hair wound in a simple braid.

Isabelle discovered an unappealing plate of cold

biscuits on the table in the kitchen. After peering under the cloth and glancing around the deserted house, she decided to forgo breakfast for the moment. Instead, she exited the back door and made her way across the dooryard and up a rise to the east of the house and the buildings toward an ancient pine that marked the place where her mother and father were buried. Once beneath the shade of the tree, she remembered how her father had sat in this place looking out over the ranch for hours at a time. A neat pile of stones had replaced the wooden cross that had marked her mother's grave. Beside it was another stack, this one with less grass growing at the edges and a slight indentation in the ground where the earth had settled, so she knew the grave to be the newer of the two.

There should be flowers, she thought through the fog of isolation that gripped her. Her mother had loved flowers. But as she knelt, she realized the ground had been well kept and the weeds pulled, so someone had respectfully cared for the graves. Kyle?

Isabelle surveyed the layout of the buildings, the stately house in need of a coat of paint, the tangle of dried vines that used to be roses growing up the corner posts. There was much to be done, inside and out, to restore the place to its former elegance, but she was up to the task.

This was her home, the only home she'd ever wanted, and nothing would discourage her. She knelt in the shade and reflected on the brief times she remembered spending with her mother, as well as her many attempts to develop a relationship with her father. She shook away those thoughts. The disappointment was behind her. She was here to move forward.

Hungry, Isabelle trekked to the kitchen and located a dusty jar of boysenberry preserves in the pantry. She made herself tea, then looked about the empty room, at a loss. Carrying a tray holding her meal onto the porch, she wished she'd brought a shawl down with her. The morning air was chilly in the shade.

She tugged her chair and the table with the tray into the sun along the railing. At school, breakfast had always been a companionably chatty affair, the girls fresh and ready for a new day. As she ate, she thought about all the girls who'd gone back to their families while she'd remained a permanent fixture at the academy, like the bust of Chopin in the upstairs music hall.

She never wanted to feel that way again, heavy with the lonely, unwanted heartache she'd borne since childhood, but it seemed she was destined to live the experience over and over. What was there about her that didn't deserve love and acceptance?

Kyle's tall, dark figure approached from the barn, and Isabelle's heart fluttered nervously. She hated the way she let him fluster her. *It wouldn't happen again today.* The sun glinted from raven black hair caught by the breeze. He climbed the stairs near the back door and approached her. "Ready for your lesson?"

His lack of convention always caught her by surprise. No polite salutation. No small talk. "The gun?" she asked.

He nodded.

She stood and gathered her tray. "I'll take these in and get it."

She returned a few minutes later, wearing her shawl and a straw hat, carrying the gun with her thumb and forefinger, arm extended before her. "Here."

He took the revolver and led the way across the yard. "You can ride?"

"I can ride." She had learned during summer outings with her aunt. Her father had never allowed her to ride here.

"We don't have any fancy saddles."

"Whatever there is will do."

They approached two saddled horses tethered near the equipment stable.

"This bay is gentle," he said, indicating the smaller of the two, a red-brown color with black mane, tail and legs.

"She's pretty." Noting the considerable height of the stirrups, she glanced around.

He pointed to a half barrel placed upside down at the corner of the stable. "Step up from there."

She did so, finding her seat, taking the reins and

adjusting her skirts to cover her legs. His mount was a beautiful combination of leopard pattern—black on white across the middle and hips, the spots larger on the rump—and dark marbled coloring, like frost on red, over the front legs.

"What kind of horse is that?" she asked, once he was in his saddle.

"Appaloosa."

"He's beautiful."

"*She's* beautiful. She's given me three colts, two of them patterned just like her." He turned the animal's head, and the bay followed.

"Where are we going?"

"Out so the shots don't scare the new horses."

Kyle rode as though he were one with the animal, while she tried to keep her teeth from jarring and her hat from flying off. Even so, she loved the clean air and bright sky, and she drank in the rich green vegetation and the abundance of birds and small animals. She'd always dreamed of days like this with her father, the two of them together, riding, sharing, building a life together.

It would never be the way she'd dreamed. She would have to settle for a life here without him.

Reaching a clearing in the midst of a stand of fragrant pines, Kyle jumped to the ground and watched her dismount less gracefully.

She tugged her skirts down in embarrassment.

He drew a rifle from a sheath on his rough-hewn

saddle, grabbed a small box from his saddlebag and gestured for her to follow.

Isabelle was used to a gentleman offering his arm, not beckoning her as though she were a dog. Swallowing her irritation, she followed.

He walked away and lined a series of rocks along a fallen log, returned and handed her the rifle. "These will be in the way." He tugged on her hat until she untied the ribbons at her throat and allowed him to remove it. He pulled her shawl from her shoulders and laid them both on the ground.

"Raise the butt to your right shoulder," he said, turning. "Squint with one eye and get the rock in line with the sight on the end of the barrel. Hold steady and squeeze the trigger."

The rifle was incredibly heavy. Isabelle brought it to her shoulder and worked to hold the barrel parallel to the ground while she peered along its length.

He stepped behind her. "Put this hand here to steady it."

He moved her hand and showed her where to place it; his body enveloped hers, his solid chest and arms circling her shoulders. Silky hair brushed her cheek, and a shiver of alarm passed along her spine. The impropriety of the intimate contact took her breath away.

"Mr. Brennan!" she said when she found air.

"What?"

"It is highly inappropriate for you to stand so close."

"No one's looking."

"Just because something is rendered in private doesn't make it any less shameful."

"You know what would be shameful?" he said near her ear.

"What?"

"For a coyote to attack you or your horse—or a renegade to take a shine to you—and for you to not know how to shoot this Winchester to protect yourself. *That* would be a shame."

A shiver ran across her shoulders—whether at his admonishing words or at his disturbing nearness and his warm breath against her neck, she didn't know.

He cupped her left hand beneath the barrel with his rough fingers. "*Otahe*—pay attention. Line the rock up with the sight. Got it?"

"I think so."

"Squeeze the trigger."

She pulled; it was harder than she'd expected, making her lose her focus on the rock. The rifle fired so loudly and with such a blow to her shoulder that she yelped and stumbled against him. A squawking red-tailed hawk burst from the grass, and tiny kinglets chirped and fluttered in the branches of the nearby trees.

He steadied her.

"Did I hit it?"

"Not quite."

Her ears rang. Her shoulder throbbed.

"Here's how to load a shell," he said, without giving her time to recover.

Isabelle listened to his softly spoken instructions, watched his graceful hands, and each time he stepped behind her, the heat from his body and the brush of his hair distracted her. After three-quarters of an hour, with her shoulder throbbing and her arms trembling, she finally hit a rock.

He proceeded to show her how to load the revolver and went through the same motions of guiding her in each step of the lesson. The revolver was more difficult to aim, but he assured her she wouldn't miss at close range.

He seemed satisfied with her progress by the time her stomach growled. Her face flushed with embarrassment, she realized as she clamped her hand over her stomach that she couldn't possibly lift her arms again.

"That's enough for today. I have to stop by Mother's sister Ma'heona'e's. She'll have something to feed us."

"I—I'm not dressed for calling."

"You're not dressed for riding or working, either."

She ignored his pointed criticism. "How do you say her name?"

"The whites call her Mae."

She tied the ribbons of her hat beneath her chin with as much dignity as she could muster and pulled on her white gloves. "Extend the courtesy of assisting me, please?"

He made a step of his laced fingers for her to reach her saddle, then mounted and led the way. How did he know which direction to turn out here? It all looked the same, sky and trees and waving grass.

Before long, a small, sturdy cabin came into view, smoke curling from the chimney. Kyle called to a woman bending over in a newly planted garden. *"Peveeseeva!"*

Smiling, she turned and raised a hand.

Kyle dismounted and stood beside the bay. "Need help?"

"I can manage." Trying not to tangle her skirts or expose her limbs, she did both and awkwardly slid to her feet without falling in a heap in the dirt. Barely.

She followed him to where the woman stood in the sun, her bare feet planted in the newly turned earth.

Kyle wore a smile when he greeted his aunt. They spoke briefly in their unfamiliar language with the quick stopping sounds between the syllables. Isabelle watched and listened in fascination. "This is Mae," he said, then, "Isabelle Cooper."

"Pleased to meet you," Isabelle said politely.

"Isabelle beautiful *he'e-ka'eskone,*" the tall, dark-haired woman said, coming forward with a warm smile and touching Isabelle's arm. "Now beautiful *kasa'eehe*."

Isabelle glanced at Kyle.

"You were a beautiful child, she says. Now you're a beautiful young woman. She speaks English, don't let her fool you."

Isabelle flushed at Mae's compliment.

"I got up with the morning star to make your *kasa'eehe* a meal," Mae said. "You will eat fried bread and turnips."

"She's not my *kasa'eehe*."

"Mr. Brennan told you we were coming?" Isabelle asked.

"Morning star tell me."

"She knows a lot of things without being told," Kyle said wryly, and followed his aunt into the cabin.

Isabelle removed her hat and shawl, tucked her gloves into her hat and hung them on a set of antlers near the door.

Mae bustled about the austere one-room structure, preparing something delicious-smelling. She tore dough from an enormous chunk, flattened it between her palms and laid it in a skillet over the flames in the fireplace.

She served the bread and vegetables on smooth wooden platters. Isabelle accepted hers and waited for a utensil.

Finally, she glanced at Kyle.

He said something to his aunt, and she produced a crude three-tonged fork.

"Thank you." Isabelle used the fork to taste her food. "This is delicious."

Mae beamed. She and Kyle ate their food with their fingers, and it took discipline not to stare. "What is this made from?" she asked, nearly finished and studying the fork.

"Bone," Kyle replied. "Antelope or deer, probably."

Isabelle finished the last mouthful with difficulty and set the fork down quickly.

"Miss Cooper likes tea," Kyle informed his aunt, a grin tugging at the corner of his lips.

"Don't go to any trouble," Isabelle insisted.

"Not trouble. Enjoy to serve tea."

"You're very kind."

A few minutes later, Mae placed three tin cups on the small table. Kyle reached for one, but she held his wrist. "That one go for Isabelle. This go for you."

One of his ebony eyebrows shot up, but he took the cup and sipped.

Warily, Isabelle accepted hers and inhaled the peculiar scent of the brew. "What is it?"

"Herbs from my garden."

The tea tasted like none she'd ever drank, but it was hot and quite good, and she finished it.

"I have to get back to work," Kyle said finally.

"You must come visit me next time," Isabelle

said to their hostess. "I will prepare lunch and tea for you."

"I will come." Mae handed Isabelle a tightly rolled packet of cloth. "Tea for you. Make muscles feel better."

Isabelle blinked in surprise. "Thank you."

She accepted Kyle's grudging assistance in climbing on the horse's back, and Mae waved them off.

"Your aunt is lovely."

"Most whites are afraid of her."

"Why?"

"Because she's a medicine woman."

"She knows how to heal people?"

"And other things."

The sun was hot, and Isabelle folded her shawl over the pommel. It had been peculiar how Mae had given Isabelle tea for aching muscles, but the woman's perception didn't frighten her.

When they arrived at the ranch, she slid from the horse gingerly, and Kyle took the bay's reins. "Tonight we talk business."

Isabelle glanced over to see Pelipa waiting for them on the side porch. "Did you tell Pelipa not to help me?"

He turned his hard gaze on her. "Do you need help?"

A confused whirl of humiliation, pride and anger kept her from replying honestly—or at all. She wasn't admitting anything he wanted her to admit.

"We are going to come to an understanding tonight.'' His steely black eyes held no compromise. The brief pleasantness of their morning ride vanished.

''Perhaps,'' she replied noncommittally.

''You don't have many choices if you want to stay.''

''Oh, I'm staying.''

His gaze moved across her face to her mouth and back to her eyes. ''Then we're definitely coming to an understanding—tonight.''

Chapter 5

If she were going to hold her own against this unyielding man, she needed to look her best and feel confident. Isabelle dressed, then frowned at the darkened burn spot on the puff sleeve of her pale rose crepe gown. She'd overheated the iron and had forgotten to place a cloth between the fabric and metal.

Once again, Pelipa had been no help, silently watching as Isabelle built the fire and singed her dress.

Belatedly, Isabelle wondered if there was going to be a meal. Kyle hadn't mentioned bringing food. He may have left her on her own. She would have to find something in the pantry.

He was standing in the dining room observing the

canary when she and Pelipa arrived. Isabelle breathed a sigh of relief at the sight of three plates on the table.

He took in her attire without expression and remained standing until she and the girl had seated themselves.

He and Pelipa picked up their forks and dug into the plate of—stew.

Isabelle stared at the beef and gravy mixture. "This is the same menu as last night."

"Harlan doesn't have much of an imagination," he replied.

She glanced up to see if he was toying with her, but his expression was unreadable, as always.

"Why do you use your fork when you eat with me and your fingers when you eat with your aunt?"

He looked up. "I honor the customs of both people when I'm in their homes."

"You see eating utensils as a custom?"

"Yes, I do. How do you see them?"

"Well, as—manners. Etiquette."

"And one person's manners are better than another's because—why? Because the person thinks their way is the only way?"

"No, because it's..." Her voice trailed off.

"Civilized?" he asked, his tone underlined with something she sensed was a bone-deep irritation.

Had she been thinking that? Did she see cultural differences in a judgmental light? She'd never had to think about it before. All the people she'd known were from similar backgrounds and held the same beliefs about manners and religion and customs.

This man challenged every axiom she'd believed in until now.

Kyle stared at the lovely white woman, secretly hoping she wasn't as high-minded and prejudiced as he feared, as the rest of her kind had proven themselves to be where the Cheyenne were concerned, and not knowing why he cared. All he cared about was that she come to her senses and sell him the ranch.

He ate the meal, speaking occasionally to Pelipa when she asked him a question. When he'd finished, he made himself a pot of coffee and retreated to the study.

Isabelle didn't show for another hour, and when she did, her fine dress was water-spotted and she carried a tray with the china pot and two cups. She set the tray on the corner of the desk. "Would you care for a cup of tea?"

"No, thanks."

She poured one full, her hand trembling, then lowered herself onto one of the overstuffed chairs, wincing as she sat but quickly masking her pained expression.

She was no doubt sore from the ride and the shooting lesson. He couldn't worry that he was being too hard on her. Rather, he needed to consider if he was being hard enough. Getting her to change her mind was tougher than he'd imagined.

"I don't think you understand the money problem," he said.

"I've considered everything you've told me," she replied. "The most outstanding debts are your wages and the cost of rebuilding the barn. We still need to replace the mares."

"And there is no way you can pay those debts. Have you looked over the books?"

"I have."

That surprised him.

"Can we let any of the men go?" she asked.

"Some good men quit a while back because they weren't getting paid. We're working with as few hands as possible now. Your father handled a big share of the work, but he's gone."

"You don't have to keep reminding me. I'm well aware that he's gone." Her brow furrowed in confusion. "I don't understand something. How could the hands not have been paid? I never saw any change in circumstances."

"Of course you didn't. Sam sent you money he couldn't spare." He eyed the pale pink gown and her jewelry. "Your feminine finery and fancy schools and trips cost the men wages and the ranch repairs. Sam was a fool."

She bristled visibly at the blunt way he'd criticized her father, but she'd needed to know the truth. Recognition and shock slowly replaced the offended expression. She blinked a few times, looked away and swallowed, as though absorbing the distressing information.

"If you take my offer, you can make a nice life for yourself in the city."

Her steady gaze lifted and met his; color rose high in her ivory cheeks. With two deft movements she lifted a hand to each ear, plucked the pearls from her lobes and dropped them on the desk. The brooch from her collar followed. "How many mares can you buy with those?" she asked.

Taken aback, he glanced from the jewelry to her determined expression. "Depends how much they're worth."

"I have more. A whole box full. We can sell them in Whitehorn. Pay the hands."

"That would take care of one problem. And per-haps even part or all of the money due me. But it won't solve getting through the next couple of sea-sons." And selling her jewelry certainly wasn't the answer he wanted. He looked aside and absently watched flames lick up the side of a log.

He'd been prepared to fall back on an alternate plan, a plan that would assure his name on the land deed, but he'd hoped it wouldn't be necessary. Now it looked like he had no other choice. And this just might be the thing to scare her off. She would either take off running or he would have what he wanted. "If you're determined to stay—"

"I am."

"Then there's one thing that would meet both our needs."

"What's that?"

"If we marry, I can run the ranch on a shoestring. Half the horses are mine, anyway. We would be putting together your land and my horses and know-how. The Big Sky would be ours—together."

She stared at him. "Marry?"

He turned to gauge her expression and nodded.

A thunderstorm swelled in the depths of her eyes. "You'll do anything to get this land, won't you?" she asked.

"Not quite anything."

She raised her chin a notch. "So, I can sleep knowing you wouldn't cut my throat during the night?"

She was goading him, and he rose to her bait. "I don't slit throats. I take scalps."

Those turbulent eyes widened, then she fixed him with a perusing but half-amused stare, the corner of her mouth threatening to tilt.

She got up and walked to the fireplace, where she gazed into the crackling fire. The flames cast a golden glow across her perfect profile.

"Is it just me you hate or all people with white skin?"

The question caught him off guard. Grateful that she wasn't looking at him, he mulled it over. "Not trusting you is more like it."

"What is it I've done to earn this mistrust?"

"How about broken treaties and broken promises?" *How about herding the Cheyenne to a desert in Oklahoma where most starved or died of disease and the rest escaped only to be shot or recaptured?* Even as he thought it, he knew in some corner of his mind that he shouldn't, but long-ingrained beliefs were difficult to mask. *How about destroying a proud, beautiful people?*

Her shoulders straightened slightly and then relaxed. "I read about Dull Knife and Fort Robinson and those horrible times in the papers," she said sadly. "You hold me personally responsible for the mistreatment of the Cheyenne?"

Of course he didn't blame her in particular. He wasn't that ignorant. But he did, in some manner he couldn't help, think she was a product of a society that believed itself above the Plains tribes. He shook his head, even though she wasn't looking.

"What about you?" she asked, as though only now wondering. "Were you among those people sent to Oklahoma?"

"My white name and the deed to my land spared me," he said. "I kept Ma'heona'e and a handful of children with me, too. I lied and told the bureau they were my mother and my children. Pelipa was one of them. Her mother and father were killed trying to return home after the army starved them at Fort Robinson."

"I'm sorry," she said, and he recognized the sincerity.

"I don't hold you responsible," he admitted. "But I can't trust you."

Finally, she turned. "All right. Let's get married."

Her swift acquiescence and the abrupt return to the original subject astounded him. He'd expected her to take offense. He'd expected her to sell and run. She never did as expected. He realigned his thinking. This direction would aid his plan just as well. Once again, she'd accepted his challenge with bravado.

A sense of relief settled over him. The Big Sky would be his at last. "All right," he said. "I wouldn't set my hopes on a church wedding, if I were you."

"Why not?"

"The people in Whitehorn don't think much of the Cheyenne."

She studied his expression. "My father was respected in these parts. We'll go into town and make arrangements."

"Take heed and don't count on the church."

She ignored him. "How soon shall we set the date?"

"As soon as possible."

"Six months?"

"Tomorrow."

She stared in disbelief. "I can't plan a wedding overnight! There are things to do. I'll need a dress. I'll need at least—at least a month."

Hand on hip, she watched him stand and move to the coffeepot hung on a wire beside the fire.

"We don't have a month," he replied. "The sooner the better." He wasn't going to give her a chance to change her mind. His name was going on the land deed without delay.

"At least a week, then. I can't be ready by tomorrow."

"A week, then. No longer."

Her gray eyes looked a little wild, perhaps at the shocking reality of what she'd hastily committed herself to. "Excuse me, please. Good night."

She gave him a preoccupied nod and hurried away.

Escaping to her room, Isabelle tamped down the barrage of chaotic thoughts that questioned her decision. As soon as he'd spoken the words, she'd known marriage was the perfect solution. Combining their interests allowed her to make her home on the Big Sky. End of deliberation. It was all she'd ever wanted, and even though the price was high, her dream was becoming a reality.

But concern took over her confidence and nagged at her sanity until she stopped ignoring it and examined the issue.

Marriage meant more than saying vows and joint ownership in property. Marriage meant intimacy, shared lives and shared beds. A flutter started in her stomach and worked its way to her limbs and her chest. Would Kyle expect them to sleep together? Would he want to consummate this union?

She had vowed to do whatever it took. There was no looking back now. She would deal with the physical aspect when the time came. But wondering certainly cost her sleep.

The following day, their trip to town was as Kyle had predicted. The local minister, though claiming to be sympathetic to their plight, refused to perform the marriage ceremony because of the anticipated reaction of his congregation. He needed his job.

Pausing only briefly outside the church, Isabelle motioned to Kyle. "Take me to the telegraph office. I'll wire my father's friend, Judge Murphy."

She did so, and they waited on separate benches outside the telegraph office for forty-five minutes until the reply came. Judge Murphy would arrive the following Saturday to perform the marriage at the ranch.

That evening, she wrote invitations, and the following day Kyle sent Tott with her to post them.

Apparently now that she was going to be staying, Kyle lifted his order that Pelipa not assist her, because the girl suddenly became helpful, showing Isabelle how to prepare a chicken as well as beef and vegetables from the root cellar. Kyle didn't join them for meals the next few evenings, and Isabelle assumed he was busy.

One morning, she opened her armoire and trunks

and grew concerned over what she would wear for her hasty wedding. Time and again she came back to an elegant white dress she'd purchased in New York, and aside from wondering if one of the hands had been denied wages so that she could purchase it, she considered the possibility of making it presentable as a wedding dress.

Remembering trunks she'd discovered in the attic years ago, she climbed the stairs with Pelipa on her heels.

Isabelle removed protective sheets and opened three trunks that had been buried in the dusty storage space. A forgotten childhood memory sprang to life as she gazed upon the contents. Her father had once discovered her wearing a feathered hat she'd taken from the items and had forbidden her to open them again.

"These were my mother's things," she said to Pelipa. "Aren't they lovely?" She held a gown against her and looked down. "She wasn't as tall as I am. I'd never get into one of them now."

"We use Mother's dress and Isabelle's dress," Pelipa said, holding up one finger on each hand. "Make one dress." She brought the two fingers together.

"That's brilliant!" Isabelle gave her a quick hug. Pelipa had, amazingly, spoken better English since Kyle had given her permission to help. "Which one?"

They sorted through the gowns and shoes and

gloves and finally Isabelle drew out an exquisite lace-trimmed creation with pearl buttons. "If I was a good enough seamstress, I could even use this silk lining," she said wistfully.

Pelipa frowned.

"If I could sew better." She mimed using a needle and thread.

Pelipa held up a hand. "Isabelle walk dress down. Pelipa bring sew better."

Wearing a wide smile, the girl tore down the attic stairs.

Puzzled, Isabelle shrugged and gathered the gown and a few other items and carried them to her room.

Not quite an hour later, Pelipa returned with an older woman in tow. "Pelipa's mother," she said by way of introduction.

The woman knew how to undo the seams of the old garment and carefully press and reuse the material, taking Isabelle's dress apart and lining it, adding the lace trim and buttons and making the gown look as though a French designer had created it.

Isabelle laughed with delight the following day when the project was finished and pressed. She gave Pelipa and her mother each a gold locket for their generous help and time. The old woman proudly wore hers home.

The day of the wedding arrived and brought sunshine. Kyle performed all his normal chores that morning, thinking of the significance of what he was about to do. He didn't take this union lightly. When he pledged to wed himself to Isabelle, he would make the vow with respect and sincerity.

But he was honest with himself. She would never have considered him as a mate if she'd had a better choice in her financial situation. There was no denying his fiery attraction. But she was white and cultured and as citified as they came. He'd be a fool to allow himself any feelings for her or any hollow hopes for a grand love to develop.

Family alliances were common among the Cheyenne, so a marriage like this wasn't unthinkable in either culture. He would take his vows seriously, but he would not kid himself. She would eventually grow bored with the hard life and head out.

As the hour neared, he rode to his cabin, bathed in the creek and dressed in the finest clothing he owned, black trousers and a soft blue doeskin shirt his aunt had made him.

On his way to the ranch, he met Judge Murphy and rode beside the man's carriage until they reached the house.

"I still can't believe Sam's gone," the man said as he stepped to the ground. He had a mane of thick silver hair that hung to his shoulders and a pointed, close-cropped white beard. "Thank you for sending me the wire."

Kyle dismounted. "I tried to let his friends know soon as I could."

"And you're marryin' little Isabelle, eh? I wonder what Sam would have thought of that."

Kyle recognized the friendly grin. "I don't think even bringing him a traditional gift of horses would have won my favor where she was concerned."

"He sure kept her away from here, didn't he?"

Kyle agreed, released his horse into a corral and instructed Tott to see to the judge's horse and those of any other guests who arrived.

Ma'heona'e sat in the shade on the porch, dressed in traditional clothing for the celebration. From her position, she was directing the layout of tables being set up in the yard. His cousins carried out her bidding, and Kyle greeted them, accepting their good-natured ribbing and good wishes.

A handful of guests arrived from Whitehorn, a fraction of the number Isabelle had invited, and soon Pelipa came and gestured for him to enter the house.

The doors to the drawing room had been opened and the furniture moved against the walls, making space for guests to stand.

A fragrant pine-bough wreath adorned the fireplace mantel, a row of lit candles on either side. Judge Murphy stood, Bible in hand, awaiting the prospective couple. He gestured for Kyle to join him.

Kyle took his place.

The resonate notes of a flute floated from the back of the room—one of his aunt's enchanted flutes, he had no doubt. The plaintive notes wafted on the warm afternoon air, a distinctive touch to an already uncommon ceremony. He glanced to see which of his cousins played and caught sight of Isabelle.

She drifted toward him like an ethereal being in a cloud of white lace. Her long-sleeved, scoop-necked dress skimmed the carpeted floor, and her white satin slippers made no sound.

She had prepared her lustrous hair in soft curls and wore a wreath of delicate baby's breath like a crown. As she drew closer, he saw the flush of color on her cheeks and the shine in her lovely storm-cloud eyes. All his thoughts of practicality fled at the sight of his exquisite bride.

Chapter 6

The vows and the legal part of the wedding took only a matter of minutes—minutes Isabelle was later hard-pressed to recall. She didn't think she had drawn a breath the entire time.

She stood on the porch among an unusual assortment of guests and sipped lemonade. It astounded Isabelle that so many of Kyle's family had come, especially after he'd shared his resentment of whites. The Cheyenne women had prepared and arranged an enormous amount of food in wooden bowls and platters on makeshift tables in the yard, and Isabelle marveled over their thoughtfulness.

She walked among the people of all ages dressed in artistically feathered, quilled and fringed buckskin

tunics, shirts and dresses. Thinking of the hardships
they had endured, their admirable talents and pleasant natures impressed her all the more. Men and
women alike wore their hair long and flowing, with
feathers or beads worked into braids. Now she understood why they were referred to as the Beautiful
People.

Isabelle marveled over the soft-looking shirt Kyle
wore. The leather had been dyed a soft blue. Long
fringe hung from the shoulders. Quill and beadwork,
in a striking geometric pattern across the shoulders,
emphasized his height and breadth.

He introduced her to the members of his family.
She couldn't pronounce their names, so he told her
the English meaning of each to make remembering
easier.

A young woman whose name meant Red Star had
a baby in a decorative cradle board on her back.
Isabelle smiled at the baby and touched his shiny
black hair, hair as silky and dark as Kyle's. Her
heart fluttered.

Would she and Kyle have beautiful children like
this together? As much as she'd tried not to concern
herself over the details they had never discussed,
these were important matters, and ignoring them
wouldn't make the situation better.

Buffalo Rib played the lovely sounding flute, and
Isabelle relaxed and enjoyed the enchanting music.
The newlyweds accepted an assortment of gifts,

from shawls, leggings and moccasins to books and candlesticks.

"It was too short notice," she whispered to Kyle. "The others from town probably had plans already."

"I don't think so," he disagreed. "They didn't come because of me. Most in town won't talk to you now."

"Well, they're narrow-minded."

"Just as some on the reservations are narrow-minded. Most of them wouldn't keep company with whites. Twenty years of killing each other does that."

She didn't know what to say, but Judge Murphy approached, and she didn't have a chance to reply. "Best wishes, my dear," he said. "I wish your father could have seen this day."

Isabelle didn't think her father would have *allowed* this day, but she smiled.

He placed his hat over his silver hair and smoothed his pointy beard, a habit she remembered from his visits to her father. "I'll be heading back to Billings before it gets dark."

"I'll hitch your horse," Kyle said, accompanying the man from the porch. A few of the guests called goodbyes before they climbed into their wagons and headed for home.

Kyle's aunt Mae silently moved beside Isabelle. "The tea made muscles better?"

"Yes, it did. Thank you."

"The magical flute was played with song just for you. Now this." She bent her head next to Isabelle's. "You must wear this."

Isabelle opened her hand and accepted the oval-shaped silver locket that Mae pressed into her palm.

"Leaves from my garden will win your husband's heart."

Isabelle touched the hammered silver, her thumbnail tracing the two running horses etched into the metal. Win her husband's heart? What did that mean?

"Put amulet on now," Mae insisted. "Wear day and night."

Not wanting to offend her, Isabelle slipped the quill chain over her head and the amulet's weight lay against her breast.

"Good." Mae's toothy smile revealed her pleasure.

If this was part of their tradition, Isabelle would go along to please Mae. "Thank you."

Mae patted her arm affectionately.

Pelipa said something in Cheyenne. Mae nodded. "Now come," she said.

Mae led Isabelle to where Kyle stood after seeing the judge off. She gestured to Spotted Feathers, and Kyle's cousin handed him a fur robe.

Gently, Mae urged Isabelle forward.

Kyle met her gaze warily. "It's a custom she feels strongly about."

Isabelle glanced at his grinning family members, her curiosity piqued.

"If we had courted, I would have placed my robe around you and we'd have taken a walk."

Isabelle read the imploring look in Mae's shining dark eyes. "Sounds all right to me."

Kyle drew the fur robe around his shoulders and held one arm out in invitation.

Isabelle took her cue and stepped to his side. He drew her close with a rock-hard arm and closed the robe around her, cocooning them in its thickness and combining the warmth of their bodies.

His family members smiled and nodded. Mae said something that sounded like a direct order.

Isabelle was keenly aware of their touching bodies as Kyle led her toward the stable where his Appaloosa and a dozen unfamiliar mounts stood, tails flicking.

Kyle paused beside his horse.

"More of the custom?" she asked.

He nodded.

She accepted his assistance onto his unsaddled horse and experienced a little jolt of shock when he climbed on behind her and reached around her shoulders for the reins.

He tossed the buffalo robe to Spotted Feathers, who rolled it and mounted his speckled horse. His wife, Red Star, waited astride a horse beside him, the baby on her back, and the others were soon mounted, as well.

Kyle turned the Appaloosa's head and urged her into the throng of fancifully dressed riders.

"Were are we going?" Isabelle asked over her shoulder.

"I guess they'll show us. Today you make your formal departure from your family to mine. A Cheyenne woman moves to her husband's lodge."

"But we won't—"

"This is just part of the ceremony," he explained. "Thank you for going along with it."

"I know it's important to your aunt. Besides, it's rather enjoyable."

Her words pleased him immeasurably. But her nearness unsettled him. Beneath the delicate floral wreath, her hair smelled of spring violets. He allowed his cheek to brush the velvety softness. She had relaxed against his chest, and her feminine scent and warmth tormented him through layers of lace and deerskin.

She hadn't seemed ashamed of the presence of his mother's people at her Christian wedding. She'd eaten the traditional feast they'd supplied and had gone along with the robe without a qualm. Was she hiding her distaste for the sake of her good manners?

So far nothing had diminished her obvious pleasure over staying at the ranch...and she'd acknowledged enjoying the ride. Kyle wouldn't admit, even to himself, how much pleasure he took from this closeness.

Walks Last called to Kyle and pointed to a

wooded area on their left. Kyle moved ahead of the others. A primitive shelter made of pine branches and tanned hides came into view.

He led the Appaloosa close, then dismounted and helped Isabelle to the ground. Her lovely gray eyes were wide with questions, but he read no fear or distaste.

Spotted Feathers handed Kyle the robe. Once again Kyle wrapped it around both of them, then he led her toward the flower-festooned bower hidden among the lodgepole pines. The other riders remained on horseback, silent observers. Needles crushed beneath the horses' hooves sent their pungent fragrance into the early evening air.

He'd seen dozens of these honeymoon shelters. A bridegroom prepared it for his wife, provisioned it for their stay and brought flowers for her pleasure. His family had observed the custom for him—probably at Ma'heona'e's direction.

Pulling aside the flap, he guided Isabelle in. She bent to accommodate her height and entered ahead of him. He turned and gave a farewell gesture to the tribe. Returning the hand sign, they turned their mounts and rode away.

With a deep breath, he entered the shaded depths behind her and laid the robe out along one side. The scent of bitterroot blossoms filled the compact and intimate area. Neither of them could stand to their full height, so he sat cross-legged on the blankets that had been spread, and she followed his example.

His bride observed the pots and bundles lining the hide walls. "What is all this?"

"Food to last several days."

"Several days!" Her eyes widened.

"It's—"

"The custom," she finished for him, with a wry grin.

"We won't stay," he added quickly. "One night should be enough to satisfy Ma'heona'e."

This time her expression did look a little fearful. "Spend the night? But I don't have anything with me."

"I'm sure all you need is here. Pelipa must have been in on this plan."

"But there's no—" Two bright pink spots appeared on her fine, high cheeks. "No facility."

"There's the whole woods," he said with a sweep of his arm.

She refused to meet his eyes.

Mindful of her maidenly blush, Kyle's heart beat too rapidly. *His bride.* The crown of tiny white blooms lent her face a sweet and completely feminine softness. The dress bared her throat and delicate collarbones. The intriguing hollow at the base of her throat pulsed rapidly, and he imagined tasting her skin there, feeling the beat of her heart against his lips.

This was dangerous thinking, and he knew better than to allow it. She might be enjoying the uniqueness of the situation for the moment, but if her upbringing and the color of her skin, as well as the fact that she was a lady, had anything to do with it, she'd soon tire of the primitive life. Her worry over the natural functions of her body proved that.

She moved across the blankets to the stacks of baskets and began a search. Holding up a porcupine's tail sewn to a strong stick with ornamental beadwork over the seams, she asked, "What's this?"

"A hairbrush."

She studied it, her expression perplexed, then went back to her exploration. In a leather bag, she found several smooth, brightly colored stones.

"A game," he said, enlightening her, before she had a chance to ask.

"Will you show me how to play tonight?"

He nodded. She examined and tasted dried fruits and berries, asking about each one. Her fascination with the cooking equipment had him showing her how the pouches and bowls and bones were used.

"Well," she said after her study was complete and everything had been neatly returned to its place. "I guess it's time I..." She scooted toward the opening. "I'll just take a brief walk." She stopped. "You don't think anyone's out there watching us, do you?"

"There's probably a guard, but he wouldn't be near enough to see you...walk."

She nodded, gathered her lace hem and disappeared.

He would have to find out who to thank for the coffeepot, he thought as he exited the shelter and built a fire from the nearby stack of sticks and logs. He filled the pot with water and added grounds. The tribe hadn't forgotten anything. They believed new-lyweds should have nothing to think about but each other.

Right now he'd be grateful for some distractions.

As a guilty afterthought, he placed a pan of water over the fire for Isabelle's tea. He was used to keeping company with cowhands and Ma'heona'e, not helpless city women. Maybe getting fired up over her muleheadedness would get him through the evening.

Twigs snapped and leaves crackled as she returned. "Something is out there!" she said, out of breath. She wore a becoming flush. "An enormous animal!"

He stood. "What kind of animal?"

"I'm not sure. Nearly as big as a horse! His eyes were so pretty and he looked right at me."

"Probably a moose."

"Yes, a moose! I saw a picture of one once. But this one was so big!"

"Might have been a bull. I have some water ready for your tea."

"That's very thoughtful of you. I'll get the tea." She started to turn, but stopped. Her gaze drifted to the fire, to his boots, then over his shoulder. "I'd like to change out of this dress and into something more comfortable. The doeskin dress I saw in one of those bundles looked so soft.''

He settled beside the fire. "I'll wait right here.''

"Well, I—um—I can't get out of this dress alone.''

"What?''

"The entire back is buttons. I can't reach them.''

"That's foolish. How did you get it on?''

She rolled her eyes. "With *help*.''

Muttering under his breath about the vain stupidity of white women, he got up and stalked toward her. "Turn around.''

"Here?'' Her voice came out as a squeak.

"Where would you have me unbutton your dress, my lady?''

"Well, we're standing right out in the open!'' She glanced around wildly, and her hands came up to her midriff defensively.

"Nobody's going to see except me, and I'll see whether we're out here or in there.''

"Yes, but—''

"Get inside.''

She ducked under the flap, and he followed.

The light had waned, and the interior had grown dim. The heavy floral scent and the extreme intimacy closed in around them.

Chapter 7

She presented her back.

Kyle raised his hand to the top of the row of buttons.

Even over the pervading bitterroot, he detected the stimulating scent of her hair, her skin—unfamiliar, exotic, arousing. For a spellbound moment, he imagined that this desirable woman loved him and that he would be making love to her this night. Here in this romantic bower, away from both their worlds, they would come together in a place with no boundaries or restrictions or prejudice.

His body reacted with a bold surge, and he had sudden difficulty breathing. The earthy vision lasted until he noted his dark hand against the snowy white lace and satin that enveloped her. A reminder that he was half Cheyenne and she was one hundred percent white. His clumsy fingers felt like tree stumps on the minute buttons. He had the dress unfastened to the middle of her back, and one side of the fabric slid to reveal her ivory skin and a lacy undergarment.

Kyle swallowed hard and continued his task. "Only a white would fashion a dress so utterly impractical."

"There's nothing practical about those beads across your shoulders, or the fringe. They're an expression of art."

"I can pull the shirt off over my head by myself."

He thought about doing just that. And pressing his heated bare skin against her revealed back, molding himself to her feminine contours, like when they'd been riding. He imagined how her body would feel and react and where he'd like to taste and touch her. Maybe she thought about it, too, because she shivered. Gooseflesh rose on her slender shoulders.

He applied himself to fumbling with the pearl buttons until the dress was completely open down the back, then with great control, he dropped his hands and ducked out of the shelter.

Isabelle clutched two fistfuls of Irish lace with trembling fingers. He was gone, but she could still feel his calluses brush her skin, his warm breath on her shoulder. If he'd been planning to consummate their marriage, it would have been right then, wouldn't it?

They'd never discussed the subject, but she'd assumed they would take on all the aspects of husband and wife. She hadn't known how she felt about that until this moment. Shamefully, she felt somewhat disappointed—and yet relieved. She barely knew the man.

But it would have to happen. Sometime. Someday.

She shrugged her arms from the sleeves, let the top of the dress fold over and stepped from the skirt. Stooping in her silk chemise and drawers, she looked for somewhere to hang the garment. Not wanting to snag it on the branches that formed the ceiling beams, she settled for spreading the dress out on one of the blankets.

Isabelle ran a palm over the lace, smoothing the silky fabric, feeling a tangible connection to her mother. She had come to Montana from Illinois, a woman out of her familiar environment among the rugged men and the extreme elements of this wild, unforgiving country.

Isabelle removed the baby's breath wreath, unpinned her hair and used the quill brush. It took some getting used to, to figure out how to hold it and run the quills through, but it did the job quite cleverly. She made a braid and tied the end with a strip of leather that had been fastening a bundle.

She removed the silver amulet, studied it curiously in the dim light for a moment, then placed it with her other things. Mae had said it would win Kyle's heart. He had a heart; it was plain by the way he interacted with his aunt and the rest of his family. But she didn't think his heart could be softened toward her. He didn't bother to hide his obvious disdain for her and her kind. And who could blame him? With what little she knew, she believed the Cheyenne had been treated abominably—and he knew far better than she.

But his parents had defied convention and put aside their differences to marry, hadn't they? She wished she knew something about them.

And what of her own parents? Had they loved each other? Her elusive memories of them as a family were of her mother laughing and her father lavishing attention. When he'd sent Isabelle away after her mother's death, she hadn't understood. Maybe she reminded him of his wife, and the sight of her had been too painful.

Maybe he'd been irrationally afraid for her well-being and couldn't bear to lose her, too. However, they could have comforted each other. She'd certainly needed comfort…and love.

Isabelle gave the dress a last fond look. Perhaps someday a daughter of hers would wear it. But that was far in the future, and she still had tonight to worry about. Her stomach quivered with growing concern. What was to happen between them this night? Unfolding the doeskin dress, she slipped it on over her head. Long fringe brushed her arms and her ankles.

He was still a stranger. But she didn't want to displease him. And neither did she want to deny herself anything good that might come of this marriage. Plenty of marriages got started this way. Her situation was not unique—except to her.

Her silk slippers looked foolish with the costume, she realized, gazing down, so she removed her stockings and garters and slipped her feet into the smaller of the two pairs of moccasins.

This marriage had never been in her plans, but then her plans had never been definite—except that she'd wanted to come back to Montana. But then Kyle's plans hadn't included her as a wife, either. Did he resent her?

A horrible thought struck her, and she stood glued to the blanket. What had this hasty arrangement done to Kyle's plans? Had there been a woman he'd wanted to marry? If so, he would resent Isabelle's interference.

When she stepped through the flap and straightened, Kyle stared from his seat beside the fire. Her cheeks flamed. "Do I look foolish?" she asked.

"Do you think Cheyenne clothing is foolish?"

"No, I—I just feel strange."

"Tomorrow you'll be home and you can wear your own clothes."

She took several hesitant steps closer to the fire.

"What kind of clothing did you picture your wife wearing on your wedding day?"

"I never thought about it."

She settled down a few feet from him. "Did you plan to marry a Cheyenne woman?"

His dark gaze studied her without expression. "Why would I?"

"Well, because you think white women are silly and useless and wear foolish clothing."

He picked up a stick and rearranged the burning embers. "Even if I had a mind to, I'm not exactly a sought-after brave."

The fact was hard to believe. He was hardworking...and handsome. She couldn't imagine the Cheyenne women not falling all over him. "Why not?"

"I'm not a brave warrior. I didn't count coup with the others. I traded with the Cheyenne and Blackfeet and Sioux, but I sold horses to the army. I wasn't sent to the reservation with them. I'm too white."

"But you saved some of their children from that awful experience. You did what you could. Surely they respect that."

"They tolerate me."

"Those there today do more than tolerate you, I believe."

He shrugged.

Isabelle could understand his refusal to participate in the wars. The blood of both nations ran in his veins, and choosing a side would be difficult—or impossible. "Tell me about your parents."

She wasn't sure if he'd answer, but he spoke almost immediately. "My mother was Ameohne'e, Walking Woman. My father was a trapper, sold beaver and wolf pelts to the whites, traded with the tribes. Hank Brennan was his name. My mother found a young raccoon caught in one of his traps. He ran across her nursing the trapped animal, crying over its suffering. He freed the raccoon and helped her care for its wounds.

"My mother sought Ma'heona'e's help," he continued. "Ma'heona'e says their father didn't want my mother to marry Hank, but it was what Ameohne'e wanted. Land was cheap back then, and Hank bought good sections and started a ranch so my mother would be close to her family."

"He loved her."

Kyle shrugged. "He had wandering feet. I was small, but I remember him being gone for long periods of time. I thought he was working. Talk later was that he had another wife in Colorado."

Isabelle's surprise must have shown on her face.

"That would have been acceptable if he'd brought her here to help my mother," he said. "Cheyenne women often suggest that their husband take another, younger wife to share the workload."

She stared at him. "I wouldn't share my husband even if I had to work like a stevedore! You don't plan to take another wife, do you?"

A grin inched up one side of his mouth, catching her by surprise.

"We had a Christian wedding," she told him firmly. Maybe he did have another woman! "Surely you don't think—"

He laughed out loud then, the outburst startling a small creature in the nearby brush that scampered across the clearing in the dusk.

Isabelle started and instinctively moved closer to Kyle, even though he was laughing at her.

"You don't want to share me?" he asked, his voice seductively low.

She looked away from the devastating smile that made her stomach flip-flop. She had no intentions of sharing him as a husband! That was—well, it was *unacceptable*. "It wouldn't be proper. Or legal."

"Depends on who you ask."

She met his unfathomable dark gaze. Once again he made her feel that everything she knew and believed in was questionable. "So where was this ranch of your father's?"

"Right here."

She glanced around the clearing. "Next to the Big Sky?"

"It *was* the Big Sky. This section is all that was left after my father sold out to yours. He left my mother and me enough land to live on and then he took off. Never saw him again after I was seven."

Finally Isabelle understood. No wonder he had

such possessive feelings. Just as she did, he felt a
kinship with the land.

"I want to learn everything I can about the
ranch," she said, pulling her knees up and wrapping
her arms around them. She rested her chin on her
forearm. "I want to learn about the horses and go
over the ledgers. I'm going to be an active partner."

"As long as you don't get in the way of anyone's
job."

She'd be working herself—how could that be interference? His insinuation was insulting.

"And don't place yourself in unnecessary danger.
Always let me know where you'll be and I'll have
someone with you."

"I don't need a nursemaid."

He leaned forward and poured himself a cup of
coffee from the dented pot. "I can't spare a nursemaid."

"You find me the most trivial creature alive,
don't you?" she asked, once again irked. "I'm not
valuable because I don't know as much about life
out here as you do. I'm in the way and I'm a nuisance. I know you'd rather I'd never come back.
You've made that very plain. My father never
wanted me here, either. I was never important to
him, either."

She stopped when she realized the burn of tears
was threatening to fracture her dignity. She blinked
and looked into the darkening woods.

The fire crackled. An animal howled in the distance, and a shiver ran up her spine.

"Your father protected you like a she-bear with a cub," he said finally. "He'd already lost your mother."

The fire warmed her skin. "I might have believed that if he'd ever visited me. Or tolerated my visits. If he'd ever done anything but send money."

"Maybe that's how he showed..."

She turned to look at him. "His love?"

He nodded.

She shrugged. "I'd have rather had a home."

With those revealing words, Kyle's perception of this woman altered so dramatically that he almost reached over and touched her to offer comfort. Had his impression of her as spoiled and pampered and greedy been based on lack of knowledge? If so, he'd done her a great injustice.

But even if he'd known her true character, he'd still have wanted the ranch...and she still wouldn't have wanted to give it up. At least he understood her desperation in a clearer light. And he didn't hold her insistence against her.

And, strangely enough, he couldn't resent her any longer, either.

But she couldn't help who and what she was. She still couldn't be trusted to stay or to be responsible. Promises and treaties and vows were like dry leaves in a brisk wind to whites.

"What more do you expect of me, besides not getting in the way?" she asked.

He studied her haughty profile in the firelight. "What do you mean?"

"Will we be—" she swallowed "—intimate?"

The word, her voice, the *idea*—hit him like a punch in the chest. What was she willing to trade— no, *sacrifice*—to make herself a home? Did she think he would treat her so callously as to hold her at arm's length and yet take her body for his own selfish pleasure? Her opinion of his character angered him—and shamed him.

"It's too soon," he replied, hoping to relieve her worry and end the discussion. "That's not the purpose of our agreement."

She didn't look at him. "But it's part of marriage."

"When and if the time is right," he insisted.

She nodded. Agreement? Understanding? He wasn't sure which.

"You know either partner can annul a marriage if it's not consummated," she said.

"I don't know what that means."

"Cancel. Either of us could cancel our marriage if we haven't been...intimate."

"I'll never do that. That would have to be your choice."

"I never will, either."

He was sure she meant it *now*. But someday... "I'll sleep out here," he said. "You stay inside."

She glanced around their darkened campsite. "I guess you've slept outside before."

"Many times."

"Do you still want to show me the game with the rocks?"

"Another night."

She stood, unconsciously smoothing the doeskin across her thighs in a sensual manner that shouldn't have affected him, but did. Especially with the question—the suggestion of intimacy freshly painted in his mind and the woods hiding them from the world.

Had she felt his hunger inside? Had she sensed the fire that raced through his veins as he stood behind her and smelled her skin and hair and saw her sleek ivory flesh? Had she expected him to do something about it then? Had she prepared herself for the possibility?

He didn't want a woman who offered herself as a sacrifice—or a trade.

He watched her disappear inside the shelter. He'd been so single-mindedly focused on obtaining the ranch that he hadn't wasted time wishing or wanting things that were out of his grasp. Today he had married Isabelle Cooper, a beautiful, intelligent, willful and utterly charming woman, united in a marriage he would never have dreamed for himself.

The untouchable young girl Sam Cooper had protected so zealously was now Kyle's mature and incredibly desirable wife.

And now, he had to ask himself...what *did* he want?

Chapter 8

Each successive day proved that Isabelle was a quick and eager student, her bookkeeping and mathematical skills far surpassing Kyle's. Every evening he joined her for dinner, and afterward they retired to the study where she showed him what she'd gone over that day and made suggestions and recommendations.

Her grasp of the business end of ranching surprised him. He would have more time to devote to the horses if she could be trusted with this work, but undoubtedly it would all fall back on him eventually.

"I've spent enough days inside," she informed him one evening. "I've been arranging things to my liking and cleaning the attic and the corners, but I'll be out to join you tomorrow morning."

He wanted to smile at the bossy way she pointed the ink pen at him, but he knew better than to let her see his amusement. If he didn't challenge her, she'd discover on her own the difficulty of the outdoor work and be able to save face.

She sat straighter, and one slim eyebrow rose, an expression he'd learned meant a defense was brewing.

He said nothing.

Isabelle rubbed at an inkstain on her finger and directed her gaze away from Kyle's. His dark, unreadable expressions wore on her nerves until she wanted to throw something at him. No one was always that stern and inscrutable. Annoying him pleased her, because then she at least got to see him react.

He'd been more distant than ever since the night of their wedding, when he'd assured her that a physical aspect to their marriage was something he was not considering. She'd felt almost foolish for being the one to voice it—to think it—to wonder in the first place.

And she'd wondered again…and again, numerous times in those days that followed. Perhaps there was something wrong with her to anticipate it. Perhaps he saw something wrong with her, and that's why he didn't initiate it.

Perhaps she'd better direct her thoughts elsewhere.

Remembering his criticism of her clothing, she dressed as sensibly as she could the following morning, and after eating sausage and biscuits with Pelipa, she made her way to the barn, where the sounds of activity drew her.

As she entered the cool interior, the potent scent of horse and hay and grain met her nostrils. She walked the center aisle, glancing at the parallel rows of facing stalls to her right, and continued toward the sound of men's voices.

In an open room on the left, Kyle and several of the hands stood or sat on kegs and sawhorses. An enormous stone forge sat cold on this day. Kyle held several tools, which he'd just taken from a bench that ran along a wall opposite an exterior doorway.

The comfortable dialogue stopped abruptly as she stepped into view. There were six of them all together, counting Kyle, Sidestep and Tott. The other three, whom she'd seen only from a distance, whipped their hats from their heads and straightened to attention as if she were a commanding officer.

"Miss Cooper," came the self-conscious murmurs.

"Mr. Tott, Mr. Sidestep," she said cordially. Their faces reddened. "I'm afraid I haven't had the pleasure of making the acquaintance of the rest of you gentlemen."

Kyle introduced the others.

"I appreciate you men remaining in spite of the fact that your wages were in arrears. I find loyalty a commendable trait."

The men glanced uncertainly at Kyle.

"She thanks you for staying on without pay," he translated, with a droll cock of one eyebrow.

Isabelle nodded. "And I want you all to go about your work just as you normally would. Nothing should change just because I'm here to help."

The men glanced at one another, over at Kyle, and took their cue to get to work.

"What's on the agenda for today?" she asked Kyle after most of them had replaced their hats and exited.

"The hands are bringing a herd in from the south pasture to the corrals this morning. Tott and I are going to be checking the animals over. We're starting with feet out here." He led the way toward the stalls.

"Feet?" she asked, hurrying to keep up.

"Check for thrush and scratches and trim hooves."

"Oh, well, you show me what to do, and I'll do it."

Tott had moved down the corridor and led a horse into the center, where he bent over beside the animal, a hoof held firmly between his knees.

"Like that," Kyle said. "Approach the horse calmly and deliberately to gain his confidence. You don't want to spook 'im. Slip his halter on and lead him out here.'' He demonstrated with a spotted mare.

Isabelle slid the bolt on a stall gate and found a halter on a nail. ''What's this one's name?''

''No name.''

''Why not?''

''Too many horses pass through here to keep track of their names,'' he replied.

She slipped the halter on and adjusted it. ''Then how do you know what to say to them?''

''It's not what you say, it's how you say it. Now lead her out here. There. Now stand facing her rear beside her front leg. They have to be trained to let you do this. You can't just try this on one of the broncs.

''Touch her shoulder and run your hand down so she knows you're going to handle her leg. Now move your hand down to grip her foot and press her shoulder with your other hand so she shifts her weight to her other leg.''

She pressed, but the enormous animal didn't budge. ''She's—uh—not going anywhere.''

''Lean against her and put your weight into it. When her weight shifts, lift the foot up off the ground and place it between your legs, just above your knee. Flex your knees, turn your toes in—''

His instructions were lost as Isabelle fought with her skirts to get the hoof between her knees. Finally she had to reach between her spread feet, grasp the back hem of her skirt, pull it up and tuck in into her waistband. The remedy bared the tops of her shoes and her calves, but she had little choice if she planned to proceed with this task. Finally she got a hoof between her knees.

"What *is* this?" she asked, her nose crinkling at the foul smell and the ghastly smear on the freshly pressed fabric of her skirt.

"Manure."

"Oh, my—" She turned her face aside and tried not to gag.

"Here, clean it off with this so you can see the bottom of her foot." He handed her an iron tool. "Run the pick gently from heel to toe, and be careful not to poke or bruise the tender spot here. If she jerks away, don't accidentally poke her."

"Clean this stuff out?" she asked. He couldn't be serious!

"I'll take over if you'd rather find something else to do."

She looked up and caught the unguarded amusement in his expression. "This is truly an important job?" she asked, not trusting him.

"Not doing it can cause disease or leg problems, sometimes faulty gaits."

Isabelle glanced over her shoulder to see Tott diligently working at the same task. She ran the pick carefully across the horse's foot as Kyle had told her.

He'd given her the most docile animals in the barn, she realized sometime later, after she'd checked three horses and he'd inspected her work. He'd finished with six or seven in the same amount of time.

Though he gave a running verbal lesson while he worked, watching Kyle was the best teacher. The horses seemed to listen, too. With his voice and his gentle, confident movements, he had earned their trust. He ran his hands over their necks and shoulders, scratched their massive foreheads and made an odd clicking sound in his throat to which they responded with perked ears.

Isabelle could have watched him forever.

Her back ached from bending over in the unnatural position, and she arched it as she observed him leading a reddish mare into her stall. The bell clanged, and the sound of horses reining in outside caught her attention.

"Dinner," Kyle said with a gesture indicating she should follow.

She let her hem down, massaged the small of her back and trudged toward the bunkhouse beside him.

The interior of the men's quarters was amazingly clean and orderly, with a large open room for cooking and dining, scarred tables and assorted benches. A few rockers and footstools were set before the fireplace at the northeast end of the room. A checkerboard sat in wait on a small, sturdy table. Open stairs led to the sleeping area above.

"This is Harlan."

She glanced at the man who wore denims and a

faded flannel shirt just like everyone else. The only sign that he was the cook was the flour dusting his scraggly gray beard.

Isabelle accepted a tin plate of beans and a bent fork and seated herself on a bench. Tins of biscuits had been placed on the tables. The men kept their distance, taking places at the opposite end from their female newcomer.

Kyle sat across from her, and his presence made her feel less like an interloper. She offered him a grateful smile.

He spared her one acknowledging nod and dug into his food.

She ate a few bites and glanced around. "Are they usually this quiet?"

"They're hungry."

She'd washed at the pump, but the odious smell remained on her skirts or in her nose and killed her appetite. She forced herself to eat the pile of salty beans and bacon so as not to offend Harlan. Kyle had been right about the man's lack of imagination, however. And she was *paying* him to supply these meals. Perhaps they could go over some menus.

One or two at a time, the hands stood and stacked their plates in a bucket beside the door.

She met Kyle's obsidian gaze.

He expected her to beg off. The thought appealed. She could come up with an excuse to change out of her smelly clothes and bathe. "What now?" she asked instead.

"I'm going to cut a few horses to break. Watch and learn."

She fell into step behind the others. "All right."

Tott and Ward had mounted horses and worked to cut a horse from the big corral and urge him through a gate into the round corral on the north end of the barn. A gleaming black horse with a gray mane broke into the space and galloped in a circle.

Isabelle took a place along the fence with the others and watched all afternoon as Kyle worked.

She'd seen her father breaking horses once, and he'd been bucked clear over the beast's head. But he hadn't taken nearly the time or the patience that Kyle showed in getting the creatures used to being handled and touched.

A tender place warmed in Isabelle's chest at the gentleness and care Kyle afforded his animals— *their* animals, she reminded herself. All this was half hers. Watching him, doubt about her ability to contribute as much to the ranch as Kyle did awakened in her mind. She lulled the discomfiting thoughts back to sleep by telling herself that none of this would be his anyway if she hadn't agreed to his proposal.

Okay, except a good share of the horses.

Horse after horse fell under Kyle's gentle submission. The last, a nervous spotted gray, fought the ropes and shied from Kyle's hands until he and Sidestep tied his feet, laid him on his side and worked the halter over his head while he fought.

This one Kyle didn't try to saddle or mount. Once he was bound and haltered, they let him stand. His eyes rolled wildly, and Isabelle could sense his fear and distress. Kyle spoke to him, touched him, rubbed him with a blanket until he calmed. Then they let him out into the big corral, where he galloped to the far side.

"Why didn't you saddle him?" she asked when Kyle approached the fence where she stood.

Kyle noted the sunburn across her nose and wished he'd thought to find her a decent hat. "Someone has tried to break him before."

"How do you know?"

"Scrapes on his shins. That scared look."

"What will you do?"

"Let him get used to me slowly. Your nose is red."

Isabelle touched her nose with one finger. "Pelipa is fixing her fried bread and vegetables for supper."

"I think I'll eat with the men," he said. "I want to stay with the chestnut mare tonight."

"The one who's close to foaling?"

He nodded.

"Why don't you let me bring you supper? Then you won't have to eat stew."

Not even stew. He remembered the beans he'd seen soaking that noon, and he wasn't about to refuse her offer. "If you wouldn't mind."

"I don't." She glanced away nervously before she said, "What would you think of me making a shopping list and having one of the hands ride into Whitehorn with me?''

That wasn't out of the ordinary. Why would she ask?

"And then," she went on, "I would like to go over a few menus with Harlan, make a few suggestions." She glanced up as though waiting for his response.

"You're asking my *opinion?*" Now *that* was out of the ordinary.

"I need to know if you think he would be offended. I truly believe the men deserve variety and good nutrition."

"You can ask the workers to do things the way you want them done," he said with a shrug. "You're the boss, too."

"And what about offending him?" she asked.

"If you make him mad, you can hire a new cook, I guess. But remember, there are worse ones." He turned and strode toward the barn.

Later Isabelle dipped hot water and sponge bathed in her room. She carried her smelly skirts to the back porch, not looking forward to having to wash them—or any of her clothing, for that matter. Another task she had to learn.

While she and Pelipa ate, the girl hinted that she'd like to visit the reservation. "You go see your friends," Isabelle encouraged her. "I don't mind an evening alone. Is it safe for you to go by yourself?"

"Pelipa know the way. Not afraid. Long Knife ride back together with Pelipa."

"Long Knife?"

The girl nodded.

"Is Long Knife your beau?"

"What is beau?"

"Gentleman caller. Sweetheart." Isabelle didn't know words to convey the idea, so she pressed her hand over her heart, fluttered her eyelashes and sighed. "Are you fond of each other?"

Pelipa giggled. "Long Knife wear many years on his face. He not a beau."

Isabelle stacked the dishes. "Oh. Well, I thought perhaps you had someone special at the reservation. You're a lovely young woman."

"Someone special is rancher son," she confided. "But he white and Kyle say not for Pelipa."

Isabelle studied the lovely girl's disillusioned expression. "I'm sorry," she said simply, understanding Kyle's feelings and yet wishing things could be different. "What's his name?"

A shy smile crept across Pelipa's face, and her bright black eyes twinkled. "William."

How sad that Kyle had discouraged her from a relationship with a white. How sad that he saw the need. Would Isabelle ever find a way past his resentment?

Scraping soap into the heated water, she paused and reflected. How surprising that she suddenly realized wanting to work her way into his trust wasn't only for reasons of their working relationship.

She'd begun to care what he thought of her...and she wanted him to care, too.

Chapter 9

The sun was setting when Isabelle carried a tray toward the barn. The long days and backbreaking work involved in keeping the ranch running had become real to her. Her contribution to the day's tasks gave her a new sense of accomplishment, and even though her body ached and her palms had blistered, she was happier than she'd ever been all those years studying and teaching in the city.

She found Kyle and the mare in one of the large stalls on the left side of the barn. He sat perched on a nail keg, a tangle of harnesses and bridles at his feet, oiling the leather with a rag, and glanced up at her arrival.

"How's she doing?" she asked.

"She's fine. I'm the nervous one."

She smiled and placed the tray on another keg. "I kept this hot for you."

"I'll wash off outside and be right back."

She offered the horse a few pieces of dried apple she'd brought and rubbed the animal's head.

"She likes you," Kyle said when he returned and sat to eat. He'd removed his hat and tied his black hair at the back of his neck. A damp lock fell across his forehead.

"I bribed her," she said.

Of course he didn't smile. He ate his meal in silence.

Isabelle rubbed the mare's shoulder and ran her palm over her distended side. "You touch them all over when you're working them. Why is that?"

He sipped coffee from the tin cup and studied her. "Getting them used to being handled."

"Her sides are sticking out so far. Does it hurt her?"

"I don't think so." He got up and came to stand beside her. "Reach under her belly. Sometimes you can feel the colt moving."

"Really?" She ran her hand along the animal's hide.

"Like this." He took her wrist firmly and stretched her left arm far beneath the horse, pressing her entire arm against the belly. "Now wait."

Kyle and Isabelle bent beneath the horse, their sides and hips touching, and after a moment, the animal's hide rippled and rolled, and she felt the muscular sensation along her limb. "I felt it! Oh, my goodness!"

She became aware of Kyle's solid, warm body where it touched hers through her clothing along her side. His strong rough hand was clamped over the back of hers, holding it to the mare's belly.

As though he, too, had become acutely aware of their closeness, Kyle's touch on her hand changed. No longer was he holding her hand in place, but he seemed to stroke her skin in nebulous discovery. Her hand trembled under the gentle caress.

As one, they straightened and stood facing each other. Kyle let her hand slide as their bodies straightened, but kept it firmly in his enormous palm. His dark gaze lowered to her fingers, pale in his dark-skinned grasp, and her attention followed. Her heart chugged like a train engine on an incline, and she experienced a quickening desire for their sweet, tentative connection to deepen.

While he studied their joined hands, she looked up and found his black lashes hiding those unreadable eyes. His features were an intriguing blend of stern angles and dramatic symmetry, his lips classically sculptured and full.

An emotion she couldn't name fluttered in her chest just looking at him, the same unidentifiable yearning she'd felt watching him with the horses, a longing utterly sweet and forlorn at the same time.

She raised her right hand and opened her palm

along the side of his face. His skin was warm and smooth, and touching him sent a tingle up her arm.

His dark gaze shot to hers, his eyes examining, weighing, boring into hers. His attention dropped to her mouth.

Isabelle's lips parted on a shaky breath.

She slid the hand against his jaw behind his neck, silky hair brushing her fingers, and raised her face expectantly.

He didn't disappoint her. Kyle lowered his head and touched those perfect lips to hers in a warm, ardent press of satiny flesh and a mingling of breaths.

He tasted like coffee…and energy. He released her hand and cupped her face, aligning, burning, drawing, tempting, until she lost herself in the feelings, wrapped her arms around his torso and pressed in closer for the deep-drawn pleasure.

One of his hands slid from her face down her neck, and his fingers brushed the sensitive skin, slid inside her collar and drew circles against her flesh.

Isabelle's weak knees left her pressed to his hard frame, her breasts crushed against his chest where his heart pounded.

He cupped her face again, more roughly this time, and held her head while he separated their mouths long enough to kiss her chin, her jaw, her neck, her ear. A shiver coursed through her body. She gripped his back less for support than to avail herself of the sensual onslaught.

His mouth returned to hers, pausing for a divine moment of expectancy as unsettling as the actual contact. Then he reclaimed her lips, and her world changed.

Tears smarted behind her eyelids; her throat constricted. She wanted to melt into him, against him, around him. She wanted to become him. She wanted...

Something subtle changed between them. Something powerful and frightening.

Almost as one they drew back, and their hooded gazes locked.

Kyle released her, then, when she swayed, had to steady her with a hand on her shoulder.

"Kyle, I—"

"Go back to the house." He withdrew his touch.

She tried to read emotion in his eyes, in his granite-hard expression, but he kept his reactions shuttered, as always.

"What's wrong?" she asked, the question burning from her aching heart. He seemed almost angry.

"Go back to the house, Isabelle." His voice was a deep rasp.

"Did I do something wrong?"

"No, I did something wrong. Now go." He picked up the tray and shoved it into her trembling hands.

Ashamed, she tore her gaze from his hard black eyes to the dirty dishes. She could still taste him, could still feel his touch on her neck, his body against hers. She still harbored the same disquieting yearning she had a minute ago.

In her mind, she went over that disorienting encounter and tried to understand what had gone wrong. Had it all been one-sided? Had she only dreamed he could feel the same way about her?

She turned her back. Rejection was something Isabelle was accustomed to. She'd been turned aside and sent away her whole life. She should have developed a thick skin for being shown she was unwanted. But this hurt as much as any of her father's rebuffs. Maybe more, because she had tried as hard as she knew how to be useful, to become the kind of wife a rancher needed.

She wanted to hold her back straight and her chin high, but her usual brave facade failed her, and she turned and exited the stall and the barn as fast as she could, striding into the darkening night before he saw the hurt. Damn him, anyway!

Why had she gone and done that? Why had she risked her heart when she knew better? Halfway to the house, the fresh injury turned to anger, and she flung the tray as hard as she could. It landed with an unsatisfactory thump in the dirt, and the tin plates clanked together. Isabelle ran forward and attacked them with the toe of her boot, sending plates and cup and silverware flying.

Kyle might not want her, damn his hide, but he couldn't send her away. The ranch was hers, and it was all she had. He might not need her, just as her father had never needed her, but there was still one thing that needed her—the ranch.

She would pour her soul into the ranch, and never again would her heart be lacerated. Isabelle ran into the house and up the stairs, not pausing for water or to say good-night to Pelipa. She closed herself in her room and nursed her humiliation and pride.

A long, sleepless time later, she pulled back a frilly curtain and gazed at the moonlit barn. Lighting a lamp, she changed her rumpled clothing, removed the pearl combs from her hair and placed them in her jewelry box.

The twinkle of silver caught her attention, and she picked up the chain and dangled the engraved amulet before the lamp.

Leaves from my garden will win your husband's heart. Mae had spoken cryptically on their wedding day. Isabelle scoffed again at the foolish hope of someone loving her. She was obviously unlovable, and a few weeds wouldn't change that.

But something bigger than her wounded self-esteem and her skeptical outlook wouldn't let her return the necklace to the velvet-lined box. She spread the quill chain wide and slipped it over her head. The amulet nestled between her breasts, almost warm against her skin.

She smiled at the fanciful girlish fantasy, and soon an indescribable peace settled over her. She was tired, and the day and her emotions had caught up with her.

She blew out the lantern, climbed into bed and fell into dream-filled slumber.

Kissing her had gone against every rational cell in his brain. He watched the light from her window disappear and admitted he could only take so much temptation.

For weeks he'd had to tamp down his reactions to her long-limbed form in her feminine clothing, ignore the sweep of her dark lashes against her pale skin and resist the enticement of the heart-kicking bow of her lips—those innocent yet seductive smiles and touches she couldn't know were eating his soul alive.

Once again entering the stall, he spread a wool blanket on a pile of straw in the corner and stretched out to chase some rest.

That kiss had sent him into a spiral of passion and confusion. She was so soft and her kiss so dizzying, it had taken an eternity for him to come to his senses. He wanted nothing more than to hold her, to enfold her and possess her.

But he couldn't allow himself to weaken. She didn't belong to him. She belonged to a glamorous life-style and a society of which he would never have any part—of which he never wanted any part. But she would. Once she came to reason and stopped playing games here, she would.

Kyle closed his eyes, though he didn't have much hope for rest. Her image had been branded on the inside of his eyelids. Her voice had become a melody that played inside his head. The smells of her skin and her hair were burned into his memory, and now that he'd tasted her, held her, he knew an aching hunger that had spread from his body to his head.

Why did it have to be her? Why did he have to want this woman when he'd never felt strongly about another in his life? Why had he fallen in love with one who wouldn't be staying? Because it would take a far stronger man than him to resist Isabelle Cooper, he admitted ruefully. And because life wasn't fair.

Chapter 10

At first he was dumbfounded by the realization that he loved a white woman. Against the mandates of his head and his beliefs, his heart had betrayed him.

At noon a couple of days later, Kyle entered the bunkhouse with the men, and his mouth watered at the savory aromas.

The table had been set properly with stoneware dishes and pitchers of milk. Two glazed hams had been sliced and placed on platters beside bowls of fluffy mashed potatoes and creamed vegetables. Loaves of crusty thick-sliced bread sat at either end of the feast.

"Whee doggie!" Tott shouted, and plunked himself down on a bench. The others quickly joined him, platters were passed and silverware clinked.

Kyle savored the delicious meal, listened to the men's profuse compliments.

Isabelle and Harlan accepted the praise, but Isabelle didn't appear as excited as Kyle had thought she should be over seeing her plans carried out. She sat in the corner chair that had become hers and ate her food without joining the men's banter.

The changes he'd seen in her these past days disturbed him. She put in as many hours as any of the hands—as Kyle himself—keeping occupied nearly round the clock. But the childlike joy he had once sensed had turned to grim determination. He felt responsible, as though he'd pulled her dreams out from under her. There hadn't been a choice, really. She would be better off once she admitted to herself that she couldn't be happy here.

He'd be better off, too. The longer she stayed, the more difficult her leaving would be. And he'd begun to dread that inevitable hour—and all the hours that would follow.

The men finished eating, noisily stacked their plates and lumbered out of the bunkhouse.

Kyle sipped his coffee. He missed her company these days—missed the optimistic twist she placed on everything. Glancing at her from the corner of his eye, he asked, "Did you go see the new foal?"

Shaking her head, she said, "I've been busy. Sidestep said he's a beauty."

"I thought you'd want to have a look at him."

"I'll look in on him when I'm over that way."

He'd been keeping an eye on her activities. She'd been clearing flower beds and the garden area all morning. The previous afternoon she'd scraped and painted the front and back doors. He'd set out to make her feel unwelcome, and he'd done his best to discourage her participation in all areas, so her sudden lack of enthusiasm about the horses shouldn't bother him. "Want to see him now?"

She got up and stacked her plate with the others at the end of the table. "Thank you, Harlan. You did an excellent job on the hams." Then to Kyle, she said, "I'd better help Harlan with the supper menu."

"You kin read me the chicken recipe later if'n you want to head out," the cook said.

"What about the dishes?"

"Washed 'em alone before you got here," he replied. "Reckon I kin still do it." He plucked stacked cups from her hand and waved her off.

She stepped outside behind Kyle. He settled his hat on his head, and they walked across the yard in uncomfortable silence.

The double-wide back doors of the barn stood open. Kyle headed in that direction. "Might as well come see him. They don't stay small long."

Obviously reluctant, she joined him in the shady barn.

Kyle opened the stall gate.

The spindly chestnut colt lay curled on the straw, the mare placidly munching oats beside him.

"You can touch him," Kyle said, noting her hesitation.

She touched the mare first, showing her hands and greeting her, then knelt close to the colt. "He's darling. He's not the same color as his mother."

She was a natural around the animals. He'd noticed from the first. "She and the sire are both quarter horses, just different coloring. I chose the sire for his muscled legs and thighs and wide hips. This year's foals will be good cow ponies."

The colt butted Isabelle's hand and nibbled at her fingers. She stroked his coat, and when he lurched to his feet, she stood back and laughed. He nuzzled his mother.

Kyle studied Isabelle's features as she watched the mother and baby. She glanced at him and dropped her gaze.

Was she remembering what had taken place here a few nights ago? Kyle had thought of little else. Or did she wonder what he'd do next to steal the smile from her lips? This one faded slowly, and it seemed as though a cloud had passed over.

Isabelle sensed the tension emanating from Kyle's body. The tangible disquiet was only tension and obviously not the attraction she'd once perceived this disquieting spark between them to mean. It was easier to stay away—easier to thwart her wild imagination when she kept her distance. She hadn't come to see the new horse until now because she was still reeling over being ordered from the barn.

She didn't want Kyle to think she would throw herself at him again. One rebuff had been enough. But neither did she want him to believe she was going to roll over and play dead. She had doubled her efforts to make herself useful. The ranch was showing improvement already.

Kyle picked up a pitchfork, scraped soiled straw to the side and spread fresh. She contemplated him while he was absorbed with the task. He didn't need the hat to mask his expressions—his granite-like facade was enough. But the hat did an even better job of preventing her from reading anything on his face. He set the fork outside the stall and rambled after a fresh bucket of water.

He'd rolled his sleeves to his elbows, and his corded arms flexed with each movement. She'd never taken so much interest in watching a man's every move, but when she was around this one she couldn't help herself. His masculine grace and efficiency appealed to her in a wholly disturbing manner.

The mare chose that moment to raise her head and press a nose against Kyle's shirtfront. Kyle paused to rake his knuckles over her forehead. Bobbing her head again, the horse knocked his hat into the straw.

One side of his mouth inched up. "Good thing for you I just cleaned that floor."

He glanced over and caught her watching him. His smile faded, and a heated awareness arced between them. Isabelle didn't understand him at all, and she hated this weakness of character, but she was drawn to him against all her self-preserving precautions.

He retrieved his hat.

Heart thudding, she rubbed her damp palms against her skirt.

He settled the hat on his head and studied her from beneath its brim.

She met his gaze, drawn to the stern but sensual set of his mouth. She would give anything for him to cross the few feet that separated them and gather her in his arms again. She was weak and foolish and would regret it later, but this artless need had a mind of its own.

Never should she have come in here with him. More than anything, she wanted him to feel something for her in return. She wanted him to accept her. Once again, she was ready to forfeit pride for a few scraps of affection and attention. Garnering her purpose, she turned and hurried from the stall.

"Isabelle!" he called behind her.

Chest aching, she kept walking.

She didn't show up at the bunkhouse for supper. But then she never used to, either. He'd assumed one reason was the food, but Harlan had prepared a savory chicken and stuffing dish that was obviously her doing. Her lack of familiarity with the men might have been a factor originally, but the hands had begun to accept her, and she seemed comfortable around them.

"Miss Cooper'll be back in an hour or so," Harlan said.

Had Kyle's face given away his thoughts? "Where did she go?"

"Didn't say. Just said she'd be gone for supper."

"The brown bay and a saddle are gone," Tott added.

Concern destroyed Kyle's appetite. The western sky had been dark with storm clouds when he'd completed his chores. Hastily, he finished the meal and pushed away from the table. Stupid woman had no idea how to take care of herself. What did she think she was doing, riding out alone? She'd been a bother since the day she'd arrived.

He hurried to the barn and a sweet melody caught his attention. He paused. From the house floated the trill of a bird, a bright, energetic warbling that carried across the landscape. Giving the house a quick once-over, he noticed the open dining room window and the cage that sat inside. That such a tiny bird could sing so loudly was remarkable—that and the fact that it seemed perfectly content in its imprisonment.

Darting for the corral, he summoned the Appaloosa and saddled it. He grabbed his rifle and a slicker and mounted, studying the ground until he found Isabelle's tracks leading east. Following them, he imagined every danger that could arise. The bay could spook and throw her. Snakes and coyotes were common, and even if she'd thought to bring the Colt, she'd never hit one. Another hour and it would be dark, and it got cold at night. Thunder rolled overhead.

Almost a half hour later, he spotted the bay standing on a grassy slope that led down to Bear Tooth Creek. The Appaloosa hadn't stopped when Kyle's boots hit the ground. He ran toward the bank.

Isabelle, sitting on her shawl on the ground, turned and leveled the barrel of the Colt on him, her eyes as wide and gray and fierce as the Montana sky.

"Kyle!" she squawked, and her shoulders sagged with relief. She lowered the gun. "You nearly frightened me to death."

"What are you doing out here?" He strode over to where she sat and glared.

"Sitting. Thinking."

"It's getting late and it's going to rain."

"I was just getting ready to head back."

"Do you know how to get back?"

"I was hoping so."

"This wasn't very smart. Something could have happened to you. You could have been lost—or hurt."

"Well, it didn't and I'm not. You're not my father, and I won't be treated like you are. There's danger everywhere. I could have been struck by a carriage in the city, too, but I wasn't."

She got to her feet, and he stared at her, rolling that twisted logic around in his head. "You have to take precautions out here."

She raised the gun.

He glanced at it and back to her stubborn face. She was the loveliest thing he'd ever seen and the most irritating person he'd ever met, though he saw her differently than when she'd first arrived. Now he understood that she was the result of the life her father had forced on her. Once she'd seen the opportunity to change and to grow, she'd done so with a determination and a spirit that he'd had to admire.

She wanted to make a place for herself here and had done all she knew how to see it happen. After seeing the determination and hard work and loyalty she'd poured into the Big Sky, he couldn't help but wonder what she would give to a man who loved her.

Perhaps she'd been willing to do just that before he built a wall between them.

Now she didn't trust him. And he understood mistrust. He took the revolver from her and tucked it in his belt. Lightning streaked, and thunder split the air. Spattering raindrops sounded on his hat and glistened on Isabelle's nose and cheeks.

He grabbed the slicker from his saddle. "Get up," he said, pointing to his horse. Taking a step from his bent knee, she arranged herself on the horse with a flurry of skirts and white petticoats.

Kyle caught her horse's reins and mounted behind

her, wrapping the slicker around them both and leading the bay.

She was as soft and erotic-smelling as he remembered, the reality better than the memory. He nudged the Appaloosa into a gallop and headed for shelter.

Isabelle would have liked to lean back into the warmth and protection of his arms, but their pace didn't afford time to relax. Her hair grew wet, and her teeth chattered by the time he drew up in front of a cabin and leaped down.

"What's this place?" she asked.

"My home." He wrapped the slicker around her. "Go in while I put the horses in the lean-to."

Obediently, she ran through the deluge to the door and entered the dark cabin.

Shivering, she stood inside until he returned and found a lantern. A golden glow illuminated the sharp angles of his tight jaw and carved brow. His glistening ebony hair dripped on the wet shirt molded to his chest.

Isabelle removed the slicker and hung it on a peg inside the door. She turned back, and Kyle was coming toward her with a stack of folded burlap toweling. "Dry your hair," he said.

"Yours is wet, too."

"I'm used to the weather."

"You're dripping all over."

He kept a length for himself, dried his hair and slipped out of his shirt. He moved to the stone fireplace, and arranged a stack of wood and lit kindling beneath. Isabelle watched the play of muscle beneath his smooth bronze skin as he performed the chore.

She hung her shawl over a wooden chair back, then scampered near the fire and waited impatiently for the flames to engulf the sticks and send heat. Careful not to stare at him, she studied the room.

A sturdy, rough-hewn table and benches sat on one side, a small cupboard and a few crates the only storage space.

The other side held a bed, its low frame fashioned from joined logs. The furs and blankets covering the mattress looked warm and comfortable. Beside the bed, a shelf held an assortment of books. Other items were stored in stacked baskets.

Two furs covered the rough plank floor before the fireplace. Like the man himself, the room was an interesting and elementary blend of cultures.

Her gaze flitted to the cabin's owner. She found him watching her. "Want dry clothes?" he asked.

She glanced at her sodden hem and spattered skirts. Her damp bodice clung uncomfortably to her skin. She raised a brow. "You have a spare gown lying about?"

"I have tunics and leggings. You can adjust them with a drawstring."

"Where would I change?"

"I'll be a gentleman and make coffee and keep my back turned." He rose, drew a bundle from beneath his bed and handed it to her. Opening the door, he darted out long enough to draw a bucket of water from the corner of the cabin.

Isabelle glanced from the clothing to his back and slowly unbuttoned her shirtwaist.

Chapter 11

Her skirt came off next, followed by her petticoats. Her chemise and drawers were dry, thank goodness, so she would leave them on beneath his soft clothing.

The leather smelled like him. She raised the tunic to her nose, and the scent created a nervous flutter in her belly.

"Let me brush your hair."

The nearness of his voice startled her. She turned her head and found him behind her. Surprisingly, she wasn't frightened or embarrassed. "You said you'd keep your back turned."

"I'm not a gentleman."

She let the clothing fall from her fingers, reached and pulled the combs and pins loose.

His palm appeared in her vision, and she placed the items within, her fingers grazing his calloused skin. He set the hair accessories on the table that held his books and picked up a quill brush, which he raised and drew through the ends of her hair. Of course, having long hair himself, he would know to start at the ends. She smiled.

He worked his way along the tresses to her scalp, and Isabelle let her head fall back in sensual pleasure.

"I remembered your hair," he said near her ear.

"What do you mean?" she asked through the seductive haze of indulgence.

"I remembered it from a time when you were here to visit your father. I saw you in the yard one afternoon, and I never forgot the way your hair shone like the fiery ball of the sun at sunset in midsummer."

That revelation took her aback. Poetic words. Revealing words. But the message behind them came into focus. He'd noticed and remembered her.

He buried his face in her hair and made a throaty sound. He lifted the tresses, and his warm breath caressed her neck as he nuzzled her skin around the quill chain. Shivers spread across her shoulders and tightened her breasts. He nipped her flesh, and her knees weakened.

As if sensing her loss of stability, he wrapped an arm across her chest and drew her against him where he easily supported her weight with his arm and his solid body.

With his other hand, he held her damp hair away from her face so he could kiss her temple, her cheek, her jaw.

"I remember you, too," she said on a shallow breath. "You were so stern-looking, so unsmiling and..." She turned in his embrace, and he didn't loosen his hold, just pressed her ardently against his body. She raised a hand to his cheek.

His black eyes smoldered. His lips parted. She'd wanted to shake him up to see him react just once, but she'd never thought to do it this way. His usually severe mask had been fractured, and desire plainly softened his features.

Isabelle smiled and drew her thumb across his lower lip.

The heat from the fire spread though the room, danced on their skin and delved through muscle and tissue to create a tremulous heat that fused them.

The nagging memory of his hurtful reaction to the kiss they'd shared in the barn stole into her thoughts, but the desire to have more of him banished the worry. Her heart and her body begged for his sweet touch, and she wouldn't be ashamed of her need. She loved him.

His fingers threaded into her hair, and her arm stole around his neck. She was tall enough to meet his kiss aggressively, and she did so with singular determination.

He banded her with an arm across her back; his other hand gripped her bottom and pulled her hips against him.

White-hot fire licked through her veins at the rush of sensation and pleasure. His tongue sought entrance, and she tasted a new and immeasurably sweet passion. Her body trembled against his.

His touch on her bottom changed to a caress, and she held her breath. Their lips parted, and as one they sighed, a mingling of breath and wonderment.

Never had anything felt so right or so perfect before. Isabelle ran her palms over his smooth shoulders, across his chest, testing and discovering and delighting.

His black eyes raked her face and dropped to the thin cotton barrier that separated them. He brought his hands up her sides and drew his thumbs across the aching crests beneath the fabric. She let her eyes drift shut to savor the achingly sweet sensation.

"I don't want to do this," he said, his voice low and gruff.

She forced her eyes open.

"If you'll regret it afterward—if you'll be ashamed for wanting me."

She shook her head to clear it. Why would she be ashamed? Did he plan to humiliate her again?

"This is where I come from," he said, and one hand left her breast to indicate the cabin. "You've met my family, and I've never claimed to be anything except what I am."

Understanding dawned slowly. "What are you that would be shameful for me to want?" she asked.

He held her gaze. "A half-breed."

Was that hard for him to say? "Is that a slur?" She raised her palm to his face and cupped his jaw. "I know you as an honest, hardworking man. A man I want to know better. The man I married. Period. Don't let other people's attitudes affect the way you see me, and I'll do the same."

"I was wrong about you," he said. He let their bodies part in order to take her hand and lead her to his bed. She sat on the edge tentatively, but he wouldn't allow shyness.

He'd been wrong about so many things, and thankfully he'd straightened his thinking before it was too late. She wasn't like his father. She wasn't even like her father. He'd seen her with his family, with Pelipa, and her heart was genuine and good.

He had resented her, along with every other white, simply because of her birth and her upbringing—just as people judged him without knowing him. By her example, she'd shown him how to let the hurts of the past go and embrace the present.

He wasn't going to waste another minute that could be spent with her, loving her. Her silky, warm skin set him on fire. He stroked her arms and untied the flimsy garment that teased him by revealing the clear outline of her nipples.

He kissed her to keep the tension high, and her burning response assured him of her excitement.

He kissed the ivory skin that was revealed as together they peeled away the last of her clothing. The amulet hung between her breasts. He touched it once, leaned to place his nose in that valley and inhale her unique scent as well as the curious fragrance of the herbs.

He kissed her breast and straightened to fill his eyes. She was more beautiful than he'd ever dreamed. And she was his wife.

He kissed her lips, and she clung to him.

He touched her body, and she opened to him.

He loved her, heart and soul, and she responded with heat and sighs and silken tremors.

When at last they joined, she cried out, and he soothed her with kisses and tender words. She drew him closer then, and he made it up to her slowly, steadily, gently, until they lay boneless and sated, his fingers still whispering across her skin in lazy circles.

It took several minutes for the hiss of steam and the smell of coffee boiling over into the flames to get his attention. Kyle rose and used a towel to remove the pot.

He poured a mug and carried it to her, amused at the blush staining her cheeks. "Not much left."

She grinned and set the cup on the floor beside the bed. "We'll share."

He stretched out beside her, curling his body around hers and dangling the amulet over her chin playfully. "Now you can't have our marriage canceled," he teased.

She went still and silent, a terrible, deafening silence he could hear.

His heart forgot to beat, and he neglected to breathe. Had she forgotten her goal in a moment of passion? Had she been planning to leave, after all?

She sat up so suddenly, her shoulder connected with his jaw and slammed his teeth together. She scooted toward the end of the bed and pulled a blanket up to cover her breasts. "Is that what this was all about?"

Kyle leaned on one elbow, rubbed his jaw and tried to detect her meaning. "What *what* was about?"

Threading one side of her tousled hair back, she glared at him, a frightening mixture of hurt and betrayal on her gentle features. Her lips were red and puffy from their kisses; he still tasted her passion.

"This!" She jabbed a finger at the bed, at his nakedness, but her attention stayed riveted on his face, as if it hurt to read betrayal there, as if she strained to read truth, hope. "You just made certain that I couldn't go have our marriage annulled." Her voice trembled on the words. "The Big Sky is yours by all rights now."

Tears glimmered on her lashes.

He almost allowed anger to push rational thought away. So this was how she trusted him. This was what she thought of him. Her mistrust cut deep.

With his next heartbeat, he remembered how he hadn't trusted her until this very night. She had every reason to question his honor and intent, especially after the way he'd bullied and provoked her. Self-preservation was a strong instinct, and no one knew that better than he did.

Inside this beautiful woman, seeking acceptance, was the insecure child that her father had created.

"I can't say I'm sorry," he admitted. "We're legally bound now."

One silvery tear slid down her cheek and pierced his heart.

"I've made you my wife. For good."

Her transparent gray eyes revealed a touch of wonder and a cloud of disbelief. The fingers she brought to her lips trembled.

"I want you, Isabelle," he said, not remembering if he'd ever spoken her name aloud before and sorry if he hadn't. He loved the sound. If he lived to be an old man, he'd never tire of saying it. "I want you to stay with me. I need you to stay with me. I was afraid I'd lose you, so I tried not to love you."

"Kyle," she said with a shaky exhale.

"What's between us here is not about the ranch. It's about us." He leaned forward and took her hand away from her mouth. He looked at his big, rough hand holding her fragile one and felt something so pure and intense, it took a moment to form words. "*Nemehotatse.* I love you," he said at last.

Tears welled in her eyes, but a hopeful smile raised the corners of her lovely mouth. "Truly?"

How could he tell her so she would understand? So she would believe? So she would know in her heart? He brought her fingers to his lips and tasted the backs with a kiss. "I could live without the ranch," he said. "I could take the horses somewhere else and start over."

He took her other hand in his and caressed them both with his thumbs.

"But I couldn't go on without you. You are...like the rain that fills the rivers and the sun that makes things grow. That's what you are to me."

"Oh, Kyle!" She threw herself against him, and he caught her, rocked her as she sobbed against his neck. He let her cry out her relief and joy while newfound assurance blossomed in both their hearts. He understood her deep-seeded need for love and acceptance. He had lived too many years without. But no more.

The blanket had worked its way down until the only thing between them was the hard knot of the silver amulet. Isabelle had grown calm, and her fingers stroked the hair at his neck.

He cupped her shoulders and held her slightly away so he could see her. She gave him a watery smile.

They talked into the night, sharing their hopes and dreams, not only for the Big Sky, but dreams for them, and for a family. She restored his faith in people, in himself.

"I'd like you to take over the bookkeeping," he said at last.

She raised a brow.

"You're better at it than I am."

"All right, I'm convinced that you love me and trust me," she said.

The first real joy he could remember feeling welled in his chest.

"You're smiling!" She touched his cheek reverently. "I love you."

The words rang through him, filling him with emotion. This time, it was he who had tears in his eyes. Tears of happiness. Of love.

Epilogue

My Beloved Husband,

Each day grows longer and each night darker without you here to experience it with me.

This is not the way I wanted to tell you this, but I shall burst if I do not share this most blessed and joyful news. The gladness and fulfillment that our love yields is unceasing! Next spring, when the mountain streams flow and the countryside bursts with new life, we will bring a new life of our own into the world. We are going to have a baby.

I think of the day we were married, and how skeptical I was about how things would turn out, and it seems like a miracle that we've reached this beautiful turn of events. The only future I could see was to keep the ranch, and you were the answer to that. You turned out to be the answer to many things— things I knew deep inside I needed and wanted, but was too afraid to dream for. How grateful I am that your determination was as great as mine, how thankful that you suggested we combine resources to keep the ranch.

If someone had told me that day as I walked toward you, wearing my mother's Irish lace and quivering with trepidation, that I would love you as much as I do this day, I would have not believed it possible. Sometimes I wonder if Mae's amulet actually had anything to do with our love, but then I think that's foolish, too, so who can really know? All that matters is that our arrangement turned out to be so much more...and now we have made a child with whom to share our love.

I shall pray for your safe travel and ex-pedient journey home so that we may cele-

brate this new and exciting chapter to our
lives in the proper manner.

I remain as always,

Your Devoted Wife, Isabelle

P.S. Your Aunt Mae says it's a son.

* * * * *

Look for THE MAGNIFICENT SEVEN,
Cheryl St.John's next book in the exciting
MONTANA MAVERICKS *series,*
in March 2001.

If you enjoyed what you just read,
then we've got an offer you can't resist!

Take 2 bestselling love stories FREE!

Plus get a FREE surprise gift!